Chairs

Chairs

1,000 Masterpieces of Modern Design, 1800 to Present

GOODMAN
FIELL

This book is dedicated to Pierre Paulin – a dear friend and a truly great designer – and his wife, Maia – a really very special person.

Published in 2012 by Goodman Fiell
An imprint of the Carlton Publishing Group
20 Mortimer Street
London W1T 3JW

Text © 2012 Charlotte & Peter Fiell
Design © 2012 Goodman Fiell

A CIP catalogue record for this book is available from the British Library

Project Concept: Charlotte & Peter Fiell
Editorial: Charlotte & Peter Fiell
Texts: Charlotte & Peter Fiell
Additional texts: Catharine Rossi
Project Editor: Isabel Wilkinson
Picture Sourcing: Charlotte & Peter Fiell, Jennifer Tilston, Isabel Wilkinson
Design: Dominic Burr
Cover Design: Alison Tutton
Indexing: Ann Barrett
Production Manager: Maria Petalidou

Printed in China
ISBN 978-1-84796-034-4

Contents

Introduction

Chairs: A Brief History

Our first survey of chairs, entitled *Modern Chairs*, was published in 1994, and was followed in 1997 by the publication of our internationally bestselling *1000 Chairs*. Over the succeeding years we have discovered, through our researches undertaken for other design-related books, notable chair designs that were not included in these earlier publications that often deserved as much recognition as the usual roster of acknowledged "modern design classics". There have also, of course, been numerous noteworthy chair designs produced in the intervening years. The enduring fascination with chairs has if anything grown over the past fifteen years, as the public has become ever-more design-literate, thanks to a growth in awareness of design matters that has been cultivated by burgeoning coverage of design in the media, on television, and in various exhibitions and publications. As design writers, we feel that now is the right time to return to the modern chair as a subject of in-depth study. To this end, *Chairs: 1,000 Masterpieces of Modern Design, 1800 to Present* is an all-new survey that traces the origins of the modern chair from its earliest Biedermeier inception to its latest "design-art" incarnations, and we hope that our readers will find the carefully chosen selection of designs in the following pages as refreshing and fascinating as it is stylistically varied.

Yes, a chair is just a chair, but it is also so much more than a useful supporting tool on which to rest, work or dine. It is not only the most ubiquitous and important design element in any domestic or office environment, but almost anyone working within the fields of design and architecture has, at some stage in their career, set themselves the challenging task of designing one. As Ludwig Mies van der Rohe (1886–1969) noted, "A chair is a very difficult object. A skyscraper is almost easier. That is why Chippendale is famous."

In comparison to any other designed object, the chair also has a unique level of interaction that not only allows a physical connection to its user but which also engenders an emotional response. Because the chair by necessity follows the contours of the human body, it also often exudes a sense of character that endears it to us as a designed artefact. Similarly the chair, because it cradles and supports the body, creates a sense of territoriality and thereby emotional possession, whilst also conveying status and hierarchy, whether in a family group or in the structure of a large corporation. But perhaps even more importantly in regard to this new historical survey, the chair reveals not only the visions of its creators but also mirrors the wider cultural context of the era in which it arose. Put simply, the evolution of the modern chair is emblematic of the wider history of modern design.

Over the last two hundred years the chair has been subject to numerous interpretations, revolutions and evolutions, yet at its heart it remains an object to sit upon, and it is this basic functional constant that has ensured its cultural longevity. Indeed, as Nicola Redway noted in the catalogue of the first Christie's auction dedicated to "The Chair" in October 1997, the story of its development "is a rich and complex tapestry of changing tastes, materials, technologies and ideologies, where no strand is a constant, except that which offers an 'invitation to repose'." Certainly, whether a chair fulfills this basic criterion successfully is almost entirely down to the skill and competence of its creator and, of course, his or her ultimate design agenda. For the chair has in recent decades become an almost totemic object of desire; an object that in some cases provocatively rides the creative fault line that exists between the worlds of fine art and functional design.

So where does the story of the modern chair begin? Ask a dozen design experts or chair aficionados this question and you will probably get a dozen different answers. The stirrings of its birth, however, can be traced back to the final years of the eighteenth century and the early years of the nineteenth century when the then-fashionable and elegant Biedermeier style introduced a new neoclassical simplification of form and ultimately construction. This reductivist tendency would eventually lead to the creation of chairs that were essentially stripped of superfluous ornamentation and as such were suited to large-scale mass production, like those manufactured by Gebrüder Thonet in Vienna during the mid-1800s. At the same time early design reformers, such as A.W.N. Pugin (1812–52) and Christopher Dresser (1834–1904), highlighted the importance of function, simplicity and fitness for purpose in regard to manufacture. Thus the seeds of the New Art were sown, a movement that would subsequently flourish throughout Europe and America, whether in the lattice-like constructions of the Charles Rennie Mackintosh (1868–1928) "Glasgow School" chairs or in the swirling back-rails of Art Nouveau chairs designed by the French architect, Hector Guimard (1867-1942) or the Belgian architect-designer, Victor Horta (1861-1947).

In Germany and Austria during the opening years of the twentieth century, an even greater wave of design reform took hold that built upon the moral underpinnings of the British Arts & Crafts Movement's adherence to fitness for purpose, truth to materials and revealed construction, and applied it to the sphere of industrial manufacture as opposed to craft production. In 1897, the Vereinigte Werkstätten für Kunst im Handwerk (United Workshops for Art in Handicraft) was founded in Munich, and the same year the Dresdner Werkstätten für Handwerkskunst (Dresden Workshops for Handicraft) was also established. The former venture – that boasted among its founding members Peter Behrens (1868–1940) and Richard Riemerschmidt (1868–1957) – sought to bring together artists, designers and architects who were committed to improving design standards and shared the belief that mass production was not only virtuous but absolutely necessary for the newly emerging modern industrial age.

The latter was founded by the furniture manufacturer Karl Schmidt, with the aim of producing furnishings designed by progressive architects and designers using the latest mechanized methods of production.

Many of the designers associated with these two design-reforming groups subsequently went on to become founding members of the Deutscher Werkbund in 1907, an association that brought together art and industry through its fostering of creative partnerships between leading Jugendstil designers and enlightened industrialists, and was formed with the objective of balancing new industrial mass production methods with a craftsmanship and quality that was sorely lacking in most mass-produced consumer goods at the time. In 1924, the Werkbund published *Form ohne Ornament* (Form Without Ornament), a hymn to functionalism that championed the beauty of the undecorated surface and the necessity of standardization for the successful manufacture of modern designed objects. The importance of the Deutscher Werkbund on the development of modern design cannot be overstated, and nor can the influence of an earlier essay entitled "Ornament und Verbrechen" (Ornament and Crime) written in 1908 by the Austro-Hungarian architect and design theorist, Adolf Loos (1870–1933). In this seminal paper, he stated, "The evolution of culture is synonymous with the removal of ornament from objects of daily use". He went on to explain how applied ornament was not only culturally debasing but also economically and socially unsound, noting, "As a rule, ornament increases the price of the object…The lack of ornament results in reduced working hours and an increased wage." Indeed, it could be argued that the Deutscher Werkbund's promotion of artistic manufactures that put theory into practice, and Loos' stridently reformist writings, not only transformed the parameters of chair design but also formed the philosophical bedrock on which the roots of modern design took hold and ultimately flourished with the 1919 foundation of the Staatliches Bauhaus in Weimar by Walter Gropius (1883-1969).

The Bauhaus not only revolutionized the teaching of art and design but also (perhaps as importantly in relation to the development of the modern chair) demonstrated through its strict ideological adherence to functionalism that new industrial methods of production could enable the mass-manufacture of truly modern furniture – modern chairs, fit for the modern man, living in the modern age. The end of the First World War the preceding year had concentrated the minds of both designers and manufacturers on the role of design in society and there was now a general feeling of urgency amongst designers associated with the Bauhaus that a radical *Neue Sachlichkeit* (New Objectivity) was needed, both in society as a whole and more specifically within the fine and applied arts. The three-dimensional realization of this new, reforming *Zeitgeist* in design was powerfully evinced during the 1920s in Marcel Breuer's series of revolutionary chairs made from tubular steel, which were highly suited to large-scale industrial production. These brutally utilitarian seating designs marked a watershed in the history of chair design and heralded a new and unequivocally modern style within the furnishing of interiors.

Although many designers in France were influenced by the designs stemming from the Bauhaus during the 1920s, the country's long tradition of superlative craftsmanship and patronage meant that their interpretation of Modernism was from a more stylistic rather than ideological standpoint and as a result the French avant-garde chair designs of the period had a distinctively chic quality. The Modernist chairs designed by René Herbst (1891–1982) or Le Corbusier (1887–1965), Pierre Jeanneret (1896–1967) and Charlotte Perriand (1903–99), for example, possessed a fashionable Parisian modishness that was totally removed from the socially inspired utilitarian doctrine of their Teutonic contemporaries. Similarly, many other French designers during the late 1920s and 1930s preferred to build on their traditional cabinetmaking heritage and continued to create opulent Art Deco furnishings using exotic and lacquered woods, such as those by Émile-Jacques Ruhlmann (1879–1933) and Jean Royère (1902–81), which their wealthy clients presumably appreciated more than the rigidly Modernist furnishings of Le Corbusier et al. But even these Art Deco chairs reflected the stylistic influence of Modernism, with their simplified and unornamented sweeping lines and use of striking geometric forms.

In 1930s America, (dubbed the "Design Decade" by *Fortune* magazine) hard-pressed manufacturers in the face of the Great Depression also sought the allure of Modernism to revitalize their product lines and catalogues. To this end they employed a new generation of professional industrial design consultants, such as Gilbert Rohde (1894–1944), Russel Wright (1904–1976), K.E.M. Weber (1889–1963) and Wolfgang Hoffmann (1900–1969) to create chairs that were in the then fashionable Moderne style using sweeping curves of tubular steel or bentwood, with deeply padded leather or vinyl-covered upholstery. This type of Art Deco chair reflected the less doctrinal approach to Modernism that was found in America, which was ultimately more fuelled by commercial goals than social concerns. The Thirties was also the golden age of Hollywood glamour, and many of the most popular movies of the time featured elegant Moderne interiors that helped to instil among the general public a desire for stylishly contemporary furnishings.

Elsewhere, the ripples of Modernism also spread their influence. In Scandinavia, for instance, it was expressed in a more humanistic way through the work of the Finnish architect Alvar Aalto (1898–1976), who rejected the hard-edged sterile aesthetic of tubular steel in favour of laminated and bent plywood in his designs for chairs, believing such "natural" materials were more suited to the human condition. This soft-edged Scandinavian approach to Modernism pioneered by Aalto had an enduring influence on later designers working in Britain and America. Indeed, the Finnish architect Eliel Saarinen's (1873–1950) directorship of the Cranbrook Academy of Arts in Michigan was to have a direct and profound impact on the next generation of American designers, many of whom trained at this influential design-teaching institution. Having been described as "America's democratic counterpart to the Bauhaus", the teaching at Cranbrook instilled in its prodigious alumni, which included Charles Eames (1907–78), Eero Saarinen (1910–61) and Ray Kaiser (later Eames, 1912–88), a deep appreciation of organic design, which had been previously pioneered by the Arts & Crafts Movement and prewar Scandinavian designers, such as Kaare Klint (1888–1954) and Alvar Aalto.

In 1940, the Department of Industrial Design at the Museum of Modern Art, New York held its influential "Organic Design in Home Furnishings" competition; sponsored by a dozen of the country's leading stores with the understanding that they would offer contracts with manufacturers to the winners of the competition's different categories. The aim of the competition, according to the event's organizer Eliot F. Noyes (1910–77), was to discover "a group of designers capable of contributing to the creation of a useful and beautiful environment for today's living". Charles Eames and Eero Saarinen's entries won first prize in two of nine categories: "Seating for a living room" and "Other furniture for a living room". Their award-winning chair designs demonstrated a new but important tendency within the design of furniture during this period: physical lightness. As the accompanying catalogue to the competition explained, "This tendency derives not only from the need to keep the weight and bulk of furnishings down as we live in smaller areas, but it is also the natural result of new techniques and new materials. Refinement

of chair design involves the economical and imaginative use of materials, while providing comfort and strength." Certainly in comparison to the overstuffed furniture that the majority of mainstream furniture manufacturers were producing, the Eames-Saarinen designs marked a new and remarkable material and visual lightening of chairs. Among the most influential seating designs of the twentieth century, this landmark series of prototypical moulded plywood chairs advanced the notion of continuous contact and support thereby allowing a greater degree of comfort. Importantly, three of the submitted designs utilized single-form seat shells for greater design unity, which were then upholstered using a thin sheet of latex rubber that provided wraparound padded comfort. Although heralding a completely new direction in modern chair design, Eames and Saarinen's progressive seating designs sadly remained as prototypes and it was not until the cessation of the Second World War that the first compound moulded plywood seat components were mass-produced.

Of course, the outbreak of war in 1939 had had a remarkable mobilising effect on research and the development of new materials and methods of production for the war effort, and these in turn found new applications within the furniture industry after the end of hostilities in 1945. For example, Charles and Ray Eames' landmark series of plywood chairs designed in 1945–46 were directly informed not only by the MoMA competition chairs of 1940, but also by their own personal wartime development of plywood leg splints and stretchers for the US military. The chairman of Herman Miller, D.J. DePree (1891–1990), the manufacturer who subsequently took over production of the chairs, described this range of moulded plywood seat furniture as: "Beautiful, comfortable, easy to move. It's unimprovable. It's a national treasure that ought to be made available." Similarly the Eameses' later revolutionary range of fibreglass shell chairs developed between 1948 and 1950 – the design concept of which can also be traced directly back to the earlier "Organic Design in Home Furnishings" competition chairs – were only realisable thanks to the greater availability of newly developed plastics and innovative production techniques that had come about because of wartime research.

Although in Europe during the immediate postwar period there was less access to new materials and state-of-the-art methods of manufacture than in America, there was a general belief that "good design" was essential for export-led recovery, which itself would lead to economic regeneration and ultimately the restoration of national pride. In Italy, for instance, designers like Gio Ponti (1891–1979) and Carlo Mollino (1905–73) used readily available materials and the skilled craftsmanship of small workshops to create modern chairs that had an undeniable élan. In the late 1940s and early 1950s, Italian designers, notably Marco Zanuso (1916–2001), also pioneered the use of a new kind of spongy foam rubber padding, which had been developed by the Pirelli Company, in the design of upholstered furniture. This led to the creation of sleek contemporary chairs that provided sculpted comfort without the need for bulky traditional springing.

During the 1950s a new sculptural confidence also emerged in the design of chairs throughout the rest of Europe and America that eventually resulted in the realization of numerous landmark designs, including Eero Saarinen's *Tulip* pedestal chair (1955–56) and Verner Panton's (1926–98) sinuous *Panton* chair (1959–60), which exploited the aesthetic and functional potential of newly available thermoplastics and production processes. At the same time, the leading furniture manufacturers in America, Herman Miller and Knoll Associates, furnished not only office spaces but also homes across the US and overseas with outstandingly modern furniture that ultimately led to an entirely new look in contemporary interior design. This groundbreaking style was predicated on carefully delineated spaces, bright blocks of colour, a refreshing sense of airiness and, of course, sculptural chairs that not only functioned well but that also had a sophisticated contemporary presence.

The 1960s, in contrast, saw a widespread cultural backlash against the perceived aesthetic diktats of "good design", especially in Britain and Italy where young designers sought to create furniture and lighting that was more in tune with the newly emerging liberal consciousness of their youthful demographic. The counterculturist rallying cry of "Turn on, tune in, drop out", popularized by the American psychologist and forthright advocate of psychedelic drugs, Dr. Timothy Leary, was a powerful reaction against the conservative homemaking world of the previous decade, and as a result the domestic landscape became a new and exciting playing field for design experimentation. In Italy, furniture producers such as Kartell, Artemide, and Zanotta functioned as idea factories encouraging designers to push the functional and formal boundaries of the latest high tech plastics, most notably shiny-surfaced ABS and PVC, to create chairs that were revolutionary in terms of their production and that expressed the new youthful Pop aesthetic and were, at times, also challenging expressions of the emerging Anti-Design movement. The generational shift of influence that occurred during this decade saw a profound change in the manufacture and purchasing of furniture. Unlike previous generations, the young hipsters of the Swinging Sixties did not necessarily want to buy a chair that would last them a lifetime or that was a sensible choice, but instead wanted something that would look cool in their groovy pads, and that could also be purchased off-the-shelf to satisfy their must-have-it-now desire for instant gratification. The craving for creative interactivity was also a powerful theme in chair design during this period, as was multi-functionality and lower and lower seat heights that enabled more casual ways of sitting or lounging.

The early 1970s saw the zenith of chair design experimentation, with the Museum of Modern Art in New York hosting the landmark and highly influential "Italy: The New Domestic Landscape" exhibition in 1972 to reflect this phenomenon. As Emilio Ambasz (1943–), the show's curator, noted in the accompanying catalogue: "It has been a long-standing assumption of the Modern Movement that if all man's products were well designed, harmony and joy would emerge eternally triumphant. Many signs from different sources are making it evident that, although good design is a necessary condition, it is not by itself sufficient to ensure the automatic solution of all the problems that precede its creation and of those that arise from it. Consequently, many designers are expanding their traditional concern for the aesthetic of the object to embrace also a concern for the aesthetic of uses to which the object will be put. Thus, the object is no longer conceived as an isolated entity... But rather as an integral part of the larger natural and socio-cultural environment."

The variety of chairs included in this exhibition revealed the diverse approaches taken by Italian designers in their pursuit of the modern chair, from Marco Zanuso and Richard Sapper's (1932–) diminutive *Model No.4999/5* child's chair (1960), the world's first ever injection-moulded plastic chair, to Gruppo G14's sinuous *Fiocco* chair (1970), with its supple stretch textile cover pulled taut over its tubular metal frame.

The oil crisis of 1973 dampened the enthusiasm of manufacturers for blue-sky creative experimentation as rising fuel prices meant the cost of plastics rocketed and a global economic recession ensued. Straitened times necessitated a return to the functional principles of the Modern Movement and a new rational sobriety came to dominate chair design and manufacture. The late 1970s, however, saw a reaction against the commercial blandness of much of what the furniture industry was producing and the sentiments of the earlier

Anti-Design movement from the late 1960s crystallized into the establishment of Studio Alchimia in 1976, which deliberately sought to produce chairs and other designed artefacts that had an intellectual foundation and were consciously anti-commercial. For instance, Alessandro Mendini's (1931–) *Spaziale* chair (1981) produced by Poltronova for Studio Alchimia had a strong totemic presence and eloquently demonstrated that the humble chair could be transformed into polemical artwork.

As the economy of the early-to-mid 1980s began to boom so a new international style emerged: Postmodernism. This new and challenging spirit in design and architecture saw a rigorous questioning of the conservative status quo of the design mainstream and its belief in the primacy of Modernism. The most influential proponent of Postmodernism in the applied arts during the early 1980s was the Memphis design collective, established by the Austrian-Italian architect Ettore Sottsass (1917–2007), which created chairs that playfully referenced past styles and revelled in the use of plastic laminates and vibrant colours and patterns. Around the same time, another branch of Postmodernism emerged as a definable grouping of similarly minded young designers that became known as Creative Salvage. Designers aligned to this new and youthful movement, such as Tom Dixon (1959–) and Ron Arad (1951–), initially used found materials to imaginatively create limited edition and one-off seating assemblages that were expressions of their individual personal creativity. Another notable designer who distanced himself from the stultifying conservatism of the mainstream was Shiro Kuramata (1934–91), who created precious, almost alchemic designs that had an innate poetic quality that transcended physical function. These kinds of Postmodern designs, although aesthetically and intellectually disparate, were hugely influential in that they collectively proved that designers could successfully work outside the industrial mainstream, and that the modern chair was the perfect platform on which to test new and challenging ideas concerning form and function.

The 1990s witnessed an ever-growing appreciation for design amongst the general public that resulted in the furniture manufacturing industry growing as a whole. Simultaneously, many of the young designers who had been working experimentally in the 1980s in a very hands-on way now came of age, having matured into very accomplished designers. Most notable were Philippe Starck (1949–), Jasper Morrison (1959–), Marc Newson (1962–), Ross Lovegrove (1958–), Ron Arad and Tom Dixon. The majority of these designers not only created limited edition works but also worked for forward-thinking manufacturers such as Cappellini, Magis and Vitra. These alliances allowed them to explore the functional possibilities offered by new materials and cutting edge technologies, enabling them to create stylish chairs for the global market that were technically and aesthetically groundbreaking, for example Jasper Morrison's *Air-Chair* (1999) and Ron Arad's *FPE* chair (1997). The popularity of contemporary design continued to build during the early 2000s with more design galleries being opened, more design weeks and events being hosted, and more television programming focused on interior design makeover shows. During this period, many well-known manufacturers also began to reintroduce long-out-of-production "design classics" back into their catalogues. Certainly, the chair was now generally acknowledged to be the ultimate vehicle through which a designer could creatively express him or herself, while at the same time the Internet allowed a greater dissemination of ideas among the design community.

The increasing availability of advanced computer-aided design software and rapid-prototyping technologies also played a crucial role in the development of chairs for manufacture, both for the mainstream and the wealthy collector, as previously undreamt of forms could now be achieved using these new digital tools. At the same time "design-art" (a term coined by the auction rooms) blossomed, being spurred on by the feeding frenzy that was simultaneously taking place in the contemporary art market. Crucially, these exclusive batch-produced limited edition designs allowed their creators to explore innovative forms, materials and processes without the usual constraint of economic viability that by necessity dominates the mainstream furniture industry. The demand for this type of furniture led to an explosion of unfettered imaginative creativity that ultimately found its most notable expressions in the modern chair. Often design-art pieces would subsequently inform chair designs modified for the mass-market by the same designers, thereby democratising cutting edge design – much like haute couture's influence on high-street fast fashion. Other designers, most notably the Campana brothers (Humberto, 1953–, and Fernando, 1961–), revitalized the notion of hand-craftsmanship within the design-art arena with their incorporation of found objects, ranging from rough off cuts of wood to plush cuddly toys. The late Nineties and "designer Noughties" also saw the unassailable rise of contemporary Dutch design, with the Breda-based furniture manufacturing company Moooi focusing on the production of chairs that often used both low- and high-tech materials in a surprisingly innovative way, from Maarten Baas' (1978–) *Smoke* armchair (2002) to Bertjan Pot (1975–) & Marcel Wanders' (1963–) *Carbon* chair (2004). Today, the field of chair design continues to be a bubbling cauldron of innovation and creative energy, which each year erupts most spectacularly during the week of the Milan Furniture Fair, thus giving us yet more interesting, unusual and contesting interpretations of this most enigmatic of designed artefacts.

There is, however, another strand of modern chair

design that is often less celebrated and certainly over-looked by collectors: the contemporary office chair. Unlike seating designs for the domestic environment, the ubiquitous task chair is by necessity a product of large-scale industrial production and has always been more concerned with functional high performance than with surface aesthetics or provocative ideological statements. Although you may not find many office chairs in the pages of glossy design magazines, the reality is that for the furniture manufacturing industry, this is where the main financial action really is. The monetary rewards of creating a highly successful, best-selling office chair are huge, but so too are the associated development costs – a groundbreaking office chair can often take years of development and millions of dollars of R&D investment. Unlike the domestic chair, the design and development of such sophisticated seating tools are not the result of a single designer's creative inspiration but the work of a highly skilled team of industrial designers, design engineers, material scientists and ergonomists. Because increasingly stringent health and safety legislation is being perpetually introduced to the workplace, employers are constantly seeking better-performing and more ergonomically responsive office chairs for their staff, such as Studio 7.5's *Setu* office chairs (2009) and Yves Béhar (1967–) & Fuseproject's *SAYL* office chair (2010). It is this understanding of the link between design and health that drives the constant search for better-performing task chairs. Indeed, the need for refined ergonomic seating solutions has never been more crucial to human well-being, especially now that the average office worker sits at a desk for, on average, between 31 and 37 hours a week, with some workers clocking up a spine-bending 48 hours a week. Ultimately, the design of chairs intended for the office environment is closely linked to human health and happiness; the more ergonomically refined the chair, the better the physical condition of the sitter. However, as

the contract seating market has become more science and engineering-based, so the vast majority of designers have been excluded from this realm of activity, and it is therefore unsurprising that many have instead chosen to go down the path of personal creative expression and hands-on experimentation in their pursuit of the ultimate modern chair.

Today, the field of chair design still remains a thriving playground for new concepts and ideas, whether it is for the domestic interior or the office environment, just as it has been for over two hundred years. And just when it seems that every form, function and material has been fully exploited, another remarkable chair is born. And that is what makes the modern chair such a fascinating phenomenon – it is open to so many and varied interpretations, yet at its core it remains what it has always been: a place of restful solace for both the body and the soul.

1800s

Nicolai Abraham Abildgaard
Klismos chair, 1790–95

The architect and painter, Nicolai Abildgaard was one of the leading figures of Danish Neoclassicism in the late eighteenth century. His remarkable sabre-legged *Klismos* chair was not only an exquisite reworking of an ancient Greek model but with its pared down form this design was also an important precursor of the modern chair. Abildgaard designed two versions of the *Klismos* chair, a mahogany version with a painted frieze, that is believed to have been designed for his own apartment in the Royal Academy of Fine Arts, and the example shown here, which though structurally simpler has among the most beautifully balanced proportions of any chair ever made.

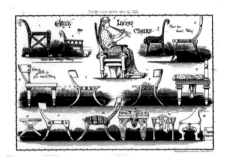

▼ *Klismos* chair, 1790–95
Mahogany, caning
Denmark

▲ Illustration by John Moyr Smith of ancient Greek furniture, *The Building News*, 1875

Gustav Friedrich Hetsch
Klismos chair, c.1840

▶ *Klismos* chair, c.1840
Walnut, textile-covered upholstery
Denmark

▼ Fashion plate showing model seated in a fashionable neo-classical chair, Ackermann's, 1823. As a style, Neoclassicism remained popular throughout the first half of the nineteenth century.

During the early years of the nineteenth century, Denmark enjoyed a glorious golden age of art and design. One of the most influential architects working in the then-fashionable Danish Empire style was Gustav Friedrich Hetsch, who had been born in Germany and educated in France. This Klismos-style chair executed after a design by him, exemplifies the simplified yet refined forms that became synonymous with Danish Biedermeier furniture of this period. Although a reworking of an ancient seating form and utilising traditional construction techniques, this chair presages the innate rationalism and functionalism of Modernism.

Dante Gabriel Rossetti & William Morris
Rossetti chair, c.1853–56

Looking like a medieval throne with its chamfered uprights and chevron motifs, the *Rossetti* chair (also known as the *Owl* chair) is a rare Pre-Raphaelite design. A pair of these high-backed chairs was designed for the bachelor "digs" that William Morris shared with Edward Burne-Jones in Red Lion Square, London. Originally the chairs' backs were decorated with scenes from Morris' poem "Sir Galahad: A Christmas Mystery" painted by Morris, Burne-Jones and their friend Dante Gabriel Rossetti. In this example, however, the painting has worn away over the intervening years to reveal the underlying plank-like structure.

◄ *Rossetti* chair, c.1853-56 ►
Deal, paint
England
(Images courtesy of Galerie Historismus)

▼ Self-portrait sketch by Edward Burne-Jones, 1857 – showing himself examining Rossetti's painting on the back of the *Rossetti* chair.

Michael Thonet
Model No. 10 rocking chair, 1866

Gebrüder Thonet manufactured its first rocking chair in 1860, however, within 12 months the firm was offering 52 different rocking chair models and over the succeeding years numerous variations of these designs were introduced. Many of Thonet's rocking chairs were highly elaborate constructions of swirling bentwood elements, however, it was one of Michael Thonet's simpler designs, the *Model No. 10*, that was the most commercially successful. This iconic rocking chair was produced from 1866 and spawned numerous imitations including versions produced by Fischel and J. & J. Kohn.

► *Model No. 10* rocking chair, 1866
Bentwood, caning
Gebrüder Thonet, Vienna, Austria

▼ Thonet catalogue page showing various rocking chair models (including the *Model No. 10*), 1870s

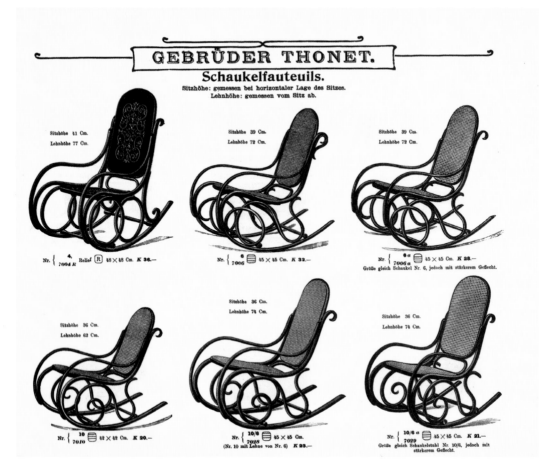

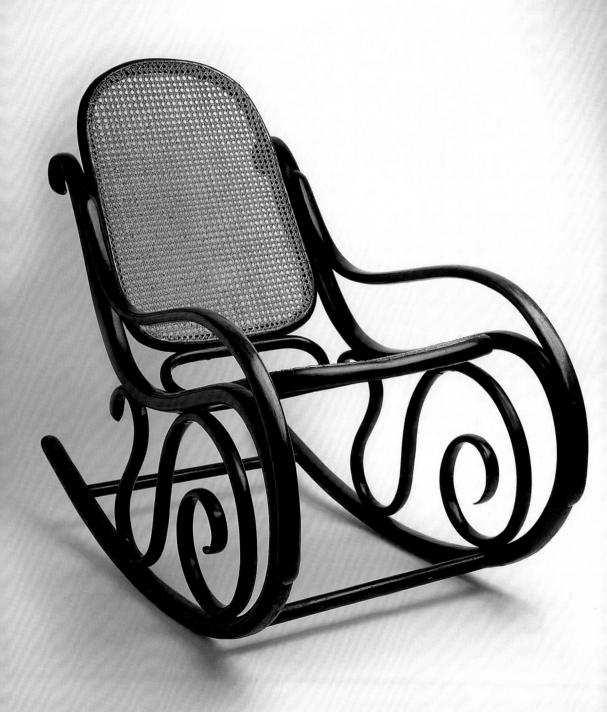

Charles Bevan
Armchair, 1860s

From the 1860s to 1880s, Charles Bevan was active as a furniture designer, producing Gothic Revival designs for his own London-based manufacturing company. He did, however, also design furnishings for the Leeds-based manufacturer, Marsh & Jones, including this robustly constructed armchair that epitomises the overt muscularity of secular Gothic Revival furniture from this period. This design also reflects the movement's reformist belief in truth to materials and revealed construction.

Armchair, 1860s
Oak, velvet-covered upholstery
Marsh & Jones, Leeds, England

Bruce Talbert (attrib)
Settle, c.1870

The design of this sturdy yet elegant oak settle is attributed to Bruce Talbert, who trained as a carver before becoming a leading Gothic Revival architect. In 1868 he published *Gothic Forms Applied to Furniture, Metal Work and Decoration for Domestic Purposes,* which he dedicated to the architect, George Edmund Street. He subsequently became one of the period's most celebrated professional decorators and also worked as a commercially successful designer for various furniture, textile, carpet and metalwork manufacturers. Robustly masculine, his "Geometric Gothic" work from the 1870s onwards can be seen as transitional in style in that it bridged Gothic Revivalism with the Aesthetic Movement.

Settle, c.1870
Oak
England

John Pollard Seddon
Chair, c.1862

A close associate of the Pre-Raphaelite Brotherhood and an intimate friend of the artist Dante Gabriel Rossetti, John Pollard Seddon trained as an architect and subsequently designed buildings as well as furniture, ceramics and tiles in the Gothic style. This chair is a good example of the robust muscularity of second phase Gothic Revivalism and was probably manufactured by the firm established by Seddon's grandfather, which supplied furniture to Buckingham Palace and Windsor Castle. This design was first displayed on the Morris, Marshall, Faulkner & Co. stand at the 1862 "London International Exhibition on Industry and Art" and subsequently a number of variations were produced including an ebonized version.

Chair, c.1862
Oak and leather brass
Thomas Seddon, London, England
(attrib.)

Christopher Dresser
Boreas chair, 1870

Regarded as the world's first industrial designer, Christopher Dresser ran a prolific London-based design studio that serviced a host of different companies producing "art manufactures". One of his most important clients was the Coalbrookdale iron foundry for which he created various designs, including this extraordinary high-backed chair made of cast-iron, which is embellished with stylized foliage decoration in the Aesthetic Movement style and a beautifully modelled roundel depicting Boreas, the Greek God of the North Wind as a child.

Boreas chair, 1870
Painted cast-iron, wood
Coalbrookdale Company,
Coalbrookdale, England

Leonard Wyburd
Thebes stool, 1884

The last quarter of the nineteenth century saw the rise of "Aestheticism" within the decorative arts, as designers looked to earlier foreign design precedents for inspiration. Needless to say, Ancient Egypt with its mystical associations was a rich source of inspiration and to this end, Arthur Liberty's famous London emporium manufactured a number of Egyptian inspired *Thebes* stools. Certainly the design of these four-legged stools was based on antique examples in the British Museum's collection, which were illustrated in *Building News* in 1875.

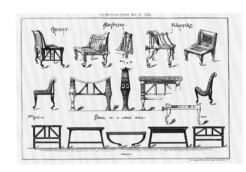

▲ Illustration by John Moyr Smoth of ancient Egyptian furniture, *The Building News*, 1875

◄ *Thebes* stool, 1884
Walnut
William Birch, High Wycombe, England (attrib.) for Liberty & Co., London, England

Ford Madox Brown
Sussex corner chair, c.1865

The Pre-Raphaelite painter, Ford Madox Brown was a founding partner of Morris, Marshall, Faulkner & Co. (est.1861) and designed various pieces of furniture and stained glass for "the Firm", including this corner chair. In accord with the prevailing Aesthetic Movement taste of ebonised furnishings, this design was part of the company's *Sussex* range of rush-seated chairs, which was inspired by earlier English vernacular antecedents.

Sussex corner seat, c.1865
Ebonized wood, rush
Morris, Marshall, Faulkner & Co. (later Morris & Co.), London, England

George Gardner
Side chair, c.1872

George Gardner of Brooklyn, New York, invented a new type of perforated three-ply veneer chair seat, which he patented on 21 May, 1872 and 3 June, 1873. Along with his brothers, he founded Gardner & Company in order to mass-produce various innovative chairs and benches incorporating his newly patented plywood seats, which were produced from a glued sandwich of thin wood veneers that were steamed under pressure in an innovative double-sided press before being dried. Operating from around 1870 until 1888, Gardner & Co. manufactured not only adult-sized chairs but also smaller ones for children and dolls.

◄ Side chair, c.1872
Wood, plywood
Gardner & Co., New York City and
Glen Gardner, New Jersey

▼ Patent for "Improvement of Chair Seats" filed by George Gardner, 1873 – this was one of many "improvements" that George Gardner patented for the manufacture of chair seats.

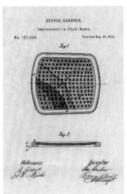

August Thonet
Model No.2 chair, c.1890

This elegant chair is a rare Thonet model that incorporates a frame made from strips of laminated wood, which would have been formed into the required shape using metal moulds, glue, heat and pressure. Unlike the majority of other designs manufactured by Thonet, this design not only employed perforated plywood for its seat but also for its back. The chair's graceful flowing lines are a result of the process used to produce it and as such it can be seen as an early example of "process-driven" design.

▲ Workers at a Thonet factory, probably in Vienna, c.1900

▶ *Model No. 2* chair, c.1890
Laminated wood, solid wood, perforated plywood
Gebrüder Thonet, Vienna, Austria

Christopher Dresser
Elephant chair, c.1880

Sometimes referred to as the *Elephant* chair, this unusual design by Christopher Dresser was intended to be used in a study and with its deeply incised zig-zag ornamentation and geometric form it reflected his interest in both Egyptian and Japanese art. Dresser also designed a number of other ebonized chairs, similarly eclectic in style, for the Art Furnishers' Alliance, a short-lived association of "art manufacturers" that he founded in 1880 in order to supply "whatever is necessary to the complete artistic furnishing of a house".

Elephant chair, c.1880
Ebonized wood
W. Booty of London (attrib.) for Art Furnishers' Alliance Co., London, England

Unattributed
Chair c.1880

Cox & Sons was a London-based ecclesiastical decorator, furniture maker and retailer located in Southampton Street, near Covent Garden. The firm commissioned various designs for furniture, ceramics, stained glass and metalwork from some of the leading designers of its day, most notably Bruce Talbert, John Moyr Smith and E.W. Godwin. With its carved and gilded Egyptian-inspired motifs, this chair reflects the popularity of historical revivalism during the last quarter of the nineteenth century.

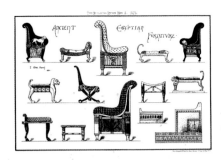

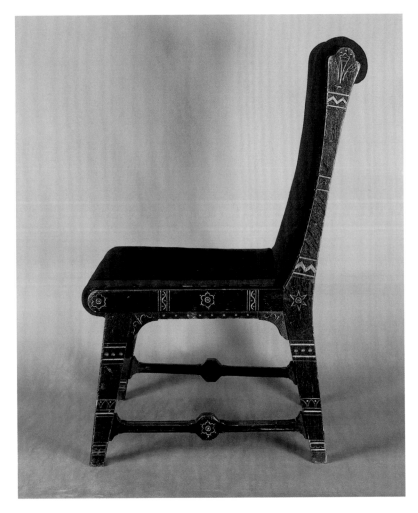

▲ Illustration by John Moyr Smith of ancient Egyptian furniture, *The Building News*, 1875

◄ Chair, c.1880
Ebonised wood, gilding
Cox & Sons, London, England

Christopher Dresser
Side chairs, c.1880

With their distinctive square-pierced backs, these side chairs designed by Christopher Dresser reflect the influence of Moorish decorative motifs, specifically the sun-filtering wooden lattice screens used in traditional Islamic architecture. Often fashionable Aesthetic Movement interiors were furnished with designs that drew inspiration from a whole host of "foreign" and seemingly exotic sources – and as such it is no surprise that Liberty & Co. also manufactured a range of furniture that incorporated similar Moorish style decoration.

Side chairs, c.1880
Ebonised mahogany, textile-covered upholstery
Chubb & Son for Art Furnishers' Alliance, London, England

Edward William Godwin
Jacobean armchair, c.1880

Apart from being influenced by Japanese and Greek historical design sources, E.W. Godwin was also interested in developing a national style and looked to Old English stylistic precedents, notably Gothic, Country Vernacular, Queen Anne, Jacobean and Georgian. One of his best-known designs, the *Jacobean* armchair was essentially a modern re-working of a traditional armchair format. Importantly, this design demonstrates that Godwin was not only concerned that his "Art Furniture" possess a harmonious beauty but also that it was practical and affordable. William Watt also manufactured an ebonized version of Godwin's *Jacobean* chair, which had a cane seat.

Jacobean armchair, c.1880
Oak, velvet-covered upholstery
Collier & Plucknett, Warwick,
England

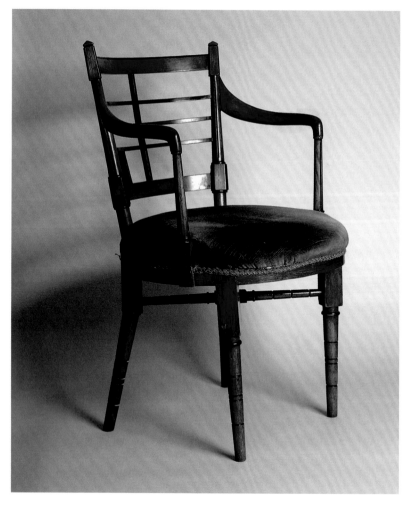

Edward William Godwin
Side chair, c.1878

E.W. Godwin described his approach to design as "judicious eclecticism". Influenced by Japanese and Chinese art, the simple motifs and bold composition of his Anglo-Japanese designs were not only inspired by his study of Hokusai Katsushika's woodblock prints but also by imported wares, such as those sold by Farmer & Rogers Oriental Warehouse. This elegant chair epitomises the refined elegance of his "Art Furniture" and was designed specifically for the 1878 Paris Exhibition.

◄ "Anglo-Japanese Furniture at Paris Exhibition by E.W. Godwin, Esq.", *The Building News*, 1878 – showing a variant of this side chair

▼ Side chair, c.1878
Ebonized wood
William Watt Artistic Furniture Warehouse, London, England

Giovanni Battista
Chiavari chair, c.1850

This type of chair was first made in the early nineteenth century in the coastal town of Chiavari, near the Port of Genova on the Italian Riviera and was originally used by fisherman. It is remarkable for being strong yet incredibly lightweight, it can literally be picked up with a single finger. The fine example, shown here, was however manufactured in Ravenna showing that this archetypal chair was also made on the eastern side of Italy as well. Interestingly, Gio Ponti was inspired by this type of generic *Chiavari* chair in the design of his well-known *Superleggera* chair from 1957.

▲ Manufacturer's label on the back of the chair

◄ *Chiavari* chair, c.1850
Cherry, cane
Gio. Battista, Ravenna, Italy

Fritz Hansen
Office chair, 1878

Fritz Hansen Snr. qualified as a journeyman cabinet-maker in his hometown of Nakskov, before moving to Copenhagen in 1872, where he registered himself as a master cabinet-maker and established a second-floor workshop. Initially specializing in lathe-turned wooden manufacturing components such as decorative table legs, balustrades and iron frames, the workshop eventually began producing its own furniture, including this simple yet stately Biedermeier style side chair. This example was used by Fritz Hansen as his own personal office chair and was the first model to be produced by the firm.

Office chair, 1878
Lacquered beech, hide-covered upholstery
Fritz Hansen, Copenhagen, Denmark

George Walton
Abingwood armchair, c.1898

Unlike George Walton's earlier Aesthetic Movement and Queen Anne style furnishings, which had an elegant historicizing refinement, his later *Abingwood* chair had a rustic presence and as such solidly predicted the increasing vernacularism of the Arts & Crafts Movement during the later Edwardian period. With its incised heart-shaped motif and traditional caquetoire form, the *Abingwood* chair was originally used in Walton's "Old English" style interior scheme for John Rowntree's Café in Scarborough and was later used in his interiors for Miss Cranston's Buchanan Street Tea Rooms in Glasgow.

Abingwood armchair, c.1898
Oak, rush
William Birch Ltd., High Wycombe, England

Charles Rennie Mackintosh
Armchair for the Argyle Street Tea Rooms, 1897

This armchair with its beautiful sweeping arm-rails that embrace the sitter was site-specifically designed for the smoking room and billiard room of the Argyle Street Tea Rooms in Glasgow. For this refurbishment project George Walton was responsible for the wall decorations, while Charles Rennie Mackintosh was commissioned to design all the furniture, which was solidly constructed in stained oak. While the resulting interiors had a homely feel, the furniture itself with its stripped down vernacularism was actually extremely progressive.

Armchair for the Argyle Street Tea Rooms, 1897
Stained oak
Scotland

Bernhard Pankok
Armchair, c.1898

A talented artist, graphic designer and furniture designer, Bernhard Pankok was one of the founders of Vereinigten Werkstätten für Kunst im Handwerk (United Workshop for Arts in Crafts) in 1897. The following year he designed this beautiful Jugendstil armchair, which was executed by this design-reforming Munich-based workshop. With its melting forms and vegetal motifs, this chair reflects the New Art Movement's desire for a greater aesthetic refinement in designs for everyday use.

Armchair, c.1898
Mahogany, textile-covered
upholstery
Vereinigte Werkstätten,
Munich, Germany
(fabric by Scherrebeker
Gobelinwirkerei)

Hector Guimard
Settee, c.1898

With its asymmetrical form, looping back and vine-like arm rail, this settee captures the organic essence of nature in its beautifully carved mahogany frame. Certainly it must have appeared strikingly innovative when it was first produced in the late nineteenth century, after decades of historical revivalism within the decorative arts. Instead, it exemplified a new direction in design with its rejection of previous period styles in favour of exaggerated whiplash lines and vegetal forms, and as such beautifully embodies the French Art Nouveau style.

Settee, c.1898
Mahogany, leather-covered
upholstery
France

Paul Hankar
Chair, c.1897

Alongside Henry van de Velde and Victor Horta, Paul Hankar is considered to be one of the greatest proponents of the Art Nouveau style in Belgium. His architecture and furniture designs were characterised by the use of sculptural forms and elemental constructions. This chair with its arching base and riveted leather straps also reveals not only the influence of the British Arts & Crafts Movement but also that of Japanese Art.

◄ Chair, c.1897
Hungarian oak, leather, metal
Brussels, Belgium
(Image courtesy of Galerie Historismus)

▼ Lithograph from "Maitres de L'Affiches" series by Paul Crespin, 1897, showing Paul Hankar at work in his studio.

Thorvald Bindesbøll
Chair for the Ny Carlsberg Glyptotek, 1898

In Denmark, Thorvald Bindesbøll was the leading practitioner of the Art Nouveau style and his idiosyncratic designs were hugely influential on the next generation of Danish designers, including Johan Rohde. Bindesbøll's chair, shown here, was designed site-specifically for the Ny Carlsberg Glyptotek, a sumptuous art gallery in Copenhagen funded by brewery profits. This design not only reflects the continuing influence of Neo-Classicism, especially Greek examples, in Scandinavian design throughout the nineteenth century, but with its unadorned surfaces also predicted the uncluttered lines of Danish Modernism.

Chair for the Ny Carlsberg Glyptotek, 1898
Mahogany, leather-covered cushion
Denmark

Louis Majorelle
Tulip armchair, 1898–99

▲ "Salle Charpentier" – a dining room designed by Alexandre Charpentier for Adrien Bénard's house in Champrosay, 1900-1901, incorporating Louis Majorelle's *Tulip* armchair

◀ *Tulip* armchair, 1898-99
Fruitwoods, velvet-covered upholstery
Louis Majorelle, Nancy, France

This beautiful armchair designed by Louis Majorelle reveals the superlative craftsmanship of the French workshops during the *fin-de-siécle* period. The side elements of this design are adorned with a pattern of stylized tulips exquisitely rendered in marquentry with a similarly floral motif being echoed in the sumptuous velvet upholstery. The armchair was incorporated into an incredible Art Nouveau dining room with oak and mahogany panelling designed by the sculptor, Alexandre Charpentier (1856–1909). This room with its elegant furnishings, including the *Tulip* fauteuil, epitomised the highly stylized organicism of the New Art movement and has since been reconstructed at the Musée d'Orsay.

1900s

Gustave Serrurier-Bovy
Armchair, 1905 & Armchair, c.1903

More than any other Belgian *fin-de-siècle* designer, Gustave Serrurier-Bovy was influenced by the British Arts & Crafts Movement's espousal of vernacularism. His armchair of 1905 reflects this with its use of oak and traditional forms, however, the proportions and motifs used have an aspect of distortion that give it a very distinctive Art Nouveau feeling. Similarly his high-backed mahogany armchair is based on a traditional chair type, yet with its sweeping lines it also exemplifies the sensual and exaggerated forms synonymous with the New Art Movement.

◄ Armchair, 1905
Oak, leather-covered
upholstery
Serrurier et Cie, Paris, France &
Brussels, Belgium
(Image courtesy of Galerie
Historismus)

► Armchair, c.1903
Mahogany, upholstery
Serrurier et Cie, Paris, France &
Brussels, Belgium
(Images courtesy of Galerie
Historismus)

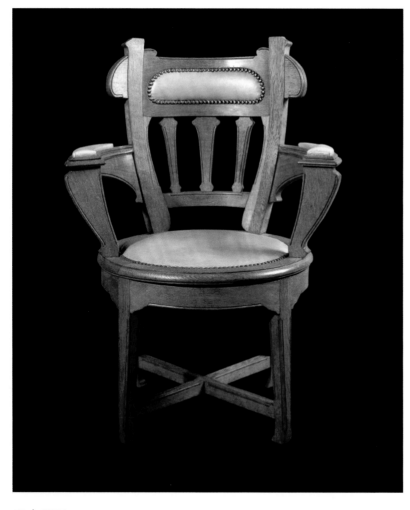

Gustave Serrurier-Bovy
Silex armchair, 1904–05

◄► *Silex* armchair, 1904–05
Poplar, painted iron
Serrurier et Cie, Paris, France &
Brussels, Belgium
(Images courtesy of Galerie
Historismus)

▼ *Silex* chair, 1904–05
Poplar, metal
Serrurier et Cie, Paris, France &
Brussels, Belgium
(Image courtesy of Galerie
Historismus)

In 1904 Gustave Serrurier-Bovy created a range of furniture for the bathroom of Château de la Cheyrelle in Dienne, which had been previously designed by his colleague, René Dulong for the Parisian banker, Pierre Felgères. This furniture made in inexpensive poplar wood was subsequently put into mass-production in 1905 and retailed as the *Silex* range. Intended to furnish the bedrooms of servants and children, this armchair and side chair, alongside the other matching designs, were inexpensive and unashamedly utilitarian.

Henry van de Velde
Chair, c.1902 & Chair, c.1903

Henry van de Velde's contribution to the development of Modern design is often undervalued, however, he was one of the most influential design-reforming figures in the early years of the twentieth century. His designs, such as the elegant side chairs shown here, had a distinctive stripped down, elemental quality when compared to the work of other furniture designers working in this period. As he noted, "ornament has no life of its own but depends on the forms and lines of the object itself, from which it receives its proper organic place." ("Was ich Will", 1901)

◄ **Chair c.1902**
Wood, textile-covered upholstery
Belgium
(Image courtesy of Galerie Historismus)

▼► **Chair, c.1903**
Mahogany, textile-covered upholstery
Belgium
(Images courtesy of Galerie Historismus, Brussels)

Henry van de Velde
Armchair 1902 & Armchair, c.1902

Born in Antwerp, Henry van de Velde was a formidable designer and influential teacher, who with his fellow countrymen Victor Horta, is widely regarded as one of the founding fathers of the Art Nouveau style. Importantly, van de Velde brought the design-reforming ideals he had formulated in Belgium to Germany, when he moved to Berlin in 1901. These chair designs reflect his desire "to replace the old symbolic elements, which have lost their effectiveness for us today, with a new, imperishable beauty..." and as such heralded the emergence of the Modern Movement.

Richard Riemerschmid
Armchair, c.1902

Richard Riemerschmid designed many chairs during his prolific career and this example is not only one of the rarest, but also one of the most beautiful with its warm-toned mahogany skillfully carved into seductively curved yet dynamic forms that are stripped of all extraneous decoration. Like other more utilitarian seating designs by Riemerschmid, this design incorporates his trademark pierced inverted-heart-shaped grip.

Armchair, c.1902
Mahogany, textile-covered upholstery
Germany
(Image courtesy of Galerie Historismus)

Peter Behrens
Armchair, 1902

This armchair designed by Peter Behrens is constructionally similar to his better-known dining chair which formed part of a suite of furniture displayed at the Berlin department store, A. Wertheim in 1902. This armed version, however, is a less utilitarian design and is also, in some ways, more formally progressive, having less decorative detailing and a more rectilinear aspect with its flat planes of polished honey-coloured wood.

Armchair, 1902
Wood, fabric-covered upholstery
Anton Blüggel, Berlin, Germany
(Images courtesy of Galerie
Historismus)

Peter Behrens
Chair for the Restaurant Jungbrunnen, 1904

This simple slatted chair was designed for the Restaurant Jungbrunnen (Fountain of Youth Restaurant), a teetotal establishment that was created for the 1904 "Internationale Kunst und Gartenbau Ausstellung" (International Art & Horticulture Exhibition) held in Düsseldorf. Around this time, Behrens who had a drink problem was going through a period of abstinence and was spearheading a temperance campaign so it is fitting that he was involved in the interior design of this socially reforming venture. The chair, shown here, is the only known surviving example of its kind.

Chair for the Restaurant
Jungbrunnen, 1904
Painted beech
Germany
(Image courtesy of Galerie
Historismus)

Gustave Serrurier-Bovy
Side chair, c.1900

After studying in Liège, Gustave Serrurier-Bovy became so interested in the work of the British designer and theorist, William Morris and the English Arts & Crafts Movement as a whole that he moved to London, where he worked as an interior designer. In 1884 he returned to Belgium and became a founding member of the "Salon de l'Esthétique" and the same year established his own shop in Liège. Apart from his British-style furniture designs, he also created some "jointed furniture" pieces, such as the chair shown here, which were innovatively based on a modular system, the elements of which could be assembled relatively easily and cheaply.

Side chair, c.1900
Oak, rush
Gustave Serrurier-Bovy, Liège, Belgium

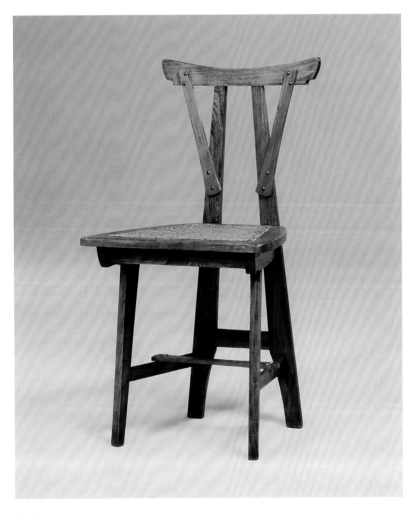

Bernard Pankok
Armchair for Haus Lange, 1901

The son of a cabinetmaker, Benhard Pankok was highly influenced by the British Arts & Crafts Movement and his designs reflected this in their rustic simplicity. This unusual vernacular-style armchair was designed specifically for the interior scheme of his first architectural commission, the home of the art historian, Professor Konrad Lange in Tübingen (1901–02). The house and its furnishings were notable for their elegance and purity and, like other works by Pankok, helped to lay the foundations for the later emergence of German Modernism.

Armchair for Haus Lange, 1901
Oak, rush
Vereinigte Werkstätten, Munich

Harvey Ellis (attrib.)
Settle, c.1903

Based on an earlier design by British architect, Mackay Hugh Baillie-Scott (published 1901), this settle with its beautiful inlaid decoration has generally been attributed to Harvey Ellis who briefly worked for Gustav Stickley from May 1903 until his untimely death the following year. Recent research by David Cathers, however, suggests that this design might have been executed by LaMont A. Warner, whose drawing of a child-sized version of this model was published in the *The Craftsman* journal in June 1903, thereby predating Ellis' first illustrations of this settle by a couple of months.

Settle, c.1903
Stained oak, copper, pewter, exotic wood
Gustav Stickley's Craftsman Workshops, Eastwood & New York, USA

Gustav Stickley
Model No. 332 armchair, c.1908

Originally retailed at $33.00, Gustav Stickley's *Model No. 332* chair epitomises the no-nonsense robustness of Mission style furnishings. Often this type of reclining chair is referred to as a "Morris Chair", in reference to a chair with an adjustable back previously designed by Philip Webb for Morris & Co. However, Stickley's design with its broad slatted construction has none of the refinement of its antecedent, rather it has a charming simplicity that harks back to America's backwoods pioneer era.

▲ Interior scheme designed by
Gustav Stickley, *The Craftsman*,
c.1905

► *Model No. 332* "Morris" reclining
chair, c.1908
Stained oak, cushion
Gustav Stickley's Craftsman
Workshops, Eastwood & New
York, USA

Charles Rennie Mackintosh
Chair for Hous'hill, 1903

In around 1903 the tearoom proprietress, Catherine Cranston and her husband, Major John Cochrane commissioned Charles Rennie Mackintosh to redesign the interiors of their home, Hous'hill. The resulting series of rooms were equipped with specially designed furniture, including this latticed-backed chair for the "white bedroom". This seating design was inspired by Japanese art and marked a transition in Mackintosh's oeuvre from the stylized organicism of his earlier furniture to more rigidly geometric forms.

Chair for Hous'hill, 1903
Stained oak, fabric-covered upholstery
Scotland

Thomas Lee
Westport chairs, 1903

Known as the *Westport* chair, this unusual design was created by Thomas Lee in 1903 for his summer cottage in Westport, New York. Christened "Uncle Tom's chair" by his family, this outdoor porch chair was made of knot-free hemlock wood. The unusually deep angles of the seat and back were set in such a way so as to provide the maximum amount of comfort. Lee's friend Harry Bunnell, whose company manufactured this famous design until c.1930, patented it in 1905. With its wide board arms and slanted construction, the ubiquitous *Westport*-style chair remains an icon of American living.

▲ Patent drawing of *Westport* chair, 1905, shown with cushions and footrest element

► *Westport* chairs, 1903
Hemlock
H.C. Bunnell, Westport (NY), USA

Adolf Loos
Knieschwimmer armchair, c.1906

Although best remembered for his *Ornament and Crime* manifesto of 1908, the architect and design theorist Adolf Loos also wrote favourably about the relaxed approach to sitting found in Britain in his publication, *Das Sitzmöbel* (1898), and how in English homes different kinds of chairs could be found in one room. Unsurprisingly his *Knieschwimmer* armchair was directly inspired by the comfortable button-upholstered "club chairs" that were so popular in America and Britain during the late nineteenth century. His lounge chair's unusual low-slung *bateau* design was also meant to assist rest and he incorporated this chair into a number of his interior schemes.

Knieschwimmer armchair, c.1906
Oak, hardwood, buttoned velvet-covered upholstery,
Friedrich Otto Schmidt, Vienna, Austria

Carlo Bugatti
Hall chair, 1900

Having trained at the Brera Academy of Fine Arts in Milan, Carlo Bugatti became one of the greatest exponents of Art Nouveau design in Italy. His sumptuous furniture is unmistakable with its intricate inlays, Moorish and Oriental references, and use of hammered metal and parchment elements. This hall chair with its extraordinary inlaid roundel-like motifs reflects Bugatti's remarkable ability to create a strong sense of opulence through a sensitive handling of different materials and a truly imaginative understanding of form.

Hall chair, 1900
Walnut copper, bone, yellow metal, ebonized wood, with brass
Carlo Bugatti, Milan, Italy

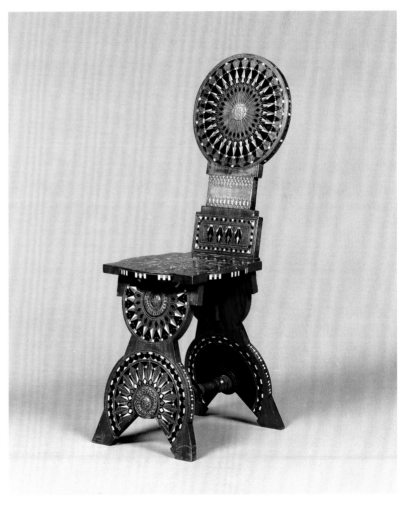

Unattributed
Model No. 9 armchair, c.1904

Although this armchair with its sweeping arms was designed in around 1904, the model did not become widely popular until some twenty years later when it was deemed to be a proto-modern masterpiece and included by Le Corbusier in many of his projects, including his seminal "Pavilion de l'Esprit Nouveau" at the "Exposition Internationale des Arts Décoratifs" in 1925 and also in his installation at the Weissenhof Siedlung in Stuttgart in 1927. Le Corbusier paid tribute to this design, which comprises only seven structural elements, stating: "this chair has nobility."

▲ Page from a J.&J. Kohn catalogue featuring a very similar model to that of Thonet's *Model No.* 9 armchair, c.1910

◄ *Model No.* 9 armchair, c.1904
Bent solid beechwood, solid wood, cane
Gebrüder Thonet, Vienna, Austria

Josef Hoffmann
Armchair, 1905

One of the first designers to introduce painted furniture into the modern interior was the Glaswegian architect, Charles Rennie Mackintosh. As a great friend of Mackintosh's, it is unsurprising the Austrian designer and architect, Josef Hoffmann also designed a number of painted chairs, including the model shown here. This design is notable for its boldly geometric, pared-down construction and lack of superfluous decoration, which can be seen to presage the reductivist tendency of later designers associated with the Modern Movement.

Armchair, 1905
Painted pine
Wiener Werkstätte, Vienna, Austria
(Images courtesy of Galerie Historismus)

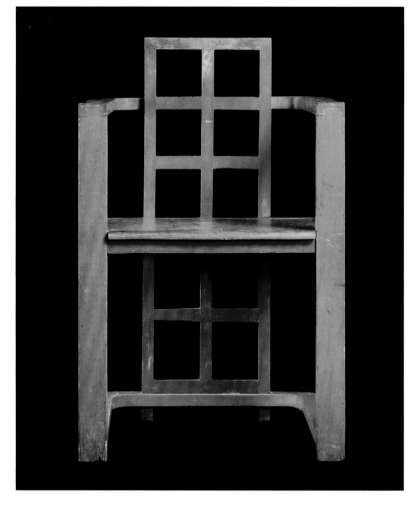

René Dulong
Armchair, 1903–04

The French architect, René Dulong and the Belgian designer, Gustave Serrurier-Bovy collaborated on a number of projects including the design of the Pavillon Bleu, a luxury restaurant at the 1900 "Exposition Universelle" that was a splendidly exuberant Art Nouveau masterpiece. Together they also founded Serrurier et Cie in 1903, which retailed their progressive designs. This proto-Modernist armchair designed by Dulong for his own private drawing room can be considered remarkably forward-looking with its highly simplified geometric construction.

Armchair, 1903–04
Ebonized wood
Serrurier et Cie, Paris, France & Brussels, Belgium
(Images courtesy of Galerie Historismus)

Richard Riemerschmid
Armchair, c.1900

The great Jugendstil architect and city planner, Richard Riemerschmid was one of the earliest pioneers of Modern design in Germany. In 1907 he became a founding member of the Deutscher Werkbund, however, even before this, his work – such as this beautiful yet reductivist armchair – can be seen as a three-dimensional realization of his design-reforming principles. With its wedge-shaped seat, body embracing arm-rail and useful C-shaped handhold, this design reflects the desire for functional forms stripped of superfluous ornament.

Armchair, c.1900
Stained oak
Fleischhauers Söhne, Nuremberg, Germany
(small image: courtesy of Galerie Historismus)

Otto Wagner
Model No. 721 armchair, c.1902

This bentwood armchair was designed by Otto Wagner and was essentially a variation of models he created specifically for two of his most famous Viennese architectural commissions: the proto-Modernist *Die Zeit* newspaper's telegraph office of 1902 and the monumental Österriche Postsparkasse (Austrian Post Office Savings Bank) of 1905–06. Like so many designs manufactured by Jacob & Josef Kohn, this chair possesses a striking modernity due to its pared-down form and absence of ornamentation. Probably intended for office usage rather than for a domestic environment, this functional chair corresponded with Wagner's belief that "Something impractical cannot be beautiful."

▲ Exterior of the Österriche
Postparkasse in Vienna designed
by Otto Wagner, 1905-06

► *Model No. 721* armchair, c.1902
Stained beech, plywood
J & J Kohn, Vienna, Austria

Wilhelm Schmidt
Armchair, 1901 & Armchair, 1902–03

◄ **Armchair, 1901**
Oak, caning, brass
Prag-Rudniker Korbwaren-
Fabrikation, Vienna, Austria

► **Armchair, 1902–03**
Oak, caning
Prag-Rudniker Korbwaren-
Fabrikation, Vienna, Austria

During its heyday from around 1900 until about 1914, Prag-Rudniker was a leading basketry and furniture manufacturer with a retail outlet on the bustling Mariahilferstrasse, Vienna's most important shopping street. Throughout this period, the company commissioned progressive furniture designs – including these delightful cane and oak armchairs – from the leading Austrian architects of the day, most notably Wilhelm Schmidt, Josef Zotti, Hans Vollmer and Koloman Moser.

Wilhelm Schmidt
Model No. 507 armchair, c.1900–05

The Viennese furniture designer, Wilhelm Schmidt created
this beautiful Secessionist chair for Prag-Rudniker
Korbwarenfabrikation, a leading manufacturer of wickerwork
that produced a number of extremely forward-looking seating
designs, including some by Josef Hoffmann and Koloman
Moser. This chair with its strong geometric form predicts
the starkly elemental designs of later Modernist design
movements, most notably De Stijl and the Bauhaus.

▲ Oak and rattan side chair
designed by Wilhelm Schmidt
for Prag-Rudniker Korbwaren-
Fabrikation, c.1905-10 - similarly
constructed to the *Model No. 507*
armchair

◄ *Model No. 507* armchair,
c.1900–05
Oak, woven cord, metal
Prag-Rudniker Korbwaren-
Fabrikation, Vienna, Austria

Charles Francis Annesley Voysey
Armchair for The Homestead, c.1905-07

This high-backed armchair was originally created for the parlour of The Homestead, a residence in Frinton-on-Sea (Essex, England) designed by the British architect Charles Voysey for Mr. A.C. Turner. Although this Arts & Crafts design has a simple slatted construction, Voysey managed to imbue it with a strong aesthetic presence through his skillful attention to detail, such as the gentle tapering of the back section and the carefully angled struts of the supporting frame.

▲ Early photograph of the interior of The Homestead, showing the armchairs in situ.

► Armchair for The Homestead, c.1905-07
Oak
England
(Image courtesy of Galerie Historismus)

Jacques Gruber
Armchairs, c.1903

After studying at the École des Beaux-Arts in Nancy and frequenting the studio of the French Symbolist painter, Gustave Moreau in Paris, Jacques Gruber returned to Nancy where he taught at his alma mater, whilst also designing vases for Daum and furniture for Majorelle. He subsequently established his own design studio specializing mainly in stained glass and furniture. These armchairs with their stylized Art Nouveau foliate motifs and almost melting organic form epitomise the output of the École de Nancy, a design-reforming alliance of like-minded designers and architects that Gruber helped to establish in 1901.

Armchairs, c.1903
Carved mahogany, leather-covered upholstery, brass
Louis Majorelle, Nancy, France

Louis Majorelle
Clématites side chairs, c.1900

With their carved and incised decoration of stylized climbing clematis, these exquisite side chairs reflect the Art Nouveau style's obsession with vegetal forms that were suitably un-historicizing for this "New Art" movement. These beautifully crafted chairs with their lace-like delicacy also reveal the extraordinary level of skill found in the Louis Majorelle's workshops, which became synonymous with the École de Nancy.

Clématites side chairs, c.1900
Walnut, textile-covered
upholstery
Louis Majorelle, Nancy, France

Frank Lloyd Wright
Slipper chair for the William E. Martin House, c.1902 & Chair, c.1902

With their strict geometric formalism, these two chairs designed by Frank Lloyd Wright in c.1902 were remarkably forward-looking for their day. Although stripped of any superfluous ornament, these practical seating solutions were "Modern" rather than "Modernist" and echoed the lines of the architectural settings for which they were intended. As Frank Lloyd Wright noted, "Form follows function – that has been misunderstood. Form and function should be one, joined in a spiritual union". These chairs are testament to this belief.

▲ Early photograph of William E. Martin House in Oak Park, Illinois

► Chair, c.1902
Oak, leather-cover upholstery
USA (J.E. Ward & Son label)

◄ *Slipper* chair for the William E. Martin House, c.1902
Oak, textile-covered upholstery
USA

Georges de Feure
Salon suite, c.1900

Georges de Feure (born, Georges van Sluÿters) initially studied
at Rijkscademie voor Beeldende Kunsten, Amsterdam, but
after becoming influenced by the work of the French Symbolist
painter, Pierre Puvis de Chavannes, he moved to Paris in 1890,
where he became a pupil of Jules Chéret. Later, he worked
for Samuel Bing, whose "L'Art Nouveau" gallery was the most
influential showcase for the New Art Movement. With its
crisply carved curvilinear and floral motifs, this salon suite
is typical of de Feure's exquisite mastery of form and with its
swelling lines reflects the very graphic nature of his work.

Salon suite, c.1900
Fruitwood, bronze, silk-covered
upholstery
France

Eliel Saarinen
Desk chair, 1901–02

The father of Eero Saarinen and the first director of the
Cranbrook Academy of Arts, Eliel Saarinen was also an
accomplished architect and designer whose work mirrored
the latest developments within these fields. At the turn
of the century, he was a leading exponent of National
Romanticism in Finland, and this desk chair with its muscular
slab-like construction reflects through its vernacularism the
movement's overwhelming desire to find an authentic national
style derived from its indigenous cultural roots.

Desk chair, 1901–02
Solid and laminated oak, leather-
covered upholstery
Executed by John Ericsson,
Helsinki, Finland

Eliel Saarinen
Chair for the State Railway Adminstration Offices, 1908–09

Just seven years after Eliel Saarinen had graduated as an architect from the University of Helsinki, he was awarded first prize in the competition to design the central railway station in Helsinki. His resulting design with its bold massing and striking neo-romantic detailing established him as a major architectural force. As part of this prestigious commission, Saarinen also designed this oak elbow chair with its distinctive horseshoe-shape back rail and perforated heart motifs. Only 14 examples of this "New Art" chair were made.

▲ Helsinki Railway Station
designed by Eliel Saarinen, 1906

► Chair for the State Railway
Administration Offices, 1908–09
Oak, oak-faced laminate
Finland

Charles Sumner Greene & Henry Mather Greene
Hall chair for the Dr. William T. Bolton House, 1906

Hall chair for the Dr. William T. Bolton House, 1906
Mahogany, ebony
Peter and John Hall Workshops,
Pasadena (CA), USA

Greene & Greene were commissioned to design a second residence by Dr. William T. Bolton, however he died before the project was completed. The house was subsequently rented to Mrs. Belle Barlow Bush who asked the brothers to design most of the remaining furniture. The dramatic proportions of this mahogany high-backed chair with its square ebony pegs and tapering slats was designed specifically for the hallway of this *Gesamtkunstwerk* (total work of art) residential project.

Charles Rohlfs
Armchairs, c.1905–08

More simplified than other furniture designs by Charles
Rohlfs, these Mission-style armchairs made of solid oak have
a stripped down elemental quality yet still retain an intrinsic
elegance with their beautiful pegged detailing and gentle
tapering planes. Epitomising the tendency for unadorned
forms found in design during the late Arts & Crafts period,
these chairs can be seen to predict the constructional
reductivism of the Modern Movement in the 1920s and 1930s.

Armchairs, c.1905–08
Oak
Charles Rohlfs' Workshop, Buffalo
(NY), USA

Victor Horta
Side chair, c.1901

The greatest proponent of the Belgian Art Nouveau style, Victor Horta's architecture was a radical departure on anything that had gone before, with its sinuous structural elements and oozing vegetal forms. His furniture was similarly remarkable, and was often conceived as part of an overall *Gesamtkunstwerk* (total work of art) scheme. For example, this side chair was reputedly designed specifically for the Hotel Sôlvay, a large town house on the Avenue Louise in Brussels and certainly with its attenuated back and crest-shaped rail echoes the architecture of this elegant private residence.

Side chair, c.1901
Mahogany, textile-covered upholstery
Belgium

Louis Majorelle
Aux Nénuphars desk chair, c.1900

A master of sculptural form, Louis Majorelle was one of the great exponents of the Art Nouveau style. Through his productive workshop, he continued the long tradition of French cabinetmaking and superlative craftsmanship in order to produce exquisite furnishings such as this desk chair with its sinuous lines and its floral ormulu mounts that almost have a melting quality that is further emphasised by the curious armrails that swoop downwards to connect with the base of the chair's back legs.

Aux Nénuphars desk chair, c.1900
Mahogany, ormolu, leather-covered upholstery
Louis Majorelle, Nancy, France

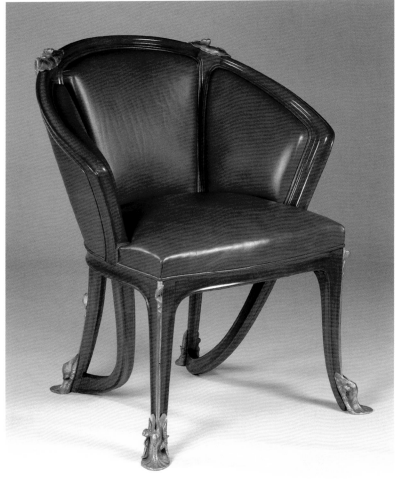

Adolf Loos
Stössler armchair, c.1900

The Viennese architect and theoretician, Adolf Loos famously wrote a manifesto entitled "Ornament and Crime" (1908) in which he expounded his utter rejection of the decorative excesses of the Art Nouveau style. As an early three-dimensional realization of his functionalist credo, this chair was designed as part of a dining suite for Eugen Stössler's apartment in Vienna. Any detail on this chair, whether it is the brass sabots or the contoured seat-pan, is informed utterly by its function.

Stössler armchair, c.1900
Walnut, brass, leather-covered upholstery
Friedrich Otto Schmidt, Vienna, Austria

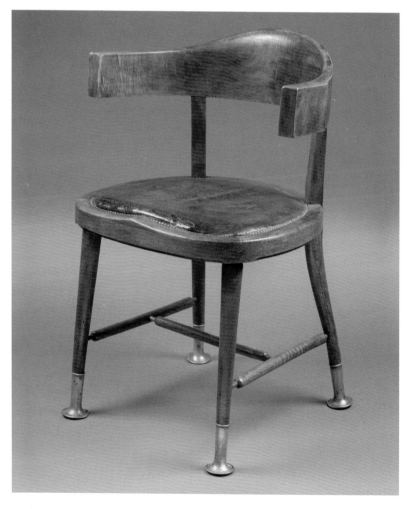

Josef Hoffman
Model No. 670 Sitzmaschine reclining chair, c.1908

The *Sitzmaschine* or "Sitting Machine" was a reworking of an adjustable chair made popular by Morris & Co., hence the reason why this type of seating is sometimes known as a "Morris Chair". With its stripped down geometric form, however, this design also predicted the practical functionalism that became a guiding principle of Modernism in the following decades. The *Sitzmaschine*, shown here, is one of the finest examples known to exist, because it retains its original horsehair-filled cushions covered in a textile designed by Hoffmann and manufactured by Johann Backhausen & Söhne in Vienna.

Model No.670 Sitzmaschine reclining chair, c.1908
Stained laminated wood, solid beech, brass, textile-covered horsehair cushions
J. & J. Kohn, Vienna, Austria

Josef Hoffmann
Fledermaus chair, 1905 & Side chair, c.1905–07

◄ *Fledermaus* chair, 1905
Stained beech bentwood, fabric-
covered upholstery
J. & J. Kohn, Vienna, Austria

► Side chair, c.1905–07
Stained beech bentwood, fabric-
covered upholstery
J. & J. Kohn, Vienna, Austria

When it was originally designed for the Cabaret Fledermaus in Vienna, this geometric chair was painted black and white. It reveals the influence of the work of Charles Rennie Mackintosh, who was a good friend of Hoffmann's, with its strong vertical and horizontal elements. Hoffmann also designed the elegant bentwood chair, shown below, that incorporates the distinctive ball-like ornament that was frequently found in other Hoffmann-designed furniture pieces. With its unusual sled-base and its continuous back, seat and leg element, it reveals a desire for constructional simplicity. This beautiful example still retains its original upholstered seat, covered in a textile also designed by Josef Hoffmann for Johann Backhausen & Söhne.

1910s

Otto Wagner
Hall chair, 1912

This simply constructed pale grey chair was originally used to furnish the entrance hall of Otto Wagner's own apartment in Vienna. Although to contemporary eyes it may seem a relatively unremarkable design, when it was first produced it would have appeared aesthetically shocking with its lack of superfluous decoration and plain lacquered finish. As a quintessential Secessionist seating design by one of its greatest architects, this chair predicted the Modern Movement's adoption of stripped down Functionalism during the following decade.

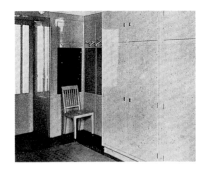

▲ Entrance hall of Otto Wagner's apartment in Vienna, c.1912

◄ Hall chair, 1912
Lacquered wood, cane, brass
Vienna, Austria

Henry van de Velde
Armchair, 1910

Although Henry van de Velde's earlier furniture often utilized oozing and abstracted organic forms, by 1910 – the year this white painted armchair was designed – the architect's work was marked by an increasing utilitarianism that predicted the rationalism of the Modern Movement. For his own apartment in Weimar, he had previously designed a simple reclining "steamer" chair (1903-04) that had a cream lacquered finish, which suggests his increasing desire during this period for less fussy and more airy Modern style interiors.

Armchair, 1910
Painted wood
Germany
(Image courtesy of Galerie Historismus)

Gerrit Rietveld
Hogestoel (Highback chair), 1919

Gerrit Rietveld's *Hogestoel* (Highback chair) was reputedly exhibited at the landmark "Staatliches Bauhaus Ausstellung" (National Bauhaus Exhibition) held in Weimar in 1923, however, there is some controversy surrounding this matter. Certainly Rietveld's armchair can be seen to share many attributes with Marcel Breuer's later *Lattenstuhl* armchair (1922) with its strong geometric formalism and use of simple planes of wood, and because of this there is some debate about who influenced whom.

Hogestoel (Highback chair), 1919
Stained and painted beech
G. van de Groeneken, De Bilt,
Netherlands
(Images courtesy of Galerie
Historismus)

Antonio Volpe
Model No. 267 rocking chair, c.1915

The Italian furniture manufacturing company, Societé Anonima Antonio Volpe was established in 1882 and by the 1910s was producing a number of innovative bentwood designs, including this unusual rocking chair – which was for many years misattributed to Josef Hoffmann. This visually dynamic design is sometimes referred to as the "Egg" because of its distinctive oval elements made from two continuous loops of bentwood that form the rocking support as well as the armrests of the chair. This rare version also incorporates a hinged footrest.

Model No. 267 rocking chair, c.1915
Bentwood, cane
Societé Anonima Antonio Volpe,
Udine, Italy

Armand Albert Rateau
Armchair, 1919–20

This exquisite design inspired by ancient curcule chairs was originally designed as a poolside chair for the Manhattan town house of George and Florence Blumenthal, who were friends and clients of Armand Albert Rateau. The seat and back of this extraordinary fauteuil are made up of numerous stylized fish made of cast bronze that are linked together to form a sculptural sling-like structure. The articulated armrests are also similarly constructed with chains of bronze scallop shells.

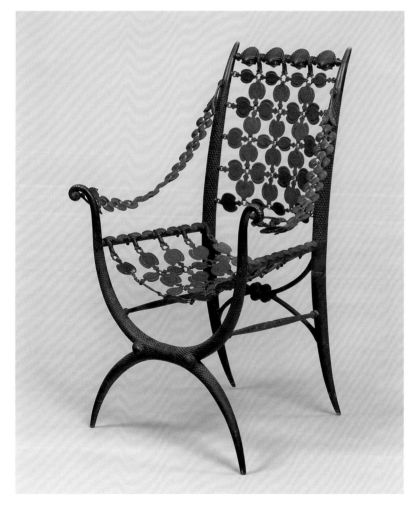

▲ Room installation of Armand Albert Rateau's designs exhibited at the Metropolitan Museum of Art, New York, 1926.

◄ Armchair, 1919–20
Cast bronze
Armand Albert Rateau, Paris, France

Hector Guimard
Side chair, 1912

Although best remembered for designing the extraordinary
Art Nouveau cast iron entrances to the Paris Métro with
their swirling organic forms, Hector Guimard was also an
accomplished furniture designer who created numerous
visually striking chairs, including the model shown here. With
its melting organic form exquisitely carved in fruitwood, this
elegantly poised model has an interesting provenance, having
originally been in the designer's possession and therefore
presumably used in his own residence.

◀ A similar chair designed by
Hector Guimard, c.1912.

▼ Side chair, 1912
Pearwood, textile-covered
upholstery
France

Harry Peach
Armchair, c.1913

Harry Peach staunchly believed that British cultural heritage should be preserved in the face of rapid industrialization, and this conviction led him to become an important design reformer aligned to the Arts and Crafts Movement as well as an early environmental campaigner. Having admired Richard Riemerschmid's cane furniture manufactured by Theodor Reimann of Dresden, Peach established Dryad Handicrafts in 1907 to produce a wide range of Modern woven cane indoor/outdoor furnishings, including this elegant armchair, using traditional craft skills and that were designed for "comfortable use" and were of "sound construction".

► Armchair, c.1913
Woven cane (painted later)
Dryad Ltd., Leicester, England

▼ Pages from the Dryad catalogue, 1913

DRYAD CANE FURNITURE

The above illustration, showing a workman weaving the back of a chair, will interest those who enjoy watching a deft craftsman at work.

Now that so many workmen are "hands," it is interesting to recall, by a modern instance, the time when "brain and hand went ever paired."

The Dryad Works commenced in February, 1907, with four craftsmen, and now employs over 50, and its productions have been exported to all parts of the world.

DAYDREAM

A RESTFUL, EASILY-MOVED LOUNGE FOR INVALIDS.
ORDER NO. 109   £4 4 0

Kaare Klint
Model No. 9662 Faaborg chair, 1914

In 1914, Kaare Klint designed this elegant classical-inspired chair for the Faaborg Museum located on the Danish island of Funen. Like other furniture designs by Klint, the Faaborg chair is a modern reworking of a historical chair type, in this case the precedent was a British Regency model. Like other Danish designers, Klint adopted an evolutionary rather than revolutionary approach to design that centred on the idea of honing existing "ideal" forms.

► *Model No. 9662 Faaborg* chair, 1914
Amboyna, oak, cane
Rud. Rasmussen, Copenhagen, Denmark

▼ *Faaborg* chairs in situ at the Faaborg Museum, c.1914

1920s

Süe et Mare
Armchairs designed for the David-Weill residence, c.1923

These beautiful armchairs by Süe et Mare were designed for the dining room of the David-Weill residence in Paris, which was also furnished with designs by Émile-Jacques Ruhlmann. With their scrolling arms and shield-like backs these chairs epitomize the stylish opulence of French Art Deco, while the richly grained mahogany literally glistening with a high-gloss French polish accentuates the sensuous forms that appear to melt into one another.

▲ Grand Salon interior by Süe et Mare, exhibited at the Paris Exposition of 1925.

◄ Armchairs designed for the David-Weill residence, c.1923
Mahogany, fabric-covered upholstery
La Compagnie des Arts Français, Paris, France

Süe et Mare
Gondole chairs, c.1924

In 1919, Louis Süe and André Mare founded the Compagnie des Arts Français, a decorating firm producing stylish contemporary furniture, lighting, wallpapers and textiles. With their scrolling carved backs and sumptuous buttoned velvet upholstery, the *Gondole* chairs reveal the exquisite level of craftsmanship achieved in the firm's workshop during this period, whilst also epitomizing the luxurious opulence of the French Art Deco style.

Gondole chairs, c.1924
Mahogany, velvet-covered upholstery
La Compagnie des Arts Français, Paris, France

Dominique
Side chair, c.1925

Founded by André Domin and Marcel Genevriere, Dominique was one of the foremost decorating firms in Paris during the 1920s and 1930s. The company was renowned for its beautifully executed Art Deco furniture that had a bold simplicity and understated luxurious quality. This gilded side chair not only typifies their firm's output with its subtly tapering legs and elegant proportions, but also reflects how formally progressive the Art Deco style could be when its protagonists adopted a pared-down reductivism.

▲ **Study interior designed by Dominique, 1920s**

◄ **Side chair, c.1925**
Gilded wood, fabric-covered upholstery
Dominique, Paris, France

Süe at Mare
Armchair, c.1925

One of the great Parisian interior decorating companies, Süe et Mare was founded in 1912. During the 1920s, the firm produced elegant Art Deco furnishings that were a sublime marriage of superlative craft skills with a sophisticated understanding of design. Utilizing exotic Brazilian rosewood (palisander), this chair epitomizes the objective of the firm's founders – André Mare and Louis Süe – to create Moderne designs that perpetuated the French workshop tradition into the twentieth century.

Armchair, c.1925
Palisander, leather-covered upholstery
Süe et Mare et la Compagnie des Arts Français, Paris, France

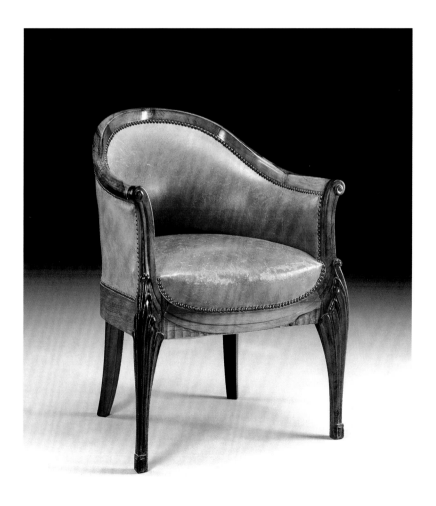

◄ ▲ *Spirales* divan, 1920–22
Rosewood-veneered wood, ivory
inlay and silk-covered upholstery
Établissements Ruhlmann et
Laurent, Paris, France

Émile-Jacques Ruhlmann
Spirales divan, 1920–22 & Daybed, c.1926

In 1917, Ruhlmann's long-established family firm joined forces with another decorating and furniture manufacturing company to establish, Établissements Ruhlmann et Laurent. The financial security that this partnership provided, gave Ruhlmann the unfettered freedom to explore his remarkable creativity and the resulting Art Deco "luxuries" included numerous seating designs, including the beautifully inlaid *Spirales* divan and the elegant daybed, shown here, veneered in *bois de violette* (kingwood).

▼ Daybed, c.1926
Kingwood-veneered wood, gilt bronze
Établissements Ruhlmann et Laurent, Paris, France

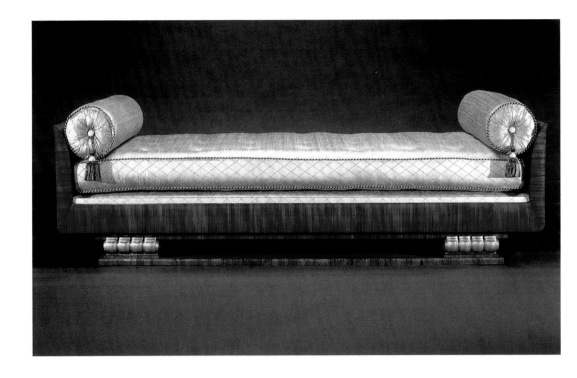

Émile-Jacques Ruhlmann
Daybed, 1925

With a productive workshop that employed over one hundred skilled craftsmen, Ruhlmann produced a plethora of furniture models from simple yet elegantly proportioned dining chairs to elaborately inlaid case pieces. He also designed a large number of daybeds, presumably for his wealthy clients to idle their days away. This two-tone silk upholstered design is one of Ruhlmann's most successful daybed models, and can be seen as a highly successful Art Deco reinterpretation of the traditional sleigh bed, also known as a *lit bateau*.

▲ Detail of postcard showing daybed, c.1925

▼ Daybed, 1925
Silk-covered upholstery, bronzed metal
Établissements Ruhlmann et Laurent, Paris, France

Émile-Jacques Ruhlmann
Chair, c.1924

A highly prolific designer of furniture that exemplified the glamour and superb refinement of French Art Deco, Émile-Jacques Rulhmann's work relied on elegant proportions and superlative execution. This side chair with its sabre-form legs and scrolling back typifies the output of his workshop, which was inspired by the classical design elements and the high level of craftsmanship found in eighteenth century furniture. Adopting these ideals Ruhlmann sought to create stylish modern designs that he described as his "precious pieces".

◄ Pochoir showing various furniture designs by Émile-Jacques Ruhlmann, 1920

▼ Chair, c.1924
Macassar ebony, bronze, fabric-covered upholstery
Établissements Ruhlmann et Laurent, Paris, France

Jules Leleu
Side chair, c.1923

An early example of Jules Leleu's design talent, this side chair also reveals the expertise of his family's workshop. Like Émile-Jacques Ruhlmann, Leleu favoured simplified forms and the use of exotic woods, and similarly his work displayed the seemingly inherent contradiction of the French Art Deco style, which attempted to reconcile tradition with modernity. Leleu skillfully resolved these opposing themes to produce visually striking "Art Moderne" designs, such as this mahogany chair with its unusual circular back section.

Side chair, c.1923
Mahogany, silk-covered upholstery
Maison Leleu, Paris, France

Jean Dunand
Armchair, c.1929

Swiss-born, Jean Dunand was a leading *décorateur* during the
1920s and 1930s and was famed for his exquisite lacquered
creations. He studied at the École des Arts Industriels (School
of Industrial Arts) in Geneva, graduating in 1896. The following
year, he was awarded a travel grant and as a result moved to
Paris to work in the atelier of Jean Dampt. By 1912, he had also
begun learning the "lost art" of Japanese lacquering from the
Japanese artist, Sougawara and subsequently established his
own workshop at 12 Rue Halle, Paris. This venture specialized
in the creation of Art Deco furnishings that incorporated this
revived artisanal craft, including this armchair with its unusual
Oriental-inspired frame that has a graduated stepped form
that has been lacquered a subtle hue of Chinese red.

Armchair, c.1929
Lacquered wood, textile-covered
upholstery
Jean Dunand, Paris, France

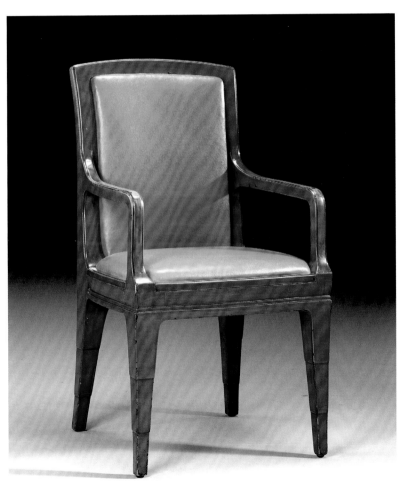

Karel Maes
Armchair, 1925

A leading Belgian abstract artist during the 1920s and 1930s, Karel Maes created dynamic geometric compositions that were not only visually powerful but also chromatically harmonic. Apart from his fine art, he also worked within the applied arts designing carpets and furniture in a similar vein, including this unusual armchair with its striking zig-zag motif. This little-known seating design with its bold elemental form was remarkably progressive for its date and certainly must be considered a Belgian Art Deco masterpiece.

Armchair, 1925
Wood, stained wood, textile-upholstery
Belgium
(Images courtesy of Galerie Historismus)

Marcel Breuer & Anton Lorenz
Model ss32 armchair, 1928

Both Hungarian-born designers who subsequently moved to Germany, Marcel Breuer and Anton Lorenz co-designed a number of Modernist chairs, including the *Model ss32*. This seating design with its gleaming Bakelite armrests has a base that is significantly deeper than Marcel Breuer's better-known *Model B33*, which presumably enhanced stability. Like other cantilevered designs, this armchair provided a good level of comfort thanks to the frame's springy resilience and the inherent give of the Eisengarn canvas seat and back.

▲ Thonet catalogue showing various tubular metal seating designs by Marcel Breuer, 1931

◄ *Model SS32* armchair, 1928
Chromed tubular steel, Eisengarn canvas, Bakelite
Desta Stahlrohrmöbel, Berlin, Germany

Marcel-Louis Baugniet
Armchair, c.1927

The Belgian artist, designer and writer, Marcel-Louis Baugniet designed this elegant tubular metal chair in the late 1920s with its upholstered seating section covered in a multi-striped fabric woven by the Belgian company, La Cambre. In 1929, Baugniet opened his own decorating business in Brussels, which subsequently produced other innovative furnishings, including the "Standax" range of dismountable furniture shown at the 1939 "Exposition Internationale des Arts et Techniques dans la Vie Moderne" in Paris.

Armchair, c.1927
Nickel-plated tubular steel, fabric-covered upholstery (Frame executed by Annoye S.A., Belgium)

Gerrit Rietveld
Military chair, 1923 & *Beugel* chair, 1927

In 1923, Rietveld was commissioned to design furniture for the Catholic Military Home in Utrecht. The resulting *Military* range, which included various chairs and tables, utilized simple wood elements to create arresting compositions of verticals and horizontals. Between 1927 and 1928, Rietveld also created another highly rationally conceived series of chairs utilizing loops of tubular metal and moulded plywood, fittingly its title *Beugel* means "loop" in Dutch. The *Beugel* model, shown here, was manufactured by the Amsterdam department store, Metz & Co., and as such is also referred to as the Metz side chair.

Military chair, 1923
Painted deal
G. van de Groenekan, De Bilt, Netherlands

Erich Dieckmann
Armchair, 1928

Erich Dieckmann was a highly accomplished furniture designer who created pieces that were characterized by the use of a rigidly pared-down geometric vocabulary of form, such as this armchair with its rectilinear design. After serving his carpentry apprenticeship at the Weimar Bauhaus, Dieckmann went on to head the carpentry workshop at the Staatliche Bauhochschule in Weimar and later taught at the Kunstgewerbeschule Burg Giebichenstein in Halle. His comprehensive range of standardized wooden furniture, including this simple chair, was highly influential.

◀ Armchair, 1928
Stained beech, stained plywood, metal screws
Hausrat GmbH, Frankfurt, Germany

▼ Armchair designed by Erich Dieckmann at the Furniture Workshop of the Staatliche Bauhochschule in Weimar, c.1926

Camille Louis Graeser
Chair for Die Wohning exhibition, 1927

The Swiss designer, Camille Graeser grew up in Stuttgart and studied under Bernhard Pankok at the city's Königlichen Kunstgewerbeschule Möbelbau und Innenarchitektur. Later, he became a member of the Deutsche Werkbund, an association of designers and manufacturers who sought to reform design by adopting rational principles, which are clearly reflected in this radically simplified dining chair. This model is one of four examples that was specifically manufactured for Mies van der Rohe's apartment building, which was part of the landmark "Werkbundausstellung Die Wohnung" exhibition held in 1927.

Chair for Die Wohning exhibition, 1927
Walnut, cane
Beutter & Lauth, Stuttgart, Germany

Donald Deskey
Chair for the Abraham & Strauss Beauty Parlor, 1929

Best known for his Art Deco furnishings and interiors created for the Radio City Music Hall in New York, Donald Deskey was one of the great pioneers of the Moderne style in America. Specifically designed for use in the beauty parlor of a major New York department store, this geometric chair by Deskey is distinguished by its simplified construction whereby the fully upholstered seat and back sections are elegantly supported on four flat aluminium sledge-like legs.

Chair for the Abraham & Strauss Beauty Parlor, 1929
Aluminium, textile-covered upholstery
Ypsilanti Reed Furniture Company, Ionia (MI), USA

Vittorio Zecchin
Armchairs, 1923

An Italian artist whose brightly hued paintings were reminiscent of Gustav Klimt's work, Vittorio Zecchin also designed glassware and furniture, including this beautiful pair of ebonized Art Deco armchairs. The chairs' incised and gilded decoration incorporates a tightly packed swirling motif of stylized fish and anemones that stylistically compliments the design's bold formal geometry and impressive visual mass.

Armchairs, 1923
Painted and lacquered wood,
textile-covered upholstery
Italy

Pierre Chareau
Model No. MF219 armchair, 1920s & Armchair, c.1925

A celebrated architect, Pierre Chareau was also a prolific furniture designer whose numerous seating designs were notable for their unusual constructions and material combinations. Offering two alternative seating positions, his *Model No. MF219* reclining armchair is not only a practical seating solution, but with its beautifully curved armrests and flaring front legs possesses an undeniable sophistication. Similarly, his almost fully upholstered armchair with its curious spiralling armrests exudes a suave modernity that has become synonymous with the French Art Deco style.

▲ Interior designed by Pierre Chareau, 1920s

▼ Armchair, c.1925
Velvet-covered upholstery, wood
Pierre Chareau, Paris, France

► Living room interior designed by
Pierre Chareau, 1920s

▼ *Model No. MF219* armchair,
c.1923
Walnut, textile-covered upholstery
Pierre Chareau, Paris, France

Erik Gunnar Asplund
Senna lounge chair, 1925

During the 1920s, Erik Gunnar Asplund was a leading proponent of Nordic Classicism, designing a number of Neoclassically inspired buildings including the Stockholm City Library (1924–28). During this period, he also designed furniture that was in a similar classicist vein – the best known design being his graceful *Senna* armchair, which was exhibited in the Swedish Pavillion at the landmark 1925 "Exposition Internationale des Arts Décoratifs et Industriels Modernes" held in Paris.

▲ Swedish Pavillion at the "Exposition Internationale des Arts Décoratifs et Industriels Modernes", Paris, 1925

◀ *Senna* lounge chair, 1925
Leather, fruitwood, brass, ivory
Sweden (later reissued by Cassina, Italy)

Josef Albers
Model No. ti244 armchair, c.1929

Having initially studied at the Bauhaus in Weimar, Josef Albers was subsequently appointed by Walter Gropius as a member of the school's teaching staff in 1923. After Marcel Breuer's departure from the institution, Albers headed the Bauhaus' furniture workshop from 1928 to 1929, and it was during this period that he designed this forward-looking armchair with its simple laminated wood frame and tilted seating section. This is an extremely rare design, with only four examples known to exist.

Model No. ti244 armchair, c.1929
Laminated beech, chromed tubular steel, textile-covered upholstery
Bauhaus Furniture Workshop, Dessau, Germany

Paul Dupré-Lafon
Desk chair, c.1929-30 & Armchairs, c.1927

Having studied at the École des Beaux-Arts in Marseilles, Paul Dupré-Lafon moved to Paris and from 1929 designed luxury accessories and furnishings for Hermès. Known as the "Millionaire's Decorator", he also specialized in the creation of Modernist furniture for Paris' wealthy elite. The lacquered armchairs and swivelling desk chair, shown here, epitomize his use of bold elemental forms to create designs that had an overt sophistication.

◄ Desk chair, c.1929-30
Ebonized wood, bronze, leather
France

▼ Armchairs, c.1927
Lacquered wood, metal, textile-covered upholstery
France

▲ Interior designed by Paul Dupré-Lafon showing lacquered wood armchairs, c.1927

Gerrit Rietveld
Stick Chair, 1924 & *Roodblauwe (Red/Blue)* chair, 1922–23

The earliest version of the *Red/Blue* chair dating from 1918 was executed in a natural wood finish, however, during the early 1920s painted versions of this revolutionary design, including a black version were produced. With its pared down construction, it was not only a veritable De Stijl masterpiece, but also an early example of standardized seating design. In 1924, Rietveld designed the similar *Stick* chair for Amsterdam pharmacist, Jacob Birza that employed rounded rather than rectangular elements for its frame and contoured seat and back sections made of moulded plywood.

▲ Multi-coloured *Roodblauwe* (Red/Blue) chair, 1922–23

► *Roodblauwe (Red/Blue)* chair, 1922–23
Painted solid beech, plywood
G. van de Groenekan, De Bilt, Netherlands

◄ *Stick* chair, 1924
Ebonized deal, plywood
G. van de Groenekan, De Bilt, Netherlands

Le Corbusier, Pierre Jeanneret & Charlotte Perriand
Model No. B302 armchair, 1927–28

Charlotte Perriand designed this elegant swivelling chair under the supervision of Le Corbusier, to be used as either a desk chair or as a dining chair. Although the design appears to be relatively utilitarian, its deeply cushioned leather back and seat give it a touch of luxurious refinement. Perriand intended the padded back-rail of the chair to provide a comfortable support "like automobile tyres" and by utilizing a state-of-the-art tubular steel frame the design speculated on the possibilities of machine production.

▲ Design for a dining room interior by Charlotte Perriand, c.1929 – featuring *Model No. B302* armchairs

◄ *Model No. B302* armchair, 1927–28
Chromed tubular steel, leather-covered upholstery
Thonet Frères, Paris, France

Ferdinand Kramer
Model No. B403 side chair, 1927

The influential German architect and civic planner, Ferdinand Kramer designed furniture for Thonet during the 1920s due to the lack of architectural commissions in this period of economic turmoil in Germany. His *Model No. B403* chair is his best-known seating design from this period and reflects both his functionalist goals as well as his understanding of ergonomics, with its subtly contoured seat and curved back section.

◄ Ebonized variant of the *B403* side chair

▼ *Model No. B403* side chair, 1927
Bent beechwood, plywood
Gebrüder Thonet, Frankenberg, Germany

Louis Sognot
Side chairs, c.1925

This elegant pair of Art Deco bedroom chairs was designed by Louis Sognot for Atelier Primavera, a high-end *atelier d'art* (art studio) established by the well-known Paris department store, Printemps. With their unadorned yet fluid lines, these stylish chairs were part of an installation exhibited by Primavera in the Pavilion du Printemps at the 1925 "Exposition des Arts Décoratifs et Industriels Modernes" held in Paris.

▼ Side chairs, c.1925
Rosewood, mahogany, textile-covered upholstery
Atelier Primavera, Paris, France

▲ Bedroom installation exhibited by Primavera at the 1925 "Exposition des Arts Décoratifs et Industriels Modernes"

Paul T. Frankl
Armchair, c.1929

During the late 1920s, Paul Frankl began creating Modernist furnishings that were distinguished by an unrelenting Art Deco geometry. Unlike the utilitarian designs emanating from the Bauhaus during this period, Frankl's designs, such as this elegant armchair, were far more luxurious and as such were an exuberant American celebration of Machine Age progress. Frankl also created a variant of this chair that incorporated tubular metal, rather than squared sectioned metal supports.

Armchair, c.1929
Nickel-plated steel, leather-covered upholstery
Frankl Galleries, New York, USA

Marcel Breuer
Model No. B3 (Wassily) armchair, 1925–27

A revolutionary use of materials, Marcel Breuer's *Model No. B3* utilized state-of-the-art tubular steel for its eye-catching yet highly functional construction. It was designed whilst Marcel Breuer was heading the furniture-making workshop at the Bauhaus in Dessau and although it was not specifically designed for his fellow tutor, Wassily Kandinsky, as is sometimes thought, the painter did admire it. It was subsequently used in his living quarters at the school, hence its other name: the *Wassily* chair. A veritable icon of the Modern movement, the *Model No. B3* – with its striking composition of strong vertical and horizontal elements – can be seen as a monochromatic three-dimensional homage to De Stijl. But its stridently modern looks were too radical for the furniture-buying public and it only really achieved notable sales success from the 1960s onwards, when public taste finally caught up with this truly radical design.

Model No. B3 Wassily armchair,
1925–27
Chromed tubular steel, Eisengarn
Standard-Möbel, Berlin, Germany
& Gebrüder Thonet, Frankenberg,
Germany (reissued by Knoll
International, New York)

Kem Weber
Chair for the Biltmore Hotel, c.1927

Completed in 1929, the famous Biltmore Hotel in Phoenix, Arizona, was designed by a former apprentice of Frank Lloyd Wright's, Albert Chase McArthur. For its interior scheme, site-specific furnishings were commissioned from not only the architect's furniture-designing brother, Warren, but also from the German émigré designer, Kem Weber, whose maple and leather armchair was used in the lobby area as well as in the hotel's suites. Importantly, this seating design echoed the linearity of the building's design with its distinctive concrete bricks.

▼ Postcard showing the lobby of the Biltmore Hotel in Phoenix, Arizona, c.1927

◄ Chair for the Biltmore Hotel, c.1927
Maple, leather-cover upholstery
USA

Émile-Jacques Ruhlmann
Francel swivelling chair, c.1929 &
Rodier swivelling armchair, c.1925–27

Although best known for his beautiful seating designs in exotic woods, Émile-Jacques Ruhlmann also designed a number of chairs that had a more overtly Modernist remit. The swivelling chair, shown below, was designed specifically for the dressing room of the French actress, Jacqueline Francel and bears little resemblance to traditional precedents, while the sumptuously padded *Rodier* swivelling desk chair reveals Ruhlmann's ability to combine Art Deco luxury with Modern functionality.

▶ *Rodier* swivelling chair,
c.1925–27
Chromed metal, macassar ebony,
leather-covered upholstery
Établissements Ruhlmann et
Laurent, Paris, France

◀ *Francel* swivelling chair, c.1929
Chromed metal, leather-covered
upholstery
Établissements Ruhlmann et
Laurent, Paris, France

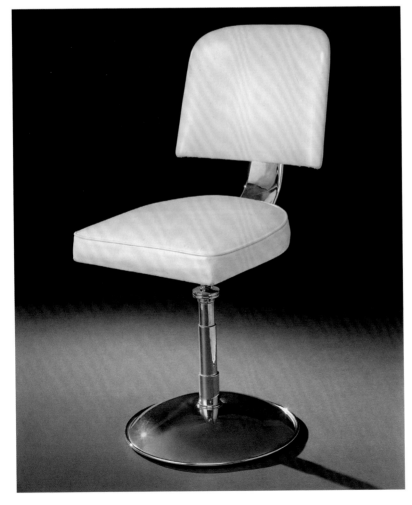

Bernhard Hoetger
Armchair, c.1927

◄ Armchair, c.1927
Oak, rush
Germany

▼► Ebonized version of Bernhard
Hoetger's armchair, c.1927 – with
incised motif on side panels
(Images courtesy of Galerie
Historismus)

Bernhard Hoetger was a leading advocate of the Expressionist style and was especially drawn to the artistic potential of handicrafts. Hoetger originally designed this chair for his own residence in Bremen, which was conceived as a totally unified *Gesamtkunstwerk* (total work of art). As an early example of "design art", this chair was a progressive statement that rejected rational standardization in favour of artistic expression. Hoetger also designed a similar oak and rush chair in 1923 for a series of workshops-cum-studios created for the selling of arts and crafts in Worpswede.

Jean Dunand
Armchair, c.1928

A leading *decorateur* working within the French Art Deco style, Jean Dunand learnt the supposedly "lost technique" of lacquering from the Japanese émigré artisan, Seizo Sugawara. The resulting lacquered furniture executed by Dunand reveals a love of bold geometry, which is emphasized not only in the slab-like construction of this luxurious armchair, but also in its jazzy Art Deco decoration.

Armchair, c.1928
Lacquered wood, part-painted
metal, silk-upholstered upholstery
Jean Dunand, Paris, France

Robert Mallet-Stevens
Armchair, 1928–30

In 1929, Ernest and Grace King accompanied by the architect Philip Maher travelled to Paris in order to find contemporary designs to refurnish their Prairie-Style summer residence, Rockledge, in Winona, Minnesota that had been designed in 1912 by Philip's father, George Washington Maher. During this buying trip, the couple purchased numerous Modernist works by the leading French *decorateurs* of the day, including this extraordinary silvered armchair by Robert Mallet-Stevens with its sling seat made of real zebra skin.

Armchair, 1928–30
Lacquered wood, zebra skin
Robert Mallet-Stevens, Paris, France

Louis Sognot
Lounge chair, c.1928

This unusual Modernist chair by the progressive French designer, Louis Sognot utilized a pair of large springs rather than a traditional sled-like base to achieve a rocking movement. Incorporating flat bands of chromed steel this rocker was certainly more forward-looking than a lot of French Art Deco seating designs, which tended to employ exotic woods rather than industrial materials in their construction.

Lounge chair, c.1928
Chromed steel, metal springs, leather-covered upholstery
France

Ludwig Mies van der Rohe
Model No. MR90 Barcelona chair, 1929

Ludwig Mies van der Rohe designed the German Pavilion for the 1929 "Exposición Internacional" held in Barcelona, Spain. Widely regarded as a Modernist architectural masterpiece, the building juxtaposed modern materials (steel and glass) with more traditional ones (marble and travertine). For its interior he designed the *Barcelona* chair, a classically inspired throne-like seat based on the ancient *sella curulis*. By combining steel and leather, Mies similarly mixed the old with the new, and in so doing created a thoroughly Modern version of the traditional leather-buttoned club chair.

Model No. MR90 Barcelona chair, 1929
Chromed steel, leather, leather-covered cushions
Berliner Metallgewerbe Josef Müller, Berlin, Germany (later reissued by Knoll Associates, USA)

◄ Contemporary interior showing various furniture pieces designed by Warren McArthur

▼ *Biltmore* lounge chairs, c.1929
Aluminium, vinyl-covered upholstery, rubber
Warren McArthur Corporation, Rome (NY), USA

Warren McArthur
Biltmore lounge chairs, c.1929 &
Biltmore reclining chaise, c.1929

A highly prolific designer and manufacturer of Machine Age furniture, Warren McArthur utilized state-of-the-art aluminum tubing in his designs. When his architect brother, Albert designed the Arizona Biltmore Hotel in Phoenix, Warren was commissioned to design various pieces of furniture for the project, including these lounge chairs and this adjustable chaise longue, which can be positioned into three different sitting angles.

Biltmore reclining chaise, c.1939
Aluminium, textile-covered upholstery, rubber
Warren McArthur Corporation, Rome (NY), USA

1930s

Émile-Jacques Ruhlmann
Model No. 278 Gonse armchairs, c.1930–32

In 1915, Émile-Jacques Ruhlmann drew in his sketchbook the concept of a low lounge chair that had arms that swept downwards and backwards to form a continuous curve of wood that incorporated the design's rear legs. He later put this elegant sketched theory into practice in his design of the *Model No.278 Gonse* armchair in the early 1930s. The armchairs shown here are extremely rare – being two of only three known extant examples that were produced in black lacquered wood – and as such were recently sold at auction for a staggering $1.4 million.

Model No. 278 Gonse
armchairs, c.1930–32
Lacquered wood, textile-covered
upholstery
Éstablissements Ruhlmann et
Laurent, Paris, France

Alvar Aalto
Model No. 21 side chair, 1933 & *Model No. 51* armchair, c.1931

In 1928, Alvar Aalto won the competition to design the Paimio Sanatorium and for this *Gesamtkunstwerk*, he subsequently created various pieces of furniture, including the *Model No. 51* armchair. The following year he designed the cantilevered *Model No. 21*, which similarly employed a moulded plywood seat. Rejecting the Modernists' doctrine of hard-edged functionalism, Aalto sought to create democratic furniture, which through the use of organic lines and natural materials was more suited to the human condition.

▼ *Model No. 51* armchair, 1932
Solid birch, moulded birch plywood
Huonekalu-Ja Rakennu-Styötehdas, Åbo, Finland
(later reissued by Artek, Helsinki, Finland)

▲ Alvar Alto at work in his studio.

◀ *Model No. 21* side chair, 1933
Laminated birch, moulded birch plywood
Huonekalu-Ja Rakennu-Styötehdas, Åbo, Finland
(later reissued by Artek, Helsinki, Finland)

Giuseppe Terragni
Armchair, c.1936

In contrast to the historicizing Novecento style advocated by the likes of Gio Ponti, the Italian Rationalists – who included among their number, Giuseppe Terragni – sought a resolutely contemporary idiom in architecture and furniture: modern design for a modern world. This simple utilitarian chair by Terragni is a variant of his *Benita* chair, which was originally designed for the Casa del Fascio in Como and which was later put into mass-production.

Armchair, c.1936
Wood, painted tubular metal
Italy

Marcel Breuer
Model No. 308 armchair, 1932

Between 1932 and 1934, Marcel Breuer designed various seating solutions that incorporated flat bands of aluminium in their constructions. The best known of these was the semi-cantilevered *Model No. 308* armchair, which was manufactured in Switzerland by Embru and retailed by the Zurich department store, Wohnbedarf. Unlike Breuer's earlier tubular metal chairs, the *Model No. 308* incorporated a padded seat and back rather than canvas or leather slings, which provided increased sitting comfort.

Model No. 308 armchair, 1932
Aluminium, ebonised wood, textile-covered upholstery
Embru-Werke, Rüti, Switzerland

Denham Maclaren
Armchair, c.1930

Denham Maclaren created a number of Modernist furniture designs, including this oak and zebra-skin armchair that he used to furnish his own apartment. As an impressive example of British Art Deco, this rare design has an understated opulence while its geometric proportions give it a reassuring sense of mass. Maclaren also designed a variant of this armchair with side panels made of thick industrial glass. During the 1930s zebra-skin was a fashionable choice of upholstery, and certainly it lent any furniture design a certain Surrealist exoticism.

◄ Armchair, c.1930
Oak, leather and zebra-skin covered upholstery
Denham, London, England

▼ Armchair with glass side panels and zebra-skin covered upholstery designed by Denham Maclaren, c.1930

Unattributed
Armchairs, 1939

Produced by Chevalier for the "L'Art du Bois" exhibition held in Paris, these stylish Art Deco armchairs with their slab-like glass panels have useful hand-holes to enable the sitter to lever themselves out of the low-slung seats. During the Art Deco era, African themes were especially popular in France and Belgium due to their colonies and as such zebra-skin upholstery would have seemed the height of exoticism. The industral glass panels with their metal fittings also gave these chairs a progressive modernity that was utterly in tune with the chic aesthetic sophistication of Parisian interiors dating from the period.

Armchairs, 1939
Glass, Chromed brass, hide-covered upholstery
Chevalier, France

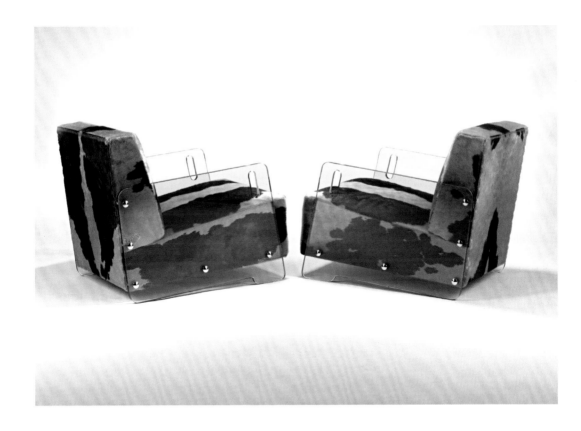

André Sornay
Bridge armchairs, 1930s

André Sornay studied at the École des Beaux-Arts in Lyons before working for his family's cabinetmaking firm, where he revitalized its output by introducing Modern designs that were distinguished by geometric forms and harmonious proportions. Like other Art Deco designers working in France, Sornay experimented with different material combinations to great effect. With these armchairs, he combined two different types of wood and also used his patented *cloutage* technique that utilised bolt-like studs to secure thin veneers onto the chairs' frames thereby becoming both a functional and decorative device.

Bridge armchairs, 1930s
Mahogany, ebony-veneer, metal
Sornay, Lyons, France

Jean-Michel Frank
Elephant chairs for the Llao-Llao Hotel, 1939

In 1936 the Argentine manufacturer, Comte signed an agreement with Jean-Michel Frank to produce his designs, as there was a ready market for his furniture among the wealthy residents of Buenos Aires. Furthering this connection, in 1939 Frank was commissioned to design some site-specific furniture for the Llao-Llao Hotel in the Patagonian resort of Bariloche. These armchairs with their spotted-deer hide coverings were used in the hotel's lobby, and were manufactured by Comte in solid native mahogany.

▲ Early photograph of the lobby of the Llao-Llao Hotel, Bariloche, Argentina

▶ *Elephant* chairs for the Llao-Llao Hotel, 1939
Mahogany, hide-covered upholstery
Comte, Buenos Aires, Argentina

Jean Prouvé
Standard chair, 1934 & *Cité* armchair, c.1933

◀ *Standard* chair, 1934
Enamelled sheet and tubular steel,
moulded plywood
Jean Prouvé, Nancy, France

▼ *Cité* armchair, c.1933
Enamelled flat steel, canvas
Jean Prouvé, Nancy, France

Jean Prouvé was a metalworker and self-taught designer/
architect, who used a hands-on trial-and-error methodology
to create furniture that had an engineered constructional
quality. This low-slung lounge chair was designed for the Cité
Universitaire in Nancy, while the stylishly utilitarian *Standard*
chair is widely considered a timeless classic; a demountable
version of this model was also produced. As Le Corbusier
noted, "Prouvé combines the soul of an engineer with that of
an architect."

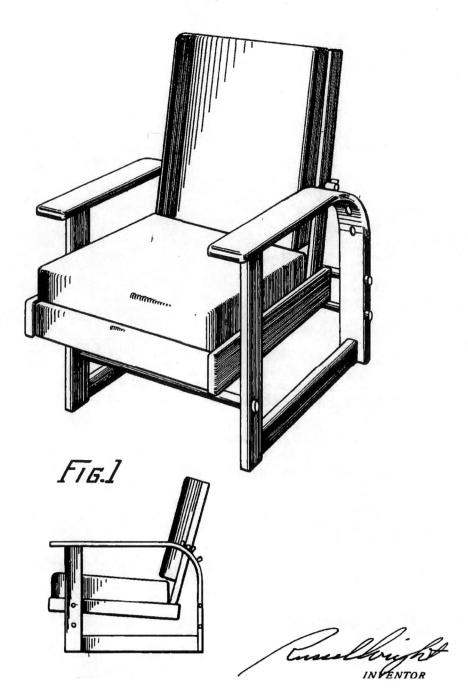

FIG.1

Russell Wright

INVENTOR

Russel Wright
American Modern sofa, 1935

Having worked for the industrial designer Norman Bel Geddes, in 1930 Russel Wright established his own studio in New York designing home furnishings and accessories for various manufacturers. Wright's Moderne products combined functionalism, Art Deco styling and Mission-style vernacularism, and were exhibited in 1932 in the "Machine Age" exhibition at the Museum of Modern Art, New York. His furniture designs, including his *American Modern* range for Conant-Ball were extremely popular being less expensive than Modern imports from Europe, and better suited to American style informal living.

◄ Patent drawing for an adjustable chair designed by Russel Wright, 1935

▼ *American Modern* sofa, 1935
Maple, textile-covered upholstery
Conant-Ball, Gardner (MA), USA

▲ *American Modern* armchair, 1935
Maple, textile-covered upholstery
Conant-Ball, Gardner (MA), USA

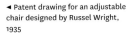

Donald Deskey & Samuel Marx
Armchair from the Marx Residence, 1939

This model was originally designed for Samuel Marx's own home and was then later used to furnish the Joseph Block residence, one of Samuel Marx's most important interior design commissions. Co-designed by Deskey and Marx, this model was also later put into mass-production by the Royal Metal Manufacturing Company of Chicago. The highly respected American textile designer and weaver, Dorothy Liebes, designed the fabric used to upholster this unusual-looking design with its tapering steel frame, and its arms and feet that terminate into atom-like balls.

Armchair from the Marx Residence, 1939
Matte chromed steel, textile-covered upholstery
Royal Metal Manufacturing Company, Chicago, USA

Donald Deskey
Lounge chair, 1933

This Art Deco design has a frame made from an unusual type of tubular steel, which has a square rather than round cross-section. Like other designs by Deskey, this chair has a visual fluidity with its looping metal frame and horseshoe-shaped backrail. As one of the main proponents of the Moderne Style during the Depression, hard-pressed manufacturers employed Deskey, including Ficks Reed, to update their product lines in order to stimulate sales in a tough marketplace.

Lounge chair, 1933
Nickeled steel, textile-covered upholstery
Ficks Reed, Cincinnati (OH), USA

Bruno Mathsson

Pernilla armchair, c.1935, *Pernilla* chair with bookrest, c.1935 & *Pernilla* lounge chair and ottoman, 1935

Like his forefathers, Bruno Mathsson was a skilled master joiner who always took a hands-on approach to design. He was, however, also a pioneering exponent of Swedish functionalism whose *Pernilla* range of chairs demonstrated that Modern design did not have to be dehumanising or overly utilitarian. As Mathsson noted, "comfortable sitting is an 'art' – it ought not to be. Instead, the making of chairs has to be done with such an 'art' that the sitting will not be any 'art'." And with the *Pernilla* chairs he clearly showed that he practiced what he preached.

▲ *Pernilla* chair with bookrest, c.1935
Laminated wood, flax webbing
Karl Mathsson, Värnamo, Sweden

► *Pernilla* lounge chair & ottoman, 1935
Laminated wood, sheepskin
Karl Mathsson, Värnamo, Sweden

◄ *Pernilla* armchair, c.1935
Laminated wood, flax webbing
Karl Mathsson, Värnamo, Sweden

Jean Royère
Desk chair, 1936

This remarkable chair was designed with a matching desk for the 1936 "Salon des Artistes Décorateurs". It is veneered in an exotic wood from Africa known as zebrawood because of its dark and light alternating stripes. Like other French designers working in the Art Deco style, Royère often used luxurious materials such as tropical woods in his Modernistic furnishings, which were stylistically far removed from the hard-edged utilitarianism emanating from 1930s Germany.

▲ Interior scheme designed by Jean Royère in the Art Deco style

◄ Desk chair, 1936
Zebrawood-veneered wood, chromed metal, hide-covered upholstery
Gouffé, Paris, France

Giuseppe Pagano Pogatsching
Armchair for l'Università Bocconi, c.1939

This beautiful chair has a remarkably elemental quality. Its frame, made from two continuous loops of laminated wood and three simple struts, supports the beautifully woven L-shaped seating section. It was originally designed site-specifically for the chancellor and vice-chancellor's offices at the University of Bocconi in Milan, a wholly integrated interior scheme that was hugely influential. Importantly, this design managed to combine a Rationalist reductive aesthetic with age-old Italian craft traditions.

Armchair for l'Università Bocconi, c.1939
Laminated wood, solid wood, woven cord
Maggioni, Varedo, Italy

Heinz & Bodo Rasch
Model No. 3138 armchair, 1930–31

In 1927, Heinz and Bodo Rasch designed a cantilevered chair, presumably inspired by the drawings of Mart Stam's earlier design shown at a meeting held a year earlier of architects taking part in the Weissenhof exhibition. Known as the *Sitzgeiststuhl*, it incorporated laminated wood and solid wood in its construction. Inspired by the mass-manufacturing possibilities offered by tubular metal, a few years later the brothers went on to design another more rationally conceived cantilevered chair, the *Model No. 3138* which incorporated this then state-of-the-art material.

Model No. 3138 armchair, 1930–31
Chromed tubular steel, ebonised beech, cane
L. & C. Arnold, Ernsbach, Germany

Jindřich Halabala
H 79 chair, 1931

A talented designer and vocal design theorist, Jindřich Halabala initially headed the Prague workshop of the Unified Corporations of Applied Arts (UCAA) – a leading innovator of Modernist furnishings in Czechoslovakia. He subsequently became the main designer at the company's headquarters in Brno and as a result created numerous furniture designs, including this highly unusual chair. Although obviously inspired by Marcel Breuer's earlier tubular metal seating designs, the *H 79* uses an inverted cantilever giving it a highly distinctive profile.

H 79 chair, 1931
Chromed tubular steel, canvas
Unified Corporations of Applied Arts (UCAA), Brno, Czechoslovakia (now Czech Republic)

Frederick Kiesler
Armchair, 1935

Born in Romania, Frederick Kiesler studied in Vienna and later was a member of the De Stijl group, before going on to become a founding director of the American Union of Decorative Artists and Craftsmen (AUDAC) in 1926. As a leading member of the design avant-garde in America he created furniture that was extremely progressive both aesthetically and functionally, such as this armchair designed for the New York apartment of Charles and Alma Mergentine.

Armchair, 1935
Chromed tubular steel, leatherette-covered upholstery
USA

Jacobus Johannes Pieter Oud
Model No. 03 armchair, 1933–34

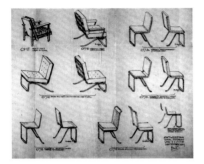

J.J.P. Oud was a leading proponent of Modernism in the Netherlands and sought through his work "poetic functionalism" that would reconcile scientific rationalism with the psychological needs of the end user. Apart from his work as an architect and city planner, Oud also created a number of functionalist designs for Metz & Co., including this Modernist armchair with its curious pedestal-cum-cantilevered base, which utilises tubular steel in a completely innovative way.

▲ Designs for various chairs by JJP Oud for Metz & Co., 1934

► *Model No. 03* armchair, 1933–34
Chromed tubular steel, leather-covered upholstery
Metz & Co., Amsterdam, Netherlands

It is good to know that when Pel nesting chairs furnish a hall they will go
on looking good — come plays, come whist drives, come dances, come
lectures — for years and years again. They are comfortable to sit upon,
and easy to stack away. The first cost is small and upkeep costs are
negligible because they are so well made. Illustrated catalogue on request.

PEL

tubular
steel nesting
chairs

MADE BY PEL LTD · OLDBURY · BIRMINGHAM · A TI COMPANY · LONDON SHOWROOMS · 15 HENRIETTA PLACE W.1

Practical Equipment Limited
Model No. SP9B stacking chair, 1936

Established in 1931, Practical Equipment Ltd. (better known as PEL) was an early British pioneer of modernist Bauhaus-style furnishings made from tubular steel. One of the firm's first commissions was for suitably modern furniture for the BBC's newly completed Broadcasting House in London (1931). It was, however, the utilitarian *Model No. SP9B* stacking chair that was perhaps the company's most commercially successful design, being employed throughout Britain in various public spaces, from church halls to schools.

▼ *Model No. SP9B* stacking chair, 1936
Tubular steel, canvas
Practical Equipment Ltd., Birmingham, England

▲ PEL advertisement showing the *Model No.RP60* stacking chair – another popular PEL model

◄ PEL advertisement showing a similar model of nesting chair being used in a public space

Ladislav Žák
Sieste armchair, 1930–31

Ladislav Žák conceived one of the most important examples of Czech functionalism, the tubular-metal *Sieste* armchair in the early 1930s using a standardised design that was inexpensive to manufacture. He originally intended this cantilevered lounge chair for small domestic units, such as those found in communes, and as such designed it to provide maximum comfort with the minimum of means. It would appear, however, that Žák's seating designs were more often used as furnishings for summer villas.

Sieste armchair, 1930–31
Chromed tubular steel, lacquered sheet iron, hand-woven fabric
Hynek Gottwald, Brandys nad Orlici, Czechoslavakia

William Lescaze
Armchair for the Philadelphia Saving Fund Society Building, c.1931

Best remembered for his uncompromisingly Modern architecture and interiors, William Lescaze was also instrumental in remodelling the look of American consumer products. In 1929, Lescaze went into partnership with fellow architect, George Howe and together they worked on a number of important projects, including the 33-storey Philadelphia Savings Fund Society skyscraper (1929–32). For this *Gesamtkunstwerk* project, Lescaze designed various pieces of furniture, including this elegantly functional armchair.

◄ Early photograph of the Philadelphia Saving Fund Society Building, 1929–32

▼ Armchair for the Philadelphia Saving Fund Society Building, c.1931
Chromed steel, tubular steel, leather-covered upholstery
USA

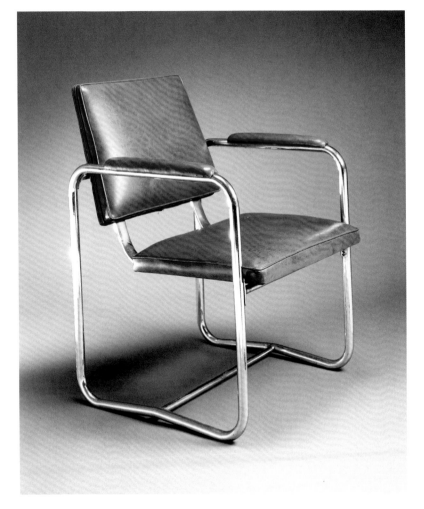

Gilbert Rohde
Armchair, 1933 & *Model No. 180* Lounge chair, 1933

In 1930, Gilbert Rohde met the founder of Herman Miller, D.J. De Pree and suggested designing a line of Modern furniture for the company to manufacture alongside its customary reproduction items. Rohde's subsequent designs for Herman Miller, including this low lounge chair with its continuous C-shaped elements that form the back and arms, were simple yet well constructed, eschewing surface decoration in favour of high quality materials. Rohde also designed resolutely Modern furniture for other firms as well, including his *Model No. 180* cantilevered lounge chair for the Troy Sunshade Company – which offered comfort not only with its deep-padded cushion but also through the springy resilience of its tubular and flat steel frame.

Armchair, 1933
Stained wood, bentwood, leather-covered upholstery
Herman Miller, Zeeland (MI), USA

Model No. 180 lounge chair, 1933
Chromed tubular metal, flat steel,
lacquered wood, leather-covered
upholstery
Troy Sunshade Co., Greenville
(OH), USA

Mart Stam
Model No. B262 chair, 1935

Mart Stam is credited with the design of the first cantilevered tubular metal chair. It would appear that during a meeting about the forthcoming Weissenhof Siedlung, Stam showed Ludwig Mies van der Rohe drawings of an early prototype chair made from gas-pipes and subsequently both Mies and Marcel Breuer created their own cantilevered chairs from tubular steel. During the late 1920s, after much legal wrangling the German courts decided in Stam's favour and awarded him the patent for his invention. The chair, shown below, is one of a number of cantilevered variants that Thonet subsequently manufactured to Stam's designs.

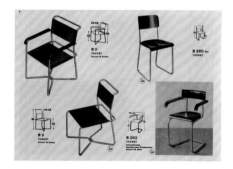

▲ Page from the Thonet catalogue showing the *Model No. B262* chair alongside seating designs by Marcel Breuer

Model No. B262 chair, 1935
Chromed tubular steel, lacquered wood
Gebrüder Thonet, Frankenberg, Germany

René Herbst
Armchair, 1930s

This extremely rare prototype armchair by René Herbst
employed state-of-the-art Bakelite for its seat, back and
armrests. This thermoset plastic, often referred to as "the
material of a thousand uses" was, however, too hard to
provide sufficient comfort and was also deemed unsuitable for
the large-scale mass-production of this innovative design. This
elegant Modernist chair is, however, an important precursor of
later plastic chairs that used other more flexible polymers that
were better suited for seating requirements.

Armchair, 1930s
Chromed tubular steel, Bakelite
France

Wolfgang Hoffmann
Lounge chair, c.1935

The son of the famous Austrian architect Josef Hoffmann, Wolfgang Hoffmann trained in Vienna, before moving to the USA in 1925. He subsequently opened his own design office on Madison Avenue and exhibited at the 1933 Chicago World's Fair, where he came to the attention of the Illinois-based furniture manufacturing company, Howell Co. From 1934 to 1942, he worked as the company's in-house designer creating numerous Moderne style chairs, including this tubular metal and leather lounge chair that epitomises the less doctrinal approach to Modernism taken by American designers.

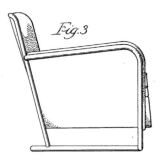

▲ Patent drawing of a similar armchair designed by Wolfgang Hoffmann, 1935.

◀ Lounge chair, c.1935
Chromed tubular steel, leather-covered upholstery
Howell Co., Geneva (Ill), USA

Kem Weber
Lounge chair, 1934

This quintessential "American Moderne" lounge chair by Kem Weber epitomises the Machine Age with its tear-drop supports made from gleaming chromed tubular metal. Unlike European Modernism that was deeply rooted in the idea of utilitarianism and social reform, American Modernism was in contrast more concerned with providing affordable luxury to the masses and a profit for the manufacturer. Interestingly, during the Depression, hard-pressed manufacturers found that if they gave their products, such as this seating design, a glamorous allure then they were more likely to sell. A variant of this chair was also produced with arching D-shaped supports.

Lounge chair, 1934
Chromed tubular steel, wood, leather-covered upholstery
Lloyd Manufacturing Company, Menominee (MI), USA

Max Stoelcker
Model No. 2200 *Frankfurter* chair, 1934–35

In 1922, Otto Stoelcker established a manufacturing plant in Southern Germany to initially produce wooden toys, and then slightly later utilitarian wooden furniture, which it marketed under the *Bombenstabil* (bomb-proof) brand reflecting its sturdy durability. In 1927 the company opened a second factory in Frankenberg to satisfy the increasing demand for its simple timeless seating designs. Around 1934, Max Stoelcker – Otto's son – developed a new model that was based on the concept of reducing a chair's parts to their most essential. Put simply, the design would have just legs, a seat, and a backrest, but other elements such as brackets would be eliminated. Patented as a "utility model", the *Model No. 2200* was to become a venerated icon of German design. Also referred to as "The Frankfurter Chair" or the "Frankfurt Kitchen Chair", this design was marketed under the slogan "New Age, New Form" and was to eventually become a ubiquitous feature of German interiors during the 1950s and 1960s .

▶ Holzindustrie GmbH catalogue
pages featuring the "bomb-proof"
Frankfurter chair, 1930s

◀ *Model No. 2200 Frankfurter*
chair, 1934–35
Wood
Holzindustrie GmbH, Ettenheim,
Germany

Lounge chair, 1931
Chromed tubular steel, wickerwork
Fritz Hansen, Allerød, Denmark

Frits Schlegel
Lounge chair, 1931 & School chair, 1930

Inspired by Bauhaus utilitarianism, the Danish architect,
Frits Schlegel designed various pieces of furniture and lighting
during the late 1920s and early 1930s that were notable for
their clean lines and inherent functionalism. His school chair
with its ergonomically contoured seat was originally designed
for the Husum School in Copenhagen, while his cantilevered
lounge chair was first exhibited at the influential design gallery,
Den Permanente in Copenhagen and was one of the first
Danish seating designs to incorporate tubular metal into
its construction.

School chair, 1930
Beech, stained bentwood
Fritz Hansen, Allerød, Denmark

Magnus Stephensen
Model No. 234 DAN chair, 1931

During the 1930s the pioneering Danish furniture manufacturer, Fritz Hansen launched its *DAN* range of chairs, which were notable for their utilitarian simplicity. Magnus Stephensen's *Model No. 234* was the bestselling design from this influential range and was produced in two backrest heights. With its appealing archetypal form, this design demonstrated that functionalism did not have to be hard-edged or emotionally sterile, but could instead evolve out of the Nordic craft tradition.

Model No. 234 DAN chair, 1931
Beech
Fritz Hansen, Allerød, Denmark

Søren Hansen
Model No. 261 DAN chair, 1932

Søren Hansen trained as a furniture-maker before entering into the management of Fritz Hansen – his family's furniture manufacturing business – in 1932, where he oversaw the firm's product development. In this capacity, he also designed a number of pieces himself over the years, including this small bentwood chair with its innovative and eye-catching arching element that forms the back section and the rear legs. Part of the successful *DAN* range of chairs, this design is believed to be Hansen's earliest design for the family firm.

Model No. 261 DAN chair, 1932
Bentwood, plywood
Fritz Hansen, Allerød, Denmark

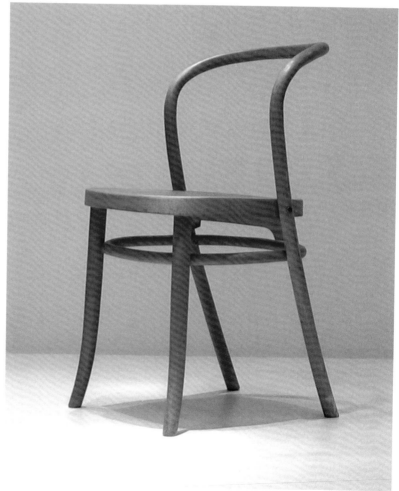

Klismos daybed, 1935
Fruitwood, leather
Saradis, Athens, Greece

Terence Harold Robsjohn-Gibbings
Klismos daybed, 1935 & *Klismos* chairs, 1935

The British-born architect, T.H. Robsjohn-Gibbings found considerable success in America as a decorator and furniture designer with his modern reinterpretations of historic furniture models. He designed his classical *Klismos* range of furniture in 1935, which with its concave backrails and elegantly tapering legs was directly inspired by Ancient Greek antecedents. After meeting the Greek cabinetmakers, Susan and Eleftherios Saridis, Robsjohn-Gibbings subsequently licensed this iconic range of furniture to be produced on an exclusive basis by their Athens-based workshop, Saridis.

Klismos chairs, 1935
Fruitwood, leather
Saridis, Athens, Greece

Warren McArthur
Tête-à-tête sofa, 1932 &
Model No. 1014 AUR armchair, c.1935

Warren McArthur was one of the leading American furniture designers during the 1930s, who helped to "glamorize" American living though his progressive seating designs such as his S-shaped *Tête-à-tête* sofa and his *Model No. 1014 AUR* armchair. In 1930, he filed a patent for an innovative means of constructing furniture, whereby the parts were held together without glue, screws or nails but instead locked together using standardised lengths of aluminium tubing and specially designed aluminium couplings. Using this revolutionary system, McArthur was able to manufacture a wide range of lightweight seating models (as well as tables, desks and dressers), that were easy to assemble and that could be transported in a knocked-down condition, and that were also eminately fashionable with their Machine Age aesthetic.

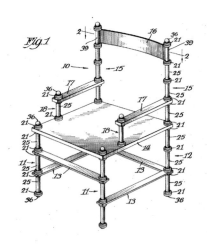

▲ Patent for innovative furniture construction filed by
Warren McArthur, 16 June 1930

▼ Interior featuring various furniture designs by Warren McArthur, 1930s

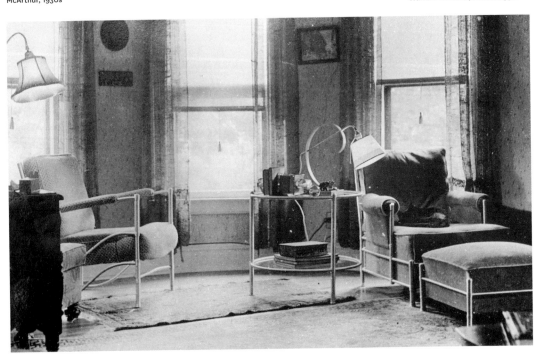

▲ *Tête-à-tête* sofa, 1932
Aluminium, textile-covered
upholstery, rubber
Warren McArthur Corporation, Los
Angeles (CA), USA

▶ *Model No. 1014 AUR* armchair,
c.1935
Aluminium, vinyl-covered
upholstery
Warren McArthur Corporation,
Rome (NY), USA

Nathan George Horwitt
Beta armchair, 1930

Nathan George Horwitt was guided as much by the issues of form and function as by a fascination of visual phenomena. In 1930 he designed the *Beta* chair for the Howell Company, which was included four years later in the landmark "Machine Art" exhibition held at the Museum of Modern Art, New York. This rare cantilevered chair employed the minimum of material yet achieved maximum visual impact with its B-shaped profile – quite simply a masterpiece of minimalism.

◀ *Beta* armchair, 1930
Painted tubular steel, leatherette-covered upholstery
Howell Manufacturing Co., St. Charles (IL), USA

▼ Patent drawings for the *Beta* armchair

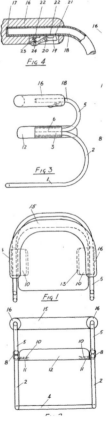

Xavier Pauchard
Model A chair, 1933

Shortly after the end of the First World War, Xaiver Pauchard established a company to produce household items from galvanized steel. In 1927, he registered the Tolix trademark and a few years later designed his well-known stackable *Model A* chair, which utilised galvanized steel in its production. Perfect for outdoor use, this inexpensive design was completely rust proof. Later in 1956, his son, Jean designed a matching armchair to compliment his father's earlier design, which is known as the *Model A56*.

Model A chair, 1934
Pressed sheet steel, tubular steel
Tolix, Autun, France

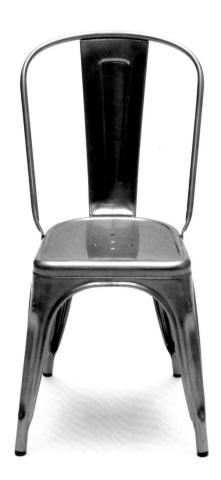

Kem Weber
Model No. LC-52 lounge chair, c.1930

A supreme example of the American Moderne style, the *Model No. LC-52* is an unashamedly opulent Art Deco design, yet ironically Kem Weber used in its construction tubular steel, a material more often associated with the utilitarian designs of European modernists than the glitzy Hollywood style found in American 1930s interiors. This chair retains its original tiger-stripped textile, however, the design was also offered in Naugahyde, a leather-look vinyl material that was patented and trademarked by Uniroyal Engineered Products in 1936.

Model No. LC-52 lounge chair, c.1930
Chromed tubular steel, fabric-covered upholstery, walnut
Lloyd Manufacturing Co., Menominee, Michigan, USA

Adrienne Gorska
Armchair, 1930

The architect and designer, Adrienne Gorska was the sister of the well-known Polish Art Deco painter, Tamara de Lempicka and certainly shared her older sibiling's artistic talents. Gorska initially studied architecture under Robert Mallet-Stevens at the Ecole Spéciale d'Architecture in Montparnasse, graduating in 1924. During the 1930s, she went on to design Modernist furniture for the Printemps department store's exclusive Atelier Primavera, including this visually bold lounge chair, which still retains its beautiful original Art Deco fabric.

Armchair, c.1930
Chromed tubular steel, textile-covered upholstery
Jean Robert Boivinet for Atelier Primavera, Paris, France

Erich Dieckmann

Model No. 8162 armchair, c.1931 &
Model No. 4218 chaise longue, c.1931

Having designed a number of severely rectilinear wooden slatted chairs in the 1920s, the following decade Dieckmann explored the functional and aesthetic potential of tubular metal. The resulting *Model No. 4218* chaise and the *Model No. 8162* armchair with their looping graphic profiles have a strong sense of dynamism that sets them apart from the majority of other tubular metal designs being produced in Germany during this period. These designs also demonstrated that Modern furnishings could at the same time be both functional and highly visually seductive.

▲► *Model No. 8162* armchair, c.1931
Nickel-plated tubular steel, laminated wood, caning
Cebaso-Stahlrohrmöbel, Ohrdruf, Germany

▼ *Model No. 4218* adjustable chaise, c.1931
Painted tubular steel, caning
D. Bamberger, Lichtenfels, Germany

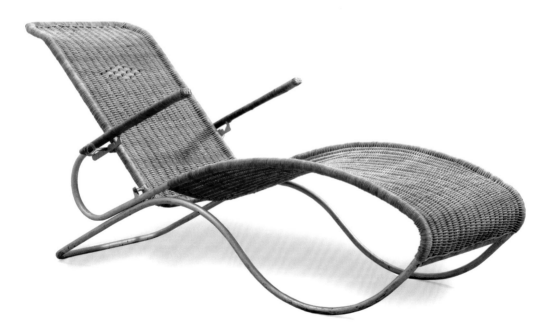

Anton Lorenz
Model No. LS22 daybed, 1931

In 1927, Anton Lorenz became managing director of Standard Möbel, a progressive furniture company founded by Marcel Breuer and Kálmán Lengyel. The following year, he established Desta, his own rival furniture manufacturing company that similarly produced designs utilising state-of-the-art tubular steel. Lorenz designed a number of furniture pieces for this venture, most notably his indoor/outdoor daybed with its continuous supporting frame. The *Model No. LS22* not only provided springy comfort, but also a remarkable physical lightness and visual transparency, which set it apart from earlier daybeds and reflected the growing concern for health and hygiene within domestic and public environments.

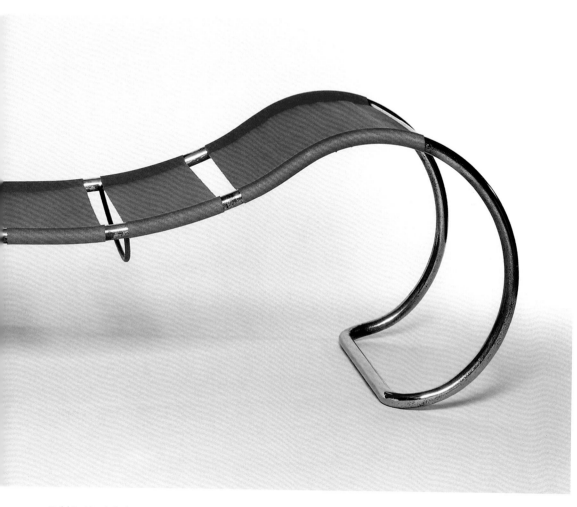

Model No. LS22 daybed, 1931
Chromed tubular steel, Eisengarn
Desta, Berlin, Germany (later
manufactured by Gebrüder Thonet,
Frankenberg, Germany)

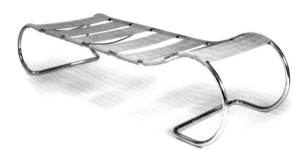

Marcel-Louis Baugniet
Armchair, 1934

Apart from being a leading proponent of abstract art in
his native Belgium, Marcel-Louis Baugniet also designed a
number of innovative chairs, including this unusual armchair
which utilises two loops of laminated wood for its supporting
structure. Having been influenced by the Modern designs
emanating from the Bauhaus, in 1930 Baugniet established his
own decorating firm in Brussels and subsequently exhibited
his furniture at the 1937 "Exposition Internationale des Arts et
Techniques dans la Vie Moderne" in Paris.

Armchair, 1934
Painted bent laminated wood,
fabric-covered upholstery
Marcel-Louis Baugniet, Brussels,
Belgium

Erich Dieckmann
Model No. 8217 armchair, c.1930

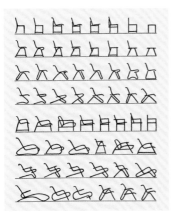

During the 1930s, Erich Dieckmann designed numerous chairs that incorporated state-of-the-art tubular steel for Cebaso-Stahlrohrmöbel, a manufacturer based in Thüringen. These chairs must have seemed startlingly avant-garde when they were introduced and often such overtly Modernist designs were too far ahead of popular taste to be widely accepted. Certainly, the *Model No. 8217* is amongst the most forward-looking of this influential group of furniture, however, with its low seat height and arching frame it is more human-centric than most German seating designs from this period.

▲ Drawing showing various seating designs by Eric Dieckmann, 1930-31

► *Model No. 8217* armchair, c.1930
Nickel-plated tubular steel, wickerwork, ebonised wood
Cebaso-Stahlrohrmöbel, Ohrdruf, Germany

René Prou
Chair, 1931

Celebrated as one of the first purveyors of the *goût moderne* (modern taste), René Prou initially worked as chief designer for the Parisian decorating company, Gouffe, before heading Bon Marché's Pomone art studio. During the 1930s, he also designed wrought-iron furniture for Edgar Brandt as well as this extraordinary side chair formed from folded sheet steel, which was decisively Modern and demonstrated the creative potential of this resolutely industrial material.

Chair, 1931
Sheet steel, leather-covered
upholstery
Labormetal, Paris, France

Jules Bouy
Armchair, c.1931

Born in France, Jules Bouy ran his own decorating firm in Brussels before emigrating in the early 1920s to New York, where he designed furniture that married French craftsmanship with American Art Deco forms. Bouy's armchair and a matching music stand executed in scrolling hand-hammered sheet steel were specially designed for the residence of the harpist, Carlos Salzedo and reflect the influence of Edgar Brandt's Art Deco ironwork, which was sold by the New York-based company, Ferrobrandt where Bouy worked.

Armchair, c.1931
Hand-hammered steel, upholstered cushion
Jules Bouy, New York, USA

Marcel Breuer
Chair for the Bryn Mawr College, 1938

Following his departure from Germany, Marcel Breuer initially moved to London where he became the design controller of Isokon, a firm that produced innovative Modern furniture using laminated wood and plywood. Subsequently relocating to the USA in 1937, Breuer was commissioned to design a range of Modern furnishings for the Bryn Mawr College in Pennsylvania, including this interesting desk chair, which like his earlier designs for Isokon was constructed of flat plywood cutouts. More humane in aesthetic than Breuer's previous tubular metal designs, this chair together with the Isokon seat furniture was tremendously influential on the following postwar generation of designers.

▲ Lounger designed by Marcel Breuer for Isokon, 1936

◄ Chair for the Bryn Mawr College, 1938
Birch
USA

Fritz Hansen
Office chair for Danish Working Environment Service, 1935

Having trained as a furniture-maker, Fritz Hansen was the third generation to work for his family's furniture manufacturing firm. Although he was mainly concerned with the production of furniture at the factory, while his brother Søren oversaw product development, Fritz was nevertheless responsible for development of this task chair. Designed in cooperation with the Danish Working Environment Service, it was manufactured with a "consideration for the human anatomy and with respect for the human position during work", and as such can be considered a very early example of an ergonomically designed office chair.

Office chair for Danish Working Environment Service, 1935
Painted tubular metal, moulded plywood
Fritz Hansen, Allerød, Denmark

Jean-Michel Frank
Armchair, c.1935 & Side chair, 1930s

◄ Armchair, c.1935
Oak, leather-covered upholstery
Jean-Michel Frank , Paris, France

► Side chair, 1930s
Cane, rattan
Jean-Michel Frank, Paris, France

Although he created thoroughly contemporary furniture, Jean-Michel Frank had a tempered approach to the design of Modern interiors and in 1935 wrote, "I believe that a less severe principle can be found – the 'mixing of styles.'" Certainly his designs, such as this oak armchair and rattan chair, could be successfully incorporated into eclectic-style interiors and the reason for this is that they were not only shaped by Frank's less doctrinal approach to Modernism, but also because they incorporated natural rather than manmade materials in their constructions.

Erik Chambert
Chair, 1930

Erik Chambert studied at the Högre Konstindustriella Skolan (University College of Arts, Crafts and Design) in Konstfack before joining his family's furniture-making business. He was responsible for the interior design of an apartment by Kurt von Schmalense that was shown at the landmark 1930 "Stockholm Exhibition", which was praised for its practical simplicity. His simple painted beech chair of 1930 similarly reflected what the design writer Helena Dahlbäck Lutteman was to later describe as his work's "humane functionalism".

Chair, 1930
Painted beech, leather
Sweden
(reissued by Kallemo, Sweden)

Charlotte Perriand
Side chairs, c.1935

Although Charlotte Perriand first came to prominence with her tubular metal Machine Age furniture designs done in collaboration with Le Corbusier and Pierre Jeanneret, during the 1930s she began exploring the use of rustic materials and the "ideal forms" honed over time that can be found in earlier vernacular seating designs. For instance, these rush-seated chairs and stools are essentially Modern re-workings of age-old country furniture typologies.

▲ Stools designed by Charlotte Perriand, c.1950 – retailed by Galerie Steph Simon

▶ Side chairs, c.1935
Ebonised oak, rushing
Sentou, France for Galerie Steph Simon

Axel Larsson
Armchair, 1937

Axel Larsson was one of the greatest proponents of Swedish Modernism, and as such he designed a living room interior for the Swedish Pavilion at the 1939 New York World's Fair. This woven-leather armchair was designed as part of this landmark installation and reflected a new Scandinavian definition of Modernism that was soft-edged and human-centric, and which also demonstrated a concern for craftsmanship and ergonomic form over pure utilitarian functionalism.

Armchair, 1937
Mahogany, leather
Svenska Mobelfrikerna, Bodafors, Sweden

Frits Henningsen
High-back wingchair, c.1939

This high-back wingchair by Frits Henningsen reflects the very Danish evolutionary approach to the design process, which seeks to hone successful historic antecedents into "ideal" Modern designs. Here the traditional gentleman's club wingchair has been transformed into a flowing sculptural entity that is ergonomically refined so as to afford the sitter maximum comfort.

High-back wingchair, c.1939
Oak, leather-covered upholstery, brass
Frits Henningsen, Copenhagen, Denmark

Gio Ponti
Chair from the Montecatini Office Building, 1938

Described in *Domus* magazine as "A Palace of Work", the Montecatini Office Building in Milan was one of Gio Ponti's first architectural commissions and it was conceived as a totally holistic work of art, which included the design of site-specific furnishings. These side chairs were part of a series of related seating designs used in the chemical company's headquarters building that incorporated standardised elements across a range of models, thus reflecting Ponti's belief in functional efficiency.

▲ Office chair and desk designed by Gio Ponti for the Montecatini office Building, 1938

◄ Chair for the Montecatini Office Building, Milan, 1938
Aluminium, vinyl, Bakelite
Kardex Italiano, Milan, Italy

Charles Eames & Eero Saarinen
Side chairs for the Kleinhans Music Hall, 1939

Although, the architect, Eliel Saarinen was responsible for the design of the Kleinhans Music Hall in Buffalo, New York, his son, Eero Saarinen and Charles Eames undertook the design of the project's site-specific furniture. These early Eames-Saarinen furniture designs explored the manufacturing potential of moulded plywood for seating shells, and as such were an important precursor of the duo's award-winning designs for the Museum of Modern Art's "Organic Design in Home Furnishings" competition held in 1940.

Side chairs for the Kleinhans Music Hall, 1939
Birch, textile-covered upholstery
USA

1940s

Charles Eames & Eero Saarinen
Side chair, 1940

Eames and Saarinen's prize-winning series of innovative seating designs for MoMa's 1940 "Organic Design in Home Furnishings" competition, employed compound-moulded plywood seat shells covered with thin latex padding, thereby providing continuous contact and support without the need for any internal springing. Amongst the most important furniture designs of the twentieth century, these revolutionary lightweight yet comfortable chairs heralded a totally new direction in Modern chair design.

► Side chair, 1940
Moulded plywood, wood, textile-covered foam rubber
USA

▼ Photograph of armchair designed by Charles Eames and Eero Saarinen for the "Organic Design in Home Furnishings Competition", 1940 – showing moulded plywood and latex construction

▼ Cover of the "Organic Design in Home Furnishings" exhibition/competition catalogue, Museum of Modern Art, New York, 1940

12

Edgar Bartolucci & Jack Waldheim
Barwa outdoor lounge chair, 1946

In 1946, Jack Waldheim and Edgar Bartolucci filed a patent for chairs which employed a supporting framework of tubular metal and a flexible wrinkle-free covering that would "resiliently support an occupant in a comfortable and relaxed position" but would "resume its original position and shape" afterwards without any sagging. Intended for outdoor use, the *Barwa* rocking lounger – its title derived from a contraction of its designers' surnames – was also an extremely stylish design that possessed an engaging graphic profile with the minimum of means.

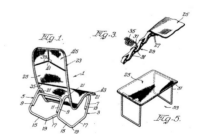

▼ *Barwa* outdoor lounge chair,
1946
Tubular aluminium, flexible canvas
Barwa Associates, Chicago (IL), USA

▲ Patent drawing of furniture designed by Edgar Bartolucci and Jack Waldheim, including a variant of their *Barwa* outdoor lounge chair

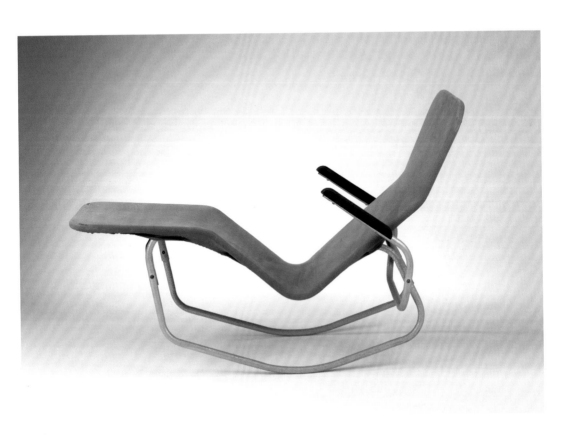

Gilbert Rohde
Model No. 3445-w lounge chair &
Model No. 3453-w ottoman, c.1940

Gilbert Rohde's furnishings for Herman Miller, including this Art Deco lounge chair and ottoman, were distinguished by clean lines and bold forms – a look that defined American Modernism during the 1940s. Significantly, Rohde's Moderne-style furniture laid the foundations on which George Nelson, and Charles and Ray Eames were able to create truly modern seating designs for this remarkably influential furniture company during the postwar years.

Model No. 3445-w lounge chair &
Model No. 3453-w ottoman, c.1940
Lacquered wood, vinyl and textile-covered upholstery
Herman Miller, Zeeland (MI), USA

Utility Furniture Advisory Committee
Model No. 3a dining chair, 1942

In 1942, the British Government's Board of Trade issued a directive outlining the criteria for wartime furniture produced under its utility regulations: "Furniture of sound construction in simple but agreeable design, for sale at reasonable prices and ensuring the maximum economy of raw materials and labour." The same year, the *Model No. 3a* dining chair with its simple construction stripped of any superfluous decoration was introduced under the Board's Utility Scheme, thereby epitomising British design reform during the wartime years.

▼ Catalogue page showing a variety of "Utility Scheme" furniture designs, c.1943, including the *Model No. 3a* dining chair

► *Model No. 3a* dining chair, 1942
Oak, moulded plywood, fabric-covered upholstery
Board of Trade Utility Furniture, London, England

LIVING ROOM

SIDEBOARD : Second Section—Model Ia
Price £10.7.0

The living room furniture is in oak. The dining chairs have loose, padded seats covered with leather cloth, in a variety of colours.

SIDEBOARD : Second Section— Model Ib
Price £10.7.0

Sideboard, with doors open, showing inside shelves. The sideboards are 4 ft. wide, 2 ft. 9 ins. high and 1 ft. 6 ins. deep.

DINING CHAIR :
Second Section—Model 3a
Price £1.9.0

DINING CHAIR :
Second Section—Model 3c
Price £1.9.0

Test load per chair:
1700 lbs.!

Only 2 aluminum lightweights can take on 5 heavyweights!

Emeco's amazing heat-treatment makes these aluminum chairs **tougher than steel!**

It's the perfect way to make the perfect chair:

Make it of workable aluminum, to form without distortion in the bends.

Then **heat treat** it to incredible strength, toughness, rigidity. So it can support nearly a ton — 1700 pounds — with less than ⅛-in. permanent distortion. So just **one** chair could support those wrestlers — **and a couple of their biggest friends!**

And anodize the surface into aluminum oxide, next to diamonds in hardness.

Result: the perfect chair (available in 7 models) . . . fantastically strong, corrosion-resistant, wipeable clean, light on its feet. **Far and away the lowest in cost**, when you measure service and length of life.

Send for a sample of aluminum "before" and "after". It supports our story as surely as it takes on the heavyweights.

AVAILABLE AS GSA STOCK ITEM
FEDERAL STOCK NO. 7110-264-5339

7110-264-5339

EMECO DIVISION
Standard Furniture Company
Hanover, Pa. 17331

Telephone E. F. Quinn, Government Administrator — (717) 637-5951

Witton C. Dinges
Model No. 1006 Navy chair, 1944

◄ Emeco advertisment
emphasising the load-bearing
potential of the company's
aluminium chairs, c.1944.

Sometimes referred to as the *Navy* chair, the *Model No. 1006* chair was commissioned by the US Navy for use on warships during the Second World War. Witton C. "Bud" Dinges, the founder of Emeco, designed the all-aluminium model, which was a translation of an archetypal wooden chair into what was then a state-of-the-art material. In fact, this rust proof chair was so durable that it far exceeded the US Navy specifications, and many of the original World War II chairs still survive. Despite its Machine-Age aesthetic, however, its production was (and still is) relatively laborious, comprising 77 different manufacturing steps.

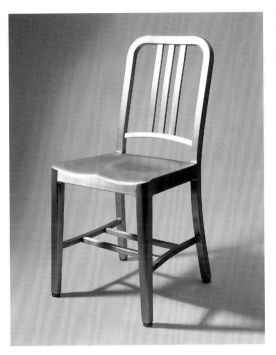

▲ *Model No. 1006 Navy* chair, 1944
Aluminium
Electric Machine and Equipment
Company (Emeco), Hannover (PA),
USA

André Arbus
Adjustable armchairs, 1949

André Arbus designed these adjustable armchairs for the music room of his own townhouse in Paris. Like other designs by him, these chairs are imbued with a refinement that harks back to earlier historic paradigms, in this case Regency campaign chairs. The exquisite detailing of these chairs, such as the looping swan-necked frame that subtly provides an integrated headrest, reflects the impressive level of craftsmanship that still existed in the French workshops even after the devastation of the Second World War.

Adjustable armchairs, 1949
Mahogany, caning, metal
France

Joaquim Tenreiro
Three-legged chair, c.1947 &
Cadeira Recurva de Espaldar Alto chairs, 1949

The son of a joiner, Joaquim Tenreiro began designing furniture in the early 1930s and by the 1940s he was creating avant-garde designs that were extremely forward-looking and led him to become rightly regarded as "the father of modern Brazilian furniture". The pair of side chairs have striking proportions, while the sculptural three-legged model shown below, is an unusual polychromatic design that was seamlessly crafted from solid strips of differently coloured native woods and is generally considered to be Tenreiro's most accomplished design.

▲ Three-legged chair, c.1947
Jacarandá, imbula, ivorywood, cabreúva
Tenreiro Móvels e Decorções, Brazil

▶ *Cadeira Recurva de Espaldar Alto* chairs, 1949
Jacarandá, cane
Tenreiro Móvels e Decorções, Brazil

Frederick Kiesler
Chair for the Art of This Century Gallery, New York, 1942

A visionary innovator, Romanian-born Frederick Kiesler was one of the foremost pioneers of modern art in America. He was also highly influential within the field of design creating a number of furniture pieces, including this ingenious sculptural chair. Designed for an installation at Peggy Guggenheim's influential Art of This Century Gallery, this multi-purpose biomorphic chair was also intended to function as a pedestal when placed on end. Significantly, with its functional flexibility this model playfully presaged the emergence of more art-based seating designs, which appeared in increasing numbers over the following decades.

▲ Photograph of Peggy
Guggenheim's Art of This Century
Gallery, c.1942

◄► Chair for the Art of This
Century Gallery, New York, 1942
Ash, linoleum
Frederick Kiesler, New York, USA

Carlo Mollino
Armchair for the Orengo House, 1949 &
Side chair for the Reale Mutua Assicurazioni offices, 1948

Carlo Mollino was a unique force in Italian postwar design, creating sculptural furniture that had an innate dynamism. His armchair from 1949 – sometimes referred to as the *Gaudí* chair because its melting form is reminiscent of the great Catalan architect's work – was originally designed as a unique piece for the Orengo House. His earlier side chair, which was specifically designed for the Reale Mutua Assicurazioni offices, had a similar construction with its three legs joined by a crosspiece element and it was also sculpted from solid wood.

► Side chair for the Reale Mutua Assicurazioni offices, 1948
Oak
Apelli & Varesio, Turin, Italy

◄ Armchair for the Orengo House, 1949
Maple, brass
Apelli & Varesio, Turin, Italy
(later reissued as a limited-edition of nine by A. Allemandi-Pinerolo, Turin, Italy)

Ico & Luisa Parisi
Sofas and lounge chairs, 1946

This stylish seating range was designed by Ico and Luisa Parisi during the immediate postwar period, and as such was probably intended more for the export market rather than the Italian domestic market. With its sculpted walnut frames, this collection of chairs and sofas was innovative in that it incorporated then state-of-the-art latex foam for its upholstery, which provided an ample level of comfort. Eliminating the need for bulky traditional springing, the utilization of latex foam also meant that seating could now be both physically and visually lighter, thereby heralding a new direction in seating design.

Sofas and lounge chairs, 1946
Walnut, textile-covered latex foam upholstery
Italy

Jean Royère
Boule sofa, 1947 & *Boule* armchairs, c.1947

Jean Royère's *Boule* sofa and armchairs are also sometimes referred to as *Ours Polaire* (Polar Bear), no doubt due to the rounded bulky forms of the suite resembling the Artic predator especially when its deep pile textile covering appears in creamy white. Although not formally trained as a designer, Royère became one of the most influential French decorators during the 1940s and 1950s thanks to his imaginative flair that allowed him to create innovative forms that were quintessentially Parisian as well as stylishly Modern.

Boule sofa, 1947
Oak, textile-covered upholstery
Jean Royère, Paris, France

► Interior designed by Jean
Royère featuring his *Boule*
armchairs

▼ *Boule* armchairs, c.1947
Oak, textile-covered upholstery
Jean Royère, Paris, France

Hans Wegner
Model No. CH27 armchair, 1949

Throughout his long and illustrious career, Hans Wegner designed numerous chairs that were remarkable for their reworking of "ideal" forms and meticulous attention to detail. His *Model No. CH27* easy chair was no exception with its inclined seat and back that provided comfort without the need for upholstered padding. This design, alongside other chairs by Wegner, epitomizes the casual sophistication of Danish Design and his uncanny ability to marry Modern forms with age-old craft skills.

Model No. CH27 armchair, 1949
Oak, woven cane
Carl Hansen & Søn, Odense, Denmark

Finn Juhl
Egypterstol (Egyptian chair), 1949

This elegant dining chair was, as its name suggests, inspired by ancient Egyptian precedents. This can be seen in particular in its distinctive sloping backrest that is supported by vertical upright elements. Like many other furniture designs by Juhl, the *Egypterstol* was produced by the talented cabinetmaker, Niels Vodder whose workshop was renowned for its supreme high quality craftsmanship. With their subtle contours and beautifully grained rosewood, a set of these chairs adorned the dining room of Juhl's own house.

Egypterstol (Egyptian chair), 1949
Rosewood, leather-covered
upholstery
Niels Vodder, Copenhagen,
Denmark

Børge Mogensen
Spoke-back chair, 1945

A modern reworking of a traditional spoke-back chair, this design was originally created by Børge Mogensen for a three-room apartment installation that he co-designed with Hans Wegner for the Copenhagen Cabinetmakers' Guild's Autumn exhibition held in 1945. Although this was one of Mogensen's earliest seating designs it was a highly accomplished piece that revealed his innate understanding of materials and demonstrated his youthful mastery of form and function.

Spoke-back chair, 1945
Walnut, fabric-covered upholstery
Fredericia Furniture A/S, Fredericia, Denmark

Ray Komai
Model No. 939 chairs, 1949

Having wooden rather than metal legs, these chairs are very rare and early versions of the *Model No. 939*, a seminal seating design that was created by Rai Komai in 1949. The model's one-piece moulded seat shell was extremely innovative in its day and pushed the physical limits of the plywood to produce a very elegant solution. In recognition of its pioneering use of plywood the *Model No. 939* received a Good Design Award from the Museum of Modern Art, New York in 1950.

Model No.939 chairs, 1949
Walnut, walnut-veneered plywood
JG Furniture Systems, Quakertown
(PA), USA

Søren Hansen
Armchair, 1943

Manufactured by Fritz Hansen, this unusual armchair was designed by the grandson of the firm's founder, Søren Hansen. Utilising moulded plywood for its distinctive curved back section, bentwood for its tilted armrests and solid wood for its legs, the form of this chair was conceived to be as ergonomically comfortable as possible. Interestingly, its back section bears a striking resemblance to the moulded plywood seat shell of Arne Jacobsen's later *3107* chair, which was launched by Fritz Hansen some twelve years later.

Armchair, 1943
Ash plywood, bentwood, solid ash
Fritz Hansen, Allerød, Denmark

Hans Wegner
Model No. 1936 lounge chair, 1948

Hans Wegner was a veritable chair-designing maestro who created numerous models that were not only functionally practical but also outstandingly aesthetically pleasing. For instance, this sculptural lounge chair designed for Fritz Hansen innovatively incorporated moulded teak-veneered plywood for its scoop-like seat and back sections giving it a strong sculptural presence. A two-seater version of this design was also produced and both the chair and sofa remained in production until the mid-1950s.

Model No. 1936 lounge chair, 1948
Teak-veneered plywood, beech
Fritz Hansen, Allerød, Denmark

Gustav Axel Berg
Torparen (The Farmer) lounge chair, 1942

Gustav Axel Berg trained as an engineer before embarking
on a career as an industrial and furniture designer. In 1933
he established his own furniture store and subsequently
exhibited his designs in the Swedish Pavilion at the 1939 New
York World's Fair. His chair designs, including the *Torparen
(The Farmer)* were based on his extensive in-depth ergonomic
research into optimum seating positions and were also highly
influential in their choice of materials – laminated wood and
hemp webbing.

▲ Low-backed variant of the
Torparen lounge chair, c.1942

◄ *Torparen* lounge chair, 1942
Laminated birch, webbing
G.A. Berg, Stockholm, Sweden

Jean Prouvé
Visiteur armchairs, 1942

The *Visiteur* armchair was first designed in 1942 and various modified versions of the design were subsequently produced, including a model with small wheels attached to the front legs. Intended as an "easy or visitors chair" this design with its tubular metal supporting frame, wooden slatted back and solid wood armrests had a bold utilitarian presence, and with its removable cushions and ergonomically angled seat and back provided a good level of comfort.

Visiteur armchairs, 1942
Oak, enamelled steel, textile-covered cushions
Ateliers Jean Prouvé, Nancy, France

Ilmari Tapiovaara
Armchair, 1947 & *Domus* armchair, 1946

Designed for the Museum of Modern Art's 1948
"International Competition for Low-Cost Furniture
Design", Ilmari Tapiovaara's leather and birch armchair
of 1947 was a rationally conceived "knock-down"
solution that was developed so that it could be easily
shipped in a disassembled state. Similarly, his *Domus*
chair was also a well-considered design that could
be stacked efficiently making it not only suitable
for public buildings, but also easy to transport and
thereby to export.

► *Domus* armchair, 1946
Solid birch, moulded plywood
Keravan Puuteollisuus, Kerava,
Finland

▼ Thonet publicity photograph
showing a stack of *Domus* chairs,
c.1946

◄ Armchair, 1947
Birch, leather
Thonet, Finland

Charles & Ray Eames
LCW prototype chair, 1945 & *LCW* chair, 1945

Amongst the most iconic chairs of all time, the *LCW* (Lounge Chair Wood) is a veritable landmark in the evolution of the Modern chair. Having developed compound-moulding plywood techniques for the manufacture of leg splints for the US Navy during the Second World War, Charles and Ray Eames applied their know-how to a range of chairs that had moulded plywood seat and back sections that provided comfort without the need for additional upholstery. The design also had the added benefit of an inherent flexibility thanks to the pioneering use of rubber shock mounts that were connected to the wood using a newly developed electronic welding technique. The development of this seating programme involved the execution of numerous prototypes (including the one shown below) until it was completely honed for mass-production, and once it was launched various models were made available including the attractive red aniline-dyed variant shown on the right.

► *LCW* chair, 1945
Aniline-dyed moulded birch plywood, rubber, metal
Evans Products Company, Venice (CA), USA for Herman Miller Furniture Co., Zeeland (MI), USA

▼ *LCW* prototype chair, 1945
Moulded plywood, rubber
Evans Products Company, Venice (CA), USA

Charles & Ray Eames
Prototype side chair, c.1944

During the development of their landmark range of plywood chairs in the mid-1940s, Charles and Ray Eames experimented with various bases, including the three-legged version shown here. Manufactured by the Molded Plywood Division of Evans Products Company, this rare variant never made it into full-scale mass-production, presumably because of stability issues. Experimental prototypes such as this are among the most highly prized by collectors today. Paradoxically, Charles Eames himself always valued the latest production models more because they were the most refined both functionally and aesthetically.

▲ Patent drawing showing another experimental leg configuration devised to be used with the standardized seat and back sections to create a tilt-back, 1947

◄ Prototype side chair, c.1944
Moulded plywood, tubular metal, rubber
Evans Products Company, Venice (CA), USA

Charles & Ray Eames
Child's chair, 1945

Fig.1

Fig.2

In 1945, Charles and Ray Eames designed this diminutive stacking chair, alongside a table, a desk and stool that were intended for children. Produced and distributed by Evans Products Company of Venice, California, this programme was available in a range of attractive stained hues: red, yellow, blue and magenta. The chair had a simple two-piece construction made of plywood, the moulding of which relied on techniques that the Eameses had earlier pioneered in their development of splints for the US Navy. In contrast to most existing children's furniture from this period, which were essentially miniature versions of adult-sized models, the Eameses' children's furniture had a playful toy-like simplicity, with, for example, the chair's folk-art inspired heart-shaped motif functioning as a useful hand-hole.

▲ "Design for a Chair", patent filed, 1946

▶ Child's chair, 1945
Aniline-dyed birch plywood
Evans Products Company, Venice (CA), USA

Charles & Ray Eames
DAW armchair, 1948–50

Charles and Ray Eames developed their *Plastic Shell Group*, in collaboration with Herman Miller, Zenith Plastics, and the engineering department of the University of California, Los Angeles. This project was based on the concept of a universal seat shell (with arms and without) that could be used with a variety of interchangeable bases to provide numerous variations. Importantly, these chairs were also the first large-scale designs to be mass produced using synthetic polymers. Introduced by Herman Miller in 1950, they were subsequently offered in a wide range of colours and interchangeable base options. This seating group – including the *DAW (Dining Armchair Wood)* – is among the most important in the history of furniture, because it introduced the concept of an integrated seating system, while successfully exploiting the manufacturing potential of plastics.

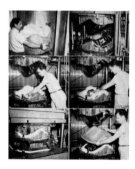

◄ Series of photographs showing the moulding of the Eameses' fibreglass seat shell, *Plastics Industry* magazine, 1950

◄ *DAW* (Dining Armchair Wood), 1948–50
Fibreglass, metal, wood
Zenith Plastics, Gardena (CA), USA
& Herman Miller, Zeeland (MI), USA

Egmont Arens
Chair, 1949–50

Best known for designing packaging and industrial products, Egmont Arens coined the term "consumer engineering", and wrote extensively on the relationship between design and marketing. Many of his products had an appealingly modern streamlined appearance, including this highly rational one-piece plastic shell chair that he designed for the General American Transportation Corporation. The ergonomic curves of the design's fiberglass seating section were informed by detailed posture studies that involved making clay impressions of variously sized posteriors. Impressively, the moulded seat shells could be mass-produced at the rate of one every five minutes.

◄ The "Posture Meter" devised by Egmont Arens using clay impressions in order to achieve as he put it, an "anthropometric design".

▼ Chair, 1949–50
Lacquered fibreglass, enamelled tubular steel
General American Transportation Corporation, Chicago (IL), USA

Edward Durrell Stone
Chaise longue, 1945–46 & Chair, 1945–46

A prominent postwar American architect, Edward Durell Stone was born in Fayetteville, Arkansas, an area known for its rustic "Ozark" cabin-style furniture. During the 1940s, he designed a line of furniture that could be best described as "Ozark Modern" for a company based in his hometown, using traditional materials and techniques but in a thoroughly modern way. Elements of the resulting chairs, chaises, stools and tables were inspired by farm implements, most notably plough handles, while their woven seats utilized local basket-weaving techniques.

▶ Chair, 1945–46
Oak, woven oak and hickory basketwork
Fulbright Industries, Fayetteville (AR), USA

▼ Chaise longue, 1945–46
Oak, woven oak and hickory basketwork
Fulbright Industries, Fayetteville (AR), USA

Frits Henningsen
Armchair, c.1940

Frits Henningsen designed furniture that was made by his own cabinetmaking workshop in Copenhagen, which was noted for its high-degree of craftsmanship and use of exotic woods. With its graceful curved lines, this armchair is an unusual hybrid design that reflects the very Danish desire to evolve "ideal forms" from earlier successful furniture types. Modern yet at the same time historicizing, this design reflects the continuing craft tradition found within Danish design during the 1940s.

Armchair, c.1940
Mahogany, leather-covered upholstery
Frits Henningsen, Copenhagen, Denmark

Alexandre Noll
Chair, c.1945

One of the twentieth century's foremost designer-makers, Alexandre Noll was not only an accomplished "form giver", but possessed a technical mastery of wood. He began working in wood in 1920 and beyond sculpture he also produced exquisitely carved and boldly formed wooden furniture, including this delightful asymmetric modern-rustic chair that looks as though it was carved for one of Goldilock's bears. Certainly, Noll delighted in exploring the plastic potential of wood and over his career designed various rough-hewn organic furniture pieces, which due to their beauty and rarity are now highly prized by collectors today.

Chair, c.1945
Sycamore
Alexandre Noll, Paris, France

Jens Risom
Model No. 652W armchair, 1941 &
Model No. 654W lounge chairs, 1941

▲ *Model No. 654W* lounge chairs,
1941
Spruce, leather webbing
Knoll Associates, New York, USA

◄ *Model No. 652W* armchair, 1941
Spruce, canvas webbing
Knoll Associates, New York, USA

The first designer to be commissioned by Knoll Associates, Jens Risom created a series of modern chairs, including the *652W* armchair and the *654W* lounge chair shown here, that were the result of a four month trip across the United States researching the type of contemporary furnishings that architects and interior designers were looking for. Because of wartime material restrictions, the chairs initially utilized army surplus parachute straps for their webbed seat sections. However, this was later replaced with either canvas or leather webbing.

Mogens Lassen
Stool, 1942

The Danish architect, Mogens Lassen became acquainted with the Modernist work of Le Corbusier during a trip to France (1927–28) and subsequently he became a leading protagonist of Danish Modernism. His best-known furniture design is this three-legged stool that was sculpted by the master cabinetmaker, K. Thomsen using imported solid teak. As a Modernist-reworking of the traditional milking stool, it is a design that reflects the long-held desire among Danish designers for "ideal forms" that are evolutionary rather than revolutionary.

Stool, 1942
Solid teak
K. Thomsen, Copenhagen, Denmark

Egon Eiermann
Model No. E10 lounge chairs, 1949

A leading architect in postwar Germany, Egon Eiermann was also a founding member of the Rat für Formgebung (German Design Council). His woven rattan *Model No. E10* lounge chair marked a departure from the prewar tubular metal aesthetic of the Bauhaus, and one hundred of these chairs were subsequently used inside and outside the German Pavillion which he designed for the 1958 Brussels World's Fair. Eiermann also designed a matching stool in 1957, however, his interest in the design possibilities of rattan went back to 1936 when he unusually created garage doors from this rather engaging natural material.

Model No. E10 lounge chairs, 1949
Woven rattan, textile-covered cushion
H. Murmann, Johannistal-Kronach, Germany (reissued by Richard Lampart)

Edward Wormley
Model No. 5499 lounge chairs, c.1949

Following a trip to Paris, where he met Le Corbusier and
Émile-Jacques Ruhlmann, Edward Wormley began designing
furniture with simple lines and unadorned surfaces. In 1931,
he was hired by the manufacturer, Dunbar to improve its
cheapest furniture line. He subsequently went on to design
around 150 pieces a year for the company, including these
elegant Mid-Century Modern lounge chairs. As the renowned
textile designer, Jack Lenor Larsen noted: "Wormley was a
major influence on American design in the mid-century" and
throughout his long career he consistently created designs
that were understated yet graceful.

Model No. 5499 lounge chairs,
c.1949
Ebonized wood, brass, textile-
covered upholstery
Dunbar Furniture Corp., Berne
(IN), USA

Harvey Probber
Sling chair, c.1948

Credited with introducing sectional modular seating into
America during the 1940s, Harvey Probber founded his own
furniture company in 1945 to produce his own progressive
designs that were characterized by clean uncluttered
geometric lines. His best-known design is the striking *Sling*
chair, which was included in the Museum of Modern Art's
"Good Design" exhibition of 1948. Interestingly, Probber
understood the importance of durability and in an interview
in 1958 described "the quality of aging gracefully" as "design's
fourth dimension."

Sling chair, c.1948
Laminated birch, textile-covered
upholstery
Harvey Probber Inc., New York
(later Fall River (MA), USA

Ralph Rapson
Model No. 657 rocking chair, c.1945

In 1945, Knoll launched the "Rapson Line", a range of five chairs by the American architect-designer, Ralph Rapson that included this remarkable rocker. Made of solid wood and army surplus webbing, this design had originally been conceived in the 1930s but was not put into mass-production until after the Second World War. The *Model No. 657* was a completely radical rethinking of how a rocking chair could be constructed and as such epitomized the playful "New Look" confidence of American postwar furniture.

Joaquim Tenreiro
Cadeira de Embalo chaise longue, c.1947

Born in Portugal, Joaquim Tenreiro came from a family of carpenters and learnt woodworking skills at a young age. He later emigrated to Brazil and during the early 1940s began creating bold geometric furniture within the Modernist idiom. In 1943, he established his own manufacturing company to produce his designs using local tropical hardwoods, including this beautiful rocking chaise longue. As a leading Brazilian furniture designer, Tenreiro was also commissioned by Oscar Niemeyer to create a number of chairs for the architect's residential projects.

Cadeira de Embalo chaise longue, c.1947
Cabrúva, cane, textile-covered cushions
Tenreiro Móveis e Decorações, Rio de Janeiro, Brazil

James Donahue
Winnipeg lounge chairs, c.1949

A.J. Donahue studied architecture at the University of Minnesota and later at Harvard University. He subsequently worked on the development of new materials at the Building Research Division of the National Research Council of Canada. Inspired by Charles and Ray Eames' moulded plywood experiments, he went on to create a single-piece plywood seating shell for his sculptural *Winnipeg* chair. This rare design was self-produced in limited numbers and because of its resemblance to George Nelson's better-known design is sometimes referred to as the "Canadian Coconut" chair.

Winnipeg lounge chairs, c.1949
Walnut plywood, textile-covered upholstery, brass
A.J. Donahue, Winnipeg, Canada

Eero Saarinen
Womb sofa, 1947–48

As head of the planning unit at Knoll Associates, Florence Knoll asked the Finnish-born architect, Eero Saarinen to design "a chair she could curl up in". The resulting *Womb* chair launched in 1948 was a landmark design that cocooned the sitter and allowed them to assume a comfortable relaxed sitting position. Importantly, this breakthrough design and the related sofa, shown here, incorporated a moulded fibreglass seat shell and foam padding that provided a high degree of comfort with the minimum of means.

Womb sofa, 1947–48
Fibreglass, chromed tubular steel, textile-covered upholstery
Knoll International, New York, USA

James Leonard
Esavian school chair, 1948

Education Supply Association Limited (ESA) specialized in fabricating schoolroom partitions and later enormous aircraft hangar doors, which were sold under the Esavian brand. During the 1940s, the company branched out into furniture manufacturing, most notably producing this stacking school chair with its cast-aluminium frame and plywood seating section. James Leonard also designed an adult-sized version and an armed model of this utilitarian chair as well as matching desks and tables for the educational market.

Esavian school chair, 1948
Cast aluminium-alloy, beech plywood
Education Supply Association Ltd., London, England

Max Bill
Tripod chair, 1949

Swiss-born, Max Bill was a veritable artistic polymath working as an architect, fine artist, typographer, industrial designer and graphic designer. All his work, however, was governed by an innate understanding of mathematical proportion, which gave it a strong sense of compositional clarity. His three-legged chair designed in 1949 was no exception with its triangular-formed seat and back elements made of blond plywood, which seemingly hover above the solid teak frame.

Tripod chair, 1949
Teak, birch laminated wood
Horgen-Glarus, Glarus,
Switzerland/Wohnnedarf AG,
Zurich, Switzerland

Richard Neutra
Armchair for the Kahn House, 1940

Born in Austria, Richard Neutra emigrated to the United States in 1923, where he briefly worked for Frank Lloyd Wright in Chicago before re-locating to California, where he famously designed numerous International Style residences. This Modernist armchair was specifically designed for the living room of the Sidney Kahn House in San Francisco, and as such echoed the building's airy geometry and understated "Californian Modern" elegance.

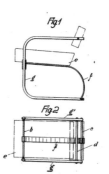

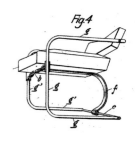

▲ Patent drawing of an earlier chair designed by Richard Neutra, 1931, with a similar geometric formal vocabulary

◄ Armchair for the Kahn House, 1940
Bent plywood, tubular steel, acrylic, textile-covered upholstery
USA

Rudolph Schindler
Dining chair for the Lechner House, 1948

Born in Vienna, Rudolph Schindler moved to Chicago in 1914 and four years later began working at Frank Lloyd Wright's Oak Park studio, where he oversaw numerous commissions. In 1922, he set up his own architectural practice in Los Angeles, and like Wright, he frequently designed site-specific furnishings for his various architectural commissions, such as this dining chair for the Richard Lechner residence in Studio City, California. Here Schindler innovatively used simple cuts of plywood to create a functional pedestal chair with dynamic planes and angles.

Dining chair for the Lechner House, 1948
Douglas fir plywood, textile-covered upholstery
USA

Pierre Jeanneret
Model No. 92 Scissor chairs, c.1947

Pierre Jeanneret was a Swiss architect and cousin of Charles-Éduoard Jeanneret, otherwise known as Le Corbusier, with whom he worked alongside Charlotte Perriand in Paris in the 1920s. Jeanneret's patented design for the *Scissor* chair was originally manufactured in France in 1947 before being put into production by the American firm Knoll in 1948 under the additional name of *Model No. 92*. Made of solid maple with an innovative circular chrome-plated steel bolt, the *Scissor* chair was Knoll's first piece of upholstered furniture.

Model No. 92 Scissor chairs, c.1947
Maple, chromed steel, cotton webbing, textile-covered cushions
France
(later by Knoll Associates, New York, USA)

Eero Saarinen
Model No. 72 chair, 1945

The Finnish born architect Eero Saarinen moved to the United States in the 1920s and started working for Knoll in 1946. His designs included the popular 1947–48 *Womb* chair whose organic form is also present in his designs for office furniture. In 1948, he filed a patent for a new office chair, which he had actually designed three years prior to this. This upholstered chair was subsequently put into production the same year by Knoll for General Motors's headquarters. The resulting *Model No. 72* and its armed variant the *Model No. 71* were available in a variety of leg combinations, seat and back colours and materials, and set a new benchmark for office seating.

▲ Knoll publicity photograph
showing the *Model No. 72* variants

▶ *Model No. 72* chair, 1945
Plywood, chromed tubular steel,
textile-covered upholstery
Knoll International, New York, USA

1950s

Jules & André Leleu
Desk chair, 1950s

This chair was created with a matching desk for an apartment in Paris, the interior scheme of which was designed by the well-known decorating firm, Maison Leleu. Unlike most desk chairs, this model managed to combine stylish good looks with functional practicalities, including a 5-star base for extra stability, a seat height-adjustment mechanism and partially padded arms for increased working comfort.

Desk chair, 1950s
Mahogany, patinated metal,
velvet-covered upholstery
Maison Leleu, Paris, France

Jacques Adnet
Lounge chairs, c.1950

Thierry Hermés was a Parisian saddle maker who founded his own eponymous company in 1837. The *maison* started out producing leather goods, but soon expanded to include the manufacture of clothing, accessories and eventually furniture. During the 1950s, Jacques Adnet designed a number of chairs for the company that exploited the firm's extraordinary leather-working skills, including these stylish lounge chairs with their distinctive faux-bamboo frames.

Lounge chairs, c.1950
Steel, brass, leather-covered upholstery
Hermès, Paris, France

Peter Hvidt & Orla Mølgaard Nielsen
AX side chair, 1950 & *Model FD-135 Boomerang* chair, 1956

During the Second World War, wood laminating techniques were advanced through among other things, the production of De Havilland's *Mosquito* combat aircraft, nicknamed the "wooden wonder". After the war, Fritz Hansen exploited the potential of this new material in its *AX* series of chairs designed by Peter Hvidt & Orla Mølgaard Nielsen – which included a side chair, an armchair, a three-seater sofa and a version with a padded leather seat. Hvidt and Mølgaard Nielsen also designed the elegant *Boomerang* chair for France & Davorksen, which possessed a similar constructional refinement.

► A variant of the *AX* chair with a padded leather seating section, c.1950

▲ ► *Model FD-135 Boomerang* chair, 1956
Teak, metal, textile-covered cushions
France & Davorksen, Hillerød, Denmark (later to become France & Søn)

◄ *AX* side chair, 1950
Laminated wood, plywood
Fritz Hansen, Allerød, Denmark

Hans Wegner
Model No. CH28 Sawbuck lounge chairs, 1951

The *Model No. CH28 Sawbuck* chair was inspired, as its title suggests, by the form of traditional "sawbucks", or as they are better known in Britain, "saw horses", devices that hold wood in place while it is being sawn. With its inverted V-shaped legs and tilted armrests, Hans Wegner's *Sawbuck* chair was actually less historicizing than many of his seating designs, which were often based on earlier vernacular seating types. Instead, this seating solution reflected a strong Danish Modernity borne out of exacting craftsmanship skills and a desire for no-nonsense practicality and comfort.

Model No. CH28 Sawbuck lounge chairs, 1951
Teak, plywood, leather or textile-covered upholstery
Carl Hansen & Søn, Valby, Denmark

Frank Lloyd Wright
Chairs for the Usonian Exhibition House, 1953

In 1936, Frank Lloyd Wright conceived a range of low cost homes, which he christened "Usonian". In tune with the harsh economic realities of the period, these houses were purposely designed with budgetary constraints in mind, having no basements, attics or superfluous decoration. Over the decades, Wright continued developing this idea of low-cost housing and in 1953 built a fully furnished Usonian House as part of an exhibition in the Guggenheim Museum's gardens, and these simple plank-like chairs with their distinctive cut-out motif formed an integral part of this scheme.

Chairs for the Usonian Exhibition House, 1953
Oak plywood, textile-covered cushion
Plycraft Products, Evergreen Park (IL), USA

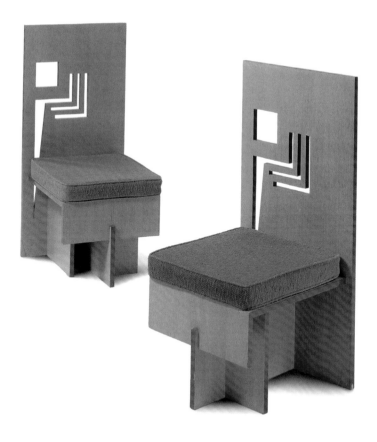

Nanna & Jørgen Ditzel
Ring chair, 1958

The *Ring* chair takes its name from the large-sized semi-circular tube shape that forms the back and arms of the armchair. It was designed in 1958 by Nanna and Jørgen Ditzel; she had previously apprenticed as a cabinetmaker and studied at the School of Arts & Crafts in Copenhagen, while he had trained as an architect. The couple set up their own design studio after marrying in 1946 and worked together until the latter's death in 1961. The chair was originally made by Kolds Savværk in Denmark and distributed in the USA by George Tanier. In 2007, it was rereleased as the *Sausage* chair by the Finnish manufacturer Artek.

RING CHAIR

DESIGNED BY *Nanna + Jørgen Ditzel*
SELECTED IN DENMARK BY
GEORGE TANIER INC
591 MADISON AVE, NEW YORK 22, N.Y. THROUGH DEALERS DECORATORS ARCHITECTS

▲ George Tanier Inc.
advertisement for the *Ring* chair,
c.1958

◄ *Ring* chair, 1958
Teak, fabric
Kolds Savværk, Kerteminde,
Denmark

Yngve Ekström
Arka chairs, c.1952

The Swedish furniture designer Yngve Ekström played a
key role in developing the modern Scandinavian style. In
1945 he founded Swedese Möbler with his brother Jerker
Ekström, which Yngve Ekström directed, designed for and
also commissioned pieces from leading designers. From the
1950s he also designed a number of pieces of furniture for the
Swedish manufacturer Stolfabriks including the *Arka* chair
from 1952. Originally made of oak and teak, this Windsor-style
chair with a low, stick-back and wide seat has been reissued
by the Swedish manufacturer Stolab in birch.

Arka chair, c.1952
Teak
Stolfabriks, Småland, Sweden

Hans J. Wegner
Teddy Bear lounge chair and ottoman, 1951

One of the greatest and most prolific chair designers of all time, Hans Wegner always used the same design process: first he would work up an idea into a drawing, then convert this into a precisely scaled model and then into a full-sized prototype. By using this workshop-based methodology, Wegner managed to thoroughly hone his ideas and the resulting designs – such as his wonderful *Teddy Bear* chair – were consistently highly resolved. Also referred to as the *Papa Bear*, this lounge chair alludes through this alternative title to the *Goldilocks* children's tale. Wegner's designs were always visually and functionally compelling, while also possessing an innate charm.

▲ A.P. Stolen brochure featuring the *Teddy Bear* lounge chair, 1950s

▼ *Teddy Bear* lounge chair and ottoman, 1951
Oak, fabric-covered upholstery
A.P. Stolen, Denmark (later P.P. Møbler)

Finn Juhl
Model No. NV-53 armchair, 1953

Made for the Cabinetmakers' Guild exhibition of 1953, the
NV-53 is a beautifully proportioned armchair that reveals
Finn Juhl's supreme mastery of wood and sculptural form.
Originally Juhl had envisioned that this chair would be covered
in cowhide, however, the master craftsman Niels Vodder with
whom he collaborated on the production of this chair and
numerous other seating designs, only ever manufactured it
with fabric-covered upholstery.

Model No. NV-53 armchair, 1953
Teak, brass, fabric-covered
upholstery
Niels Vodder, Copenhagen, Denmark

Pierre Paulin
Model No. F157 Oyster chair, 1954

A maestro of chair design, Pierre Paulin was renowned for creating innovative seating solutions that offered superlative comfort. Although less known than some of his later designs, the *Oyster* is nevertheless extremely resolved both in aesthetic and functional terms. With its simple chromed metal base, this design has a minimalist quality, which makes its upholstered, body embracing seat shell appear to be almost weightless, as though it is floating.

▲ Artifort promotional photograph of the *Model No. F157 Oyster* lounge chair, c.1955

◄ *Model No. F157 Oyster* lounge chair, 1954
Jersey-covered upholstery, wood, springing, chromed tubular metal
Artifort, Maastrict, Netherlands

Pierluigi Giordani
Lounge chair and Sofa, c.1955

The Italian architect, Pierluigi Giordani – like his fellow
countrymen, Gio Ponti and Carlo Mollino – created furniture
that expressed the sculptural biomorphic bravado and almost
animalistic poise of Italian furniture design during the postwar
period. Presumably drawing inspiration from the earlier
Art Nouveau style as well as Surrealism, Giordani's suite of
furniture had an almost oozing, melting quality with its arching
armrests not only gently cradling the sitter's elbows but also
giving the overall impression that at any moment, or indeed
at even the slightest provocation, these characterful chairs
and sofa could potentially become animated and scuttle out
of the room.

Lounge chair and Sofa, c.1955
Walnut, velvet-covered
upholstery, brass
Italy

Lucien Engels
Lounge chair, c.1954

In 1950, the architects, Lucien Engels and Roger de Winter received a commission to design a new recreational building in the popular Belgian seaside resort of Oostduinkerke. For this project, Engels also site-specifically designed this low-seated armchair that echoed the building's form and colour palette. Although only thirty of these chairs were made, the design can be seen to reflect the idealism and optimism of the socialistic political mood of the Continent during the postwar period.

Lounge chair, c.1954
Birch, ebonized birch, painted metal
Belgium

Willy Guhl
Loop rocking chair, 1954

Designed as a weather-resistant chair for the garden, the *Loop* was moulded from a newly developed reinforced concrete material known as Eternit, which was produced for the house-construction industry as slabs that could be pressed into the required forms while in its moist unset state. As an inexpensive composite building material, Eternit was ideal for the production of outdoor furniture because it offered incredible durability, high tensile strength and required no supporting structural element. Conceived as a single-piece looped form, Guhl's chair had a strong sculptural quality and achieved its creator's desire of "achieving the optimum with minimum effort".

▲ Eternit publicity photograph
showing *Loop* chair being used,
1950s

► *Loop* rocking chair, 1954
Eternit fibre-reinfornced concrete
with surface sealant
Eternit AG, Niederurnen - reissued
by WB Form, Switzerland

George Nelson
DAF chair, c.1956

One of the great innovators of American design, George Nelson created technically cutting-edge furniture that was always not only ergonomically refined but also aesthetically surprising. This visually striking armchair has a moulded fiberglass seat shell that provided comfort without upholstery. The seat shell rests on a distinctive pedestal base with tapering "swag legs" made of 16-gauge steel. The overall sculptural effect expresses an understated yet stylish Mid-Century Modern sophistication.

◄ *DAF* chair, c.1956
Fibreglass, chromed steel
Herman Miller Inc., Zeeland (MI), USA

▼ Herman Miller brochure showing *DAF* chair and the flexi-backed *MAA* chair, c.1956

Niko Kralj
Rex folding chair, 1952

A pioneer of industrial design in his native Yugoslavia, Niko Kralj graduated as an architect before heading the design bureau of a furniture factory in Duplica. His *Rex* armchair of 1952 was the first Slovenian chair created for the mass-market. Incorporating an innovative perforated moulded plywood construction, this Cold War design afforded greater comfort than other wooden folding chairs thanks to its ergonomic curves. A rocking version was also available.

Rex folding armchair, 1952
Moulded plywood
Lowenstein, Duplica, Yugoslavia
(Slovenia)

Sol Bloom
Scoop chair, 1950

Sol Bloom's design for the high-backed *Scoop* chair was included in the Museum of Modern Art's first "Good Design" exhibition in New York in 1950. It was shown alongside other wrought iron furniture by designers such as Eero Saarinen and was part of a fashion for wrought iron furniture in the domestic interior at this time. In these designs, the metal's appealing malleability, sturdiness and practicality was matched with the clean lines of the Modernist aesthetic, that is also seen in Bloom's *Catch-It-All* wire mesh stand from the same year.

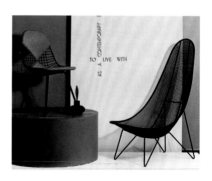

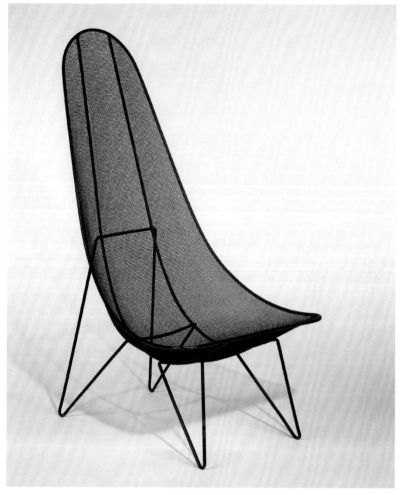

▲ "Good Design" display featuring Sol Bloom's *Scoop* chair, 1950

◄ *Scoop* chair, 1950
Enamelled metal wire mesh, metal rods
New Directions Furniture, Houston, USA

Egon Eiermann
Model No. *E20* chair, 1957

Egon Eiermann was responsible for creating eight
interconnecting steel and glass pavilions for the German
section at the landmark Expo 58 exhibition, also known as the
Brussels World's Fair held in 1958. For this prestigious project
he also created the wickerwork *E20* chair specifically for the
pavilions' outside areas. With its flaring basket form, this chair
had a charming sculptural quality whilst also being relatively
inexpensive to produce through its utilization of low-tech
materials and manufacturing processes.

Model No. E20 chair, 1957
Lacquered wicker
Heinrich Murmann, Johannisthal,
Germany

Verner Panton
Model 276 S chair, 1956

Although Verner Panton designed this eye-catching cantilevered chair in 1956, it wasn't actually put into production until the mid-60s. Presumably it not only took time to develop the moulding technology sufficiently, but also for the public's taste to catch up to Panton's forward-looking Pop aesthetic. Significantly, this single material/single form chair can be seen as an important precursor of its more famous younger brother – the ubiquitous plastic *Panton* chair.

◄ *Model 276 S* chair, 1956
Lacquered moulded plywood
A. Sommer, Germany for Gebrüder Thonet

▼ A rare variant of the *S* chair, c.1956

Lina Bo Bardi
Bowl chair, 1956

Born in Italy, Lina Bo Bardi studied architecture in Rome and worked in Gio Ponti's office, prior to establishing her own Milan-based design practice. She subsequently moved with her husband to Brazil and became a leading figure within the country's design and architecture community. Her best-known design, the *Bowl* chair, consists of a simple metal frame onto which a hemispherical seating bowl rests, the position of which can be adjusted to suit the user's requirements.

▲ Early publicity photograph showing the *Bowl* chair in use, 1950s

▶ *Bowl* chair, 1956
Painted iron, aluminium, fabric-covered foam upholstery
Italy

Paul McCobb
Chairs, c.1955

Paul McCobb was one of the most influential designers in America during the postwar period with his sleek contemporary furniture designs being distinguished by a simple pared-down aesthetic. These ladder-back dining chairs with their straightforward dowel connections and plain iron frames reflected the American desire for unfussy contemporary furnishings that had an inherent practicality.

Chairs, c.1955
Iron, birch
Winchendon Furniture
Company, Winchendon (MA), USA

Russel Wright
Samsonite folding chair, c.1953

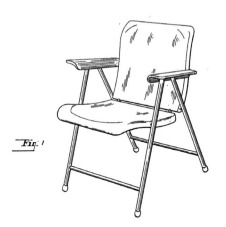

Fig. 1

Although Shwayder Brothers Inc. was better known for its production of trunks and Samsonite suitcases, the company also produced folding chairs and tables – either for card-playing or patio use. One of its most successful folding chairs was designed by Russel Wright (patented in 1953) and utilized pressed metal seat and back sections that were painted. The model shown here, however, is a rare variation that is slightly less utilitarian in that it incorporated moulded plywood instead.

◄ Patent drawing of the *Samsonite* folding chair, 1953

▼ *Samsonite* folding chair, c.1953
Birch plywood, enamelled steel
Shwayder Brothers Inc., Denver (CO), USA

Marco Zanuso
Senior armchair, 1951 & *Lady* sofa, 1951

Epitomising the stylish new look of postwar Italian design, Marco Zanuso's elegant *Senior* armchair was one of the first seating designs to use latex foam in its construction. This new wonder material of the period eliminated the need for bulky traditional springing, thereby allowing contours that had previously been unattainable in seating design. Incredibly innovative in its day, the *Lady* sofa and its matching chair were awarded first prize at the 1951 Milan Triennale, and even now their charming, retro-yet-contemporary appeal endures.

◄ *Senior* armchair, 1951,
Wood, elasticated strapping,
chromed tubular metal, textile-
covered latex foam upholstery
Arflex, Milan, Italy

▼ *Lady* sofa, 1951,
Wood, elasticated strapping,
chromed tubular metal, textile-
covered latex foam upholstery
Arflex, Milan, Italy

▲ Arflex advertisement, 1950s,
featuring the *Lady* chair and the
Senior chair

Marco Zanuso
Sleep-O-Matic sofa, 1954

Having developed foam rubber padding and elasticated webbing suitable for furnishings, Pirelli founded a new furniture manufacturing division, Arflex, in 1948 to produce sleek contemporary designs using these innovative new materials. One of the most successful of these was Marco Zanuso's *Sleep-o-matic* sofa, which won a Gold medal at the X Milan Triennale in 1954 for its pioneering use of state-of-the-art materials and its innovative construction that allowed it to be easily converted into a comfortable bed.

Sleep-O-Matic sofa, 1954
Metal, textile-covered foam
upholstery
Arflex, Meda, Italy

Carlo Mollino
Chair for the Casa Editrice Lattes, 1953

Designed for the Turin headquarters building of the Lattes publishing house, this lightweight side chair exploited the expressive potential of moulded plywood with its slender elements formed into sensuous arching curves. Certainly Carlo Mollino was a truly gifted designer who created furnishings that were not only inventive in terms of their constructions but that were also boundary pushing in relation to their aesthetics. For the Lattes project, Mollino also designed various other chairs, tables, desks and lighting that similarly pushed the formal limits of the materials they employed.

Chair for the Casa Editrice Lattes, 1953
Moulded plywood, brass, textile-covered upholstery
Apelli & Varesio, Turin, Italy
(Images courtesy of Galerie Historismus, Brussels)

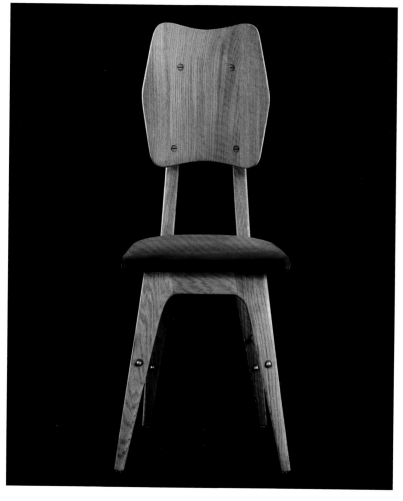

Finn Juhl
Lounge chairs, 1955

The Danish architect and designer, Finn Juhl created beautifully crafted wooden furniture that became synonymous with the term "Danish Modern" during the 1940s and 1950s. These lounge chairs with their wonderful combination of teak, leather and caning revealed the extraordinary ability that Juhl possessed to create harmoniously balanced designs that had an understated sophistication. Interestingly this design also had the added benefit of an adjustable leather strap that allowed the backrest to be positioned into varying angles thereby providing an extra degree of comfort.

▲ Design for lounge chairs by Finn Juhl, 1955

▼ Lounge chairs, 1955
Teak, caning, brass, leather-covered upholstery
Niels Vodder, Copenhagen, Denmark

Edward Wormley
Chaise longue, c.1956

As a young and gifted designer, Edward J. Wormley began working for the Dunbar Furniture Company in 1931. He remained the company's design director for over three decades and created a plethora of furnishings that were notable for their careful detailing and casual functionality – such as this elegant chaise longue. As Wormley noted, "Furniture is needed for practical reasons, and because it must be there, it may as well be as pleasant as possible to look at, and in a less definable psychological way, comforting to the spirit."

Chaise longue, c.1956
Mahogany, cane, metal
Dunbar Furniture Company, Berne (IN), USA

Gio Ponti
Distex lounge chair, 1953 & Lounge chairs, 1950s

◄ *Distex* lounge chair, 1953
Textile-covered upholstery,
lacquered walnut
Cassina, Meda, Italy

▼ Lounge chairs, 1950s
Textile-covered upholstery,
walnut, brass
Italy
(for M. Singer & Sons, USA)

The *Distex* lounge chair, sometimes referred to as *Model No. 807*, was one of the most commercially successful designs that Gio Ponti created for Cassina. It was also one of his most visually stunning designs and with its unusual faceted planes the chair epitomizes the elegant sophistication of Italian furniture during the 1950s. The open-armed lounge chairs designed by Ponti around the same time, were made in Italy for the American company M. Singer & Sons and also possess a similar stylish élan and employed a comparable angular geometry.

Yngve Ekström
Lamino armchair, 1956

A leading figure within Swedish design, Yngve Ekström created the visually striking *Lamino* chair in 1956. With its elegant ergonomic form made of a laminated wood frame and a canvas backing, this easy chair offered a soft-edged interpretation of Modernism that was utterly in keeping with the more casual lifestyles of the mid-1950s. With its beautiful flaring armrests and sinuous back that echoes the line of the human spine, the *Lamino* is a veritable Scandinavian design classic, being named "The Best Swedish Furniture Design of the Century" in 1999 and also winning the I.M.M Cologne Award for best design in 2003. The design is still manufactured by Swedese Möbler, a company founded by Yngve Ekström with his brother, Jerker and Sven Bertil Sjöqvist in 1945.

► Yngve Ekström inspecting a *Lamino* armchair, 1950s

▼ *Lamino* armchair, 1956
Laminated plywood, sheepskin, canvas
Swedese Möbler, Vaggeryd, Sweden

Dan Johnson
Model No. 50B Gazelle lounge chair & *Model No. 30W Gazelle* armchair, 1956

These chairs are part of the *Gazelle* furniture collection by the artist and designer Dan Johnson in 1956 and are his best-known designs. The American-born Johnson lived in Italy in the 1950s until moving back to the USA in 1962, an internationalism that was reflected in the *Gazelle* furniture itself. Production took place at the Dan Johnson Studio that had been set up in Rome, before moving to Foligno (then Tormini) in northern Italy, and distributed by the Californian firm Arch Industries. The latter's closure and the furniture's high production costs account for their rarity, as less than 150 pieces were ever made. Originally available with walnut or bronze frames, in 2008 Brown Jordan put cast-aluminium versions into production.

► *Gazelle* chair with bronze frame, c.1956

◄ *Model No. 50B Gazelle* lounge chair, 1956
Walnut, cane, brass
Dan Johnson Studio, Rome, Italy

► *Model No. 30W armchair*, 1956
Walnut, cane, brass
Dan Johnson Studio, Rome, Italy

Jean Prouvé
Model No. 352 Direction chair, c.1951

As a young man, Jean Prouvé worked as an artisan blacksmith and this formative experience was to profoundly influence his later career as an architect and furniture designer. For him, there was "no difference between the construction of an item of furniture and that of a house" and as such he used the same rational process-driven methodology. For instance, his *Model No. 352 Direction* armchair and its variation shown here, reveals a somewhat rough-and-ready approach to design that can also be found in his buildings.

Model No. 352 Direction chair, c.1951
Enamelled metal, wood, vinyl-
covered upholster
Ateliers Jean Prouvé, Nency, France

Jean Prouvé
Bridge armchair, c.1953

Jean Prouvé designed the *Bridge* armchair as essentially
an executive director's chair. With its bold utilitarianism
that utilized industrial materials, namely sheet and tubular
steel, this design had a stylish machine aesthetic that could
be traced back to an earlier seating design, the *Standard*
chair. Although employing a similar construction, the *Bridge*
armchair was, however, produced in far lower quantities than
its utilitarian yet stylish precusor.

Bridge armchair, c.1953
Sheet steel, tubular steel, oak,
leather-covered upholstery
Les Ateliers Jean Prouvé, Nancy,
France

Gio Ponti
Lounge chair, c.1955

A virtuoso form-giver as well as a highly accomplished furniture designer, Gio Ponti designed numerous chairs during his long and prolific career, including this elegant lounge chair for Cassina. Ponti often incorporated triangular and diamond forms within his designs, as in this armchair, which gave his work a dynamic tension and a modish angularity that came to epitomize the cool edgy stylishness of Italian postwar design.

▲ Rocking chair by Gio Ponti for Cassina, c.1950 – photographed without cushions, this design employed similar angular forms

◄ Lounge chair, c.1955
Walnut, webbing, fabric-covered seat cushion
Cassina, Meda, Italy

Poul Volther
Pyramid chair, 1958

With its visually striking segmented back, the *Pyramid* lounge chair can be seen as a direct precursor of Paul Volther's better-known *Corona* chair from 1964. This rare seating design with its curved back elements cradles the user in upholstered ergonomic comfort and predicts the growing sculptural confidence that was to emerge in Scandinavian design during the 1960s. The *Pyramid* chair was produced by the Allerød-based family-run furniture workshop established by the two brothers, Ejnar and Lars Peder Petersen in 1953, which is now better known as the Danish furniture manufacturing company, PP Møbler.

Pyramid chair, 1958
Solid oak, oak faced plywood,
fabric-covered upholstery
PP Møbler, Allerød, Denmark

Taichiro Nakai
Sofa, 1954

The Japanese designer, Taichiro Nakai's eye-catching sofa consists of a wooden frame with an off-centre upholstered back and expansive, curving L-shaped seat. It is an early example of collaboration between an international designer and an Italian manufacturer, as it was the result of Nakai's successful entry to the inaugural *Selettiva di Cantù* competition. Nakai entered a complete set of living room furniture for the competition, in which winning designs were manufactured by local producers and put on display in the town of Cantù, near Milan, in 1955.

Sofa, 1954
Wood, velvet-covered upholstery
Consorzio La Permanente Mobili,
Cantù, Italy

Folke Jansson
Arabesk sofa and chair, c.1955

The curving cutout back and riotous yellow and black
textile pattern make the *Arabesk* one of the more exuberant
examples of post-war Scandinavian design. Designed by the
Swedish designer Folke Jansson in 1955, the chair and sofa
were originally manufactured by Wingrantz Möbelindustri
AB in a limited production run of 50 chairs and four sofas
between 1955 and 1958, and then later in Denmark by Fritz
Hansen. Originally made of hand-carved wood, the chair is
now produced by the Italian manufacturer Matrix International
with a metal frame and expanded foam padding.

Arabesk sofa and chair, c.1955
Wood, foam rubber, fabric
Wingrantz Möbelindustri AB,
Skövde, Sweden

Tapio Wirkkala
Model No. 9019 Nikke chair, 1958

One of the greatest form-givers of the twentieth century, Tapio Wirkkala possessed a remarkable understanding of materials and ergonomics that directly informed his work. During the early 1950s, he developed an innovative method of gluing alternating layers of birch and teak together that allowed him to create a patterned laminate with different coloured striations, as utilized in the seat section of his beautiful *Nikke* chair of 1958. He also used this simple yet visually striking technique in his design of sculptural bowls and tables.

Model No. 9019 Nikke chair, 1958
Laminated birch, laminated teak, chromed tubular steel
Asko Oy, Helsinki, Finland

Marco Zanuso & Richard Sapper
Lambda chair, 1963

With its L-shaped seat section, the *Lambda* chair's name makes reference to the eleventh letter of the Greek alphabet. Weighing just five kilos, this elegant side chair won a prestigious Compasso d'Oro award for its innovative stamped sheet-metal construction and was subsequently shown at MoMA's landmark 1972 "New Domestic Landscape" exhibition.

Lambda chair, 1963
Enamelled pressed-forged sheet metal, plastic
Gavina, Bologna, Italy

Florence Knoll
Sofa, c.1952

With its clean lines and innate functionalism, this innovative sofa had a pivoting mechanism that allowed the back section to swing out and away from its seating/mattress section so as to provide a large bed. Like other designs by Florence Knoll, this simple elemental design had an understated contemporary sophistication that reflected her extraordinary understanding of spatial composition.

Sofa, c.1952
Enamelled steel, textile-covered upholstery
Knoll Associates, New York, USA

Mabel Hutchinson
Daybed, 1955

Mabel Hutchinson's design for a daybed with wooden legs
and a two-part wooden back is punctuated with two rows
of identically-sized circles that add to its contemporary,
modernist appearance. Hutchinson was an independent artist,
sculptor and furniture maker from West Coast America, whose
other designs for wooden furniture include a chest, sideboard
and pair of doors. Her designs, which were included in the
California Design exhibitions held between 1954 and 1976 at
the Pasadena Art Museum, cemented Hutchinson's place in
the Californian post-war design scene.

Daybed, 1955
Walnut-veneered plywood,
upholstery
Mabel Hutchinson, California, USA

100, The Slim Multi-Position Contour Chair, with the foot rest that disappears,* designed by Vladimir Kagan.

*PATENT PENDING

K A G A N - D R E Y F U S S

125 EAST 57 STREET, NEW YORK 22, NY · SEND $1 FOR NEW TRI-FORM CATALOG

Vladimir Kagan
Contour sofa and chair, 1950s

According to Kagan's website, "Sensuously formed designs that warmly enfold a person in elegant comfort typify the classic chair designs of Vladimir Kagan". Certainly the *Contour* range can be seen as the classic Kagan collection, which includes this sofa and high-backed chair. Combining sculptural forms with comfortable padded upholstery, these Kagan designs have a distinctive dynamic poise with their swooping armrests and swept-back rear legs.

► *Contour* sofa, c.1959
Walnut, fabric-coved upholstery
Kagan-Dreyfuss Inc., New York, USA

◄ Kagan-Dreyfuss Inc. advertisement featuring the *Slim Multiposition Contour* chair with footrest, 1950s

► *Contour* high-back lounge chair, c.1952
Walnut, fabric-coved upholstery
Kagan-Dreyfuss Inc., New York, USA

▲ *Model No. 503 Wing* lounge
chair and ottoman, 1952
Walnut, fabric-covered upholstery
Kagan-Dreyfuss Inc.,
New York, USA

Vladimir Kagan

Model No. 503 Wing lounge chair and ottoman, 1952,
Model No. 176SC sofa, 1952 & *Contour* chaise longue, c.1952

Effortlessly tasteful and casually sophisticated, Vladimir
Kagan's furniture marked a highpoint in the realm of American
home furnishings during the 1950s. Whether it was his
undulating chaise longue, his elegant *Wing* chair or his
gracefully curved sofa with its "floating" back, Kagan's work
epitomized a stylish Mid-Century Modernity that abandoned
the socialist inspired utilitarianism of earlier Modern
Movement protagonists, whilst also demonstrating a new
sculptural confidence within post-war design.

► *Contour* chaise longue, c.1952
Walnut, fabric-covered upholstery
Kagan-Dreyfuss Inc., New York, USA

▼ *Model No. 176C* sofa, c.1952
Walnut, fabric-covered upholstery
Kagan-Dreyfuss Inc., New York, USA

Charles & Ray Eames
Model No. 670 lounge chair, 1956

Charles and Ray Eames' *Model No. 670* lounge chair is one of the best-known seating designs of all time. Its segmented moulded plywood construction was a refined evolution of an earlier prototypical design they had created for the Museum of Modern Art's "Organic Design in Home Furnishings" competition held in 1940. With its ample proportions, rosewood veneer and down-filled buttoned leather cushions, it was also their first chair design developed for the luxury end of the home furnishings market. Normally the *Model No. 670* was upholstered in black leather giving it a rather masculine feel, and certainly it was Charles Eames' intention that the chair was to possess the "warm receptive look of a well-used first baseman's mitt". The design, however, was also produced in other colours, most notably in brown and white, and also occasionally in bright red.

Model No. 670 lounge chair, 1956
Cast aluminium, rosewood-faced moulded plywood, leather-covered cushions
Herman Miller, Zeeland (MI), USA

Ib & Jørgen Rasmussen
Kevi office chair, 1958

Twin brothers, Ib and Jørgen Rasmussen both studied
architecture at The Royal Danish Academy of Fine Arts, before
founding their own studio in 1957. The following year they
were commissioned to design a villa for Bent Harlang, a main
shareholder and manager of the furniture manufacturing
company, Kevi A/S. The outcome was so successful that he
subsequently asked the brothers to design chairs for the
company. The resulting *Kevi* multi-purpose office chairs were
truly revolutionary in their design, especially after 1965 with
the addition of Jørgen's innovative *Kevi Wheel*, a double-wheel
castor that allowed the chairs to glide smoothly over the floor.

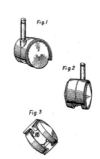

◄ Patent drawing of revolutionary
Kevi castor invented in 1965

▼ Variant of *Kevi* office chair, 1970s

◄ *Kevi* office chair, 1958
(redesigned 1973)
Aluminium, plastic
Kevi A/S, Glostrup, Denmark
(later Engelbrechts,
Copenhagen, Denmark)

Ilmari Tapiovaara
Aslak armchair, 1957

Belonging to the functionalist camp within the Scandinavian design community, Ilmari Tapiovaara sought to create products that were rationally conceived for mass-production. To this end, he designed the *Domus* armchair in 1946, which had a solid birch frame and moulded plywood seat and back. He subsequently went on to design a variant of this well-known chair called the *Aslak* that was even more suited to large-scale production with its distinctive moulded laminated wood armrests that swoop down to form the rear legs.

▲ Ilmari Tapiovaara shown holding the *Lukki 1* chair designed for Lukkiseppo Oy, 1952, a precursor of his later and better-known, *Aslak* chair

► *Aslak* armchair, 1957
Laminated maple, plywood, metal screws
Asko Oy, Helsinki, Finland

Ilmari Tapiovaara
Pirkka chair, 1955 & *Mademoiselle* chairs, 1956

Throughout his design career, Ilmari Tapiovaara pursued the goal of the "ideal" chair and to this end designed a number of models that were based on earlier vernacular precedents. For instance, his *Mademoiselle* chair and *Pirkka* chair are both modern re-workings of traditional wooden chairs that had been functionally honed over the decades, if not centuries. He also designed a rocking version of the *Mademoiselle* lounge chair as well as the later *Crinolette* armchair which was similarly constructed. He also executed variants of the *Pirkka* chair, including a low stool, a bar stool and a bench. These simple and honestly constructed seating models had a timeless functionality as well as an engaging homely quality.

▲ *Crinolette* armchairs designed by Ilmari Tapiovaara for Asko Oy, c.1961

◄ *Pirkka* chair, 1955
Pine, lacquered birch
Laukaan Puu, Finland
(reissued by Artek)

► *Mademoiselle* chairs, 1956
Lacquered birch
Asko Oy, Finland
(reissued by Artek)

Pierre Jeanneret
Kangourou lounge chair, c.1956 & armchair, c.1956

India's first modern planned city, Chandigarh was designed by Le Corbusier and his cousin, Pierre Jeanneret. Apart from planning the city and designing numerous public buildings for it, Jeanneret and Le Corbusier also created site-specific furnishings for the project. For instance, this rosewood and woven cane lounge chair was used in a number of the city's buildings, including the General Hospital's main reception area. Jeanneret's bamboo armchair, also shown here, was a more experimental seating design made for his own personal use that similarly employed Indian local materials and craft skills.

▲ Pierre Jeanneret at home in Chandigarh, c.1956

► Armchair, c.1956
Bamboo
India

▼ *Kangourou* lounge chair, c.1956
Rosewood, caning
India

George Nakashima
Lounge chair, 1958 & *Long Chair* lounger, 1951

▲ *Long Chair* lounger, 1951
Walnut, canvas webbing
George Nakashima, New Hope
(PA), USA

◄ Lounge chair, 1958
Walnut, textile-covered upholstery
Widdicomb, Grand Rapids (MI),
USA

George Nakashima studied architecture at the University of Washington, MIT and L'Ecole Americaine des Beaux Arts, Fontainebleau, before working in Antonin Raymond's offices in Tokyo (Japan) and Pondicherry (India). At the outbreak of the Second World War, he returned to the USA where he was sent to a Japanese internment camp, but through Raymond's intervention he was moved to work on a farm in Bucks County, where he subsequently designed and built his own house and workshop. There he created modern furnishings, such as the lounger and armchair shown here, that were informed by the time-honoured craft-skills of Japan.

Antti Nurmesniemi
Sauna stools, 1952

The sauna is an absolutely integral part of Finnish cultural
life, being used as a place for socialising as well as relaxation.
It is, therefore, unsurprising that it was a Finnish designer,
Antti Nurmesniemi, who designed what has to be seen as
the ultimate sauna stool. This horseshoe-shaped design
was originally created for the Palace Hotel in Helsinki and
incorporated a laminated birch seat that was ergonomically
contoured for presumably sweaty posteriors.

Sauna stools, 1952
Laminated birch, teak
G. Soderstrom, Helsinki, Finland

Sori Yanagi
Elephant stool, 1954

One of the leading Japanese designers working during the post-war period, Sori Yanagi's work was widely exhibited abroad. Having founded the Yanagi Industrial Design Institute in 1952, he designed numerous landmark housewares and furniture designs, including the lightweight and stackable *Elephant* stool. This simple yet sculptural design was intended for both indoor and outdoor use and was originally made of fibreglass, however, it has been recently reissued by Vitra in polypropylene.

Elephant stool, 1954
Fibreglass
Kotobuki, Japan
(reissued by Vitra)

Sergio Conti, Marisa Forlani & Luciano Grassi
Armchairs, 1955

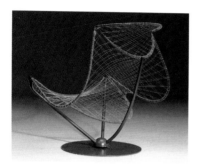

These rare armchairs innovatively incorporated a web of crisscrossing nylon strands to provide an efficient seating support, while also giving the design a dynamic presence. When they were first launched in the mid-1950s, they must have seemed startlingly radical to an audience used to heavily upholstered furnishings. Certainly these armchairs have an exceptional visual lightness that gives the impression that at any moment they could flutter away. Conti, Forlani and Grassi also designed another chair called *Farfalla* (meaning butterfly in Italian) that similarly employed strands of strong near-transparent nylon.

▲ *Farfalla* chair designed for Conti, Forlani & Grassi for Poali, 1954

◄► Armchairs, 1955
Tubular iron, nylon string, metal
Paoli, Florence

Harry Bertoia
Bird lounge chair, 1952, *Model No. 420C* chair &
Model No. 425 child's chair, c.1952

◄ *Bird* lounge chair, 1952
Rislan-bonded welded steel, textile
covered-upholstery
Knoll Associates, New York, USA

As a sculptor, Harry Bertoia was a talented form-giver who created a number of acclaimed chairs made of industrial wire rods that were welded together to form supporting mesh-like seat shells. Apart from his well-known *Bird* lounge chair (shown here) and his *Diamond* chair, he also designed a simple side chair, the *Model No. 420C*, as well as a smaller child-sized version, known as the *Model No. 425*. This functional and highly durable seating range with its sled-like bases must have seemed revolutionary when it was first launched and certainly the individual designs enlivened any interior with their stylishly contemporary sculptural presence.

▲ Knoll advertisement featuring
the *Model No. 425* child's chair,
1950s

► *Model No. 420C* chair & *Model
No. 425* child's chair, c.1952
Chromed steel rod, textile-covered
cushions
Knoll Associates, New York, USA

Poul Kjærholm
The Bow chair, 1952

Poul Kjærholm experimented with flag halyard in the design of several chairs, including perhaps most successfully *The Bow* chair for Fritz Hansen. With its simple laminated wood construction that incorporates a supporting frame made of just two bow-shaped elements and two tapering elements, the design has a strong elemental quality. The chair's seat and back sections were originally offered in either red or black flag halyard.

The Bow chair, 1952
Laminate wood, flag halyard
Fritz Hansen, Allerød, Denmark

Verner Panton
Bachelor chair, 1956

Verner Panton's *Bachelor* chair was designed so that its frame could be easily dismantled and the entire chair could be packed into a cardboard box making it highly transportable. This flat-pack design was especially popular among younger people and as such presaged the more youth-based and nomadic furnishings of the 1960s. The design was available with and without arms and also came with a matching footrest and table.

Batchelor chair, 1956
Tubular metal, poplin
Fritz Hansen, Allerød, Denmark

Ernest Race
Heron lounge chair, 1955

Designed by Ernest Race in 1955, the angular, steel-framed *Heron* lounge chair exemplifies the designer's research into combining steel rod structures with upholstery. Race was one of the most prominent British designers of the immediate post-war period, and is best known for the *Antelope* and *Springbok* chairs he designed for the 1951 Festival of Britain. Designed with an optional headrest cushion and accompanying footstool, the *Heron* was produced by Race Furniture Ltd., which had been co-founded by Race and the engineer J.W. Noel Jordan in 1946.

RACE FURNITURE · LONDON

write for free illustrated catalogue of our full range
22 Union Road Clapham SW4; Telephone Macaulay 3217

▲ Race furniture brochure featuring the *Heron* lounge chair, 1950s

◄ *Heron* lounge chair, 1955
Steel, aluminium, latex foam upholstery, webbing
Race Furniture, London, United Kingdom

Ico Parisi
Model No. 813 lounge chairs, 1953

The architect and designer Ico Parisi collaborated with his wife Luisa Parisi from the late 1940s in their La Ruota studio in native Como, where in the 1930s he had worked for the Rationalist architect Giuseppe Terragni. The *Model No. 813* chair from 1953 is the best-known of several designs by Parisi that Cassina manufactured in the 1950s, such as the similarly curvaceous *Model No. 812* sofa from the same year. Also known as the *Uova* for its egg-shaped form, the lounge chair exemplifies the popularity of organic-shaped forms in the 1950s and was praised by fellow architect Gio Ponti as a "marvel".

▼ *Model No. 813* lounge chairs, 1953
Enamelled brass, upholstery
Cassina, Meda, Italy

► *Model No. 812* sofa, 1953
Enamelled brass, upholstery
Cassina, Meda, Italy

Franco Campo & Carlo Graffi
Lounge chairs, 1951

Franco Campo and Carlo Graffi studied architecture under the Turinese architect Carlo Mollino and worked in his studio before setting up their own practice in the late 1950s. Their flamboyant design for this high-backed lounge chair reflects Mollino's influence on the two designers, to whom their designs are often erroneously attributed, and exemplifies their similarly "Turinese Baroque" style. The moulded maple wood chair was produced by the Turinese workshop Apelli & Varesio who also manufactured much of Mollino's furniture.

Lounge chairs, 1951
Maple, velvet-covered upholstery, rubber
Apelli & Varesio, Turin, Italy

Franco Campo & Carlo Graffi
Stool, 1953

Designed in 1953, this stool is unusual for both its form and the felt-coated steel that makes up the shell seat. Its combination of industrial materials with a decadent velvet cushion, wing-shaped seat and spiked brass legs exemplifies the organic and surreal qualities of Campo and Graffi's "Turinese Baroque" style. While the architects worked together throughout the 1950s, first in Carlo Mollino's studio and then in their own practice, there is speculation that the stool was possibly designed by Graffi alone.

▲ Early publicity photograph of Campo & Graffi's stool, 1950s

► Stool, 1953
Felt coated steel, brass, velvet-covered cushion
Manufacturer unknown, Italy

Hans Wegner
Model No. FH-4103 Heart chair, 1952 & *Model No. 50* task chair, 1955

One of the great seating designers of his generation, Hans Wegner was adept at creating chairs that had an inherent "rightness" – a sublime combination of materials, functionality and aesthetics. For instance, his three-legged *Heart* chair could not only be stacked efficiently but also when several were used around a circular table they fit snuggly thereby eliminating a sense of clutter. His *Model No. 50* swivelling task chair was likewise a highly considered design with its continuous yoke-shaped back-and-arm rail subtly contoured to provide ergonomic comfort.

▶ *Model No. 50* task chair, 1955
Teak, chromed steel, leather-covered upholstery
Johannes Hansen, Copenhagen, Denmark

◀ *Model No. FH-4103 Heart* chair, 1952
Teak
Fritz Hansen, Allerød, Denmark

Frits Henningsen
Easy chair, c.1950

Like his earlier wingback chair from the late 1930s, Frits Henningsen's easy chair has a sensual organic form that reflects the designer's superlative cabinetmaking skills. An example of this high-backed recliner in mahogany and black-leather was used in Henningsen's own office. With its beautifully curved frame, this design reflects the understated elegance of Danish mid-century design, which remains today as popular as it ever was.

Easy chair, c.1950
Oak, leather-covered
upholstery
Frits Henningsen, Copenhagen,
Denmark

Arne Jacobsen
Egg chair and ottoman, 1957–58

Instantly identifiable, the *Egg* chair is a truly iconic mid-century seating design that was as sculptural as it was functional. Originally designed as part of the unified furnishing scheme for the SAS Royal Hotel in Copenhagen, the *Egg* and its matching footstool have an engaging organic form that comfortably cradle the body. One of the keys to the longevity of its appeal is that the *Egg* chair works in almost any interior setting, whether ultra-modern or antique, while its high-quality manufacture ensures a robust physical durability.

Egg chair & ottoman, 1957–58
Aluminium, fibreglass, leather-covered upholstery
Fritz Hansen, Allerød, Denmark

Renzo Zavanella
Sofa, lounge chairs and armchair for the Mediterraneo Hotel, 1950

The Milanese architect and designer Renzo Zavanella conceived this series of organic, surreal-shaped chairs as part of his commission to design the interiors and furniture of the Mediterraneo Hotel in San Remo, Italy. The hotel included decoration by artists such as Lucio Fontana, with whom Zavanella collaborated on designs for a number of cemetery monuments. In *Domus* magazine the architect Gio Ponti noted how the furniture combined a nineteenth century form with twentieth century abstraction, indicative of the influence of sculpture on furniture design at the time.

Sofa, lounge chairs and armchair for the Mediterraneo Hotel, 1950
Walnut, velvet upholstery
Manufacturer unknown, Italy

Lucian Ercolani
Child's stacking chair, 1957

Ercol was set up in the furniture making area of High Wycombe in 1920 by the Italian Lucian Ercolani, who had moved to England in 1895. Designed in 1957, this stacking child's chair demonstrates his particular expertise in steam bending elm, a hardwood previously considered too difficult to process in this manner. Designed for schools and meeting rooms, the chair is innovative for its vertical stacking system. Despite being overtaken in popularity by polypropylene chairs in the 1960s, in the early 2000s the chair was reissued as part of the Ercol Originals collection.

Child's stacking chair, 1957
Beech, elm
Ercol, Princes Risborough, Great Britain

Lucian Ercolani
Butterfly chair, 1958

Designed in 1958, the curving back and seat of the *Butterfly* chair demonstrate the expertise of Lucian Ercolani in his development of thick wooden laminates for his furniture designs for Ercol. The chair echoes the pared down aesthetic of Scandinavian furniture that was hugely popular at the time and combines traditional and modern design with its Windsor chair-shaped base and steam-bent form. Although manufacture of the *Butterfly* chair ceased in the 1980s, in the early 2000s it was re-issued as part of Ercol Originals collection.

Butterfly chair, 1958
Beech, elm
Ercol, Princes Risborough, Great Britain

Arne Jacobsen
Model No. 3105 chair, 1955 &
Model No. 3102 chair, 1955

The *Model No. 3102* was originally designed as a school chair, however, it had a drawback in that it could not be stacked, yet despite this oversight it must be considered an elegant and accomplished design from Jacobsen's comprehensive series of plywood chairs developed during the mid-1950s. In contrast the *Model No. 3105* was stackable and as such was mass-produced in three child sizes as well as in an adult variant. This simple yet elegant chair was used by students at the Munkegaard School, an International Style building designed by Jacobsen, completed in 1957, that consisted of pavilions linked by airy glass corridors.

▼► *Model No. 3105* chair, 1955
Stained moulded plywood, tubular steel, rubber
Fritz Hansen, Allerød, Denmark

▲ right ▶ *Model No. 3102* chair,
1955
Moulded plywood, tubular steel,
rubber
Fritz Hansen, Allerød, Denmark

Arne Jacobsen
Model No. 3103 chair, 1955

After the success of his seminal *Ant* side chair of 1952, Arne Jacobsen created a number of variant designs with similar continous seat and back sections shaped from moulded plywood, including the stackable *3103*. With its distinctive T-shaped back section, this elegant side chair could be attached to a number of different bases and was available in a number of different veneers and coloured finishes. Fritz Hansen also manufactured a diminutive version of the *3103* for children.

◄ *Model No. 3103* chair, 1955
Teak-faced moulded plywood, lacquered tubular metal, rubber
Fritz Hansen, Allerød, Denmark

▼ Fritz Hansen publicity photogrphs of the *Model No. 3103* chair, 1950s – including a fixed pedestal variant

André Bloc
Bellevue chair, 1951

The French architect, André Bloc was highly influenced by the work of the sculptor, Hans Arp and his abstraction of the human body. This S-shaped chair designed for Bellevue, Bloc's own home in Meudon, France, reflects this artistic inspiration with its continuous seat element and dynamic flowing lines. Although a V-shaped metal base supports this eye-catching sculptural element, Bloc's *Bellevue* chair can be seen as an important precursor of Verner Panton's revolutionary single-piece plywood *S-chair* of 1956.

Bellevue chair, 1951
Beech-faced plywood,
enamelled steel
André Bloc, Meudon, France

Adrien Claude
Armchair, c.1950

During the early 1950s, there were a number of French designers who exploited the functional and aesthetic potential of perforated metal for the manufacture of contemporary "New Look" furnishings. Adrien Claude's armchair is perhaps the most visually striking of these seating designs with its continuous S-shaped seating element of perforated aluminium that bends around to provide an integral headrest. Eminently suitable for outdoor use, this design allowed rain to drain efficiently through the holes.

Armchair, c.1950
Tubular steel, perforated aluminium, rubber
Meubles Artistiques Modernes, Paris, France

Egon Eiermann
Model No. SE68 chair, 1950

Egon Eiermann's *Model No. SE68* chair can be seen as a highly rational Teutonic answer to the Eameses' earlier plywood group of chairs. Utilising standardized seat and back sections of compound moulded plywood Eiermann combined them with a large variety of bases to create a comprehensive seating system, from dining chairs to office chairs – including the *Model No. SE40* task chair which became the ubiquitous chair used in German architectural offices. Despite their lack of upholstery, the design's ergonomic contours of these chairs provided a satisfying level of comfort.

Model No. SE68 chair, 1950
Moulded plywood, chromed tubular steel
Wilde + Spieth, Esslingen, Germany

Edward Wormley
Sofa, c.1956

The American furniture designer, Edward Wormley designed numerous chairs and sofas for the Indiana-based manufacturer, Dunbar, that accorded with his belief that "Modernism means freedom – freedom to mix, to choose, to change, to embrace the new but to hold fast to what is good". With its clean Modern lines, this sofa that was originally designed in the mid-1950s is typical of his output, however, this example is enlivened with its sumptuous covering of multi-coloured *Caravan* velvet designed in 1962 by Anita Askild for Jack Lenor Larsen Inc.

Sofa, c.1956
Walnut, velvet-covered upholstery
Dunbar, Berne (IN), USA

Cees Braakman
Model No. FB03 lounge chairs, 1954

The Dutch designer, Cees Braakman created these low-slung
lounge chairs using Z-shaped elements cut from sheets of
laminated wood that provided the two main supports for
the design's seat and back sections. Like Marcel Breuer's
earlier use of this relatively utilitarian material, Braakman
demonstrated that it was possible to create dynamic cutout
forms that could be used to assemble highly functional yet
inexpensive furniture, which also possessed a striking
visual presence.

Model No. FB03 lounge chairs, 1954
Laminated birch,
fabric-covered upholstery
UMS-Pastoe, Utrecht,
The Netherlands

Friso Kramer
Result side chair, 1958

Having studied interior architecture at Amsterdam's Instituut voor Kunstnijverheidsonderwijs (Institute for Education in Arts and Crafts), Friso Kramer subsequently worked from 1948 until 1963 as a designer for De Cirkel, a manufacturer of steel furnishings that was a subsidiary of the Ahrend group. During this tenure, he notably designed a number of multifunctional chairs as well as various desks and tables. His *Result* chair from 1958 was, however, his most interesting design thanks to its dynamic profile that belied its innate functionality. Kramer also designed a matching teacher's desk to accompany this practical chair with its sleek industrial aesthetic recalling Jean Prouvé's earlier and similarly stylish seating designs.

Result side chair, 1958
Moulded plywood, enamelled steel
De Cirkel, Zwanenburg,
Netherlands

Gerrit Thomas Rietveld
Mondial chair, 1957

The distinctive k-shaped profile of the *Mondial* chair came
with optional armrests and was designed by Gerrit Rietveld
with his son Wim Rietveld for the Dutch pavilion at the 1958
Brussels Expo, which he co-designed with J.H. van den Broek,
J.B. Bakema, J. Boks and F.P.J. Peutz. Rietveld had designed
the chair's seat and back to be made from a single sheet of
pressed aluminium. While the prototype was made of steel
and aluminium, in the production version the aluminium
section was swapped for two sheets of glass-reinforced
polyester. Due to subsequent developments in welding
technology, the manufacturer Rietveld by Rietveld's re-edition
of the chair is able to follow Gerrit Rietveld's original design.

▲ Gerrit Rietveld with a model of
his 1948 Core House

◄ *Mondial* chair, 1957
Glass-reinforced polyster,
lacquered metal
W.H. Gispen, Rotterdam, The
Netherlands

Paul László
Chair, 1950s

Paul László was a Hungarian born architect who worked in Europe before emigrating to California in the 1930s, where he designed interiors for celebrities, luxury shops and casinos. This combination of European Modernism and Hollywood glamour is evident in this chair, one of a small number designed for the Los Angeles headquarters of the McCulloch Corporation, a chainsaw manufacturer. The company's tool-based brand identity is picked up in the wrench-shaped back stretcher, while its logo has been monogrammed onto the rear of the two cushions that make up the chair back.

Chair, 1950s
Tubular steel, brass, leather-covered upholstery
Manufacturer unknown, USA

Vittorio Nobili
Medea chair & armchair, 1955

The architect Vittorio Nobili's design for the *Medea* chair comprised a singleform compound moulded plywood seat shell. Bending a single piece of plywood in such a way, over two geometric planes, was a major technical achievement. The chair was designed in a number of patented versions, available with or without arms, and with a loose cushion or with padded latex foam upholstery. In 1956 Nobili's design was nominated for the prestigious *Compasso D'Oro* (Golden Compass) industrial design award that had been established by the Italian department store La Rinascente two years earlier on the idea of the architects Gio Ponti and Alberto Rosselli.

Medea chair & armchair, 1955
Bent laminated wood, teak veneer, clear lacquer, painted tubular steel
Fratelli Tagliabue, Meda, Italy

Eddie Harlis
Model No. ST 664 chair, 1955

Eddie Harlis initially trained as a carpenter and later studied at the Werkkunstschule in Hildesheim. From 1953, he worked as a designer of furniture and interiors, designing for among others, Thonet, COR, Kaufeld and Profilia. His eye-catching *Model No. ST 664* chair is rightly regarded as an icon of post-war design in Germany with its extraordinary one-piece seat-shell that took the moulding possibilities of plywood with complex curves to an unprecedented level. With its splayed metal rod base the chair also reflected the spiky 1950s sputnik-aesthetic.

Model No. ST 664 chair, 1955
Moulded plywood, lacquered metal
Gebrüder Thonet, Frankenberg, Germany

Arne Jacobsen
Drop chair, 1958 & *The Pot* chairs, 1958

◄ *Drop* chair, 1958
Steel, moulded polyurethane foam,
leather
Fritz Hansen, Allerød, Denmark

▼ *The Pot* chairs, 1958
Steel, moulded polyurethane foam,
leather
Fritz Hansen, Allerød, Denmark

Like his iconic *Swan* and *Egg* chairs, Arne Jacobsen used
a type of polyurethane foam known as "styropore" in the
construction of *The Pot* and the *Drop* chairs. These designs
were similarly created site-specifically for Arne Jacobsen's
landmark SAS Royal Hotel in Copenhagen, where they
adorned the bar and the so-called Orchid Room. Essentially
a Modernist reworking of the traditional tub chair, *The Pot* is
extremely comfortable thanks to its low-slung ergonomic form
that cradles the body and allows the sitter to comfortably
rest their arms on the padded edge of the seat-shell. Likewise,
the *Drop* chair has an organic form that very comfortably
embraces the sitter

Gio Ponti
Chairs, 1950s

In the late 1940s the Milanese architect Gio Ponti set out to design the lightest chair possible. Inspired by the nineteenth century ladderback, straw-seated *Chiavari* chair, Ponti designed a number of versions over a near ten-year period, some of which were manufactured by Cassina, including the stylish pair of chairs shown below. While most of these designs remained prototypes, in 1951 Ponti unveiled the *Leggera* chair at the ninth *Triennale di Milano* which Cassina put into production the following year, and which led to the famous *Superleggera* chair in 1957, which is still manufactured today.

▶ Cassina publicity photograph demonstrating the physical lightness of the *Superleggera* chair by Gio Ponti, 1957

▼ Chairs, 1950s
Ash, rush
Cassina, Meda, Italy

Ico Parisi
Model No. 839 armchair, 1954

In 1947 Ico Parisi and his wife Luisa founded a studio known
as La Ruota that specialized in interior design as well as the
creation of furnishings that had a sophisticated yet modern
elegance. Their subsequent work, including the *Model No. 839*
armchair designed for Cassina, literally came to define the
shape of post-war Italian design and was widely celebrated
in the design journals of the day. Exploiting the formal and
functional potential of moulded plywood, tubular steel and
foam upholstery, the *839* was a lightweight yet comfortable
seating solution that was awarded the *Compasso d'Oro* in 1955.

Model No. 839 armchair, 1954
Enamelled tubular metal,
moulded plywood, textile-covered
upholstery
Cassina, Meda, Italy

Carlo De Carli
Model No. 683 chair, 1954

In 1954 the prestigious Compasso d'Oro prize for design and manufacturing excellence was awarded for the first time. Amongst the winners was Carlo de Carli who received this coveted accolade for the design of his *Model No. 683* side chair, which had an elegant and sinuous frame made of solid ash that supported its back and seating sections, which were innovatively constructed of moulded plywood. This prize-winning chair also received the Diploma of Honour at the tenth Milan Triennale as well as the Museum of Modern Art's Good Design prize in New York.

Model No. 683 chair, 1954
Ash, moulded plywood, brass
Cassina, Meda, Italy

Gastone Rinaldi
Lounge chair, 1954

Born in Padua, Gastone Rinaldi designed various metal chairs, school desks, lounge chairs and sofas for his father's firm, Rima. He also exhibited at the Milan Triennale in 1951, where Rima was reputedly the first Italian manufacturing company to propose utilising latex foam as an upholstery material supported by an internal framework of tubular metal. Three years later, Rinaldi designed this elegantly poised lounge chair, which incorporated this innovative type of structure that allowed him to create dynamic sculptural yet also extremely comfortable forms.

Lounge chair, 1954
Wood, tubular metal, textile-covered latex-foam upholstery
Rima, Padua, Italy

Gianfranco Frattini
Model No. 831 lounge chairs, 1955

Like so many chairs designed in Italy during the mid-1950s, Gianfranco Frattini's *831* incorporated state-of-the-art latex-foam for its upholstery, thereby allowing padded comfort without too much bulk. These stylish lounge chairs were also demountable to allow easy "boxed" transportation, which would have made them highly suitable for the all-important export market, which was a key element of Italy's remarkable economic expansion, referred to as *il miracolo economico*, that took place during the post-war period.

Model No. 831 lounge chairs, 1955
Ash plywood, brass, vinyl-covered latex-foam upholstery
Cassina, Meda, Italy

Osvaldo Borsani
Model No. S88 folding chairs, c.1955

The Italian architect Osvaldo Borsani designed the *S88* chair in c.1955 for Tecno, the furniture manufacturer that he established with his twin brother Fulgenzio Borsani in 1953. While not as complex as his better-known *P40* chaise longue and *D70* sofa, the *S88* was equally technically sophisticated. The articulated chair consists of a steel frame structure with hinged splayed legs and a plywood seat and back that fold into each other to form a virtually flat, compact shape.

▼ *Model No. S88* folding chairs,
c.1955
Teak-faced plywood, steel
Tecno, Milan, Italy

▲ Tecno publicity photograph
showing the *Model No. S88* chair
being folded

Vittorio Gregotti, Lodovico Meneghetti & Giotto Stoppino
Armchair, 1954

The architects Vittorio Gregotti, Lodovico Meneghetti and Giotto Stoppino founded Architetti Associati in Novara in 1953, before relocating their practice to nearby Milan until its closure in the late 1960s. Consisting of a series of plywood shapes slotted together into a fanned-out design, this was one of a number of plywood furniture pieces the architects designed in the 1950s as part of their interest in modularity and mass production. The highly structural chair was produced by SIM in Novara who would also produce their Neoliberty *Cavour* chair from 1960.

◄ SIM publicity photograph showing armchair with seat cushion, 1950s

▼ Armchair, 1954
Laminated and birch-faced plywood, cushion
SIM, Novara, Milan

Charles & Ray Eames
Aluminum Group lounge chair, 1958

This example of an *Aluminum Group* lounge chair is a rare pre-production model, which has a sling seat made from a textile designed by Alexander Girard; in contrast to the later mass-produced variant that utilized a padded and ribbed sling often made of Naugahyde. The *Aluminum Group* was Charles Eames' response to the lack of availability of high-quality outdoor furniture, and as such was sometimes referred to as the "Indoor Outdoor Group" or "Leisure Line". This influential range of seating took three years to develop and incorporated an innovative way of invisibly attaching the sling seat to the frame. Ironically, although intended for outside use, it was almost exclusively used in office environments.

◄► *Aluminum Group* lounge chair, 1958
Aluminium, plastic-coated aluminium, textile upholstery
Herman Miller, Zeeland (MI), USA

▼ Early publicity photograph showing *Aluminum Group* furniture being used outside, as was originally intended, c.1958

Paulo Mendes da Rocha
Paulistano chair, 1957

The Brazilian architect Paulo Mendes da Rocha conceived
the *Paulistano* for the Paulistano Athletics Club in Sao Paolo,
for which he also designed the gymnasium. The structure's
Brazilian Brutalist aesthetic is also evident in the chair, which
is made of a single length of bent tubular steel with a sling
seat that can be adjusted by moving the material up and down
the frame. Only ever produced in small runs, since 2004 the
Brazilian producer Objekto has manufactured the chair with a
canvas or leather seat.

► Design sketches for the
Paulistano chair, 1957

▼ *Paulistano* chair, 1957
Tubular steel, canvas (and later
leather)
Brazil
(later by Objekto, Brazil)

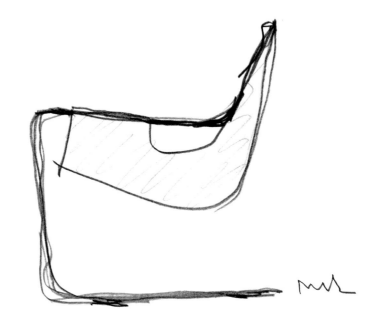

Hans Brattrud
Scandia lounge chairs, 1957

A veritable icon of Norwegian design, Hans Brattrud's *Scandia* chair range was originally designed while he was still studying at the Oslo National Academy of the Arts. Technically innovative, the *Scandia* chairs utilized thin strips of moulded plywood to create contoured and continuous seating sections that were supported on simple metal rod frames or pedestal bases. Normally the chairs were then used with cushions or sheepskins to give them a greater degree of comfort.

Scandia lounge chairs, 1957
Moulded plywood, metal rod
Hove Mobler, Norway (later produced by Fjordfiesta)

Ole Wanscher

T chairs, 1957

A student of Kaare Klint, the Danish designer Ole Wanscher, like his mentor, created furniture that was inspired by earlier historic designs and that was notable for its exquisitely balanced proportions. His elegant teak and leather *T* chair from the late 1950s was a thoroughly modern reworking of the Ancient Egyptian *Klismos* chair and exemplified the Danish Mid-Century Modern look.

T chairs, 1957
Mahogany, leather
A.J. Iversen, Copenhagen, Denmark

Eero Saarinen
Model No. 151 Tulip chair, 1955–56

In an attempt to clear up the visual clutter or as he put it the "slum of legs" around a table, Eero Saarinen created his famous *Tulip* chair with its elegant pedestal base. This landmark seating design was not only an attempt to clarify aesthetics, but also an exercise in design unity. Although Saarinen was unable to achieve his ultimate goal of creating a single material/single form chair because of the limits of then-current plastics technology, the *Tulip* chair and armchair were hugely influential and as such marked a new sculptural confidence within the design of seating.

▲ Florence Knoll with Eero Saarinen discussing his design for a pedestal base, c.1955

◄ *Model No. 151 Tulip* chair, 1955–56
Moulded fiberglass, plastic-coated aluminium, textile-covered cushion
Knoll Associates, New York, USA

▼ *Tulips* armchairs and stool by Eero Saarinen for Knoll Associates, 1955–56

Verner Panton
Model No. C1 chair, 1959

This is an extremely rare version of Verner Panton's C1 chair, which has a cone-shaped base rather than the simple metal X-base pedestal that was used on the more common serial production model. Indeed, only a few examples of this visually dynamic seating design appear to have been manufactured or have managed to survive the intervening years. With its hemispherical seat section delicately balanced over its splaying conical base, this stridently geometric chair gives the impression that it is defying the laws of gravity and as a result has a striking sculptural quality.

Model No. C1 chair, 1959
Painted steel, textile-covered
upholstery
Plus-Linje, Copenhagen, Denmark

Verner Panton
Heart chair, 1959

Verner Panton stated, "Most people spend their lives living in dreary, beige conformity, mortally afraid of using colors. The main purpose of my work is to provoke people into using their imagination and make their surroundings more exciting." Certainly, his highly sculptural *Heart* chair from the late 1950s with its brightly coloured upholstery and its strong graphic profile must have seemed like a breath of fresh air in comparison to the prevailing mainstream taste for muted earth tones and wood. This stunning design was an evolution of his well-known *Cone* chair created the previous year. Another variant of this earlier design was Panton's equally striking *Model No. K4 Pyramid* chair.

▲ *Model No. K4 Pyrmaid* chair designed by Verner Panton for Plus-Linje, c.1959

► *Heart* chair, 1959
Stainless steel, textile-covered upholstery
Plus-Linje, Copenhagen, Denmark
(reissued by Vitra)

Erwine & Estelle Laverne
Lily chairs, 1957

Erwine and Estelle Laverne both studied painting under Hans Hoffman (1880–1966) at the Art Students League in New York, prior to establishing their own design company, Laverne Originals, which promoted a modern, highly artistic look for the home. Their New York showroom was notable for its sense of uncluttered space, which was further enhanced by the introduction of their *Invisible Group* of sculptural, transparent acrylic chairs in 1957. This range, which included the *Lily* chair, was remarkably organic in form, and had a spatial lightness that predicted the more art-based furniture designs of the following decade.

► Laverne Originals advertisement for the "Invisible" Chair, c.1960

▼ *Lily* chairs, 1957
PMMA, textile-covered cushion
Laverne Originals, New York, USA

The next sound you hear will not be a mother screaming.

The "Invisible" Chair® by Laverne washes cleaner than the child. it is oblivious to cats, dogs, canapés and coffee. It is very comfortable; the recommended chair for reading Proust or watching "Open End." In crowded rooms it seems to take no space, delighting all who see it.

WITH COLOR CUSHION. ABOUT $280. OTHER "INVISIBLES" FROM ABOUT $190. AT FINE STORES OR WRITE LAVERNE INC., 160 E. 57 ST. N.Y. 22

Verner Panton
Panton chair, 1959–60

The cantilevered *Panton* chair was the first ever single-material, single-piece injection moulded plastic chair and this highly sculptural seat has since become a much-loved and celebrated icon of twentieth century design. It took years to develop and a huge financial commitment from its manufacturer, Vitra to overcome the plastic-moulding technological challenges that eventually allowed for its full-scale production. After initially using rigid cold-pressed GRP (glass-reinforced polyester) and then moulded Baydur (polyurethane hard foam), in 1971 the design was modified to include strengthening ribs under its seat, which enabled it to be injection-moulded in Luran S – BASF's acrylonitrile-styrene-acrylate (ASA), which was the ideal material for the chair's mass-production. In fact this change of polymer heralded the advent of the one-shot plastic monobloc chair.

◄ Early Vitra publicity photograph featuring the *Panton* chair, c.1960

▼► *Panton* chair, 1959–60
Fibreglass-reinforced polyester (1967); polyurethane hard foam (PU) (1968–71); acrylonitrile-styrene-acrylate (ASA) (1971–79); polypropylene (PP) or polyurethane hard foam (PU) (1990 to present)
Manufacturer: Vitra GmbH, Weil am Rhein, German

Vico Magistretti
Model No. 892 Carimate armchair, 1959

In 1959, Vico Magistretti and Guido Veneziani designed a stylish sport clubhouse for a new residential development in Carimate, some 20 miles outside of Milan. For this project, Magistretti also specially created the *Carimate* chair, a boldly modern and brightly coloured reworking of a traditional rush-seated peasant chair. Amply proportioned, this stylish armchair was extremely influential and was subsequently used in restaurants and cafés throughout Italy and Europe, and also spawned numerous imitations.

Model No. 892 Carimate armchair, 1959
Painted wood, rushing
Cassina, Meda, Italy

Børge Mogensen
Model No. 2254 Runner chair and ottoman, 1958

Like his mentor Kaare Klint, Børge Mogensen created numerous furniture designs, most of which were based on earlier vernacular "ideal" furniture typologies. In 1955 he began designing for Fredericia Furniture A/S and subsequently created various notable chairs for the company, including the *Runner* chair which rather than being a modern re-working of an earlier type of seating, had instead a frame made from simple square-shaped elements that supported the seating section. Unpretentious, lightweight and practical, this armchair, with its adjustable back and headrest, predicted the pared-down aesthetic of later seating designs from Scandinavia in the 1970s.

Model No. 2254 Runner chair and ottoman, 1958
Oak, textile-covered upholstery
Fredericia Furniture, Fredericia, Denmark

Isamu Noguchi & Isamu Kenmochi *Bamboo Basket* chair, 1951
Isamu Kenmochi Chair, c.1959

In 1950 Isamu Noguchi made his first post-war trip to Japan, and whilst there saw a proposal for a chair that had been devised by fellow designer, Isamu Kenmochi, which incorporated traditional bamboo basket weaving techniques for its seat and back sections. Inspired by this prototypical design, Noguchi set to work to design an alternative base for it and the resulting looping metal rod support – which is reminiscent of the frame used by Jorge Ferrari Hardoy for his well-known *Butterfly* chair for Knoll – gave the overall design an engaging visual rhythm and a sculptural presence. Kenmochi later designed a similarly constructed chair (shown to the right) that also reflected the synthesis of Eastern craft skills with Western chair forms.

► Chair, c.1959
Woven bambo, metal rod
Japan

▼ *Bamboo Basket* chair, 1951
Woven bamboo, metal rod
Japan

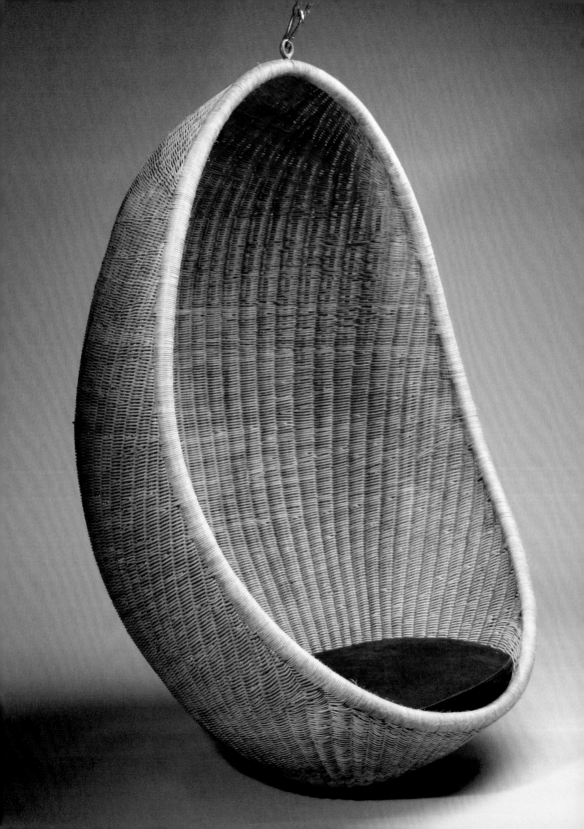

Nanna & Jørgen Ditzel
Egg hanging chair, 1957

Egg hanging chair, 1957
Woven rattan, tubular steel
Bonacina Pierantonio,
Giussano, Italy & Yamakawa
Rattan Industry PT, Tokyo,
Japan

Although designed in the late 1950s, Nanna & Jørgen Ditzel's *Egg* chair became an omnipresent feature of interiors during the 1960s. Suspended from the ceiling, the *Egg* chair had a youthful quality that invited playful interaction. The couple also designed a number of other wickerwork seating designs, notably for R. Wengler of Copenhagen. After she was tragically widowed in 1961, Nanna continued to design eye-catching furniture on her own, including her delightful children's *Toadstool* from 1962.

◄ Nanna & Jørgen Ditzel's daughter seated in an *Egg* hanging chair

▼ Nanna & Jørgen Ditzel's daughter with the Kolds Savværk *Toadstools*, 1962

◄ *Wire Cone* chairs around a matching *Cone* table (1958), also manufactured by Plus-Linje

◄ *Model No. K2 Wire Cone* chair, 1959
Galvanized and chromed steel, textile-covered cushion
Plus-Linje, Copenhagen, Denmark

Verner Panton
Model No. K2 Wire Cone chair, 1958 & *Model No. T5 Peacock* chair, 1959–60

Essentially a hemispherical basket made from a lattice of steel rods placed on a cylinder of similar construction the *Peacock* chair's sitting position could be easily adjusted by altering the angle of the upper element on the base. Padded with seven colorful cushions, the visually impactful *Peacock* chair was one of a number of chairs designed by Verner Panton that utilized this relatively simple type of welded steel rod construction to dramatic effect. Panton also used this type of construction for his well-known *Wire Cone* chair – a re-interpretation of his earlier textile-covered *Cone* chair – which was notable for its strong op art associations.

Model No. T5 Peacock chair, 1959–60
Galvanized steel, textile-covered cushions
Plus-Linje, Copenhagen, Denmark

1960s

la possiamo
lasciare in
giardino perché
tanto non si
sciupa

neanche
l'automobile
riesci a
romperla

nell' acqua
ci stá bene e
quando é
sporca la
laviamo noi

Marco Zanuso & Richard Sapper
Model No. 4999 stacking child's chair, 1960

The *Model No. 4999* was the first chair in the world to be made entirely of injection-moulded plastic. However, because it was still relatively difficult to injection mould large items during the 1960s, the chair's ribbed seating section was fabricated separately from its four cylindrical legs, which slotted into the seat. Its designers playfully conceived this chair almost as a lightweight building block that could be stacked one on top of the other. Significantly, the *Model No. 4999* chair was a radical departure from existing children's seating, which up to this point had essentially been diminutive versions of adult-sized chairs.

▼ *Model No. 4999* stacking child's chair, 1960
High-density polyethylene (later polypropylene)
Kartell, Noviglio, Italy

▲ Kartell publicity photograph showing child with stacked *Model No. 4999* chairs, c.1960

◄ Kartell advertisement for the *Model No. 4999* child's chair, c.1960

Angelo Mangiarotti
Model No. 1110 chair, 1961

The Italian architect, Angelo Mangiarotti was a master form-giver whose innovative furniture, lighting and buildings were characterized by an engineering logic and bold sculptural forms that had an undeniable poetic presence. His *Model No. 1110* easy chair for Cassina typified his o uvre with its elegantly splayed cast aluminium base supporting the fully upholstered seat section that innovatively utilized polystyrene foam in its single-piece monocoque construction.

Model No. 1110 chair, 1961
Aluminium, leather-covered polystyrene
Cassina, Meda, Italy

Renato Toso, Roberto Pamio & Noti Massari
Lara sectional sofa, 1968

The *Lara* sofa was one of a number of modular seating
systems produced by Italian manufacturers in the 1960s that
built on the new formal possibilities of polyurethane foam
to create informal, youth-orientated furniture. Composed
of two curving, irregular shaped sections that fit together
like a jigsaw, the *Lara* sofa was designed by three Venetian
architects, Roberto Pamio, Renato Toso and Noti Massari
and produced by Stilwood, a local furniture manufacturer
founded in 1964.

Lara sectional sofa, 1968
Polyurethane foam, leather
Stilwood, Pordenone, Italy

Marco Zanuso
Regent armchairs, 1960

Like Marco Zanuso's earlier latex-foam upholstered seating for Arflex, the *Regent* armchair also had a strong sculptural quality and used a minimal amount of upholstery to provide maximum comfort. The curious disc-like feet of this design also give it a space-age feeling that predicts the popularity of Sci-Fi-style designs in Italy during the late 1960s. Its low seat height also reflected the increasingly informal lifestyle of the early 1960s

Regent armchairs, 1960
Enamelled metal, painted wood, textile-covered foam upholstery
Arflex, Italy

Gio Ponti
High-backed armchair, lounge chairs and sofa, 1960–64

This group of seating was initially designed for the lobby of the stylish Hotel Parco dei Principi, Sorrento (1960), Gio Ponti's extraordinary *Gesamtkunstwerk* overlooking the Mediterranean Sea. The examples shown here, strikingly upholstered in two-tone leather, were created for the later Hotel Parco dei Principi in Rome (1964), which was a similarly chic and wholly integrated composition of greenish hues. Providing modish comfort, this furniture group had subtle space-age connotations that presaged the iconoclastic work of later Italian designers.

High-backed armchair, lounge chairs and sofa, 1960–64
Wodd, ebonized wood, brass, leather- and suede-covered upholstery
Cassina, Italy

Pierre Paulin
Concorde chairs, 1966, *Face à Face* seating unit, 1967–69 & *Dos à Dos* seating unit, 1967–69

Originally created for Air France's Concorde Lounge at Charles de Gaulle Airport, these elegant *Concorde* chairs designed by Pierre Paulin in 1966 were extremely comfortable with their backs' "spine lines" echoing the contours of the human body to provide the optimum support while waiting for a flight. Following on from the success of his airport seating, Paulin was subsequently commissioned by Mobiler National to research and develop other seating concepts destined for public spaces, such as those in the Louvre. Similarly sinuous, the resulting *Face à Face* (initially titled the *Relax* chaise) and *Dos à Dos* seating typified Paulin's work: fluid lines, perfectly balanced proportions, comfortable seating positions and a strong sculptural presence.

▶ *Face à Face* seating unit, 1967–69
Metal, jersey-covered foam upholstery
Perimeter, Paris, France (produced as a limited edition in 2008)

◀ *Concorde* chairs, 1966
Chromed-plated steel, rubber, jersey-covered foam upholstery
Artifort, Maastricht, Netherlands

▶ *Dos à Dos* seating unit, 1967–69
Metal, jersey-covered foam upholstery
Perimeter, Paris, France (produced as a limited edition in 2008)

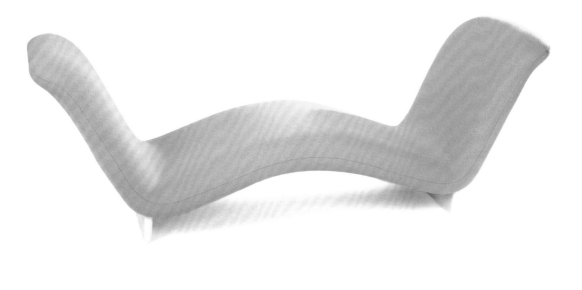

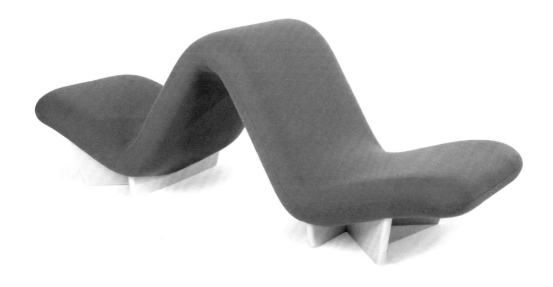

Eugenio Gerli
Model No. S-83 chairs, 1962

During the 1960s, Eugenio Gerli co-designed with Osvaldo Borsani a number of innovative office furniture designs for the Milanese manufacturer, Tecno. He also created designs for the firm that were more suited to domestic settings, such as his stylish *Model No. S-83* dining chair, notable for its rich-toned wooden seat and back sections and elegantly tapering supports that gave it a distinctive Milanese sophistication. Interestingly, the chair utilized a layer of rubber to connect the seat to the frame.

Model No. S-83 chairs, 1962
Enamelled steel, rosewood-veneered moulded plywood, rubber
Tecno, Milan, Italy

Poul Kjaerholm
Model No. PK9 chair, 1960

Unlike most Danish furniture designers, Poul Kjaerholm preferred the Modernists' material of choice – steel – rather than wood. Strict formal geometry as well as a high level of detailing also distinguished his designs. His tripod-based *Model No. PK9* chair, sometimes referred to as "the Tulip chair" thanks to its elegant form, incorporated a sculptural seat shell made of fiberglass that was fully upholstered in leather. Suitable for both office and domestic settings, this elegant chair had a very Danish refinement that married harmonious proportions with superlative craftsmanship.

Model No. PK9 chair, 1960
Steel, fiberglass, leather
E. Kold Christensen, Copenhagen, Denmark (later by Fritz Hansen)

Ingmar Relling
Siesta chair & ottoman, 1965

Ingmar Relling trained at Statens Håndverks- og Kunsthøgskole (National School of Arts and Crafts) in Oslo, prior to becoming one of Norway's leading furniture designers. His well-known *Siesta* chair was awarded first prize in The Norwegian Furniture Council Competition in 1965 and today is generally regarded as a veritable icon of Nordic design. This comfortable, lightweight, resilient and durable design was not only informed by ergonomic studies but also by Relling's innate understanding of construction. A high-backed version of this quintessentially Scandinavian design was also produced

Siesta chair & ottoman, 1965
Laminated beech, canvas, leather-cover cushions
Vestlandske Møbelfabrikk AS, Ikornnes, Norway (later manufactured by Rybo, Øystese, Norway)

Geoffrey Harcourt

Model No. F590 lounge chair & *Model No. P510* ottoman, 1967

Geoffrey Harcourt trained at the Royal College of Art, London, where he was awarded a silver medal in 1960 for a chair design that was subsequently put into production by the Dutch furniture manufacturer, Artifort. He went on to create numerous other sculptural and extremely comfortable seating designs for the firm, including the *Model No. F590* lounge chair, which with its distinctive buttoning has a rather inviting luxuriant appeal.

▲ *Model No. F584* chair designed by Geoffrey Harcourt for Artifort, 1967

▼ *Model No. F590* lounge chair & *Model No. P510* ottoman, 1967
Enamelled metal, leather-covered upholstery
Artifort, Maastricht, Netherlands

Ebert Wels
Folding chair, 1960s

Little is known about this chair or its designer, Ebert Wels.
However, it is an interesting Yugoslavian-manufactured design
that is similar to Hans Wegner's *Model No. JH512* folding chair
(1949). Although some sources cite its year of design as 1928,
it is generally believed that this Soviet-made chair actually
post-dates Wegner's better-known design, and certainly it was
being retailed in Yugoslavia during the 1960s. Wels' folding
chair incorporates two simple curved wood elements that
have integrated handholds and it also employs woven rope to
create a comfortable seating support.

Folding chair, 1960s
Cherry, woven rope
Yugoslavia

Arne Jacobsen
Model No. 4235 Catherine chair, 1962

Part of the University of Oxford, St. Catherine's College was designed by Arne Jacobsen as a *Gesamtkunstwerk* or wholly integrated environment, which not only included the striking Modernist glass and concrete building (1964–66) and garden but also interiors with specially designed furnishings, from cutlery to lighting. Each of the student's rooms was furnished with Jacobsen's simple *Catherine* side chair, which was constructed from a sturdy frame of bent laminated wood and a gently contoured moulded plywood seat and back. Fritz Hansen later produced in 1978 an armed version of this design that similarly accorded with Jacobsen's belief that, "when a thing is practical and functional, it is beautiful as well."

▲ Photograph of a student's room at St. Catherine's College, Oxford, 1960s

► *Model No. 4235 Catherine* chair, 1962
Laminated wood, plywood
Fritz Hansen, Allerød, Denmark

Antti Nurmesniemi *Model No. 001 Triennale* chair, 1960
Antti & Vuokko Nurmesniemi *Model No. 001* chaise, 1968

One of the great pioneers of modern Finnish design, Antti Nurmesniemi's seating solutions are characterized by an elegant and timeless sophistication, as well as a strong graphic profile that gives them a powerful and easily recognisable visual presence. His *Model No. 001* chair won a gold medal at the XII Milan Triennale exhibition in 1960; while his later chaise longue was upholstered with an eye-catching stripy stretch jersey created by his wife, the acclaimed textile-designer, Vuokko Eskolin-Nurmesniemi. Promoting a humanistic approach to Modernism, Nurmesniemi believed, "Design is a language of cultural policy that has reached a material form."

► *Model No. 001 Triennale* chair, 1960
Leather-covered upholstery, chromed tubular metal
J. Merivaara, Helsinki, Finland
(reissued by Piiroinen, Finland)

▼ *Model No. 001* chaise longue, 1968
Textile-covered upholstery, tubular metal, metal
Vuokko, Helsinki, Finalnd

Preben Fabricius & Jørgen Kastholm
Bird armchairs, 1964

Preben Fabricius and Jørgen Kastholm met while studying at the School of Interior Design, Copenhagen and subsequently founded their own studio in 1961. During the 1960s, they created various furniture designs that were predicated on the use of innovative yet ergonomic forms, including the sculptural *Bird* armchair with swivelling base – which was also sometimes referred to as the *Tulip* chair. A higher backed version of this elegant design was also produced that was similarly fully upholstered in stylish brown or black leather.

▲ High-backed variant of the *Bird* chair

◄ *Bird* armchairs, 1964
Aluminium, leather-covered upholstery
Alfred Kill International, Baden-Württemberg, Germany

Preben Fabricius & Jørgen Kastholm
Scimitar chair, 1962

Preben Fabricius and Jørgen Kastholm's *Scimitar* chair was first shown at the "New Forms" exhibition held at the Charlotteborg Museum, Copenhagen in 1963. As its title suggests the sweeping form of a Middle Eastern sword inspired this design and certainly the shape of its steel base echoes the form of the Muslim crescent. As the catalogue of the Whitechapel Art Gallery's 1970 "Modern Chairs" exhibition also noted, "The thrust of this chair, with its shallow bucket seat carried on a single bar of solid steel, suggests the inspiration of a tractor seat."

Scimitar chair, 1962
Steel, leather-covered upholstery
Ivan Schlechter, Copenhagen,
Denmark

Robin Day
Polypropylene chair, 1962–63

◄► *Polypropylene* chair, 1962–63
Injection-molded polypropylene,
enamelled tubular metal
Hille, United Kingdom

In 1962, Robin Day designed his ubiquitous plastic stacking chair, which became the best-selling institutional/school chair of all time with around 14 million having so far been sold worldwide. Extraordinarily tough yet lightweight and easy to transport, the *Polypropylene* armchair was designed five years later and was more suited to domestic interiors. The upholstered version of the armchair was also widely used for airport beam seating. A veritable classic of British design, the *Polyprop* (as it is commonly called) was the first mass-produced chair to incorporate an injection-molded polypropylene seat shell.

▲ Hille publicity photograph showing the *Polypropylene* range of chairs with various different bases, 1960s

Maurice Burke
Mushroom chair, 1965

◄ Arkana publicity photograph
promoting Maurice Burke's
Mushroom Collection, 1969

Showcased at the Interplas '69 exhibition, Maurice Burke's
Mushroom was the first British chair to be made using
rotational moulding – a then state-of-the-art plastic moulding
technique. This progressive Space-Age design also utilized
in its manufacture high-impact polystyrene that had been
recently developed by BP Plastics, which was coated with
a tough butyrate finish for added durability. This highly
sculptural double-shelled design also had a hollow cavity,
which was filled with polyurethane foam to give it extra ballast.
A matching armchair and table were also produced.

► *Mushroom* chair, 1965
Butyrate-finished polystyrene,
polyurethane foam
Arkana Designs Ltd., Bath, England

▼ Patent drawing of Maurice
Burke's *Mushroom* chair, filed 1968

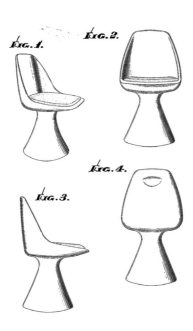

Günter Ferdinand Ris & Herbert Selldorff
Sunball garden chair, 1969–71

This truly extraordinary chair with its eye-catching spherical form was intended for outdoor use. Its visor-like elements could be drawn down completely to provide a total enclosed pod-like space for privacy or to keep out of the rain. While inside the upholstered section was generously proportioned to accommodate two sitters. The adjustable seating section could also be transformed into a daybed and additionally the design incorporated clamp-on trays, a built-in light and loudspeakers.

Sunball garden chair, 1969-71
Fibreglass, aluminium, textile-covered upholstery
Rosenthal, Selb, Germany

Eero Aarnio
Bubble chair, 1968

Like a gigantic soap bubble suspended in mid-air, Eero Aarnio's *Bubble* chair was an eye-catching and innovative design that exploited the structural and aesthetic potential of transparent plastic. As Aarnio explains, "After I had made the *Ball* chair I wanted to have the light inside it and so I had the idea of a transparent ball where light comes from all directions. The only suitable material is acrylic which is heated and blown into shape like a soap bubble. Since I knew that the dome-shaped skylights are made in this way I contacted the manufacturer and asked if it would be technically possible to blow a bubble that is bigger than a hemisphere. The answer was 'yes'."

▲ *Ball (Globe)* chair designed by
Eero Aarnio for Asko, 1963-65

▶ *Bubble* chair, 1968
Acrylic, steel
Asko, Finland (later produced by
Adelta)

Henning Larsen
Model No. 9230 armchairs, 1967

Henning Larsen studied at the Academy of Fine Arts in Copenhagen as well as the Architectural Association in London and the MIT School of Architecture in Boston, before founding his own office in 1959. Since then he has designed numerous landmark buildings including the visually striking and newly completed Copenhagen Opera House. Apart from his architecture, Larsen has also designed lighting and furniture, most notably his forward-looking *Model No. 9230* chair for Fritz Hansen from the mid-60s with its innovative sculptural yet pared-down construction that reveals both his skillful mastery of form and materials.

Model No. 9230 armchairs, 1967
Steel, leather
Fritz Hansen, Allerød, Denmark

Poul Kjaerholm
Model No. PK12 armchair, 1962

Although he initially trained as a carpenter, Poul Kjaerholm preferred, unlike other Danish furniture designers, to use metal rather than wood with which to create his elegant seating designs, which are characterized by a distinctive geometric refinement. His *Model No. PK12* armchair has a stylish minimal simplicity with its two arch-like elements of gleaming tubular metal supporting the D-shaped leather-covered seat, and as such predicted the tendency in the early-to-mid 1970s for neo-rational Modernist furnishings.

Model No. PK12 armchair, 1962
Chromed steel, leather-covered upholstery
E. Kold Christensen, Hellerup, Denmark

Pierre Paulin
Model No. 675 Butterfly chair, 1963 & Model No. F444 armchair, 1963

◄ *Model No. 675 Butterfly* chair,
1963
Tubular steel, metal rod, leather
Artifort, Maastricht, Netherlands

▼ *Model No. F444* armchair, 1963
Stainless steel, leather
Artifort, Maastricht, Netherlands

Although best known for his sculptural seating designs that utilized soft padded foam upholstery, Pierre Paulin also designed these two chairs that instead incorporated leather slings into their constructions. The *Butterfly* used a cat's cradle-like support made of narrow-gauge tubular steel and metal rod onto which two slings of leather were attached, while the *F444* armchair had a seating sling made from three pieces of joined saddle leather that fitted over its stainless steel frame. Unlike his foam upholstered seating designs, these two chairs actually looked better and became more comfortable with repeated use as the leather became softer over time and took on an attractive patina.

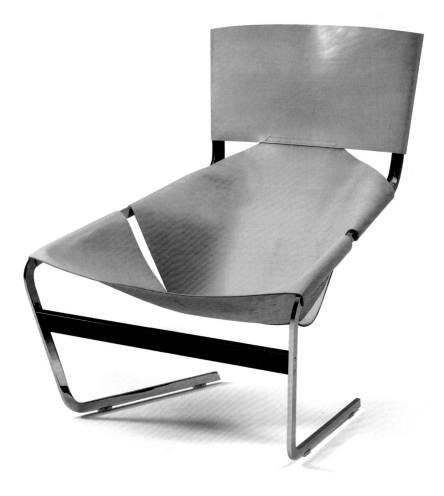

Börge Lindau & Bo Lindekrantz
Model No. S70 barstool, 1968

The Bauhaus-inspired *S70* series of barstools with its continuous loop of tubular steel, which gave it such a distinctive S-shaped profile, marked a new Neo-Rationalist direction in Swedish design. Highly successful in terms of sales both at home and abroad, this stacking, lightweight and practical barstool brought widespread recognition for its young designers, Börge Lindau and Bo Lindekrantz, who went on to design numerous other innovative seating solutions for Lammhults over the suceeding decades.

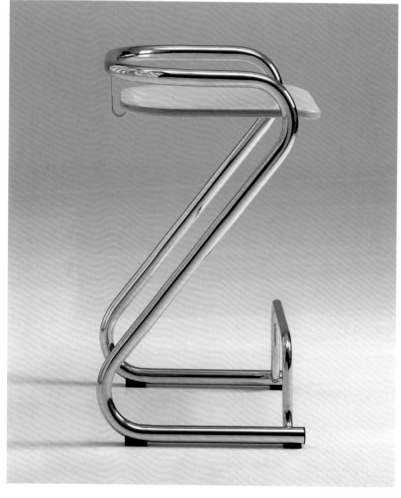

▲ Low variant of the *Model No. S70* stool designed by Börge Lindau and Bo Lindekrantz for Lammhults Möbel, c.1968

◄ *Model No. S70* barstool, 1968
Tubular steel, plywood
Lammhults Möbel, Lammhult, Sweden

Erik Magnussen
Zdown folding chair, 1968

Although Erik Magnussen was awarded the Lunning Prize in 1967 for his ceramics, the following year he demonstrated his ability to work within other product categories with his design of the folding *Zdown* chair. This highly functional seating solution was available with either a canvas or leather sling seat and back, and utilized a two-part frame made of tubular steel that incorporated a "bayonet lock" connection. Inherently springy, this chair provided a good level of comfort and was originally intended for public spaces, such as hotel foyers and reception areas, although it worked equally well in more domestic settings.

▲ Engelbrechts publicity photograph of *Zdown* chairs in a contemporary interior setting

► *Zdown* folding chair, 1968
Chromed tubular steel, leather
Torben Ørskov, Denmark
(Reissued by Engelbrechts)

Gionatan De Pas, Donato D'Urbino & Paolo Lomazzi
Blow armchairs, 1967

While numerous inflatible chairs and sofas appeared in the 1960s – a period of intense design experimentation – the *Blow* chair by De Pas, D'Urbino and Lomazzi, stands out not only as the first mass-produced inflatable chair from Italy, but also as one of the most commercially successful and widely disseminated seating designs of the period. A veritable icon of Pop culture, the *Blow* chair's expendability playfully dismissed the traditional associations of furniture with costliness and permanence. Heralding a more youthful and carefree spirit in design and manufacture, the *Blow* chair celebrated the ephemeral novelty as well as the aesthetic and functional potential made possible by new polymers.

Blow chair, 1967
Polyvinyl chloride (PVC)
Zanotta, Milan, Italy

Giovanni Travasa
Foglia armchairs, 1968

The origins of Vittorio Bonacina can be traced back to 1889, when Giovanni Bonacina established a business in Lurago D'Erba and began importing rattan from South-East Asia and applied this "new" material to two local craft traditions: basket-weaving and furniture making. During the 1950s and 1960s, his son Vittorio employed various talented designers to create more contemporary style models for the family-run business, such as the *Foglia* armchair by Giovanni Travasa. As its title suggests, a leaf inspired the elegant cantilevered form of this rattan chair.

Foglia armchairs, 1968
Woven rattan
Vittorio Bonacina, Como, Italy

Franco Albini & Franca Helg
Primavera chair, 1967

In 1950 Vittorio Bonacina began his collaboration with the Milanese architect and designer, Franco Albini in order to create contemporary designs for his family's rattan furniture manufacturing business. The first success of this alliance was the *Margherita* chair (1950), which won a prestigious Gold Medal at the 1951 Milan Triennale. Following on from this achievement, Albini created a number of other models for the firm including the dramatic *Primavera* chair, which was co-designed with Franca Helg.

Primavera chair, 1967
Woven rattan
Vittorio Bonacina, Como, Italy

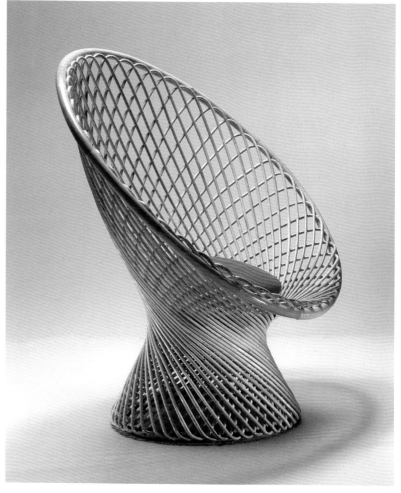

Eero Aarnio
Stools, c.1962 & Chair and ottoman, 1962

Known for his pioneering development of iconoclastic plastic chairs during the mid-to-late 1960s, the Finnish designer Eero Aarnio also explored the furniture manufacturing potential of natural materials and traditional Finnish basket-making skills. During the early sixties, he created a number of notable seating designs made of wickerwork supported on bamboo frames, including this circular tub chair and these barrel-like stools. He also created a matching sofa to compliment these sculptural designs, which can be seen to formally presage his later Space-Age seating designs.

Stools, c.1962
Wicker
Eero Aarnio, Finland

▶ Publicity photograph showing various wicker stools designed by Eero Aarnio, c.1962

▼ Chair and ottoman, 1962
Wicker, bamboo
Eero Aarnio, Finland

Isamu Kenmochi
Model No. C-3150 Rattan Round chair, 1960

Isamu Kenmochi created a number of interesting sculptural seating designs, including several utilising traditional Japanese bamboo and rattan weaving skills. His *Rattan Round* chair was essentially an Eastern interpretation of the traditional Western tub chair, and as such reflected the increasing synthesis of the two cultures during the postwar period. Traditionally in Japan, tatami floor mats had been used as seating and chairs were generally viewed as a rather suspect Western import, however, Kenmochi embraced the concept of "the Western chair" in order to create, as he put it, "Japanese Modern" furniture. This not only aided the so-called "modernization" of Japanese design in the 1960s, but enabled Kenmochi to export his designs abroad.

Model No. C-3150 Rattan Round chair, 1960
Woven rattan, textile-covered cushion
Yamakawa Rattan Co. Ltd., Japan (later by Y.M.K. Co. Ltd., Tokyo, Japan)

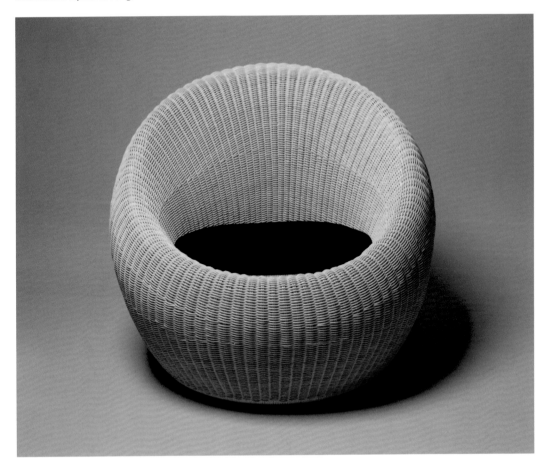

Gruppo Dam
Baffo chair, 1969

The progressive Milanese design group, Gruppo DAM (Designer Associati Milano) created a number of innovative seating designs, including the *Baffo* chair. With its simple tubular metal cross-stretchered frame and thick Bulgarian leather sling, this design might at first appear to predict the return to the more sombre and architectonic approach to seating design that was to manifest itself in Italian design during the mid-to-late 1970s, however, its title which translates as "whiskers" suggests this was probably not its creators' original intention.

Baffo chair, 1969
Chromed tubular steel, leather
Busnelli, Milan, Italy

Charles & Ray Eames
La Fonda side chair, 1961

Charles and Ray Eames and their talented design team, including Don Albinson, specially designed a side chair and an armchair for the La Fonda del Sol restaurant in New York City's famous Time-Life Building, the stylish interior of which was designed by Alexander Girard. The *La Fonda* chairs employed similar seat shells to the Eameses' earlier fiberglass chairs of 1948–50, however, at the request of Girard the backs of the chairs were lowered so that they were closer to the level of the table tops. These abbreviated seat shells were upholstered and then supported on an elegant four-column pedestal aluminum base.

▲ Contemporary photograph showing *La Fonda* armchairs within an interior setting, c.1961

◄ *La Fonda* side chair, 1961
Vinyl-covered upholstery, gel-coated fiberglass, aluminum, rubber
Herman Miller, Zeeland (MI), USA

► Early prototype of the *La Fonda* side chair, c.1961

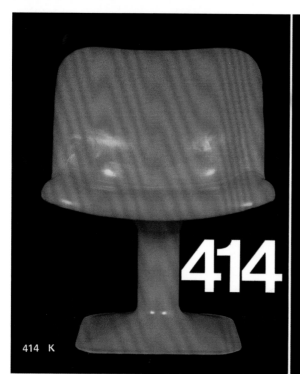

414 K

415

415 A

Haimi

415 P

Yrjo Kukkapuro
Model No. 415 chairs, 1964

◄ Haimi Oy brochure featuring the
Model No. 415 chair, c.1964

▼ *Model No. 415* chairs, 1964
Fibreglass, leather-covered
upholstery
Haimi Oy, Helsinki, Finland

Yrjo Kukkapuro designed a number of innovative chairs using
fiberglass seat shells, most notably his large *Karuselli* rocking
chair of 1964–65. Having a similar Pop aesthetic, his series
of dining/working chairs created for Haimi Oy during the
mid-1960s – which included the *Model No. 415* shown here –
employed two different seat shells (side version and armed
version) which could then be attached to three different
pedestal bases – the resulting chairs had a strong graphic
profile and reflected the Finnish love of bold sculptural shapes.

Ahti Kotikoski
Anatomia chair, 1968

In 1968 the Finnish furniture manufacturer Asko Oy held a furniture design competition and the *Anatomia* chair won first prize. As the jury noted, Ahti Kotikoski "examined the anatomy of the chair by using himself and his friends as guinea pigs. In this way an exceptional chair was formed that, when considering its sitting comfort, construction and cost, approaches some universal trends." A long forgotten design classic, this chair possesses that bold graphic quality that came to characterize Finnish design during the 1960s and 1970s.

Anatomia chair, 1968
Fibreglass, leather-covered
upholstery
Asko Oy, Lahti, Finland
(later by Artekno for Pro Feel
Design, Espoo, Finland)

Giancarlo Piretti
Model No. DSC 106 chair, 1965

Although Giancarlo Piretti is best known for his funky plastic furnishings from the 1960s and 1970s, he also designed the more sombre and rationally conceived *Model No. DSC 106* chair, which stacked very efficiently making it perfect for contract use. This design was a highly durable seating solution that also came in an upholstered version, and it is a tribute to its functional longevity that it is still in production nearly 50 years after it was first launched.

Model No. DSC 106 chair, 1965
Cast aluminium, moulded plywood
Anonima Castelli, Milan, Italy

Isamu Kenmochi
Kashiwado chair, 1961

Initially designed for a hotel lobby, this chunky chair is made of cedar, a wood not usually associated with furniture making because of its tendency to break, however, here it is used as solid pieces that are carefully joined together, which means the construction has the necessary strength. The beautiful grain of the wood is further enhanced by the use of the traditional *uzukuri* process, which involves the heating of the wood in order to darken its hue. This all-wood chair was named after the Sumo wrestler, Kashiwado, when he became *Yokozuna* ("horizontal rope", the highest rank of grand champion) in November 1961.

Kashiwado chair, 1961
Japanese cedar
Tendo, Tendō (Yamagata Prefecture), Japan

Jens Quistgaard
Stock armchairs, 1965

A personal favourite, the *Stock* armchair is perhaps the most exquisitely crafted chair from the 1960s and certainly one of the most stylish. Jens Harald Quistgaard was a self-taught craftsman whose design skills were exemplary, and his *Stock* armchair with its perfectly articulated back reveals all the distinctive trademarks of his *oeuvre*, the use of fluid lines and almost melting forms, the unusual combination of relatively exotic materials and above all, an extraordinary level of precision and detailing – is is, quite simply, a sublime *tour de force* of design.

Stock armchairs, 1965
Polished steel, solid rosewood,
suede-covered upholstery
Nissen, Langaa, Denmark

Grete Jalk Lounge chairs, 1968
Charlotte Perriand *Sandoz* bench, 1962

▲ *Sandoz* bench, 1962
Iroko mahogany, texile-covered
upholstery and cushions
Produced exclusively for Sandoz
Pharmaceutical
Laboratories, Rueil Malmaison,
France

◀ Lounge chairs, 1968
Birch plywood, textile-covered
upholstery
France & Son, Denmark

During the 1960s, there was a definable trend towards wooden furniture that had a sculptural and elemental simplicity, such as the bench site-specifically designed by Charlotte Perriand for the Sandoz Pharmaceutical Laboratories with its strong horizontal and vertical elements. Another design that also shared a similar essentialist and pared-down aesthetic was Grete Jalk's lounge chair from 1968, which had an extremely simple yet effective construction made of just four pieces of birch veneered and upholstered plywood.

Illum Wikkelsø
Lounge chair, c.1960

After studying at the School of Arts & Crafts in Copenhagen, Illum Wikkelsø worked for the well-known cabinetmaker Jacob Kjaer. He then subsequently joined the architectural office of Peter Hvidt and Orla Mølegaard-Nielsen, where he designed "Danish Modern" furnishings that were beautifully crafted and exquisitely proportioned. Although he is best known for his wooden furniture pieces, Wikkelsø also created this highly sculptural lounge chair, which with its striking upholstered seating section reveals a growing Pop sensibility in Nordic design during the early 1960s.

Lounge chair, c.1960
Chromed steel, textile-covered upholstery
Denmark

Gosta Berg & Stenerik Eriksson
Seagull chair and ottoman, 1968

A relatively rare design, the *Seagull* chair is a sculptural *tour-de-force* with its dynamic sweeping lines that are dictated by ergonomic considerations. Providing all-round comfort with its pillow-like headrest and its angled footstool that is subtly contoured, this luxuriant seating solution reflects a different side of Danish design that is more akin to the work of Verner Panton than the beautifully crafted solid wood furniture that is generally associated with Scandinavian design.

Seagull chair & ottoman, 1968
Steel, fabric-covered foam
upholstery
Fritz Hansen, Allerød, Denmark

Preben Fabricius & Jørgen Kastholm
Model No. FK82 lounge chair, 1968 & Skater chair, 1968

The cabinetmaker, Preben Fabricius and the blacksmith
Jørgen Kastholm began their collaboration in 1961, however
unlike most of their Danish contemporaries they preferred
using steel and leather to wood in their design of modern
furniture. In 1965, their work was spotted at a furniture fair
held in Frederica by the German manufacturer, Alfred Kill,
who subsequently put many of their designs into production,
including the Model No. FK82 (sometimes referred to as
the X-chair thanks to its simple yet dynamic frame). Also
designed in 1968, the Skater chair had a similarly sleek
Modernist aesthetic with its combination of gleaming steel
and contoured leather.

▲ Technical working drawings of
the Skater chair showing front and
side views

► Skater chair, 1968
Chromed steel, leather-covered
upholstery
Alfred Kill International, Germany
(later produced by Lange
Production)

◄ Model No. FK82 lounge chair,
1968
Chromed steel, leather
Kill International, Germany (later
produced by Lange Production)

Achille & Pier Giacomo Castiglioni
Tric folding chair, 1965 & *Ginevra* folding armchair, 1965

A modern re-working of an earlier chair dating from 1904 that was produced by Gebrüder Thonet, the *Tric* folding chair exemplified the Castiglioni brothers ability to create designs that had a strong visual presence as well as an innate functionality. Importantly, this design, together with its armed version known as the *Ginevra*, predicted the move away from the exuberant anything-goes Pop aesthetic of the 1960s to the more restrained Neo-Modernist sensibility of the mid-1970s.

◄ *Tric* folding chair, 1965
Painted solid wood, plywood
BBB Bonacina, Meda, Italy (later known as BBB Emmebonacina)

▼ *Ginevra* folding armchair, 1965
Painted solid wood, plywood
BBB Bonacina, Meda, Italy
(later known as BBB Emmebonacina)

Hans Wegner
Model No. PP701 armchair, 1965

Hans Wegner can be considered the chair designer's chair designer – a veritable maestro of seating design. The *Model No. PP701* armchair reflects his skillful ability to combine a variety of materials – in this case, tubular steel, wood and leather – into a cohesive design that has an inherent rightness. The subtle angle of the seat, the gentle contours of the C-shaped back-rail and the slight splaying of the legs were all incorporated to enhance the design's functionality. And it is this sublime attention to functional considerations that also give the design its understated, almost transparent, aesthetic.

Model No. PP701 armchair, 1965
Tubular steel, maple, leather-covered upholstery
PP Møbler, Allerød, Denmark

Gae Aulenti
Sgarsul rocking chair, 1962

In the early 1960s the Italian architect Gae Aulenti was a leading figure in Neoliberty, the movement that reacted against the dominant Modernist ethos by promoting a return to historical styles. This is apparent in the looping curves of the *Sgarsul* rocking chair that Aulenti designed for Poltronova in 1962 that referenced both Art Nouveau (called "Liberty" in Italy) and Thonet's nineteenth century bentwood chairs. The chair's name also reflects the movement's interest in regional, place-rooted design, as *Sgarsul* comes from the Neapolitan word for street urchin.

▲ Early publicity photograph showing the *Sgarsul* rocking chair in an interior setting, c.1962

◀ *Sgarsul* rocking chair, 1962
Lacquered bentwood, leather-covered upholstery
Poltronova, Pistoia, Italy

Joe Colombo
Superleggera chair, 1964

The *Superleggera* chair was designed by Joe Colombo in 1964 for the Italian manufacturer B-Line. Originally named the *Supercomfort*, the chair was renamed due to "superlight" design. Its slender frame consists of two curved, cutout walnut veneer sheets that are combined with an ergonomically designed seat and back with removable padded sections with concealed plastic splints designed to maximize comfort. The chair was subsequently manufactured in sheet steel and named *LEM*, short for Lunar Excursion Module, due to its space-age appearance.

Superleggera chair, 1964
Walnut, leather-covered
polyurethane foam upholstery, PVC
B-Line, Vicenza, Italy

Henry Massonnet
Tam Tam stool, 1967

Launched in 1968, Henry Massonnet's *Tam Tam* stool enjoyed enormous sales success during the 1970s, thanks to a magazine article featuring Brigitte Bardot sitting on one, which of course made it appear instantly stylish to the wider public. The ensuing sales of this practical and inexpensive stool were astonishing – 12 million units were sold in the five years following its creation. Much of its success, however, lay in the fact that the *Tam Tam* was extremely cheap to manufacture, thanks to its highly rational three-piece construction made entirely of injection-moulded polypropylene.

Tam Tam stool, 1967
Polypropylene
Stamp, Nurieux, France

Walter Papst
Model No. 404/4 outdoor chair & stool, 1961

After studying at the Muthesius-Werkkunstschule in Kiel, Walter Papst established his own Cologne-based design office in 1957. He was one of the first designers in Germany to experiment with the design potential of GRP (fiberglass) developing furniture from this reinforced plastic that utilized shell-like self-supporting constructions. In 1961, he created this simple yet elegant fiberglass chair and stool, intended for outdoor use. He also designed a matching two-seater bench and table, which was similarly produced by Mauser-Werke.

Model No. 404/4 outdoor chair &
stool, 1961
Glass-reinforced polyester
Mauser-Werke, Waldeck, Germany

Stacy Dukes
Efebino & *Efebo* stools, 1966

◄ Artemide catalogue page featuring the *Efebino* and *Efebo* stools, 1960s

▼ *Efebino* & *Efebo* stools, 1966
Glass-reinforced polyester
Artemide, Milan, Italy

In 1963, the County of Los Angeles Public Library system asked Frank Bros., a retail furniture store in Long Beach, California, to supply children's seating for their library. The American designer Stacy Dukes undertook the project, developing several models and prototypes, resulting in a final mould and a number of fibreglass castings. Despite having this firm order, however, no local manufacturer could be found, and eventually in 1966 Artemide in Italy put the *Efebino* and *Efebo* stools into production. As Dukes noted, "The style of the times, the means of production, the expectations of both the designer and audience led naturally to the completed configuration, in which the lines would never stop, never straighten, or become mechanical. The natural, organic form is derived from the free flow of the line, inviting the viewer to trace the form with his fingertips."

Luigi Colani
Gartenmöbel-Kollektion lounger and chair, 1967

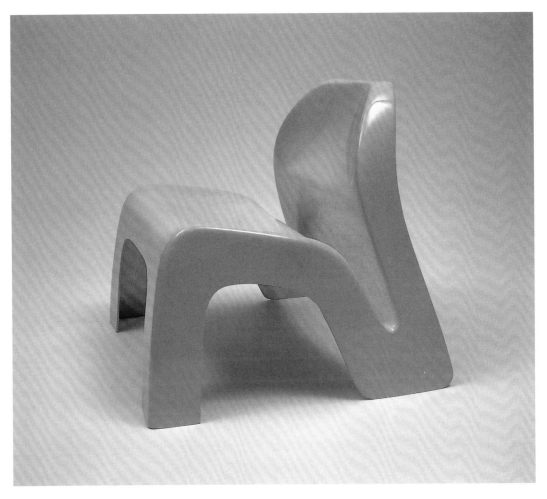

Luigi Colani was a visionary designer who sculpted plastics into sensuous and futuristic organic forms. His pioneering *Gartenmöbel-Kollektion* programme of fibreglass garden furniture from 1967 comprised the chair and sun lounger, shown here, as well as another chair, a bench and a table. Also sometimes referred to as the *Gardenparty* range, these weatherproof designs with their fluid lines were designed to drain rainwater and introduced a sculptural Space Age aesthetic to the realm of outdoor furniture.

Gartenmöbel-Kollektion
lounger and chair, 1967
Painted fibreglass
Heinz Essmann, Schotmar-Lippe,
Germany

Rodolfo Bonetto
Boomerang chair, 1968

Despite no formal training as a designer, Rodolfo Bonetto worked in both furniture and industrial design for companies including Pininfarina and Fiat from the late 1950s. Bonetto's curvaceous *Boomerang* chair is characteristic of his approach to design that combined Modernist austerity with humourous touches. The polyurethane foam form is supported by an internal steel structure and has two angled steel strips on either side. These give the *Boomerang* chair its name and act as a coupling mechanism to join individual chairs together into a settee formation.

Boomerang chair, 1968
Chromed steel, steel, textile-covered polyurethane foam upholstery
B-Line, Vicenza, Italy

Luigi Colani
TV-Relax recliner, 1968

With a background in automotive design, the German born designer Luigi Colani worked in America and France before returning to his native Berlin in 1954. From 1968 to 1969 Colani was employed as an in-house designer at Kusch & Co., for which he designed the *TV-Relax* recliner as part of the *Meereskolletion* (Ocean collection). This organically shaped chair, which has a fibreglass supporting core fully upholstered in stretch jersey-covered polyurethane foam, exemplifies Colani's approach to design that combined his interest in nature-derived forms, what he called "bio-design", with the sensuous curves of the human body.

TV-Relax recliner, 1968
Fibreglass, textile-covered
polyurethane foam upholstery
Kusch & Co, Hallenberg,
Germany

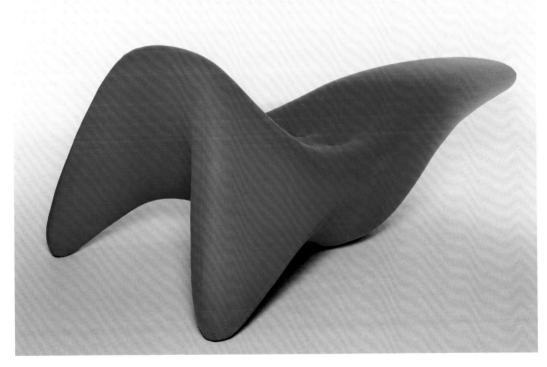

Bernard Rancillac
Éléphant chair, 1966

The French artist and designer Bernard Rancillac designed the *Éléphant* chair in 1966. Rancillac's design combines a welded steel base with a one-piece seat and back that explored the formal potential of glass-reinforced polyester (GRP). As its name suggests, the chair's unusual form takes its inspiration from the shape of an elephant's head, the trunk forming the seat and leg-rest of the chair. Initially produced in a small edition by Galerie Lacloche in Paris, in 1985 Michel Roudillon re-editioned the *Éléphant* in a range of five different colours.

Éléphant chair, 1966
Steel, glass-reinforced polyester
Galerie Lacloche, Paris, France
(later by Michel Roudillon, Paris)

Liisi Beckmann
Karelia chair, 1966

The *Karelia* chair is one of the most well-known designs of
Liisi Beckmann, a Finnish designer who moved to Italy in the
1950s and who was active in Milan's design scene. Her chair
was put into production in 1966 by Zanotta, who subsequently
reissued in the design in 2007. With its ribbed profile and
bright colours, the *Karelia's* playful form appealed to children
and adults alike, and had a removable cover available in a
variety of materials and hues.

Karelia chair, 1966
Vinyl-covered polyurethane foam
Zanotta, Nova Milanese, Italy

Rossi Molinari
Toy chair, 1968

The *Toy* chair was moulded from a single sheet of acrylic and
came in three different colour choices: clear, fluorescent pink
or yellow. A simple hemispherical depression in the plastic
provided a seat, which was then softened with a padded
cushion. Like a large plaything inviting interaction, this design
was youthfully lighthearted and reflected the engaging Pop
spirit of the era in which it was created.

Toy chair, 1968
Acrylic, upholstered cushion
Totem, Grisignano di Zocco, Italy

Lella & Massimo Vignelli
Saratoga armchair, 1964

In 1964, Lella and Massimo Vignelli designed their stylishly sophisticated yet boxy *Saratoga* furniture line for Poltronova, which was a comprehensive range that included not only the cube-like chair, shown here, but also a matching sofa, a low coffee table and various storage units. With its glossy planes skinned in gleaming polyester lacquer and its unrelenting hard edge geometry, the *Saratoga* range was designed to have a built-in look and as such was hugely influential within the furnishings market, establishing according to the Vignellis, "a trend for years to come".

Saratoga armchair, 1964
Polyester lacquered wood, leather-covered cushions
Poltronova, Montale, Italy

Pedro Friedeberg
Hand Foot chair, c.1960 & *Hand* chair, c.1965

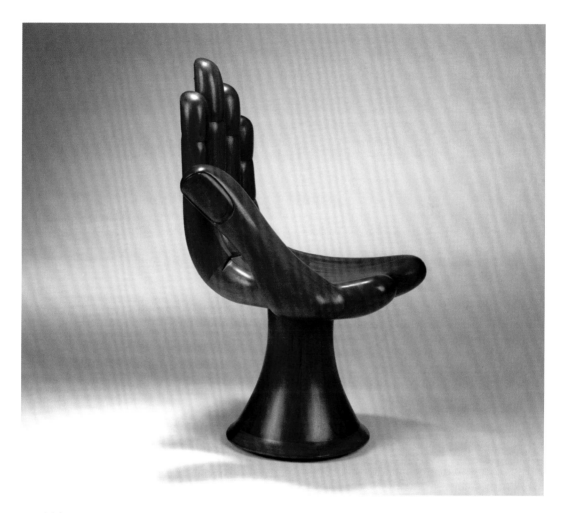

▲ *Hand* chair, c.1965
Mahogany
Pedro Friedeberg, Mexico City,
Mexico

◄ *Hand Foot* chair, c.1960
Gilded and lacquered mahogany
Pedro Friedeberg, Mexico City,
Mexico

Born in Florence, the Mexican artist Pedro Friedeberg created fantastical surrealist paintings often imbued with symbolic meaning and peppered with occult motifs. He also designed similarly bizarre furnishings, most notably his series of *Hand* chairs that cradled the sitter in their gigantic outsized palms. In many cultures the hand is a symbol of strength and support, and this presumably attracted Friedeberg to choose it as a theme he returned to over and over again.

Angiolo Giuseppe Fronzoni
Fronzoni '64 chair, 1964

The Italian minimalist designer, editor and educator Angiolo Giuseppe Fronzoni worked across various design disciplines, including graphics, exhibition design and interior design. He also created this starkly geometric chair as part of his *Fronzoni '64* collection for the Italian manufacturer Cappellini. The chair's square-sectioned tubular metal frame and lacquered wood seat was available in black or white, a sober colour palette found throughout his work that reflected a design ideology based on the elimination of all excess in order to get to the essence of things.

Fronzoni '64 chair, 1964
Metal, lacquered wood
Cappellini, Mariano Comense, Italy

Roger Tallon
Zombie chair, 1967

***Zombie* chair, 1967**
ABS, vinyl-covered upholstery,
tubular steel, flat steel
France

In the early 1960s the highly talented French designer, Roger Tallon created a number of "personalized" versions of his eye-catching *Zombie* chair, which were made from brightly painted bent plywood. He subsequently simplified the design so that it could be serially produced, such as the example shown here. The "body" of Tallon's chair was made of yellow or orange ABS plastic, while its target-like back cushion was upholstered in vinyl. This totemic design is a quintessentially Pop design that is more about emotional character than functional comfort, and it has an endearing playful quality that absolutely characterizes the *zeitgeist* of the period.

Roger Tallon
Module 400 armchair, 1965

In 1965 Roger Tallon designed an "adjustable helicoid spiral staircase", known as the *M400* that incorporated modular polished steel steps that were attached to a central column. The same year, he also designed his *Module 400* range of chairs that similarly incorporated a standardized element, in this case an elegant supporting pedestal base made of highly polished aluminium. This extensive seating programme, which included the armchair shown here, also innovatively utilized sheets of textured industrial foam often used for noise dampening and packaging.

Module 400 armchair, 1965
Aluminium, polyester foam
Jacques Lacloche, Paris, France

Peter Karpf
Wing chair, 1968

With its innovative bentwood construction, Peter Karpf's dramatic design for the *Wing* chair represents the Danish furniture designer's research into the technical and formal possibilities of plywood in the 1960s. Available in a black or red painted finish, Karpf's expressive use of the material in the *Wing* chair echoes earlier chairs by fellow Danish designers Grete Jalk and Arne Jacobsen, both of whom Karpf had worked for, while the cat's cradle design of the cord chair back echoes the stringed forms of earlier Modernist sculpture.

Wing chair, 1968
Lacquered plywood, cord
Christensen & Larsen, Denmark

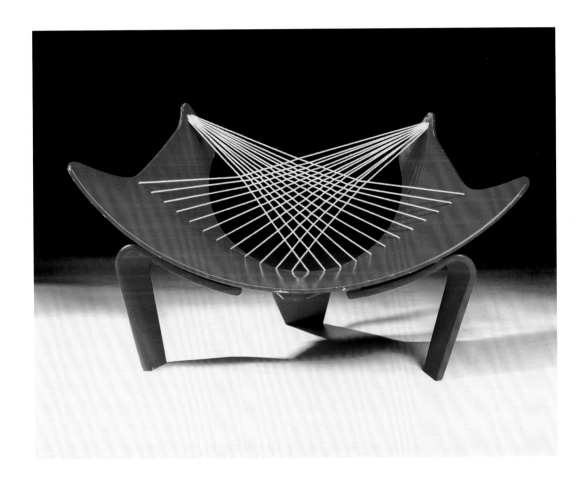

Pierre Paulin
Model No. F163 Little Tulip chair, 1965

The *Little Tulip* chair with its petal-like elements has an inviting character and a strong sculptural profile, which ensures that it looks good in any setting. It is also extremely comfortable like other seating designs by Pierre Paulin, who more than any other chair designer was able to obtain the optimum level of supporting comfort, whilst also creating bold Space-Age forms that were not only suitable for both the contract and the domestic markets, but still to this day have an enduring timeless appeal. The *Little Tulip* was also functionally adaptable in that it could be used for sitting and relaxing, as well as for dining.

▲ Artifort publicity photograph of the *Little Tulip* chair, c.1965

▼ *Model No. F163 Little Tulip* chair, 1965
Chromed metal, textile-covered polyurethane foam upholstery
Artifort, Maastricht, The Netherlands

Verner Panton
Model No. S401 chairs, 1963

Although not as well known as other seating designs by Verner Panton, the *Model No. S401* chair was a radical departure when it was first launched in 1967 with its boldly segmented seating section swivelling on its circular metal base. The matching *Model No. S400* footstool and *Model No. S402* high-backed chair were similarly constructed, and similarly provided a high degree of comfort through their use of stretch jersey-covered polyurethane foam.

Model No. S401 easy chairs, 1963
Chromed metal, tubular steel, fabric-covered foam upholstery
Gebrüder Thonet, Frankenberg, Germany

Pierre Paulin
Le Chat chair, 1967

An extremely comfortable seating solution, the *Le Chat* lounge chair as its title suggests had a form that recalled the arching back of a cat. With its low seat-height, this design offered a more casual sitting position, which suited the laid-back lifestyle of the late 1960s. Although in tune with the Flower Power sentiments of the period, this design – like other chairs and sofas created by Paulin for Artifort – was also highly aesthetically refined and brought a new sculptural confidence to the design of seating. The example, shown below, is upholstered in a psychedelic stretch-jersey textile designed by the American textile designer, Jack Lenor Larsen.

▲ Turner Ltd. advertisement showing various seating designs by Pierre Paulin, 1960s

▼ *Le Chat* chair, 1967
Steel, stretch jersey-covered polyurethane foam upholstery
Artifort, Maastricht, Netherlands

Pierre Paulin
Model No. 582 Ribbon chair, 1965

Perhaps the most comfortable seating solution in the world, the *Ribbon* chair is a loop of upholstered foam that gently cradles the body and provides superlative ergonomic support. Highly sculptural, the *Ribbon* chair remains a very bold aesthetic statement, especially when upholstered, as shown here, in psychedelic stretch-jersey fabric specially designed by Jack Lenor Larsen. Despite its blatant Space-Age connotations, this remarkable chair has an enduring appeal thanks to its seductive and inviting organic form.

Model No. 582 Ribbon chair, 1965
Steel, lacquered pressed wood, stretch jersey-covered polyurethane foam upholstery
Artifort, Maastricht, Netherlands

Pierre Paulin
Amphys modular seating system, 1968 & *Mushroom* sofa, 1960

Pierre Paulin's undulating *Amphys* seating system was sold
in modular units, which could be joined together to form
a continuous seating unit of whatever length required. The
articulated base made of lacquered steel held the three fabric-
covered foam seating elements in place and the final desired
shape was determined by adjusting the position of these
base elements. Paulin's *Mushroom* loveseat was similarly
eye-catching, especially when upholstered in psychedelic
stretch-jersey fabric designed by Jack Lenor Larsen. Both
these designs were not only supremely comfortable but also
epitomized the experimental nature of design in the 1960s,
both in terms of form and pattern.

Mushroom sofa, 1960
Tubular steel, stretch jersey-
covered polyurethane foam
upholstery
Artlfort, Maastricht,
The Netherlands

► *Amphys* modular seating
system, 1968
Lacquered steel, textile-
covered polyurethane foam
Alpha International Mobilier,
Paris, France

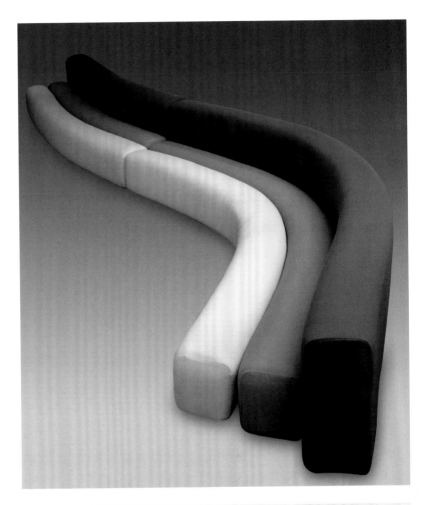

► Alpha International Mobilier
brochure showing various
configurations of the *Amphys*
seating system, c.1968

Alexander Girard
Model No. 66301 lounge chairs, 1967

◄ Herman Miller brochure for the *Girard Group*, c.1967, showing different models and textile options

▼ *Model No. 66301* lounge chairs, 1967
Aluminium, textile-covered upholstery
Herman Miller, Zeeland (MI), USA

In 1965, Alexander Girard was hired by Braniff Airlines to oversee the re-design of every aspect of the company's appearance, from the aircraft interiors and airport lounges to the ticket counters and ground equipment. The venture was officially termed "The End of the Plain Plane" and also included the creation of a comprehensive new furniture range developed in conjunction with Herman Miller. Marketed as the *Girard Group*, the furniture range included a number of tables as well as a wide variety of seating options, such as the stylish *Model No. 66301* lounge chairs, shown here, that are upholstered in their original Girard-designed textiles, including a pattern known as *Toolstripe*.

Giancarlo Piretti
Plona folding chair, 1969

In 1969, Giancarlo Piretti designed his ubiquitous *Plia* folding chair with its transparent seat and back. The same year, he also designed another less well-known but nonetheless important chair, the *Plona*. Larger than the *Plia*, this attention-grabbing foldable design came with either a smoky acrylic seating section or a soft vinyl sling-like seat, as shown here. Incorporating the same folding mechanism that Piretti used for the *Plia*, the *Plona*, although a relatively large lounge chair could be folded down into a very compact space when not in use.

Plona folding chair, 1969
Aluminium, vinyl, plastic
Anonima Castelli, Ozzano
Dell'Emilia, Italy

Hans Wegner
Hammock chaise longue, 1967

As its title suggests, Hans Wegner was inspired by a hammock in his design of this elegant chaise longue with its cradling support of woven flag halyard attached to a simple frame of moulded plywood and supported by M-shaped legs. The design was also provided with a leather-covered pillow for extra comfort as well as a natural sheepskin that could be used for additional padding. This chaise longue's clean lines, subtle organic contours and exquisite craftsmanship reflects the pared-down simplicity and inherent practicality that have become synonymous with the term, Scandinavian Modernism.

Hammock chaise longue, 1967
Oak plywood, flag halyard, copper, leather cushion
Getama, Gedsted, Denmark

George Nakashima
Conoid lounge chair, 1968

George Nakashima desired to create practical designs without "style" but that had a connection to nature, for as he noted, "To be intimate with nature in its multifaceted moods is one of the greatest experiences of life". Certainly, his low-seated *Conoid* lounge chair reflected this with its subtly angled frame made of solid wood. Harking back to Mission style furniture and using native woods, Nakashima's design had a comforting familiarity yet at the same time was also unequivocally modern.

Conoid lounge chair, 1968
American black walnut, hickory,
textile-covered cushion
George Nakashima, New Hope
(PA), USA

Mitsumasa Sugasawa
Heron rocking chair, 1966

While working as Tendo's in-house designer and development manager, Mitsumasa Sugasawa created this elegant rocking chair and matching ottoman that skillful utilized the company's high-grade plywood, known as "koma", which had an excellent strength-to-weight ratio. The well-known Japanese/American artist-designer, Isamu Noguchi habitually used this visually striking rocking chair is his sculpture studio, with its subtly contoured frame echoing the form of the human body to provide functional comfort within a refined sculptural form.

Heron rocking chair, 1966
Teak plywood, leather-covered upholstery
Tendo, Tendō (Yamagata Prefecture), Japan

Daisaku Choh & Junzo Sakakura Architecture Institute
Teiza-Isu chair, 1960

The Kabuki actor, Koushirou Matumoto asked his friend Daisaku Choh, one of Japan's most respected furniture designers who was then in charge of the Junzo Sakakura Architecture Institute, if he could design a chair for his mother that she could relax in but which, at the same time, would not damage her tatami. The resulting design, also sometimes known as the *Sakakura* chair, with its wide sled-like base distributes the sitter's weight evenly so as to avoid damaging flooring mats. This icon of Japanese design was initially launched at the XII Milan Triennale in 1960, and the following year it was put into mass-production by Tendo.

Teiza-Isu chair, 1960
Oak plywood, fabric-covered upholstery
Tendo, Tendō (Yamagata Prefecture), Japan

Nguyen Manh Khanh
Chair, c.1968, Lounger, c.1968, *Apollo* chairs & *Venus* child's chair, 1968

The Paris-based Vietnamese designer, Nguyen Manh Khanh adopted the name Quasar while in his twenties believing it to be "more modern and universal". His designs for affordable inflatable furniture were similarly forward-looking and accorded with the carefree and youthful zeitgeist of the 1960s. He not only created the designs shown here, but also a daybed, a block-like armchair and a circular ottoman, all of which were manufactured by the British company, Ultralite Ltd. According to José Manser in *Design* magazine (January 1968), Quasar's "throwaway" designs were the first inflatable furnishings to be retailed in Britain. Their individual blow-up PVC elements were linked together using metal rings and could be filled with air or water.

▲ **Lounger, c.1968**
PVC
Ultralight Ltd., UK

◀ **Chair, c.1968**
PVC
Ultralight Ltd., UK

▶ *Apollo* **chairs &** *Venus* **child's chair, 1968**
PVC
Ultralight Ltd., UK

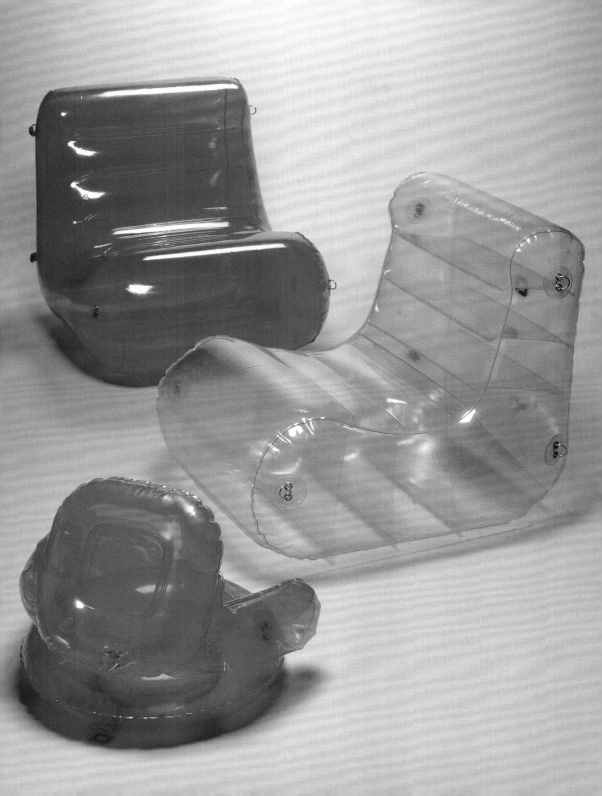

Jean-Pierre LaPorte
Girolle chair, 1969

The *Girolle* chair was designed in 1969 by the French designer
Jean-Pierre Laporte. In his youth Laporte was a frequent
visitor to the workshops of Thonet France, where his father
worked, and it is one of several chairs he designed for the
firm. Made from a single sheet of glass-reinforced polyester,
the sculptural chair takes its name from the mushroom, also
known as a chanterelle, and exemplifies the widespread
experimentation with synthetic materials and unconventional
forms at this time. In 2010 the chair was reissued by Galerie
Edouard Edwards.

Girolle chair, 1969
Glass-reinforced polyester
Thonet France, Paris, France

Gerd Lange
Model No. DSM400K Nova chair, 1967

Gerd Lange designed the *Model No. DSM400K Nova* chair, better known as the *Swing* chair, for Drabert, one of a number of manufacturers for whom the German designer conceived contract furniture and lighting following the opening of his design studio in 1961. The bestselling, lightweight, stackable chair was made from a tubular steel frame with a seat and back made from a single sheet of polyamid. An interlocking mechanism was also produced that enabled the creation of fixed rows of *Nova* chairs. Extremely comfortable thanks to its frame's inherent give, the design came with optional padded seat and back sections (as shown here) to further enhance the sitting experience.

◄ Atelier International advertisement for the *Nova* chair, 1970 – Atelier International manufactured the design under license in the USA

▼ *Model No. DSM400K Nova* chair, 1967
Tubular steel, polyamide, textile-covered upholstery
Drabert, Minden, Germany

Alberto Rosselli
Play chair, 1969 & *Jumbo* chair, 1969

Alberto Rosselli began promoting industrial materials and methods of manufacture in the 1950s and the experimental, futuristic forms of the moulded fiberglass *Play* and *Jumbo* chairs from 1969 were the result of his research into the use of thermoset plastic materials in design. The hollow, cube-shaped *Play* chair had open sides and was intended to be lined up in a row. The lightweight *Jumbo* chair, one of Rosselli's best known designs, appears to be a closed form but has an open back intended for the storage of books and magazines.

Play chair, 1969 &
Jumbo chair, 1969
Glass-reinforced polyester
Saporiti, Besnate, Verona, Italy

Shiro Kuramata
Luminous chair, 1969

The Japanese designer Shiro Kuramata designed the moulded acrylic *Luminous* chair in 1969. The luminous effect of the translucent, ghostly white chair is the result of a light concealed within the chair that was informed by the designer's attempt to design light itself, into a form that the user then sits on. Produced in a limited edition of 30, the chair's combination of a Pop form and avant-garde thinking is characteristic of Kuramata's philosophical approach to design, which could also be seen in his *Luminous* table of the same year.

Luminous chair, 1969
Moulded acrylic
Ishimaru Co. Ltd, Tokyo, Japan

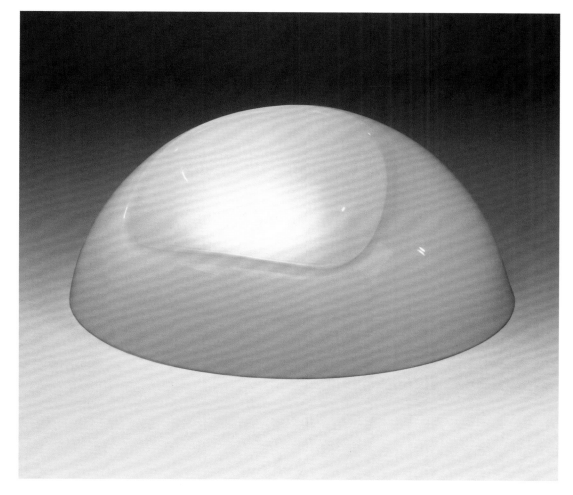

Gunnar Magnusson
Apollo chair, 1967

One of Iceland's leading furniture designers, Gunnar Magnusson studied furniture and interior design in Copenhagen, prior to establishing his own Reykjavik-based design studio in 1963. Four years later he designed his moulded plywood *Apollo* chair, which was directly inspired by the staging sections of NASA's *Saturn V* moon rocket used for the Apollo space mission, hence its title. The design was based on simple geometric shapes and, as Magnusson observed, the constructional concept of "a central point and two types of curves".

Apollo chair, 1967
Moulded plywood, textile-covered upholstery
Kristján Siggeirsson, Reykjavik, Iceland

Helgi Hallgrímsson
Rocking chair, 1968

Helgi Hallgrímsson studied at the School of Industrial Art, Copenhagen, where his classmates included Hans Wegner, Børge Mogensen and Jens Risom – all of whom went on to become famous furniture designers. After graduating, Hallgrimsson returned to his native Iceland and established his own design office in Reykjavik in 1938. From 1941 to 1946, he also ran his own furniture workshop that manufactured his designs, including this rocking chair with its distinctive two-tone upholstery and visually striking frame made of imported teak – there being no locally grown wood available due to Iceland's harsh climatic conditions.

Rocking chair, 1968
Teak, textile-covered upholstery
FHI, Reykjavik, Iceland

Fabio Lenci
Chain lounge chair, 1967

This stylish and extremely comfortable armchair has a sling of sausage-like rolls of padded leather that is attached to its glass side panels with two aluminium connectors. Lenci's combination of materials give the chair a distinctive Neo-Deco look, which was to eventually become so popular during the early 1970s. Like so many other progressive European designs, Stendig distributed this visually dramatic chair in the United States.

Chain lounge chair, 1967
Glass, aluminium, leather-covered upholstery
Bernini, Ceriano Laghetto, Italy

Cini Boeri
Bicia armchair, 1969

In keeping with the more casual lifestyle of the 1960s, the *Bicia* affords the user a low sitting position that is quite literally laid-back. With a bold graphic profile reminiscent of abstracted cloud forms, the lounger is highly sculptural, and reflects the playful and experimental nature of Italian design during the Pop era. This comfortable design was made from varying densities of polyurethane foam. It came with fully removable covers, and was available in a wide range of colours.

▲ Arflex publicity photograph promoting the *Bicia* armchair, c.1969

▼ *Bicia* armchair, 1969
Fibreglass, leather-covered polyurethane foam upholstery
Arflex, Milan, Italy

Gaetano Pesce
Up-3 Chair, 1969

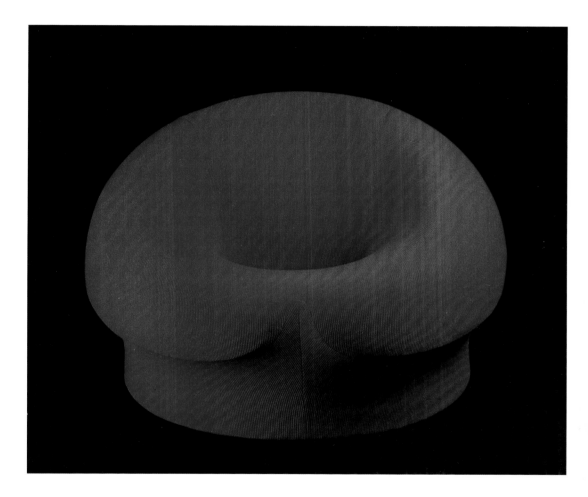

▲ *Up-3* chair, 1969
Jersey-covered polyurethane foam
C&B Italia, Como, Italy

◄ Salvador Dali with the *Up Series*
seating collection, c.1969

The *Up Series* quite literally turned the act of buying furniture into a home "happening". This range comprised seven different models, six of which – including the *Up-3*, the form of which was inspired by the tip of a phallus – were made of squishy polyurethane foam covered in stretch jersey fabric. The individual pieces were compressed and vacuum-packed into PVC envelopes, which when opened allowed the designs to dramatically bounce into life.

Verner Panton
Kleeblatt-Sofa, 1969 & *3D Carpet* seating units, c.1969–70

◄ *Kleeblatt-Sofa*
(*Cloverleaf Sofa*), 1969
Rigid polyurethane foam, cold-
formed polyuretance foam, Dralon
textile
Metzeler Schaum, Germany/Mira-X,
Switzerland

▼ *3D Carpet* seating units,
c.1969–70
Rigid polyurethane foam, cold-
formed polyurethane foam, Dralon
textile
Germany

This undulating cloverleaf-shaped sectional sofa reflects
Verner Panton's interest in creating comfortably functional
yet highly sculptural forms. Almost functioning as a standalone seating pit, this "shagadelic" seating solution was
completely upholstered in deep-pile twisted Dralon. It was
initially conceived for the landmark "Visiona II" exhibition for
Bayer held during the Cologne Furniture Fair in 1970, where
Panton created a series of extraordinary room installations
that were futuristic "Phantasy" Space-Age projections. Also
displayed in this landmark installation was Panton's *3D Carpet*
seating unit – that looks like an animated rippling floor rug –
and which like the sofa had a sculptural undulating profile that
invited playful interaction.

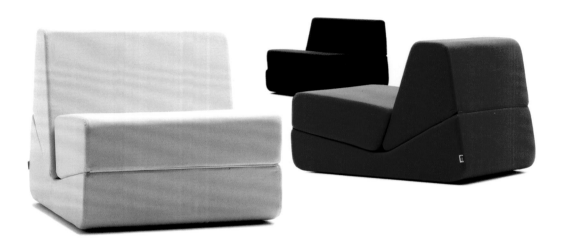

Jonathan Du Pas, Donato D'Urbino & Paolo Lomazzi
Galeotta chair, 1967 & *Gomma* armchair, 1967

▲ *Gomma* armchair, 1967
Textile-covered polyurethane foam
BBB Emmebonacina, Spilimbergo,
Italy

◄ *Galeotta* chair, 1967
Textile-covered polyurethane foam
BBB Emmebonacina, Spilimbergo,
Italy

During the 1960s and 1907s, Jonathan Du Pas, Donato D'Urbino and Paolo Lomazzi created innovative furniture and temporary architecture that utilized advanced industrial technologies. Although best remembered for their inflatable *Blow* chair made of PVC, the Milanese design trio also designed the multi-functional *Galeotta* chair, the title of which translates into English as "galoot", a slang word for a lazy fellow, which is rather fitting given that the design can be configured into a low slouching couch. They also designed the highly sculptural *Gomma* armchair with its useful removable covers, which as its name suggests utilized foam rubber for its curvaceous and seductive form.

Jonathan De Pas, Donato D'Urbino & Paolo Lomazzi
Carrera seating system and chair, 1969

Carrera was designed in 1969 by Jonathan De Pas, Donato D'Urbino and Paolo Lomazzi, three young Italian architects who had set up a design practice in Milan in 1966. The modular seating system was composed of a number of straight and curvilinear polyurethane foam shapes with removable covers that could be arranged into any number of combinations. Its open-ended design and elementary, soft shapes were characteristic of the architects' youth-orientated approach to design most famously seen in their inflatable *Blow* chair, produced by Zanotta in 1967. A matching stand alone *Carrera* chair was also manufactured, as seen to the right.

Carrera modular seating system and chair, 1969
Polyurethane foam, stretch fabric cover
BBB EmmeBonacina, Meda, Italy

1970s

Steen Østergaard
Model No. 290 chair, 1970

► *Model No. 290* chair, 1970
Glass-reinforced polyamide, textile-covered cushion
France & Son for Cado, Aarhus, Denmark

After the success of the *Panton* chair, many other designers were inspired to create similar single-form/single-material chairs made in a variety of different thermoplastic compounds. One of the most successful of these was Steen Østergaard's seminal range of seating for Cado, which included the *Model No. 290* chair. In fact, this sinuous chair can be considered a more resolved design than Verner Panton's, because it used less material, stacked more efficiently and, perhaps most importantly, was infinitely more comfortable to sit in.

▲ Cado publicity photograph showing Steen Østergaard's *Model No.290* chair stacked on a purpose-designed dolly, c.1970

Steen Østergaard
Model No. 291 armchair, c.1970

Steen Østergaard's *Model No. 291* armchair was made of injection-moulded glass-reinforced polyamide – a tough-wearing composite material. Together with Østergaard's matching *Model No. 265* lounge chair and *Model No. 290* side chair, this elegant cantilevered plastic armchair provided, according to the journal *Design from Scandinavia*, "comfortable seating in a timeless design appropriate to any setting". Lightweight yet strong, the *Model No. 291* could also be stacked, though not as efficiently as the side version, and had a flexible resilience that afforded the sitter a high level of comfort with the minimum of padding.

▲ Cado promotional photograph showing the *Model No. 265* lounge chair and matching ottoman, c.1970

◄► *Model No. 291* armchair, c.1970
Glass-reinforced polyamide, textile-covered cushion
France & Son for Cado, Aarhus, Denmark

Stefan Wewerka
Classroom chair, c.1970

An early example of "design art", Stefan Wewerka's quirky *Classroom* chair was originally titled the *Vertreterstuhl* (Representative's Chair) and was designed as part of a "classroom" installation for the Galerie Müller in Cologne in 1971. This asymmetrical chair-sculpture was seen there by Axel Bruchhaüser and was subsequently used by his company, Tecta, as an "eyecatcher" for a tradeshow and was also produced as a limited edition by Galerie Mikro in Berlin. Importantly, this intentionally absurd design with its skewed form revealed, according to an exhibition catalogue of Tecta designs, "what is left when a chair is deprived of its *raison d'être*: its seat function".

Classroom chair, c.1970
Painted wood
Galerie Mikro, Berlin, Germany

Nanda Vigo
Due Più chair, 1971

One of the most interesting Italian furniture and lighting designers of the 1970s, Nanda Vigo had previously worked with Gio Ponti and Lucio Fontana. Her distinctive work had a powerful visual artistry and a stark elemental quality, as evinced in her *Due Più* (Two More) chair from 1971 with its frame made of gleaming tubular metal onto which two upholstered rollers were attached. The design's shaggy faux fur covering contrasted with its hard-edged chromed metal supporting structure to create a strong aesthetic tension.

Due Più chair, 1971
Chromed tubular steel, faux fur-covered upholstery
Conconi, Italy

Gruppo G14
Fiocco lounge chair, 1970 & *Argine* chair, c.1970

◄ *Fiocco* lounge chair, 1970
Tubular metal, stretch jersey textile
Busnelli, Milan, Italy

▼ *Argine* chair, c.1970
Self-skinning polyurethane foam,
cord
Busnelli, Milan, Italy

Gruppo G14 was a radical design group founded by Gianfranco Facchetti, Umberto Orsoni, Gianni Pareschi, Giuseppe Pensotti and Roberto Ubaldi that created a number of formally and structurally innovative seating designs during the early 1970s. Their *Fiocco* lounge chair with its sinuous organic form used a tubular metal support sheathed in a removable cover made of stretch fabric, while the surrealistic *Argine* chair incorporated naturalistic-looking "pebbles" made from self-skinning polyurethane foam that were encased in a net of white cord.

Arne Jacobsen
Model No. 3208 Seagull armchair, 1970

An evolution of Arne Jacobsen's successful *7 Series* seating range, the *Seagull* chair had a more overtly sculptural form with its comma-shaped armrests reminding one of an Alexander Calder mobile. Launched at the Danish furniture fair in 1970, it was subsequently used to furnish Arne Jacobsen's headquarters building for the Danmarks Nationalbank. However, the design's distinctive curves were difficult to mass-produce because they required a substantial amount of pressure during the moulding process and as a result its production was discontinued after only a short while. This design has, however, recently been put back into production and has since been rechristened *The Lily*.

▲ Fritz Hansen publicity photograph showing back view of the *Model No. 3208 Seagull* armchair, c.1970

◄ *Model No. 3208 Seagull* armchair, 1970
Lacquered moulded plywood, chromed tubular steel
Fritz Hansen, Allerød, Denmark

George Nakashima
New armchairs, 1970

A modern re-working of a historic English armchair known as the *Windsor* chair, George Nakashima's *New* armchairs reflected not only the enduring appeal of vernacular typologies but also the widespread "return to craft" movement that happened in the 1970s. Lovingly crafted in his workshop in New Hope, Pennsylvania, these elegant chairs with their lathe-turned uprights and shallow dish seats revealed a high-degree of skilled workmanship as well as an attuned sense of harmonious proportion.

New armchairs, 1970
Walnut, hickory
George Nakashima, New Hope
(PA), USA

Terje Ekstrøm
Ekstrem chair, 1972

The ergonomically refined *Ekstrem* chair was originally designed in 1972, however, it was not actually put into production until 1984, presumably because its proto-Post-Modern sculptural aesthetic was a little too far ahead of popular taste, especially in the Scandinavian countries. Nevertheless, it became a much-lauded icon of Norwegian design during the 1980s thanks as much to its bold appearance as to its functional and comfortable versatility. Unlike much seating designed from a human factors standpoint, the *Ekstrem* chair was a static design that was not responsive to the sitter's movements, however, this was not a failing because instead its open structure allowed for multiple sitting positions that all supported the sitter in back-easing comfort.

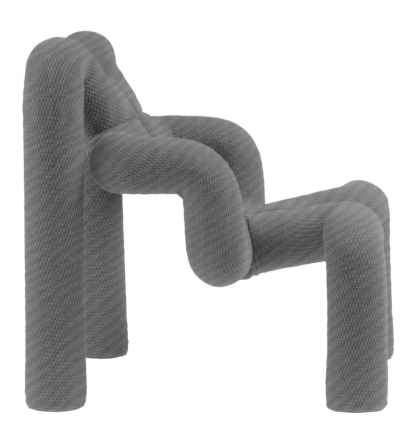

Ekstrem chair, 1972
Tubular metal, textile-covered polyurethane foam upholstery
Hjellegjerde Møbler, Norway (later by Stokke, Norway and then Variér Furniture, Norway)

Peter Opsvik & Hans Christian Mengshoel
Balans Variable sitting tool, 1979

Most conventional chairs are fundamentally objects of inactivity that support the sitter in essentially one static position, which is actually not particularly good for anyone's postural health. Instead, it is much better for human wellbeing to have a chair or seat that actually promotes movement as well as a variation in seating position. To this end, the concept for the *Balans Variable* sitting tool was originally conceived by Hans Christian Mengshoel and then subsequently designed into a three-dimensional reality by Peter Opsvik. As *the* original kneeling stool, the *Balans Variable* was highly influential in its promotion of "active sitting". Its balanced seating position not only keeps the curvature of the spine in its correct natural position but additionally helps to work the abdominal and back muscles, whilst also improving circulation and oxygen levels.

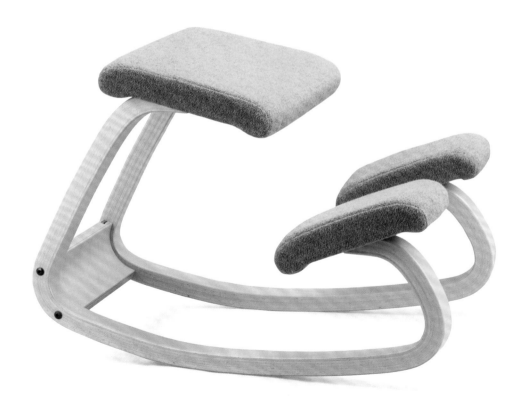

Niels Jørgen Haugesen
X-Line chair, 1977

Niels Jorgen Haugesen studied cabinetmaking at the School of Arts & Crafts in Copenhagen and later worked for Arne Jacobsen from 1966 to 1971. Unlike most Danish designers whose material of choice was wood, Haugesen preferred to experiment with the formal potential of metal. When his stackable *X-Line* chair was first launched in 1977, it was instantly heralded as a design classic and certainly its utilization of 8mm steel rods and perforated steel not only gave it a visually distinctive form but also an engaging and then very fashionable high-tech minimalist aesthetic.

X-Line chair, 1977
Chromed or powder-coated steel rod,
perforated steel
Bent Krogh, Skanderborg, Denmark

Fred Scott
Supporto task chair, 1976

One of the first chairs to be wholly informed by rigorous
ergonomic considerations, Fred Scott's *Supporto* was one of
the most successful office chairs to be designed in the late
1970s and it is testament to its enduring appeal that this
icon of British design is still in production over thirty years
after its original launch. The design was, and still is, offered
in a low-backed armed version (shown here), a high-backed
model, a narrow-backed side variant as well as armed and
unarmed drafting stools. In 1991, the International Federation
of Architects named this award-winning design as "the chair
that most influenced modern office seating".

◄ Hille publicity photograph
featuring high-backed and low-
backed *Supporto* task chairs with
enamelled black finish, c.1979

▼ *Supporto* task chair, 1976
Polished aluminium, leather-
covered upholstery
Hille, High Wycombe, UK
(later by Supporto, Bude, UK)

Ettore Sottsass
Harlow chair, 1971

The title of this chair makes reference to the 1930s platinium blonde silver-screen goddess, Jean Harlow and certainly it has a strong Neo-Deco Moderne aesthetic, which predicts the Post-Modern referencing of past styles in the late 1970s and early 1980s. Its simple, Pop-Deco form also reflects Sottsass's early involvement in the Radical Design Movement alongside the groups Archizoom Associati and Superstudio, several of whose designs were also manufactured by Poltronova. Available in a number of colours and upholstery fabrics, Sottsass also designed the accompanying *Harlow* dining table, which combined the chair's cast aluminium base with a smoked glass top.

Harlow chair, 1971
Cast aluminium, fabric-covered upholstery
Poltronova, Pistoia, Italy

Studio 65
Attica chair, 1972

9 attica
1000 esemplari

Design: STUDIO 65

Designed by Studio 65 in 1972, the *Attica* chair for Gufram exemplifies their ironic, Pop-inspired approach to design. With its form based on a truncated fluted Roman column, the chair makes refererence to Classical architecture just like their *Baby-Lonia* puzzle sculpture. Painted white, *Attica* was designed to look like real stone but was made of polyurethane foam, a play between nature and artifice seen in other Gufram products at this time such as Piero Gilardi's *Sassi* (Rocks) from 1968.

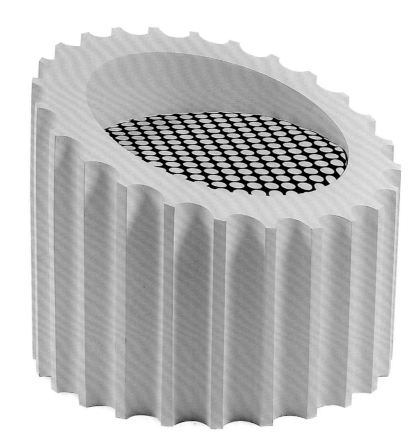

▲ Gufram brochure, 1972,
featuring the *Attica* chair

► *Attica* chair, 1972
Polyurethane foam
Gufram, Turin, Italy

Peter Ghyczy
Model No. GN2 armchair, 1970

Although Peter Ghyczy is best known for his *Gartenei* (Garden Egg) chair, he also designed other furniture for outdoor use including the visually striking stacking *Model No. GN2* lounge chair, which was included in Reuter's *Form + Life Collection*. From 1968 to 1972, Ghyczy designed a number of seating designs for this progressive German plastics company that incorporated fibreglass constructions and which were not only sculptural but also highly functional. Recently Ghyczy's own company has put the classic and amply proportioned *Model No. GN2* armchair back into production.

Model No. GN2 armchair, 1970
Fibreglass
Reuter Produkts, Germany

Gae Aulenti
Model No. 4794 armchair, 1972

Gae Aulenti was an adherent of Ernesto Roger's belief that the architect should adopt a unified approach that encompasses everything "from the spoon to the city". In 1968, she began designing showrooms for Fiat in Milan, Turin, Zurich, Brussels and Geneva – for this prestigious project she also created special lighting and furniture, which included the amply proportioned *Model No. 4794* armchair. For this seating design, which was primarily intended for waiting areas, Aulenti smoothed the rigid plastic into seductively curved forms.

Model No. 4794 armchair, 1972
Rigid expanded polyurethane
Kartell, Milan, Italy

Mario Bellini
Teneride chair, 1970

Launched in 1970, the *Teneride* chair by Mario Bellini marked a revolutionary new ergonomic direction in office seating. Significantly, this highly sculptural design could be adjusted to suit the individual sitter's personal seating requirements. Made of self-skinning polyurethane foam, this extraordinary design was not only comfortable but also rotated on its circular base. Ahead of its time, the *Teneride* reflected an optimistic vision of the future that was to sadly end with the subsequent oil-crisis of the early 1970s.

▲ Cassina publicity photograph featuring a black example of the *Teneride* chair, 1970

◄ *Teneride* chair, 1970
Self-skinning polyurethane foam, enamelled metal
Cassina, Meda, Italy

Studio 65
Chiocciola sectional sofa, 1972

The *Chiocciola* sectional sofa was one of a number of designs that the Turinese group Studio 65 designed for Gufram in the 1970s that were characterized by their playful references to architectural history. The sections of *Chiocciola* were based on the scroll-shaped leaf of the Mediterranean acanthus plant, a motif extensively used in ancient Greek and Roman art and architecture. Around this time, this iconoclasitc design group also created the *Baby-Lonia*, a sculptural puzzle of columns, cornices and pediments.

▲ *Baby-Lonia* puzzle sculpture designed by Studio 65 for Gufram, 1973

▶ *Chiocciola* sectional sofa, 1972
Fabric-cover polyurethane foam
Gufram, Turin, Italy

Ueli & Susi Berger
Boxing Glove chairs, c.1970

Normally Swiss design is associated with a rather austere form of Modernism, however, Ueli and Susi Berger's *Boxing Glove* chair was quite the opposite: a Pop design that like other seating designs from the late 1960s and early 1970s playfully subverted our notion of what a chair could be by using outsized and out-of-context forms. The origins of the chair's manufacturer, De Sede, can be traced to a saddler's workshop, and it was only in the mid-1960s that the workshop began to produce leather furniture, which became renowned for its high-level of craftsmanship.

Boxing Glove chairs, c.1970
Leather-covered upholstery, cord
De Sede, Klingnau,
Switzerland

Boris Tobacoff
Sphère armchairs, 1971

Little is known about Boris Tobacoff, the designer of these remarkable armchairs that have a glitzy glamour that is quintessentially Seventies. With their smoky acrylic seat sections supported on cantilevered bases these chairs have a dynamic form that also gives them a comfort-providing springy resilience. Tobacoff also created a dining chair variant of this design as well as various tables that also employed sculptural chromed steel bases.

Sphère armchairs, 1971
Chromed steel, acrylic, vinyl-covered cushion
Mobilier Modulaire Moderne, Paris, France

Tobia & Afra Scarpa
Soriana chairs and sofa, 1970

The quintessential 1970s lounge suite, the *Soriana* group designed by Tobia and Afra Scarpa in 1970, comprised an armchair, an ottoman, a two-seater sofa and a three-seater sofa. With its low-slung seat height and sumptuously padded buttoned-leather, the sofa was a modern and perhaps even rather louche reworking of the traditional Chesterfield sofa. Spawning numerous imitations, the casually relaxed *Soriana* range was superbly comfortable thanks to all that squishy foam upholstery.

Soriana sofa, 1970,
Chromed metal, leather-covered polyurethane foam upholstery
Cassina, Meda, Italy

▲ *Soriana* chairs, 1970
Chromed metal, leather-covered
polyurethane foam upholstery
Cassina, Meda, Italy

► Cassina publicity photograph of
the *Soriana* seating group, c.1970

Frank Gehry
Easy Edges chair and ottoman, 1972 & *Easy Edges* nesting chairs, 1972

The Pritzker-winning architect, Frank Gehry is renowned for his dynamic landmark buildings, however, he first found success as a designer of cardboard furniture in the early 1970s with his *Easy Edges* range of 14 pieces. Made from layers of corrugated cardboard, these designs demonstrated that a simple low-cost material could be re-imagined to create inexpensive and recyclable furnishings that were not only functional but also aesthetically pleasing. Despite the range's success, Gehry withdrew it from production after only a few months fearing that his ascendency as a furniture designer would eclipse his potential career as an architect.

▲ Publicity photograph showing Gehry's *Easy Edges* chair, ottoman and bed in an interior setting, 1972

▼ *Easy Edges* chair & ottoman, 1972
Laminated corrugated cardboard
Jack Brogan, Los Angeles, USA

▲ *Easy Edges* nesting chairs, 1972
Laminated corrugated cardboard
Jack Brogan, Los Angeles, USA

▶ Publicity photograph showing
two chairs and a table from the
Easy Edges range, 1972

Gaetano Pesce
Golgotha chairs, 1972

Gaetano Pesce designed the limited edition *Golgotha* chair for Braccio di Ferro, a small experimental firm he established with the Italian manufacturer Cassina. To make the chair, a resin-impregnated fiberglass cloth was draped over an elementary chair-shaped mould and sat on until dry, its wrinkled surface bearing the imprint of the clothed human body. Named after the site of Christ's crucifixion, and resembling the Turin shroud, the chair's disturbing imagery was intended to illustrate Pesce's pessimistic view of society at the time.

Golgotha chairs, 1972
Resin soaked fibreglass cloth,
Dacron filling
Braccio di Ferro, Genoa, Italy

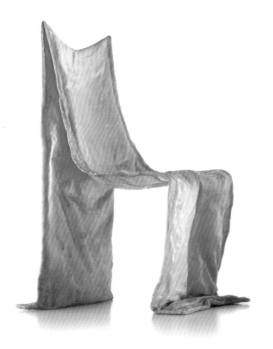

José Zanine Caldas
Namoradeira rocking chairs, c.1970

Following the military coup in Brazil in 1964, José Zanine Caldas lost his teaching position at the University of Brasilia and retreated to the Bahia coastal town of Nova Viçosa, where inspired by the work of local boat-builders, he began chiselling furniture from solid logs. Incorporating native woods, including acajou, vinhático and pequi, these designs have an elemental quality and an impressive visual mass, such as these angular one-armed rocking chairs shown below.

Namoradeira rocking chairs,
c.1970
Solid vinhático wood
José Zanine Caldas, Nova Viçosa,
Brazil

Tobia Scarpa & Afra Scarpa
Africa chairs, 1975

After the plastic-fantastic days of the 1960s, the '70s saw a return to wood and leather as the materials of choice for many furniture designers. To this end, Tobia and Afra Scarpa designed the *Africa* chair, which produced a visual *tour-de-force* through the innovative combination of layers of rosewood and ebony that created a stunning polychromatic effect. With its strong graphic outline and almost totemic presence, the *Africa* chair was the key piece of the Scarpas' *Artona* collection, a range that helped launch the Maxalto furnishing brand for B&B Italia.

▲ *Africa* chairs, 1975,
Rosewood, ebony, leather, brass
Maxalto/B&B Italia, Novedrate, Italy

►*Africa* chairs shown with matching table

Vico Magistretti
Maralunga sofa, armchair and ottoman, 1973

▲ *Maralunga* sofa, armchair and
ottoman, 1973
Steel, textile-covered upholstery
Cassina, Meda, Italy

► Cassina publicity photograph
of the *Maralunga* armchair and
ottoman, 1970s, showing the
articulation of the adjustable
seat back

During the 1970s there was a move towards deep-padded,
squishy foam-filled upholstered seating that provided
exceptional comfort. Vico Magistretti's *Maralunga* range was
one of the most successful of this new generation of seating
and had the added benefit of incorporating a back section
that could be articulated to provide an even greater level of
comfort. For instance, when the back was raised it provided a
useful headrest that allowed a slouched sitting position.

Jorge Zalszupin
Sofa and armchair, 1970

Born in Poland, Jorge Zalszupin moved to Brazil after the Second World War and embraced his adopted nation's post-war utopic enthusiasm for modern architecture and design. His furniture, such as this sculptural sofa, is typified by the use of local exotic woods, graceful yet strong lines and a distinctive sculptural sensibility. Zalszupin was a founding member of the design collective, L'Atelier, which not only manufactured this sofa but also produced a matching chair (shown to the right) and other seating designs by him.

▼ Sofa, 1970
Rosewood-veneered plywood, painted metal, chromed metal, leather-covered cushions
L'Atelier, São Paulo, Brazil

► Amrchair, 1970
Rosewood-veneered plywood, painted metal, chromed metal (shown without cushions)
L'Atelier, São Paulo, Brazil

Verner Panton
Model No. 125 T Pantanova reclining chair &
Model No. 126 S Pantanova ottoman, 1971

The *Pantanova* range, or as it was sometimes known the *Series 100*, was a comprehensive furniture programme designed by Verner Panton in the early 1970s. Constructed of frames of parallel wire rods, the seating designs – including the reclining chair and ottoman shown here – as well as the related tables, shelving system and planters had an interesting optical quality that reflected the influence of Op Art during this period. The designs were originally conceived for the Varna Restaurant in Aarhus, however, they were subsequently put into successful mass-production by Fritz Hansen.

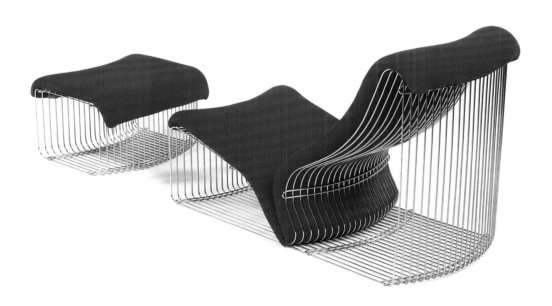

Milo Baughman
Chaise longue, c.1970

Established in 1953, Thayer Coggin was committed from its outset to the production of contemporary yet classic furnishings for the US home market. The same year the firm began its association with the progressive furniture designer, Milo Baughman, a collaboration that lasted for over half-a-century. One of the most interesting results of this enduring relationship was this remarkable chaise longue with its undulating wave-like seat section supported on a minimalist base made of bronze.

▼ Chaise longue, c.1970
Bronze, textile-covered upholstery
Thayer Coggin, High Point (NC),
USA

► Armchair designed by Milo Baughman for Thayer Coggin, 1970s, with a similar geometric supporting frame

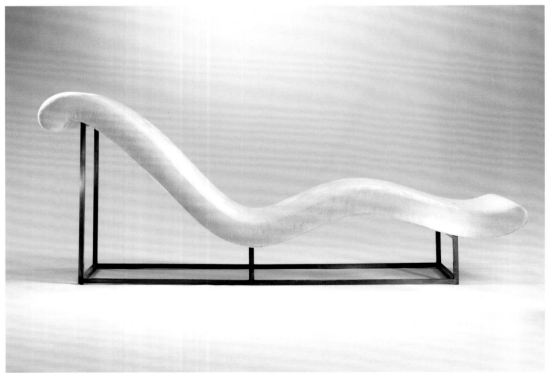

Burkhard Vogtherr
Vario Pilo sectional seating system, 1970

During the late 1960s and early 1970s, the German company, Rosenthal – better known for its fine china – manufactured a number of highly progressive seating designs, including Burkhard Vogtherr's snaking sectional sofa which was made up of separate elements that could be combined into various configurations. In fact there were four different sized and shaped elements (only three are shown here), including a high-backed version and another that could be used as a terminating armrest.

Vario Pilo sectional seating system, 1970
Plastic, textile-covered upholstery
Rosenthal, Selb, Germany

Isao Hosoe
Bau chairs, 1972

Although born in Tokyo, Isao Hosoe has lived and worked in Italy since 1967. From 1967 to 1974 he worked at Studio Ponti-Fornaroli-Rosselli with the architect Alberto Rosselli, who himself created a number of pioneering plastic seating designs. It was during this period that Hosoe similarly explored the manufacturing potential of newly available plastics for the creation of innovative seating products that challenged the traditional notions of what a chair could or should look like. The resulting *Bau* chair with its inverted F shaped profile was a progressive single form/single material design made of injection-moulded ABS, which nested into one another rather than stacked one on top of the other.

Bau chairs, 1972
ABS
Bilumen, Milan, Italy

Pierre Paulin
Model No. 275 sectional sofa, 1974

During the early 1970s, like other designers working within the furniture arena, Pierre Paulin became interested in the idea of modular seating solutions, whereby a repeating single element could be combined with others to create a furniture system. The 275 sectional sofa, shown here, utilized seven padded L-shaped seating elements that were securely attached to a wood and steel base. These elements were also used by Artifort to create smaller sofa units with either three or five elements.

Model No. 275 sectional sofa, 1974
Painted wood, enamelled steel, textile-covered foam upholstery
Artifort, Maastricht, Netherlands

Vico Magistretti
Vicario armchair, 1971

Following on from the development of his *Selene* side chair and *Gaudi* armchair for Artemide, Magistretti created the amply proportioned *Vicario* in 1971. As the first large-scale, single-piece plastic armchair to be moulded in a single material, it was an impressive accomplishment. Rationally conceived through a process driven approach to design, Magistretti adopted a W-shaped sectional profile for the legs of this chair giving the design extra structural strength and stability while also conferring lightness.

Vicario armchair, 1971
Glass-reinforced polyester
Artemide, Pregnana Milanese, Italy

Claudio Salocchi
Appoggio stool, 1971

During the 1970s, the Italian manufacturer, Sormani became well known for producing innovative seating designs that were both functionally and visually contesting. Claudio Salocchi's *Appoggio* stool, for instance, can really be considered more of a seating tool than a traditional chair with its inverted T-shaped seat section. Interestingly, the design's title translates into English as "support", and certainly its ergonomic pared-down form does support the body with the absolute minimum of means.

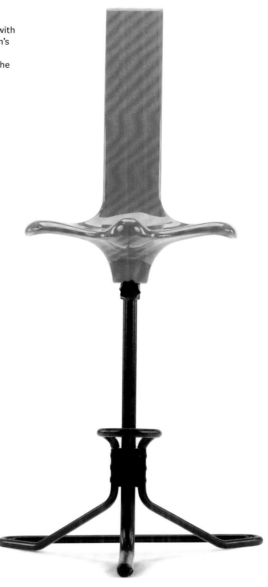

Appoggio stool, 1971
ABS, painted tubular metal
Sormani, Arosio, Italy

Facciamo progetti per il presente.

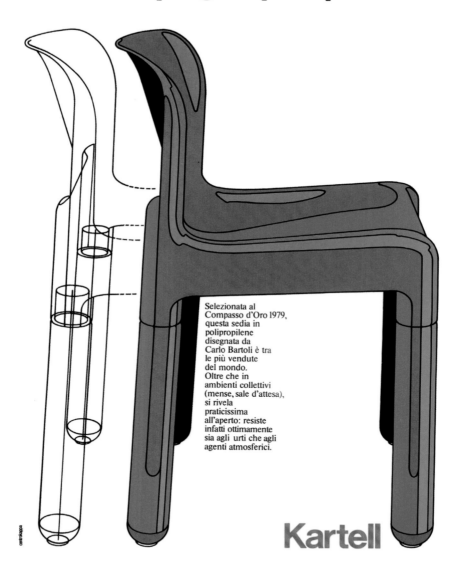

Selezionata al
Compasso d'Oro 1979,
questa sedia in
polipropilene
disegnata da
Carlo Bartoli è tra
le più vendute
del mondo.
Oltre che in
ambienti collettivi
(mense, sale d'attesa),
si rivela
praticissima
all'aperto: resiste
infatti ottimamente
sia agli urti che agli
agenti atmosferici.

Kartell

Carlo Bartoli
Model No. 4875 chair, 1974

◄ Kartell advertisment for the
Model No. 4875 chair, c.1979

► *Model No. 4875* chair, 1974
Polypropylene
Kartell, Milan, Italy

Although not as well known as other landmark plastic
chairs manufactured by Kartell during the 1960s and 1970s,
Carlo Bartoli's *Model No. 4875* chair was a highly innovative
design. Made entirely of polypropylene, it was selected for
a prestigious Compasso d'Oro award in 1979. The design's
seat section was moulded separately from the legs, which
individually slotted into the main element. Highly durable, this
practical and comfortable chair was originally intended for
dining and also for use in waiting areas.

Alexander Begge
Casalino 2004 chair, 1970–71

Since the dawn of industrialization, designers have striven to create objects with fewer components and materials, knowing that greater unity and simplicity in design facilitate high-volume manufacture, production efficiency and enhanced profitability. For furniture designers, this has meant the dogged pursuit of the one-piece, one-material chair, preferably made of plastics. One of the most successful of these was the *Casalino* chair created by the German designer, Alexander Begge, who whilst working at the Casala furniture factory had a vision of "a wisp of fog" that inspired the development of this award-winning design with its graceful flowing profile and distinctive cutout base.

Casalino 2004 chair, 1970–71
Glass-reinforced polyamide
Casala Meubelen Nederland,
Culemborg, Netherlands

Luigi Colani
Swivelling armchair, c.1971

Sometimes referred to as *The Lusch Chair* after its German manufacturer, this Space-Age armchair is perhaps Luigi Colani's most sculpturally dynamic yet practical seating solution. Its protruding arm-rail encircles the back section to produce a strong visual fluidity, while the seat shell elegantly tapers down to form the pedestal that swivels on a plastic-covered X-shaped base. Another version of this design incorporated a circular white base.

Swivelling armchair, c.1971
Fibreglass, plasticized metal
Lusch, Bielefeld, Germany

Fred Scott
Elephant chair, 1972

Fred Scott designed a number of innovative seating solutions for Hille, including the *Elephant* chair, which has the look of a well-padded hide. This visually striking and extremely comfortable design innovatively exploited the formal and structural potential of new plastic materials – in this case, squishy moulded polyurethane foam that was glued onto a supporting shell made of rigid fiberglass. Sculptural and low-slung, the *Elephant* chair was perfectly in tune with the increasingly casual lifestyle of the early 1970s.

▲ Hille publicity photograph showing the front view of the *Elephant* chair, 1972

◄ *Elephant* chair, 1972
Steel, fiberglass, textile-covered polyurethane foam upholstery
Hille International, High Wycombe, England

Kwok Hoi Chan
Limande lounge chairs, 1970

Although, these lounge chairs reflect the early 1970s predilection for steel and leather, it is highly unusual to find a cantilevered seating design made of tubular metal that is on such a commodious scale. The design's title translates into English as "dab" (a type of edible flatfish), however, it is more often known as the *Lemon Sole* chair. Certainly the design's wide-splayed form and the springy resilience of the frame makes it look as though it could flap into life at any moment.

Limande **lounge chairs, 1970,**
Chromed tubular steel, leather-covered upholstery
Steiner, Paris, France

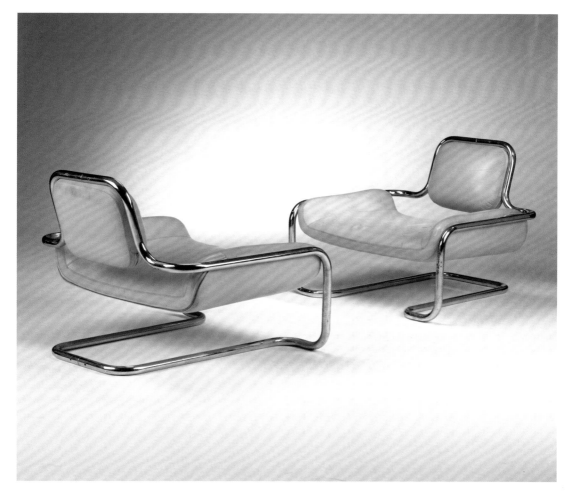

Pierre Vandel
Vertebra armchairs, 1970s

During the 1970s, the Paris-based designer/maker, Pierre Vandel created stylish Neo-Deco furnishings as well as more contemporary pieces, such as his visually striking *Vertebra* armchairs. These chairs have seven rib-like steel-backed sections that are supported on a simple column of steel that terminates into a double u-shaped base – the overall effect is unashamedly high-tech and overtly masculine, yet at the same time these striking chairs are also highly sculptural.

Vertebra armchairs, 1970s
Steel, leather-covered upholstery
Pierre Vandel, Paris, France

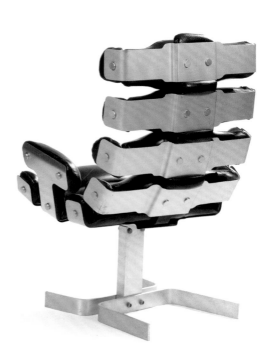

Cini Boeri
Botolo chair, 1973

Cini Boeri's *Botolo* chair has an innovative construction that is made up of three large-gauge metal tubes that conceal within their bases three castors that allow the chair to glide or roll with ease across a floor. This freewheeling chair possesses a disco-like glamour with its shiny columnar legs of chromed-metal and reflects the very architectonic nature of Milanese furniture design during the early 1970s.

Botolo chair, 1973
Chromed tubular metal, fabric-covered foam upholstery, recessed castors
Arflex, Meda, Italy

Verner Panton
Amoebe chairs, 1970

In 1970 Verner Panton created a landmark installation for the "Visiona II" exhibition in Cologne, which comprised a number of new seating designs, including the *Amoebe* chair. The title of this progressive seating design made reference to its globular organic form that was constructed of jersey-covered foam upholstery that was internally supported by a tubular metal frame. The design's low seating position reflected the more casual lifestyle of the late 1960s and early 1970s, while its highly sculptural form demonstrated the increasing shift away from traditional chair forms to more poetic and expressive shapes within the domestic environment.

Amoebe chairs, 1970
Tubular metal, textile-covered upholstery

Pedro Friedeberg
Centipede chair, 1972

Italian-born, Pedro Friedeberg emigrated to Mexico with his parents as a child and subsequently studied architecture at the Universidad Iberoamericana under the guidance of Mathias Goeritz who encourage him to create architectural fantasies. In 1960 he joined the Dadaist group, Los Hartos and his art became increasingly influenced by Surrealism and Symbolism. These aspects were also displayed in his seating designs, such as the *Centipede* chair that takes the form of a traditional Thonet café chair richly embellished with carved hands and feet.

Centipede chair, 1972
Gilded and painted wood, caning
Pedro Friedeberg, Mexico City, Mexico

Ettore Sottsass
Tappeto Volante chair and sofa, 1974

Ettore Sottsass designed the exotic, mystical *Tappeto Volante* (Flying Carpet) sofa at the height of the Radical Design movement that challenged the tenets of Modernism and the values of Italy's consumer society. The architect's designs from this period were fuelled by his desire to forge a relationship with objects that went beyond consumerist desire and were heavily influenced by his visits to both California and India in the early 1960s. This is most evident in the sofa's elementary forms in deep, bold colours and simple, striking patterns that reference both Eastern iconography and American Pop Art.

Tappeto Volante sofa and chair, 1974
Stained beechwood, jersey-covered upholstery, velvet, carpet
Caimi Brevetti, Nova Milanese, Italy

Ubald Klug
Model No. DS 1025 Terazza sofa, 1973

This unusual sofa almost looks like terraces cut into a mountainside, hence its name. Certainly, the design has a distinctly topographic look with its layered leather-upholstery sections placed on top of each other to create an undulating island-like seating statement. The *Terazza* sofa predicted the return to leather as a material of choice for seating designers during the 1970s, however, rarely has this natural material been used to create such a dynamic sculptural form.

Model No. DS 1025 Terazza sofa, 1973
Leather-covered upholstery
De Sede, Klingnau, Switzerland

Luigi Colani
Modular seating unit, c.1970

Not only an accomplished form-giver but also a highly
inventive designer, Luigi Colani has produced numerous
innovative furniture designs during his long and prolific career.
With this modular unit comprising nine upholstered elements,
he re-imagined the traditional sofa into a low-slung seating
landscape that reflected the more casual and carefree lifestyle
of the early 1970s.

Modular seating unit, c.1970
Textile-covered foam
upholstery, rubber, plastic
Rosenthal, Selb, Germany

Verner Panton
System 1-2-3 armchair, 1973 &
System 1-2-3 Model G linked armchairs, 1973

Verner Panton's *System 1-2-3* was his most comprehensive seating range comprising numerous models with a variety of different seat heights and bases. The armchair shown to the left is an extremely rare version that has a swivelling five-star wooden base and padded armrests. The range was also offered in a startling array of upholstery options, including a "deluxe" leather variant. Extremely comfortable and very stylish, the *System 1-2-3* was not only used in domestic interiors but also within office environments and other public spaces.

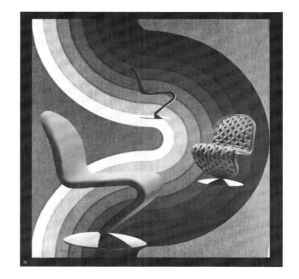

► Page from a special issue of *Mobilia* magazine showing various *System 1-2-3* models, 1970s

◄ *System 1-2-3* armchair, 1973
Tubular steel, stretch textile upholstery, wood, rubber
Fritz Hansen, Allerød, Denmark

► *System 1-2-3 Model G* linked armchairs, 1973
Tubular steel, stretch textile upholstery, polypropylene
Fritz Hansen, Allerød, Denmark

Maria Pergay
Ring chair, c.1970 & Lounge chair, c.1970

Maria Pergay combined dynamic sculptural forms with a functional consideration in order to create stunning seating designs cut from sheet steel, which functioned rather like serially produced "design-art" multiples. Certainly her *Ring* chair made from concentric circles of metal and her undulating lounge chair captured the stylishly arty *zeitgeist* of 70s France and as such were favoured by an impressive roster of clients including Salvador Dali, Pierre Cardin and King Fahd of Saudi Arabia.

► Lounge chair, c.1970
Stainless steel
Design Steel, Paris, France

▼ *Ring* chair, c.1970
Stainless steel
Design Steel, Paris, France

Oscar Niemeyer
Rio rocking chair, 1978

Brazil's most celebrated architect, Oscar Niemeyer has also designed progressive furniture that like his buildings possesses a visual and constructional bravado. Produced in Brazil by the Japanese furniture manufacturer, Tendo, the *Rio* rocking chair had a wonderful looping profile, and thanks to its plywood supporting elements has a springy resilience that provides comfort without additional padding.

Rio rocking chair, 1978
Ash moulded plywood, caning, rubber, metal, leather-covered cushion
Tendo Brasiliera, Brazil

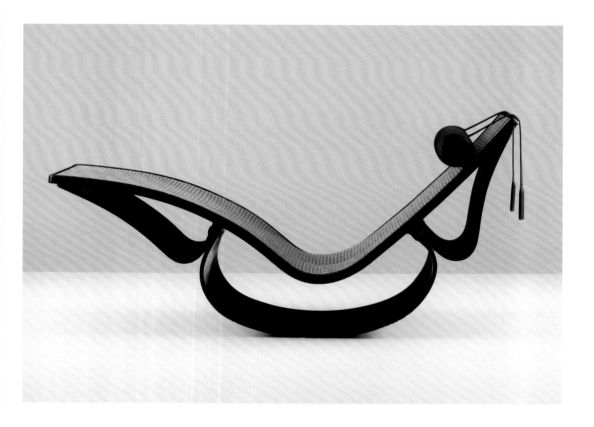

Oscar Niemeyer
Model No. ON1 Brasilia lounge chair, c.1971

During the late 1960s, the Brazilian architect, Oscar Niemeyer opened an office in Paris and subsequently began designing furniture, including the *Brasilia* chair and ottoman, which was produced by Mobilier de France. Like the *Rio* rocking chaise, this springy chair was used to furnish Communist Party headquarters throughout the world. Reputedly the forms of Niemeyer's furniture were intended to echo the contours of the female body as well as the hills of Rio de Janeiro.

Model No. ON1 Brasilia lounge chair, c.1971
Stainless steel, leather-covered upholstery, plastic
Mobilier de France, Paris, France

Randall Buhk
Model No. 451 executive office chair, 1970

Although obviously influenced by Charles Pollock's earlier office chair for Knoll, Randall Buhk's *Model No. 451* executive office chair with its distinctive buttoned leather upholstery was itself an innovative design that became a bestseller for its manufacturer, Steelcase Inc. Buhk subsequently designed numerous other office chairs for the company during the 1970s, which were variations of this successful open-armed model. Its buttoned leather seat harks back to the club chairs of yesteryear and as such gives it a very masculine quality.

FIG. I.

FIG. 2.

▲ Patent drawing of the *Model No. 451* executive office chair

◄ *Model No. 451* executive office chair, 1970
Enamelled metal, plastic, leather-covered upholstery
Steelcase Inc., Grand Rapids (MI), USA

Emilio Ambasz & Giancarlo Piretti
Dorsal office chairs, 1978

▶ Patent drawing of the *Dorsal*
office chair

▼ *Dorsal* office chairs, 1978
Thermoplastic, textile-covered
upholstery
KI, Green Bay (WI), USA
(and also by Intermobel)

FIG. 2

Emilio Ambasz and Giancarlo Piretti developed a number of
office seating solutions together that were notable for their
pioneering use of ergonomic data. Their *Dorsal* range included
various models intended for office and institutional use and
had flexible backrests that provided enhanced comfort. As
Ambasz notes, "Employing ergonomic and orthopedic research
in its automatically functioning backrest and in its overall
configuration of interrelated parts, *Dorsal* relaxes the sitter's
body. The minimal design becomes a part of the worker in
motion rather than an overwhelming visible structure.
The chair disappears during use, becoming a moving part
of the worker."

1980s

Henri Massonnet
Stacking chair, 1980

In 1973 Henry Massonnet designed the *Boston* chair, reputedly the first ever single-piece injection-moulded chair made of polypropylene. He subsequently designed a number of other monobloc garden chairs, including the model shown here, which were manufactured by his company, Stamp. This functional and inexpensive stacking garden chair embellished with its creator's signature provided comfort and stability with the minimum use of material, while its fluid form allowed rainwater to easily drain. This humble mass-produced plastic chair accorded with Massonnet's credo: "Innovative ingenuity coupled with a dynamic approach".

▲ Patent drawings of Stacking chair, filed 1982

◄► Stacking chair, 1980
Polypropylene
Stamp, Nurieux, France

Jonas Bohlin
Concrete chair, 1981

As a reaction to Swedish functionalism as well as a wry comment on it, Jonas Bohlin's *Concrete* chair was first shown in 1981 at his degree show at the Konstfack (the National College of Art and Design) in Stockholm and immediately caused both an uproar and a sensation. Intended to be a "design-art" piece rather than a functional piece of furniture, the *Concrete* chair was an early and highly influential example of Scandinavian Postmodernism.

Concrete chair, 1981
Tubular steel, concrete
Källemo, Värnamo, Sweden

Rei Kawakubo
No.1 chair, 1983

Although better known for her work in the world of avant-garde fashion, Rei Kawakubo – the founder of Comme des Garçons – has also designed a number of furniture pieces for her company, including this minimalist metal chair. Stripped on any extraneous ornamentation, the design has a strong Zen-like quality that is reminiscent of the poetic work of her fellow countryman and designer, Shiro Kuramata.

No.1 chair, 1983
Zinc-plated steel
Pallucco Italia for Commes des Garçons, Tokyo, Japan

Gaetano Pesce
Dalila II chair, 1980

By using plastics in an almost artisanal manner, Gaetano Pesce has managed to imbue his designs with a charming handcrafted individuality. In 1980, he designed the *Dalila II* side chair and *Dalila III* armchair to compliment his *Sansone* table. This furniture group was inspired by the biblical story of Samson's love for the treacherous but delectable Delilah. These sensuously anthropomorphic chairs with their undulating profiles expressed the incredible plasticity of synthetic polymers, as well as the soft roundness of the female body.

▲ Cassina publicity photograph of *Dalila III* chair, 1980

◄ *Dalila II* chair, 1980
Epoxy-coated rigid polyurethane foam (PU)
Cassina, Meda, Italy

Philippe Starck
Starck chair, 1984

During the mid-1980s the short-lived Matt Black style emerged within the design world, which was characterized by an industrial aesthetic, a monochrome palette and an overt sense of masculinity. Reflecting this phenomenon, Philippe Starck's *Starck* chair from 1984 incorporated a simple enamel-coated tubular metal frame onto which a perforated synthetic rubber seat was attached using a series of metal springs. Despite its pared down minimalistic form, this chair was surprisingly comfortable thanks to its seat's springy resilience.

Starck chair, 1984
Enamelled tubular metal, synthetic rubber, springs
Baleri, Milan, Italy

Giovanni Offredi
Inlay dining chairs, 1980

During the late 1970s and early 1980s, Saporiti Italia manufactured a number of elegant and comfortable seating designs by the architect and furniture designer, Giovanni Offredi. His *Inlay* dining chairs, shown here, are typical of his oeuvre, being sleekly stylish and having an almost architectonic quality. With its simple inverted T-shape chromed steel elements supporting the fully upholstered seat shell, this design has a visual and structural clarity with a distinctive Neomodernism about it.

Inlay dining chairs, 1980
Chromed steel, anodized aluminium, leather-covered upholstery
Saporiti Italia, Besnate, Italy

Shiro Kuramata
Hal 2 side chair, 1987 & *Hal 3* barstool, 1987

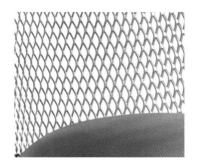

Using stainless steel mesh, an inexpensive and blatantly industrial material, Shiro Kuramata managed to create a number of highly poetic and beautiful seating designs, most notably his *How High the Moon* armchair and sofa. His *Hal 3* also utilized steel mesh for its arching and curved back section. In so doing, Kuramata redefined the aesthetics of the humble barstool. Kuramata also created variants of this visually appealing design, including the *Hal 2* side chair (shown here), the *Hal* armchair and the *Big Hal* lounge chair, which had a small table attached to it.

Hal 2 side chair, 1987 &
Hal 3 barstool, 1987
Enamelled steel, stainless steel,
plastic
Terada Tokkojo, Japan

Pierre Sala
Piranha chair, 1983

Pierre Sala was the director of the Theatre de la Potinière in Paris and later became a furniture designer for Furnitur. His visually striking *Piranha* chair with its stylized bite marks was a playful Postmodern design that was manufactured in a limited edition of 250 pieces. Sala also produced other similarly humorous designs, including his *Clairefontaine* table and chairs that incorporated giant crayons for their legs.

Piranha chair, 1983
Lacquered wood
France

Alessandro Mendini
Spaziale chair, 1981

The *Spaziale* chair was one of six designs by Alessandro Mendini that transformed the humble chair into an emblematic artwork. At its launch, a series of drawings showing this iconic collection identified this specific design as the *Sedia Aderivo* (Complied Chair) and accompanied it with the byline "decorate your life inimitably". Certainly, this design has a totemic presence that emphasizes that a chair is not necessarily just a chair, but can also be a polemical symbol.

▲ Drawing of the *Lassù* chair – an earlier design by Alessandro Mendini from 1974 that was symbolically destroyed by fire the same year

► *Spaziale* chair, 1981
Lacquered wood
Poltronova for Studio Alchimia, Milan, Italy (limited edition of six)

Robert Venturi
Art Nouveau chair, 1982, *Queen Anne* chair, 1984 &
Chippendale chair, 1984

◄ *Art Nouveau* chair, 1982
Laminate-faced bent laminated
wood, nylon
Knoll International, New York, USA

► *Chippendale* chair, 1984
Laminate-faced bent laminated
wood, nylon
Knoll International, New York, USA

▼ *Queen Anne* chair, 1984
Laminate-faced bent laminated
wood, nylon
Knoll International, New York, USA

Known for his famous quip "less is a bore", the Princeton-educated architect, Robert Venturi, was one of the great proponents of Postmodernism, while his seminal book *Learning from Las Vegas* (1972) became required reading for architecture and design professionals. Putting theory into practice, between 1974 and 1984 he designed the *Venturi Collection* for Knoll. The furniture group comprising nine chairs, a sofa and various tables playfully and irreverently referenced American and European furniture history. These "clichéd simplifications of furniture forms", as Knoll put it, essentially caricatured historic styles, and as such poked fun at the intellectualized veneration that surrounded them.

Michele De Lucchi
Riviera chair, 1981

The furniture designs created by Michele De Lucchi for Memphis are highly distinctive, with strong geometric lines and utilizing unusual combinations of colours. For instance, his *Riviera* chair of 1981 was a startlingly Postmodern statement, provocatively countering the perceived notions of what a chair should look like in a humorous, light-hearted way, through the use of relatively low-tech materials and production methods.

Riviera chair, 1981
Laminate vinyl-covered, padded upholstery, lacquered tubular metal
Memphis, Milan, Italy

Jonas Bohlin
Concave chaise longue, 1983

One of the great pioneers of Scandinavian Postmodernism,
Jonas Bohlin created a number of seating designs that pushed
both functional and aesthetic conventions, such as his well-
known *Concrete* chair. Just as visually striking but doubtlessly
more comfortable, Bohlin's *Concave* chaise longue was, like
the *Concrete,* manufactured by Källemo. This striking design
with its highly graphic profile incorporated seven curved cutout struts of plywood, mounted on a steel base that acted as
a cradling support for two simple segmented blocks of foam
and a head-rest.

Concave **chaise longue, 1983**
Painted plywood, painted steel,
textile-covered upholstery
Källemo, Värnamo, Sweden

George Sowden
Mamounia chair, 1985

The British designer George Sowden designed the *Mamounia* chair for the third collection presented by Memphis, the Milan-based design collective set up by renowned architect Ettore Sottsass in 1980. Sowden contributed a number of furniture designs to Memphis, all of which made use of plastic laminates and loud patterns in line with the group's brash, Neo-kitsch style. The boldly patterned fabric used to upholster the chair was designed by the French designer Nathalie Du Pasquier, who collaborated with Sowden on a number of Memphis projects.

◄ Design drawing of the *Mamounia* chair, 1985

▼ *Mamounia* chair, 1985
Lacquered wood, plastic laminate, felt
Memphis, Milan, Italy.

Marco Zanini
Roma armchair, 1986

The Italian architect Marco Zanini designed furniture, ceramics and glassware for Memphis. He had been working with founding member Ettore Sottsass since the 1970s and in 1980 became a partner of the architecture practice Sottsass Associati. Zanini designed the throne-like, moulded fibreglass *Roma* armchair for Memphis's third collection in 1986, and with its bright metallic coloured finish and unconventional form it became a quintessential Memphis piece. Bold forms and bright colours, often combined in clashing combinations, were also used by Zanini for his *Dublin* sofa (1981) and the *Colorado* teapot (1983), also created for Memphis.

Roma **armchair, 1986**
Glass-reinforced polyester
Memphis, Milan, Italy

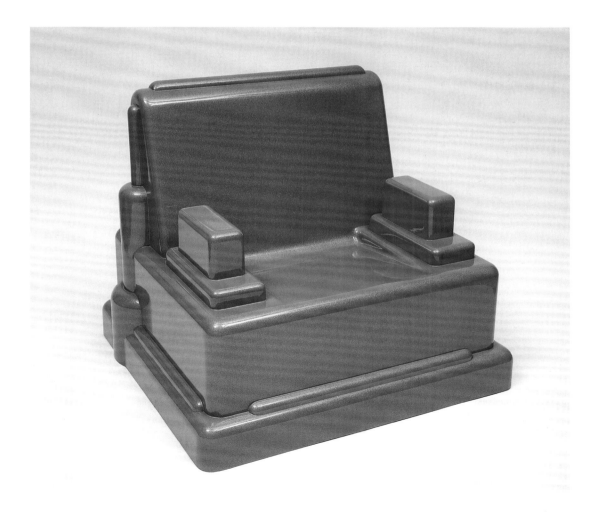

Michele de Lucchi
Lido sofa, 1982

The architect Michele de Lucchi had been involved in Italy's radical design movement and a member of Studio Alchymia before he set up Memphis with Ettore Sottsass in 1980. De Lucchi designed the playful, cartoonish *Lido* sofa for the second Memphis collection in 1982, and its multi-coloured upholstery and use of striped plastic laminate corresponds with the group's provocative challenge to Italian design's reputation for good taste.

Lido sofa, 1982
Plastic laminate, lacquered wood, metal, upholstery
Memphis, Milan, Italy

Masanori Umeda
Tawaraya seating pit, 1981

The Japanese designer Masanori Umeda was one of several non-Italian members of Memphis, reflecting Ettore Sottsass's ambition for Memphis to be the "New International Style". The *Tawaraya* is one of Memphis's most recognisable designs, following its use in a publicity shot of the founding members piled into the boxing ring. Designed for a number of uses including seating, sleeping and as a "conversation pit", the multi-functionality and unusual typology of the *Tawaraya* exemplifies how Memphis challenged existing conventions of both form and function in furniture design.

▲ Ettore Sottsass with other founding members of Memphis, 1981

▼ *Tawaraya* seating pit, 1981
Wood, metal, plastic, tatami mats, cushions, glass
Memphis, Milan, Italy

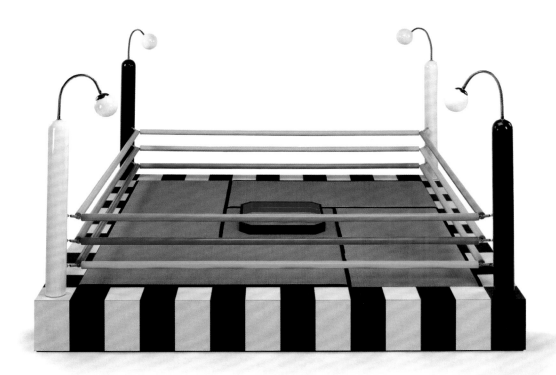

Shigeru Uchida
Nirvana chair, 1981

Since the 1980s, Shigeru Uchida has created highly poetic designs that successfully synthesize the aesthetic traditions of both the East and the West. His curious *Nirvana* chair with its squiggly base gives a gravity-defying illusion that a mess of uncoiled rope is supporting the rest of the chair. A bona fide icon of Japanese design, this chair exemplifies the playfulness and tongue-in-cheek humour of early 1980s Postmodernism.

Nirvana chair, 1981
Enamelled steel, brass-plated steel, fabric-covered upholstery
Japan

Andrea Branzi
Animali Domestici bench, 1985

During the mid-1980s a "Neo-Primitive" tendency arose in design that was perhaps best expressed by Andrea Branzi's *Animali Domestici* furniture collection. Evolving from the Arte Povera movement of the late 1960s, Branzi's designs – including this bench – incorporated "found" tree branches and were intended as contemplative objects that functioned as domestic pets. As Andrea and Nicoletta Branzi explained, "The difference between a domestic animal and a trained (or tamed) one lies in the fact that the latter is the outcome of an unnatural and violent attitude, while the domestic animal establishes the dream of a loving relationship with man."

Animali Domestici bench, 1985
Painted MDF, tree branches
Zabro, Milan, Italy

Shiro Kuramata
How High the Moon sofa, 1986-87

Named after a 1940s jazz song, Shiro Kuramata based the minimalist design of his *How High the Moon* sofa on a traditional upholstered settee. The Japanese designer transformed this heavy, stuffy form into a seemingly ephemeral and weightless construction through the use of steel mesh (expanded metal). This challenge to convention is characteristic of Kuramata's approach to design in the 1980s, when the designer became well known for his poetic interpretation of industrial materials, such as the acrylic and aluminium *Miss Blanche* chair (1988).

How High the Moon sofa, 1986-87
Nickel-plated expanded steel mesh (expanded metal), nickel-plated steel
Ishimaru Co Ltd., Tokyo, Japan for Idée, Japan

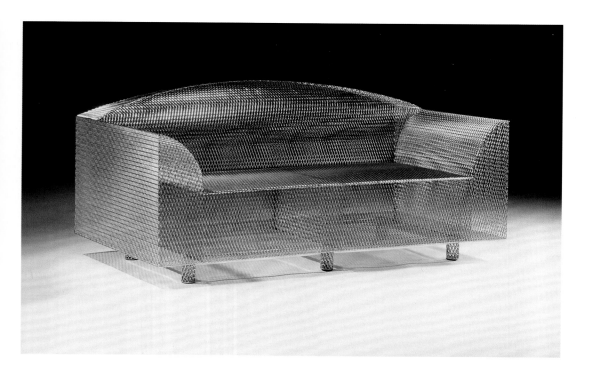

Forrest Myers
Gilder chair, 1988

The American artist and designer Forrest Myers had been producing objects that straddled the boundary between functional design and abstract sculpture throughout the 1980s. Designed in 1988, the *Gilder* chair was the first of a number of coiled wire armchairs that this highly skilled metalworker produced. It demonstrated the influence of Alexander Calder's wire sculptures and the paintings of Jackson Pollock on Myers's work and its free form composition echoes his interest in jazz music.

Gilder chair, 1988
Anodized aluminium
Forest Myers, New York, USA

Shiro Kuramata
Sofa with Arms armchair, 1982 & *Sedia Seduta* armchair, 1984

This curiously titled chair was one of several designs created by Shiro Kuramata for the Italian manufacturer Cappellini that fused the gracious aesthetics of the East with design typologies from the West. Sometimes called the *Tubular Pipe* armchair, this constructionally simple yet elegantly refined design was also originally offered as a two-seater sofa. Kuramata's other seating design shown to the right, the *Sedia Seduta* armchair from 1984, similarly demonstrates his mastery of poetic composition and his ability to eloquently define the space surrounding an object.

▶ *Sedia Seduta* armchair, 1984
Suede-finish ABS resin board, enamelled aluminium, chromed steel
Ishimaru Co., Tokyo, Japan

▼ *Sofa with Arms*, 1982
Textile-upholstered polyurethane foam and chromed tubular metal
Cappellini, Mariano Comense, Italy

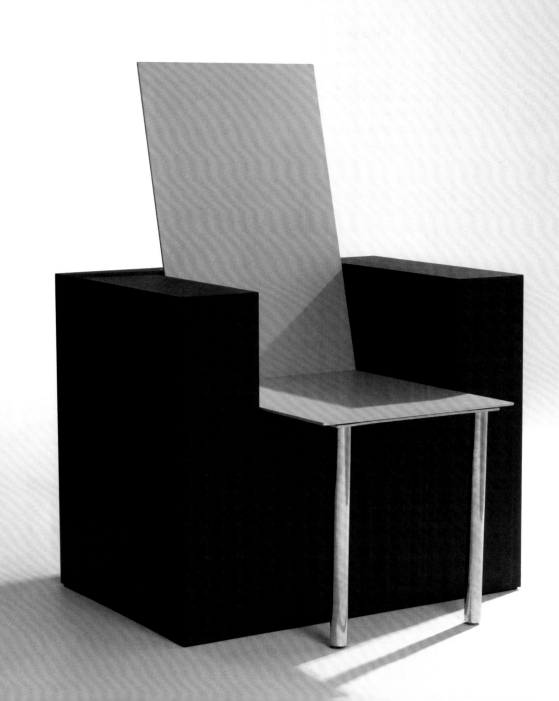

Shiro Kuramata
KoKo chair, 1986 & *Three-legged* chair, c.1987

Since the 1920s, tubular steel has been the favoured material of many chair designers in their pursuit of low-cost, mass-producible and practical seating. In contrast, Shiro Kuramata used utilitarian metal tubing to create more overtly poetic designs, such as the *Koko* chair and *Three-legged* chair. With their simple, low-tech constructions, these designs have a distinctive sculptural and elemental character that is in keeping with the traditional pared-down Japanese aesthetic.

► *Three-legged* chair, c.1987
Chromed tubular steel, laminated oak
Ishimaru Co., Tokyo, Japan

▼ *Koko* chair, 1986
Chromed tubular steel, wood, textile-covered upholstery
Cappellini, Milan, Italy

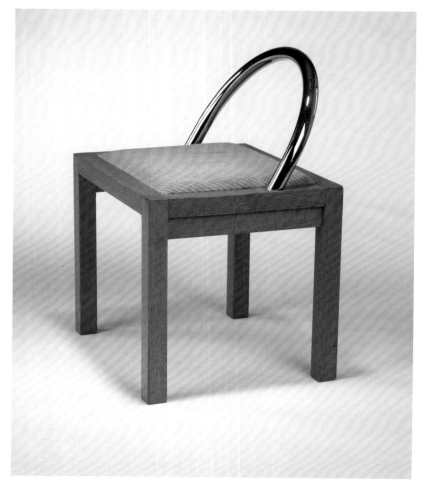

Mark Brazier-Jones
Lyre chair, 1986

One of Brazier-Jones' earliest designs and an early example from the Creative Salvage movement, the *Lyre* chair is an assemblage of welded metal elements that include a lyre-and-book back and an artist's palette seat, which are supported by a sword and an axe head. The chair also bears the designer's signature on the book-shaped component. This lyrical design was an early example of limited edition "design-art" and as such marked a new, poetic direction in contemporary furniture design.

Lyre chair, 1986
Cast iron, wrought iron
Mark Brazier-Jones, London,
England

Caroline Schlyter
Lilla H chair, 1989

While studying sculpture at the Konstfack (University College of Arts and Design) in Stockholm, Caroline Schlyter designed her *Lilla H* chair moulded from a single piece of plywood. The name meaning "little h" makes reference to the chair's h-shaped profile. As she explains, "My aim was to create a clean, unbroken line and avoid joints and connecting details... I enjoy playing with the line and exploring the border between volume and void – the shape the line creates, two-dimensionally and three-dimensionally in the architectural space." She has also designed other furniture pieces with similar one-piece moulded plywood constructions.

▼ *Lilla H* chair, 1989
Moulded birch plywood
Caroline Schlyter, Stockholm, Sweden

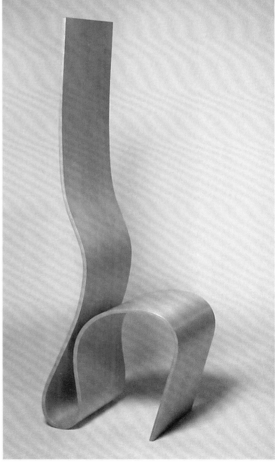

▲ Other furniture pieces designed by Caroline Schlyter – all fabricated from moulded birch plywood

Pelikan Design
Café chair, 1988

Niels Gammelgaard and Lars Mathiesen established Pelikan Design in 1978 and have since designed a number of interesting chairs typified by a no-nonsense, functionalist minimalism. Their stackable *Café* chair with its water-draining split seat pan thoughtfully utilized durable galvanized steel and weatherproof rubber. As the designers noted, "Why not accept that weather isn't forgiving? Why not use materials that like wind, rain, snow and hail? Like hot galvanized steel and rubber. Why not make it really heavy and make it look even better if left outside? Why not make a crack in the seat so that the rain water or the melting snow runs off it?".

◄ *Café* chair, 1988
Galvanized tubular steel, rubber
Fritz Hansen, Allerød, Denmark

▼ Fritz Hansen brochure images of the *Café* chair, 1988

Ettore Sottsass
Mandarin chairs, 1986

FIG. 2

FIG. I

Although during the 1980s Ettore Sottsass became widely celebrated for his bold, colourful and flamboyantly idiosyncratic Postmodern furniture designs for Memphis, he also designed more rational furniture as well, such as the *Mandarin* chair for Knoll International. Intended for corporate office spaces, the *Mandarin* was a highly functional design, yet with its colourful and highly distinctive arm-rail that wraps around the seating section this chair brought a little bit of much needed Postmodern playfulness into the office environment.

▲ Patent drawing of the *Mandarin* chair

► *Mandarin* chairs, 1986
Enamelled tubular steel, textile-covered upholstery
Knoll International, New York, USA

Ron Arad
Well Tempered chair, 1986

Designed for the Vitra Edition series, the *Well Tempered* chair represents Arad's first commission to produce a design for serial industrial production. Based on the luxurious curves of the traditional club chair, the sheet metal chair derives its name from the tempering process involved, a heat treatment which endows the steel with a memory so that it returns to its original shape following bending and welding. An early example from his *Volume* series, Arad developed the *Well Tempered's* simple, looping folds into the more technically complex, closed form of his later *Big Easy* chair (1988).

Well Tempered chair, 1986
Tempered sheet steel
Vitra, Weil am Rhein, Germany

Jasper Morrison
Ply-Chair, 1988

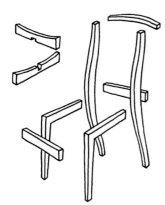

In the late 1980s and 1990s Jasper Morrison became a prominent figure in the New Simplicity movement that rebelled against the excesses of Postmodern design. The simplicity of the British designer's *Ply-Chair* reflects his highly minimalist approach to design, which is characterized by its repeated reference to pure, archetypal forms. Morrison originally designed the *Ply-Chair* as part of his installation for *Some New Items for the Home* at the DAAD Gallery in Berlin in 1998, and Vitra subsequently put it into production along with several other items from the show.

▲ Exploded drawing of construction

► *Ply-Chair*, 1988
Birch-veneered plywood
Vitra, Weil am Rhein, Germany

Ron Arad
Little Heavy chair, 1989 & *Big Easy* armchair, 1988

◄ *Little Heavy* chair, 1989
Beaten and welded mild steel
One Off Ltd, London, UK

► Polished steel variant of the
Little Heavy chair, 1989

▼ *Big Easy* armchair, 1988
Beaten and welded mild steel
One Off Ltd, London, UK

Tel Aviv-born Ron Arad was one of a number of "designer-makers" working in London in the 1980s whose self-made designs were characterized by their rough and ready appearance and use of salvaged materials. Designed as part of Arad's *Volume* series, the hollow, ballooning forms of the *Little Heavy* and *Big Easy* armchairs demonstrate his interest in the formal possibilities of welded and polished metal. Both chairs were manufactured by One Off, the company set up by Arad in 1981 with his business partner, Caroline Thorman.

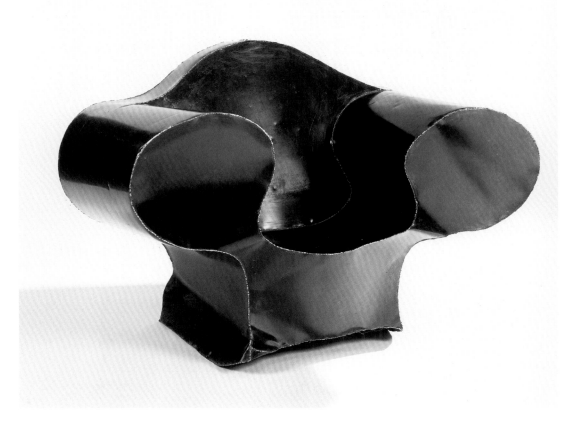

Philippe Starck
Dr Sonderbar armchair, 1983

An early seating design by Philippe Starck, the *Dr Sonderbar* has an almost Japanese simplicity with its tubular metal frame supporting a curved seat of perforated steel. Like other chairs by Starck, it playfully challenges the notion of the traditional chair form, while its evocative title – which in English means "Doctor Strange" – was consciously used to enhance the design's personality and thereby its emotional appeal.

Dr Sonderbar armchair, 1983
Chromed steel, plastic
XO, Servon, France

Philippe Starck
Hi-Glob stool, 1988

The *Hi Glob* stool is part of a family of seating – that also included two chairs, the *Dr Glob* and the *Miss Glob* – created by the French maestro of design, Philippe Starck, for Kartell. Combining a durable and colourful polypropylene seat with a powder-coated tubular steel frame ensuring that the design was strong and hardwearing, despite its elegantly slender profile. The waterproof design's success lay in the fact that it could be used in bar and office environments, while also being attractive enough to use within domestic settings.

▲ Page from Kartell catalogue showing various models from Starck's *Glob* series

► *Hi-Glob* stool, 1988
Epoxy-polyester powder coated tubular steel, polypropylene
Kartell, Meda, Italy

Alessandro Mendini & Alessandro Guerriero
Ollo chairs, 1988

Part of Studio Alchimia's extensive *Ollo* Collection, these chairs were designed by Alessandro Mendini in collaboration with Alessandro Guerriero. They are simply constructed from three pieces of laminate that are screen-printed with black and white motifs incorporating abstract symbols of columns and arches. This irreverent use of classical architectural motifs as decorative ornament is typical of Alchimia's desire to produce provocative work that questioned the elevated status of classical design and architecture.

► Cover of *Ollo* review, c.1988

▼ *Ollo* chairs, 1988
Silk-screened laminate
Consorzio Esposizione Mobili, Italy
for Studio Alchimia, Milan, Italy

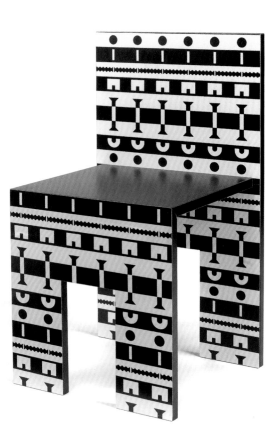

oIIo

RIVISTA SENZA MESSAGGIO DIRETTA DA ALESSANDRO MENDINI

ALCHIMIA

Mark Robson
GRP chair, 1989

While studying furniture design at the Royal College of Art, Mark Robson created his sculptural *GRP* chair – made of glass-reinforced polyester (fibreglass) – for his final project. The prototype of this forward-looking organic design was developed by building it up around an actual human, thereby allowing its forms to correlate exactly with the curves of the body. Possibly the ultimate posing chair, this limited-edition design was widely published in contemporary design journals and importantly predicted the blobular forms that would become so popular during the late 1990s and 2000s.

GRP chair, 1989
Glass-reinforced polyester
Mark Robson for Fiell, London, UK

Marc Newson
Embryo chair, 1988

Australian-born Marc Newson lived and worked in Tokyo from 1987 to 1991, and during this period he created a number of forward-looking furniture designs for Idée, a progressive manufacturing company and design store founded by Japanese entrepreneur, Teruo Kurosaki. In this body of work, the *Embryo* chair stands out for its playful organic form and its blatant futuristic connotations. This three-legged biomorphic chair with its beautifully engineered detailing and soft curvaceous lines also has a characterful presence that is testimony to Newson's ability to create forms imbued with an engaging emotional connection.

Embryo chair, 1988
Chromed tubular steel, aluminium, neoprene-covered polyurethane foam upholstery
Idée, Tokyo, Japan

1990s

Mark Brazier-Jones
San Demas lounge chair, 1992

Perhaps Mark Brazier-Jones's most iconic design and certainly his best-known chair, the *San Demas* – with its distinctive cast wings, snakeheads and claw-like feet – is a thoroughly modern reinterpretation of a French Empire chair. With its Masonic symbolism, it is a design that exudes a sense of imperial power as well as otherworldly mysticism.

San Demas lounge chair, 1992
Aluminium, leather-covered upholstery
Mark Brazier-Jones, Buntingford, England

Tejo Remy
Rag chair, 1991

Designed for his graduation show in 1991, two years later
Tejo Remy's *Rag* chair was selected for the first Droog Design
collection, unveiled at the Milan Furniture Fair in 1993. Made of
discarded rags banded together with metal straps, each chair
is unique – the owner can even choose their own clothes to be
recycled into the design. Remy's chair is an early example of
the Dutch conceptual design movement that emerged in the
early 1990s, whose challenge to the aesthetic and ideals of
industrial production significantly impacted design practice
on an international scale.

▲ Publicity photograph showing
various views of the *Rag* chair,
1991

◄ *Rag* chair, 1991
Recycled rags, steel strips
Droog, Amsterdam, The
Netherlands

Mats Theselius
Aluminium chair, 1990

One of the preeminent proponents of Scandinavian Postmodernism in the early 1990s, Mats Theselius designed furniture that often combined historic stylistic references with materials associated with industrial modernism to create works that had an innate poetry and visual intrigue. For instance, his *Aluminium* chair was a reinterpretation of the traditional tub chair and had an almost Steampunk quality with its exposed rivets holding the aluminium onto the chair's wooden body.

Aluminium chair, 1990
Wood, aluminium, leather-
covered upholstery
Källemo, Värnamo, Sweden

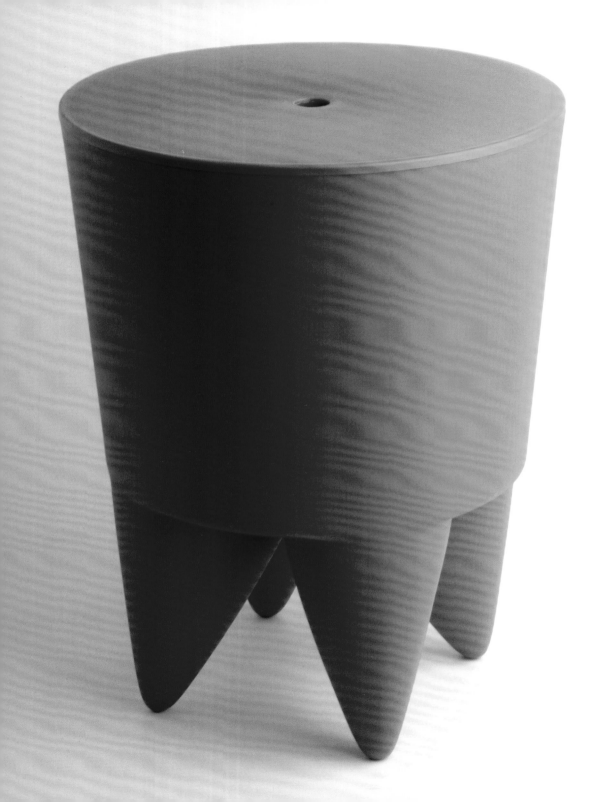

Philippe Starck
Bubu 1er stool, 1991 & *Prince AHA* stools, 1996

◄ *Bubu 1er* stool, 1991
Polypropylene
XO, Servon, France

► *Prince AHA* stools, 1996
Polypropylene
Kartell, Milan, Italy

One of the best-selling designs of the 1990s, Philippe Starck's playful *Bubu* stool possesses a whimsical humour that epitomizes the designer's tongue-in-cheek approach to design. This highly useful and inexpensive "container stool" has a simple construction of two injection-moulded elements made of colourful and robust polypropylene. Starck's hourglass shaped *Prince AHA* is also made of durable polypropylene and similarly has a dual function, being suitable for use as a side table as well as a stool.

Jane Atfield
RCP2 armchair, 1992

While studying at the Royal College of Art (London), Jane Atfield designed a chair made of imported recycled plastic – one of the first plastic designs made from consumer waste. She subsequently acquired an old plywood press, which she used to develop her own recycled plastic material made from discarded detergent containers, shampoo bottles and yoghurt pots. She then used the resulting mottled sheets of recycled plastic to create her first *RCP2* chair in 1992. She subsequently put this influential design into batch-production, manufacturing not only the armed model (shown here) but also side and child-sized variants as well.

RCP2 armchair, 1992
Recycled polyethylene sheet
Made of Waste, London, UK

Humberto & Fernando Campana
Favela armchair, 1991

Inspired by the ramshackle buildings found in the notorious
shanty town favelas of São Paulo, the Campana brothers
created their first *Favela* chair using scraps of wood found
on the streets of one of the city's slum districts. This poetic
and intricately fabricated design was subsequently put into
production by the progressive Italian furniture manufacturing
company, Edra, in 2003. Each one of these chairs is unique
with the off-cuts of wood being glued and nailed by hand
to create the design's self-supporting structure. An outdoor
version of this influential chair is also available in teak.

Favela armchair, 1991
Wood
Edra, Perignano, Italy

Ross Lovegrove
Air One chair, 1999

Made of expanded polypropylene beaded foam, the *Air One* chair demonstrates how a material that is mainly used for the disposable packaging of electronics and white goods can, with a little bit of imagination, be creatively reapplied to the construction of stylish furniture. The self-supporting structure of the *Air One* is extremely lightweight yet strong, whilst also impermeable to water and fully recyclable.

Air One chair, 1999
Expanded polypropylene
Edra, Perignano, Italy

Marcel Wanders
Knotted chair, 1996

Marcel Wanders designed the *Knotted* chair for the Dutch collective Droog Design in 1996. While its hand-knotted macramé appearance reflects the group's craftsmanlike aesthetic, the design is the result of Dry Tech, a technologically advanced collaboration between Droog and the Aviation and Space Laboratory of Delft University of Technology. To make the lightweight chair, the fibres are knotted together and soaked in epoxy resin, before the form is draped over a mould to dry and harden. Wanders made the first versions of the chair himself, before Cappellini put it into production in 2005.

▲ *Fishnet* chair designed by Marcel Wanders and produced by Marcel Wanders Studio, 2001. A limited edition evolution of the *Knotted* chair

► *Knotted* chair, 1996
Carbon and aramid fibre cord, epoxy resin
Cappellini, Mariano Comense, Italy

Philippe Starck
La Marie chair, 1998

◄ *La Marie* chair, 1998
Polycarbonate
Kartell, Noviglio, Italy

▼ Photograph by James Moore
for the *Kartell: 150 items 150
artworks* book by Franca
Sozzani & Luca Stoppini, 2003,
showing the *La Marie* chair

Philippe Starck's *La Marie* chair marked a huge technical breakthrough in plastic chair manufacture, being the world's first completely transparent chair formed from a single moulding of polycarbonate. Although its form was based on an archetypal four-legged chair, it was a truly advanced design created in a completely automated factory. The crystal-clear transparency of the polycarbonate gave the design a visual lightness that belied its robust structural strength. The *La Marie* was the first of several "invisible" chairs that Starck created for Kartell as part of the highly successful *Ghost* series.

Marc Newson
Coast chair, 1995

With its combination of oak and polyurethane foam, Marc Newson's *Coast* dining chair reflects the designer's interest in combining old and new materials at this time. Newson likens the unusual shape of the back and seat of the chair to a TV screen, and its form typifies the futuristic, sci-fi appearance of much of his work. The Australian designer conceived the chair for London's Coast restaurant, one of a number of restaurant interiors that Newson designed in the 1990s. Originally available in a limited edition of 130, in 2002 Magis put a polypropylene and glass-reinforced polyester version of the chair into production.

▲ Later edition of the *Coast* chair manufactured in polypropylene and glass-reinforced polyester by Magis, 2002

◄ *Coast* chair, 1995
Oak, coated polyurethane foam
Magis, Torre di Mosto, Italy

Marc Newson
Komed chair, 1996

As with his *Coast* chair, Marc Newson's design for the *Komed* chair was also the result of a commission to design a restaurant interior, the Osman restaurant in the KOMED Media Park in Cologne. Newson designed an orange fabric version for the restaurant, and another in white leather for the restaurant Canteen in Soho, New York. The chair's biomorphic shape can also be found in some of his other designs such as his earlier *Lockheed Lounge* and *Felt* chair from 1994.

Komed chair, 1996
Brushed tubular steel, textile-covered upholstery
Marc Newson Ltd., London, England

Tom Dixon
Fat armchair, 1991

Tom Dixon first emerged on the London design scene in the 1980s. This largely self-taught designer became known for his use of welded steel, a process he had learnt when trying to repair his motorbike. The Italian manufacturer Cappellini was an early champion of Dixon's work, putting first his *S* chair and then the *Fat* armchair into production. Originally made to order, Dixon and Cappellini worked together to adapt the design for mass-production. In comparison to the hand-woven *S* chair, the woven rush used for the chair's seat, arms and back was machine produced.

Fat armchair, 1991
Steel rod, rush upholstery
Cappellini, Mariano Comense, Italy

Mark Newson
Wicker chair, 1990

Born in Sydney, Marc Newson lived in Tokyo between 1987 and 1991, where he designed a number of chairs for the Japanese manufacturer Idée, including the *Embryo* chair in 1988 and the *Wicker* chair in 1990. Newson recalls being sent to Idée's rural factory to experiment with wicker material before hitting on the design for the *Wicker* chair, which combines his characteristic organic aesthetic with a high level of traditional craftsmanship. No longer in production, each *Wicker* chair was hand-woven and took four hundred hours to make.

Wicker chair, 1990
Wicker, brushed aluminium, polished aluminium
Idée, Tokyo, Japan

Vico Magistretti
Maui armchair, 1997

Vico Magistretti designed the *Maui* chair when he was a
venerable seventy-seven years old and certainly he brought
to its development a lifetime's design experience. Practical,
comfortable and affordable, this elegant design with its robust
polypropylene seat shell subsequently went on to become
one of the most commercially successful chairs of the late
1990s and early 2000s. The reason for its success lay in its
functionality, durability and stackability, as well as its choice
of eleven attractive matt colour options, all of which gave it a
versatility that allowed it to be as much at home in a domestic
environment as in a public space or office environment.

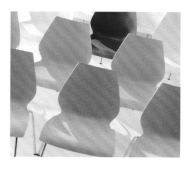

▲ Kartell publicity photograph
of the *Maui* side chair in various
colours

◄ *Maui* armchair, 1997
Chromed tubular metal,
polypropylene
Kartell, Meda, Italy

Sigurdur Gustafsson
Tango chairs, 1997

The Icelandic born architect-designer, Sigurdur Gustafsson began designing furniture for the progressive Swedish manufacturer, Källemo in 1997. The same year he created his eye-catching *Tango* chair, which confusingly was originally entitled the *Red Baron* chair. This unusual design with its distinctive Z-shaped element that forms the chair's curving back-rail and supporting rear leg was produced as a limited edition of forty-nine pieces. Its single offset front leg further heightens this quirky design's delightful sense of gravity-defying imbalance.

Tango **chairs, 1997**
Lacquered tubular steel, lacquered wood
Källemo, Värnamo, Sweden

Niels Gammelgaard
Nevil chair, 1993

Niels Gammelgaard began designing for the Swedish democratic furnishing company IKEA in 1975 and has since then created numerous pieces for the firm that are notable for their unpretentious practicality and simple uncluttered lines. One of his most successful and interesting designs has been the swivelling *Nevil* chair, which proved that it was possible to produce a very low-cost task chair that also looked great and functioned well, and in so doing eloquently demonstrated yet again that affordable good design is an achievable goal.

Nevil chair, 1993
Enamelled tubular metal,
polypropylene
IKEA, Älmhult, Sweden

Jurgen Bey & Kan Konings
Kokon chair, 1997

A key part of the Dutch designer Jurgen Bey's concept-led design practice is based on the transformation of everyday objects through unusual combinations of the new and the found or reclaimed. With the *Kokon* (Cocoon) chair, designed in 1997 with Kan Konings, discarded chairs have been tightly covered – or cocooned – with spun PVC, giving the chairs a new, smooth elastic skin. Part of Bey's *Skin* series, the *Kokon* was a result of the Dry Tech project (that also led to Marcel Wanders's *Knotted* chair), and was subsequently put into production by Droog in 1999.

▲ Photograph showing *Kokon* chair and other designs from the *Skin* series, c.1997

▼ *Kokon* chair, 1997
Wood, PVC
Droog, Amsterdam, The Netherlands

Ron Arad
Uncut chair, 1997 & *Tom Vac* chair, 1999

◄ *Uncut* chair, 1997
Vacuum-formed anodized
aluminium, tubular stainless steel
One-Off Ltd., London, England

▼ *Tom Vac* chair, 1999
Injection-moulded polypropylene,
tubular steel
Vitra, Weil am Rhein, Germany

The origins of the stackable *Tom Vac* chair lie in a commission
Ron Arad received from *Domus* magazine to design an
installation for the 1997 Milan Furniture Fair. Soon after, Arad
reused the vacuum-forming machine he had purchased to
manufacture the chairs for the Domus installation, to produce
a brand new design with a corrugated aluminium shell. In 1999
Vitra put an injection-moulded plastic version of this chair,
entitled *Tom Vac*, into production and since then there have
been several multi-coloured variations, including swivelling
and rocking models and a weather-resistant outdoor version.

Shiro Kuramata
Feather stool, 1990

Establishing his own Tokyo design studio in 1965, Shiro Kuramata was at the forefront of Japanese design creativity and became widely acclaimed for his ability to combine the Japanese concept of artistic unity with Western low and high cultural influences. Creating poetic furniture that had an almost alchemic quality he revelled in juxtaposing disparate materials in order to create a sense of otherworldly dynamism. For instance, in the design of his *Feather* stool he suspended feathers in an icy block of acrylic, thereby contrasting the weightlessness of the floating plumes with the weighty materiality of the solid polymer, creating a rare sense of transcendent lightness and transparency.

Feather stool, 1990
Acrylic, aluminium, feathers
Ishimaru Co., Tokyo, Japan

Ilkka Suppanen & Pasi Kolhonen
Airbag chair, 1997

Ilkka Suppanen studied architecture at the Technical University of Helsinki and then interior and furniture design at the University of Art and Design Helsinki. In 1997 he established, with three other designers, the award-winning Snowcrash design co-operative. For this venture, he and Pasi Kolhonen co-designed the inflatable *Airbag* chair, made from materials normally associated with the manufacture of high-performance sports equipment. A highly versatile design that could be used indoors and outdoors, it had adjustable straps that also allowed the back's angle to be adjusted to such an extent that it could even be converted into a mattress.

Airbag chair, 1997
Woven nylon, plastic
Snowcrash, Stockholm,
Sweden

Stefano Giovannoni
Bombo barstools, 1997

One of the most commercially successful seating ranges of the late 1990s and early 2000s, the *Bombo* family of chairs, stools and tables reflected the new sculptural confidence that emerged in furniture design during this period. One of the reasons for its success is Stefano Giovannoni's ability to create designs that have an emotionally engaging character. With its soft-edged look the *Bombo* – or, as its title translates into English, "the bumblebee" – seems to invite the sitter into the comforting embrace of its moulded plastic curves.

▲ *Bombo* chairs designed by Stefano Giovannoni for Magis, 1999

◄ *Bombo* barstool, 1997
Chromed steel, ABS
Magis, Torre di Mosto, Italy

Ron Arad
FPE chair, 1997

Like other chairs manufactured by Kartell, the *FPE* is made without a single human hand touching it, as it is transformed from plastic pellets to a ready-to-ship boxed product. Its title is an abbreviation of *Fantastic Plastic Elastic*, which eloquently describes the attributes of this lightweight and flexible stacking chair. Its seating section is made from a flat strip of smooth, batch-dyed polypropylene. This is automatically slotted into an extruded tubular aluminium profile, and is then bent in a special curved machine to form a resilient supporting frame.

FPE chair, 1997
Polypropylene, varnished
aluminium
Kartell, Noviglio, Italy

Alberto Meda
Meda chair, 1996

Having trained as a design engineer, Alberto Meda worked as the technical manager of Kartell before founding his own industrial design office. His inherent understanding of manufacturing processes and engineering means that his innovative designs are highly resolved both in terms of ergonomic functionality and mass-production viability. For instance, his *Meda* chair is responsive to the human body's movements, but unlike other task chairs it does not rely on overly complex mechanisms to achieve this. Also, instead of using bulky upholstery, an elasticized textile cover is stretched taut over the back frame to provide a flexible and comfortable support with the minimum of means.

Meda chair, 1996
Aluminium, plastic, elasticized mesh, textile-covered upholstery
Vitra, Weil am Rhein, Germany

Ross Lovegrove
Spin chair, 1997

Inspired by the seat-shell form of George Nelson's *Swag-Leg* office chairs from 1958, the *Spin* chair can be seen as Ross Lovegrove's personal homage to the work of this great American mid-century designer. Although it is unupholstered, the *Spin* – with its fluid lines and soft curves – provides a good level of comfort thanks to Lovegrove's innate understanding of ergonomics. Using an eye-catching combination of opaque and translucent polypropylene for its seat-shell, the *Spin* is offered in three different and attractive colour choices: translucent white, blue or yellow. Driade also produces a stackable four-legged armchair and beam variants of this design.

Spin chair, 1997
Painted aluminium, polypropylene
Driade, Milan, Italy

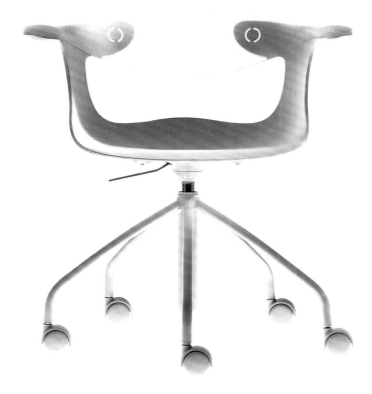

Antonio Citterio
T-Chair, 1994

The Italian architect Antonio Citterio designed his first office chair for the German furniture manufacturer Vitra in 1988. His 1994 design for the *T-Chair* has a patented synchronized mechanism that moves with the body to support it in any position. This technologically advanced, highly ergonomic design is made of moulded polyurethane foam upholstery to maximize comfort and support. The seat depth, back and arm rests can all be adjusted to meet the user's individual needs.

T-Chair, 1994
Aluminium, textile-covered polyurethane foam upholstery, polypropylene
Vitra, Weil am Rhein, Germany

Niels Diffrient
Freedom office chair, 1999

Designed by ergonomic design pioneer Niels Diffrient in 1999, the *Freedom* office chair is seen to have set a new benchmark for environmentally friendly, ergonomic office chair design. Made largely of either recycled or recyclable materials, by 2009 over a million of the lightweight, self-adjusting chairs had been sold worldwide. The chair is manufactured by Humanscale, a company set up in the 1970s that took its name from a series of booklets on ergonomics co-written by Diffrient.

▲ *Freedom Family* range of office seating, 1999

► *Freedom* office chair, 1999
Aluminium, steel, plastic
Humanscale, New York, USA

Jasper Morrison
Low Pad chair, 1999

Elegantly refined, the *Low Pad* lounge chair is an accomplished *tour-de-force* of cool functional essentialism. Equally at home in a stylish domestic interior or a trendy office environment, this design is a contemporary take on iconic Modernist club chair designs, such as Ludwig Mies van der Rohe's seminal *Barcelona* chair from the 1920s. Upholstered in either fabric or leather, the *Low Pad* has a comfortable ergonomic "spine-line" and is also available with armrests.

Low Pad chair, 1999
Stainless steel, plywood, leather-covered upholstery
Cappellini, Arosio, Italy

Jasper Morrison
Air-Chair, 1999

The virtually indestructible *Air-Chair* is a highly rational one piece/one material construction made of polypropylene strengthened with glass fibre. Using a state-of-the-art technique, nitrogen gas is injected at high pressure during the plastic moulding process. This reduces the length of the production cycle and also introduces an internal cavity so that less material is used in fabrication. Relatively lightweight, this elegant stackable indoor/outdoor design is also easy to carry and transport.

▲ Magis publicity image of the *Air-Chair* showing different colour options and stackability, 1999

▼ *Air-Chair,* 1999
Gas-assisted, injection-moulded polypropylene, glass fibre
Magis, Motta di Livenza, Italy

2000s

Shin & Tomoko Azumi
LEM stool, 2000

The Azumis described their phenomenally successful *LEM* height-adjustable stool as "a loop... floating in air". As one of the most influential seating designs of the Noughties, it became an almost omnipresent feature of both public and domestic interiors thanks to its understated minimalism and practical functionality. It received the Design Product of the Year FX Award in 2000, as well as a Good Design award from Japan's Industrial Design Promotion Organization in 2001.

▲ Computer rendering of *LEM* stools showing view from above, 2000

▼ *LEM* stool, 2000
Chromed steel, plywood, beech or walnut veneer
La Palma, Cadoneghe, Italy

Ross Lovegrove
Go armchair, 2001

Ross Lovegrove's highly innovative *Go* chair from 2001 is the world's first chair to be made of magnesium. It was made with a pressure die-casting process, a technology developed in the car industry, which enabled the chair's elegant yet futuristic form to take shape. The frame is powder-coated in silver or white, with a seat in grey or white polycarbonate or maple veneer. Selected on its release as one of *Time* magazine's designs of the year, *Go* exemplifies Lovegrove's approach that combines advanced technology with an aesthetic he describes as "organic essentialism".

Go chair, 2001
Powder-coated magnesium,
polycarbonate/maple veneer
Bernhardt Design, Lenoir, USA

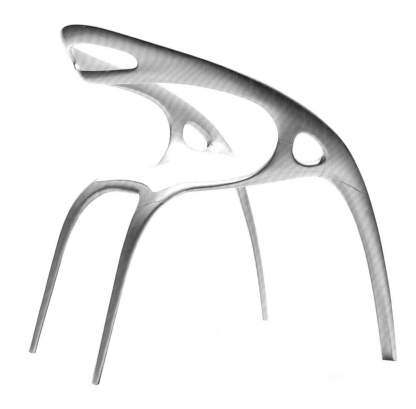

Werner Aisslinger
Nic chair, 2001

Designed in 2001, Werner Aisslinger's cantilevered *Nic*
chair is made of air-moulded plastic, the edges of which are
hollow like the chair's tubular steel legs. It took three years
of development before the chair went into production in
2004 with the Italian manufacturer Magis, one of only two
companies in the world capable at the time of undertaking
the chair's complex manufacturing process. The seat of this
functional design can be placed upright on a tabletop edge to
facilitate floor cleaning, and the chair can also be easily taken
apart for space efficient transportation.

▲ Computer rendering of *Nic*
chair, 2001

◄ *Nic* chair, 2001
Air-moulded polypropylene with
glass fibre, chromed steel
Magis, Torre di Mosto, Italy

Studio 7.5
Mirra office chair, 2003

The Studio 7.5 design group bases its designs on the close observation of how workers react to working environments and its research into how this can be improved through product innovation. The *Mirra* chair was based on the concept of "a chair that would react with passive adjustability". The result was an award-winning, humancentric, high-performance design with a flexible back, a woven suspension seat and a "harmonic" tilt that is made of 33% recycled materials and is 96% recyclable.

▲ Detail of perforated seat back

► *Mirra* office chair, 2003
Steel, Capron nylon, Airweave textile
Herman Miller, Zeeland (MI), USA

Louise Campbell
Prince chair, 2001

Designed in 2001, the *Prince* chair was Louise Campbell's submission for a competition to design a chair for the Crown Prince Frederick of Denmark. The Danish furniture designer translated the Prince's reputation for combining tradition with innovation into the chair's design and manufacture. It has a lace-like pattern made by water and laser-cutting the neoprene and a felt seat that acts as the chair's upholstery. Although the chair did not win the competition, in 2005 it was put into production by the Danish manufacturer Hay.

▲ Photograph showing the manufacture of the *Prince* chair, 2000s

▼ *Prince* chair, 2001
Powder-coated steel, neoprene rubber, felt
Hay, Horsens, Denmark

Mark Robson
Fly chair, 2003

After graduating in furniture design from the Royal College of Art, Mark Robson began working for the French furniture manufacturer, Allibert, in Grenoble. Apart from his designs for this behemoth of a company of the ubiquitous monobloc garden chair, Robson has also created a few less utilitarian seating designs for other manufacturers, most notably his *Fly* chair for Zanotta. A super lightweight design, the *Fly* is made from a continuous loop of carbon fibre onto which is connected a mesh of fine stretch fabric. This combination of high-tech materials allows the user to adopt numerous comfortable sitting and reclining positions with the absolute minimum of means.

Fly chair, 2003
Varnished carbon fibre,
Quota textile
Zanotta, Milan, Italy

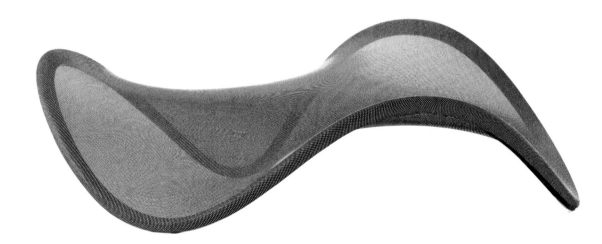

Marcel Wanders
VIP chair, 2000

Marcel Wanders conceived the *VIP* chair as part of his design for the Dutch Pavilion's Royal Wing Room at the Hanover World Expo in 2000. The room included a woodland ice rink on which forty-four of the armchairs were placed. The flared legs concealed the chair's castors, making it seem as if the chair was ice skating in a gesture typical of the Dutch designer's familiar yet subversive approach. In the same year the chair was put into production by Moooi, the Dutch manufacturer of which Wanders is Creative Director.

VIP chair, 2000
Foam covered steel frame, Nylon/
upholstered steel
Moooi, Amsterdam, The
Netherlands

Zaha Hadid
Moraine sofa, 2000

In 2000, the award-winning architect Zaha Hadid created the *Z-scape* range of furniture for Sawaya & Moroni, which included the *Moraine* seating unit. These sculptural and visually striking furniture pieces were, according to their designer, "conceptually derived from dynamic landscape formations and designed to coexist as a single mass or reconstituted fragments". Unlike traditional furniture, these pieces with their vibrant fluid forms were also intended to introduce "an element of strangeness and indeterminacy" into an interior and as such were not particularly informed by functional or ergonomic requirements.

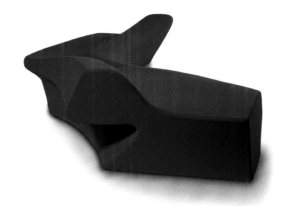

Moraine sofa, 2000
Metal, textile-covered
upholstery
Sawaya & Moroni, Milan, Italy

Patrick Norguet
Rive Droite chair, 2001 & *Rainbow* chair, 2000

Patrick Norguet has an astonishing eye for colour, which is evinced in his remarkable *Rainbow* chair made from a bold spectrum of glowing acrylic slabs that are joined together using ultrasound technology. Having close links with the fashion industry having worked for Louis Vuitton, Lanvin, Guerlain and Christian Dior, Norguet has also sought out collaborative projects; for example, his *Rive Droite* chair is enlivened with a choice of textile covering designed by Emilio Pucci. Norguet's seating designs not only have a fashionable sophistication, but an undeniable sculptural presence that lift them out of the ordinary and into the extraordinary.

▲ *Rive Droite* chair, 2001
Plywood, steel, textile-covered upholstery
Cappellini, Milan, Italy

► *Rainbow* chair, 2000
Acrylic resin
Cappellini, Milan, Italy

Philippe Starck
Louis Ghost armchair, 2002

One of the best-selling seating designs during the first decade of the twenty-first century with over 100,000 units being sold in the first year after its launch, the *Louis Ghost* armchair is a sophisticated and quirky interpretation of a classic Louis XV style chair from the 18th century. The crystal-clear acrylic gives this Postmodern design a jewel-like quality, and emphasises the idea that plastic can be a noble material. Like so many designs by Starck, this stylish single material, single form armchair has a distinctive identity that makes it so visually engaging.

▲ Kartell publicity photograph showing a stack of *Louis Ghost* armchairs, c.2002

◄ *Louis Ghost* armchair, 2002
Acrylic (PMMA)
Kartell, Milan, Italy

Philippe Starck
Ero/s/ chair, 2001

With its jewel-like seat shell of transparent acrylic, the *Ero/s/* chair is not only a technically sophisticated solution, but also an elegant yet functional one. It has a choice of bases: either an elegant aluminium pedestal that harks back to Eero Saarinen's 1950s *Tulip* chair, or a chromed rod version reminiscent of the famous "Eiffel Tower" bases used by Charles and Ray Eames in their *Plastic Shell Group* chairs. This blending of retro and modern helps to imbue this visually seductive design with familiar associations and thereby emotional resonance.

▲ Detail showing the *Ero/s/* chair's seat connection

► *Ero/s/* chair, 2001
Batch-dyed or transparent PMMA, die-cast aluminium or chromed steel
Kartell, Milan, Italy

Patrick Norguet
Apollo chair, 2002

Unquestionably a master of form, Patrick Norguet creates simple elemental shapes for his furniture pieces that have a very distinctive graphic quality. His *Apollo* chair for Artifort, for instance, has an angled C-shaped seating section that ergonomically embraces the user in foam-padded comfort. Reminiscent of some of Pierre Paulin's earlier seating designs for Artifort, the *Apollo* incorporates a simple metal pedestal base and likewise has a dramatic sculptural quality. In 2004, Norguet created the *Little Apollo*, which has a similar shaped seat shell but which is supported on a sled-like metal rod base.

▲ *Little Apollo* chair designed by Patrick Norguet for Artifort, 2004

◄ *Apollo* chair, 2002
Plywood, steel, textile-covered upholstery
Artifort, Maastricht, Netherlands

Michael Young
Avalon chair, 2010

Hong-Kong-based British designer Michael Young has, throughout his career, married cutting-edge technologies with simple elemental forms to create products that have a formal and functional logic. His furniture designs are often imbued with a minimalism that is playful rather than austere. Young's *Avalon* chair, produced by Swedish manufacturer Swedese, is essentially a modern reworking of a traditional tub chair stripped down to its bare essentials. Thoughtfully considered, it has a concealed 360° swivelling steel disc base with an automatic return for enhanced user performance, and comes with an optional "shoe-protecting" base made of ABS.

Avalon chair, 2010
Tubular steel, steel, textile-covered
foam upholstery, ABS
Swedese, Vaggeryd, Sweden

Tokujin Yoshioka
Honey-Pop armchair, 2001

The Japanese designer Tokujin Yoshioka designed the *Honey-Pop* armchair in 2001 using paper glued together into a honeycomb formation, like a Chinese lantern or Christmas decoration. Folded flat, the paper opens out in a concertina pattern and the seat takes the shape of the first person to sit on it. Handmade in the designer's Tokyo studio, the pure white chair is only available in a limited edition of 300. Driade subsequently commissioned Yoshioka to design a solid version suitable for serial production, which led to the rotationally moulded polyethylene *Tokyo-Pop* chair in 2002, and ultimately the elegant *Tokyo-Pop* chaise shown to the right.

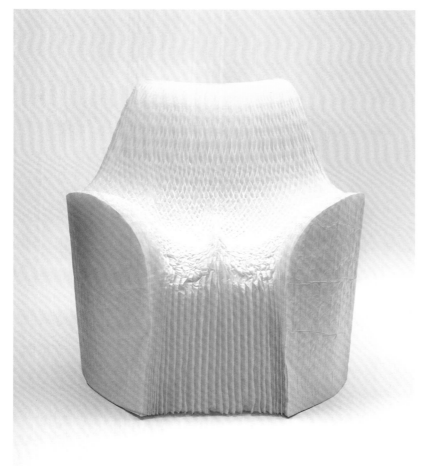

▲ *Tokyo Pop* chaise designed by Tokujin Yoshioka for Driade, 2002

◄ *Honey-Pop* armchair, 2001
Glassine paper
Tokujin Yoshioka Design, Tokyo, Japan.

Mathias Bengtsson
Slice chair, 2000

Looking like a three-dimensional topographical map, Mathias Bengtsson's *Slice* chair is innovatively constructed from layers of laser-cut aluminium using CAD/CAM technology. The resulting armchair appears like a rocky cliff face that has been shrunk down to human scale. Although never intended to function as a truly comfortable piece of furniture, this "design-art" chair has an undeniably powerful sculptural presence.

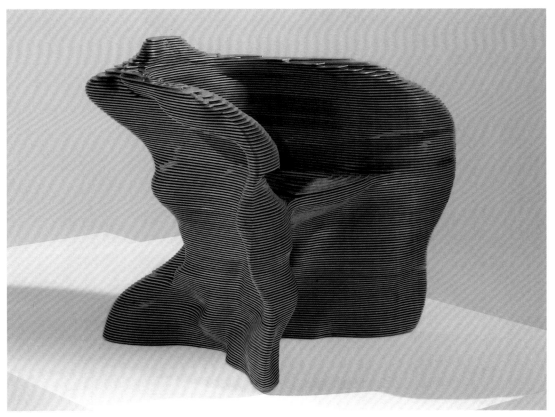

Slice chair, 2000
Laser-cut aluminium
Mathias Bengtsson, London, UK

Fernando & Humberto Campana
Sushi chair, 2002

As the Campana brothers explain, "In the favelas of Brazil, they make mats and bedspreads of all sorts simply by overlapping pieces of fabric. We began with this and we thought of sushi. Textiles of different types all rolled together." Their resulting *Sushi* chair manufactured by Edra was made from an assortment of fabric off-cuts and strips of carpet underlay that were rolled together and supported on an underlying and invisible metal structure in order to create a colourful layered effect. Each example uses a slightly different combination of materials and is therefore unique.

Sushi chair, 2002
Metal, polyurethane, felt, textile
Edra, Perigano, Italy

Fernando & Humberto Campana
Corallo armchair, 2004

Described by the Campana brothers as "a three-dimensional scribble", the generously proportioned *Corallo* armchair is made of irregularly woven steel wire that is shaped by hand to "resemble the sprawling coral reefs found off the coast of Brazil". After the frameless wire construction has been soldered and bent, it is then carefully smoothed to eliminate any rough edges and an epoxy coating is applied. This weatherproof finish has an almost silky tactility and its bright reddish-orange hue further enhances the impression of growing coral. Like other furniture designs by the Campana brothers, the *Corallo* demonstrates that even the simplest of materials can be imaginatively shaped into surprising and inventive forms that have an appealing artistic resonance.

Corallo armchair, 2004
Epoxy-coated steel wire
Edra, Perigano, Italy

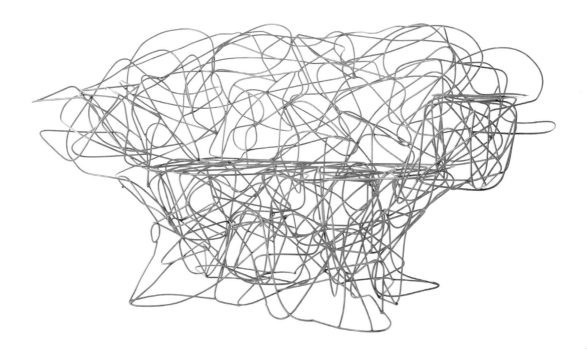

Maarten Baas
Smoke dining chair, 2002 & *Smoke* armchair, 2002

◄ *Smoke* dining chair, 2002
Epoxy-finished burnt wood,
leather-covered upholstery
Moooi, Breda, Netherlands

Maarten Baas is one of the leading lights of contemporary Dutch design who creates work that is infused with a playful eccentricity. His *Smoke* dining chair and armchair, for instance, are made from the controlled burning of antique-style reproduction chairs. The chairs' charred surfaces are then sealed in a durable epoxy coating and upholstered in black leather. This manufacturing process not only ensures that the beauty and character of the burnt wood are transformed into a long-lasting material, but also means that each example is unique. The resulting effect is visually powerful, possessing an inherent aesthetic tension that juxtaposes the antique with a contemporary Postmodern sensibility.

◄ ▲ *Smoke* armchair, 2002
Epoxy-finished burnt wood,
leather-covered upholstery
Moooi, Breda, Netherlands

Komplot Design
NON chairs, 2000

Komplot Design was established in 1987 by the Danish designers Boris Berlin and Poul Christiansen, who have since gone on to create a number of landmark seating designs that are notable for their interesting use of materials. Their stacking *NON* chair is a geometrically refined monobloc seating design that is moulded from a single shot of PUR-rubber. It can be used indoors or outdoors and has a surprising level of comfort thanks to the inherent flexibility of rubber. As Berlin and Christiansen noted, "The rubber chair is an archetype for a chair, not a designed chair, just a chair."

▲ Computer rendering showing a grouping of *NON* chairs

► Computer rendering showing underside of the *NON* chair's seat

◄ *NON* chairs, 2000
PUR-rubber
Källemo AB, Värnamo, Sweden

Fernando & Humberto Campana

Sushi IV chair, c.2003, *Sonia Diniz* chair, c.2003 &
Sushi sofa, 2003

The Campana brothers are renowned for their ability to
take relatively ordinary materials and transform them into
absolutely extraordinary designs that push both functional
and aesthetic boundaries. With this series of seating designs,
they utilized multi-coloured pieces of felt that were coiled
together and then cut like sushi, hence their name. The
resulting effect is a bright explosion of colour that would
enliven any room, and that looks wonderful in a gallery-
type space.

▼ *Sonia Diniz* chair, c.2003
Felt, textiles, plastic, EVA, steel
Estudio Campana, São Paulo, Brazil

▲ *Sushi* sofa, 2003
Felt, textiles, plastic,
EVA, steel
Campana Objetos, São Paulo, Brazil

▶ *Sushi IV* chair, c.2003
Felt, textiles, plastic,
EVA, steel
Campana Objetos, São Paulo, Brazil

Jerszy Seymour
Easy chair, 2004

The *Easy* chair from 2004 is one of Jerszy Seymour's best-known designs. Made of injection-moulded polypropylene with added glass fibre, the lightweight, playful stacking chair is available in a number of bright colours and exemplifies the designer's humorous yet technologically innovative approach to design. The *Easy* chair also demonstrates Seymour's interest in experimenting with the flowing materiality and form-giving potential of plastics. The chair is part of the Museum of Modern Art's permanent collection, as is the accompanying *Easy* table from 2006.

▲ Magis publicity image showing stack of *Easy* chairs

◄ *Easy* chair, 2004
Glass fibre reinforced polypropylene
Magis, Torre di Mosto, Italy

Karim Rashid
Butterfly chair, 2003

Karim Rashid's *Butterfly* chair has an endearing retro pop appeal, with the high-gloss brightly coloured surfaces of its seat shell, which is made of two-toned injection-moulded ABS. The seat and its reverse are available in seven different contrasting colours and give this practical stacking chair a distinctive look that typifies Rashid's colourful and playful approach to design. With its soft curves, this design provides a good degree of ergonomic comfort and is an affordable seating solution that reflects Rashid's unique visual language.

Butterfly chair, 2003
Chromed tubular steel, ABS
Magis, Torre di Mosto, Italy

René Holten
Ondo sofa, 2003

René Holten initially studied architecture at the Academy of Arts in Maastricht before training as an industrial designer at the renowned Eindhoven Design Academy, where he graduated *cum laude* in 1993. The same year he established his own design office and four years later created the *DoDo* chair, his first design for Artifort, which won the prize for best Dutch Furniture Design in 1998. He has since created a number of sculptural furniture pieces for Artifort, including his simple yet striking *Ondo* sofa with its flowing wave-like lines. Like other products made by Artifort, this elegant sofa is not only remarkable for the high quality of its manufacture but is also extremely comfortable.

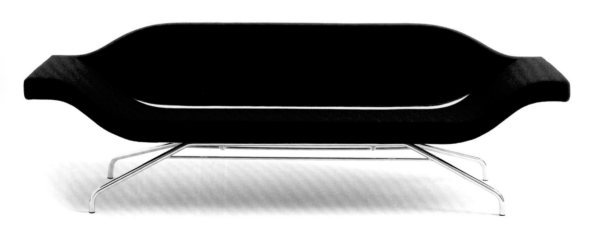

Ondo sofa, 2003
Chromed tubular steel, textile-covered upholstery
Artifort, Maastricht, Netherlands

Fredrik Mattson
Innovation C chair, 2001

Fredrik Mattson's *Innovation C* swivelling chair is a multifunctional seating solution that invites the user to choose their own way of sitting on it as it has no obvious back or front. The backrest can also be used as a laptop table, transforming the chair into a compact workstation. The original intention of the design was that it could be used in various different environments from airport lounges and waiting rooms, to libraries and schools, but it works equally well in a domestic setting. The *Innovation C* chair is an cutting-edge and thoughtful piece reflecting Mattson's belief that designing is a bit like raising children; both products and kids need love and affection to produce a sense of self-confidence.

Innovation C chair, 2001
Stainless steel, moulded
polyurethane foam
Blå Station, Åhus, Sweden

Ingvar Kamprad
Three legged stool, 2004

In 2004, Habitat (then owned by IKEA) developed its first *VIP* collection, while under the art direction of Tom Dixon. For this venture the firm asked various celebrities to design a range of objects that wereput into production. By far the most noteworthy of these was the *Three legged* stool by Ingvar Kamprad, the founder of IKEA, who – needless to say – had a real understanding of the design process, unlike the majority of the other VIP "designers" that took part in the project. With a form based on a traditional milking stool used in rural Sweden, this affordable design had an inherent rightness and with its removable screw-in legs could be sold as a flat-pack.

Three legged stool, 2004
Painted wood
Habitat, London, England

Jasper Morrison
Cork Family stools, 2004

Cork is one of the most eco-friendly materials one can use for the design of furniture, as it is the bark of the tree rather than the actual tree that is used. In fact the harvesting of cork trees is usually limited to nine-year cycles, which means the same tree can be productive for generations. Here, Jasper Morrison has utilized this wonderful light-but-strong natural resource for the design of three small, robust stools, which have flexible functionality – they can also be used as side tables.

Cork Family stools, 2004
Natural cork
Vitra, Weil am Rhein, Germany

Bertjan Pot & Marcel Wanders
Carbon chair, 2004

Although various furniture designers – from Alberto Meda to Philippe Starck – have used a woven matrix of carbon fibre in order to create a lightweight yet strong chair, Bertjan Pot and Marcel Wanders did something a little different by using individual strands of fibre instead for their creation of the *Carbon* chair. Their innovative technique involved combining loosely interwoven fibre strands with epoxy resin, which when dried formed a stable and extremely strong self-supporting structure that not only had a captivating visual lightness, but also an endearing crafted sensibility.

Carbon chair, 2004
Carbon fibre, epoxy resin
Moooi, Breda, Netherlands

Roderick Vos
Ayu chair, 2002

The Dutch designer Roderick Vos had a great-grandfather who not only built windmills, but in his spare time wove traditional farmhouse chairs, while his grandfather was a trained cabinet-maker and his father was an interior architect – so you could say furniture design is in Vos' blood. After studying at the acclaimed Design Academy in Eindhoven, he subsequently worked in Ingo Maurer's studio in Munich and also for Kenji Ekuan's office, GK Industrial Design Associates, in Tokyo. He subsequently spent six years living and working on the Indonesian island of Java, renowned for its production of rattan furnishings. Vos has designed several chairs woven in this natural material, however perhaps the most interesting is his eye-catching *Ayu* chair for Driade, which redefined the aesthetic parameters of the humble wicker chair with its soft undulating and thoroughly contemporary ergonomic form.

Ayu chair, 2002
Painted tubular steel, wickerwork
Driade, Milan, Italy

Konstantin Grcic
Chair One concrete base chairs, 2004 &
Chair One stacking chair, 2004

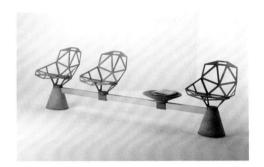

This innovative seating range utilizes an unusual and highly distinctive formal language of design that is characterized by the use of flat planes and faceted forms. Despite this, these chairs – which are constructed almost like a football – are surprisingly comfortable and have the added benefit of being suitable for indoor or outdoor use. As Grcic explains, "Given the chance to work with aluminium casting I thought that I should take it all the way. The more we worked on the models the more we learnt to understand the structural logic behind what we were doing."

▲ Beam configuration of the *Chair One* range

► *Chair One* stacking chair, 2004
Polyester powder-coated cast aluminium, titanium
Magis, Torre di Mosto, Italy

◄ *Chair One* concrete base chairs, 2004
Polyester powder-coated cast aluminium, concrete, titanium
Magis, Torre di Mosto, Italy

Franco Poli
Loom chair, 2006

The Italian designer Franco Poli notes: "a designer's background should be as wide as possible. It should include scientific, humanistic and technical aspects". For him the starting point of any design concept is an in-depth understanding of geometry. For his *Loom* chair, he utilised a sling of thick leather that he had ingeniously and uniformly perforated with a new high-frequency cutting machine. The resulting flexible mesh not only overcame the limited physical dimensions of a piece of leather in terms of both width and length, but also provided a comfortable and breathable support for the human body.

Loom chair, 2006
Steel, leather, plastic
Matteograssi, Giussano, Italy

Thomas Feichtner

FX10 chair, 2006

The name *FX10* was originally used for a ski binding that Thomas Feichtner had previously designed for the Austrian ski maker Fischer. Because he felt his approach to the chair's design was similar and its form reminded him of ski bindings, he decided to give this lounge chair the same name. Its dramatic planed surfaces are achieved by using individual block-like components upholstered in leather, which, as its creator explains, are then "put together to form a whole, like the ice blocks of an igloo... Since no seams and no time-consuming sewing are necessary, the lounge chair is produced quickly and, moreover, is easy to repair simply by exchanging a surface".

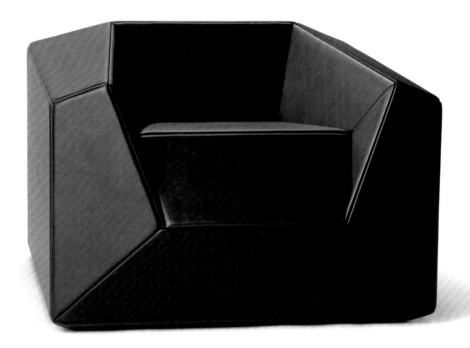

FX10 chair, 2006
Wood, leather-covered upholstery
Neue Wiener Werkstätte, Vienna,
Austria

Johannes Foersom & Peter Hiort-Lorenzen
Imprint chair, 2006

Johannes Foersom and Peter Hiort-Lorenzen's revolutionary *Imprint* chair has a seat shell made of compressed plant fibre, a material developed by the duo that makes use of waste products from the timber industry, such as treetops, roots and branches. As they explain, "We wanted to create fibre matting with aesthetic qualities, cellulose felt decorated with fibres from bark and spruce, from chopped up newsprint. It took us three years. Only then did we begin to 'shape'. And then the main goal was primarily to stress the material. A dome shaped seat shell did this best. And most comfortably." The chair's seat shell is not only highly ecologically sustainable but also has an engaging flecked surface that invites tactile interaction.

▲ Another variant of the *Imprint* chair, 2006

◄ *Imprint* chair, 2006
Ash, compressed cellulose fibres
Lammhults Möbel, Lammhult, Sweden

Andreas Ostwald & Klaus Nolting
Cox chair, 2005

La Palma specialize in the manufacture of beautiful plywood furniture that is notable for its exquisitely thin profiles and precise detailing. The *Cox* chair has a compound moulded plywood seat shell that is produced using a special three-dimensional malleable 6mm veneer, developed by the German-based company Reholz. Pushing the constructional possibilities of plywood to the limit, this beautiful chair swivels on a sandblasted steel base and received a Design Plus award in 2005 for its use of innovative technology.

▲ Design drawing of the *Cox* chair, 2005

▶ *Cox* chair, 2005
Moulded plywood, stainless steel
La Palma, Cadoneghe, Italy

Hannes Wettstein
Tototo chair, 2007

Hannes Wettstein was one of the most influential Swiss designers of his generation, whose career was sadly all too brief. He approached the design process from a highly pragmatic viewpoint and as such his designs not only functioned well, but also had a stripped down quality that resulted from his purging of any extraneous and superfluous detailing. For example, his *Tototo* chair is a stackable, single-form/single-material seating design that is as perfectly suited for outdoor use as it is for indoor use, thanks to its employment of highly durable and fully recyclable polypropylene. This essentialist design with its distinctive slanting armrests eloquently demonstrates that it is quite possible to create a monobloc chair – a one-shot plastic chair – that is both elegant and functional.

Tototo chair, 2007
Polypropylene
Max Design, Bagnaria Arsa, Italy

Lievore Altherr Molina
Leaf outdoor chaise longue and chairs, 2005

Comprising a chaise longue, a lounge chair and two side chairs, the *Leaf* collection offers, according to its manufacturer, "contemporary comfort inspired by nature". With their structure echoing the veining of leaves, the natural habitat for these chairs is in the garden, and in the right light they throw evocatively leaf-like shadows. These spectacular designs come with optional cushions to provide greater comfort.

Leaf outdoor chaise longue & chairs, 2005
Enamelled steel
Arper, Monastier di Treviso, Italy

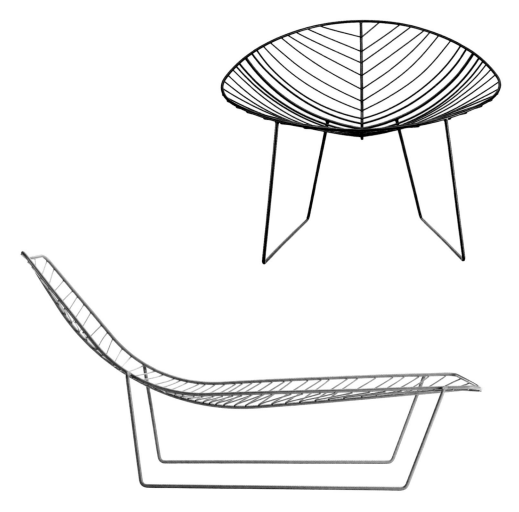

Tokujin Yoshioka
Pane chair, 2003-06

Inspired by an article in the *National Geographic* on the technological possibilities of newly developed fibres, Tokujin Yoshioka decided to create a chair from a translucent and malleable material known as thermoplastic polyester elastomer (TPEE). The resulting *Pane* chair – the title meaning "bread" in Italian – uses a similar process to that used to produce a loaf. Yoshioka rolled sections of TPEE into a chair-like form, encased it in a paper tube and then baked it in a 104°C oven. The resulting sponge-like structure was achieved through the material's expansion on heating and subsequent hardening on cooling, which allowed it to become self-supporting; the fibres memorized the chair's form. This inventive seating solution was showcased at an installation hosted by Moroso at the Milan Furniture Fair in 2007.

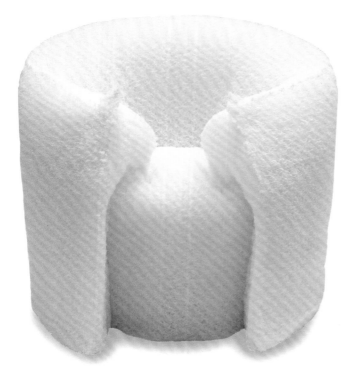

► Installation of *Pane* chairs hosted by Moroso in Milan, 2007

◄ ▲ *Pane* chair, 2003-06
Polyester elastomer fibre
Tokujin Yoshioka for Moroso, Cavalicco, Italy

Nendo
Cabbage chair, c.2008

Large quantities of paper are used for the production of pleated textiles, such as those used by fashion designer Issey Miyake for his beautiful garments. Normally this by-product is then discarded or recycled once it has served its manufacturing purpose. Nendo, however, used this waste paper at Issey Miyake's behest to create the beautiful *Cabbage* chair. The method used to create the design involved rolling the pleated paper into a cylinder and then making a vertical cut halfway down one side, and then carefully peeling back the layers one at the time – almost like leaves on a cabbage. The resulting design not only has a captivating fragile beauty but also accords with that old maxim "waste not, want not".

Cabbage chair, c.2008
Paper
Nendo, Tokyo, Japan

Naoto Fukasawa
Chair, 2007

In 2007, Vitra launched a new "Vitra Edition" collection that included specially commissioned pieces by some of the world's leading furniture designers. Among these, one of the most interesting creations was Naoto Fukasawa's *Chair*. A sculptural block of material, the *Chair* was produced in a variety of materials, including marble, redwood, acrylic, felt, wickerwork, concrete, attaché case metal and hay. This limited-editon collection of nine chairs was inspired by the work of the American psychologist, James J. Gibson who put forward the concept of "affordances", which centres on the relationship between animals (including humans) and their surrounding environments. Fukasawa believes that people are given "affordances" throughout their daily lives by the objects they encounter, often on a subliminal level. To engender this phenomenon even further Fukasawa adopted a form that was essentially a primitive, abstracted distillation of "chairness" that helped to emphasize the unique intrinsic qualities of the different materials used.

▲ Photograph showing the nine different variations of *Chair*, 2007

◄ *Chair*, 2007
Acrylic
Vitra, Weil am Rhein, Germany

Fernando & Humberto Campana
Shark & Dolphin chair, 2004 & *Alligator* chair, 2004

Fernando and Humberto Campana designed the *Alligator* and *Shark & Dolphin* banquete chairs in 2004. The limited edition designs are among a number of chairs made from plush animals serially produced in the brothers' São Paulo studio for the Moss Gallery in New York. The kitsch toy animals illustrate the Campanas' preference for using everyday, found materials and objects from Brazilian life and culture, including rubber hosing and string, which they then transform into richly decorative objects that deliberately play on the contrast between high and low cultures and technologies.

▼ *Alligator* chair, 2004
Stuffed toy animals, metal
Estudio Campana, São Paulo, Brazil

► *Shark & Dolphin* chair, 2004
Stuffed toy animals, metal
Estudio Campana, São Paulo, Brazil

Sebastian Brajkovic
Lathe VIII chair, 2008

Sebastian Brajkovic designed his first *Lathe* chair for his final project at the Design Academy Eindhoven in 2006. As with the rest of the Dutch designer's series of *Lathe* chairs and tables, *Lathe VIII* combines elements from the past and present. The chair's stretched nineteenth century style and embroidered pattern are inspired by a Photoshop tool that allows you to stretch pixels to any length. Produced in a limited edition, Brajkovic rotated historical chair forms to achieve the *Lathe's* stretched shape, before casting it in bronze.

Lathe VIII chair, 2008
Bronze with a nitric-acid burned patina, embroidered textile-covered upholstery
Sebastian Brajkovic, Amsterdam, The Netherlands

Giovanni Pagnotta
Vortex chair, 2006

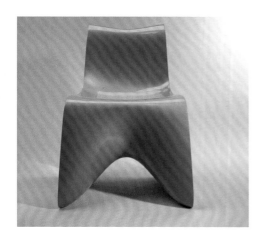

Giovanni Pagnotta studied architecture at the Parsons School of Design and later at Yale University, where he received the prestigious Eero Saarinen Memorial Scholarship. Since then, he has worked as a materials-led designer exploring the constructional possibilities offered by high-tech composites – such as carbon fibre – mainly in the development of furniture. As he notes, "What feeds my soul is the challenge of deciphering the secrets of a particular material and translating those discoveries into something unexpected and beautiful." Certainly his *Vortex* chair, made from a continuous loop of carbon fibre, pushes the furthermost structural boundaries of this remarkably lightweight yet incredibly strong material, and in so doing Pagnotta has also created a very beautiful object in its own right. A polyethylene variant of this design – known as the *Mi* chair – is also in production and is fully recyclable.

Vortex chair, 2006
Enamel-finished carbon fibre,
Self-produced

Patrick Jouin
Solid C2 chair, 2004

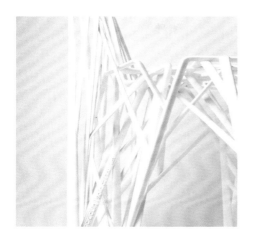

First exhibited at the "Maison & Objet" show in Paris in 2004, Patrick Jouin's *Solid* collection was produced in collaboration with MGX, the design division of Materialise N.V., a leading developer of rapid-prototyping techniques. For this design a process known as stereolithography was used, which essentially builds up the three-dimensional design from a computer model using layers of curable photopolymer resin. This process allows for the creation of highly complex shapes that would be unimaginable using any other method of manufacture. Essentially, the *Solid C2* chair was "grown" in a stereolithography machine, enabling Jouin to create a functional seating design from ribbon-like strands of resin that are woven together to form a complex structure sufficiently strong to bear the weight of a human body.

▲ Detail of *Solid C2* chair

► *Solid C2* chair, 2004
Epoxy resin
MGX by Materialise, Leuven, Belgium

Komplot Design
Nobody chair, 2007

Komplot Design was set up by Danish designers Poul Christiansen and Boris Berlin in 1987. Their 2007 design for this lightweight, stackable chair has the appearance of a piece of cloth draped over a chair, yet as the name suggests, there is "no body" underneath the material. The first industrially produced all-textile chair, *Nobody* is made of two layers of thermo-pressed PET felt, a completely recyclable material normally used for water bottles. Moulded in a single process using a technique borrowed from the car industry, the *Nobody* chair won the Best Nordic Product Design accolade in 2008.

▲ Design sketch of *Nobody* chair, 2007

▼ *Nobody* chair, 2007
Polymer fibre, PET felt mat
Hay, Horsens, Denmark

Satyendra Pakhalé
Fish chair, 2004

Describing himself as a cultural nomad, Satyendra Pakhalé believes that "Design is a universal poetry" and seeks through his work to find solutions that have an engaging cultural content. As happy to use state-of-the-art high-tech processes as much as age-old low-tech production methods, his work often has a strong sculptural quality as evinced by his *Fish* chair for Cappellini, the form of which was inspired by the Universally recognised abstract symbol for a fish. This small-scale and lightweight seating solution is made entirely of rotationally moulded thermoplastic, which means it can be used either indoors or outdoors.

Fish chair, 2004
Thermoplastic
Cappellini, Milan, Italy

Martin Azúa & Gerard Moliné
Flod stool, 2008

Designed by Martin Azúa and Gerard Moliné, the *Flod* stool hails a renaissance of sculptural forms in contemporary Spanish design. With its tilted seat and integrated footrest, this one-piece stool keeps the sitter's posture ergonomically correct and, therefore, provides a good level of comfort. Available in four muted colours – black, grey, red and yellow – this design is virtually indestructible and is eminently suitable for outdoor usage.

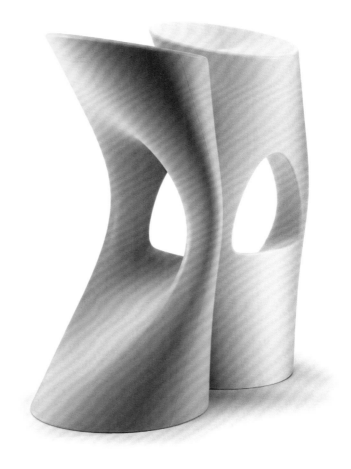

Flod stool, 2008
Rotationally moulded
polypropylene
Mobles 114, Barcelona, Spain

Konstanin Grcic
MYTO stacking chair, 2007

The German chemical company BASF invited Konstantin Grcic to design a product incorporating their newly developed Ultradur(R) High Speed plastic, the formula of which can be changed to make it either very flexible or robustly rigid. Combining state-of-the-art technology with sophisticated design, the resulting *MYTO* cantilevered chair uses the minimum amount of material to achieve the maximum effect.

MYTO stacking chair, 2007
Ultradur(R) High Speed plastic
Plank Collezioni, Ora, Italy

Jean-Marie Massaud
Terminal 1 daybed, 2008

The French designer Jean-Marie Massaud designed the fluid, graceful *Terminal 1* daybed to function as both an armchair and a chaise longue. Massaud established his first studio in 1996 before founding Studio Massaud in 2000, in the process expanding his practice from furniture and industrial design to include architecture and branding. This multidisciplinarity is evident in the architectural, landscaped quality of the chair in which the seat floats over four steel supports. *Terminal 1* is available in a variety of monochrome hues, with surface variation produced by the seat's shiny underside and matt varnished top.

Terminal 1 **daybed, 2008**
Matt varnished tubular steel, glossy
varnished polyurethane
B&B Italia, Novedrate, Italy

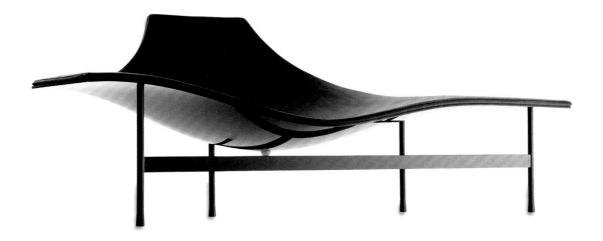

Thomas Heatherwick
Spun chair, 2010

The British designer Thomas Heatherwick designed the *Spun* chair in 2010 for the Italian manufacturer Magis. The highly sculptural chair looks like a spinning top, in which the user can either rock in a sideways motion, or spin around in a complete circle. The plastic chair is made by the rotational moulding process, its rippled surface making the chair look like it is moving even when stationary. In 2010 Heatherwick designed a limited edition spun steel and copper version of this visually compelling chair for the London gallery, Haunch of Venison.

Spun chair, 2010
Rotational-moulded polyethylene
Magis, Torre di Mosto, Italy

Brodie Neill
Reverb chair, 2009

Designed in 2009, the *Reverb* chair is made of a wire frame network of mirror-polished steel rods. The chair was designed by London-based, Australian designer Brodie Neill for the Apartment Gallery and shown during the London Design Festival in 2009. As its name indicates, the inspiration for this expressive, mushroom-shaped chair with its distinctive conical geometry comes from the reverberation of sound, a combination of technology and craftsmanship that is evident throughout the chair. Neill also produced a solid version of this design using nickel-plated sheet aluminium.

Reverb chair, 2009
Polished stainless steel rods
Brodie Neill, London, England

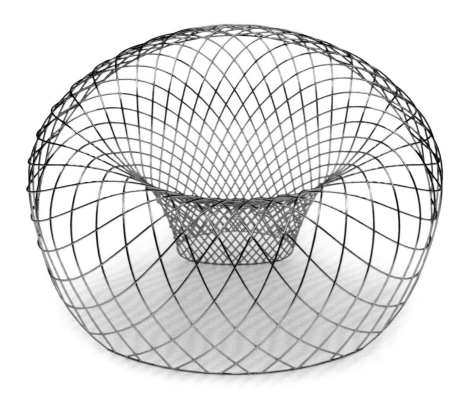

Tom Dixon & Artek Studio
Bambu chair, 2007

Launched in 2007, the *Bambu* chair – designed by Artek Studio, under the direction of Tom Dixon – reflected a new ecological direction in furniture design. Moulded from laminated bamboo, this chair was more environmentally sustainable than its wooden or plastic contemporaries because bamboo is a remarkably fast-growing and easily renewable natural resource. The design also possessed a notable physical lightness as well as a pleasing grain-like surface.

Bambu chair, 2007
Laminated bamboo
Artek, Helsinki, Finland

Ronan & Erwan Bouroullec
Steelwood chair, 2007

The *Steelwood* chair is a marriage of two traditional materials that are used to create a simple yet eye-catching design that is not only comfortable but is also intended to age more attractively than its plastic contemporaries – with the wood acquiring a delicate patina over time. The subtle curvature of the steel frame requires ten successive stamping stages in its production, and it is this element that gives the design its distinctively simple yet elegant aesthetic.

Steelwood chair, 2007
Beech, epoxy-painted steel
Magis, Torre di Mosto, Italy

Ronan & Erwan Bouroullec
Slow armchair, 2007

The French brothers Erwan and Ronan Bouroullec designed the *Slow* armchair in 2007. For this design they were inspired by the technological possibilities of new fabrics to combine strength with elasticity. Stretched over the tubular metal frame like a stocking, the translucent material maintains its shape to make a comfortable, supportive and lightweight chair. Available in a variety of colours and designed with an accompanying ottoman, the *Slow* chair's generous, welcoming shape echoes historical designs such as Eero Saarinen's *Womb* chair for Knoll from 1948

Slow armchair, 2007
Elasticated textile mesh, lacquered metal, tubular aluminium, textile-covered cushion
Vitra, Weil am Rhein, Germany

Ron Arad
Voido rocking chair, 2006 & *MT* rocking chair, 2005

In 2005 Ron Arad created the sculptural *MT* rocking chair for Driade using the rotational moulding process. He subsequently evolved its looping form into the *Voido* rocking chair the following year. Suitable for indoor or outdoor use, this serially produced design is manufactured using blow-moulding – a plastic-moulding process that allows for the creation of hollow plastic objects. These 21st century rocking chairs were realized using advanced computer-aided design technologies, which facilitate the creation of complex forms that are both sculptural and functional.

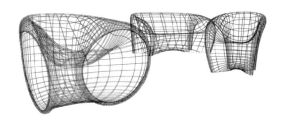

◀ *Voido* rocking chair, 2006
Blow-moulded polyethylene
Magis, Torre di Mosto, Italy

▼ *MT* rocking chair, 2005
Rotationally moulded polyethylene
Driade, Milan, Italy

▲ Computer-generated three-dimensional models of the *MT* rocking chair, c.2005

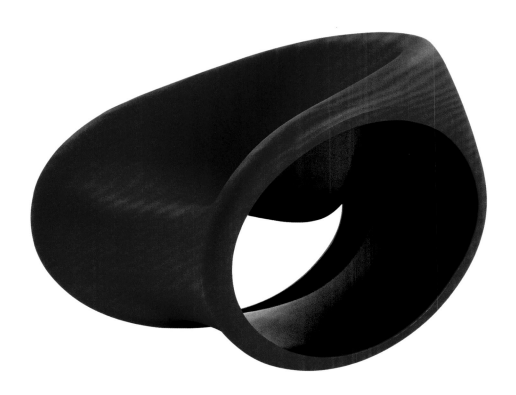

Greg Lynn
Ravioli chair, 2005

The American architect and theorist, Greg Lynn explores the possibilities of digital technology in the design and manufacture of his products, furniture and architecture projects. Designed in 2005, the biomorphic curves of the *Ravioli* chair play on the form of the conventional upholstered armchair, and display the blob-like forms characteristic of his computer-led architecture practice. The *Ravioli* chair was designed with an accompanying ottoman, and when joined together they create an architectural, landscaped form.

Ravioli chair, 2005
Glass-reinforced polyester,
textile-covered polyurethane foam
upholstery.
Vitra, Weil am Rhein, Germany

Ron Arad
Clover chair, 2007

The sculptural, organic-shaped *Clover* chair was designed by Ron Arad for the Italian manufacturer Driade in 2007. As its name suggests, Arad's design for the shape of the plastic chair takes its inspiration from the lucky four-leaf clover, a combination of nature and Pop that continues into the choice of colours available; white, green and orange. Made of polyethylene, the rotationally moulded monobloc chair is suitable for both indoor and outdoor use.

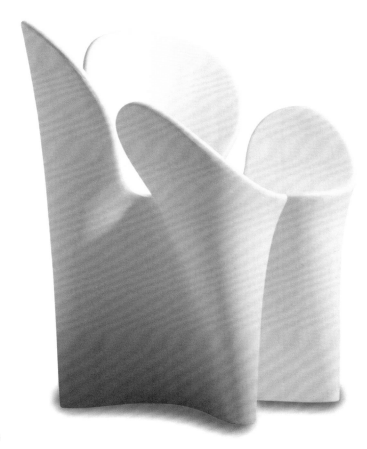

Clover chair, 2007
Rotationally moulded polyethylene
Driade, Piacenza, Italy

Edward Barber & Jay Osgerby
De La Warr chair, 2005

Edward Barber and Jay Osgerby originally designed this chair
site-specifically for the newly renovated De La Warr Pavilion
at Bexhill-On-Sea – a Modernist architectural masterpiece
overlooking the Sussex coastline designed by Erich
Mendelsohn and Serge Chermayeff in 1935. Known as the *De La
Warr* chair, the chair's fluid yet modernistic form was intended
to contrast with the severe and uncompromising rectilinearity
of the building. Another interesting feature of this design is
its distinctive skid back leg component, a response to the
designers' observation that most chairs are mainly seen from
the back yet all too often designers do not overly concern
themselves with the look of a chair's rear elevation.

De La Warr chair, 2005
Powder-coated aluminium, tubular
steel
Established & Co., London, UK

Ross Lovegrove
Supernatural chair, 2005 & *Supernatural* armchair, 2006

Ross Lovegrove's goal is to create "fat-free" designs that intelligently employ materials in a thoughtful and relevant way. For example, his stackable indoor/outdoor *Supernatural* chair was the result of his desire to lighten the mass of a chair's structure to produce a model weighing less than 2.5 kilograms. The form of the chair originated from the flow patterns of the polymer when it cools in the mould, resulting in a sufficiently rigid structure as well as a highly pleasing sensual organicism.

▲ *Supernatural* chair, 2005
Gas-injection-moulded, fibreglass-reinforced polypropylene
Moroso, Udine, Italy

▼ *Supernatural* armchair, 2006
Gas-injection-moulded, fibreglass-reinforced polypropylene
Moroso, Udine, Italy

Michael Young
4-a chair, 2010

Part of Michael Young's "Works in China" collection, the *4-a* chair was originally created for the SML restaurant group in Hong Kong. Fascinated by the production techniques used by Chinese firms, Young notes, "I realised that if I could capture the engineering skills employed by local industry and put that depth of knowledge in aluminium research into furniture design using a similar mass-produced nature, I could design a state-of-the-art and relevant chair." Fully recyclable, this durable chair offers a sustainable alternative to the ubiquitous plastic monobloc chair.

4-a chair, 2010
Aluminium, leather
DD-3, Hong Kong

Naoto Fukasawa
Déjà-vu chair, 2007

Japanese designer Naoto Fukasawa is renowned for his ability to infuse poetry into everyday objects. His *Déjà-vu* chair is a lyrical Postmodern homage to the ubiquitous, anonymously designed four-legged wooden chair. Although Fukasawa's design adopts the same construction as an ordinary chair, its choice of materials is a drastic departure from tradition; combining polished extruded aluminium legs and a polished die-cast aluminium seat with a backrest made of either oak, black or white ABS, or polished die-cast aluminium.

Déjà-vu chair, 2007
Extruded aluminium, die-cast
aluminium, injection-moulded
ABS or wood
Magis, Torre di Mosta, Italy

Naoto Fukasawa
Grande Papilio armchair, 2009

A sculpturally pleasing and visually unified design, the *Grande Papilio* is a twenty-first century reinterpretation and highly abstracted rendition of the historic wing chair. With its sensuous fluid lines, it invites the viewer to take a comforting seat and unwind in its cradling curves. It also swivels 360 degrees to further enhance its user experience, while a matching ottoman provides even further relaxation potential.

Grande Papilio **armchair, 2009**
Steel, aluminium, plastic, textile-covered upholstery
B&B Italia, Novedrate, Italy

Greg Benson & Jeff Taly
Cricket chair, 2010

Founded in 2003, Loll Design specialises in the manufacture of outdoor furniture made from recycled materials. For instance, its *Cricket* chair is made from sturdy ⅝ inch thick 100% recycled plastic, which requires no maintenance whatsoever, no matter how long it sits outside in the wind, rain or sun. This simple and practical chair with its slightly angled back is part of Loll Design's *Alfresco* collection (which includes five other chairs and six table options), which won the 2010 Innovative Green Design Award from *New York House* magazine.

Cricket chair, 2010
Recycled plastic
Loll Design, Duluth (MN), USA

Roger Conill Esteve
Benicassim chair, 2010

The dramatic *Benicassim* chair by the Spanish designer and blacksmith, Roger Conill Esteve looks as though it has just exploded violently and vividly recalls the artist Cornelia Parker's *Cold Dark Matter: An Exploded View* installation (1991) that was memorably comprised of suspended fragments from an exploded shed. Named after the Spanish resort that hosts a well-known music festival each summer, this chair certainly looks as though it has survived some devastating apocalyptic event and its resulting strong sculptural presence is, perhaps, a wry commentary on the increasing atomisation of our world. The *Benicassim* chair is produced in Oko's forge without any template so each example is unique.

Benicassim chair, 2010
Solid iron, sheet iron
Oko, Barcelona, Spain

KiBiSi
Shanghay chair, 2010

The *Shanghay* bench was specifically designed for the Danish Pavilion at the Shanghai World Expo 2010. Initially it was conceived as a continuous 264m long "social bench" that orbited the pavilion's inside and outside spaces. The project was a collaboration between the Copenhagen-based KiBiSi design group and the architectural firm, BIG and Jeppe Hein. KiBiSi's *Shanghay* chair was designed the same year and was similarly composed of four moulded plywood components that are folded to create a simple form that merges the legs with the seat section. Easy to disassemble and reassemble, the components come in a variety of colours thereby allowing the purchaser a degree of personal customization.

Shanghay chair, 2010
Painted moulded plywood
Hay, Horsens, Denmark

Martino Gamper
100 Chairs in a 100 Days, 2006-07

The Italian designer, Martino Gamper creates what can be best described as mutant chairs, remade from elements of existing chairs – many of which are acknowledged design classics – as well as other found elements including musical instruments, vehicles, lights and other odds and ends. Between 2006 and 2007, he made 100 chairs in 100 days, which were subsequently exhibited, to critical acclaim, in a large Victorian terraced house in London's Cromwell Place. These hybrid designs are essentially three-dimensional furniture collages that fuse designs from different periods together, lending the resulting series of chairs an engaging quirkiness and a refreshing Postmodern irreverence.

▲ *100 Chairs in a 100 Days* exhibition held at 5 Cromwell Place, London, 2007

▶ *Olympia* chair for *100 Chairs in a 100 Days*, 2007
Existing chairs
Martino Gamper, London, England

◀ *Omback* chair for *100 Chairs in a 100 Days*, 2007
Existing chairs
Martino Gamper, London, England

Clockwise: *Sonet Butterfly, Back Issue, Backside, Gymnastic* **chairs for** *100 Chairs in a 100 Days*, 2007
Existing chairs
Martino Gamper, London, England

Clockwise: *Black Skirt, Ch'Air No.9, Mono Suede, Arne Cubista* chairs for *100 Chairs in a 100 Days*, 2007
Existing chairs
Martino Gamper, London, England

Barber Osgerby
Tip Ton chair, 2011

Edward Barber and Jay Osgerby set up their own design studio in 1996 following their graduation from the Royal College of Art. Their *Tip Ton* chair, designed in 2011 for Vitra, is a lightweight, stackable, single material/single form chair that is injection-moulded in polypropylene. The chair's name refers to its two seating positions. *Tip Ton* has a forward tilt action, enabled by the angled bottom rail of the sled base that tips forward nine degrees to allow the user to lean forward in a more comfortable and ergonomically correct way.

Tip Ton chair, 2011
Polypropylene
Vitra, Weil am Rhein, Germany

Patricia Urquiola
Husk chair, 2011

The *Husk* chair was designed in 2011 by Patricia Urquiola, a Spanish designer who lives and works in Milan. Manufactured by B&B Italia, the chair's shell seat and back are made of moulded recycled plastic. It is available in a variety of sizes with either a spoked swivel or fixed rectangular base. The *Husk* chair is upholstered with soft padded cushions in either fabric or leather, the quilted design of which epitomises the chair's balance between soft curves and rigid geometry that is characteristic of Urquola's approach.

Husk chair, 2011
Recycled plastic, oak, textile-covered cushion
B&B Italia, Novedrate, Italy

Harri Koskinen
Lento chair, 2006

The Finnish designer, Harri Koskinen is one of the great form-givers of his generation of designers. His *Lento* chair designed for Artek reflects his ability to create simple yet attractive forms that have an underlying functional logic. The nipped-in waist of this understated seating design, for example, assists with the fabrication of the plywood seat section and helps avoid material deformation during the moulding process. The design's title in Finnish means "flight" and certainly the *Lento* has a physical and visual lightness.

Lento chair, 2006
Lacquered birch plywood,
laminated birch
Artek, Helsinki, Finland

Blasius Osko & Oliver Deichmann
Clip chair, 2006

This remarkable folding lounge chair was inspired by a small, foldable basket that Blasius Osko and Oliver Deichmann came across in a Bulgarian market, which had "single slats [that] were beaded on ropes to form two hinged surfaces, which could be transformed into a curved three-dimensional object." The designers subsequently honed this innovative mechanism to create their own highly original *Clip* chair, which when opened provides an ample seating space, and when closed creates an interesting sculptural object.

Clip chair, 2006
Lacquered wenge
Moooi, Breda, Netherlands

Niels Diffrient
Diffrient World office chair, 2009

Niels Diffrient is one of the world's most accomplished designers of ergonomic office seating. Having studied at the Cranbrook Academy of Art, he subsequently worked in Marco Zanuso's Milanese studio and then later for Henry Dreyfuss Associates, an industrial design consultancy renowned for its pioneering work in human factors design. In 1980, Diffrient established his own design office and has since designed numerous groundbreaking office chairs, including the ergonomically refined *Diffrient World* chair that incorporates a flexible but supportive form-sensing mesh seat and back, weighs just 25 pounds, is 97% recyclable and has only eight major elements meaning that far less raw materials and far fewer manufacturing processes are used in its manufacture.

Diffrient World
office chair, 2009
Steel, plastic,
elasticated mesh
Humanscale, New York, USA

Studio 7.5
Setu office chairs, 2009

Burkhard Schmitz, Claudia Plikat, and Carola Zwick founded a design partnership in 1992. Because of the recent fall of the Berlin Wall they had difficulty finding suitable accommodation, and briefly used a 7.5 ton truck as a mobile office instead – hence their studio's name. Since then the studio has become renowned for its development of high performance humancentric office seating, such as their *Setu* chairs with their flexible and responsive spine-echoing frames and their seats made of an elastomeric textile that readily conforms to the sitter's contours, thereby providing a high level of ergonomic comfort.

Setu office chairs, 2009
Aluminium, plastic, steel, elastomeric textile
Herman Miller, Zeeland (MI), USA

Naoto Fukasawa
Hiroshima armchair, 2008

Naoto Fukasawa has won numerous awards for his elegant understated designs that delicately synthesize the aesthetic sensibilities of East and West. They are born of his desire to transpose human consciousness into design; to create effortless products that can be used intuitively and spontaneously, or as he puts it "without thought". His *Hiroshima* chair reflects his goal of finding a natural and ideal solution to problem solving, with its familiar though pared-down form and its beautiful crafted detailing that satisfy both the hand and the eye.

Hiroshima armchair, 2008
Solid oak or birch
Maruni, Hiroshima, Japan

Industrial Facility
Branca armchair, 2010

The *Branca* chair was designed in 2010 by Sam Hecht, Kim Colin and Ippei Matsumoto of the London-based practice Industrial Facility. The design is inspired by the irregular growth of tree branches – *branca* is the Italian word for branch. Its elegant simplicity belies the complex manufacture, which combines robotic CNC machinery with hand-shaping and finishing by the Italian manufacturer Mattiazzi's craftsmen. *Branca* won the furniture category in the Design Musuem's Brit Insurance Design of the Year awards in 2011. Industrial Facility has subsequently designed the accompanying *Branca* table for Mattiazzi.

Branca chair, 2010
Ash
Mattiazzi, San Giovanni al Natisone, Italy

Ronan & Erwan Bouroullec
Worknest office chair, 2006

The Bouroullec brothers have created numerous notable designs over the past decade, some of which are manufactured by the progressive furniture manufacturing company, Vitra. One of their most accomplished designs is their *Worknest* office chair, which was born of the desire to create a task chair that unlike other models did not employ, as the Bouroullecs put it, a visual language "with obvious references to robots and technology" but was instead more humancentric with its soft accommodating curves and skin-like textile covering.

Worknest office chair, 2006
Aluminium, fibreglass-reinforced polyamide, upholstery-covered polyurethane foam
Vitra, Weil am Rhein, Switzerland

Yves Béhar & Fuseproject
Sayl office chair, 2010

Designed by Yves Béhar and his Fuseproject studio, *Sayl* is an affordable, ergonomic line of office chairs. The award-winning chair's frameless back and vertical support is inspired by the Golden Gate suspension bridge in San Francisco, where Fuseproject is based. *Sayl's* name is a play on the sailing ships that pass under the bridge and the "y" a reference to the shape of the back support that adapts to the individual's shape and movements. In this design, Béhar aimed to minimize the amount of materials and components used, an approach he calls "Eco-Dematerialization".

Sayl office chair, 2010
Injection-moulded urethane back, steel, textile-covered foam upholstery
Herman Miller, Zeeland (MI), USA

Rolf Sachs
Spitting Image chair and armchair, 2008 & *a,b,c* chair, 2008

Rolf Sachs creates furniture, lighting and objects that have an almost alchemic quality. Indeed, his West London studio is more like an ideas laboratory than a conventional design office, while his resulting designs have an engaging personality that is born from his emotive approach to design. As he explains, "I want every aspect of my collections to have warmth, integrity and, of course, always character. I aim to create designs that demonstrate abstract, rather than decorative ideas, governed by emotion and intellect." His *Spitting Image* chairs made of amber-coloured cast resin and his *a,b,c* chair executed in grey slate quarried in Kirby-in-Furness are reinterpretations of what Sachs' describes as the "Frankfurt Administration Chair", a model informed by functional requirements dating from the 1930s that is, as he put it, "a model of practicality for a mercantile society".

▶ *a,b,c* chair, 2008
Slate
Rolf Sachs, London, England

◀▶ *Spitting Image* chair &
armchair, 2008
Cast urethane resin
Rolf Sachs, London, England

Rolf Sachs
Second Thoughts armchair, 2009 &
Dirty Thoughts armchair, 2009

◄ *Second Thoughts* armchair,
2009
Carbon-fibre, Kevlar, bonding resin
Rolf Sachs, London, England

▼ *Dirty Thoughts* armchair, 2009
Carbon-fibre, Kevlar, bonding
resin, paint
Rolf Sachs, London, England

For these limited edition chairs, Rolf Sachs draped resin-soaked carbon-fibre and Kevlar over everyday plastic garden chairs to dramatic effect. The resulting imprints thanks to the inherent strength of these lightweight materials provided the chairs' self-supporting structures. Paradoxically something so ubiquitous and emotionally sterile as a mass-produced plastic monobloc chair has essentially provided a mould for these limited edition designs that have an inherent artistic preciousness and as Sachs puts it, "a soul". First shown in 2010 in an exhibition entitled "Flawless/Imperfection" at the Studio Visconti in Milan, the *Dirty Thoughts* chair with its splashes of paint makes a nostalgic reference back to the school art room, while its roughness and imperfections give it a personality and character as well as a unique individuality.

Niels van Eijk & Miriam van der Lubbe
M-Furniture listening chair & armchair, 2011

The *M-Furniture* collection was created for the interior spaces
of the Muziekgebouw (music hall) in Eindhoven, which was
re-designed by Niels van Eijk and Miriam van der Lubbe in
collaboration with Philips Ambient Experience Design in
2011. As an award-winning, entirely site-specifically designed
project, Van Eijk and Van der Lubbe not only designed the
furniture and fittings for the building but also special carpets,
crockery, clothing and even cufflinks. The *M-Furniture*
collection comprised an armchair, a bench, a sofa, a stool, a
love seat and a listening chair with a music-emitting hood.
All of these pieces were based on a modular system, the
distinctive elements of which were fittingly inspired by the
flight cases used to safely transport musical instruments.

► Foyer area of the Muziekgebouw
in Eindhoven, 2011

◄ ▲ *M-Furniture* listening chair &
armchair, 2011
Lacquered fibreglass, textile-
covered polyurethane foam
upholstery
Lensvelt, Breda, Netherlands

Doshi Levien
Capo chair, 2011

Designed in 2011, the *Capo* (leader) chair is the first collaboration between Cappellini and Doshi Levien, a London-based studio set up by the Anglo-Indian couple Nipa Doshi and Jonathan Levien in 2000. The chair's cantilevered arms and tall, broad back envelops the sitter and is designed to endow them with an appearance of boss-like importance. Inspired by the image of a well-dressed gentleman in a felt hat, the chair is available in a variety of colours and upholstery options including leather and felt.

Capo chair, 2011
Tubular steel, felt
Cappellini, Mariano Comense, Italy

Dror Benshetrit
Tron armchair, 2011

Born in Tel Aviv and educated at the Design Academy
Eindhoven in the Netherlands, in 2002 Dror Benshetrit set up
his own practice in New York. His design for the *Tron* armchair
was inspired by the 2011 remake of the groundbreaking
1980s Disney film. Its jagged surfaces combine the form of
a traditional club chair with the angular terrain of the film's
off-grid "Outlands". Made entirely of recycled plastic (linear
polyethylene) in a single piece, the rotational moulded chair
was the result of a partnership between Cappellini and Walt
Disney Signature.

Tron armchair, 2011
Rotational-moulded recycled
polyethylene
Cappellini, Mariano Comense, Italy

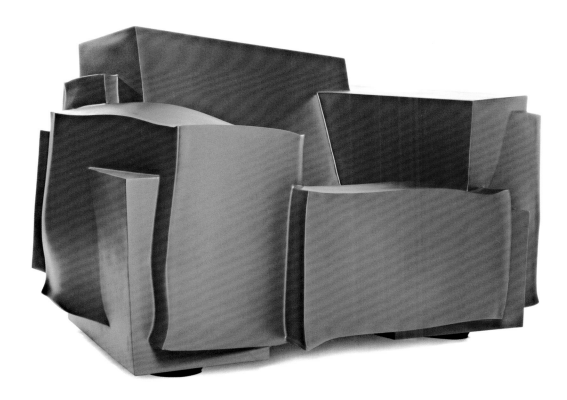

Studio Drift
Ghost Queen Chair, 2011

Ralph Nauta and Lonneke Gordijn of Studio Drift based the concept of their *Ghost Collection* on the forms derived from earlier historic seating precedents. As they explain, "During our shape research we stumbled upon the Dutch Queens' chair collection and learned about a fascinating history", that showed the powerful link between the form of a chair and its user's status. The milky spectral form encased in the *Ghost Queen Chair* has been created using a unique three-dimensional technique to create a subsurface "drawing" set within the solid acrylic structure of the chair.

Ghost Queen Chair, 2011
Acrylic
Studio Drift, Amsterdam, the Netherlands (for Patrick Brillet Fine Art, London)

Zaha Hadid & Patrik Schumacher
Z-Chair, 2011

Z-Chair, 2011
Polished stainless steel
Sawaya & Moroni, Milan, Italy

Over the last three decades, Zaha Hadid has created buildings and objects that have a strong dynamism and distinctive gestural quality. Her *Z-Chair* – co-designed with Patrik Schumacher for Sawaya & Moroni – is a looping zig-zig of polished steel that has a remarkable sense of fluidity and energetic tension and as such echoes the calligraphic quality of her two-dimensional sketches. Produced as a limited-edition of twenty-four chairs, the *Z-Chair* is a visually striking piece that as its manufacturer notes reflects on the "discourse between form and function, elegance and utility, differentiation and continuity". Its smooth curves contrast with its angular corners, while its profile courses from wide gleaming surfaces to thin streams of metal, which give the overall composition a gravity-defying sculptural presence.

Werner Aisslinger
Chair Farm, 2012

Chair Farm, 2012
Bamboo
Werner Aisslinger, Berlin, Germany

At the Milan Furniture Fair in 2012, one of the most intriguing exhibits was Werner Aisslinger's *Chair Farm* installation at Ventura Lambrate, which speculated on the possibility of quite literally growing a chair. Using a Meccano-style metal framework, living bamboo was encouraged to grow into a chair form inside a heated greenhouse. The resulting chair might be a little unrefined, yet even given this, it sends a powerful and thought-provoking message about the nature of production and consumption. Certainly this utopian vision projected a new concept for the future of design that is towards the increasing use of renewable materials and more sustainable local solutions that have an underlying eco-responsibility. So go on: "Plant yourself a chair..."

Index

Bibliography

Selected Bibliography

Bröhan, T. & Berg, T., *Avantgarde Design 1880–1930*, Taschen GmbH, Cologne, 1994

Bruchhäuser, A., *Der Kragstuhl*, Stuhlmuseum Burg Beverungen, Berlin, 1986

Byars, M., *The Design Encyclopedia*, Museum of Modern Art, New York, 2004

Decelle, P., Hennebert, D. & Loze, P., *L'Utopie du Tout Plastique 1960-1973*, Fondation Pour L'Architecture, Brussels, 1994

Eidelberg, M. (ed.), *Design 1935–1960: What Modern Was*, Le Musée des Arts Décoratifs de Montreal/ Harry N. Abrams, Inc., New York, 1991

Fiell, C. & Fiell, P, *1000 Chairs*, Taschen GmbH, Cologne, 1997

Fiell, C. & Fiell, P, *Design Now*, Taschen GmbH, Cologne, 2007

Fiell, C. & Fiell, P, *Design of the 20th Century*, Taschen GmbH, Cologne, 1999

Fiell, C. & Fiell, P, *Designing the 21st Century*, Taschen GmbH, Cologne, 2002

Fiell, C. & Fiell, P, *Domus* (Volumes I-XII), Taschen GmbH, Cologne, 2006

Fiell, C. & Fiell, P., *Industrial Design A-Z*, Taschen GmbH, Cologne, 2000

Fiell, C. & Fiell, P., *Plastic Dreams: Synthetic Visions in Design*, Fiell Publishing Limited, London, 2009

Larrabee, E. & Vignelli, M., *Knoll Design*, Harry N. Abrams, Inc., New York, 1981

Nelson, G., *Chairs*, Whitney Publications Inc., New York, 1953

Neuhart, J. & M., Eames, R., *Eames Design: The Work of the Office of Charles & Ray Eames*, Harry N. Abrams, Inc., New York, 1989

Oda, Noritsugu, *Danish Chairs*, Korinsha Press, Tokyo, 1996

Olivares, J., *A Taxonomy of Office Chairs*, Phaidon Press, London, 2011

Ostergard, D., *Bent Wood and Metal Furniture: 1850–1946*, The American Federation of Arts, New York, 1987

Remmele, M., et al., *Verner Panton: The Collected Works*, Vitra Design Museum, 2001

Vegesack, A. von, *Deutsche Stahlrohr-Möbel: 650 Modelle aus Katalogen*, Bangert Verlag, Munich, 1986

Exhibition Catalogues

Library of Congress & Vitra Design Museum, *The Work of Charles and Ray Eames: A Legacy of Invention*, Harry N. Abrams, Inc., New York, 2005

Museum of Modern Art, *Italy: The New Domestic Landscape*, Museum of Modern Art, New York, 1972

Die Neue Sammlung, Staatliches Museum für Angewandte Kunst, *Plastics + Design*, Die Neue Sammlung, Staatliche Museum für angewandte Kunst, Munich, 1997

Vitra Design Museum, *100 Masterpieces from the Vitra Design Museum Collection*, Vitra Design Museum, Weil am Rhein, 1996

The Whitechapel Art Gallery, *Modern Chairs: 1918–1970*, Lund Humphries, London, 1970

Picture credits

ARFLEX, MILAN: 505 (both);ARPER, MONASTI ER DI TREVISO: 696, 697; ARTEK, HELSINKI: 288 (bottom), 334, 716 (both), 717, 738; ARTCURIAL, BRIEST: 482 (bottom); ARTIFORT, MAASTRICHT: Front Cover, 292 (both), 406, 414, 419 (both), 435, 482 (top), 484 (bottom), 485, 668 (both), 682 (both); B&B ITALIA, NOVEDRATE: 713, 728, 737; BBB EMMABONCINA, SPILIMBERGO: 460, 510 (both), 511, 512, 513; BENT KROGH, SKANDERBORG: 528 (both); B-LINE, VICENZA: 463, 470 (both); BLÅ STATION, ÅHUS: 683; BLOOMBERG, AMSTERDAM: 285 (left + bottom), 372 (both), 445, 475, 546 (top), 547; BONHAMS, LONDON: 413 (top), 507, 560, 616; BRODIE NEILL, LONDON: 715; CAPPELLINI, MARIANO COMENSE: 478, 602, 607 (both), 619, 636, 652, 664, 665, 710 (both), 752, 753; CASSINA, MEDA: 349 (bottom), 377, 378 (both), 379, 410, 534 (both), 539 (bottom), 542, 546 (bottom), 584 (top); CITY FURNITURE, GHENT: 420 (both); CHRISTIE'S IMAGES, LONDON: 21, 27, 28, 35, 42, 43, 45, 64, 65, 66, 67, 68, 70, 79, 84 (bottom), 85, 86–87, 88 (both images), 89 (bottom), 92, 93 (both images), 96, 104, 105 (both images), 109, 115, 116 (both images), 121, 130, 132 (bottom), 138 (top), 140, 141 (bottom), 141 (top), 142 (bottom), 147, 151, 153 (both images), 155, 163, 166, 167 (bottom), 175 (bottom), 181, 205, 216, 217, 219 (both), 224, 236, 237 (bottom), 238, 242, 243 (bottom), 244, 250 (bottom), 251, 254 (both), 262, 263, 264, 282, 286 (bottom), 289, 295 (bottom), 300 (right), 317, 321, 336 (bottom), 337, 339, 343 (top), 348 (bottom), 363, 380, 383 (right), 393 (bottom), 396, 397 (all), 402, 404 (bottom), 413 (bottom), 431 (top), 432, 481, 501, 522, 523, 529 (right), 535 (bottom), 536, 541 (top), 545 (bottom), 590, 591 (both), 596, 597 (bottom), 600, 602, 613 (bottom); DOROTHEUM, VIENNA: 2, 40 (both images), 80 (bottom), 94, 97, 100, 110, 148, 162, 184, 211 (bottom), 299, 300, 320, 352, 373 (right); DRIADE, MILAN: 649, 670 (top), 687, 721 (both), 723 (bottom); EDRA, PERIGNANO: 629, 672, 673; EMECO, HANOVER: 232; ENGELBRECHTS, COPENHAGEN: 332 (bottom left + middle right), 437 (both); ERCOL FURNITURE LTD, PRINCES RISBOROUGH: 358 (left); ESTABLISHED & SONS, LONDON: 724 (both); ESTUDIO CAMPANA, SÃO PAULO: 703 (both); FIELL ARCHIVE, LONDON (non-archival images: photographer: PAUL CHAVE): 6, 16–17, 24, 25, 30 (top), 32, 36 (top), 39 (right), 50, 72 (left), 73, 95 (both images), 106 (both images), 107, 118 (top), 119 (left), 128 (left), 134 (top), 140, 142 (top), 160, 161 (top), 174 (courtesy of David Tatham), 182, 183 (left), 183 (right) 207 (courtesy of David Tatham), 226 (both), 230 (both), 231, 233 (both), 258 (all images), 259 (left), 274, 284 (Courtesy of David Tatham), 288 (top), 297 (top), 298 (top), 305 (top), 326, 333 (top), 341, 345 (both), 358 (right), 359 (both), 365 (both), 368, 369 (both), 385 (bottom), 395, 398, 409 (bottom left + right), 426, 427 (both), 428, 436 (top), 443 (top), 446 (Courtesy of Graham Mancha), 447 (top), 448, 462 (top), 464, 465, 466 (photo: Francis Jacoby – Courtesy of Philippe Decelle/Plasticarium, Brussels), 467 (bottom – photo: Francis Jacoby – Courtesy of Philippe Decelle/Plasticarium, Brussels), 467 (top), 468 (photo: Francis Jacoby – Courtesy of Philippe Decelle/Plasticarium, Brussels), 469 (photo: Francis Jacoby – Courtesy of Philippe Decelle/Plasticarium, Brussels), 479 (photo: Francis Jacoby – Courtesy of Philippe Decelle/Plasticarium, Brussels), 484 (top), 487 (bottom), 490, 491, 499 (both), 502, 503, 506, 514, 517, 518, 519 (both), 530 (Courtesy of Daniel Ostroff Collection), 531 (top), 532 (photo: Francis Jacoby – Courtesy of Philippe Decelle/Plasticarium, Brussels), 533 (photo: Francis Jacoby – Courtesy of Philippe Decelle/Plasticarium, Brussels), 540 (top), 541 (bottom), 554 (both), 557, 558 (both), 570, 571 (top), 576 (bottom – photo: Anthony Oliver), 578, 580 (left), 581, 584 (bottom – photo: Francis Jacoby – Courtesy of Philippe Decelle/Plasticarium, Brussels), 585 (both), 595 (photo: Francis Jacoby – Courtesy of Philippe Decelle/Plasticarium, Brussels), 608 (left), 615 (both), 617, 618, 620, 626, 627 (photo: Francis Jacoby – Courtesy of Philippe Decelle/Plasticarium, Brussels), 653 (bottom left + bottom right), 684 (both); FJORDFIESTA, MOLDE: 388 (bottom); FREDERICIA FURNITURE A/S, FREDERICIA: 246 (both), 399; FRITZ HANSEN, ALLERØD: 41 (both images), 194 (both), 195, 196 (both), 197 (both), 215, 248 (both), 249 (both), 285 (top), 346 (both), 347 (both), 360, 361 (all), 362 (all), 421 (both), 524 (both), 608 (right top + right bottom); GALERIE HISTORISMUS, BRUSSELS: 18, 31 (left), 23, 46 (left), 52, 53, 54, 55 (both images), 56 (both images), 57, 58, 59, 60, 61 (both images), 62, 63, 74 (both images), 75 (both images), 76 (right), 81 (bottom), 101, 102 (both images), 122, 123, 149 (both), 307 (both); GEORGE SOWDEN, MILAN: 594 (top); GIOVANNI PAGNOTTA, NEW YORK: 706 (both); GRAHAM MANCHA (www.mancha.demon.co.uk): 451 (both); GUFRAM, TURIN: 531; HARRIS LINDSAY, LONDON: 245 (photo: Mark French), 389; HARRIS LINDSAY, LONDON/KUNSTINDUSTRIMUSEET, COPENHAGEN: 20, 47; HASLAM & WHITEWAY, LONDON: 34, 36 (bottom), 38, 39 (left); HAY, HORSENS: 708, 709; HERMAN MILLER, ZEELAND: 330, 331, 659 (both), 741, 745 (both); HILLE, HIGH WYCOMBE: 529 (left), 560 (top); HISTORICAL DESIGN, NEW YORK: 31, 152, 171 (top), 186 (both images), 187, 294, 371 (top), 520, 521; HUMANSCALE, NEW YORK: 651 (both), 740; IKEA, ÄLMHULT: 640; JANE ATFIELD, LONDON: 628; JASPER MORRISON, LONDON: 611; JURGEN BEY/STUDIO MAKKINK & BEY, ROTTERDAM: 641 (bottom); KÄLLEMO, VÄRNAMO: 218, 582, 593, 625 (both), 639, 676, 677 (both); KARTELL, NOVIGLIO: 408, 409 (top left), 556, 632, 633 (photo: James Moore), 638 (both), 647 (both), 666 (both), 667 (both); KI, GREEN BAY: 577; KIBISI, COPENHAGEN: 731 (both); KNOLL INTERNATIONAL, NEW YORK: 279 (both), 344, 390, 391 (both), 609 (bottom); LA PALMA, CADONEGHE: 656 (both), 692 (both); LANGE PRODUCTION, COPENHAGEN: 458 (both), 459; LENSVELT, BREDA: 750 (both), 751; LILLIAN KIESLER, NEW YORK: 237 (top); LOLL DESIGN, DULUTH: 729; MAGIS, TORRE DI MOSTO: 634 (top), 646 (both), 653 (top), 654, 658 (both), 680 (both), 681 (both), 688, 689 (both), 714, 718 (both), 720, 727 (both); MAISON GERARD, NEW YORK: 113, 114 (bottom), 117, 118 (bottom), 120; MARK BRAZIER-JONES, BUNTINGFORD: 606 (both), 622, 623; MARTINO GAMPER, LONDON: 732, 733 (both), 734 (all), 735 (all); MARUNI, HIROSHIMA: 742 (all); MATHIAS BENGTSSON, LONDON: 671 (top); MATTEOGRASSI, GIUSSANO: 690; MATTIAZZI, SAN GIOVANNI AL NATISONE: 743; MAX DESIGN, BAGNARIA ARSA: 694, 695; MEMPHIS SRL, MILAN: 597; MICHAEL YOUNG, HONG KONG: 726 (both); MOBLES 114, BARCELONA: 711 (both); MODERNITY, STOCKHOLM: 319 (left);MOOOI, AMERSTERDAM: 662 (both), 674 (all), 675, 686 (both), 739; MOROSO, UDINE: 724 (both); NANNA DITZEL, COPENHAGEN: 403 (both); NENDO, TOKYO: 700, 701; OBJEKTO, SÃO PAULO: 386, 387 (both); ONE-OFF LTD, LONDON: 642; PATRICK JOUIN, PARIS: 707 (both); PERIMETER, PARIS: 415 (both); PHILLIPS DE PURY & COMPANY, LONDON: 77 (bottom), 80 (top right), 125, 126, 127 (bottom), 128 (right), 129, 135, 136, 138 (bottom), 152 (bottom), 158–159, 164, 168, 169, 176, 180, 185 (right), 201 (top), 202 (left), 206 (both), 208–209 (both images), 210, 227, 235 (top), 259 (right), 260, 261, 266, 271, 276 (bottom), 277, 293 (both), 316 (both), 318 (bottom), 371 (bottom), 393 (top), 405, 471 (bottom), 472, 483, 487, 498, 520 (top), 553, 566, 567, 572, 573, 574, 589, 610, 612, 613 (top), 631 (bottom), 671 (bottom), 678, 679 (both); PIIROINEN, SALO: 423; PLANK COLLEZIONI, ORA: 712; PLASTICARIUM, BRUSSELS: 496 (both), 497, 500, 552; POLTRONOVA, MONTALE: 589 (top); PP MØBLER, ALLERØD: 461; PRO FEEL DESIGN, ESPOO: 450; QUITTENBAUM, MUNICH: 177, 178, 247, 267, 429 (right), 559; RMN – COLLECTION OF MUSÉE D'ORSAY, PARIS: 48 (photo: R. G. Ojeda), 49 (photo: Hervé Lewandowski); ROGER CONILL ESTEVE, BARCELONA: 730; ROLF SACHS, LONDON: 746, 747, 748, 749; ROSS LOVEGROVE/STUDIO X, LONDON (photo: John Ross): 630 (both), 657; RYBO, ØYSTESE: 418;SAWAYA & MORONI, MILAN: 663 (both), 755 ; SEBASTIAN BRAJKOVIC, AMSTERDAM: 704, 705; SNOWCRASH, STOCKHOLM: 645 (both); SOTHEBY'S PICTURE LIBRARY, LONDON: 26, 29, 37, 44, 71, 72 (right), 83, 90, 91, 112, 119 (right), 133 (bottom), 137 (bottom), 139, 143, 145 (bottom), 146, 150, 234, 286 (top), 287, 290 (bottom), 291, 301 (bottom), 319 (bottom), 322 (both), 370 (bottom), 375, 411, 422, 430, 431 (bottom), 433, 540 (bottom), 543, 562, 565, 589 (bottom), 594 (bottom), 637; STANZA DEL RE, MILAN: 33, 98, 103; STOELCKER, ETTENHEIM: 192, 193 (bottom); STUDIO DRIFT, AMSTERDAM/PATRICK BRILLET LTD, LONDON: 754 (both); SWEDESE MÖBLER, VAGGERYD: 312, 313, 669 (both); TEJO REMY, UTRECHT: 624 (top); TENDO JAPAN, TENDO: 452, 494, 495; THAYER COGGIN, HIGH POINT: 550 (top); THE ISAMU NOGUCHI FOUNDATION AND GARDEN MUSEUM, NEW YORK: 400, 401, 444; THOMAS FEICHTNER, VIENNA: 691 (both); THONET GMBH, FRANKENBERG: 33 (top), 124 (top), 188 (top); TOKUJIN YOSHIOKA STUDIO, TOKYO: 670 (bottom), 698 (both), 699; TOLIX, AUTUN: 203; TORSTEN BRÖHAN: 144; V&A IMAGES, LONDON: 32 (left); VARIÉR FURNITURE, SKODJE: 526 (both), 527 (both); VITRA, WEIL AM RHEIN: 564, 643, 648, 650, 685, 702 (both), 719 (both), 722 (both), 736, 744; VITTORIO BONACINA, COMO: 440 (both), 441 (both); VON ZEZSCHWITZ KUNST UND DESIGN GMBH, MUNICH: 179, 333 (bottom), 592; WERNER AISSLINGER, BERLIN: 756, 757; WHITECHAPEL ART GALLERY, LONDON: 164 (right); WRIGHT, CHICAGO: 30 (bottom), 69 (bottom), 76 (left), 78, 81 (top), 82, 131, 134 (bottom), 156, 165, 171 (bottom), 172, 173, 175 (top), 188, 189, 190, 191, 198, 199, 201 (bottom), 204, 212, 213, 214 (bottom), 220, 221, 222 (both), 223, 228 (bottom), 229, 235 (bottom), 240 (both), 241, 252 (left), 253, 255, 256 (left), 257 (bottom), 265, 268, 269, 270, 272, 273, 275, 278, 280, 283, 296 (left), 298 (bottom), 302, 303 (bottom), 304, 305 (bottom), 306, 308 (bottom), 309, 310, 311, 314, 315 (both), 318 (top), 323, 324, 325, 327 (both), 328, 329 (both), 335 (bottom), 338, 340, 342, 343 (bottom), 349 (top), 350, 351, 353, 354, 355, 356 (both), 357, 364, 366, 367, 374, 376, 381, 382 (bottom), 384, 385 (top), 388 (top), 394, 404 (top), 412, 416, 417, 424 (both), 425 (both), 434, 442, 443 (bottom), 447 (bottom), 449, 453, 454, 455, 456, 457, 462, 471 (top), 474, 476, 477, 480, 486, 488 (both), 489, 492, 493 (both), 504, 508, 509, 525, 537, 538, 539 (top), 544–545 (main), 548 (both), 549 (bottom), 550 (bottom), 551, 555, 561, 563, 568, 569, 571 (bottom), 575, 580 (right), 586, 587 (both), 588, 589, 601, 604, 605, 624 (bottom), 631 (top), 634 (bottom), 635 (both), 644; XO, SERVON: 614 (both); ZANOTTA, MILAN: 438, 439, 473, 661; Additional draft entries researched & supplied by Catharine Rossi: pages: 278, 279, 288, 289, 298, 315, 320, 321, 325, 348, 349, 350, 351, 356, 358, 359, 370, 371, 372, 376, 382, 383, 386, 398, 411, 462, 463, 470, 471, 472, 473, 478, 481, 498, 499, 500, 501, 513, 530, 542, 566, 594, 595, 596, 597, 600, 601, 610, 611, 613, 631, 634, 636, 637, 643, 650, 651, 657, 658, 660, 662, 666, 680, 703, 705, 709, 713, 714, 715, 719, 722, 723, 736, 737, 743, 745, 752, 753

Acknowledgements

We would like to offer our heartfelt thanks to everyone involved in this project, including Jennifer Tilston and Isabel Wilkinson for their excellent picture researching skills, Dominic Burr for his graphic design layout and his good-natured can-do attitude, Catharine Rossi for her editorial research, Alison Tutton for her cover design, Gemma Maclagan-Ram for her proofreading, Paul Chave for his new photography, and of course all the many designers, manufacturers, collectors, dealers, auction houses, and image libraries that have made this enormous project possible. With extra special thanks to:

Richard Wright of Wright, Chicago
Roberto Polo of Galerie Historismus, Brussels
Philippe Decelle of Plasticarium, Brussels
Dr Gerti Draxler of Dorotheum, Vienna
David Tatham of David Tatham Modern Design, London
Chiara & Giovanni Renzi of Stanza del Re, Milan
Joanna Ling & Sue Daly of Sotheby's Picture Library, London
Laura Nixey of Christie's Images, London
Michael Whiteway of Haslam & Whiteway, London
Christopher Knight of Maison Gérard, New York
Denis Gallion & Daniel Morris of Historical Design Inc., New York
Patrick Brillet of The Apartment Gallery, London
The Isamu Noguchi Foundation and Garden Museum, New York
Arthur Floss of Quittenbaum, Munich
Fiona McGovern of Phillips de Pury, London
Dr Graham Dry of Von Zezschwitz, Munich
Andrew Duncanson, Isaac Pineus and Maria Wermelin of Modernity, Stockholm
Patricia Keurentjes of Bloomberry, Amsterdam

Structure of the Book

The book contains 30 chapters covering all topics—from basic to advanced—in JavaFX. Chapters are arranged in an order that aids you to quickly learn JavaFX. I have used an incremental approach to teach JavaFX, assuming no prior GUI development knowledge. Each chapter starts with a section introducing the topic to be discussed in the chapter. Each section contains a bit of background of the features being discussed, followed with code snippets and a complete program.

What You Will Learn

This book will help you to learn:

- What JavaFX 8 is and its history

- How to develop rich-client desktop applications using JavaFX 8

- How to use properties, collections, colors, and styles

- How to use controls and handle events to build modern GUI applications

- How to use advanced controls such as TreeView, TableView, and TreeTableViev.

- How to access web pages in JavaFX applications

- How to draw 2D and 3D shapes and apply effects and transformations

- How to create animations and charts using the JavaFX 8 APIs

- How to add audios and videos to your applications

- How to create GUIs in JavaFX using FXML

- How to provide the printing capabilities using the JavaFX Print API

Who Is This Book for?

Learn JavaFX 8 was written for Java developers, with beginning to intermediate level Java skills, who want to learn how to develop modern desktop GUI applications using JavaFX 8.

Source code for this book may be downloaded from `www.apress.com/9781484211434`; errata can be submitted and viewed via the same link.

Please direct all your questions and comments for the author to `ksharan@jdojo.com`.

CHAPTER 1

■ ■ ■

Getting Started

In this chapter, you will learn:

- What JavaFX is

- The history of JavaFX

- How to write your first JavaFX application

- How to use the NetBeans Integrated Development Environment to work with a JavaFX application

- How to pass parameters to a JavaFX application

- How to launch a JavaFX application

- The life cycle of a JavaFX application

- How to terminate a JavaFX Application

What Is JavaFX?

JavaFX is an open source Java-based framework for developing rich client applications. It is comparable to other frameworks on the market such as Adobe Flex and Microsoft Silverlight. JavaFX is also seen as the successor of Swing in the arena of graphical user interface (GUI) development technology in Java platform. The JavaFX library is available as a public Java application programming interface (API). JavaFX contains several features that make it a preferred choice for developing rich client applications:

- JavaFX is written in Java, which enables you to take advantage of all Java features such as multithreading, generics, and lambda expressions. You can use any Java editor of your choice, such as NetBeans, to author, compile, run, debug, and package your JavaFX application.

- JavaFX supports data binding through its libraries.

- JavaFX code can be written using any Java virtual machine (JVM)-supported scripting languages such as Visage, Groovy, and Scala.

- JavaFX offers two ways to build a user interface (UI): using Java code and using FXML. FXML is an XML-based scriptable markup language to define a UI declaratively. Oracle provides a tool called Scene Builder, which is a visual editor for FXML.

- JavaFX provides a rich set of multimedia support such as playing back audios and videos. It takes advantage of available codecs on the platform.

- JavaFX lets you embed web content in the application.

- JavaFX provides out-of-the-box support for applying effects and animations, which are important for developing gaming applications. You can achieve sophisticated animations by writing a few lines of code.

Behind the JavaFX API lies a number of components to take advantage of the Java native libraries and the available hardware and software. JavaFX components are shown in Figure 1-1.

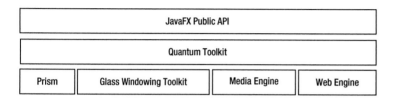

Figure 1-1. *Components of the JavaFX platform*

The GUI in JavaFX is constructed as a *scene graph*. A scene graph is a collection of visual elements, called nodes, arranged in a hierarchical fashion. A scene graph is built using the public JavaFX API. Nodes in a scene graph can handle user inputs and user gestures. They can have effects, transformations, and states. Types of nodes in a scene graph include simple UI controls such as buttons, text fields, two-dimensional (2D) and three-dimensional (3D) shapes, images, media (audio and video), web content, and charts.

Prism is a hardware-accelerated graphics pipeline used for rendering the scene graph. If hardware-accelerated rendering is not available on the platform, Java 2D is used as the fallback rendering mechanism. For example, before using Java 2D for rending, it will try using DirectX on Windows and OpenGL on Mac Linux and embedded platforms.

The *Glass Windowing Toolkit* provides graphics and windowing services such as windows and the timer using the native operating system. The toolkit is also responsible for managing event queues. In JavaFX, event queues are managed by a single, operating system–level thread called *JavaFX Application Thread*. All user input events are dispatched on the JavaFX Application Thread. JavaFX requires that a live scene graph must be modified only on the JavaFX Application Thread.

Prism uses a separate thread, other than the JavaFX Application Thread, for the rendering process. It accelerates the process by rendering a frame while the next frame is being processed. When a scene graph is modified, for example, by entering some text in the text field, Prism needs to re-render the scene graph. Synchronizing the scene graph with Prism is accomplished using an event called a *pulse* event. A pulse event is queued on the JavaFX Application Thread when the scene graph is modified and it needs to be re-rendered. A pulse event is an indication that the scene graph is not in sync with the rendering layer in Prism, and the latest frame at the Prism level should be rendered. Pulse events are throttled at 60 frames per second maximum.

The media engine is responsible for providing media support in JavaFX, for example, playing back audios and videos. It takes advantage of the available codecs on the platform. The media engine uses a separate thread to process media frames and uses the JavaFX Application Thread to synchronize the frames with the scene graph. The media engine is based on *GStreamer*, which is an open source multimedia framework.

The web engine is responsible for processing web content (HTML) embedded in a scene graph. Prism is responsible for rendering the web contents. The web engine is based on *WebKit*, which is an open source web browser engine. HTML5, Cascading Style Sheets (CSS), JavaScript, and Document Object Model (DOM) are supported.

Quantum toolkit is an abstraction over the low-level components of Prism, Glass, Media Engine, and Web Engine. It also facilitates coordination between low-level components.

■ **Note**   Throughout this book, it is assumed that you have intermediate-level knowledge of the Java programming language. Familiarity with the new features in Java 8 such as lambda expressions and Time API is also assumed.

History of JavaFX

JavaFX was originally developed by Chris Oliver at SeeBeyond and it was called F3 (Form Follows Function). F3 was a Java scripting language for easily developing GUI applications. It offered declarative syntax, static typing, type inference, data binding, animation, 2D graphics, and Swing components. SeeBeyond was bought by Sun Microsystems and F3 was renamed JavaFX in 2007. Oracle acquired Sun Microsystems in 2010. Oracle then open sourced JavaFX in 2013.

The first version of JavaFX was released in the fourth quarter of 2008. The current release for JavaFX is version 8.0. The version number jumped from 2.2 to 8.0. From Java 8, the version numbers of Java SE and JavaFX will be the same. The major versions for Java SE and JavaFX will be released at the same time as well. Table 1-1 contains a list of releases of JavaFX. Starting with the release of Java SE 8, JavaFX is part of the Java SE runtime library. From Java 8, you do not need any extra set up to compile and run your JavaFX programs.

Table 1-1. *JavaFX Releases*

Release Date	Version	Comments
Q4, 2008	JavaFX 1.0	It was the initial release of JavaFX. It used a declaration language called JavaFX Script to write the JavaFX code.
Q1, 2009	JavaFX 1.1	Support for JavaFX Mobile was introduced.
Q2, 2009	JavaFX 1.2	
Q2, 2010	JavaFX 1.3	
Q3, 2010	JavaFX 1.3.1	
Q4, 2011	JavaFX 2.0	Support for JavaFX script was dropped. It used the Java language to write the JavaFX code. Support for JavaFX Mobile was dropped.
Q2, 2012	JavaFX 2.1	Support for Mac OS for desktop only was introduced.
Q3, 2012	JavaFX 2.2	
Q1, 2014	JavaFX 8.0	JavaFX version jumped from 2.2 to 8.0. JavaFX and Java SE versions will match from Java 8.

System Requirements

You need to have the following software installed on your computer:

- Java Development Kit 8
- NetBeans IDE 8.0 or later

It is not necessary to have the NetBeans IDE to compile and run the programs in this book. However, the NetBeans IDE has special features for creating, running, and packaging JavaFX applications to make developers' lives easier. You can use any other IDE, for example, Eclipse, JDeveloper, or IntelliJ IDEA.

JavaFX Runtime Library

All JavaFX classes are packaged in a Java Archive (JAR) file named jfxrt.jar. The JAR file is located in the jre\lib\ext directory under the Java home directory.

If you compile and run JavaFX programs on the command line, you do not need to worry about setting the JavaFX runtime JAR file in the CLASSPATH. Java 8 compiler (the javac command) and launcher (the java command) automatically include the JavaFX runtime JAR file in the CLASSPATH.

The NetBeans IDE automatically includes the JavaFX runtime JAR file in the CLASSPATH when you create a Java or JavaFX project. If you are using an IDE other than NetBeans, you may need to include jfxrt. jar in the IDE CLASSPATH to compile and run a JavaFX application from inside the IDE.

JavaFX Source Code

Experienced developers sometimes prefer to look at the source code of the JavaFX library to learn how things are implemented behind the scenes. Oracle provides the JavaFX source code. The Java 8 installation copies the source in the Java home directory. The file name is javafx-src.zip. Unzip the file to a directory and use your favorite Java editor to open the source code.

Your First JavaFX Application

Let's write your first JavaFX application. It should display the text "Hello JavaFX" in a window. I will take an incremental, step-by-step approach to explain how to develop this first application. I will add as few lines of code as possible, and then, explain what the code does and why it is needed.

Creating the *HelloJavaFX* Class

A JavaFX application is a class that must inherit from the Application class that is in the javafx. application package. You will name your class HelloFXApp and it will be stored in the com.jdojo.intro package. Listing 1-1 shows the initial code for the HelloFXApp class. Note that the HelloFXApp class will not compile at this point. You will fix it in the next section.

Listing 1-1. Inheriting Your JavaFX Application Class from the `javafx.application.Application` Class

```
// HelloFXApp.java
package com.jdojo.intro;

import javafx.application.Application;

public class HelloFXApp extends Application {
        // Application logic goes here
}
```

The program includes a package declaration, an import statement, and a class declaration. There is nothing like JavaFX in the code. It looks like any other Java program. However, you have fulfilled one of the requirements of the JavaFX application by inheriting the `HelloFXApp` class from the `Application` class.

Overriding the *start()* Method

If you try compiling the `HelloFXApp` class, it will result in the following compile-time error: *HelloFXApp is not abstract and does not override abstract method start(Stage) in Application.* The error is stating that the `Application` class contains an abstract `start(Stage stage)` method, which has not been overridden in the `HelloFXApp` class. As a Java developer, you know what to do next: you either declare the `HelloFXApp` class as abstract or provide an implementation for the `start()` method. Here let's provide an implementation for the `start()` method. The `start()` method in the `Application` class is declared as follows:

```
public abstract void start(Stage stage) throws java.lang.Exception
```

Listing 1-2 shows the revised code for the `HelloFXApp` class that overrides the `start()` method.

Listing 1-2. Overriding the `start()` Method in Your JavaFX Application Class

```
// HelloFXApp.java
package com.jdojo.intro;

import javafx.application.Application;
import javafx.stage.Stage;

public class HelloFXApp extends Application {
        @Override
        public void start(Stage stage) {
                // The logic for starting the application goes here
        }
}
```

In the revised code, you have incorporated two things:

- You have added one more `import` statement to import the `Stage` class from the `javafx.stage` package.

- You have implemented the `start()` method. The `throws` clause for the method is dropped, which is fine by the rules for overriding methods in Java.

The start() method is the entry point for a JavaFX application. It is called by the JavaFX application launcher. Notice that the start() method is passed an instance of the Stage class, which is known as the *primary stage* of the application. You can create more stages as necessary in your application. However, the primary stage is always created by the JavaFX runtime for you.

▪ **Tip**   Every JavaFX application class must inherit from the Application class and provide the implementation for the start(Stage stage) method.

Showing the Stage

Similar to a stage in the real world, a JavaFX stage is used to display a scene. A scene has visuals—such as text, shapes, images, controls, animations, and effects—with which the user may interact, as is the case with all GUI-based applications.

In JavaFX, the primary stage is a container for a scene. The stage look-and-feel is different depending on the environment your application is run in. You do not need to take any action based on the environment because the JavaFX runtime takes care of all the details for you. For example, if the application runs as a desktop application, the primary stage will be a window with a title bar and an area to display the scene; if the application runs an applet in a web browser, the primary stage will be an embedded area in the browser window.

The primary stage created by the application launcher does not have a scene. You will create a scene for your stage in the next section.

You must show the stage to see the visuals contained in its scene. Use the show() method to show the stage. Optionally, you can set a title for the stage using the setTitle() method. The revised code for the HelloFXApp class is shown in Listing 1-3.

Listing 1-3. Showing the Primary Stage in Your JavaFX Application Class

```
// HelloFXApp.java
package com.jdojo.intro;

import javafx.application.Application;
import javafx.stage.Stage;

public class HelloFXApp extends Application {
        @Override
        public void start(Stage stage) {
                // Set a title for the stage
                stage.setTitle("Hello JavaFX Application");

                // Show the stage
                stage.show();
        }
}
```

Launching the Application

You are now ready to run your first JavaFX application. You can use one of the following two options to run it:

- It is not necessary to have a main() method in the class to start a JavaFX application. When you run a Java class that inherits from the Application class, the java command launches the JavaFX application if the class being run does not contain the main() method.

- If you include a main() method in the JavaFX application class inside the main() method, call the launch() static method of the Application class to launch the application. The launch() method takes a String array as an argument, which are the parameters passed to the JavaFX application.

If you are using the first option, you do not need to write any additional code for the HelloFXApp class. If you are using the second option, the revised code for the HelloFXApp class with the main() method will be as shown in Listing 1-4.

Listing 1-4. The HelloFXApp JavaFX Application Without a Scene

```
// HelloFXApp.java
package com.jdojo.intro;

import javafx.application.Application;
import javafx.stage.Stage;

public class HelloFXApp extends Application {
    public static void main(String[] args) {
        // Launch the JavaFX application
        Application.launch(args);
    }

    @Override
    public void start(Stage stage) {
        stage.setTitle("Hello JavaFX Application");
        stage.show();
    }
}
```

The main() method calls the launch() method, which will do some setup work and call the start() method of the HelloFXApp class. Your start() method sets the title for the primary stage and shows the stage. Compile the HelloFXApp class using the following command:

```
javac com/jdojo/intro/HelloFXApp.java
```

Run the HelloFXApp class using the following command, which will display a window with a title bar as shown in Figure 1-2:

```
java com.jdojo.intro.HelloFXApp
```

Figure 1-2. *The HelloFXApp JavaFX Application Without a Scene*

The main area of the window is empty. This is the content area in which the stage will show its scene. Because you do not have a scene for your stage yet, you will see an empty area. The title bar shows the title that you have set in the start() method.

You can close the application using the Close menu option in the window title bar. Use Alt + F4 to close the window in Windows. You can use any other option to close the window as provided by your platform.

■ **Tip** The launch() method of the Application class does not return until all windows are closed or the application exits using the Platform.exit() method. The Platform class is in the javafx.application package.

You haven't seen anything exciting in JavaFX yet! You need to wait for that until you create a scene in the next section.

Adding the *main()* Method

As described in the previous section, the Java 8 launcher (the java command) does not require a main() method to launch a JavaFX application. If the class that you want to run inherits from the Application class, the java command launches the JavaFX application by automatically calling the Application.launch() method for you.

If you are using the NetBeans IDE to create the JavaFX project, you do not need to have a main() method to launch your JavaFX application if you run the application by running the JavaFX project. However, the NetBeans IDE requires you to have a main() method when you run the JavaFX application class as a file, for example, by selecting the HelloFXApp file, right-clicking it, and selecting the Run File option from the menu.

Some IDEs still require the main() method to launch a JavaFX application. All examples in this chapter will include the main() method that will launch the JavaFX applications.

Adding a Scene to the Stage

An instance of the Scene class, which is in the javafx.scene package, represents a scene. A stage contains one scene, and a scene contains visual contents.

The contents of the scene are arranged in a tree-like hierarchy. At the top of the hierarchy is the *root* node. The root node may contain child nodes, which in turn may contain their child nodes, and so on. You must have a root node to create a scene. You will use a VBox as the root node. VBox stands for vertical box, which arranges its children vertically in a column. The following statement creates a VBox:

```
VBox root = new VBox();
```

■ **Tip** Any node that inherits from the javafx.scene.Parent class can be used as the root node for a scene. Several nodes, known as layout panes or containers such as VBox, HBox, Pane, FlowPane, GridPane, or TilePane can be used as a root node. Group is a special container that groups its children together.

A node that can have children provides a getChildren() method that returns an ObservableList of its children. To add a child node to a node, simply add the child node to the ObservableList. The following snippet of code adds a Text node to a VBox:

```
// Create a VBox node
VBox root = new VBox();

// Create a Text node
Text msg = new Text("Hello JavaFX");

// Add the Text node to the VBox as a child node
root.getChildren().add(msg);
```

The Scene class contains several constructors. You will use the one that lets you specify the root node and the size of the scene. The following statement creates a scene with the VBox as the root node, with 300px width and 50px height:

```
// Create a scene
Scene scene = new Scene(root, 300, 50);
```

You need to set the scene to the stage by calling the setScene() method of the Stage class:

```
// Set the scene to the stage
stage.setScene(scene);
```

That's it. You have completed your first JavaFX program with a scene. Listing 1-5 contains the complete program. The program displays a window as shown in Figure 1-3.

Listing 1-5. A JavaFX Application with a Scene Having a Text Node

```java
// HelloFXAppWithAScene.java
package com.jdojo.intro;

import javafx.application.Application;
import javafx.scene.Scene;
import javafx.scene.layout.VBox;
import javafx.scene.text.Text;
import javafx.stage.Stage;

public class HelloFXAppWithAScene extends Application {
        public static void main(String[] args) {
                Application.launch(args);
        }

        @Override
        public void start(Stage stage) {
                Text msg = new Text("Hello JavaFX");
                VBox root = new VBox();
                root.getChildren().add(msg);

                Scene scene = new Scene(root, 300, 50);
                stage.setScene(scene);
                stage.setTitle("Hello JavaFX Application with a Scene");
                stage.show();
        }
}
```

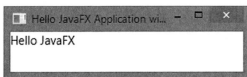

Figure 1-3. *A JavaFX application with a scene having a Text node*

Improving the *HelloFX* Application

JavaFX is capable of doing much more than you have seen so far. Let's enhance the first program and add some more user interface elements such as buttons and text fields. This time, the user will be able to interact with the application. Use an instance of the Button class to create a button as shown:

```java
// Create a button with "Exit" text
Button exitBtn = new Button("Exit");
```

When a button is clicked, an `ActionEvent` is fired. You can add an `ActionEvent` handler to handle the event. Use the `setOnAction()` method to set an `ActionEvent` handler for the button. The following statement sets an `ActionEvent` handler for the button. The handler terminates the application. You can use a lambda expression or an anonymous class to set the `ActionEvent` handler. The following snippet of code shows both approaches:

```
// Using a lambda expression
exitBtn.setOnAction(e -> Platform.exit());

// Using an anonymous class
import javafx.event.ActionEvent;
import javafx.event.EventHandler;
...
exitBtn.setOnAction(new EventHandler<ActionEvent>() {
        @Override
        public void handle(ActionEvent e) {
                Platform.exit();
        }
});
```

The program in Listing 1-6 shows how to add more nodes to the scene. The program uses the `setStyle()` method of the `Label` class to set the fill color of the `Label` to blue. I will discuss using CSS in JavaFX later.

Listing 1-6. Interacting with Users in a JavaFX Application

```
// ImprovedHelloFXApp.java
package com.jdojo.intro;

import javafx.application.Application;
import javafx.application.Platform;
import javafx.scene.Scene;
import javafx.scene.control.Button;
import javafx.scene.control.Label;
import javafx.scene.control.TextField;
import javafx.scene.layout.VBox;
import javafx.stage.Stage;

public class ImprovedHelloFXApp extends Application {
        public static void main(String[] args) {
                Application.launch(args);
        }

        @Override
        public void start(Stage stage) {
                Label nameLbl = new Label("Enter your name:");
                TextField nameFld = new TextField();

                Label msg = new Label();
                msg.setStyle("-fx-text-fill: blue;");
```

```
                // Create buttons
                Button sayHelloBtn = new Button("Say Hello");
                Button exitBtn = new Button("Exit");

                // Add the event handler for the Say Hello button
                sayHelloBtn.setOnAction(e -> {
                        String name = nameFld.getText();
                        if (name.trim().length() > 0) {
                                msg.setText("Hello " + name);
                        } else {
                                msg.setText("Hello there");
                        }
                });

                // Add the event handler for the Exit button
                exitBtn.setOnAction(e -> Platform.exit());

                // Create the root node
                VBox root = new VBox();

                // Set the vertical spacing between children to 5px
                root.setSpacing(5);

                // Add children to the root node
                root.getChildren().addAll(nameLbl, nameFld, msg, sayHelloBtn, exitBtn);

                Scene scene = new Scene(root, 350, 150);
                stage.setScene(scene);
                stage.setTitle("Improved Hello JavaFX Application");
                stage.show();
        }
}
```

The improved HelloFX program displays a window as shown in Figure 1-4. The window contains two labels, a text field, and two buttons. A VBox is used as the root node for the scene. Enter a name in the text field and click the Say Hello button to see a hello message. Clicking the Say Hello button without entering a name displays the message Hello there. The application displays a message in a Label control. Click the Exit button to exit the application.

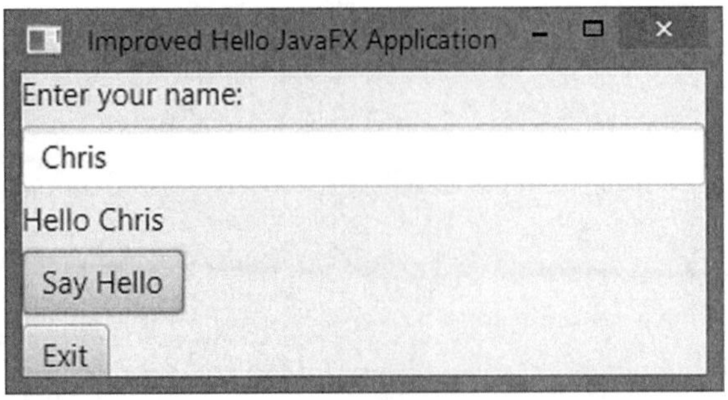

Figure 1-4. *A JavaFX Application with few controls in its scene*

Using the NetBeans IDE

You can use the NetBeans IDE to create, compile, package, and run new JavaFX applications. The source code used in this book is available with a NetBeans project.

Creating a New JavaFX Project

Use the following steps to create a new JavaFX project:

1. Select the New Project... menu option from the File menu. Alternatively, use the keyboard shortcut Ctrl + Shift + N.

2. A New Project dialog appears as shown in Figure 1-5. From the Categories list, select JavaFX. From the Projects list, select JavaFX Application. Click the Next button.

3. The New JavaFX Application dialog appears as shown in Figure 1-6. Enter the details of the project such as project name and location. The Create Application Class check box is checked by default. You can enter the full-qualified name of the JavaFX application in the box next to the check box. NetBeans will create the class and add the initial code for you. When you run the project from inside the IDE, this class is run. You can change this class later.

4. Click the Finish button when you are done.

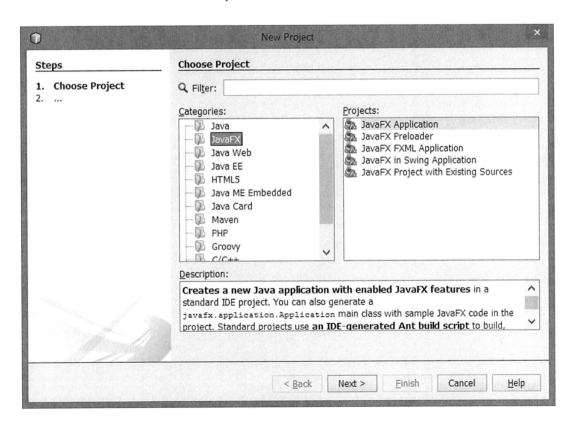

Figure 1-5. *The New Project dialog*

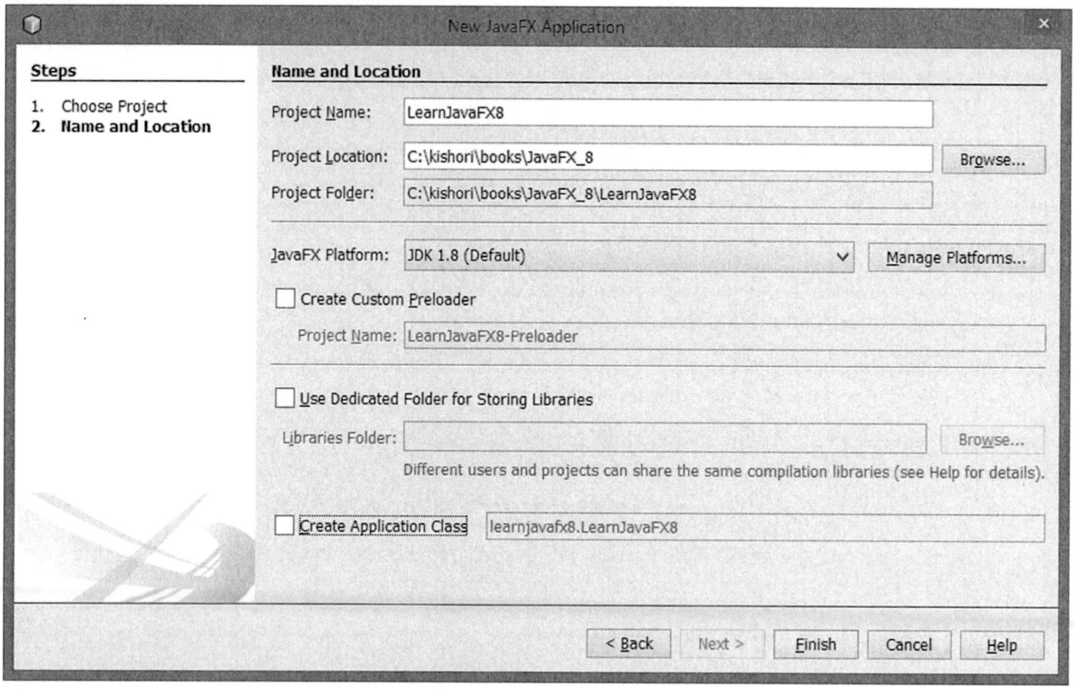

Figure 1-6. The New JavaFX Application dialog

Opening an Existing JavaFX Project

The source code for this book is provided with a NetBeans project. You can use the following steps to open the project. If you have not downloaded the source code for this book, please do so before proceeding.

1. From inside the NetBeans IDE, select the Open Project… menu option from the File menu. Alternatively, use the keyboard shortcut Ctrl + Shift + O.

2. An Open Project dialog appears. Navigate to the directory containing the downloaded source code for this book. You should see the project LearnJavaFX8, as shown in Figure 1-7. Select the project name and click the Open Project button. The project should appear in the IDE.

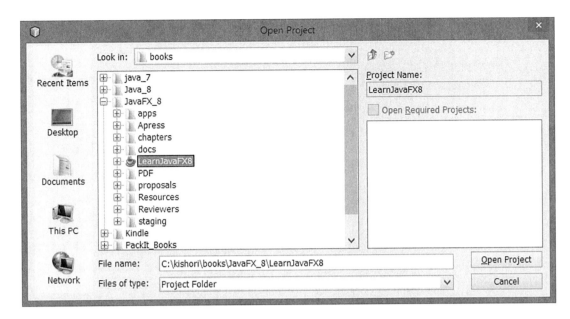

Figure 1-7. *The Open Project dialog*

Running a JavaFX Project from the NetBeans IDE

You can compile and run a JavaFX application from inside the NetBeans IDE. You have the options to run a Java application in one of three ways:

- Run as a standalone desktop application

- Run as a WebStart

- Run in a browser

By default, NetBeans runs a JavaFX application as a standalone desktop application. You can change the way your application is run on the project properties page under the Run category. To access the project properties page, select your project in the IDE, right-click, and select the Properties menu option. The Project Properties dialog box appears. Select the Run item from the Categories tree. Enter the desired Run properties for your project on the right side of the screen.

Passing Parameters to a JavaFX Application

Like a Java application, you can pass parameters to a JavaFX application. There are two ways to pass parameters to a JavaFX application:

- On the command line for a standalone application

- In a Java Network Launching Protocol (JNLP) file for an applet and WebStart application

The Parameters class, which is a static inner class of the Application class, encapsulates the parameters passed to a JavaFX application. It divides parameters into three categories:

- Named parameters
- Unnamed parameters
- Raw parameters (a combination of named and unnamed parameters)

You need to use the following three methods of the Parameters class to access the three types of parameters:

- Map<String, String> getNamed()
- List<String> getUnnamed()
- List<String> getRaw()

A parameter can be named or unnamed. A named parameter consists of a (name, value) pair. An unnamed parameter consists of a single value. The getNamed() method returns a Map<String, String> that contains the key-value pairs of the name parameters. The getUnnamed() method returns a List<String> where each element is an unnamed parameter value.

You pass only named and unnamed parameters to a JavaFX application. You do not pass raw type parameters. The JavaFX runtime makes all parameters, named and unnamed, passed to an application available as a List<String> through the getRaw() method of the Parameters class. The following discussion will make the distinction between the returned values from the three methods clear.

The getParameters() method of the Application class returns the reference of the Application. Parameters class. The reference to the Parameters class is available in the init() method of the Application class and the code that executes afterward. The parameters are not available in the constructor of the application as it is called before the init() method. Calling the getParameters() method in the constructor returns null.

The program in Listing 1-7 reads all types of parameters passed to the application and displays them in a TextArea. A TextArea is a UI node that displays multiple lines of text.

Listing 1-7. Accessing Parameters Passed to a JavaFX Application

```
// FXParamApp.java
package com.jdojo.intro;

import java.util.List;
import java.util.Map;
import javafx.application.Application;
import javafx.scene.Group;
import javafx.scene.Scene;
import javafx.scene.control.TextArea;
import javafx.stage.Stage;

public class FXParamApp extends Application {
        public static void main(String[] args) {
                Application.launch(args);
        }
```

```
@Override
public void start(Stage stage) {
        // Get application parameters
        Parameters p = this.getParameters();
        Map<String, String> namedParams = p.getNamed();
        List<String> unnamedParams = p.getUnnamed();
        List<String> rawParams = p.getRaw();

        String paramStr = "Named Parameters: " + namedParams + "\n" +
                "Unnamed Parameters: " + unnamedParams + "\n" +
                "Raw Parameters: " + rawParams;

        TextArea ta = new TextArea(paramStr);
        Group root = new Group(ta);
        stage.setScene(new Scene(root));
        stage.setTitle("Application Parameters");
        stage.show();
    }
}
```

Let's look at a few cases of passing the parameters to the FXParamApp class. The output mentioned in the following cases is displayed in the TextArea control in the window when you run the FXParamApp class.

Case 1

The class is run as a standalone application using the following command:

```
java com.jdojo.stage.FXParamApp Anna Lola
```

The above command passes no named parameters and two unnamed parameters: Anna and Lola. The list of the raw parameters will contain the two unnamed parameters. The output will be as shown:

```
Named Parameters: {}
Unnamed Parameters: [Anna, Lola]
Raw Parameters: [Anna, Lola]
```

Case 2

The class is run as a standalone application using the command:

```
java com.jdojo.stage.FXParamApp Anna Lola width=200 height=100
```

The above command passes no named parameters even though it seems that the last two parameters would be passed as named parameters. Using an equals (=) sign in a parameter value on the command line does not make the parameter a named parameter. The next case explains how to pass named parameters from the command line.

It passes four unnamed parameters: Anna, Lola, width=200, and height=100. The list of the raw parameters will contain the four unnamed parameters. The output will be as shown:

```
Named Parameters: {}
Unnamed Parameters: [Anna, Lola, width=200, height=100]
Raw Parameters: [Anna, Lola, width=200, height=100]
```

Case 3

To pass a named parameter from the command line, you need to precede the parameter with exactly two hyphens (--). That is, a named parameter should be entered in the form:

```
--key=value
```

The class is run as a standalone application using the command:

```
java com.jdojo.stage.FXParamApp Anna Lola --width=200 --height=100
```

The above command passes two named parameters: width=200 and height=100. It passes two unnamed parameters: Anna and Lola. The list of the raw parameters will contain four elements: two named parameters and two unnamed parameters. Named parameter values in the raw parameter list are preceded by two hyphens. The output will be as shown:

```
Named Parameters: {height=100, width=200}
Unnamed Parameters: [Anna, Lola]
Raw Parameters: [Anna, Lola, --width=200, --height=100]
```

Case 4

The class FXParamApp is run as an applet or a WebStart application. In these cases, you have different ways to specify the named and unnamed parameters. However, they are accessed inside the application in the same way. Note that when a named parameter is accessed using the getRaw() method, it is preceded by two hyphens. However, you do not add two hyphens before a named parameter when you specify it in web and WebStart deployment files.

The partial content of a JNLP file to start the FXParamApp application using WebStart is shown below. It specifies two named and two unnamed parameters:

```
<?xml version="1.0" encoding="utf-8"?>
<jnlp spec="1.0" xmlns:jfx="http://javafx.com" href="FX_NetBeans_Only.jnlp">
...
        <jfx:javafx-desc ... >
                <fx:param name="width" value="200"/>
                <fx:param name="height" value="100"/>
                <fx:argument>Anna</fx:argument>
                <fx:argument>Lola</fx:argument>
        </jfx:javafx-desc>
</jnlp>
```

Launching a JavaFX Application

Earlier I touched on the topic of launching the JavaFX application while developing the JavaFX first application. This section gives more details on launching a JavaFX application.

Every JavaFX application class inherits from the Application class. The Application class is in the javafx.application package. It contains a static launch() method. Its sole purpose is to launch a JavaFX application. It is an overloaded method with the following two variants:

- static void launch(Class<? extends Application> appClass, String... args)

- static void launch(String... args)

Notice that you do not create an object of your JavaFX application class to launch it. The JavaFX runtime creates an object of your application class when the launch() method is called.

■ **Tip** Your JavaFX application class must have a no-args constructor, otherwise a runtime exception will be thrown when an attempt is made to launch it.

The first variant of the launch() method is clear. You pass the class reference of your application class as the first argument, and the launch() method will create an object of that class. The second argument is comprised of the command-line arguments passed to the application. The following snippet of code shows how to use the first variant of the launch() method:

```
public class MyJavaFXApp extends Application {
        public static void main(String[] args) {
                Application.launch(MyJavaFXApp.class, args);
        }

        // More code goes here
}
```

The class reference passed to the launch() method does not have to be of the same class from which the method is called. For example, the following snippet of code launches the MyJavaFXApp application class from the MyAppLauncher class, which does not extend the Application class:

```
public class MyAppLauncher {
        public static void main(String[] args) {
                Application.launch(MyJavaFXApp.class, args);
        }

        // More code goes here
}
```

The second variant of the launch() method takes only one argument, which is the command-line argument passed to the application. Which JavaFX application class does it use to launch the application? It attempts to find the application class name based on the caller. It checks the class name of the code that calls it. If the method is called as part of the code for a class that inherits from the Application class, directly or indirectly, that class is used to launch the JavaFX application. Otherwise, a runtime exception is thrown. Let's look at some examples to make this rule clear.

In the following snippet of code, the launch() method detects that it is called from the main() method of the MyJavaFXApp class. The MyJavaFXApp class inherits from the Application class. Therefore, the MyJavaFXApp class is used as the application class:

```
public class MyJavaFXApp extends Application {
        public static void main(String[] args) {
                Application.launch(args);
        }

        // More code goes here
}
```

In the following snippet of code, the launch() method is called from the main() method of the Test class. The Test does not inherit from the Application class. Therefore, a runtime exception is thrown, as shown in the output below the code:

```
public class Test {
        public static void main(String[] args) {
                Application.launch(args);
        }

        // More code goes here
}
```

```
Exception in thread "main" java.lang.RuntimeException: Error: class Test is not a subclass
of javafx.application.Application
        at javafx.application.Application.launch(Application.java:211)
        at Test.main(Test.java)
```

In the following snippet of code, the launch() method detects that it is called from the run() method of the MyJavaFXApp$1 class. Note that MyJavaFXApp$1 class is an anonymous inner class generated by the compiler, which is a subclass of the Object class, not the Application class, and it implements the Runnable interface. Because the call to the launch() method is contained within the MyJavaFXApp$1 class, which is not a subclass of the Application class, a runtime exception is thrown, as shown in the output that follows the code:

```
public class MyJavaFXApp extends Application {
        public static void main(String[] args) {
                Thread t = new Thread(new Runnable() {
                        public void run() {
                                Application.launch(args);
                        }
                });

                t.start();
        }

        // More code goes here
}
```

```
Exception in thread "Thread-0" java.lang.RuntimeException: Error: class MyJavaFXApp$1 is
not a subclass of javafx.application.Application
        at javafx.application.Application.launch(Application.java:211)
        at MyJavaFXApp$1.run(MyJavaFXApp.java)
        at java.lang.Thread.run(Thread.java:722)
```

Now that you know how to launch a JavaFX application, it's time to learn the best practice in launching a JavaFX application: limit the code in the main() method to only one statement that launches the application, as shown in the following code:

```
public class MyJavaFXApp extends Application {
    public static void main(String[] args) {
        Application.launch(args);

        // Do not add any more code in this method
    }

    // More code goes here
}
```

▨ **Tip**   The launch() method of the Application class must be called only once, otherwise, a runtime exception is thrown. The call to the launch() method blocks until the application is terminated. It is not always necessary to have a main() method to launch a JavaFX application. A JavaFX packager synthesizes one for you. For example, when you use the NetBeans IDE, you do not need to have a main() method, and if you have one, NetBeans ignores it.

The Life Cycle of a JavaFX Application

JavaFX runtime creates several threads. At different stages in the application, threads are used to perform different tasks. In this section, I will only explain those threads that are used to call methods of the Application class during its life cycle. The JavaFX runtime creates, among other threads, two threads:

- JavaFX-Launcher
- JavaFX Application Thread

The launch() method of the Application class create these threads. During the lifetime of a JavaFX application, the JavaFX runtime calls the following methods of the specified JavaFX Application class in order:

- The no-args constructor
- The init() method
- The start() method
- The stop() method

The JavaFX runtime creates an object of the specified `Application` class on the JavaFX Application Thread. The JavaFX Launcher Thread calls the `init()` method of the specified `Application` class. The `init()` method implementation in the `Application` class is empty. You can override this method in your application class. It is not allowed to create a `Stage` or a `Scene` on the JavaFX Launcher Thread. They must be created on the JavaFX Application Thread. Therefore, you cannot create a `Stage` or a `Scene` inside the `init()` method. Attempting to do so throws a runtime exception. It is fine to create UI controls, for example, buttons or shapes.

The JavaFX Application Thread calls the `start(Stage stage)` method of the specified `Application` class. Note that the `start()` method in the `Application` class is declared `abstract`, and you must override this method in your application class.

At this point, the `launch()` method waits for the JavaFX application to finish. When the application finishes, the JavaFX Application Thread calls the `stop()` method of the specified `Application` class. The default implementation of the `stop()` method is empty in the `Application` class. You will have to override this method in your `application` class to perform your logic when your application stops.

The code in Listing 1-8 illustrates the life cycle of a JavaFX application. It displays an empty stage. You will see the first three lines of the output when the stage is shown. You will need to close the stage to see the last line of the output.

Listing 1-8. The Life Cycle of a JavaFX Application

```java
// FXLifeCycleApp.java
package com.jdojo.intro;

import javafx.application.Application;
import javafx.scene.Group;
import javafx.scene.Scene;
import javafx.stage.Stage;

public class FXLifeCycleApp extends Application {
        public FXLifeCycleApp() {
                String name = Thread.currentThread().getName();
                System.out.println("FXLifeCycleApp() constructor: " + name);
        }

        public static void main(String[] args) {
                Application.launch(args);
        }

        @Override
        public void init() {
                String name = Thread.currentThread().getName();
                System.out.println("init() method: " + name);
        }

        @Override
        public void start(Stage stage) {
                String name = Thread.currentThread().getName();
                System.out.println("start() method: " + name);
```

```
            Scene scene = new Scene(new Group(), 200, 200);
            stage.setScene(scene);
            stage.setTitle("JavaFX Application Life Cycle");
            stage.show();
    }

    @Override
    public void stop() {
            String name = Thread.currentThread().getName();
            System.out.println("stop() method: " + name);
    }
}
```

```
FXLifeCycleApp() constructor: JavaFX Application Thread
init() method: JavaFX-Launcher
start() method: JavaFX Application Thread
stop() method: JavaFX Application Thread
```

Terminating a JavaFX Application

A JavaFX application may be terminated explicitly or implicitly. You can terminate a JavaFX application explicitly by calling the Platform.exit() method. When this method is called, after or from within the start() method, the stop() method of the Application class is called, and then the JavaFX Application Thread is terminated. At this point, if there are only daemon threads running, the JVM will exit. If this method is called from the constructor or the init() method of the Application class, the stop() method may not be called.

■ **Tip**   A JavaFX application may be run in web browsers. Calling the Platform.exit() method in web environments may not have any effect.

A JavaFX application may be terminated implicitly, when the last window is closed. This behavior can be turned on and turned off using the static setImplicitExit(boolean implicitExit) method of the Platform class. Passing true to this method turns this behavior on. Passing false to this method turns this behavior off. By default, this behavior is turned on. This is the reason that in most of the examples so far, applications were terminated when you closed the windows. When this behavior is turned on, the stop() method of the Application class is called before terminating the JavaFX Application Thread. Terminating the JavaFX Application Thread does not always terminate the JVM. The JVM terminates if all running nondaemon threads terminate. If the implicit terminating behavior of the JavaFX application is turned off, you must call the exit() method of the Platform class to terminate the application.

Summary

JavaFX is an open source Java-based GUI framework that is used to develop rich client applications. It is the successor of Swing in the arena of GUI development technology on the Java platform.

The GUI in JavaFX is shown in a stage. A stage is an instance of the Stage class. A stage is a window in a desktop application and an area in the browser in a web application. A stage contains a scene. A scene contains a group of nodes (graphics) arranged in a tree-like structure.

A JavaFX application inherits from the Application class. The JavaFX runtime creates the first stage called the primary stage and calls the start() method of the application class passing the reference of the primary stage. The developer needs to add a scene to the stage and make the stage visible inside the start() method.

You can launch a JavaFX application using the launch() method of the Application class. If you run a Java class that inherits from the application class, which would be a JavaFX application class, the java command automatically launches the JavaFX application for you.

During the lifetime of a JavaFX application, the JavaFX runtime calls predefined methods of the JavaFX Application class in a specific order. First, the no-args constructor of the class is called, followed by calls to the init() and start() methods. When the application terminates, the stop() method is called.

You can terminate a JavaFX application by calling the Platform.exit() method. Calling the Platform.exit() method when the application is running in a web browser as an applet may not have any effects.

The next chapter will introduce you to properties and binding in JavaFX.

CHAPTER 2

■ ■ ■

Properties and Bindings

In this chapter, you will learn:

- What a property is in JavaFX

- How to create a property object and use it

- The class hierarchy of properties in JavaFX

- How to handle the invalidation and change events in a property object

- What a binding is in JavaFX and how to use unidirectional and bidirectional bindings

- About the high-level and low-level binding API in JavaFX

This chapter discusses the properties and binding support in Java and JavaFX. If you have experience using the JavaBeans API for properties and binding, you can skip the first few sections, which discuss the properties and binding support in Java, and start with the section "Understanding Properties in JavaFX."

What Is a Property?

A Java class can contain two types of members: *fields* and *methods*. Fields represent the state of objects and they are declared private. Public methods, known as *accessors*, or *getters* and *setters*, are used to read and modify private fields. In simple terms, a Java class that has public accessors, for all or part of its private fields, is known as a Java *bean*, and the accessors define the properties of the bean. Properties of a Java bean allow users to customize its state, behavior, or both.

Java beans are observable. They support property change notification. When a public property of a Java bean changes, a notification is sent to all interested listeners.

In essence, Java beans define reusable components that can be assembled by a builder tool to create a Java application. This opens the door for third parties to develop Java beans and make them available to others for reuse.

A property can be read-only, write-only, or read/write. A ready-only property has a getter but no setter. A write-only property has a setter but no getter. A read/write property has a getter and a setter.

Java IDEs and other builder tools (e.g., a GUI layout builder), use introspection to get the list of properties of a bean and let you manipulate those properties at design time. A Java bean can be visual or nonvisual. Properties of a bean can be used in a builder tool or programmatically.

The JavaBeans API provides a class library, through the `java.beans` package, and naming conventions to create and use Java beans. The following is an example of a `Person` bean with a read/write name property. The `getName()` method (the getter) returns the value of the name field. The `setName()` method (the setter) sets the value of the name field:

```
// Person.java
package com.jdojo.binding;

public class Person {
        private String name;

        public String getName() {
                return name;
        }

        public void setName(String name) {
                this.name = name;
        }
}
```

By convention, the names of the getter and setter methods are constructed by appending the name of the property, with the first letter in uppercase, to the words *get* and *set*, respectively. The getter method should not take any parameters, and its return type should be the same as the type of the field. The setter method should take a parameter whose type should be the same as the type of the field, and its returns type should be void.

The following snippet of code manipulates the name property of a `Person` bean programmatically:

```
Person p = new Person();
p.setName("John Jacobs");
String name = p.getName();
```

Some object-oriented programming languages, for example, C#, provide a third type of class member known as a *property*. A property is used to read, write, and compute the value of a private field from outside the class. C# lets you declare a `Person` class with a `Name` property as follows:

```
// C# version of the Person class
public class Person {
        private string name;

        public string Name {
                get { return name; }
                set { name = value; }
        }
}
```

In C#, the following snippet of code manipulates the name private field using the `Name` property; it is equivalent to the previously shown Java version of the code:

```
Person p = new Person();
p.Name = "John Jacobs";
string name = p.Name;
```

26

If the accessors of a property perform the routine work of returning and setting the value of a field, C# offers a compact format to define such a property. You do not even need to declare a private field in this case. You can rewrite the Person class in C# as shown here:

```
// C# version of the Person class using the compact format
public class Person {
        public string Name { get; set; }
}
```

So, what is a property? A *property* is a publicly accessible attribute of a class that affects its state, behavior, or both. Even though a property is publicly accessible, its use (read/write) invokes methods that hide the actual implementation to access the data. Properties are observable, so interested parties are notified when its value changes.

■ **Tip**   In essence, properties define the public state of an object that can be read, written, and observed for changes. Unlike other programming languages, such as C#, properties in Java are not supported at the language level. Java support for properties comes through the JavaBeans API and design patterns. For more details on properties in Java, please refer to the JavaBeans specification, which can be downloaded from http://www.oracle.com/technetwork/java/javase/overview/spec-136004.html.

Apart from simple properties, such as the name property of the Person bean, Java also supports *indexed*, *bound*, and *constrained* properties. An indexed property is an array of values that are accessed using indexes. An indexed property is implemented using an array data type. A bound property sends a notification to all listeners when it is changed. A constrained property is a bound property in which a listener can veto a change.

What Is a Binding?

In programming, the term *binding* is used in many different contexts. Here I want to define it in the context of *data binding*. Data binding defines a relation between data elements (usually variables) in a program to keep them synchronized. In a GUI application, data binding is frequently used to synchronize the elements in the data model with the corresponding UI elements.

Consider the following statement, assuming that x, y, and z are numeric variables:

```
x = y + z;
```

The above statement defines a binding between x, y, and z. When it is executed, the value of x is synchronized with the sum of y and z. A binding also has a time factor. In the above statement, the value of x is bound to the sum of y and z and is valid at the time the statement is executed. The value of x may not be the sum of y and z before and after the above statement is executed.

Sometimes it is desired for a binding to hold over a period. Consider the following statement that defines a binding using listPrice, discounts, and taxes:

```
soldPrice = listPrice - discounts + taxes;
```

For this case, you would like to keep the binding valid forever, so the sold price is computed correctly, whenever listPrice, discounts, or taxes change.

In the above binding, listPrice, discounts, and taxes are known as *dependencies*, and it is said that soldPrice is bound to listPrice, discounts, and taxes.

For a binding to work correctly, it is necessary that the binding is notified whenever its dependencies change. Programming languages that support binding provide a mechanism to register listeners with the dependencies. When dependencies become invalid or they change, all listeners are notified. A binding may synchronize itself with its dependencies when it receives such notifications.

A binding can be an *eager binding* or a *lazy binding*. In an eager binding, the bound variable is recomputed immediately after its dependencies change. In a lazy binding, the bound variable is not recomputed when its dependencies change. Rather, it is recomputed when it is read the next time. A lazy binding performs better compared to an eager binding.

A binding may be *unidirectional* or *bidirectional*. A unidirectional binding works only in one direction; changes in the dependencies are propagated to the bound variable. A bidirectional binding works in both directions. In a bidirectional binding, the bound variable and the dependency keep their values synchronized with each other. Typically, a bidirectional binding is defined only between two variables. For example, a bidirectional binding, x = y and y = x, declares that the values of x and y are always the same.

Mathematically, it is not possible to define a bidirectional binding between multiple variables uniquely. In the above example, the sold price binding is a unidirectional binding. If you want to make it a bidirectional binding, it is not uniquely possible to compute the values of the list price, discounts, and taxes when the sold price is changed. There are an infinite number of possibilities in the other direction.

Applications with GUIs provide users with UI widgets, for example, text fields, check boxes, and buttons, to manipulate data. The data displayed in UI widgets have to be synchronized with the underlying data model and vice versa. In this case, a bidirectional binding is needed to keep the UI and the data model synchronized.

Understanding Bindings Support in JavaBeans

Before I discuss Java FX properties and binding, let's take a short tour of binding support in the JavaBeans API. You may skip this section if you have used the JavaBeans API before.

Java has supported binding of bean properties since its early releases. Listing 2-1 shows an Employee bean with two properties, name and salary.

Listing 2-1. An Employee Java Bean with Two Properties Named name and salary

```java
// Employee.java
package com.jdojo.binding;

import java.beans.PropertyChangeListener;
import java.beans.PropertyChangeSupport;

public class Employee {
        private String name;
        private double salary;
        private PropertyChangeSupport pcs = new PropertyChangeSupport(this);

        public Employee() {
                this.name = "John Doe";
                this.salary = 1000.0;
        }
```

```java
    public Employee(String name, double salary) {
            this.name = name;
            this.salary = salary;
    }

    public String getName() {
            return name;
    }

    public void setName(String name) {
            this.name = name;
    }

    public double getSalary() {
            return salary;
    }

    public void setSalary(double newSalary) {
            double oldSalary = this.salary;
            this.salary = newSalary;

            // Notify the registered listeners about the change
            pcs.firePropertyChange("salary", oldSalary, newSalary);
    }

    public void addPropertyChangeListener(PropertyChangeListener listener) {
            pcs.addPropertyChangeListener(listener);
    }

    public void removePropertyChangeListener(PropertyChangeListener listener) {
            pcs.removePropertyChangeListener(listener);
    }

    @Override
    public String toString() {
            return "name = " + name + ", salary = " + salary;
    }
}
```

Both properties of the Employee bean are read/write. The salary property is also a bound property. Its setter generates property change notifications when the salary changes.

Interested listeners can register or deregister for the change notifications using the addPropertyChangeListener() and removePropertyChangeListener() methods. The PropertyChangeSupport class is part of the JavaBeans API that facilitates the registration and removal of property change listeners and firing of the property change notifications.

Any party interested in synchronizing values based on the salary change will need to register with the Employee bean and take necessary actions when it is notified of the change.

Listing 2-2 shows how to register for salary change notifications for an Employee bean. The output below it shows that salary change notification is fired only twice, whereas the setSalary() method is called three times. This is true because the second call to the setSalary() method uses the same salary amount as the first call and the PropertyChangeSupport class is smart enough to detect that. The example also shows how you would bind variables using the JavaBeans API. The tax for an employee is computed based on a tax percentage. In the JavaBeans API, property change notifications are used to bind the variables.

Listing 2-2. An EmployeeTest Class that Tests the Employee Bean for Salary Changes

```java
// EmployeeTest.java
package com.jdojo.binding;

import java.beans.PropertyChangeEvent;

public class EmployeeTest {
    public static void main(String[] args) {
        final Employee e1 = new Employee("John Jacobs", 2000.0);

        // Compute the tax
        computeTax(e1.getSalary());

        // Add a property change listener to e1
        e1.addPropertyChangeListener(EmployeeTest::handlePropertyChange);

        // Change the salary
        e1.setSalary(3000.00);
        e1.setSalary(3000.00); // No change notification is sent.
        e1.setSalary(6000.00);
    }

    public static void handlePropertyChange(PropertyChangeEvent e) {
        String propertyName = e.getPropertyName();

        if ("salary".equals(propertyName)) {
            System.out.print("Salary has changed. ");
            System.out.print("Old:" + e.getOldValue());
            System.out.println(", New:" + e.getNewValue());
             computeTax((Double)e.getNewValue());
        }
    }

    public static void computeTax(double salary) {
        final double TAX_PERCENT = 20.0;
        double tax = salary * TAX_PERCENT/100.0;
        System.out.println("Salary:" + salary + ", Tax:" + tax);
    }
}
```

```
Salary:2000.0, Tax:400.0
Salary has changed. Old:2000.0, New:3000.0
Salary:3000.0, Tax:600.0
Salary has changed. Old:3000.0, New:6000.0
Salary:6000.0, Tax:1200.0
```

Understanding Properties in JavaFX

JavaFX supports properties, events, and binding through *properties* and *binding* APIs. Properties support in JavaFX is a huge leap forward from the JavaBeans properties.

All properties in JavaFX are observable. They can be observed for invalidation and value changes. There can be read/write or read-only properties. All read/write properties support binding.

In JavaFX, a property can represent a value or a collection of values. This chapter covers properties that represent a single value. I will cover properties representing a collection of values in Chapter 3.

In JavaFX, properties are objects. There is a property class hierarchy for each type of property. For example, the IntegerProperty, DoubleProperty, and StringProperty classes represent properties of int, double, and String types, respectively. These classes are abstract. There are two types of implementation classes for them: one to represent a read/write property and one to represent a wrapper for a read-only property. For example, the SimpleDoubleProperty and ReadOnlyDoubleWrapper classes are concrete classes whose objects are used as read/write and read-only double properties, respectively.

Below is an example of how to create an IntegerProperty with an initial value of 100:

```
IntegerProperty counter = new SimpleIntegerProperty(100);
```

Property classes provide two pairs of getter and setter methods: get()/set() and getValue()/ setValue(). The get() and set() methods get and set the value of the property, respectively. For primitive type properties, they work with primitive type values. For example, for IntegerProperty, the return type of the get() method and the parameter type of the set() method are int. The getValue() and setValue() methods work with an object type; for example, their return type and parameter type are Integer for IntegerProperty.

■ **Tip**   For reference type properties, such as StringProperty and ObjectProperty<T>, both pairs of getter and setter work with an object type. That is, both get() and getValue() methods of StringProperty return a String, and set() and setValue() methods take a String parameter. With autoboxing for primitive types, it does not matter which version of getter and setter is used. The getValue() and setValue() methods exist to help you write generic code in terms of object types.

The following snippet of code uses an IntegerProperty and its get() and set() methods. The counter property is a read/write property as it is an object of the SimpleIntegerProperty class:

```
IntegerProperty counter = new SimpleIntegerProperty(1);
int counterValue = counter.get();
System.out.println("Counter:" + counterValue);

counter.set(2);
counterValue = counter.get();
System.out.println("Counter:" + counterValue);
```

```
Counter:1
Counter:2
```

Working with read-only properties is a bit tricky. A ReadOnlyXXXWrapper class wraps two properties of XXX type: one read-only and one read/write. Both properties are synchronized. Its getReadOnlyProperty() method returns a ReadOnlyXXXProperty object.

The following snippet of code shows how to create a read-only Integer property. The idWrapper property is read/write, whereas the id property is read-only. When the value in idWrapper is changed, the value in id is changed automatically:

```
ReadOnlyIntegerWrapper idWrapper = new ReadOnlyIntegerWrapper(100);
ReadOnlyIntegerProperty id = idWrapper.getReadOnlyProperty();

System.out.println("idWrapper:" + idWrapper.get());
System.out.println("id:" + id.get());

// Change the value
idWrapper.set(101);

System.out.println("idWrapper:" + idWrapper.get());
System.out.println("id:" + id.get());
```

```
idWrapper:100
id:100
idWrapper:101
id:101
```

■ **Tip** Typically, a wrapper property is used as a private instance variable of a class. The class can change the property internally. One of its methods returns the read-only property object of the wrapper class, so the same property is read-only for the outside world.

You can use seven types of properties that represent a single value. The base classes for those properties are named as XXXProperty, read-only base classes are named as ReadOnlyXXXProperty, and wrapper classes are named as ReadOnlyXXXWrapper. The values for XXX for each type are listed in Table 2-1.

Table 2-1. *List of Property Classes that Wrap a Single Value*

Type	XXX Value
int	Integer
long	Long
float	Float
double	Double
boolean	Boolean
String	String
Object	Object

A property object wraps three pieces of information:

- The reference of the bean that contains it

- A name

- A value

When you create a property object, you can supply all or none of the above three pieces of information. Concrete property classes, named like SimpleXXXProperty and ReadOnlyXXXWrapper, provide four constructors that let you supply combinations of the three pieces of information. The following are the constructors for the SimpleIntegerProperty class:

```
SimpleIntegerProperty()
SimpleIntegerProperty(int initialValue)
SimpleIntegerProperty(Object bean, String name)
SimpleIntegerProperty(Object bean, String name, int initialValue)
```

The default value for the initial value depends on the type of the property. It is zero for numeric types, false for boolean types, and null for reference types.

A property object can be part of a bean or it can be a standalone object. The specified bean is the reference to the bean object that contains the property. For a standalone property object, it can be null. Its default value is null.

The name of the property is its name. If not supplied, it defaults to an empty string.

The following snippet of code creates a property object as part of a bean and sets all three values. The first argument to the constructor of the SimpleStringProperty class is this, which is the reference of the Person bean, the second argument—"name"—is the name of the property, and the third argument— "Li"—is the value of the property:

```
public class Person {
        private StringProperty name = new SimpleStringProperty(this, "name", "Li");
        // More code goes here...
}
```

Every property class has getBean() and getName() methods that return the bean reference and the property name, respectively.

Using Properties in JavaFX Beans

In the previous section, you saw the use of JavaFX properties as standalone objects. In this section, you will use them in classes to define properties. Let's create a Book class with three properties: ISBN, title, and price, which will be modeled using JavaFX properties classes.

In JavaFX, you do not declare the property of a class as one of the primitive types. Rather, you use one of the JavaFX property classes. The title property of the Book class will be declared as follows. It is declared private as usual:

```
public class Book {
        private StringProperty title = new SimpleStringProperty(this, "title", "Unknown");
}
```

You declare a public getter for the property, which is named, by convention, as XXXProperty, where XXX is the name of the property. This getter returns the reference of the property. For our title property, the getter will be named titleProperty as shown below:

```
public class Book {
        private StringProperty title = new SimpleStringProperty(this, "title", "Unknown");

        public final StringProperty titleProperty() {
                return title;
        }
}
```

The above declaration of the Book class is fine to work with the title property, as shown in the following snippet of code that sets and gets the title of a book:

```
Book b = new Book();
b.titleProperty().set("Harnessing JavaFX 8.0");
String title = b.titleProperty().get();
```

According to the JavaFX design patterns, and not for any technical requirements, a JavaFX property has a getter and a setter that are similar to the getters and setters in JavaBeans. The return type of the getter and the parameter type of the setter are the same as the type of the property value. For example, for StringProperty and IntegerProperty, they will be String and int, respectively. The getTitle() and setTitle() methods for the title property are declared as follows:

```
public class Book {
        private StringProperty title = new SimpleStringProperty(this, "title", "Unknown");

        public final StringProperty titleProperty() {
                return title;
        }

        public final String getTitle() {
                return title.get();
        }

        public final void setTitle(String title) {
                this.title.set(title);
        }
}
```

Note that the getTitle() and setTitle() methods use the title property object internally to get and set the title value.

■ **Tip** By convention, getters and setters for a property of a class are declared final. Additional getters and setters, using JavaBeans naming convention, are added to make the class interoperable with the older tools and frameworks that use the old JavaBeans naming conventions to identify the properties of a class.

The following snippet of code shows the declaration of a read-only ISBN property for the Book class:

```
public class Book {
        private ReadOnlyStringWrapper ISBN = new ReadOnlyStringWrapper
        (this, "ISBN", "Unknown");

        public final String getISBN() {
                return ISBN.get();
        }

        public final ReadOnlyStringProperty ISBNProperty() {
                return ISBN.getReadOnlyProperty();
        }

        // More code goes here...
}
```

Notice the following points about the declaration of the read-only ISBN property:

- It uses the ReadOnlyStringWrapper class instead of the SimpleStringProperty class.

- There is no setter for the property value. You may declare one; however, it must be private.

- The getter for the property value works the same as for a read/write property.

- The ISBNProperty() method uses ReadOnlyStringProperty as the return type, not ReadOnlyStringWrapper. It obtains a read-only version of the property object from the wrapper object and returns the same.

For the users of the Book class, its ISBN property is read-only. However, it can be changed internally, and the change will be reflected in the read-only version of the property object automatically.

Listing 2-3 shows the complete code for the Book class.

Listing 2-3. A Book Class with Two Read/Write and a Read-Only Properties

```
// Book.java
package com.jdojo.binding;

import javafx.beans.property.DoubleProperty;
import javafx.beans.property.ReadOnlyStringProperty;
import javafx.beans.property.ReadOnlyStringWrapper;
import javafx.beans.property.SimpleDoubleProperty;
import javafx.beans.property.SimpleStringProperty;
import javafx.beans.property.StringProperty;

public class Book {
        private StringProperty title = new SimpleStringProperty(this, "title", "Unknown");
        private DoubleProperty price = new SimpleDoubleProperty(this, "price", 0.0);
        private ReadOnlyStringWrapper ISBN = new ReadOnlyStringWrapper(this, "ISBN", "Unknown");

        public Book() {
        }
```

```java
        public Book(String title, double price, String ISBN) {
                this.title.set(title);
                this.price.set(price);
                this.ISBN.set(ISBN);
        }

        public final String getTitle() {
                return title.get();
        }

        public final void setTitle(String title) {
                this.title.set(title);
        }

        public final StringProperty titleProperty() {
                return title;
        }

        public final double getprice() {
                return price.get();
        }

        public final void setPrice(double price) {
                this.price.set(price);
        }

        public final DoubleProperty priceProperty() {
                return price;
        }

        public final String getISBN() {
                return ISBN.get();
        }

        public final ReadOnlyStringProperty ISBNProperty() {
                return ISBN.getReadOnlyProperty();
        }
}
```

Listing 2-4 tests the properties of the Book class. It creates a Book object, prints the details, changes some properties, and prints the details again. Note the use of the ReadOnlyProperty parameter type for the printDetails() method. All property classes implement, directly or indirectly, the ReadOnlyProperty interface.

The toString() methods of the property implementation classes return a well-formatted string that contains all relevant pieces of information for a property. I did not use the toString() method of the property objects because I wanted to show you the use of the different methods of the JavaFX properties.

Listing 2-4. A Test Class to Test Properties of the Book Class

```java
// BookPropertyTest.java
package com.jdojo.binding;

import javafx.beans.property.ReadOnlyProperty;

public class BookPropertyTest {
        public static void main(String[] args) {
                Book book = new Book("Harnessing JavaFX", 9.99, "0123456789");

                System.out.println("After creating the Book object...");

                // Print Property details
                printDetails(book.titleProperty());
                printDetails(book.priceProperty());
                printDetails(book.ISBNProperty());

                // Change the book's properties
                book.setTitle("Harnessing JavaFX 8.0");
                book.setPrice(9.49);

                System.out.println("\nAfter changing the Book properties...");

                // Print Property details
                printDetails(book.titleProperty());
                printDetails(book.priceProperty());
                printDetails(book.ISBNProperty());
        }

        public static void printDetails(ReadOnlyProperty<?> p) {
                String name = p.getName();
                Object value = p.getValue();
                Object bean = p.getBean();
                String beanClassName = (bean == null)? "null":bean.getClass().getSimpleName();
                String propClassName = p.getClass().getSimpleName();

                System.out.print(propClassName);
                System.out.print("[Name:" + name);
                System.out.print(", Bean Class:" + beanClassName);
                System.out.println(", Value:" + value + "]");
        }
}
```

```
After creating the Book object...
SimpleStringProperty[Name:title, Bean Class:Book, Value:Harnessing JavaFX]
SimpleDoubleProperty[Name:price, Bean Class:Book, Value:9.99]
ReadOnlyPropertyImpl[Name:ISBN, Bean Class:Book, Value:0123456789]

After changing the Book properties...
SimpleStringProperty[Name:title, Bean Class:Book, Value:Harnessing JavaFX 8.0]
SimpleDoubleProperty[Name:price, Bean Class:Book, Value:9.49]
ReadOnlyPropertyImpl[Name:ISBN, Bean Class:Book, Value:0123456789]
```

Lazily Instantiating Property Objects

Compared to simple JavaBeans properties, JavaFX properties are more powerful. Their power comes from their observable and binding features at a price that every JavaFX property is an object. If you consider ten instances of a JavaFX class with 50 properties, you will have 500 objects in memory. However, not all properties use their advanced features. Most of them will be used as JavaBeans properties, using only getters and setters, or they will just use their default values. When it is likely that a JavaFX property will rarely use its advanced features, the property object may be instantiated lazily to optimize memory usage. The optimization comes at a price of adding a few extra lines of code.

The following are the two use cases where you can lazily instantiate a property:

- When the property will use its default value in most of the cases

- When the property will not use its observable and binding features in most cases

Consider a Monitor class with a screenType property whose default value is "flat". This falls into the first category, because most of the monitors are flat and will use the default value for the screenType property. Listing 2-5 shows the declaration of the Monitor class.

Listing 2-5. A Monitor Class that Uses the Default Value for Its screenType Property Most of the Time

```java
// Monitor.java
package com.jdojo.binding;

import javafx.beans.property.StringProperty;
import javafx.beans.property.SimpleStringProperty;

public class Monitor {
        public static final String DEFAULT_SCREEN_TYPE = "flat";
        private StringProperty screenType;

        public String getScreenType() {
                return (screenType == null) ? DEFAULT_SCREEN_TYPE : screenType.get();
        }

        public void setScreenType(String newScreenType) {
                if (screenType != null || !DEFAULT_SCREEN_TYPE.equals(newScreenType)) {
                        screenTypeProperty().set(newScreenType);
                }
        }

        public StringProperty screenTypeProperty() {
                if (screenType == null) {
                        screenType = new SimpleStringProperty(this, "screenType",
                                        DEFAULT_SCREEN_TYPE);
                }

                return screenType;
        }
}
```

The Monitor class declares a static variable DEFAULT_SCREEN_TYPE, which is initialized to the default value of the screen type. It declares a StringProperty, which is not instantiated at the time of declaration. It is instantiated later, when needed.

The getScreenType() method checks if the screenType property has been instantiated. If not, it returns the default value. Otherwise, it returns the value stored in the property object.

The setScreenType() method checks if the property object has already been instantiated or the property being set is other than the default value. If either one is true, it gets the property object using the screenTypeProperty() method, which will instantiate the property object, if needed, and sets the new property value.

The screenTypeProperty() method instantiates the property object the first time it is called.

This design for the Monitor class will work as intended only if its users do not call the screenTypeProperty() method until they really need the advanced features of the property. Consider the following snippet of code:

```
Monitor m = new Monitor();
String st = m.screenTypeProperty().get(); // Instantiates the property object
```

The above snippet of code instantiates a screenType property object, even though the user only wants to get the value of the property. The code should be rewritten as follows to delay the instantiation of the property object:

```
Monitor m = new Monitor();
String st = m.getScreenType(); // Does not instantiate the property object
```

Properties in the second category are used without advanced features in most of the cases. Listing 2-6 shows the declaration of an Item class that instantiates the property object when it is needed.

Listing 2-6. An Item Class that Rarely Uses Advanced Features of Its weight Property

```
// Item.java
package com.jdojo.binding;

import javafx.beans.property.DoubleProperty;
import javafx.beans.property.SimpleDoubleProperty;

public class Item {
        private DoubleProperty weight;
        private double _weight = 150;

        public double getWeight() {
                return (weight == null)?_weight:weight.get();
        }

        public void setWeight(double newWeight) {
                if (weight == null) {
                        _weight = newWeight;
                }
                else {
                        weight.set(newWeight);
                }
        }

        public DoubleProperty weightProperty() {
                if (weight == null) {
                        weight = new SimpleDoubleProperty(this, "weight", _weight);
                }
                return weight;
        }
}
```

The Item class declares an extra variable, _weight, which is used to hold the value of the weight property until the property object is instantiated. Unlike the Monitor class, changing the weight property does not instantiate the property object. It is instantiated when the weightProperty() method is called.

■ **Tip**   The approach used for instantiating a property object, eager or lazy, depends on the situation at hand. The fewer the number of properties in a class, the more likely all of them will be used, and you should be fine with eager instantiation. The more the number of properties in a class, the more likely fewer of them will be used, and you should go for lazy instantiation if the performance of your application matters.

Understanding the Property Class Hierarchy

It is important to understand a few core classes and interfaces of the JavaFX properties and binding APIs before you start using them. Figure 2-1 shows the class diagram for core interfaces of the properties API. You will not need to use these interfaces directly in your programs. Specialized versions of these interfaces and the classes that implement them exist and are used directly.

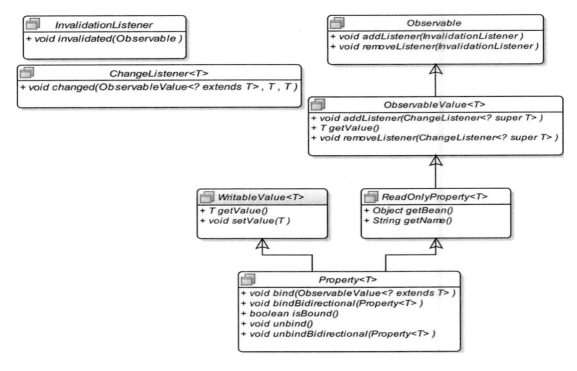

Figure 2-1. *A class diagram for core interfaces in the JavaFX property API*

Classes and interfaces in the JavaFX properties API are spread across different packages. Those packages are javafx.beans, javafx.beans.binding, javafx.beans.property, and javafx.beans.value.

The Observable interface is at the top of the properties API. An Observable wraps content, and it can be observed for invalidations of its content. The Observable interface has two methods to support this. Its addListener() method lets you add an InvalidationListener. The invalidated() method of the InvalidationListener is called when the content of the Observable becomes invalid. An InvalidationListener can be removed using its removeListener() method.

■ **Tip**   All JavaFX properties are observable.

An Observable should generate an invalidation event only when the status of its content changes from valid to invalid. That is, multiple invalidations in a row should generate only one invalidation event. Property classes in the JavaFX follow this guideline.

■ **Tip**   The generation of an invalidation event by an Observable does not necessarily mean that its content has changed. All it means is that its content is invalid for some reason. For example, sorting an ObservableList may generate an invalidation event. Sorting does not change the contents of the list; it only reorders the contents.

The ObservableValue interface inherits from the Observable interface. An ObservableValue wraps a value, which can be observed for changes. It has a getValue() method that returns the value it wraps. It generates invalidation events and change events. Invalidation events are generated when the value in the ObservableValue is no longer valid. Change events are generated when the value changes. You can register a ChangeListener to an ObservableValue. The changed() method of the ChangeListener is called every time the value of its value changes. The changed() method receives three arguments: the reference of the ObservableValue, the old value, and the new value.

An ObservableValue can recompute its value lazily or eagerly. In a lazy strategy, when its value becomes invalid, it does not know if the value has changed until the value is recomputed; the value is recomputed the next time it is read. For example, using the getValue() method of an ObservableValue would make it recompute its value if the value was invalid and if it uses a lazy strategy. In an eager strategy, the value is recomputed as soon as it becomes invalid.

To generate invalidation events, an ObservableValue can use lazy or eager evaluation. A lazy evaluation is more efficient. However, generating change events forces an ObservableValue to recompute its value immediately (an eager evaluation) as it has to pass the new value to the registered change listeners.

The ReadOnlyProperty interface adds getBean() and getName() methods. Their use was illustrated in Listing 2-4. The getBean() method returns the reference of the bean that contains the property object. The getName() method returns the name of the property. A read-only property implements this interface.

A WritableValue wraps a value that can be read and set using its getValue() and setValue() methods, respectively. A read/write property implements this interface.

The `Property` interface inherits from `ReadOnlyProperty` and `WritableValue` interfaces. It adds the following five methods to support binding:

- `void bind(ObservableValue<? extends T> observable)`
- `void unbind()`
- `void bindBidirectional(Property<T> other)`
- `void unbindBidirectional(Property<T> other)`
- `boolean isBound()`

The `bind()` method adds a unidirectional binding between this `Property` and the specified `ObservableValue`. The `unbind()` method removes the unidirectional binding for this `Property`, if one exists.

The `bindBidirectional()` method creates a bidirectional binding between this `Property` and the specified `Property`. The `unbindBidirectional()` method removes a bidirectional binding.

Note the difference in the parameter types for the `bind()` and `bindBidirectional()` methods. A unidirectional binding can be created between a `Property` and an `ObservableValue` of the same type as long as they are related through inheritance. However, a bidirectional binding can only be created between two properties of the same type.

The `isBound()` method returns `true` if the `Property` is bound. Otherwise, it returns `false`.

▪ **Tip** All read/write JavaFX properties support binding.

Figure 2-2 shows a partial class diagram for the integer property in JavaFX. The diagram gives you an idea about the complexity of the JavaFX properties API. You do not need to learn all of the classes in the properties API. You will use only a few of them in your applications.

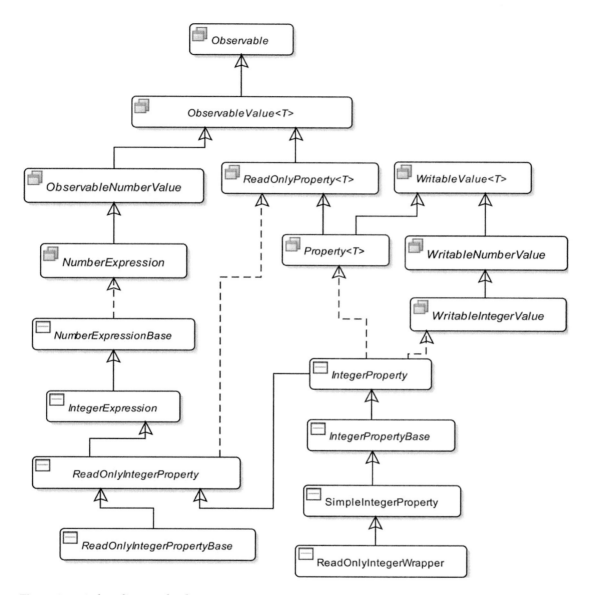

Figure 2-2. *A class diagram for the integer property*

Handling Property Invalidation Events

A property generates an invalidation event when the status of its value changes from valid to invalid for the first time. Properties in JavaFX use lazy evaluation. When an invalid property becomes invalid again, an invalidation event is not generated. An invalid property becomes valid when it is recomputed, for example, by calling its get() or getValue() method.

Listing 2-7 provides the program to demonstrate when invalidation events are generated for properties. The program includes enough comments to help you understand its logic. In the beginning, it creates an IntegerProperty named counter:

```
IntegerProperty counter = new SimpleIntegerProperty(100);
```

An InvalidationListener is added to the counter property:

```
counter.addListener(InvalidationTest::invalidated);
```

Note that the above statement uses a lambda expression and a method reference, which are features of Java 8. If you are not familiar with lambda expressions, you can compare the above statement to the following snippet of code, which uses an anonymous inner class:

```
import javafx.beans.InvalidationListener;
...
counter.addListener(new InvalidationListener() {
        @Override
        public void invalidated(Observable prop) {
                InvalidationTest.invalidated(prop);
        }});
```

When you create a property object, it is valid. When you change the counter property to 101, it fires an invalidation event. At this point, the counter property becomes invalid. When you change its value to 102, it does not fire an invalidation event, because it is already invalid. When you use the get() method to read the counter value, it becomes valid again. Now you set the same value, 102, to the counter, which does not fire an invalidation event, as the value did not really change. The counter property is still valid. At the end, you change its value to a different value, and sure enough, an invalidation event is fired.

■ **Tip**   You are not limited to adding only one invalidation listener to a property. You can add as many invalidation listeners as you need. Once you are done with an invalidation listener, make sure to remove it by calling the removeListener() method of the Observable interface; otherwise, it may lead to memory leaks. Please refer to the section "Avoiding Memory Leaks in Listeners" for more details on how to avoid memory leaks.

Listing 2-7. Testing Invalidation Events for Properties

```
// InvalidationTest.java
package com.jdojo.binding;

import javafx.beans.Observable;
import javafx.beans.property.IntegerProperty;
import javafx.beans.property.SimpleIntegerProperty;

public class InvalidationTest {
        public static void main(String[] args) {
                IntegerProperty counter = new SimpleIntegerProperty(100);

                // Add an invalidation listener to the counter property
                counter.addListener(InvalidationTest::invalidated);
```

```
            System.out.println("Before changing the counter value-1");
            counter.set(101);
            System.out.println("After changing the counter value-1");

            /* At this point counter property is invalid and further changes
               to its value will not generate invalidation events.
             */
            System.out.println("\nBefore changing the counter value-2");
            counter.set(102);
            System.out.println("After changing the counter value-2");

            // Make the counter property valid by calling its get() method
            int value = counter.get();
            System.out.println("Counter value = " + value);

            /* At this point counter property is valid and further changes
               to its value will generate invalidation events.
             */
            // Try to set the same value
            System.out.println("\nBefore changing the counter value-3");
            counter.set(102);
            System.out.println("After changing the counter value-3");

            // Try to set a different value
            System.out.println("\nBefore changing the counter value-4");
            counter.set(103);
            System.out.println("After changing the counter value-4");
    }

    public static void invalidated(Observable prop) {
            System.out.println("Counter is invalid.");
    }
}
```

```
Before changing the counter value-1
Counter is invalid.
After changing the counter value-1

Before changing the counter value-2
After changing the counter value-2
Counter value = 102

Before changing the counter value-3
After changing the counter value-3

Before changing the counter value-4
Counter is invalid.
After changing the counter value-4
```

Handling Property Change Events

You can register a ChangeListener to receive notifications about property change events. A property change event is fired every time the value of a property changes. The changed() method of a ChangeListener receives three values: the reference of the property object, the old value, and the new value.

Let's run a similar test case for testing property change events as was done for invalidation events in the previous section. Listing 2-8 has the program to demonstrate change events that are generated for properties.

Listing 2-8. Testing Change Events for Properties

```java
// ChangeTest.java
package com.jdojo.binding;

import javafx.beans.property.IntegerProperty;
import javafx.beans.property.SimpleIntegerProperty;
import javafx.beans.value.ObservableValue;

public class ChangeTest {
    public static void main(String[] args) {
        IntegerProperty counter = new SimpleIntegerProperty(100);

        // Add a change listener to the counter property
        counter.addListener(ChangeTest::changed);

        System.out.println("\nBefore changing the counter value-1");
        counter.set(101);
        System.out.println("After changing the counter value-1");

        System.out.println("\nBefore changing the counter value-2");
        counter.set(102);
        System.out.println("After changing the counter value-2");

        // Try to set the same value
        System.out.println("\nBefore changing the counter value-3");
        counter.set(102); // No change event is fired.
        System.out.println("After changing the counter value-3");

        // Try to set a different value
        System.out.println("\nBefore changing the counter value-4");
        counter.set(103);
        System.out.println("After changing the counter value-4");
    }

    public static void changed(ObservableValue<? extends Number> prop,
                               Number oldValue,
                               Number newValue) {
        System.out.print("Counter changed: ");
        System.out.println("Old = " + oldValue + ", new = " + newValue);
    }
}
```

```
Befor changing the counter value-1
Counter changed: Old = 100, new = 101
After changing the counter value-1

Before changing the counter value-2
Counter changed: Old = 101, new = 102
After changing the counter value-2

Before changing the counter value-3
After changing the counter value-3

Before changing the counter value-4
Counter changed: Old = 102, new = 103
After changing the counter value-4
```

In the beginning, the program creates an IntegerProperty named counter:

```
IntegerProperty counter = new SimpleIntegerProperty(100);
```

There is a little trick in adding a ChangeListener. The addListener() method in the IntegerPropertyBase class is declared as follows:

```
void addListener(ChangeListener<? super Number> listener)
```

This means that if you are using generics, the ChangeListener for an IntegerProperty must be written in terms of the Number class or a superclass of the Number class. Three ways to add a ChangeListener to the counter property are shown below:

```
// Method-1: Using generics and the Number class
counter.addListener(new ChangeListener<Number>() {
        @Override
        public void changed(ObservableValue<? extends Number> prop,
                            Number oldValue,
                            Number newValue) {
            System.out.print("Counter changed: ");
            System.out.println("Old = " + oldValue + ", new = " + newValue);
        }});

// Method-2: Using generics and the Object class
counter.addListener( new ChangeListener<Object>() {
        @Override
        public void changed(ObservableValue<? extends Object> prop,
                            Object oldValue,
                            Object newValue) {
            System.out.print("Counter changed: ");
            System.out.println("Old = " + oldValue + ", new = " + newValue);
        }});
```

```
// Method-3: Not using generics. It may generate compile-time warnings.
counter.addListener(new ChangeListener() {
        @Override
        public void changed(ObservableValue prop,
                            Object oldValue,
                            Object newValue) {
            System.out.print("Counter changed: ");
            System.out.println("Old = " + oldValue + ", new = " + newValue);
        }});
```

Listing 2-8 uses the first method, which makes use of generics; as you can see, the signature of the changed() method in the ChangeTest class matches with the changed() method signature in method-1. I have used a lambda expression with a method reference to add a ChangeListener as shown:

```
counter.addListener(ChangeTest::changed);
```

The output above shows that a property change event is fired when the property value is changed. Calling the set() method with the same value does not fire a property change event.

Unlike generating invalidation events, a property uses an eager evaluation for its value to generate change events, because it has to pass the new value to the property change listeners. The next section discusses how a property object evaluates its value, if it has both invalidation and change listeners.

Avoiding Memory Leaks in Listeners

When you add an invalidation listener to an Observable, the Observable stores a strong reference to the listener. Like an Observable, an ObservableValue also keeps a strong reference to the registered change listeners. In a short-lived small application, you may not notice any difference. However, in a long-running big application, you may encounter memory leaks. The cause of the memory leaks is the strong reference to the listeners being stored in the observed objects, even though you do not need those listeners anymore.

■ **Tip** Memory leaks happens when the property object holding the strong reference to the listeners outlives the need to use the listeners. If you do not need listeners, and at the same time the property object holding their strong references becomes eligible for garbage collection, memory leaks may not occur.

The solution is to remove the listeners using removeListener() method when you do not need them. Implementing this solution may not always be easy. The main problem in implementing this is in deciding when to remove the listener. Sometimes multiple paths may exist, adding complexity to the solution, when listeners may need to be removed.

Listing 2-9 shows a simple use case, where a change listener is added, used, and removed. It creates an IntegerProperty named counter as a static variable. In the main() method, it calls the addListener() method that adds a change listener to the counter property, changes the value of counter to fire a change event, as shown in the output, and finally, it removes the change listener. The main() method changes the value of counter again, which does not fire any change events, because the change listener has already been removed. This is a use case where everything worked as expected.

Listing 2-9. Removing Listeners When They Are Not Needed

```java
// CleanupListener.java
package com.jdojo.binding;

import javafx.beans.property.IntegerProperty;
import javafx.beans.property.SimpleIntegerProperty;
import javafx.beans.value.ChangeListener;
import javafx.beans.value.ObservableValue;

public class CleanupListener {
        public static IntegerProperty counter = new SimpleIntegerProperty(100);

        public static void main(String[] args) {
                // Add a change listener to the property
                ChangeListener<Number> listener = CleanupListener::changed;
                counter.addListener(listener);

                // Change the counter value
                counter.set(200);

                // Remove the listener
                counter.removeListener(listener);

                // Will not fire change event as change listener has
                // already been removed.
                counter.set(300);
        }

        public static void changed(ObservableValue<? extends Number> prop,
                                Number oldValue,
                                Number newValue) {
                System.out.print("Counter changed: ");
                System.out.println("old = " + oldValue + ", new = " + newValue);
        }
}
```

```
Counter changed: old = 100, new = 200
```

The program in Listing 2-10 shows a variation of the program in Listing 2-9. In the addStrongListener() method, you have added a change listener to the counter property but did not remove it. The second line in the output proves that even after the addStrongListener() method finishes executing, the counter property is still holding the reference to the change listener you had added. After the addStrongListener() method is finished, you do not have a reference to the change listener variable, because it was declared as a local variable. Therefore, you do not even have a way to remove the listener. This use case shows, though trivially, the intrinsic nature of memory leaks while using invalidation and change listeners with properties.

Listing 2-10. Simulating Memory Leaks Because Listeners Were Not Removed

```java
// StrongListener.java

package com.jdojo.binding;

import javafx.beans.property.IntegerProperty;
import javafx.beans.property.SimpleIntegerProperty;
import javafx.beans.value.ChangeListener;
import javafx.beans.value.ObservableValue;

public class StrongListener {
        public static IntegerProperty counter = new SimpleIntegerProperty(100);

        public static void main(String[] args) {
                // Add a change listener to the property
                addStrongListener();

                // Change counter value. It will fire a change event.
                counter.set(300);
        }

        public static void addStrongListener() {
                ChangeListener<Number> listener = StrongListener::changed;
                counter.addListener(listener);

                // Change the counter value
                counter.set(200);
        }

        public static void changed(ObservableValue<? extends Number> prop,
                                Number oldValue,
                                Number newValue) {
                System.out.print("Counter changed: ");
                System.out.println("old = " + oldValue + ", new = " + newValue);
        }
}
```

```
Counter changed: old = 100, new = 200
Counter changed: old = 200, new = 300
```

The solution is to use weak listeners, which are garbage collected automatically. A weak listener is an instance of the WeakListener interface. JavaFX provides two implementation classes of the WeakListener interface that can be used as invalidation and change listeners: WeakInvalidationListener and WeakChangeListener classes. Figure 2-3 shows a class diagram for these classes. Note that a WeakListener interface has one method that tells whether the listener has been garbage collected. I will discuss change listeners in the rest of this section. However, this discussion applies to the invalidation listener as well.

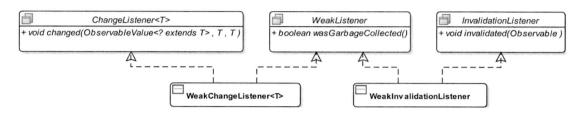

Figure 2-3. *A class diagram for WeakChangeListener and WeakInvalidationListener*

A WeakChangeListener is a wrapper for a ChangeListener. It has only one constructor that accepts an instance of a ChangeListener. The following snippet of code shows how to create and use a WeakChangeListener:

```
ChangeListener<Number> cListener = create a change listener...
WeakChangeListener<Number> wListener = new WeakChangeListener(cListener);

// Add a weak change listener, assuming that counter is a property
counter.addListener(wListener);
```

You might be happy to see the above snippet of code in the hope that you have found an easy solution to the big issue of memory leaks. However, this solution is not as elegant as it seems. You need to keep a strong reference of the change listener around as long as you do not want it to be garbage collected. In the above snippet of code, you will need to keep the reference cListener around until you know that you no longer need to listen to the change event. Isn't this similar to saying that you need to remove the listener when you do not need it? The answer is yes and no. The answer is yes, because you do need to take an action to clean up the listener. But the answer is also no, because you may design your logic to store the reference of the change listener in an object that is scoped in such a way that the change listener goes out of scope the same time you do not need it.

The program in Listing 2-11 shows, using a trivial use case, how to use a weak change listener. It is a slight variation of the previous two programs. It declares three static variables: a counter property, a WeakChangeListener, and a ChangeListener. The addWeakListener() method creates a change listener, stores its reference to the static variable, wraps it in a weak change listener, and adds it to the counter property. The counter property is changed at the end.

The main() method changes the counter property several times. It also tries to invoke garbage collection, using System.gc(), and prints a message to check if the change listener has been garbage collected. As long as you keep a strong reference to the change listener in the changeListener static variable, the change listener is not garbage collected. After you set it to null and then invoke the garbage collection again, the change listener will be garbage collected. The last change in the counter property, inside the main() method, did not fire a change event as the change listener had already been removed automatically, as it was wrapped in a weak change listener.

Listing 2-11. Using a Weak Change Listener

```
// WeakListener.java
package com.jdojo.binding;

import javafx.beans.property.IntegerProperty;
import javafx.beans.property.SimpleIntegerProperty;
import javafx.beans.value.ChangeListener;
import javafx.beans.value.ObservableValue;
import javafx.beans.value.WeakChangeListener;

public class WeakListener {
        public static IntegerProperty counter = new SimpleIntegerProperty(100);
        public static WeakChangeListener<Number> weakListener ;
        public static ChangeListener<Number> changeListener;

        public static void main(String[] args) {
                // Add a weak change listener to the property
                addWeakListener();

                // It will fire a change event
                counter.set(300);

                // Try garbage collection
                System.gc();

                // Check if change listener got garbage collected
                System.out.println("Garbage collected: " +
                                        weakListener.wasGarbageCollected());

                // It will fire a change event
                counter.set(400);

                // You do not need a strong reference of the change listener
                changeListener = null;

                // Try garbage collection
                System.gc();

                // Check if the change listener got garbage collected
                System.out.println("Garbage collected: " +
                                        weakListener.wasGarbageCollected());

                // It will not fire a change event, if it was garbage collected
                counter.set(500);
        }

        public static void addWeakListener() {
                // Keep a strong reference to the change listener
                changeListener = WeakListener::changed;
```

```
            // Wrap the change listener inside a weak change listener
            weakListener = new WeakChangeListener<>(changeListener);

            // Add weak change listener
            counter.addListener(weakListener);

            // Change the value
            counter.set(200);
        }

        public static void changed(ObservableValue<? extends Number> prop,
                                   Number oldValue,
                                   Number newValue) {
            System.out.print("Counter changed: ");
            System.out.println("old = " + oldValue + ", new = " + newValue);
        }
}
```

```
Counter changed: old = 100, new = 200
Counter changed: old = 200, new = 300
Garbage collected: false
Counter changed: old = 300, new = 400
Garbage collected: false
Counter changed: old = 400, new = 500
```

Handling Invalidation and Change Events

You need to consider performance when you have to decide between using invalidation listeners and change listeners. Generally, invalidation listeners perform better than change listeners. The reason is twofold:

- Invalidation listeners make it possible to compute the value lazily.
- Multiple invalidations in a row fire only one invalidation event.

However, which listener you use depends on the situation at hand. A rule of thumb is that if you read the value of the property inside the invalidation event handler, you should use a change listener instead. When you read the value of a property inside an invalidation listener, it triggers the recomputation of the value, which is automatically done before firing a change event. If you do not need to read the value of a property, use invalidation listeners.

Listing 2-12 has a program that adds an invalidation listener and a change listener to an IntegerProperty. This program is a combination of Listing 2-7 and Listing 2-8. The output below it shows that when the property value changes, both events, invalidation and change, are always fired. This is because a change event makes a property valid immediately after the change, and the next change in the value fires an invalidation event, and of course, a change event too.

Listing 2-12. Testing Invalidation and Change Events for Properties Together

```java
// ChangeAndInvalidationTest.java
package com.jdojo.binding;

import javafx.beans.Observable;
import javafx.beans.property.IntegerProperty;
import javafx.beans.property.SimpleIntegerProperty;
import javafx.beans.value.ObservableValue;

public class ChangeAndInvalidationTest {
        public static void main(String[] args) {
                IntegerProperty counter = new SimpleIntegerProperty(100);

                // Add an invalidation listener to the counter property
                counter.addListener(ChangeAndInvalidationTest::invalidated);

                // Add a change listener to the counter property
                counter.addListener(ChangeAndInvalidationTest::changed);

                System.out.println("Before changing the counter value-1");
                counter.set(101);
                System.out.println("After changing the counter value-1");

                System.out.println("\nBefore changing the counter value-2");
                counter.set(102);
                System.out.println("After changing the counter value-2");

                // Try to set the same value
                System.out.println("\nBefore changing the counter value-3");
                counter.set(102);
                System.out.println("After changing the counter value-3");

                // Try to set a different value
                System.out.println("\nBefore changing the counter value-4");
                counter.set(103);
                System.out.println("After changing the counter value-4");
        }

        public static void invalidated(Observable prop) {
                System.out.println("Counter is invalid.");
        }

        public static void changed(ObservableValue<? extends Number> prop,
                                Number oldValue,
                                Number newValue) {
                System.out.print("Counter changed: ");
                System.out.println("old = " + oldValue + ", new = " + newValue);
        }
}
```

```
Before changing the counter value-1
Counter is invalid.
Counter changed: old = 100, new = 101
After changing the counter value-1

Before changing the counter value-2
Counter is invalid.
Counter changed: old = 101, new = 102
After changing the counter value-2

Before changing the counter value-3
After changing the counter value-3

Before changing the counter value-4
Counter is invalid.
Counter changed: old = 102, new = 103
After changing the counter value-4
```

Using Bindings in JavaFX

In JavaFX, a binding is an expression that evaluates to a value. It consists of one or more observable values known as its *dependencies*. A binding observes its dependencies for changes and recomputes its value automatically. JavaFX uses lazy evaluation for all bindings. When a binding is initially defined or when its dependencies change, its value is marked as invalid. The value of an invalid binding is computed when it is requested next time, usually using its get() or getValue() method. All property classes in JavaFX have built-in support for binding.

Let's look at a quick example of binding in JavaFX. Consider the following expression that represents the sum of two integers x and y:

```
x + y
```

The expression, x + y, represents a binding, which has two dependencies: x and y. You can give it a name sum as:

```
sum = x + y
```

To implement the above logic in JavaFX, you create two IntegerProperty variables: x and y:

```
IntegerProperty x = new SimpleIntegerProperty(100);
IntegerProperty y = new SimpleIntegerProperty(200);
```

The following statement creates a binding named sum that represents the sum of x and y:

```
NumberBinding sum = x.add(y);
```

A binding has an isValid() method that returns true if it is valid; otherwise, it returns false. You can get the value of a NumberBinding using the methods intValue(), longValue(), floatValue(), and doubleValue() as int, long, float, and double, respectively.

The program in Listing 2-13 shows how to create and use a binding based on the above discussion. When the sum binding is created, it is invalid and it does not know its value. This is evident from the output. Once you request its value, using the sum.initValue() method, it computes its value and marks itself as valid. When you change one of its dependencies, it becomes invalid until you request its value again.

Listing 2-13. Using a Simple Binding

```
// BindingTest.java
package com.jdojo.binding;

import javafx.beans.binding.NumberBinding;
import javafx.beans.property.IntegerProperty;
import javafx.beans.property.SimpleIntegerProperty;

public class BindingTest {
        public static void main(String[] args) {
                IntegerProperty x = new SimpleIntegerProperty(100);
                IntegerProperty y = new SimpleIntegerProperty(200);

                // Create a binding: sum = x + y
                NumberBinding sum = x.add(y);

                System.out.println("After creating sum");
                System.out.println("sum.isValid(): " + sum.isValid());

                // Let us get the value of sum, so it computes its value and
                // becomes valid
                int value = sum.intValue();

                System.out.println("\nAfter requesting value");
                System.out.println("sum.isValid(): " + sum.isValid());
                System.out.println("sum = " + value);

                // Change the value of x
                x.set(250);

                System.out.println("\nAfter changing x");
                System.out.println("sum.isValid(): " + sum.isValid());

                // Get the value of sum again
                value = sum.intValue();

                System.out.println("\nAfter requesting value");
                System.out.println("sum.isValid(): " + sum.isValid());
                System.out.println("sum = " + value);
        }
}
```

```
After creating sum
sum.isValid(): false

After requesting value
sum.isValid(): true
sum = 300

After changing x
sum.isValid(): false

After requesting value
sum.isValid(): true
sum = 450
```

A binding, internally, adds invalidation listeners to all of its dependencies (Listing 2-14). When any of its dependencies become invalid, it marks itself as invalid. An invalid binding does not mean that its value has changed. All it means is that it needs to recompute its value when the value is requested next time.

In JavaFX, you can also bind a property to a binding. Recall that a binding is an expression that is synchronized with its dependencies automatically. Using this definition, a bound property is a property whose value is computed based on an expression, which is automatically synchronized when the dependencies change. Suppose you have three properties, x, y, and z, as follows:

```
IntegerProperty x = new SimpleIntegerProperty(10);
IntegerProperty y = new SimpleIntegerProperty(20);
IntegerProperty z = new SimpleIntegerProperty(60);
```

You can bind the property z to an expression, x + y, using the bind() method of the Property interface as follows:

```
z.bind(x.add(y));
```

Note that you cannot write z.bind(x + y) as the + operator does not know how to add the values of two IntegerProperty objects. You need to use the binding API, as you did in the above statement, to create a binding expression. I will cover the details of the binding API shortly.

Now, when x, y, or both change, the z property becomes invalid. The next time you request the value of z, it recomputes the expression x.add(y) to get its value.

You can use the unbind() method of the Property interface to unbind a bound property. Calling the unbind() method on an unbound or never bound property has no effect. You can unbind the z property as follows:

```
z.unbind();
```

After unbinding, a property behaves as a normal property, maintaining its value independently. Unbinding a property breaks the link between the property and its dependencies.

Listing 2-14. Binding a Property

```java
// BoundProperty.java
package com.jdojo.binding;

import javafx.beans.property.IntegerProperty;
import javafx.beans.property.SimpleIntegerProperty;

public class BoundProperty {
    public static void main(String[] args) {
        IntegerProperty x = new SimpleIntegerProperty(10);
        IntegerProperty y = new SimpleIntegerProperty(20);
        IntegerProperty z = new SimpleIntegerProperty(60);
        z.bind(x.add(y));
        System.out.println("After binding z: Bound = " + z.isBound() +
                        ", z = " + z.get());

        // Change x and y
        x.set(15);
        y.set(19);
        System.out.println("After changing x and y: Bound = " + z.isBound() +
                        ", z = " + z.get());
        // Unbind z
        z.unbind();

        // Will not affect the value of z as it is not bound to x and y anymore
        x.set(100);
        y.set(200);
        System.out.println("After unbinding z: Bound = " + z.isBound() +
                        ", z = " + z.get());
    }
}
```

```
After binding z: Bound = true, z = 30
After changing x and y: Bound = true, z = 34
After unbinding z: Bound = false, z = 34
```

Unidirectional and Bidirectional Bindings

A binding has a direction, which is the direction in which changes are propagated. JavaFX supports two types of binding for properties: *unidirectional binding* and *bidirectional binding*. A unidirectional binding works only in one direction; changes in dependencies are propagated to the bound property and not vice versa. A bidirectional binding works in both directions; changes in dependencies are reflected in the property and vice versa.

The bind() method of the Property interface creates a unidirectional binding between a property and an ObservableValue, which could be a complex expression. The bindBidirectional() method creates a bidirectional binding between a property and another property of the same type.

Suppose that x, y, and z are three instances of `IntegerProperty`. Consider the following bindings:

```
z = x + y
```

In JavaFX, the above binding can only be expressed as a unidirectional binding as follows:

```
z.bind(x.add(y));
```

Suppose you were able to use bidirectional binding in the above case. If you were able to change the value of z to 100, how would you compute the values of x and y in the reverse direction? For z being 100, there are an infinite number of possible combinations for x and y, for example, (99, 1), (98, 2), (101, -1), (200, -100), and so on. Propagating changes from a bound property to its dependencies is not possible with predictable results. This is the reason that binding a property to an expression is allowed only as a unidirectional binding.

Unidirectional binding has a restriction. Once a property has a unidirectional binding, you cannot change the value of the property directly; its value must be computed automatically based on the binding. You must unbind it before changing its value directly. The following snippet of code shows this case:

```
IntegerProperty x = new SimpleIntegerProperty(10);
IntegerProperty y = new SimpleIntegerProperty(20);
IntegerProperty z = new SimpleIntegerProperty(60);
z.bind(x.add(y));

z.set(7878); // Will throw a RuntimeException
```

To change the value of z directly, you can type the following:

```
z.unbind();  // Unbind z first
z.set(7878); // OK
```

Unidirectional binding has another restriction. A property can have only one unidirectional binding at a time. Consider the following two unidirectional bindings for a property z. Assume that x, y, z, a, and b are five instances of `IntegerProperty`:

```
z = x + y
z = a + b
```

If x, y, a, and b are four different properties, the bindings shown above for z are not possible. Think about x = 1, y = 2, a = 3, and b = 4. Can you define the value of z? Will it be 3 or 7? This is the reason that a property can have only one unidirectional binding at a time.

Rebinding a property that already has a unidirectional binding unbinds the previous binding. For example, the following snippet of code works fine:

```
IntegerProperty x = new SimpleIntegerProperty(1);
IntegerProperty y = new SimpleIntegerProperty(2);
IntegerProperty a = new SimpleIntegerProperty(3);
IntegerProperty b = new SimpleIntegerProperty(4);
IntegerProperty z = new SimpleIntegerProperty(0);
```

```
z.bind(x.add(y));
System.out.println("z = " + z.get());

z.bind(a.add(b)); // Will unbind the previous binding
System.out.println("z = " + z.get());
```

```
z = 3
z = 7
```

A bidirectional binding works in both directions. It has some restrictions. It can only be created between properties of the same type. That is, a bidirectional binding can only be of the type x = y and y = x, where x and y are of the same type.

Bidirectional binding removes some restrictions that are present for unidirectional binding. A property can have multiple bidirectional bindings at the same time. A bidirectional bound property can also be changed independently; the change is reflected in all properties that are bound to this property. That is, the following bindings are possible, using the bidirectional bindings:

```
x = y
x = z
```

In the above case, the values of x, y, and z will always be synchronized. That is, all three properties will have the same value, after the bindings are established. You can also establish bidirectional bindings between x, y, and z as follows:

```
x = z
z = y
```

Now a question arises. Will both of the above bidirectional bindings end up having the same values in x, y, and z? The answer is no. The value of the right-hand operand (see the above expressions for example) in the last bidirectional binding is the value that is contained by all participating properties. Let me elaborate this point. Suppose x is 1, y is 2, and z is 3, and you have the following bidirectional bindings:

```
x = y
x = z
```

The first binding, x = y, will set the value of x equal to the value of y. At this point, x and y will be 2. The second binding, x = z, will set the value of x to be equal to the value of z. That is, x and z will be 3. However, x already has a bidirectional binding to y, which will propagate the new value 3 of x to y as well. Therefore, all three properties will have the same value as that of z. The program in Listing 2-15 shows how to use bidirectional bindings.

Listing 2-15. Using Bidirectional Bindings

```
// BidirectionalBinding.java
package com.jdojo.binding;

import javafx.beans.property.IntegerProperty;
import javafx.beans.property.SimpleIntegerProperty;
```

```java
public class BidirectionalBinding {
        public static void main(String[] args) {
                IntegerProperty x = new SimpleIntegerProperty(1);
                IntegerProperty y = new SimpleIntegerProperty(2);
                IntegerProperty z = new SimpleIntegerProperty(3);

                System.out.println("Before binding:");
                System.out.println("x=" + x.get() + ", y=" + y.get() + ", z=" + z.get());

                x.bindBidirectional(y);
                System.out.println("After binding-1:");
                System.out.println("x=" + x.get() + ", y=" + y.get() + ", z=" + z.get());

                x.bindBidirectional(z);
                System.out.println("After binding-2:");
                System.out.println("x=" + x.get() + ", y=" + y.get() + ", z=" + z.get());

                System.out.println("After changing z:");
                z.set(19);
                System.out.println("x=" + x.get() + ", y=" + y.get() + ", z=" + z.get());

                // Remove bindings
                x.unbindBidirectional(y);
                x.unbindBidirectional(z);
                System.out.println("After unbinding and changing them separately:");
                x.set(100);
                y.set(200);
                z.set(300);
                System.out.println("x=" + x.get() + ", y=" + y.get() + ", z=" + z.get());
        }
}
```

```
Before binding:
x=1, y=2, z=3
After binding-1:
x=2, y=2, z=3
After binding-2:
x=3, y=3, z=3
After changing z:
x=19, y=19, z=19
After unbinding and changing them separately:
x=100, y=200, z=300
```

Unlike a unidirectional binding, when you create a bidirectional binding, the previous bindings are not removed because a property can have multiple bidirectional bindings. You must remove all bidirectional bindings using the unbindBidirectional() method, calling it once for each bidirectional binding for a property, as shown here:

```
// Create bidirectional bindings
x.bindBidirectional(y);
x.bindBidirectional(z);

// Remove bidirectional bindings
x.unbindBidirectional(y);
x.unbindBidirectional(z);
```

Understanding the Binding API

Previous sections gave you a quick and simple introduction to bindings in JavaFX. Now it's time to dig deeper and understand the binding API in detail. The binding API is divided into two categories:

- High-level binding API
- Low-level binding API

The high-level binding API lets you define binding using the JavaFX class library. For most use cases, you can use the high-level binding API.

Sometimes the existing API is not sufficient to define a binding. In those cases, the low-level binding API is used. In low-level binding API, you derive a binding class from an existing binding class and write your own logic to define a binding.

The High-Level Binding API

The high-level binding API consists of two parts: the Fluent API and the Bindings class. You can define bindings using only the Fluent API, only the Bindings class, or by combining the two. Let's look at both parts, first separately and then together.

Using the Fluent API

The Fluent API consists of several methods in different interfaces and classes. The API is called *Fluent* because the method names, their parameters, and return types have been designed in such a way that they allow writing the code fluently. The code written using the Fluent API is more readable as compared to code written using nonfluent APIs. Designing a fluent API takes more time. A fluent API is more developer friendly and less designer friendly. One of the features of a fluent API is *method chaining*; you can combine separate method calls into one statement. Consider the following snippet of code to add three properties x, y, and z. The code using a nonfluent API might look as follows:

```
x.add(y);
x.add(z);
```

Using a Fluent API, the above code may look as shown below, which gives readers a better understanding of the intention of the writer:

```
x.add(y).add(z);
```

Figure 2-4 shows a class diagram for the `IntegerBinding` and `IntegerProperty` classes. The diagram has omitted some of the interfaces and classes that fall into the `IntegerProperty` class hierarchy. Class diagrams for `long`, `float`, and `double` types are similar.

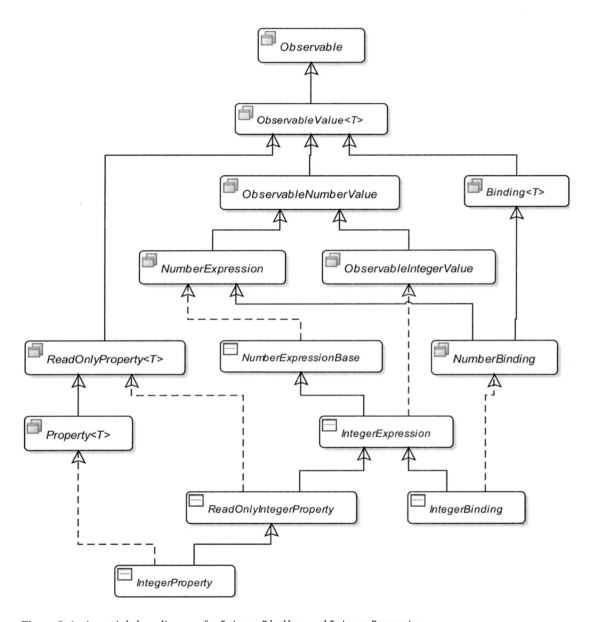

Figure 2-4. *A partial class diagram for `IntegerBinding` and `IntegerProperty`*

Classes and interfaces from the ObservableNumberValue and Binding interfaces down to the IntegerBinding class are part of the fluent binding API for the int data type. At first it may seem as if there were many classes to learn. Most of the classes and interfaces exist in properties and binding APIs to avoid boxing and unboxing of primitive values. To learn the fluent binding API, you need to focus on XXXExpression and XXXBinding classes and interfaces. The XXXExpression classes have the methods that are used to create binding expressions.

The *Binding* Interface

An instance of the Binding interface represents a value that is derived from one or more sources known as dependencies. It has the following four methods:

- public void dispose()
- public ObservableList<?> getDependencies()
- public void invalidate()
- public boolean isValid()

The dispose() method, whose implementation is optional, indicates to a Binding that it will no longer be used, so it can remove references to other objects. The binding API uses weak invalidation listeners internally, making the call to this method unnecessary.

The getDependencies() method, whose implementation is optional, returns an unmodifiable ObservableList of dependencies. It exists only for debugging purposes. This method should not be used in production code.

A call to the invalidate() method invalidates a Binding. The isValid() method returns true if a Binding is valid. Otherwise, it returns false.

The *NumberBinding* Interface

The NumberBinding interface is a marker interface whose instance wraps a numeric value of int, long, float, or double type. It is implemented by DoubleBinding, FloatBinding, IntegerBinding, and LongBinding classes.

The *ObservableNumberValue* Interface

An instance of the ObservableNumberValue interface wraps a numeric value of int, long, float, or double type. It provides the following four methods to get the value:

- double doubleValue()
- float floatValue()
- int intValue()
- long longValue()

You used the intValue() method provided in Listing 2-13 to get the int value from a NumberBinding instance. The code you use would be:

```
IntegerProperty x = new SimpleIntegerProperty(100);
IntegerProperty y = new SimpleIntegerProperty(200);

// Create a binding: sum = x + y
NumberBinding sum = x.add(y);
int value = sum.intValue(); // Get the int value
```

The *ObservableIntegerValue* Interface

The ObservableIntegerValue interface defines a get() method that returns the type specific int value.

The *NumberExpression* Interface

The NumberExpression interface contains several convenience methods to create bindings using a fluent style. It has over 50 methods, and most of them are overloaded. These methods return a Binding type such as NumberBinding, BooleanBinding, and so on. Table 2-2 lists the methods in the NumberExpression interface. Most of the methods are overloaded. The table does not show the method arguments.

Table 2-2. *Summary of the Methods in the NumberExpression Interface*

Method Name	Return Type	Description
add() subtract() multiply() divide()	NumberBinding	These methods create a new NumberBinding that is the sum, difference, product, and division of the NumberExpression, and a numeric value or an ObservableNumberValue.
greaterThan() greaterThanOrEqualTo() isEqualTo() isNotEqualTo() lessThan() lessThanOrEqualTo()	BooleanBinding	These methods create a new BooleanBinding that stores the result of the comparison of the NumberExpression and a numeric value or an ObservableNumberValue. Method names are clear enough to tell what kind of comparisons they perform.
negate()	NumberBinding	It creates a new NumberBinding that is the negation of the NumberExpression.
asString()	StringBinding	It creates a StringBinding that holds the value of the NumberExpression as a String object. This method also supports locale-based string formatting.

The methods in the NumberExpression interface allow for mixing types (int, long, float, and double) while defining a binding, using an arithmetic expression. When the return type of a method in this interface is NumberBinding, the actual returned type would be of IntegerBinding, LongBinding, FloatBinding, or DoubleBinding. The binding type of an arithmetic expression is determined by the same rules as the Java programming language. The results of an expression depend on the types of the operands. The rules are as follows:

- If one of the operands is a double, the result is a double.

- If none of the operands is a double and one of them is a float, the result is a float.

- If none of the operands is a double or a float and one of them is a long, the result is a long.

- Otherwise, the result is an int.

Consider the following snippet of code:

```
IntegerProperty x = new SimpleIntegerProperty(1);
IntegerProperty y = new SimpleIntegerProperty(2);
NumberBinding sum = x.add(y);
int value = sum.intValue();
```

The number expression x.add(y) involves only int operands (x and y are of int type). Therefore, according to the above rules, its result is an int value and it returns an IntegerBinding object. Because the add() method in the NumberExpression specifies the return type as NumberBinding, a NumberBinding type is used to store the result. You have to use the intValue() method from the ObservableNumberValue interface. You can rewrite the above snippet of code as follows:

```
IntegerProperty x = new SimpleIntegerProperty(1);
IntegerProperty y = new SimpleIntegerProperty(2);

// Casting to IntegerBinding is safe
IntegerBinding sum = (IntegerBinding)x.add(y);
int value = sum.get();
```

The NumberExpressionBase class is an implementation of the NumberExpression interface. The IntegerExpression class extends the NumberExpressionBase class. It overrides methods in its superclass to provide a type-specific return type.

The program in Listing 2-16 creates a DoubleBinding that computes the area of a circle. It also creates a DoubleProperty and binds it to the same expression to compute the area. It is your choice whether you want to work with Binding objects or bound property objects. The program shows you both approaches.

Listing 2-16. Computing the Area of a Circle from Its Radius Using Fluent Binding API

```
// CircleArea.java
package com.jdojo.binding;

import javafx.beans.binding.DoubleBinding;
import javafx.beans.property.DoubleProperty;
import javafx.beans.property.SimpleDoubleProperty;
```

```
public class CircleArea {
        public static void main(String[] args) {
                DoubleProperty radius = new SimpleDoubleProperty(7.0);

                // Create a binding for computing arae of the circle
                DoubleBinding area = radius.multiply(radius).multiply(Math.PI);

                System.out.println("Radius = " + radius.get() +
                                ", Area = " + area.get());

                // Change the radius
                radius.set(14.0);
                System.out.println("Radius = " + radius.get() +
                                ", Area = " + area.get());

                // Create a DoubleProperty and bind it to an expression
                // that computes the area of the circle
                DoubleProperty area2 = new SimpleDoubleProperty();
                area2.bind(radius.multiply(radius).multiply(Math.PI));
                System.out.println("Radius = " + radius.get() +
                                ", Area2 = " + area2.get());
        }
}
```

```
Radius = 7.0, Area = 153.93804002589985
Radius = 14.0, Area = 615.7521601035994
Radius = 14.0, Area2 = 615.7521601035994
```

The *StringBinding* Class

The class diagram containing classes in the binding API that supports binding of String type is depicted in Figure 2-5.

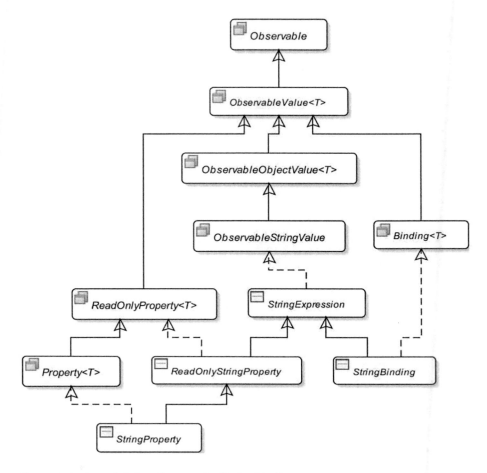

Figure 2-5. *A partial class diagram for* StringBinding

The ObservableStringValue interface declares a get() method whose return type is String. The methods in the StringExpression class let you create binding using a fluent style. Methods are provided to concatenate an object to the StringExpression, compare two strings, check for null, among others. It has two methods to get its value: getValue() and getValueSafe(). Both return the current value. However, the latter returns an empty String when the current value is null.

The program in Listing 2-17 shows how to use StringBinding and StringExpression classes. The concat() method in the StringExpression class takes an Object type as an argument. If the argument is an ObservableValue, the StringExpression is updated automatically when the argument changes. Note the use of the asString() method on the radius and area properties. The asString() method on a NumberExpression returns a StringBinding.

Listing 2-17. Using StringBinding and StringExpression

```java
// StringExpressionTest.java
package com.jdojo.binding;

import java.util.Locale;
import javafx.beans.binding.StringExpression;
import javafx.beans.property.DoubleProperty;
import javafx.beans.property.SimpleDoubleProperty;
import javafx.beans.property.SimpleStringProperty;
import javafx.beans.property.StringProperty;

public class StringExpressionTest {
        public static void main(String[] args) {
                DoubleProperty radius = new SimpleDoubleProperty(7.0);
                DoubleProperty area = new SimpleDoubleProperty(0);
                StringProperty initStr = new SimpleStringProperty("Radius = ");

                // Bind area to an expression that computes the area of the circle
                area.bind(radius.multiply(radius).multiply(Math.PI));

                // Create a string expression to describe the circle
                StringExpression desc = initStr.concat(radius.asString())
                                        .concat(", Area = ")
                                        .concat(area.asString(Locale.US, "%.2f"));

                System.out.println(desc.getValue());

                // Change the radius
                radius.set(14.0);
                System.out.println(desc.getValue());
        }
}
```

```
Radius = 7.0, Area = 153.94
Radius = 14.0, Area = 615.75
```

The *ObjectExpression* and *ObjectBinding* Classes

Now it's time for ObjectExpression and ObjectBinding classes to create bindings of any type of objects. Their class diagram is very similar to that of the StringExpression and StringBinding classes. The ObjectExpression class has methods to compare objects for equality and to check for null values. The program in Listing 2-18 shows how to use the ObjectBinding class.

Listing 2-18. Using the ObjectBinding Class

```java
// ObjectBindingTest.java
package com.jdojo.binding;

import javafx.beans.binding.BooleanBinding;
import javafx.beans.property.ObjectProperty;
import javafx.beans.property.SimpleObjectProperty;
```

```java
public class ObjectBindingTest {
        public static void main(String[] args) {
                Book b1 = new Book("J1", 90, "1234567890");
                Book b2 = new Book("J2", 80, "0123456789");
                ObjectProperty<Book> book1 = new SimpleObjectProperty<>(b1);
                ObjectProperty<Book> book2 = new SimpleObjectProperty<>(b2);

                // Create a binding that computes if book1 and book2 are equal
                BooleanBinding isEqual = book1.isEqualTo(book2);
                System.out.println(isEqual.get());

                book2.set(b1);
                System.out.println(isEqual.get());
        }
}
```

```
false
true
```

The *BooleanExpression* and *BooleanBinding* Classes

The BooleanExpression class contains methods such as and(), or(), and not() that let you use boolean logical operators in an expression. Its isEqualTo() and isNotEqualTo() methods let you compare a BooleanExpression with another ObservableBooleanValue. The result of a BooleanExpression is true or false.

The program in Listing 2-19 shows how to use the BooleanExpression class. It creates a boolean expression, x > y && y <> z, using a fluent style. Note that the greaterThan() and isNotEqualTo() methods are defined in the NumberExpression interface. The program only uses the and() method from the BooleanExpression class.

Listing 2-19. Using BooleanExpression and BooleanBinding

```java
// BooelanExpressionTest.java
package com.jdojo.binding;

import javafx.beans.binding.BooleanExpression;
import javafx.beans.property.IntegerProperty;
import javafx.beans.property.SimpleIntegerProperty;

public class BooelanExpressionTest {
        public static void main(String[] args) {
                IntegerProperty x = new SimpleIntegerProperty(1);
                IntegerProperty y = new SimpleIntegerProperty(2);
                IntegerProperty z = new SimpleIntegerProperty(3);

                // Create a boolean expression for x > y && y <> z
                BooleanExpression condition = x.greaterThan(y).and(y.isNotEqualTo(z));

                System.out.println(condition.get());
```

```
        // Make the condition true by setting x to 3
        x.set(3);
        System.out.println(condition.get());
    }
}
```

```
false
true
```

Using Ternary Operation in Expressions

The Java programming language offers a ternary operator, (condition?value1:value2), to perform a ternary operation of the form *when-then-otherwise*. The JavaFX binding API has a When class for this purpose. The general syntax of using the When class is shown here:

```
new When(condition).then(value1).otherwise(value2)
```

The condition must be an ObservableBooleanValue. When the condition evaluates to true, it returns value1. Otherwise, it returns value2. The types of value1 and value2 must be the same. Values may be constants or instances of ObservableValue.

Let's use a ternary operation that returns a String even or odd depending on whether the value of an IntegerProperty is even or odd, respectively. The Fluent API does not have a method to compute modulus. You will have to do this yourself. Perform an integer division by 2 on an integer and multiply the result by 2. If you get the same number back, the number is even. Otherwise, the number is odd. For example, using an integer division, (7/2)*2, results in 6, and not 7. Listing 2-20 provides the complete program.

Listing 2-20. Using the When Class to Perform a Ternary Operation

```
// TernaryTest.java
package com.jdojo.binding;

import javafx.beans.binding.When;
import javafx.beans.property.IntegerProperty;
import javafx.beans.property.SimpleIntegerProperty;
import javafx.beans.binding.StringBinding;

public class TernaryTest {
    public static void main(String[] args) {
        IntegerProperty num = new SimpleIntegerProperty(10);
        StringBinding desc = new When(num.divide(2).multiply(2).isEqualTo(num))
                    .then("even")
                    .otherwise("odd");

        System.out.println(num.get() + " is " + desc.get());

        num.set(19);
        System.out.println(num.get() + " is " + desc.get());
    }
}
```

```
10 is even
19 is odd
```

Using the *Bindings* Utility Class

The Bindings class is a helper class to create simple bindings. It consists of more than 150 static methods. Most of them are overloaded with several variants. I will not list or discuss all of them. Please refer to the online JavaFX API documentation to get the complete list of methods. Table 2-3 lists the methods of the Bindings class and their descriptions. It has excluded methods belonging to collections binding.

Table 2-3. *Summary of Methods in the Bindings Class*

Method Name	Description
add() subtract() multiple() divide()	They create a binding by applying an arithmetic operation, indicated by their names, on two of its arguments. At least one of the arguments must be an ObservableNumberValue. If one of the arguments is a double, its return type is DoubleBinding; otherwise, its return type is NumberBinding.
and()	It creates a BooleanBinding by applying the boolean and to two of its arguments.
bindBidirectional() unbindBidirectional()	They create and delete a bidirectional binding between two properties.
concat()	It returns a StringExpression that holds the value of the concatenation of its arguments. It takes a varargs argument.
convert()	It returns a StringExpression that wraps its argument.
createXXXBinding()	It lets you create a custom binding of XXX type, where XXX could be Boolean, Double, Float, Integer, String, and Object.
equal() notEqual() equalIgnoreCase() notEqualIgnoreCase()	They create a BooleanBinding that wraps the result of comparing two of its arguments being equal or not equal. Some variants of the methods allow passing a tolerance value. If two arguments are within the tolerance, they are considered equal. Generally, a tolerance value is used to compare floating-point numbers. The ignore case variants of the methods work only on String type.
format()	It creates a StringExpression that holds the value of multiple objects formatted according to a specified format String.
greaterThan() greaterThanOrEqual() lessThan() lessThanOrEqual()	They create a BooleanBinding that wraps the result of comparing arguments.
isNotNull isNull	They create a BooleanBinding that wraps the result of comparing the argument with null.
max() min()	They create a binding that holds the maximum and minimum of two arguments of the method. One of the arguments must be an ObservableNumberValue.
negate()	It creates a NumberBinding that holds the negation of an ObservableNumberValue.

(continued)

Table 2-3. (*continued*)

Method Name	Description
not()	It creates a BooleanBinding that holds the inverse of an ObservableBooleanValue.
or()	It creates a BooleanBinding that holds the result of applying the conditional or operation on its two ObservableBooleanValue arguments.
selectXXX()	It creates a binding to select a nested property. The nested property may be of the type a.b.c. The value of the binding will be c. The classes and properties involved in the expression like a.b.c must be public. If any part of the expression is not accessible, because they are not public or they do not exist, the default value for the type, for example, null for Object type, an empty String for String type, 0 for numeric type, and false for boolean type, is the value of the binding. (Later I will discuss an example of using the select() method.)
when()	It creates an instance of the When class taking a condition as an argument.

Most of our examples using the Fluent API can also be written using the Bindings class. The program in Listing 2-21 is similar to the one in Listing 2-17. It uses the Bindings class instead of the Fluent API. It uses the multiply() method to compute the area and the format() method to format the results. There may be several ways of doing the same thing. For formatting the result, you can also use the Bindings.concat() method, as shown here:

```
StringExpression desc = Bindings.concat("Radius = ", radius.asString(Locale.US, "%.2f"),
                        ", Area = ", area.asString(Locale.US, "%.2f"));
```

Listing 2-21. Using the Bindings Class

```
// BindingsClassTest.java
package com.jdojo.binding;

import java.util.Locale;
import javafx.beans.binding.Bindings;
import javafx.beans.binding.StringExpression;
import javafx.beans.property.DoubleProperty;
import javafx.beans.property.SimpleDoubleProperty;

public class BindingsClassTest {
    public static void main(String[] args) {
        DoubleProperty radius = new SimpleDoubleProperty(7.0);
        DoubleProperty area = new SimpleDoubleProperty(0.0);

        // Bind area to an expression that computes the area of the circle
        area.bind(Bindings.multiply(Bindings.multiply(radius, radius), Math.PI));
```

```
                // Create a string expression to describe the circle
                StringExpression desc = Bindings.format(Locale.US,
                                        "Radius = %.2f, Area = %.2f", radius, area);

                System.out.println(desc.get());

                // Change the radius
                radius.set(14.0);
                System.out.println(desc.getValue());
        }
}
```

```
Radius = 7.00, Area = 153.94
Radius = 14.00, Area = 615.75
```

Let's look at an example of using the selectXXX() method of the Bindings class. It is used to create a binding for a nested property. In the nested hierarchy, all classes and properties must be public. Suppose you have an Address class that has a zip property and a Person class that has an addr property. The classes are shown in Listing 2-22 and Listing 2-23, respectively.

Listing 2-22. An Address Class

```
// Address.java
package com.jdojo.binding;

import javafx.beans.property.SimpleStringProperty;
import javafx.beans.property.StringProperty;

public class Address {
        private StringProperty zip = new SimpleStringProperty("36106");

        public StringProperty zipProperty() {
                return zip;
        }
}
```

Listing 2-23. An Person Class

```
// Person.java
package com.jdojo.binding;

import javafx.beans.property.ObjectProperty;
import javafx.beans.property.SimpleObjectProperty;

public class Person {
        private ObjectProperty<Address> addr = new SimpleObjectProperty(new Address());

        public ObjectProperty<Address> addrProperty() {
                return addr;
        }
}
```

Suppose you create an ObjectProperty of the Person class as follows:

```
ObjectProperty<Person> p = new SimpleObjectProperty(new Person());
```

Using the Bindings.selectString() method, you can create a StringBinding for the zip property of the addr property of the Person object as shown here:

```
// Bind p.addr.zip
StringBinding zipBinding = Bindings.selectString(p, "addr", "zip");
```

The above statement gets a binding for the StringProperty zip, which is a nested property of the addr property of the object p. A property in the selectXXX() method may have multiple levels of nesting. You can have a selectXXX() call like:

```
StringBinding xyzBinding = Bindings.selectString(x, "a", "b", "c", "d");
```

■ **Note**   JavaFX 2.2 API documentation states that Bindings.selectString() returns an empty String if any of its property arguments is inaccessible. However, the runtime returns null.

Listing 2-24 shows the use of the selectString() method. The program prints the values of the zip property twice: once for its default value and once for its changed value. At the end, it tries to bind a nonexistent property p.addr.state. Binding to a nonexistent property is not a runtime error. When I ran the program in the latest Java Development Kit 8 release, accessing the property p.addr.state resulted in a runtime NoSuchMethodException that seems to be a bug; earlier it returned null without throwing the exception.

Listing 2-24. Using the selectXXX() Method of the Bindings Class

```java
// BindNestedProperty.java
package com.jdojo.binding;

import javafx.beans.binding.Bindings;
import javafx.beans.binding.StringBinding;
import javafx.beans.property.ObjectProperty;
import javafx.beans.property.SimpleObjectProperty;
import javafx.beans.property.SimpleStringProperty;
import javafx.beans.property.StringProperty;

public class BindNestedProperty {
        public static class Address {
                private StringProperty zip = new SimpleStringProperty("36106");

                public StringProperty zipProperty() {
                        return zip;
                }
```

```java
            public String getZip() {
                    return zip.get();
            }

            public void setZip(String newZip) {
                    zip.set(newZip);
            }
    }

    public static class Person {
            private ObjectProperty<Address> addr =
                            new SimpleObjectProperty(new Address());

            public ObjectProperty<Address> addrProperty() {
                    return addr;
            }

            public Address getAddr() {
                    return addr.get();
            }

            public void setZip(Address newAddr) {
                    addr.set(newAddr);
            }
    }

    public static void main(String[] args) {
            ObjectProperty<Person> p = new SimpleObjectProperty(new Person());

            // Bind p.addr.zip
            StringBinding zipBinding = Bindings.selectString(p, "addr", "zip");
            System.out.println(zipBinding.get());

            // Change the zip
            p.get().addrProperty().get().setZip("35217");
            System.out.println(zipBinding.get());

            // Bind p.addr.state, which does not exist
            StringBinding stateBinding = Bindings.selectString(p, "addr", "state");
            System.out.println(stateBinding.get());
    }
}
```

```
36106
35217
null
```

Combining the Fluent API and the *Bindings* Class

While using the high-level binding API, you can use the fluent and Bindings class APIs in the same binding expression. The following snippet of code shows this approach:

```
DoubleProperty radius = new SimpleDoubleProperty(7.0);
DoubleProperty area = new SimpleDoubleProperty(0);

// Combine the Fluent API and Bindings class API
area.bind(Bindings.multiply(Math.PI, radius.multiply(radius)));
```

Using the Low-Level Binding API

The high-level binding API is not sufficient in all cases. For example, it does not provide a method to compute the square root of an Observable number. If the high-level binding API becomes too cumbersome to use or it does not provide what you need, you can use the low-level binding API. It gives you power and flexibility at the cost of a few extra lines of code. The low-level API allows you to use the full potential of the Java programming language to define bindings.

Using the low-level binding API involves the following three steps:

1. Create a class that extends one of the binding classes. For example, if you want to create a DoubleBinding, you need to extend the DoubleBinding class.

2. Call the bind() method of the superclass to bind all dependencies. Note that all binding classes have a bind() method implementation. You need to call this method passing all dependencies as arguments. Its argument type is a varargs of Observable type.

3. Override the computeValue() method of the superclass to write the logic for your binding. It calculates the current value of the binding. Its return type is the same as the type of the binding, for example, it is double for a DoubleBinding, String for a StringBinding, and so forth.

Additionally, you can override some methods of the binding classes to provide more functionality to your binding. You can override the dispose() method to perform additional actions when a binding is disposed. The getDependencies() method may be overridden to return the list of dependencies for the binding. Overriding the onInvalidating() method is needed if you want to perform additional actions when the binding becomes invalid.

Consider the problem of computing the area of a circle. The following snippet of code uses the low-level API to do this:

```
final DoubleProperty radius = new SimpleDoubleProperty(7.0);
DoubleProperty area = new SimpleDoubleProperty(0);

DoubleBinding areaBinding = new DoubleBinding() {
        {
                this.bind(radius);
        }
```

```
        @Override
        protected double computeValue() {
                double r = radius.get();
                double area = Math.PI * r * r;
                return area;
        }
};
```

```
area.bind(areaBinding); // Bind the area property to the areaBinding
```

The above snippet of code creates an anonymous class, which extends the DoubleBinding class. It calls the bind() method, passing the reference of the radius property. An anonymous class does not have a constructor, so you have to use an instance initializer to call the bind() method. The computeValue() method computes and returns the area of the circle. The radius property has been declared final, because it is being used inside the anonymous class.

The program in Listing 2-25 shows how to use the low-level binding API. It overrides the computeValue() method for the area binding. For the description binding, it overrides the dispose(), getDependencies(), and onInvalidating() methods as well.

Listing 2-25. Using the Low-Level Binding API to Compute the Area of a Circle

```
// LowLevelBinding.java
package com.jdojo.binding;

import java.util.Formatter;
import java.util.Locale;
import javafx.beans.binding.DoubleBinding;
import javafx.beans.binding.StringBinding;
import javafx.beans.property.DoubleProperty;
import javafx.beans.property.SimpleDoubleProperty;
import javafx.collections.FXCollections;
import javafx.collections.ObservableList;

public class LowLevelBinding {
        public static void main(String[] args) {
                final DoubleProperty radius = new SimpleDoubleProperty(7.0);
                final DoubleProperty area = new SimpleDoubleProperty(0);

                DoubleBinding areaBinding = new DoubleBinding() {
                        {
                                this.bind(radius);
                        }

                        @Override
                        protected double computeValue() {
                                double r = radius.get();
                                double area = Math.PI * r *r;
                                return area;
                        }
                };
```

```
        // Bind area to areaBinding
        area.bind(areaBinding);

        // Create a StringBinding
        StringBinding desc = new StringBinding() {
                {
                        this.bind(radius, area);
                }

                @Override
                protected String computeValue() {
                        Formatter f = new Formatter();
                        f.format(Locale.US, "Radius = %.2f, Area = %.2f",
                                radius.get(), area.get());
                        String desc = f.toString();
                        return desc;
                }

                @Override
                public ObservableList<?> getDependencies() {
                        return FXCollections.unmodifiableObservableList(
                                FXCollections.observableArrayList(radius, area));
                }

                @Override
                public void dispose() {
                        System.out.println("Description binding is disposed.");
                }

                @Override
                protected void onInvalidating() {
                        System.out.println("Description is invalid.");
                }
        };

        System.out.println(desc.getValue());

        // Change the radius
        radius.set(14.0);
        System.out.println(desc.getValue());
    }
}
```

```
Radius = 7.00, Area = 153.94
Description is invalid.
Radius = 14.00, Area = 615.75
```

Using Bindings to Center a Circle

Let's look at an example of a JavaFX GUI application that uses bindings. You will create a screen with a circle, which will be centered on the screen, even after the screen is resized. The circumference of the circle will touch the closer sides of the screen. If the width and height of the screen is the same, the circumference of the circle will touch all four sides of the screen.

Attempting to develop the screen, with a centered circle, without bindings is a tedious task. The Circle class in the javafx.scene.shape package represents a circle. It has three properties—centerX, centerY, and radius—of the DoubleProperty type. The centerX and centerY properties define the (x, y) coordinates of the center of the circle. The radius property defines the radius of the circle. By default, a circle is filled with black color.

You create a circle with centerX, centerY, and radius set to the default value of 0.0 as follows:

```
Circle c = new Circle();
```

Next, add the circle to a group and create a scene with the group as its root node as shown here:

```
Group root = new Group(c);
Scene scene = new Scene(root, 150, 150);
```

The following bindings will position and size the circle according to the size of the scene:

```
c.centerXProperty().bind(scene.widthProperty().divide(2));
c.centerYProperty().bind(scene.heightProperty().divide(2));
c.radiusProperty().bind(Bindings.min(scene.widthProperty(), scene.heightProperty())
                        .divide(2));
```

The first two bindings bind the centerX and centerY of the circle to the middle of the width and height of the scene, respectively. The third binding binds the radius of the circle to the half (see divide(2)) of the minimum of the width and the height of the scene. That's it! The binding API does the magic of keeping the circle centered when the application is run.

Listing 2-26 has the complete program. Figure 2-6 shows the screen when the program is initially run. Figure 2-7 shows the screen when the screen is stretched horizontally. Try stretching the screen vertically and you will notice that the circumference of the circle touches only the left and right sides of the screen.

Listing 2-26. Using the Binding API to Keep a Circle Centered in a Scene

```
// CenteredCircle.java
package com.jdojo.binding;

import javafx.application.Application;
import javafx.beans.binding.Bindings;
import javafx.scene.Group;
import javafx.scene.Scene;
import javafx.scene.shape.Circle;
import javafx.stage.Stage;

public class CenteredCircle extends Application {
        public static void main(String[] args) {
                Application.launch(args);
        }
```

```
    @Override
    public void start(Stage stage) {
            Circle c = new Circle();
            Group root = new Group(c);
            Scene scene = new Scene(root, 100, 100);

            // Bind the centerX, centerY, and radius to the scene width and height
            c.centerXProperty().bind(scene.widthProperty().divide(2));
            c.centerYProperty().bind(scene.heightProperty().divide(2));
            c.radiusProperty().bind(Bindings.min(scene.widthProperty(),
                                            scene.heightProperty())
                                 .divide(2));

            // Set the stage properties and make it visible
            stage.setTitle("Binding in JavaFX");
            stage.setScene(scene);
            stage.sizeToScene();
            stage.show();
    }
}
```

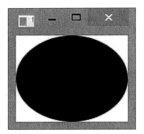

Figure 2-6. *The screen when the* CenteredCircle *program is initially run*

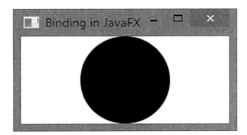

Figure 2-7. *The screen when the screen for the* CenteredCircle *program is stretched horizontally*

81

Summary

A Java class may contain two types of members: fields and methods. Fields represent the state of its objects and they are declared private. Public methods, known as accessors, or getters and setters, are used to read and modify private fields. A Java class having public accessors for all or part of its private fields is known as a Java bean, and the accessors define the properties of the bean. Properties of a Java bean allow users to customize its state, behavior, or both.

JavaFX supports properties, events, and binding through properties and binding APIs. Properties support in JavaFX is a huge leap forward from the JavaBeans properties. All properties in JavaFX are observable. They can be observed for invalidation and value changes. You can have read/write or read-only properties. All read/write properties support binding. In JavaFX, a property can represent a value or a collection of values.

A property generates an invalidation event when the status of its value changes from valid to invalid for the first time. Properties in JavaFX use lazy evaluation. When an invalid property becomes invalid again, an invalidation event is not generated. An invalid property becomes valid when it is recomputed.

In JavaFX, a binding is an expression that evaluates to a value. It consists of one or more observable values known as its dependencies. A binding observes its dependencies for changes and recomputes its value automatically. JavaFX uses lazy evaluation for all bindings. When a binding is initially defined or when its dependencies change, its value is marked as invalid. The value of an invalid binding is computed when it is requested next time. All property classes in JavaFX have built-in support for binding.

A binding has a direction, which is the direction in which changes are propagated. JavaFX supports two types of binding for properties: unidirectional binding and bidirectional binding. A unidirectional binding works only in one direction; changes in dependencies are propagated to the bound property, not vice versa. A bidirectional binding works in both directions; changes in dependencies are reflected in the property and vice versa.

The binding API in JavaFX is divided into two categories: high-level binding API and low-level binding API. The high-level binding API lets you define binding using the JavaFX class library. For most use cases, you can use the high-level binding API. Sometimes, the existing API is not sufficient to define a binding. In those cases, the low-level binding API is used. In low-level binding API, you derive a binding class from an existing binding class and write your own logic to define the binding.

The next chapter will introduce you to observable collections in JavaFX.

CHAPTER 3

Observable Collections

In this chapter, you will learn:

- What observable collections in JavaFX are
- How to observe observable collections for invalidations and changes
- How to use observable collections as properties

What Are Observable Collections?

Observable collections in JavaFX are extensions to collections in Java. The *collections* framework in Java has the List, Set, and Map interfaces. JavaFX adds the following three types of observable collections that may be observed for changes in their contents:

- An observable list
- An observable set
- An observable map

JavaFX supports these types of collections through three new interfaces:

- ObservableList
- ObservableSet
- ObservableMap

These interfaces inherit from List, Set, and Map from the java.util package. In addition to inheriting from the Java collection interfaces, JavaFX collection interfaces also inherit the Observable interface. All JavaFX observable collection interfaces and classes are in the javafx.collections package. Figure 3-1 shows a partial class diagram for the ObservableList, ObservableSet, and ObservableMap interfaces.

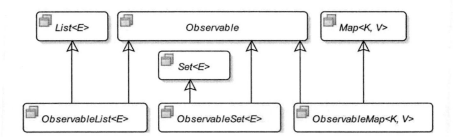

Figure 3-1. *A partial class diagram for observable collection interfaces in JavaFX*

The observable collections in JavaFX have two additional features:

- They support invalidation notifications as they are inherited from the Observable interface.

- They support change notifications. You can register change listeners to them, which are notified when their contents change.

The javafx.collections.FXCollections class is a utility class to work with JavaFX collections. It consists of all static methods.

JavaFX does not expose the implementation classes of observable lists, sets, and maps. You need to use one of the factory methods in the FXCollections class to create objects of the ObservableList, ObservableSet, and ObservableMap interfaces.

■ **Tip**   In simple terms, an observable collection in JavaFX is a list, set, or map that may be observed for invalidation and content changes.

Understanding *ObservableList*

An ObservableList is a java.util.List and an Observable with change notification features. Figure 3-2 shows the class diagram for the ObservableList interface.

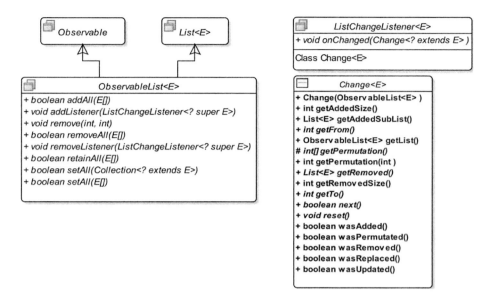

Figure 3-2. *A class diagram for the* ObservableList *interface*

The addListener() and removeListener() methods in the ObservableList interface allow you to add and remove ListChangeListeners, respectively. Other methods perform operations on the list, which affect multiple elements.

If you want to receive notifications when changes occur in an ObservableList, you need to add a ListChangeListener interface whose onChanged() method is called when a change occurs in the list. The Change class is a static inner class of the ListChangeListener interface. A Change object contains a report of the changes in an ObservableList. It is passed to the onChanged() method of the ListChangeListener. I will discuss list change listeners in detail later in this section.

You can add or remove invalidation listeners to or from an ObservableList using the following two methods that it inherits from the Observable interface:

- void addListener(InvalidationListener listener)

- void removeListener(InvalidationListener listener)

Note that an ObservableList contains all of the methods of the List interface as it inherits them from the List interface.

■ **Tip**   JavaFX library provides two classes named FilteredList and SortedList that are in the javafx.collections.transformation package. A FilteredList is an ObservableList that filters its contents using a specified Predicate. A SortedList sorts its contents. I will not discuss these classes in this chapter. All discussions of observable lists apply to the objects of these classes as well.

Creating an *ObservableList*

You need to use one of the following factory methods of the FXCollections class to create an ObservableList:

- `<E> ObservableList<E> emptyObservableList()`

- `<E> ObservableList<E> observableArrayList()`

- `<E> ObservableList<E> observableArrayList(Collection<? extends E> col)`

- `<E> ObservableList<E> observableArrayList(E... items)`

- `<E> ObservableList<E> observableList(List<E> list)`

- `<E> ObservableList<E> observableArrayList(Callback<E, Observable[]> extractor)`

- `<E> ObservableList<E> observableList(List<E> list, Callback<E, Observable[]> extractor)`

The emptyObservableList() method creates an empty, unmodifiable ObservableList. Often, this method is used when you need an ObservableList to pass to a method as an argument and you do not have any elements to pass to that list. You can create an empty ObservableList of String as follows:

```
ObservableList<String> emptyList = FXCollections.emptyObservableList();
```

The observableArrayList() method creates an ObservableList backed by an ArrayList. Other variants of this method create an ObservableList whose initial elements can be specified in a Collection as a list of items or as a List.

The last two methods in the above list create an ObservableList whose elements can be observed for updates. They take an extractor, which is an instance of the Callback<E, Observable[]> interface. An extractor is used to get the list of Observable values to observe for updates. I will cover the use of these two methods in the "Observing an ObservableList for Updates" section.

Listing 3-1 shows how to create observable lists and how to use some of the methods of the ObservableList interface to manipulate the lists. At the end, it shows how to use the concat() method of the FXCollections class to concatenate elements of two observable lists.

Listing 3-1. Creating and Manipulating Observable Lists

```java
// ObservableListTest.java
package com.jdojo.collections;

import javafx.collections.FXCollections;
import javafx.collections.ObservableList;

public class ObservableListTest {
    public static void main(String[] args) {
        // Create a list with some elements
        ObservableList<String> list = FXCollections.observableArrayList("one", "two");
        System.out.println("After creating list: " + list);

        // Add some more elements to the list
        list.addAll("three", "four");
        System.out.println("After adding elements: " + list);
```

```
                    // You have four elements. Remove the middle two
                    // from index 1 (inclusive) to index 3 (exclusive)
                    list.remove(1, 3);
                    System.out.println("After removing elements: " + list);

                    // Retain only the element "one"
                    list.retainAll("one");
                    System.out.println("After retaining \"one\": " + list);

                    // Create another ObservableList
                    ObservableList<String> list2 =
                            FXCollections.<String>observableArrayList("1", "2", "3");

                    // Set list2 to list
                    list.setAll(list2);
                    System.out.println("After setting list2 to list: " + list);

                    // Create another list
                    ObservableList<String> list3 =
                            FXCollections.<String>observableArrayList("ten", "twenty", "thirty");

                    // Concatenate elements of list2 and list3
                    ObservableList<String> list4 = FXCollections.concat(list2, list3);
                    System.out.println("list2 is " + list2);
                    System.out.println("list3 is " + list3);
                    System.out.println("After concatenating list2 and list3:" + list4);
        }
}
```

```
After creating list: [one, two]
After adding elements: [one, two, three, four]
After removing elements: [one, four]
After retaining "one": [one]
After setting list2 to list: [1, 2, 3]
list2 is [1, 2, 3]
list3 is [ten, twenty, thirty]
After concatenating list2 and list3:[1, 2, 3, ten, twenty, thirty]
```

Observing an *ObservableList* for Invalidations

You can add invalidation listeners to an ObservableList as you do to any Observable. Listing 3-2 shows how to use an invalidation listener with an ObservableList.

■ **Tip**   In the case of the ObservableList, the invalidation listeners are notified for every change in the list, irrespective of the type of a change.

Listing 3-2. Testing Invalidation Notifications for an `ObservableList`

```java
// ListInvalidationTest.java
package com.jdojo.collections;

import javafx.beans.Observable;
import javafx.collections.FXCollections;
import javafx.collections.ObservableList;

public class ListInvalidationTest {
        public static void main(String[] args) {
                // Create a list with some elements
                ObservableList<String> list =
                        FXCollections.observableArrayList("one", "two");

                // Add an InvalidationListener to the list
                list.addListener(ListInvalidationTest::invalidated);

                System.out.println("Before adding three.");
                list.add("three");
                System.out.println("After adding three.");

                System.out.println("Before adding four and five.");
                list.addAll("four", "five");
                System.out.println("Before adding four and five.");

                System.out.println("Before replacing one with one.");
                list.set(0, "one");
                System.out.println("After replacing one with one.");
        }

        public static void invalidated(Observable list) {
                System.out.println("List is invalid.");
        }
}
```

```
Before adding three.
List is invalid.
After adding three.
Before adding four and five.
List is invalid.
Before adding four and five.
Before replacing one with one.
List is invalid.
After replacing one with one.
```

Observing an *ObservableList* for Changes

Observing an ObservableList for changes is a bit tricky. There could be several kinds of changes to a list. Some of the changes could be exclusive, whereas some can occur along with other changes. Elements of a list can be permutated, updated, replaced, added, and removed. You need to be patient in learning this topic because I will cover it in bits and pieces.

You can add a change listener to an ObservableList using its addListener() method, which takes an instance of the ListChangeListener interface. The changed() method of the listeners is called every time a change occurs in the list. The following snippet of code shows how to add a change listener to an ObservableList of String. The onChanged() method is simple; it prints a message on the standard output when it is notified of a change:

```
// Create an observable list
ObservableList<String> list = FXCollections.observableArrayList();

// Add a change listener to the list
list.addListener(new ListChangeListener<String>() {
        @Override
        public void onChanged(ListChangeListener.Change<? extends String> change) {
                System.out.println("List has changed.");
        }
});
```

Listing 3-3 contains the complete program showing how to detect changes in an ObservableList. It uses a lambda expression with a method reference, which are features of Java 8, to add a change listener. After adding a change listener, it manipulates the list four times, and the listener is notified each time, as is evident from the output that follows.

Listing 3-3. Detecting Changes in an ObservableList

```
// SimpleListChangeTest.java
package com.jdojo.collections;

import javafx.collections.FXCollections;
import javafx.collections.ListChangeListener;
import javafx.collections.ObservableList;

public class SimpleListChangeTest {
        public static void main(String[] args) {
                // Create an observable list
                ObservableList<String> list = FXCollections.observableArrayList();

                // Add a change listener to the list
                list.addListener(SimpleListChangeTest::onChanged);
```

```
                // Manipulate the elements of the list
                list.add("one");
                list.add("two");
                FXCollections.sort(list);
                list.clear();
        }

        public static void onChanged(ListChangeListener.Change<? extends String> change) {
                System.out.println("List has changed");
        }
}
```

```
List has changed.
List has changed.
List has changed.
List has changed.
```

Understanding the *ListChangeListener.Change* Class

Sometimes you may want to analyze changes to a list in more detail rather than just knowing that the list has changed. The ListChangeListener.Change object that is passed to the onChanged() method contains a report to a change performed on the list. You need to use a combination of its methods to know the details of a change. Table 3-1 lists the methods in the ListChangeListener.Change class with their categories.

Table 3-1. Methods in the ListChangeListener.Change Class

Method	Category
ObservableList<E> getList()	General
boolean next()	Cursor movement
void reset()	
boolean wasAdded()	Change type
boolean wasRemoved()	
boolean wasReplaced()	
boolean wasPermutated()	
boolean wasUpdated()	
int getFrom()	Affected range
int getTo()	
int getAddedSize()	Addition
List<E> getAddedSubList()	
List<E> getRemoved()	Removal
int getRemovedSize()	
int getPermutation(int oldIndex)	Permutation

The getList() method returns the source list after changes have been made. A ListChangeListener. Change object may report a change in multiple chunks. This may not be obvious at first. Consider the following snippet of code:

```
ObservableList<String> list = FXCollections.observableArrayList();

// Add a change listener here...

list.addAll("one", "two", "three");
list.removeAll("one", "three");
```

In this code, the change listener will be notified twice: once for the addAll() method call and once for the removeAll() method call. The ListChangeListener.Change object reports the affected range of indexes. In the second change, you remove two elements that fall into two different ranges of indexes. Note that there is an element "two" between the two removed elements. In the second case, the Change object will contain a report of two changes. The first change will contain the information that, at index 0, the element "one" has been removed. Now, the list contains only two elements with the index 0 for the element "two" and index 1 for the element "three". The second change will contain the information that, at index 1, the element "three" has been removed.

A Change object contains a cursor that points to a specific change in the report. The next() and reset() methods are used to control the cursor. When the onChanged() method is called, the cursor points before the first change in the report. Calling the next() method the first time moves the cursor to the first change in the report. Before attempting to read the details for a change, you must point the cursor to the change by calling the next() method. The next() method returns true if it moves the cursor to a valid change. Otherwise, it returns false. The reset() method moves the cursor before the first change. Typically, the next() method is called in a while-loop, as shown in the following snippet of code:

```
ObservableList<String> list = FXCollections.observableArrayList();
...
// Add a change listener to the list
list.addListener(new ListChangeListener<String>() {
        @Override
        public void onChanged(ListChangeListener.Change<? extends String> change) {
                while(change.next()) {
                        // Process the current change here...
                }
        }
});
```

In the change type category, methods report whether a specific type of change has occurred. The wasAdded() method returns true if elements were added. The wasRemoved() method returns true if elements were removed. The wasReplaced() method returns true if elements were replaced. You can think of a replacement as a removal followed by an addition at the same index. If wasReplaced() returns true, both wasRemoved() and wasAdded() return true as well. The wasPermutated() method returns true if elements of a list were permutated (i.e., reordered) but not removed, added, or updated. The wasUpdated() method returns true if elements of a list were updated.

Not all five types of changes to a list are exclusive. Some changes may occur simultaneously in the same change notification. The two types of changes, permutations and updates, are exclusive. If you are interested in working with all types of changes, your code in the onChanged() method should look as follows:

```
public void onChanged(ListChangeListener.Change change) {
        while (change.next()) {
                if (change.wasPermutated()) {
                        // Handle permutations
                }
                else if (change.wasUpdated()) {
                        // Handle updates
                }
                else if (change.wasReplaced()) {
                        // Handle replacements
                }
                else {
                        if (change.wasRemoved()) {
                                // Handle removals
                        }
                        else if (change.wasAdded()) {
                                // Handle additions
                        }
                }
        }
}
```

In the affected range type category, the getFrom() and getTo() methods report the range of indexes affected by a change. The getFrom() method returns the beginning index and the getTo() method returns the ending index plus one. If the wasPermutated() method returns true, the range includes the elements that were permutated. If the wasUpdated() method returns true, the range includes the elements that were updated. If the wasAdded() method returns true, the range includes the elements that were added. If the wasRemoved() method returns true and the wasAdded() method returns false, the getFrom() and getTo() methods return the same number—the index where the removed elements were placed in the list.

The getAddedSize() method returns the number of elements added. The getAddedSubList() method returns a list that contains the elements added. The getRemovedSize() method returns the number of elements removed. The getRemoved() method returns an immutable list of removed or replaced elements. The getPermutation(int oldIndex) method returns the new index of an element after permutation. For example, if an element at index 2 moves to index 5 during a permutation, the getPermutation(2) will return 5.

This completes the discussion about the methods of the ListChangeListener.Change class. However, you are not done with this class yet! I still need to discuss how to use these methods in actual situations, for example, when elements of a list are updated. I will cover handling updates to elements of a list in the next section. I will finish this topic with an example that covers everything that was discussed.

Observing an *ObservableList* for Updates

In the "Creating an *ObservableList*" section, I had listed the following two methods of the FXCollections class that create an ObservableList:

- `<E> ObservableList<E> observableArrayList(Callback<E, Observable[]> extractor)`

- `<E> ObservableList<E> observableList(List<E> list, Callback<E, Observable[]> extractor)`

If you want to be notified when elements of a list are updated, you need to create the list using one of these methods. Both methods have one thing in common: They take a Callback<E,Observable[]> object as an argument. The Callback<P,R> interface is in the javafx.util package. It is defined as follows:

```
public interface Callback<P,R> {
        R call(P param)
}
```

The Callback<P,R> interface is used in situations where further action is required by APIs at a later suitable time. The first generic type parameter specifies the type of the parameter passed to the call() method and the second one specifies the returns type of the call() method.

If you notice the declaration of the type parameters in Callback<E,Observable[]>, the first type parameter is E, which is the type of the elements of the list. The second parameter is an array of Observable. When you add an element to the list, the call() method of the Callback object is called. The added element is passed to the call() method as an argument. You are supposed to return an array of Observable from the call() method. If any of the elements in the returned Observable array changes, listeners will be notified of an "update" change for the element of the list for which the call() method had returned the Observable array.

Let's examine why you need a Callback object and an Observable array to detect updates to elements of a list. A list stores references of its elements. Its elements can be updated using their references from anywhere in the program. A list does not know that its elements are being updated from somewhere else. It needs to know the list of Observable objects, where a change to any of them may be considered an update to its elements. The call() method of the Callback object fulfills this requirement. The list passes every element to the call() method. The call() method returns an array of Observable. The list watches for any changes to the elements of the Observable array. When it detects a change, it notifies its change listeners that its element associated with the Observable array has been updated. The reason this parameter is named *extractor* is that it extracts an array of Observable for an element of a list.

Listing 3-4 shows how to create an ObservableList that can notify its change listeners when its elements are updated.

Listing 3-4. Observing a List for Updates of Its Elements

```
// ListUpdateTest.java
package com.jdojo.collections;

import java.util.List;
import javafx.beans.Observable;
import javafx.beans.property.IntegerProperty;
import javafx.beans.property.SimpleIntegerProperty;
import javafx.collections.FXCollections;
import javafx.collections.ListChangeListener;
import javafx.collections.ObservableList;
import javafx.util.Callback;
```

```java
public class ListUpdateTest {
        public static void main(String[] args) {
                // Create an extractor for IntegerProperty.
                Callback<IntegerProperty, Observable[]> extractor = (IntegerProperty p) -> {
                                // Print a message to know when it is called
                                System.out.println("The extractor is called for " + p);

                                // Wrap the parameter in an Observable[] and return it
                                return new Observable[]{p};
                        };

                // Create an empty observable list with a callback to extract the
                // observable values for each element of the list
                ObservableList<IntegerProperty> list =
                        FXCollections.observableArrayList(extractor);

                // Add two elements to the list
                System.out.println("Before adding two elements...");
                IntegerProperty p1 = new SimpleIntegerProperty(10);
                IntegerProperty p2 = new SimpleIntegerProperty(20);
                list.addAll(p1, p2); // Will call the call() method of the
                                     // extractor - once for p1 and once for p2.
                System.out.println("After adding two elements...");

                // Add a change listener to the list
                list.addListener(ListUpdateTest::onChanged);

                // Update p1 from 10 to 100, which will trigger
                // an update change for the list
                p1.set(100);
        }

        public static void onChanged(
                ListChangeListener.Change<? extends IntegerProperty> change) {
                System.out.println("List is " + change.getList());

                // Work on only updates to the list
                while (change.next()) {
                        if (change.wasUpdated()) {
                                // Print the details of the update
                                System.out.println("An update is detected.");

                                int start = change.getFrom();
                                int end = change.getTo();
                                System.out.println("Updated range:
                                [" + start + ", " + end + "]");
```

```
                        List<? extends IntegerProperty> updatedElementsList;
                        updatedElementsList = change.getList().subList(start, end);

                        System.out.println("Updated elements: " + updatedElementsList);
                    }
                }
            }
        }
    }
```

```
Before adding two elements...
The extractor is called for IntegerProperty [value: 10]
The extractor is called for IntegerProperty [value: 20]
After adding two elements...
List is [IntegerProperty [value: 100], IntegerProperty [value: 20]]
An update is detected.
Updated range: [0, 1]
Updated elements: [IntegerProperty [value: 100]]
```

The `main()` method of the `ListUpdateTest` class creates an extractor that is an object of the `Callback<IntegerProperty, Observable[]>` interface. The `call()` method takes an `IntegerProperty` argument and returns the same by wrapping it in an `Observable` array. It also prints the object that is passed to it.

The extractor is used to create an `ObservableList`. Two `IntegerProperty` objects are added to the list. When the objects are being added, the `call()` method of the extractor is called with the object being added as its argument. This is evident from the output. The `call()` method returns the object being added. This means that the list will watch for any changes to the object (the `IntegerProperty`) and notify its change listeners of the same.

A change listener is added to the list. It handles only updates to the list. At the end, you change the value for the first element of the list from 10 to 100 to trigger an update change notification.

A Complete Example of Observing an *ObservableList* for Changes

This section provides a complete example that shows how to handle the different kinds of changes to an `ObservableList`.

Our starting point is a `Person` class as shown in Listing 3-5. Here you will work with an `ObservableList` of `Person` objects. The `Person` class has two properties: `firstName` and `lastName`. Both properties are of the `StringProperty` type. Its `compareTo()` method is implemented to sort `Person` objects in ascending order by the first name then by the last name. Its `toString()` method prints the first name, a space, and the last name.

Listing 3-5. A Person Class with Two Properties Named `firstName` and `lastName`

```java
// Person.java
package com.jdojo.collections;

import javafx.beans.property.SimpleStringProperty;
import javafx.beans.property.StringProperty;

public class Person implements Comparable<Person> {
        private StringProperty firstName = new SimpleStringProperty();
        private StringProperty lastName = new SimpleStringProperty();

        public Person() {
                this.setFirstName("Unknown");
                this.setLastName("Unknown");
        }

        public Person(String firstName, String lastName) {
                this.setFirstName(firstName);
                this.setLastName(lastName);
        }

        public final String getFirstName() {
                return firstName.get();
        }

        public final void setFirstName(String newFirstName) {
                firstName.set(newFirstName);
        }

        public StringProperty firstNameProperty() {
                return firstName;
        }

        public final String getLastName() {
                return lastName.get();
        }

        public final void setLastName(String newLastName) {
                lastName.set(newLastName);
        }

        public StringProperty lastNameProperty() {
                return lastName;
        }
```

```java
        @Override
        public int compareTo(Person p) {
                // Assume that the first and last names are always not null
                int diff = this.getFirstName().compareTo(p.getFirstName());
                if (diff == 0) {
                        diff = this.getLastName().compareTo(p.getLastName());
                }

                return diff;
        }

        @Override
        public String toString() {
                return getFirstName() + " " + getLastName();
        }
}
```

The PersonListChangeListener class, as shown in Listing 3-6, is a change listener class. It implements the onChanged() method of the ListChangeListener interface to handle all types of change notifications for an ObservableList of Person objects.

Listing 3-6. A Change Listener for an ObservableList of Person Objects

```java
// PersonListChangeListener.java
package com.jdojo.collections;

import java.util.List;
import javafx.collections.ListChangeListener;

public class PersonListChangeListener implements ListChangeListener<Person> {
        @Override
        public void onChanged(ListChangeListener.Change<? extends Person> change) {
                while (change.next()) {
                        if (change.wasPermutated()) {
                                handlePermutated(change);
                        }
                        else if (change.wasUpdated()) {
                            handleUpdated(change);
                        }
                        else if (change.wasReplaced()) {
                            handleReplaced(change);
                        }
                        else {
                                if (change.wasRemoved()) {
                                    handleRemoved(change);
                                }
                                else if (change.wasAdded()) {
                                    handleAdded(change);
                                }
                        }
                }
        }
```

```java
        public void handlePermutated(ListChangeListener.Change<? extends Person> change) {
                System.out.println("Change Type: Permutated");
                System.out.println("Permutated Range: " + getRangeText(change));
                int start = change.getFrom();
                int end = change.getTo();
                for(int oldIndex = start; oldIndex < end; oldIndex++) {
                        int newIndex = change.getPermutation(oldIndex);
                        System.out.println("index[" + oldIndex + "] moved to " +
                                            "index[" + newIndex + "]");
                }
        }

        public void handleUpdated(ListChangeListener.Change<? extends Person> change) {
                System.out.println("Change Type: Updated");
                System.out.println("Updated Range : " + getRangeText(change));
                System.out.println("Updated elements are: " +
                        change.getList().subList(change.getFrom(), change.getTo()));
        }

        public void handleReplaced(ListChangeListener.Change<? extends Person> change) {
                System.out.println("Change Type: Replaced");

                // A "replace" is the same as a "remove" followed with an "add"
                handleRemoved(change);
                handleAdded(change);
        }

        public void handleRemoved(ListChangeListener.Change<? extends Person> change) {
                System.out.println("Change Type: Removed");

                int removedSize = change.getRemovedSize();
                List<? extends Person> subList = change.getRemoved();

                System.out.println("Removed Size: " + removedSize);
                System.out.println("Removed Range: " + getRangeText(change));
                System.out.println("Removed List: " + subList);
        }

        public void handleAdded(ListChangeListener.Change<? extends Person> change) {
                System.out.println("Change Type: Added");

                int addedSize = change.getAddedSize();
                List<? extends Person> subList = change.getAddedSubList();

                System.out.println("Added Size: " + addedSize);
                System.out.println("Added Range: " + getRangeText(change));
                System.out.println("Added List: " + subList);
        }

        public String getRangeText(ListChangeListener.Change<? extends Person> change) {
                return "[" + change.getFrom() + ", " + change.getTo() + "]";
        }
}
```

The ListChangeTest class, as shown in Listing 3-7, is a test class. It creates an ObservableList with an extractor. The extractor returns an array of firstName and lastName properties of a Person object. That means when one of these properties is changed, a Person object as an element of the list is considered updated and an update notification will be sent to all change listeners. It adds a change listener to the list. Finally, it makes several kinds of changes to the list to trigger change notifications. The details of a change notification are printed on the standard output.

This completes one of the most complex discussions about writing a change listener for an ObservableList. Aren't you glad that JavaFX designers didn't make it more complex?

Listing 3-7. Testing an ObservableList of Person Objects for All Types of Changes

```
// ListChangeTest.java
package com.jdojo.collections;

import javafx.beans.Observable;
import javafx.collections.FXCollections;
import javafx.collections.ObservableList;
import javafx.util.Callback;

public class ListChangeTest {
        public static void main(String[] args) {
                Callback<Person, Observable[]> cb =
                        (Person p) -> new Observable[] {
                                p.firstNameProperty(),
                                p.lastNameProperty()
                        };

                // Create a list
                ObservableList<Person> list = FXCollections.observableArrayList(cb);

                // Add a change listener to the list
                list.addListener(new PersonListChangeListener());

                Person p1 = new Person("Li", "Na");
                System.out.println("Before adding " + p1 + ": " + list);
                list.add(p1);
                System.out.println("After adding " + p1 + ": " + list) ;

                Person p2 = new Person("Vivi", "Gin");
                Person p3 = new Person("Li", "He");
                System.out.println("\nBefore adding " + p2 + " and " + p3 + ": " + list);
                list.addAll(p2, p3);
                System.out.println("After adding " + p2 + " and " + p3 + ": " + list);

                System.out.println("\nBefore sorting the list:" + list);
                FXCollections.sort(list);
                System.out.println("After sorting the list:" + list);

                System.out.println("\nBefore updating " + p1 + ": " + list);
                p1.setLastName("Smith");
                System.out.println("After updating " + p1 + ": " + list);
```

```
                    Person p = list.get(0);
                    Person p4 = new Person("Simon", "Ng");
                    System.out.println("\nBefore replacing " + p +
                                         " with " + p4 + ": " + list);
                    list.set(0, p4);
                    System.out.println("After replacing " + p + " with " + p4 + ": " + list);

                    System.out.println("\nBefore setAll(): " + list);
                    Person p5 = new Person("Lia", "Li");
                    Person p6 = new Person("Liz", "Na");
                    Person p7 = new Person("Li", "Ho");
                    list.setAll(p5, p6, p7);
                    System.out.println("After setAll(): " + list);

                    System.out.println("\nBefore removeAll(): " + list);
                    list.removeAll(p5, p7); // Leave p6 in the list
                    System.out.println("After removeAll(): " + list);
            }
    }
```

```
Before adding Li Na: []
Change Type: Added
Added Size: 1
Added Range: [0, 1]
Added List: [Li Na]
After adding Li Na: [Li Na]

Before adding Vivi Gin and Li He: [Li Na]
Change Type: Added
Added Size: 2
Added Range: [1, 3]
Added List: [Vivi Gin, Li He]
After adding Vivi Gin and Li He: [Li Na, Vivi Gin, Li He]

Before sorting the list:[Li Na, Vivi Gin, Li He]
Change Type: Permutated
Permutated Range: [0, 3]
index[0] moved to index[1]
index[1] moved to index[2]
index[2] moved to index[0]
After sorting the list:[Li He, Li Na, Vivi Gin]

Before updating Li Na: [Li He, Li Na, Vivi Gin]
Change Type: Updated
Updated Range : [1, 2]
Updated elements are: [Li Smith]
After updating Li Smith: [Li He, Li Smith, Vivi Gin]
```

```
Before replacing Li He with Simon Ng: [Li He, Li Smith, Vivi Gin]
Change Type: Replaced
Change Type: Removed
Removed Size: 1
Removed Range: [0, 1]
Removed List: [Li He]
Change Type: Added
Added Size: 1
Added Range: [0, 1]
Added List: [Simon Ng]
After replacing Li He with Simon Ng: [Simon Ng, Li Smith, Vivi Gin]

Before setAll(): [Simon Ng, Li Smith, Vivi Gin]
Change Type: Replaced
Change Type: Removed
Removed Size: 3
Removed Range: [0, 3]
Removed List: [Simon Ng, Li Smith, Vivi Gin]
Change Type: Added
Added Size: 3
Added Range: [0, 3]
Added List: [Lia Li, Liz Na, Li Ho]
After setAll(): [Lia Li, Liz Na, Li Ho]

Before removeAll(): [Lia Li, Liz Na, Li Ho]
Change Type: Removed
Removed Size: 1
Removed Range: [0, 0]
Removed List: [Lia Li]
Change Type: Removed
Removed Size: 1
Removed Range: [1, 1]
Removed List: [Li Ho]
After removeAll(): [Liz Na]
```

Understanding *ObservableSet*

If you survived learning the ObservableList and list change listeners, learning about the ObservableSet will be easy! Figure 3-3 shows the class diagram for the ObservableSet interface.

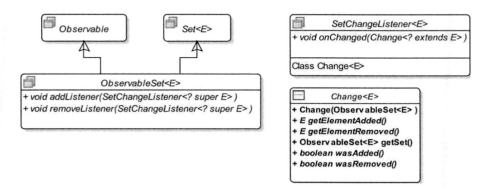

Figure 3-3. *A class diagram for the* ObservableSet *interface*

It inherits from the Set and Observable interfaces. It supports invalidation and change notifications and it inherits the methods for the invalidation notification support from the Observable interface. It adds the following two methods to support change notifications:

- void addListener(SetChangeListener<? super E> listener)

- void removeListener(SetChangeListener<? super E> listener)

An instance of the SetChangeListener interface listens for changes in an ObservableSet. It declares a static inner class named Change, which represents a report of changes in an ObservableSet.

■ **Note** A set is an unordered collection. This section shows the elements of several sets in outputs. You may get a different output showing the elements of sets in a different order than shown in those examples.

Creating an *ObservableSet*

You need to use one of the following factory methods of the FXCollections class to create an ObservableSet:

- <E> ObservableSet<E> observableSet(E... elements)

- <E> ObservableSet<E> observableSet(Set<E> set)

- <E> ObservableSet<E> emptyObservableSet()

The first method lets you specify initial elements for the set. The second method lets you create an ObservableSet that is backed by the specified set. Mutations performed on the ObservableSet are reported to the listeners. Mutations performed directly on the backing set are not reported to the listeners. The third method creates an empty unmodifiable observable set. Listing 3-8 shows how to create ObservableSets.

Listing 3-8. Creating ObservableSets

```
// ObservableSetTest.java
package com.jdojo.collections;

import java.util.HashSet;
import java.util.Set;
import javafx.collections.FXCollections;
import javafx.collections.ObservableSet;

public class ObservableSetTest {
        public static void main(String[] args) {
                // Create an ObservableSet with three initial elements
                ObservableSet<String> s1 = FXCollections.observableSet("one", "two", "three");
                System.out.println("s1: " + s1);

                // Create a Set, and not an ObservableSet
                Set<String> s2 = new HashSet<String>();
                s2.add("one");
                s2.add("two");
                System.out.println("s2: " + s2);

                // Create an ObservableSet backed by the Set s2
                ObservableSet<String> s3 = FXCollections.observableSet(s2);
                s3.add("three");
                System.out.println("s3: " + s3);
        }
}
```

```
s1: [one, two, three]
s2: [one, two]
s3: [one, two, three]
```

Observing an *ObservableSet* for Invalidations

You can add invalidation listeners to an ObservableSet. It fires an invalidation event when elements are added or removed. Adding an already existing element does not fire an invalidation event. Listing 3-9 shows how to use an invalidation listener with an ObservableSet.

Listing 3-9. Testing Invalidation Notifications for an ObservableSet

```
// SetInvalidationTest.java
package com.jdojo.collections;

import javafx.beans.Observable;
import javafx.collections.FXCollections;
import javafx.collections.ObservableSet;
```

```
public class SetInvalidationTest {
        public static void main(String[] args) {
                // Create a set with some elements
                ObservableSet<String> set = FXCollections.observableSet("one", "two");

                // Add an InvalidationListener to the set
                set.addListener(SetInvalidationTest::invalidated);

                System.out.println("Before adding three.");
                set.add("three");
                System.out.println("After adding three.");

                System.out.println("\nBefore adding four.");
                set.add("four");
                System.out.println("After adding four.");

                System.out.println("\nBefore adding one.");
                set.add("one");
                System.out.println("After adding one.");

                System.out.println("\nBefore removing one.");
                set.remove("one");
                System.out.println("After removing one.");

                System.out.println("\nBefore removing 123.");
                set.remove("123");
                System.out.println("After removing 123.");
        }

        public static void invalidated(Observable set) {
                System.out.println("Set is invalid.");
        }
}
```

```
Before adding three.
Set is invalid.
After adding three.

Before adding four.
Set is invalid.
After adding four.

Before adding one.
After adding one.

Before removing one.
Set is invalid.
After removing one.

Before removing 123.
After removing 123.
```

Observing an *ObservableSet* for Changes

An ObservableSet can be observed for changes. You need to add a SetChangeListener whose onChanged() method is called for every addition or removal of elements. It means if you use methods like addAll() or removeAll() on an ObservableSet, which affects multiple elements, multiple change notifications will be fired—one for each element added or removed.

An object of the SetChangeListener.Change class is passed to the onChanged() method of the SetChangeListener interface. The SetChangeListener.Change class is a static inner class of the SetChangeListener interface with the following methods:

- boolean wasAdded()
- boolean wasRemoved()
- E getElementAdded()
- E getElementRemoved()
- ObservableSet<E> getSet()

The wasAdded() and wasRemoved() methods return true if an element was added and removed, respectively. Otherwise, they return false. The getElementAdded() and getElementRemoved() methods return the element that was added and removed, respectively. The getElementAdded() method returns null if removal of an element triggers a change notification. The getElementRemoved() method returns null if addition of an element triggers a change notification. The getSet() method returns the source ObservableSet on which the changes are performed.

The program in Listing 3-10 shows how to observe an ObservableSet for changes.

Listing 3-10. Observing an ObservableSet for Changes

```
// SetChangeTest.java
package com.jdojo.collections;

import java.util.HashSet;
import java.util.Set;
import javafx.collections.FXCollections;
import javafx.collections.ObservableSet;
import javafx.collections.SetChangeListener;

public class SetChangeTest {
        public static void main(String[] args) {
                // Create an observable set with some elements
                ObservableSet<String> set = FXCollections.observableSet("one", "two");

                // Add a change lisetener to the set
                set.addListener(SetChangeTest::onChanged);

                set.add("three"); // Fires an add change event

                // Will not fire a change event as "one" already exists in the set
                set.add("one");
```

```
                    // Create a Set
                    Set<String> s = new HashSet<>();
                    s.add("four");
                    s.add("five");

                    // Add all elements of s to set in one go
                    set.addAll(s); // Fires two add change events

                    set.remove("one"); // Fires a removal change event
                    set.clear();       // Fires four removal change events
            }

        public static void onChanged(SetChangeListener.Change<? extends String> change) {
                if (change.wasAdded()) {
                        System.out.print("Added: " + change.getElementAdded());
                } else if (change.wasRemoved()) {
                        System.out.print("Removed: " + change.getElementRemoved());
                }

                System.out.println(", Set after the change: " + change.getSet());
        }
}
```

```
Added: three, Set after the change: [three, two, one]
Added: four, Set after the change: [four, one, two, three]
Added: five, Set after the change: [four, one, five, two, three]
Removed: one, Set after the change: [four, five, two, three]
Removed: four, Set after the change: [five, two, three]
Removed: five, Set after the change: [two, three]
Removed: two, Set after the change: [three]
Removed: three, Set after the change: []
```

Understanding *ObservableMap*

Figure 3-4 shows the class diagram for the ObservableMap interface. It inherits from the Map and Observable interfaces. It supports invalidation and change notifications. It inherits the methods for the invalidation notification support from the Observable interface and it adds the following two methods to support change notifications:

- void addListener(MapChangeListener<? super K, ? super V> listener)

- void removeListener(MapChangeListener<? super K, ? super V> listener)

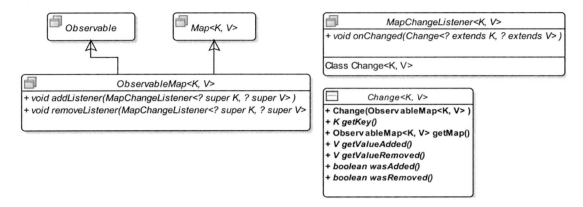

Figure 3-4. *A class diagram for the* ObservableMap *interface*

An instance of the MapChangeListener interface listens for changes in an ObservableMap. It declares a static inner class named Change, which represents a report of changes in an ObservableMap.

Creating an *ObservableMap*

You need to use one of the following factory methods of the FXCollections class to create an ObservableMap:

- <K,V> ObservableMap<K, V> observableHashMap()

- <K,V> ObservableMap<K, V> observableMap(Map<K, V> map)

- <K,V> ObservableMap<K,V> emptyObservableMap()

The first method creates an empty observable map that is backed by a HashMap. The second method creates an ObservableMap that is backed by the specified map. Mutations performed on the ObservableMap are reported to the listeners. Mutations performed directly on the backing map are not reported to the listeners. The third method creates an empty unmodifiable observable map. Listing 3-11 shows how to create ObservableMaps.

Listing 3-11. Creating ObservableMaps

```
// ObservableMapTest.java
package com.jdojo.collections;

import java.util.HashMap;
import java.util.Map;
import javafx.collections.FXCollections;
import javafx.collections.ObservableMap;
```

```java
public class ObservableMapTest {
    public static void main(String[] args) {
        ObservableMap<String, Integer> map1 = FXCollections.observableHashMap();

        map1.put("one", 1);
        map1.put("two", 2);
        System.out.println("Map 1: " + map1);

        Map<String, Integer> backingMap = new HashMap<>();
        backingMap.put("ten", 10);
        backingMap.put("twenty", 20);

        ObservableMap<String, Integer> map2 = FXCollections.
        observableMap(backingMap);
        System.out.println("Map 2: " + map2);
    }
}
```

```
Map 1: {two=2, one=1}
Map 2: {ten=10, twenty=20}
```

Observing an *ObservableMap* for Invalidations

You can add invalidation listeners to an ObservableMap. It fires an invalidation event when a new (key, value) pair is added, the value for an existing key is changed, or a (key, value) pair is removed. Invalidation events are fired once for every affected (key, value) pair. For example, if you call the clear() method on an observable map that has two entries, two invalidation events are fired. Listing 3-12 shows how to use an invalidation listener with an ObservableMap.

Listing 3-12. Testing Invalidation Notifications for an ObservableMap

```java
// MapInvalidationTest.java
package com.jdojo.collections;

import javafx.beans.Observable;
import javafx.collections.FXCollections;
import javafx.collections.ObservableMap;

public class MapInvalidationTest {
    public static void main(String[] args) {
        ObservableMap<String, Integer> map = FXCollections.observableHashMap();

        // Add an InvalidationListener to the map
        map.addListener(MapInvalidationTest::invalidated);

        System.out.println("Before adding (\"one\", 1)");
        map.put("one", 1);
        System.out.println("After adding (\"one\", 1)");
```

```
            System.out.println("\nBefore adding (\"two\", 2)");
            map.put("two", 2);
            System.out.println("After adding (\"two\", 2)");

            System.out.println("\nBefore adding (\"one\", 1)");

            // Adding the same (key, value) does not trigger an invalidation event
            map.put("one", 1);
            System.out.println("After adding (\"one\", 1)");

            System.out.println("\nBefore adding (\"one\", 100)");

            // Adding the same key with different value triggers invalidation event
            map.put("one", 100);
            System.out.println("After adding (\"one\", 100)");

            System.out.println("\nBefore calling clear()");
            map.clear();
            System.out.println("After calling clear()");
    }

    public static void invalidated(Observable map) {
            System.out.println("Map is invalid.");
    }
}
```

```
Before adding ("one", 1)
Map is invalid.
After adding ("one", 1)

Before adding ("two", 2)
Map is invalid.
After adding ("two", 2)

Before adding ("one", 1)
After adding ("one", 1)

Before adding ("one", 100)
Map is invalid.
After adding ("one", 100)

Before calling clear()
Map is invalid.
Map is invalid.
After calling clear()
```

Observing an *ObservableMap* for Changes

An ObservableMap can be observed for changes by adding a MapChangeListener. The onChanged() method of map change listeners is called for every addition and removal of a (key, value) pair and for a change in the value of an existing key.

An object of the MapChangeListener.Change class is passed to the onChanged() method of the MapChangeListener interface. MapChangeListener.Change is a static inner class of the MapChangeListener interface with the following methods:

- boolean wasAdded()

- boolean wasRemoved()

- K getKey()

- V getValueAdded()

- V getValueRemoved()

- ObservableMap<K,V> getMap()

The wasAdded() method returns true if a (key, value) pair is added. The wasRemoved() method returns true if a (key, value) pair is removed. If the value for an existing key is replaced, both methods return true for the same change event. Replacing the value of a key is treated as a removal of the (key, oldValue) pair followed by an addition of a new (key, newValue) pair.

The getKey method returns the key associated with the change. If it is a removal, the key returned by this method does not exist in the map when the change is reported. The getValueAdded() method returns the new key value for an addition. For a removal, it returns null. The getValueRemoved() method returns the old value of the removed key. This is null if and only if the value was added to the key that was not previously in the map. The getMap() method returns the source ObservableMap on which the changes are performed.

Listing 3-13 shows how to observe an ObservableMap for changes.

Listing 3-13. Observing an ObservableMap for Changes

```java
// MapChangeTest.java
package com.jdojo.collections;

import javafx.collections.FXCollections;
import javafx.collections.MapChangeListener;
import javafx.collections.ObservableMap;

public class MapChangeTest {
    public static void main(String[] args) {
        ObservableMap<String, Integer> map = FXCollections.observableHashMap();

        // Add an MapChangeListener to the map
        map.addListener(MapChangeTest::onChanged);

        System.out.println("Before adding (\"one\", 1)");
        map.put("one", 1);
        System.out.println("After adding (\"one\", 1)");
```

```
                System.out.println("\nBefore adding (\"two\", 2)");
                map.put("two", 2);
                System.out.println("After adding (\"two\", 2)");

                System.out.println("\nBefore adding (\"one\", 3)");

                // Will remove ("one", 1) and add("one", 3)
                map.put("one", 3);
                System.out.println("After adding (\"one\", 3)");

                System.out.println("\nBefore calling clear()");
                map.clear();
                System.out.println("After calling clear()");
        }

        public static void onChanged(
                MapChangeListener.Change<? extends String, ? extends Integer> change) {
                if (change.wasRemoved()) {
                        System.out.println("Removed (" + change.getKey() + ", " +
                                        change.getValueRemoved() + ")");
                }

                if (change.wasAdded()) {
                        System.out.println("Added (" + change.getKey() + ", " +
                                        change.getValueAdded() + ")");
                }
        }
}
```

```
Before adding ("one", 1)
Added (one, 1)
After adding ("one", 1)

Before adding ("two", 2)
Added (two, 2)
After adding ("two", 2)

Before adding ("one", 3)
Removed (one, 1)
Added (one, 3)
After adding ("one", 3)

Before calling clear()
Removed (one, 3)
Removed (two, 2)
After calling clear()
```

Properties and Bindings for JavaFX Collections

The ObservableList, ObservableSet, and ObservableMap collections can be exposed as Property objects. They also support bindings using high-level and low-level binding APIs. Property objects representing single values were discussed in Chapter 2. Make sure you have read that chapter before proceeding in this section.

Understanding *ObservableList* Property and Binding

Figure 3-5 shows a partial class diagram for the ListProperty class. The ListProperty class implements the ObservableValue and ObservableList interfaces. It is an observable value in the sense that it wraps the reference of an ObservableList. Implementing the ObservableList interface makes all of its methods available to a ListProperty object. Calling methods of the ObservableList on a ListProperty has the same effect as if they were called on the wrapped ObservableList.

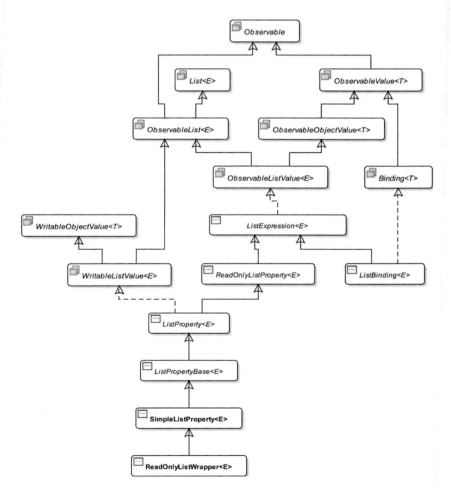

Figure 3-5. *A partial class diagram for the ListProperty class*

You can use one of the following constructors of the SimpleListProperty class to create an instance of the ListProperty:

- SimpleListProperty()

- SimpleListProperty(ObservableList<E> initialValue)

- SimpleListProperty(Object bean, String name)

- SimpleListProperty(Object bean, String name, ObservableList<E> initialValue)

One of the common mistakes in using the ListProperty class is not passing an ObservableList to its constructor before using it. A ListProperty must have a reference to an ObservableList before you can perform a meaningful operation on it. If you do not use an ObservableList to create a ListProperty object, you can use its set() method to set the reference of an ObservableList. The following snippet of code generates an exception:

```
ListProperty<String> lp = new SimpleListProperty<String>();

// No ObservableList to work with. Generates an exception.
lp.add("Hello");
```

```
Exception in thread "main" java.lang.UnsupportedOperationException
        at java.util.AbstractList.add(AbstractList.java:148)
        at java.util.AbstractList.add(AbstractList.java:108)
        at javafx.beans.binding.ListExpression.add(ListExpression.java:262)
```

■ **Tip**   Operations performed on a ListProperty that wraps a null reference are treated as if the operations were performed on an immutable empty ObservableList.

The following snippet of code shows how to create and initialize a ListProperty before using it:

```
ObservableList<String> list1 = FXCollections.observableArrayList();
ListProperty<String> lp1 = new SimpleListProperty<String>(list1);
lp1.add("Hello");

ListProperty<String> lp2 = new SimpleListProperty<String>();
lp2.set(FXCollections.observableArrayList());
lp2.add("Hello");
```

Observing a *ListProperty* for Changes

You can attach three types of listeners to a ListProperty:

- An InvalidationListener

- A ChangeListener

- A ListChangeListener

All three listeners are notified when the reference of the ObservableList, which is wrapped in the ListProperty, changes or the content of the ObservableList changes. When the content of the list changes, the changed() method of ChangeListeners receives the reference to the same list as the old and new value. If the wrapped reference of the ObservableList is replaced with a new one, this method receives references of the old list and the new list. To handle the list change events, please refer to the "Observing an *ObservableList* for Changes" section in this chapter.

The program in Listing 3-14 shows how to handle all three types of changes to a ListProperty. The list change listener handles the changes to the content of the list in a brief and generic way. Please refer to the "Observing an *ObservableList* for Changes" section in this chapter on how to handle the content change events for an ObservableList in detail.

Listing 3-14. Adding Invalidation, Change, and List Change Listeners to a ListProperty

```
// ListPropertyTest.java
package com.jdojo.collections;

import javafx.beans.Observable;
import javafx.beans.property.ListProperty;
import javafx.beans.property.SimpleListProperty;
import javafx.beans.value.ObservableValue;
import javafx.collections.FXCollections;
import javafx.collections.ListChangeListener;
import javafx.collections.ObservableList;

public class ListPropertyTest {
        public static void main(String[] args) {
                // Create an observable list property
                ListProperty<String> lp =
                new SimpleListProperty<>(FXCollections.observableArrayList());

                // Add invalidation, change, and list change listeners
                lp.addListener(ListPropertyTest::invalidated);
                lp.addListener(ListPropertyTest::changed);
                lp.addListener(ListPropertyTest::onChanged);

                System.out.println("Before addAll()");
                lp.addAll("one", "two", "three");
                System.out.println("After addAll()");

                System.out.println("\nBefore set()");

                // Replace the wrapped list with a new one
                lp.set(FXCollections.observableArrayList("two", "three"));
                System.out.println("After set()");

                System.out.println("\nBefore remove()");
                lp.remove("two");
                System.out.println("After remove()");
        }
```

```
        // An invalidation listener
        public static void invalidated(Observable list) {
                System.out.println("List property is invalid.");
        }

        // A change listener
        public static void changed(ObservableValue<? extends ObservableList<String>> observable,
                                ObservableList<String> oldList,
                                ObservableList<String> newList) {
            System.out.print("List Property has changed.");
            System.out.print(" Old List: " + oldList);
            System.out.println(", New List: " + newList);
        }

        // A list change listener
        public static void onChanged(ListChangeListener.Change<? extends String> change) {
            while (change.next()) {
                    String action = change.wasPermutated() ? "Permutated"
                                    : change.wasUpdated() ? "Updated"
                                    : change.wasRemoved() && change.wasAdded() ? "Replaced"
                                    : change.wasRemoved() ? "Removed" : "Added";

                    System.out.print("Action taken on the list: " + action);
                    System.out.print(". Removed: " + change.getRemoved());
                    System.out.println(", Added: " + change.getAddedSubList());
            }
        }
    }
}
```

```
Before addAll()
List property is invalid.
List Property has changed. Old List: [one, two, three], New List: [one, two, three]
Action taken on the list: Added. Removed: [], Added: [one, two, three]
After addAll()

Before set()
List property is invalid.
List Property has changed. Old List: [one, two, three], New List: [two, three]
Action taken on the list: Replaced. Removed: [one, two, three], Added: [two, three]
After set()

Before remove()
List property is invalid.
List Property has changed. Old List: [three], New List: [three]
Action taken on the list: Removed. Removed: [two], Added: []
After remove()
```

Binding the *size* and *empty* Properties of a *ListProperty*

A ListProperty exposes two properties, size and empty, which are of type ReadOnlyIntegerProperty and ReadOnlyBooleanProperty, respectively. You can access them using the sizeProperty() and emptyProperty() methods. The size and empty properties are useful for binding in GUI applications. For example, the model in a GUI application may be backed by a ListProperty, and you can bind these properties to the text property of a label on the screen. When the data changes in the model, the label will be updated automatically through binding. The size and empty properties are declared in the ListExpression class.

The program in Listing 3-15 shows how to use the size and empty properties. It uses the asString() method of the ListExpression class to convert the content of the wrapped ObservableList to a String.

Listing 3-15. Using the size and empty Properties of a ListProperty Object

```
// ListBindingTest.java
package com.jdojo.collections;

import javafx.beans.property.ListProperty;
import javafx.beans.property.SimpleListProperty;
import javafx.beans.property.SimpleStringProperty;
import javafx.beans.property.StringProperty;
import javafx.collections.FXCollections;

public class ListBindingTest {
        public static void main(String[] args) {
                ListProperty<String> lp =
                        new SimpleListProperty<>(FXCollections.observableArrayList());

                // Bind the size and empty properties of the ListProperty
                // to create a description of the list
                StringProperty initStr = new SimpleStringProperty("Size: " );
                StringProperty desc = new SimpleStringProperty();
                desc.bind(initStr.concat(lp.sizeProperty())
                                .concat(", Empty: ")
                                .concat(lp.emptyProperty())
                                .concat(", List: ")
                                .concat(lp.asString()));

                System.out.println("Before addAll(): " + desc.get());
                lp.addAll("John", "Jacobs");
                System.out.println("After addAll(): " + desc.get());
        }
}
```

```
Before addAll(): Size: 0, Empty: true, List: []
After addAll(): Size: 2, Empty: false, List: [John, Jacobs]
```

Methods to support high-level binding for a list property are in the `ListExpression` and `Bindings` classes. Low-level binding can be created by subclassing the `ListBinding` class. A `ListProperty` supports two types of bindings:

- Binding the reference of the `ObservableList` that it wraps

- Binding the content of the `ObservableList` that it wraps

The `bind()` and `bindBidirectional()` methods are used to create the first kind of binding. The program in Listing 3-16 shows how to use these methods. As shown in the output below, notice that both list properties have the reference of the same `ObservableList` after binding.

Listing 3-16. Binding the References of List Properties

```java
// BindingListReference.java
package com.jdojo.collections;

import javafx.beans.property.ListProperty;
import javafx.beans.property.SimpleListProperty;
import javafx.collections.FXCollections;

public class BindingListReference {

    public static void main(String[] args) {
        ListProperty<String> lp1 =
            new SimpleListProperty<>(FXCollections.observableArrayList());
        ListProperty<String> lp2 =
            new SimpleListProperty<>(FXCollections.observableArrayList());

        lp1.bind(lp2);

        print("Before addAll():", lp1, lp2);
        lp1.addAll("One", "Two");
        print("After addAll():", lp1, lp2);

        // Change the reference of the ObservableList in lp2
        lp2.set(FXCollections.observableArrayList("1", "2"));
        print("After lp2.set():", lp1, lp2);

        // Cannot do the following as lp1 is a bound property
        // lp1.set(FXCollections.observableArrayList("1", "2"));
        // Unbind lp1
        lp1.unbind();
        print("After unbind():", lp1, lp2);

        // Bind lp1 and lp2 bidirectionally
        lp1.bindBidirectional(lp2);
        print("After bindBidirectional():", lp1, lp2);

        lp1.set(FXCollections.observableArrayList("X", "Y"));
        print("After lp1.set():", lp1, lp2);
    }
```

117

```java
    public static void print(String msg, ListProperty<String> lp1, ListProperty<String> lp2) {
        System.out.println(msg);
        System.out.println("lp1: " + lp1.get() + ", lp2: " + lp2.get() +
                        ", lp1.get() == lp2.get(): " + (lp1.get() == lp2.get()));
        System.out.println("--------------------------");
    }
}
```

```
Before addAll():
lp1: [], lp2: [], lp1.get() == lp2.get(): true
--------------------------
After addAll():
lp1: [One, Two], lp2: [One, Two], lp1.get() == lp2.get(): true
--------------------------
After lp2.set():
lp1: [1, 2], lp2: [1, 2], lp1.get() == lp2.get(): true
--------------------------
After unbind():
lp1: [1, 2], lp2: [1, 2], lp1.get() == lp2.get(): true
--------------------------
After bindBidirectional():
lp1: [1, 2], lp2: [1, 2], lp1.get() == lp2.get(): true
--------------------------
After lp1.set():
lp1: [X, Y], lp2: [X, Y], lp1.get() == lp2.get(): true
--------------------------
```

The bindContent() and bindContentBidirectional() methods let you bind the content of the ObservableList that is wrapped in a ListProperty to the content of another ObservableList in one direction and both directions, respectively. Make sure to use the corresponding methods, unbindContent() and unbindContentBidirectional(), to unbind contents of two observable lists.

■ **Tip** You can also use methods of the Bindings class to create bindings for references and contents of observable lists.

It is allowed, but not advisable, to change the content of a ListProperty whose content has been bound to another ObservableList. In such cases, the bound ListProperty will not be synchronized with its target list. Listing 3-17 shows examples of both types of content binding.

Listing 3-17. Binding Contents of List Properties

```java
// BindingListContent.java
package com.jdojo.collections;

import javafx.beans.property.ListProperty;
import javafx.beans.property.SimpleListProperty;
import javafx.collections.FXCollections;

public class BindingListContent {

    public static void main(String[] args) {
        ListProperty<String> lp1 =
            new SimpleListProperty<>(FXCollections.observableArrayList());
        ListProperty<String> lp2 =
            new SimpleListProperty<>(FXCollections.observableArrayList());

        // Bind the content of lp1 to the content of lp2
        lp1.bindContent(lp2);

        /* At this point, you can change the content of lp1. However,
         * that will defeat the purpose of content binding, because the
         * content of lp1 is no longer in sync with the content of lp2.
         * Do not do this:
         * lp1.addAll("X", "Y");
         */
        print("Before lp2.addAll():", lp1, lp2);
        lp2.addAll("1", "2");
        print("After lp2.addAll():", lp1, lp2);

        lp1.unbindContent(lp2);
        print("After lp1.unbindContent(lp2):", lp1, lp2);

        // Bind lp1 and lp2 contents bidirectionally
        lp1.bindContentBidirectional(lp2);

        print("Before lp1.addAll():", lp1, lp2);
        lp1.addAll("3", "4");
        print("After lp1.addAll():", lp1, lp2);

        print("Before lp2.addAll():", lp1, lp2);
        lp2.addAll("5", "6");
        print("After lp2.addAll():", lp1, lp2);
    }

    public static void print(String msg, ListProperty<String> lp1, ListProperty<String> lp2) {
        System.out.println(msg + " lp1: " + lp1.get() + ", lp2: " + lp2.get());
    }
}
```

```
Before lp2.addAll(): lp1: [], lp2: []
After lp2.addAll(): lp1: [1, 2], lp2: [1, 2]
After lp1.unbindContent(lp2): lp1: [1, 2], lp2: [1, 2]
Before lp1.addAll(): lp1: [1, 2], lp2: [1, 2]
After lp1.addAll(): lp1: [1, 2, 3, 4], lp2: [1, 2, 3, 4]
Before lp2.addAll(): lp1: [1, 2, 3, 4], lp2: [1, 2, 3, 4]
After lp2.addAll(): lp1: [1, 2, 3, 4, 5, 6], lp2: [1, 2, 3, 4, 5, 6]
```

Binding to Elements of a List

ListProperty provides so many useful features that I can keep discussing this topic for at least 50 more pages! I will wrap this topic up with one more example.

It is possible to bind to a specific element of the ObservableList wrapped in a ListProperty using one of the following methods of the ListExpression class:

- ObjectBinding<E> valueAt(int index)

- ObjectBinding<E> valueAt(ObservableIntegerValue index)

The first version of the method creates an ObjectBinding to an element in the list at a specific index. The second version of the method takes an index as an argument, which is an ObservableIntegerValue that can change over time. When the bound index in the valueAt() method is outside the list range, the ObjectBinding contains null.

Let's use the second version of the method to create a binding that will bind to the last element of a list. Here you can make use of the size property of the ListProperty in creating the binding expression. The program in Listing 3-18 shows how to use the valueAt() method. Note that this program throws an ArrayIndexOutOfBoundsException when run using Java Development Kit 8 Build 25. It did not throw an exception before and it does not throw an exception in Java Development Kit 9's early access build.

Listing 3-18. Binding to the Elements of a List

```java
// BindingToListElements.java
package com.jdojo.collections;

import javafx.beans.binding.ObjectBinding;
import javafx.beans.property.ListProperty;
import javafx.beans.property.SimpleListProperty;
import javafx.collections.FXCollections;

public class BindingToListElements {
    public static void main(String[] args) {
        ListProperty<String> lp =
                new SimpleListProperty<>(FXCollections.observableArrayList());

        // Create a binding to the last element of the list
        ObjectBinding<String> last = lp.valueAt(lp.sizeProperty().subtract(1));
        System.out.println("List:" + lp.get() + ", Last Value: " + last.get());
```

```
            lp.add("John");
            System.out.println("List:" + lp.get() + ", Last Value: " + last.get());

            lp.addAll("Donna", "Geshan");
            System.out.println("List:" + lp.get() + ", Last Value: " + last.get());

            lp.remove("Geshan");
            System.out.println("List:" + lp.get() + ", Last Value: " + last.get());

            lp.clear();
            System.out.println("List:" + lp.get() + ", Last Value: " + last.get());
        }
}
```

```
List:[], Last Value: null
List:[John], Last Value: John
List:[John, Donna, Geshan], Last Value: Geshan
List:[John, Donna], Last Value: Donna
List:[], Last Value: null
```

Understanding *ObservableSet* Property and Binding

A SetProperty object wraps an ObservableSet. Working with a SetProperty is very similar to working with a ListProperty. I are not going to repeat what has been discussed in the previous sections about properties and bindings of an ObservableList. The same discussions apply to properties and bindings of ObservableSet. The following are the salient points to remember while working with a SetProperty:

- The class diagram for the SetProperty class is similar to the one shown in Figure 3-5 for the ListProperty class. You need to replace the word "List" with the word "Set" in all names.

- The SetExpression and Bindings classes contain methods to support high-level bindings for set properties. You need to subclass the SetBinding class to create low-level bindings.

- Like the ListProperty, the SetProperty exposes the size and empty properties.

- Like the ListProperty, the SetProperty supports bindings of the reference and the content of the ObservableSet that it wraps.

- Like the ListProperty, the SetProperty supports three types of notifications: invalidation notifications, change notifications, and set change notifications.

- Unlike a list, a set is an unordered collection of items. Its elements do not have indexes. It does not support binding to its specific elements. Therefore, the SetExpression class does not contain a method like valueAt() as the ListExpression class does.

You can use one of the following constructors of the SimpleSetProperty class to create an instance of the SetProperty:

- SimpleSetProperty()

- SimpleSetProperty(ObservableSet<E> initialValue)

- SimpleSetProperty(Object bean, String name)

- SimpleSetProperty(Object bean, String name, ObservableSet<E> initialValue)

The following snippet of code creates an instance of the SetProperty and adds two elements to the ObservableSet that the property wraps. In the end, it gets the reference of the ObservableSet from the property object using the get() method:

```
// Create a SetProperty object
SetProperty<String> sp = new SimpleSetProperty<String>(FXCollections.observableSet());

// Add two elements to the wrapped ObservableSet
sp.add("one");
sp.add("two");

// Get the wrapped set from the sp property
ObservableSet<String> set = sp.get();
```

The program in Listing 3-19 demonstrates how to use binding with SetProperty objects.

Listing 3-19. Using Properties and Bindings for Observable Sets

```
// SetBindingTest.java
package com.jdojo.collections;

import javafx.beans.property.SetProperty;
import javafx.beans.property.SimpleSetProperty;
import javafx.beans.property.SimpleStringProperty;
import javafx.beans.property.StringProperty;
import javafx.collections.FXCollections;

public class SetBindingTest {
        public static void main(String[] args) {
                SetProperty<String> sp1 =
                        new SimpleSetProperty<>(FXCollections.observableSet());

                // Bind the size and empty properties of the SetProperty
                // to create a description of the set
                StringProperty initStr = new SimpleStringProperty("Size: " );
                StringProperty desc = new SimpleStringProperty();
                desc.bind(initStr.concat(sp1.sizeProperty())
                                .concat(", Empty: ")
                                .concat(sp1.emptyProperty())
                                .concat(", Set: " )
                                .concat(sp1.asString())
                        );
```

```
                System.out.println("Before sp1.add(): " + desc.get());
                sp1.add("John");
                sp1.add("Jacobs");
                System.out.println("After sp1.add(): " + desc.get());

                SetProperty<String> sp2 =
                        new SimpleSetProperty<>(FXCollections.observableSet());

                // Bind the content of sp1 to the content of sp2
                sp1.bindContent(sp2);
                System.out.println("Called sp1.bindContent(sp2)...");

                /* At this point, you can change the content of sp1. However,
                 * that will defeat the purpose of content binding, because the
                 * content of sp1 is no longer in sync with the content of sp2.
                 * Do not do this:
                 * sp1.add("X");
                 */
                print("Before sp2.add():", sp1, sp2);
                sp2.add("1");
                print("After sp2.add():", sp1, sp2);

                sp1.unbindContent(sp2);
                print("After sp1.unbindContent(sp2):", sp1, sp2);

                // Bind sp1 and sp2 contents bidirectionally
                sp1.bindContentBidirectional(sp2);

                print("Before sp2.add():", sp1, sp2);
                sp2.add("2");
                print("After sp2.add():", sp1, sp2);
        }

        public static void print(String msg, SetProperty<String> sp1, SetProperty<String> sp2) {
                System.out.println(msg + " sp1: " + sp1.get() + ", sp2: " + sp2.get());
        }
}
}
```

```
Before sp1.add(): Size: 0, Empty: true, Set: []
After sp1.add(): Size: 2, Empty: false, Set: [Jacobs, John]
Called sp1.bindContent(sp2)...
Before sp2.add(): sp1: [], sp2: []
After sp2.add(): sp1: [1], sp2: [1]
After sp1.unbindContent(sp2): sp1: [1], sp2: [1]
Before sp2.add(): sp1: [1], sp2: [1]
After sp2.add(): sp1: [1, 2], sp2: [2, 1]
```

Understanding *ObservableMap* Property and Binding

A MapProperty object wraps an ObservableMap. Working with a MapProperty is very similar to working with a ListProperty. I are not going to repeat what has been discussed in the previous sections about properties and bindings of an ObservableList. The same discussions apply to properties and bindings of ObservableMap. The following are the salient points to remember while working with a MapProperty:

- The class diagram for the MapProperty class is similar to the one shown in Figure 3-5 for the ListProperty class. You need to replace the word "List" with the word "Map" in all names and the generic type parameter <E> with <K, V>, where K and V stand for the key type and value type, respectively, of entries in the map.

- The MapExpression and Bindings classes contain methods to support high-level bindings for map properties. You need to subclass the MapBinding class to create low-level bindings.

- Like the ListProperty, the MapProperty exposes size and empty properties.

- Like the ListProperty, the MapProperty supports bindings of the reference and the content of the ObservableMap that it wraps.

- Like the ListProperty, the MapProperty supports three types of notifications: invalidation notifications, change notifications, and map change notifications.

- The MapProperty supports binding to the value of a specific key using its valueAt() method.

Use one of the following constructors of the SimpleMapProperty class to create an instance of the MapProperty:

- SimpleMapProperty()

- SimpleMapProperty(Object bean, String name)

- SimpleMapProperty(Object bean, String name, ObservableMap<K,V> initialValue)

- SimpleMapProperty(ObservableMap<K,V> initialValue)

The following snippet of code creates an instance of the MapProperty and adds two entries. In the end, it gets the reference of the wrapped ObservableMap using the get() method:

```
// Create a MapProperty object
MapProperty<String, Double> mp =
        new SimpleMapProperty<String, Double>(FXCollections.observableHashMap());

// Add two entries to the wrapped ObservableMap
mp.put("Ken", 8190.20);
mp.put("Jim", 8990.90);

// Get the wrapped map from the mp property
ObservableMap<String, Double> map = mp.get();
```

The program in Listing 3-20 shows how to use binding with MapProperty objects. It shows the content binding between two maps. You can also use unidirectional and bidirectional simple binding between two map properties to bind the references of the maps they wrap.

Listing 3-20. Using Properties and Bindings for Observable Maps

```java
// MapBindingTest.java
package com.jdojo.collections;

import javafx.beans.binding.ObjectBinding;
import javafx.beans.property.MapProperty;
import javafx.beans.property.SimpleMapProperty;
import javafx.beans.property.SimpleStringProperty;
import javafx.beans.property.StringProperty;
import javafx.collections.FXCollections;

public class MapBindingTest {
        public static void main(String[] args) {
                MapProperty<String, Double> mp1 =
                        new SimpleMapProperty<>(FXCollections.observableHashMap());

                // Create an object binding to bind mp1 to the value of the key "Ken"
                ObjectBinding<Double> kenSalary = mp1.valueAt("Ken");
                System.out.println("Ken Salary: " + kenSalary.get());

                // Bind the size and empty properties of the MapProperty
                // to create a description of the map
                StringProperty initStr = new SimpleStringProperty("Size: " );
                StringProperty desc = new SimpleStringProperty();
                desc.bind(initStr.concat(mp1.sizeProperty())
                                .concat(", Empty: ")
                                .concat(mp1.emptyProperty())
                                .concat(", Map: " )
                                .concat(mp1.asString())
                                .concat(", Ken Salary: ")
                                .concat(kenSalary));

                System.out.println("Before mp1.put(): " + desc.get());

                // Add some entries to mp1
                mp1.put("Ken", 7890.90);
                mp1.put("Jim", 9800.80);
                mp1.put("Lee", 6000.20);
                System.out.println("After mp1.put(): " + desc.get());

                // Create a new MapProperty
                MapProperty<String, Double> mp2 =
                new SimpleMapProperty<>(FXCollections.observableHashMap());

                // Bind the content of mp1 to the content of mp2
                mp1.bindContent(mp2);
                System.out.println("Called mp1.bindContent(mp2)...");
```

125

```
            /* At this point, you can change the content of mp1. However,
             * that will defeat the purpose of content binding, because the
             * content of mp1 is no longer in sync with the content of mp2.
             * Do not do this:
             * mp1.put("k1", 8989.90);
             */
            System.out.println("Before mp2.put(): " + desc.get());
            mp2.put("Ken", 7500.90);
            mp2.put("Cindy", 7800.20);
            System.out.println("After mp2.put(): " + desc.get());
        }
}
```

```
Ken Salary: null
Before mp1.put(): Size: 0, Empty: true, Map: {}, Ken Salary: null
After mp1.put(): Size: 3, Empty: false, Map: {Jim=9800.8, Lee=6000.2, Ken=7890.9}, Ken
Salary: 7890.9
Called mp1.bindContent(mp2)...
Before mp2.put(): Size: 0, Empty: true, Map: {}, Ken Salary: null
After mp2.put(): Size: 2, Empty: false, Map: {Cindy=7800.2, Ken=7500.9}, Ken Salary: 7500.9
```

Summary

JavaFX extends the collections framework in Java by adding support for observable lists, sets, and maps that are called observable collections. An observable collection is a list, set, or map that may be observed for invalidation and content changes. Instances of the ObservableList, ObservableSet, and ObservableMap interfaces in the javafx.collections package represent observable interfaces in JavaFX. You can add invalidation and change listeners to instances of these observable collections.

The FXCollections class is a utility class to work with JavaFX collections. It consists of all static methods. JavaFX does not expose the implementation classes of observable lists, sets, and maps. You need to use one of the factory methods in the FXCollections class to create objects of the ObservableList, ObservableSet, and ObservableMap interfaces.

JavaFX library provides two classes named FilteredList and SortedList that are in the javafx.collections.transformation package. A FilteredList is an ObservableList that filters its contents using a specified Predicate. A SortedList sorts its contents.

The next chapter will discuss how to create and customize stages in JavaFX applications.

CHAPTER 4

■ ■ ■

Managing Stages

In this chapter, you will learn:

- How to get details of screens such as their number, resolutions, and dimensions
- What a stage is in JavaFX and how to set bounds and styles of a stage
- How to move an undecorated stage
- How to set the modality and opacity of a stage
- How to resize a stage and how to show a stage in full-screen mode

Knowing the Details of Your Screens

The Screen class in the javafx.stage package is used to get the details, for example, dots-per-inch (DPI) setting and dimensions of user screens (or monitors). If multiple screens are hooked up to a computer, one of the screens is known as the primary screen and others as nonprimary screens. You can get the reference of the Screen object for the primary monitor using the static getPrimary() method of the Screen class with the following code:

```
// Get the reference to the primary screen
Screen primaryScreen = Screen.getPrimary();
```

The static getScreens() method returns an ObservableList of Screen objects:

```
ObservableList<Screen> screenList = Screen.getScreens();
```

You can get the resolution of a screen in DPI using the getDpi() method of the Screen class as follows:

```
Screen primaryScreen = Screen.getPrimary();
double dpi = primaryScreen.getDpi();
```

You can use the getBounds() and getVisualBounds() methods to get the bounds and visual bounds, respectively. Both methods return a Rectangle2D object, which encapsulates the (x, y) coordinates of the upper-left and the lower-right corners, the width, and the height of a rectangle. The getMinX() and getMinY() methods return the x and y coordinates of the upper-left corner of the rectangle, respectively. The getMaxX() and getMaxY() methods return the x and y coordinates of the lower-right corner of the rectangle, respectively. The getWidth() and getHeight() methods return the width and height of the rectangle, respectively.

The bounds of a screen cover the area that is available on the screen. The visual bounds represent the area on the screen that is available for use, after taking into account the area used by the native windowing system such as task bars and menus. Typically, but not necessarily, the visual bounds of a screen represents a smaller area than its bounds.

If a desktop spans multiple screens, the bounds of the nonprimary screens are relative to the primary screen. For example, if a desktop spans two screens with the (x, y) coordinates of the upper-left corner of the primary screen at (0, 0) and its width 1600, the coordinates of the upper-left corner of the second screen would be (1600, 0).

The program in Listing 4-1 prints the screens details when it was run on a Windows desktop with two screens. You may get a different output. Notice the difference in height for bounds and visual bounds for one screen and not for the other. The primary screen displays a task bar at the bottom that takes away some part of the height from the visual bounds. The nonprimary screen does not display a task bar, and therefore, its bounds and visual bounds are the same.

▪ **Tip** Although it is not mentioned in the API documentation for the Screen class, you cannot use this class until the JavaFX launcher has started. That is, you cannot get screen descriptions in a non-JavaFX application. This is the reason that you would write the code in the start() method of a JavaFX application class. There is no requirement that the Screen class needs to be used on the JavaFX Application Thread. You could also write the same code in the init() method of your class.

Listing 4-1. Accessing Screens Details

```java
// ScreenDetailsApp.java
package com.jdojo.stage;

import javafx.application.Application;
import javafx.application.Platform;
import javafx.collections.ObservableList;
import javafx.geometry.Rectangle2D;
import javafx.stage.Screen;
import javafx.stage.Stage;

public class ScreenDetailsApp extends Application  {
        public static void main(String[] args) {
                Application.launch(args);
        }

        public void start(Stage stage) {
                ObservableList<Screen> screenList = Screen.getScreens();
                System.out.println("Screens Count: " + screenList.size());

                // Print the details of all screens
                for(Screen screen: screenList) {
                        print(screen);
                }

                Platform.exit();
        }
```

```
        public void print(Screen s) {
                System.out.println("DPI: " + s.getDpi());

                System.out.print("Screen Bounds: ");
                Rectangle2D bounds = s.getBounds();
                print(bounds);

                System.out.print("Screen Visual Bounds: ");
                Rectangle2D visualBounds = s.getVisualBounds();
                print(visualBounds);
                System.out.println("----------------------");
        }

        public void print(Rectangle2D r) {
                System.out.format("minX=%.2f, minY=%.2f, width=%.2f, height=%.2f%n",
                                r.getMinX(), r.getMinY(), r.getWidth(), r.getHeight());
        }
}
```

```
Screens Count: 2
DPI: 96.0
Screen Bounds: minX=0.00, minY=0.00, width=1680.00, height=1050.00
Screen Visual Bounds: minX=0.00, minY=0.00, width=1680.00, height=1022.00
----------------------
DPI: 96.0
Screen Bounds: minX = 1680.00, minY=0.00, width= 1680.00, height=1050.00
Screen Visual Bounds: minX = 1680.00, minY=0.00, width= 1680.00, height=1050.0
----------------------
```

What Is a Stage?

A stage in JavaFX is a top-level container that hosts a scene, which consists of visual elements. The Stage class in the javafx.stage package represents a stage in a JavaFX application. The primary stage is created by the platform and passed to the start(Stage s) method of the Application class. You can create additional stages as needed.

■ **Tip** A stage in a JavaFX application is a top-level container. This does not mean that it is always displayed as a separate window. For example, in a web environment, the primary stage of a JavaFX application is embedded inside the browser window.

Figure 4-1 shows the class diagram for the Stage class, which inherits from the Window class. The Window class is the superclass for several window-line container classes. It contains the basic functionalities that are common to all types of windows (e.g., methods to show and hide the window, set x, y, width, and height properties, set the opacity of the window, etc.). The Window class defines x, y, width, height, and opacity properties. It has show() and hide() methods to show and hide a window, respectively. The setScene() method of the Window class sets the scene for a window. The Stage class defines a close() method, which has the same effect as calling the hide() method of the Window class.

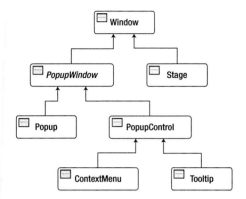

Figure 4-1. *The class diagram for the Stage class*

A Stage object must be created and modified on the JavaFX Application Thread. Recall that the start() method of the Application class is called on the JavaFX Application Thread, and a primary Stage is created and passed to this method. Note that the primary stage that is passed the start() method is not shown. You need to call the show() method to show it.

Several aspects of working with stages need to be discussed. I will handle them one by one from the basic to the advanced level in the sections that follow.

Showing the Primary Stage

Let's start with the simplest JavaFX application, as shown in Listing 4-2. The start() method has no code. When you run the application, you do not see a window, nor do you see output on the console. The application runs forever. You will need to use the system-specific keys to cancel the application. If you are using Windows, use your favorite key combination Ctrl + Alt + Del to activate the task manager! If you are using the command prompt, use Ctrl + C.

Listing 4-2. An Ever-Running JavaFX Application

```
// EverRunningApp.java
package com.jdojo.stage;

import javafx.application.Application;
import javafx.stage.Stage;

public class EverRunningApp extends Application {
    public static void main(String[] args) {
        Application.launch(args);
    }

    @Override
    public void start(Stage stage) {
        // Do not write any code here
    }
}
```

To determine what is wrong with the program in Listing 4-2, you need to understand what the JavaFX application launcher does. Recall that JavaFX Application Thread is terminated when the `Platform.exit()` method is called or the last shown stage is closed. The JVM terminates when all nondaemon threads die. JavaFX Application Thread is a nondaemon thread. The `Application.launch()` method returns when the JavaFX Application Thread terminates. In the above example, there is no way to terminate the JavaFX Application Thread. This is the reason the application runs forever.

Using the `Platform.exit()` method in the `start()` method will fix the problem. The modified code for the `start()` method is shown in Listing 4-3. When you run the program, it exits without doing anything meaningful.

Listing 4-3. A Short-Lived JavaFX Application

```
// ShortLivedApp.java
package com.jdojo.stage;

import javafx.application.Application;
import javafx.application.Platform;
import javafx.stage.Stage;

public class ShortLivedApp extends Application {
        public static void main(String[] args) {
                Application.launch(args);
        }

        @Override
        public void start(Stage stage) {
                Platform.exit(); // Exit the application
        }
}
```

Let's try to fix the ever-running program by closing the primary stage. You have only one stage when the `start()` method is called and closing it should terminate the JavaFX Application Thread. Let's modify the `start()` method of the EverRunningApp with the following code:

```
@Override
public void start(Stage stage) {
        stage.close(); // Close the only stage you have
}
```

Even with this code for the `start()` method, the EverRunningApp runs forever. The `close()` method does not close the stage if the stage is not showing. The primary stage was never shown. Therefore, adding a `stage.close()` call to the `start()` method did not do any good. The following code for the `start()` method would work. However, this will cause the screen to flicker as the stage is shown and closed:

```
@Override
public void start(Stage stage) {
        stage.show();  // First show the stage
        stage.close(); // Now close it
}
```

▪ **Tip** The close() method of the Stage class has the same effect as calling the hide() method of the Window class. The JavaFX API documentation does not mention that attempting to close a not showing window has no effect.

Setting the Bounds of a Stage

The bounds of a stage consist of four properties: x, y, width, and height. The x and y properties determine the location (or position) of the upper-left corner of the stage. The width and height properties determine its size. In this section, you will learn how to position and size a stage on the screen. You can use the getters and setters for these properties to get and set their values.

Let's start with a simple example as shown in Listing 4-4. The program sets the title for the primary stage before showing it. When you run this code, you would see a window with the title bar, borders, and an empty area. If other applications are open, you can see their content through the transparent area of the stage. The position and size of the window are decided by the platform.

▪ **Tip** When a stage does not have a scene and its position and size are not set explicitly, its position and size are determined and set by the platform.

Listing 4-4. Displaying a Stage with No Scene and with the Platform Default Position and Size

```java
// BlankStage.java
package com.jdojo.stage;

import javafx.application.Application;
import javafx.stage.Stage;

public class BlankStage extends Application {
    public static void main(String[] args) {
        Application.launch(args);
    }

    @Override
    public void start(Stage stage) {
        stage.setTitle("Blank Stage");
        stage.show();
    }
}
```

Let's modify the logic a bit. Here you will set an empty scene to the stage without setting the size of the scene. The modified start() method would look as follows:

```
import javafx.scene.Group;
import javafx.scene.Scene;
...
@Override
public void start(Stage stage) {
        stage.setTitle("Stage with an Empty Scene");
        Scene scene = new Scene(new Group());
        stage.setScene(scene);
        stage.show();
}
```

Notice that you have set a Group with no children nodes as the root node for the scene, because you cannot create a scene without a root node. When you run the program in Listing 4-4 with the above code as its start() method, the position and size of the stage are determined by the platform. This time, the content area will have a white background, because the default background color for a scene is white.

Let's modify the logic again. Here let's add a button to the scene. The modified start() method would be as follows:

```
import javafx.scene.control.Button;
...
@Override
public void start(Stage stage) {
        stage.setTitle("Stage with a Button in the Scene");
        Group root = new Group(new Button("Hello"));
        Scene scene = new Scene(root);
        stage.setScene(scene);
        stage.show();
}
```

When you run the program in Listing 4-4 with the above code as its start() method, the position and size of the stage are determined by the computed size of the scene. The content area of the stage is wide enough to show the title bar menus or the content of the scene, whichever is bigger. The content area of the stage is tall enough to show the content of the scene, which in this case has only one button. The stage is centered on the screen, as shown in Figure 4-2.

Figure 4-2. *A stage with a scene that contains a button where the size of the scene is not specified*

Let's add another twist to the logic by adding a button to the scene and set the scene width and height to 300 and 100, respectively, as follows:

```
@Override
public void start(Stage stage) {
        stage.setTitle("Stage with a Sized Scene");
        Group root = new Group(new Button("Hello"));
        Scene scene = new Scene(root, 300, 100);
        stage.setScene(scene);
        stage.show();
}
```

When you run the program in Listing 4-4 with the above code as its start() method, the position and size of the stage are determined by the specified size of the scene. The content area of the stage is the same as the specified size of the scene. The width of the stage includes the borders on the two sides, and the height of the stage includes the height of the title bar and the bottom border. The stage is centered on the screen, as shown in Figure 4-3.

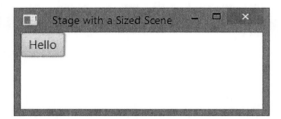

Figure 4-3. *A stage with a scene with a specified size*

Let's add one more twist to the logic. You will set the size of the scene and the stage using the following code:

```
@Override
public void start(Stage stage) {
        stage.setTitle("A Sized Stage with a Sized Scene");
        Group root = new Group(new Button("Hello"));
        Scene scene = new Scene(root, 300, 100);
        stage.setScene(scene);
        stage.setWidth(400);
        stage.setHeight(100);
        stage.show();
}
```

When you run the program in Listing 4-4 with the above code as its start() method, the position and size of the stage are determined by the specified size of the stage. The stage is centered on the screen and it will then look like the one shown in Figure 4-4.

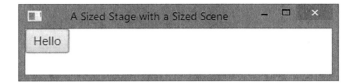

Figure 4-4. *A sized stage with a sized scene*

■ **Tip** The default centering of a stage centers it horizontally on the screen. The y coordinate of the upper-left corner of the stage is one-third of the height of the screen minus the height of the stage. This is the logic used in the `centerOnScreen()` method in the `Window` class.

Let me recap the rules for positioning and resizing a stage. If you do not specify the bounds of a stage and:

- It has no scene, its bounds are determined by the platform.

- It has a scene with no visual nodes, its bounds are determined by the platform. In this case, the size of the scene is not specified.

- It has a scene with some visual nodes, its bounds are determined by the visual nodes in the scene. In this case, the size of the scene is not specified and the stage is centered in the screen.

- It has a scene and the size of the scene is specified, its bounds are determined by the specified size of the scene. The stage is centered on the screen.

If you specify the size of the stage but not its position, the stage is sized according the set size and centered on the screen, irrespective of the presence of a scene and the size of the scene. If you specify the position of the stage (x, y coordinates), it is positioned accordingly.

■ **Tip** If you want to set the width and height of a stage to fit the content of its scene, use the `sizeToScene()` method of the `Window` class. The method is useful if you want to synchronize the size of a stage with the size of its scene after modifying the scene at runtime. Use the `centerOnScreen()` method of the `Window` class to center the stage on the screen.

If you want to center a stage on the screen horizontally as well as vertically, use the following logic:

```
Rectangle2D bounds = Screen.getPrimary().getVisualBounds();
double x = bounds.getMinX() + (bounds.getWidth() - stage.getWidth())/2.0;
double y = bounds.getMinY() + (bounds.getHeight() - stage.getHeight())/2.0;
stage.setX(x);
stage.setY(y);
```

Be careful in using the above snippet of code. It makes use of the size of the stage. The size of a stage is not known until the stage is shown for the first time. Using the above logic before a stage is shown will not really center the stage on the screen. The following start() method of a JavaFX application will not work as intended:

```
@Override
public void start(Stage stage) {
        stage.setTitle("A Truly Centered Stage");
        Group root = new Group(new Button("Hello"));
        Scene scene = new Scene(root);
        stage.setScene(scene);

        // Wrong!!!! Use the logic shown below after the stage.show() call
        // At this point, stage width and height are not known. They are NaN.
        Rectangle2D bounds = Screen.getPrimary().getVisualBounds();
        double x = bounds.getMinX() + (bounds.getWidth() - stage.getWidth())/2.0;
        double y = bounds.getMinY() + (bounds.getHeight() - stage.getHeight())/2.0;
        stage.setX(x);
        stage.setY(y);

        stage.show();
}
```

Initializing the Style of a Stage

The area of a stage can be divided into two parts: content area and decorations. The content area displays the visual content of its scene. Typically, decorations consist of a title bar and borders. The presence of a title bar and its content varies depending on the type of decorations provided by the platform. Some decorations provide additional features rather than just an aesthetic look. For example, a title bar may be used to drag a stage to a different location; buttons in a title bar may be used to minimize, maximize, restore, and close a stage; or borders may be used to resize a stage.

In JavaFX, the style attribute of a stage determines its background color and decorations. Based on styles, you can have the following five types of stages in JavaFX:

- Decorated

- Undecorated

- Transparent

- Unified

- Utility

A *decorated* stage has a solid white background and platform decorations. An *undecorated* stage has a solid white background and no decorations. A *transparent* stage has a transparent background and no decorations. A *unified* stage has platform decorations and no border between the client area and decorations; the client area background is unified with the decorations. To see the effect of the unified stage style, the scene should be filled with Color.TRANSPARENT. Unified style is a conditional feature. A *utility* stage has a solid white background and minimal platform decorations.

■ **Tip** The style of a stage specifies only its decorations. The background color is controlled by its scene background, which is solid white by default. If you set the style of a stage to TRANSPARENT, you will get a stage with a solid white background, which is the background of the scene. To get a truly transparent stage, you will need to set the background color of the scene to null using its setFill() method.

You can set the style of a stage using the initStyle(StageStyle style) method of the Stage class. The style of a stage must be set before it is shown for the first time. Setting it the second time, after the stage has been shown, throws a runtime exception. By default, a stage is decorated.

The five types of styles for a stage are defined as five constants in the StageStyle enum:

- StageStyle.DECORATED
- StageStyle.UNDECORATED
- StageStyle.TRANSPARENT
- StageStyle.UNIFIED
- StageStyle.UTILITY

Listing 4-5 shows how to use these five styles for a stage. In the start() method, you need to uncomment only one statement at a time, which initializes the style of the stage. You will use a VBox to display two controls: a Label and a Button. The Label displays the style of the stage. The Button is provided to close the stage, because not all styles provide a title bar with a close button. Figure 4-5 shows the stage using four styles. The contents of windows in the background can be seen through a transparent stage. This is the reason that when you use the transparent style, you will see more content that has been added to the stage.

Listing 4-5. Using Different Styles for a Stage

```java
// StageStyleApp.java
package com.jdojo.stage;

import javafx.application.Application;
import javafx.scene.Scene;
import javafx.scene.control.Button;
import javafx.scene.control.Label;
import javafx.scene.layout.VBox;
import javafx.scene.paint.Color;
import javafx.stage.Stage;
import javafx.stage.StageStyle;
import static javafx.stage.StageStyle.DECORATED;
import static javafx.stage.StageStyle.UNDECORATED;
import static javafx.stage.StageStyle.TRANSPARENT;
import static javafx.stage.StageStyle.UNIFIED;
import static javafx.stage.StageStyle.UTILITY;

public class StageStyleApp extends Application {
    public static void main(String[] args) {
        Application.launch(args);
    }
```

```
    @Override
    public void start(Stage stage) {
            // A label to display the style type
            Label styleLabel = new Label("Stage Style");

            // A button to close the stage
            Button closeButton = new Button("Close");
            closeButton.setOnAction(e -> stage.close());

            VBox root = new VBox();
            root.getChildren().addAll(styleLabel, closeButton);
            Scene scene = new Scene(root, 100, 70);
            stage.setScene(scene);

            // The title of the stage is not visible for all styles.
            stage.setTitle("The Style of a Stage");

            /* Uncomment one of the following statements at a time */
            this.show(stage, styleLabel, DECORATED);
            //this.show(stage, styleLabel, UNDECORATED);
            //this.show(stage, styleLabel, TRANSPARENT);
            //this.show(stage, styleLabel, UNIFIED);
            //this.show(stage, styleLabel, UTILITY);
    }

    private void show(Stage stage, Label styleLabel, StageStyle style) {
            // Set the text for the label to match the style
            styleLabel.setText(style.toString());

            // Set the style
            stage.initStyle(style);

            // For a transparent style, set the scene fill to null. Otherwise, the
            // content area will have the default white background of the scene.
            if (style == TRANSPARENT) {
                    stage.getScene().setFill(null);
                    stage.getScene().getRoot().setStyle(
                            "-fx-background-color: transparent");
            } else if(style == UNIFIED) {
                    stage.getScene().setFill(Color.TRANSPARENT);
            }

            // Show the stage
            stage.show();
    }
}
```

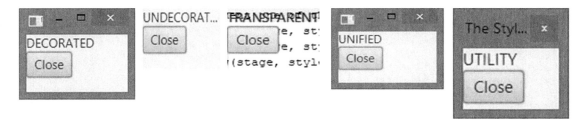

Figure 4-5. *A stage using different styles*

Moving an Undecorated Stage

You can move a stage to a different location by dragging its title bar. In an undecorated or transparent stage, a title bar is not available. You need to write a few lines of code to let the user move this kind of stage by dragging the mouse over the scene area. Listing 4-6 shows how to write the code to support dragging of a stage. If you change the stage to be transparent, you will need to drag the stage by dragging the mouse over only the message label, as the transparent area will not respond to the mouse events.

This example uses mouse event handling. I will cover event handling in detail in Chapter 9. It is briefly presented here to complete the discussion on using different styles of a stage.

Listing 4-6. Dragging a Stage

```java
// DraggingStage.java
package com.jdojo.stage;

import javafx.application.Application;

import javafx.scene.Scene;
import javafx.scene.control.Button;
import javafx.scene.control.Label;
import javafx.scene.input.MouseEvent;
import javafx.scene.layout.VBox;

import javafx.stage.Stage;
import javafx.stage.StageStyle;

public class DraggingStage extends Application {
        private Stage stage;
        private double dragOffsetX;
        private double dragOffsetY;

        public static void main(String[] args) {
                Application.launch(args);
        }

        @Override
        public void start(Stage stage) {
                // Store the stage reference in the instance variable to
                // use it in the mouse pressed event handler later.
                this.stage = stage;
```

```
            Label msgLabel = new Label("Press the mouse button and drag.");
            Button closeButton = new Button("Close");
            closeButton.setOnAction(e -> stage.close());

            VBox root = new VBox();
            root.getChildren().addAll(msgLabel, closeButton);

            Scene scene = new Scene(root, 300, 200);

            // Set mouse pressed and dragged even handlers for the scene
            scene.setOnMousePressed(e -> handleMousePressed(e));
            scene.setOnMouseDragged(e -> handleMouseDragged(e));

            stage.setScene(scene);
            stage.setTitle("Moving a Stage");
            stage.initStyle(StageStyle.UNDECORATED);
            stage.show();
    }

    protected void handleMousePressed(MouseEvent e) {
            // Store the mouse x and y coordinates with respect to the
            // stage in the reference variables to use them in the drag event
            this.dragOffsetX = e.getScreenX() - stage.getX();
            this.dragOffsetY = e.getScreenY() - stage.getY();
    }

    protected void handleMouseDragged(MouseEvent e) {
            // Move the stage by the drag amount
            stage.setX(e.getScreenX() - this.dragOffsetX);
            stage.setY(e.getScreenY() - this.dragOffsetY);
    }
}
```

The following snippet of code adds the mouse pressed and mouse dragged event handlers to the scene:

```
scene.setOnMousePressed(e -> handleMousePressed(e));
scene.setOnMouseDragged(e -> handleMouseDragged(e));
```

When you press the mouse in the scene (except the button area), the handleMousePressed() method is called. The getScreenX() and getScreenY() methods of the MouseEvent object return the x and y coordinates of the mouse with respect to the upper-left corner of the screen. Figure 4-6 shows a diagrammatic view of the coordinate systems. It shows a thin border around the stage. However, when you run the example code, you will not see any border. This is shown here to distinguish the screen area from the stage area. You store the x and y coordinates of the mouse with respect to the stage upper-left corner in instance variables.

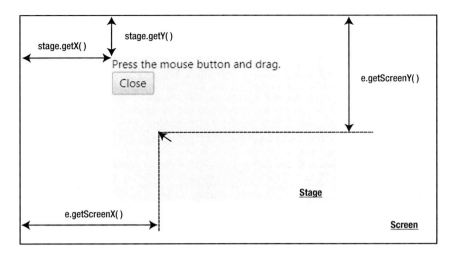

Figure 4-6. *Computing the mouse coordinates with respect to the stage*

When you drag the mouse, the handleMouseDragged() method is called. The method computes and sets the position of the stage using the position of the mouse when it was pressed and its position during the drag.

Initializing Modality of a Stage

In a GUI application, you can have two types of windows: modal and modeless. When a modal window is displayed, the user cannot work with other windows in the application until the modal window is dismissed. If an application has multiple modeless windows showing, the user can switch between them at any time.

JavaFX has three types of modality for a stage:

- None
- Window modal
- Application modal

Modality of a stage is defined by one of the following three constants in the Modality enum in the javafx.stage package:

- NONE
- WINDOW_MODAL
- APPLICATION_MODEL

You can set the modality of a stage using the initModality(Modality m) method of the Stage class as follows:

```
// Create a Stage object and set its modality
Stage stage = new Stage();
stage.initModality(Modality.WINDOW_MODAL);

/* More code goes here.*/

// Show the stage
stage.show();
```

■ **Tip** The modality of a stage must be set before it is shown. Setting the modality of a stage after it has been shown throws a runtime exception. Setting the modality for the primary stage also throws a runtime exception.

A Stage can have an owner. An owner of a Stage is another Window. You can set an owner of a Stage using the initOwner(Window owner) method of the Stage class. The owner of a Stage must be set before the stage is shown. The owner of a Stage may be null, and in this case, it is said that the Stage does not have an owner. Setting an owner of a Stage creates an owner-owned relationship. For example, a Stage is minimized or hidden if its owner is minimized or hidden, respectively.

The default modality of a Stage is NONE. When a Stage with the modality NONE is displayed, it does not block any other windows in the application. It behaves as a modeless window.

A Stage with the WINDOW_MODAL modality blocks all windows in its owner hierarchy. Suppose there are four stages: s1, s2, s3, and s4. Stages s1 and s4 have modalities set to NONE and do not have an owner; s1 is the owner of s2; s2 is the owner of s3. All four stages are displayed. If s3 has its modality set to WINDOW_MODAL, you can work with s3 or s4, but not with s2 and s1. The owner-owned relationship is defined as s1 to s2 to s3. When s3 is displayed, it blocks s2 and s1, which are in its owner hierarchy. Because s4 is not in the owner hierarchy of s3, you can still work with s4.

■ **Tip** The modality of WINDOW_MODAL for a stage that has no owner has the same effect as if the modality is set to NONE.

If a Stage with its modality set to APPLICATION_MODAL is displayed, you must work with the Stage and dismiss it before you can work with any other windows in the application. Continuing with the same example from the previous paragraph of displaying four stages, if you set the modality of s4 to APPLICATION_MODAL, the focus will be set to s4 and you must dismiss it before you can work with other stages. Notice that an APPLICATION_MODAL stage blocks all other windows in the same application, irrespective of the owner-owned relationships.

Listing 4-7 shows how to use different modalities for a stage. It displays the primary stage with six buttons. Each button opens a secondary stage with a specified modality and owner. The text of the buttons tells you what kind of secondary stage they will open. When the secondary stage is shown, try clicking on the primary stage. When the modality of the secondary stage blocks the primary stage, you will not be able to work with the primary stage; clicking the primary stage will set the focus back to the secondary stage.

Listing 4-7. Using Different Modalities for a Stage

```java
// StageModalityApp.java
package com.jdojo.stage;

import javafx.application.Application;
import javafx.scene.Scene;
import javafx.scene.control.Button;
import javafx.scene.control.Label;
import javafx.scene.layout.VBox;
import javafx.stage.Stage;
import javafx.stage.Modality;
import static javafx.stage.Modality.NONE;
import static javafx.stage.Modality.WINDOW_MODAL;
```

```java
import static javafx.stage.Modality.APPLICATION_MODAL;
import javafx.stage.Window;

public class StageModalityApp extends Application {
    public static void main(String[] args) {
        Application.launch(args);
    }

    @Override
    public void start(Stage stage) {
        /* Buttons to display each kind of modal stage */
        Button ownedNoneButton = new Button("Owned None");
        ownedNoneButton.setOnAction(e -> showDialog(stage, NONE));

        Button nonOwnedNoneButton = new Button("Non-owned None");
        nonOwnedNoneButton.setOnAction(e -> showDialog(null, NONE));

        Button ownedWinButton = new Button("Owned Window Modal");
        ownedWinButton.setOnAction(e -> showDialog(stage, WINDOW_MODAL));

        Button nonOwnedWinButton = new Button("Non-owned Window Modal");
        nonOwnedWinButton.setOnAction(e -> showDialog(null, WINDOW_MODAL));

        Button ownedAppButton = new Button("Owned Application Modal");
        ownedAppButton.setOnAction(e -> showDialog(stage, APPLICATION_MODAL));

        Button nonOwnedAppButton = new Button("Non-owned Application Modal");
        nonOwnedAppButton.setOnAction(e -> showDialog(null, APPLICATION_MODAL));

        VBox root = new VBox();
        root.getChildren().addAll(ownedNoneButton, nonOwnedNoneButton,
                                  ownedWinButton, nonOwnedWinButton,
                                  ownedAppButton, nonOwnedAppButton);
        Scene scene = new Scene(root, 300, 200);
        stage.setScene(scene);
        stage.setTitle("The Primary Stage");
        stage.show();
    }

    private void showDialog(Window owner, Modality modality) {
        // Create a Stage with specified owner and modality
        Stage stage = new Stage();
        stage.initOwner(owner);
        stage.initModality(modality);

        Label modalityLabel = new Label(modality.toString());
        Button closeButton = new Button("Close");
        closeButton.setOnAction(e -> stage.close());
```

```
            VBox root = new VBox();
            root.getChildren().addAll(modalityLabel, closeButton);
            Scene scene = new Scene(root, 200, 100);
            stage.setScene(scene);
            stage.setTitle("A Dialog Box");
            stage.show();
        }
}
```

Setting the Opacity of a Stage

The opacity of a stage determines how much you can see through the stage. You can set the opacity of a stage using the setOpacity(double opacity) method of the Window class. Use the getOpacity() method to get the current opacity of a stage.

The opacity value ranges from 0.0 to 1.0. Opacity of 0.0 means the stage is fully translucent; opacity of 1.0 means the stage is fully opaque. Opacity affects the entire area of a stage, including its decorations. Not all JavaFX runtime platforms are required to support opacity. Setting opacity on the JavaFX platforms that do not support opacity has no effect. The following snippet of code sets the opacity of a state to half-translucent:

```
Stage stage = new Stage();
stage.setOpacity(0.5); // A half-translucent stage
```

Resizing a Stage

You can set whether a user can or cannot resize a stage by using its setResizable(boolean resizable) method. Note that a call to the setResizable() method is a *hint* to the implementation to make the stage resizable. By default, a stage is resizable. Sometimes, you may want to restrict the use to resize a stage within a range of width and height. The setMinWidth(), setMinHeight(), setMaxWidth(), and setMaxHeight() methods of the Stage class let you set the range within which the user can resize a stage.

■ **Tip** Calling the setResizable(false) method on a Stage object prevents the user from resizing the stage. You can still resize the stage programmatically.

It is often required to open a window that takes up the entire screen space. To achieve this, you need to set the position and size of the window to the available visual bounds of the screen. Listing 4-8 provides the program to illustrate this. It opens an empty stage, which takes up the entire visual area of the screen.

Listing 4-8. Opening a Stage to Take Up the Entire Available Visual Screen Space

```
// MaximizedStage.java
package com.jdojo.stage;

import javafx.application.Application;
import javafx.geometry.Rectangle2D;
import javafx.scene.Group;
import javafx.scene.Scene;
```

```
import javafx.stage.Screen;
import javafx.stage.Stage;

public class MaximizedStage extends Application {
        public static void main(String[] args) {
                Application.launch(args);
        }

        @Override
        public void start(Stage stage) {
                stage.setScene(new Scene(new Group()));
                stage.setTitle("A Maximized Stage");

                // Set the position and size of the stage equal to the position and
                // size of the screen
                Rectangle2D visualBounds = Screen.getPrimary().getVisualBounds();
                stage.setX(visualBounds.getMinX());
                stage.setY(visualBounds.getMinY());
                stage.setWidth(visualBounds.getWidth());
                stage.setHeight(visualBounds.getHeight());

                // Show the stage
                stage.show();
        }
}
```

Showing a Stage in Full-Screen Mode

The Stage class has a fullScreen property that specified whether a stage should be displayed in full-screen mode. The implementation of full-screen mode depends on the platform and profile. If the platform does not support full-screen mode, the JavaFX runtime will simulate it by displaying the stage maximized and undecorated. A stage may enter full-screen mode by calling the setFullScreen(true) method. When a stage enters full-screen mode, a brief message is displayed about how to exit the full-screen mode: You will need to press the ESC key to exit full-screen mode. You can exit full-screen mode programmatically by calling the setFullScreen(false) method. Use the isFullScreen() method to check if a stage is in full-screen mode.

Showing a Stage and Waiting for It to Close

You often want to display a dialog box and suspend further processing until it is closed. For example, you may want to display a message box to the user with options to click yes and no buttons, and you want different actions performed based on which button is clicked by the user. In this case, when the message box is displayed to the user, the program must wait for it to close before it executes the next sequence of logic. Consider the following pseudo-code:

```
Option userSelection = messageBox("Close", "Do you want to exit?", YESNO);
if (userSelection == YES) {
        stage.close();
}
```

In this pseudo-code, when the messageBox() method is called, the program needs to wait to execute the subsequent if statement until the message box is dismissed.

The show() method of the Window class returns immediately, making it useless to open a dialog box in the above example. You need to use the showAndWait() method, which shows the stage and waits for it to close before returning to the caller. The showAndWait() method stops processing the current event temporarily and starts a nested event loop to process other events.

■ **Tip** The showAndWait() method must be called on the JavaFX Application Thread. It should not be called on the primary stage or a runtime exception will be thrown.

You can have multiple stages open using the showAndWait() method. Each call to the method starts a new nested event loop. A specific call to the method returns to the caller when all nested event loops created after this method call have terminated.

This rule may be confusing in the beginning. Let's look at an example to explain this in detail. Suppose you have three stages: s1, s2, and s3. Stage s1 is opened using the call s1.showAndWait(). From the code in s1, stage s2 is opened using the call s2.showAndWait(). At this point, there are two nested event loops: one created by s1.showAndWait() and another by s2.showAndWait(). The call to s1.showAndWait() will return only after both s1 and s2 have been closed, irrespective of the order they were closed. The s2.showAndWait() call will return after s2 has been closed.

Listing 4-9 contains a program that will allow you to play with the showAndWait() method call using multiple stages. The primary stage is opened with an Open button. Clicking the Open button opens a secondary stage using the showAndWait() method. The secondary stage has two buttons—Say Hello and Open—which will, respectively, will print a message on the console and open another secondary stage. A message is printed on the console before and after the call to the showAndWait() method. You need to open multiple secondary stages, print messages by clicking the Say Hello button, close them in any order you want, and then look at the output on the console.

Listing 4-9. Playing with showAndWait() Call

```
// ShowAndWaitApp.java
package com.jdojo.stage;

import javafx.application.Application;
import javafx.scene.Scene;
import javafx.scene.control.Button;
import javafx.scene.layout.VBox;
import javafx.stage.Stage;

public class ShowAndWaitApp extends Application {
        protected static int counter = 0;
        protected Stage lastOpenStage;

        public static void main(String[] args) {
                Application.launch(args);
        }
```

```
    @Override
    public void start(Stage stage) {
            VBox root = new VBox();
            Button openButton = new Button("Open");
            openButton.setOnAction(e -> open(++counter));
            root.getChildren().add(openButton);
            Scene scene = new Scene(root, 400, 400);
            stage.setScene(scene);
            stage.setTitle("The Primary Stage");
            stage.show();

            this.lastOpenStage = stage;
    }

    private void open(int stageNumber) {
            Stage stage = new Stage();
            stage.setTitle("#" + stageNumber);

            Button sayHelloButton = new Button("Say Hello");
            sayHelloButton.setOnAction(
                    e -> System.out.println("Hello from #" + stageNumber));

            Button openButton = new Button("Open");
            openButton.setOnAction(e -> open(++counter));

            VBox root = new VBox();
            root.getChildren().addAll(sayHelloButton, openButton);
            Scene scene = new Scene(root, 200, 200);
            stage.setScene(scene);
            stage.setX(this.lastOpenStage.getX() + 50);
            stage.setY(this.lastOpenStage.getY() + 50);
            this.lastOpenStage = stage;

            System.out.println("Before stage.showAndWait(): " + stageNumber);

            // Show the stage and wait for it to close
            stage.showAndWait();

            System.out.println("After stage.showAndWait(): " + stageNumber);
    }
}
```

■ **Tip** JavaFX does not provide a built-in window that can be used as a dialog box (a message box or a prompt window). You can develop one by setting the appropriate modality for a stage and showing it using the showAndWait() method.

147

Summary

The Screen class in the javafx.stage package is used to obtain the details, such as the DPI setting and dimensions, of the user's screens hooked to the machine running the program. If multiple screens are present, one of the screens is known as the primary screen and the others are the nonprimary screens. You can get the reference of the Screen object for the primary monitor using the static getPrimary() method of the Screen class.

A stage in JavaFX is a top-level container that hosts a scene, which consists of visual elements. The Stage class in the javafx.stage package represents a stage in a JavaFX application. The primary stage is created by the platform and passed to the start(Stage s) method of the Application class. You can create additional stages as needed.

A stage has bounds that comprise its position and size. The bounds of a stage are defined by its four properties: x, y, width, and height. The x and y properties determine the location (or position) of the upper-left corner of the stage. The width and height properties determine its size.

The area of a stage can be divided into two parts: content area and decorations. The content area displays the visual content of its scene. Typically, decorations consist of a title bar and borders. The presence of a title bar and its content vary depending on the type of decorations provided by the platform. You can have five types of stages in JavaFX: decorated, undecorated, transparent, unified, and utility.

JavaFX allows you to have two types of windows: modal and modeless. When a modal window is displayed, the user cannot work with other windows in the application until the modal window is dismissed. If an application has multiple modeless windows showing, the user can switch between them at any time. JavaFX defines three types of modality for a stage: none, window modal, and application modal. A stage with none as its modality is modeless window. A stage with window modal as its modality blocks all windows in its owner hierarchy. A stage with application modal as its modality blocks all other windows in the application.

The opacity of a stage determines how much you can see through the stage. You can set the opacity of a stage using its setOpacity(double opacity) method. The opacity value ranges from 0.0 to 1.0. Opacity of 0.0 means the stage is fully translucent; the opacity of 1.0 means the stage is fully opaque. Opacity affects the entire area of a stage, including its decorations.

You can set a hint whether a user can resize a stage by using its setResizable(boolean resizable) method. The setMinWidth(), setMinHeight(), setMaxWidth(), and setMaxHeight() methods of the Stage class let you set the range within which the user can resize a stage. A stage may enter full-screen mode by calling its setFullScreen(true) method.

You can use the show() and showAndWait() methods of the Stage class to show a stage. The show() method shows the stage and returns, whereas the showAndWait() method shows the stage and blocks until the stage is closed.

The next chapter will show you how to create scenes and work with scene graphs.

CHAPTER 5

■ ■ ■

Making Scenes

In this chapter, you will learn:

- What a scene and a scene graph are in a JavaFX application
- About different rendering modes of a scene graph
- How to set the cursor for a scene
- How to determine the focus owner in a scene
- How to use the Platform and HostServices classes

What Is a Scene?

A *scene* represents the visual contents of a stage. The Scene class in the javafx.scene package represents a scene in a JavaFX program. A Scene object is attached to, at the most, one stage at a time. If an already attached scene is attached to another stage, it is first detached from the previous stage. A stage can have, at the most, one scene attached to it at any time.

A scene contains a scene graph that consists of visual nodes. In this sense, a scene acts as a container for a scene graph. A scene graph is a tree data structure whose elements are known as *nodes*. Nodes in a scene graph form a parent-child hierarchical relationship. A node in a scene graph is an instance of the javafx.scene.Node class. A node can be a branch node or a leaf node. A branch node can have children nodes, whereas a leaf node cannot. The first node in a scene graph is called the *root* node. The root node can have children nodes; however, it never has a parent node. Figure 5-1 shows the arrangement of nodes in a scene graph. Branch nodes are shown in rounded rectangles and leaf nodes in rectangles.

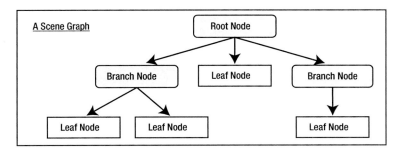

Figure 5-1. The arrangement of nodes in a scene graph

The JavaFX class library provides many classes to represent branch and leaf nodes in a scene graph. The Node class in the javafx.scene package is the superclass of all nodes in a scene graph. Figure 5-2 shows a partial class diagram for classes representing nodes.

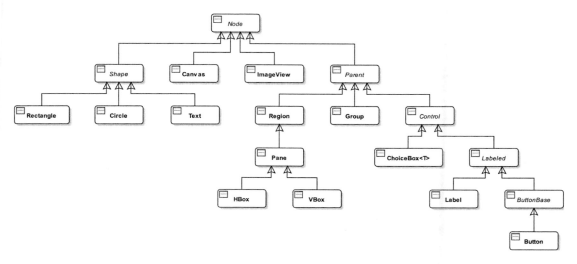

Figure 5-2. *A partial class diagram for the* javafx.scene.Node *class*

A scene always has a root node. If the root node is resizable, for example, a Region or a Control, it tracks the size of the scene. That is, if the scene is resized, the resizable root node resizes itself to fill the entire scene. Based on the policy of a root node, the scene graph may be laid out again when the size of the scene changes.

A Group is a nonresizable Parent node that can be set as the root node of a scene. If a Group is the root node of a scene, the content of the scene graph is clipped by the size of the scene. If the scene is resized, the scene graph is not laid out again.

Parent is an abstract class. It is the base class for all branch nodes in a scene graph. If you want to add a branch node to a scene graph, use objects of one of its concrete subclasses, for example, Group, Pane, HBox, or VBox. Classes that are subclasses of the Node class, but not the Parent class, represent leaf nodes, for example, Rectangle, Circle, Text, Canvas, or ImageView. The root node of a scene graph is a special branch node that is the topmost node. This is the reason you use a Group or a VBox as the root node while creating a Scene object. I will discuss classes representing branch and leaf nodes in detail in Chapters 10 and 12. Table 5-1 lists some of the commonly used properties of the Scene class.

Table 5-1. *Commonly Used Properties of the Scene Class*

Type	Name	Property and Description
ObjectProperty<Cursor>	cursor	It defines the mouse cursor for the Scene.
ObjectProperty<Paint>	fill	It defines the background fill of the Scene.
ReadOnlyObjectProperty<Node>	focusOwner	It defines the node in the Scene that owns the focus.
ReadOnlyDoubleProperty	height	It defines the height of the Scene.
ObjectProperty<Parent>	root	It defines the root Node of the scene graph.
ReadOnlyDoubleProperty	width	It defines the width of the Scene.
ReadOnlyObjectProperty<Window>	window	It defines the Window for the Scene.
ReadOnlyDoubleProperty	x	It defines the horizontal location of the Scene on the Window.
ReadOnlyDoubleProperty	y	It defines the vertical location of the Scene on the window.

Graphics Rendering Modes

The scene graph plays a vital role in rendering the content of a JavaFX application on the screen. Typically, two types of APIs are used to render graphics on a screen:

- Immediate mode API

- Retained mode API

In immediate mode API, the application is responsible for issuing the drawing commands when a frame is needed on the screen. The graphics are drawn directly on the screen. When the screen needs to be repainted, the application needs to reissue the drawing commands to the screen. Java2D is an example of the immediate mode graphics-rendering API.

In retained mode API, the application creates and attaches drawing objects to a graph. The graphics library, not the application code, retains the graph in memory. Graphics are rendered on the screen by the graphics library when needed. The application is responsible only for creating the graphic objects—the "what" part; the graphics library is responsible for storing and rendering the graphics—the "when" and "how" parts. Retained mode rendering API relieves developers of writing the logic for rendering the graphics. For example, adding or removing part of a graphic from a screen is simple by adding or removing a graphic object from the graph using high-level APIs; the graphics library takes care of the rest. In comparison to the immediate mode, retained mode API uses more memory, as the graph is stored in memory. The JavaFX scene graph uses retained mode APIs.

You might think that using immediate mode API would always be faster than using retained mode API because the former renders graphics directly on the screen. However, using retained mode API opens the door for optimizations by the class library that is not possible in the immediate mode where every developer is in charge of writing the logic as to what and when it should be rendered.

Figures 5-3 and 5-4 illustrate how immediate and retained mode APIs work, respectively. They show how a text, Hello, and a hexagon are drawn on the screen using the two APIs.

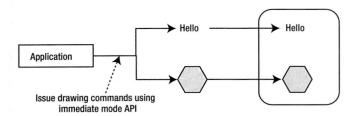

Figure 5-3. *An illustration of the immediate mode API*

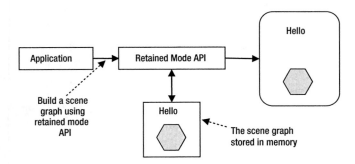

Figure 5-4. *An illustration of the retained mode API*

Setting the Cursor for a Scene

An instance of the javafx.scene.Cursor class represents a mouse cursor. The Cursor class contains many constants, for example, HAND, CLOSED_HAND, DEFAULT, TEXT, NONE, WAIT, for standard mouse cursors. The following snippet of code sets the WAIT cursor for a scene:

```
Scene scene;
...
scene.setCursor(Cursor.WAIT);
```

You can also create and set a custom cursor to a scene. The cursor(String name) static method of the Cursor class returns a standard cursor if the specified name is the name of a standard cursor. Otherwise, it treats the specified name as a URL for the cursor bitmap. The following snippet of code creates a cursor from a bitmap file named mycur.png, which is assumed to be in the CLASSPATH:

```
// Create a Cursor from a bitmap
URL url = getClass().getClassLoader().getResource("mycur.png");
Cursor myCur = Cursor.cursor(url.toExternalForm());
scene.setCursor(myCur);

// Get the WAIT standard cursor using its name
Cursor waitCur = Cursor.cursor("WAIT")
scene.setCursor(waitCur);
```

The Focus Owner in a Scene

Only one node in a scene can be the focus owner. The focusOwner property of the Scene class tracks the Node class that has the focus. Note that the focusOwner property is read-only. If you want a specific node in a scene to be the focus owner, you need to call the requestFocus() method of the Node class.

You can use the getFocusOwner() method of the Scene class to get the reference of the node having the focus in the scene. A scene may not have a focus owner, and in that case, the getFocusOwner() method returns null. For example, a scene does not have a focus owner when it is created but is not attached to a window.

It is important to understand the distinction between a focus owner and a node having focus. Each scene may have a focus owner. For example, if you open two windows, you will have two scenes and you can have two focus owners. However, only one of the two focus owners can have the focus at a time. The focus owner of the active window will have the focus. To check if the focus owner node also has the focus, you need to use the focused property of the Node class. The following snippet of code shows the typical logic in using the focus owner:

```
Scene scene;
...
Node focusOwnerNode = scene.getFocusOwner();
if (focusOwnerNode == null) {
        // The scene does not have a focus owner
}
else if (focusOwnerNode.isFocused()) {
        // The focus owner is the one that has the focus
}
else {
        // The focus owner does not have the focus
}
```

Using Builder Classes

JavaFX provides two classes for creating and configuring objects that constitute the building blocks of a scene graph. One class is named after the type of object that the class represents; another with the former class name suffixed with the word "Builder." For example, Rectangle and RectangleBuilder classes exist to work with rectangles, Scene and SceneBuilder classes exist to work with scenes, and so on.

■ **Note** As of JavaFX 8, builder classes have been deprecated and they are not visible in the API documentation. This section is provided in case you need to maintain JavaFX code written in the older version such as version 2. Do not use the builder classes in JavaFX 8 or later. If you do not have to look at older version of JavaFX code, you can skip this section.

Builder classes provide three types of methods:

- They have a `create()` static method to create an instance of the builder class.

- They contain methods to set properties. Method names are the same as the property names that they set.

- They have a `build()` method that returns the object of the class for which the builder class exists. For example, the `build()` method of the `RectangleBuilder` class returns an object of the `Rectangle` class.

Builder classes are designed to use method chaining. Their methods to configure properties return the same builder instance. Assuming that p1 and p2 are properties of an object of XXX type, the following statement uses the builder class to create an object of the XXX type. It sets the properties p1 and p2 to v1 and v2, respectively:

```
XXX x = XXXBuilder.create()
        .p1(v1)
        .p2(v2)
        .build();
```

The following snippet of code creates a rectangle, using the `Rectangle` class, with (x, y) coordinates at (10, 20), with a width of 100px and a height of 200px. It also sets the fill property to red:

```
Rectangle r1 = new Rectangle(10, 20, 100, 200);
r1.setFill(Color.RED);
```

You can use the `RectangleBuilder` class to create the same rectangle:

```
Rectangle r1 = RectangleBuilder.create()
               .x(10)
               .y(20)
               .width(100)
               .height(200)
               .fill(Color.RED)
               .build();
```

Using builder classes requires longer code; however, it is more readable compared to using constructors to set the properties. Another advantage of builder classes is that they can be reused to build objects with slightly different properties. Suppose you want to create multiple rectangles with a 100px width and a 200px height, filled with the color red. However, they have different x and y coordinates. You can do so with the following code:

```
// Create a partially configured RectangleBuilder
RectangleBuilder builder = RectangleBuilder.create()
                           .width(100)
                           .height(200)
                           .fill(Color.RED);

// Create a Rectangles at (10, 20) and (120, 20) using the builder
Rectangle r3 = builder.x(10).y(20).build();
Rectangle r4 = builder.x(120).y(20).build();
```

The program in Listing 5-1 constructs a scene graph using builder classes. It adds a Label and a Button to a VBox. It also sets an action event handler for the button. The resulting screen is shown in Figure 5-5.

Listing 5-1. Using Builder Classes to Construct Scene Graphs

```java
// BuilderApp.java
package com.jdojo.scene;

import javafx.application.Application;
import javafx.application.Platform;
import javafx.scene.Scene;
import javafx.scene.SceneBuilder;
import javafx.scene.control.ButtonBuilder;
import javafx.scene.control.LabelBuilder;
import javafx.scene.layout.VBoxBuilder;
import javafx.stage.Stage;

public class BuilderApp extends Application {
        public static void main(String[] args) {
                Application.launch(args);
        }

        @Override
        public void start(Stage stage) {
                Scene scene = SceneBuilder.create()
                                .width(300)
                                .height(100)
                                .root(VBoxBuilder.create()
                                    .children(LabelBuilder.create()
                                                .text("Hello Builder")
                                                .build(),
                                                ButtonBuilder.create()
                                                .text("Exit")
                                                .onAction(e -> Platform.exit())
                                                .build()
                                            )
                                    .build()
                                )
                                .build();

                stage.setScene(scene);
                stage.setTitle("Using Builder Classes");
                stage.show();
        }
}
```

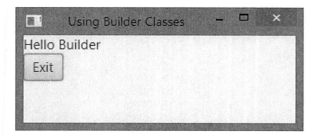

Figure 5-5. *A screen whose scene graph is created using builder classes*

If you used JavaFX script, which was removed from JavaFX version 2.0, you may be inclined to use builder classes for building scenes. If you have been using Swing/AWT, you may be comfortable using constructors and setters instead. The examples in this book do not use builder classes.

Table 5-2. *Methods of the Platform Class*

Method	Description
void exit()	It terminates a JavaFX application.
boolean isFxApplicationThread()	It returns true if the calling thread is the JavaFX Application Thread. Otherwise, it returns false.
boolean isImplicitExit()	It returns the value of the implicit implicitExit attribute of the application. If it returns true, it means that the application will terminate after the last window is closed. Otherwise, you need to call the exit() method of this class to terminate the application.
boolean isSupported(ConditionalFeature feature)	It returns true if the specified conditional feature is supported by the platform. Otherwise, it returns false.
void runLater(Runnable runnable)	It executes the specified Runnable on the JavaFX Application Thread. The timing of the execution is not specified. The method posts the Runnable to an event queue and returns immediately. If multiple Runnables are posted using this method, they are executed in the order they are submitted to the queue.
void setImplicitExit(boolean value)	It sets the implicitExit attribute to the specified value.

Understanding the *Platform* Class

The Platform class in the javafx.application package is a utility class used to support platform-related functionalities. It consists of all static methods, which are listed in Table 5-2.

The runLater() method is used to submit a Runnable task to an event queue, so it is executed on the JavaFX Application Thread. JavaFX allow developers to execute some of the code only on the JavaFX Application Thread. Listing 5-2 creates a task in the init() method that is called on the JavaFX Launcher Thread. It uses the Platform.runLater() method to submit the task to be executed on the JavaFX Application Thread later.

■ **Tip**   Use the `Platform.runLater()` method to execute a task that is created on a thread other than the JavaFX Application Thread but needs to run on the JavaFX Application Thread.

Listing 5-2. Using the `Platform.runLater()` Method

```
// RunLaterApp.java
package com.jdojo.scene;

import javafx.application.Application;
import javafx.application.Platform;
import javafx.scene.Group;
import javafx.scene.Scene;
import javafx.stage.Stage;

public class RunLaterApp extends Application {
        public static void main(String[] args) {
                Application.launch(args);
        }

        @Override
        public void init() {
                System.out.println("init(): " + Thread.currentThread().getName());

                // Create a Runnable task
                Runnable task = () -> System.out.println("Running the task on the "
                                + Thread.currentThread().getName());

                // Submit the task to be run on the JavaFX Aplication Thread
                Platform.runLater(task);
        }

        @Override
        public void start(Stage stage) throws Exception {
                stage.setScene(new Scene(new Group(), 400, 100));
                stage.setTitle("Using Platform.runLater() Method");
                stage.show();
        }
}
```

```
init(): JavaFX-Launcher
Running the task on the JavaFX Application Thread
```

Some features in a JavaFX implementation are optional (or conditional). They may not be available on all platforms. Using an optional feature on a platform that does not support the feature does not result in an error; the optional feature is simply ignored. Optional features are defined as enum constants in the `ConditionalFeature` enum in the `javafx.application` package, as listed in Table 5-3.

Table 5-3. *Constants Defined in the ConditionalFeature Enum*

Enum Constant	Description
EFFECT	Indicates the availability of filter effects, for example, reflection, shadow, etc.
INPUT_METHOD	Indicates the availability of text input method.
SCENE3D	Indicates the availability of 3D features.
SHAPE_CLIP	Indicates the availability of clipping of a node against an arbitrary shape.
TRANSPARENT_WINDOW	Indicates the availability of the full window transparency.

Suppose your JavaFX application uses 3D GUI on user demand. You can write your logic for enabling 3D features as shown in the following code:

```
import javafx.application.Platform;
import static javafx.application.ConditionalFeature.SCENE3D;
...
if (Platform.isSupported(SCENE3D)) {
        // Enable 3D features
}
else {
        // Notify the user that 3D features are not available
}
```

Knowing the Host Environment

The HostServices class in the javafx.application package provides services related to the launching environment (desktop, web browser, or WebStart) hosting the JavaFX application. You cannot create an instance of the HostServices class directly. The getHostServices() method of the Application class returns an instance of the HostServices class. The following is an example of how to get an instance of HostServices inside a class that inherits from the Application class:

```
HostServices host = getHostServices();
```

The HostServices class contains the following methods:

- String getCodeBase()
- String getDocumentBase()
- JSObject getWebContext()
- String resolveURI(String base, String relativeURI)
- void showDocument(String uri)

The getCodeBase() method returns the code base uniform resource identifier (URI) of the application. In a stand-alone mode, it returns the URI of the directory that contains the JAR file used to launch the application. If the application is launched using a class file, it returns an empty string. If the application is launched using a JNLP file, it returns the value for the specified code base parameter in the JNLP file.

The getDocumentBase() method returns the URI of the document base. In a web environment, it returns the URI of the web page that contains the application. If the application is launched using WebStart, it returns the code base parameter specified in the JNLP file. It returns the URI of the current directory for application launched in stand-alone mode.

The getWebContext() method returns a JSObject that allows a JavaFX application to interact with the JavaScript objects in a web browser. If the application is not running in a web page, it returns null. You can use the eval() method of the JSObject to evaluate a JavaScript expression from inside your JavaFX code. The following snippet of code displays an alert box using the window.alert() function. If the application runs in a nonweb environment, it shows a JavaFX modal stage instead:

```
HostServices host = getHostServices();
JSObject js = host.getWebContext();
if (js == null) {
        Stage s = new Stage(StageStyle.UTILITY);
        s.initModality(Modality.WINDOW_MODAL);
        s.setTitle("FX Alert");

        Scene scene = new Scene(new Group(new Label("This is an FX alert!")));
        s.setScene(scene);
        s.show();
}
else {
        js.eval("window.alert('This is a JavaScript alert!')");
}
```

The resolveURI() method resolves the specified relative URI with respect to the specified base URI and returns the resolved URI.

The showDocument() method opens the specified URI in a new browser window. Depending on the browser preference, it may open the URI in a new tab instead. This method can be used in a stand-alone mode as well as in a web environment. The following snippet of code opens the Yahoo! home page:

```
getHostServices().showDocument("http://www.yahoo.com");
```

The program in Listing 5-3 uses all of the methods of the HostServices class. It shows a stage with two buttons and host details. One button opens the Yahoo! home page and another shows an alert box. The output shown on the stage will vary depending on how the application is launched.

Listing 5-3. Knowing the Details of the Host Environment for a JavaFX Application

```
// KnowingHostDetailsApp.java
package com.jdojo.scene;

import java.util.HashMap;
import java.util.Map;
import javafx.application.Application;
import javafx.application.HostServices;
import javafx.scene.Group;
import javafx.scene.Scene;
import javafx.scene.control.Button;
import javafx.scene.control.Label;
import javafx.scene.layout.VBox;
import javafx.stage.Modality;
```

```java
import javafx.stage.Stage;
import javafx.stage.StageStyle;
import netscape.javascript.JSObject;

public class KnowingHostDetailsApp extends Application {
        public static void main(String[] args) {
                Application.launch(args);
        }

        @Override
        public void start(Stage stage) {
                String yahooURL = "http://www.yahoo.com";
                Button openURLButton = new Button("Go to Yahoo!");
                openURLButton.setOnAction(e -> getHostServices().showDocument(yahooURL));

                Button showAlert = new Button("Show Alert");
                showAlert.setOnAction(e -> showAlert());

                VBox root = new VBox();

                // Add buttons and all host related details to the VBox
                root.getChildren().addAll(openURLButton, showAlert);

                Map<String, String> hostdetails = getHostDetails();
                for(Map.Entry<String, String> entry : hostdetails.entrySet()) {
                        String desc = entry.getKey() + ": " + entry.getValue();
                        root.getChildren().add(new Label(desc));
                }

                Scene scene = new Scene(root);
                stage.setScene(scene);
                stage.setTitle("Knowing the Host");
                stage.show();
        }

        protected Map<String, String> getHostDetails() {
                Map<String, String> map = new HashMap<>();
                HostServices host = this.getHostServices();

                String codeBase = host.getCodeBase();
                map.put("CodeBase", codeBase);

                String documentBase = host.getDocumentBase();
                map.put("DocumentBase", documentBase);

                JSObject js = host.getWebContext();
                map.put("Environment", js == null?"Non-Web":"Web");

                String splashImageURI = host.resolveURI(documentBase, "splash.jpg");
                map.put("Splash Image URI", splashImageURI);

                return map;
        }
```

```
    protected void showAlert() {
            HostServices host = getHostServices();
            JSObject js = host.getWebContext();
            if (js == null) {
                    Stage s = new Stage(StageStyle.UTILITY);
                    s.initModality(Modality.WINDOW_MODAL);

                    Label msgLabel = new Label("This is an FX alert!");
                    Group root = new Group(msgLabel);
                    Scene scene = new Scene(root);
                    s.setScene(scene);

                    s.setTitle("FX Alert");
                    s.show();
            }
            else {
                    js.eval("window.alert('This is a JavaScript alert!')");
            }
    }
}
```

Summary

A scene represents the visual contents of a stage. The Scene class in the javafx.scene package represents a scene in a JavaFX program. A Scene object is attached to at the most one stage at a time. If an already-attached scene is attached to another stage, it is first detached from the previous stage. A stage can have at the most one scene attached to it at any time.

A scene contains a scene graph that consists of visual nodes. In this sense, a scene acts as a container for a scene graph. A scene graph is a tree data structure whose elements are known as nodes. Nodes in a scene graph form a parent-child hierarchical relationship. A node in a scene graph is an instance of the javafx.scene.Node class. A node can be a branch node or a leaf node. A branch node can have children nodes, whereas a leaf node cannot. The first node in a scene graph is called the root node. The root node can have children nodes; however, it never has a parent node.

An instance of the javafx.scene.Cursor class represents a mouse cursor. The Cursor class contains many constants, for example, HAND, CLOSED_HAND, DEFAULT, TEXT, NONE, WAIT, for standard mouse cursors. You can set a cursor for the scene using the setCursor() method of the Scene class.

Only one node in a scene can be the focus owner. The read-only focusOwner property of the Scene class tracks the node that has the focus. If you want a specific node in a scene to be the focus owner, you need to call the requestFocus() method of the Node class. Each scene may have a focus owner. For example, if you open two windows, you will have two scenes and you may have two focus owners. However, only one of the two focus owners can have the focus at a time. The focus owner of the active window will have the focus. To check if the focus owner node also has the focus, you need to use the focused property of the Node class.

The Platform class in the javafx.application package is a utility class used to support platform-related functionalities. It contains methods for terminating the application, checking if the code being executed is executed on the JavaFX Application Thread, and so on.

The HostServices class in the javafx.application package provides services related to the launching environment (desktop, web browser, or WebStart) hosting the JavaFX application. You cannot create an instance of the HostServices class directly. The getHostServices() method of the Application class returns an instance of the HostServices class.

The next chapter will discuss nodes in detail.

CHAPTER 6

■ ■ ■

Understanding Nodes

In this chapter, you will learn:

- What a node is in JavaFX
- About the Cartesian coordinate system
- About the bounds and bounding box of nodes
- How to set the size of a node and how to position a node
- How to store user data in a node
- What a managed node is
- How to transform node's bounds between coordinate spaces

What Is a Node?

Chapter 5 introduced you to scenes and scene graphs. A scene graph is a tree data structure. Every item in a scene graph is called a *node*. An instance of the javafx.scene.Node class represents a node in the scene graph. Note that the Node class is an abstract class, and several concrete classes exist to represent specific type of nodes.

A node can have subitems (also called children), and these node are called branch nodes. A branch node is an instance of the Parent, whose concrete subclasses are Group, Region, and WebView. A node that does cannot have subitems is called a *leaf node*. Instances of classes such as Rectangle, Text, ImageView, and MediaView are examples of leaf nodes. Only a single node within each scene graph tree will have no parent, which is referred to as the *root node*. A node may occur at the most once anywhere in the scene graph.

A node may be created and modified on any thread if it is not yet attached to a scene. Attaching a node to a scene and subsequent modification must occur on the JavaFX Application Thread.

A node has several types of bounds. Bounds are determined with respect to different coordinate systems. The next section will discuss the Cartesian coordinate system in general; the following section explains how Cartesian coordinate systems are used to compute the bounds of a node in JavaFX.

The Cartesian Coordinate System

If you have studied (and still remember) the Cartesian coordinate system from your coordinate geometry class in high school, you may skip this section.

The Cartesian coordinate system is a way to define each point on a 2D plane uniquely. Sometimes it is also known as a *rectangular coordinate system*. It consists of two perpendicular, directed lines known as the x axis and the y axis. The point where the two axes intersect is known as the *origin*.

A point in a 2D plane is defined using two values known as its x and y coordinates. The x and y coordinates of a point are its perpendicular distances from the y axis and x axis, respectively. Along an axis, the distance is measured as positive on one side from the origin and as negative on the other side. The origin has (x, y) coordinates, such as (0, 0). The axes divide the plane into four quadrants. Note that the 2D plane itself is infinite and so are the four quadrants. The set of all points in a Cartesian coordinate system defines the *coordinate space* of that system.

Figure 6-1 shows an illustration of the Cartesian coordinate system. It shows a point P having x and y coordinates of x1 and y1. It shows the type of values for the x and y coordinates in each quadrant. For example, the upper right quadrant shows (+, +), meaning that both x and y coordinates for all points in this quadrant will have positive values.

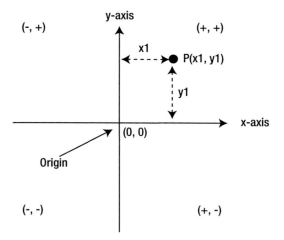

Figure 6-1. *A two-dimensional Cartesian coordinate system used in coordinate geometry*

A transformation is a mapping of points in a coordinate space to themselves, preserving distances and directions between them. Several types of transformations can be applied to points in a coordinate space. Some examples of transformation types are *translation, rotation, scaling,* and *shearing.*

In a translation transformation, a fixed pair of numbers is added to the coordinates of all points. Suppose you want to apply translation to a coordinate space by (a, b). If a point had coordinates (x, y) before translation, it will have the coordinate of (x + a, y + b) after translation.

In a rotation transformation, the axes are rotated around a pivot point in the coordinate space and the coordinates of points are mapped to the new axes. Figure 6-2 shows examples of translation and rotation transformations.

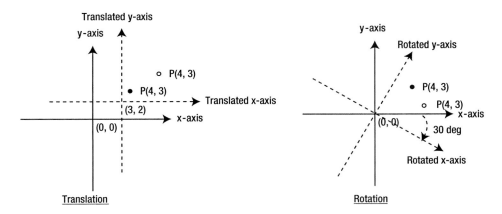

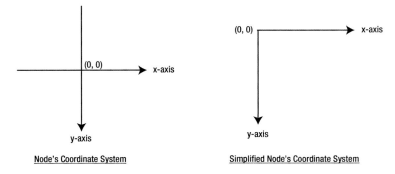

Figure 6-2. *Examples of translation and rotation transformations*

In Figure 6-2, axes before the transformations are shown in solid lines, and axes after the transformations are shown in dashed lines. Note that the coordinates of the point P at (4, 3) remains the same in the translated and rotated coordinate spaces. However, the coordinates of the point relative to the original coordinate space change after the transformation. The point in the original coordinate space is shown in a solid black fill color, and in the transformed coordinate space, it is shown without a fill color. In the rotation transformation, you have used the origin as the pivot point. Therefore, the origins for the original and the transformed coordinate space are the same.

Cartesian Coordinate System of a Node

Each node in a scene graph has its own coordinate system. A node uses a Cartesian coordinate system that consists of an x axis and a y axis. In computer systems, the values on the x axis increase to the right and the values on y axis increase downward, as shown in Figure 6-3. Typically, when showing the coordinate system of nodes, the negative sides of the x axis and y axis are not shown, even though they always exist. The simplified version of the coordinate system is shown on the right part of Figure 6-3. A node can have negative x and y coordinates.

Figure 6-3. *The coordinate system of nodes*

In a typical GUI application, nodes are placed within their parents. A root node is the ultimate parent of all nodes and it is placed inside a scene. The scene is placed inside a stage and the stage is placed inside a screen. Each element comprising a window, from nodes to the screen, has its own coordinate system, as shown in Figure 6-4.

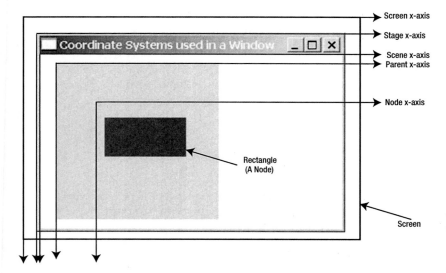

Figure 6-4. *Coordinate systems of all elements comprising a GUI window*

The outermost rectangular area with a thick black border is the screen. The rest is a JavaFX stage with a region and a rectangle. The region has a light-gray background color and a rectangle has a blue background color. The region is the parent of the rectangle. This simple window uses five coordinate spaces as indicated in Figure 6-4. I have labeled only the x axes. All y axes are vertical lines meeting the respective x axes at their origins.

What are the coordinates of the upper left corner of the rectangle? The question is incomplete. The coordinates of a point are defined relative to a coordinate system. As shown in Figure 6-4, you have five coordinate systems at play, and hence, five coordinate spaces. Therefore, you must specify the coordinate system in which you want to know the coordinates of the upper left corner of the rectangle. In a node's coordinate system, they are (10, 15); in a parent's coordinate system, they are (40, 45); in a scene's coordinate system, they are (60, 55); in a stage's coordinate system, they are (64, 83); in a screen's coordinate system, they are (80, 99).

The Concept of Bounds and Bounding Box

Every node has a geometric shape and it is positioned in a coordinate space. The size and the position of a node are collectively known as its *bounds*. The bounds of a node are defined in terms of a bounding rectangular box that encloses the entire geometry of the node. Figure 6-5 shows a triangle, a circle, a rounded rectangle, and a rectangle with a solid border. Rectangles around them, shown with a dashed border, are the bounding boxes for those shapes (nodes).

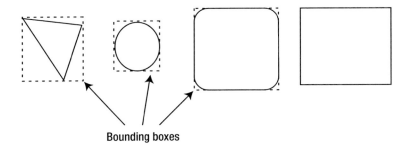

Bounding boxes

Figure 6-5. *The bounding rectangular box defining the geometric shape of nodes*

The area (area in a 2D space and volume in a 3D space) covered by the geometric shape of a node and its bounding box may be different. For example, for the first three nodes in Figure 6-5, counting from the left, the areas of the nodes and their bounding boxes are different. However, for the last rectangle, without rounded corners, its area and that of its bounding box are the same.

An instance of the `javafx.geometry.Bounds` class represents the bounds of a node. The Bounds class is an abstract class. The BoundingBox class is a concrete implementation of the Bounds class. The Bounds class is designed to handle bounds in a 3D space. It encapsulates the coordinates of the upper left corner with the minimum depth in the bounding box and the width, height, and depth of the bounding box. The methods `getMinX()`, `getMinY()`, and `getMinZ()` are used to get the coordinates. The three dimensions of the bounding box are accessed using the `getWidth()getHeight()`, and `getDepth()` methods. The Bounds class contains the `getMaxX()` `getMaxY()` and `getMaxZ()` methods that return the coordinates of the lower right corner, with the maximum depth, in the bounding box.

In a 2D space, the `minX` and `minY` define the x and y coordinates of the upper left corner of the bounding box, respectively, and the `maxX` and `maxY` define the x and y coordinates of the lower right corner, respectively. In a 2D space, the values of the z coordinate and the depth for a bounding box are zero. Figure 6-6 shows the details of a bounding box in a 2D coordinate space.

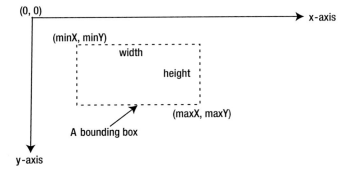

Figure 6-6. *The makings of a bounding box in a 2D space*

The Bounds class contains `isEmpty()`, `contains()`, and `intersects()` utility methods. The `isEmpty()` method returns true if any of the three dimensions (width, height, or depth) of a Bounds is negative. The `contains()` method lets you check if a Bounds contains another Bounds, a 2D point, or a 3D point. The `intersects()` method lets you check if the interior of a Bounds intersects the interior of another Bounds, a 2D point, or a 3D point.

Knowing the Bounds of a Node

So far, I have covered topics such as coordinate systems, bounds, and bounding boxes related to a node. That discussion was to prepare you for this section, which is about knowing the bounds of a node. You might have guessed (though incorrectly) that the Node class should have a getBounds() method to return the bounds of a node. It would be great if it were that simple! In this section, I will discuss the details of different types of bounds of a node. In the next section, I will walk you through some examples.

Figure 6-7 shows a button with the text "Close" in three forms.

Figure 6-7. *A button with and without an effect and a transformation*

The first one, starting from the left, has no effects or transformations. The second one has a drop shadow effect. The third one has a drop shadow effect and a rotation transformation. Figure 6-8 shows the bounding boxes representing the bounds of the button in those three forms. Ignoring the coordinates for now, you may notice that the bounds of the button change as effects and transformations are applied.

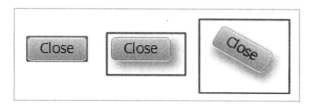

Figure 6-8. *A button with and with an effect and a transformation with bounding boxes*

A node in a scene graph has three types of bounds defined as three read-only properties in the Node class:

- layoutBounds
- boundsInLocal
- boundsInParent

When you are trying to understand the three types of the bounds of a node, you need to look for three points:

- How the (minX, minY) values are defined. They define the coordinates of the upper left corner of the bounding box described by the Bounds object.

- Remember that coordinates of a point are always defined relative to a coordinate space. Therefore, pay attention to the coordinate space in which the coordinates, as described in the first step, are defined.

- What properties of the node—geometry, stroke, effects, clip, and transformations—are included in a particular type of bounds.

Figure 6-9 shows the properties of a node contributing to the bounds of a node. They are applied from left to right in order. Some node types (e.g., Circle, Rectangle) may have a nonzero stroke. A nonzero stroke is considered part of the geometry of a node for computing its bounds.

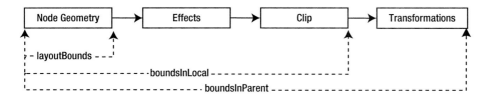

Figure 6-9. *Factors contributing to the size of a node*

Table 6-1 lists the properties that contribute to a particular type of the bounds of a node and the coordinate space in which the bounds are defined. The boundsInLocal and boundsInParent of a node are also known as its *physical bounds* as they correspond to the physical properties of the node. The layoutBounds of a node is known as the *logical bounds* as it is not necessarily tied to the physical bounds of the node. When the geometry of a node is changed, all bounds are recomputed.

Table 6-1. *Contributing Properties to the Bounds of a Node*

Bounds Type	Coordinate Space	Contributors
layoutBounds	Node (Untransformed)	Geometry of the node Nonzero stroke
boundsInLocal	Node (Untransformed)	Geometry of the node Nonzero stroke Effects Clip
boundsInParent	Parent	Geometry of the node Nonzero stroke Effects Clip Transformations

■ **Tip**   The boundsInLocal and BoundsInParent are known as physical or visual bounds as they correspond to how the node looks visually. The layoutBounds is also known as the *logical bounds* as it does not necessarily correspond to the physical bounds of the node.

The *layoutBounds* Property

The layoutBounds property is computed based on the geometric properties of the node in the *untransformed* local coordinate space of the node. Effects, clip, and transformations are not included. Different rules, depending on the resizable behavior of the node, are used to compute the coordinates of the upper left corner of the bounding box described by the layoutBounds:

- For a resizable node (a Region, a Control, and a WebView), the coordinates for the upper left corner of the bounding box are always set to (0, 0). For example, the (minX, minY) values in the layoutBounds property are always (0, 0) for a button.

- For a nonresizable node (a Shape, a Text, and a Group), the coordinates of the upper left corner of the bounding box are computed based on the geometric properties. For a shape (a rectangle, a circle, etc.) or a Text, you can specify the (x, y) coordinates of a specific point in the node relative to the untransformed coordinate space of the node. For example, for a rectangle, you can specify the (x, y) coordinates of the upper left corner, which become the (x, y) coordinates of the upper left corner of the bounding box described by its layoutBounds property. For a circle, you can specify the centerX, centerY, and radius properties, where centerX and centerY are the x and y coordinates of the center of the circle, respectively. The (x, y) coordinates of the upper left corner of the bounding box described by the layoutBounds for a circle are computed as (centerX - radius, centerY - radius).

The width and height in layoutBounds are the width and height of the node. Some nodes let you set their width and height; but some compute them automatically for you and let you override them.

Where do you use the layoutBounds property of a node? Containers allocate spaces to lay out child nodes based on their layoutBounds. Let's look at an example as shown in Listing 6-1. It displays four buttons in a VBox. The first button has a drop shadow effect. The third button has a drop shadow effect and a 30-degree rotation transformation. The second and the fourth buttons have no effect or transformation. The resulting screen is shown in Figure 6-10. The output shows that irrespective of the effect and transformation, all buttons have the same layoutBounds values. The size (width and height) in the layoutBounds objects for all buttons is determined by the text of the button and the font, which is the same for all buttons. The output may differ on your platform.

Listing 6-1. Accessing the layoutBounds of Buttons with and without Effects

```java
// LayoutBoundsTest.java
package com.jdojo.node;

import javafx.application.Application;
import javafx.scene.Scene;
import javafx.scene.control.Button;
import javafx.scene.effect.DropShadow;
import javafx.scene.layout.VBox;
import javafx.stage.Stage;

public class LayoutBoundsTest extends Application {
    public static void main(String[] args) {
        Application.launch(args);
    }
```

```
        @Override
        public void start(Stage stage) {
                Button b1 = new Button("Close");
                b1.setEffect(new DropShadow());

                Button b2 = new Button("Close");

                Button b3 = new Button("Close");
                b3.setEffect(new DropShadow());
                b3.setRotate(30);

                Button b4 = new Button("Close");

                VBox root = new VBox();
                root.getChildren().addAll(b1, b2, b3, b4);

                Scene scene = new Scene(root);
                stage.setScene(scene);
                stage.setTitle("Testing LayoutBounds");
                stage.show();

                System.out.println("b1=" + b1.getLayoutBounds());
                System.out.println("b2=" + b2.getLayoutBounds());
                System.out.println("b3=" + b3.getLayoutBounds());
                System.out.println("b4=" + b4.getLayoutBounds());
        }
}
```

```
b1=BoundingBox [minX:0.0, minY:0.0, minZ:0.0, width:57.0, height:23.0, depth:0.0,
maxX:57.0, maxY:23.0, maxZ:0.0]
b2=BoundingBox [minX:0.0, minY:0.0, minZ:0.0, width:57.0, height:23.0, depth:0.0,
maxX:57.0, maxY:23.0, maxZ:0.0]
b3=BoundingBox [minX:0.0, minY:0.0, minZ:0.0, width:57.0, height:23.0, depth:0.0,
maxX:57.0, maxY:23.0, maxZ:0.0]
b4=BoundingBox [minX:0.0, minY:0.0, minZ:0.0, width:57.0, height:23.0, depth:0.0,
maxX:57.0, maxY:23.0, maxZ:0.0]
```

Figure 6-10. *The layoutBounds property does not include the effects and transformations*

Sometimes you may want to include the space needed to show the effects and transformations of a node in its layoutBounds. The solution for this is easy. You need to wrap the node in a Group and the Group in a container. Now the container will query the Group for its layoutBounds. The layoutBounds of a Group is the union of the boundsInParent for all its children. Recall that (see Table 6-1) the boundsInParent of a node includes the space needed for showing effects and transformation of the node. If you change the statement

```
root.getChildren().addAll(b1, b2, b3, b4);
```

in Listing 6-1 to

```
root.getChildren().addAll(new Group(b1), b2, new Group(b3), b4);
```

the resulting screen is shown in Figure 6-11. This time, VBox allocated enough space for the first and the third groups to account for the effect and transformation applied to the wrapped buttons.

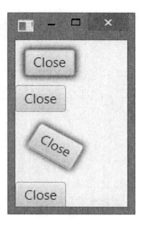

Figure 6-11. *Using a Group to allocate space for effects and transformations of a node*

■ **Tip**   The layoutBounds of a node is computed based on the geometric properties of a node. Therefore, you should not bind such properties of a node to an expression that includes the layoutBounds of the node.

The *boundsInLocal* Property

The boundsInLocal property is computed in the untransformed coordinate space of the node. It includes the geometric properties of the node, effects, and clip. Transformations applied to a node are not included.

Listing 6-2 prints the layoutBounds and boundsInLocal of a button. The boundsInLocal property includes the drop shadow effect around the button. Notice that the coordinates of the upper left corner of the bounding box defined by the layoutBounds are (0.0, 0.0) and they are (-9.0, -9.0) for the boundsInLocal. The output may be a bit different on different platforms as the size of nodes is computed automatically based on the platform running the program.

Listing 6-2. Accessing the boundsInLocal Property of a Node

```java
// BoundsInLocalTest.java
package com.jdojo.node;

import javafx.application.Application;
import javafx.scene.Scene;
import javafx.scene.control.Button;
import javafx.scene.effect.DropShadow;
import javafx.scene.layout.VBox;
import javafx.stage.Stage;

public class BoundsInLocalTest extends Application {
        public static void main(String[] args) {
                Application.launch(args);
        }

        @Override
        public void start(Stage stage) {
                Button b1 = new Button("Close");
                b1.setEffect(new DropShadow());

                VBox root = new VBox();
                root.getChildren().addAll(b1);

                Scene scene = new Scene(root);
                stage.setScene(scene);
                stage.setTitle("Testing LayoutBounds");
                stage.show();

                System.out.println("b1(layoutBounds)=" + b1.getLayoutBounds());
                System.out.println("b1(boundsInLocal)=" + b1.getBoundsInLocal());
        }
}
```

```
b1(layoutBounds)=BoundingBox [minX:0.0, minY:0.0, minZ:0.0, width:57.0, height:23.0,
depth:0.0, maxX:57.0, maxY:23.0, maxZ:0.0]
b1(boundsInLocal)=BoundingBox [minX:-9.0, minY:-9.0, minZ:0.0, width:75.0, height:42.0,
depth:0.0, maxX:66.0, maxY:33.0, maxZ:0.0]
```

When do you use the boundsInLocal of a node? You would use boundsInLocal when you need to include the effects and the clip of a node. Suppose you have a Text node with a reflection and you want to center it vertically. If you use the layoutBounds of the Text node, it will only center the text portion of the node and would not include the reflection. If you use the boundsInLocal, it will center the text with its reflection. Another example would be checking for collisions of balls that have effects. If a collision between two balls occurs when one ball moves inside the bounds of another ball that include their effects, use the boundsInLocal for the balls. If a collision occurs only when they intersect their geometric boundaries, use the layoutBounds.

The *boundsInParent* Property

The boundsInParent property of a node is in the coordinate space of its parent. It includes the geometric properties of the node, effects, clip, and transformations. It is rarely used directly in code.

Bounds of a Group

The computation of layoutBounds, boundsInLocal, and boundsInParent for a Group is different from that of a node. A Group takes on the collection bounds of its children. You can apply effects, clip, and transformations separately on each child of a Group. You can also apply effects, clip, and transformations directly on a Group and they are applied to all of its children nodes.

The layoutBounds of a Group is the union of the boundsInParent of all its children. It includes effects, clip, and transformations applied directly to the children. It does not include effects, clip, and transformations applied directly to the Group. The boundsInLocal of a Group is computed by taking its layoutBounds and including the effects and clip applied directly to the Group. The boundsInParent of a Group is computed by taking its boundsInLocal and including the transformations applied directly to the Group.

When you want to allocate space for a node that should include effects, clip, and transformations, you need to try wrapping the node in a Group. Suppose you have a node with effects and transformations and you only want to allocate layout space for its effects, not its transformations. You can achieve this by applying the effects on the node and wrapping it in a Group, and then applying the transformations on the Group.

A Detailed Example on Bounds

In this section, I will walk you through an example to show how the bounds of a node are computed. You will use a rectangle and its different properties, effects, and transformations in this example.

Consider the following snippet of code that creates a 50 by 20 rectangle and places it at (0, 0) in the local coordinate space of the rectangle. The resulting rectangle is shown in Figure 6-12, which shows the axes of the parent and the untransformed local axes of the node (the rectangle in this case), which are the same at this time:

```
Rectangle r = new Rectangle(0, 0, 50, 20);
r.setFill(Color.GRAY);
```

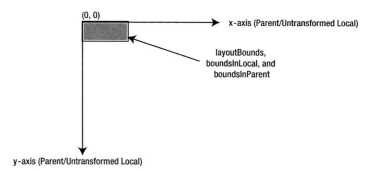

Figure 6-12. *A 50 by 20 rectangle placed at (0, 0) with no effects and transformations*

Three types of bounds of the rectangle are the same, as follows:

```
layoutBounds[minX=0.0, minY=0.0, width=50.0, height=20.0]
boundsInLocal[minX=0.0, minY=0.0, width=50.0, height=20.0]
boundsInParent[minX=0.0, minY=0.0, width=50.0, height=20.0]
```

Let's modify the rectangle to place it at (75, 50) as follows:

```
Rectangle r = new Rectangle(75, 50, 50, 20);
```

The resulting node is shown in Figure 6-13.

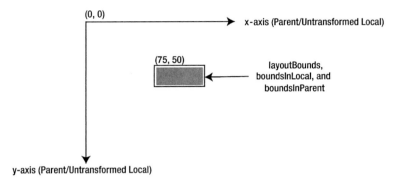

Figure 6-13. *A 50 by 20 rectangle placed at (75, 50) with no effects and transformations*

The axes for the parent and the node are still the same. All bounds are the same, as follows: The upper left corner of all bounding boxes have moved to (75, 50) with the same width and height:

```
layoutBounds[minX=75.0, minY=50.0, width=50.0, height=20.0]
boundsInLocal[minX=75.0, minY=50.0, width=50.0, height=20.0]
boundsInParent[minX=75.0, minY=50.0, width=50.0, height=20.0]
```

Let's modify the rectangle and give it a drop shadow effect, as follows:

```
Rectangle r = new Rectangle(75, 50, 50, 20);
r.setEffect(new DropShadow());
```

The resulting node is shown in Figure 6-14.

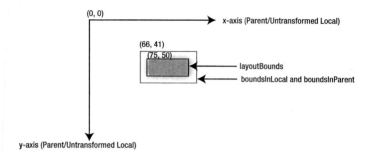

Figure 6-14. *A 50 by 20 rectangle placed at (75, 50) with a drop shadow and no transformations*

The axes for the parent and the node are still the same. Now, the layoutBounds did not change. To accommodate the drop shadow effect, the boundsInLocal and boundsInParent have changed and they have the same values. Recall that the boundsInLocal is defined in the untransformed coordinate space of the node and the boundsInParent in the coordinate space of the parent. In this case, both coordinate spaces are the same. Therefore, the same values for the two bounds define the same bounding box. The values for the bounds are as follows:

```
layoutBounds[minX=75.0, minY=50.0, width=50.0, height=20.0]
boundsInLocal[minX=66.0, minY=41.0, width=68.0, height=38.0]
boundsInParent[minX=66.0, minY=41.0, width=68.0, height=38.0]
```

Let's modify the previous rectangle to have a (x, y) translation of (150, 75) as follows:

```
Rectangle r = new Rectangle(75, 50, 50, 20);
r.setEffect(new DropShadow());
r.getTransforms().add(new Translate(150, 75));
```

The resulting node is shown in Figure 6-15. A transformation (a translation, in this case) transforms the coordinate space of the node, and as a result, you see the node being transformed. In this case, you have three coordinate spaces to consider: the coordinate space of the parent, and the untransformed and transformed coordinate spaces of the node. The layoutBounds and boundsInParent are relative to the untransformed local coordinate space of the node. The boundsInParent is relative to the coordinate space of the parent. Figure 6-15 shows all coordinate spaces at play. The values for the bounds are as follows:

```
layoutBounds[minX=75.0, minY=50.0, width=50.0, height=20.0]
boundsInLocal[minX=66.0, minY=41.0, width=68.0, height=38.0]
boundsInParent[minX=216.0, minY=116.0, width=68.0, height=38.0]
```

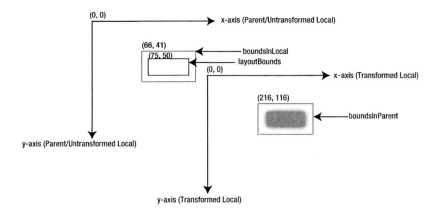

Figure 6-15. *A 50 by 20 rectangle placed at (75, 50) with a drop shadow and a (150, 75) translation*

Let's modify the rectangle to have a (x, y) translation of (150, 75) and a 30-degree clockwise rotation:

```
Rectangle r = new Rectangle(75, 50, 50, 20);
r.setEffect(new DropShadow());
r.getTransforms().addAll(new Translate(150, 75), new Rotate(30));
```

The resulting node is shown in Figure 6-16. Notice that the translation and rotation have been applied to the local coordinate space of the rectangle and the rectangle appears in the same position relative to its transformed local coordinate axes. The layoutBounds and boundsInLocal remained the same because you did not change the geometry of the rectangle and the effects. The boundsInParent has changed because you added a rotation. The values for the bounds are as follows:

```
layoutBounds[minX=75.0, minY=50.0, width=50.0, height=20.0]
boundsInLocal[minX=66.0, minY=41.0, width=68.0, height=38.0]
boundsInParent[minX=167.66, minY=143.51, width=77.89, height=66.91]
```

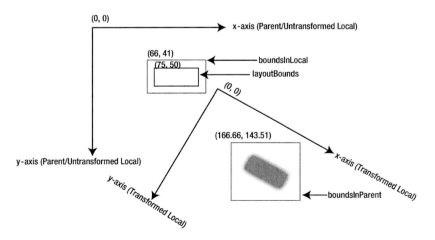

Figure 6-16. *A 50 by 20 rectangle placed at (75, 50) with a drop shadow, a (150, 75) translation, and a 30-degree clockwise rotation*

As the last example, you will add scale and shear transformations to the rectangle:

```
Rectangle r = new Rectangle(75, 50, 50, 20);
r.setEffect(new DropShadow());
r.getTransforms().addAll(new Translate(150, 75), new Rotate(30),
                    new Scale(1.2, 1.2), new Shear(0.30, 0.10));
```

The resulting node is shown in Figure 6-17.

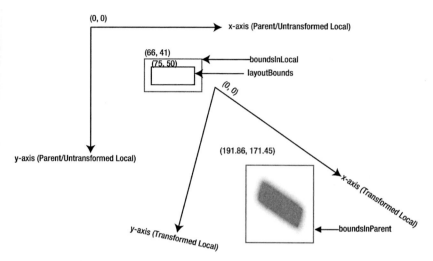

Figure 6-17. *A 50 by 20 rectangle placed at (75, 50) with a drop shadow, a (150, 75) translation, a 30-degree clockwise rotation, a 1.2 in x and y scales, and a 0.30 x shear and 0.10 y shear*

Notice that only boundsInParent has changed. The values for the bounds are as follows:

```
layoutBounds[minX=75.0, minY=50.0, width=50.0, height=20.0]
boundsInLocal[minX=66.0, minY=41.0, width=68.0, height=38.0]
boundsInParent[minX=191.86, minY=171.45, width=77.54, height=94.20]
```

For a beginner, it is not easy to grasp the concepts behind different types of bounds of a node. A beginner is one who is learning something for the first time. I started out as a beginner while learning about bounds. During the learning process, another beautiful concept and hence its implementation in a JavaFX program came about. The program, which is a very detailed demo application, helps you understand visually how bounds are affected by changing the state of a node. You can save the scene graph with all coordinate axes. You can run the NodeBoundsApp class as shown in Listing 6-3 to see all the examples in this section in action.

Listing 6-3. Computing the Bounds of a Node

```
// NodeBoundsApp.java
package com.jdojo.node;
...
public class NodeBoundsApp extends Application {
        // The code for this class is not included here as it is very big.
        // Please refer to the source code. You can download the source code
        // for all programs in this book from http://www.apress.com/source-code
}
```

Positioning a Node Using *layoutX* and *layoutY*

If you do not understand the details and the reasons behind the existence of all layout-related properties, laying out nodes in JavaFX is as confusing as it can get. The Node class has two properties, layoutX and layoutY, to define translation of its coordinate space along the x axis and y axis, respectively. The Node class has translateX and translateY properties that do the same thing. The final translation of the coordinate space of a node is the sum of the two:

```
finalTranslationX = layoutX + translateX
finalTranslationY = layoutY + translateY
```

Why do you have two properties to define translations of the same kind? The reason is simple. They exist to achieve the similar results in different situations. Use layoutX and layoutY to position a node for a stable layout. Use translateX and translateY to position a node for a dynamic layout, for example, during animation.

It is important to keep in mind that the layoutX and layoutY properties do not specify the final position of a node. They are translations applied to the *coordinate space* of the node. You need to factor the minX and minY values of the layoutBounds when you compute the value of layoutX and layoutY to position a node at a particular position. To position the upper left corner of the bounding box of a node at finalX and finalY, use the following formula:

```
layoutX = finalX - node.getLayoutBounds().getMinX()
layoutY = finalY - node.getLayoutBounds().getMinY()
```

■ **Tip** The Node class has a convenience method, relocate(double finalX, double finalY), to position the node at the (finalX, finalY) location. The method computes and sets the layoutX and layoutY values correctly, taking into account the minX and minY values of the layoutBounds. To avoid errors and misplacement of nodes, I prefer using the relocate() method over the setLayoutX() and setLayoutY() methods.

Sometimes setting the layoutX and layoutY properties of a node may not position them at the desired location inside its parent. If you are caught in this situation, check the parent type. Most parents, which are the subclasses of the Region class, use their own positioning policy, ignoring the layoutX and layoutY settings of their children. For example, HBox and VBox use their own positioning policy and they will ignore the layoutX and layoutY values for their children.

The following snippet of code will ignore the layoutX and layoutY values for two buttons, as they are placed inside a VBox that uses its own positioning policy. The resulting layout is shown in Figure 6-18.

```
Button b1 = new Button("OK");
b1.setLayoutX(20);
b1.setLayoutY(20);

Button b2 = new Button("Cancel");
b2.setLayoutX(50);
b2.setLayoutY(50);

VBox vb = new VBox();
vb.getChildren().addAll(b1, b2);
```

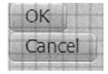

Figure 6-18. *Two buttons using layoutX and layoutY properties and placed inside a VBox*

If you want to have full control on positioning a node within its parent, use a Pane or a Group. A Pane is a Region, which does not position its children. You will need to position the children using the layoutX and layoutY properties. The following snippet of code will lay out two buttons as shown in Figure 6-19, which shows the coordinate grid in which lines are placed 10px apart.

```
Button b1 = new Button("OK");
b1.setLayoutX(20);
b1.setLayoutY(20);

Button b2 = new Button("Cancel");
b2.setLayoutX(50);
b2.setLayoutY(50);

Group parent = new Group(); //Or. Pane parent = new Pane();
parent.getChildren().addAll(b1, b2);
```

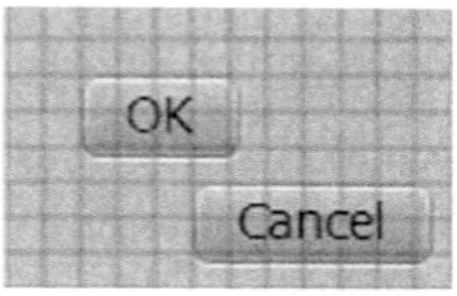

Figure 6-19. *Two buttons using layoutX and layoutY properties and placed inside a Group or a Pane*

Setting the Size of a Node

Every node has a size (width and height), which may be changed. That is, every node can be resized. There are two types of nodes: *resizable* nodes and *nonresizable* nodes. Aren't the previous two sentences contradictory? The answer is yes and no. It is true that every node has the potential to be resized. However, by a resizable node, it is meant that a node can be resized by its parent during layout. For example, a button is a resizable node and a rectangle is a nonresizable node. When a button is placed in a container, for example, in an HBox, the HBox determines the best size for the button. The HBox resizes the button depending on how much space is needed for the button to display and how much space is available to the HBox. When a rectangle is placed in an HBox, the HBox does not determine its size; rather, it uses the size of the rectangle specified by the application.

■ **Tip** A resizable node can be resized by its parent during a layout. A nonresizable node is not resized by its parent during a layout. If you want to resize a nonresizable node, you need to modify its properties that affect its size. For example, to resize a rectangle, you need to change its width and height properties. Regions, Controls, and WebView are examples of resizable nodes. Group, Text, and Shapes are examples of nonresizable nodes.

How do you know if a node is resizable? The `isResizable()` method in the Node class returns `true` for a resizable node; it returns `false` for a nonresizable node.

The program in Listing 6-4 shows the behavior of resizable and nonresizable nodes during a layout. It adds a button and a rectangle to an HBox. After you run the program, make the stage shorter in width. The button becomes smaller up to a point when it displays an ellipsis (...). The rectangle remains the same size all the time. Figure 6-20 shows the stage at three different points during resizing.

Listing 6-4. A Button and a Rectangle in an HBox

```java
// ResizableNodeTest.java
package com.jdojo.node;

import javafx.application.Application;
import javafx.scene.Scene;
import javafx.scene.control.Button;
import javafx.scene.layout.HBox;
import javafx.scene.paint.Color;
import javafx.scene.shape.Rectangle;
import javafx.stage.Stage;

public class ResizableNodeTest extends Application {
        public static void main(String[] args) {
                Application.launch(args);
        }

        @Override
        public void start(Stage stage) {
                Button btn = new Button("A big button");
                Rectangle rect = new Rectangle(100, 50);
                rect.setFill(Color.WHITE);
                rect.setStrokeWidth(1);
                rect.setStroke(Color.BLACK);

                HBox root = new HBox();
                root.setSpacing(20);
                root.getChildren().addAll(btn, rect);

                Scene scene = new Scene(root);
                stage.setScene(scene);
                stage.setTitle("Resizable Nodes");
                stage.show();

                System.out.println("btn.isResizable(): " + btn.isResizable());
                System.out.println("rect.isResizable(): " + rect.isResizable());
        }
}
```

```
btn.isResizable(): true
rect.isResizable(): false
```

Figure 6-20. *A button and a rectangle shown in full size and after resizing the stage*

Resizable Nodes

The actual size of a resizable node is determined by two things:

- The sizing policy of the container in which the node is placed
- The sizing range specified by the node itself

Each container has a resizing policy for its children. I will discuss the resizing policy of containers in Chapter 10. A resizable node may specify a range for its size (width and height), which should be taken into account by an *honoring* container for laying out the node. A resizable node specifies three types of sizes that constitute the range of its size:

- Preferred size
- Minimum size
- Maximum size

The *preferred size* of a node is its ideal width and height to display its contents. For example, a button in its preferred size would be big enough to display all its contents, based on the current properties such as the image, text, font, and text wrapping. The *minimum size* of a node is the smallest width and height that it would like to have. For example, a button in its minimum size would be big enough to display the image and an ellipsis for its text. The *maximum size* of a node is the largest width and height that it would like to have. In the case of a button, the maximum size of a button is the same as its preferred size. Sometimes you may want to extend a node to an unlimited size. In those cases, the maximum width and height are set to `Double.MAX_VALUE`.

Most of the resizable nodes compute their preferred, minimum, and maximum sizes automatically, based on their contents and property settings. These sizes are known as their *intrinsic sizes*. The `Region` and `Control` classes define two constants that act as sentinel values for the intrinsic sizes of nodes. Those constants are:

- `USE_COMPUTED_SIZE`
- `USE_PREF_SIZE`

Both constants are of `double` type. The values for `USE_COMPUTED_SIZE` and `USE_PREF_SIZE` are -1 and `Double.NEGATIVE_INFINITY`, respectively. It was not documented as to why the same constants were defined twice. Maybe the designers did not want to move them up in the class hierarchy, as they do not apply to all types of nodes.

If the size of a node is set to the sentinel value `USE_COMPUTED_SIZE`, the node will compute that size automatically based on its contents and properties settings. The `USE_PREF_SIZE` sentinel value is used to set the minimum and maximum sizes if they are the same as the preferred size.

The Region and Control classes have six properties of the DoubleProperty type to define preferred, minimum, and maximum values for their width and height:

- prefWidth
- prefHeight
- minWidth
- minHeight
- maxWidth
- maxHeight

By default, these properties are set to the sentinel value USE_COMPUTED_SIZE. That means, nodes compute these sizes automatically. You can set one of these properties to override the intrinsic size of a node. For example, you can set the preferred, minimum, and maximum width of a button to be 50 pixels as follows:

```
Button btn = new Button("Close");
btn.setPrefWidth(50);
btn.setMinWidth(50);
btn.setMaxWidth(50);
```

The above snippet of code sets preferred, minimum, and maximum widths of the button to the same value that makes the button horizontally nonresizable.

The following snippet of code sets the minimum and maximum widths of a button to the preferred width, where the preferred width itself is computed internally:

```
Button btn = new Button("Close");
btn.setMinWidth(Control.USE_PREF_SIZE);
btn.setMaxWidth(Control.USE_PREF_SIZE);
```

■ **Tip**   In most cases, the internally computed values for preferred, minimum, and maximum sizes of nodes are fine. Use these properties to override the internally computed sizes only if they do not meet the needs of your application. If you need to bind the size of a node to an expression, you would need to bind the prefWidth and prefHeight properties.

How do you get the actual preferred, minimum, and maximum sizes of a node? You might guess that you can get them using the getPrefWidth(), getPrefHeight(), getMinWidth(), getMinHeight(), getMaxWidth(), and getMaxHeight() methods. But you should not use these methods to get the actual sizes of a node. These sizes may be set to the sentinel values and the node will compute the actual sizes internally. These methods return the sentinel values or the override values. Listing 6-5 creates two buttons and overrides the preferred intrinsic width for one of them to 100 pixels. The resulting screen is shown in Figure 6-21. The output below proves that these methods are not very useful to learn the actual sizes of a node for layout purposes.

Listing 6-5. Using getXXXWidth() and getXXXHeight() Methods of Regions and Controls

```java
// NodeSizeSentinelValues.java
package com.jdojo.node;

import javafx.application.Application;
import javafx.scene.Scene;
import javafx.scene.control.Button;
import javafx.scene.layout.VBox;
import javafx.stage.Stage;

public class NodeSizeSentinelValues extends Application {
        public static void main(String[] args) {
                Application.launch(args);
        }

        @Override
        public void start(Stage stage) {
                Button okBtn = new Button("OK");
                Button cancelBtn = new Button("Cancel");

                // Override the intrinsic width of the cancel button
                cancelBtn.setPrefWidth(100);

                VBox root = new VBox();
                root.getChildren().addAll(okBtn, cancelBtn);

                Scene scene = new Scene(root);
                stage.setScene(scene);
                stage.setTitle("Overriding Node Sizes");
                stage.show();

                System.out.println("okBtn.getPrefWidth(): " + okBtn.getPrefWidth());
                System.out.println("okBtn.getMinWidth(): " + okBtn.getMinWidth());
                System.out.println("okBtn.getMaxWidth(): " + okBtn.getMaxWidth());

                System.out.println("cancelBtn.getPrefWidth(): " + cancelBtn.getPrefWidth());
                System.out.println("cancelBtn.getMinWidth(): " + cancelBtn.getMinWidth());
                System.out.println("cancelBtn.getMaxWidth(): " + cancelBtn.getMaxWidth());
        }
}
```

```
okBtn.getPrefWidth(): -1.0
okBtn.getMinWidth(): -1.0
okBtn.getMaxWidth(): -1.0
cancelBtn.getPrefWidth(): 100.0
cancelBtn.getMinWidth(): -1.0
cancelBtn.getMaxWidth(): -1.0
```

Figure 6-21. *Buttons using sentinel and override values for their widths*

To get the actual sizes of a node, you need to use the following methods in the Node class. Note that the Node class does not define any properties related to sizes. The size-related properties are defined in the Region, Control, and other classes.

- `double prefWidth(double height)`
- `double prefHeight(double width)`
- `double minWidth(double height)`
- `double minHeight(double width)`
- `double maxWidth(double height)`
- `double maxHeight(double width)`

Here you can see another twist in getting the actual sizes of a node. You need to pass the value of its height to get its width and vice versa. For most nodes in JavaFX, width and height are independent. However, for some nodes, the height depends on the width and vice versa. When the width of a node depends on its height or vice versa, the node is said to have a *content bias*. If the height of a node depends on its width, the node has a *horizontal content bias*. If the width of a node depends on its height, the node has a *vertical content bias*. Note that a node cannot have both horizontal and vertical content biases, which will lead to a circular dependency.

The getContentBias() method of the Node class returns the content bias of a node. Its return type is the javafx.geometry.Orientation enum type, which has two constants: HORIZONTAL and VERTICAL. If a node does not have a content bias, for example, Text or ChoiceBox, the method returns null.

All controls that are subclasses of the Labeled class, for example, Label, Button, or CheckBox, have a HORIZONTAL content bias when they have the text wrapping property enabled. For some nodes, their content bias depends on their orientation. For example, if the orientation of a FlowPane is HORIZONTAL, its content bias is HORIZONTAL; if its orientation is VERTICAL, its content bias is VERTICAL.

You are supposed to use the above-listed six methods to get the sizes of a node for layout purposes. If a node type does not have a content bias, you need to pass -1 to these methods as the value for the other dimension. For example, a ChoiceBox does not have a content bias, and you would get its preferred size as follows:

```
ChoiceBox choices = new ChoiceBox();
...
double prefWidth = choices.prefWidth(-1);
double prefHeight = choices.prefHeight(-1);
```

For those nodes that have a content bias, you need to pass the biased dimension to get the other dimension. For example, for a button, which has a HORIZONTAL content bias, you would pass -1 to get its width, and you would pass its width value to get its height as follows:

```
Button b = new Button("Hello JavaFX");

// Enable text wrapping for the button, which will change its
// content bias from null (default) to HORIZONTAL
b.setWrapText(true);
...
double prefWidth = b.prefWidth(-1);
double prefHeight = b.prefHeight(prefWidth);
```

If a button does not have the text wrap property enabled, you can pass -1 to both methods prefWidth() and prefHeight(), as it would not have a content bias.

The generic way to get the width and height of a node for layout purposes is outlined as follows. The code shows how to get the preferred width and height, and the code would be similar to get minimum and maximum width and height of a node:

```
Node node = get the reference of of the node;
...
double prefWidth = -1;
double prefHeight = -1;

Orientation contentBias = b.getContentBias();

if (contentBias == HORIZONTAL) {
        prefWidth = node.prefWidth(-1);
        prefHeight = node.prefHeight(prefWidth);
} else if (contentBias == VERTICAL) {
        prefHeight = node.prefHeight(-1);
        prefWidth = node.prefWidth(prefHeight);
} else {
        // contentBias is null
        prefWidth = node.prefWidth(-1);
        prefHeight = node.prefHeight(-1);
}
```

Now you know how to get the specified values and the actual values for the preferred, minimum, and maximum sizes of a node. These values indicate the range for the size of a node. When a node is laid out inside a container, the container tries to give the node its preferred size. However, based on the container's policy and the specified size of the node, the node may not get its preferred size. Instead, an honoring container will give a node a size that is within its specified range. This is called the *current size*. How do you get the current size of a node? The Region and Control classes define two *read-only* properties, width and height, that hold the values for the current width and height of a node.

Now let's see all these methods in action. Listing 6-6 places a button in an HBox, prints different types of sizes for the button, changes some properties, and prints the sizes of the button again. The output below shows that as the preferred width of the button becomes smaller, its preferred height becomes bigger.

Listing 6-6. Using Different Size-Related Methods of a Node

```java
// NodeSizes.java
package com.jdojo.node;

import javafx.application.Application;
import javafx.scene.Scene;
import javafx.scene.control.Button;
import javafx.scene.layout.HBox;
import javafx.stage.Stage;

public class NodeSizes extends Application {
        public static void main(String[] args) {
                Application.launch(args);
        }

        @Override
        public void start(Stage stage) {
                Button btn = new Button("Hello JavaFX!");

                HBox root = new HBox();
                root.getChildren().addAll(btn);

                Scene scene = new Scene(root);
                stage.setScene(scene);
                stage.setTitle("Sizes of a Node");
                stage.show();

                // Print button's sizes
                System.out.println("Before changing button properties:");
                printSizes(btn);

                // Change button's properties
                btn.setWrapText(true);
                btn.setPrefWidth(80);
                stage.sizeToScene();

                // Print button's sizes
                System.out.println("\nAfter changing button properties:");
                printSizes(btn);

        }

        public void printSizes(Button btn) {
                System.out.println("btn.getContentBias() = " + btn.getContentBias());

                System.out.println("btn.getPrefWidth() = " + btn.getPrefWidth() +
                                ", btn.getPrefHeight() = " + btn.getPrefHeight());

                System.out.println("btn.getMinWidth() = " + btn.getMinWidth() +
                                ", btn.getMinHeight() = " + btn.getMinHeight());
```

```
            System.out.println("btn.getMaxWidth() = " + btn.getMaxWidth() +
                          ", btn.getMaxHeight() = " + btn.getMaxHeight());

            double prefWidth = btn.prefWidth(-1);
            System.out.println("btn.prefWidth(-1) = " + prefWidth +
                    ", btn.prefHeight(prefWidth) = " + btn.prefHeight(prefWidth));

            double minWidth = btn.minWidth(-1);
            System.out.println("btn.minWidth(-1) = " + minWidth +
                    ", btn.minHeight(minWidth) = " + btn.minHeight(minWidth));

            double maxWidth = btn.maxWidth(-1);
            System.out.println("btn.maxWidth(-1) = " + maxWidth +
                    ", btn.maxHeight(maxWidth) = " + btn.maxHeight(maxWidth));

            System.out.println("btn.getWidth() = " + btn.getWidth() +
                          ", btn.getHeight() = " + btn.getHeight());
        }
    }
```

```
Before changing button properties:
btn.getContentBias() = null
btn.getPrefWidth() = -1.0, btn.getPrefHeight() = -1.0
btn.getMinWidth() = -1.0, btn.getMinHeight() = -1.0
btn.getMaxWidth() = -1.0, btn.getMaxHeight() = -1.0
btn.prefWidth(-1) = 107.0, btn.prefHeight(prefWidth) = 22.8984375
btn.minWidth(-1) = 37.0, btn.minHeight(minWidth) = 22.8984375
btn.maxWidth(-1) = 107.0, btn.maxHeight(maxWidth) = 22.8984375
btn.getWidth() = 107.0, btn.getHeight() = 23.0

After changing button properties:
btn.getContentBias() = HORIZONTAL
btn.getPrefWidth() = 80.0, btn.getPrefHeight() = -1.0
btn.getMinWidth() = -1.0, btn.getMinHeight() = -1.0
btn.getMaxWidth() = -1.0, btn.getMaxHeight() = -1.0
btn.prefWidth(-1) = 80.0, btn.prefHeight(prefWidth) = 39.796875
btn.minWidth(-1) = 37.0, btn.minHeight(minWidth) = 22.8984375
btn.maxWidth(-1) = 80.0, btn.maxHeight(maxWidth) = 39.796875
btn.getWidth() = 80.0, btn.getHeight() = 40.0
```

The list of methods to get or set sizes of resizable nodes is not over. There are some convenience methods that can be used to perform the same task as the methods discussed in this section. Table 6-2 lists the size-related methods with their defining classes and usage.

Table 6-2. *Size-Related Methods of Resizable Nodes*

Methods/Properties	Defining Class	Usage
Properties: prefWidth prefHeight minWidth minHeight maxWidth maxHeight	Region, Control	They define the preferred, minimum, and maximum sizes. They are set to sentinel values by default. Use them to override the default values.
Methods: double prefWidth(double h) double prefHeight(double w) double minWidth(double h) double minHeight(double w) double maxWidth(double h) double maxHeight(double w)	Node	Use them to get the actual sizes of nodes. Pass -1 as the argument if the node does not have a content bias. Pass the actual value of the other dimension as the argument if the node has a content bias. Note that there are no corresponding properties to these methods.
Properties: width height	Region, Control	These are *read-only* properties that hold the current width and height of resizable nodes.
Methods: void setPrefSize(double w, double h) void setMinSize(double w, double h) void setMaxSize(double w, double h)	Region, Control	These are convenience methods to override the default computed width and height of nodes.
Methods: void resize(double w, double h)	Node	It resizes a node to the specified width and height. It is called by the parent of the node during a layout. You should not call this method directly in your code. If you need to set the size of a node, use the setMinSize(), setPrefSize(), or setMaxSize() methods instead. This method has no effect on a nonresizable node.
Methods: void autosize()	Node	For a resizable node, it sets the layout bounds to its current preferred width and height. It takes care of the content bias. This method has no effect on a nonresizable node.

Nonresizable Nodes

Nonresizable nodes are not resized by their parents during layout. However, you can change their sizes by changing their properties. Nonresizable nodes (e.g., all shapes) have different properties that determine their sizes. For example, the width and height of a rectangle, the radius of a circle, and the (startX, startY) and (endX, endY) of a line determine their sizes.

There are several size-related methods defined in the Node class. Those methods have no effect when they are called on nonresizable nodes or they return their current size. For example, calling the resize(double w, double h) method of the Node class on a nonresizable node has no effect. For a nonresizable node, the prefWidth(double h), minWidth(double h), and maxWidth(double h) methods in the Node class return its layoutBounds width; whereas prefHeight(double w), minHeight(double w), and maxHeight(double w) methods return its layoutBounds height. Nonresizable nodes do not have content bias. Pass -1 to all these methods as the argument for the other dimension.

Storing User Data in a Node

Every node maintains an observable map of user-defined properties (key/value pairs). You can use it to store any useful information. Suppose you have a TextField that lets the user manipulate a person's name. You can store the originally retrieved person's name from the database as the property of the TextField. You can use the property later to reset the name or to generate an UPDATE statement to update the name in the database. Another use of the properties would be to store micro help text. When a node receives the focus, you can read its micro help property and display it, for example, in a status bar, to help the user understand the use of the node.

The getProperties() method of the Node class returns an ObservableMap<Object, Object> in which you can add or remove properties for the node. The following snippet of code adds a property "originalData" with a value "Advik" to a TextField node:

```
TextField nameField = new TextField();
...
ObservableMap<Object, Object> props = nameField.getProperties();
props.put("originalData", "Advik");
```

The following snippet of code reads the value of the "originalData" property from the nameField node:

```
ObservableMap<Object, Object> props = nameField.getProperties();
if (props.containsKey("originalData")) {
        String originalData = (String)props.get("originalData");
} else {
        // originalData property is not set yet
}
```

The Node class has two convenience methods, setUserData(Object value) and getUserData(), to store a user-defined value as a property for a node. The value specified in the setUserData() method uses the same ObservableMap to store the data that are returned by the getProperties() method. The Node class uses an internal Object as the key to store the value. You need to use the getUserData() method to get the value that you store using the setUserData() method, as follows:

```
nameField.setUserData("Saved"); // Set the user data
...
String userData = (String)nameField.getUserData(); // Get the user data
```

▨ **Tip** You cannot access the user data of a node directly except by using the getUserData() method. Because it is stored in the same ObservableMap returned by the getProperties() method, you can get to it indirectly by iterating through the values in that map.

The Node class has a hasProperties() method. It tests if a node has properties. Its implementation seems to be wrong as of JavaFX version 2.2. The Node class creates an ObservableMap to store properties lazily. It is created when you call the getProperties() of setUserData() method for the first time. The implementation of the hasProperties() method returns true if the internal ObservableMap object has been created. It does not check if the internal map has any key/value pair in it:

```
TextField nameField = new TextField();
System.out.println(nameField.hasProperties());
ObservableMap<Object, Object> props = nameField.getProperties();
System.out.println(nameField.hasProperties());
```

```
false
true
```

The above snippet of code should print false twice. However, it prints true for the second time because you have called the getProperties() method, which is wrong. Your nameField node still has no properties. Let's see if this would get fixed in the later version.

What Is a Managed Node?

The Node class has a managed property, which is of type BooleanProperty. By default, all nodes are managed. The laying out of a managed node is managed by its parent. A Parent node takes into account the layoutBounds of all its managed children when it computes its own size. A Parent node is responsible for resizing its managed resizable children and positioning them according to its layout policy. When the layoutBounds of a managed child changes, the relevant part of the scene graph is relaid out.

If a node is unmanaged, the application is solely responsible for laying it out (computing its size and position). That is, a Parent node does not lay out its unmanaged children. Changes in the layoutBounds of an unmanaged node do not trigger the relayout above it. An unmanaged Parent node acts as a *layout root*. If a child node calls the Parent.requestLayout() method, only the branch rooted by the unmanaged Parent node is relaid out.

■ **Tip**   Contrast the visible property of the Node class with its managed property. A Parent node takes into account the layoutBounds of all its invisible children for layout purposes and ignores the unmanaged children.

When would you use an unmanaged node? Typically, you do not need to use unmanaged nodes in applications because they need additional work on your part. However, just know that they exist and you can use them, if needed.

You can use an unmanaged node when you want to show a node in a container without the container considering its layoutBounds. You will need to size and position the node yourself. Listing 6-7 demonstrates how to use unmanaged nodes. It uses an unmanaged Text node to display a micro help when a node has the focus. The node needs to have a property named "microHelpText". When the micro help is shown, the layout for the entire application is not disturbed as the Text node to show the micro help is an unmanaged node. You place the node at an appropriate position in the focusChanged() method. The program registers a change listener to the focusOwner property of the scene, so you show or hide the micro help Text node when the focus inside the scene changes. The resulting screens, when two different nodes have focus, are shown in Figure 6-22. Note that positioning the Text node, in this example, was easy as all nodes were inside the same parent node, a GridPane. The logic to position the Text node becomes complex if nodes are placed inside different parents.

Listing 6-7. Using an Unmanaged Text Node to Show Micro Help

```
// MicroHelpApp.java
package com.jdojo.node;

import javafx.application.Application;
import javafx.application.Platform;
import javafx.beans.value.ObservableValue;
import javafx.geometry.VPos;
import javafx.scene.Node;
import javafx.scene.Scene;
import javafx.scene.control.Button;
import javafx.scene.control.Label;
import javafx.scene.control.TextField;
import javafx.scene.layout.GridPane;
import javafx.scene.paint.Color;
import javafx.scene.text.Font;
import javafx.scene.text.Text;
import javafx.stage.Stage;

public class MicroHelpApp extends Application {
        // An instance variable to store the Text node reference
        private Text helpText = new Text();

        public static void main(String[] args) {
                Application.launch(args);
        }

        @Override
        public void start(Stage stage) {
                TextField fName = new TextField();
                TextField lName = new TextField();
                TextField salary = new TextField();

                Button closeBtn = new Button("Close");
                closeBtn.setOnAction(e -> Platform.exit());

                fName.getProperties().put("microHelpText", "Enter the first name");
                lName.getProperties().put("microHelpText", "Enter the last name");
                salary.getProperties().put("microHelpText",
                                        "Enter a salary greater than $2000.00.");

                // The help text node is unmanaged
                helpText.setManaged(false);
                helpText.setTextOrigin(VPos.TOP);
                helpText.setFill(Color.RED);
                helpText.setFont(Font.font(null, 9));
                helpText.setMouseTransparent(true);

                // Add all nodes to a GridPane
                GridPane root = new GridPane();
```

192

```
        root.add(new Label("First Name:"), 1, 1);
        root.add(fName, 2, 1);
        root.add(new Label("Last Name:"), 1, 2);
        root.add(lName, 2, 2);

        root.add(new Label("Salary:"), 1, 3);
        root.add(salary, 2, 3);
        root.add(closeBtn, 3, 3);
        root.add(helpText, 4, 3);

        Scene scene = new Scene(root, 300, 100);

        // Add a change listener to the scene, so you know when the focus owner
        // changes and display the micro help
        scene.focusOwnerProperty().addListener(
                (ObservableValue<? extends Node> value, Node oldNode, Node newNode)
                        -> focusChanged(value, oldNode, newNode));
        stage.setScene(scene);
        stage.setTitle("Showing Micro Help");
        stage.show();
    }

    public void focusChanged(ObservableValue<? extends Node> value,
                        Node oldNode, Node newNode) {
        // Focus has changed to a new node
        String microHelpText = (String)newNode.getProperties().get("microHelpText");

        if (microHelpText != null && microHelpText.trim().length() > 0)  {
                helpText.setText(microHelpText);
                helpText.setVisible(true);

                // Position the help text node
                double x = newNode.getLayoutX() +
                        newNode.getLayoutBounds().getMinX() -
                        helpText.getLayoutBounds().getMinX();
                double y = newNode.getLayoutY() +
                        newNode.getLayoutBounds().getMinY() +
                        newNode.getLayoutBounds().getHeight() -
                        helpText.getLayoutBounds().getMinX();

                helpText.setLayoutX(x);
                helpText.setLayoutY(y);
                helpText.setWrappingWidth(newNode.getLayoutBounds().getWidth());
        }
        else {
                helpText.setVisible(false);
        }
    }
}
```

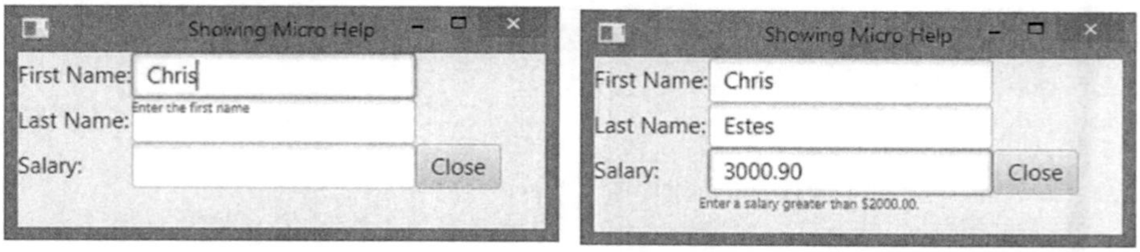

Figure 6-22. *Using an unmanaged Text node to show micro help*

Sometimes you may want to use the space that is used by a node if the node becomes invisible. Suppose you have an HBox with several buttons. When one of the buttons becomes invisible, you want to slide all buttons from right to left. You can achieve a slide-up effect in VBox. Achieving sliding effects in HBox and VBox (or any other containers with relative positioning) is easy by binding the managed property of the node to the visible property. Listing 6-8 shows how to achieve the slide-left feature in an HBox. It displays four buttons. The first button is used to make the third button, b2, visible and invisible. The managed property of the b2 button is bound to its visible property:

```
b2.managedProperty().bind(b2.visibleProperty());
```

When the b2 button is made invisible, it becomes unmanaged, and the HBox does not use its layoutBounds in computing its own layoutBounds. This makes the b3 button slide to the left. Figure 6-23 shows two screenshots when the application is run.

Listing 6-8. Simulating the Slide-Left Feature Using Unmanaged Nodes

```java
// SlidingLeftNodeTest.java
package com.jdojo.node;

import javafx.application.Application;
import javafx.beans.binding.When;
import javafx.scene.Scene;
import javafx.scene.control.Button;
import javafx.scene.layout.HBox;
import javafx.stage.Stage;

public class SlidingLeftNodeTest extends Application {
        public static void main(String[] args) {
                Application.launch(args);
        }

        @Override
        public void start(Stage stage) {
                Button b1 = new Button("B1");
                Button b2 = new Button("B2");
                Button b3 = new Button("B3");
                Button visibleBtn = new Button("Make Invisible");

                // Add an action listener to the button to make b2 visible
                // if it is invisible and invisible if it is visible
                visibleBtn.setOnAction(e -> b2.setVisible(!b2.isVisible()));
```

```
        // Bind the text property of the button to the visible
        // property of the b2 button
        visibleBtn.textProperty().bind(new When(b2.visibleProperty())
                        .then("Make Invisible")
                        .otherwise("Make Visible"));

        // Bind the managed property of b2 to its visible property
        b2.managedProperty().bind(b2.visibleProperty());

        HBox root = new HBox();
        root.getChildren().addAll(visibleBtn, b1, b2, b3);

        Scene scene = new Scene(root);
        stage.setScene(scene);
        stage.setTitle("Sliding to the Left");
        stage.show();
    }
}
```

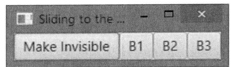 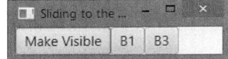

Figure 6-23. *Simulating the slide-left feature for B2 button*

Transforming Bounds between Coordinate Spaces

I have already covered coordinate spaces used by nodes. Sometimes you may need to translate a Bounds or a point from one coordinate space to another. The Node class contains several methods to support this. The following transformations of a Bounds or a point are supported:

- Local to parent
- Local to scene
- Parent to local
- Scene to local

The localToParent() method transforms a Bounds or a point in the local coordinate space of a node to the coordinate space of its parent. The localToScene() method transforms a Bounds or a point in the local coordinate space of a node to the coordinate space of its scene. The parentToLocal() method transforms a Bounds or a point in the coordinate space of the parent of a node to the local coordinate space of the node. The sceneToLocal() method transforms a Bounds or a point in the coordinate space of the scene of a node to the local coordinate space of the node. All methods have three overloaded versions; one version takes a Bounds as an argument and returns the transformed Bounds; another version takes a Point2D as an argument and returns the transformed Point2D; another version takes the x and y coordinates of a point and returns the transformed Point2D.

195

These methods are sufficient to transform the coordinate of a point in one coordinate space to another within a scene graph. Sometimes you may need to transform the coordinates of a point in the local coordinate space of a node to the coordinate space of the stage or screen. You can achieve this using the x and y properties of the Scene and Stage classes. The (x, y) properties of a scene define the coordinates of the top left corner of the scene in the coordinate space of its stage. The (x, y) properties of a stage define the coordinates of the top left corner of the stage in the coordinate space of the screen. For example, if (x1, y1) is a point in the coordinate space of the scene, (x1 + x2, y1 + y2) defines the same point in the coordinate space of the state, where x2 and y2 are the x and y properties of the stage, respectively. Apply the same logic to get the coordinate of a point in the coordinate space of the screen.

Let's look at an example that uses transformations between the coordinate spaces of a node, its parent, and its scene. A scene has three Labels and three TextFields placed under different parents. A red, small circle is placed at the top left corner of the bounding box of the node that has the focus. As the focus changes, the position of the circle needs to be computed, which would be the same as the position of the top left corner of the current node, relative to the parent of the circle. The center of the circle needs to coincide with the top left corner of the node that has the focus. Figure 6-24 shows the stage when the focus is in the first name and last name nodes. Listing 6-9 has the complete program to achieve this.

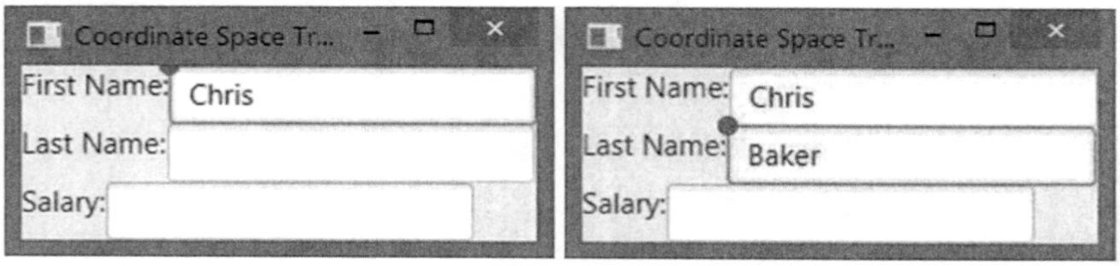

Figure 6-24. *Using coordinate space transformations to move a circle to a focused node*

The program has a scene consisting of three Labels and TextFields. A pair of a Label and a TextField is placed in an HBox. All HBoxes are placed in a VBox. An unmanaged Circle is placed in the VBox. The program adds a change listener to the focusOwner property of the scene to track the focus change. When the focus changes, the circle is placed at the top left corner of the node that has the focus.

The placeMarker() contains the main logic. It gets the (x, y) coordinates of the top left corner of the bounding box of the node in focus in the local coordinate space:

```
double nodeMinX = newNode.getLayoutBounds().getMinX();
double nodeMinY = newNode.getLayoutBounds().getMinY();
```

It transforms the coordinates of the top left corner of the node from the local coordinate space to the coordinate space of the scene:

```
Point2D nodeInScene = newNode.localToScene(nodeMinX, nodeMinY);
```

Now the coordinates of the top left corner of the node are transformed from the coordinate space of the scene to the coordinate space of the circle, which is named marker in the program:

```
Point2D nodeInMarkerLocal = marker.sceneToLocal(nodeInScene);
```

Finally, the coordinate of the top left corner of the node is transformed to the coordinate space of the parent of the circle:

```
Point2D nodeInMarkerParent = marker.localToParent(nodeInMarkerLocal);
```

At this point, the nodeInMarkerParent is the point (the top left corner of the node in focus) relative to the parent of the circle. If you relocate the circle to this point, you will place the top left corner of the bounding box of the circle to the top left corner of the node in focus:

```
marker.relocate(nodeInMarkerParent.getX(), nodeInMarkerParent.getY())
```

If you want to place the center of the circle to the top left corner of the node in focus, you will need to adjust the coordinates accordingly:

```
marker.relocate(nodeInMarkerParent.getX() + marker.getLayoutBounds().getMinX(),
                nodeInMarkerParent.getY() + marker.getLayoutBounds().getMinY());
```

Listing 6-9. Transforming the Coordinates of a Point from One Coordinate Space to Another

```java
// CoordinateConversion.java
package com.jdojo.node;

import javafx.application.Application;
import javafx.geometry.Point2D;
import javafx.scene.Node;
import javafx.scene.Scene;
import javafx.scene.control.Label;
import javafx.scene.control.TextField;
import javafx.scene.layout.HBox;
import javafx.scene.layout.VBox;
import javafx.scene.paint.Color;
import javafx.scene.shape.Circle;
import javafx.stage.Stage;

public class CoordinateConversion extends Application {
        // An instance variable to store the reference of the circle
        private Circle marker;

        public static void main(String[] args) {
                Application.launch(args);
        }

        @Override
        public void start(Stage stage) {
                TextField fName = new TextField();
                TextField lName = new TextField();
                TextField salary = new TextField();
```

```
                // The Circle node is unmanaged
                marker = new Circle(5);
                marker.setManaged(false);
                marker.setFill(Color.RED);
                marker.setMouseTransparent(true);

                HBox hb1 = new HBox();
                HBox hb2 = new HBox();
                HBox hb3 = new HBox();
                hb1.getChildren().addAll(new Label("First Name:"), fName);
                hb2.getChildren().addAll(new Label("Last Name:"), lName);
                hb3.getChildren().addAll(new Label("Salary:"), salary);

                VBox root = new VBox();
                root.getChildren().addAll(hb1, hb2, hb3, marker);

                Scene scene = new Scene(root);

                // Add a focus change listener to the scene
                scene.focusOwnerProperty().addListener(
                            (prop, oldNode, newNode) -> placeMarker(newNode));

                stage.setScene(scene);
                stage.setTitle("Coordinate Space Transformation");
                stage.show();
        }

        public void placeMarker(Node newNode) {
                double nodeMinX = newNode.getLayoutBounds().getMinX();
                double nodeMinY = newNode.getLayoutBounds().getMinY();
                Point2D nodeInScene = newNode.localToScene(nodeMinX, nodeMinY);
                Point2D nodeInMarkerLocal = marker.sceneToLocal(nodeInScene);
                Point2D nodeInMarkerParent = marker.localToParent(nodeInMarkerLocal);

                // Position the circle approperiately
                marker.relocate(nodeInMarkerParent.getX()
                            + marker.getLayoutBounds().getMinX(),
                            nodeInMarkerParent.getY()
                            + marker.getLayoutBounds().getMinY());
        }
}
```

Summary

A scene graph is a tree data structure. Every item in a scene graph is called a node. An instance of the javafx.scene.Node class represents a node in the scene graph. A node can have subitems (also called children) and such a node is called a branch node. A branch node is an instance of the Parent class whose concrete subclasses are Group, Region, and WebView. A node that cannot have subitems is called a leaf node. Instances of classes such as Rectangle, Text, ImageView, and MediaView are examples of leaf nodes. Only a single node within each scene graph tree will have no parent, which is referred to as the root node. A node may occur at the most once anywhere in the scene graph.

A node may be created and modified on any thread if it is not yet attached to a scene. Attaching a node to a scene and subsequent modification must occur on the JavaFX Application Thread. A node has several types of bounds. Bounds are determined with respect to different coordinate systems. A node in a scene graph has three types of bounds: layoutBounds, boundsInLocal, and boundsInParent.

The layoutBounds property is computed based on the geometric properties of the node in the *untransformed* local coordinate space of the node. Effects, clip, and transformations are not included. The boundsInLocal property is computed in the untransformed coordinate space of the node. It includes the geometric properties of the node, effects, and clip. Transformations applied to a node are not included. The boundsInParent property of a node is in the coordinate space of its parent. It includes the geometric properties of the node, effects, clip, and transformations. It is rarely used directly in code.

The computation of layoutBounds, boundsInLocal, and boundsInParent for a Group is different from that of a node. A Group takes on the collection bounds of its children. You can apply effects, clip, and transformations separately on each child of a Group. You can also apply effects, clip, and transformations directly on a Group and they are applied to all its children nodes. The layoutBounds of a Group is the union of the boundsInParent of all its children. It includes effects, clip, and transformations applied directly to the children. It does not include effects, clip, and transformations applied directly to the Group. The boundsInLocal of a Group is computed taking its layoutBounds and including the effects and clip applied directly to the Group. The boundsInParent of a Group is computed by taking its boundsInLocal and including the transformations applied directly to the Group.

Every node maintains an observable map of user-defined properties (key/value pairs). You can use it to store any useful information. A node can be managed or unmanaged. A managed node is laid out by its parent, whereas the application is responsible for laying out an unmanaged node.

The next chapter will discuss how to use colors in JavaFX.

CHAPTER 7

■ ■ ■

Playing with Colors

In this chapter, you will learn:

- How colors are represented in JavaFX
- What different color patterns are
- How to use image pattern
- How to use linear color gradient
- How to use radial color gradient

Understanding Colors

In JavaFX, you can specify color for text and background color for regions. You can specify a color as a uniform color, an image pattern, or a color gradient. A uniform color uses the same color to fill the entire region. An image pattern lets you fill a region with an image pattern. A color gradient defines a color pattern in which the color varies along a straight line from one color to another. The variation in a color gradient can be linear or radial. I will present examples using all color types in this chapter. Figure 7-1 shows the class diagram for color-related classes in JavaFX. All classes are included in the javafx.scene.paint package.

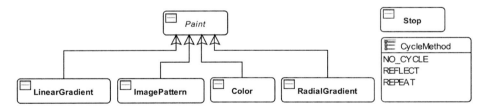

Figure 7-1. The class diagram of color-related classes in JavaFX

The Paint class is an abstract class and it is the base class for other color classes. It contains only one static method that takes a String argument and returns a Paint instance. The returned Paint instance would be of the Color, LinearGradient, or RadialGradient class, as shown in the following code:

```
public static Paint valueOf(String value)
```

You will not use the valueOf() method of the Paint class directly. It is used to convert the color value read in a String from the CSS files. The following snippet of code creates instances of the Paint class from Strings:

```
// redColor is an instance of the Color class
Paint redColor = Paint.valueOf("red");

// aLinearGradientColor is an instance of the LinearGradient class
Paint aLinearGradientColor = Paint.valueOf("linear-gradient(to bottom right, red, black)" );

// aRadialGradientColor is an instance of the RadialGradient class
Paint aRadialGradientColor =
    Paint.valueOf("radial-gradient(radius 100%, red, blue, black)");
```

A uniform color, an image pattern, a linear color gradient, and a radial color gradient are instances of the Color, ImagePattern, LinearGradient, and RadialGradient classes, respectively. The Stop class and the CycleMethod enum are used while working with color gradients.

■ **Tip** Typically, methods for setting the color attribute of a node take the Paint type as an argument, allowing you to use any of the four color patterns.

Using the Color Class

The Color class represents a solid uniform color from the RGB color space. Every color has an alpha value defined between 0.0 to 1.0 or 0 to 255. An alpha value of 0.0 or 0 means the color is completely transparent, and an alpha value of 1.0 or 255 denotes a completely opaque color. By default, the alpha value is set to 1.0. You can have an instance of the Color class in three ways:

- Using the constructor
- Using one of the factory methods
- Using one of the color constants declared in the Color class

The Color class has only one constructor that lets you specify the RGB and opacity in the range of 1,0 and 1.0:

```
public Color(double red, double green, double blue, double opacity)
```

The following snippet of code creates a completely opaque blue color:

```
Color blue = new  Color(0.0, 0.0, 1.0, 1.0);
```

You can use the following static methods in the Color class to create Color objects. The double values need to be between 0.0 and 1.0 and int values between 0 and 255:

- Color color(double red, double green, double blue)
- Color color(double red, double green, double blue, double opacity)
- Color hsb(double hue, double saturation, double brightness)

- Color hsb(double hue, double saturation, double brightness, double opacity)

- Color rgb(int red, int green, int blue)

- Color rgb(int red, int green, int blue, double opacity)

The valueOf() and web() factory methods let you create Color objects from strings in web color value formats. The following snippet of code creates blue Color objects using different string formats:

```
Color blue = Color.valueOf("blue");
Color blue = Color.web("blue");
Color blue = Color.web("#0000FF");
Color blue = Color.web("0X0000FF");
Color blue = Color.web("rgb(0, 0, 255)");
Color blue = Color.web("rgba(0, 0, 255, 0.5)"); // 50% transparent blue
```

The Color class defines about 140 color constants, for example, RED, WHITE, TAN, BLUE, among others. Colors defined by these constants are completely opaque.

Using the *ImagePattern* Class

An image pattern lets you fill a shape with an image. The image may fill the entire shape or use a tiling pattern. Here are the steps you would use to get an image pattern:

1. Create an Image object using an image from a file.

2. Define a rectangle, known as the anchor rectangle, relative to the upper left corner of the shape to be filled.

The image is shown in the anchor rectangle and is then resized to fit the anchor rectangle. If the bounding box for the shape to be filled is bigger than that of the anchor rectangle, the anchor rectangle with the image is repeated within the shape in a tiling pattern.

You can create an object of the ImagePattern using one of its constructors:

- ImagePattern(Image image)

- ImagePattern(Image image, double x, double y, double width, double height, boolean proportional)

The first constructor fills the entire bounding box with the image without any pattern. The second constructor lets you specify the x and y coordinates, width, and height of the anchor rectangle. If the proportional argument is true, the anchor rectangle is specified relative to the bounding box of the shape to be filled in terms of a unit square. If the proportional argument is false, the anchor rectangle is specified in the local coordinate system of the shape. The following two calls to the two constructors would produce the same result:

```
ImagePatterm ip1 = new ImagePattern(anImage);
ImagePatterm ip2 = new ImagePattern(anImage, 0.0, 0.0, 1.0, 1.0, true);
```

For the example here, you will use the image shown in Figure 7-2. It is a 37px by 25px blue rounded rectangle. It can be found in the resources/picture/blue_rounded_rectangle.png file under the source code folder.

Figure 7-2. *A blue rounded rectangle*

Using that file, let's create an image pattern, using the following code:

```
Image img = create the image object...
ImagePattern p1 = new ImagePattern(img, 0, 0, 0.25, 0.25, true);
```

The last argument in the ImagePattern constructor set to true makes the bounds of the anchor rectangle, 0, 0, 0.25, and 0.25, to be interpreted proportional to the size of the shape to be filled. The image pattern will create an anchor rectangle at (0, 0) of the shape to be filled. Its width and height will be 25% of the shape to be filled. This will make the anchor rectangle repeat four times horizontally and four times vertically. If you use the following code with the above image pattern, it will produce a rectangle as shown in Figure 7-3.

```
Rectangle r1 = new Rectangle(100, 50);
r1.setFill(p1);
```

Figure 7-3. *Filling a rectangle with an image pattern*

If you use the same image pattern to fill a triangle with the following snippet of code, the resulting triangle will look like the one shown in Figure 7-4.

```
Polygon triangle = new Polygon(50, 0, 0, 50, 100, 50);
triangle.setFill(p1);
```

Figure 7-4. *Filling a triangle with an image pattern*

How would you fill a shape completely with an image without having a tiling pattern? You would need to use an ImagePattern with the proportional argument set to true. The center of the anchor rectangle should be at (0, 0) and its width and height should be set to 1 as follows:

```
// An image pattern to completely fill a shape with the image
ImagePatterm ip = new ImagePattern(yourImage, 0.0, 0.0, 1.0, 1.0, true);
```

The program in Listing 7-1 shows how to use an image pattern. The resulting screen is shown in Figure 7-5. Its init() method loads an image in an Image object and stores it in an instance variable. If the image file is not found in the CLASSPATH, it prints an error message and quits.

Listing 7-1. Using and Image Pattern to Fill Different Shapes

```java
// ImagePatternApp.java
package com.jdojo.color;

import java.net.URL;
import javafx.application.Application;
import javafx.application.Platform;
import javafx.scene.Scene;
import javafx.scene.image.Image;
import javafx.scene.layout.HBox;
import javafx.scene.paint.ImagePattern;
import javafx.scene.shape.Circle;
import javafx.scene.shape.Rectangle;
import javafx.stage.Stage;

public class ImagePatternApp extends Application {
        private Image img;

        public static void main(String[] args) {
                Application.launch(args);
        }

        @Override
        public void init() {
                // Create an Image object
                final String IMAGE_PATH = "resources/picture/blue_rounded_rectangle.png";
                URL url = this.getClass().getClassLoader().getResource(IMAGE_PATH);
                if (url == null) {
                        System.out.println(IMAGE_PATH + " file not found in CLASSPATH");
                        Platform.exit();
                        return;
                }
                img = new Image(url.toExternalForm());
        }

        @Override
        public void start(Stage stage) {
                // An anchor rectangle at (0, 0) that is 25% wide and 25% tall
                // relative to the rectangle to be filled
                ImagePattern p1 = new ImagePattern(img, 0, 0, 0.25, 0.25, true);
                Rectangle r1 = new Rectangle(100, 50);
                r1.setFill(p1);

                // An anchor rectangle at (0, 0) that is 50% wide and 50% tall
                // relative to the rectangle to be filled
                ImagePattern p2 = new ImagePattern(img, 0, 0, 0.5, 0.5, true);
                Rectangle r2 = new Rectangle(100, 50);
                r2.setFill(p2);
```

```
// Using absolute bounds for the anchor rectangle
ImagePattern p3 = new ImagePattern(img, 40, 15, 20, 20, false);
Rectangle r3 = new Rectangle(100, 50);
r3.setFill(p3);

// Fill a circle
ImagePattern p4 = new ImagePattern(img, 0, 0, 0.1, 0.1, true);
Circle c = new Circle(50, 50, 25);
c.setFill(p4);

HBox root = new HBox();
root.getChildren().addAll(r1, r2, r3, c);

Scene scene = new Scene(root);
stage.setScene(scene);

stage.setTitle("Using Image Patterns");
stage.show();
    }
}
```

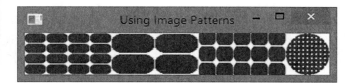

Figure 7-5. *Filling different shapes with image patterns*

Understanding Linear Color Gradient

A linear color gradient is defined using an axis known as a *gradient line*. Each point on the gradient line is of a different color. All points on a line that is perpendicular to the gradient line have the same color, which is the color of the point of intersection between the two lines. The gradient line is defined by a starting point and an ending point. Colors along the gradient line are defined at some points on the gradient line, which are known as *stop-color points* (or stop points). Colors between two stop points are computed using interpolation.

The gradient line has a direction, which is from the starting point to the ending point. All points on a line perpendicular to the gradient line that pass through a stop point will have the color of the stop point. For example, suppose you have defined a stop point P1 with a color C1. If you draw a line perpendicular to the gradient line passing through the point P1, all points on that line will have the color C1.

Figure 7-6 shows the details of the elements constituting a linear color gradient. It shows a rectangular region filled with a linear color gradient. The gradient line is defined from the left side to the right side. The starting point has a white color and the ending point has a black color. On the left side of the rectangle, all points have the white color, and on the right side, all points have the black color. In between the left and the right sides, the color varies between white and black.

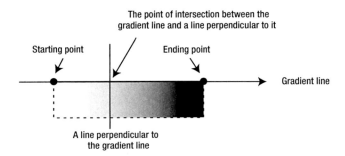

Figure 7-6. *The details of a linear color gradient*

Using the *LinearGradient* Class

In JavaFX, an instance of the LinearGradient class represents a linear color gradient. The class has the following two constructors. The types of their last arguments are different:

- LinearGradient(double startX, double startY, double endX, double endY, boolean proportional, CycleMethod cycleMethod, List<Stop> stops)

- LinearGradient(double startX, double startY, double endX, double endY, boolean proportional, CycleMethod cycleMethod, Stop... stops)

The startX and startY arguments define the x and y coordinates of the starting point of the gradient line. The endX and endY arguments define the x and y coordinates of the starting point of the gradient line.

The proportional argument affects the way the coordinates of the starting and ending points are treated. If it is true, the starting and ending points are treated relative to a unit square. Otherwise, they are treated as absolute value in the local coordinate system. The use of this argument needs a little more explanation.

Typically, a color gradient is used to fill a region, for example, a rectangle. Sometimes, you know the size of the region and sometimes you will not. The value of this argument lets you specify the gradient line in relative or absolute form. In relative form, the region is treated as a unit square. That is, the coordinates of the upper left and the lower right corners are (0.0, 0.0) and (1.0, 1.0), respectively. Other points in the regions will have x and y coordinates between 0.0 and 1.0. Suppose you specify the starting point as (0.0, 0.0) and the ending point as (1.0, 0.0). It defines a horizontal gradient line from the left to right. The starting and ending points of (0.0, 0.0) and (0.0, 1.0) define a vertical gradient line from top to bottom. The starting and ending points of (0.0, 0.0) and (0.5, 0.0) define a horizontal gradient line from left to middle of the region.

When the proportional argument is false, the coordinate values for the starting and ending points are treated as absolute values with respect to the local coordinate system. Suppose you have a rectangle of width 200 and height 100. The starting and ending points of (0.0, 0.0) and (200.0, 0.0) define a horizontal gradient line from left to right. The starting and ending points of (0.0, 0.0) and (200.0, 100.0) define a diagonal gradient line from the top left corner to the bottom right corner.

The cycleMethod argument defines how the regions outside the color gradient bounds, defined by the starting and ending points, should be filled. Suppose you define the starting and ending points with the proportional argument set to true as (0.0, 0.0) and (0.5, 0.0), respectively. This covers only the left half of the region. How should the right half of the region be filled? You specify this behavior using the cycleMethod argument. Its value is one of the enum constants defined in the CycleMethod enum:

- CycleMethod.NO_CYCLE

- CycleMethod.REFLECT

- CycleMethod.REPEAT

The cycle method of NO_CYCLE fills the remaining region with the terminal color. If you have defined color a stop point only from the left to the middle of a region, the right half will be filled with the color that is defined for the middle of the region. Suppose you define a color gradient for only the middle half of a region, leaving the 25% at the left side and 25% at the right side undefined. The NO_CYCLE method will fill the left 25% region with the color that is defined at the 25% distance from left and the right 25% region with the color defined at the 25% distance from right. The color for the middle 50% will be determined by the color-stop points.

The cycle method of REFLECT fills the remaining regions by reflecting the color gradient, as start-to-end and end-to-start, from the nearest filled region. The cycle method of REPEAT repeats the color gradient to fill the remaining region.

The stops argument defines the color-stop points along the gradient line. A color-stop point is represented by an instance of the Stop class, which has only one constructor:

```
Stop(double offset, Color color)
```

The offset value is between 0.0 and 1.0. It defines the relative distance of the stop point along the gradient line from the starting point. For example, an offset of 0.0 is the starting point, an offset of 1.0 is the ending point, an offset of 0.5 is in the middle of the starting and ending points, and so forth. You define at least two stop points with two different colors to have a color gradient. There are no limits on the number of stop points you can define for a color gradient.

That covers the explanation for the arguments of the LinearGradient constructors. So let's look at some examples on how to use them.

The following snippet of code fills a rectangle with a linear color gradient, as shown in Figure 7-7:

```
Stop[] stops = new Stop[]{new Stop(0, Color.WHITE), new Stop(1, Color.BLACK)};
LinearGradient lg = new LinearGradient(0, 0, 1, 0, true, NO_CYCLE, stops);
Rectangle r = new Rectangle(200, 100);
r.setFill(lg);
```

Figure 7-7. *A horizontal linear color gradient with two stop points: white at starting and black at ending point*

You have two color-stop points. The stop point in the beginning is colored white and that of the end is colored black. The starting point (0, 0) and ending point (1, 0) define a horizontal gradient from left to right. The proportional argument is set to true, which means the coordinate values are interpreted as relative to a unit square. The cycle method argument, which is set to NO_CYCLE, has no effect in this case as your gradient bounds cover the entire region. In the above code, if you want to set the proportional argument value to false, to have the same effect, you would create the LinearGradient object as follows. Note the use of 200 as the x coordinate for the ending point to denote the end of the rectangle width:

```
LinearGradient lg = new LinearGradient(0, 0, 200, 0, false, NO_CYCLE, stops);
```

Let's look at another example. The resulting rectangle after running the following snippet of code is shown in Figure 7-8:

```
Stop[] stops = new Stop[]{new Stop(0, Color.WHITE), new Stop(1, Color.BLACK)};
LinearGradient lg = new LinearGradient(0, 0, 0.5, 0, true, NO_CYCLE, stops);
Rectangle r = new Rectangle(200, 100);
r.setFill(lg);
```

Figure 7-8. *A horizontal linear color gradient with two stop points: white at starting and black at midpoint*

In this code, you have made a slight change. You defined a horizontal gradient line, which starts at the left side of the rectangle and ends in the middle. Note the use of (0.5, 0) as the coordinates for the ending point. This leaves the right half of the rectangle with no color gradient. The cycle method is effective in this case as its job is to fill the unfilled regions. The color at the middle of the rectangle is black, which is defined by the second stop point. The NO_CYCLE value uses the terminal black color to fill the right half of the rectangle.

Let's look at a slight variant of the previous example. You change the cycle method from NO_CYCLE to REFLECT, as shown in the following snippet of code, which results in a rectangle as shown in Figure 7-9. Note that the right half region (the region with undefined gradient) is the reflection of the left half:

```
Stop[] stops = new Stop[]{new Stop(0, Color.WHITE), new Stop(1, Color.BLACK)};
LinearGradient lg = new LinearGradient(0, 0, 0.5, 0, true, REFLECT, stops);
Rectangle r = new Rectangle(200, 100);
r.setFill(lg);
```

Figure 7-9. *A horizontal linear color gradient with two stop points: white at starting and black at midpoint and REFLECT as the cycle method*

Let's make a slight change in the previous example so the ending point coordinate covers only one-tenth of the width of the rectangle. The code is as follows, and the resulting rectangle is shown in Figure 7-10. The right 90% of the rectangle is filled using the REFLECT cycle method by alternating end-to-start and start-to-end color patterns:

```
Stop[] stops = new Stop[]{new Stop(0, Color.WHITE), new Stop(1, Color.BLACK)};
LinearGradient lg = new LinearGradient(0, 0, 0.1, 0, true, REFLECT, stops);
Rectangle r = new Rectangle(200, 100);
r.setFill(lg);
```

Figure 7-10. *A horizontal linear color gradient with two stop points: white at starting and black at one-tenth point and REFLECT as the cycle method*

Now let's look at the effect of using the REPEAT cycle method. The following snippet of code uses an ending point at the middle of the width of the rectangle and a cycle method of REPEAT. This results in a rectangle as shown in Figure 7-11. If you set the ending point to one-tenth of the width in this example, it will result in a rectangle as shown in Figure 7-12.

```
Stop[] stops = new Stop[]{new Stop(0, Color.WHITE), new Stop(1, Color.BLACK)};
LinearGradient lg = new LinearGradient(0, 0, 0.5, 0, true, REPEAT, stops);
Rectangle r = new Rectangle(200, 100);
r.setFill(lg);
```

Figure 7-11. *A horizontal linear color gradient with two stop points: white at starting and black at midpoint and REPEAT as the cycle method*

Figure 7-12. *A horizontal linear color gradient with two stop points: white at starting and black at one-tenth point and REPEAT as the cycle method*

You could also define more than two stop points, as shown in the following snippet of code. It divides the distance between the starting and the ending points on the gradient line into four segments, each by 25% of the width. The first segment (from left) will have colors between red and green, the second between green and blue, the third between blue and orange, and the fourth between orange and yellow. The resulting rectangle is shown in Figure 7-13. If you are reading a printed copy of the book, you may not see the colors.

```
Stop[] stops = new Stop[]{new Stop(0, Color.RED),
                         new Stop(0.25, Color.GREEN),
                         new Stop(0.50, Color.BLUE),
                         new Stop(0.75, Color.ORANGE),
                         new Stop(1, Color.YELLOW)};
LinearGradient lg = new LinearGradient(0, 0, 1, 0, true, NO_CYCLE, stops);
Rectangle r = new Rectangle(200, 100);
r.setFill(lg);
```

Figure 7-13. *A horizontal linear color gradient with five stop points*

You are not limited to defining only horizontal color gradients. You can define a color gradient with a gradient line with any angle. The following snippet of code creates a gradient from the top left corner to the bottom right corner. Note that when the proportional argument is true, (0, 0) and (1, 1) define the (x, y) coordinates of the top left and bottom right corners of the region:

```
Stop[] stops = new Stop[]{new Stop(0, Color.WHITE), new Stop(1, Color.BLACK)};
LinearGradient lg = new LinearGradient(0, 0, 1, 1, true, NO_CYCLE, stops);
Rectangle r = new Rectangle(200, 100);
r.setFill(lg);
```

The following snippet of code defines a gradient line between (0, 0) and (0.1, 0.1) points. It uses the REPEAT cycle method to fill the rest of the region. The resulting rectangle is shown in Figure 7-14.

```
Stop[] stops = new Stop[]{new Stop(0, Color.WHITE), new Stop(1, Color.BLACK)};
LinearGradient lg = new LinearGradient(0, 0, 0.1, 0.1, true, REPEAT, stops);
Rectangle r = new Rectangle(200, 100);
r.setFill(lg);
```

Figure 7-14. *An angled linear color gradient with two stop points: white at the starting point (0, 0) and black at the ending point (0.1, 0.1) with REPEAT as the cycle method*

Defining Linear Color Gradients Using a String Format

You can also specify a linear color gradient in string format using the static method valueOf(String colorString) of the LinearGradient class. Typically, the string format is used to specify a linear color gradient in a CSS file. It has the following syntax:

```
linear-gradient([gradient-line], [cycle-method], color-stops-list)
```

The arguments within square brackets ([and]) are optional. If you do not specify an optional argument, the comma that follows also needs to be excluded. The default value for the gradient-line argument is "to bottom." The default value for the cycle-method argument is NO_CYCLE. You can specify the gradient line in two ways:

- Using two points—the starting point and the ending point

- Using a side or s corner

The syntax for using two points for the gradient line is:

```
from point-1 to point-2
```

The coordinates of the points may be specified in percentage of the area or in actual measurement in pixels. For a 200px wide by 100px tall rectangle, a horizontal gradient line may be specified in the following two ways:

```
from 0% 0% to 100% 0%
```

or

```
from 0px 0px to 200px 0px
```

The syntax for using a side or a corner is:

```
to side-or-corner
```

The side-or-corner value may be top, left, bottom, right, top left, bottom left, bottom right, or top right. When you define the gradient line using a side or a corner, you specify only the ending point. The starting point is inferred. For example, the value "to top" infers the starting point as "from bottom"; the value "to bottom right" infers the starting point as "from top left," and so forth. If the gradient-line value is missing, it defaults to "to bottom."

The valid values for the cycle-method are repeat and reflect. If it is missing, it defaults to NO_CYCLE. It is a runtime error to specify the value of the cycle-method argument as NO_CYCLE. If you want it to be NO_CYCLE, simply omit the cycle-method argument from the syntax.

The color-stops-list argument is a list of color stops. A color stop consists of a web color name and, optionally, a position in pixels or percentage from the starting point. Examples of lists of color stops are:

- white, black

- white 0%, black 100%

- white 0%, yellow 50%, blue 100%

- white 0px, yellow 100px, red 200px

When you do not specify positions for the first and the last color stops, the positions for the first one defaults to 0% and the second one to 100%. So, the color stop lists "white, black" and "white 0%, black 100%" are fundamentally the same.

If you do not specify positions for any of the color stops in the list, they are assigned positions in such a way that they are evenly placed between the starting point and the ending point. The following two lists of color stops are the same:

- white, yellow, black, red, green

- white 0%, yellow 25%, black 50%, red 75%, green 100%

You can specify positions for some color stops in a list and not for others. In this case, the color stops without positions are evenly spaced between the preceding and following color stops with positions. The following two lists of color stops are the same:

- white, yellow, black 60%, red, green

- white 0%, yellow 30%, black 50%, red 80%, green 100%

If a color stop in a list has its position set less than the position specified for any previous color stops, its position is set equal to the maximum position set for the previous color stops. The following list of color stops sets 10% for the third color stop, which is less than the position of the second color stop (50%):

white, yellow 50%, black 10%, green

This will be changed at runtime to use 50% for the third color stop as follows:

white 0%, yellow 50%, black 50%, green 100%

Now let's look at some examples. The following string will create a linear gradient from top to bottom with NO_CYCLE as the cycle method. Colors are white and black at the top and bottom, respectively:

linear-gradient(white, black)

This value is the same as

linear-gradient(to bottom, white, black)

The following snippet of code will create a rectangle as shown in Figure 7-15. It defines a horizontal color gradient with the ending point midway through the width of the rectangle. It uses repeat as the cycle method:

```
String value = "from 0px 0px to 100px 0px, repeat, white 0%, black 100%";
LinearGradient lg2 = LinearGradient.valueOf(value);
Rectangle r2 = new Rectangle(200, 100);
r2.setFill(lg2);
```

Figure 7-15. *Creating a linear color gradient using the string format*

The following string value for a linear color gradient will create a diagonal gradient from the top left corner to the bottom right corner filling the area with white and black colors:

```
"to bottom right, white 0%, black 100%"
```

Understanding Radial Color Gradient

In a radial color gradient, colors start at a single point, transitioning smoothly outward in a circular or elliptical shape. The shape, let's say a circle, is defined by a center point and a radius. The starting point of colors is known as the *focus point of the gradient*. The colors change along a line, starting at the focus point of the gradient, in all directions until the periphery of the shape is reached. A radial color gradient is defined using three components:

- A gradient shape (the center and radius of the of the gradient circle)
- A focus point that has the first color of the gradient
- Color stops

The focus point of the gradient and the center point of the gradient shape may be different. Figure 7-16 shows the components of a radial color gradient. The figure shows two radial gradients: In the left side, the focus point and the center point are located at the same place; in the right side, the focus point is located horizontally right to the center point of the shape.

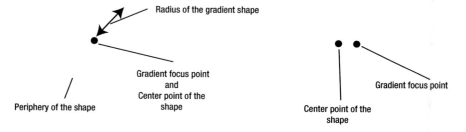

Figure 7-16. *Elements defining a radial color gradient*

The focus point is defined in terms of a focus angle and a focus distance, as shown in Figure 7-17. The focus angle is the angle between a horizontal line passing through the center point of the shape and a line joining the center point and the focus point. The focus distance is the distance between the center point of the shape and the focus point of the gradient.

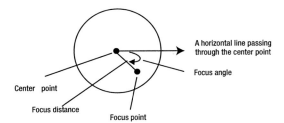

Figure 7-17. *Defining a focus point in a radial color gradient*

The list of color stops determines the value of the color at a point inside the gradient shape. The focus point defines the 0% position of the color stops. The points on the periphery of the circle define the 100% position for the color stops. How would you determine the color at a point inside the gradient circle? You would draw a line passing through the point and the focus point. The color at the point will be interpolated using the nearest color stops on each side of the point on the line.

Using the *RadialGradient* Class

An instance of the RadialGradient class represents a radial color gradient. The class contains the following two constructors that differ in the types of their last argument:

- RadialGradient(double focusAngle, double focusDistance, double centerX, double centerY, double radius, boolean proportional, CycleMethod cycleMethod, List<Stop> stops)

- RadialGradient(double focusAngle, double focusDistance, double centerX, double centerY, double radius, boolean proportional, CycleMethod cycleMethod, Stop... stops)

The focusAngle argument defines the focus angle for the focus point. A positive focus angle is measured clockwise from the horizontal line passing through the center point and the line connecting center point and the focus point. A negative value is measured counterclockwise.

The focusDistance argument is specified in terms of the percentage of the radius of the circle. The value is clamped between -1 and 1. That is, the focus point is always inside the gradient circle. If the focus distance sets the focus point outside the periphery of the gradient circle, the focus point that is used is the point of intersection of the periphery of the circle and the line connecting the center point and the set focus point.

The focus angle and the focus distance can have positive and negative values. Figure 7-18 illustrates this: it shows four focus points located at 80% distance, positive and negative, from the center point and at a 60-degree angle, positive and negative.

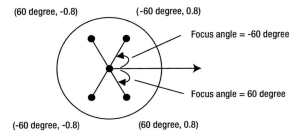

Figure 7-18. *Locating a focus point with its focus angle and focus distance*

The centerX and centerY arguments define the x and y coordinates of the center point, respectively, and the radius argument is the radius of the gradient circle. These arguments can be specified relative to a unit square (between 0.0 and 1.0) or in pixels.

The proportional argument affects the way the values for the coordinates of the center point and radius are treated. If it is true, they are treated relative to a unit square. Otherwise, they are treated as absolute values in the local coordinate system. For more details on the use of the proportional argument, please refer to the section "Using the *LinearGradient* Class" earlier in this chapter.

■ **Tip**   JavaFX lets you create a radial gradient of a circular shape. However, when the region to be filled by a radial color gradient has a nonsquare bounding box (e.g., a rectangle) and you specify the radius of the gradient circle relative to the size of the shape to be filled, JavaFX will use an elliptical radial color gradient. This is not documented in the API documentation of the RadialGradient class. I will present an example of this kind shortly.

The cycleMethod and stops arguments have the same meaning as described earlier in the section on using the LinearGradient class. In a radial color gradient, stops are defined along lines connecting the focus point and points on the periphery of the gradient circle. The focus point defines the 0% stop point and the points on the circle periphery define 100% stop points.

Let's look at some examples of using the RadialGradient class. The following snippet of code produces a radial color gradient for a circle as shown in Figure 7-19:

```
Stop[] stops = new Stop[]{new Stop(0, Color.WHITE), new Stop(1, Color.BLACK)};
RadialGradient rg = new RadialGradient(0, 0, 0.5, 0.5, 0.5, true, NO_CYCLE, stops);
Circle c = new Circle(50, 50, 50);
c.setFill(rg);
```

Figure 7-19. *A radial color gradient with the same center point and focus point*

The zero value for the focus angle and focus distance locates the focus point at the center of the gradient circle. A true proportional argument interprets the center point coordinates (0.5, 0.5) as (25px, 25px) for the 50 by 50 rectangular bounds of the circle. The radius value of 0.5 is interpreted as 25px, and that places the center of the gradient circle at the same location as the center of the circle to fill. The cycle method of NO_CYCLE has no effect in this case as the gradient circle fills the entire circular area. The color stop at the focus point is white and at the periphery of the gradient circle it is black.

The following snippet of code specifies the radius of the gradient circle as 0.2 of the circle to be filled. This means that it will use a gradient circle of 10px (0.2 multiplied by 50px, which is the radius of the circle to be filled). The resulting circle is shown in Figure 7-20. The region of the circle beyond the 0.2 of its radius has been filled with the color black, as the cycle method was specified as NO_CYCLE:

```
Stop[] stops = new Stop[]{new Stop(0, Color.WHITE), new Stop(1, Color.BLACK)};
RadialGradient rg = new RadialGradient(0, 0, 0.5, 0.5, 0.2, true, NO_CYCLE, stops);
Circle c = new Circle(50, 50, 50);
c.setFill(rg);
```

Figure 7-20. A radial color gradient with the same center point and focus point having a gradient circle with a radius of 0.20

Now let's use the cycle method of REPEAT in the above snippet of code. The resulting circle is shown in Figure 7-21.

```
Stop[] stops = new Stop[]{new Stop(0, Color.WHITE), new Stop(1, Color.BLACK)};
RadialGradient rg = new RadialGradient(0, 0, 0.5, 0.5, 0.2, true, REPEAT, stops);
Circle c = new Circle(50, 50, 50);
c.setFill(rg);
```

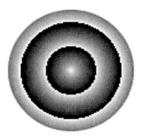

Figure 7-21. A radial color gradient with the same center point and focus point, a gradient circle with a radius of 0.20, and the cycle method as REPEAT

So now let's use a different center point and focus point. Use a 60-degree focus angle and 0.2 times the radius as the focus distance as in the following code. The resulting circle is shown in Figure 7-22. Notice the 3D effect you get by moving the focus point away from the center point.

```
Stop[] stops = new Stop[]{new Stop(0, Color.WHITE), new Stop(1, Color.BLACK)};
RadialGradient rg = new RadialGradient(60, 0.2, 0.5, 0.5, 0.2, true, REPEAT, stops);
Circle c = new Circle(50, 50, 50);
c.setFill(rg);
```

Figure 7-22. A radial color gradient using different center and focus points

Now let's fill a rectangular region (nonsquare) with a radial color gradient. The code for this effect follows and the resulting rectangle is shown in Figure 7-23. Notice the elliptical gradient shape used by JavaFX. You have specified the radius of the gradient as 0.5 and the proportional argument as true. Since your rectangle is 200px wide and 100px tall, it results in two radii: one along the x-axis and one along the y-axis, giving rise to an ellipse. The radii along the x and y axes are 100px and 50px, respectively.

```
Stop[] stops = new Stop[]{new Stop(0, Color.WHITE), new Stop(1, Color.BLACK)};
RadialGradient rg = new RadialGradient(0, 0, 0.5, 0.5, 0.5, true, REPEAT, stops);
Rectangle r = new Rectangle(200, 100);
r.setFill(rg);
```

Figure 7-23. A rectangle filled with a radial color gradient with a proportional argument value of true

If you want a rectangle to be filled with a color gradient of a circular shape rather than elliptical shape, you should specify the proportional argument as false and the radius value will be treated in pixels. The following snippet of code produces a rectangle, as shown in Figure 7-24:

```
Stop[] stops = new Stop[]{new Stop(0, Color.WHITE), new Stop(1, Color.BLACK)};
RadialGradient rg = new RadialGradient(0, 0, 100, 50, 50, false, REPEAT, stops);
Rectangle r = new Rectangle(200, 100);
r.setFill(rg);
```

Figure 7-24. *A rectangle filled with a radial color gradient with a proportional argument value of false*

How can you fill a triangle or any other shape with a radial color gradient? The shape of a radial gradient, circular or elliptical, depends on the several conditions. Table 7-1 shows the combinations of the criteria that will determine the shape of a radial color gradient.

Table 7-1. *Criteria Used to Determine the Shape of a Radial Color Gradient*

Proportional Argument	Bounding Box for the Filled Region	Gradient Shape
true	Square	Circle
true	Nonsquare	Ellipse
false	Square	Circle
false	Nonsquare	Circle

I should emphasize here that, in the above discussion, I am talking about the bounds of the regions to be filled, not the region. For example, suppose you want to fill a triangle with a radial color gradient. The bounds of the triangle will be determined by its width and height. If the triangle has the same width and height, its bounds take a square region. Otherwise, its bounds take a rectangular region.

The following snippet of code fills a triangle with vertices (0.0, 0.0), (0.0, 100.0), and (100.0, 100.0). Notice that the bounding box for this triangle is a 100px by 100px square. The resulting triangle is the left one shown in Figure 7-25.

```
Stop[] stops = new Stop[]{new Stop(0, Color.WHITE), new Stop(1, Color.BLACK)};
RadialGradient rg = new RadialGradient(0, 0, 0.5, 0.5, 0.2, true, REPEAT, stops);
Polygon triangle = new Polygon(0.0, 0.0, 0.0, 100.0, 100.0, 100.0);
triangle.setFill(rg);
```

100px X 100px   200px X 100px

Figure 7-25. *Filling triangles with radial color gradients of circular and elliptical shapes*

219

The triangle in the right side of Figure 7-25 uses a rectangular bounding box of 200px by 100px, which is produced by the following snippet of code. Notice that the gradient uses an elliptical shape:

```
Polygon triangle = new Polygon(0.0, 0.0, 0.0, 100.0, 200.0, 100.0);
```

Finally, let's look at an example of using multiple color stops with the focus point on the periphery of the circle, as shown in Figure 7-26. The code to produce the effect is as follows:

```
Stop[] stops = new Stop[]{new Stop(0, Color.WHITE),
                          new Stop(0.40, Color.GRAY),
                          new Stop(0.60, Color.TAN),
                          new Stop(1, Color.BLACK)};
RadialGradient rg = new RadialGradient(-30, 1.0, 0.5, 0.5, 0.5, true, REPEAT, stops);
Circle c = new Circle(50, 50, 50);
c.setFill(rg);
```

Figure 7-26. *Using multiple color stops in a radial color gradient*

Defining Radial Color Gradients in String Format

You can also specify a radial color gradient in string format by using the static method valueOf(String colorString) of the RadialGradient class. Typically, the string format is used to specify a radial color gradient in a CSS file. It has the following syntax:

```
radial-gradient([focus-angle], [focus-distance], [center], radius, [cycle-method],
color-stops-list)
```

The arguments within square brackets are optional. If you do not specify an optional argument, the comma that follows needs to be excluded as well.

The default value for focus-angle and focus-distance is 0. You can specify the focus angle in degrees, radians, gradians, and turns. The focus distance is specified as a percentage of the radius. Examples are as follows:

- focus-angle 45.0deg
- focus-angle 0.5rad
- focus-angle 30.0grad
- focus-angle 0.125turn
- focus-distance 50%

The center and radius arguments are specified in a percentage relative to the region being filled or in absolute pixels. You cannot specify one argument in a percentage and the other in pixels. Both must be specified in the same unit. The default value for center is (0, 0) in the unit. Examples are as follows:

- center 50px 50px, radius 50px

- center 50% 50%, radius 50%

The valid values for the cycle-method argument are repeat and reflect. If this is not specified, it defaults to NO_CYCLE.

A list of color stops is specified using colors and their positions. Positions are specified as a percentage of distance on a line from the focus point to the periphery of the shape of the gradient. Please refer to the earlier discussion on specifying the color stops in a linear color gradient for more details. Examples are as follows:

- white, black

- white 0%, black 100%

- red, green, blue

- red 0%, green 80%, blue 100%

The following snippet of code will produce a circle, as shown in Figure 7-27:

```
String colorValue = "radial-gradient(focus-angle 45deg, focus-distance 50%, " +
                    "center 50% 50%, radius 50%, white 0%, black 100%)";
RadialGradient rg = RadialGradient.valueOf(colorValue);
Circle c = new Circle(50, 50, 50);
c.setFill(rg);
```

Figure 7-27. *Using string format for specifying a radial color gradient*

Summary

In JavaFX, you can specify text color and background color for regions. You can specify a color as a uniform color, an image pattern, or a color gradient. A uniform color uses the same color to fill the entire region. An image pattern lets you fill a region with an image pattern. A color gradient defines a color pattern in which the color varies along a straight line from one color to another. The variation in a color gradient can be linear or radial. All classes are included in the javafx.scene.paint package.

The `Paint` class is an abstract class and it is the base class for other color classes. A uniform color, an image pattern, a linear color gradient, and a radial color gradient are instances of the `Color`, `ImagePattern`, `LinearGradient`, and `RadialGradient` classes, respectively. The `Stop` class and the `CycleMethod` enum are used when working with color gradients. You can specify colors using instances of one of these classes or in string forms. When you use a CSS to style nodes, you specify colors using string forms.

An image pattern lets you fill a shape with an image. The image may fill the entire shape or use a tiling pattern.

A linear color gradient is defined using an axis known as a gradient line. Each point on the gradient line is of a different color. All points on a line that is perpendicular to the gradient line have the same color, which is the color of the point of intersection between the two lines. The gradient line is defined by a starting point and an ending point. Colors along the gradient line are defined at some points on the gradient line, which are known as stop-color points (or stop points). Colors between two stop points are computed using interpolation. The gradient line has a direction, which is from the starting point to the ending point. All points on a line perpendicular to the gradient line that passes through a stop point will have the color of the stop point. For example, suppose you have defined a stop point P1 with a color C1. If you draw a line perpendicular to the gradient line passing through the point P1, all points on that line will have the color C1.

In a radial color gradient, colors start at a single point, transitioning smoothly outward in a circular or elliptical shape. The shape is defined by a center point and a radius. The starting point of colors is known as the focus point of the gradient. The colors change along a line, starting at the focus point of the gradient, in all directions until the periphery of the shape is reached.

The next chapter will show you how to style nodes in a scene graph using CSS.

CHAPTER 8

▪ ▪ ▪

Styling Nodes

In this chapter, you will learn:

- What a cascading style sheets is
- The difference between styles, skins, and themes
- Naming conventions of cascading style sheets styles in JavaFX
- How to add style sheets to a scene
- How to use and override the default style sheet in a JavaFX application
- How to add inline styles for a node
- About the different types of cascading style sheet properties
- About cascading style sheets style selectors
- How to look up nodes in a scene graph using cascading style sheets selectors
- How to use compiled style sheets

What Is a Cascading Style Sheet?

A cascading style sheet (CSS) is a language used to describe the presentation (the look or the style) of UI elements in a GUI application. CSS was primarily developed for use in web pages for styling HTML elements. It allows for the separation of the presentation from the content and behavior. In a typical web page, the content and presentation are defined using HTML and CSS, respectively.

JavaFX allows you to define the look (or the style) of JavaFX applications using CSS. You can define UI elements using JavaFX class libraries or FXML and use CSS to define their look.

CSS provides the syntax to write rules to set the visual properties. A rule consists of a *selector* and a set of *property-value* pairs. A selector is a string that identifies the UI elements to which the rules will be applied. A property-value pair consists of a property name and its corresponding value separated by a colon (:). Two property-value pairs are separated by a semicolon (;). The set of property-value pairs is enclosed within curly braces ({ }) preceded by the selector. An example of a rule in CSS is as follows:

```
.button {
        -fx-background-color: red;
        -fx-text-fill: white;
}
```

223

Here, .button is a selector, which specifies that the rule will apply to all buttons; -fx-background-color and -fx-text-fill are property names with their values set to red and white, respectively. When the above rule is applied, all buttons will have the red background color and white text color.

■ **Tip**   Using CSS in JavaFX is similar to using CSS with HTML. If you have worked with CSS and HTML before, the information in this chapter will sound familiar. Prior experience with CSS is not necessary to understand how to use CSS in JavaFX. This chapter covers all of the necessary material to enable you to use CSS in JavaFX.

What are Styles, Skins, and Themes?

A CSS rule is also known as a *style*. A collection of CSS rules is known as a *style sheet. Styles, skins,* and *themes* are three related, and highly confused, concepts.

Styles provide a mechanism to separate the presentation and content of UI elements. They also facilitate grouping of visual properties and their values, so they can be shared by multiple UI elements. JavaFX lets you create styles using JavaFX CSS.

Skins are collections of application-specific styles, which define the appearance of an application. *Skinning* is the process of changing the appearance of an application (or the skin) on the fly. JavaFX does not provide a specific mechanism for skinning. However, using the JavaFX CSS and JavaFX API, available for the Scene class and other UI-related classes, you can provide skinning for your JavaFX application easily.

Themes are visual characteristics of an operating system that are reflected in the appearance of UI elements of all applications. For example, changing the theme on the Windows operating system changes the appearance of UI elements in all applications that are running. To contrast skins and themes, skins are application specific, whereas themes are operating system specific. It is typical to base skins on themes. That is, when the current theme is changed, you would change the skin of an application to match the theme. JavaFX has no direct support for themes.

A Quick Example

Let's look at a simple, though complete, example of using style sheets in JavaFX. You will set the background color and text color of all buttons to red and white, respectively. The code for the styles is shown in Listing 8-1.

Listing 8-1. The Content of the File buttonstyles.css

```
.button {
    -fx-background-color: red;
    -fx-text-fill: white;
}
```

Save the content of Listing 8-1 in a buttonstyles.css file under the resources\css directory. You can place the file in any other directory; however, make sure that you change the file path accordingly. Finally, place the resources\css directory in the application CLASSPATH.

A scene contains an ObservableList of string URLs of styles sheets. You can get the reference of the ObservableList using the getStylesheets() method of the Scene class. The following snippet of code adds the URL for the buttonstyles.css style sheet to the scene:

```
Scene scene;
...
scene.getStylesheets().add("resources/css/buttonstyles.css");
```

Listing 8-2 contains the complete program, which shows three buttons with a red background and white text. If you get the following warning message and do not see the buttons in red background with white text, it indicates that you have not placed the resources\css directory in the CLASSPATH.

```
WARNING: com.sun.javafx.css.StyleManager loadStylesheetUnPrivileged Resource
"resources/css/buttonstyles.css" not found.
```

If one of the CLASSPATH entries is C:\abc\xyz, you need to place the buttonstyles.css file under the C:\abc\xyz\resources\css directory.

Listing 8-2. Using a Style Sheet to Change the Background and Text Colors for Buttons

```java
// ButtonStyleTest.java
package com.jdojo.style;

import javafx.application.Application;
import javafx.scene.Scene;
import javafx.scene.control.Button;
import javafx.scene.layout.HBox;
import javafx.stage.Stage;

public class ButtonStyleTest extends Application {
        public static void main(String[] args) {
                Application.launch(args);
        }

        @Override
        public void start(Stage stage) {
                Button yesBtn = new Button("Yes");
                Button noBtn = new Button("No");
                Button cancelBtn = new Button("Cancel");

                HBox root = new HBox();
                root.getChildren().addAll(yesBtn, noBtn, cancelBtn);

                Scene scene = new Scene(root);

                // Add a style sheet to the scene
                scene.getStylesheets().add("resources/css/buttonstyles.css");

                stage.setScene(scene);
                stage.setTitle("Styling Buttons");
                stage.show();
        }
}
```

Naming Conventions in JavaFX CSS

JavaFX uses slightly different naming conventions for the CSS style classes and properties. CSS style class names are based on the simple names of the JavaFX classes representing the node in a scene graph. All style class names are lowercased. For example, the style class name is button for the Button class. If the class name for the JavaFX node consists of multiple words, for example, TextField, a hyphen is inserted between two words to get the style class name. For example, the style classes for the TextField and CheckBox classes are text-field and check-box, respectively.

▪ **Tip** It is important to understand the difference between a JavaFX class and a CSS style class. A JavaFX class is a Java class, for example, javafx.scene.control.Button. A CSS style class is used as a selector in a style sheet, for example, button in Listing 8-1.

Property names in JavaFX styles start with -fx-. For example, the property name font-size in normal CSS styles becomes -fx-font-size in JavaFX CSS style. JavaFX uses a convention to map the style property names to the instance variables. It takes an instance variable; it inserts a hyphen between two words; if the instance variable consists of multiple words, it converts the name to the lowercase and prefixes it with -fx-. For example, for an instance variable named textAlignment, the style property name would be -fx-text-alignment.

Adding Style Sheets

You can add multiple style sheets to a JavaFX application. Style sheets are added to a scene or parents. Scene and Parent classes maintain an observable list of string URLs linking to style sheets. Use the getStylesheets() method in the Scene and Parent classes to get the reference of the observable list and add additional URLs to the list. The following code would accomplish this:

```
// Add two style sheets, ss1.css and ss2.css to a scene
Scene scene = ...
scene.getStylesheets().addAll("resources/css/ss1.css", "resources/css/ss2.css");

// Add a style sheet, vbox.css, to a VBox (a Parent)
VBox root = new VBox();
root.getStylesheets().add("vbox.css");
```

How are the string URLs for a style sheet resolved? You can specify a style sheet URL in three forms:

- A relative URL, for example, "resources/css/ss1.css"

- An absolute URL with no scheme or authority, for example, "/resources/css/ss1.css"

- An absolute URL, for example, "http://jdojo.com/resources/css/ss1.css" and "file:/C:/css/ss2.css"

The first two types of URLs are resolved the same way. They are resolved relative to the base URL of the ClassLoader of the concrete class that extends the Application class. This needs a little explanation. Suppose you have a com.jdojo.style.FXApp class, which extends the Application class and it is the main application class for your JavaFX application. To resolve the style sheets URLs correctly, you need to place your style sheet files in the same directory that contains the com/jdojo/style/FXApp.class file.

If you have problems accessing your style sheets using the above technique, you can use the absolute URLs. You can also use class's getResource() method or the ClassLoader of a class to get the URL of your style sheet. The following snippet of code uses the base URL of the ClassLoader of the Test class to resolve the relative URL of the style sheet:

```
Scene scene;
...
String urlString = Test.class.getClassLoader()
                    .getResource("resources/css/hjfx.css")
                    .toExternalForm();
scene.getStylesheets().add(urlString);
```

Default Style Sheet

In previous chapters you developed JavaFX applications with UI elements without the use of any style sheets. However, JavaFX runtime was always using a style sheet behind the scenes. The style sheet is named Modena.css, which is known as the *default style sheet* or the *user-agent style sheet*. The default look that you get for a JavaFX application is defined in the default style sheet.

The modena.css file is packaged in the JavaFX runtime jfxrt.jar file. If you want to know the details of how styles are set for specific nodes, you need to look at the modena.css file. You can extract this file using the following command:

```
jar -xf jfxrt.jar com/sun/javafx/scene/control/skin/modena/modena.css
```

This command places the modena.css file in the com\sun\javafx\scene\control\skin\modena directory under the current directory. Note that the jar command is in the JAVA_HOME\bin directory.

Prior to JavaFX 8, Caspian was the default style sheet. Caspian is defined in the jfxrt.jar file in the file named com/sun/javafx/scene/control/skin/caspian/caspian.css. In JavaFX 8, Modena is the default style sheet. The Application class defines two String constants named STYLESHEET_CASPIAN and STYLESHEET_MODENA to represent the two themes. Use the following static methods of the Application class to set and get the application-wide default style sheet:

- public static void setUserAgentStylesheet(String url)
- public static String getUserAgentStylesheet()

Use the setUserAgentStylesheet(String url) method to set an application–wide default. A value of null will restore the platform default style sheet, for example, Modena on JavaFX 8 and Caspian on the prior versions. The following statement sets Caspian as the default style sheet:

```
Application.setUserAgentStylesheet(Application.STYLESHEET_CASPIAN);
```

Use the getUserAgentStylesheet() method to return the current default style sheet for the application. If one of the built-in style sheet is the default, it returns null.

Adding Inline Styles

CSS styles for a node in a scene graph may come from style sheets or an inline style. In the previous section, you learned how to add style sheets to the Scene and Parent objects. In this section, you will learn how to specify an inline style for a node.

The Node class has a style property that is of StringProperty type. The style property holds the inline style for a node. You can use the setStyle(String inlineStyle) and getStyle() methods to set and get the inline style of a node.

There is a difference between a style in a style sheet and an inline style. A style in a style sheet consists of a selector and a set of property-value pairs, and it may affect zero or more nodes in a scene graph. The number of nodes affected by a style in a style sheet depends on the number of nodes that match the selector of the style. An inline style does not contain a selector. It consists of only set property-value pairs. An inline style affects the node on which it is set. The following snippet of code uses an inline style for a button to display its text in red and bold:

```
Button yesBtn = new Button("Yes");
yesBtn.setStyle("-fx-text-fill: red; -fx-font-weight: bold;");
```

Listing 8-3 displays six buttons. It uses two VBox instances to hold three buttons. It places both VBox instances into an HBox. Inline styles are used to set a 4.0px blue border for both VBox instances. The inline style for the HBox sets a 10.0px navy border. The resulting screen is shown in Figure 8-1.

Listing 8-3. Using Inline Styles

```java
// InlineStyles.java
package com.jdojo.style;

import javafx.application.Application;
import javafx.geometry.Insets;
import javafx.scene.Scene;
import javafx.scene.control.Button;
import javafx.scene.layout.HBox;
import javafx.scene.layout.VBox;
import javafx.stage.Stage;

public class InlineStyles extends Application {
        public static void main(String[] args) {
                Application.launch(args);
        }

        @Override
        public void start(Stage stage) {
                Button yesBtn = new Button("Yes");
                Button noBtn = new Button("No");
                Button cancelBtn = new Button("Cancel");

                // Add an inline style to the Yes button
                yesBtn.setStyle("-fx-text-fill: red; -fx-font-weight: bold;");
```

```
Button openBtn = new Button("Open");
Button saveBtn = new Button("Save");
Button closeBtn = new Button("Close");

VBox vb1 = new VBox();
vb1.setPadding(new Insets(10, 10, 10, 10));
vb1.getChildren().addAll(yesBtn, noBtn, cancelBtn);

VBox vb2 = new VBox();
vb2.setPadding(new Insets(10, 10, 10, 10));
vb2.getChildren().addAll(openBtn, saveBtn, closeBtn);

// Add a border to VBoxes using an inline style
vb1.setStyle("-fx-border-width: 4.0; -fx-border-color: blue;");
vb2.setStyle("-fx-border-width: 4.0; -fx-border-color: blue;");

HBox root = new HBox();
root.setSpacing(20);
root.setPadding(new Insets(10, 10, 10, 10));
root.getChildren().addAll(vb1, vb2);

// Add a border to the HBox using an inline style
root.setStyle("-fx-border-width: 10.0; -fx-border-color: navy;");

Scene scene = new Scene(root);
stage.setScene(scene);
stage.setTitle("Using Inline Styles");
stage.show();
    }
}
```

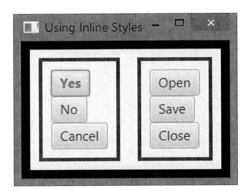

Figure 8-1. A button, two VBox instances, and an HBox using inline styles

Priorities of Styles for a Node

In a JavaFX application, it is possible, and very common, for the visual properties of nodes to come from multiple sources. For example, the font size of a button can be set by the JavaFX runtime, style sheets can be added to the parent and the scene of the button, an inline style can be set for the button, and programmatically can be added using the setFont(Font f) method. If the value for the font size of a button is available from multiple sources, JavaFX uses a rule to decide the source whose value is to be used.

Consider the following snippet of code along with the stylespriorities.css style sheet whose content is shown in Listing 8-4:

```
Button yesBtn = new Button("Yes");
yesBtn.setStyle("-fx-font-size: 16px");
yesBtn.setFont(new Font(10));

Scene scene = new Scene(yesBtn);
scene.getStylesheets().addAll("resources/css/stylespriorities.css");
...
```

Listing 8-4. The Content of stylespriorities.css File

```
.button {
        -fx-font-size: 24px;
        -fx-font-weight: bold;
}
```

What will be the font size of the button? Will it be the default font size set by the JavaFX runtime, 24px, declared in the stylespriorities.css, 16px set by the inline style, or 10px set by the program using the setFont() method? The correct answer is 16px, which is set by the inline style.

The JavaFX runtime uses the following priority rules to set the visual properties of a node. The source with a higher priority that has a value for a property is used:

- Inline style (the highest priority)
- Parent style sheets
- Scene style sheets
- Values set in the code using JavaFX API
- User agent style sheets (the lowest priority)

The style sheet added to the parent of a node is given higher priority than the style sheets added to the scene. This enables developers to have custom styles for different branches of the scene graph. For example, you can use two style sheets that set properties of buttons differently: one for buttons in the scene and one for buttons in any HBox. Buttons in an HBox will use styles from its parent, whereas all other buttons will use styles from the scene.

The values set using the JavaFX API, for example, setFont() method, have the second lowest priority.

■ **Note** It is a common mistake to set the same properties of a node in a style sheet and code using the Java API. In that case, the styles in the style sheet win and developers spend countless hours trying to find the reasons why the properties set in the code are not taking effect.

The lowest priority is given to style sheets used by the user agent. What is a user agent? A user agent, in general, is a program that interprets a document and applies style sheets to the document to format, print, or read. For example, a web browser is a user agent that applies default formatting to HTML documents. In our case, the user agent is the JavaFX runtime, which uses the caspian.css style sheet for providing the default look for all UI nodes.

■ **Tip**   The default font size that is inherited by nodes is determined by the system font size. Not all nodes use fonts. Fonts are used by only those nodes that display text, for example, a Button or a CheckBox. To experiment with the default font, you can change the system font and check it in code using the getFont() method of those nodes.

Listing 8-5 demonstrates the priority rules for choosing a style from multiple sources. It adds the style sheet, as shown in Listing 8-4, to the scene. The resulting screen is shown in Figure 8-2.

Listing 8-5. Testing Priorities of Styles for a Node

```java
// StylesPriorities.java
package com.jdojo.style;

import javafx.application.Application;
import javafx.scene.Scene;
import javafx.scene.control.Button;
import javafx.scene.layout.HBox;
import javafx.scene.text.Font;
import javafx.stage.Stage;

public class StylesPriorities extends Application {
        public static void main(String[] args) {
                Application.launch(args);
        }

        @Override
        public void start(Stage stage) {
                Button yesBtn = new Button("Yes");
                Button noBtn = new Button("No");
                Button cancelBtn = new Button("Cancel");

                // Change the font size for the Yes button
                // using two methods: inline style and JavaFX API
                yesBtn.setStyle("-fx-font-size: 16px");
                yesBtn.setFont(new Font(10));

                // Change the font size for the No button using the JavaFX API
                noBtn.setFont(new Font(8));

                HBox root = new HBox();
                root.setSpacing(10);
                root.getChildren().addAll(yesBtn, noBtn, cancelBtn);
```

```
        Scene scene = new Scene(root);

        // Add a style sheet to the scene
        scene.getStylesheets().addAll("resources/css/stylespriorities.css");

        stage.setScene(scene);
        stage.setTitle("Styles Priorities");
        stage.show();
    }
}
```

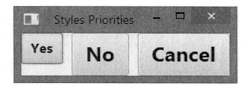

Figure 8-2. *Nodes using styles from different sources*

The font size value for the Yes button comes from four sources:

- Inline style (16px)
- Style sheet added to the scene (24px)
- JavaFX API (10px)
- Default font size set by the user agent (the JavaFX runtime)

The Yes button gets a 16px font size from its inline style, because that has the highest priority. The font size value for the No button comes from three sources:

- Style sheet added to the scene (24px)
- JavaFX API (10px)
- Default font size set by the user agent (the JavaFX runtime)

The No button gets a 24px font size from the style sheet added to the scene because that has the highest priority among the three available sources.

The font size value for the Cancel button comes from two sources:

- Style sheet added to the scene (24px)
- Default font size set by the user agent (the JavaFX runtime)

The Cancel button gets a 24px font size from the style sheet added to the scene, because that has the highest priority between the two available sources. The text for all buttons are shown in bold, because you have used the "-fx-font-weight: bold;" style in the style sheet and this property value is not overridden by any other sources.

At this point, several questions may arise in your mind:

- How do you let the Cancel button use the default font size that is set by the JavaFX runtime?

- How do you use one font size (or any other properties) for buttons if they are inside an HBox and use another font size if they are inside a VBox?

You can achieve all these and several other effects using appropriate selectors for a style declared in a style sheet. I will discuss different types of selectors supported by JavaFX CSS shortly.

Inheriting CSS Properties

JavaFX offers two types of inheritance for CSS properties:

- Inheritance of CSS property types

- Inheritance of CSS property values

In the first type of inheritance, all CSS properties declared in a JavaFX class are inherited by all its subclasses. For example, the Node class declares a cursor property and its corresponding CSS property is -fx-cursor. Because the Node class is the superclass of all JavaFX nodes, the -fx-cursor CSS property is available for all node types.

In the second type of inheritance, a CSS property for a node may inherit its value from its parent. The parent of a node is the container of the node in the scene graph, not its JavaFX superclass. The values of some properties of a node are inherited from its parent by default, and for some, the node needs to specify explicitly that it wants to inherit the values of the properties from its parent.

You can specify inherit as the value for a CSS property of a node if you want the value to be inherited from its parent. If a node inherits a CSS property from its parent by default, you do not need to do anything, that is, you do not even need to specify the property value as inherit. If you want to override the inherited value, you need to specify the value explicitly (overriding the parent's value).

Listing 8-6 demonstrates how a node inherits the CSS properties of its parent. It adds two buttons, OK and Cancel, to HBox. The following CSS properties are set on the parent and the OK button. No CSS properties are set on the Cancel button:

```
/* Parent Node (HBox)*/
-fx-cursor: hand;
-fx-border-color: blue;
-fx-border-width: 5px;

/* Child Node (OK Button)*/
-fx-border-color: red;
-fx-border-width: inherit;
```

The -fx-cursor CSS property is declared in the Node class and is inherited by all nodes by default. The HBox overrides the default value and overrides it to the HAND cursor. Both the OK and Cancel buttons inherit the HAND cursor value for their -fx-cursor from their parent, HBox. When you point your mouse to the area occupied by the HBox and these buttons, your mouse pointer will change to a HAND cursor. You can use the "-fx-cursor: inherit" style on the OK and Cancel buttons to achieve the same functionality you get by default.

Border-related CSS properties are not inherited by nodes by default. The HBox sets its -fx-border-color to blue and -fx-border-width to 5px. The OK button sets its -fx-border-color to red and -fx-border-width to inherit. The inherit value will make the -fx-border-width of the OK button to inherit from its parent (the HBox), which is 5px. Figure 8-3 shows the changes after adding this coding.

Listing 8-6. Inheriting CSS Properties from the Parent Node

```java
// CSSInheritance.java
package com.jdojo.style;

import javafx.application.Application;
import javafx.scene.Scene;
import javafx.scene.control.Button;
import javafx.scene.layout.HBox;
import javafx.stage.Stage;

public class CSSInheritance extends Application {
    public static void main(String[] args) {
        Application.launch(args);
    }

    @Override
    public void start(Stage stage) {
        Button okBtn = new Button("OK");
        Button cancelBtn = new Button("Cancel");

        HBox root = new HBox(10); // 10px spacing
        root.getChildren().addAll(okBtn, cancelBtn);

        // Set styles for the OK button and its parent HBox
        root.setStyle("-fx-cursor: hand;-fx-border-color: blue;-fx-border-width: 5px;");
        okBtn.setStyle("-fx-border-color: red;-fx-border-width: inherit;");

        Scene scene = new Scene(root);
        stage.setScene(scene);
        stage.setTitle("CSS Inheritance");
        stage.show();
    }
}
```

Figure 8-3. *A button inheriting its border width and cursor CSS properties from its parent*

■ **Tip** A node inherits -fx-cursor, -fx-text-alignment, and -fx-font CSS properties from its parent by default.

Types of CSS Properties

All values in Java (and in JavaFX as well) have a type. The values of CSS properties set in styles also have types. Each type of value has a different syntax. JavaFX CSS supports the following types:

- inherit
- boolean
- string
- number
- angle
- point
- color-stop
- URI
- effect
- font
- paint

Note that the CSS types have nothing to do with Java types. They can only be used in specifying the values in CSS style sheets or inline styles. The JavaFX runtime takes care of parsing and converting these types to appropriate JavaFX types before assigning them to nodes.

The *inherit* Type

You have seen an example of the use of the inherit type in the previous section. It is used to inherit the value of a CSS property for a node from its parent.

The *boolean* Type

You can specify the boolean type values as true or false. They can also be specified as strings: "true" or "false". The following style sets the -fx-display-caret CSS property of a TextField node to false:

```
.text-field {
    -fx-display-caret: false;
}
```

The *string* Type

String values can be enclosed in single quotes or double quotes. If the string value is enclosed in double quotes, a double quote as part of the value should be escaped, such as \" or \22. Similarly, a single quote as part of the string value enclosed in single quotes must be escaped, such as \' or \27. The following style uses strings to set the skin and font properties. It encloses the string value for the skin property in double quotes and the font family for the font property in single quotes:

```
.my-control {
    -fx-skin: "com.jdojo.MySkin";
    -fx-font: normal bold 20px 'serif';
}
```

235

■ **Tip**　A string value cannot contain a newline directly. To embed a newline in a string value, use the escape sequence \A or \00000a.

The *number* Type

Number values may be represented as integers or real numbers. They are specified using the decimal number format. The following style sets the opacity to 0.60:

```
.my-style {
        -fx-opacity: 0.60;
}
```

The value of a CSS property denoting a size can be specified using a number following by a unit of length. The unit of length can be px (pixels), mm (millimeters), cm (centimeters), in (inches), pt (points), pc (picas), em, or ex. A size can also be specified using the percentage of a length, for example, the width or height of a node. If a unit of a percentage is specified, it must immediately follow the number, for example, 12px, 2em, 80%:

```
.my-style {
        -fx-font-size: 12px;
        -fx-background-radius: 0.5em;
        -fx-border-width: 5%;
}
```

The *angle* Type

An angle is specified using a number and a unit. The unit of an angle can be deg (degrees), rad (radians), grad (gradients), or turn (turns). The following style sets the -fx-rotate CSS property to 45 degrees:

```
.my-style {
        -fx-rotate: 45deg;
}
```

The *point* Type

A point is specified using x and y coordinates. It can be specified using two numbers separated by whitespaces, for example, 0 0, 100, 0, 90 67, or in percentage form, for example, 2% 2%. The following style specifies a linear gradient color from the point (0, 0) to (100, 0):

```
.my-style {
        -fx-background-color: linear-gradient(from 0 0 to 100 0, repeat, red, blue);
}
```

The *color-stop* Type

A color-stop is used to specify color at a specific distance in linear or radial color gradients. A color-stop consists of a color and a stop distance. The color and the distance are separated by whitespaces. The stop distance may be specified as a percentage, for example 10%, or as a length, for example, 65px. Some examples of color-stops are white 0%, yellow 50%, yellow 100px. Please refer to Chapter 7 for more details on how to use color-stops in colors.

The *URI* Type

A URI can be specified using the url(<address>) function. A relative <address> is resolved relative to the location of the CSS file:

```
.image-view {
        -fx-image: url("http://jdojo.com/myimage.png");
}
```

The *effect* Type

Drop shadow and inner shadow effects can be specified for nodes using CSS styles using the dropshadow() and innershadow() CSS functions, respectively. Their signature are:

- dropshadow(<blur-type>, <color>, <radius>, <spread>, <x-offset>, <y-offset>)

- innershadow(<blur-type>, <color>, <radius>, <choke>, <x-offset>, <y-offset>)

The <blur-type> value can be Gaussian, one-pass-box, three-pass-box, or two-pass-box. The color of the shadow is specified in <color>. The <radius> value specifies the radius of the shadow blur kernel between 0.0 and 127.0. The spread/choke of the shadow is specified between 0.0 and 1.0. The last two parameters specify the shadow offsets in pixels in x and y directions. The following styles show how to specify the values for the -fx-effect CSS property:

```
.drop-shadow-1 {
        -fx-effect: dropshadow(gaussian, gray, 10, 0.6, 10, 10);
}

.drop-shadow-2 {
        -fx-effect: dropshadow(one-pass-box, gray, 10, 0.6, 10, 10);
}

.inner-shadow-1 {
        -fx-effect: innershadow(gaussian, gray, 10, 0.6, 10, 10);
}
```

The *font* Type

A font consists of four attributes: family, size, style, and weight. There are two ways to specify the font CSS property:

- Specify the four attributes of a font separately using the four CSS properties: -fx-font-family, -fx-font-size, -fx-font-style, and -fx-font-weight.

- Use a shorthand CSS property -fx-font to specify all four attributes as one value.

The font family is a string value that can be the actual font family available on the system, for example, "Arial", "Times", or generic family names, for example, "serif", "sans-serif", "monospace".

The font size can be specified in units such as px, em, pt, in, cm. If the unit for the font size is omitted, px (pixels) is assumed.

The font style can be normal, italic, or oblique.

The font weight can be specified as normal, bold, bolder, lighter, 100, 200, 300, 400, 500, 600, 700, 800, or 900.

The following style sets the font attributes separately:

```
.my-font-style {
        -fx-font-family: "serif";
        -fx-font-size: 20px;
        -fx-font-style: normal;
        -fx-font-weight: bolder;
}
```

Another way to specify the font property is to combine all four attributes of the font into one value and use the -fx-font CSS property. The syntax for using the -fx-font property is:

```
-fx-font: <font-style> <font-weight> <font-size> <font-family>;
```

The following style uses the -fx-font CSS property to set the font attributes:

```
.my-font-style {
        -fx-font: italic bolder 20px "serif";
}
```

The *paint* Type

A paint type value specifies a color, for example, the fill color of a rectangle or the background color of a button. You can specify a color value in the following ways:

- Using the linear-gradient() function

- Using the radial-gradient() function

- Using various color values and color functions

Please refer to Chapter 7 for a complete discussion on how to specify gradient colors in string format using the linear-gradient() and radial-gradient() functions. These functions are used to specify color gradients. The following style shows how to use these functions:

```
.my-style {
        -fx-fill: linear-gradient(from 0% 0% to 100% 0%, black 0%, red 100%);
        -fx-background-color: radial-gradient(radius 100%, black, red);
}
```

You can specify a solid color in several ways:

- Using named colors

- Using looked-up colors

- Using the rgb() and rgba() functions

- Using red, green, blue (RGB) hexadecimal notation

- Using the hsb() or hsba() function

- Using color functions: derive() and ladder()

You can use predefined color names to specify the color values, for example, red, blue, green, or aqua:

```
.my-style {
        -fx-background-color: red;
}
```

You can define a color as a CSS property on a node or any of its parents and, later, look it up by name, when you want to use its value. The following styles define a color named my-color and refer to it later:

```
.root {
        my-color: black;
}

.my-style {
        -fx-fill: my-color;
}
```

You can use the rgb(red, green, blue) and the rgba(red, green, blue, alpha) functions to define colors in terms of RGB components:

```
.my-style-1 {
        -fx-fill: rgb(0, 0, 255);
}

.my-style-2 {
        -fx-fill: rgba(0, 0, 255, 0.5);
}
```

You can specify a color value in the #rrggbb or #rgb format, where rr, gg, and bb are the values for red, green, and blue components, respectively, in hexadecimal format. Note that you need to specify the three components using two digits or one hexadecimal digit. You cannot specify some components in one hexadecimal digit and others in two:

```
.my-style-1 {
        -fx-fill: #0000ff;
}

.my-style-2 {
        -fx-fill: #0bc;
}
```

You can specify a color value in hue, saturation, brightness (HSB) color components using the hsb(hue, saturation, brightness) or hsba(hue, saturation, brightness, alpha) function:

```
.my-style-1 {
        -fx-fill: hsb(200, 70%, 40%);
}

.my-style-2 {
        -fx-fill: hsba(200, 70%, 40%, 0.30);
}
```

You can compute colors from other colors using the derive() and ladder() functions. The JavaFX default CSS, caspian.css, uses this technique. It defines some base colors and derives other colors from the base colors.

The derive function takes two parameters:

```
derive(color, brightness)
```

The derive() function derives a brighter or darker version of the specified color. The brightness value ranges from -100% to 100%. A brightness of -100% means completely black, 0% means no change in brightness, and 100% means completely white. The following style will use a version of red that is 20% darker:

```
.my-style {
        -fx-fill: derive(red, -20%);
}
```

The ladder() function takes a color and one or more color-stops as parameters:

```
ladder(color, color-stop-1, color-stop-2, ...)
```

Think of the ladder() function as creating a gradient using the color-stops and then using the brightness of the specified color to return the color value. If the brightness of the specified color is x%, the color at the x% distance from the beginning of the gradient will be returned. For example, for 0% brightness, the color at the 0.0 end of the gradient is returned; for 40% brightness, the color at the 0.4 end of the gradient is returned.

Consider the following two styles:

```
.root {
        my-base-text-color: red;
}
```

```
.my-style {
        -fx-text-fill: ladder(my-base-text-color, white 29%, black 30%);
}
```

The ladder() function will return the color white or black depending on the brightness of the my-base-text-color. If its brightness is 29% or lower, white is returned; otherwise, black is returned. You can specify as many color-stops as you want in the ladder() function to choose from a variety of colors depending on the brightness of the specified color.

You can use this technique to change the color of a JavaFX application on the fly. The default style sheet, caspian.css, defines some base colors and uses the derive() and ladder() functions to derive other colors of different brightnesses. You need to redefine the base colors in your style sheet for the root class to make an application-wide color change.

Specifying Background Colors

A node (a Region and a Control) can have multiple background fills, which are specified using three properties:

- `-fx-background-color`
- `-fx-background-radius`
- `-fx-background-insets`

The `-fx-background-color` property is a list of comma-separated color values. The number of colors in the list determines the number of rectangles that will be painted. You need to specify the radius values for four corners and insets for four sides, for each rectangle, using the other two properties. The number of color values must match the number of radius values and inset values.

The `-fx-background-radius` property is a list of a comma-separated set of four radius values for the rectangles to be filled. A set of radius values in the list may specify only one value, for example, 10, or four values separated by whitespaces, for example, 10 5 15 20. The radius values are specified for the top-left, top-right, bottom-right, and bottom-left corners in order. If only one radius value is specified, the same radius value is used for all corners.

The `-fx-background-insets` property is a list of a comma-separated set of four inset values for the rectangles to be filled. A set of inset values in the list may specify only one value, for example, 10, or four values separated by whitespaces, for example, 10 5 15 20. The inset values are specified for the top, right, bottom, and left sides in order. If only one inset value is specified, the same inset value is used for all sides.

Let's look at an example. The following snippet of code creates a Pane, which is a subclass of the Region class:

```
Pane pane = new Pane();
pane.setPrefSize(100, 100);
```

Figure 8-4 shows how the Pane looks when the following three styles are supplied:

```
.my-style-1 {
        -fx-background-color: gray;
        -fx-background-insets: 5;
        -fx-background-radius: 10;
}

.my-style-2 {
        -fx-background-color: gray;
        -fx-background-insets: 0;
        -fx-background-radius: 0;
}

.my-style-3 {
        -fx-background-color: gray;
        -fx-background-insets: 5 10 15 20;
        -fx-background-radius: 10 0 0 5;
}
```

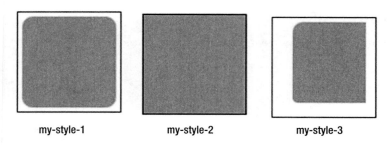

| my-style-1 | my-style-2 | my-style-3 |

Figure 8-4. *A Pane with three different background fills*

All three styles use a gray fill color, which means that only one rectangle will be drawn. The first style uses a 5px inset on all four sides, and a radius of 10px for all corners. The second style uses a 0px inset and a 0px radius, which makes the fill rectangle occupy the entire area of the pane. The third style uses a different inset on each side: 5px on the top, 10px on the right, 15px on the bottom, and 20px on the left. Notice the different unfilled background on each side for the third style. The third style also sets different values for the radius of four corners: 10px for the top-left, 0px for the top-right, 0px for the bottom-right, and 5px for the bottom-left. Notice that if the radius of a corner is 0px, the two sides at the corner meet at 90 degrees.

If you apply the following style to the same pane, the background will be filled as shown in Figure 8-5:

```
.my-style-4 {
        -fx-background-color: red, green, blue;
        -fx-background-insets: 5 5 5 5, 10 15 10 10, 15 20 15 15;
        -fx-background-radius: 5 5 5 5, 0 0 10 10, 0 20 5 10;
}
```

Figure 8-5. *A pane with three background fills with different radius and inset values*

The style uses three colors and, therefore, three background rectangles will be painted. The background rectangles are painted in the order they are specified in the style: red, green, and blue. The inset and radius values are specified in the same order as the colors. The style uses the same value for insets and radii for the red color. You can replace the set of four similar values with one value; that is, 5 5 5 5 in the above style can be replaced with 5.

Specifying Borders

A node (a Region and a Control) can have multiple borders through CSS. A border is specified using five properties:

- `-fx-border-color`
- `-fx-border-width`

- `-fx-border-radius`
- `-fx-border-insets`
- `-fx-border-style`

Each property consists of a comma-separated list of items. Each item may consist of a set of values, which are separated by whitespaces.

Border Colors

The number of items in the list for the `-fx-border-color` property determines the number of borders that are painted. The following style will paint one border with the red color:

```
-fx-border-color: red;
```

The following style specifies a set of red, green, blue, and aqua colors to paint the borders on top, right, bottom, and left sides, respectively. Note that it still results in only one border, not four borders, with different colors on four sides:

```
-fx-border-color: red green blue aqua;
```

The following style specifies two sets of border colors:

```
-fx-border-color: red green blue aqua, tan;
```

The first set consists of four colors, `red green blue aqua`, and the second set consists of only one color, `tan`. It will result in two borders. The first border will be painted with different colors on four sides; the second border will use the same color on all four sides.

■ **Tip** A node may not be rectangular in shape. In that case, only the first border color (and other properties) in the set will be used to paint the entire border.

Border Widths

You can specify the width for borders using the `-fx-border-width` property. You have an option to specify different widths for all four sides of a border. Different border widths are specified for top, right, bottom, and left sides in order. If the unit for the width value is not specified, pixel is used.

The following style specifies one border with all sides painted in red in 2px width:

```
-fx-border-color: red;
-fx-border-width: 2;
```

The following style specifies three borders, as determined by the three sets of colors specified in the `-fx-border-color` property. The first two borders use different border widths of four sides. The third border uses the border width of 3px on all sides:

```
-fx-border-color: red green blue black, tan, aqua;
-fx-border-width: 2 1 2 2, 2 2 2 1, 3;
```

Border Radii

You can specify the radius values for four corners of a border using the `-fx-border-radius` property. You can specify the same radius value for all corners. Different radius values are specified for top-left, top-right, bottom-right, and bottom-left corners in order. If the unit for the radius value is not specified, pixel is used.

The following style specifies one border in red, 2px width, and 5px radii on all four corners:

```
-fx-border-color: red;
-fx-border-width: 2;
-fx-border-radius: 5;
```

The following style specifies three borders. The first two borders use different radius values for four corners. The third border uses the radius value of 0px for all corners:

```
-fx-border-color: red green blue black, tan, aqua;
-fx-border-width: 2 1 2 2, 2 2 2 1, 3;
-fx-border-radius: 5 2 0 2, 0 2 0 1, 0;
```

Border Insets

You can specify the inset values for four sides of a border using the `-fx-border-insets` property. You can specify the same inset value for all sides. Different inset values are specified for top, right, bottom, and left sides in order. If the unit for the inset value is not specified, pixel is used.

The following style specifies one border in red, 2px width, 5px radius, and 20px inset on all four sides:

```
-fx-border-color: red;
-fx-border-width: 2;
-fx-border-radius: 5;
-fx-border-insets: 20;
```

The following style specifies three borders with insets 10px, 20px, and 30px on all sides:

```
-fx-border-color: red green blue black, tan, aqua;
-fx-border-width: 2 1 2 2, 2 2 2 1, 3;
-fx-border-radius: 5 2 0 2, 0 2 0 1, 0;
-fx-border-insets: 10, 20, 30;
```

■ **Tip** An inset is the distance from the side of the node at which the border will be painted. The final location of the border also depends of other properties, for example, `-fx-border-width` and `-fx-border-style`.

Border Styles

The `-fx-border-style` property defines the style of a border. Its value may contain several parts as follows:

```
-fx-border-style: <dash-style> [phase <number>] [<stroke-type>] [line-join <line-join-value>]
[line-cap <line-cap-value>]
```

The value for <dash-style> can be none, solid, dotted, dashed, or segments(<number>, <number>...). The value for <stroke-type> can be centered, inside, or outside. The value for <line-join-value> can be miter <number>, bevel, or round. The value for <line-cap-value> can be square, butt, or round.

The simplest border style would be to specify just the value for the <dash-style>:

```
-fx-border-style: solid;
```

The segments() function is used to have a border with a pattern using alternate dashes and gaps:

```
-fx-border-style: segments(dash-length, gap-length, dash-length, ...);
```

The first argument to the function is the length of the dash; the second argument is the length of the gap, and so on. After the last argument, the pattern repeats itself from the beginning. The following style will paint a border with a pattern of a 10px dash, a 5px gap, a 10px dash, and so on:

```
-fx-border-style: segments(10px, 5px);
```

You can pass as many dashes and gap segments to the function as you want. The function expects you to pass an even number of values. If you pass an odd number of values, this will result in values that are concatenated to make them even in number. For example, if you use segments(20px, 10px, 5px), it is the same as if you passed segments(20px, 10px, 5px, 20px, 10px, 5px).

The phase parameter is applicable only when you use the segments() function. The number following the phase parameter specifies the offset into the dashed pattern that corresponds to the beginning of the stroke. Consider the following style:

```
-fx-border-style: segments(20px, 5px) phase 10.0;
```

It specifies the phase parameter as 10.0. The length of the dashing pattern is 25px. The first segment will start at 10px from the beginning of the pattern. That is, the first dash will only be 10px in length. The second segment will be a 5px gap followed by a 20px dash, and so on. The default value for phase is 0.0.

The <stroke-type> has three valid values: centered, inside, and outside. Its value determines where the border is drawn relative to the inset. Assume that you have a 200px by 200px region. Assume that you have specified the top inset as 10px and a top border width of 4px. If <stroke-type> is specified as centered, the border thickness at the top will occupy the area from the eighth pixel to the 12th pixel from the top boundary of the region. For <stroke-type> as inside, the border thickness will occupy the area from the 10th pixel to 14th pixel. For <stroke-type> as outside, the border thickness at the top will occupy the area from the sixth pixel to the tenth pixel.

You can specify how the two segments of the borders are joined using the line-join parameter. Its value can be miter, bevel, or round. If you specify the value of line-join as miter, you need to pass a miter limit value. If the specified miter limit is less than the miter length, a bevel join is used instead. Miter length is the distance between the inner point and the outer point of a miter join. Miter length is measured in terms of the border width. The miter limit parameter specifies how far the outside edges of two meeting border segments can extend to form a miter join. For example, suppose the miter length is 5 and you specify the miter limit as 4, a bevel join is used; however, if you specify a miter limit greater than 5, a miter join is used. The following style uses a miter limit of 30:

```
-fx-border-style: solid line-join miter 30;
```

The value for the line-cap parameter specifies how the start and end of a border segment are drawn. The valid values are square, butt, and round. The following style specified a line-cap of round:

```
-fx-border-style: solid line-join bevel 30 line-cap round;
```

Let's look at some examples. Figure 8-6 shows four instances of the Pane class of 100px by 50px, when the following styles are applied to them:

```
.my-style-1 {
        -fx-border-color: black;
        -fx-border-width: 5;
        -fx-border-radius: 0;
        -fx-border-insets: 0;
        -fx-border-style: solid line-join bevel line-cap square;
}

.my-style-2 {
        -fx-border-color: red, black;
        -fx-border-width: 5, 5;
        -fx-border-radius: 0, 0;
        -fx-border-insets: 0, 5;
        -fx-border-style: solid inside, dotted outside;
}

.my-style-3 {
        -fx-border-color: black, black;
        -fx-border-width: 1, 1;
        -fx-border-radius: 0, 0;
        -fx-border-insets: 0, 5;
        -fx-border-style: solid centered, solid centered;
}

.my-style-4 {
        -fx-border-color: red black red black;
        -fx-border-width: 5;
        -fx-border-radius: 0;
        -fx-border-insets: 0;
        -fx-border-style: solid line-join bevel line-cap round;
}
```

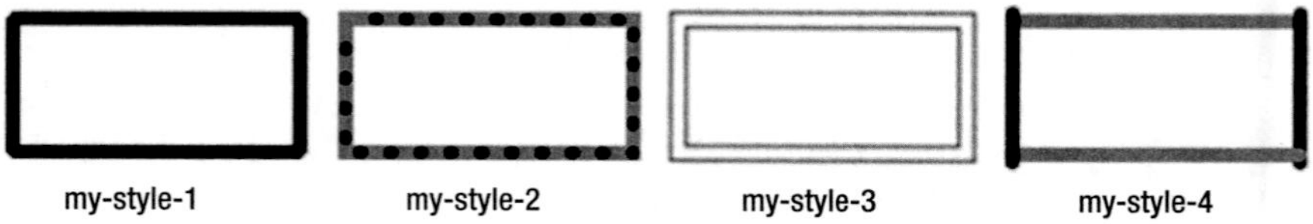

my-style-1   my-style-2   my-style-3   my-style-4

Figure 8-6. *Using border styles*

Notice that the second style achieves overlapping of two borders, one in solid red and one in dotted black, by specifying the appropriate insets and stroke type (inside and outside). Borders are drawn in the order they are specified. It is important that you draw the solid border first in this case; otherwise, you would not see the dotted border. The third one draws two borders, giving it the look of a double border type.

■ **Tip** A Region can also have a background image and a border image specified through CSS. Please refer to the *JavaFX CSS Reference Guide*, which is available online, for more details. Many other CSS styles are supported by nodes in JavaFX. The styles for those nodes will be discussed later in this book.

Understanding Style Selectors

Each style in a style sheet has an associated *selector* that identifies the nodes in the scene graph to which the associated JavaFX CSS property values are applied. JavaFX CSS supports several types of selectors: class selectors, pseudo-class selectors, ID selectors, among others. Let's look at some of these selector types briefly.

Using Class Selectors

The Node class defines a styleClass variable that is an ObservableList<String>. Its purpose is to maintain a list of JavaFX style class names for a node. Note that the JavaFX class name and the style class name of a node are two different things. A JavaFX class name of a node is a Java class name, for example, javafx.scene.layout.VBox, or simply VBox, which is used to create objects of that class. A style class name of a node is a string name that is used in CSS styling.

You can assign multiple CSS class names to a node. The following snippet of code assigns two style class names, "hbox" and "myhbox", to an HBox:

```
HBox hb = new HBox();
hb.getStyleClass().addAll("hbox", "myhbox");
```

A style class selector applies the associated style to all nodes, which have the same style class name as the name of the selector. A style class selector starts with a period followed by the style class name. Note that the style class names of nodes do not start with a period.

Listing 8-7 shows the content of a style sheet. It has two styles. Both styles use style class selectors because both of them start with a period. The first style class selector is "hbox", which means it will match all nodes with a style class named hbox. The second style uses the style class name as button. Save the style sheet in a file named resources\css\styleclass.css in the CLASSPATH.

Listing 8-7. A Style Sheet with Two Style Class Selectors Named hbox and button

```
.hbox {
        -fx-border-color: blue;
        -fx-border-width: 2px;
        -fx-border-radius: 5px;
        -fx-border-insets: 5px;
        -fx-padding: 10px;
        -fx-spacing: 5px;
        -fx-background-color: lightgray;
        -fx-background-insets: 5px;
}

.button {
        -fx-text-fill: blue;
}
```

Listing 8-8 has the complete program to demonstrate the use of the style class selectors hbox and button. The resulting screen is shown in Figure 8-7.

Listing 8-8. Using Style Class Selectors in Code

```java
// StyleClassTest.java
package com.jdojo.style;

import javafx.application.Application;
import javafx.application.Platform;
import javafx.scene.Scene;
import javafx.scene.control.Button;
import javafx.scene.control.Label;
import javafx.scene.control.TextField;
import javafx.scene.layout.HBox;
import javafx.stage.Stage;

public class StyleClassTest extends Application {
        public static void main(String[] args) {
                Application.launch(args);
        }

        @Override
        public void start(Stage stage) {
                Label nameLbl = new Label("Name:");
                TextField nameTf = new TextField("");
                Button closeBtn  = new Button("Close");
                closeBtn.setOnAction(e -> Platform.exit());

                HBox root = new HBox();
                root.getChildren().addAll(nameLbl, nameTf, closeBtn);

                // Set the styleClass for the HBox to "hbox"
                root.getStyleClass().add("hbox");

                Scene scene = new Scene(root);
                scene.getStylesheets().add("resources/css/styleclass.css");

                stage.setScene(scene);
                stage.setTitle("Using Style Class Selectors");
                stage.show();
        }
}
```

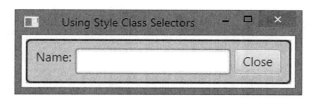

Figure 8-7. *An HBox using border, padding, spacing, and background color from a style sheet*

Notice that you have set the style class name for the HBox (named root in the code) to "hbox", which will apply CSS properties to the HBox from the style with the class selector hbox. The text color of the Close button is blue because of the second style with the style class selector button. You did not set the style class name for the Close button to "button". The Button class adds a style class, which is named "button", to all its instances. This is the reason that the Close button was selected by the button style class selector.

Most of the commonly used controls in JavaFX have a default style class name. You can add more style class names if needed. The default style class names are constructed from the JavaFX class names. The JavaFX class name is converted to lowercase and a hyphen is inserted in the middle of two words. If the JavaFX class name consists of only one word, the corresponding default style class name is created by just converting it to lowercase. For example, the default style class name is button for Button, label for Label, hyperlink for Hyperlink, text-field for TextField, text-area for TextArea, check-box for CheckBox.

JavaFX container classes, for example, Region, Pane, HBox, VBox, do not have a default style class name. If you want to style them using style class selectors, you need to add a style class name to them. This is the reason that you had to add a style class name to the HBox that you used in Listing 8-8 to use the style class selector.

▨ **Tip**   Style class names in JavaFX are case-sensitive.

Sometimes you might need to know the default style class name of a node to use it in a style sheet. There are three ways to determine the default style class name of a JavaFX node:

- Guess it using the described rules to form the default style class name from the JavaFX class name;

- Use the online *JavaFX CSS Reference Guide* to look up the name;

- Write a small piece of code.

The following snippet of code shows how to print the default style class name for the Button class. Change the name of the JavaFX node class, for example, from Button to TextField, to print the default style class name for other types of nodes:

```
Button btn = new Button();
ObservableList<String> list = btn.getStyleClass();

if (list.isEmpty()) {
        System.out.println("No default style class name");
} else {
        for(String styleClassName : list) {
                System.out.println(styleClassName);
        }
}
```

```
button
```

Class Selector for the *root* Node

The root node of a scene is assigned a style class named "root". You can use the root style class selector for CSS properties that are inherited by other nodes. The root node is the parent of all nodes in a scene graph. Storing CSS properties in the root node is preferred because they can be looked up from any node in the scene graph.

Listing 8-9 shows the content of a style sheet saved in a file resources\css\rootclass.css. The style with the root class selector declares two properties: -fx-cursor and -my-button-color. The -fx-cursor property is inherited by all nodes. If this style sheet is attached to a scene, all nodes will have a HAND cursor unless they override it. The -my-button-color property is a look-up property, which is looked up in the second style to set the text color of buttons.

Listing 8-9. The Content of the Style Sheet with Root as a Style Class Selector

```
.root {
        -fx-cursor: hand;
        -my-button-color: blue;
}

.button {
        -fx-text-fill: -my-button-color;
}
```

Run the program in Listing 8-10 to see the effects of these changes. Notice that you get a HAND cursor when you move the mouse anywhere in the scene, except over the name text field. This is because the TextField class overrides the -fx-cursor CSS property to set it to the TEXT cursor.

Listing 8-10. Using the Root Style Class Selector

```
// RootClassTest.java
package com.jdojo.style;

import javafx.application.Application;
import javafx.scene.Scene;
import javafx.scene.control.Button;
import javafx.scene.control.Label;
import javafx.scene.control.TextField;
import javafx.scene.layout.HBox;
import javafx.stage.Stage;

public class RootClassTest extends Application {
        public static void main(String[] args) {
                Application.launch(args);
        }

        @Override
        public void start(Stage stage) {
                Label nameLbl = new Label("Name:");
                TextField nameTf = new TextField("");
                Button closeBtn = new Button("Close");
```

```
        HBox root = new HBox();
        root.getChildren().addAll(nameLbl, nameTf, closeBtn);

        Scene scene = new Scene(root);
        /* The root variable is assigned a default style class name "root" */

        scene.getStylesheets().add("resources/css/rootclass.css");

        stage.setScene(scene);
        stage.setTitle("Using the root Style Class Selector");
        stage.show();
    }
}
```

Using ID Selectors

The Node class has an id property of the StringProperty type, which can be used to assign a unique id to each node in a scene graph. Maintaining the uniqueness of an id in a scene graph is the responsibility of the developer. It is not an error to set a duplicate id for a node.

You do not use the id property of a node directly in your code, except when you are setting it. It is mainly used for styling nodes using ID selectors. The following snippet of code sets the id property of a Button to "closeBtn":

```
Button b1 = new Button("Close");
b1.setId("closeBtn");
```

An ID selector in a style sheet is preceded by the pound (#) sign. Note that the ID value set for a node does not include the # sign. Listing 8-11 shows the content of a style sheet, which contains two styles, one with a class selector ".button" and one with an ID selector "#closeButton". Save the content of Listing 8-11 in a file called resources\css\idselector.css in the CLASSPATH. Figure 8-8 shows the results after the program is run.

Listing 8-11. A Style Sheet that Uses a Class Selector and an ID Selector

```
.button {
        -fx-text-fill: blue;
}

#closeButton {
        -fx-text-fill: red;
}
```

Listing 8-12 presents the program that uses the style sheet in Listing 8-11. The program creates three buttons. It sets the ID for a button to "closeButton". The other two buttons do not have an ID. When the program is run, the Close button's text is in red, whereas the other two have blue text.

Listing 8-12. Using ID Selector in a Style Sheet

```java
// IDSelectorTest.java
package com.jdojo.style;

import javafx.application.Application;
import javafx.scene.Scene;
import javafx.scene.control.Button;
import javafx.scene.layout.HBox;
import javafx.stage.Stage;

public class IDSelectorTest extends Application {
        public static void main(String[] args) {
                Application.launch(args);
        }

        @Override
        public void start(Stage stage) {
                Button openBtn = new Button("Open");
                Button saveBtn = new Button("Save");

                Button closeBtn = new Button("Close");
                closeBtn.setId("closeButton");

                HBox root = new HBox();
                root.getChildren().addAll(openBtn, saveBtn, closeBtn);

                Scene scene = new Scene(root);
                scene.getStylesheets().add("resources/css/idselector.css");

                stage.setScene(scene);
                stage.setTitle("Using ID selectors");
                stage.show();
        }
}
```

Figure 8-8. Buttons using class and ID selectors

Did you notice a conflict in the styles for the Close button? All buttons in JavaFX are assigned a default style class named button, so does the Close button. The Close button also has an ID that matches with the ID style selector. Therefore, both selectors in the style sheet match the Close button. In cases where there are multiple selectors matching a node, JavaFX uses the *specificity of selectors* to determine which selector will be used. In cases where a class selector and an ID selector are used, the ID selector has higher specificity. This is the reason that the ID selector matched the Close button, not the class selector.

■ **Tip** CSS uses complex rules to calculate the specificity of selectors. Please refer to
http://www.w3.org/TR/CSS21/cascade.html#specificity for more details.

Combining ID and Class Selectors

A selector can use the combination of a style class and an ID. In this case, the selector matches all nodes with the specified style class and ID. Consider the following style:

```
#closeButton.button {
        -fx-text-fill: red;
}
```

The selector #closeButton.button matches all nodes with a closeButton ID and a button style class. You can also reverse the order:

```
.button#closeButton {
        -fx-text-fill: red;
}
```

Now it matches all nodes with a button style class and a closeButton ID.

The Universal Selector

An asterisk (*) is used as a universal selector, which matches any node. The universal selector has the lowest specificity. The following style uses the universal selector to set the text fill property of all nodes to blue:

```
* {
        -fx-text-fill: blue;
}
```

When the universal selector does not appear by itself, it can be ignored. For example, the selectors *.button and .button are the same.

Grouping Multiple Selectors

If the same CSS properties apply to multiple selectors, you have two choices:

- You can use multiple styles by duplicating the property declarations.
- You can group all selectors into one style, separating the selectors by a comma.

Suppose you want to set the button and label classes text fill color to blue. The following code uses two styles with the duplicate property declarations:

```
.button {
        -fx-text-fill: blue;
}
.label {
        -fx-text-fill: blue;
}
```

The two styles can be combined into one style as follows:

```
.button, .label {
        -fx-text-fill: blue;
}
```

Descendant Selectors

A descendant selector is used to match nodes that are descendants of another node in the scene graph. A descendant selector consists of two or more selectors separated by whitespaces. The following style uses a descendant selector:

```
.hbox .button {
        -fx-text-fill: blue;
}
```

It will select all nodes that have a button style class and are descendants of a node with an hbox style class. The term *descendant* in this context means a child at any level (immediate or nonimmediate).

A descendant selector comes in handy when you want to style parts of JavaFX controls. Many controls in JavaFX consist of subnodes, which are JavaFX nodes. In the *JavaFX CSS Reference Guide*, those subnodes are listed as substructures. For example, a CheckBox consists of a LabeledText (not part of the public API) with a style class name of text and a StackPane with a style class name of box. The box contains another StackPane with the style class name of mark. You can use these pieces of information for the substructure of the CheckBox class to style the subparts. The following styles use descendant selectors to set the text color of all CheckBox instances to blue and the box to a dotted border:

```
.check-box .text {
        -fx-fill: blue;
}
```

```
.check-box .box {
        -fx-border-color: black;
        -fx-border-width: 1px;
        -fx-border-style: dotted;
}
```

Child Selectors

A child selector matches a child node. It consists of two or more selectors separated by the greater than sign (>). The following style matches all nodes with a button style class, which are the children of a node with an hbox style class:

```
.hbox > .button {
        -fx-text-fill: blue;
}
```

■ **Tip**   CSS supports other types of selectors, for example, sibling selectors and attribute selectors. JavaFX CSS does not support them yet.

State-Based Selectors

State-based selectors are also known as *pseudo-class* selectors. A pseudo-class selector matches nodes based on their current states, for example, matching a node that has focus or matching text input controls that are read-only. A pseudo-class is preceded by a colon and is appended to an existing selector. For example, .button:focused is a pseudo-class selector that matches a node with the button style class name that also has the focus; #openBtn:hover is another pseudo-class selector that matches a node with the ID #openBtn, when the mouse hovers over the node. Listing 8-13 presents the content of a style sheet that has a pseudo-class selector. It changes the text color to red when the mouse hovers over the node. When you add this style sheet to a scene, all buttons will change their text color to red when the mouse hovers over them.

Listing 8-13. A Style Sheet with a Pseudo-class Selector

```
.button:hover {
        -fx-text-fill: red;
}
```

JavaFX CSS does not support the :first-child and :lang pseudo-classes that are supported by CSS. JavaFX does not support *pseudo-elements* that allow you to style the content of nodes (e.g., the first line in a TextArea). Table 8-1 contains a partial list of the pseudo-classes supported by JavaFX CSS. Please refer to the online *JavaFX CSS Reference Guide* for the complete list of pseudo-classes supported by JavaFX CSS.

Table 8-1. *Some Pseudo-classes Supported by JavaFX CSS*

Pseudo-class	Applies to	Description
disabled	Node	It applies when the node is disabled.
focused	Node	It applies when the node has the focus.
hover	Node	It applies when the mouse hovers over the node.
pressed	Node	It applies when the mouse button is clicked over the node.
show-mnemonic	Node	It applies when the mnemonic should be shown.
cancel	Button	It applies when the Button would receive VK_ESC if the event is not consumed.
default	Button	It applies when the Button would receive VK_ENTER if the event is not consumed.
empty	Cell	It applies when the Cell is empty.
filled	Cell	It applies when the Cell is not empty.
selected	Cell, CheckBox	It applies when the node is selected.
determinate	CheckBox	It applies when the CheckBox is in a determinate state.
indeterminate	CheckBox	It applies when the CheckBox is in an indeterminate state.
visited	Hyperlink	It applies when the Hyperlink has been visited.
horizontal	ListView	It applies when the node is horizontal.
vertical	ListView	It applies when the node is vertical.

Using JavaFX Class Names as Selectors

It is allowed, but not recommended, to use the JavaFX class name as a type selector in a style. Consider the following content of a style sheet:

```
HBox {
        -fx-border-color: blue;
        -fx-border-width: 2px;
        -fx-border-insets: 10px;
        -fx-padding: 10px;
}

Button {
        -fx-text-fill: blue;
}
```

Notice that a type selector differs from a class selector in that the former does not start with a period. A class selector is the JavaFX class name of the node without any modification (HBOX and HBox are not the same). If you attach a style sheet with the above content to a scene, all HBox instances will have a border and all Button instances will have blue text.

It is not recommended to use the JavaFX class names as type selectors because the class name may be different when you subclass a JavaFX class. If you depend on the class name in your style sheet, the new classes will not pick up your styles.

Looking Up Nodes in a Scene Graph

You can look up a node in a scene graph by using a selector. Scene and Node classes have a lookup(String selector) method, which returns the reference of the first node found with the specified selector. If no node is found, it returns null. The methods in two classes work a little differently. The method in the Scene class searches the entire scene graph. The method in the Node class searches the node on which it is called and its subnodes. The Node class also has a lookupAll(String selector) method that returns a Set of all Nodes that are matched by the specified selector, including the node on which this method is called and its subnode.

The following snippet of code shows how to use the look-up methods using ID selectors. However, you are not limited to using only ID selectors in these methods. You can use all selectors that are valid in JavaFX:

```
Button b1 = new Button("Close");
b1.setId("closeBtn");
VBox root = new VBox();
root.setId("myvbox");
root.getChildren().addAll(b1);
Scene scene = new Scene(root, 200, 300);
...
Node n1 = scene.lookup("#closeBtn");        // n1 is the reference of b1
Node n2 = root.lookup("#closeBtn");         // n2 is the reference of b1
Node n3 = b1.lookup("#closeBtn");           // n3 is the reference of b1
Node n4 = root.lookup("#myvbox");           // n4 is the reference of root
Node n5 = b1.lookup("#myvbox");             // n5 is null
Set<Node> s = root.lookupAll("#closeBtn");  // s contains the reference of b1
```

Using Compiled Style Sheets

When packaging JavaFX projects, you can convert the CSS files into binary form to improve the runtime performance of your application. The `.css` files are converted to `.bss` files. You can convert CSS files into binary form using the `javafxpackager` tool with `-createbss` command:

```
javafxpackager -createbss -srcfiles mystyles.css -outdir compiledcss
```

If you are using the NetBeans IDE, you can select the Project Properties ➤ Build ➤ Packaging ➤ Binary Encode JavaFX CSS Files property, which will convert all your CSS files into BSS files while packaging your project.

Summary

CSS is a language used to describe the presentation of UI elements in a GUI application. It was primarily used in web pages for styling HTML elements and separating presentation from contents and behavior. In a typical web page, the content and presentation are defined using HTML and CSS, respectively.

JavaFX allows you to define the look of JavaFX applications using CSS. You can define UI elements using JavaFX class libraries or FXML, and use CSS to define their look.

A CSS rule is also known as a style. A collection of CSS rules is known as a style sheet. Skins are collections of application-specific styles, which define the appearance of an application. Skinning is the process of changing the appearance of an application (or the skin) on the fly. JavaFX does not provide a specific mechanism for skinning. Themes are visual characteristics of an operating system that are reflected in the appearance of UI elements of all applications. JavaFX has no direct support for themes.

You can add multiple style sheets to a JavaFX application. Style sheets are added to a scene or parents. Scene and Parent classes maintain an observable list of string URLs linking to style sheets.

JavaFX 8 use a default style sheet called Modena. Prior to JavaFX 8, the default style sheet was called Caspian. You can still use the Caspian style sheet as the default in JavaFX 8 using the static method `setUserAgentStylesheet(String url)` of the Application class. You can refer to the Caspian and Modena stylesheets' URLs using the constants named `STYLESHEET_CASPIAN` and `STYLESHEET_MODENA` defined in the Application class.

It is common for the visual properties of nodes to come from multiple sources. The JavaFX runtime uses the following priority rules to set the visual properties of a node: inline style (the highest priority), parent style sheets, scene style sheets, values set in the code using JavaFX API, and user agent style sheets (the lowest priority).

JavaFX offers two types of inheritance for CSS properties: CSS property types and CSS property values. In the first type of inheritance, all CSS properties declared in a JavaFX class are inherited by all its subclasses. In the second type of inheritance, a CSS property for a node may inherit its value from its parent. The parent of a node is the container of the node in the scene graph, not its JavaFX superclass.

Each style in a style sheet has a selector that identifies the nodes in the scene graph to which the style is applied. JavaFX CSS supports several types of selectors: class selectors and most of them work the same way they do in web browsers. You can look up a node in a scene graph by using a selector and the `lookup(String selector)` method of the Scene and Node classes.

The next chapter will discuss how to handle events in a JavaFX application.

CHAPTER 9

■ ■ ■

Event Handling

In this chapter, you will learn:

- What an event is
- What an event source, an event target, and event type are
- About the event processing mechanism
- How to handle events using event filters and event handlers
- How to handle mouse events, key events, and window events

What Is an Event?

In general, the term *event* is used to describe an occurrence of interest. In a GUI application, an event is an occurrence of a user interaction with the application. Clicking the mouse and pressing a key on the keyboard are examples of events in a JavaFX application.

An event in JavaFX is represented by an object of the javafx.event.Event class or any of its subclasses. Every event in JavaFX has three properties:

- An event source
- An event target
- An event type

When an event occurs in an application, you typically perform some processing by executing a piece of code. The piece of code that is executed in response to an event is known as an *event handler* or an *event filter*. I will clarify the difference between these shortly. For now, think of both as a piece of code and I will refer to both of them as event handlers. When you want to handle an event for a UI element, you need to add event handlers to the UI element, for example, a Window, a Scene, or a Node. When the UI element detects the event, it executes your event handlers.

The UI element that calls event handlers is the source of the event for those event handlers. When an event occurs, it passes through a chain of event dispatchers. The source of an event is the current element in the event dispatcher chain. The event source changes as the event passes through one dispatcher to another in the event dispatcher chain.

The event target is the destination of an event. The event target determines the route through which the event travels during its processing. Suppose a mouse click occurs over a Circle node. In this case, the Circle node is the event target of the mouse-clicked event.

The event type describes the type of the event that occurs. Event types are defines in a hierarchical fashion. Each event type has a name and a supertype.

The three properties that are common to all events in JavaFX are represented by objects of three different classes. Specific events define additional event properties; for example, the event class to represent a mouse event adds properties to describe the location of the mouse cursor, state of the mouse buttons, among others. Table 9-1 lists the classes and interfaces involved in event processing. JavaFX has an event delivery mechanism that defines the details of the occurrence and processing of events. I will discuss all of these in detail in subsequent sections.

Table 9-1. *Classes Involved in Event Processing*

Name	Class/Interface	Description
Event	Class	An instance of this class represents an event. Several subclasses of the Event class exist to represent specific types of events.
EventTarget	Interface	An instance of this interface represents an event target.
EventType	Class	An instance of this class represents an event type, for example, mouse pressed, mouse released, mouse moved.
EventHandler	Interface	An instance of this interface represents an event handler or an event filter. Its handle() method is called when the event for which it has been registered occurs.

Event Class Hierarchy

Classes representing events in JavaFX are arranged in hierarchical fashion through class inheritance. Figure 9-1 shows a partial class diagram for the Event class. The Event class is at the top of the class hierarchy and it inherits from java.util.EventObject class, which is not shown in the diagram.

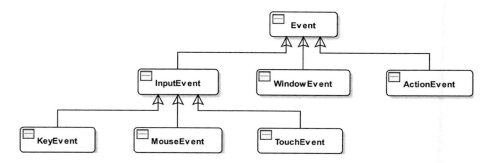

Figure 9-1. *A partial class hierarchy for the javafx.event.Event class*

Subclasses of the Event class represent specific types of events. Sometimes a subclass of the Event class is used to represent a generic event of some kind. For example, the InputEvent class represents a generic event to indicate a user input event, whereas the KeyEvent and MouseEvent classes represent specific input events such as the user input from the keyboard and mouse, respectively. An object of the WindowEvent class represents an event of a window, for example, showing and hiding of the window. An object of the ActionEvent is used to represent several kinds of events denoting some type of action, for example, firing a button or a menu item. Firing of a button may happen if the user clicks it with the mouse, presses some keys, or touches it on the touch screen.

The Event class provides properties and methods that are common to all events. The getSource() method returns an Object, which is the source of the event. The Event class inherits this method from the EventObject class. The getTarget() method returns an instance of the EventTarget interface, which is the target of the event. The getEventType() method returns an object of the EventType class, which indicates the type of the event.

The Event class contains consume() and isConsumed() methods. As noted before, an event travels from one element to another in an event-dispatching chain. Calling the consume() method on an Event object indicates that the event has been consumed and no further processing is required. After the consume() method is called, the event does not travel to the next element in the event-processing chain. The isConsumed() method returns true if the consume() method has been called, otherwise, it returns false.

Specific Event subclasses define more properties and methods. For example, the MouseEvent class defines getX() and getY() methods that return the x and y coordinates of the mouse cursor relative to the source of the event. I'll explain the details of the methods in event-specific classes when I discuss them later in this chapter or subsequent chapters.

Event Targets

An *event target* is a UI element (not necessarily just Nodes) that can respond to events. Technically, a UI element that wants to respond to events must implement the EventTarget interface. That is, in JavaFX, implementing the EventTarget interface makes a UI element eligible to be an event target.

The Window, Scene, and Node classes implement the EventTarget interface. This means that all nodes, including windows and scenes, can respond to events. The classes for some UI elements, for example, Tab, TreeItem, and MenuItem, do not inherit from the Node class. They can still respond to events because they implement the EventTarget interface. If you develop a custom UI element, you will need to implement this interface if you want your UI element to respond to events.

The responsibility of an event target is to build a chain of event dispatchers, which is also called the *event route*. An *event dispatcher* is an instance of the EventDispatcher interface. Each dispatcher in the chain can affect the event by handling and consuming. An event dispatcher in the chain can also modify the event properties, substitute the event with a new event, or chain the event route. Typically, an event target route consists of dispatchers associated with all UI elements in the container-child hierarchy. Suppose you have a Circle node placed in an HBox, which is placed in a Scene. The Scene is added to a Stage. If the mouse is clicked on the Circle, the Circle becomes the event target. The Circle builds an event dispatcher chain whose route will be, from head to tail, the Stage, Scene, HBox, and Circle.

Event Types

An instance of the EventType class defines an event type. Why do you need a separate class to define event types? Aren't separate event classes, for example, KeyEvent, MouseEvent, for each event sufficient to define event types? Can't you distinguish one event from another based on the event class? The EventType class is used to further classify the events within an event class. For example, the MouseEvent class only tells us that the user has used the mouse. It does not tell us the details of the mouse use, for example, whether the mouse was pressed, released, dragged, or clicked. The EventType class is used to classify these subevent types of an event. The EventType class is a generic class whose type parameter is defined as follows:

```
EventType<T extends Event>
```

Event types are hierarchical. They are hierarchical by implementation, not by class inheritance. Each event type has a name and a supertype. The getName() and getSuperType() methods in the EventType class return the name and supertype of an event type. The constant Event.ANY, which is the same as the constant EventType.ROOT, is the supertype of all events in JavaFX. Figure 9-2 shows a partial list of some event types that have been predefined in some event classes.

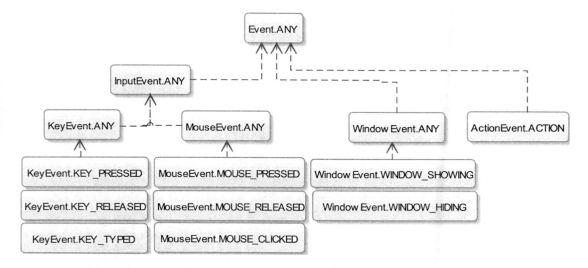

Figure 9-2. *A partial list of predefined event types for some event classes*

Note that the arrows in the diagram do not denote class inheritance. They denote dependencies. For example, the InputEvent.ANY event type depends on the Event.ANY event type, as the latter is the supertype of the former.

An event class, which has subevent types, defines an ANY event type. For example, the MouseEvent class defines an ANY event type that represents a mouse event of any type, for example, mouse released, mouse clicked, mouse moved. MOUSE_PRESSED and MOUSE_RELEASED are other event types defined in the MouseEvent class. The ANY event type in an event class is the supertype of all other event types in the same event class. For example, the MouseEvent.ANY event type is the supertype of MOUSE_RELEASED and MOUSE_PRESSED mouse events.

Event Processing Mechanism

When an event occurs, several steps are performed as part of the event processing:

- Event target selection
- Event route construction
- Event route traversal

Event Target Selection

The first step in the event processing is the selection of the event target. Recall that an event target is the destination node of an event. The event target is selected based on the event type.

For mouse events, the event target is the node at the mouse cursor. Multiple nodes can be available at the mouse cursor. For example, you can have a circle placed over a rectangle. The topmost node at the mouse cursor is selected as the event target.

The event target for key events is the node that has focus. How a node gets the focus depends on the type of the node. For example, a TextField may gain focus by clicking the mouse inside it or using the focus traversal keys such as Tab or Shift + Tab on the Windows format. Shapes such as Circles or Rectangles do not get focus by default. If you want them to receive key events, you can give them focus by calling the requestFocus() method of the Node class.

JavaFX supports touch and gesture events on touch-enabled devices. A touch event is generated by touching a touch screen. Each touch action has a point of contact called a *touch point*. It is possible to touch a touch screen with multiple fingers, resulting in multiple touch points. Each state of a touch point, for example, pressed, released, and so forth, generates a touch event. The location of the touch point determines the target of the touch event. For example, if the location of the touch event is a point within a circle, the circle becomes the target of the touch event. In case of multiple nodes at the touch point, the topmost node is selected as the target.

Users can interact with a JavaFX application using gestures. Typically, a gesture on a touch screen and a track pad consists of multiple touch points with touch actions. Examples of gesture events are rotating, scrolling, swiping, and zooming. A rotating gesture is performed by rotating two fingers around each other. A scrolling gesture is performed by dragging a finger on touch screen. A swiping gesture is performed by dragging a finger (or multiple fingers) on the touch screen in one direction. A zooming gesture is performed to scale a node by dragging two fingers apart or closer.

The target for gesture events are selected depending on the type of gesture. For direct gestures, for example, gestures performed on touch screens, the topmost node at the center point of all touch points at the start of the gesture is selected as the event target. For indirect gestures, for example, gestures performed on a track pad, the topmost node at the mouse cursor is selected as the event target.

Event Route Construction

An event travels through event dispatchers in an event dispatch chain. The event dispatch chain is the *event route*. The initial and default routes for an event are determined by the event target. The default event route consists of the container-children path starting at the stage to the event target node.

Suppose you have placed a Circle and a Rectangle in an HBox and the HBox is the root node of the Scene of a Stage. When you click the Circle, the Circle becomes the event target. The Circle constructs the default event route, which is the path starting at the stage to the event target (the Circle).

In fact, an event route consists of event dispatchers that are associated with nodes. However, for all practical and understanding purposes, you can think of the event route as the path comprising the nodes. Typically, you do not deal with event dispatchers directly.

Figure 9-3 shows the event route for the mouse-clicked event. The nodes on the event route have been shown in gray background fills. The nodes on the event route are connected by solid lines. Note that the Rectangle that is part of the scene graph is not part of the event path when the Circle is clicked.

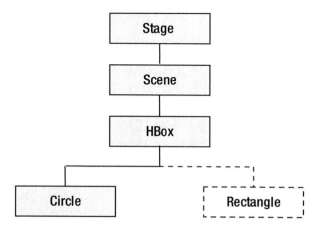

Figure 9-3. *Construction of the default event route for an event*

An event dispatch chain (or event route) has a *head* and a *tail*. In Figure 9-3, the Stage and the Circle are the head and the tail of the event dispatch chain, respectively. The initial event route may be modified as the event processing progresses. Typically, but not necessarily, the event passes through all nodes in its route twice during the event traversal step, as described in the next section.

Event Route Traversal

An event route traversal consists of two phases:

- Capture phase
- Bubbling phase

An event travels through each node in its route twice: once during the capture phase and once during the bubbling phase. You can register event filters and event handlers to a node for specific events types. The event filters and event handlers registered to a node are executed as the event passes through the node during the capture phase and the bubbling phase, respectively. The event filters and handlers are passed in the reference of the current node as the source of the event. As the event travels from one node to another, the event source keeps changing. However, the event target remains the same from the start to the finish of the event route traversal.

During the route traversal, a node can consume the event in event filters or handlers, thus completing the processing of the event. Consuming an event is simply calling the consume() method on the event object. When an event is consumed, the event processing is stopped, even though some of the nodes in the route were not traversed at all.

Event Capture Phase

During the capture phase, an event travels from the head to the tail of its event dispatch chain. Figure 9-4 shows the traveling of a mouse-clicked event for the Circle in our example in the capture phase. The down arrows in the figure denote the direction of the event travel. As the event passes through a node, the registered event filters for the node are executed. Note that the event capture phase executes only event filters, not event handlers, for the current node.

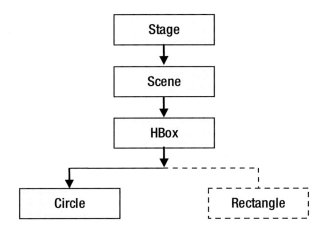

Figure 9-4. *The event capture phase*

In Figure 9-4, the event filters for the Stage, Scene, HBox, and Circle are executed in order, assuming none of the event filters consumes the event.

You can register multiple event filters for a node. If the node consumes the event in one of its event filters, its other event filters, which have not been executed yet, are executed before the event processing stops. Suppose you have registered five event filters for the Scene in our example, and the first event filter that is executed consumes the event. In this case, the other four event filters for the Scene will still be executed. After executing the fifth event filter for the Scene, the event processing will stop, without the event traveling to the remaining nodes (HBox and Circle).

In the event capture phase, you can intercept events (and provide a generic response) that are targeted at the children of a node. For example, you can add event filters for the mouse-clicked event to the Stage in our example to intercept all mouse-clicked events for all its children. You can block events from reaching their targets by consuming the event in event filters for a parent node. For example, if you consume the mouse-clicked event in a filter for the Stage, the event will not reach its target, in our example, the Circle.

Event Bubbling Phase

During the bubbling phase, an event travels from the tail to the head of its event dispatch chain. Figure 9-5 shows the traveling of a mouse-clicked event for the Circle in the bubbling phase.

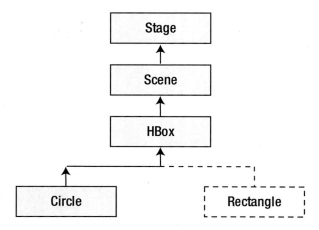

Figure 9-5. *The event bubbling phase*

The up arrows in Figure 9-5 denote the direction of the event travel. As the event passes through a node, the registered event handlers for the node are executed. Note that the event bubbling phase executes event handlers for the current node, whereas the event capture phase executes the event filters.

In our example, the event handlers for the Circle, HBox, Scene, and Stage are executed in order, assuming none of the event filters consumes the event. Note that the event bubbling phase starts at the target of the event and travels up to the topmost parent in the parent-children hierarchy.

You can register multiple event handlers for a node. If the node consumes the event in one of its event handlers, its other event handlers, which have not been executed yet, are executed before the event processing stops. Suppose you have registered five event handlers for the Circle in our example, and the first event handler that is executed consumes the event. In this case, the other four event handlers for the Circle will still be executed. After executing the fifth event handler for the Circle, the event processing will stop, without the event traveling to the remaining nodes (HBox, Scene, and Stage).

Typically, event handlers are registered to target nodes to provide a specific response to events. Sometimes event handlers are installed on parent nodes to provide a default event response for all its children. If an event target decides to provide a specific response to the event, it can do so by adding event handlers and consuming the event, thus blocking the event from reaching the parent nodes in the event bubbling phase.

Let's look at a trivial example. Suppose you want to display a message box to the user when he clicks anywhere inside a window. You can register an event handler to the window to display the message box. When the user clicks inside a circle in the window, you want to display a specific message. You can register an event handler to the circle to provide the specific message and consume the event. This will provide a specific event response when the circle is clicked, whereas for other nodes, the window provides a default event response.

Handling Events

Handling an event means executing the application logic in response to the occurrence of the event. The application logic is contained in the event filters and handlers, which are objects of the EventHandler interface, as shown in the following code:

```
public interface EventHandler<T extends Event> extends EventListener
        void handle(T event);
}
```

The EventHandler class is a generic class in the javafx.event package. It extends the EventListener marker interface, which is in the java.util package. The handle() method receives the reference of the event object, for example, the reference of the KeyEvent, MouseEvent, among others.

Both event filters and handlers are objects of the same EventHandler interface. You cannot tell whether an EventHandler object is an event filter or an event handler by just looking at it. In fact, you can register the same EventHandler object as event filters as well as handlers at the same time. The distinction between the two is made when they are registered to a node. Nodes provide different methods to register them. Internally, nodes know whether an EventHandler object was registered as an event filter or a handler. Another distinction between them is made based on the event traversal phase in which they are called. During the event capture phase, the handle() method of registered filters is called, whereas the handle() method of registered handlers is called in the event bubbling phase.

▪ Tip In essence, handling an event means writing the application logic for EventHandler objects and registering them to nodes as event filters, handlers, or both.

Creating Event Filters and Handlers

Creating event filters and handlers is as simple as creating objects of the class that implement the EventHandler interface. Before Java 8, you would use inner classes to create event filters and handlers, as in the following code:

```
EventHandler<MouseEvent> aHandler = new EventHandler<MouseEvent>() {
        @Override
        public void handle(MouseEvent e) {
                /* Event handling code goes here */
        }
};
```

Starting in Java 8, using lambda expressions is the best choice for creating the event filters and handlers, as in the following code:

```
EventHandler<MouseEvent> aHandler = e -> /* Event handling code goes here */;
```

I use lambda expressions in this book to create event filters and handlers. If you are not familiar with lambda expressions in Java 8, I suggest you learn at least the basics so you can understand the event handling code.

The following snippet of code creates a MouseEvent handler. It prints the type of the mouse event that occurs:

```
EventHandler<MouseEvent> mouseEventHandler =
        e -> System.out.println("Mouse event type: " + e.getEventType());
```

Registering Event Filters and Handlers

If you want a node to process events of specific types, you need to register event filters and handlers for those event types to the node. When the event occurs, the handle() method of the registered event filters and handlers for the node are called following the rules discussed in the previous sections. If the node is no longer interested in processing the events, you need to unregister the event filters and handlers from the node. Registering and unregistering event filters and handlers are also known as adding and removing event filters and handlers, respectively.

JavaFX provides two ways to register and unregister event filters and handlers to nodes:

- Using the addEventFilter(), addEventHandler(), removeEventFilter(), and removeEventHandler() methods

- Using the onXXX convenience properties

Using *addXXX()* and *removeXXX()* Methods

You can use the addEventFilter() and addEventHandler() methods to register event filters and handlers to nodes, respectively. These methods are defined in the Node class, Scene class, and Window class. Some classes (e.g., MenuItem and TreeItem) can be event targets; however, they are not inherited from the Node class. The classes provide only the addEventHandler() method for event handlers registration, such as:

- <T extends Event> void addEventFilter(EventType<T> eventType, EventHandler<? super T> eventFilter)

- <T extends Event> void addEventHandler(EventType<T> eventType, EventHandler<? super T> eventHandler)

These methods have two parameters. The first parameter is the event type and the second is an object of the EventHandler interface.

You can handle mouse-clicked events for a Circle using the following snippet of code:

```
import javafx.scene.shape.Circle;
import javafx.event.EventHandler;
import javafx.scene.input.MouseEvent;
...
Circle circle = new Circle (100, 100, 50);

// Create a MouseEvent filter
EventHandler<MouseEvent> mouseEventFilter =
                  e -> System.out.println("Mouse event filter has been called.");

// Create a MouseEvent handler
EventHandler<MouseEvent> mouseEventHandler =
                  e -> System.out.println("Mouse event handler has been called.");

// Register the MouseEvent filter and handler to the Circle
// for mouse-clicked events
circle.addEventFilter(MouseEvent.MOUSE_CLICKED, mouseEventFilter);
circle.addEventHandler(MouseEvent.MOUSE_CLICKED, mouseEventHandler);
```

This code creates two EventHandler objects, which prints a message on the console. At this stage, they are not event filters or handlers. They are just two EventHandler objects. Note that giving the reference variables names and printing messages that use the words filter and handler does not make any difference in their status as filters and handlers. The last two statements register one of the EventHandler objects as an event filter and another as an event handler; both are registered for the mouse-clicked event.

Registering the same EventHandler object as event filters as well as handlers is allowed. The following snippet of code uses one EventHandler object as the filter and handler for the Circle to handle the mouse-clicked event:

```
// Create a MouseEvent EventHandler object
EventHandler<MouseEvent> handler =
        e -> System.out.println("Mouse event filter or handler has been called.");

// Register the same EventHandler object as the MouseEvent filter and handler
// to the Circle for mouse-clicked events
circle.addEventFilter(MouseEvent.MOUSE_CLICKED, handler);
circle.addEventHandler(MouseEvent.MOUSE_CLICKED, handler);
```

■ **Tip** You can add multiple event filters and events for a node using the addEventFilter() and addEventHandler() methods. You need to call these methods once for every instance of the event filters and handlers that you want to add.

Listing 9-1 has the complete program to demonstrate the handling of the mouse-clicked events of a Circle object. It uses an event filter and an event handler. Run the program and click inside the circle. When the circle is clicked, the event filter is called first, followed by the event handler. This is evident from the output. The mouse-clicked event occurs every time you click any point inside the circle. If you click outside the circle, the mouse-clicked event still occurs; however, you do not see any output because you have not registered event filters or handlers on the HBox, Scene, and Stage.

Listing 9-1. Registering Event Filters and Handlers

```
// EventRegistration.java
package com.jdojo.event;

import javafx.application.Application;
import javafx.event.EventHandler;
import javafx.scene.Scene;
import javafx.scene.input.MouseEvent;
import javafx.scene.layout.HBox;
import javafx.scene.paint.Color;
import javafx.scene.shape.Circle;
import javafx.stage.Stage;

public class EventRegistration extends Application {
        public static void main(String[] args) {
                Application.launch(args);
        }

        @Override
        public void start(Stage stage) {
                Circle circle = new Circle (100, 100, 50);
                circle.setFill(Color.CORAL);
```

```
                    // Create a MouseEvent filter
                    EventHandler<MouseEvent> mouseEventFilter =
                            e -> System.out.println("Mouse event filter has been called.");

                    // Create a MouseEvent handler
                    EventHandler<MouseEvent> mouseEventHandler =
                            e -> System.out.println("Mouse event handler has been called.");

                    // Register the MouseEvent filter and handler to the Circle
                    // for mouse-clicked events
                    circle.addEventFilter(MouseEvent.MOUSE_CLICKED, mouseEventFilter);
                    circle.addEventHandler(MouseEvent.MOUSE_CLICKED, mouseEventHandler);

                    HBox root = new HBox();
                    root.getChildren().add(circle);
                    Scene scene = new Scene(root);
                    stage.setScene(scene);
                    stage.setTitle("Registering Event Filters and Handlers");
                    stage.show();
                    stage.sizeToScene();
            }
}
```

```
Mouse event filter has been called.
Mouse event handler has been called.
...
```

To unregister an event filter and an event handler, you need to call the removeEventFilter() and removeEventHandler() methods, respectively:

- `<T extends Event> void removeEventFilter(EventType<T> eventType, EventHandler<? super T> eventFilter)`

- `<T extends Event> void removeEventHandler(EventType<T> eventType, EventHandler<? super T> eventHandler)`

The following snippet of code adds and removes an event filter to a Circle, and later, it removes them. Note that once an EventHandler is removed from a node, its handle() method is not called when the event occurs:

```
// Create a MouseEvent EventHandler object
EventHandler<MouseEvent> handler =
        e -> System.out.println("Mouse event filter or handler has been called.");

// Register the same EventHandler object as the MouseEvent filter and handler to the Circle
// for mouse-clicked events
circle.addEventFilter(MouseEvent.MOUSE_CLICKED, handler);
circle.addEventHandler(MouseEvent.MOUSE_CLICKED, handler);

...
```

```
// At a later stage, when you are no longer interested in handling the mouse
// clicked event for the Circle, unregister the event filter and handler
circle.removeEventFilter(MouseEvent.MOUSE_CLICKED, handler);
circle.removeEventHandler(MouseEvent.MOUSE_CLICKED, handler);
```

Using *onXXX* Convenience Properties

The Node, Scene, and Window classes contain event properties to store event handlers of some selected event types. The property names use the event type pattern. They are named as onXXX. For example, the onMouseClicked property stores the event handler for the mouse-clicked event type; the onKeyTyped property stores the event handler for the key-typed event, and so on. You can use the setOnXXX() methods of these properties to register event handlers for a node. For example, use the setOnMouseClicked() method to register an event handler for the mouse-clicked event and use the setOnKeyTyped() method to register an event handler for the key-typed event, and so on. The setOnXXX() methods in various classes are known as convenience methods for registering event handlers.

You need to remember some points about the onXXX convenience properties:

- They only support the registration of event handlers, not event filters. If you need to register event filters, use the addEventFilter() method.

- They only support the registration of *one event handler* for a node. Multiple event handlers for a node may be registered using the addEventHandler() method.

- These properties exist only for the commonly used events for a node type. For example, the onMouseClicked property exists in the Node and Scene classes, but not the Window class; the onShowing property exists in the Window class, but not in the Node and Scene classes.

The program in Listing 9-2 works the same as the program in Listing 9-1. This time, you have used the onMouseClicked property of the Node class to register the mouse-clicked event handler for the circle. Notice that to register the event filter, you have to use the addEventFilter() method as before. Run the program and click inside the circle. You will get the same output you got when running the code in Listing 9-1.

Listing 9-2. Using the Convenience Event Handler Properties

```java
// EventHandlerProperties.java
package com.jdojo.event;

import javafx.application.Application;
import javafx.event.EventHandler;
import javafx.scene.Scene;
import javafx.scene.input.MouseEvent;
import javafx.scene.layout.HBox;
import javafx.scene.paint.Color;
import javafx.scene.shape.Circle;
import javafx.stage.Stage;

public class EventHandlerProperties extends Application {
        public static void main(String[] args) {
                Application.launch(args);
        }
```

```
        @Override
        public void start(Stage stage) {
                Circle circle = new Circle (100, 100, 50);
                circle.setFill(Color.CORAL);

                HBox root = new HBox();
                root.getChildren().add(circle);
                Scene scene = new Scene(root);
                stage.setScene(scene);
                stage.setTitle("Using convenience event handler properties");
                stage.show();
                stage.sizeToScene();

                // Create a MouseEvent filter
                EventHandler<MouseEvent> eventFilter =
                        e -> System.out.println("Mouse event filter has been called.");

                // Create a MouseEvent handler
                EventHandler<MouseEvent> eventHandler =
                        e -> System.out.println("Mouse event handler has been called.");

                // Register the filter using the addEventFilter() method
                circle.addEventFilter(MouseEvent.MOUSE_CLICKED, eventFilter);

                // Register the handler using the setter method for
                // the onMouseCicked convenience event property
                circle.setOnMouseClicked(eventHandler);
        }
}
```

The convenience event properties do not provide a separate method to unregister the event handler. Setting the property to null unregisters the event handler that has already been registered:

```
// Register an event handler for the mouse-clicked event
circle.setOnMouseClicked(eventHandler);

...

// Later, when you are no longer interested in processing the mouse-clicked event,
// unregister it.
circle.setOnMouseClicked(null);
```

Classes that define the onXXX event properties also define getOnXXX() getter methods that return the reference of the registered event handler. If no event handler is set, the getter method returns null.

Execution Order of Event Filters and Handlers

There are some execution order rules for event filters and handlers for both similar and different nodes:

- Event filters are called before event handlers. Event filters are executed from the topmost parent to the event target in the parent-child order. Event handlers are executed in the reverse order of the event filters. That is, the execution of the event handlers starts at the event target and moves up in the child-parent order.

- For the same node, event filters and handlers for a specific event type are called before the event filters and handlers for generic types. Suppose you have registered event handlers to a node for MouseEvent.ANY and MouseEvent.MOUSE_CLICKED. Event handlers for both event types are capable of handling mouse-clicked events. When the mouse is clicked on the node, the event handler for the MouseEvent.MOUSE_CLICKED event type is called before the event handler for the MouseEvent.ANY event type. Note that a mouse-pressed event and a mouse-released event occur before a mouse-clicked event occurs. In our example, these events will be handled by the event handler for the MouseEvent.ANY event type.

- The order in which the event filters and handlers for the same event type for a node are executed is not specified. There is one exception to this rule. Event handlers registered to a node using the addEventHandler() method are executed before the event handlers registered using the setOnXXX() convenience methods.

Listing 9-3 demonstrates the execution order of the event filters and handlers for different nodes. The program adds a Circle and a Rectangle to an HBox. The HBox is added to the Scene. An event filter and an event handler are added to the Stage, Scene, HBox, and Circle for the mouse-clicked event. Run the program and click anywhere inside the circle. The output shows the order in which filters and handlers are called. The output contains the event phase, type, target, source, and location. Notice that the source of the event changes as the event travels from one node to another. The location is relative to the event source. Because every node uses its own local coordinate system, the same point, where the mouse is clicked, has different values for (x, y) coordinates relative to different nodes.

Listing 9-3. Execution Order for Event Filters and Handlers

```
// CaptureBubblingOrder.java
package com.jdojo.event;

import javafx.application.Application;
import javafx.event.EventHandler;
import javafx.geometry.Insets;
import javafx.scene.Scene;
import javafx.scene.input.MouseEvent;
import javafx.scene.layout.HBox;
import javafx.scene.paint.Color;
import javafx.scene.shape.Circle;
import javafx.scene.shape.Rectangle;
import javafx.stage.Stage;
import static javafx.scene.input.MouseEvent.MOUSE_CLICKED;
```

If you click the rectangle, you will notice that the output shows the same path for the event through its parents as it did for the circle. The event still passes through the rectangle, which is the event target. However, you do not see any output, because you have not registered any event filters or handlers for the rectangle to output any message. You can click at any point outside the circle and rectangle to see the event target and the event path.

273

```java
public class CaptureBubblingOrder extends Application {
        public static void main(String[] args) {
                Application.launch(args);
        }

        @Override
        public void start(Stage stage) {
                Circle circle = new Circle (50, 50, 50);
                circle.setFill(Color.CORAL);

                Rectangle rect = new Rectangle(100, 100);
                rect.setFill(Color.TAN);

                HBox root = new HBox();
                root.setPadding(new Insets(20));
                root.setSpacing(20);
                root.getChildren().addAll(circle, rect);

                Scene scene = new Scene(root);

                // Create two EventHandlders
                EventHandler<MouseEvent> filter = e -> handleEvent("Capture", e);
                EventHandler<MouseEvent> handler = e -> handleEvent("Bubbling", e);

                // Register filters
                stage.addEventFilter(MOUSE_CLICKED, filter);
                scene.addEventFilter(MOUSE_CLICKED, filter);
                root.addEventFilter(MOUSE_CLICKED, filter);
                circle.addEventFilter(MOUSE_CLICKED, filter);

                // Register handlers
                stage.addEventHandler(MOUSE_CLICKED, handler);
                scene.addEventHandler(MOUSE_CLICKED, handler);
                root.addEventHandler(MOUSE_CLICKED, handler);
                circle.addEventHandler(MOUSE_CLICKED, handler);

                stage.setScene(scene);
                stage.setTitle("Event Capture and Bubbling Execution Order");
                stage.show();
        }

        public void handleEvent(String phase, MouseEvent e) {
                String type = e.getEventType().getName();
                String source = e.getSource().getClass().getSimpleName();
                String target = e.getTarget().getClass().getSimpleName();

                // Get coordinates of the mouse cursor relative to the event source
                double x = e.getX();
                double y = e.getY();
```

```
                System.out.println(phase + ": Type=" + type +
                                ", Target=" + target + ", Source=" +  source +
                                ", location(" + x + ", " + y + ")");
        }
}
```

Listing 9-4 demonstrates the execution order of event handlers for a node. It displays a circle. It registers three event handlers for the circle:

- One for the MouseEvent.ANY event type

- One for the MouseEvent.MOUSE_CLICKED event type using the addEventHandler() method

- One for the MouseEvent.MOUSE_CLICKED event type using the setOnMouseClicked() method

Run the program and click inside the circle. The output shows the order in which three event handlers are called. The order will be similar to that presented in the discussion at the beginning of the section.

Listing 9-4. Order of Execution of Event Handlers for a Node

```
// HandlersOrder.java
package com.jdojo.event;

import javafx.application.Application;
import javafx.scene.Scene;
import javafx.scene.input.MouseEvent;
import javafx.scene.layout.HBox;
import javafx.scene.paint.Color;
import javafx.scene.shape.Circle;
import javafx.stage.Stage;

public class HandlersOrder extends Application {
        public static void main(String[] args) {
                Application.launch(args);
        }

        @Override
        public void start(Stage stage) {
                Circle circle = new Circle(50, 50, 50);
                circle.setFill(Color.CORAL);

                HBox root = new HBox();
                root.getChildren().addAll(circle);
                Scene scene = new Scene(root);

                /* Register three handlers for the circle that can handle mouse-clicked events */
                // This will be called last
                circle.addEventHandler(MouseEvent.ANY, e -> handleAnyMouseEvent(e));
```

```
                // This will be called first
                circle.addEventHandler(MouseEvent.MOUSE_CLICKED,
                                e -> handleMouseClicked("addEventHandler()", e));

                // This will be called second
                circle.setOnMouseClicked(e -> handleMouseClicked("setOnMouseClicked()", e));

                stage.setScene(scene);
                stage.setTitle("Execution Order of Event Handlers of a Node");
                stage.show();
        }

        public void handleMouseClicked(String registrationMethod, MouseEvent e) {
                System.out.println(registrationMethod
                                + ": MOUSE_CLICKED handler detected a mouse click.");
        }

        public void handleAnyMouseEvent(MouseEvent e) {
                // Print a message only for mouse-clicked events, ignoring
                // other mouse events such as mouse-pressed, mouse-released, etc.
                if (e.getEventType() == MouseEvent.MOUSE_CLICKED) {
                        System.out.println("MouseEvent.ANY handler detected a mouse click.");
                }
        }
}
```

```
addEventHandler(): MOUSE_CLICKED handler detected a mouse click.
setOnMouseClicked(): MOUSE_CLICKED handler detected a mouse click.
MouseEvent.ANY handler detected a mouse click.
```

Consuming Events

An event is consumed by calling its consume() method. The event class contains the method and it is inherited by all event classes. Typically, the consume() method is called inside the handle() method of the event filters and handlers.

Consuming an event indicates to the event dispatcher that the event processing is complete and that the event should not travel any farther in the event dispatch chain. If an event is consumed in an event filter of a node, the event does not travel to any child node. If an event is consumed in an event handler of a node, the event does not travel to any parent node.

All event filters or handlers for the consuming node are called, irrespective of which filter or handler consumes the event. Suppose you have registered three event handlers for a node and the event handler, which is called first, consumes the event. In this case, the other two event handlers for the node are still called.

If a parent node does not want its child nodes to respond to an event, it can consume the event in its event filter. If a parent node provides a default response to an event in an event handler, a child node can provide a specific response and consume the event, thus suppressing the default response of the parent.

Typically, nodes consume most input events after providing a default response. The rule is that all event filters and handlers of a node are called, even if one of them consumes the event. This makes it possible for developers to execute their event filters and handlers for a node even if the node consumes the event.

The code in Listing 9-5 shows how to consume an event. Figure 9-6 shows the screen when you run the program.

Listing 9-5. Consuming Events

```
// ConsumingEvents.java
package com.jdojo.event;

import javafx.application.Application;
import javafx.event.EventHandler;
import javafx.geometry.Insets;
import javafx.scene.Scene;
import javafx.scene.control.CheckBox;
import javafx.scene.input.MouseEvent;
import static javafx.scene.input.MouseEvent.MOUSE_CLICKED;
import javafx.scene.layout.HBox;
import javafx.scene.paint.Color;
import javafx.scene.shape.Circle;
import javafx.scene.shape.Rectangle;
import javafx.stage.Stage;
```

Figure 9-6. *Consuming events*

The program adds a Circle, a Rectangle, and a CheckBox to an HBox. The HBox is added to the scene as the root node. An event handler is added to the Stage, Scene, HBox, and Circle. Notice that you have a different event handler for the Circle, just to keep the program logic simple. When the check box is selected, the event handler for the circle consumes the mouse-clicked event, thus preventing the event from traveling up to the HBox, Scene, and Stage. If the check box is not selected, the mouse-clicked event on the circle travels from the Circle to the HBox, Scene, and Stage. Run the program and, using the mouse, click the different areas of the scene to see the effect. Notice that the mouse-clicked event handler for the HBox, Scene, and Stage are executed, even if you click a point outside the circle, because they are in the event dispatch chain of the clicked nodes.

```
public class ConsumingEvents extends Application {
        private CheckBox consumeEventCbx = new CheckBox("Consume Mouse Click at Circle");

        public static void main(String[] args) {
                Application.launch(args);
        }
```

```java
    @Override
    public void start(Stage stage) {
            Circle circle = new Circle (50, 50, 50);
            circle.setFill(Color.CORAL);

            Rectangle rect = new Rectangle(100, 100);
            rect.setFill(Color.TAN);

            HBox root = new HBox();
            root.setPadding(new Insets(20));
            root.setSpacing(20);
            root.getChildren().addAll(circle, rect, consumeEventCbx);

            Scene scene = new Scene(root);

            // Register mouse-clicked event handlers to all nodes,
            // except the rectangle and checkbox
            EventHandler<MouseEvent> handler = e -> handleEvent(e);
            EventHandler<MouseEvent> circleMeHandler = e -> handleEventforCircle(e);

            stage.addEventHandler(MOUSE_CLICKED, handler);
            scene.addEventHandler(MOUSE_CLICKED, handler);
            root.addEventHandler(MOUSE_CLICKED, handler);
            circle.addEventHandler(MOUSE_CLICKED, circleMeHandler);

            stage.setScene(scene);
            stage.setTitle("Consuming Events");
            stage.show();
    }

    public void handleEvent(MouseEvent e) {
            print(e);
    }

    public void handleEventforCircle(MouseEvent e) {
            print(e);
            if (consumeEventCbx.isSelected()) {
                    e.consume();
            }
    }

    public void print(MouseEvent e) {
            String type = e.getEventType().getName();
            String source = e.getSource().getClass().getSimpleName();
            String target = e.getTarget().getClass().getSimpleName();

            // Get coordinates of the mouse cursor relative to the event source
            double x = e.getX();
            double y = e.getY();
```

```
                System.out.println("Type=" + type + ", Target=" + target +
                        ", Source=" +  source +
                        ", location(" + x + ", " + y + ")");
        }
}
```

Clicking the check box does not execute the mouse-clicked event handlers for the HBox, Scene, and Stage, whereas clicking the rectangle does. Can you think of a reason for this behavior? The reason is simple. The check box has a default event handler that takes a default action and consumes the event, preventing it from traveling up the event dispatch chain. The rectangle does not consume the event, allowing it to travel up the event dispatch chain.

■ **Tip**   Consuming an event by the event target in an event filter has no effect on the execution of any other event filters. However, it prevents the event bubbling phase from happening. Consuming an event in the event handlers of the topmost node, which is the head of the event dispatch chain, has no effect on the event processing at all.

Handling Input Events

An input event indicates a user input (or a user action), for example, clicking the mouse, pressing a key, touching a touch screen, and so forth. JavaFX supports many types of input events. Figure 9-7 shows the class diagram for some of the classes that represent input event. All input event–related classes are in the javafx.scene.input package. The InputEvent class is the superclass of all input event classes. Typically, nodes execute the user-registered input event handlers before taking the default action. If the user event handlers consume the event, nodes do not take the default action. Suppose you register key-typed event handlers for a TextField, which consume the event. When you type a character, the TextField will not add and display it as its content. Therefore, consuming input events for nodes gives you a chance to disable the default behavior of the node. In next sections, I will discuss mouse and key input events.

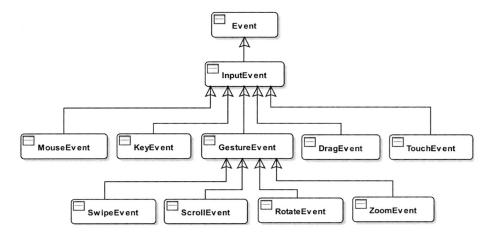

Figure 9-7. *Class hierarchy for some input events*

Handling Mouse Events

An object of the MouseEvent class represents a mouse event. The MouseEvent class defines the following mouse-related event types constants. All constants are of the type EventType<MouseEvent>. The Node class contains the convenience onXXX properties for most of the mouse event types that can be used to add one event handler of a specific mouse event type for a node:

- ANY: It is the supertype of all mouse event types. If a node wants to receive all types of mouse events, you would register handlers for this type. The InputEvent.ANY is the supertype of this event type.

- MOUSE_PRESSED: Pressing a mouse button generates this event. The getButton() method of the MouseEvent class returns the mouse button that is responsible for the event. A mouse button is represented by the NONE, PRIMARY, MIDDLE, and SECONDARY constants defined in the MouseButton enum.

- MOUSE_RELEASED: Releasing a mouse button generates this event. This event is delivered to the same node on which the mouse was pressed. For example, you can press a mouse button on a circle, drag the mouse outside the circle, and release the mouse button. The MOUSE_RELEASED event will be delivered to the circle, not the node on which the mouse button was released.

- MOUSE_CLICKED: This event is generated when a mouse button is clicked on a node. The button should be pressed and released on the same node for this event to occur.

- MOUSE_MOVED: Moving the mouse without pressing any mouse buttons generates this event.

- MOUSE_ENTERED: This event is generated when the mouse enters a node. The event capture and bubbling phases do not take place for this event. That is, event filters and handlers of the parent nodes of the event target of this event are not called.

- MOUSE_ENTERED_TARGET: This event is generated when the mouse enters a node. It is a variant of the MOUSE_ENTERED event type. Unlike the MOUSE_ENTER event, the event capture and bubbling phases take place for this event.

- MOUSE_EXITED: This event is generated when the mouse leaves a node. The event capture and bubbling phases do not take place for this event, that is, it is delivered only to the target node.

- MOUSE_EXITED_TARGET: This event is generated when the mouse leaves a node. It is a variant of the MOUSE_EXITED event type. Unlike the MOUSE_EXITED event, the event capture and bubbling phases take place for this event.

- DRAG_DETECTED: This event is generated when the mouse is pressed and dragged over a node over a platform-specific distance threshold.

- MOUSE_DRAGGED: Moving the mouse with a pressed mouse button generates this event. This event is delivered to the same node on which the mouse button was pressed, irrespective of the location of the mouse pointer during the drag.

Getting Mouse Location

The MouseEvent class contains methods to give you the location of the mouse when a mouse event occurs. You can obtain the mouse location relative to the coordinate systems of the event source node, the scene, and the screen. The getX() and getY() methods give the (x, y) coordinates of the mouse relative to the event source node. The getSceneX() and getSceneY() methods give the (x, y) coordinates of the mouse relative to the scene to which the node is added. The getScreenX() and getScreenY() methods give the (x, y) coordinates of the mouse relative to the screen to which the node is added.

Listing 9-6 contains the program to show how to use the methods in the MouseEvent class to know the mouse location. It adds a MOUSE_CLICKED event handler to the stage, and the stage can receive the notification when the mouse is clicked anywhere in its area. Run the program and click anywhere in the stage, excluding its title bar if you are running it on the desktop. Each mouse click prints a message describing the source, target, and location of the mouse relative to the source, scene, and screen.

Listing 9-6. Determining the Mouse Location During Mouse Events

```java
// MouseLocation.java
package com.jdojo.event;

import javafx.application.Application;
import javafx.geometry.Insets;
import javafx.scene.Scene;
import javafx.scene.input.MouseEvent;
import javafx.scene.layout.HBox;
import javafx.scene.paint.Color;
import javafx.scene.shape.Circle;
import javafx.scene.shape.Rectangle;
import javafx.stage.Stage;

public class MouseLocation extends Application {
        public static void main(String[] args) {
                Application.launch(args);
        }

        @Override
        public void start(Stage stage) {
                Circle circle = new Circle (50, 50, 50);
                circle.setFill(Color.CORAL);

                Rectangle rect = new Rectangle(100, 100);
                rect.setFill(Color.TAN);

                HBox root = new HBox();
                root.setPadding(new Insets(20));
                root.setSpacing(20);
                root.getChildren().addAll(circle, rect);
```

```
            // Add a MOUSE_CLICKED event handler to the stage
            stage.addEventHandler(MouseEvent.MOUSE_CLICKED, e -> handleMouseMove(e));

            Scene scene = new Scene(root);
            stage.setScene(scene);
            stage.setTitle("Mouse Location");
            stage.show();
        }

    public void handleMouseMove(MouseEvent e) {
            String source = e.getSource().getClass().getSimpleName();
            String target = e.getTarget().getClass().getSimpleName();

            // Mouse location relative to the event source
            double sourceX = e.getX();
            double sourceY = e.getY();

            // Mouse location relative to the scene
            double sceneX = e.getSceneX();
            double sceneY = e.getSceneY();

            // Mouse location relative to the screen
            double screenX = e.getScreenX();
            double screenY = e.getScreenY();

            System.out.println("Source=" +  source + ", Target=" + target +
                            ", Location:" +
                            " source(" + sourceX + ", " + sourceY + ")" +
                            ", scene(" + sceneX + ", " + sceneY + ")" +
                            ", screen(" + screenX + ", " + screenY + ")");
        }
}
```

Representing Mouse Buttons

Typically, a mouse has three buttons. You will also find some that have only one or two buttons. Some platforms provide ways to simulate the missing mouse buttons. The MouseButton enum in the javafx.scene.input package contains constants to represent mouse button. Table 9-2 contains the list of constants defined in the MouseButton enum.

Table 9-2. *Constants for the MouseButton Enum*

MouseButton Enum Constant	Description
NONE	It represents no button.
PRIMARY	It represents the primary button. Usually it is the left button in the mouse.
MIDDLE	It represents the middle button.
SECONDARY	It represents the secondary button. Usually it is the right button in the mouse.

The location of the primary and second mouse buttons depends on the mouse configuration. Typically, for right-handed users, the left and right buttons are configured as the primary and secondary buttons, respectively. For the left-handed users, the buttons are configured in the reverse order. If you have a two-button mouse, you do not have a middle button.

State of Mouse Buttons

The MouseEvent object that represents a mouse event contains the state of the mouse buttons at the time the event occurs. The MouseEvent class contains many methods to report the state of mouse buttons. Table 9-3 contains a list of such methods with their descriptions.

Table 9-3. Methods Related to the State of Mouse Buttons in the MouseEvent Class

Method	Description
MouseButton getButton()	It returns the mouse button responsible for the mouse event.
int getClickCount()	It returns the number of mouse clicks associated with the mouse event.
boolean isPrimaryButtonDown()	It returns true if the primary button is currently pressed. Otherwise, it returns false.
boolean isMiddleButtonDown()	It returns true if the middle button is currently pressed. Otherwise, it returns false.
boolean isSecondaryButtonDown()	It returns true if the secondary button is currently pressed. Otherwise, it returns false.
boolean isPopupTrigger()	It returns true if the mouse event is the pop-up menu trigger event for the platform. Otherwise, it returns false.
boolean isStillSincePress()	It returns true if the mouse cursor stays within a small area, which is known as the system-provided hysteresis area, between the last mouse-pressed event and the current mouse event.

In many circumstances, the getButton() method may return MouseButton.NONE, for example, when a mouse event is triggered on a touch screen by using the fingers instead of a mouse or when a mouse event, such as a mouse-moved event, is not triggered by a mouse button.

It is important to understand the difference between the getButton() method and other methods, for example, isPrimaryButtonDown(), which returns the pressed state of buttons. The getButton() method returns the button that triggers the event. Not all mouse events are triggered by buttons. For example, a mouse-move event is triggered when the mouse moves, not by pressing or releasing a button. If a button is not responsible for a mouse event, the getButton() method returns MouseButton.NONE. The isPrimaryButtonDown() method returns true if the primary button is currently pressed, whether or not it triggered the event. For example, when you press the primary button, the mouse-pressed event occurs. The getButton() method will return MouseButton.PRIMARY because this is the button that triggered the mouse-pressed event. The isPrimaryButtonDown() method returns true because this button is pressed when the mouse-pressed event occurs. Suppose you keep the primary button pressed and you press the secondary button. Another mouse-pressed event occurs. However, this time, the getButton() returns MouseButton.SECONDARY and both isPrimaryButtonDown() and isSecondaryButtonDown() methods return true, because both of these buttons are in the pressed state at the time of the second mouse-pressed event.

A *pop-up* menu, also known as a *context*, *contextual*, or *shortcut* menu, is a menu that gives a user a set of choices that are available in a specific context in an application. For example, when you click the right mouse button in a browser on the Windows platform, a pop-up menu is displayed. Different platforms trigger pop-up menu events differently upon use of a mouse or keyboard. On the Windows platform, typically it is a right-mouse click or Shift + F10 key press.

The isPopupTrigger() method returns true if the mouse event is the pop-up menu trigger event for the platform. Otherwise, it returns false. If you perform an action based on the returned value of this method, you need to use it in both mouse-pressed and mouse-released events. Typically, when this method returns true, you let the system display the default pop-up menu.

■ **Tip**   JavaFX provides a *context menu event* that is a specific type of input event. It is represented by the ContextMenuEvent class in the javafx.scene.input package. If you want to handle context menu events, use ContextMenuEvent.

Hysteresis in GUI Applications

Hysteresis is a feature that allows user inputs to be within a range of time or location. The time range within which user inputs are accepted is known as the *hysteresis time*. The area in which user inputs are accepted is known as the *hysteresis area*. Hysteresis time and area are system dependent. For example, modern GUI applications provide features that are invoked by double-clicking a mouse button. A time gap exists between two clicks. If the time gap is within the hysteresis time of the system, two clicks are considered a double-click. Otherwise, they are considered two separate single clicks.

Typically, during a mouse-click event, the mouse is moved by a very tiny distance between the mouse-pressed and mouse-released events. Sometimes it is important to take into account the distance the mouse is moved during a mouse click. The isStillSincePress() method returns true if the mouse stays in the system-provided hysteresis area since the last mouse-pressed event and the current event. This method is important when you want to consider a mouse-drag action. If this method returns true, you may ignore mouse drags as the mouse movement is still within the hysteresis distance from the point where the mouse was last pressed.

State of Modifier Keys

A modifier key is used to change the normal behavior of other keys. Some examples of modifier keys are Alt, Shift, Ctrl, Meta, Caps Lock, and Num Lock. Not all platforms support all modifier keys. The Meta key is present on Mac, not on Windows. Some systems let you simulate the functionality of a modifier key even if the modifier key is physically not present, for example, you can use the Windows key on Windows to work as the Meta key. The MouseEvent method contains methods to report the pressed state of some of the modifier keys when the mouse event occurs. Table 9-4 lists the methods related to the modifier keys in the MouseEvent class.

Table 9-4. *Methods, Related to the State of Modifier Keys, in the* MouseEvent *Class*

Method	Description
boolean isAltDown()	It returns true if the Alt key is down for this mouse event. Otherwise, it returns false.
boolean isControlDown()	It returns true if the Ctrl key is down for this mouse event. Otherwise, it returns false.
boolean isMetaDown()	It returns true if the Meta key is down for this mouse event. Otherwise, it returns false.
boolean isShiftDown()	It returns true if the Shift key is down for this mouse event. Otherwise, it returns false.
boolean isShortcutDown()	It returns true if the platform-specific shortcut key is down for this mouse event. Otherwise, it returns false. The shortcut modifier key is the Ctrl key on Windows and Meta key on Mac.

Picking Mouse Events on Bounds

The Node class has a pickOnBounds property to control the way mouse events are picked (or generated) for a node. A node can have any geometric shape, whereas its bounds always define a rectangular area. If the property is set to true, the mouse events are generated for the node if the mouse is on the perimeter or inside of its bounds. If the property is set to false, which is the default value, mouse events are generated for the node if the mouse is on the perimeter or inside of its geometric shape. Some nodes, such as the Text node, have the default value for the pickOnBounds property set to true.

Figure 9-8 shows the perimeter for the geometric shape and bounds of a circle. If the pickOnBounds property for the circle is false, the mouse event will not be generated for the circle if the mouse is one of the four areas in the corners that lie between the perimeter of the geometric shape and bounds.

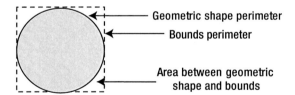

Figure 9-8. *Difference between the geometric shape and bounds of a circle*

Listing 9-7 contains the program to show the effects of the pickOnBounds property of a Circle node. It displays a window as shown in Figure 9-9. The program adds a Rectangle and a Circle to a Group. Note that the Rectangle is added to the Group before the Circle to keep the former below the latter in Z-order.

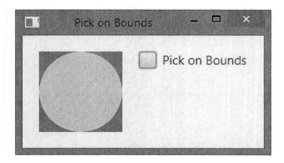

Figure 9-9. *Demonstrating the effects of the pickOnBounds property of a Circle node*

The Rectangle uses red as the fill color, whereas light gray is used as the fill color for the Circle. The area in red is the area between the perimeters of the geometric shape and bounds of the Circle.

You have a check box that controls the pickOnBounds property of the circle. If it is selected, the property is set to true. Otherwise, it is set to false.

When you click the gray area, Circle always picks up the mouse-clicked event. When you click the red area with the check box unselected, the Rectangle picks up the event. When you click the red area with the check box selected, the Circle picks up the event. The output shows who picks up the mouse-clicked event.

Listing 9-7. Testing the Effects of the pickOnBounds Property for a Circle Node

```java
// PickOnBounds.java
package com.jdojo.event;

import javafx.application.Application;
import javafx.event.ActionEvent;
import javafx.geometry.Insets;
import javafx.scene.Group;
import javafx.scene.Scene;
import javafx.scene.control.CheckBox;
import javafx.scene.input.MouseEvent;
import javafx.scene.layout.HBox;
import javafx.scene.paint.Color;
import javafx.scene.shape.Circle;
import javafx.scene.shape.Rectangle;
import javafx.stage.Stage;

public class PickOnBounds extends Application {
        private CheckBox pickonBoundsCbx = new CheckBox("Pick on Bounds");
        Circle circle = new Circle(50, 50, 50, Color.LIGHTGRAY);

        public static void main(String[] args) {
                Application.launch(args);
        }
```

```java
    @Override
    public void start(Stage stage) {
            Rectangle rect = new Rectangle(100, 100);
            rect.setFill(Color.RED);

            Group group = new Group();
            group.getChildren().addAll(rect, circle);

            HBox root = new HBox();
            root.setPadding(new Insets(20));
            root.setSpacing(20);
            root.getChildren().addAll(group, pickonBoundsCbx);

            // Add MOUSE_CLICKED event handlers to the circle and rectangle
            circle.setOnMouseClicked(e -> handleMouseClicked(e));
            rect.setOnMouseClicked(e -> handleMouseClicked(e));

            // Add an Action handler to the checkbox
            pickonBoundsCbx.setOnAction(e -> handleActionEvent(e));

            Scene scene = new Scene(root);
            stage.setScene(scene);
            stage.setTitle("Pick on Bounds");
            stage.show();
    }

    public void handleMouseClicked(MouseEvent e) {
            String target = e.getTarget().getClass().getSimpleName();
            String type = e.getEventType().getName();
            System.out.println(type + " on " + target);
    }

    public void handleActionEvent(ActionEvent e) {
            if (pickonBoundsCbx.isSelected()) {
                    circle.setPickOnBounds(true);
            } else {
                    circle.setPickOnBounds(false);
            }
    }
}
```

Mouse Transparency

The Node class has a mouseTransparent property to control whether or not a node and its children receive mouse events. Contrast the pickOnBounds and mouseTransparent properties: The former determines the area of a node that generates mouse events, and the latter determines whether or not a node and its children generate mouse events, irrespective of the value of the former. The former affects only the node on which it is set; the latter affects the node on which it is set and all its children.

The code in Listing 9-8 shows the effects of the mouseTransparent property of a Circle. This is a variant of the program in Listing 9-7. It displays a window that is very similar to the one shown in Figure 9-9. When the check box MouseTransparency is selected, it sets the mouseTransparent property of the circle to true. When the check box is unselected, it sets the mouseTransparent property of the circle to false.

Click the circle, in the gray area, when the check box is selected and all mouse-clicked events will be delivered to the rectangle. This is because the circle is mouse transparent and it lets the mouse events pass through. Unselect the check box, and all mouse-clicks in the gray area are delivered to the circle. Note that clicking the red area always delivers the event to the rectangle, because the pickOnBounds property for the circle is set to false by default. The output shows the node that receives the mouse-clicked events.

Listing 9-8. Testing the Effects of the mouseTransparent Property for a Circle Node

```java
// MouseTransparency.java
package com.jdojo.event;

import javafx.application.Application;
import javafx.event.ActionEvent;
import javafx.geometry.Insets;
import javafx.scene.Group;
import javafx.scene.Scene;
import javafx.scene.control.CheckBox;
import javafx.scene.input.MouseEvent;
import javafx.scene.layout.HBox;
import javafx.scene.paint.Color;
import javafx.scene.shape.Circle;
import javafx.scene.shape.Rectangle;
import javafx.stage.Stage;

public class MouseTransparency extends Application {
        private CheckBox mouseTransparentCbx = new CheckBox("Mouse Transparent");
        Circle circle = new Circle(50, 50, 50, Color.LIGHTGRAY);

        public static void main(String[] args) {
                Application.launch(args);
        }

        @Override
        public void start(Stage stage) {
                Rectangle rect = new Rectangle(100, 100);
                rect.setFill(Color.RED);

                Group group = new Group();
                group.getChildren().addAll(rect, circle);

                HBox root = new HBox();
                root.setPadding(new Insets(20));
                root.setSpacing(20);
                root.getChildren().addAll(group, mouseTransparentCbx);

                // Add MOUSE_CLICKED event handlers to the circle and rectangle
                circle.setOnMouseClicked(e -> handleMouseClicked(e));
                rect.setOnMouseClicked(e -> handleMouseClicked(e));
```

```
            // Add an Action handler to the checkbox
            mouseTransparentCbx.setOnAction(e -> handleActionEvent(e));

            Scene scene = new Scene(root);
            stage.setScene(scene);
            stage.setTitle("Mouse Transparency");
            stage.show();
    }

    public void handleMouseClicked(MouseEvent e) {
            String target = e.getTarget().getClass().getSimpleName();
            String type = e.getEventType().getName();
            System.out.println(type + " on " + target);
    }

    public void handleActionEvent(ActionEvent e) {
            if (mouseTransparentCbx.isSelected()) {
                    circle.setMouseTransparent(true);
            } else {
                    circle.setMouseTransparent(false);
            }
    }
}
```

Synthesized Mouse Events

A mouse event can be generated using several types of devices, such as a mouse, track pad, or touch screen. Some actions on a touch screen generate mouse events, which are considered *synthesized mouse events*. The isSynthesized() method of the MouseEvent class returns true if the event is synthesized from using a touch screen. Otherwise, it returns false.

When a finger is dragged on a touch screen, it generates both a scrolling gesture event and a mouse-drag event. The return value of the isSynthesized() method can be used inside the mouse-drag event handlers to detect if the event is generated by dragging a finger on a touch screen or by dragging a mouse.

Handling Mouse Entered and Exited Events

Four mouse event types deal with events when the mouse enters or exits a node:

- MOUSE_ENTERED
- MOUSE_EXITED
- MOUSE_ENTERED_TARGET
- MOUSE_EXITED_TARGET

You have two sets of event types for mouse-entered and mouse-exited events. One set contains two types called MOUSE_ENTERED and MOUSE_EXITED and another set contains MOUSE_ENTERED_TARGET and MOUSE_EXITED_TARGET. They both have something in common, such as when they are triggered. They differ in their delivery mechanisms. I will discuss all of them this section.

When the mouse enters a node, a MOUSE_ENTERED event is generated. When the mouse leaves a node, a MOUSE_EXITED event is generated. These events do not go through the capture and bubbling phases. That is, they are delivered directly to the target node, not to any of its parent nodes.

289

> ■ **Tip** The MOUSE_ENTERED and MOUSE_EXITED events do not participate in the capture and bubbling phases. However, all event *filters* and *handlers* are executed for the target following the rules for event handling.

The program in Listing 9-9 shows how mouse-entered and mouse-exited events are delivered. The program displays a window as shown in Figure 9-10. It shows a circle with gray fill inside an HBox. Event handlers for mouse-entered and mouse-exited events are added to the HBox and the Circle. Run the program and move the mouse in and out of the circle. When the mouse enters the white area in the window, its MOUSE_ENTERED event is delivered to the HBox. When you move the mouse in and out of the circle, the output shows that the MOUSE_ENTERED and MOUSE_EXITED events are delivered only to the Circle, not to the HBox. Notice that in the output the source and target of these events are always the same, proving that the capture and bubbling phases do not occur for these events. When you move the mouse in and out of the circle, keeping it in the white area, the MOUSE_EXITED event for the HBox does not fire, as the mouse stays on the HBox. To fire the MOUSE_EXITED event on the HBox, you will need to move the mouse outside the scene area, for example, outside the window or over the title bar of the window.

Listing 9-9. Testing Mouse-Entered and Mouse-Exited Events

```java
// MouseEnteredExited.java
package com.jdojo.event;

import javafx.application.Application;
import javafx.geometry.Insets;
import javafx.scene.Scene;
import javafx.scene.input.MouseEvent;
import javafx.scene.layout.HBox;
import javafx.scene.paint.Color;
import javafx.scene.shape.Circle;
import javafx.event.EventHandler;
import javafx.stage.Stage;
import static javafx.scene.input.MouseEvent.MOUSE_ENTERED;
import static javafx.scene.input.MouseEvent.MOUSE_EXITED;

public class MouseEnteredExited  extends Application {
        public static void main(String[] args) {
                Application.launch(args);
        }

        @Override
        public void start(Stage stage) {
                Circle circle = new Circle (50, 50, 50);
                circle.setFill(Color.GRAY);

                HBox root = new HBox();
                root.setPadding(new Insets(20));
                root.setSpacing(20);
                root.getChildren().addAll(circle);
```

```
            // Create a mouse event handler
            EventHandler<MouseEvent> handler = e -> handle(e);

            // Add mouse-entered and mouse-exited event handlers to the HBox
            root.addEventHandler(MOUSE_ENTERED, handler);
            root.addEventHandler(MOUSE_EXITED, handler);

            // Add mouse-entered and mouse-exited event handlers to the Circle
            circle.addEventHandler(MOUSE_ENTERED, handler);
            circle.addEventHandler(MOUSE_EXITED, handler);

            Scene scene = new Scene(root);
            stage.setScene(scene);
            stage.setTitle("Mouse Entered and Exited Events");
            stage.show();
    }

    public void handle(MouseEvent e) {
            String type = e.getEventType().getName();
            String source = e.getSource().getClass().getSimpleName();
            String target = e.getTarget().getClass().getSimpleName();
            System.out.println("Type=" + type + ", Target=" + target +
                            ", Source=" +  source);
    }
}
```

```
Type=MOUSE_ENTERED, Target=HBox, Source=HBox
Type=MOUSE_ENTERED, Target=Circle, Source=Circle
Type=MOUSE_EXITED, Target=Circle, Source=Circle
Type=MOUSE_ENTERED, Target=Circle, Source=Circle
Type=MOUSE_EXITED, Target=Circle, Source=Circle
Type=MOUSE_EXITED, Target=HBox, Source=HBox
...
```

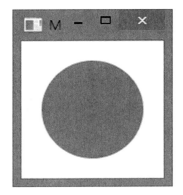

Figure 9-10. *Demonstrating mouse-entered and mouse-exited events*

The MOUSE_ENTERED and MOUSE_EXITED event types provide the functionality needed in most cases. Sometimes you need these events to go through the normal capture and bubbling phases, so parent nodes can apply filters and provide default responses. The MOUSE_ENTERED_TARGET and MOUSE_EXITED_TARGET event types provide these features. They participate in the event capture and bubbling phases.

The MOUSE_ENTERED and MOUSE_EXITED event types are subtypes of the MOUSE_ENTERED_TARGET and MOUSE_EXITED_TARGET event types. A node interested in the mouse-entered event of its children should add event filters and handlers for the MOUSE_ENTERED_TARGET type. The child node can add MOUSE_ENTERED, MOUSE_ENTERED_TARGET, or both event filters and handlers. When the mouse enters the child node, parent nodes receive the MOUSE_ENTERED_TARGET event. Before the event is delivered to the child node, which is the target node of the event, the event type is changed to the MOUSE_ENTERED type. Therefore, in the same event processing, the target node receives the MOUSE_ENTERED event, whereas all its parent nodes receive the MOUSE_ENTERED_TARGET event. Because the MOUSE_ENTERED event type is a subtype of the MOUSE_ENTERED_TARGET type, either type of event handler on the target can handle this event. The same would apply to the mouse-exited event and its corresponding event types.

Sometimes, inside the parent event handler, it is necessary to distinguish the node that fires the MOUSE_ENTERED_TARGET event. A parent node receives this event when the mouse enters the parent node itself or any of its child nodes. You can check the target node reference, using the getTarget() method of the Event class, for equality with the reference of the parent node, inside the event filters and handlers, to know whether or not the event was fired by the parent.

The program in Listing 9-10 shows how to use the mouse-entered-target and mouse-exited-target events. It adds a Circle and a CheckBox to an HBox. The HBox is added to the Scene. It adds the mouse-entered-target and mouse-exited-target event filters to the HBox and event handlers to the Circle. It also adds mouse-entered and mouse-exited event handlers to the Circle. When the check box is selected, events are consumed by the HBox, so they do not reach the Circle. Below are a few observations when you run the program:

- With the check box unselected, when the mouse enters or leaves the Circle, the HBox receives the MOUSE_ENTERED_TARGET and MOUSE_EXITED_TARGET events. The Circle receives the MOUSE_ENTERED and MOUSE_EXITED events.

- With the check box selected, the HBox receives the MOUSE_ENTERED_TARGET and MOUSE_EXITED_TARGET events and consumes them. The Circle does not receive any events.

- When the mouse enters or leaves the HBox, the white area in the window, the HBox receives the MOUSE_ENTERED and MOUSE_EXITED events, because the HBox is the target of the event.

Play with the application by moving the mouse around, selecting and unselecting the check box. Look at the output to get a feel for how these events are processed.

Listing 9-10. Using the Mouse-Entered-Target and Mouse-Exited-Target Events

```
// MouseEnteredExitedTarget.java
package com.jdojo.event;

import javafx.application.Application;
import javafx.event.EventHandler;
import javafx.geometry.Insets;
import javafx.scene.Scene;
import javafx.scene.control.CheckBox;
import javafx.scene.input.MouseEvent;
import static javafx.scene.input.MouseEvent.MOUSE_ENTERED;
import static javafx.scene.input.MouseEvent.MOUSE_EXITED;
```

```java
import static javafx.scene.input.MouseEvent.MOUSE_ENTERED_TARGET;
import static javafx.scene.input.MouseEvent.MOUSE_EXITED_TARGET;
import javafx.scene.layout.HBox;
import javafx.scene.paint.Color;
import javafx.scene.shape.Circle;
import javafx.stage.Stage;

public class MouseEnteredExitedTarget extends Application {
        private CheckBox consumeCbx = new CheckBox("Consume Events");

        public static void main(String[] args) {
                Application.launch(args);
        }

        @Override
        public void start(Stage stage) {
                Circle circle = new Circle(50, 50, 50);
                circle.setFill(Color.GRAY);

                HBox root = new HBox();
                root.setPadding(new Insets(20));
                root.setSpacing(20);
                root.getChildren().addAll(circle, consumeCbx);

                // Create mouse event handlers
                EventHandler<MouseEvent> circleHandler = e -> handleCircle(e);
                EventHandler<MouseEvent> circleTargetHandler =
                                e -> handleCircleTarget(e);
                EventHandler<MouseEvent> hBoxTargetHandler = e -> handleHBoxTarget(e);

                // Add mouse-entered-target and mouse-exited-target event
                // handlers to HBox
                root.addEventFilter(MOUSE_ENTERED_TARGET, hBoxTargetHandler);
                root.addEventFilter(MOUSE_EXITED_TARGET, hBoxTargetHandler);

                // Add mouse-entered-target and mouse-exited-target event
                // handlers to the Circle
                circle.addEventHandler(MOUSE_ENTERED_TARGET, circleTargetHandler);
                circle.addEventHandler(MOUSE_EXITED_TARGET, circleTargetHandler);

                // Add mouse-entered and mouse-exited event handlers to the Circle
                circle.addEventHandler(MOUSE_ENTERED, circleHandler);
                circle.addEventHandler(MOUSE_EXITED, circleHandler);

                Scene scene = new Scene(root);
                stage.setScene(scene);
                stage.setTitle("Mouse Entered Target and Exited Target Events");
                stage.show();
        }
```

```
        public void handleCircle(MouseEvent e) {
                print(e, "Circle Handler");
        }

        public void handleCircleTarget(MouseEvent e) {
                print(e, "Circle Target Handler");
        }

        public void handleHBoxTarget(MouseEvent e) {
                print(e, "HBox Target Filter");
                if (consumeCbx.isSelected()) {
                        e.consume();
                        System.out.println("HBox consumed the " + e.getEventType() + " event");
                }
        }

        public void print(MouseEvent e, String msg) {
                String type = e.getEventType().getName();
                String source = e.getSource().getClass().getSimpleName();
                String target = e.getTarget().getClass().getSimpleName();
                System.out.println(msg + ": Type=" + type +
                                        ", Target=" + target +
                                        ", Source=" + source);
        }
}
```

Handling Key Events

A key event is a type of input event that denotes the occurrence of a keystroke. It is delivered to the node that has focus. An instance of the KeyEvent class, which is declared in the javafx.scene.input package, represents a key event. Key pressed, key released, and key typed are three types of key events. Table 9-5 lists all of the constants in the KeyEvent class, which represent key event types.

Table 9-5. Constants in the KeyEvent Class to Represent Key Event Types

Constant	Description
ANY	It is the supertype of other key events types.
KEY_PRESSED	It occurs when a key is pressed.
KEY_RELEASED	It occurs when a key is released.
KEY_TYPED	It occurs when a Unicode character is entered.

▓ **Tip** It may not be obvious that shapes, for example circles or rectangles, can also receive key events. The criterion for a node to receive key events is that the node should have focus. By default, shapes are not part of the focus traversal chain and mouse clicks do not bring focus to them. Shape nodes can get focus by calling the requestFocus() method.

The key-pressed and key-released events are lower-level events compared to the key-typed event; they occur with a key press and release, respectively, and depend of the platform and keyboard layout.

The key-typed event is a higher-level event. Generally, it does not depend on the platform and keyboard layout. It occurs when a Unicode character is typed. Typically, a key press generates a key-typed event. However, a key release may also generate a key-typed event. For example, when using the Alt key and number pad on Windows, a key-typed event is generated by the release of the Alt key, irrespective of the number of keystrokes entered on the number pad. A key-typed event can also be generated by a series of key presses and releases. For example, the character A is entered by pressing Shift + A, which includes two key presses (Shift and A). In this case, two key presses generate one key-typed event. Not all key presses or releases generate key-typed events. For example, when you press a function key (F1, F2, etc.) or modifier keys (Shift, Ctrl, etc.), no Unicode character is entered, and hence, no key-typed event is generated.

The KeyEvent class maintains three variables to describe the keys associated with the event: code, text, and character. These variables can be accessed using the getter methods in the KeyEvent class as listed in Table 9-6.

Table 9-6. *Methods in the KeyEvent Class Returning Key Details*

Method	Valid for	Description
KeyCode getCode()	KEY_PRESSED KEY_RELEASED	The KeyCode enum contains a constant to represent all keys on the keyboard. This method returns the KeyCode enum constant that is associated with the key being pressed or released. For the key-typed events, it always returns KeyCode.UNDEFINED, because the key-typed event may not necessarily be triggered by a single keystroke.
String getText()	KEY_PRESSED KEY_RELEASED	It returns a String description of the KeyCode associated with the key-pressed and key-released events. It always returns an empty string for the key-typed events.
String getCharacter()	KEY_TYPED	It returns a character or a sequence of character associated with a key-typed event as a String. For the key-pressed and key-released events, it always returns KeyEvent.CHAR_UNDEFINED.

It is interesting to note that the return type of the getCharacter() method is String, not char. The design is intentional. Unicode characters outside the basic multilingual plane cannot be represented in one character. Some devices may produce multiple characters using a single keystroke. The return type of String for the getCharacter() method covers these odd cases.

The KeyEvent class contains isAltDown(), isControlDown(), isMetaDown(), isShiftDown(), and isShortcutDown() methods that let you check whether modifier keys are down when a key event occurs.

Handling Key-pressed and Key-released Events

Key-pressed and key-released events are handled simply by adding the event filters and handlers to nodes for the KEY_PRESED and KEY_RELEASED event types. Typically you use these events to know which keys were pressed or released and to perform an action. For example, you can detect the F1 function key press and display a custom Help window for the node in focus.

The program in Listing 9-11 shows how to handle key-pressed and key-released events. It displays a Label and a TextField. When you run the program, the TextField has focus. Notice the following points when you use keystrokes while running this program:

- Press and release some keys. Output will show the details of events as they occur. A key-released event does not occur for every key-pressed event.

- The mapping between key-pressed and key-released events is not one-to-one. There may be no key-released event for a key-pressed event (refer to the next item). There may be one key-released event for several key-pressed events. This can happen when you keep a key pressed for a longer period. Sometimes you do it to type the same character multiple times. Press the A key and hold it for some time and then release it. This will generate several key-pressed events and only one key-released event.

- Press the F1 key. It will display the Help window. Notice that pressing the F1 key does not generate an output for a key-released event, even after you release the key. Can you think of the reason for this? On the key-pressed event, the Help window is displayed, which grabs the focus. The TextField on the main window no longer has focus. Recall that the key events are delivered to the node that has focus, and only one node can have focus in a JavaFX application. Therefore, the key-released event is delivered to the Help window, not the TextField.

Listing 9-11. Handling Key-pressed and Key-released Events

```java
// KeyPressedReleased.java
package com.jdojo.event;

import javafx.application.Application;
import javafx.geometry.Insets;
import javafx.scene.Scene;
import javafx.scene.control.Label;
import javafx.scene.control.TextField;
import javafx.scene.input.KeyCode;
import javafx.scene.input.KeyEvent;
import static javafx.scene.input.KeyEvent.KEY_PRESSED;
import javafx.scene.layout.HBox;
import javafx.scene.text.Text;
import javafx.stage.Stage;

public class KeyPressedReleased extends Application {
    public static void main(String[] args) {
        Application.launch(args);
    }

    @Override
    public void start(Stage stage) {
        Label nameLbl = new Label("Name:");
        TextField nameTfl = new TextField();

        HBox root = new HBox();
        root.setPadding(new Insets(20));
        root.setSpacing(20);
        root.getChildren().addAll(nameLbl, nameTfl);
```

```
        // Add key pressed and released events to the TextField
        nameTfl.setOnKeyPressed(e -> handle(e));
        nameTfl.setOnKeyReleased(e -> handle(e));

        Scene scene = new Scene(root);
        stage.setScene(scene);
        stage.setTitle("Key Pressed and Released Events");
        stage.show();
    }

    public void handle(KeyEvent e) {
        String type = e.getEventType().getName();
        KeyCode keyCode = e.getCode();
        System.out.println(type + ": Key Code=" + keyCode.getName() +
                           ", Text=" + e.getText());

        // Show the help window when the F1 key is pressed
        if (e.getEventType() == KEY_PRESSED && e.getCode() == KeyCode.F1) {
            displayHelp();
            e.consume();
        }
    }

    public void displayHelp() {
        Text helpText = new Text("Please enter a name.");
        HBox root = new HBox();
        root.setStyle("-fx-background-color: yellow;");
        root.getChildren().add(helpText);

        Scene scene = new Scene(root, 200, 100);
        Stage helpStage = new Stage();
        helpStage.setScene(scene);
        helpStage.setTitle("Help");
        helpStage.show();
    }
}
```

Handling the Key-typed Event

The typical use of the key-typed event is to detect specific keystrokes to prevent some characters from being entered. For example, you may allow users to only enter letters in a name field. You can do so by consuming all key-typed events for the field associated with all nonletters.

The program in Listing 9-12 shows a Label and a TextField. It adds a key-typed event handler to the TextField, which consumes the event if the character typed is not a letter. Otherwise, it prints the character typed on the standard output. Run the program. You should be able to enter letters in the TextField. When you press any nonletter keys, for example, 1, 2, 3, nothing happens.

This example is not a correct solution to stop users from entering nonletter characters. For example, users can still paste nonletters using the context menu (right-click on Windows) or using the keyboard shortcut Ctrl + V. The correct solution lies in detecting and handling the event on the TextField that is generated, irrespective of the method used. For now, this example serves the purpose of showing how to use key-typed events.

Listing 9-12. Using the Key-typed Event

```java
// KeyTyped.java
package com.jdojo.event;

import javafx.application.Application;
import javafx.geometry.Insets;
import javafx.scene.Scene;
import javafx.scene.control.Label;
import javafx.scene.control.TextField;
import javafx.scene.input.KeyEvent;
import javafx.scene.layout.HBox;
import javafx.stage.Stage;

public class KeyTyped extends Application {
        public static void main(String[] args) {
                Application.launch(args);
        }

        @Override
        public void start(Stage stage) {
                Label nameLbl = new Label("Name:");
                TextField nameTfl = new TextField();

                HBox root = new HBox();
                root.setPadding(new Insets(20));
                root.setSpacing(20);
                root.getChildren().addAll(nameLbl, nameTfl);

                // Add key-typed event to the TextField
                nameTfl.setOnKeyTyped(e -> handle(e));

                Scene scene = new Scene(root);
                stage.setScene(scene);
                stage.setTitle("Key Typed Event");
                stage.show();
        }

        public void handle(KeyEvent e) {
                // Consume the event if it is not a letter
                String str = e.getCharacter();
                int len = str.length();
                for(int i = 0; i < len; i++) {
                        Character c = str.charAt(i);
                        if (!Character.isLetter(c)) {
                                e.consume();
                        }
                }
```

```
                // Print the details if it is not consumed
                if (!e.isConsumed()) {
                        String type = e.getEventType().getName();
                        System.out.println(type + ": Character=" + e.getCharacter());
                }
        }
}
```

Handling Window Events

A window event occurs when a window is shown, hidden, or closed. An instance of the WindowEvent class in the javafx.stage package represents a window event. Table 9-7 lists the constants in the WindowEvent class.

Table 9-7. *Constants in the WindowEvent Class to Represent Window Event Types*

Constant	Description
ANY	It is the supertype of all other window event types.
WINDOW_SHOWING	It occurs just before the window is shown.
WINDOW_SHOWN	It occurs just after the window is shown.
WINDOW_HIDING	It occurs just before the window is hidden.
WINDOW_HIDDEN	It occurs just after the window is hidden.
WINDOW_CLOSE_REQUEST	It occurs when there is an external request to close this window.

The window-showing and window-shown events are straightforward. They occur just before and after the window is shown. Event handlers for the window-showing event should have time-consuming logic, as it will delay showing the window to the user, and hence, degrading the user experience. Initializing some window-level variables is a good example of the kind of code you need to write in this event. Typically, the window-shown event sets the starting direction for the user, for example, setting focus to the first editable field on the window, showing alerts to the user about the tasks that need his attention, among others.

The window-hiding and window-hidden events are counterparts of the window-showing and window-shown events. They occur just before and after the window is hidden.

The window-close-request event occurs when there is an external request to close the window. Using the Close menu from the context menu or the Close icon in the window title bar or pressing Alt + F4 key combination on Windows is considered an external request to close the window. Note that closing a window programmatically, for example, using the close() method of the Stage class or Platform.exit() method, is not considered an external request. If the window-close-request event is consumed, the window is not closed.

The program in Listing 9-13 shows how to use all window events. You may get a different output than that shown below the code. It adds a check box and two buttons to the primary stage. If the check box is unselected, external requests to close the window are consumed, thus preventing the window from closing. The Close button closes the window. The Hide button hides the primary window and opens a new window, so the user can show the primary window again.

The program adds event handlers to the primary stage for window event types. When the show() method on the stage is called, the window-showing and window-shown events are generated. When you click the Hide button, the window-hiding and window-hidden events are generated. When you click the button on the pop-up window to show the primary window, the window-showing and window-shown events are generated again. Try clicking the Close icon on the title bar to generate the window-close-request event. If the Can Close Window check box is not selected, the window is not closed. When you use the Close button to close the window, the window-hiding and window-hidden events are generated, but not the window-close-request event, as it is not an external request to close the window.

Listing 9-13. Using Window Events

```java
// WindowEventApp.java
package com.jdojo.event;

import javafx.application.Application;
import javafx.event.EventType;
import javafx.geometry.Insets;
import javafx.scene.Scene;
import javafx.scene.control.Button;
import javafx.scene.control.CheckBox;
import javafx.scene.layout.HBox;
import javafx.stage.Stage;
import javafx.stage.WindowEvent;
import static javafx.stage.WindowEvent.WINDOW_CLOSE_REQUEST;

public class WindowEventApp  extends Application {
        private CheckBox canCloseCbx = new CheckBox("Can Close Window");

        public static void main(String[] args) {
                Application.launch(args);
        }

        @Override
        public void start(Stage stage) {
                Button closeBtn = new Button("Close");
                closeBtn.setOnAction(e -> stage.close());

                Button hideBtn = new Button("Hide");
                hideBtn.setOnAction(e -> {showDialog(stage); stage.hide(); });

                HBox root = new HBox();
                root.setPadding(new Insets(20));
                root.setSpacing(20);
                root.getChildren().addAll(canCloseCbx, closeBtn, hideBtn);

                // Add window event handlers to the stage
                stage.setOnShowing(e -> handle(e));
                stage.setOnShown(e -> handle(e));
                stage.setOnHiding(e -> handle(e));
                stage.setOnHidden(e -> handle(e));
                stage.setOnCloseRequest(e -> handle(e));

                Scene scene = new Scene(root);
                stage.setScene(scene);
                stage.setTitle("Window Events");
                stage.show();
        }
```

```
        public void handle(WindowEvent e) {
                // Consume the event if the CheckBox is not selected
                // thus preventing the user from closing the window
                EventType<WindowEvent> type = e.getEventType();
                if (type == WINDOW_CLOSE_REQUEST && !canCloseCbx.isSelected()) {
                        e.consume();
                }

                System.out.println(type + ": Consumed=" + e.isConsumed());
        }

        public void showDialog(Stage mainWindow) {
                Stage popup = new Stage();

                Button closeBtn = new Button("Click to Show Main Window");
                closeBtn.setOnAction(e -> { popup.close(); mainWindow.show();});

                HBox root = new HBox();
                root.setPadding(new Insets(20));
                root.setSpacing(20);
                root.getChildren().addAll(closeBtn);

                Scene scene = new Scene(root);
                popup.setScene(scene);
                popup.setTitle("Popup");
                popup.show();
        }
}
```

```
WINDOW_SHOWING: Consumed=false
WINDOW_SHOWN: Consumed=false
WINDOW_HIDING: Consumed=false
WINDOW_HIDDEN: Consumed=false
WINDOW_SHOWING: Consumed=false
WINDOW_SHOWN: Consumed=false
WINDOW_CLOSE_REQUEST: Consumed=true
```

Summary

In general, the term event is used to describe an occurrence of interest. In a GUI application, an event is an occurrence of a user interaction with the application such as clicking the mouse, pressing a key on the keyboard, and so forth. An event in JavaFX is represented by an object of the javafx.event.Event class or any of its subclasses. Every event in JavaFX has three properties: an event source, an event target, and an event type.

When an event occurs in an application, you typically perform some processing by executing a piece of code. The piece of code that is executed in response to an event is known as an event handler or an event filter. When you want to handle an event for a UI element, you need to add event handlers to the UI element, for example, a Window, a Scene, or a Node. When the UI element detects the event, it executes your event handlers.

The UI element that calls event handlers is the source of the event for those event handlers. When an event occurs, it passes through a chain of event dispatchers. The source of an event is the current element in the event dispatcher chain. The event source changes as the event passes through one dispatcher to another in the event dispatcher chain. The event target is the destination of an event, which determines the route the event travels through during its processing. The event type describes the type of the event that occurs. They are defined in a hierarchical fashion. Each event type has a name and a supertype.

When an event occurs, the following three steps are performed in order: event target selection, event route construction, and event route traversal. An event target is the destination node of the event that is selected based on the event type. An event travels through event dispatchers in an event dispatch chain. The event dispatch chain is the event route. The initial and default route for an event is determined by the event target. The default event route consists of the container-children path starting at the stage to the event target node.

An event route traversal consists of two phases: capture and bubbling. An event travels through each node in its route twice: once during the capture phase and once during the bubbling phase. You can register event filters and event handlers to a node for specific events types. The event filters and event handlers registered to a node are executed as the event passes through the node during the capture and the bubbling phases, respectively.

During the route traversal, a node can consume the event in event filters or handlers, thus completing the processing of the event. Consuming an event is simply calling the consume() method on the event object. When an event is consumed, the event processing is stopped, even though some of the nodes in the route were not traversed at all.

Interaction of the user with the UI elements using the mouse, such as clicking, moving, or pressing the mouse, triggers a mouse event. An object of the MouseEvent class represents a mouse event.

A key event denotes the occurrence of a keystroke. It is delivered to the node that has focus. An instance of the KeyEvent class represents a key event. Key pressed, key released, and key typed are three types of key events.

A window event occurs when a window is shown, hidden, or closed. An instance of the WindowEvent class in the javafx.stage package represents a window event.

The next chapter discusses layout panes that are used as containers for other controls and nodes.

CHAPTER 10

■ ■ ■

Understanding Layout Panes

In this chapter, you will learn:

- What a layout pane is
- Classes in JavaFX representing layout panes
- How to add children to layout panes
- Utility classes such as Insets, HPos, VPos, Side, Priority, etc.
- How to use a Group to layout nodes
- How to work with Regions and its properties
- How to use different types of layout panes such as HBox, VBox, FlowPane, BorderPane, StackPane, TilePane, GridPane, AnchorPane, and TextFlow

What Is a Layout Pane?

You can use two types of layouts to arrange nodes in a scene graph:

- Static layout
- Dynamic layout

In a static layout, the position and size of nodes are calculated once, and they stay the same as the window is resized. The user interface looks good when the window has the size for which the nodes were originally laid out.

In a dynamic layout, nodes in a scene graph are laid out every time a user action necessitates a change in their position, size, or both. Typically, changing the position or size of one node affects the position and size of all other nodes in the scene graph. The dynamic layout forces the recomputation of the position and size of some or all nodes as the window is resized.

Both static and dynamic layouts have advantages and disadvantages. A static layout gives developers full control on the design of the user interface. It lets you make use of the available space as you see fit. A dynamic layout requires more programming work, and the logic is much more involved. Typically, programming languages supporting GUI: for example, JavaFX, supports dynamic layouts through libraries. Libraries solve most of the use-cases for dynamic layouts. If they do not meet your needs, you must do the hard work to roll out your own dynamic layout.

A *layout pane* is a node that contains other nodes, which are known as its children (or child nodes). The responsibility of a layout pane is to lay out its children, whenever needed. A layout pane is also known as a *container* or a *layout container*.

A layout pane has a *layout policy* that controls how the layout pane lays out its children. For example, a layout pane may lay out its children horizontally, vertically, or in any other fashion.

JavaFX contains several layout-related classes, which are the topic of discussion in this chapter. A layout pane performs two things:

- It computes the position (the x and y coordinates) of the node within its parent.

- It computes the size (the width and height) of the node.

For a 3D node, a layout pane also computes the z coordinate of the position and the depth of the size.

The layout policy of a container is a set of rules to compute the position and size of its children. When I discuss containers in this chapter, pay attention to the layout policy of the containers as to how they compute the position and size of their children. A node has three sizes: preferred size, minimum size, and maximum size. Most of the containers attempt to give its children their preferred size. The actual (or current) size of a node may be different from its preferred size. The current size of a node depends on the size of the window, the layout policy of the container, and the expanding and shrinking policy for the node, etc.

Layout Pane Classes

JavaFX contains several container classes. Figure 10-1 shows a class diagram for the container classes. A container class is a subclass, direct or indirect, of the Parent class.

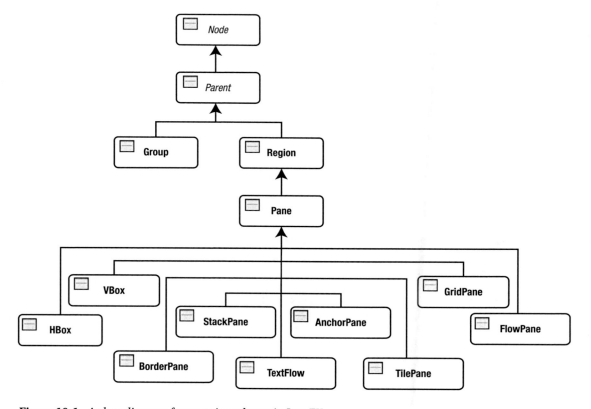

Figure 10-1. *A class diagram for container classes in JavaFX*

A Group lets you apply effects and transformations to all its children collectively. The Group class is in the javafx.scene package.

Subclasses of the Region class are used to lay out children. They can be styled with CSS. The Region class and most of its subclasses are in the javafx.scene.layout package.

It is true that a container needs to be a subclass of the Parent class. However, not all subclasses of the Parent class are containers. For example, the Button class is a subclass of the Parent class; however, it is a control, not a container. A node must be added to a container to be part of a scene graph. The container lays out its children according to its layout policy. If you do not want the container to manage the layout for a node, you need to set the managed property of the node to false. Please refer to the chapter on *Understanding Nodes* for more details and examples on managed and unmanaged nodes.

A node can be a child node of only one container at a time. If a node is added to a container while it is already the child node of another container, the node is removed from the first container before being added to the second one. Oftentimes, it is necessary to nest containers to create a complex layout. That is, you can add a container to another container as a child node.

The Parent class contains three methods to get the list of children of a container:

- protected ObservableList<Node> getChildren()

- public ObservableList<Node> getChildrenUnmodifiable()

- protected <E extends Node> List<E> getManagedChildren()

The getChildren() method returns a modifiable ObservableList of the child nodes of a container. If you want to add a node to a container, you would add the node to this list. This is the most commonly used method for container classes. We have been using this method to add children to containers such as Group, HBox, VBox, etc., from the very first program.

Notice the protected access for the getChildren() method. If a subclass of the Parent class does not want to be a container, it will keep the access for this method as protected. For example, control-related classes (Button, TextField, etc.) keep this method as protected, so you cannot add child nodes to them. A container class overrides this method and makes it public. For example, the Group and Pane classes expose this method as public.

The getChildrenUnmodifiable() method is declared public in the Parent class. It returns a read-only ObservableList of children. It is useful in two scenarios:

- You need to pass the list of children of a container to a method that should not modify the list.

- You want to know what makes up a control, which is not a container.

The getManagedChildren() method has the protected access. Container classes do not expose it as public. They use it internally to get the list of managed children, during layouts. You will use this method to roll out your own container classes.

Table 10-1 has brief descriptions of the container classes. We will discuss them in detail with examples in subsequent sections.

Table 10-1. *List of Container Classes*

Container Class	Description
Group	A Group applies effects and transformations collectively to all its children.
Pane	It is used for absolute positioning of its children.
HBox	It arranges its children horizontally in a single row.
VBox	It arranges its children vertically in a single column.
FlowPane	It arranges its children horizontally or vertically in rows or columns. If they do not fit in a single row or column, they are wrapped at the specified width or height.
BorderPane	It divides its layout area in the top, right, bottom, left, and center regions and places each of its children in one of the five regions.
StackPane	It arranges its children in a back-to-front stack.
TilePane	It arranges its children in a grid of uniformly sized cells.
GridPane	It arranges its children in a grid of variable sized cells.
AnchorPane	It arranges its children by anchoring their edges to the edges of the layout area.
TextFlow	It lays out rich text whose content may consist of several Text nodes.

Adding Children to a Layout Pane

A container is meant to contain children. You can add children to a container when you create the container object or after creating it. All container classes provide constructors that take a var-args Node type argument to add the initial set of children. Some containers provide constructors to add an initial set of children and set initial properties for the containers.

You can also add children to a container at any time after the container is created. Containers store their children in an observable list, which can be retrieved using the getChildren() method. Adding a node to a container is as simple as adding a node to that observable list. The following snippet of code shows how to add children to an HBox when it is created and after it is created.

```
// Create two buttons
Button okBtn = new Button("OK");
Button cancelBtn = new Button("Cancel");

// Create an HBox with two buttons as its children
HBox hBox1 = new HBox(okBtn, cancelBtn);

// Create an HBox with two buttons with 20px horizontal spacing between them
double hSpacing = 20;
HBox hBox2 = new HBox(hSpacing, okBtn, cancelBtn);

// Create an empty HBox, and afterwards, add two buttons to it
HBox hBox3 = new HBox();
hBox3.getChildren().addAll(okBtn, cancelBtn);
```

■ **Tip** When you need to add multiple child nodes to a container, use the `addAll()` method of the `ObservableList` rather than using the `add()` method multiple times.

Utility Classes and Enums

While working with layout panes, you will need to use several classes and enums that are related to spacing and directions. These classes and enums are not useful when used stand-alone. They are always used as properties for nodes. This section describes some of these classes and enums.

The Insets Class

The `Insets` class represents inside offsets in four directions: top, right, bottom, and left, for a rectangular area. It is an immutable class. It has two constructors – one lets you set the same offset for all four directions and another lets you set different offsets for each direction.

- `Insets(double topRightBottomLeft)`

- `Insets(double top, double right, double bottom, double left)`

The `Insets` class declares a constant, `Insets.EMPTY`, to represent a zero offset for all four directions. Use the `getTop()`, `getRight()`, `getBottom()`, and `getLeft()` methods to get the value of the offset in a specific direction.

It is a bit confusing to understand the exact meaning of the term *insets* by looking at the description of the `Insets` class. Let us discuss its meaning in detail in this section. We talk about insets in the context of two rectangles. An inset is the distance between the same edges (from top to top, from left to left, etc.) of two rectangles. There are four inset values – one for each side of the rectangles. An object of the `Insets` class stores the four distances. Figure 10-2 shows two rectangles and the insets of the inner rectangle relative to the outer rectangle.

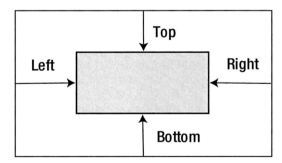

Figure 10-2. *Insets of a rectangular area relative to another rectangular area*

It is possible for two rectangles to overlap instead of one to be contained fully within another. In this case, some inset values may be positive and some negative. Inset values are interpreted relative to a reference rectangle. To interpret an inset value correctly, it is required that you get the position of the reference rectangle, its edge, and the direction in which the inset needs to be measured. The context where the term "insets" is used should make these pieces of information available. In the figure, we can define the same insets relative to the inner or outer rectangle. The inset values would not change. However, the reference rectangle and the direction in which the insets are measured (to determine the sign of the inset values) will change.

Typically, in JavaFX, the term insets and the Insets object are used in four contexts:

- Border insets

- Background insets

- Outsets

- Insets

In the first two contexts, insets mean the distances between the edges of the layout bounds and the inner edge of the border or the inner edge of the background. In these contents, insets are measured inwards from the edges of the layout bounds. A negative value for an inset means a distance measured outward from the edges of the layout bounds.

A border stroke or image may fall outside of the layout bounds of a Region. Outsets are the distances between the edges of the layout bounds of a Region and the outer edges of its border. Outsets are also represented as an Insets object.

Javadoc for JavaFX uses the term insets several times to mean the sum of the thickness of the border and the padding measured inward from all edges of the layout bounds. Be careful interpreting the meaning of the term insets when you encounter it in Javadoc.

The HPos Enum

The HPos enum defines three constants: LEFT, CENTER, and RIGHT, to describe the horizontal positioning and alignment.

The VPos Enum

The constants of the VPos enum describe vertical positioning and alignment. It has four constants: TOP, CENTER, BASELINE, and BOTTOM.

The Pos Enum

The constants in the Pos enum describe vertical and horizontal positioning and alignment. It has constants for all combinations of VPos and HPos constants. Constants in Pos enum are BASELINE_CENTER, BASELINE_LEFT, BASELINE_RIGHT, BOTTOM_CENTER, BOTTOM_LEFT, BOTTOM_RIGHT, CENTER, CENTER_LEFT, CENTER_RIGHT, TOP_CENTER, TOP_LEFT, and TOP_RIGHT. It has two methods – getHpos() and getVpos() – that return objects of HPos and VPos enum types, describing the horizontal and vertical positioning and alignment, respectively.

The HorizontalDirection Enum

The HorizontalDirection enum has two constants, LEFT and RIGHT, which denote directions to the left and right, respectively.

The VerticalDirection Enum

The `VerticalDirection` enum has two constants, `UP` and `DOWN`, which denote up and down directions, respectively.

The Orientation Enum

The `Orientation` enum has two constants, `HORIZONTAL` and `VERTICAL`, which denote horizontal and vertical orientations, respectively.

The Side Enum

The `Side` enum has four constants: `TOP`, `RIGHT`, `BOTTOM`, and `LEFT`, to denote the four sides of a rectangle.

The Priority Enum

Sometimes, a container may have more or less space available than required to layout its children using their preferred sizes. The `Priority` enum is used to denote the priority of a node to grow or shrink when its parent has more or less space. It contains three constants: `ALWAYS`, `NEVER`, and `SOMETIMES`. A node with the `ALWAYS` priority always grows or shrinks as the available space increases or decreases. A node with `NEVER` priority never grows or shrinks as the available space increases or decreases. A node with `SOMETIMES` priority grows or shrinks when there are no other nodes with `ALWAYS` priority or nodes with `ALWAYS` priority could not consume all the increased or decreased space.

Understanding Group

A `Group` has features of a container; for example, it has its own layout policy, coordinate system, and it is a subclass of the `Parent` class. However, its meaning is best reflected by calling it a *collection of nodes* or a *group*, rather than a *container*. It is used to manipulate a collection of nodes as a single node (or as a group). Transformations, effects, and properties applied to a `Group` are applied to all nodes in the `Group`.

A `Group` has its own layout policy, which does not provide any specific layout to its children, except giving them their preferred size:

- It renders nodes in the order they are added.

- It does not position its children. All children are positioned at (0, 0) by default. You need to write code to position child nodes of a `Group`. Use the `layoutX` and `layoutY` properties of the children nodes to position them within the `Group`.

- By default, it resizes all its children to their preferred size. The auto-sizing behavior can be disabled by setting its `autoSizeChildren` property to false. Note that if you disable the auto-sizing property, all nodes, except shapes, will be invisible as their size will be zero, by default.

A `Group` does not have a size of its own. It is not resizable directly. Its size is the collective bounds of its children. Its bounds change, as the bounds of any or all of its children change. The chapter on *Understanding Nodes* explains how different types of bounds of a `Group` are computed.

Creating a Group Object

You can use the no-args constructor to create an empty Group.

```
Group emptyGroup = new Group();
```

Other constructors of the Group class let you add children to the Group. One constructor takes a Collection<Node> as the initial children; another takes a var-args of the Node type.

```
Button smallBtn = new Button("Small Button");
Button bigBtn = new Button("This is a big button");

// Create a Group with two buttons using its var-args constructor
Group group1 = new Group(smallBtn, bigBtn);

List<Node> initailList = new ArrayList<>();
initailList.add(smallBtn);
initailList.add(bigBtn);

// Create a Group with all Nodes in the initialList as its children
Group group2 = new Group(initailList);
```

Rendering Nodes in a Group

Children of a Group are rendered in the order they are added. The following snippet of code, when displayed in a stage, looks as shown in Figure 10-3.

```
Button smallBtn = new Button("Small button");
Button bigBtn = new Button("This is a big button");
Group root = new Group();
root.getChildren().addAll(smallBtn, bigBtn);
Scene scene = new Scene(root);
```

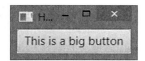

Figure 10-3. *Rendering order of the children in a Group: first smaller and second bigger*

Notice that we have added two buttons to the Group. Only one of the buttons is shown. The smaller button is rendered first because it is the first one in the collection. The bigger button is rendered covering the smaller button. Both buttons exist. One is just hidden under another. If we swap the order in which buttons are added, using the following statement, the resulting screen would be as shown in Figure 10-4. Notice that the left part of the bigger button is covered by the smaller button and the right part is still showing.

```
// Add the bigger button first
root.getChildren().addAll(bigBtn, smallBtn);
```

Figure 10-4. *Rendering order of the children in a Group: first bigger and second smaller*

■ **Tip** If you do not want nodes in a Group to overlap, you need to set their positions.

Positioning Nodes in a Group

You can position child nodes in a Group by assigning them absolute positions using the layoutX and layoutY properties of the nodes. Alternatively, you can use binding API to position them relative to other nodes in the Group.

Listing 10-1 shows how to use the absolute and relative positioning in a Group. Figure 10-5 shows the resulting screen. The program adds two buttons (*OK* and *Cancel)* to the Group. The *OK* button uses absolute positioning; it is placed at (10, 10). The Cancel button is placed relative to the *OK* button; its vertical position is the same as the *OK* button; its horizontal position is 20px after the right edge of the *OK* button. Notice the use of the *Fluent Binding API* to accomplish the relative positioning for the *Cancel* button.

Listing 10-1. Laying Out Nodes in a Group

```java
// NodesLayoutInGroup.java
package com.jdojo.container;

import javafx.application.Application;
import javafx.beans.binding.NumberBinding;
import javafx.scene.Group;
import javafx.scene.Scene;
import javafx.scene.control.Button;
import javafx.stage.Stage;

public class NodesLayoutInGroup extends Application {
        public static void main(String[] args) {
                Application.launch(args);
        }

        @Override
        public void start(Stage stage) {
                // Create two buttons
                Button okBtn = new Button("OK");
                Button cancelBtn = new Button("Cancel");

                // Set the location of the OK button
                okBtn.setLayoutX(10);
                okBtn.setLayoutY(10);
```

```
                    // Set the location of the Cancel botton relative to the OK button
                    NumberBinding layoutXBinding =
                            okBtn.layoutXProperty().add(okBtn.widthProperty().add(10));
                    cancelBtn.layoutXProperty().bind(layoutXBinding);
                    cancelBtn.layoutYProperty().bind(okBtn.layoutYProperty());

                    Group root = new Group();
                    root.getChildren().addAll(okBtn, cancelBtn);

                    Scene scene = new Scene(root);
                    stage.setScene(scene);
                    stage.setTitle("Positioning Nodes in a Group");
                    stage.show();
        }
}
```

Figure 10-5. *A Group with two buttons using relative positions*

Applying Effects and Transformations to a Group

When you apply effects and transformations to a Group, they are automatically applied to all of its children. Setting a property, for example, the disable or opacity property, on a Group, sets the property on all of its children.

Listing 10-2 shows how to apply effects, transformations, and states to a Group. The program adds two buttons to the Group. It applies a rotation transformation of 10 degrees, a drop shadow effect, and opacity of 80%. Figure 10-6 shows that the transformation, effect, and state applied to the Group are applied to all of its children (two buttons in this case).

Listing 10-2. Applying Effects and Transformations to a Group

```
// GroupEffect.java
package com.jdojo.container;

import javafx.application.Application;
import javafx.scene.Group;
import javafx.scene.Scene;
import javafx.scene.control.Button;
import javafx.scene.effect.DropShadow;
import javafx.stage.Stage;

public class GroupEffect extends Application {
        public static void main(String[] args) {
                Application.launch(args);
        }
```

```
        @Override
        public void start(Stage stage) {
                // Create two buttons
                Button okBtn = new Button("OK");
                Button cancelBtn = new Button("Cancel");

                // Set the locations of the buttons
                okBtn.setLayoutX(10);
                okBtn.setLayoutY(10);
                cancelBtn.setLayoutX(80);
                cancelBtn.setLayoutY(10);

                Group root = new Group();
                root.setEffect(new DropShadow()); // Set a drop shadow effect
                root.setRotate(10);                // Rotate by 10 degrees clockwise
                root.setOpacity(0.80);             // Set the opacity to 80%

                root.getChildren().addAll(okBtn, cancelBtn);

                Scene scene = new Scene(root);
                stage.setScene(scene);
                stage.setTitle("Applying Transformations and Effects to a Group");
                stage.show();
        }
}
```

Figure 10-6. *Two buttons in a Group after effects, transformations, and states are applied to the Group*

Styling a Group with CSS

The Group class does not offer much CSS styling. All CSS properties for the Node class are available for the Group class: for example, -fx-cursor, -fx-opacity, -fx-rotate, etc. A Group cannot have its own appearance such as padding, backgrounds, and borders.

Understanding Region

Region is the base class for all layout panes. It can be styled with CSS. Unlike Group, it has its own size. It is resizable. It can have a visual appearance, for example, with padding, multiple backgrounds, and multiple borders. You do not use the Region class directly as a layout pane. If you want to roll out your own layout pane, extend the Pane class, which extends the Region class.

■ **Tip** The Region class is designed to support the CSS3 specification for backgrounds and borders, as they are applicable to JavaFX. The specification for "CSS Backgrounds and Borders Module Level 3" can be found online at http://www.w3.org/TR/2012/CR-css3-background-20120724/.

By default, a Region defines a rectangular area. However, it can be changed to any shape. The drawing area of a Region is divided into several parts. Depending on the property settings, a Region may draw outside of its layout bounds. Parts of a Region:

- Backgrounds (fills and images)

- Content Area

- Padding

- Borders (strokes and images)

- Margin

- Region Insets

Figure 10-7 shows parts of a Region. The margin is not directly supported as of JavaFX 2. You can get the same effect by using Insets for the border.

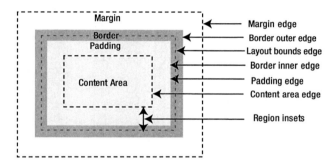

Figure 10-7. *Different parts of a Region*

A region may have a background that is drawn first. The content area is the area where the content of the Region (e.g., controls) are drawn.

Padding is an optional space around the content area. If the padding has a zero width, the padding edge and the content area edge are the same.

The border area is the space around the padding. If the border has a zero width, the border edge and the padding edge are the same.

Margin is the space around the border. Padding and margin are very similar. The only difference between them is that the margin defines the space around the outside edge of the border, whereas the padding defines the space around the inside edge of the border. Margins are supported for controls when they are added to panes, for example, HBox, VBox, etc. However, margins are not directly supported for a Region directly.

The content area, padding, and borders affect the layout bounds of the Region. You can draw borders outside the layout bounds of a Region, and those borders will not affect the layout bounds of the Region. Margin does not affect the layout bounds of the Region.

The distance between the edge of the layout bounds of the Region and its content area defines the insets for the Region. The Region class computes its insets automatically based on its properties. It has a read-only insets property that you can read to know its insets. Note that a layout container would need to know the area in which to place its children, and they can compute the content area knowing the layout bounds and insets.

■ **Tip** The background fills, background images, border strokes, border images, and content of a Region are drawn in order.

Setting Backgrounds

A Region can have a background that consists of fills, images, or both. A fill consists of a color, radii for four corners, and insets on four sides. Fills are applied in the order they are specified. The color defines the color to be used for painting the background. The radii define the radii to be used for corners; set them to zero if you want rectangular corners. The insets define the distance between the sides of the Region and the outer edges of the background fill. For example, an inset of 10px on top means that a horizontal strip of 10px inside the top edge of the layout bounds will not be painted by the background fill. An inset for the fill may be negative. A negative inset extends the painted area outside of the layout bounds of the Region; and in this case, the drawn area for the Region extends beyond its layout bounds.

The following CSS properties define the background fill for a Region.

- -fx-background-color
- -fx-background-radius
- -fx-background-insets

The following CSS properties fill the entire layout bounds of the Region with a red color.

```
-fx-background-color: red;
-fx-background-insets: 0;
-fx-background-radius: 0;
```

The following CSS properties use two fills.

```
-fx-background-color: lightgray, red;
-fx-background-insets: 0, 4;
-fx-background-radius: 4, 2;
```

The first fill covers the entire Region (see 0px insets) with a light gray color; it uses a 4px radius for all four corners, making the Region look like a rounded rectangle. The second fill covers the Region with a red color; it uses a 4px inset on all four sides, which means that 4px from the edges of the Region are not painted by this fill, and that area will still have the light gray color used by the first fill. A 2px radius for all four corners is used by the second fill.

Starting from JavaFX 8, you can also set the background of a Region in code using Java objects. An instance of the Background class represents the background of a Region. The class defines a Background.EMPTY constant to represent an empty background (no fills and no images).

■ **Tip** A Background object is immutable. It can be safely used as the background of multiple Regions.

A Background object has zero or more fills and images. An instance of the BackgroundFill class represents a fill; an instance of the BackgroundImage class represents an image.

The Region class contains a background property of the ObjectProperty<Background> type. The background of a Region is set using the setBackground(Background bg) method.

The following snippet of code creates a Background object with two BackgroundFill objects. Setting this to a Region produces the same effects of drawing a background with two fills as shown in the above snippet of code using the CSS style. Notice that the Insets and CornerRadii classes are used to define the insets and the radius for corners for the fills.

```
import javafx.geometry.Insets;
import javafx.scene.layout.Background;
import javafx.scene.layout.BackgroundFill;
import javafx.scene.layout.CornerRadii;
import javafx.scene.paint.Color;
...
BackgroundFill lightGrayFill =
        new BackgroundFill(Color.LIGHTGRAY, new CornerRadii(4), new Insets(0));

BackgroundFill redFill = new BackgroundFill(Color.RED, new CornerRadii(2), new Insets(4));

// Create a Background object with two BackgroundFill objects
Background bg = new Background(lightGrayFill, redFill);
```

The program in Listing 10-3 shows how to set the background for a Pane, which is a Region, using both the CSS properties and the Background object. The resulting screen is shown in Figure 10-8. The getCSSStyledPane() method creates a Pane, adds a background with two fills using CSS, and returns the Pane. The getObjectStyledPane() method creates a Pane, adds a background with two fills using Java classes, and returns the Pane. The start() method adds the two Panes to another Pane and positions them side-by-side.

Listing 10-3. Using Background Fills as the Background for a Region

```
// BackgroundFillTest.java
package com.jdojo.container;

import javafx.application.Application;
import javafx.geometry.Insets;
import javafx.scene.Scene;
import javafx.scene.layout.Background;
import javafx.scene.layout.BackgroundFill;
import javafx.scene.layout.CornerRadii;
import javafx.scene.layout.Pane;
import javafx.scene.paint.Color;
import javafx.stage.Stage;
```

```java
public class BackgroundFillTest extends Application {
        public static void main(String[] args) {
                Application.launch(args);
        }

        @Override
        public void start(Stage stage) {
                Pane p1 = this.getCSSStyledPane();
                Pane p2 = this.getObjectStyledPane();

                p1.setLayoutX(10);
                p1.setLayoutY(10);

                // Place p2 20px right to p1
                p2.layoutYProperty().bind(p1.layoutYProperty());
                p2.layoutXProperty().bind(p1.layoutXProperty().add(p1.widthProperty()).
                add(20));

                Pane root = new Pane(p1, p2);
                root.setPrefSize(240, 70);
                Scene scene = new Scene(root);
                stage.setScene(scene);
                stage.setTitle("Setting Background Fills for a Region");
                stage.show();
                stage.sizeToScene();
        }

        public Pane getCSSStyledPane() {
                Pane p = new Pane();
                p.setPrefSize(100, 50);
                p.setStyle("-fx-background-color: lightgray, red;"
                                + "-fx-background-insets: 0, 4;"
                                + "-fx-background-radius: 4, 2;");

                return p;
        }

        public Pane getObjectStyledPane() {
                Pane p = new Pane();
                p.setPrefSize(100, 50);

                BackgroundFill lightGrayFill =
                        new BackgroundFill(Color.LIGHTGRAY, new CornerRadii(4),
                        new Insets(0));

                BackgroundFill redFill =
                        new BackgroundFill(Color.RED, new CornerRadii(2), new Insets(4));
```

```
        // Create a Background object with two BackgroundFill objects
        Background bg = new Background(lightGrayFill, redFill);
        p.setBackground(bg);

        return p;
    }
}
```

Figure 10-8. *Two Panes having identical backgrounds set: one using CSS and one using Java objects*

The following CSS properties define the background image for a Region.

- -fx-background-image

- -fx-background-repeat

- -fx-background-position

- -fx-background-size

The -fx-background-image property is a CSS URL for the image. The -fx-background-repeat property indicates how the image will be repeated (or not repeated) to cover the drawing area of the Region. The -fx-background-position determines how the image is positioned with the Region. The -fx-background-size property determines the size of the image relative to the Region.

The following CSS properties fill the entire layout bounds of the Region with a red color.

```
-fx-background-image: URL('your_image_url_goes_here');
-fx-background-repeat: space;
-fx-background-position: center;
-fx-background-size: cover;
```

The following snippet of code and the above set of the CSS properties will produce identical effects when they are set on a Region.

```
import javafx.scene.image.Image;
import javafx.scene.layout.Background;
import javafx.scene.layout.BackgroundImage;
import javafx.scene.layout.BackgroundPosition;
import javafx.scene.layout.BackgroundRepeat;
import javafx.scene.layout.BackgroundSize;
...
Image image = new Image("your_image_url_goes_here");
BackgroundSize bgSize = new BackgroundSize(100, 100, true, true, false, true);
```

```
BackgroundImage bgImage = new BackgroundImage(image,
                                    BackgroundRepeat.SPACE,
                                    BackgroundRepeat.SPACE,
                                    BackgroundPosition.DEFAULT,
                                    bgSize);

// Create a Background object with an BackgroundImage object
Background bg = new Background(bgImage);
```

Setting Padding

The padding of a Region is the space around its content area. The Region class contains a padding property of the ObjectProperty<Insets> type. You can set separate padding widths for each of the four sides.

```
// Create an HBox
HBox hb = new HBox();

// A uniform padding of 10px around all edges
hb.setPadding(new Insets(10));

// A non-uniform padding: 2px top, 4px right, 6px bottom, and 8px left
hb.setPadding(new Insets(2, 4, 6, 8));
```

Setting Borders

A Region can have a border, which consists of strokes, images, or both. If strokes and images are not present, the border is considered empty. Strokes and images are applied in the order they are specified; all strokes are applied before images. Before JavaFX 8, you could set the border only using CSS. Starting JavaFX 8, you also set the border using the Border class in code.

■ **Note** We will use the phrases, "the edges of a Region" and "the layout bounds of a Region," in this section, synonymously, which mean the edges of the rectangle defined by the layout bounds of the Region.

A stroke consists of five properties:

- A color
- A style
- A width
- Radii for four corners
- Insets on four sides

The color defines the color to be used for the stroke. You can specify four different colors for the four sides.

The style defines the style for the stroke: for example, solid, dashed, etc. The style also defines the location of the border relative to its insets: for example, inside, outside, or centered. You can specify four different styles for the four sides.

The radii define the radii for corners; set them to zero if you want rectangular corners.

The width of the stroke defines its thickness. You can specify four different widths for the four sides.

The insets of a stroke define the distance from the sides of the layout bounds of the Region where the border is drawn. A positive value for the inset for a side is measured inward from the edge of the Region. A negative value of the inset for a side is measured outward from the edge of the Region. An inset of zero on a side means the edge of the layout bounds itself. It is possible to have positive insets for some sides (e.g., top and bottom) and negative insets for others (e.g., right and left). Figure 10-9 shows the positions of positive and negative insets relative to the layout bounds of a Region. The rectangle in solid lines is the layout bounds of a Region, and the rectangles in dashed lines are the insets lines.

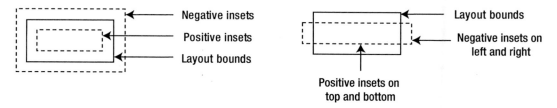

Figure 10-9. *Positions of positive and negative insets relative to the layout bounds*

The border stroke may be drawn inside, outside, or partially inside and partially outside the layout bounds of the Region. To determine the exact position of a stroke relative to the layout bounds, you need to look at its two properties: *insets* and *style*.

- If the style of the stroke is inside, the stroke is drawn inside the insets.

- If the style is outside, it is drawn outside the insets.

- If the style is centered, it is drawn half inside and half outside the insets.

Figure 10-10 shows some examples of the border positions for a Region. The rectangle in dashed lines indicates the layout bounds of the Region. Borders are shown in a light gray color. The label below each Region shows the some details of the border properties (e.g., style, insets, and width).

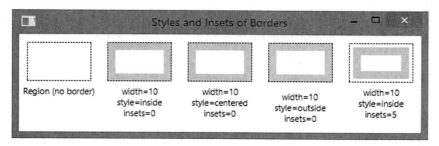

Figure 10-10. *Examples of determining the position of a border based on its style and insets*

The following CSS properties define border strokes for a Region.

- -fx-border-color

- -fx-border-style

- -fx-border-width

- -fx-border-radius

- -fx-border-insets

The following CSS properties draw a border with a stroke of 10px in width and red in color. The outside edge of the border will be the same as the edges of the Region as we have set insets and style as zero and inside, respectively. The border will be rounded on the corners as we have set the radii for all corners to 5px.

```
-fx-border-color: red;
-fx-border-style: solid inside;
-fx-border-width: 10;
-fx-border-insets: 0;
-fx-border-radius: 5;
```

The following CSS properties use two strokes for a border. The first stroke is drawn inside the edges of the Region and the second one outside.

```
-fx-border-color: red, green;
-fx-border-style: solid inside, solid outside;
-fx-border-width: 5, 2 ;
-fx-border-insets: 0, 0;
-fx-border-radius: 0, 0;
```

■ **Tip**　The part of the border drawn outside the edges of the Region does not affect its layout bounds. The part of the border drawn outside the edges of the Region is within the layout bounds of the Region. In other words, the border area that falls inside the edges of a Region influences the layout bounds for that Region.

So far, we have discussed the insets for strokes of a border. A border also has *insets* and *outsets*, which are computed automatically based on the properties for its strokes and images. The distance between the edges of the Region and the inner edges of its border, considering all strokes and images that are drawn *inside* the edges of the Region, is known as the *insets of the border*. The distance between the edges of the Region and the outer edges of its border, considering all strokes and images that are drawn *outside* the edges of the Region, is known as the *outsets of the border*. You must be able to differentiate between the insets of a stroke and insets/outsets a border. The insets of a stroke determine the location where the stroke is drawn, whereas the insets/outsets of a border tell you how far the border extends inside/outside of the edges of the Region. Figure 10-11 shows how the insets and outsets of a border are computed. The dashed line shows the layout bounds of a Region, which has a border with two strokes: one in red and one in green. The following styles, when set on a 150px X 50px Region, results in the border as shown in Figure 10-11.

```
-fx-background-color: white;
-fx-padding: 10;
-fx-border-color: red, green, black;
-fx-border-style: solid inside, solid outside, dashed centered;
-fx-border-width: 10, 8, 1;
-fx-border-insets: 12, -10, 0;
-fx-border-radius: 0, 0, 0;
```

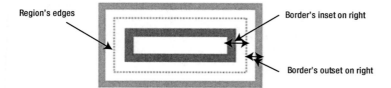

Figure 10-11. *Relationship between insets/outsets of a border and the layout bounds of a Region*

The insets of the border are 22px on all four sides, which is computed (10px + 12px) by adding the 10px width of the red border drawn inside 12px (insets) from the edges of the Region. The outsets of the border are 18px on all four sides, which is computed (8px + 10px) by adding the 8px width of the green border drawn outside 10px (-10 insets) from the edges of the Region.

Starting from JavaFX 8, you can also set the border of a Region in code using Java objects. An instance of the Border class represents the border of a Region. The class defines a Border.EMPTY constant to represent an empty border (no strokes and no images).

■ **Tip** A Border object is immutable. It can be safely used for multiple Regions.

A Border object has zero or more strokes and images. The Border class provides several constructors that take multiple strokes and images as arguments. The Region class contains a border property of the ObjectProperty<Border> type. The border of a Region is set using the setBorder(Border b) method.

An instance of the BorderStroke class represents a stroke; an instance of the BorderImage class represents an image. The BorderStroke class provides constructors to set the style of the stroke. The following are the two commonly used constructors. The third constructor allows you to set different color and style of strokes on four sides.

- BorderStroke(Paint stroke, BorderStrokeStyle style, CornerRadii radii, BorderWidths widths)

- BorderStroke(Paint stroke, BorderStrokeStyle style, CornerRadii radii, BorderWidths widths, Insets insets)

The BorderStrokeStyle class represents the style of a stroke. The BorderWidths class represents widths of a stroke on all four sides of a border. It lets you set the widths as absolute values or as a percentage of the dimensions of the Region. The following snippet of code creates a Border and sets it to a Pane.

```
BorderStrokeStyle style = new BorderStrokeStyle(StrokeType.INSIDE,
                                                StrokeLineJoin.MITER,
                                                StrokeLineCap.BUTT,
                                                10,
                                                0,
                                                null);
BorderStroke stroke = new BorderStroke(Color.GREEN,
                                       style,
                                       CornerRadii.EMPTY,
                                       new BorderWidths(8),
                                       new Insets(10));
```

```
Pane p = new Pane();
p.setPrefSize(100, 50);
Border b = new Border(stroke);
p.setBorder(b);
```

The Border class provides getInsets() and getOutsets() methods that return the insets and outsets for the Border. Both methods return an Insets object. Remember that the insets and outsets for a Border are different from insets of strokes. They are computed automatically based on the insets and styles for strokes and images that a Border has.

You can get all strokes and all images of a Border using its getStrokes() and getImages() methods, which return List<BorderStroke> and List<BorderImage>, respectively. You can compare two Border objects and two BorderStroke objects for equality using their equals() method.

Listing 10-4 demonstrates how to create and set a border to a Pane. It displays a screen with two Panes. One Pane is styled using CSS and another using a Border object. The Panes look similar to the one shown in Figure 10-11. The program prints the insets and outsets for the borders and checks whether both borders are the same or not. Both borders use three strokes. The getCSSStyledPane() method returns a Pane styled with CSS; the getObjectStyledPane() method returns a Pane styled using a Border object.

Listing 10-4. Using Strokes as the Border for a Region

```
// BorderStrokeTest.java
package com.jdojo.container;

import java.util.ArrayList;
import java.util.List;
import javafx.application.Application;
import javafx.geometry.Insets;
import javafx.scene.Scene;
import javafx.scene.layout.Background;
import javafx.scene.layout.Border;
import javafx.scene.layout.BorderStroke;
import javafx.scene.layout.BorderStrokeStyle;
import javafx.scene.layout.BorderWidths;
import javafx.scene.layout.CornerRadii;
import javafx.scene.layout.Pane;
import javafx.scene.paint.Color;
import javafx.scene.shape.StrokeLineCap;
import javafx.scene.shape.StrokeLineJoin;
import javafx.scene.shape.StrokeType;
import javafx.stage.Stage;

public class BorderStrokeTest extends Application {
        public static void main(String[] args) {
                Application.launch(args);
        }

        @Override
        public void start(Stage stage) {
                Pane p1 = this.getCSSStyledPane();
                Pane p2 = this.getObjectStyledPane();
```

```
        // Place p1 and p2
        p1.setLayoutX(20);
        p1.setLayoutY(20);
        p2.layoutYProperty().bind(p1.layoutYProperty());
        p2.layoutXProperty().bind(
                        p1.layoutXProperty().add(p1.widthProperty()).add(40));

        Pane root = new Pane(p1, p2);
        root.setPrefSize(300, 120);
        Scene scene = new Scene(root);
        stage.setScene(scene);
        stage.setTitle("Setting Background Fills for a Region");
        stage.show();

        // Print borders details
        printBorderDetails(p1.getBorder(), p2.getBorder());
    }

    public Pane getCSSStyledPane() {
        Pane p = new Pane();
        p.setPrefSize(100, 50);
        p.setStyle("-fx-padding: 10;" +
                        "-fx-border-color: red, green, black;" +
                        "-fx-border-style: solid inside, solid outside, dashed
                        centered;" +
                        "-fx-border-width: 10, 8, 1;" +
                        "-fx-border-insets: 12, -10, 0;" +
                        "-fx-border-radius: 0, 0, 0;");

        return p;
    }

    public Pane getObjectStyledPane() {
        Pane p = new Pane();
        p.setPrefSize(100, 50);
        p.setBackground(Background.EMPTY);
        p.setPadding(new Insets(10));

        // Create three border strokes
        BorderStroke redStroke = new BorderStroke(Color.RED,
                        BorderStrokeStyle.SOLID,
                        CornerRadii.EMPTY,
                        new BorderWidths(10),
                        new Insets(12));

        BorderStrokeStyle greenStrokeStyle = new BorderStrokeStyle(StrokeType.OUTSIDE,
                        StrokeLineJoin.MITER,
                        StrokeLineCap.BUTT,
                        10,
                        0,
                        null);
```

```
        BorderStroke greenStroke = new BorderStroke(Color.GREEN,
                    greenStrokeStyle,
                    CornerRadii.EMPTY,
                    new BorderWidths(8),
                    new Insets(-10));

        List<Double> dashArray = new ArrayList<>();
        dashArray.add(2.0);
        dashArray.add(1.4);

        BorderStrokeStyle blackStrokeStyle
                    = new BorderStrokeStyle(StrokeType.CENTERED,
                            StrokeLineJoin.MITER,
                            StrokeLineCap.BUTT,
                            10,
                            0,
                            dashArray);
        BorderStroke blackStroke = new BorderStroke(Color.BLACK,
                    blackStrokeStyle,
                    CornerRadii.EMPTY,
                    new BorderWidths(1),
                    new Insets(0));

        // Create a Border object with three BorderStroke objects
        Border b = new Border(redStroke, greenStroke, blackStroke);
        p.setBorder(b);

        return p;
    }

    private void printBorderDetails(Border cssBorder, Border objectBorder) {
        System.out.println("cssBorder insets:" + cssBorder.getInsets());
        System.out.println("cssBorder outsets:" + cssBorder.getOutsets());
        System.out.println("objectBorder insets:" + objectBorder.getInsets());
        System.out.println("objectBorder outsets:" + objectBorder.getOutsets());

        if (cssBorder.equals(objectBorder)) {
                System.out.println("Borders are equal.");
        } else {
                System.out.println("Borders are not equal.");
        }
    }
}
```

```
cssBorder insets:Insets [top=22.0, right=22.0, bottom=22.0, left=22.0]
cssBorder outsets:Insets [top=18.0, right=18.0, bottom=18.0, left=18.0]
objectBorder insets:Insets [top=22.0, right=22.0, bottom=22.0, left=22.0]
objectBorder outsets:Insets [top=18.0, right=18.0, bottom=18.0, left=18.0]
Borders are equal.
```

Using an image for a border is not as straightforward as using a stroke. An image defines a rectangular area; so does a Region. A border is drawn around a Region in an area called the border image area. The border area of a Region may be the entire area of the Region; it may be partly or fully inside or outside of the Region. The insets on four edges of the Region define the border image area. To make an image a border around a Region, both the border image area and the image are divided into nine regions: four corners, four sides, and a middle. The border area is divided into nine parts by specifying widths on all four sides, top, right, bottom, and left. The width is the width of the border along those sides. The image is also sliced (divided) into nine regions by specifying the slice width for each side. Figure 10-12 shows a Region, the border image area with its nine regions, an image and its nine regions (or slices). In the figure, the border image area is the same as the area of the Region.

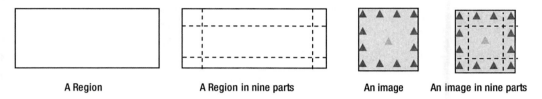

| A Region | A Region in nine parts | An image | An image in nine parts |

Figure 10-12. *Slicing a Region and an image into nine parts*

■ **Tip** The border image is not drawn if a Region uses a shape other than a rectangular shape.

Note that the four widths from the edges, while dividing a border area and an image, do not necessarily have to be uniform. For example, you can specify widths as 2px on top, 10px on right, 2px on bottom, and 10px on left.

After you have divided the border image area and the image into nine regions, you need to specify properties that control the positioning and resizing behavior of the image slices. Each of nine slices of the image has to be positioned and fit inside its corresponding part in the border image area. For example, the image slice in the upper left corner of the image has to fit in the upper-left corner part of the border image area. The two components, an image slice and its corresponding border image slice, may not be of the same size. You will need to specify how to fill the region in the border image area (scale, repeat, etc.) with the corresponding image slice. Typically, the middle slice of the image is discarded. However, if you want to fill the middle region of the border image area, you can do so with the middle slice of the image.

In Figure 10-12, the boundaries of the Region and the border image area are the same. Figure 10-13 has examples in which the boundaries of the border image area fall inside and outside of the boundary of the Region. It is possible that some regions of the border image area fall outside of the Region and some inside.

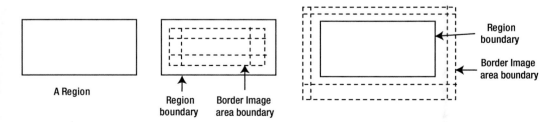

Figure 10-13. *Relationship between the area of a Region and the border image area*

The following CSS properties define border images for a Region.

- -fx-border-image-source
- -fx-border-image-repeat
- -fx-border-image-slice
- -fx-border-image-width
- -fx-border-image-insets

The -fx-border-image-source property is a CSS URL for the image. For multiple images, use a comma-separated list of CSS URLs of images.

The -fx-border-image-repeat property specifies how a slice of the image will cover the corresponding part of the Region. You can specify the property separately for the x-axis and y-axis. Valid values:

- no-repeat
- repeat
- round
- space

The no-repeat value specifies that the image slice should be scaled to fill the area without repeating it. The repeat value specifies that the image should be repeated (tiled) to fill the area. The round value specifies that the image should be repeated (tiled) to fill the area using a whole number of tiles, and if necessary, scale the image to use the whole number of tiles. The space value specifies that the image should be repeated (tiled) to fill the area using a whole number of tiles without scaling the image and by distributing the extra space uniformly around the tiles.

The -fx-border-image-slice property specifies inward offsets from the top, right, bottom, and left edges of the image to divide it into nine slices. The property can be specified as a number literal or a percentage of the side of the image. If the word fill is present in the value, the middle slice of the image is preserved and is used to fill the middle region of the border image area; otherwise, the middle slice is discarded.

The -fx-border-image-width property specifies the inward offsets from four sides of the border image area to divide the border image area into nine regions. Note that we divide the border image area into nine regions, not the Region. The property can be specified as a number literal or a percentage of the side of the border image area.

The -fx-border-image-insets property specifies the distance between the edges of the Region and the edges of the border image area on four sides. A positive inset is measured from the edge of the Region toward its center. A negative inset is measured outward from the edge of the Region. In Figure 10-13, the border image area for the Region in the middle has positive insets, whereas the border image area for the Region (third from the left) has negative insets.

Let us look at some examples of using images as a border. In all examples, we will use the image shown in Figure 10-12 as a border for a 200px X 70px Pane.

Listing 10-5 contains the CSS and Figure 10-14 shows the resulting Panes when the -fx-border-image-repeat property is set to no-repeat, repeat, space, and round. Notice that we have set the -fx-border-image-width and the -fx-border-image-slice properties to the same value of 9px. This will cause the corner slices to fit exactly into the corners of the border image area. The middle region of the border image area is not filled because we have not specified the fill value for the -fx-border-image-slice property. We have used a stroke to draw the boundary of the Pane.

Listing 10-5. Using an Image as a Border Without Filling the Middle Region

```
-fx-border-image-source: url('image_url_goes_here') ;
-fx-border-image-repeat: no-repeat;
-fx-border-image-slice: 9;
-fx-border-image-width: 9;
-fx-border-image-insets: 10;
-fx-border-color: black;
-fx-border-width: 1;
-fx-border-style: dashed inside;
```

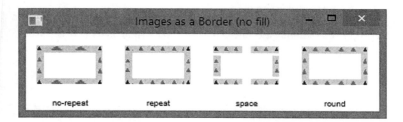

Figure 10-14. Using different values for repeat without the fill value for slice property

Listing 10-6 contains the CSS, which is a slight variation of Listing 10-5. Figure 10-15 shows the resulting Panes. This time, the middle region of the border image area is filled because we have specified the fill value for the -fx-border-image-slice property.

Listing 10-6. Using an Image as a Border Filling the Middle Region

```
-fx-border-image-source: url('image_url_goes_here') ;
-fx-border-image-repeat: no-repeat;
-fx-border-image-slice: 9 fill;
-fx-border-image-width: 9;
-fx-border-image-insets: 10;
-fx-border-color: black;
-fx-border-width: 1;
-fx-border-style: dashed inside;
```

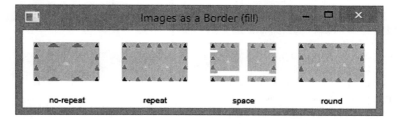

Figure 10-15. Using different values for repeat with the fill value for the slice property

The BorderImage class, which is immutable, represents a border image in a Border. All properties for the border image are specified in the constructor:

```
BorderImage(Image image,
            BorderWidths widths,
            Insets insets,
            BorderWidths slices,
            boolean filled,
            BorderRepeat repeatX,
            BorderRepeat repeatY)
```

The BorderRepeat enum contains STRETCH, REPEAT, SPACE, and ROUND constants that are used to indicate how the image slices are repeated in the x and y directions to fill the regions of the border image area. They have the same effect of specifying no-repeat, repeat, space, and round in CSS.

```
BorderWidths regionWidths = new BorderWidths(9);
BorderWidths sliceWidth = new BorderWidths(9);
boolean filled = false;
BorderRepeat repeatX = BorderRepeat.STRETCH;
BorderRepeat repeatY = BorderRepeat.STRETCH;
BorderImage borderImage = new BorderImage(new Image("image_url_goes_here"),
                                          regionWidths,
                                          new Insets(10),
                                          sliceWidth,
                                          filled,
                                          repeatX,
                                          repeatY);
```

Listing 10-7 has a program that creates the border using CSS and Java classes. The resulting screen is shown in Figure 10-16. The left and right Panes are decorated with the same borders: one uses CSS and another Java classes.

Listing 10-7. Using Strokes and Images as a Border

```
// BorderImageTest.java
package com.jdojo.container;

import java.net.URL;
import java.util.ArrayList;
import java.util.List;
import javafx.application.Application;
import javafx.geometry.Insets;
import javafx.scene.Scene;
import javafx.scene.image.Image;
import javafx.scene.layout.Background;
import javafx.scene.layout.Border;
import javafx.scene.layout.BorderImage;
import javafx.scene.layout.BorderRepeat;
import javafx.scene.layout.BorderStroke;
import javafx.scene.layout.BorderStrokeStyle;
import javafx.scene.layout.BorderWidths;
import javafx.scene.layout.CornerRadii;
```

```java
import javafx.scene.layout.Pane;
import javafx.scene.paint.Color;
import javafx.scene.shape.StrokeLineCap;
import javafx.scene.shape.StrokeLineJoin;
import javafx.scene.shape.StrokeType;
import javafx.stage.Stage;

public class BorderImageTest extends Application {
        public static void main(String[] args) {
                Application.launch(args);
        }

        @Override
        public void start(Stage stage) {
                // Get the URL of the image
                String imagePath = "resources/picture/border_with_triangles.jpg";
                URL imageURL = getClass().getResource(imagePath);
                String imageURLString = imageURL.toExternalForm();

                Pane p1 = this.getCSSStyledPane(imageURLString);
                Pane p2 = this.getObjectStyledPane(imageURLString);

                // Place p1 and p2
                p1.setLayoutX(20);
                p1.setLayoutY(20);
                p2.layoutYProperty().bind(p1.layoutYProperty());
                p2.layoutXProperty().bind(p1.layoutXProperty().add(p1.widthProperty()).add(20));

                Pane root = new Pane(p1, p2);
                root.setPrefSize(260, 100);

                Scene scene = new Scene(root);
                stage.setScene(scene);
                stage.setTitle("Strokes and Images as a Border");
                stage.show();
        }

        public Pane getCSSStyledPane(String imageURL) {
                Pane p = new Pane();
                p.setPrefSize(100, 70);
                p.setStyle("-fx-border-image-source: url('" + imageURL + "') ;" +
                        "-fx-border-image-repeat: no-repeat;" +
                        "-fx-border-image-slice: 9;" +
                        "-fx-border-image-width: 9;" +
                        "-fx-border-image-insets: 10;" +
                        "-fx-border-color: black;" +
                        "-fx-border-width: 1;" +
                        "-fx-border-style: dashed inside;");

                return p;
        }
}
```

```java
public Pane getObjectStyledPane(String imageURL) {
        Pane p = new Pane();
        p.setPrefSize(100, 70);
        p.setBackground(Background.EMPTY);

        // Create a BorderImage object
        BorderWidths regionWidths = new BorderWidths(9);
        BorderWidths sliceWidth = new BorderWidths(9);
        boolean filled = false;
        BorderRepeat repeatX = BorderRepeat.STRETCH;
        BorderRepeat repeatY = BorderRepeat.STRETCH;
        BorderImage borderImage = new BorderImage(new Image(imageURL),
                                            regionWidths,
                                            new Insets(10),
                                            sliceWidth,
                                            filled,
                                            repeatX,
                                            repeatY);

        // Set the Pane's boundary with a dashed stroke
        List<Double> dashArray = new ArrayList<>();
        dashArray.add(2.0);
        dashArray.add(1.4);
        BorderStrokeStyle blackStrokeStyle =
                new BorderStrokeStyle(StrokeType.INSIDE,
                                StrokeLineJoin.MITER,
                                StrokeLineCap.BUTT,
                                10,
                                0,
                                dashArray);
        BorderStroke borderStroke = new BorderStroke(Color.BLACK,
                                            blackStrokeStyle,
                                            CornerRadii.EMPTY,
                                            new BorderWidths(1),
                                            new Insets(0));

        // Create a Border object with a stroke and an image
        BorderStroke[] strokes = new BorderStroke[] { borderStroke };
        BorderImage[] images = new BorderImage[] { borderImage };
        Border b = new Border(strokes, images);

        p.setBorder(b);

        return p;
    }
}
```

Figure 10-16. *Creating a border with a strike and an image using CSS and Java classes*

Setting Margins

Setting margins on a Region is not supported directly. Most layout panes support margins for their children. If you want margins for a Region, add it to a layout pane, for example, an HBox, and use the layout pane instead of the Region.

```
Pane p1 = new Pane();
p1.setPrefSize(100, 20);

HBox box = new HBox();

// Set a margin of 10px around all four sides of the Pane
HBox.setMargin(p1, new Insets(10));
box.getChildren().addAll(p1);
```

Now, use box instead of p1 to get the margins around p1.

Understanding Panes

Pane is a subclass class of the Region class. It exposes the getChildren() method of the Parent class, which is the superclass of the Region class, This means that instances of the Pane class and its subclasses can add any children.

A Pane provides the following layout features:

- It can be used when absolute positioning is needed. By default, it positions all its children at (0, 0). You need to set the positions of the children explicitly.

- It resizes all resizable children to their preferred sizes.

By default, a Pane has minimum, preferred, and maximum sizes. Its minimum width is the sum of the left and right insets; its minimum height is the sum of the top and bottom insets. Its preferred width is the width required to display all its children at their current x location with their preferred widths; its preferred height is the height required to display all its children at their current y location with their preferred heights. Its maximum width and height are set to Double.MAX_VALUE.

The program in Listing 10-8 shows how to create a Pane, add two Buttons to it, and how to position the Buttons. The resulting screen is shown in Figure 10-17. The Pane uses a border to show the area it occupies in the screen. Try resizing the window, and you will find that the Pane shrinks and expands.

Listing 10-8. Using Panes

```java
// PaneTest.java
package com.jdojo.container;

import javafx.application.Application;
import javafx.scene.Scene;
import javafx.scene.control.Button;
import javafx.scene.layout.Pane;
import javafx.stage.Stage;

public class PaneTest extends Application {
        public static void main(String[] args) {
                Application.launch(args);
        }

        @Override
        public void start(Stage stage) {
                Button okBtn = new Button("OK");
                Button cancelBtn = new Button("Cancel");
                okBtn.relocate(10, 10);
                cancelBtn.relocate(60, 10);

                Pane root = new Pane();
                root.getChildren().addAll(okBtn, cancelBtn);
                root.setStyle("-fx-border-style: solid inside;" +
                                "-fx-border-width: 3;" +
                                "-fx-border-color: red;");

                Scene scene = new Scene(root);
                stage.setScene(scene);
                stage.setTitle("Using Panes");
                stage.show();
        }
}
```

Figure 10-17. *A pane with two Buttons*

A Pane lets you set its preferred size:

```java
Pane root = new Pane();
root.setPrefSize(300, 200); // 300px wide and 200px tall
```

You can tell the Pane to compute its preferred size based on its children sizes by resetting its preferred width and height to the computed width and height.

```
Pane root = new Pane();

// Set the preferred size to 300px wide and 200px tall
root.setPrefSize(300, 200);

/* Do some processing... */

// Set the default preferred size
root.setPrefSize(Region.USE_COMPUTED_SIZE, Region.USE_COMPUTED_SIZE);
```

■ **Tip**   A Pane does not clip its content; its children may be displayed outside its bounds.

Understanding HBox

An HBox lays out its children in a single horizontal row. It lets you set the horizontal spacing between adjacent children, margins for any children, resizing behavior of children, etc. It uses 0px as the default spacing between adjacent children. The default width of the content area and HBox is wide enough to display all its children at their preferred widths, and the default height is the largest of the heights of all its children.

You cannot set the locations for children in an HBox. They are automatically computed by the HBox. You can control the locations of children to some extent by customizing the properties of the HBox and setting constraints on the children.

Creating HBox Objects

Constructors of the HBox class let you create HBox objects with or without specifying the spacing and initial set of children.

```
// Create an empty HBox with the default spacing (0px)
HBox hbox1 = new HBox();

// Create an empty HBox with a 10px spacing
HBox hbox2 = new HBox(10);

// Create an HBox with two Buttons and a 10px spacing
Button okBtn = new Button("OK");
Button cancelBtn = new Button("Cancel");
HBox hbox3 = new HBox(10, okBtn, cancelBtn);
```

The program in Listing 10-9 shows how to use an HBox. It adds a Label, a TextField, and two Buttons to an HBox. Spacing between adjacent children is set to 10px. A padding of 10px is used to maintain a distance between the edges of the HBox and the edges of its children. The resulting window is shown in Figure 10-18.

Listing 10-9. Using the HBox Layout Pane

```java
// HBoxTest.java
package com.jdojo.container;

import javafx.application.Application;
import javafx.scene.Scene;
import javafx.scene.control.Button;
import javafx.scene.control.Label;
import javafx.scene.control.TextField;
import javafx.scene.layout.HBox;
import javafx.stage.Stage;

public class HBoxTest extends Application {
        public static void main(String[] args) {
                Application.launch(args);
        }

        @Override
        public void start(Stage stage) {
                Label nameLbl = new Label("Name:");
                TextField nameFld = new TextField();
                Button okBtn = new Button("OK");
                Button cancelBtn = new Button("Cancel");

                HBox root = new HBox(10); // 10px spacing
                root.getChildren().addAll(nameLbl, nameFld, okBtn, cancelBtn);
                root.setStyle("-fx-padding: 10;" +
                                "-fx-border-style: solid inside;" +
                                "-fx-border-width: 2;" +
                                "-fx-border-insets: 5;" +
                                "-fx-border-radius: 5;" +
                                "-fx-border-color: blue;");

                Scene scene = new Scene(root);
                stage.setScene(scene);
                stage.setTitle("Using HBox");
                stage.show();
        }
}
```

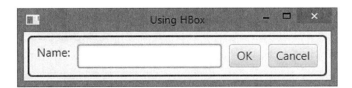

Figure 10-18. *An HBox with a Label, a TextField, and two Buttons*

HBox Properties

The HBox class declares three properties as listed in Table 10-2.

Table 10-2. *Properties Declared in the HBox Class*

Property	Type	Description
alignment	ObjectProperty<Pos>	It specifies the alignment of children relative to the content area of the HBox. The fillHeight property is ignored if the vertical alignment is set to BASELINE. The default value is Pos.TOP_LEFT.
fillHeight	BooleanProperty	It specifies whether the resizable children are resized to fill the full height of the HBox or they are given their preferred heights. This property is ignored, if the vertical alignment is set to BASELINE. The default value is true.
spacing	DoubleProperty	It specifies the horizontal spacing between adjacent children. The default value is zero.

The Alignment Property

Using the alignment property is simple. It specifies how children are aligned within the content area of the HBox. By default, an HBox allocates just enough space for its content to lay out all children at their preferred size. The effect of the alignment property is noticeable when the HBox grows bigger than its preferred size.

The program in Listing 10-10 uses an HBox with two Buttons. It sets the alignment of the HBox to Pos.BOTTOM_RIGHT. It sets the preferred size of the HBox a little bigger than needed to accommodate all its children, so you can see the effect of the alignment. The resulting window is shown in Figure 10-19. When you resize the window, the children stay aligned in the bottom-right area.

Listing 10-10. Using HBox Alignment Property

```java
// HBoxAlignment.java
package com.jdojo.container;

import javafx.application.Application;
import javafx.geometry.Pos;
import javafx.scene.Scene;
import javafx.scene.control.Button;
import javafx.scene.layout.HBox;
import javafx.stage.Stage;

public class HBoxAlignment extends Application {
    public static void main(String[] args) {
        Application.launch(args);
    }

    @Override
    public void start(Stage stage) {
        Button okBtn = new Button("OK");
        Button cancelBtn = new Button("Cancel");
```

```
        HBox hbox = new HBox(10);
        hbox.setPrefSize(200, 100);
        hbox.getChildren().addAll(okBtn, cancelBtn);

        // Set the alignment to bottom right
        hbox.setAlignment(Pos.BOTTOM_RIGHT);

        hbox.setStyle("-fx-padding: 10;" +
                      "-fx-border-style: solid inside;" +
                      "-fx-border-width: 2;" +
                      "-fx-border-insets: 5;" +
                      "-fx-border-radius: 5;" +
                      "-fx-border-color: blue;");

        Scene scene = new Scene(hbox);
        stage.setScene(scene);
        stage.setTitle("Using HBox Alignment Property");
        stage.show();
    }
}
```

Figure 10-19. *An HBox with two Buttons and alignment property set to Pos.BOTTOM_RIGHT*

The fillHeight Property

The fillHeight property specifies whether the HBox expands its children vertically to fill the height of its content area or keeps them to their preferred height. Note that this property affects only those child nodes that allow for the vertical expansion. For example, by default, the maximum height of a Button is set to its preferred height, and a Button does become taller than its preferred width in an HBox, even if vertical space is available. If you want a Button to expand vertically, set its maximum height to Double.MAX_VALUE. By default, a TextArea is set to expand. Therefore, a TextArea inside an HBox will become taller as the height of the HBox is increased. If you do not want the resizable children to fill the height of the content area of an HBox, set the fillHeight property to false.

■ **Tip**   The preferred height of the content area of an HBox is the largest of the preferred height of its children. Resizable children fill the full height of the content area, provided their maximum height property allows them to expand. Otherwise, they are kept at their preferred height.

The program in Listing 10-11 shows how the fillHeight property affects the height of the children of an HBox. It displays some controls inside an HBox. A TextArea can grow vertically by default. The maximum height of the *Cancel* button is set to Double.MAX_VALUE, so it can grow vertically. A CheckBox is provided to change the value of the fillHeight property of the HBox. The initial window is shown in Figure 10-20. Notice that the Ok button has the preferred height, whereas the *Cancel* button expends vertically to fill the height of the content area as determined by the TextArea. Resize the window to make it taller and change the fillHeight property using the CheckBox; the TextArea and the *Cancel* button expands and shrinks vertically.

Listing 10-11. Using the fillHeight Property of an HBox

```java
// HBoxFillHeight.java
package com.jdojo.container;

import javafx.application.Application;
import javafx.scene.Scene;
import javafx.scene.control.Button;
import javafx.scene.control.CheckBox;
import javafx.scene.control.Label;
import javafx.scene.control.TextArea;
import javafx.scene.layout.HBox;
import javafx.stage.Stage;

public class HBoxFillHeight extends Application {
        public static void main(String[] args) {
                Application.launch(args);
        }

        @Override
        public void start(Stage stage) {
                HBox root = new HBox(10); // 10px spacing

                Label descLbl = new Label("Description:");
                TextArea desc = new TextArea();
                desc.setPrefColumnCount(10);
                desc.setPrefRowCount(3);

                Button okBtn = new Button("OK");
                Button cancelBtn = new Button("Cancel");

                // Let the Cancel button expand vertically
                cancelBtn.setMaxHeight(Double.MAX_VALUE);

                CheckBox fillHeightCbx = new CheckBox("Fill Height");
                fillHeightCbx.setSelected(true);

                // Add an event handler to the CheckBox, so the user can set the
                // fillHeight property using the CheckBox
                fillHeightCbx.setOnAction(e ->
                                root.setFillHeight(fillHeightCbx.isSelected()));
```

```
            root.getChildren().addAll(
                                    descLbl, desc, fillHeightCbx, okBtn,
                                    cancelBtn);
            root.setStyle("-fx-padding: 10;" +
                        "-fx-border-style: solid inside;" +
                        "-fx-border-width: 2;" +
                        "-fx-border-insets: 5;" +
                        "-fx-border-radius: 5;" +
                        "-fx-border-color: blue;");

            Scene scene = new Scene(root);
            stage.setScene(scene);
            stage.setTitle("Using HBox fillHeight Property");
            stage.show();
        }
}
```

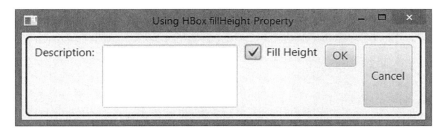

Figure 10-20. *An HBox with some control, where the user can change the fillHeight property*

The Spacing Property

The spacing property specifies the horizontal distance between adjacent children in an HBox. By default, it is set to 0px. It can be set in constructors or using the setSpacing() method.

Setting Constraints for Children in HBox

HBox supports two types of constraints, *hgrow* and *margin*, which can be set on each child node individually. The hgrow constraint specifies whether a child node expands horizontally when additional space is available. The margin constraint specifies space outside the edges of a child node. The HBox class provides setHgrow() and setMargin() static methods to specify these constraints. You can use null with these methods to remove the constraints individually. Use the clearConstraints(Node child) method to remove both constraints for a child node at once.

Letting Children Grow Horizontally

By default, the children in an HBox get their preferred widths. If the HBox is expanded horizontally, its children may get the additional available space, provided their hgrow priority is set to grow. If an HBox is expanded horizontally and none of its children has its hgrow constraint set, the additional space is left unused.

The hgrow priority for a child node is set using the setHgrow() static method of the HBox class by specifying the child node and the priority.

```
HBox root = new HBox(10);
TextField nameFld = new TextField();

// Let the TextField always grow horizontally
root.setHgrow(nameFld, Priority.ALWAYS);
```

To reset the hgrow priority of a child node, use null as the priority.

```
// Stop the TextField from growing horizontally
root.setHgrow(nameFld, null);
```

The program in Listing 10-12 shows how to set the priority of a TextField to Priority.ALWAYS, so it can take all the additional horizontal space when the HBox is expanded. Figure 10-21 shows the initial and expanded windows. Notice that all controls, except the TextField, stayed at their preferred widths, after the window is expanded horizontally.

Listing 10-12. Letting a TextField Grow Horizontally

```
// HBoxHGrow.java
package com.jdojo.container;

import javafx.application.Application;
import javafx.scene.Scene;
import javafx.scene.control.Button;
import javafx.scene.control.Label;
import javafx.scene.control.TextField;
import javafx.scene.layout.HBox;
import javafx.scene.layout.Priority;
import javafx.stage.Stage;

public class HBoxHGrow extends Application {
        public static void main(String[] args) {
                Application.launch(args);
        }

        @Override
        public void start(Stage stage) {
                Label nameLbl = new Label("Name:");
                TextField nameFld = new TextField();

                Button okBtn = new Button("OK");
                Button cancelBtn = new Button("Cancel");

                HBox root = new HBox(10);
                root.getChildren().addAll(nameLbl, nameFld, okBtn, cancelBtn);

                // Let the TextField always grow horizontally
                HBox.setHgrow(nameFld, Priority.ALWAYS);
```

```
                 root.setStyle("-fx-padding: 10;" +
                               "-fx-border-style: solid inside;" +
                               "-fx-border-width: 2;" +
                               "-fx-border-insets: 5;" +
                               "-fx-border-radius: 5;" +
                               "-fx-border-color: blue;");

                 Scene scene = new Scene(root);
                 stage.setScene(scene);
                 stage.setTitle("Using Horizontal Grow Priority in an HBox");
                 stage.show();
        }
}
```

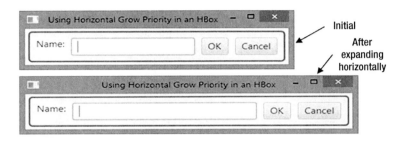

Figure 10-21. *An HBox with a TextField set to always grow horizontally*

Setting Margins for Children

Margins are extra spaces added outside the edges of a node. The following snippet of code shows how to add margins to the children of an HBox.

```
Label nameLbl = new Label("Name:");
TextField nameFld = new TextField();
Button okBtn = new Button("OK");
Button cancelBtn = new Button("Cancel");

HBox hbox = new HBox(nameLbl, nameFld, okBtn, cancelBtn);

// Set a margin for all children:
// 10px top, 2px right, 10px bottom, and 2px left
Insets margin = new Insets(10, 2, 10, 2);
HBox.setMargin(nameLbl, margin);
HBox.setMargin(nameFld, margin);
HBox.setMargin(okBtn, margin);
HBox.setMargin(cancelBtn, margin);
```

You can remove the margin from a child node by setting the margin value to null.

```
// Remove margins for okBtn
HBox.setMargin(okBtn, null);
```

■ **Tip**   Be careful when using the `spacing` property of the `HBox` and the margin constraint on its children. Both will add to the horizontal gap between adjacent children. If you want margins applied, keep the horizontal spacing between children uniform, and set the right and left margins for children to zero.

Understanding VBox

A VBox lays out its children in a single vertical column. It lets you set the vertical spacing between adjacent children, margins for any children, resizing behavior of children, etc. It uses 0px as the default spacing between adjacent children. The default height of the content area of a VBox is tall enough to display all its children at their preferred heights, and the default width is the largest of the widths of all its children.

You cannot set the locations for children in a VBox. They are automatically computed by the VBox. You can control the locations of children to some extent by customizing the properties of the VBox and setting constraints on the children.

Working with a VBox is similar to working with an HBox with a difference that they work in opposite directions. For example, in an HBox, the children fills the height of the content area by default, and in a VBox, children fill the width of the content by default; an HBox lets you set hgrow constraints on a child node and a VBox lets you set the vgrow constraint.

Creating VBox Objects

Constructors of the VBox class let you create VBox objects with or without specifying the spacing and initial set of children.

```
// Create an empty VBox with the default spacing (0px)
VBox vbox1 = new VBox();

// Create an empty VBox with a 10px spacing
VBox vbox2 = new VBox(10);

// Create a VBox with two Buttons and a 10px spacing
Button okBtn = new Button("OK");
Button cancelBtn = new Button("Cancel");
VBox vbox3 = new VBox(10, okBtn, cancelBtn);
```

The program in Listing 10-13 shows how to use a VBox. It adds a Label, a TextField, and two Buttons to a VBox. Spacing between adjacent children is set to 10px. A padding of 10px is used to maintain a distance between the edges of the VBox and the edges of its children. The resulting window is shown in Figure 10-22.

Listing 10-13. Using the VBox Layout Pane

```java
// VBoxTest.java
package com.jdojo.container;

import javafx.application.Application;
import javafx.scene.Scene;
import javafx.scene.control.Button;
import javafx.scene.control.Label;
import javafx.scene.control.TextField;
import javafx.scene.layout.VBox;
import javafx.stage.Stage;

public class VBoxTest extends Application {
        public static void main(String[] args) {
                Application.launch(args);
        }

        @Override
        public void start(Stage stage) {
                Label nameLbl = new Label("Name:");
                TextField nameFld = new TextField();
                Button okBtn = new Button("OK");
                Button cancelBtn = new Button("Cancel");

                VBox root = new VBox(10); // 10px spacing
                root.getChildren().addAll(nameLbl, nameFld, okBtn, cancelBtn);
                root.setStyle("-fx-padding: 10;" +
                                "-fx-border-style: solid inside;" +
                                "-fx-border-width: 2;" +
                                "-fx-border-insets: 5;" +
                                "-fx-border-radius: 5;" +
                                "-fx-border-color: blue;");

                Scene scene = new Scene(root);
                stage.setScene(scene);
                stage.setTitle("Using VBox");
                stage.show();
        }
}
```

Figure 10-22. *A VBox with a Label, a TextField, and two Buttons*

VBox Properties

The VBox class declares three properties as listed in Table 10-3.

Table 10-3. *Properties Declared in the VBox Class*

Property	Type	Description
alignment	ObjectProperty<Pos>	It specifies the alignment of children relative to the content area of the VBox. The default value is Pos.TOP_LEFT.
fillWidth	BooleanProperty	It specifies whether the resizable children are resized to fill the full width of the VBox or they are given their preferred widths. The default value is true.
spacing	DoubleProperty	It specifies the vertical spacing between adjacent children. The default value is zero.

The Alignment Property

Using the alignment property is simple. It specifies how children are aligned within the content area of the VBox. By default, a VBox allocates just enough space for its content to lay out all children at their preferred size. The effect of the alignment property is noticeable when the VBox grows bigger than its preferred size.

The program in Listing 10-14 uses a VBox with two Buttons. It sets the alignment of the VBox to Pos.BOTTOM_RIGHT. It sets the preferred size of the VBox a little bigger than needed to accommodate all its children, so you can see the effect of the alignment. The resulting window is shown in Figure 10-23. When you resize the window, the children stay aligned in the bottom-right area.

Listing 10-14. Using VBox Alignment Property

```java
// VBoxAlignment.java
package com.jdojo.container;

import javafx.application.Application;
import javafx.geometry.Pos;
import javafx.scene.Scene;
import javafx.scene.control.Button;
import javafx.scene.layout.VBox;
import javafx.stage.Stage;

public class VBoxAlignment extends Application {
        public static void main(String[] args) {
                Application.launch(args);
        }

        @Override
        public void start(Stage stage) {
                Button okBtn = new Button("OK");
                Button cancelBtn = new Button("Cancel");

                VBox vbox = new VBox(10);
                vbox.setPrefSize(200, 100);
                vbox.getChildren().addAll(okBtn, cancelBtn);

                // Set the alignment to bottom right
                vbox.setAlignment(Pos.BOTTOM_RIGHT);

                vbox.setStyle("-fx-padding: 10;" +
                                "-fx-border-style: solid inside;" +
                                "-fx-border-width: 2;" +
                                "-fx-border-insets: 5;" +
                                "-fx-border-radius: 5;" +
                                "-fx-border-color: blue;");

                Scene scene = new Scene(vbox);
                stage.setScene(scene);
                stage.setTitle("Using VBox Alignment Property");
                stage.show();
        }
}
```

Figure 10-23. *A VBox with two Buttons and alignment property set to Pos.BOTTOM_RIGHT*

The fillWidth Property

The fillWidth property specifies whether the VBox expands its children horizontally to fill the width of its content area or keeps them to their preferred height. Note that this property affects only those child nodes that allow for the horizontal expansion. For example, by default, the maximum width of a Button is set to its preferred width, and a Button does become wider than its preferred width in a VBox, even if horizontal space is available. If you want a Button to expand horizontally, set its maximum width to Double.MAX_VALUE. By default, a TextField is set to expand. Therefore, a TextField inside a VBox will become wider as the width of the VBox is increased. If you do not want the resizable children to fill the width of the content area of a VBox, set the fillWidth property to false. Run the program in Listing 10-13 and try expanding the window horizontally. The TextField will expand horizontally as the window expands.

■ **Tip** The preferred width of the content area of a VBox is the largest of the preferred width of its children. Resizable children fill the full width of the content area, provided their maximum width property allows them to expand. Otherwise, they are kept at their preferred width.

It is often needed in a GUI application that you need to arrange a set of Buttons in a vertical column and make them the same size. You need to add the buttons to a VBox and set the maximum width of all buttons to Double.MAX_VALUE so they can grow to match the width of the widest button in the group. The program in Listing 10-15 shows how to achieve this. Figure 10-24 shows the window.

Listing 10-15. Using the fillWidth Property of a VBox

```
// VBoxFillWidth.java
package com.jdojo.container;

import javafx.application.Application;
import javafx.scene.Scene;
import javafx.scene.control.Button;
import javafx.scene.layout.VBox;
import javafx.stage.Stage;

public class VBoxFillWidth extends Application {
        public static void main(String[] args) {
                Application.launch(args);
        }
```

```
        @Override
        public void start(Stage stage) {
                Button b1 = new Button("New");
                Button b2 = new Button("New Modified");
                Button b3 = new Button("Not Modified");
                Button b4 = new Button("Data Modified");

                // Set the max width of the buttons to Double.MAX_VALUE,
                // so they can grow horizontally
                b1.setMaxWidth(Double.MAX_VALUE);
                b2.setMaxWidth(Double.MAX_VALUE);
                b3.setMaxWidth(Double.MAX_VALUE);
                b4.setMaxWidth(Double.MAX_VALUE);

                VBox root = new VBox(10, b1, b2, b3, b4);
                root.setStyle("-fx-padding: 10;" +
                                "-fx-border-style: solid inside;" +
                                "-fx-border-width: 2;" +
                                "-fx-border-insets: 5;" +
                                "-fx-border-radius: 5;" +
                                "-fx-border-color: blue;");

                Scene scene = new Scene(root);
                stage.setScene(scene);
                stage.setTitle("Using VBox fillWidth Property");
                stage.show();
        }
}
```

Figure 10-24. *A VBox with some control, where the user can change the fillWidth property*

When you expand the VBox horizontally in Listing 10-16, all buttons grow to fill the available extra space. To prevent the buttons growing when the VBox expands in the horizontal direction, you can add the VBox in an HBox and add the HBox to the scene.

■ **Tip** You can create powerful visual effects by nesting HBox and VBox layout panes. You can also add buttons (or any other types of nodes) in a column in a GridPane to make them the same size. Please refer to the *Understanding GridPane* section for more details.

The Spacing Property

The spacing property specifies the vertical distance between adjacent children in a VBox. By default, it is set to 0px. It can be set in the constructors or using the setSpacing() method.

Setting Constraints for Children in VBox

VBox supports two types of constraints, *vgrow* and *margin*, that can be set on each child node individually. The vgrow constraint specifies whether a child node expands vertically when additional space is available. The margin constraint specifies space outside the edges of a child node. The VBox class provides setVgrow() and setMargin() static methods to specify these constraints. You can use null with these methods to remove the constraints individually. Use the clearConstraints(Node child) method to remove both constraints for a child node at once.

Letting Children Grow Vertically

By default, the children in a VBox get their preferred heights. If the VBox is expanded vertically, its children may get the additional available space, provided their vgrow priority is set to grow. If a VBox is expanded vertically and none of its children has its vgrow constraint set, the additional space is left unused.

The vgrow priority for a child node is set using the setVgrow() static method of the VBox class by specifying the child node and the priority.

```
VBox root = new VBox(10);
TextArea desc = new TextArea();

// Let the TextArea always grow vertically
root.setVgrow(desc, Priority.ALWAYS);
```

To reset the vgrow priority of a child node, use null as the priority.

```
// Stop the TextArea from growing horizontally
root.setVgrow(desc, null);
```

The program in Listing 10-16 shows how to set the priority of a TextArea to Priority.ALWAYS, so it can take all the additional vertical space when the VBox is expanded. Figure 10-25 shows the initial and expanded windows. Notice that the Label stays at its preferred height, after the window is expanded vertically.

Listing 10-16. Letting a TextArea Grow Vertically

```java
// VBoxVGrow.java
package com.jdojo.container;

import javafx.application.Application;
import javafx.scene.Scene;
import javafx.scene.control.Label;
import javafx.scene.control.TextArea;
import javafx.scene.layout.Priority;
import javafx.scene.layout.VBox;
import javafx.stage.Stage;

public class VBoxVGrow extends Application {
        public static void main(String[] args) {
                Application.launch(args);
        }

        @Override
        public void start(Stage stage) {
                Label descLbl = new Label("Descrption:");
                TextArea desc = new TextArea();
                desc.setPrefColumnCount(10);
                desc.setPrefRowCount(3);

                VBox root = new VBox(10);
                root.getChildren().addAll(descLbl, desc);

                // Let the TextArea always grow vertically
                VBox.setVgrow(desc, Priority.ALWAYS);

                root.setStyle("-fx-padding: 10;" +
                                        "-fx-border-style: solid inside;" +
                                        "-fx-border-width: 2;" +
                                        "-fx-border-insets: 5;" +
                                        "-fx-border-radius: 5;" +
                                        "-fx-border-color: blue;");

                Scene scene = new Scene(root);
                stage.setScene(scene);
                stage.setTitle("Using Vertical Grow Priority in a VBox");
                stage.show();
        }
}
```

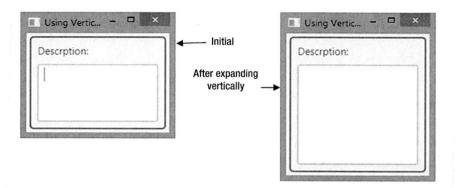

Figure 10-25. *A VBox with a TextArea set to always grow vertically*

Setting Margin for Children

You can set margins for the children of a VBox using its setMargin() static method.

```
Button okBtn = new Button("OK");
Button cancelBtn = new Button("Cancel");
VBox vbox = new VBox(okBtn, cancelBtn);

// Set margins for OK and cancel buttons
Insets margin = new Insets(5);
VBox.setMargin(okBtn, margin);
VBox.setMargin(cancelBtn, margin);
...
// Remove margins for okBtn
VBox.setMargin(okBtn, null);
```

Understanding FlowPane

A FlowPane is a simple layout pane that lays out its children in rows or columns wrapping at a specified width or height. It lets its children flow horizontally or vertically, and hence the name "flow pane." You can specify a preferred wrap length, which is the preferred width for a horizontal flow and the preferred height for a vertical flow, where the content is wrapped. A FlowPane is used in situations where the relative locations of children are not important: for example, displaying a series of pictures or buttons. A FlowPane gives all its children their preferred sizes. Rows and columns may be of different heights and widths. You can customize the vertical alignments of children in rows and the horizontal alignments of children in columns.

■ **Tip**   Children in a horizontal FlowPane may be arranged in rows from left to right or right to left, which is controlled by the nodeOrientation property declared in the Node class. The default value for this property is set to NodeOrientation.LEFT_TO_RIGHT. If you want the children to flow right to left, set the property to NodeOrientation.RIGHT_TO_LEFT. This applies to all layout panes that arrange children in rows (e.g., HBox, TilePane, etc.).

The orientation of a FlowPane, which can be set to horizontal or vertical, determines the direction of the flow for its content. In a horizontal FlowPane, the content flows in rows. In a vertical FlowPane, the content flows in columns. Figure 10-26 and Figure 10-27 show a FlowPane with ten buttons. The buttons are added in the order they have been labeled. That is, Button 1 is added before Button 2. The FlowPane in Figure 10-26 has a horizontal orientation, whereas the FlowPane in Figure 10-27 has a vertical orientation. By default, a FlowPane has a horizontal orientation.

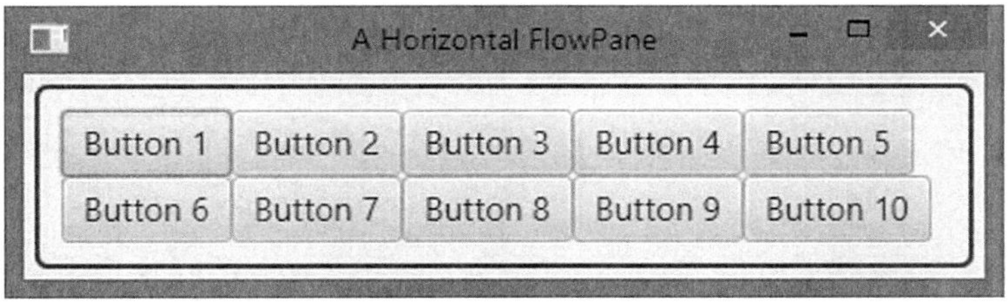

Figure 10-26. *A horizontal flow pane showing ten buttons*

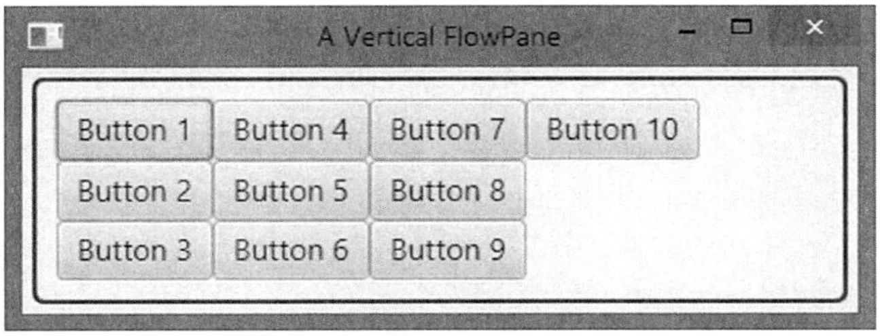

Figure 10-27. *A vertical flow pane showing ten buttons*

Creating FlowPane Objects

The FlowPane class provides several constructors to create FlowPane objects with a specified orientation (horizontal or vertical), a specified horizontal and vertical spacing between children, and a specified initial list of children.

```
// Create an empty horizontal FlowPane with 0px spacing
FlowPane fpane1 = new FlowPane();

// Create an empty vertical FlowPane with 0px spacing
FlowPane fpane2 = new FlowPane(Orientation.VERTICAL);

// Create an empty horizontal FlowPane with 5px horizontal and 10px vertical spacing
FlowPane fpane3 = new FlowPane(5, 10);

// Create an empty vertical FlowPane with 5px horizontal and 10px vertical spacing
FlowPane fpane4 = new FlowPane(Orientation.VERTICAL, 5, 10);

// Create a horizontal FlowPane with two Buttons and 0px spacing
FlowPane fpane5 = new FlowPane(new Button("Button 1"), new Button("Button 2"));
```

The program in Listing 10-17 shows how to create a FlowPane and add children. It adds ten Buttons and uses 5px horizontal and 10px vertical gaps. The window is shown in Figure 10-28.

Listing 10-17. Using a Horizontal FlowPane

```java
// FlowPaneTest.java
package com.jdojo.container;

import javafx.application.Application;
import javafx.scene.Scene;
import javafx.scene.control.Button;
import javafx.scene.layout.FlowPane;
import javafx.stage.Stage;

public class FlowPaneTest extends Application {
        public static void main(String[] args) {
                Application.launch(args);
        }

        @Override
        public void start(Stage stage) {
                double hgap = 5;
                double vgap = 10;
                FlowPane root = new FlowPane(hgap, vgap);

                // Add ten buttons to the flow pane
                for(int i = 1; i <= 10; i++) {
                        root.getChildren().add(new Button("Button " + i));
                }

                root.setStyle("-fx-padding: 10;" +
                                "-fx-border-style: solid inside;" +
                                "-fx-border-width: 2;" +
                                "-fx-border-insets: 5;" +
                                "-fx-border-radius: 5;" +
                                "-fx-border-color: blue;");

                Scene scene = new Scene(root);
                stage.setScene(scene);
                stage.setTitle("A Horizontal FlowPane");
                stage.show();
        }
}
```

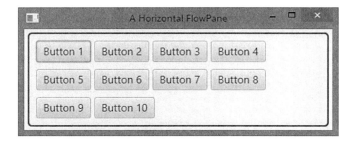

Figure 10-28. *A horizontal pane with ten buttons using 5px hgap and 10px vgap*

FlowPane Properties

Table 10-4 lists several FlowPane class properties that are used to customize the layout of its children.

Table 10-4. *The List of Properties Declared in the FlowPane Class*

Property	Type	Description
alignment	ObjectProperty<Pos>	It specifies the alignment of rows and columns relative to the content area of the FlowPane. The default value is Pos.TOP_LEFT.
rowValignment	ObjectProperty<VPos>	It specifies the vertical alignment of the children within each row in a horizontal FlowPane. It is ignored for a vertical FlowPane.
columnHalignment	ObjectProperty<HPos>	It specifies the horizontal alignment of the children within each column in a vertical FlowPane. It is ignored for a horizontal FlowPane.
hgap, vgap	DoubleProperty	They specify the horizontal and vertical gaps between children. The default is zero.
orientation	ObjectProperty<Orientation>	It specifies the orientation of the FlowPane. It defaults to HORIZONTAL.
prefWrapLength	DoubleProperty	It is the preferred width in a horizontal FlowPane and the preferred height in a vertical FlowPane where the content should wrap. The default is 400.

The Alignment Property

The alignment property of a FlowPane controls the alignment of its content. A Pos value contains a vertical alignment (vpos) and horizontal alignment (hpos). For example, Pos.TOP_LEFT has the vertical alignment as top and horizontal alignment as left. In a horizontal FlowPane, each row is aligned using the hpos value of the alignment and rows (the entire content) is aligned using the vpos value. In a vertical FlowPane, each column is aligned using the vpos value of the alignment and the columns (the entire content) are aligned using the hpos value.

The program in Listing 10-18 displays three FlowPaness in an HBox. Each FlowPane has a different alignment. The Text node in each FlowPane displays the alignment used. Figure 10-29 shows the window.

Listing 10-18. Using the Alignment Property of the FlowPane

```java
// FlowPaneAlignment.java
package com.jdojo.container;

import javafx.application.Application;
import javafx.geometry.Pos;
import javafx.scene.Scene;
import javafx.scene.control.Button;
import javafx.scene.layout.FlowPane;
import javafx.scene.layout.HBox;
import javafx.scene.text.Text;
import javafx.stage.Stage;

public class FlowPaneAlignment extends Application {
        public static void main(String[] args) {
                Application.launch(args);
        }

        @Override
        public void start(Stage stage) {
                FlowPane fp1 = createFlowPane(Pos.BOTTOM_RIGHT);
                FlowPane fp2 = createFlowPane(Pos.BOTTOM_LEFT);
                FlowPane fp3 = createFlowPane(Pos.CENTER);

                HBox root = new HBox(fp1, fp2, fp3);
                Scene scene = new Scene(root);
                stage.setScene(scene);
                stage.setTitle("FlowPane Alignment");
                stage.show();
        }

        private FlowPane createFlowPane(Pos alignment) {
                FlowPane fp = new FlowPane(5, 5);
                fp.setPrefSize(200, 100);
                fp.setAlignment(alignment);
                fp.getChildren().addAll(new Text(alignment.toString()),
                                        new Button("Button 1"),
                                        new Button("Button 2"),
                                        new Button("Button 3"));

                fp.setStyle("-fx-padding: 10;" +
                            "-fx-border-style: solid inside;" +
                            "-fx-border-width: 2;" +
                            "-fx-border-insets: 5;" +
                            "-fx-border-radius: 5;" +
                            "-fx-border-color: blue;");

                return fp;
        }
}
```

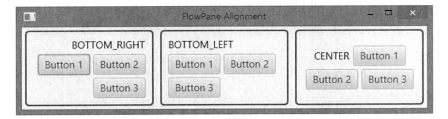

Figure 10-29. *Flow:Panes using different alignments for their contents*

The rowValignment and columnHalignment Properties

A FlowPane lays out its children at their preferred sizes. Rows and columns could be of different sizes.
You can align children in each row or column using the rowValignment and columnHalignment properties.

In a horizontal FlowPane, children in one row may be of different heights. The height of a row is the largest of the preferred heights of all children in the row. The rowValignment property lets you specify the vertical alignment of children in each row. Its value could be set to one of the constants of the VPos enum: BASELINE, TOP, CENTER, and BOTTOM. If the maximum height value of a child node allows for vertical expansion, the child node will be expanded to fill the height of the row. If the rowValignment property is set to VPos.BASELINE, children are resized to their preferred height instead of expanding to fill the full height of the row.

In a vertical FlowPane, children in one column may be of different widths. The width of a column is the largest of the preferred widths of all children in the column. The columnHalignment property lets you specify the horizontal alignment of children in each column. Its value could be set to one of the constants of the HPos enum: LEFT, RIGHT, and CENTER. If the maximum width value of a child node allows for horizontal expansion, the child node will be expanded to fill the width of the column.

The program in Listing 10-19 creates three FlowPanes and adds them to an HBox. Figure 10-30 shows the window. The first two FlowPanes have horizontal orientations and the last one has a vertical orientation. The row and column alignments are displayed in the Text node and the orientations for the FlowPane are displayed in the TextArea node.

Listing 10-19. Using Row and Column Alignments in a FlowPane

```java
// FlowPaneRowColAlignment.java
package com.jdojo.container;

import javafx.application.Application;
import javafx.geometry.HPos;
import javafx.geometry.Orientation;
import static javafx.geometry.Orientation.HORIZONTAL;
import static javafx.geometry.Orientation.VERTICAL;
import javafx.geometry.VPos;
import javafx.scene.Scene;
import javafx.scene.control.TextArea;
import javafx.scene.layout.FlowPane;
import javafx.scene.layout.HBox;
import javafx.scene.text.Text;
import javafx.stage.Stage;
```

```java
public class FlowPaneRowColAlignment extends Application {
        public static void main(String[] args) {
                Application.launch(args);
        }

        @Override
        public void start(Stage stage) {
                FlowPane fp1 = createFlowPane(HORIZONTAL, VPos.TOP, HPos.LEFT);
                FlowPane fp2 = createFlowPane(HORIZONTAL, VPos.CENTER, HPos.LEFT);
                FlowPane fp3 = createFlowPane(VERTICAL, VPos.CENTER, HPos.RIGHT);

                HBox root = new HBox(fp1, fp2, fp3);
                Scene scene = new Scene(root);
                stage.setScene(scene);
                stage.setTitle("FlowPane Row and Column Alignment");
                stage.show();
        }

        private FlowPane createFlowPane(Orientation orientation,
                                        VPos rowAlign,
                                        HPos colAlign) {
                // Show the row or column alignment value in a Text
                Text t = new Text();
                if (orientation == Orientation.HORIZONTAL) {
                        t.setText(rowAlign.toString());
                } else {
                        t.setText(colAlign.toString());
                }

                // Show the orientation of the FlowPane in a TextArea
                TextArea ta = new TextArea(orientation.toString());
                ta.setPrefColumnCount(5);
                ta.setPrefRowCount(3);

                FlowPane fp = new FlowPane(orientation, 5, 5);
                fp.setRowValignment(rowAlign);
                fp.setColumnHalignment(colAlign);
                fp.setPrefSize(175, 130);
                fp.getChildren().addAll(t, ta);
                fp.setStyle("-fx-padding: 10;" +
                                "-fx-border-style: solid inside;" +
                                "-fx-border-width: 2;" +
                                "-fx-border-insets: 5;" +
                                "-fx-border-radius: 5;" +
                                "-fx-border-color: blue;");

                return fp;
        }
}
```

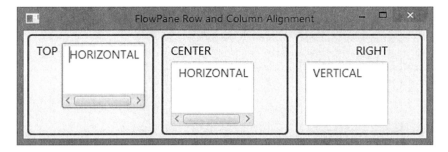

Figure 10-30. *FlowPanes using different row and column alignments*

The hgap and vgap Properties

Using the hgap and vgap properties is straightforward. In a horizontal FlowPane, the hgap property specifies the horizontal spacing between adjacent children in a row and the vgap property specifies the spacing between adjacent rows. In a vertical FlowPane, the hgap property specifies the horizontal spacing between adjacent columns and the vgap property specifies the spacing between adjacent children in a column. You can set these properties in the constructors or using the setter methods. We have been using these properties in our examples discussed in this section.

```
// Create a FlowPane with 5px hgap and 10px vgap
FlowPane fpane = new FlowPane(5, 10);
...
// Change the hgap to 15px and vgap to 25px
fpane.setHgap(15);
fpane.setVgap(25);
```

The Orientation Property

The orientation property specifies the flow of content in a FlowPane. If it is set to Orientation.HORIZONTAL, which is the default value, the content flows in rows. If it is set to Orientation.VERTICAL, the content flows in columns. You can specify the orientation in the constructors or using the setter method.

```
// Create a horizontal FlowPane
FlowPane fpane = new FlowPane();
...
// Change the orientation of the FlowPane to vertical
fpane.setOrientation(Orientation.VERTICAL);
```

The prefWrapLength Property

The prefWrapLength property is the preferred width in a horizontal FlowPane or the preferred height in a vertical FlowPane where content should wrap. This is only used to compute the preferred size of the FlowPane. It defaults to 400. Treat the value of this property as a hint to resize your FlowPane. Suppose you set this value to less than the largest preferred width or height of a child node. In this case, this value will not be respected, as a row cannot be shorter than the widest child node in a horizontal FlowPane or a column cannot be shorter than the tallest child node in a vertical FlowPane. If 400px is too wide or tall for your FlowPane, set this value to a reasonable value.

357

Content Bias of a FlowPane

Notice that the number of rows in a horizontal FlowPane depends on its width and the number of columns in a vertical FlowPane depends on its height. That is, a horizontal FlowPane has a horizontal content bias and a vertical FlowPane has a vertical content bias. Therefore, when you are getting the size of a FlowPane, make sure to take into account its content bias.

Understanding BorderPane

A BorderPane divides its layout area into five regions: top, right, bottom, left, and center. You can place at most one node in each of the five regions. Figure 10-31 shows five Buttons placed in the five regions of the BorderPane – one Button in each region. The Buttons have been labeled the same as their regions in which they are placed. Any of the regions may be null. If a region is null, no space is allocated for it.

Figure 10-31. *Five regions of a BorderPane*

In a typical Windows application, a screen uses the five regions to places its content.

- A menu or a toolbar at the top
- A status bar at the bottom
- A navigation panel on the left
- Additional information on the right
- Main content in the center

A BorderPane satisfies all the layout requirements for a typical Windows-based GUI screen. This is the reason that a BorderPane is most often used as the root node for a scene. Typically, you have more than five nodes in a window. If you have more than one node to place in one of the five regions of a BorderPane, add the nodes to a layout pane: for example, an HBox, a VBox, etc., and then add the layout pane to the desired region of the BorderPane.

A BorderPane uses the following resizing policies for its children:

- The children in the top and bottom regions are resized to their preferred heights. Their widths are extended to fill the available extra horizontal space, provided the maximum widths of the children allow extending their widths beyond their preferred widths.

- The children in the right and left regions are resized to their preferred widths. Their heights are extended to fill the extra vertical space, provided the maximum heights of the children allow extending their heights beyond their preferred heights.

- The child node in the center will fill the rest of the available space in both directions.

Children in a BorderPane may overlap if it is resized to a smaller size than its preferred size. The overlapping rule is based on the order in which the children are added. The children are drawn in the order they are added. This means that a child node may overlap all child nodes added prior to it. Suppose regions are populated in the order of right, center, and left. The left region may overlap the center and right regions, and the center region may overlap the right region.

■ **Tip**   You can set the alignments for all children within their regions. You can set the margins for children. As with all layout panes, you can also style a BorderPane with CSS.

Creating BorderPane Objects

The BorderPane class provides constructors to create BorderPane objects with or without children.

```
// Create an empty BorderPane
BorderPane bpane1 = new BorderPane();

// Create a BorderPane with a TextArea in the center
TextArea center = new TextArea();
BorderPane bpane2 = new BorderPane(center);

// Create a BorderPane with a Text node in each of the five regions
Text center = new Text("Center");
Text top = new Text("Top");
Text right = new Text("Right");
Text bottom = new Text("Bottom");
Text left = new Text("Left");
BorderPane bpane3 = new BorderPane(center, top, right, bottom, left);
```

The BorderPane class declares five properties named top, right, bottom, left, and center that store the reference of five children in the five regions. Use the setters for these properties to add a child node to any of the five regions. For example, use the setTop(Node topChild) method to add a child node to the top region. To get the reference of the children in any of the five regions, use the getters for these properties. For example, the getTop() method returns the reference of the child node in the top region.

```
// Create an empty BorderPane and add a text node in each of the five regions
BorderPane bpane = new BorderPane();
bpane.setTop(new Text("Top"));
bpane.setRight(new Text("Right"));
bpane.setBottom(new Text("Bottom"));
bpane.setLeft(new Text("Left"));
bpane.setCenter(new Text("Center"));
```

■ **Tip**   Do not use the ObservableList<Node>, which is returned by the getChildren() method of the BorderPane, to add children to a BorderPane. The children added to this list are ignored. Use the top, right, bottom, left, and center properties instead.

The program in Listing 10-20 shows how to create a BorderPane and add children. It adds children to the right, bottom, and center regions. Two Labels, a TextField, and a TextArea are added to the center region. A VBox with two buttons are added to the right region. A Label to show the status is added to the bottom region. The top and left regions are set to null. The BorderPane is set as the root node for the scene. Figure 10-32 shows the window.

Listing 10-20. Using the BorderPane Layout Pane

```java
// BorderPaneTest.java
package com.jdojo.container;

import javafx.application.Application;
import javafx.geometry.Insets;
import javafx.scene.Node;
import javafx.scene.Scene;
import javafx.scene.control.Button;
import javafx.scene.control.Label;
import javafx.scene.control.TextArea;
import javafx.scene.control.TextField;
import javafx.scene.layout.BorderPane;
import javafx.scene.layout.HBox;
import javafx.scene.layout.Priority;
import javafx.scene.layout.VBox;
import javafx.stage.Stage;

public class BorderPaneTest extends Application {
        public static void main(String[] args) {
                Application.launch(args);
        }

        @Override
        public void start(Stage stage) {
                // Set the top and left child nodes to null
                Node top = null;
                Node left = null;

                // Build the content nodes for the center region
                VBox center = getCenter();

                // Create the right child node
                Button okBtn = new Button("Ok");
                Button cancelBtn = new Button("Cancel");

                // Make the OK and cancel buttons the same size
                okBtn.setMaxWidth(Double.MAX_VALUE);
                VBox right = new VBox(okBtn, cancelBtn);
                right.setStyle("-fx-padding: 10;");

                // Create the bottom child node
                Label statusLbl = new Label("Status: Ready");
                HBox bottom = new HBox(statusLbl);
                BorderPane.setMargin(bottom, new Insets(10, 0, 0, 0));
```

```
                bottom.setStyle("-fx-background-color: lavender;" +
                            "-fx-font-size: 7pt;" +
                            "-fx-padding: 10 0 0 0;" );

                BorderPane root = new BorderPane(center, top, right, bottom, left);
                root.setStyle("-fx-background-color: lightgray;");

                Scene scene = new Scene(root);
                stage.setScene(scene);
                stage.setTitle("Using a BorderPane");
                stage.show();
        }

        private VBox getCenter() {
                // A Label and a TextField in an HBox
                Label nameLbl = new Label("Name:");
                TextField nameFld = new TextField();
                HBox.setHgrow(nameFld, Priority.ALWAYS);
                HBox nameFields = new HBox(nameLbl, nameFld);

                // A Label and a TextArea
                Label descLbl = new Label("Description:");
                TextArea descText = new TextArea();
                descText.setPrefColumnCount(20);
                descText.setPrefRowCount(5);
                VBox.setVgrow(descText, Priority.ALWAYS);

                // Box all controls in a VBox
                VBox center = new VBox(nameFields, descLbl, descText);

                return center;
        }
}
```

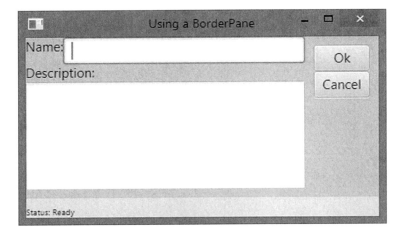

Figure 10-32. *A BorderPane using some controls in its top, right, bottom, and center regions*

BorderPane Properties

The BorderPane class declares five properties: top, right, bottom, left, and center. They are of the ObjectProperty<Node> type. They store the reference of the child node nodes in the five regions of the BorderPane. Use the setters of these properties to add children to the BorderPane. Use the getters of properties to get the reference of the child node in any regions.

Recall that not all of the five regions in a BorderPane need to have nodes. If a region does not a node, no space is allocated for it. Use null to remove a child node from a region. For example, setTop(null) will remove the already added node to the top region. By default, all regions have null nodes as their child nodes.

Setting Constraints for Children in BorderPane

A BorderPane allows you to set alignment and margin constraints on individual children. The alignment for a child node is defined relative to its region. The default alignments:

- Pos.TOP_LEFT for the top child node
- Pos.BOTTOM_LEFT for the bottom child node
- Pos.TOP_LEFT for the left child node
- Pos.TOP_RIGHT for the right child node
- Pos.CENTER for the center child node

Use the setAlignment(Node child, Pos value) static method of the BorderPane class to set the alignment for children. The getAlignment(Node child) static method returns the alignment for a child node.

```
BorderPane root = new BorderPane();
Button top = new Button("OK");
root.setTop(top);

// Place the OK button in the top right corner (default is top left)
BorderPane.setAlignment(top, Pos.TOP_RIGHT);
...
// Get the alignment of the top node
Pos alignment = BorderPane.getAlignment(top);
```

Use the setMargin(Node child, Insets value) static method of the BorderPane class to set the margin for the children. The getMargin(Node child) static method returns the margin for a child node.

```
// Set 10px margin around the top child node
BorderPane.setMargin(top, new Insets(10));
...
// Get the margin of the top child node
Insets margin = BorderPane.getMargin(top);
```

Use null to reset the constraints to the default value. Use the clearConstraints(Node child) static method of the BorderPane to reset all constraints for a child at once.

```
// Clear the alignment and margin constraints for the top child node
BorderPane.clearConstraints(top);
```

Understanding StackPane

A StackPane lays out its children in a stack of nodes. It is simple to use. However, it provides a powerful means to overlay nodes. Children are drawn in the order they are added. That is, the first child node is drawn first; the second child node is drawn next, etc. For example, overlaying text on a shape is as easy as using a StackPane: add the shape as the first child node and the text as the second child node. The shape will be drawn first followed by the text, which makes it seem as if the text is a part of the shape.

Figure 10-33 shows a window with a StackPane set as the root node for its scene. A Rectangle shape and a Text node with text "A Rectangle" are added to the StackPane. The Text is added last, which overlays the Rectangle. The outer border is the border of the StackPane. The dashed inner border is the border of the Rectangle.

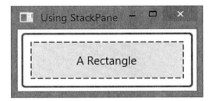

Figure 10-33. *A Text node overlaying a Rectangle in a StackPane*

■ **Tip**   You can create very appealing GUI using StackPanes by overlaying different types of nodes. You can overlay text on an image to get an effect as if the text were part of the image. And you can overlay different types of shapes to create a complex shape. Remember that the node that overlays other nodes is added last to the StackPane.

The preferred width of a StackPane is the width of its widest children. Its preferred height is the height of its tallest children. StackPane does clip its content. Therefore, its children may be drawn outside its bounds.

A StackPane resizes its resizable children to fill its content area, provided their maximum size allows them to expand beyond their preferred size. By default, a StackPane aligns all its children to the center of its content area. You can change the alignment for a child node individually or for all children to use the same alignment.

Creating StackPane Objects

The StackPane class provides constructors to create objects with or without children.

```
// Create an empty StackPane
StackPane spane1 = new StackPane();

// Add a Rectangle and a Text to the StackPane
Rectangle rect = new Rectangle(200, 50);
rect.setFill(Color.LAVENDER);
Text text = new Text("A Rectangle");
spane1.getChildren().addAll(rect, text);
```

```
// Create a StackPane with a Rectangle and a Text
StackPane spane2 = new StackPane(RectangleBuilder.create()
                                     .width(200)
                                     .height(50)
                                     .fill(Color.LAVENDER)
                                     .build(),
                          new Text("A Rectangle")));
```

The program in Listing 10-21 shows how to create a StackPane. It adds a Rectangle and a Text to a StackPane. The Rectangle is added first, and therefore it is overlaid with the Text. Figure 10-33 shows the window.

Listing 10-21. Using StackPane

```java
// StackPaneTest.java
package com.jdojo.container;

import javafx.application.Application;
import javafx.scene.Scene;
import javafx.scene.layout.StackPane;
import javafx.scene.shape.Rectangle;
import javafx.scene.text.Text;
import javafx.stage.Stage;

public class StackPaneTest extends Application {
        public static void main(String[] args) {
                Application.launch(args);
        }

        @Override
        public void start(Stage stage) {
                // Create a Rectangle and a Text
                Rectangle rect = new Rectangle(200, 50);
                rect.setStyle("-fx-fill: lavender;" +
                                "-fx-stroke-type: inside;" +
                                "-fx-stroke-dash-array: 5 5;" +
                                "-fx-stroke-width: 1;" +
                                "-fx-stroke: black;" +
                                "-fx-stroke-radius: 5;");

                Text text = new Text("A Rectangle");

                // Create a StackPane with a Rectangle and a Text
                StackPane root = new StackPane(rect, text);
                root.setStyle("-fx-padding: 10;" +
                                "-fx-border-style: solid inside;" +
                                "-fx-border-width: 2;" +
                                "-fx-border-insets: 5;" +
                                "-fx-border-radius: 5;" +
                                "-fx-border-color: blue;");
```

```
            Scene scene = new Scene(root);
            stage.setScene(scene);
            stage.setTitle("Using StackPane");
            stage.show();
        }
}
```

You must add the children to a StackPane in a specific order to create the desired overlay. Children are drawn in the order they exist in the list. The following two statements will not get the same results.

```
// Overlay a Text on a Rectangle
spane1.getChildren().addAll(rect, text);

// Overlay a Rectangle on a Text
spane1.getChildren().addAll(text, rect);
```

If the Text is smaller than the Rectangle, overlaying the Rectangle on the Text will hide the Text. If the Text size is bigger than the Rectangle, the part of the Text outside the Rectangle bounds will be visible.

The program in Listing 10-22 shows how the overlay rules work in a StackPane. The createStackPane() method creates a StackPane with a Rectangle and a Text. It takes the text for the Text node, the opacity of the Rectangle, and a boolean value indicating whether the Rectangle should be added first to the StackPane. The start method creates five StackPanes and adds them to an HBox. Figure 10-34 shows the window.

- In the first StackPane, the text is overlaid on the rectangle. The rectangle is drawn first and the text second. Both are visible.

- In the second StackPane, the rectangle is overlaid on the text. The text is hidden behind the rectangle as the rectangle is drawn over the text and it is bigger than the text.

- In the third StackPane, the rectangle is overlaid on the text. Unlike the second StackPane, the text is visible because we have set the opacity for the rectangle to 0.5, which makes it is 50% transparent.

- In the fourth StackPane, the rectangle is overlaid on a big text. The opacity of the rectangle is 100%. Therefore, we see only the part of the text that is outside the bounds of the rectangle.

- In the fifth StackPane, the rectangle is overlaid on a big text. The opacity of the rectangle is 50%. We can see the entire text. The visibility of the text within the bounds of the rectangle is 50% and that of outside the bounds is 100%.

Listing 10-22. Overlaying Rules in a StackPane

```
// StackPaneOverlayTest.java
package com.jdojo.container;

import javafx.application.Application;
import javafx.scene.Scene;
import javafx.scene.layout.HBox;
import javafx.scene.layout.StackPane;
import javafx.scene.shape.Rectangle;
```

```
import javafx.scene.text.Text;
import javafx.stage.Stage;

public class StackPaneOverlayTest  extends Application {
        public static void main(String[] args) {
                Application.launch(args);
        }

        @Override
        public void start(Stage stage) {
                StackPane textOverRect = createStackPane("Hello", 1.0, true);
                StackPane rectOverText = createStackPane("Hello", 1.0, false);
                StackPane transparentRectOverText = createStackPane("Hello", 0.5, false);
                StackPane rectOverBigText = createStackPane("A bigger text", 1.0, false);
                StackPane transparentRectOverBigText = createStackPane("A bigger text",
                                                                0.5, false);

                // Add all StackPanes to an HBox
                HBox root = new HBox(textOverRect,
                                       rectOverText,
                                       transparentRectOverText,
                                       rectOverBigText,
                                       transparentRectOverBigText);

                Scene scene = new Scene(root);
                stage.setScene(scene);
                stage.setTitle("Overlaying Rules in StackPane");
                stage.show();
        }

        public StackPane createStackPane(String str, double rectOpacity, boolean rectFirst) {
                Rectangle rect = new Rectangle(60, 50);
                rect.setStyle("-fx-fill: lavender;" + "-fx-opacity: " + rectOpacity + ";");

                Text text = new Text(str);

                // Create a StackPane
                StackPane spane = new StackPane();

                // add the Rectangle before the Text if rectFirst is true.
                // Otherwise add the Text first
                if (rectFirst) {
                        spane.getChildren().addAll(rect, text);
                } else {
                    spane.getChildren().addAll(text, rect);
                }
```

```
        spane.setStyle("-fx-padding: 10;" +
                       "-fx-border-style: solid inside;" +
                       "-fx-border-width: 2;" +
                       "-fx-border-insets: 5;" +
                       "-fx-border-radius: 5;" +
                       "-fx-border-color: blue;");

        return spane;
    }
}
```

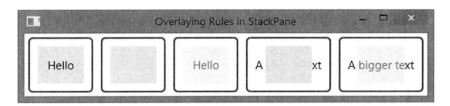

Figure 10-34. *Overlaying a Rectangle on a Text and vice versa*

StackPane Properties

The StackPane class has an alignment property of the ObjectProperty<Pos> type. The property defines the default alignment of all children within the content area of the StackPane. By default, its value is set to Pos.CENTER, which means that all children, by default, are aligned in the center of the content area of the StackPane. This is what we have seen in our previous examples. If you do not want the default alignment for all children, you can change it to any other alignment value. Note that changing the value of the alignment property sets the default alignment for all children.

Individual children may override the default alignment by setting its alignment constraint. We will discuss how to set the alignment constraint on a child node in the next section.

StackPane has several other uses besides overlaying nodes. Whenever you have a requirement to align a node or a collection of nodes in a specific position, try using a StackPane. For example, if you want to display text in the center of your screen, use a StackPane with a Text node as the root node of the scene. The StackPane takes care of keeping the text in the center as the window is resized. Without a StackPane, you will need to use binding to keep the text positioned in the center of the window.

The program in Listing 10-23 uses five StackPanes in an HBox. Each StackPane has a Rectangle overlaid with a Text. The alignment for the StackPane, and hence for all its children, is used as the text for the Text node. Figure 10-35 shows the window. Notice that the Rectangles in StackPanes are bigger than the Texts. Therefore, the Rectangles occupy the entire content area of the StackPanes and they seem not to be affected by the alignment property.

Listing 10-23. Using the Alignment Property of a StackPane

```
// StackPaneAlignment.java
package com.jdojo.container;

import javafx.application.Application;
import javafx.geometry.Pos;
import javafx.scene.Scene;
import javafx.scene.layout.HBox;
```

```java
import javafx.scene.layout.StackPane;
import javafx.scene.paint.Color;
import javafx.scene.shape.Rectangle;
import javafx.scene.text.Text;
import javafx.stage.Stage;

public class StackPaneAlignment extends Application {
        public static void main(String[] args) {
                Application.launch(args);
        }

        @Override
        public void start(Stage stage) {
                StackPane topLeft = createStackPane(Pos.TOP_LEFT);
                StackPane topRight = createStackPane(Pos.TOP_RIGHT);
                StackPane bottomLeft = createStackPane(Pos.BOTTOM_LEFT);
                StackPane bottomRight = createStackPane(Pos.BOTTOM_RIGHT);
                StackPane center = createStackPane(Pos.CENTER);

                double spacing = 10.0;
                HBox root = new HBox(spacing,
                                        topLeft,
                                        topRight,
                                        bottomLeft,
                                        bottomRight,
                                        center);

                Scene scene = new Scene(root);
                stage.setScene(scene);
                stage.setTitle("Using StackPane");
                stage.show();
        }

        public StackPane createStackPane(Pos alignment) {
                Rectangle rect = new Rectangle(80, 50);
                rect.setFill(Color.LAVENDER);

                Text text = new Text(alignment.toString());
                text.setStyle("-fx-font-size: 7pt;");

                StackPane spane = new StackPane(rect, text);
                spane.setAlignment(alignment);
                spane.setStyle("-fx-padding: 10;" +
                                "-fx-border-style: solid inside;" +
                                "-fx-border-width: 2;" +
                                "-fx-border-insets: 5;" +
                                "-fx-border-radius: 5;" +
                                "-fx-border-color: blue;");
                return spane;
        }
}
```

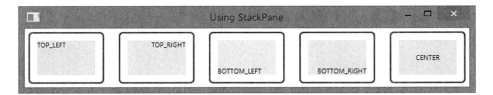

Figure 10-35. *StackPanes using different alignment values*

Setting Constraints for Children

A StackPane allows you to set alignment and margin constraints on individual children. The alignment for a child node is defined relative to the content area of the StackPane.

You should be able to differentiate between the alignment property of a StackPane and the alignment constraint on its children. The alignment property affects all children. Its value is used to align children by default. The alignment constraint on a child node overrides the default alignment value set by the alignment property. The alignment constraint on a child node affects the alignment of only that child node, whereas the alignment property affects all child nodes. When a child node is drawn, JavaFX uses the alignment constraint of the child node for aligning it within the content area of the StackPane. If its alignment constraint is not set, the alignment property of the StackPane is used.

■ **Tip**   The default value for the alignment property of StackPane is Pos.CENTER. The default value for the alignment constraint for children is null.

Use the setAlignment(Node child, Pos value) static method of the StackPane class to set the alignment constraints for children. The getAlignment(Node child) static method returns the alignment for a child node.

```
// Place a Text node in the top left corner of the StackPane
Text topLeft = new Text("top-left");
StackPane.setAlignment(topLeft, Pos.TOP_LEFT);
StackPane root = new StackPane(topLeft);
...
// Get the alignment of the topLeft node
Pos alignment = StackPane.getAlignment(topLeft);
```

Listing 10-24. Using the Alignment Constraints for Children in a StackPane

```
// StackPaneAlignmentConstraint.java
package com.jdojo.container;

import javafx.application.Application;
import javafx.geometry.Pos;
import javafx.scene.Scene;
import javafx.scene.layout.StackPane;
import javafx.scene.paint.Color;
```

```
import javafx.scene.shape.Rectangle;
import javafx.scene.text.Text;
import javafx.stage.Stage;

public class StackPaneAlignmentConstraint extends Application {
        public static void main(String[] args) {
                Application.launch(args);
        }

        @Override
        public void start(Stage stage) {
                Rectangle rect = new Rectangle(200, 60);
                rect.setFill(Color.LAVENDER);

                // Create a Text node with the default CENTER alignment
                Text center = new Text("Center");

                // Create a Text node with a TOP_LEFT alignemnt constraint
                Text topLeft = new Text("top-left");
                StackPane.setAlignment(topLeft, Pos.TOP_LEFT);

                // Create a Text node with a BOTTOM_LEFT alignemnt constraint
                Text bottomRight = new Text("bottom-right");
                StackPane.setAlignment(bottomRight, Pos.BOTTOM_RIGHT);

                StackPane root = new StackPane(rect, center, topLeft, bottomRight);
                root.setStyle("-fx-padding: 10;" +
                                "-fx-border-style: solid inside;" +
                                "-fx-border-width: 2;" +
                                "-fx-border-insets: 5;" +
                                "-fx-border-radius: 5;" +
                                "-fx-border-color: blue;");

                Scene scene = new Scene(root);
                stage.setScene(scene);
                stage.setTitle("StackPane Alignment Constraint");
                stage.show();
        }
}
```

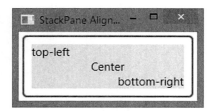

Figure 10-36. *Children using different alignment constraints in a StackPane*

Use the setMargin(Node child, Insets value) static method of the StackPane class to set the margin for children. The getMargin(Node child) static method returns the margin for a child node.

```
// Set 10px margin around the topLeft child node
StackPane.setMargin(topLeft, new Insets(10));
...
// Get the margin of the topLeft child node
Insets margin = StackPane.getMargin(topLeft);
```

Use null to reset the constraints to the default value. Use the clearConstraints(Node child) static method of the StackPane to reset all constraints for a child at once.

```
// Clear the alignment and margin constraints for the topLeft child node
StackPane.clearConstraints(topLeft);
```

After you clear all constraints for a child node, it will use the current value of the alignment property of the StackPane as its alignment and 0px as the margins.

Understanding TilePane

A TilePane lays out its children in a grid of uniformly sized cells, known as tiles. TilePanes work similar to FlowPanes with one difference: In a FlowPane, rows and columns can be of different heights and widths, whereas in a TilePane, all rows have the same heights and all columns have the same widths. The width of the widest child node and the height of the tallest child node are the default widths and heights of all tiles in a TilePane.

The orientation of a TilePane, which can be set to horizontal or vertical, determines the direction of the flow for its content. By default, a TilePane has a horizontal orientation. In a horizontal TilePane, the content flows in rows. The content in rows may flow from left to right (the default) or from right to left. In a vertical TilePane, the content flow in columns. Figures 10-37, 10-38, and 10-26 show horizontal and vertical TilePanes.

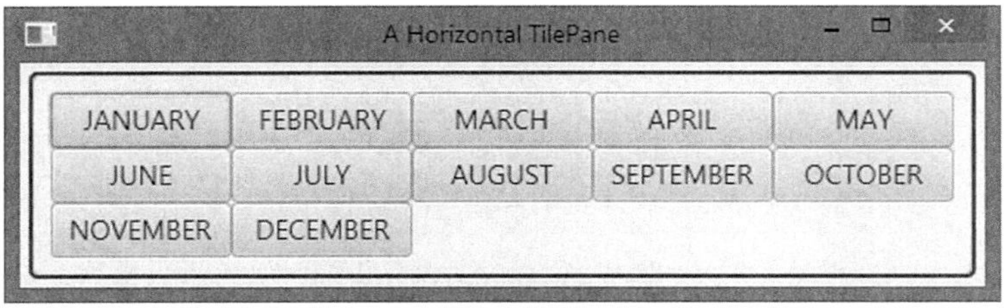

Figure 10-37. *A horizontal TilePane showing months in a year*

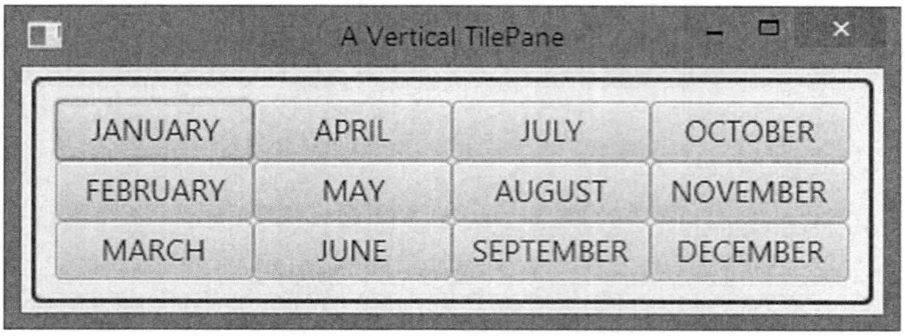

Figure 10-38. *A vertical TilePane showing months in a year*

You can customize the layout in a TilePane using its properties or setting constraints on individual children:

- You can override the default size of tiles.

- You can customize the alignment of the entire content of a TilePane within its content area, which defaults to Pos.TOP_LEFT.

- You can also customize the alignment of each child node within its tile, which defaults to Pos.CENTER.

- You specify the spacing between adjacent rows and columns, which defaults to 0px.

- You can specify the preferred number of columns in a horizontal TilePane and the preferred number of rows in a vertical TilePane. The default values for the preferred number of rows and columns are five.

Creating TilePane Objects

The TilePane class provides several constructors to create TilePane objects with a specified orientation (horizontal or vertical), a specified horizontal and vertical spacing between children, and a specified initial list of children.

```
// Create an empty horizontal TilePane with 0px spacing
TilePane tpane1 = new TilePane();

// Create an empty vertical TilePane with 0px spacing
TilePane tpane2 = new TilePane(Orientation.VERTICAL);

// Create an empty horizontal TilePane with 5px horizontal
// and 10px vertical spacing
TilePane tpane3 = new TilePane(5, 10);

// Create an empty vertical TilePane with 5px horizontal
// and 10px vertical spacing
TilePane tpane4 = new TilePane(Orientation.VERTICAL, 5, 10);

// Create a horizontal TilePane with two Buttons and 0px spacing
TilePane tpane5 = new TilePane(new Button("Button 1"), new Button("Button 2"));
```

The program in Listing 10-25 shows how to create a TilePane and add children. It uses the Month enum from the java.time package to get the names of ISO months. Note that java.time package was added in Java 8. The resulting window is the same as shown in Figure 10-37.

Listing 10-25. Using TilePane

```java
// TilePaneTest.java
package com.jdojo.container;

import java.time.Month;
import javafx.application.Application;
import javafx.scene.Scene;
import javafx.scene.control.Button;
import javafx.scene.layout.TilePane;
import javafx.stage.Stage;

public class TilePaneTest extends Application {
        public static void main(String[] args) {
                Application.launch(args);
        }

        @Override
        public void start(Stage stage) {
                double hgap = 5.0;
                double vgap = 5.0;
                TilePane root = new TilePane(hgap, vgap);
                root.setPrefColumns(5);

                // Add 12 Buttons - each having the name of the 12 months
                for(Month month: Month.values()) {
                        Button b = new Button(month.toString());
                        b.setMaxHeight(Double.MAX_VALUE);
                        b.setMaxWidth(Double.MAX_VALUE);
                        root.getChildren().add(b);
                }

                root.setStyle("-fx-padding: 10;" +
                                "-fx-border-style: solid inside;" +
                                "-fx-border-width: 2;" +
                                "-fx-border-insets: 5;" +
                                "-fx-border-radius: 5;" +
                                "-fx-border-color: blue;");

                Scene scene = new Scene(root);
                stage.setScene(scene);
                stage.setTitle("A Horizontal TilePane");
                stage.show();
        }
}
```

You can modify the code in Listing 10-25 to get the window in Figure 10-38. You need to specify the orientation of the TilePane as Orientation.VERTICAL and use three as the preferred number of rows.

```
import javafx.geometry.Orientation;
...
double hgap = 5.0;
double vgap = 5.0;
TilePane root = new TilePane(Orientation.VERTICAL, hgap, vgap);
root.setPrefRows(3);
```

TilePane Properties

The TilePane class contains several properties, as listed in Table 10-5, which let you customize the layout of its children.

Table 10-5. *The List of Properties Declared in the TilePane Class*

Property	Type	Description
alignment	ObjectProperty<Pos>	It specifies the alignment of the content of the TilePane relative to its content area. It defaults to Pos.TOP_LEFT.
tileAlignment	ObjectProperty<Pos>	It specifies the default alignment of all children within their tiles. It defaults to Pos.CENTER.
hgap, vgap	DoubleProperty	The hgap property specifies the horizontal gap between adjacent children in a row. The vgap property specifies the vertical gap between adjacent children in a column. The default is zero for both properties.
orientation	ObjectProperty<Orientation>	It specifies the orientation of the TilePane – horizontal or vertical. It defaults to HORIZONTAL.
prefRows	IntegerProperty	It specifies the preferred number of rows for a vertical TilePane. It is ignored for a horizontal TilePane.
prefColumns	IntegerProperty	It specifies the preferred number of columns for a horizontal TilePane. It is ignored for a vertical TilePane.
prefTileWidth	DoubleProperty	It specifies the preferred width of each tile. The default is to use the width of the widest children.
prefTileHeight	DoubleProperty	It specifies the preferred height of each tile. The default is to use the height of the tallest children.
tileHeight	ReadOnlyDoubleProperty	It is a read-only property that stores the actual height of each tile.
tileWidth	ReadOnlyDoubleProperty	It is a read-only property that stores the actual width of each tile.

The Alignment Property

The alignment property of a TilePane controls the alignment of its content within its content area. You can see the effects of this property when the size of the TilePane is bigger than its content. The property works the same way as the alignment property for the FlowPane. Please refer to the description of the alignment property for FlowPane for more details and illustrations.

The tileAlignment Property

The tileAlignment property specifies the default alignment of children within their tiles. Note that this property affects children smaller than the size of tiles. This property affects the default alignment of all children within their tiles. This can be overridden on individual children by setting their alignment constraints. The program in Listing 10-26 shows how to use the tileAlignment property. It shows display windows, as shown in Figure 10-39, with two TilePanes – one has the tileAlignment property set to Pos.CENTER and another Pos.TOP_LEFT.

Listing 10-26. Using the TileAlignment Property of TilePane

```
// TilePaneTileAlignment.java
package com.jdojo.container;

import javafx.application.Application;
import javafx.geometry.Pos;
import javafx.scene.Scene;
import javafx.scene.control.Button;
import javafx.scene.layout.HBox;
import javafx.scene.layout.TilePane;
import javafx.stage.Stage;

public class TilePaneTileAlignment extends Application {
        public static void main(String[] args) {
                Application.launch(args);
        }

        @Override
        public void start(Stage stage) {
                TilePane tileAlignCenter = createTilePane(Pos.CENTER);
                TilePane tileAlignTopRight = createTilePane(Pos.TOP_LEFT);

                HBox root = new HBox(tileAlignCenter, tileAlignTopRight);
                root.setFillHeight(false);
                Scene scene = new Scene(root);
                stage.setScene(scene);
                stage.setTitle("The tileAlignment Property for TilePane");
                stage.show();
        }
```

```
public TilePane createTilePane(Pos tileAlignment) {
    Button[] buttons = new Button[] {new Button("Tile"),
                                     new Button("are"),
                                     new Button("aligned"),
                                     new Button("at"),
                                     new Button(tileAlignment.toString())};

    TilePane tpane = new TilePane(5, 5, buttons);
    tpane.setTileAlignment(tileAlignment);
    tpane.setPrefColumns(3);
    tpane.setStyle("-fx-padding: 10;" +
                   "-fx-border-style: solid inside;" +
                   "-fx-border-width: 2;" +
                   "-fx-border-insets: 5;" +
                   "-fx-border-radius: 5;" +
                   "-fx-border-color: blue;");
    return tpane;
    }
}
```

Figure 10-39. *Using the tileAlignment property*

The hgap and vgap Properties

The hgap and vgap properties specify the spacing between adjacent columns and adjacent rows. They default to zero. They can be specified in the constructors or using the setHgap(double hg) and setVgap(double vg) methods of the TilePane.

The Orientation Property

The orientation property specifies the flow of content in a TilePane. If it is set to Orientation.HORIZONTAL, which is the default value, the content flows in rows. If it is set to Orientation.VERTICAL, the content flows in columns. You can specify the orientation in the constructors or using the setter method.

```
// Create a horizontal TilePane
TilePane tpane = new TilePane();
...
// Change the orientation of the TilePane to vertical
tpane.setOrientation(Orientation.VERTICAL);
```

The prefRows and prefColumns Properties

The prefRows property specifies the preferred number of rows for a vertical TilePane. It is ignored for a horizontal TilePane.

The prefColumns specifies the preferred number of columns for a horizontal TilePane. It is ignored for a vertical TilePane.

The default values for prefRows and prefColumns is 5. It is recommended that you use a sensible value for these properties.

Note that these properties are only used to compute the preferred size of the TilePane. If the TilePane is resized to a size other than its preferred size, these values may not reflect the actual number of rows or columns. In Listing 10-26, we have specified three as the preferred number of columns. If you resize the window displayed by Listing 10-26 to a smaller width, you may get only one or two columns, and the number of rows will increase accordingly.

■ **Tip**   Recall the prefWrapLength property of the FlowPane that is used to determine the preferred width or height of the FlowPane. The prefRows and prefColumns properties serve the same purpose in a TilePane, as does the prefWrapLength in a FlowPane.

The prefTileWidth and prefTileHeight Properties

A TilePane computes the preferred size of its tiles based on the widest and the tallest children. You can override the computed width and height of tiles using the prefTileWidth and prefTileHeight properties. They default to Region.USE_COMPUTED_SIZE. The TilePane attempts to resize its children to fit in the tile size, provided their minimum and maximum size allows them to be resized.

```
// Create a TilePane and set its preferred tile width and height to 40px
TilePane tpane = new TilePane();
tpane.setPrefTileWidth(40);
tpane.setPrefTileHeight(40);
```

The tileWidth and tileHeight Properties

The tileWidth and tileHeight properties specify the actual width and height of each tile. They are read-only properties. If you specify the prefTileWidth and prefTileHeight properties, they return their values. Otherwise, they return the computed size of tiles.

Setting Constraints for Children in TilePane

A TilePane allows you to set alignment and margin constraints on individual children. The alignment for a child node is defined within the tile that contains the child node.

You should be able to differentiate between the three:

- The alignment property of a TilePane

- The tileAlignment property of the TilePane

- The alignment constraint on individual children of the TilePane

The `alignment` property is used to align the content (all children) within the content area of the TilePane. It affects the content of TilePane as a whole.

The `tileAlignment` property is used to align all children within their tiles by default. Modifying this property affects all children.

The alignment constraint on a child node is used to align the child node within its tile. It affects only the child node on which it is set. It overrides the default alignment value for the child node that is set using the `tileAlignment` property of the TilePane.

■ **Tip**   The default value for the `tileAlignment` property of a TilePane is Pos.CENTER. The default value for the alignment constraint for children is `null`.

Use the `setAlignment(Node child, Pos value)` static method of the TilePane class to set the alignment constraints for the children. The `getAlignment(Node child)` static method returns the alignment for a child node.

```
// Place a Text node in the top left corner in a tile
Text topLeft = new Text("top-left");
TilePane.setAlignment(topLeft, Pos.TOP_LEFT);

TilePane root = new TilePane();
root.getChildren().add(topLeft);
...
// Get the alignment of the topLeft node
Pos alignment = TilePane.getAlignment(topLeft);
```

The program in Listing 10-27 adds five buttons to a TilePane. The button labeled "Three" uses a custom tile alignment constraint of Pos.BOTTOM_RIGHT. All other buttons use the default tile alignment, which is Pos.CENTER. Figure 10-40 shows the window.

Listing 10-27. Using the Alignment Constraints for Children in a TilePane

```
// TilePaneAlignmentConstraint.java
package com.jdojo.container;

import javafx.application.Application;
import javafx.geometry.Pos;
import javafx.scene.Scene;
import javafx.scene.control.Button;
import javafx.scene.layout.TilePane;
import javafx.stage.Stage;

public class TilePaneAlignmentConstraint extends Application {
        public static void main(String[] args) {
                Application.launch(args);
        }
```

```
        @Override
        public void start(Stage stage) {
                Button b12 = new Button("One\nTwo");
                Button b3 = new Button("Three");
                Button b4 = new Button("Four");
                Button b5 = new Button("Five");
                Button b6 = new Button("Six");

                // Set the tile alignment constraint on b3 to BOTTOM_RIGHT
                TilePane.setAlignment(b3, Pos.BOTTOM_RIGHT);

                TilePane root = new TilePane(b12, b3, b4, b5, b6);
                root.setPrefColumns(3);
                root.setStyle("-fx-padding: 10;" +
                                "-fx-border-style: solid inside;" +
                                "-fx-border-width: 2;" +
                                "-fx-border-insets: 5;" +
                                "-fx-border-radius: 5;" +
                                "-fx-border-color: blue;");

                Scene scene = new Scene(root);
                stage.setScene(scene);
                stage.setTitle("Using Alignment Constraints in TilePane");
                stage.show();
        }
}
```

Figure 10-40. *Children using different alignment constraints in a TilePane*

Use the setMargin(Node child, Insets value) static method of the TilePane class to set the margin for children. The getMargin(Node child) static method returns the margin for a child node.

```
// Set 10px margin around the topLeft child node
TilePane.setMargin(topLeft, new Insets(10));
...
// Get the margin of the topLeft child node
Insets margin = TilePane.getMargin(topLeft);
```

Use null to reset the constraints to the default value. Use the clearConstraints(Node child) static method of the TilePane to reset all constraints for a child at once.

```
// Clear the tile alignment and margin constraints for the topLeft child node
TilePane.clearConstraints(topLeft);
```

After you clear all constraints for a child node, it will use the current value of the tileAlignment property of the TilePane as its alignment and 0px as the margins.

Understanding GridPane

GridPane is one of the most powerful layout panes. With power comes complexity. Therefore, it is also a bit complex to learn.

A GridPane lays out its children in a dynamic grid of cells arranged in rows and columns. The grid is dynamic because the number and size of cells in the grid are determined based on the number of children. They depend on the constraints set on children. Each cell in the grid is identified by its position in the column and row. The indexes for columns and rows start at 0. A child node may be placed anywhere in the grid spanning more than one cell. All cells in a row are of the same height. Cells in different rows may have different heights. All cells in a column are of the same width. Cells in different columns may have different widths. By default, a row is tall enough to accommodate the tallest child node in it. A column is wide enough to accommodate the widest child node in it. You can customize the size of each row and column. GridPane also allows for vertical spacing between rows and horizontal spacing between columns.

GridPane does not show the grid lines by default. For debug purposes, you can show the grid lines. Figure 10-41 shows three instances of the GridPane. The first GridPane shows only the grid lines and no child nodes. The second GridPane shows the cell positions, which are identified by row and column indexes. In the figure, (cM, rN) means the cell at the (M+1)th column and the (N+1)th row. For example, (c3, r2) means the cell at the 4th column and the 3rd row. The third GridPane shows six buttons in the grid. Five of the buttons spans one row and one column; one of them spans two rows and one column.

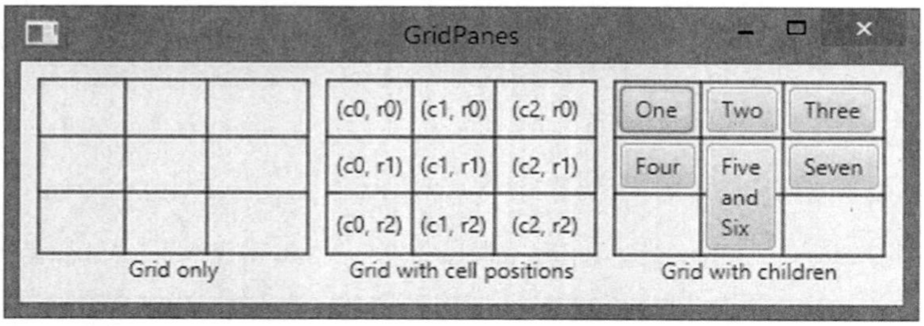

Figure 10-41. *GridPanes with grid only, with cell positions, and with children placed in the grid*

In a GridPane, rows are indexed from top to bottom. The top row has an index of 0. Columns are indexed from left to right or from right to left. If the nodeOrientation property for the GridPane is set to LEFT_TO_RIGHT, the leftmost column has index 0. If it is set to RIGHT_TO_LEFT, the rightmost column has an index of 0. The second grid in Figure 10-41 shows the leftmost column having an index of 0, which means that its nodeOrientation property is set from LEFT_TO_RIGHT.

■ **Tip** A question that is often asked about the GridPane is, "How many cells, and of what sizes, do we need to lay out children in a GridPane?" The answer is simple but sometimes perplexing to beginners. You specify the cell positions and cell spans for the children. GridPane will figure out the number of cells (rows and columns) and their sizes for you. That is, GridPane computes the number of cells and their sizes based on the constraints that you set for the children.

Creating GridPane Objects

The GridPane class contains a no-args constructor. It creates an empty GridPane with 0px spacing between rows and columns, placing the children, which need to be added later, at the top-left corner within its content area.

```
GridPane gpane = new GridPane();
```

Making Grid Lines Visible

The GridPane class contains a gridLinesVisible property of the BooleanProperty type. It controls the visibility of the grid lines. By default, it is set to false and the grid lines are invisible. It exists for debugging purposes only. Use it when you want to see the positions of children in the grid.

```
GridPane gpane = new GridPane();
gpane.setGridLinesVisible(true); // Make grid lines visible
```

Adding Children to GridPane

Like most of the other layout panes, a GridPane stores its children in an ObservableList<Node> whose reference is returned by the getChildren() method. You should not add children to the GridPane directly to the list. Rather, you should use one of the convenience methods to add children to the GridPane. You should specify constraints for children when you add them to a GridPane. The minimum constraints would be the column and row indexes to identify the cell in which they are placed.

Let us first see the effect of adding the children directly to the observable list of the GridPane. Listing 10-28 contains the program that directly adds three buttons to the list of children of a GridPane. Figure 10-42 shows the window. Notice that the buttons overlap. They are all placed in the same cell (c0, r0). They are drawn in the order they are added to the list.

■ **Tip** In a GridPane, by default, all children are added in the first cell (c0, r0) spanning only one column and one row, thus overlapping each other. They are drawn in the order they are added.

Listing 10-28. Adding Children to the List of Children for a GridPane Directly

```
// GridPaneChildrenList.java
package com.jdojo.container;

import javafx.application.Application;
import javafx.scene.Scene;
import javafx.scene.control.Button;
import javafx.scene.layout.GridPane;
import javafx.stage.Stage;

public class GridPaneChildrenList extends Application {
        public static void main(String[] args) {
                Application.launch(args);
        }

        @Override
        public void start(Stage stage) {
                Button b1 = new Button("One One One One One");
                Button b2 = new Button("Two Two Two");
                Button b3 = new Button("Three");

                GridPane root = new GridPane();

                // Add three buttons to the list of children of the GridPane directly
                root.getChildren().addAll(b1, b2, b3);

                root.setStyle("-fx-padding: 10;" +
                                "-fx-border-style: solid inside;" +
                                "-fx-border-width: 2;" +
                                "-fx-border-insets: 5;" +
                                "-fx-border-radius: 5;" +
                                "-fx-border-color: blue;");

                Scene scene = new Scene(root);
                stage.setScene(scene);
                stage.setTitle("Adding Children to a GridPane");
                stage.show();
        }
}
```

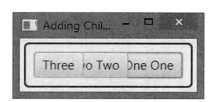

Figure 10-42. Three buttons added to the list of children for a GridPane directly

There are two ways of fixing the problem of overlapping children in Listing 10-28:

- We can set the position in which they are placed, before or after adding them to the list.

- We can use convenience methods of the GridPane class that allow specifying the positions, among other constraints, while adding children to the GridPane.

Setting Positions of Children

You can set the column and row indexes for a child node using one of the following three static methods of the GridPane class.

- `public static void setColumnIndex(Node child, Integer value)`

- `public static void setRowIndex(Node child, Integer value)`

- `public static void setConstraints(Node child,int columnIndex, int rowIndex)`

The program in Listing 10-29 is a modified version of the program in Listing 10-28. It adds the column and row indexes to three buttons, so they are positioned in separate columns in one row. Figure 10-43 shows the window.

Listing 10-29. Setting Positions for Children in a GridPane

```java
// GridPaneChildrenPositions.java
package com.jdojo.container;

import javafx.application.Application;
import javafx.scene.Scene;
import javafx.scene.control.Button;
import javafx.scene.layout.GridPane;
import javafx.stage.Stage;

public class GridPaneChildrenPositions extends Application {
        public static void main(String[] args) {
                Application.launch(args);
        }

        @Override
        public void start(Stage stage) {
                Button b1 = new Button("One One One One One");
                Button b2 = new Button("Two Two Two");
                Button b3 = new Button("Three");

                GridPane root = new GridPane();

                // Add three buttons to the list of children of the GridPane directly
                root.getChildren().addAll(b1, b2, b3);

                // Set the cells the buttons
                GridPane.setConstraints(b1, 0, 0); // (c0, r0)
                GridPane.setConstraints(b2, 1, 0); // (c1, r0)
                GridPane.setConstraints(b3, 2, 0); // (c2, r0)
```

```
            root.setStyle("-fx-padding: 10;" +
                          "-fx-border-style: solid inside;" +
                          "-fx-border-width: 2;" +
                          "-fx-border-insets: 5;" +
                          "-fx-border-radius: 5;" +
                          "-fx-border-color: blue;");

            Scene scene = new Scene(root);
            stage.setScene(scene);
            stage.setTitle("Setting Positions for Children in a GridPane");
            stage.show();
    }
}
```

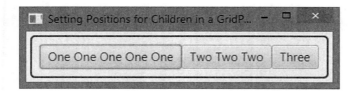

Figure 10-43. *Three buttons added to a GridPane directly and then their position set*

Using Convenience Methods to Add Children

The GridPane class contains the following convenience methods to add children with constraints.

- void add(Node child, int columnIndex, int rowIndex)

- void add(Node child, int columnIndex, int rowIndex, int colspan,int rowspan)

- void addRow(int rowIndex, Node... children)

- void addColumn(int columnIndex, Node... children)

The add() methods let you add a child node specifying the column index, row index, column span, and row span.

The addRow() method adds the specified children in a row identified by the specified rowIndex. Children are added sequentially. If the row already contains children, the specified children are appended sequentially. For example, if the GridPane has no children in the specified row, it will add the first child node at column index 0, the second at column index 1, etc. Suppose the specified row already has two children occupying column indexes 0 and 1. The addRow() method will add children starting at column index 2.

■ **Tip** All children added using the addRow() method spans only one cell. Row and column spans for a child node can be modified using the setRowSpan(Node child, Integer value) and setColumnSpan(Node child, Integer value) static methods of the GridPane class. When you modify the row and column spans for a child node, make sure to update row and column indexes of the affected children so they do not overlap.

The addColumn() method adds the specified children sequentially in a column identified by the specified columnIndex. This method adds children to a column the same way the addRow() method adds children to a row.

The following snippet code creates three GridPanes and adds four buttons to them using three different ways. Figure 10-44 shows one of the GridPanes. All of them will look the same.

```
// Add a child node at a time
GridPane gpane1 = new GridPane();
gpane1.add(new Button("One"), 0, 0);          // (c0, r0)
gpane1.add(new Button("Two"), 1, 0);          // (c1, r0)
gpane1.add(new Button("Three"), 0, 1);        // (c0, r1)
gpane1.add(new Button("Four"), 1, 1);         // (c1, r1)

// Add a row at a time
GridPane gpane2 = new GridPane();
gpane2.addRow(0, new Button("One"), new Button("Two"));
gpane2.addRow(1, new Button("Three"), new Button("Four"));

// Add a column at a time
GridPane gpane3 = new GridPane();
gpane3.addColumn(0, new Button("One"), new Button("Three"));
gpane3.addColumn(1, new Button("Two"), new Button("Four"));
```

Figure 10-44. *A GridPane with four buttons*

Specifying Row and Column Spans

A child node may span more than one row and column, which can be specified using the rowSpan and colSpan constraints. By default, a child node spans one column and one row. These constraints can be specified while adding the child node or later using any of the following methods in the GridPane class.

- void add(Node child, int columnIndex, int rowIndex, int colspan, int rowspan)

- static void setColumnSpan(Node child, Integer value)

- static void setConstraints(Node child, int columnIndex, int rowIndex, int columnspan, int rowspan)

The setConstraints() method is overloaded. Other versions of the method also let you specify the column/row span.

The GridPane class defines a constant named REMAINING that is used for specifying the column/row span. It means that the child node spans the remaining columns or remaining rows.

The following snippet of code adds a `Label` and a `TextField` to the first row. It adds a `TextArea` to the first column of the second row with its colSpan as REMAINING. This makes the `TextArea` occupy two columns because there are two columns created by the controls added to the first row. Figure 10-45 shows the window.

```
// Create a GridPane and set its background color to lightgray
GridPane root = new GridPane();
root.setGridLinesVisible(true);
root.setStyle("-fx-background-color: lightgray;");

// Add a Label and a TextField to the first row
root.addRow(0, new Label("First Name:"), new TextField());

// Add a TextArea in the second row to span all columns in row 2
TextArea ta = new TextArea();
ta.setPromptText("Enter your resume here");
ta.setPrefColumnCount(10);
ta.setPrefRowCount(3);
root.add(ta, 0, 1, GridPane.REMAINING, 1);
```

Figure 10-45. *A TextArea Using GridPane.REMAINING as the colSpan value*

Suppose you add two more children in the first column to occupy the third and fourth columns.

```
// Add a Label and a TextField to the first row
root.addRow(0, new Label("Last Name:"), new TextField());
```

Now, the number of columns has increased from two to four. This will make the `TextArea` occupy four columns as we set its colSpan as REMAINING. Figure 10-46 shows the new window.

Figure 10-46. *A TextArea using GridPane.REMAINING as the colSpan value*

Creating Forms Using GridPanes

GridPane is best suited for creating forms. Let us build a form using a GridPane. The form will be similar to the one shown in Figure 10-32 that was created using a BorderPane. Our new form will look as shown in Figure 10-47. The figure shows two instances of the window: the form with children (on the left) and the form with grid only (on the right). The form with grid only is shown, so you can visualize the positions and spans of the children within the grid.

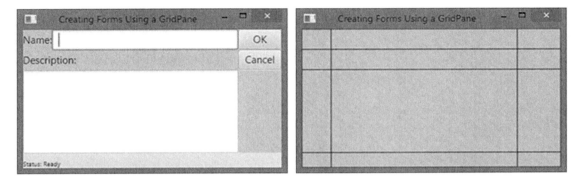

Figure 10-47. *A GridPane with some controls to create a form*

The grid will have three columns and four rows. It has seven children.

- A Label, a TextField, and an *OK* button in the first row
- A Label and a Cancel button in the second row
- A TextArea in the third row
- A Label in the fourth row

The following snippet of code creates all children.

```
// A Label and a TextField
Label nameLbl = new Label("Name:");
TextField nameFld = new TextField();

// A Label and a TextArea
Label descLbl = new Label("Description:");
TextArea descText = new TextArea();
descText.setPrefColumnCount(20);
descText.setPrefRowCount(5);

// Two buttons
Button okBtn = new Button("OK");
Button cancelBtn = new Button("Cancel");
```

All children in the first row span only one cell. The "Description" Label in the second row spans two columns (c0 and c1) and the *Cancel* button only one column. The TextArea in the third row spans two columns (c0 and c1). The Label in the fourth row spans three columns (c0, c1, and c1). The following snippet of code places all children in the grid.

```
// Create a GridPane
GridPane root = new GridPane();

// Add children to the GridPane
root.add(nameLbl, 0, 0, 1, 1);    // (c0, r0, colspan=1, rowspan=1)
root.add(nameFld, 1, 0, 1, 1);    // (c1, r0, colspan=1, rowspan=1)
root.add(descLbl, 0, 1, 3, 1);    // (c0, r1, colspan=3, rowspan=1)
root.add(descText, 0, 2, 2, 1);   // (c0, r2, colspan=2, rowspan=1)
root.add(okBtn, 2, 0, 1, 1);      // (c2, r0, colspan=1, rowspan=1)
root.add(cancelBtn, 2, 1, 1, 1);  // (c2, r1, colspan=1, rowspan=1)

// Let the status bar start at column 0 and take up all remaning columns
// (c0, r3, colspan=REMAININg, rowspan=1)
root.add(statusBar, 0, 3, GridPane.REMAINING, 1);
```

If we add the GridPane to a scene, it will give us the desired look of the form, but not the desired resizing behavior. The children will not resize correctly on resizing the window. We need to specify the correct resizing behavior for some of the children.

- The *OK* and *Cancel* buttons should be of the same size.

- The TextField to enter name should expand horizontally.

- The TextArea to enter the description should expand horizontally and vertically.

- The Label used as the status bar at the bottom should expand horizontally.

Making the *OK* and *Cancel* buttons the same size is easy. By default, a GridPane resizes its children to fill their cells, provided the maximum size of the children allows it. The maximum size of a Button is clamped to its preferred size. We need to set the maximum size of the *OK* button big enough, so it can expand to fill the width of its cell, which would be the same as the preferred width of the widest node in its column (the *Cancel* button).

```
// The max width of the OK button should be big enough, so it can fill the
// width of its cell
okBtn.setMaxWidth(Double.MAX_VALUE);
```

By default, the rows and columns in a GridPane stay at their preferred size when the GridPane is resized. Their horizontal and vertical grow constraints specify how they grow when additional space is available. To let the name, description, and status bar fields grow when the GridPane is expanded, we will set their hgrow and vgrow constraints appropriately.

```
// The name field in the first row should grow horizontally
GridPane.setHgrow(nameFld, Priority.ALWAYS);
```

```
// The description field in the third row should grow vertically
GridPane.setVgrow(descText, Priority.ALWAYS);
```

```
// The status bar in the last row should fill its cell
statusBar.setMaxWidth(Double.MAX_VALUE);
```

When the GridPane is expanded horizontally, the second column, occupied by the name field, grows by taking the extra available width. It makes the description and status bar fields fill the extra width generated in the second column.

When the GridPane is expanded vertically, the third row, occupied by the description field, grows by taking the extra available height. The maximum size of a TextArea is unbounded. That is, it can grow to fill the available space in both directions. The program in Listing 10-30 contains the complete code.

Listing 10-30. Using a GridPane to Create Forms

```java
// GridPaneForm.java
package com.jdojo.container;

import javafx.application.Application;
import javafx.scene.Scene;
import javafx.scene.control.Button;
import javafx.scene.control.Label;
import javafx.scene.control.TextArea;
import javafx.scene.control.TextField;
import javafx.scene.layout.GridPane;
import javafx.scene.layout.Priority;
import javafx.stage.Stage;

public class GridPaneForm extends Application {
        public static void main(String[] args) {
                Application.launch(args);
        }

        @Override
        public void start(Stage stage) {
                // A Label and a TextField
                Label nameLbl = new Label("Name:");
                TextField nameFld = new TextField();

                // A Label and a TextArea
                Label descLbl = new Label("Description:");
                TextArea descText = new TextArea();
                descText.setPrefColumnCount(20);
                descText.setPrefRowCount(5);

                // Two buttons
                Button okBtn = new Button("OK");
                Button cancelBtn = new Button("Cancel");

                // A Label used as a status bar
                Label statusBar = new Label("Status: Ready");
                statusBar.setStyle("-fx-background-color: lavender;" +
                                "-fx-font-size: 7pt;" +
                                "-fx-padding: 10 0 0 0;");

                // Create a GridPane and set its background color to lightgray
                GridPane root = new GridPane();
                root.setStyle("-fx-background-color: lightgray;");
```

```
        // Add children to the GridPane
        root.add(nameLbl, 0, 0, 1, 1);    // (c0, r0, colspan=1, rowspan=1)
        root.add(nameFld, 1, 0, 1, 1);    // (c1, r0, colspan=1, rowspan=1)
        root.add(descLbl, 0, 1, 3, 1);    // (c0, r1, colspan=3, rowspan=1)
        root.add(descText, 0, 2, 2, 1);   // (c0, r2, colspan=2, rowspan=1)
        root.add(okBtn, 2, 0, 1, 1);      // (c2, r0, colspan=1, rowspan=1)
        root.add(cancelBtn, 2, 1, 1, 1);  // (c2, r1, colspan=1, rowspan=1)
        root.add(statusBar, 0, 3, GridPane.REMAINING, 1);

        /* Set constraints for children to customize their resizing behavior */

        // The max width of the OK button should be big enough,
        // so it can fill the width of its cell
        okBtn.setMaxWidth(Double.MAX_VALUE);

        // The name field in the first row should grow horizontally
        GridPane.setHgrow(nameFld, Priority.ALWAYS);

        // The description field in the third row should grow vertically
        GridPane.setVgrow(descText, Priority.ALWAYS);

        // The status bar in the last should fill its cell
        statusBar.setMaxWidth(Double.MAX_VALUE);

        Scene scene = new Scene(root);
        stage.setScene(scene);
        stage.setTitle("Creating Forms Using a GridPane");
        stage.show();
    }
}
```

GridPane Properties

The GridPane class contains several properties, as listed in Table 10-6, to customize its layout.

Table 10-6. *The List of Properties Declared in the GridPane Class*

Property	Type	Description
alignment	ObjectProperty<Pos>	It specifies the alignment of the grid (the content of the GridPane) relative to its content area. It defaults to Pos.TOP_LEFT.
gridLinesVisible	BooleanProperty	It is recommend to be used for debug purposes only. It controls whether grid lines are visible or not. It defaults to false.
hgap, vgap	DoubleProperty	They specify the gaps between adjacent columns and rows. The hgap property specifies the horizontal gap between adjacent columns. The vgap property specifies the vertical gap between adjacent rows. They default to zero.

The Alignment Property

The alignment property of a GridPane controls the alignment of its content within its content area. You can see the effects of this property when the size of the GridPane is bigger than its content. The property works the same way as the alignment property for the FlowPane. Please refer to the description of the alignment property for FlowPane for more details and illustrations.

The gridLinesVisible Property

When the gridLinesVisible is set to true, the grid lines in a GridPane are made visible. Otherwise, they are invisible. You should use this feature only for debug purposes only.

```
GridPane gpane = new GridPane();
gpane.setGridLinesVisible(true); // Make grid lines visible
```

Sometimes, you may want to show the grid without showing the children to get an idea on how the grid is formed. You can do so by making all children invisible. The GridPane computes the size of the grid for all managed children irrespective of their visibility.

The following snippet of code creates a GridPane and sets the gridLinesVisible property to true. It creates four Buttons, makes them invisible, and adds them to the GridPane. Figure 10-48 shows the window when the GridPane is added to a scene as the root node.

```
GridPane root = new GridPane();

// Make the grid lines visible
root.setGridLinesVisible(true);

// Set the padding to 10px
root.setStyle("-fx-padding: 10;");

// Make the gridLInes
Button b1 = new Button("One");
Button b2 = new Button("Two");
Button b3 = new Button("Three");
Button b4 = new Button("Four and Five");

// Make all children invisible to see only grid lines
b1.setVisible(false);
b2.setVisible(false);
b3.setVisible(false);
b4.setVisible(false);

// Add children to the GridPane
root.addRow(1, b1, b2);
root.addRow(2, b3, b4);
```

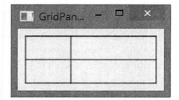

Figure 10-48. *A GridPane showing the grid without children*

The hgap and vgap Properties

You can specify spacing between adjacent columns and rows using the hgap and vgap properties, respectively. By default, they are zero. The program in Listing 10-31 uses these properties of a GridPane. The grid lines are visible to show the gaps clearly. Figure 10-49 shows the window.

Listing 10-31. Using the hgap and vgap Properties of a GridPane

```
// GridPaneHgapVgap.java
package com.jdojo.container;

import javafx.application.Application;
import javafx.scene.Scene;
import javafx.scene.control.Button;
import javafx.scene.control.Label;
import javafx.scene.control.TextField;
import javafx.scene.layout.GridPane;
import javafx.stage.Stage;

public class GridPaneHgapVgap extends Application {
        public static void main(String[] args) {
                Application.launch(args);
        }

        @Override
        public void start(Stage stage) {
                Label fnameLbl = new Label("First Name:");
                TextField fnameFld = new TextField();
                Label lnameLbl = new Label("Last Name:");
                TextField lnameFld = new TextField();
                Button okBtn = new Button("OK");
                Button cancelBtn = new Button("Cancel");

                // The Ok button should fill its cell
                okBtn.setMaxWidth(Double.MAX_VALUE);

                // Create a GridPane and set its background color to lightgray
                GridPane root = new GridPane();
                root.setGridLinesVisible(true); // Make grid lines visible
                root.setHgap(10); // hgap = 10px
                root.setVgap(5);  // vgap = 5px
                root.setStyle("-fx-padding: 10;-fx-background-color: lightgray;");
```

```
        // Add children to the GridPane
        root.addRow(0, fnameLbl, fnameFld, okBtn);
        root.addRow(1, lnameLbl, lnameFld, cancelBtn);

        Scene scene = new Scene(root);
        stage.setScene(scene);
        stage.setTitle("Using hgap and vgap Properties for a GridPane");
        stage.show();
    }
}
```

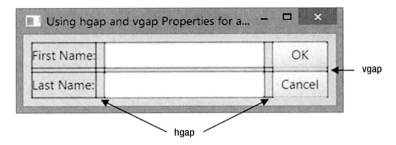

Figure 10-49. *A GridPane using hgap and vgap properties*

Customizing Columns and Rows

You can customize columns and rows in a GridPane using column and row constraints. For example, for a column/row, you can specify:

- How the width/height should be computed. Should it be computed based on its content, a fixed width/height, or a percentage of the available width/height?

- Should the children fill the width/height of the column/row?

- Should the column/row grow when the GridPane is resized larger than its preferred width/height?

- How should the children in a column/row be aligned within its layout area (cells)?

An object of the ColumnConstraints class represents constraints for a column and an object of the RowConstraints class represents constraints for a row. Both classes declare several properties that represent the constraints. Tables 10-7 and 10-8 list the properties with a brief description for the ColumnConstraints and RowConstraints classes.

Table 10-7. *The List of Properties for the ColumnConstraints Class*

Property	Type	Description
fillWidth	BooleanProperty	It specifies whether the children in the column are expanded beyond their preferred width to fill the width of the column. The default value is true.
halignment	ObjectProperty <HPos>	It specifies the default horizontal alignment of the children in a column. Its default value is null. By default, all children in a column are horizontally aligned to HPos.LEFT. An individual child node in the column may override this constraint.
hgrow	ObjectProperty <Priority>	It specifies the horizontal grow priority for the column. This property is used to give additional space to the column when the GridPane is resized larger than its preferred width. If the percentWidth property is set, the value for this property is ignored.
minWidth, prefWidth, maxWidth	DoubleProperty	They specify the minimum, preferred, and maximum widths of the column. If the percentWidth property is set, the values for these properties are ignored.
		The default values for these properties are set to USE_COMPUTED_SIZE. By default, the minimum width of a column is the largest of the minimum widths of children in the column; the preferred width is the largest of the preferred widths of children in the column; and, the maximum width is the smallest of the maximum widths of children in the column.
percentWidth	DoubleProperty	It specifies the width percentage of the column relative to the width of the content area of the GridPane. If it is set to a value greater than zero, the column is resized to have the width that is this percentage of the available width of the GridPane. If this property is set, the minWidth, prefWidth, maxWidth, and hgrow properties are ignored.

Table 10-8. *Properties for the RowConstraints Class*

Property	Type	Description
fillHeight	BooleanProperty	It specifies whether the children in the row are expanded beyond their preferred height to fill the height of the row. The default value is true.
valignment	ObjectProperty <HPos>	It specifies the default vertical alignment of the children in a row. Its default value is null. By default, all children in a row are vertically aligned to VPos.CENTER. An individual child node in the row may override this constraint.
vgrow	ObjectProperty <Priority>	It specifies the vertical grow priority for the row. This property is used to give additional space to the row when the GridPane is resized larger than its preferred height. If the percentHeight property is set, the value for this property is ignored.

(continued)

Table 10-8. (*continued*)

Property	Type	Description
minHeight, prefHeight, maxHeight	DoubleProperty	They specify the minimum, preferred, and maximum heights of the row. If the percentHeight property is set, the values for these properties are ignored.
		The default values for these properties are set to USE_COMPUTED_SIZE. By default, the minimum height of a row is the largest of the minimum heights of children in the row; the preferred height is the largest of the preferred heights of children in the row; and, the maximum height is the smallest of the maximum heights of children in the row.
percentHeight	DoubleProperty	It specifies the height percentage of the row relative to the height of the content area of the GridPane. If it is set to a value greater than zero, the row is resized to have the height that is this percentage of the available height for the GridPane. If this property is set, the minHeight, prefHeight, maxHeight, and vgrow properties are ignored.

The ColumnConstraints and RowConstraints classes provide several constructors to create their objects. Their no-args constructors create their objects with default property values.

```
// Create a ColumnConstraints object with default property values
ColumnConstraints cc1 = new ColumnConstraints();

// Set the percentWidth to 30% and horizontal alignment to center
cc1.setPercentWidth(30);
cc1.setHalignment(HPos.CENTER);
```

If you want to create a fixed width/height column/row, you can use one of the convenience contractors.

```
// Create a ColumnConstraints object with a fixed column width of 100px
ColumnConstraints cc2 = new ColumnConstraints(100);

// Create a RowConstraints object with a fixed row height of 80px
RowConstraints rc2 = new RowConstraints(80);
```

If you want to achieve the same effect of having a fixed width column, you can do so by setting the preferred width to the desired fixed width value and setting the minimum and maximum widths to use the preferred width as shown below.

```
// Create a ColumnConstraints object with a fixed column width of 100px
ColumnConstraints cc3 = new ColumnConstraints();
cc3.setPrefWidth(100);
cc3.setMinWidth(Region.USE_PREF_SIZE);
cc3.setMaxWidth(Region.USE_PREF_SIZE);
```

The following snippet of code sets the column width to 30% of the GridPane width and the horizontal alignment for the children in the column as center.

```
ColumnConstraints cc4 = new ColumnConstraints();
cc4.setPercentWidth(30);                    // 30% width
cc4.setHalignment(HPos.CENTER);
```

In a GridPane, the width/height of different columns/rows may be computed differently. Some columns/row may set percent width/height, some fixed sizes, and some may choose to compute their sizes based on their content. The percent size is given the first preference in allocating the space. For example, if two columns set their widths based on percentage and one uses a fixed width, the available width will be allocated first to the two columns using the percentage width, and then, to the column using the fixed width.

■ **Tip**   It is possible that the sum of the percentage width/height of all columns/rows exceeds 100. For example, it is permissible to set the percentage width of columns in a GridPane to 30%, 30%, 30%, and 30%. In this case, the percentage value is used as weights and each of the four columns will be given one-fourth (30/120) of the available width. As an another example, if columns use 30%, 30%, 60%, and 60% as percentage width, they will be treated as weights, allocating them one-sixth (30/180), one-sixth (30/180), one-third (60/180), and one-third (60/180) of the available width, respectively.

A GridPane stores the constraints for columns and rows in ObservableList of ColumnConstraints and RowConstraints. You can obtain the reference of the lists using the getColumnConstraints() and getRowConstraints() methods. The element at a particular index in the list stores the constraints object for the column/row at the same index in the GridPane. The first element in the list, for example, stores the column/row constraints for the first column/row, the second elements for the second column/row, etc. It is possible to set the column/row constraints for some column/row, not for others. In this case, the constraints for column/row for which the column/row constraints are absent will be computed based on the default values. The following snippet of code creates three ColumnConstraints objects, sets their properties, and adds them to the list of column constraints of a GridPane. Using RowConstraints objects for setting row constraints would use the similar logic.

```
// Set the fixed width to 100px
ColumnConstraints cc1 = new ColumnConstraints(100);

// Set the percent width to 30% and horizontal alignment to center
ColumnConstraints cc2 = new ColumnConstraints();
cc2.setPercentWidth(30);
cc1.setHalignment(HPos.CENTER);

// Set the percent width to 50%
ColumnConstraints cc3 = new ColumnConstraints();
cc3.setPercentWidth(30);

// Add all column constraints to the column constraints list
GridPane root = new GridPane();
root.getColumnConstraints().addAll(cc1, cc2, cc3);
```

The program in Listing 10-32 uses column and row constraints to customize columns and rows in a GridPane. Figure 10-50 shows the window, after it is resized.

Listing 10-32. Using Column and Row Constraints in a GridPane

```java
// GridPaneColRowConstraints.java
package com.jdojo.container;

import javafx.application.Application;
import javafx.geometry.HPos;
import javafx.geometry.VPos;
import javafx.scene.Scene;
import javafx.scene.control.Button;
import javafx.scene.layout.ColumnConstraints;
import javafx.scene.layout.GridPane;
import javafx.scene.layout.RowConstraints;
import javafx.stage.Stage;

public class GridPaneColRowConstraints extends Application {
        public static void main(String[] args) {
                Application.launch(args);
        }

        @Override
        public void start(Stage stage) {
                GridPane root = new GridPane();
                root.setStyle("-fx-padding: 10;");
                root.setGridLinesVisible(true);

                // Add children
                for (int row = 0; row < 3; row++) {
                        for (int col = 0; col < 3; col++) {
                                Button b = new Button(col + " " + row);
                                root.add(b, col, row);
                        }
                }

                // Set the fixed width for the first column to 100px
                ColumnConstraints cc1 = new ColumnConstraints(100);

                // Set the percent width for the second column to 30% and
                // the horizontal alignment to center
                ColumnConstraints cc2 = new ColumnConstraints();
                cc2.setPercentWidth(35);
                cc2.setHalignment(HPos.CENTER);

                // Set the percent width for the third column to 50%
                ColumnConstraints cc3 = new ColumnConstraints();
                cc3.setPercentWidth(35);
```

```
        // Add all column constraints to the column constraints list
        root.getColumnConstraints().addAll(cc1, cc2, cc3);

        // Create two RowConstraints objects
        RowConstraints rc1 = new RowConstraints();
        rc1.setPercentHeight(35);
        rc1.setValignment(VPos.TOP);

        RowConstraints rc2 = new RowConstraints();
        rc2.setPercentHeight(35);
        rc2.setValignment(VPos.BOTTOM);

        // Add RowConstraints for the first two rows
        root.getRowConstraints().addAll(rc1, rc2);

        Scene scene = new Scene(root);
        stage.setScene(scene);
        stage.setTitle("Setting Column/Row Constraints");
        stage.show();
    }
}
```

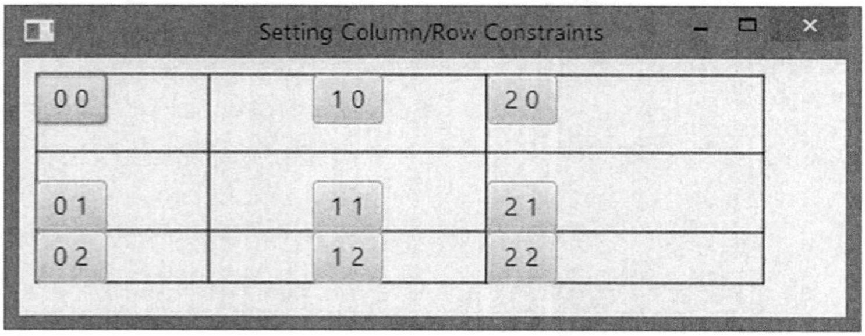

Figure 10-50. *A GridPane using column and row constraints*

The first column width is set to 100px fixed width. Each of the second and third columns is set to occupy 35% of the width. If the needed width (35% + 35% + 100px) is less than the available width, the extra width will be left unused, as has been shown in the figure. The horizontal alignment for the first column is set to center, so all buttons in the first column are horizontally aligned in the center. The buttons in the other two columns use left as the horizontal alignment, which is the default setting. We have three rows. However, the program adds constraints for only the first two rows. The constraints for the third row will be computed based on its content.

When you set column/row constraints, you cannot skip some columns/rows in the middle. That is, you must set the constraints for columns/rows sequentially starting from the first column/row. Setting null for a constraint's object throws a NullPointerException at runtime. If you want to skip setting custom constraints for a row/column in the list, set it to a constraints object that is created using the no-args constructor, which will use the default settings. The following snippet of code sets the column constraints for the first three columns. The second column uses default settings for the constraints.

```
// With 100px fied width
ColumnConstraints cc1 = new ColumnConstraints(100);

// Use all default settings
ColumnConstraints defaultCc2 = new ColumnConstraints();

// With 200px fied width
ColumnConstraints cc3 = new ColumnConstraints(200);

GridPane gpane = new GridPane();
gpane.getColumnConstraints().addAll(cc1, defaultCc2, cc3);
```

■ **Tip** Some column/row constraints set on a column/row can be overridden by children in the column/row individually. Some constraints can be set on children in a column/row and may affect the entire column/row. We will discuss these situations in the next section.

Setting Constraints on Children in GridPane

Table 10-9 lists the constraints that can be set for the children in a GridPane. We have already discussed the column/row index and span constraints. We will discuss the rest in this section. The GridPane class contains two sets of static methods to set these constraints:

- The setConstraints() methods
- The setXxx(Node child, CType cvalue) methods, where Xxx is the constraint name and CType is its type

To remove a constraint for a child node, set it to null

Table 10-9. *List of Constraints That Can Be Set for the Children in a GridPane*

Constraint	Type	Description
columnIndex	Integer	It is the column index where the layout area of the child node starts. The first column has the index 0. The default value is 0.
rowIndex	Integer	It is the row index where the layout area of the child node starts. The first row has the index 0. The default value is 0.
columnSpan	Integer	It is the number of columns the layout area of a child node spans. The default is 1.
rowSpan	Integer	It is the number of columns the layout area of a child node spans. The default is 1.
halignment	HPos	It specifies the horizontal alignment of the child node within its layout area.
valignment	VPos	It specifies the vertical alignment of the child node within its layout area.
hgrow	Priority	It specifies the horizontal grow priority of the child node.
vgrow	Priority	It specifies the vertical grow priority of the child node.
margin	Insets	It specifies the margin space around the outside of the layout bounds of the child node.

The halignment and valignment Constraints

The halignment and valignment constraints specify the alignment of a child node within its layout area. They default to HPos.LEFT and VPos.CENTER. They can be set on column/row affecting all children. Children may set them individually. The final value applicable to a child node depends of some rules:

- When they are not set for column/row and not for the child node, the child node will use the default values.

- When they are set for column/row and not for the child node, the child node will use the value set for the column/row.

- When they are set for column/row and for the child node, the child node will use the value set for it, not the value set for the column/row. In essence, a child node can override the default value or the value set for the column/row for these constraints.

The program in Listing 10-33 demonstrates the rules mentioned above. Figure 10-51 shows the window. The program adds three buttons to a column. The column constraints override the default value of HPos.LEFT for the halignment constraints for the children and set it to HPos.RIGHT. The button labeled "Two" overrides this setting to HPos.CENTER. Therefore, all buttons in the column are horizontally aligned to the right, except the button labeled "Two," which is aligned to the center. We set constraints for all three rows. The first and the second rows set valignment to VPos.TOP. The third row leaves the valignment to the default that is VPos.CENTER. The button with the label "One" overrides the valignment constraint set on the first row to set it to VPos.BOTTOM. Notice that all children follow the above thee rules to use the valignment and halignment constraints.

Listing 10-33. Using the halignment and valignment Constraints for Children in a GridPane

```
// GridPaneHValignment.java
package com.jdojo.container;

import javafx.application.Application;
import javafx.geometry.HPos;
import javafx.geometry.VPos;
import javafx.scene.Scene;
import javafx.scene.control.Button;
import javafx.scene.layout.ColumnConstraints;
import javafx.scene.layout.GridPane;
import javafx.scene.layout.RowConstraints;
import javafx.stage.Stage;

public class GridPaneHValignment extends Application {
        public static void main(String[] args) {
                Application.launch(args);
        }

        @Override
        public void start(Stage stage) {
                GridPane root = new GridPane();
                root.setStyle("-fx-padding: 10;");
                root.setGridLinesVisible(true);
```

```
// Add three buttons to a column
Button b1 = new Button("One");
Button b2 = new Button("Two");
Button b3 = new Button("Three");
root.addColumn(0, b1, b2, b3);

// Set the column constraints
ColumnConstraints cc1 = new ColumnConstraints(100);
cc1.setHalignment(HPos.RIGHT);
root.getColumnConstraints().add(cc1);

// Set the row constraints
RowConstraints rc1 = new RowConstraints(40);
rc1.setValignment(VPos.TOP);

RowConstraints rc2 = new RowConstraints(40);
rc2.setValignment(VPos.TOP);

RowConstraints rc3 = new RowConstraints(40);
root.getRowConstraints().addAll(rc1, rc2, rc3);

// Override the halignment for b2 set in the column
GridPane.setHalignment(b2, HPos.CENTER);

// Override the valignment for b1 set in the row
GridPane.setValignment(b1, VPos.BOTTOM);

Scene scene = new Scene(root);
stage.setScene(scene);
stage.setTitle("halignemnt and valignment Constraints");
stage.show();
    }
}
```

Figure 10-51. *Children overriding the halignment and valignment constraints in a GridPane*

The hgrow and vgrow Constraints

The hgrow and vgrow constraints specify the horizontal and vertical grow priorities for the entire column and row, even though it can be set for children individually. These constraints can also be set using the ColumnConstraints and RowConstraints objects for columns and rows. By default, columns and rows do not grow. The final value for these constraints for a column/row is computed using the following rules:

- If the constraints are not set for the column/row and are not set for any children in the column/row, the column/row does not grow if the GridPane is resized to a larger width/height than the preferred width/height.

- If the constraints are set for the column/row, the values set in the ColumnConstraints and RowConstraints objects for hgrow and vgrow are used, irrespective of whether the children set these constraints or not.

- If the constraints are not set for the column/row, the maximum values for these constraints set for children in the column/row are used for the entire column/row. Suppose a column has three children and no column constraints have been set for the column. The first child node sets the hgrow to Priority.NEVER; the second to Priority.ALWAYS; and the third to Priority.SOMETIMES. In this case, the maximum of the three priorities would be Priority.ALWAYS, which will be used for the entire column. The ALWAYS priority has the highest value, SOMETIMES the second highest, and NEVER the lowest.

- If a column/row is set to have a fixed or percentage width/height, the hgrow/vgrow constraints will be ignored.

The program in Listing 10-34 demonstrates the above rules. Figure 10-52 shows the window when it is expanded horizontally. Notice that the second column grows, but not the first column. The program adds six buttons arranged in two columns. The first column sets the hgrow constraints to Priority.NEVER. The hgrow value set by the column takes priority; the first column does not grow when the GridPane is expanded horizontally. The second column does not use column constraints. The children in this column use three different types of priorities: ALWAYS, NEVER, and SOMETIMES. The maximum of the three priorities is ALWAYS, which makes the second column grow horizontally.

Listing 10-34. Using the hgrow Constraints for Columns and Rows in a GridPane

```
// GridPaneHVgrow.java
package com.jdojo.container;

import javafx.application.Application;
import javafx.scene.Scene;
import javafx.scene.control.Button;
import javafx.scene.layout.ColumnConstraints;
import javafx.scene.layout.GridPane;
import javafx.scene.layout.Priority;
import javafx.stage.Stage;

public class GridPaneHVgrow extends Application {
        public static void main(String[] args) {
                Application.launch(args);
        }
```

```java
    @Override
    public void start(Stage stage) {
        GridPane root = new GridPane();
        root.setStyle("-fx-padding: 10;");
        root.setGridLinesVisible(true);

        // Add three buttons to a column
        Button b1 = new Button("One");
        Button b2 = new Button("Two");
        Button b3 = new Button("Three");
        Button b4 = new Button("Four");
        Button b5 = new Button("Five");
        Button b6 = new Button("Six");

        root.addColumn(0, b1, b2, b3);
        root.addColumn(1, b4, b5, b6);

        // Set the column constraints
        ColumnConstraints cc1 = new ColumnConstraints();
        cc1.setHgrow(Priority.NEVER);
        root.getColumnConstraints().add(cc1);

        // Set three different hgrow priorities for children in the second
        // column. The highest priority, ALWAYS, will be used.
        GridPane.setHgrow(b4, Priority.ALWAYS);
        GridPane.setHgrow(b5, Priority.NEVER);
        GridPane.setHgrow(b6, Priority.SOMETIMES);

        Scene scene = new Scene(root);
        stage.setScene(scene);
        stage.setTitle("hgrow and vgrow Constraints");
        stage.show();
    }
}
```

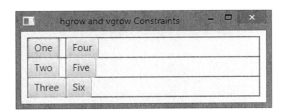

Figure 10-52. *Columns and children using the hgrow constraint in a GridPane*

403

The Margin Constraints

Use the setMargin(Node child, Insets value) static method of the GridPane class to set the margin (the space around the layout bounds) for children. The getMargin(Node child) static method returns the margin for a child node.

```
// Set 10px margin around the b1 child node
GridPane.setMargin(b1, new Insets(10));
...
// Get the margin of the b1 child node
Insets margin = GridPane.getMargin(b1);
```

Use null to reset the margin to the default value, which is zero.

Clearing All Constraints

Use the clearConstraints(Node child) static method of the GridPane class to reset all constraints (columnIndex, rowIndex, columnSpan, rowSpan, halignment, valignment, hgrow, vgrow, margin) for a child at once.

```
// Clear all constraints for the b1 child node
GridPane.clearConstraints(b1);
```

Understanding AnchorPane

An AnchorPane lays out its children by anchoring the four edges of its children to its own four edges at a specified distance. Figure 10-53 shows a child node inside an AnchorPane with an anchor distance specified on all four sides.

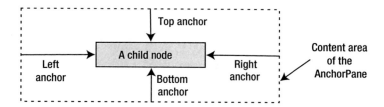

Figure 10-53. *The four side constraints for a child node in an AnchorPane*

An AnchorPane may be used for two purposes:

- For aligning children along one or more edges of the AnchorPane

- For stretching children when the AnchorPane is resized

The specified distance between the edges of the children and the edges of the AnchorPane is called the *anchor* constraint for the sides it is specified. For example, the distance between the top edge of the children and the top edge of the AnchorPane is called topAnchor *constraint*, etc. You can specify at most four anchor constraints for a child node: topAnchor, rightAnchor, bottomAnchor, and leftAnchor.

When you anchor a child node to the two opposite edges (top/bottom or left/right), the children are resized to maintain the specified anchor distance as the AnchorPane is resized.

▪ **Tip** Anchor distance is measured from the edges of the content area of the `AnchorPane` and the edges of the children. That is, if the `AnchorPane` has a border and padding, the distance is measured from the inner edges the insets (border + padding).

Creating AnchorPane Objects

You can create an empty `AnchorPane` using the no-args constructor:

```
AnchorPane apane1 = new AnchorPane();
```

You can also specify the initial list of children for the `AnchorPane` when you create it, like so:

```
Button okBtn = new Button("OK");
Button cancelBtn = new Button("Cancel");
AnchorPane apane2 = new AnchorPane(okBtn, cancelBtn);
```

You can add children to an `AnchorPane` after you create it, like so:

```
Button okBtn = new Button("OK");
Button cancelBtn = new Button("Cancel");
AnchorPane apane3 = new AnchorPane();
apane3.getChildren().addAll(okBtn, cancelBtn);
```

You need to keep two points in mind while working with an `AnchorPane`:

- By default, an `AnchorPane` places its children at (0, 0). You need to specify anchor constraints for the children to anchor them to one or more edges of the `AnchorPane` at a specified distance.

- The preferred size of the `AnchorPane` is computed based on the children preferred sizes and their anchor constraints. It adds the preferred width, left anchor, and right anchor for each child node. The child having maximum of this value determines the preferred width of the `AnchorPane`. It adds the preferred height, left anchor, and right anchor for each child node. The child having the maximum of this value determines the preferred height of the `AnchorPane`. It is possible that children will overlap. Children are drawn in the order they are added.

The program in Listing 10-35 adds two buttons to an `AnchorPane`. One button has a long label and another has a short label. The button with the long label is added first, and hence, it is drawn first. The second button is drawn second, which overlays the first button as shown in Figure 10-54. The figure shows two views of the window: one when the program is run and another when the window is resized. Both buttons are placed at (0, 0). This program does not take advantage of the anchoring features of the `AnchorPane`.

Listing 10-35. Using Default Positions in an AnchorPane

```
// AnchorPaneDefaults.java
package com.jdojo.container;

import javafx.application.Application;
import javafx.scene.Scene;
import javafx.scene.control.Button;
import javafx.scene.layout.AnchorPane;
import javafx.stage.Stage;

public class AnchorPaneDefaults extends Application {
        public static void main(String[] args) {
                Application.launch(args);
        }

        @Override
        public void start(Stage stage) {
                Button bigBtn = new Button("This is a big button.");
                Button smallBtn = new Button("Small button");

                // Create an AnchorPane with two buttons
                AnchorPane root = new AnchorPane(bigBtn, smallBtn);

                Scene scene = new Scene(root);
                stage.setScene(scene);
                stage.setTitle("Using Defaults in AnchorPane");
                stage.show();
        }
}
```

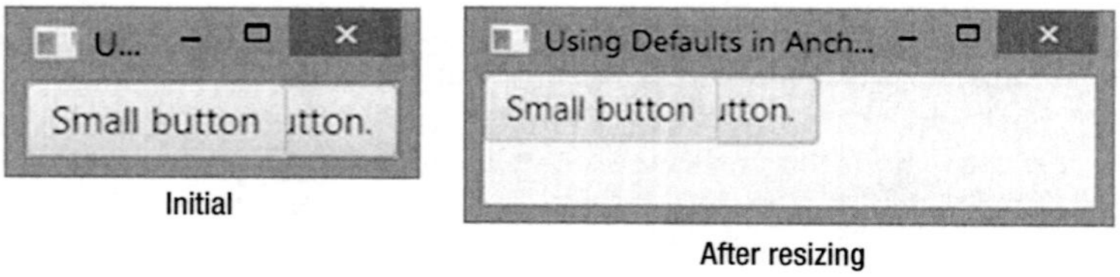

Figure 10-54. *An AnchorPane with two Buttons without having anchor constraints specified*

Setting Constraints for Children in AnchorPane

Table 10-10 lists the constraints that can be set for the children in a GridPane. Note that the anchor distance is measured from the edges of the content area of the AnchorPane, not the edges of the layout bounds. Recall that a Region has padding and border insets between the edges of the content area and the layout bounds.

Table 10-10. *The List of Constraints That Can Be Set for the Children in a GridPane*

Constraint	Type	Description
topAnchor	Double	It specifies the distance between the top edge of the content area of the AnchorPane and the top edge of the child node.
rightAnchor	Double	It specifies the distance between the right edge of the content area of the AnchorPane and the right edge of the child node.
bottomAnchor	Double	It specifies the distance between the bottom edge of the content area of the AnchorPane and the bottom edge of the child node.
leftAnchor	Double	It specifies the distance between the left edge of the content area of the AnchorPane and the left edge of the child node.

The AnchorPane class contains four static methods that let you set the values for the four anchor constraints. To remove a constraint for a child node, set it to null

```
// Create a Button and anchor it to top and left edges at 10px from each
Button topLeft = new Button("Top Left");
AnchorPane.setTopAnchor(topLeft, 10.0);  // 10px from the top edge
AnchorPane.setLeftAnchor(topLeft, 10.0); // 10px from the left edge

AnchorPane root = new AnchorPane(topLeft);
```

Use the clearConstraints(Node child) static method to clear the values for all four anchor constraints for a child node.

The setXxxAnchor(Node child, Double value) method takes a Double value as its second parameters. Therefore, you must pass a double value or a Double object to these methods. When you pass a double value, the autoboxing feature of Java will box the value into a Double object for you. A common mistake is to pass an int value:

```
Button b1 = new Button("A button");
AnchorPane.setTopAnchor(b1, 10); // An error: 10 is an int, not a double
```

The above code generates an error:

```
Error(18): error: method setTopAnchor in class AnchorPane cannot be applied to given types;
```

The error is generated because we have passed 10 as the second argument. The value 10 is an int literal, which is boxed to an Integer object, not a Double object. Changing 10 to 10D or 10.0 will make it a double value and will fix the error.

The program in Listing 10-36 adds two Buttons to an AnchorPane. The first button has its top and left anchors set. The second button has its bottom and right anchors set. Figure 10-55 shows the window in two states: one when the program is run and another when the window is resized. The initial size of the window is not wide enough to display both buttons, so the buttons overlap. The JavaFX runtime computes the width of the content area of the window based on the preferred size of the bottom-right button, which has the maximum preferred width, and its right anchor value. The figure also shows the window after it is resized. You need to set a sensible preferred size for an AnchorPane, so all children are visible without overlapping.

Listing 10-36. Using an AnchorPane to Align Children to Its Corners

```java
// AnchorPaneTest.java
package com.jdojo.container;

import javafx.application.Application;
import javafx.scene.Scene;
import javafx.scene.control.Button;
import javafx.scene.layout.AnchorPane;
import javafx.stage.Stage;

public class AnchorPaneTest extends Application {
        public static void main(String[] args) {
                Application.launch(args);
        }

        @Override
        public void start(Stage stage) {
                Button topLeft = new Button("Top Left");
                AnchorPane.setTopAnchor(topLeft, 10.0);
                AnchorPane.setLeftAnchor(topLeft, 10.0);

                Button bottomRight = new Button("Botton Right");
                AnchorPane.setBottomAnchor(bottomRight, 10.0);
                AnchorPane.setRightAnchor(bottomRight, 10.0);

                AnchorPane root = new AnchorPane();
                root.getChildren().addAll(topLeft, bottomRight);
                root.setStyle("-fx-padding: 10;" +
                                "-fx-border-style: solid inside;" +
                                "-fx-border-width: 2;" +
                                "-fx-border-insets: 5;" +
                                "-fx-border-radius: 5;" +
                                "-fx-border-color: blue;");

                Scene scene = new Scene(root);
                stage.setScene(scene);
                stage.setTitle("Using an AnchorPane");
                stage.show();
        }
}
```

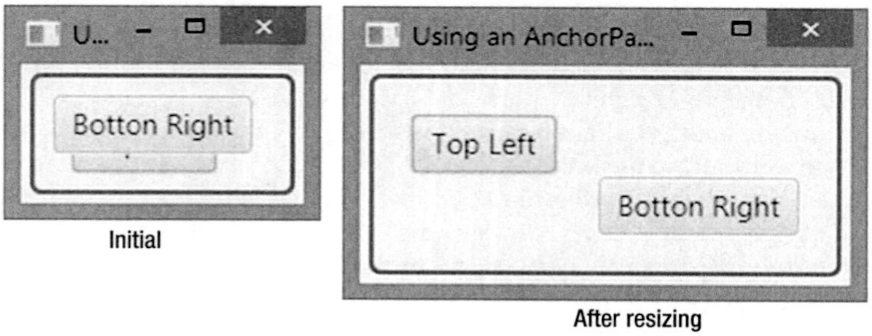

Initial

After resizing

Figure 10-55. *Two Buttons in an AnchorPane aligned at top-left and bottom-right corners*

When a child node in an AnchorPane is anchored to opposite edges, for example, top/bottom or left/right, the AnchorPane stretches the child node to maintaining the specified anchors.

The program in Listing 10-37 adds a button to an AnchorPane and anchors it to the left and right edges (opposite edges) using an anchor of 10px from each edge. This will make the button stretch when the AnchorPane is resized to a width larger than its preferred width. The button is also anchored to the top edge. Figure 10-56 shows the initial and resized windows.

Listing 10-37. Anchoring Children to Opposite Sides in an AnchorPane

```
// AnchorPaneStretching.java
package com.jdojo.container;

import javafx.application.Application;
import javafx.scene.Scene;
import javafx.scene.control.Button;
import javafx.scene.layout.AnchorPane;
import javafx.stage.Stage;

public class AnchorPaneStretching extends Application {
        public static void main(String[] args) {
                Application.launch(args);
        }

        @Override
        public void start(Stage stage) {
                Button leftRight = new Button("A button");
                AnchorPane.setTopAnchor(leftRight, 10.0);
                AnchorPane.setLeftAnchor(leftRight, 10.0);
                AnchorPane.setRightAnchor(leftRight, 10.0);

                AnchorPane root = new AnchorPane();
                root.getChildren().addAll(leftRight);
                root.setStyle("-fx-padding: 10;" +
                                "-fx-border-style: solid inside;" +
                                "-fx-border-width: 2;" +
                                "-fx-border-insets: 5;" +
                                "-fx-border-radius: 5;" +
                                "-fx-border-color: blue;");

                Scene scene = new Scene(root);
                stage.setScene(scene);
                stage.setTitle("Streching Children in an AnchorPane");
                stage.show();
        }
}
```

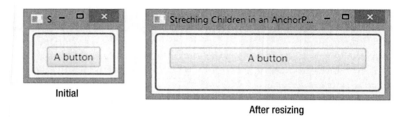

Initial

After resizing

Figure 10-56. *An AnchorPane with a Button anchored to Oopposite sides*

Understanding TextFlow

A TextFlow layout pane is designed to display rich text. The rich text is composed of multiple Text nodes. The TextFlow combines the text in all Text nodes to display in a single text flow. A new line character ('\n') in the text of the Text child nodes indicates the start of a new paragraph. The text is wrapped at the width of the TextFlow.

A Text node has its position, size, and wrapping width. However, when it is added to a TextFlow pane, these properties are ignored. Text nodes are placed one after another wrapping them when necessary. A Text node in e TextFlow may span multiple lines in a TextFlow, whereas in a Text node it is displayed in only one line. Figure 10-57 shows a window with a TextFlow as its root node.

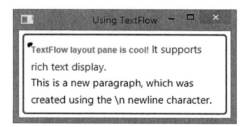

Figure 10-57. *A TextFlow showing rich text*

The TextFlow is especially designed to display rich text using multiple Text nodes. However, you are not limited to adding only Text nodes to a TextFlow. You can add any other nodes to it, for example: Buttons, TextFields, etc. Nodes other than Text nodes are displayed using their preferred sizes.

■ **Tip**   You can think of a TextFlow very similar to a FlowPane. Like a FlowPane, a TextFlow lays out its children in a flow from one end to another by treating Text nodes differently. When a Text node is encountered past its width boundary, it breaks the text of the Text node at its width and displays the remaining text in the next line.

Creating TextFlow Objects

Unlike the classes for other layout panes, the TextFlow class is in the javafx.scene.text package where all other text related classes exist.

You can create an empty TextFlow using the no-args constructor:

```
TextFlow tflow1 = new TextFlow ();
```

You can also specify the initial list of children for the TextFlow when you create it:

```
Text tx1 = new Text("TextFlow layout pane is cool! ");
Text tx2 = new Text("It supports rich text display.");
TextFlow tflow2 = new TextFlow(tx1, tx2);
```

You can add children to a TextFlow after you create it.

```
Text tx1 = new Text("TextFlow layout pane is cool! ");
Text tx2 = new Text("It supports rich text display.");
TextFlow tflow3 = new TextFlow();
tflow3.getChildren().addAll(tx1, tx2);
```

The program in Listing 10-38 shows how to use a TextFlow. It adds three Text nodes to a TextFlow. The text in the third Text node starts with a newline character (\n), which starts a new paragraph. The program sets the preferred width of the TextFlow to 300px and the line spacing to 5px. Figure 10-58 shows the window. When you resize the window, the TextFlow redraws the text wrapping, if necessary, at the new width.

Listing 10-38. Using the TextFlow Layout Pane to Display Rich Text

```java
// TextFlowTest.java
package com.jdojo.container;

import javafx.application.Application;
import javafx.scene.Scene;
import javafx.scene.paint.Color;
import javafx.scene.text.Font;
import javafx.scene.text.FontWeight;
import javafx.scene.text.Text;
import javafx.scene.text.TextFlow;
import javafx.stage.Stage;

public class TextFlowTest extends Application {
        public static void main(String[] args) {
                Application.launch(args);
        }

        @Override
        public void start(Stage stage) {
                // Create three Text nodes
                Text tx1 = new Text("TextFlow layout pane is cool! ");
                tx1.setFill(Color.RED);
                tx1.setFont(Font.font("Arial", FontWeight.BOLD, 12));
```

```
                Text tx2 = new Text("It supports rich text display.");
                tx2.setFill(Color.BLUE);

                Text tx3 = new Text("\nThis is a new paragraph, which was " +
                                "created using the \\n newline character.");

                // Create a TextFlow object with the three Text nodes
                TextFlow root = new TextFlow(tx1, tx2, tx3);

                // Set the preferred width and line spacing
                root.setPrefWidth(300);
                root.setLineSpacing(5);

                root.setStyle("-fx-padding: 10;" +
                                "-fx-border-style: solid inside;" +
                                "-fx-border-width: 2;" +
                                "-fx-border-insets: 5;" +
                                "-fx-border-radius: 5;" +
                                "-fx-border-color: blue;");

                Scene scene = new Scene(root);
                stage.setScene(scene);
                stage.setTitle("Using TextFlow");
                stage.show();
        }
}
```

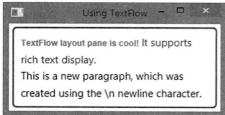

Figure 10-58. *Several Text nodes displayed in a TextFlow as rich text*

A TextFlow also lets you embed nodes other than Text nodes. You can create a form to display text mixed with other types of nodes that users can use. The program in Listing 10-39 embeds a pair of RadioButtons, a TextField, and a Button to a TextFlow to create an online form with text. Users can use these nodes to interact with the form.

Figure 10-59 shows the window. At the time of testing this example, the RadioButtons and TextField nodes did not gain focus using the mouse. Use the Tab key to navigate to these nodes and the spacebar to select a RadioButton.

Listing 10-39. Embedding Nodes Other Than Text Nodes in a TextFlow

```java
// TextFlowEmbeddingNodes.java
package com.jdojo.container;

import javafx.application.Application;
import javafx.scene.Scene;
import javafx.scene.control.Button;
import javafx.scene.control.RadioButton;
import javafx.scene.control.TextField;
import javafx.scene.control.ToggleGroup;
import javafx.scene.text.Text;
import javafx.scene.text.TextFlow;
import javafx.stage.Stage;

public class TextFlowEmbeddingNodes extends Application {
        public static void main(String[] args) {
                Application.launch(args);
        }

        @Override
        public void start(Stage stage) {
                Text tx1 = new Text("I, ");

                RadioButton rb1 = new RadioButton("Mr.");
                RadioButton rb2 = new RadioButton("Ms.");
                rb1.setSelected(true);

                ToggleGroup group = new ToggleGroup();
                rb1.setToggleGroup(group);
                rb2.setToggleGroup(group);

                TextField nameFld = new TextField();
                nameFld.setPromptText("Your Name");

                Text tx2 = new Text(", acknowledge the receipt of this letter...\n\n" +
                                "Sincerely,\n\n");

                Button submitFormBtn = new Button("Submit Form");

                // Create a TextFlow object with all nodes
                TextFlow root = new TextFlow(tx1, rb1, rb2, nameFld, tx2, submitFormBtn);

                // Set the preferred width and line spacing
                root.setPrefWidth(350);
                root.setLineSpacing(5);
                root.setStyle("-fx-padding: 10;" +
                                "-fx-border-style: solid inside;" +
                                "-fx-border-width: 2;" +
                                "-fx-border-insets: 5;" +
                                "-fx-border-radius: 5;" +
                                "-fx-border-color: blue;");
```

```
                    Scene scene = new Scene(root);
                    stage.setScene(scene);
                    stage.setTitle("Creating Forms Using TextFlow");
                    stage.show();
            }
    }
```

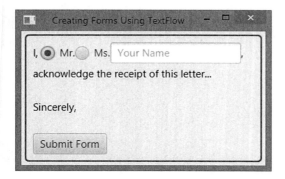

Figure 10-59. *Nodes other than Text nodes embedded in a TextFlow*

TextFlow Properties

The TextFlow class contains two properties, as listed in Table 10-11, to customize its layout.

Table 10-11. *The List of Properties Declared in the GridPane Class*

Property	Type	Description
lineSpacing	DoubleProperty	It specifies the vertical space between lines. Its default value is 0px.
textAlignment	ObjectProperty <TextAlignment>	It specifies the alignment of the content of the TextFlow. Its value is one of the constants of the TextAlignment enum: LEFT, RIGHT, CENTER, and JUSTIFY. Its default value is LEFT.

The lineSpacing property specifies the vertical space (in pixel) between lines in a TextFlow. We have used it in our previous examples.

```
TextFlow tflow = new TextFlow();
tflow.setLineSpacing(5); // 5px lineSpacing
```

The textAlignment property specifies the alignment of the overall content of the TextFlow. By default, the content is aligned to the left. Figure 10-60 shows the window for the program in Listing 10-39 when the following statement is added after the TextFlow object is created in the program.

```
// Set the textAlignment to CENTER
root.setTextAlignment(TextAlignment.CENTER);
```

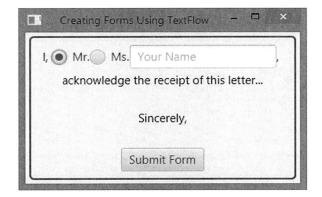

Figure 10-60. *A TextFlow using CENTER as its textAlignment*

Setting Constraints for Children in TextFlow

TextFlow does not allow you to add any constraints to its children, not even a margin.

Snapping to Pixel

Figure 10-61 shows a screen of a device that is five pixels wide and five pixels tall. A circle in the figure represents a pixel. A coordinate (0, 0) is mapped to the upper-left corner of the upper-left pixel. The center of the upper-left pixel maps to the coordinates (0.5, 0.5). All integer coordinates fall in the corners and cracks between the pixels. In the figure, solid lines are drawn through the cracks of pixels and dashed lines through the centers of the pixels.

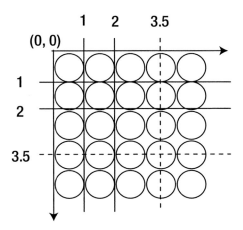

Figure 10-61. *A 5X5 pixel region on the screen*

In JavaFX, coordinates can be specified in floating-point numbers: for example, 0.5, 6.0, etc., which lets you represent any part of a pixel. If the floating-point number is an integer (e.g., 2.0, 3.0, etc.), it will represent corners of the pixel.

A Region using floating-point numbers as coordinates will not align exactly at the pixel boundary and its border may look fuzzy. The Region class contains a snapToPixel property to address this issue. By default, it is set to true and a Region adjusts the position, spacing, and size values of its children to an integer to match the pixel boundaries, resulting in crisp boundaries for the children. If you do not want a Region to adjust these values to integers, set the snapToPixel property to false.

Summary

A *layout pane* is a node that contains other nodes, which are known as its children (or child nodes). The responsibility of a layout pane is to lay out its children, whenever needed. A layout pane is also known as a *container* or a *layout container*. A layout pane has a *layout policy* that controls how the layout pane lays out its children. For example, a layout pane may lay out its children horizontally, vertically, or in any other fashion. JavaFX contains several layout-related classes. A layout pane computes the position and size of its children. The layout policy of a layout pane is a set of rules to compute the position and size of its children.

Objects of the following classes represent layout panes: HBox, VBox, FlowPane, BorderPane, StackPane, TilePane, GridPane, AnchorPane, and TextFlow. All layout pane classes inherits from the Pane class.

A Group has features of a container; for example, it has its own layout policy, coordinate system, and it is a subclass of the Parent class. However, its meaning is best reflected by calling it a *collection of nodes* or a *group*, rather than a *container*. It is used to manipulate a collection of nodes as a single node (or as a group). Transformations, effects, and properties applied to a Group are applied to all nodes in the Group. A Group has its own layout policy, which does not provide any specific layout to its children, except giving them their preferred size.

An HBox lays out its children in a single horizontal row. It lets you set the horizontal spacing between adjacent children, margins for any children, resizing behavior of children, etc. It uses 0px as the default spacing between adjacent children. The default width of the content area and HBox is wide enough to display all its children at their preferred widths and the default height is the largest of the heights of all its children.

A VBox lays out its children in a single vertical column. It lets you set the vertical spacing between adjacent children, margins for any children, resizing behavior of children, etc. It uses 0px as the default spacing between adjacent children. The default height of the content area of a VBox is tall enough to display all its children at their preferred heights, and the default width is the largest of the widths of all its children.

A FlowPane is a simple layout pane that lays out its children in rows or columns wrapping at a specified width or height. It lets its children flow horizontally or vertically, and hence the name "flow pane." You can specify a preferred wrap length, which is the preferred width for a horizontal flow and the preferred height for a vertical flow, where the content is wrapped. A FlowPane is used in situations where the relative locations of children are not important: for example, displaying a series of pictures or buttons.

A BorderPane divides its layout area into five regions: top, right, bottom, left, and center. You can place at most one node in each of the five regions. The children in the top and bottom regions are resized to their preferred heights. Their widths are extended to fill the available extra horizontal space, provided the maximum widths of the children allow extending their widths beyond their preferred widths. The children in the right and left regions are resized to their preferred widths. Their heights are extended to fill the extra vertical space, provided the maximum heights of the children allow extending their heights beyond their preferred heights. The child node in the center will fill the rest of the available space in both directions.

A StackPane lays out its children in a stack of nodes. It provides a powerful means to overlay nodes. Children are drawn in the order they are added.

A TilePane lays out its children in a grid of uniformly sized cells, known as tiles. TilePanes work similar to FlowPanes with one difference: In a FlowPane, rows and columns can be of different heights and widths, whereas in a TilePane, all rows have the same heights and all columns have the same widths. The width of the widest child node and the height of the tallest child node are the default widths and heights of all tiles in a TilePane. The orientation of a TilePane, which can be set to horizontal or vertical, determines the direction of the flow for its content. By default, a TilePane has a horizontal orientation.

A GridPane lays out its children in a dynamic grid of cells arranged in rows and columns. The grid is dynamic because the number and size of cells in the grid are determined based on the number of children. They depend on the constraints set on children. Each cell in the grid is identified by its position in the column and row. The indexes for columns and rows start at 0. A child node may be placed anywhere in the grid spanning more than one cell. All cells in a row are of the same height. Cells in different rows may have different heights. All cells in a column are of the same width. Cells in different columns may have different widths. By default, a row is tall enough to accommodate the tallest child node in it. A column is wide enough to accommodate the widest child node in it. You can customize the size of each row and column. GridPane also allows for vertical spacing between rows and horizontal spacing between columns. For debug purposes, you can show the grid lines. Figure 10-41 shows three instances of the GridPane.

An AnchorPane lays out its children by anchoring the four edges of its children to its own four edges at a specified distance. An AnchorPane may be used for aligning children along one or more edges of the AnchorPane or for stretching children when the AnchorPane is resized.

The specified distance between the edges of the children and the edges of the AnchorPane is called the *anchor* constraint for the sides it is specified. When you anchor a child node to the two opposite edges (top/bottom or left/right), the children are resized to maintain the specified anchor distance as the AnchorPane is resized.

A TextFlow layout pane is designed to display rich text. The rich text is composed of multiple Text nodes. The TextFlow combines the text in all Text nodes to display in a single text flow. A new line character ('\n') in the text of the Text child nodes indicates the start of a new paragraph. The text is wrapped at the width of the TextFlow.

CHAPTER 11

■ ■ ■

Model-View-Controller Pattern

In this chapter, you will learn:

- What the model-view-controller pattern is

- What other variants of the model-view-controller pattern are, such as the model-view-presenter pattern

- How to develop a JavaFX application using the model-view-presenter pattern

What Is the Model-View-Controller Pattern?

JavaFX lets you create applications using GUI components. A GUI application performs three tasks: accepts inputs from the user, processes the input, and displays outputs. A GUI application contains two types of code:

- Domain code that deals with domain-specific data and business rules

- Presentation code that deals with manipulating user interface widgets

It is often required that the same data in a specific domain be presented in different forms. For example, you may have a web interface using HTML and a desktop interface using JavaFX to present the same data. For easy maintenance of the application code, it is often necessary to divide the application into two logical modules where one module contains presentation code and another domain code (domain-specific business logic and data). The division is made in such a way that the presentation module can see the domain module, but not vice versa. This type of division supports multiple presentations with the same domain code.

Model-view-controller (MVC) pattern is the oldest and the most popular pattern to model GUI applications to facilitate such a division. The MVC pattern consists of three components: *model*, *view*, and *controller*. Figure 11-1 shows a pictorial view of the MVC components and the interactions among them.

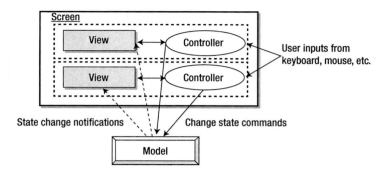

Figure 11-1. *Interaction between participants in the classic MVC pattern*

In MVC, the *model* consists of the domain objects that model the real world problems. The *view* and *controller* consist of the presentation objects that deal with the presentation such as input, output, and user interactions with GUI elements. The controller accepts the inputs from the users and decides what to do with it. That is, the user interacts with the controller directly. The view displays the output on the screen. Each view is associated with a unique controller and vice versa. Each widget on the screen is a view, which has a corresponding controller. Therefore, there are typically multiple view-controller pairs in a GUI screen. The model is not aware of any specific views and controllers. However, views and controllers are model specific. The controller commands the model to modify its state. The views and model always stay in sync. The model notifies views about changes in its state, so views can display the updated data. The model-to-view interaction is facilitated through an *observer* pattern. Keep in mind that the model is fully unaware of any specific views. The model provides a way for views to subscribe to its state change notifications. Any interested views subscribe to the model to receive state change notifications. The model notifies all views that had subscribed whenever a model's state changes.

What has been described so far about the MVC pattern is the original concept of MVC that was used in developing user interfaces in Smalltalk-80 language that was created in 1980. There have been many variants of Smalltalk. The concept in MVC that the presentation and domain logic should be separated in a GUI application still holds true. However, in MVC, dividing the responsibilities between three components had issues. Which component, for example, will have the logic to update the attributes of the view, such as changing the view color or disabling it, that depend on the state of the model? Views can have their own states. A list that displays a list of items has the index of the currently selected item. The selected index is the state of the view, not the model. A model may be associated with several views at one time, and it is not the responsibility of the model to store the state of all views.

The issues of which component in MVC has the responsibility of storing the view logic and state led to another variant of MVC called the Application Model MVC (AM-MVC). In AM-MVC, a new component, called *Application Model*, is introduced between the model and the view/controller. Its purpose is to contain presentation logic and the state, thus solving the issue of which component keeps the presentation logic and the state in the original MVC. The model in MVC is decoupled from the view, and this is also true in AM-MVC. Both use the same observer technique to keep the view and the model in sync. In AM-MVC, the Application Model was supposed to keep the view-related logic but was not allowed to access the view directly. This resulted in bulky and ugly code when the Application Model had to update the view attributes. Figure 11-2 shows a pictorial view of the AM-MVC components and the interactions among them.

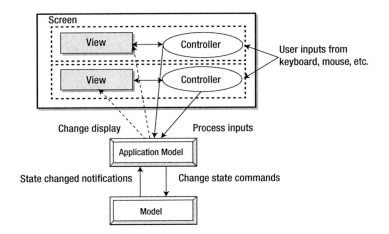

Figure 11-2. *Interaction among participants in the AM-MVC pattern*

Later, modern graphical operating systems like Microsoft Windows and Mac OS offered native widgets, which users can interact with directly. These widgets combined the functions of the view and controller into one. This led to another variant of MVC, called the model-view-presenter (MVP) pattern. Modern widgets also support data binding, which helps keep the view and model in sync with fewer lines of code. Figure 11-3 shows a pictorial view of the MVP components and the interactions among them.

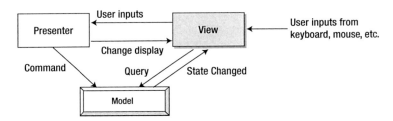

Figure 11-3. *Interactions among participants in the MVP pattern*

In MVC, each widget on the screen is a view, and it has its own unique controller. In MPV, the view is composed of several widgets. The view intercepts the inputs from the user and hands over the control to the presenter. Note that the view does not react to the user inputs. It only intercepts them. The view is also responsible for displaying the data from the model.

The presenter is notified by the view about the user inputs. It determines how to react to the user's input. The presenter is responsible for the presentation logic, manipulating the view, and issuing commands to the model. Once the presenter modifies the model, the view is updated using the observer pattern, as was done in MVC.

The model is responsible for storing domain-specific data and logic. Like MVC, it is independent of any views and presenters. The presenter commands the model to change, and the view updates itself when it receives *state-changed* notifications from the model.

There are some variants of MVP as well. They vary in the responsibility of the view and the presenter. In one variant, the view is responsible for all view-related logic without the help of the presenter. In another variant, the view is responsible for all the simple logic that can be handled declaratively, except when the logic is complex, which is handled by the presenter. In another variant, the presenter handles all view-related logic and manipulates the view. This variant is called *passive view MVP* in which the view is unaware of the model. Figure 11-4 shows a pictorial view of the components in MVP passive view and the interactions among them.

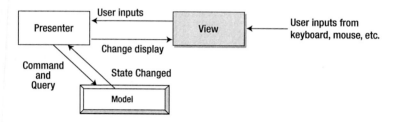

Figure 11-4. *Interactions among the participants in the passive view MVP pattern*

The concept of MVC that the presentation logic should be separated from the domain logic has been around for over 30 years, and it is going to stay in one form or another. All variants of MVC have been attempting to achieve the same function of what the classic MVC did, though in different ways. The variants vary from the classic MVC in the responsibilities of their components. When someone talks about MVC in a GUI application design, make sure you understand which variant of MVC is used and which components perform which tasks.

A Model-View-Presenter Example

This section presents a detailed example that uses the MVP pattern.

The Requirements

For the example here, you will develop a GUI application that will let the user enter the details of a person, validate the data, and save it. The form should contain:

- Person ID field: An autogenerated unique noneditable field

- First name field: An editable text field

- Last name field: An editable text field

- Birth date: An editable text field

- Age category: An autocomputed noneditable field based on the birth date

- Save button: A button to save the data

- Close button: A button to close the window

The personal data should be validated against the following rules:

- The first and last names must be at least one character long.

- If a birth date is entered, it must not be a future date.

The Design

Three classes will represent the three components of an MVP:

- Person class
- PersonView and PersonPresenter classes

The Person class represents the model, the PersonView class the view, and the PersonPresenter class the presenter. As required by the MVP pattern, the Person class will be agnostic about the PersonView and the PersonPresenter classes. The PersonView and the PersonPresenter classes will interact with each other and they will use the Person class directly.

Let's divide the classes related to the model and the view logically by placing them in different Java packages. The com.jdojo.mvc.model package will contain model-related classes, and the com.jdojo.mvc.view package will contain the view-related classes. Figure 11-5 shows the finished window.

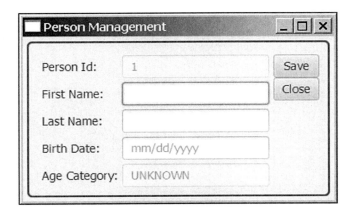

Figure 11-5. *The initial screenshot of the person management window*

The Implementation
The Model

Listing 11-1 contains the complete code for the Person class. The Person class contains the code for the domain data and the business rules. In real life you might want to separate the two into multiple classes. However, for a small application like this, let's keep them in one class.

Listing 11-1. The Person Class Used as the Model

```
// Person.java
package com.jdojo.mvc.model;

import java.time.LocalDate;
import java.time.temporal.ChronoUnit;
import java.util.ArrayList;
import java.util.List;
import java.util.concurrent.atomic.AtomicInteger;
import javafx.beans.property.ObjectProperty;
import javafx.beans.property.ReadOnlyIntegerWrapper;
```

```java
import javafx.beans.property.SimpleObjectProperty;
import javafx.beans.property.SimpleStringProperty;
import javafx.beans.property.StringProperty;
import javafx.beans.property.ReadOnlyIntegerProperty;

public class Person {
        // An enum for age categories
        public enum AgeCategory {
                BABY, CHILD, TEEN, ADULT, SENIOR, UNKNOWN
        };

        private final ReadOnlyIntegerWrapper personId =
                new ReadOnlyIntegerWrapper(this, "personId", personSequence.incrementAndGet());
        private final StringProperty firstName =
                 new SimpleStringProperty(this, "firstName", null);
        private final StringProperty lastName =
                 new SimpleStringProperty(this, "lastName", null);
        private final ObjectProperty<LocalDate> birthDate =
                new SimpleObjectProperty<>(this, "birthDate", null);

        // Keeps track of last generated person id
        private static AtomicInteger personSequence = new AtomicInteger(0);

        public Person() {
                this(null, null, null);
        }

        public Person(String firstName, String lastName, LocalDate birthDate) {
                this.firstName.set(firstName);
                this.lastName.set(lastName);
                this.birthDate.set(birthDate);
        }

        /* personId Property */
        public final int getPersonId() {
                return personId.get();
        }

        public final ReadOnlyIntegerProperty personIdProperty() {
                return personId.getReadOnlyProperty();
        }

        /* firstName Property */
        public final String getFirstName() {
                return firstName.get();
        }

        public final void setFirstName(String firstName) {
                firstNameProperty().set(firstName);
        }
```

```java
public final StringProperty firstNameProperty() {
        return firstName;
}

/* lastName Property */
public final String getLastName() {
        return lastName.get();
}

public final void setLastName(String lastName) {
        lastNameProperty().set(lastName);
}

public final StringProperty lastNameProperty() {
        return lastName;
}

/* birthDate Property */
public final LocalDate getBirthDate() {
        return birthDate.get();
}

public final void setBirthDate(LocalDate birthDate) {
        birthDateProperty().set(birthDate);
}

public final ObjectProperty<LocalDate> birthDateProperty() {
        return birthDate;
}

/* Domain specific business rules */
public boolean isValidBirthDate(LocalDate bdate) {
        return isValidBirthDate(bdate, new ArrayList<>());
}

/* Domain specific business rules */
public boolean isValidBirthDate(LocalDate bdate, List<String> errorList) {
        if (bdate == null) {
                return true;
        }

        // Birth date cannot be in the future
        if (bdate.isAfter(LocalDate.now())) {
                errorList.add("Birth date must not be in future.");
                return false;
        }

        return true;
}
```

```java
        /* Domain specific business rules */
        public boolean isValidPerson(List<String> errorList) {
                return isValidPerson(this, errorList);
        }

        /* Domain specific business rules */
        public boolean isValidPerson(Person p, List<String> errorList) {
                boolean isValid = true;

                String fn = p.firstName.get();
                if (fn == null || fn.trim().length() == 0) {
                        errorList.add("First name must contain minimum one character.");
                        isValid = false;
                }

                String ln = p.lastName.get();
                if (ln == null || ln.trim().length() == 0) {
                        errorList.add("Last name must contain minimum one character.");
                        isValid = false;
                }

                if (!isValidBirthDate(this.birthDate.get(), errorList)) {
                        isValid = false;
                }

                return isValid;
        }

        /* Domain specific business rules */
        public AgeCategory getAgeCategory() {
                if (birthDate.get() == null) {
                        return AgeCategory.UNKNOWN;
                }

                long years = ChronoUnit.YEARS.between(birthDate.get(), LocalDate.now());
                if (years >= 0 && years < 2) {
                        return AgeCategory.BABY;
                } else if (years >= 2 && years < 13) {
                        return AgeCategory.CHILD;
                } else if (years >= 13 && years <= 19) {
                        return AgeCategory.TEEN;
                } else if (years > 19 && years <= 50) {
                        return AgeCategory.ADULT;
                } else if (years > 50) {
                        return AgeCategory.SENIOR;
                } else {
                        return AgeCategory.UNKNOWN;
                }
        }
```

```java
        /* Domain specific business rules */
        public boolean save(List<String> errorList) {
                boolean isSaved = false;
                if (isValidPerson(errorList)) {
                        System.out.println("Saved " + this.toString());
                        isSaved = true;
                }

                return isSaved;
        }

        @Override
        public String toString() {
                return "[personId=" + personId.get() +
                        ", firstName=" + firstName.get() +
                        ", lastName=" + lastName.get() +
                        ", birthDate=" + birthDate.get() + "]";
        }
}
```

The Person class declares an AgeCategory enum to represents different ages:

```java
public enum AgeCategory {BABY, CHILD, TEEN, ADULT, SENIOR, UNKNOWN};
```

The person ID, first name, last name, and birth date are represented by JavaFX properties. The personId property is declared read-only and it is autogenerated. Relevant setter and getter methods are provided for these properties.

The isValidBirthDate() and isValidPerson() methods are included to perform domain-specific validations. The getAgeCategory() method belongs to the Person class as it computes the age category of a person based on his birth date. I have made up some date ranges to divide the age of a person into different categories. You may be tempted to add this method to the view. However, you would then need to duplicate the logic inside this method for each view. The method uses the model data and computes a value. It knows nothing about views, so it belongs to the model, not to the view.

The save() method saves the personal data. The save method is trivial; it simply displays a message on the standard output if the personal data are valid. In a real world application, it would save the data to a database or a file.

The View

The PersonView class shown in Listing 11-2 represents the view in this application. It is mainly responsible for displaying the data in the model.

Listing 11-2. The PersonView Class Used as the View

```java
// PersonView.java
package com.jdojo.mvc.view;

import com.jdojo.mvc.model.Person;
import java.time.LocalDate;
import java.time.format.DateTimeFormatter;
import javafx.scene.control.Button;
```

427

```java
import javafx.scene.control.Label;
import javafx.scene.control.TextField;
import javafx.scene.layout.GridPane;
import javafx.scene.layout.VBox;

public class PersonView extends GridPane {
        private final Person model;

        // Labels
        Label personIdLbl = new Label("Person Id:");
        Label fNameLbl = new Label("First Name:");
        Label lNameLbl = new Label("Last Name:");
        Label bDateLbl = new Label("Birth Date:");
        Label ageCategoryLbl = new Label("Age Category:");

        // Fields
        TextField personIdFld = new TextField();
        TextField fNameFld = new TextField();
        TextField lNameFld = new TextField();
        TextField bDateFld = new TextField();
        TextField ageCategoryFld = new TextField();

        // Buttons
        Button saveBtn = new Button("Save");
        Button closeBtn = new Button("Close");

        // Date format
        String dateFormat;

        public PersonView(Person model, String dateFormat) {
                this.model = model;
                this.dateFormat = dateFormat;
                layoutForm();
                initFieldData();
                bindFieldsToModel();
        }

        private void initFieldData() {
                // Id and names are populated using bindings.
                // Populate birth date and age category
                syncBirthDate();
        }

        private void layoutForm() {
                this.setHgap(5);
                this.setVgap(5);

                this.add(personIdLbl, 1, 1);
                this.add(fNameLbl, 1, 2);
                this.add(lNameLbl, 1, 3);
                this.add(bDateLbl, 1, 4);
                this.add(ageCategoryLbl, 1, 5);
```

```java
            this.add(personIdFld, 2, 1);
            this.add(fNameFld, 2, 2);
            this.add(lNameFld, 2, 3);
            this.add(bDateFld, 2, 4);
            this.add(ageCategoryFld, 2, 5);

            // Add buttons and make them the same width
            VBox buttonBox = new VBox(saveBtn, closeBtn);
            saveBtn.setMaxWidth(Double.MAX_VALUE);
            closeBtn.setMaxWidth(Double.MAX_VALUE);

            this.add(buttonBox, 3, 1, 1, 5);

            // Disable the personId field
            personIdFld.setDisable(true);
            ageCategoryFld.setDisable(true);

            // Set the prompt text for the birth date field
            bDateFld.setPromptText(dateFormat.toLowerCase());
    }

    public void bindFieldsToModel() {
            personIdFld.textProperty().bind(model.personIdProperty().asString());
            fNameFld.textProperty().bindBidirectional(model.firstNameProperty());
            lNameFld.textProperty().bindBidirectional(model.lastNameProperty());
    }

    public void syncBirthDate() {
            LocalDate bdate = model.getBirthDate();
            if (bdate != null) {
                    bDateFld.setText(bdate.format(DateTimeFormatter.
                    ofPattern(dateFormat)));
            }

            syncAgeCategory();
    }

    public void syncAgeCategory() {
            ageCategoryFld.setText(model.getAgeCategory().toString());
    }
}
```

The PersonView class inherits from the GridPane class. It contains an instance variable for each UI component. Its constructor takes the model (an instance of the Person class) and a date format as arguments. The date format is the format used to display the birth date. Note that the format for the birth date is view specific and it should be part of the view as such. The model knows nothing about the format in which the birth date is displayed by views.

The initFieldData() method initializes the view with the data. I used JavaFX bindings to bind the data in UI nodes to the model data except for the birth date and age category fields. This method synchronizes the birth date and the age category fields with the model. The layoutForm() method lays out the UI nodes in the grid pane. The bindFieldsToModel() method binds the person ID, first name, and last name TextFields to the corresponding data fields in the model, so they stay in sync. The syncBirthDate() method reads the birth date from the model, formats it, and displays it in the view. The syncAgeCategory() method synchronizes the age category field, which is computed by the model based on the birth date.

Notice that the view, the PersonView class, does not know about the presenter, the PersonPresenter class. So how will the view and the presenter communicate? The role of a presenter is mainly to get the user's inputs from the view and act upon them. The presenter will have a reference to the view. It will add event listeners to the view, so it is notified when the data in the view change. In the event handlers, the presenter takes control and processes the inputs. If the application requires a reference to the presenter in the view, you can have that as an argument to the constructor of the view class. Alternatively, you can provide a setter method in the view class to set the presenter.

The Presenter

The PersonPresenter class shown in Listing 11-3 represents the presenter in this application. It is mainly responsible for intercepting the new input in the view and processing it. It communicates directly with the model and the view.

Listing 11-3. The PersonPresenter Class Used as the Presenter

```java
// PersonPresenter.java
package com.jdojo.mvc.view;

import com.jdojo.mvc.model.Person;
import java.time.LocalDate;
import java.time.format.DateTimeFormatter;
import java.time.format.DateTimeParseException;
import java.util.ArrayList;
import java.util.List;
import javafx.beans.value.ObservableValue;
import javafx.scene.Node;
import javafx.scene.Scene;
import javafx.scene.control.Button;
import javafx.scene.control.Label;
import javafx.scene.layout.StackPane;
import javafx.scene.layout.VBox;
import javafx.stage.Modality;
import javafx.stage.Stage;
import javafx.stage.StageStyle;

public class PersonPresenter {
        private final Person model;
        private final PersonView view;

        public PersonPresenter(Person model, PersonView view) {
                this.model = model;
                this.view = view;
                attachEvents();
        }

        private void attachEvents() {
                // We need to detect the birth date change when the bDate field loses
                // focus or the user presses the Enter key while it still has focus
```

```java
        view.bDateFld.setOnAction(e -> handleBirthDateChange());
        view.bDateFld.getScene().focusOwnerProperty()
                            .addListener(this::focusChanged);

        // Save the data
        view.saveBtn.setOnAction(e -> saveData());

        // Close the window when the Close button is pressed
        view.closeBtn.setOnAction(e -> view.getScene().getWindow().hide());
}

public void focusChanged(ObservableValue<? extends Node> value,
                        Node oldNode,
                        Node newNode) {

        // The birth date field has lost focus
        if (oldNode == view.bDateFld) {
                handleBirthDateChange();
        }
}

private void handleBirthDateChange() {
        String bdateStr = view.bDateFld.getText();
        if (bdateStr == null || bdateStr.trim().equals("")) {
                model.setBirthDate(null);
                view.syncBirthDate();
        } else {
                try {
                        DateTimeFormatter formatter = DateTimeFormatter.
                        ofPattern(view.dateFormat);
                        LocalDate bdate = LocalDate.parse(bdateStr, formatter);

                        List<String> errorList = new ArrayList<>();
                        if (model.isValidBirthDate(bdate, errorList)) {
                                model.setBirthDate(bdate);
                                view.syncAgeCategory();
                        } else {
                                this.showError(errorList);
                                view.syncBirthDate();
                        }
                }
                catch (DateTimeParseException e) {
                        // Birth date is not in the specified date format
                        List<String> errorList = new ArrayList<>();
                        errorList.add("Birth date must be in the " +
                                        view.dateFormat.toLowerCase() + " format.");
                        this.showError(errorList);

                        // Refresh the view
                        view.syncBirthDate();
                }
        }
}
```

```java
        private void saveData() {
                List<String> errorList = new ArrayList<>();
                boolean isSaved = model.save(errorList);
                if (!isSaved) {
                        this.showError(errorList);
                }
        }

        public void showError(List<String> errorList) {
                String msg = "";
                if (errorList.isEmpty()) {
                        msg = "No message to display.";
                } else {
                        for (String s : errorList) {
                                msg = msg + s + "\n";
                        }
                }

                Label msgLbl = new Label(msg);
                Button okBtn = new Button("OK");
                VBox root = new VBox(new StackPane(msgLbl), new StackPane(okBtn));
                root.setSpacing(10);

                Scene scene = new Scene(root);
                Stage stage = new Stage(StageStyle.UTILITY);
                stage.initModality(Modality.WINDOW_MODAL);
                stage.setScene(scene);
                stage.initOwner(view.getScene().getWindow());

                // Set the Action listener for the OK button
                 okBtn.setOnAction(e -> stage.close());

                stage.setTitle("Error");
                stage.sizeToScene();
                stage.showAndWait();
        }
}
```

The constructor of the PersonPresenter class takes the model and the view as arguments. The attachEvents() method attaches event handlers to the UI components of the view. In this example you are not interested in intercepting all inputs in the view. But you are interested in the birth date changes and the clicking of the Save and Close buttons. You do not want to detect all edit changes in the birth date field. If you are interested in all changes in the birth date field, you would need to add a change listener for its text property. You want to detect changes only when the user is done entering the birth date. For this reason:

- You attach a focus listener to the scene and detect if the birth date has lost the focus.

- You attach an action listener to the birth date field, so you intercept the Enter key press while the field has focus.

This validates and refreshes the birth date and age category whenever the birth date field loses focus or the Enter key is pressed while focus is still in the field.

The `handleBirthDateChange()` method handles a change in the birth date field. It validates the birth date format before updating the model. It displays an error message to the user if the birth date is not valid. Finally, it tells the view to update the birth date and age category.

The `saveData()` method is called when the user clicks the Save button, and it commands the model to save the data. The `showError()` method does not belong to the presenter. Here you added it instead of creating a new view class. It is used to display an error message.

Putting Them Together

Let's put the model, view, and presenter together to use them in an application. The program in Listing 11-4 creates the model, view, and presenter, glues them together, and displays the view in a window as shown in Figure 11-5. Notice that the view must be attached to a scene before the presenter is created. It is required because the presenter attaches a focus change listener to the scene. Creating the presenter before adding the view to the scene will result in a `NullPointerException`.

Listing 11-4. The `PersonApp` Class Uses the Model, View, and Presenter to Create a GUI Application

```java
// PersonApp.java
package com.jdojo.mvc;

import com.jdojo.mvc.view.PersonView;
import com.jdojo.mvc.view.PersonPresenter;
import com.jdojo.mvc.model.Person;
import javafx.application.Application;
import javafx.scene.Scene;
import javafx.stage.Stage;

public class PersonApp extends Application {
        public static void main(String[] args) {
                Application.launch(args);
        }

        @Override
        public void start(Stage stage) {
                Person model = new Person();
                String dateFormat = "MM/dd/yyyy";
                PersonView view = new PersonView(model, dateFormat);

                // Must set the scene before creating the presenter that uses
                // the scene to listen for the focus change
                Scene scene = new Scene(view);

                PersonPresenter presenter = new PersonPresenter(model, view);
                view.setStyle("-fx-padding: 10;" +
                                "-fx-border-style: solid inside;" +
                                "-fx-border-width: 2;" +
```

```
                        "-fx-border-insets: 5;" +
                        "-fx-border-radius: 5;" +
                        "-fx-border-color: blue;");

        stage.setScene(scene);
        stage.setTitle("Person Management");
        stage.show();
    }
}
```

Summary

It is often required that the same domain data be presented in different forms. For example, you may have a web interface using HTML and a desktop interface using JavaFX to present the same data. For easy maintenance of the application code, it is often necessary to divide the application into two logical modules where one module contains presentation code and another domain code (domain-specific business logic and data). The division is made in such a way that the presentation module can see the domain module, but not vice versa. This type of division supports multiple presentations with the same domain code. The MVC pattern is the oldest and the most popular pattern to model GUI applications to facilitate such a division. The MVC pattern consists of three components: model, view, and controller.

In MVC, the model consists of the domain objects that model the real world problems. The view and controller consist of the presentation objects that deal with the presentation such as input, output, and user interactions with GUI elements. The controller accepts the inputs from the users and decides what to do with them. That is, the user interacts with the controller directly. The view displays the output on the screen. Each view is associated with a unique controller and vice versa. Each widget on the screen is a view, which has a corresponding controller. In MVC, dividing the responsibilities between three components created issues. Which component, for example, would have the logic to update the attributes of the view, such as changing the view color or disabling it, that depend on the state of the model?

The issues for which component in MVC has the responsibility storing the view logic and the state led to another variant of MVC called the Application Model MVC. In AM-MVC, a new component, called the Application Model, was introduced between the model and the view/controller. Its purpose is to contain presentation logic and the state, thus solving the issue of which component keeps the presentation logic and state in the original MVC.

Later, modern graphical operating systems like Microsoft Windows and Mac OS offered native widgets, which users can interact with directly. These widgets combined the functions of the view and controller into one. This led to another variant of MVC, called the model-view-presenter pattern.

In MVC, each widget on the screen is a view and it has its unique controller. In MVP, the view is composed of several widgets. The view intercepts the inputs from the user and hands over the control to the presenter. Note that the view does not react to the user's inputs; it only intercepts them. The presenter is notified by the view about the user's inputs and determines how to react to them. The presenter is responsible for the presentation logic, manipulating the view, and issuing commands to the model. Once the presenter modifies the model, the view is updated using the observer pattern, as was done in MVC.

There are some variants of MVP as well. They vary in the responsibility of the view and the presenter. In one variant, the view is responsible for all view-related logic without the help of the presenter. In another variant, the view is responsible for all the simple logic that can be handled declaratively, except when the logic is complex, which is handled by the presenter. In another variant, the presenter handles all view-related logic and manipulates the view. This variant is called passive view MVP, in which the view is unaware of the model.

The next chapter will introduce you to controls that are used to build the view in JavaFX applications.

CHAPTER 12

■ ■ ■

Understanding Controls

In this chapter, you will learn:

- What a control is in Java

- About classes whose instances represent controls in JavaFX

- About controls such as Label, Button, CheckBox, RadioButton, Hyperlink, ChoiceBox, ComboBox, ListView, ColorPicker, DatePicker, TextField, TextArea, and Menu

- How to style controls using a CSS

- How to use the FileChooser and DirectoryChooser dialogs

What Is a Control?

JavaFX lets you create applications using GUI components. An application with a GUI performs three tasks:

- Accepts inputs from the user through input devices such as a keyboard or a mouse

- Processes the inputs (or takes actions based on the input)

- Displays outputs

The UI provides a means to exchange information in terms of input and output between an application and its users. Entering text using a keyboard, selecting a menu item using a mouse, clicking a button, or other actions are examples of providing input to a GUI application. The application displays outputs on a computer monitor using text, charts, dialog boxes, and so forth.

Users interact with a GUI application using graphical elements called *controls* or *widgets*. Buttons, labels, text fields, text area, radio buttons, and check boxes are a few examples of controls. Devices like a keyboard, a mouse, and a touch screen are used to provide input to controls. Controls can also display output to the users. Controls generate events that indicate an occurrence of some kind of interaction between the user and the control. For example, pressing a button using a mouse or a spacebar generates an action event indicating that the user has pressed the button.

JavaFX provides a rich set of easy-to-use controls. Controls are added to layout panes that position and size them. Layout panes were discussed in Chapter 10. This chapter discusses how to use the controls available in JavaFX.

Typically, the MVP pattern (discussed in Chapter 11) is used to develop a GUI application in JavaFX. MVP requires you to have at least three classes and place your business logic in a certain way and in certain classes. Generally, this bloats the application code, although for the right reason. This chapter will focus on the different types of controls, not on learning the MVP pattern. You will embed classes required for MVP patterns into one class to keep the code brief and save a lot of space in this book as well!

Understanding Control Classes Hierarchy

Each control in JavaFX is represented by an instance of a class. If multiple controls share basic features, they inherit from a common base class. Control classes are included in the `javafx.scene.control` package. A control class is a subclass, direct or indirect, of the `Control` class, which in turn inherits from the `Region`. Recall that the `Region` class inherits from the `Parent` class. Therefore, technically, a `Control` is also a `Parent`. All our discussions about the `Parent` and `Region` classes in the previous chapters also apply to all control-related classes.

A `Parent` can have children. Typically, a control is composed of another node (sometimes, multiple nodes), which is its child node. Control classes do not expose the list of its children through the `getChildren()` method, and therefore, you cannot add any children to them.

Control classes expose the list of their internal unmodifiable children through the `getChildrenUnmodifiable()` method, which returns an `ObservableList<Node>`. You are not required to know about the internal children of a control to use the control. However, if you need the list of their children, the `getChildrenUnmodifiable()` method will give you that.

Figure 12-1 shows a class diagram for classes of some commonly used controls. The list of control classes is a lot bigger than the one shown in the class diagram.

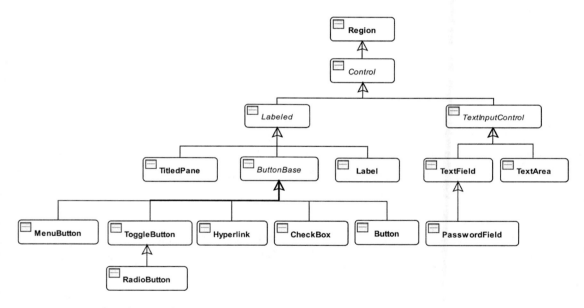

Figure 12-1. *A class diagram for control classes in JavaFX*

The `Control` class is the base class for all controls. It declares three properties, as shown in Table 12-1, that are common to all controls.

Table 12-1. *Properties Declared in the Control Class*

Property	Type	Description
contextMenu	ObjectProperty<ContextMenu>	Specifies the content menu for the control.
skin	ObjectProperty<Skin<?>>	Specifies the skin for the control.
tooltip	ObjectProperty<Tooltip>	Specifies the tool tip for the control.

The contextMenu property specifies the context menu for the control. A context menu gives a list of choices to the user. Each choice is an action that can be taken on the control in its current state. Some controls have their default context menus. For example, a TextField, when right-clicked, displays a context menu with choices like Undo, Cut, Copy, and Paste. Typically, a context menu is displayed when the user presses a combination of keys (e.g., Shift + F10 on Windows) or clicks the mouse (right-click on Windows) when the control has focus. I will revisit the contextMenu property when I discuss the text input controls.

At the time of this writing, JavaFX doesn't allow access or customization of the default context menu for controls. The contextMenu property is null even if the control has a default context menu. When you set the contextMenu property, it replaces the default context for the control. Note that not all controls have a default context menu and a context menu is not suitable for all controls. For example, a Button control does not use a context menu.

The visual appearance of a control is known as its *skin*. A skin responds to the state changes in a control by changing its visual appearance. A skin is represented by an instance of the Skin interface. The Control class implements the Skinnable interface, giving all controls the ability to use a skin.

The skin property in the Control class specifies the custom skin for a control. Developing a new skin is not an easy task. For the most part, you can customize the appearance of a control using CSS styles. All controls can be styled using CSS. The Control class implements the Styleable interface, so all controls can be styled. Please refer to Chapter 8 for more details on how to use a CSS. I will discuss some commonly used CSS attributes for some controls in this chapter.

Controls can display a short message called a *tool tip* when the mouse hovers over the control for a short period. An object of the Tooltip class represents a tool tip in JavaFX. The tooltip property in the Control class specifies the tool tip for a control.

Labeled Controls

A labeled control contains a read-only textual content and optionally a graphic as part of its UI. Label, Button, CheckBox, RadioButton, and Hyperlink are some examples of labeled controls in JavaFX. All labeled controls are inherited, directly or indirectly, from the Labeled class, which is declared abstract. The Labeled class inherits from the Control class. Figure 12-2 shows a class diagram for labeled controls. Some of the classes have been left out in the diagram for brevity.

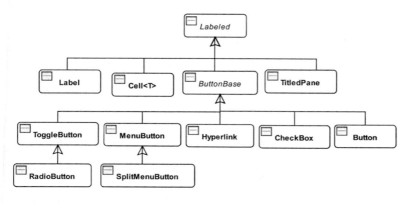

Figure 12-2. *A class diagram for labeled control classes*

The Labeled class declares text and graphic properties to represent the textual and graphic contents, respectively. It declares several other properties to deal with the visual aspects of its contents, for example, alignment, font, padding, and text wrapping. Table 12-2 contains the list of those properties with their brief descriptions. I will discuss some of these properties in the subsequent sections.

Table 12-2. *Properties Declared in the Labeled Class*

Property	Type	Description
alignment	ObjectProperty<Pos>	It specifies the alignment of the content of the control within the content area. Its effect is visible when the content area is bigger than the content (text + graphic). The default value is Pos.CENTER_LEFT.
contentDisplay	ObjectProperty<ContentDisplay>	It specifies positioning of the graphic relative to the text.
ellipsisString	StringProperty	It specifies the string to display for the ellipsis when the text is truncated because the control has a smaller size than the preferred size. The default value is "..." for most locales. Specifying an empty string for this property does not display an ellipsis string in truncated text.
font	ObjectProperty<Font>	It specifies the default font for the text.
graphic	ObjectProperty<Node>	It specifies an optional icon for the control.
graphicTextGap	DoubleProperty	It specifies the amount of text between the graphic and text.
labelPadding	ReadOnlyObjectProperty<Insets>	It is the padding around the content area of the control. By default, it is Insets.EMPTY.

(continued)

Table 12-2. (*continued*)

Property	Type	Description
lineSpacing	DoubleProperty	It specifies the space between adjacent lines when the control displays multiple lines.
mnemonicParsing	BooleanProperty	It enables or disables text parsing to detect a mnemonic character. If it is set to true, the text for the control is parsed for an underscore (_) character. The character following the first underscore is added as the mnemonic for the control. Pressing the Alt key on Windows computers highlights mnemonics for all controls.
textAlignment	ObjectProperty<TextAlignment>	It specifies the text alignment within the text bounds for multiline text.
textFill	ObjectProperty<Paint>	It specifies the text color.
textOverrun	ObjectProperty<OverrunStyle>	It specifies how to display the text when the text content exceeds the available space.
text	StringProperty	It specifies the text content.
underline	BooleanProperty	It specifies whether the text content should be underlined.
wrapText	BooleanProperty	It specifies whether the text should be wrapped if the text cannot be displayed in one line.

Positioning Graphic and Text

The contentDisplay property of labeled controls specifies the positioning of the graphic relative to the text. Its value is one of the constants of the ContentDisplay enum: TOP, RIGHT, BOTTOM, LEFT, CENTER, TEXT_ONLY, and GRAPHIC_ONLY. If you do not want to display the text or the graphic, you can use the GRAPHIC_ONLY and TEXT_ONLY values instead of setting the text to an empty string and the graphic to null. Figure 12-3 shows the effects of using different values for the contentDisplay property of a Label. The Label uses Name: as the text and a blue rectangle as the graphic. The value for the contentDisplay property is displayed at the bottom of each instance.

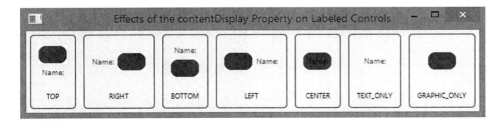

Figure 12-3. *Effects of the* contentDisplay *property on labeled controls*

Understanding Mnemonics and Accelerators

Labeled controls support keyboard *mnemonics*, which is also known as a *keyboard shortcut* or *keyboard indicator*. A mnemonic is a key that sends an ActionEvent to the control. The mnemonic key is often pressed in combination with a modifier key such as an Alt key. The modifier key is platform dependent; however, it is usually an Alt key. For example, suppose you set the C key as a mnemonic for a Close button. When you press Alt + C, the Close button is activated.

Finding the documentation about mnemonics in JavaFX is not easy. It is buried in the documentation for the Labeled and Scene classes. Setting a mnemonic key for a labeled control is easy. You need to precede the mnemonic character with an underscore in the text content and make sure that the mnemonicParsing property for the control is set to true. The first underscore is removed and the character following it is set as the mnemonic for the control. For some labeled controls, the mnemonic parsing is set to true by default, and for others, you will need to set it.

■ **Tip**   Mnemonics are not supported on all platforms. Mnemonic characters in the text for controls are not underlined, at least on Windows, until the Alt key is pressed.

The following statement will set the C key as the mnemonic for the Close button:

```
// For Button, mnemonic parsing is true by default
Button closeBtn = new Button("_Close");
```

When you press the Alt key, the mnemonic characters for all controls are underlined and pressing the mnemonic character for any controls will set focus to the control and send it an ActionEvent.

JavaFX provides the following four classes in the javafx.scene.input package to set mnemonics for all types of controls programmatically:

- Mnemonic
- KeyCombination
- KeyCharacterCombination
- KeyCodeCombination

An object of the Mnemonic class represents a mnemonic. An object of the KeyCombination class, which is declared abstract, represents the key combination for a mnemonic. The KeyCharacterCombination and KeyCodeCombination classes are subclasses of the KeyCombination class. Use the former to construct a key combination using a character; use the latter to construct a key combination using a key code. Note that not all keys on the keyboard represent characters. The KeyCodeCombination class lets you create a key combination for any key on the keyboard.

The Mnemonic object is created for a node and is added to a Scene. When the Scene receives an unconsumed key event for the key combination, it sends an ActionEvent to the target node.

The following snippet of code achieves the same result that was achieved using one statement in the above example:

```
Button closeBtn = new Button("Close");

// Create a KeyCombination for Alt + C
KeyCombination kc = new KeyCodeCombination(KeyCode.C, KeyCombination.ALT_DOWN);
```

```
// Create a Mnemonic object for closeBtn
Mnemonic mnemonic = new Mnemonic(closeBtn, kc);

Scene scene = create a scene...;
scene.addMnemonic(mnemonic); // Add the mnemonic to the scene
```

The KeyCharacterCombination class can also be used to create a key combination for Alt + C:

```
KeyCombination kc = new KeyCharacterCombination("C", KeyCombination.ALT_DOWN);
```

The Scene class supports accelerator keys. An accelerator key, when pressed, executes a Runnable task. Notice the difference between mnemonics and accelerator keys. A mnemonic is associated with a control, and pressing its key combination sends an ActionEvent to the control. An accelerator key is not associated with a control, but rather to a task. The Scene class maintains an ObservableMap<KeyCombination, Runnable>, whose reference can be obtained using the getAccelerators() method.

The following snippet of code adds an accelerator key (Ctrl + X on Windows and Meta + X on Mac) to a Scene, which closes the window associated with the Scene. The SHORTCUT key represents the shortcut key on the platform—Ctrl on Windows and Meta on Mac:

```
Scene scene = create a scene object...;
...
KeyCombination kc = new KeyCodeCombination(KeyCode.X,
                                    KeyCombination.SHORTCUT_DOWN);
Runnable task = () -> scene.getWindow().hide();
scene.getAccelerators().put(kc, task);
```

The program in Listing 12-1 shows how to use mnemonics and accelerator keys. Press Alt + 1 and Alt + 2 to activate Button 1 and Button 2, respectively. Pressing these buttons changes the text for the Label. Pressing the shortcut key + X will close the window.

Listing 12-1. Using Mnemonics and Accelerator Keys

```
// MnemonicTest.java
package com.jdojo.control;

import javafx.application.Application;
import javafx.scene.Scene;
import javafx.scene.control.Button;
import javafx.scene.control.Label;
import javafx.scene.input.KeyCode;
import javafx.scene.input.KeyCodeCombination;
import javafx.scene.input.KeyCombination;
import javafx.scene.input.Mnemonic;
import javafx.scene.layout.VBox;
import javafx.stage.Stage;

public class MnemonicTest  extends Application {
        public static void main(String[] args) {
                Application.launch(args);
        }
```

```java
@Override
public void start(Stage stage) {
        VBox root = new VBox();
        root.setSpacing(10);
        root.setStyle("-fx-padding: 10;" +
                        "-fx-border-style: solid inside;" +
                        "-fx-border-width: 2;" +
                        "-fx-border-insets: 5;" +
                        "-fx-border-radius: 5;" +
                        "-fx-border-color: blue;");

        Scene scene = new Scene(root);
        Label msg = new Label("Press Ctrl + X on Windows \nand " +
                                        "\nMeta + X on Mac to close the window");
        Label lbl = new Label("Press Alt + 1 or Alt + 2");

        // Use Alt + 1 as the mnemonic for Button 1
        Button btn1 = new Button("Button _1");
        btn1.setOnAction(e -> lbl.setText("Button 1 clicked!"));

        // Use Alt + 2 as the mnemonic key for Button 2
        Button btn2 = new Button("Button 2");
        btn2.setOnAction(e -> lbl.setText("Button 2 clicked!"));
        KeyCombination kc = new KeyCodeCombination(KeyCode.DIGIT2,
                                                    KeyCombination.ALT_DOWN);
        Mnemonic mnemonic = new Mnemonic(btn2, kc);
        scene.addMnemonic(mnemonic);

        // Add an accelarator key to the scene
        KeyCombination kc4 =
                new KeyCodeCombination(KeyCode.X, KeyCombination.SHORTCUT_DOWN);
        Runnable task = () -> scene.getWindow().hide();
        scene.getAccelerators().put(kc4, task);

        // Add all children to the VBox
        root.getChildren().addAll(msg, lbl, btn1, btn2);

        stage.setScene(scene);
        stage.setTitle("Using Mnemonics and Accelerators");
        stage.show();
    }
}
```

Understanding the *Label* Control

An instance of the Label class represents a label control. As the name suggest, a Label is simply a label that is used to identify or describe another component on a screen. It can display a text, an icon, or both. Typically, a Label is placed next to (to the right or left) or at the top of the node it describes.

A Label is not focus traversable. That is, you cannot set the focus to a Label using the Tab key. A Label control does not generate any interesting events that are typically used in an application.

A Label control can also be used to display text in situations where it is acceptable to truncate the text if enough space is not available to display the entire text. Please refer to the API documentation on the textOverrun and ellipsisString properties of the Labeled class for more details on how to control the text truncation behavior in a Label control.

Figure 12-4 shows a window with two Label controls with text First Name: and Last Name:. The Label with the text First Name: is an indicator for the user that he should enter a first name in the field that is placed right next to it. A similar argument goes for the Last Name: Label control.

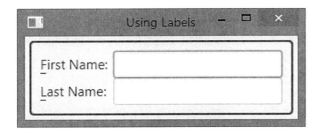

Figure 12-4. *A window with two Label controls*

The Label class has a very useful labelFor property of ObjectProperty<Node> type. It is set to another node in the scene graph. A Label control can have a mnemonic. Mnemonic parsing for Label controls is set to false by default. When you press the mnemonic key for a Label, the focus is set to the labelFor node for that Label. The following snippet of code creates a TextField and a Label. The Label sets a mnemonic, enables mnemonic parsing, and sets the TextField as its labelFor property. When the Alt + F keys are pressed, focus is moved to the TextField:

```
TextField fNameFld = new TextField();
Label fNameLbl = new Label("_First Name:"); // F is mnemonic
fNameLbl.setLabelFor(fNameFld);
fNameLbl.setMnemonicParsing(true);
```

The program in Listing 12-2 produces the screen shown in Figure 12-4. Press Alt + F and Alt + L to shift focus between the two TextField controls.

Listing 12-2. Using the Label Control

```
// LabelTest.java
package com.jdojo.control;

import javafx.application.Application;
import javafx.scene.Scene;
import javafx.scene.control.Label;
import javafx.scene.control.TextField;
import javafx.scene.layout.GridPane;
import javafx.stage.Stage;

public class LabelTest extends Application {
        public static void main(String[] args) {
                Application.launch(args);
        }
```

```
@Override
public void start(Stage stage) {
        TextField fNameFld = new TextField();
        Label fNameLbl = new Label("_First Name:");
        fNameLbl.setLabelFor(fNameFld);
        fNameLbl.setMnemonicParsing(true);

        TextField lNameFld = new TextField();
        Label lNameLbl = new Label("_Last Name:");
        lNameLbl.setLabelFor(lNameFld);
        lNameLbl.setMnemonicParsing(true);

        GridPane root = new GridPane();
        root.addRow(0, fNameLbl, fNameFld);
        root.addRow(1, lNameLbl, lNameFld);
        root.setStyle("-fx-padding: 10;" +
                        "-fx-border-style: solid inside;" +
                        "-fx-border-width: 2;" +
                        "-fx-border-insets: 5;" +
                        "-fx-border-radius: 5;" +
                        "-fx-border-color: blue;");

        Scene scene = new Scene(root);
        stage.setScene(scene);
        stage.setTitle("Using Labels");
        stage.show();
    }
}
```

Understanding Buttons

JavaFX provides three types of controls that represent buttons:

- Buttons to execute commands

- Buttons to make choices

- Buttons to execute commands as well as make choices

All button classes inherit from the ButtonBase class. Please refer to Figure 12-2 for a class diagram. All types of buttons support the ActionEvent. Buttons trigger an ActionEvent when they are activated. A button can be activated in different ways, for example, by using a mouse, a mnemonic, an accelerator key, or other key combinations.

A button that executes a command when activated is known as a *command button*. The Button, Hyperlink, and MenuButton classes represent command buttons. A MenuButton lets the user execute a command from a list of commands. Buttons used for presenting different choices to users are known as *choice buttons*. The ToggleButton, CheckBox, and RadioButton classes represent choice buttons. The third kind of button is a hybrid of the first two kinds. They let users execute a command or make choices. The SplitMenuButton class represents a hybrid button.

> ■ **Tip** All buttons are labeled controls. Therefore, they can have a textual content, a graphic, or both. All types of buttons are capable of firing an `ActionEvent`.

Understanding Command Buttons

You have already used command buttons in several instances, for example, a Close button to close a window. In this section, I will discuss buttons that are used as command buttons.

Understanding the Button Control

An instance of the `Button` class represents a command button. Typically, a `Button` has text as its label and an `ActionEvent` handler is registered to it. The `mnemonicParsing` property for the `Button` class is set to true by default.

A `Button` can be in one of three modes:

- A normal button

- A default button

- A cancel button

For a normal button, its `ActionEvent` is fired when the button is activated. For a default button, the `ActionEvent` is fired when the Enter key is pressed and no other node in the scene consumes the key press. For a cancel button, the `ActionEvent` is fired when the Esc key is pressed and no other node in the scene consumes the key press.

By default, a `Button` is a normal button. The default and cancel modes are represented by the `defaultButton` and `cancelButton` properties. You would set one of these properties to true to make a button a default or cancel button. By default, both properties are set to false.

The following snippet of code creates a normal `Button` and adds an `ActionEvent` handler. When the button is activated, for example, by clicking using a mouse, the `newDocument()` method is called:

```
// A normal button
Button newBtn = new Button("New");
newBtn.setOnAction(e -> newDocument());
```

The following snippet of code creates a default button and adds an `ActionEvent` handler. When the button is activated, the `save()` method is called. Note that a default `Button` is also activated by pressing the Enter key if no other node in the scene consumes the key press:

```
// A default button
Button saveBtn = new Button("Save");
saveBtn.setDefaultButton(true); // Make it a default button
saveBtn.setOnAction(e -> save());
```

The program in Listing 12-3 creates a normal button, a default button, and a cancel button. It adds an ActionEvent listener to all three buttons. Notice that all buttons have a mnemonic (e.g., N for the New button). When the buttons are activated, a message is displayed in a Label. You can activate the buttons by different means:

- Clicking on buttons

- Setting focus to the buttons using the Tab key and pressing the spacebar

- Pressing Alt key and their mnemonics

- Pressing the Enter key to activate the Save button

- Pressing Esc key to activate the Cancel button

No matter how you activate the buttons, their ActionEvent handler is called. Typically, the ActionEvent handler for a button contains the command for the button.

Listing 12-3. Using the Button Class to Create Command Buttons

```
// ButtonTest.java
package com.jdojo.control;

import javafx.application.Application;
import javafx.scene.Scene;
import javafx.scene.control.Button;
import javafx.scene.control.Label;
import javafx.scene.layout.HBox;
import javafx.scene.layout.VBox;
import javafx.stage.Stage;

public class ButtonTest extends Application {
        Label msgLbl = new Label("Press Enter or Esc key to see the message");

        public static void main(String[] args) {
                Application.launch(args);
        }

        @Override
        public void start(Stage stage) {
                // A normal button with N as its mnemonic
                Button newBtn = new Button("_New");
                newBtn.setOnAction(e -> newDocument());

                // A default button with S as its mnemonic
                Button saveBtn = new Button("_Save");
                saveBtn.setDefaultButton(true);
                saveBtn.setOnAction( e -> save());

                // A cancel button with C as its mnemonic
                Button cancelBtn = new Button("_Cancel");
                cancelBtn.setCancelButton(true);
                cancelBtn.setOnAction(e -> cancel());
```

```
            HBox buttonBox = new HBox(newBtn, saveBtn, cancelBtn);
            buttonBox.setSpacing(15);
            VBox root = new VBox(msgLbl, buttonBox);
            root.setSpacing(15);
            root.setStyle("-fx-padding: 10;" +
                          "-fx-border-style: solid inside;" +
                          "-fx-border-width: 2;" +
                          "-fx-border-insets: 5;" +
                          "-fx-border-radius: 5;" +
                          "-fx-border-color: blue;");

            Scene scene = new Scene(root);
            stage.setScene(scene);
            stage.setTitle("Command Buttons");
            stage.show();
    }

    public void newDocument() {
            msgLbl.setText("Creating a new document...");
    }

    public void save() {
            msgLbl.setText("Saving...");
    }

    public void cancel() {
            msgLbl.setText("Cancelling...");
    }
}
```

■ **Tip** It is possible to set more than one button in a scene as a default or cancel button. However, only the first one is used. It is poor designing to declare multiple buttons as default and cancel buttons in a scene. By default, JavaFX highlights the default button with a light shade of color to give it a unique look. You can customize the appearance of default and cancel buttons using CSS styles. Setting the same button as a default button and a cancel button is also allowed, but it is a sign of bad design when this is done.

The default CSS style-class name for a Button is button. The Button class supports two CSS pseudo-classes: default and cancel. You can use these pseudo-classes to customize the look for default and cancel buttons. The following CSS style will set the text color for default buttons to blue and cancel buttons to gray:

```
.button:default {
       -fx-text-fill: blue;
}

.button:cancel {
       -fx-text-fill: gray;
}
```

447

■ **Tip**   You can use CSS styles to create stylish buttons. Please visit the web site at `http://fxexperience.com/2011/12/styling-fx-buttons-with-css/` for examples.

Understanding the Hyperlink Control

An instance of the Hyperlink class represents a hyperlink control, which looks like a hyperlink in a web page. In a web page, a hyperlink is used to navigate to another web page. However, in JavaFX, an ActionEvent is triggered when a Hyperlink control is activated, for example, by clicking it, and you are free to perform any action in the ActionEvent handler.

A Hyperlink control is simply a button styled to look like a hyperlink. By default, mnemonic parsing is off. A Hyperlink control can have focus, and by default, it draws a dashed rectangular border when it has focus. When the mouse cursor hovers over a Hyperlink control, the cursor changes to a hand and its text is underlined.

The Hyperlink class contains a visited property of BooleanProperty type. When a Hyperlink control is activated for the first time, it is considered "visited" and the visited property is set to true automatically. All visited hyperlinks are shown in a different color than the not visited ones. You can also set the visited property manually using the setVisited() method of the Hyperlink class.

The following snippet of code creates a Hyperlink control with the text "JDojo" and adds an ActionEvent handler for the Hyperlink. When the Hyperlink is activated, the www.jdojo.com web page is opened in a WebView, which is another JavaFX control to display a web page. I will discuss the WebView control in Chapter 16; here I will use it without any explanation:

```
Hyperlink jdojoLink = new Hyperlink("JDojo");
WebView webview = new WebView();
jdojoLink.setOnAction(e -> webview.getEngine().load("http://www.jdojo.com"));
```

The program in Listing 12-4 adds three Hyperlink controls to the top region of a BorderPane. A WebView control is added in the center region. When you click one of the hyperlinks, the corresponding web page is displayed.

Listing 12-4.   Using the Hyperlink Control

```
// HyperlinkTest.java
package com.jdojo.control;

import javafx.application.Application;
import javafx.geometry.Pos;
import javafx.scene.Scene;
import javafx.scene.control.Hyperlink;
import javafx.scene.layout.BorderPane;
import javafx.scene.layout.HBox;
import javafx.scene.web.WebView;
import javafx.stage.Stage;

public class HyperlinkTest extends Application {
        private WebView webview;

        public static void main(String[] args) {
                Application.launch(args);
        }
```

```
@Override
public void start(Stage stage) {
        // Must create a WebView object from the JavaFX Application Thread
        webview = new WebView();

        // Create some hyperlinks
        Hyperlink jdojoLink = new Hyperlink("JDojo");
        jdojoLink.setOnAction(e -> loadPage("http://www.jdojo.com"));

        Hyperlink yahooLink = new Hyperlink("Yahoo!");
        yahooLink.setOnAction(e -> loadPage("http://www.yahoo.com"));

        Hyperlink googleLink = new Hyperlink("Google");
        googleLink.setOnAction(e -> loadPage("http://www.google.com"));

        HBox linkBox = new HBox(jdojoLink, yahooLink, googleLink);
        linkBox.setSpacing(10);
        linkBox.setAlignment(Pos.TOP_RIGHT);

        BorderPane root = new BorderPane();
        root.setTop(linkBox);
        root.setCenter(webview);

        Scene scene = new Scene(root);
        stage.setScene(scene);
        stage.setTitle("Using Hyperlink Controls");
        stage.show();
}

public void loadPage(String url) {
        webview.getEngine().load(url);
}
}
```

Understanding the *MenuButton* Control

A MenuButton control looks like a button and behaves like a menu. When it is activated (by clicking or other means), it shows a list of options in the form of a pop-up menu. The list of options in the menu is maintained in an ObservableList<MenuItem> whose reference is returned by the getItems() method. To execute a command when a menu option is selected, you need to add the ActionEvent handler to the MenuItems.

The following snippet of code creates a MenuButton with two MenuItems. Each menu item has an ActionEvent hander attached to it. Figure 12-5 shows the MenuButton in two states: not showing and showing.

```
// Create two menu items with an ActionEvent handler.
// Assume that the loadPage() method exists
MenuItem jdojo = new MenuItem("JDojo");
jdojo.setOnAction(e -> loadPage("http://www.jdojo.com"));

MenuItem yahoo = new MenuItem("Yahoo");
yahoo.setOnAction(e -> loadPage("http://www.yahoo.com"));
```

449

```
// Create a MenuButton and the two menu items
MenuButton links = new MenuButton("Visit");
links.getItems().addAll(jdojo, yahoo);
```

Figure 12-5. *A MenuButton in not showing and showing states*

The MenuButton class declares two properties:

- popupSide
- showing

The popupSide property is of the ObjectProperty<Side> type and the showing property is of the ReadOnlyBooleanProperty type.

The popupSide property determines which side of the menu should be displayed. Its value is one of the constants in the Side enum: TOP, LEFT, BOTTOM, and RIGHT. The default value is Side.BOTTOM. An arrow in the MenuItem shows the direction set by the popupSide property. The arrow in Figure 12-5 is pointing downward, indicating that the popupSide property is set to Side.BOTTOM. The menu is opened in the direction set in the popupSide property only if space is available to display the menu in that side. If space is not available, the JavaFX runtime will make a smart decision as to which side the menu should be displayed. The value of the showing property is true when the pop-up menu is showing. Otherwise, it is false.

The program in Listing 12-5 creates an application using a MenuButton control that works similar to the one in Listing 12-4 that used Hyperlink control. Run the application, click the Visit MenuButton at the top right of the window, and select a page to open.

Listing 12-5. Using the MenuButton Control

```
// MenuButtonTest.java
package com.jdojo.control;

import javafx.application.Application;
import javafx.geometry.Pos;
import javafx.scene.Scene;
import javafx.scene.control.MenuButton;
import javafx.scene.control.MenuItem;
import javafx.scene.layout.BorderPane;
import javafx.scene.web.WebView;
import javafx.stage.Stage;

public class MenuButtonTest extends Application {
        private WebView webview;

        public static void main(String[] args) {
                Application.launch(args);
        }
```

```java
@Override
public void start(Stage stage) {
        // Must create a WebView object from the JavaFX Application Thread
        webview = new WebView();

        MenuItem jdojo = new MenuItem("JDojo");
        jdojo.setOnAction(e -> loadPage("http://www.jdojo.com"));

        MenuItem yahoo = new MenuItem("Yahoo");
        yahoo.setOnAction(e -> loadPage("http://www.yahoo.com"));

        MenuItem google = new MenuItem("Google");
        google.setOnAction(e -> loadPage("http://www.google.com"));

        // Add menu items to the MenuButton
        MenuButton links = new MenuButton("Visit");
        links.getItems().addAll(jdojo, yahoo, google);

        BorderPane root = new BorderPane();
        root.setTop(links);
        BorderPane.setAlignment(links, Pos.TOP_RIGHT);
        root.setCenter(webview);

        Scene scene = new Scene(root);
        stage.setScene(scene);
        stage.setTitle("Using MenuButton Controls");
        stage.show();
}

public void loadPage(String url) {
        webview.getEngine().load(url);
}
}
```

Understanding Choice Buttons

JavaFX provides several controls to make one or more selections from a list of available choices:

- ToggleButton
- CheckBox
- RadioButton

■ **Tip** JavaFX also provides ChoiceBox, ComboBox, and ListView controls to allow the user to make a selection from multiple available choice. I will discuss these controls in a separate section.

All three controls are labeled controls and they help you present multiple choices to the user in different formats. The number of available choices may vary from two to N, where N is a number greater than two.

Selection from the available choices may be mutually exclusive. That is, the user can only make one selection from the list of choices. If the user changes the selection, the previous selection is automatically deselected. For example, the list of gender selection with three choices, Male, Female, and Unknown, is mutually exclusive. The user must select only one of the three choices, not two or more of them. The ToggleButton and RadioButton controls are typically used in this case.

There is a special case of selection where the number of choices is two. In this case, the choices are of boolean type: true or false. Sometimes, it is also referred to as a *Yes/No* or *On/Off* choice. The ToggleButton and CheckBox controls are typically used in this case.

Sometimes the user can have multiple selections from a list of choices. For example, you may present the user with a list of hobbies to choose zero or more hobbies from the list. The ToggleButton and CheckBox controls are typically used in this case.

Understanding the *ToggleButton* Control

ToggleButton is a two-state button control. The two states are *selected* and *unselected*. Its selected property indicates whether it is selected. The selected property is true when it is in the selected state. Otherwise, it is false. When it is in the selected state, it stays depressed. You can toggle between the selected and unselected states by pressing it, and hence it got the name ToggleButton. For ToggleButtons, mnemonic parsing is enabled by default.

Figure 12-6 shows four toggle buttons with Spring, Summer, Fall, and Winter as their labels. Two of the toggle buttons, Spring and Fall, are selected and the other two are unselected.

Figure 12-6. *A window showing four toggle buttons*

You create a ToggleButton the same way you create a Button, using the following code:

```
ToggleButton springBtn = new ToggleButton("Spring");
```

A ToggleButton is used to select a choice, not to execute a command. Typically, you do not add ActionEvent handlers to a ToggleButton. Sometimes you can use a ToggleButton to start or stop an action. For that, you will need to add a ChangeListener for its selected property.

■ **Tip** The ActionEvent handler for a ToggleButton is invoked every time you click it. Notice that the first click selects a ToggleButton and the second click deselects it. If you select and deselect a ToggleButton, the ActionEvent handler will be called twice.

Toggle buttons may be used in a group from which zero or one ToggleButton can be selected. To add toggle buttons to a group, you need to add them to a ToggleGroup. The ToggleButton class contains a toggleGroup property. To add a ToggleButton to a ToggleGroup, set the toggleGroup property of the ToggleButton to the group. Setting the toggleGroup property to null removes a ToggleButton from the group. The following snippet of code creates four toggle buttons and adds them to a ToggleGroup:

```
ToggleButton springBtn = new ToggleButton("Spring");
ToggleButton summerBtn = new ToggleButton("Summer");
ToggleButton fallBtn = new ToggleButton("Fall");
ToggleButton winterBtn = new ToggleButton("Winter");

// Create a ToggleGroup
ToggleGroup group = new ToggleGroup();

// Add all ToggleButtons to the ToggleGroup
springBtn.setToggleGroup(group);
summerBtn.setToggleGroup(group);
fallBtn.setToggleGroup(group);
winterBtn.setToggleGroup(group);
```

Each ToggleGroup maintains an ObservableList<Toggle>. Note that Toggle is an interface that is implemented by the ToggleButton class. The getToggles() method of the ToggleGroup class returns the list of Toggles in the group. You can add a ToggleButton to a group by adding it to the list returned by the getToggles() method. The above snippet of code may be rewritten as follows:

```
ToggleButton springBtn = new ToggleButton("Spring");
ToggleButton summerBtn = new ToggleButton("Summer");
ToggleButton fallBtn = new ToggleButton("Fall");
ToggleButton winterBtn = new ToggleButton("Winter");

// Create a ToggleGroup
ToggleGroup group = new ToggleGroup();

// Add all ToggleButtons to the ToggleGroup
group.getToggles().addAll(springBtn, summerBtn, fallBtn, winterBtn);
```

The ToggleGroup class contains a selectedToggle property that keeps track of the selected Toggle in the group. The getSelectedToggle() method returns the reference of the Toggle that is selected. If no Toggle is selected in the group, it returns null. Add a ChangeListener to this property if you are interested in tracking the change in selection inside a ToggleGroup.

■ **Tip**   You can select zero or one ToggleButton in a ToggleGroup. Selecting a ToggleButton in a group deselects the already selected ToggleButton. Clicking an already selected ToggleButton in a group deselects it, leaving no ToggleButton in the group selected.

The program in Listing 12-6 adds four toggle buttons to a ToggleGroup. You can select none or at the most one ToggleButton from the group. Figure 12-7 shows two screenshots: one when there is no selection and one when the ToggleButton with the label Summer is selected. The program adds a ChangeListener to the group to track the change in selection and displays the label of the selected ToggleButton in a Label control.

453

Figure 12-7. *Four toggle buttons in a ToggleGroup allowing selection of one button at a time*

Listing 12-6. Using Toggle Buttons in a ToggleGroup and Tracking the Selection

```java
// ToggleButtonTest.java
package com.jdojo.control;

import javafx.application.Application;
import javafx.beans.value.ObservableValue;
import javafx.scene.Scene;
import javafx.scene.control.Label;
import javafx.scene.control.Labeled;
import javafx.scene.control.Toggle;
import javafx.scene.control.ToggleButton;
import javafx.scene.control.ToggleGroup;
import javafx.scene.layout.HBox;
import javafx.scene.layout.VBox;
import javafx.stage.Stage;

public class ToggleButtonTest extends Application {
        Label userSelectionMsg = new Label("Your selection: None");

        public static void main(String[] args) {
                Application.launch(args);
        }

        @Override
        public void start(Stage stage) {
                // Create four ToggleButtons
                ToggleButton springBtn = new ToggleButton("Spring");
                ToggleButton summerBtn = new ToggleButton("Summer");
                ToggleButton fallBtn = new ToggleButton("Fall");
                ToggleButton winterBtn = new ToggleButton("Winter");

                // Add all ToggleButtons to a ToggleGroup
                ToggleGroup group = new ToggleGroup();
                group.getToggles().addAll(springBtn, summerBtn, fallBtn, winterBtn);

                // Track the selection changes and display the currently selected season
                group.selectedToggleProperty().addListener(this::changed);

                Label msg = new Label("Select the season you like:");
```

```
                // Add ToggleButtons to an HBox
                HBox buttonBox = new HBox(springBtn, summerBtn, fallBtn, winterBtn);
                buttonBox.setSpacing(10);

                VBox root = new VBox(userSelectionMsg, msg, buttonBox);
                root.setSpacing(10);
                root.setStyle("-fx-padding: 10;" +
                              "-fx-border-style: solid inside;" +
                              "-fx-border-width: 2;" +
                              "-fx-border-insets: 5;" +
                              "-fx-border-radius: 5;" +
                              "-fx-border-color: blue;");

                Scene scene = new Scene(root);
                stage.setScene(scene);
                stage.setTitle("Using ToggleButtons in a Group");
                stage.show();
        }

        // A change listener to track the selection in the group
        public void changed(ObservableValue<? extends Toggle> observable,
                            Toggle oldBtn,
                            Toggle newBtn) {
                String selectedLabel = "None";
                if (newBtn != null ) {
                        selectedLabel = ((Labeled)newBtn).getText();
                }

                userSelectionMsg.setText("Your selection: " + selectedLabel);
        }
}
```

Understanding the *RadioButton* Control

An instance of the RadioButton class represents a radio button. It inherits from the ToggleButton class. Therefore, it has all of the features of a toggle button. A radio button is rendered differently compared to a toggle button. Like a toggle button, a radio button can be in one of the two states: *selected* and *unselected*. Its selected property indicates its current state. Like a toggle button, its mnemonic parsing is enabled by default. Like a toggle button, it also sends an ActionEvent when it is selected and unselected. Figure 12-8 shows a RadioButton with Summer as its text in selected and unselected states.

In unselected State   In selected State

Figure 12-8. *Showing a radio button in selected and unselected states*

There is a significant difference in the use of radio buttons compared to the use of toggle buttons. Recall that when toggle buttons are used in a group, there may not be any selected toggle button in the group. When radio buttons are used in a group, there must be one selected radio button in the group. Unlike a toggle button, clicking a selected radio button in a group does not unselect it. To enforce the rule that one radio button must be selected in a group of radio buttons, one radio button from the group is selected programmatically by default.

■ **Tip**   Radio buttons are used when the user must make a selection from a list of choices. Toggle buttons are used when the user has an option to make one selection or no selection from a list of choices.

The program in Listing 12-7 shows how to use radio buttons inside a ToggleGroup. Figure 12-9 shows the window with the results of running the code. The program is very similar to the previous program that used toggle buttons. With the following code, Summer is set as the default selection:

```
// Select the default season as Summer
summerBtn.setSelected(true);
```

You set the default season in the radio button after you have added the change listener to the group, so the message to display the selected season is updated correctly.

Listing 12-7. Using Radio Buttons in a ToggleGroup and Tracking the Selection

```
// RadioButtonTest.java
package com.jdojo.control;

import javafx.application.Application;
import javafx.beans.value.ObservableValue;
import javafx.scene.Scene;
import javafx.scene.control.Label;
import javafx.scene.control.Labeled;
import javafx.scene.control.Toggle;
import javafx.scene.control.RadioButton;
import javafx.scene.control.ToggleGroup;
import javafx.scene.layout.HBox;
import javafx.scene.layout.VBox;
import javafx.stage.Stage;

public class RadioButtonTest extends Application {
        Label userSelectionMsg = new Label("Your selection: None");

        public static void main(String[] args) {
                Application.launch(args);
        }

        @Override
        public void start(Stage stage) {
                // Create four RadioButtons
                RadioButton springBtn = new RadioButton("Spring");
                RadioButton summerBtn = new RadioButton("Summer");
```

```java
        RadioButton fallBtn = new RadioButton("Fall");
        RadioButton winterBtn = new RadioButton("Winter");

        // Add all RadioButtons to a ToggleGroup
        ToggleGroup group = new ToggleGroup();
        group.getToggles().addAll(springBtn, summerBtn, fallBtn, winterBtn);

        // Track the selection changes and display the currently selected season
        group.selectedToggleProperty().addListener(this::changed);

        // Select the default season as Summer
        summerBtn.setSelected(true);

        Label msg = new Label("Select the season you like the most:");

        // Add RadioButtons to an HBox
        HBox buttonBox = new HBox(springBtn, summerBtn, fallBtn, winterBtn);
        buttonBox.setSpacing(10);

        VBox root = new VBox(userSelectionMsg, msg, buttonBox);
        root.setSpacing(10);
        root.setStyle("-fx-padding: 10;" +
                     "-fx-border-style: solid inside;" +
                     "-fx-border-width: 2;" +
                     "-fx-border-insets: 5;" +
                     "-fx-border-radius: 5;" +
                     "-fx-border-color: blue;");

        Scene scene = new Scene(root);
        stage.setScene(scene);
        stage.setTitle("Using RadioButtons in a Group");
        stage.show();
    }

    // A change listener to track the selection in the group
    public void changed(ObservableValue<? extends Toggle> observable,
                    Toggle oldBtn,
                    Toggle newBtn) {
        String selectedLabel = "None";
        if (newBtn != null ) {
            selectedLabel = ((Labeled)newBtn).getText();
        }
        userSelectionMsg.setText("Your selection: " + selectedLabel);
    }
}
```

Figure 12-9. *Four radio buttons in a* `ToggleGroup`

Understanding the *CheckBox* Control

CheckBox is a three-state selection control: *checked, unchecked,* and *undefined.* The undefined state is also known as an *indeterminate* state. A CheckBox supports a selection of three choices: true/false/unknown or yes/no/unknown. Usually, a CheckBox has text as a label, but not a graphic (even though it can). Clicking a CheckBox transitions it from one state to another cycling through three states.

A box is drawn for a CheckBox. In the unchecked state, the box is empty. A tick mark (or a check mark) is present in the box when it is in the checked state. In the undefined state, a horizontal line is present in the box. Figure 12-10 shows a CheckBox labeled Hungry in its three states.

Figure 12-10. *Showing a check box in unchecked, checked, and undefined states*

By default, the CheckBox control supports only two states: *checked* and *unchecked.* The `allowIndeterminate` property specifies whether the third state (the undefined state) is available for selection. By default, it is set to false:

```
// Create a CheckBox that supports checked and unchecked states only
CheckBox hungryCbx = new CheckBox("Hungry");

// Create a CheckBox and configure it to support three states
CheckBox agreeCbx = new CheckBox("Hungry");
agreeCbx.setAllowIndeterminate(true);
```

The CheckBox class contains `selected` and `indeterminate` properties to track its three states. If the indeterminate property is true, it is in the undefined state. If the indeterminate property is false, it is defined and it could be in a checked or unchecked state. If the indeterminate property is false and the selected property is true, it is in a checked state. If the indeterminate property is false and the selected property is false, it is in an unchecked state. Table 12-3 summarizes the rules for determining the state of a check box.

Table 12-3. *Determining the State of a Check Box Based on Its Indeterminate and Selected Properties*

indeterminate	selected	State
false	true	Checked
false	false	Unchecked
true	true/false	Undefined

Sometimes you may want to detect the state transition in a check box. Because a check box maintains the state information in two properties, you will need to add a ChangeListener to both properties. An ActionEvent is fired when a check box is clicked. You can also use an ActionEvent to detect a state change in a check box. The following snippet of code shows how to use two ChangeListeners to detect a state change in a CheckBox. It is assumed that the changed() method and the rest of the code are part of the same class:

```
// Create a CheckBox to support three states
CheckBox agreeCbx = new CheckBox("I agree");
agreeCbx.setAllowIndeterminate(true);

// Add a ChangeListener to the selected and indeterminate properties
agreeCbx.selectedProperty().addListener(this::changed);
agreeCbx.indeterminateProperty().addListener(this::changed);
...
// A change listener to track the selection in the group
public void changed(ObservableValue<? extends Boolean> observable,
                    Boolean oldValue,
                    Boolean newValue) {
    String state = null;
    if (agreeCbx.isIndeterminate()) {
            state = "Undefined";
    } else if (agreeCbx.isSelected()) {
            state = "Checked";
    } else {
            state = "Unchecked";
    }
    System.out.println(state);
}
```

The program in Listing 12-8 shows how to use CheckBox controls. Figure 12-11 shows the window that results from running this code. The program creates two CheckBox controls. The Hungry CheckBox supports only two states. The I agree CheckBox is configured to support three states. When you change the state for the I agree CheckBox by clicking it, the Label at the top displays the description of the state.

Listing 12-8. Using the CheckBox Control

```java
// CheckBoxTest.java
package com.jdojo.control;

import javafx.application.Application;
import javafx.beans.value.ObservableValue;
import javafx.scene.Scene;
import javafx.scene.control.Label;
import javafx.scene.control.CheckBox;
import javafx.scene.layout.VBox;
import javafx.stage.Stage;

public class CheckBoxTest extends Application {
        Label userSelectionMsg = new Label("Do you agree? No");
        CheckBox agreeCbx;

        public static void main(String[] args) {
                Application.launch(args);
        }

        @Override
        public void start(Stage stage) {
                // Create a CheckBox to support only two states
                CheckBox hungryCbx = new CheckBox("Hungry");

                // Create a CheckBox to support three states
                agreeCbx = new CheckBox("I agree");
                agreeCbx.setAllowIndeterminate(true);

                // Track the state change for the "I agree" CheckBox
                // Text for the Label userSelectionMsg will be updated
                agreeCbx.selectedProperty().addListener(this::changed);
                agreeCbx.indeterminateProperty().addListener(this::changed);

                VBox root = new VBox(userSelectionMsg, hungryCbx, agreeCbx);
                root.setSpacing(20);
                root.setStyle("-fx-padding: 10;" +
                                "-fx-border-style: solid inside;" +
                                "-fx-border-width: 2;" +
                                "-fx-border-insets: 5;" +
                                "-fx-border-radius: 5;" +
                                "-fx-border-color: blue;");

                Scene scene = new Scene(root, 200, 130);
                stage.setScene(scene);
                stage.setTitle("Using CheckBoxes");
                stage.show();
        }
```

```
        // A change listener to track the state change in agreeCbx
        public void changed(ObservableValue<? extends Boolean> observable,
                            Boolean oldValue,
                            Boolean newValue) {
            String msg;
            if (agreeCbx.isIndeterminate()) {
                msg = "Not sure";
            } else if (agreeCbx.isSelected()) {
                msg = "Yes";
            } else {
                    msg = "No";
            }
            this.userSelectionMsg.setText("Do you agree? " + msg);
        }
}
```

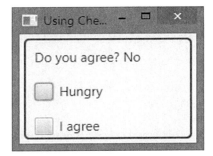

Figure 12-11. *Two check boxes: one uses two states and one uses three states*

The default CSS style-class name for a CheckBox is check-box. The CheckBox class supports three CSS pseudo-classes: selected, determinate, and indeterminate. The selected pseudo-class applies when the selected property is true. The determinate pseudo-class applies when the indeterminate property is false. The indeterminate pseudo-class applies when the indeterminate property is true.

The CheckBox control contains two substructures: box and mark. You can style them to change their appearance. You can change the background color and border for the box and you can change the color and shape of the tick mark. Both box and mark are an instance of StackPane. The tick mark is shown giving a shape to the StackPane. You can change the shape for the mark by supplying a different shape in a CSS. By changing the background color of the mark, you change the color of the tick mark. The following CSS will show the box in tan and tick mark in red:

```
.check-box .box {
        -fx-background-color: tan;
}

.check-box:selected .mark {
    -fx-background-color: red;
}
```

Understanding the Hybrid *Button* Control

With our definitions of different button types, a SplitMenuButton falls under the hybrid category. It combines the features of a pop-up menu and a command button. It lets you select an action like a MenuButton control and execute a command like a Button control. The SplitMenuButton class inherits from the MenuButton class.

A SplitMenuButton is divided into two areas: the action area and the menu-open area. When you click in the action area, ActionEvent is fired. The registered ActionEvent handlers execute the command. When the menu-open area is clicked, a menu is shown from which the user will select an action to execute. Mnemonic parsing for SplitMenuButton is enabled by default.

Figure 12-12 shows a SplitMenuButton in two states. The picture on the left shows it in the collapsed state. In the picture on the right, it shows the menu items. Notice the vertical line dividing the control in two halves. The half containing the text Home is the action area. The other half containing the down arrow is the menu-open area.

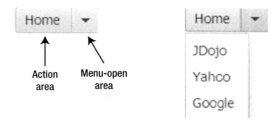

Figure 12-12. *A SplitMenuButton in the collapsed and showing states*

You can create a SplitMenuButton with menu items or without them using its constructors with the following code:

```
// Create an empty SplitMenuItem
SplitMenuButton splitBtn = new SplitMenuButton();
splitBtn.setText("Home"); // Set the text as "Home"

// Create MenuItems
MenuItem jdojo = new MenuItem("JDojo");
MenuItem yahoo = new MenuItem("Yahoo");
MenuItem google = new MenuItem("Google");

// Add menu items to the MenuButton
splitBtn.getItems().addAll(jdojo, yahoo, google);
```

You need to add an ActionEvent handler to execute an action when the SplitMenuButton is clicked in the action area:

```
// Add ActionEvent handler when "Home" is clicked
splitBtn.setOnAction(e -> /* Take some action here */);
```

The program in Listing 12-9 shows how to use a SplitMenuButton. It adds a SplitMenuButton with the text Home and three menu items in the top right region of a BorderPane. A WebView is added in the center region. When you click Home, the www.jdojo.com web page is opened. When you select a web site using the menu by clicking the down arrow, the corresponding web site is opened. The program is very similar to the ones you developed earlier using MenuButton and Hyperlink controls.

Listing 12-9. Using the SplitMenuButton Control

```java
// SplitMenuButtonTest.java
package com.jdojo.control;

import javafx.application.Application;
import javafx.geometry.Pos;
import javafx.scene.Scene;
import javafx.scene.control.MenuItem;
import javafx.scene.control.SplitMenuButton;
import javafx.scene.layout.BorderPane;
import javafx.scene.web.WebView;
import javafx.stage.Stage;

public class SplitMenuButtonTest extends Application {
        private WebView webview;

        public static void main(String[] args) {
                Application.launch(args);
        }

        @Override
        public void start(Stage stage) {
                // Must create a WebView object from the JavaFX Application Thread
                webview = new WebView();

                MenuItem jdojo = new MenuItem("JDojo");
                jdojo.setOnAction(e -> loadPage("http://www.jdojo.com"));

                MenuItem yahoo = new MenuItem("Yahoo");
                yahoo.setOnAction(e -> loadPage("http://www.yahoo.com"));

                MenuItem google = new MenuItem("Google");
                google.setOnAction(e -> loadPage("http://www.google.com"));

                // Create a SplitMenuButton
                SplitMenuButton splitBtn = new SplitMenuButton();
                splitBtn.setText("Home");

                // Add menu items to the SplitMenuButton
                splitBtn.getItems().addAll(jdojo, yahoo, google);

                // Add ActionEvent handler when "Home" is clicked
                splitBtn.setOnAction(e -> loadPage("http://www.jdojo.com"));

                BorderPane root = new BorderPane();
                root.setTop(splitBtn);
                BorderPane.setAlignment(splitBtn, Pos.TOP_RIGHT);
                root.setCenter(webview);
```

```
            Scene scene = new Scene(root);
            stage.setScene(scene);
            stage.setTitle("Using SplitMenuButton Controls");
            stage.show();
    }

    public void loadPage(String url) {
            webview.getEngine().load(url);
    }
}
```

Making Selections from a List of Items

In the previous sections, you have seen how to present users with a list of items, for example, using toggle buttons and radio buttons. Toggle and radio buttons are easier to use because all options are always visible to the users. However, they use a lot of space on the screen. Think about using radio buttons to show the names of all 50 states in the United States to the user. It would take a lot of space. Sometimes none of the available items in the list is suitable for selection, so you will want to give users a chance to enter a new item that is not in the list.

JavaFX provides some controls that let users select an item(s) from a list of items. They take less space compared to buttons. They provide advanced features to customize their appearance and behaviors. I will discuss the following such controls in subsequent sections:

- ChoiceBox

- ComboBox

- ListView

- ColorPicker

- DatePicker

ChoiceBox lets users select an item from a small list of predefined items. ComboBox is an advanced version of ChoiceBox. It has many features, for example, the ability to be editable or change the appearance of the items in the list, which are not offered in ChoiceBox. ListView provides users an ability to select multiple items from a list of items. Typically, all or more than one item in a ListView is visible to the user all the time. ColorPicker lets users select a color from a standard color palette or define a custom color graphically. DatePicker lets users select a date from a calendar pop-up. Optionally, users can enter a date as text. ComboBox, ColorPicker, and DatePicker have the same superclass ComboBoxBase.

Understanding the *ChoiceBox* Control

ChoiceBox is used to let a user select an item from a small list of items. The items may be any type of objects. ChoiceBox is a parameterized class. The parameter type is the type of the items in its list. If you want to store mixed types of items in a ChoiceBox, you can use its raw type, as shown in the following code:

```
// Create a ChoiceBox for any type of items
ChoiceBox seasons = new ChoiceBox();

// Create a ChoiceBox for String items
ChoiceBox<String> seasons = new ChoiceBox<String>();
```

You can specify the list items while creating a ChoiceBox with the following code:

```
ObservableList<String> seasonList = FXCollections.<String>observableArrayList(
                                "Spring", "Summer", "Fall", "Winter");
ChoiceBox<String> seasons = new ChoiceBox<>(seasonList);
```

After you create a ChoiceBox, you can add items to its list of items using the items property, which is of the ObjectProperty<ObservableList<T>> type in which T is the type parameter for the ChoiceBox. The following code will accomplish this:

```
ChoiceBox<String> seasons = new ChoiceBox<>();
seasons.getItems().addAll("Spring", "Summer", "Fall", "Winter");
```

Figure 12-13 shows a choice box in four different states. It has four names of seasons in the list of items. The first picture (labeled #1) shows it in its initial state when there is no selection. The user can open the list of items using the mouse or the keyboard. Clicking anywhere inside the control opens the list of items in a pop-up window, as shown in the picture labeled #2. Pressing the down arrow key when the control has focus also opens the list of items. You can select an item from the list by clicking it or using the up/down arrow and the Enter key. When you select an item, the pop-up window showing the items list is collapsed and the selected item is shown in the control, as shown in the picture labeled #3. The picture labeled #4 shows the control when an item is selected (Spring in this case) and the list items are shown. The pop-up window displays a check mark with the item already selected in the control. Table 12-4 lists the properties declared in the ChoiceBox class.

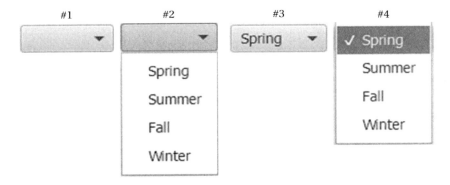

Figure 12-13. *A choice box in different states*

Table 12-4. *Properties Declared in the ChoiceBox Class*

Property	Type	Description
converter	ObjectProperty <StringConverter<T>>	It serves as a converter object whose toString() method is called to get the string representation of the items in the list.
items	ObjectProperty <ObservableList<T>>	It is the list of choices to display in the ChoiceBox.
selectionModel	ObjectProperty <SingleSelectionModel<T>>	It serves as a selection model that keeps track of the selections in a ChoiceBox.
showing	ReadOnlyBooleanProperty	Its true value indicates that the control is showing the list of choices to the user. Its false value indicates that the list of choices is collapsed.
value	ObjectProperty<T>	It is the selected item in the ChoiceBox.

■ **Tip**   You are not limited to showing the items list using the mouse or keyboard. You can show and hide the list programmatically using the show() and hide() methods, respectively.

The value property of the ChoiceBox stores the selected item in the control. Its type is ObjectProperty<T>, where T is the type parameter for the control. If the user has not selected an item, its value is null. The following snippet of code sets the value property:

```
// Create a ChoiceBox for String items
ChoiceBox<String> seasons = new ChoiceBox<String>();
seasons.getItems().addAll("Spring", "Summer", "Fall", "Winter");

// Get the selected value
String selectedValue = seasons.getValue();

// Set a new value
seasons.setValue("Fall");
```

When you set a new value using the setValue() method, the ChoiceBox selects the specified value in the control if the value exists in the list of items. It is possible to set a value that does not exist in the list of items. In that case, the value property contains the newly set item, but the control does not show it. The control keeps showing the previously selected item, if any. When the new item is later added to the list of items, the control shows the item set in the value property.

The ChoiceBox needs to track the selected item and its index in the list of items. It uses a separate object, called the *selection model*, for this purpose. The ChoiceBox class contains a selectionModel property to store the item selection details. ChoiceBox uses an object of the SingleSelectionModel class as its selection model, but you can use your own selection model. The default selection model works in almost all cases. The selection model provides you selection-related functionality:

- It lets you select an item using the index of the item in the list.

- It lets you select the first, next, previous, or last item in the list.

- It lets you clear the selection.

- Its selectedIndex and selectedItem properties track the index and value of the selected item. You can add a ChangeListener to these properties to handle a change in selection in a ChoiceBox. When no item is selected, the selected index is -1 and the selected item is null.

The following snippet of code forces a value in a ChoiceBox by selecting the first item in the list by default:

```
ChoiceBox<String> seasons = new ChoiceBox<>();
seasons.getItems().addAll("Spring", "Summer", "Fall", "Winter", "Fall");

// Select the first item in the list
seasons.getSelectionModel().selectFirst();
```

Use the selectNext() method of the selection model to select the next item from the list. Calling the selectNext() method when the last item is already selected has no effect. Use the selectPrevious() and selectLast() methods to select the previous and the last item in the list, respectively. The select(int index) and select(T item) methods select an item using the index and value of the item, respectively. Note that you can also use the setValue() method of the ChoiceBox to select an item from the list by its value. The clearSelection() method of the selection model clears the current selection, returning the ChoiceBox to a state as if no item had been selected.

The program in Listing 12-10 displays a window as shown in Figure 12-14. It uses a ChoiceBox with a list of four seasons. By default, the program selects the first season from the list. The application forces the user to select one season name by selecting one by default. It adds ChangeListeners to the selectedIndex and selectedItem properties of the selection model. They print the details of the selection change on the standard output. The current selection is shown in a Label control whose text property is bound to the value property of the ChoiceBox. Select a different item from the list and watch the standard output and the window for the details.

Listing 12-10. Using ChoiceBox with a Preselected Item

```
// ChoiceBoxTest.java
package com.jdojo.control;

import javafx.application.Application;
import javafx.beans.value.ObservableValue;
import javafx.scene.Scene;
import javafx.scene.control.ChoiceBox;
import javafx.scene.control.Label;
import javafx.scene.layout.GridPane;
import javafx.stage.Stage;

public class ChoiceBoxTest extends Application {
        public static void main(String[] args) {
                Application.launch(args);
        }
```

```java
@Override
public void start(Stage stage) {
        Label seasonLbl = new Label("Select a Season:");
        ChoiceBox<String> seasons = new ChoiceBox<>();
        seasons.getItems().addAll("Spring", "Summer", "Fall", "Winter");

        // Select the first season from the list
        seasons.getSelectionModel().selectFirst();

        // Add ChangeListeners to track change in selected index and item. Only
        // one listener is necessary if you want to track change in selection
        seasons.getSelectionModel().selectedItemProperty()
                                .addListener(this::itemChanged);
        seasons.getSelectionModel().selectedIndexProperty()
                                .addListener(this::indexChanged);

        Label selectionMsgLbl = new Label("Your selection:");
        Label selectedValueLbl = new Label("None");

        // Bind the value property to the text property of the Label
        selectedValueLbl.textProperty().bind(seasons.valueProperty());

        // Display controls in a GridPane
        GridPane root = new GridPane();
        root.setVgap(10);
        root.setHgap(10);
        root.addRow(0, seasonLbl, seasons);
        root.addRow(1, selectionMsgLbl, selectedValueLbl);
        root.setStyle("-fx-padding: 10;" +
                        "-fx-border-style: solid inside;" +
                        "-fx-border-width: 2;" +
                        "-fx-border-insets: 5;" +
                        "-fx-border-radius: 5;" +
                        "-fx-border-color: blue;");

        Scene scene = new Scene(root);
        stage.setScene(scene);
        stage.setTitle("Using ChoiceBox Controls");
        stage.show();
}

// A change listener to track the change in selected item
public void itemChanged(ObservableValue<? extends String> observable,
                        String oldValue,
                        String newValue) {
        System.out.println("Itemchanged: old = " + oldValue + ",
                        new = " + newValue);
}
```

```
        // A change listener to track the change in selected index
        public void indexChanged(ObservableValue<? extends Number> observable,
                                 Number oldValue,
                                 Number newValue) {
            System.out.println("Indexchanged: old = " + oldValue + ", new = " + newValue);
        }
}
```

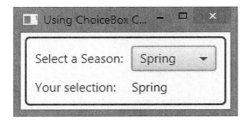

Figure 12-14. *A choice box with a preselected item*

Using Domain Objects in *ChoiceBox*

In the previous example, you used String objects as items in the choice box. You can use any object type as items. ChoiceBox calls the toString() method of every item and displays the returned value in the pop-up list. The following snippet of code creates a choice box and adds four Person objects as its items. Figure 12-15 shows the choice box in the showing state. Notice the items are displayed using the String object returned from toString() method of the Person class.

```
import com.jdojo.mvc.model.Person;
import javafx.scene.control.ChoiceBox;
...
ChoiceBox<Person> persons = new ChoiceBox<>();
persons.getItems().addAll(new Person("John", "Jacobs", null),
                          new Person("Donna", "Duncan", null),
                          new Person("Layne", "Estes", null),
                          new Person("Mason", "Boyd", null));
```

```
[personId=1, firstName=John, lastName=Jacobs, birthDate=null]
[personId=2, firstName=Donna, lastName=Duncan, birthDate=null]
[personId=3, firstName=Layne, lastName=Estes, birthDate=null]
[personId=4, firstName=Mason, lastName=Boyd, birthDate=null]
```

Figure 12-15. *A choice box showing four Person objects as its list of items*

Typically, the toString() method of an object returns a String that represents the state of the object. It is not meant to provide a customized string representation of the object to be displayed in a choice box. The ChoiceBox class contains a converter property. It is an ObjectProperty of the StringConverter<T> type. A StringConverter<T> object acts as a converter from the object type T to a string and vice versa. The class is declared abstract, as in the following snippet of code:

```java
public abstract class StringConverter<T> {
        public abstract String toString(T object);
        public abstract T fromString(String string);
}
```

The toString(T object) method converts the object of type T to a string. The fromString(String string) method converts a string to a T object.

By default, the converter property in a choice box is null. If it is set, the toString(T object) method of the converter is called to get the list of items instead of the toString() method of the class of the item. The PersonStringConverter class shown in Listing 12-11 can act as a converter in a choice box. Notice that you are treating the argument string in the fromString() method as the name of a person and trying to construct a Person object from it. You do not need to implement the fromString() method for a choice box. It will be used in a ComboBox, which I will discuss next. The ChoiceBox will use only the toString(Person p) method.

Listing 12-11. A Person to String Converter

```java
// PersonStringConverter.java
package com.jdojo.control;

import com.jdojo.mvc.model.Person;
import javafx.util.StringConverter;

public class PersonStringConverter extends StringConverter<Person> {
        @Override
        public String toString(Person p) {
                return p == null? null : p.getLastName() + ", " + p.getFirstName();
        }

        @Override
        public Person fromString(String string) {
                Person p = null;
                if (string == null) {
                        return p;
                }

                int commaIndex = string.indexOf(",");
                if (commaIndex == -1) {
                        // Treat the string as first name
                        p = new Person(string, null, null);
                } else {
```

```
                    // Ignoring string bounds check for brevity
                    String firstName = string.substring(commaIndex + 2);
                    String lastName = string.substring(0, commaIndex);
                    p = new Person(firstName, lastName, null);
            }

            return p;
        }
}
```

The following snippet of code uses a converter in a ChoiceBox to convert Person objects in its list of items to strings. Figure 12-16 shows the choice box in the showing state.

```
import com.jdojo.mvc.model.Person;
import javafx.scene.control.ChoiceBox;
...
ChoiceBox<Person> persons = new ChoiceBox<>();

// Set a converter to convert a Person object to a String object
persons.setConverter(new PersonStringConverter());

// Add five person objects to the ChoiceBox
persons.getItems().addAll(new Person("John", "Jacobs", null),
                          new Person("Donna", "Duncan", null),
                          new Person("Layne", "Estes", null),
                          new Person("Mason", "Boyd", null));
```

Figure 12-16. *Person objects using a converter in a choice box*

Allowing Nulls in *ChoiceBox*

Sometimes a choice box may allow the user to select null as a valid choice. This can be achieved by using null as an item in the list of choices, as shown in the following code:

```
ChoiceBox<String> seasons = new ChoiceBox<>();
seasons.getItems().addAll(null, "Spring", "Summer", "Fall", "Winter");
```

The above snippet of code produces a choice box as shown in Figure 12-17. Notice that the null item is shown as an empty space.

Figure 12-17. *Null as a choice in a choice box*

It is often required that the null choice be shown as a custom string, for example, "[None]". This can be accomplished using a converter. In the previous section, you used a converter to customize the choices for Person objects. Here you will use the converter to customize the choice item for null. You can do both in one converter as well. The following snippet of code uses a converter with a ChoiceBox to convert a null choice as "[None]". Figure 12-18 shows the resulting choice box.

```
ChoiceBox<String> seasons = new ChoiceBox<>();
seasons.getItems().addAll(null, "Spring", "Summer", "Fall", "Winter");

// Use a converter to convert null to "[None]"
seasons.setConverter(new StringConverter<String>() {
        @Override
        public String toString(String string) {
                return (string == null) ? "[None]" : string;
        }

        @Override
        public String fromString(String string) {
                return string;
        }
});
```

Figure 12-18. *A null choice in a choice box converted as* `"[None]"`

Using Separators in *ChoiceBox*

Sometimes you may want to separate choices into separate groups. Suppose you want to show fruits and cooked items in a breakfast menu, and you want to separate one from the other. You would use an instance of the Separator class to achieve this. It appears as a horizontal line in the list of choices. A Separator is not selectable. The following snippet of code creates a choice box with one of its items as a Separator. Figure 12-19 shows the choice box in the showing state.

```
ChoiceBox breakfasts = new ChoiceBox();
breakfasts.getItems().addAll("Apple", "Banana", "Strawberry",
                        new Separator(),
                        "Apple Pie", "Donut", "Hash Brown");
```

Figure 12-19. *A choice box using a separator*

Styling a *ChoiceBox* with CSS

The default CSS style-class name for a ChoiceBox is choice-box. The ChoiceBox class supports a showing CSS pseudo-class, which applies when the showing property is true.

The ChoiceBox control contains two substructures: open-button and arrow. You can style them to change their appearance. Both are instances of StackPane. ChoiceBox shows the selected item in a Label. The list of choices are shown in a ContextMenu whose ID is set to choice-box-popup-menu. Each choice is displayed in a menu item whose IDs are set to choice-box-menu-item. The following styles customize the ChoiceBox control. Currently, there is no way to customize the pop-up menu for an individual choice box. The style will affect all instances of ChoiceBox control at the level (scene or layout pane) at which it is set.

```
/* Set the text color and font size for the selected item in the control */
.choice-box .label {
        -fx-text-fill: blue;
        -fx-font-size: 8pt;
}

/* Set the text color and text font size for choices in the popup list */
#choice-box-menu-item * {
        -fx-text-fill: blue;
        -fx-font-size: 8pt;
}

/* Set background color of the arrow */
.choice-box .arrow {
        -fx-background-color: blue;
}

/* Set the background color for the open-button area */
.choice-box .open-button {
    -fx-background-color: yellow;
}

/* Change the background color of the popup */
#choice-box-popup-menu {
        -fx-background-color: yellow;
}
```

■ **Tip** There is a bug in applying the styles to the ChoiceBox pop-up. Styles are not effective until the pop-up is opened twice.

Understanding the *ComboBox* Control

ComboBox is used to let a user select an item from a list of items. You can think of ComboBox as an advanced version of ChoiceBox. ComboBox is highly customizable. The ComboBox class inherits from ComboBoxBase class, which provides the common functionality for all ComboBox-like controls, such as ComboBox, ColorPicker, and DatePicker. If you want to create a custom control that will allow users to select an item from a pop-up list, you need to inherit your control from the ComboBoxBase class.

The items list in a ComboBox may comprise any type of objects. ComboBox is a parameterized class. The parameter type is the type of the items in the list. If you want to store mixed types of items in a ComboBox, you can use its raw type, as in the following code:

```
// Create a ComboBox for any type of items
ComboBox seasons = new ComboBox();

// Create a ComboBox for String items
ComboBox<String> seasons = new ComboBox<String>();
```

You can specify the list items while creating a ComboBox, as in the following code:

```
ObservableList<String> seasonList = FXCollections.<String>observableArrayList(
                                    "Spring", "Summer", "Fall", "Winter");
ComboBox<String> seasons = new ComboBox<>(seasonList);
```

After you create a combo box, you can add items to its list of items using the items property, which is of the ObjectProperty<ObservableList<T>> type, in which T is the type parameter for the combo box, as in the following code:

```
ComboBox<String> seasons = new ComboBox<>();
seasons.getItems().addAll("Spring", "Summer", "Fall", "Winter");
```

Like ChoiceBox, ComboBox needs to track the selected item and its index in the list of items. It uses a separate object, called *selection model*, for this purpose. The ComboBox class contains a selectionModel property to store the item selection details. ComboBox uses an object of the SingleSelectionModel class as its selection model. The selection model lets you select an item from the list of items and lets you add ChangeListeners to track changes in index and item selections. Please refer to the section "Understanding the *ChoiceBox* Control" for more details on using a selection model.

Unlike ChoiceBox, ComboBox can be editable. Its editable property specifies whether or not it is editable. By default, it is not editable. When it is editable, it uses a TextField control to show the selected or entered item. The editor property of the ComboBox class stores the reference of the TextField and it is null if the combo box is not editable, as shown in the following code:

```
ComboBox<String> breakfasts = new ComboBox<>();

// Add some items to choose from
breakfasts.getItems().addAll("Apple", "Banana", "Strawberry");

// By making the control editable, let users enter an item
breakfasts.setEditable(true);
```

ComboBox has a value property that stores the currently selected or entered value. Note that when a user enters a value in an editable combo box, the entered string is converted to the item type T of the combo box. If the item type is not a string, a StringConverter<T> is needed to convert the String value to type T. I will present an example of this shortly.

You can set a prompt text for a combo box that is displayed when the control is editable, it does not have focus, and its value property is null. The prompt text is stored in the promptText property, which is of the StringProperty type, as in the following code:

```
breakfasts.setPromptText("Select/Enter an item"); // Set a prompt text
```

The ComboBox class contains a placeholder property, which stores a Node reference. When the items list is empty or null, the placeholder node is shown in the pop-up area. The following snippet of code sets a Label as a placeholder:

```
Label placeHolder = new Label("List is empty.\nPlease enter an item");
breakfasts.setPlaceholder(placeHolder);
```

The program in Listing 12-12 creates two ComboBox controls: seasons and breakfasts. The combo box having the list of seasons is not editable. The combo box having the list of breakfast items is editable. Figure 12-20 shows the screenshot when the user selected a season and entered a breakfast item, Donut, which is not in the list of breakfast items. A Label control displays the user selection. When you enter a new value in the breakfast combo box, you need to change the focus, press the Enter key, or open the pop-up list to refresh the message Label.

Listing 12-12. Using ComboBox Controls

```
// ComboBoxTest.java
package com.jdojo.control;

import javafx.application.Application;
import javafx.beans.property.SimpleStringProperty;
import javafx.beans.property.StringProperty;
import javafx.scene.Scene;
import javafx.scene.control.ComboBox;
import javafx.scene.control.Label;
import javafx.scene.layout.HBox;
import javafx.scene.layout.VBox;
import javafx.stage.Stage;

public class ComboBoxTest extends Application {
        public static void main(String[] args) {
                Application.launch(args);
        }

        @Override
        public void start(Stage stage) {
                Label seasonsLbl = new Label("Season:");
                ComboBox<String> seasons = new ComboBox<>();
                seasons.getItems().addAll("Spring", "Summer", "Fall", "Winter");

                Label breakfastsLbl = new Label("Breakfast:");
                ComboBox<String> breakfasts = new ComboBox<>();
                breakfasts.getItems().addAll("Apple", "Banana", "Strawberry");
                breakfasts.setEditable(true);

                // Show the user's selection in a Label
                Label selectionLbl = new Label();
                StringProperty str = new SimpleStringProperty("Your selection: ");
                selectionLbl.textProperty().bind(str.concat("Season=")
                                                .concat(seasons.valueProperty())
                                                .concat(", Breakfast=")
                                                .concat(breakfasts.valueProperty()));
```

```
            HBox row1 = new HBox(seasonsLbl, seasons, breakfastsLbl, breakfasts);
            row1.setSpacing(10);
            VBox root = new VBox(row1, selectionLbl);
            root.setSpacing(10);
            root.setStyle("-fx-padding: 10;" +
                        "-fx-border-style: solid inside;" +
                        "-fx-border-width: 2;" +
                        "-fx-border-insets: 5;" +
                        "-fx-border-radius: 5;" +
                        "-fx-border-color: blue;");

            Scene scene = new Scene(root);
            stage.setScene(scene);
            stage.setTitle("Using ComboBox Controls");
            stage.show();
    }
}
```

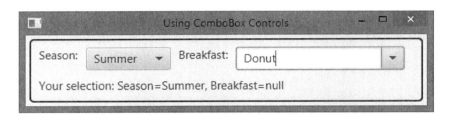

Figure 12-20. *Two ComboBox controls: one noneditable and one editable*

Detecting Value Change in *ComboBox*

Detecting an item change in a noneditable combo box is easily performed by adding a ChangeListener to the selectedIndex or selectedItem property of its selection model. Please refer to the "Understanding the *ChoiceBox* Control" section for more details.

You can still use a ChangeListener for the selectedItem property to detect when the value in an editable combo box changes by selecting from the items list or entering a new value. When you enter a new value, the selectedIndex property does not change because the entered value does not exist in the items list.

Sometimes you want to perform an action when the value in a combo box changes. You can do so by adding an ActionEvent handler, which is fired when the value changes by any means. You would do this by setting it programmatically, selecting from items list, or entering a new value, as in the following code:

```
ComboBox<String> list = new ComboBox<>();
list.setOnAction(e -> System.out.println("Value changed"));
```

Using Domain Objects in Editable *ComboBox*

In an editable ComboBox<T> where T is something other than String, you must set the converter property to a valid StringConverter<T>. Its toString(T object) method is used to convert the item object to a string to show it in the pop-up list. Its fromString(String s) method is called to convert the entered string to an item object. The value property is updated with the item object converted from the entered string. If the entered string cannot be converted to an item object, the value property is not updated.

477

The program in Listing 12-13 shows how to use a StringConverter in a combo box, which uses domain objects in its items list. The ComboBox uses Person objects. The PersonStringConverter class, as shown in Listing 12-11, is used as the StringConverter. You can enter a name in the format LastName, FirstName or FirstName in the ComboBox and press the Enter key. The entered name will be converted to a Person object and shown in the Label. The program ignores the error checking in name formatting. For example, if you enter Kishori as the name, it displays null, Kishori in the Label. The program adds a ChangeListener to the selectedItem and selectedIndex properties of the selection model to track the selection change. Notice that when you enter a string in the ComboBox, a change in selectedIndex property is not reported. An ActionEvent handler for the ComboBox is used to keep the values in the combo box and the text in the Label in sync.

Listing 12-13. Using a StringConverter in a ComboBox

```java
// ComboBoxWithConverter.java
package com.jdojo.control;

import com.jdojo.mvc.model.Person;
import javafx.application.Application;
import javafx.beans.value.ObservableValue;
import javafx.scene.Scene;
import javafx.scene.control.ComboBox;
import javafx.scene.control.Label;
import javafx.scene.layout.GridPane;
import javafx.stage.Stage;

public class ComboBoxWithConverter extends Application {
        Label userSelectionMsgLbl = new Label("Your selection:");
        Label userSelectionDataLbl = new Label("");

        public static void main(String[] args) {
                Application.launch(args);
        }

        @Override
        public void start(Stage stage) {
                Label personLbl = new Label("Select/Enter Person:");
                ComboBox<Person> persons = new ComboBox<>();
                persons.setEditable(true);
                persons.setConverter(new PersonStringConverter());
                persons.getItems().addAll(new Person("John", "Jacobs", null),
                                        new Person("Donna", "Duncan", null),
                                        new Person("Layne", "Estes", null),
                                        new Person("Mason", "Boyd", null));

                // Add ChangeListeners to the selectedItem and selectedIndex
                // properties of the selection model
                persons.getSelectionModel().selectedItemProperty()
                                        .addListener(this::personChanged);
                persons.getSelectionModel().selectedIndexProperty()
                                        .addListener(this::indexChanged);

                // Update the message Label when the value changes
                persons.setOnAction(e -> valueChanged(persons));
```

```
        GridPane root = new GridPane();
        root.addRow(0, personLbl, persons);
        root.addRow(1, userSelectionMsgLbl, userSelectionDataLbl);
        root.setStyle("-fx-padding: 10;" +
                      "-fx-border-style: solid inside;" +
                      "-fx-border-width: 2;" +
                      "-fx-border-insets: 5;" +
                      "-fx-border-radius: 5;" +
                      "-fx-border-color: blue;");

        Scene scene = new Scene(root);
        stage.setScene(scene);
        stage.setTitle("Using StringConverter in ComboBox");
        stage.show();
    }

    public void valueChanged(ComboBox<Person> list) {
        Person p = list.getValue();
        String name = p.getLastName() + ", " + p.getFirstName();
        userSelectionDataLbl.setText(name);
    }

    // A change listener to track the change in item selection
    public void personChanged(ObservableValue<? extends Person> observable,
                              Person oldValue,
                              Person newValue) {
        System.out.println("Itemchanged: old = " + oldValue +
                           ", new = " + newValue);
    }

    // A change listener to track the change in index selection
    public void indexChanged(ObservableValue<? extends Number> observable,
                             Number oldValue,
                             Number newValue) {
        System.out.println("Indexchanged: old = " + oldValue + ",
                           new = " + newValue);
    }
}
```

Customizing the Height of Pop-up List

By default, ComboBox shows only ten items in the pop-up list. If the number of items is more than ten, the pop-up list shows a scrollbar. If the number of items is less than ten, the height of the pop-up list is shortened to show only the available items. The visibleRowCount property of the ComboBox controls how many rows are visible in the pop-up list, as in the following code:

```
ComboBox<String> states = new ComboBox<>();
...
// Show five rows in the popup list
states.setVisibleRowCount(5);
```

Using Nodes as Items in *ComboBox*

A combo box has two areas:

- Button area to display the selected item

- Pop-up area to display the items list

Both areas use ListCells to display items. A ListCell is a Cell. A Cell is a Labeled control to display some form of content that may have text, a graphic, or both. The pop-up area is a ListView that contains an instance of ListCell for each item in the list. I will discuss ListView in the next section.

Elements in the items list of a combo box can be of any type, including Node type. It is not recommended to add instances of the Node class directly to the items list. When nodes are used as items, they are added as the graphic to the cells. Scene graphics need to follow the rule that a node cannot be displayed in two places at the same time. That is, a node must be inside one container at a time. When a node from the items list is selected, the node is removed from the pop-up ListView cell and added to the button area. When the pop-up is displayed again, the selected node is not shown in the list as it is already showing in the button area. To avoid this inconsistency in display, avoid using nodes directly as items in a combo box.

Figure 12-21 show three views of a combo box created using the following snippet of code. Notice that the code adds three instances of HBox, which is a node to the items list. The figure labeled #1 shows the pop-up list when it is opened for the first time, and you see all three items correctly. The figure labeled #2 shows after the second item is selected and you see the correct item in the button area. At this time, the second item in the list, an HBox with a rectangle, was removed from the cell in the ListView and added to the cell in the button area. The figure labeled #3 shows the pop-up list when it is open for the second time. At this time, the second item is missing from the list because it is already selected. This problem was discussed in the previous paragraph.

```
Label shapeLbl = new Label("Shape:");
ComboBox<HBox> shapes = new ComboBox<>();
shapes.getItems().addAll(new HBox(new Line(0, 10, 20, 10), new Label("Line")),
                new HBox(new Rectangle(0, 0, 20, 20), new Label("Rectangle")),
                new HBox(new Circle(20, 20, 10), new Label("Circle")));
```

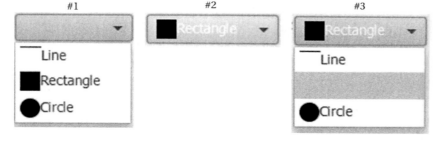

Figure 12-21. *Three views of a combo box with nodes in the items list*

You can fix the display issue that occurs when you use nodes as items. The solution is to add nonnode items in the list and supply a cell factory to create the desired node inside the cell factory. You need to make sure that the nonnode items will provide enough pieces of information to create the node you wanted to insert. The next section explains how to use a cell factory.

Using a Cell Factory in *ComboBox*

The ComboBox class contains a cellFactory property, which is declared as follows:

```
public ObjectProperty<Callback<ListView<T>, ListCell<T>>> cellFactory;
```

Callback is an interface in the javafx.util package. It has a call() method that takes an argument of type P and returns and object of type R, as in the following code:

```
public interface Callback<P,R> {
        public R call(P param);
}
```

The declaration of the cellFactory property states that it stores a Callback object whose call() method receives a ListView<T> and returns a ListCell<T>. Inside the call() method, you create an instance of the ListCell<T> class and override the updateItem(T item, boolean empty) method of the Cell class to populate the cell.

Let's use a cell factory to display nodes in the button area and the pop-up area of a combo box. Listing 12-14 will be our starting point. It declares a StringShapeCell class, which inherits from the ListCell<String> class. You need to update its content in its updateItem() method, which is automatically called. The method receives the item, which in this case is String, and a boolean argument indicating whether the cell is empty. Inside the method, you call the method in the superclass first. You derive a shape from the string argument and set the text and graphic in the cell. The shape is set as the graphic. The getShape() method returns a Shape from a String.

Listing 12-14. A Custom ListCell that Displays a Shape and Its Name

```
// StringShapeCell.java
package com.jdojo.control;

import javafx.scene.control.ListCell;
import javafx.scene.shape.Circle;
import javafx.scene.shape.Line;
import javafx.scene.shape.Rectangle;
import javafx.scene.shape.Shape;

public class StringShapeCell extends ListCell<String> {
        @Override
        public void updateItem(String item, boolean empty) {
                // Need to call the super first
                super.updateItem(item, empty);

                // Set the text and graphic for the cell
                if (empty) {
                        setText(null);
                        setGraphic(null);
                } else {
                        setText(item);
                        Shape shape = this.getShape(item);
                        setGraphic(shape);
                }
        }
```

```
        public Shape getShape(String shapeType) {
                Shape shape = null;
                switch (shapeType.toLowerCase()) {
                        case "line":
                                shape = new Line(0, 10, 20, 10);
                                break;
                        case "rectangle":
                                shape = new Rectangle(0, 0, 20, 20);
                                break;
                        case "circle":
                                shape = new Circle(20, 20, 10);
                                break;
                        default:
                                shape = null;
                }
                return shape;
        }
}
```

The next step is to create a Callback class, as shown in Listing 12-15. The program in this listing is very simple. Its call() method returns an object of the StringShapeCell class. The class will act as a cell factory for ComboBox.

Listing 12-15. A Callback Implementation for Callback<ListView<String>, ListCell<String>>

```
// ShapeCellFactory.java
package com.jdojo.control;

import javafx.scene.control.ListCell;
import javafx.scene.control.ListView;
import javafx.util.Callback;

public class ShapeCellFactory implements Callback<ListView<String>, ListCell<String>> {
        @Override
        public ListCell<String> call(ListView<String> listview) {
                return new StringShapeCell();
        }
}
```

The program in Listing 12-16 shows how to use a custom cell factory and button cell in a combo box. The program is very simple. It creates a combo box with three String items. It sets an object of the ShapeCellFactory as the cell factory, as in the following code:

```
// Set the cellFactory property
shapes.setCellFactory(new ShapeCellFactory());
```

Setting the cell factory is not enough in this case. It will only resolve the issue of displaying the shapes in the pop-up area. When you select a shape, it will display the String item, not the shape, in the button area. To make sure, you see the same item in the list for selection and after you select one, you need to set the buttonCell property, as in the following code:

```
// Set the buttonCell property
shapes.setButtonCell(new StringShapeCell());
```

Notice the use of the StringShapeCell class in the buttonCell property and ShapeCellFactory class.

Run the program in Listing 12-16. You should be able to select a shape from the list and the shape should be displayed in the combo box correctly. Figure 12-22 shows three views of the combo box.

Listing 12-16. Using a Cell Factory in a Combo Box

```java
// ComboBoxCellFactory.java
package com.jdojo.control;

import javafx.application.Application;
import javafx.scene.Scene;
import javafx.scene.control.ComboBox;
import javafx.scene.control.Label;
import javafx.scene.layout.HBox;
import javafx.stage.Stage;

public class ComboBoxCellFactory extends Application {
        public static void main(String[] args) {
                Application.launch(args);
        }

        @Override
        public void start(Stage stage) {
                Label shapeLbl = new Label("Shape:");
                ComboBox<String> shapes = new ComboBox<>();
                shapes.getItems().addAll("Line", "Rectangle", "Circle");

                // Set the cellFactory property
                shapes.setCellFactory(new ShapeCellFactory());

                // Set the buttonCell property
                shapes.setButtonCell(new StringShapeCell());

                HBox root = new HBox(shapeLbl, shapes);
                root.setStyle("-fx-padding: 10;" +
                                "-fx-border-style: solid inside;" +
                                "-fx-border-width: 2;" +
                                "-fx-border-insets: 5;" +
                                "-fx-border-radius: 5;" +
                                "-fx-border-color: blue;");

                Scene scene = new Scene(root);
                stage.setScene(scene);
                stage.setTitle("Using CellFactory in ComboBox");
                stage.show();
        }
}
```

Figure 12-22. *Three views of a combo box with a cell factory*

Using a custom cell factory and button cell in a combo box gives you immense power to customize the look of the pop-up list and the selected item. If using a cell factory looks hard or confusing to you, keep in mind that a cell is a Labeled control and you are setting the text and graphic in that Labeled control inside the updateItem() method. The Callback interface comes into play because the ComboBox control needs to give you a chance to create a cell when it needs it. Otherwise, you would have to know how many cells to create and when to create them. There is nothing more to it.

The ComboBoxBase class provides four properties that can also be used with ComboBox:

- onShowing

- onShown

- onHiding

- onHidden

These properties are of the type ObjectProperty<EventHandler<Event>>. You can set an event handler to these properties, which will be called before the pop-up list is shown, after it is shown, before it is hidden, and after it is hidden. For example, the onShowing event handlers are handy when you want to customize the pop-up list just before it is shown.

Styling *ComboBox* with CSS

The default CSS style-class name for a ComboBox is combo-box. A combo box contains several CSS substructures, as shown in Figure 12-23.

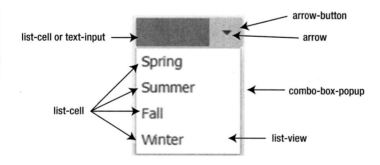

Figure 12-23. *Substructures of a combo box that can be styled separately using CSS*

The CSS names for the substructure are:

- arrow-button
- list-cell
- text-input
- combo-box-popup

An arrow-button contains a substructure called arrow. Both arrow-button and arrow are instances of StackPane. The list-cell area represents the ListCell used to show the selected item in a noneditable combo box. The text-input area is the TextField used to show the selected or entered item in an editable combo box. The combo-box-popup is the Popup control that shows the pop-up list when the button is clicked. It has two substructures: list-view and list-cell. The list-view is the ListView control that shows the list of items, and list-cell represents each cell in the ListView. The following CSS styles customize the appearance of some substructures of ComboBox:

```
/* The ListCell that shows the selected item in a non-editable ComboBox */
.combo-box .list-cell {
        -fx-background-color: yellow;
}

/* The TextField that shows the selected item in an editable ComboBox */
.combo-box .text-input {
        -fx-background-color: yellow;
}

/* Style the arrow button area */
.combo-box .arrow-button {
        -fx-background-color: lightgray;
}

/* Set  the text color in the popup list for ComboBox to blue */
.combo-box-popup .list-view .list-cell {
        -fx-text-fill: blue;
}
```

Understanding the *ListView* Control

ListView is used to allow a user to select one item or multiple items from a list of items. Each item in ListView is represented by an instance of the ListCell class, which can be customized. The items list in a ListView may contain any type of objects. ListView is a parameterized class. The parameter type is the type of the items in the list. If you want to store mixed types of items in a ListView, you can use its raw type, as shown in the following code:

```
// Create a ListView for any type of items
ListView seasons = new ListView();

// Create a ListView for String items
ListView<String> seasons = new ListView<String>();
```

You can specify the list items while creating a ListView, as in the following code:

```
ObservableList<String> seasonList = FXCollections.<String>observableArrayList(
                                "Spring", "Summer", "Fall", "Winter");
ListView<String> seasons = new ListView<>(seasonList);
```

After you create a ListView, you can add items to its list of items using the items property, which is of the ObjectProperty<ObservableList<T>> type in which T is the type parameter for the ListView, as in the following code:

```
ListView<String> seasons = new ListView<>();
seasons.getItems().addAll("Spring", "Summer", "Fall", "Winter");
```

ListView sets its preferred width and height, which are normally not the width and height that you want for your control. It would have helped developers if the control had provided a property such as visibleItemCount. Unfortunately, the ListView API does not support such a property. You need to set them to reasonable values in your code, as follows:

```
// Set preferred width = 100px and height = 120px
seasons.setPrefSize(100, 120);
```

If the space needed to display items is larger than what is available, a vertical, a horizontal, or both scrollbars are automatically added.

The ListView class contains a placeholder property, which stores a Node reference. When the items list is empty or null, the placeholder node is shown in the list area of the ListView. The following snippet of code sets a Label as a placeholder:

```
Label placeHolder = new Label("No seasons available for selection.");
seasons.setPlaceholder(placeHolder);
```

ListView offers a scrolling feature. Use the scrollTo(int index) or scrollTo(T item) method to scroll to a specified index or item in the list. The specified index or item is made visible, if it is not already visible. The ListView class fires a ScrollToEvent when scrolling takes place using the scrollTo() method or by the user. You can set an event handler using the setOnScrollTo() method to handle scrolling.

Each item in a ListView is displayed using an instance of the ListCell class. In essence, a ListCell is a labeled control that is capable of displaying text and a graphic. Several subclasses of ListCell exist to give ListView items a custom look. ListView lets you specify a Callback object as a *cell factory*, which can create custom list cells. A ListView does not need to create as many ListCell objects as the number items. It can have only as many ListCell object as the number of visible items on the screen. As items are scrolled, it can reuse the ListCell objects to display different items. Figure 12-24 shows a class diagram for ListCell-related classes.

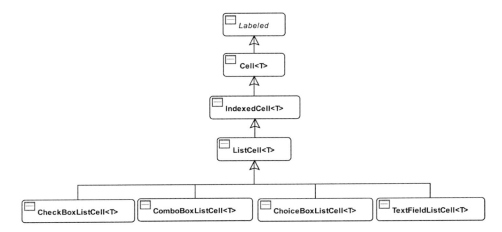

Figure 12-24. *A class diagram for* ListCell*-related classes*

Cells are used as building blocks in different types of controls. For example, ListView, TreeView, and TableView controls use cells in one form or another to display and edit their data. The Cell class is the superclass for all cells. You can override its updateItem(T object, boolean empty) and take full control of how the cell is populated. This method is called automatically by these controls when the item in the cell needs to be updated. The Cell class declares several useful properties: editable, editing, empty, item, and selected. When a Cell is empty, which means it is not associated with any data item, its empty property is true.

The IndexedCell class adds an index property, which is the index of the item in the underlying model. Suppose a ListView uses an ObservableList as a model. The list cell for the second item in the ObservableList will have index 1 (index starts at 0). The cell index facilitates customization of cells based on their indices, for example, using different colors for cells at odd and even index cells. When a cell is empty, its index is -1.

Orientation of a *ListView*

The items in a ListView may be arranged vertically in a single column (default) or horizontally in a single row. It is controlled by the orientation property, as shown in the following code:

```
// Arrange list of seasons horizontally
seasons.setOrientation(Orientation.HORIZONTAL);
```

Figure 12-25 shows two instances of ListView: one uses vertical orientation and one horizontal orientation. Notice that the odd and even rows or columns have different background colors. This is the default look of the ListView. You can change the appearance using a CSS. Please refer to the "Styling ListView with CSS" section for details.

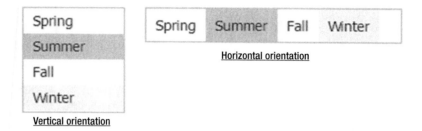

Vertical orientation

Horizontal orientation

Figure 12-25. *Two instances of* ListView *having the same items but different orientations*

Selection Model in *ListView*

ListView has a selection model that stores the selected state of its items. Its selectionModel property stores the reference of the selection model. By default, it uses an instance of the MultipleSelectionModel class. You can use a custom selection model, however, that is rarely needed. The selection model can be configured to work in two modes:

- Single selection mode
- Multiple selection mode

In single selection mode, only one item can be selected at a time. If an item is selected, the previously selected item is deselected. By default, a ListView supports single selection mode. An item can be selected using a mouse or a keyboard. You can select an item using a mouse-click. Using a keyboard to select an item requires that the ListView has focus. You can use the up/down arrow in a vertical ListView and the left/right arrow in a horizontal ListView to select items.

In multiple selection mode, multiple items can be selected at a time. Using only a mouse lets you select only one item at a time. Clicking an item selects the item. Clicking an item with the Shift key pressed selects all contiguous items. Clicking an item with the Ctrl key pressed selects a deselected item and deselects a selected item. You can use the up/down or left/right arrow key to navigate and the Ctrl key with the spacebar or Shift key with the spacebar to select multiple items. If you want a ListView to operate in multiple selection mode, you need to set the selectionMode property of its selection model, as in the following code:

```
// Use multiple selection mode
seasons.getSelectionModel().setSelectionMode(SelectionMode.MULTIPLE);

// Set it back to single selection mode, which is the default for a ListView
seasons.getSelectionModel().setSelectionMode(SelectionMode.SINGLE);
```

The MultipleSelectionModel class inherits from the SelectionModel class, which contains selectedIndex and selectedItem properties.

The selectedIndex property is -1 if there is no selection. In single selection mode, it is the index of the currently selected item. In multiple selection mode, it is the index of the last selected item. In multiple selection mode, use the getSelectedIndices() method that returns a read-only ObservableList<Integer> containing the indices of all selected items. If you are interested in listening for selection change in a ListView, you can add a ChangeListener to the selectedIndex property or a ListChangeListener to the ObservableList returned by the getSelectedIndices() method.

The selectedItem property is null if there is no selection. In single selection mode, it is the currently selected item. In multiple selection mode, it is the last selected item. In multiple selection mode, use the getSelectedItems() method that returns a read-only ObservableList<T> containing all selected items. If you are interested in listening for selection change in a ListView, you can add a ChangeListener to the selectedItem property or a ListChangeListener to the ObservableList<T> returned by the getSelectedItems() method.

The selection model of ListView contains several methods to select items in different ways:

- The selectAll() method selects all items.

- The selectFirst() and selectLast() methods select the first item and the last item, respectively.

- The selectIndices(int index, int... indices) method selects items at the specified indices. Indices outside the valid range are ignored.

- The selectRange(int start, int end) method selects all indices from the start index (inclusive) to the end index (exclusive).

- The clearSelection() and clearSelection(int index) methods clear all selection and the selection at the specified index, respectively.

The program in Listing 12-17 demonstrates how to use the selection model of a ListView for making selections and listening for selection change events. Figure 12-26 shows the window that results from running this code. Run the application and use a mouse or buttons on the window to select items in the ListView. The selection details are displayed at the bottom.

Listing 12-17. Using ListView Selection Model

```
// ListViewSelectionModel.java
package com.jdojo.control;

import javafx.application.Application;
import javafx.beans.value.ObservableValue;
import javafx.collections.ObservableList;
import javafx.scene.Scene;
import javafx.scene.control.Button;
import javafx.scene.control.Label;
import javafx.scene.control.ListView;
import javafx.scene.control.SelectionMode;
import javafx.scene.layout.GridPane;
import javafx.scene.layout.VBox;
import javafx.stage.Stage;

public class ListViewSelectionModel extends Application {
        private ListView<String> seasons;
        private final Label selectedItemsLbl = new Label("[None]");
        private final Label lastSelectedItemLbl = new Label("[None]");

        public static void main(String[] args) {
                Application.launch(args);
        }

        @Override
        public void start(Stage stage) {
                Label seasonsLbl = new Label("Select Seasons:");
                seasons = new ListView<>();
                seasons.setPrefSize(120, 120);
                seasons.getItems().addAll("Spring", "Summer", "Fall", "Winter");
```

489

```java
// Enable multiple selection
seasons.getSelectionModel().setSelectionMode(SelectionMode.MULTIPLE);

// Add a selection change listener
seasons.getSelectionModel()
        .selectedItemProperty()
        .addListener(this::selectionChanged);

// Add some buttons to assist in selection
Button selectAllBtn = new Button("Select All");
selectAllBtn.setOnAction(e -> seasons.getSelectionModel().selectAll());

Button clearAllBtn = new Button("Clear All");
clearAllBtn.setOnAction(
        e -> seasons.getSelectionModel().clearSelection());

Button selectFirstBtn = new Button("Select First");
selectFirstBtn.setOnAction(
        e -> seasons.getSelectionModel().selectFirst());

Button selectLastBtn = new Button("Select Last");
selectLastBtn.setOnAction(e -> seasons.getSelectionModel().selectLast());

Button selectNextBtn = new Button("Select Next");
selectNextBtn.setOnAction(e -> seasons.getSelectionModel().selectNext());

Button selectPreviousBtn = new Button("Select Previous");
selectPreviousBtn.setOnAction(
        e -> seasons.getSelectionModel().selectPrevious());

// Let all buttons expand as needed
selectAllBtn.setMaxWidth(Double.MAX_VALUE);
clearAllBtn.setMaxWidth(Double.MAX_VALUE);
selectFirstBtn.setMaxWidth(Double.MAX_VALUE);
selectLastBtn.setMaxWidth(Double.MAX_VALUE);
selectNextBtn.setMaxWidth(Double.MAX_VALUE);
selectPreviousBtn.setMaxWidth(Double.MAX_VALUE);

// Display controls in a GridPane
GridPane root = new GridPane();
root.setHgap(10);
root.setVgap(5);

// Add buttons to two VBox objects
VBox singleSelectionBtns = new VBox(selectFirstBtn, selectNextBtn,
                                selectPreviousBtn, selectLastBtn);
VBox allSelectionBtns = new VBox(selectAllBtn, clearAllBtn);
root.addColumn(0, seasonsLbl, seasons);
root.add(singleSelectionBtns, 1, 1, 1, 1);
root.add(allSelectionBtns, 2, 1, 1, 1);
```

```
            // Add controls to display the user selection
            Label selectionLbl = new Label("Your selection:");
            root.add(selectionLbl, 0, 2);
            root.add(selectedItemsLbl, 1, 2, 2, 1);

            Label lastSelectionLbl = new Label("Last selection:");
            root.add(lastSelectionLbl, 0, 3);
            root.add(lastSelectedItemLbl, 1, 3, 2, 1);

            root.setStyle("-fx-padding: 10;" +
                        "-fx-border-style: solid inside;" +
                        "-fx-border-width: 2;" +
                        "-fx-border-insets: 5;" +
                        "-fx-border-radius: 5;" +
                        "-fx-border-color: blue;");

            Scene scene = new Scene(root);
            stage.setScene(scene);
            stage.setTitle("Using ListView Selection Model");
            stage.show();
    }

    // A change listener to track the change in item selection
    public void selectionChanged(ObservableValue<? extends String> observable,
                             String oldValue,
                             String newValue) {
            String lastItem = (newValue == null)?"[None]":"[" + newValue + "]";
            lastSelectedItemLbl.setText(lastItem);

            ObservableList<String> selectedItems =
                                seasons.getSelectionModel().getSelectedItems();
            String selectedValues =
                    (selectedItems.isEmpty())?"[None]":selectedItems.toString();
            this.selectedItemsLbl.setText(selectedValues);
    }
}
```

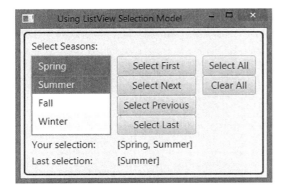

Figure 12-26. *A ListView with several buttons to make selections*

Using Cell Factory in *ListView*

Each item in a ListView is displayed in an instance of ListCell, which a Labeled control. Recall that a Labeled control contains text and a graphic. The ListView class contains a cellFactory property that lets you use custom cells for its items. The property type is ObjectProperty<Callback<ListView<T>,ListCell<T>>>. The reference of the ListView is passed to the call() method of the Callback object and it returns an instance of the ListCell class. In a large ListView, say 1,000 items, the ListCell returned from the cell factory may be reused. The control needs to create only the number of cells that are visible. Upon scrolling, it may reuse the cells that went out of the view to display newly visible items. The updateItem() method of the ListCell receives the reference of the new item.

By default, a ListView calls the toString() method of its items and it displays the string in its cell. In the updateItem() method of your custom ListCell, you can populate the text and graphic for the cell to display anything you want in the cell based on the item in that cell.

■ **Tip** You used a custom cell factory for the pop-up list of the combo box in the previous section. The pop-up list in a combo box uses a ListView. Therefore, using a custom cell factory in a ListView would be the same as discussed in the earlier combo box section.

The program in Listing 12-18 shows how to use a custom cell factory to display the formatted names of Person items. Figure 12-27 shows the resulting window after running the code. The snippet of code in the program creates and sets a custom cell factory. The updateItem() method of the ListCell formats the name of the Person object and adds a serial number that is the index of the cell plus one.

Listing 12-18. Using a Custom Cell Factory for ListView

```
// ListViewDomainObjects.java
package com.jdojo.control;

import com.jdojo.mvc.model.Person;
import javafx.application.Application;
import javafx.scene.Scene;
import javafx.scene.control.Label;
import javafx.scene.control.ListCell;
import javafx.scene.control.ListView;
import javafx.scene.layout.HBox;
import javafx.stage.Stage;
import javafx.util.Callback;

public class ListViewDomainObjects extends Application {
        public static void main(String[] args) {
                Application.launch(args);
        }

        @Override
        public void start(Stage stage) {
                ListView<Person> persons = new ListView<>();
                persons.setPrefSize(150, 120);
```

```
persons.getItems().addAll(new Person("John", "Jacobs", null),
                     new Person("Donna", "Duncan", null),
                     new Person("Layne", "Estes", null),
                     new Person("Mason", "Boyd", null));

// Add a custom cell factory to display formatted names of persons
persons.setCellFactory(
        new Callback<ListView<Person>,ListCell<Person>>() {
        @Override
        public ListCell<Person> call(ListView<Person> listView) {
                return new ListCell<Person>() {
                        @Override
                        public void updateItem(Person item, boolean empty) {
                                // Must call super
                                super.updateItem(item, empty);

                                int index = this.getIndex();
                                String name = null;

                                // Format name
                                if (item == null || empty) {
                                        // No action to perform
                                } else {
                                        name = (index + 1) + ". " +
                                                item.getLastName() + ", " +
                                                item.getFirstName();
                                }

                                this.setText(name);
                                setGraphic(null);
                        }
                };
}});

HBox root = new HBox(new Label("Persons:"), persons);
root.setSpacing(20);
root.setStyle("-fx-padding: 10;" +
                "-fx-border-style: solid inside;" +
                "-fx-border-width: 2;" +
                "-fx-border-insets: 5;" +
                "-fx-border-radius: 5;" +
                "-fx-border-color: blue;");

Scene scene = new Scene(root);
stage.setScene(scene);
stage.setTitle("Using ListView Cell Factory");
stage.show();
    }
}
```

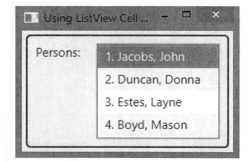

Figure 12-27. *A* ListView *displaying* Person *objects in its list of items using a custom cell factory*

Using Editable *ListView*

The ListView control offers many customizations, and one of them is its ability to let users edit the items. You need to set two properties for a ListView before it can be edited:

- Set the editable property of the ListView to true.

- Set the cellFactory property of the ListView to a cell factory that produces an editable ListCell.

Select a cell and click to start editing. Alternatively, press the spacebar when a cell has focus to start editing. If a ListView is editable and has an editable cell, you can also use the edit(int index) method of the ListView to edit the item in the cell at the specified index.

■ **Tip** The ListView class contains a read-only editingIndex property. Its value is the index of the item being edited. Its value is -1 if no item is being edited.

JavaFX provides cell factories that let you edit a ListCell using TextField, ChoiceBox, ComboBox, and CheckBox. You can create a custom cell factory to edit cells in some other way. Instances of the TextFieldListCell, ChoiceBoxListCell, ComboBoxListCell, and CheckBoxListCell classes, as list cells in a ListView, provide editing support. These classes are included in the javafx.scene.control.cell package.

Using a *TextField* to Edit *ListView* Items

An instance of the TextFieldListCell is a ListCell that displays an item in a Label when the item is not being edited and in a TextField when the item is being edited. If you want to edit a domain object to a ListView, you will need to use a StringConverter to facilitate the two-way conversion. The forListView() static method of the TextFieldListCell class returns a cell factory configured to be used with String items. The following snippet of code shows how to set a TextField as the cell editor for a ListView:

```
ListView<String> breakfasts = new ListView<>();
...
breakfasts.setEditable(true);
```

```
// Set a TextField as the editor
Callback<ListView<String>, ListCell<String>> cellFactory =
        TextFieldListCell.forListView();
breakfasts.setCellFactory(cellFactory);
```

The following snippet of code shows how to set a TextField as the cell editor with a converter for a ListView that contains Person objects. The converter used in the code was shown in Listing 12-11. The converter object will be used to convert a Person object to a String for displaying and a String to a Person object after editing.

```
ListView<Person> persons = new ListView<>();
...
persons.setEditable(true);

// Set a TextField as the editor.
// Need to use a StringConverter for Person objects.
StringConverter<Person> converter = new PersonStringConverter();
Callback<ListView<Person>, ListCell<Person>> cellFactory
        = TextFieldListCell.forListView(converter);
persons.setCellFactory(cellFactory);
```

The program in Listing 12-19 shows how to edit a ListView item in a TextField. It uses a ListView of domain objects (Person) and a ListView of String objects. After running the program, double-click on any items in the two ListViews to start editing. When you are done editing, press the Enter key to commit the changes.

Listing 12-19. Using an Editable ListView

```
// ListViewEditing.java
package com.jdojo.control;

import com.jdojo.mvc.model.Person;
import javafx.application.Application;
import javafx.scene.Scene;
import javafx.scene.control.Label;
import javafx.scene.control.ListCell;
import javafx.scene.control.ListView;
import javafx.scene.control.cell.TextFieldListCell;
import javafx.scene.layout.GridPane;
import javafx.stage.Stage;
import javafx.util.Callback;
import javafx.util.StringConverter;

public class ListViewEditing extends Application {
        public static void main(String[] args) {
                Application.launch(args);
        }

        @Override
        public void start(Stage stage) {
                ListView<String> breakfasts = getBreakfastListView();
                ListView<Person> persons = getPersonListView();
```

495

```java
                GridPane root = new GridPane();
                root.setHgap(20);
                root.setVgap(10);
                root.add(new Label("Double click an item to edit."), 0, 0, 2, 1);
                root.addRow(1, new Label("Persons:"), new Label("Breakfasts:"));
                root.addRow(2, persons, breakfasts);
                root.setStyle("-fx-padding: 10;" +
                             "-fx-border-style: solid inside;" +
                             "-fx-border-width: 2;" +
                             "-fx-border-insets: 5;" +
                             "-fx-border-radius: 5;" +
                             "-fx-border-color: blue;");

                Scene scene = new Scene(root);
                stage.setScene(scene);
                stage.setTitle("Using ListView Cell Factory");
                stage.show();
        }

        public ListView<Person> getPersonListView() {
                ListView<Person> persons = new ListView<>();
                persons.setPrefSize(200, 120);
                persons.setEditable(true);
                persons.getItems().addAll(new Person("John", "Jacobs", null),
                                          new Person("Donna", "Duncan", null),
                                          new Person("Layne", "Estes", null),
                                          new Person("Mason", "Boyd", null));

                // Set a TextField cell factory to edit the Person items. Also use a
                // StringConverter to convert a String to a Person and vice-versa
                StringConverter<Person> converter = new PersonStringConverter();
                Callback<ListView<Person>, ListCell<Person>> cellFactory =
                        TextFieldListCell.forListView(converter);
                persons.setCellFactory(cellFactory);

                return persons;
        }

        public ListView<String> getBreakfastListView() {
                ListView<String> breakfasts = new ListView<>();
                breakfasts.setPrefSize(200, 120);
                breakfasts.setEditable(true);
                breakfasts.getItems().addAll("Apple", "Banana", "Donut", "Hash Brown");

                // Set a TextField cell factory to edit the String items
                Callback<ListView<String>, ListCell<String>> cellFactory =
                        TextFieldListCell.forListView();
                breakfasts.setCellFactory(cellFactory);

                return breakfasts;
        }
}
```

Using a *ChoiceBox*/*ComboBox* to Edit *ListView* Items

An instance of the ChoiceBoxListCell is a ListCell that displays an item in a Label when the item is not being edited and in a ChoiceBox when the item is being edited. If you want to edit a domain object to a ListView, you will need to use a StringConverter to facilitate two-way conversion. You need to supply the list of items to show in the choice box. Use the forListView() static method of the ChoiceBoxListCell class to create a cell factory. The following snippet of code shows how to set a choice box as the cell editor for a ListView:

```
ListView<String> breakfasts = new ListView<>();
...
breakfasts.setEditable(true);

// Set a cell factory to use a ChoiceBox for editing
ObservableList<String> items =
        FXCollections.<String>observableArrayList("Apple", "Banana", "Donut", "Hash Brown");
breakfasts.setCellFactory(ChoiceBoxListCell.forListView(items));
```

The program in Listing 12-20 uses a choice box to edit items in a ListView. Double-click an item in a cell to start editing. In edit mode, the cell becomes a choice box. Click the arrow to show the list of items to select. Using a combo box for editing is similar to using a choice box.

Listing 12-20. Using a ChoiceBox for Editing Items in a ListView

```java
// ListViewChoiceBoxEditing.java
package com.jdojo.control;

import javafx.application.Application;
import javafx.collections.FXCollections;
import javafx.collections.ObservableList;
import javafx.scene.Scene;
import javafx.scene.control.Label;
import javafx.scene.control.ListView;
import javafx.scene.control.SelectionMode;
import javafx.scene.control.cell.ChoiceBoxListCell;
import javafx.scene.layout.VBox;
import javafx.stage.Stage;

public class ListViewChoiceBoxEditing extends Application {
        public static void main(String[] args) {
                Application.launch(args);
        }

        @Override
        public void start(Stage stage) {
                ListView<String> breakfasts = new ListView<>();
                breakfasts.setPrefSize(200, 120);
                breakfasts.setEditable(true);
                breakfasts.getSelectionModel().setSelectionMode(SelectionMode.MULTIPLE);
```

497

```
                    // Let the user select a maximum of four breakfast items
                    breakfasts.getItems().addAll("[Double click to select]",
                                                 "[Double click to select]",
                                                 "[Double click to select]",
                                                 "[Double click to select]");

                    // The breakfast items to select from
                    ObservableList<String> items = FXCollections.<String>observableArrayList(
                                        "Apple", "Banana", "Donut", "Hash Brown");

                    // Set a ChoiceBox cell factory for editing
                    breakfasts.setCellFactory(ChoiceBoxListCell.forListView(items));

                    VBox root = new VBox(new Label("Double click an item to select."),
                                         new Label("Breakfasts:"),
                                         breakfasts);
                    root.setSpacing(10);
                    root.setStyle("-fx-padding: 10;" +
                                  "-fx-border-style: solid inside;" +
                                  "-fx-border-width: 2;" +
                                  "-fx-border-insets: 5;" +
                                  "-fx-border-radius: 5;" +
                                  "-fx-border-color: blue;");

                    Scene scene = new Scene(root);
                    stage.setScene(scene);
                    stage.setTitle("Using ListView Cell Factory");
                    stage.show();
        }
}
```

Using a Check Box to Edit *ListView* Items

The CheckBoxListCell class provides the ability to edit a ListCell using a check box. It draws a check box in the cell, which can be selected or deselected. Note that the third state, the *indeterminate* state, of the check box is not available for selection while using a check box to edit ListView items.

Using a check box to edit ListView items is a little different. You need to provide the CheckBoxListCell class with an ObservableValue<Boolean> object for each item in the ListView. Internally, the observable value is bound bidirectionally to the selected state of the check box. When the user selects or deselects an item in the ListView using the check box, the corresponding ObservableValue object is updated with a true or false value. If you want to know which item is selected, you will need to keep the reference of the ObservableValue object.

Let's redo our earlier breakfast example using a check box. The following snippet of code creates a map and adds all items as a key and a corresponding ObservableValue item with false value. Using a false value, you want to indicate that the items will be initially deselected:

```
Map<String, ObservableValue<Boolean>> map = new HashMap<>();
map.put("Apple", new SimpleBooleanProperty(false));
map.put("Banana", new SimpleBooleanProperty(false));
map.put("Donut", new SimpleBooleanProperty(false));
map.put("Hash Brown", new SimpleBooleanProperty(false));
```

Now, you create an editable `ListView` with all keys in the map as its items:

```
ListView<String> breakfasts = new ListView<>();
breakfasts.setEditable(true);

// Add all keys from the map as items to the ListView
breakfasts.getItems().addAll(map.keySet());
```

The following snippet of code creates a `Callback` object. Its `call()` method returns the `ObservableValue` object for the specified `item` passed to the `call()` method. The `CheckBoxListCell` class will call the `call()` method of this object automatically:

```
Callback<String, ObservableValue<Boolean>> itemToBoolean = (String item) -> map.get(item);
```

Now it is time to create and set a cell factory for the `ListView`. The `forListView()` static method of the `CheckBoxListCell` class takes a `Callback` object as an argument. If your `ListView` contains domain objects, you can also provide a `StringConverter` to this method, using the following code:

```
// Set the cell factory
breakfasts.setCellFactory(CheckBoxListCell.forListView(itemToBoolean));
```

When the user selects or deselects an item using the check box, the corresponding `ObservableValue` in the map will be updated. To know whether an item in the `ListView` is selected, you need to look at the value in the `ObservableValue` object for that item.

The program in Listing 12-21 shows how to use a check box to edit items in a `ListView`. Figure 12-28 shows the resulting window after running the code. Select items using a mouse. Pressing the Print Selection button prints the selected items on the standard output.

Listing 12-21. Using a Check Box to Edit `ListView` Items

```
// ListViewCheckBoxEditing.java
package com.jdojo.control;

import java.util.HashMap;
import java.util.Map;
import javafx.application.Application;
import javafx.beans.property.SimpleBooleanProperty;
import javafx.beans.value.ObservableValue;
import javafx.scene.Scene;
import javafx.scene.control.Button;
import javafx.scene.control.Label;
import javafx.scene.control.ListView;
import javafx.scene.control.SelectionMode;
import javafx.scene.control.cell.CheckBoxListCell;
import javafx.scene.layout.VBox;
import javafx.stage.Stage;
import javafx.util.Callback;
```

```java
public class ListViewCheckBoxEditing extends Application {
        Map<String, ObservableValue<Boolean>> map = new HashMap<>();

        public static void main(String[] args) {
                Application.launch(args);
        }

        @Override
        public void start(Stage stage) {
                // Populate the map with ListView items as its keys and
                // their selected state as the value
                map.put("Apple", new SimpleBooleanProperty(false));
                map.put("Banana", new SimpleBooleanProperty(false));
                map.put("Donut", new SimpleBooleanProperty(false));
                map.put("Hash Brown", new SimpleBooleanProperty(false));

                ListView<String> breakfasts = new ListView<>();
                breakfasts.setPrefSize(200, 120);
                breakfasts.setEditable(true);
                breakfasts.getSelectionModel().setSelectionMode(SelectionMode.MULTIPLE);

                // Add all keys from the map as items to the ListView
                breakfasts.getItems().addAll(map.keySet());

                // Create a Callback object
                Callback<String, ObservableValue<Boolean>> itemToBoolean =
                        (String item) -> map.get(item);

                // Set the cell factory
                breakfasts.setCellFactory(CheckBoxListCell.forListView(itemToBoolean));

                Button printBtn = new Button("Print Selection");
                printBtn.setOnAction(e -> printSelection());

                VBox root = new VBox(new Label("Breakfasts:"), breakfasts, printBtn);
                root.setSpacing(10);
                root.setStyle("-fx-padding: 10;" +
                                "-fx-border-style: solid inside;" +
                                "-fx-border-width: 2;" +
                                "-fx-border-insets: 5;" +
                                "-fx-border-radius: 5;" +
                                "-fx-border-color: blue;");

                Scene scene = new Scene(root);
                stage.setScene(scene);
                stage.setTitle("Using ListView Cell Factory");
                stage.show();
        }
```

```
        public void printSelection() {
                System.out.println("Selected items: ");
                for(String key: map.keySet()) {
                        ObservableValue<Boolean> value = map.get(key);
                        if (value.getValue()) {
                                System.out.println(key);
                        }
                }

                System.out.println();
        }
}
```

Figure 12-28. *A ListView with a check box for editing its items*

Handling Events While Editing a *ListView*

An editable ListView fires three kinds of events:

- An editStart event when the editing starts
- An editCommit event when the edited value is committed
- An editcancel event when the editing is cancelled

The ListView class defines a ListView.EditEvent<T> static inner class to represent edit-related event objects. Its getIndex() method returns the index of the item that is edited. The getNewValue() method returns the new input value. The getSource() method returns the reference of the ListView firing the event. The ListView class provides onEditStart, onEditCommit, and onEditCancel properties to set the event handlers for these methods.

The following snippet of code adds an editStart event hander to a ListView. The handler prints the index that is being edited and the new item value:

```
ListView<String> breakfasts = new ListView<>();
...
breakfasts.setEditable(true);
breakfasts.setCellFactory(TextFieldListCell.forListView());
```

```
// Add an editStart event handler to the ListView
breakfasts.setOnEditStart(e ->
                System.out.println("Edit Start: Index=" + e.getIndex() +
                                ", item  = " + e.getNewValue())));
```

Listing 12-22 contains a complete program to show how to handle edit-related events in a ListView. Run the program and double-click an item to start editing. After changing the value, press Enter to commit editing or Esc to cancel editing. Edit-related event handlers print messages on the standard output.

Listing 12-22. Handling Edit-Related Events in a ListView

```java
// ListViewEditEvents.java
package com.jdojo.control;

import javafx.application.Application;
import javafx.scene.Scene;
import javafx.scene.control.Label;
import javafx.scene.control.ListView;
import javafx.scene.control.cell.TextFieldListCell;
import javafx.scene.layout.HBox;
import javafx.stage.Stage;

public class ListViewEditEvents extends Application {
        public static void main(String[] args) {
                Application.launch(args);
        }

        @Override
        public void start(Stage stage) {
                ListView<String> breakfasts = new ListView<>();
                breakfasts.setPrefSize(200, 120);
                breakfasts.getItems().addAll("Apple", "Banana", "Donut", "Hash Brown");
                breakfasts.setEditable(true);
                breakfasts.setCellFactory(TextFieldListCell.forListView());

                // Add Edit-related event handlers
                breakfasts.setOnEditStart(this::editStart);
                breakfasts.setOnEditCommit(this::editCommit);
                breakfasts.setOnEditCancel(this::editCancel);

                HBox root = new HBox(new Label("Breakfast:"), breakfasts);
                root.setSpacing(20);
                root.setStyle("-fx-padding: 10;" +
                                "-fx-border-style: solid inside;" +
                                "-fx-border-width: 2;" +
                                "-fx-border-insets: 5;" +
                                "-fx-border-radius: 5;" +
                                "-fx-border-color: blue;");
```

```
                Scene scene = new Scene(root);
                stage.setScene(scene);
                stage.setTitle("Using ListView Edit Events");
                stage.show();
        }

        public void editStart(ListView.EditEvent<String> e) {
                System.out.println("Edit Start: Index=" + e.getIndex() +
                                    ", Item=" + e.getNewValue());
        }

        public void editCommit(ListView.EditEvent<String> e) {
                System.out.println("Edit Commit: Index=" + e.getIndex() +
                                    ", Item=" + e.getNewValue());
        }

        public void editCancel(ListView.EditEvent<String> e) {
                System.out.println("Edit Cancel: Index=" + e.getIndex() +
                                    ", Item=" + e.getNewValue());
        }
}
```

Styling *ListView* with CSS

The default CSS style-class name for a ListView is list-view and for ListCell it is list-cell. The ListView class has two CSS pseudo-classes: horizontal and vertical. The -fx-orientation CSS property controls the orientation of the ListView, which can be set to *horizontal* or *vertical*.

You can style a ListView as you style any other controls. Each item is displayed in an instance of ListCell. ListCellprovides several CSS pseudo-classes:

- empty
- filled
- selected
- odd
- even

The empty pseudo-class applies when the cell is empty. The filled pseudo-class applies when the cell is not empty. The selected pseudo-class applies when the cell is selected. The odd and even pseudo-classes apply to cells with an odd and even index, respectively. The cell representing the first item is index 0 and it is considered an even cell.

The following CSS styles will highlight even cells with tan and odd cells with light gray:

```
.list-view .list-cell:even {
    -fx-background-color: tan;
}

.list-view .list-cell:odd {
    -fx-background-color: lightgray;
}
```

Developers often ask how to remove the default alternate cell highlighting in a ListView. In the modena.css file, the default background color for all list cells is set to -fx-control-inner-background, which is a CSS-derived color. For all odd list cells, the default color is set to derive(-fx-control-inner-background,-5%). To keep the background color the same for all cells, you need to override the background color of odd list cells as follows:

```
.list-view .list-cell:odd {
    -fx-background-color: -fx-control-inner-background;
}
```

This only solves half of the problem; it only takes care of the background colors of the list cells in a normal state inside a ListView. A list cell can be in several states, for example, focused, selected, empty, or filled. To completely address this, you will need to set the appropriate background colors for list cells for all states. Please refer to the modena.css file for a complete list of states that you will need to modify the background colors for list cells.

The ListCell class supports an -fx-cell-size CSS property that is the height of the cells in a vertical ListView and the width of cells in a horizontal ListView.

The list cell could be of the type ListCell, TextFieldListCell, ChoiceBoxListCell, ComboBoxListCell, or CheckBoxListCell. The default CSS style-class names for subclasses of ListCell are text-field-list-cell, choice-box-list-cell, combo-box-list-cell, and check-box-list-cell. You can use these style class names to customize their appearance. The following CSS style will show the TextField in an editable ListView in yellow background:

```
.list-view .text-field-list-cell .text-field {
        -fx-background-color: yellow;
}
```

Understanding the *ColorPicker* Control

ColorPicker is a combo box–style control that is especially designed for users to select a color from a standard color palette or create a color using a built-in color dialog. The ColorPicker class inherits from the ComboBoxBase<Color> class. Therefore, all properties declared in the ComboBoxBase class apply to the ColorPicker control as well. I have discussed several of these properties earlier in the "Understanding the *ComboBox* Control" section. If you want to know more about those properties, please refer to that section. For example, the editable, onAction, showing, and value properties work the same way in a ColorPicker as they do in a combo box. A ColorPicker has three parts:

- ColorPicker control
- Color palette
- Custom color dialog

A ColorPicker control consists of several components, as shown in Figure 12-29. You can customize their looks. The color indicator is a rectangle displaying the current color selection. The color label displays the color in text format. If the current selection is one of the standard colors, the label displays the color name. Otherwise, it displays the color value in hex format. Figure 12-30 shows a ColorPicker control and its color palette.

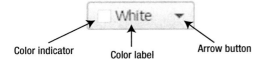

Color indicator   Color label   Arrow button

Figure 12-29. *Components of a ColorPicker control*

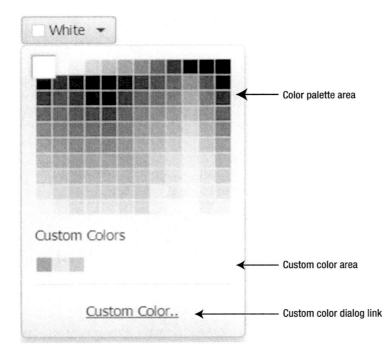

Color palette area

Custom color area

Custom color dialog link

Figure 12-30. *ColorPicker control and its color palette dialog box*

The color palette is shown as a pop-up when you click the arrow button in the control. The color palette consists of three areas:

- A color palette area to show a set of standard colors
- A custom colors area showing the list of custom colors
- A hyperlink to open the custom color dialog box

The color palette area shows a set of predefined standard colors. If you click one of the colors, it closes the pop-up and sets the selected color as the value for the ColorPicker control.

The custom color area shows a set of custom colors. When you open this pop-up for the first time, this area is absent. There are two ways to get colors in this area. You can load a set of custom colors or you can build and save custom colors using the custom color dialog box.

When you click the Custom Color... hyperlink, a custom color dialog box, as shown in Figure 12-31, is displayed. You can use HSB, RGB, or Web tab to build a custom color using one of these formats. You can also define a new color by selecting a color from the color area or the color vertical bar, which are on the left side of the dialog box. When you click the color area and the color bar, they show a small circle and rectangle to denote the new color. Clicking the Save button selects the custom color in the control and saves it to display later in the custom color area when you open the pop-up again. Clicking the Use button selects the custom color for the control.

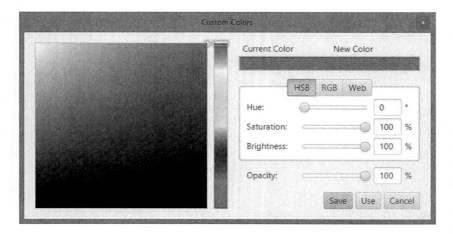

Figure 12-31. *Custom color dialog box of* ColorPicker

Using the *ColorPicker* Control

The ColorPicker class has two constructors. One of them is the default constructor and the other takes the initial color as an argument. The default constructor uses white as the initial color, as in the following code:

```
// Create a ColorPicker control with an initial color of white
ColorPicker bgColor1 = new ColorPicker();

// Create a ColorPicker control with an initial color of red
ColorPicker bgColor2 = new ColorPicker(Color.RED);
```

The value property of the control stores the currently selected color. Typically, the value property is set when you select a color using the control. However, you can also set it directly in your code, as follows:

```
ColorPicker bgColor = new ColorPicker();
...
// Get the selected color
Color selectedCOlor = bgColor.getValue();

// Set the ColorPicker color to yellow
bgColor.setValue(Color.YELLOW);
```

The getCustomColors() method of the ColorPicker class returns a list of custom colors that you save in the custom colors dialog box. Note that custom colors are saved only for the current session and the current ColorPicker control. If you need to, you can save custom colors in a file or database and load them on startup. You will have to write some code to achieve this:

```
ColorPicker bgColor = new ColorPicker();
...
// Load two custom colors
bgColor.getCustomColors().addAll(Color.web("#07FF78"), Color.web("#C2F3A7"));
...
// Get all custom colors
ObservableList<Color> customColors = bgColor.getCustomColors();
```

Typically, when a color is selected in a ColorPicker, you want to use the color for other controls. When a color is selected, the ColorPicker control generates an ActionEvent. The following snippet of code adds an ActionEvent handler to a ColorPicker. When a color is selected, the handler sets the new color as the fill color of a rectangle:

```
ColorPicker bgColor = new ColorPicker();
Rectangle rect = new Rectangle(0, 0, 100, 50);

// Set the selected color in the ColorPicker as the fill color of the Rectangle
bgColor.setOnAction(e -> rect.setFill(bgColor.getValue()));
```

The program in Listing 12-23 shows how to use ColorPicker controls. When you select a color using the ColorPicker, the fill color for the rectangle is updated.

Listing 12-23. Using the ColorPicker Control

```
// ColorPickerTest.java
package com.jdojo.control;

import javafx.application.Application;
import javafx.scene.Scene;
import javafx.scene.control.ColorPicker;
import javafx.scene.control.Label;
import javafx.scene.layout.HBox;
import javafx.scene.paint.Color;
import javafx.scene.shape.Rectangle;
import javafx.stage.Stage;

public class ColorPickerTest extends Application {
        public static void main(String[] args) {
                Application.launch(args);
        }

        @Override
        public void start(Stage stage) {
                ColorPicker bgColor = new ColorPicker(Color.RED);
```

```
                    // A Rectangle to show the selected color from the color picker
                    Rectangle rect = new Rectangle(0, 0, 100, 50);
                    rect.setFill(bgColor.getValue());
                    rect.setStyle("-fx-stroke-width: 2; -fx-stroke: black;");

                    // Add an ActionEvent handler to the ColorPicker, so you change
                    // the fill color for the rectangle when you pick a new color
                    bgColor.setOnAction(e -> rect.setFill(bgColor.getValue()));

                    HBox root = new HBox(new Label("Color:"), bgColor, rect);
                    root.setSpacing(10);
                    root.setStyle("-fx-padding: 10;" +
                                  "-fx-border-style: solid inside;" +
                                  "-fx-border-width: 2;" +
                                  "-fx-border-insets: 5;" +
                                  "-fx-border-radius: 5;" +
                                  "-fx-border-color: blue;");

                    Scene scene = new Scene(root);
                    stage.setScene(scene);
                    stage.setTitle("Using ColorPicker Controls");
                    stage.show();
        }
}
```

The ColorPicker control supports three looks: combo-box look, button look, and split-button look. Combo-box look is the default look. Figure 12-32 shows a ColorPicker in these three looks, respectively.

Figure 12-32. Three looks of a ColorPicker

The ColorPicker class contains two string contents that are the CSS style-class name for the button and split-button looks. The constants are:

- STYLE_CLASS_BUTTON
- STYLE_CLASS_SPLIT_BUTTON

If you want to change the default look of a ColorPicker, add one of the above constants as its style class, as follows:

```
// Use default combo-box look
ColorPicker cp = new ColorPicker(Color.RED);

// Change the look to button
cp.getStyleClass().add(ColorPicker.STYLE_CLASS_BUTTON);

// Change the look to split-button
cp.getStyleClass().add(ColorPicker.STYLE_CLASS_SPLIT_BUTTON);
```

■ **Tip** It is possible to add both STYLE_CLASS_BUTTON and STYLE_CLASS_SPLIT_BUTTON as style classes for a ColorPicker. In such a case, the STYLE_CLASS_BUTTON is used.

Styling *ColorPicker* with CSS

The default CSS style-class name for a ColorPicker is color-picker. You can style almost every part of a ColorPicker, for example, color indicator, color label, color palette dialog, and custom color dialog. Please refer to the modena.css file for complete reference.

The -fx-color-label-visible CSS property of the ColorPicker sets whether the color label is visible or not. Its default value is true. The following code makes the color label invisible:

```
.color-picker {
        -fx-color-label-visible: false;
}
```

The color indicator is a rectangle, which has a style class name of picker-color-rect. The color label is a Label, which has a style class name of color-picker-label. The following code shows the color label in blue and sets a 2px thick black stroke around the color indicator rectangle:

```
.color-picker .color-picker-label {
        -fx-text-fill: blue;
}

.color-picker .picker-color .picker-color-rect {
        -fx-stroke: black;
        -fx-stroke-width: 2;
}
```

The style class name for the color palette is color-palette. The following code hides the Custom Colors... hyperlink on the color palette:

```
.color-palette .hyperlink {
        visibility: hidden;
}
```

Understanding the *DatePicker* Control

DatePicker is a combo-box style control. The user can enter a date as text or select a date from a calendar. The calendar is displayed as a pop-up for the control, as shown in Figure 12-33. The DatePicker class inherits from the ComboBoxBase<LocalDate> class. All properties declared in the ComboBoxBase class are also available to the DatePicker control.

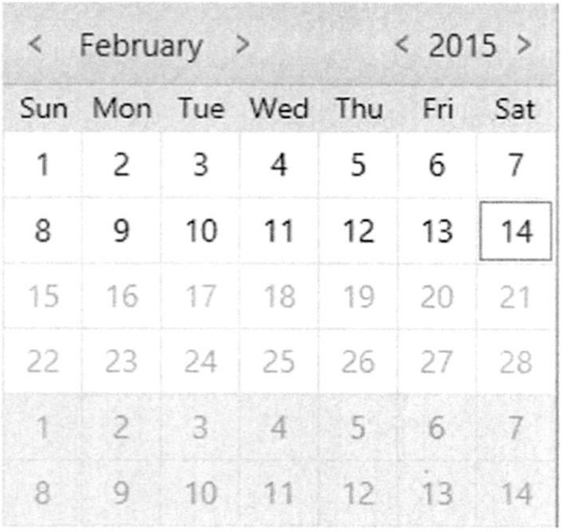

Figure 12-33. *Calendar pop-up for a DatePicker control*

The first row of the pop-up displays the month and year. You can scroll through months and years using the arrows. The second row displays the short names of weeks. The first column displays the week number of the year. By default, the week numbers column is not displayed. You can use the context menu on the pop-up to display it or you can set the showWeekNumbers property of the control to show it.

The calendar always displays dates for 42 days. Dates not applicable to the current month are disabled for selection. Each day cell is an instance of the DateCell class. You can provide a cell factory to use your custom cells. You will have an example of using a custom cell factory later.

Right-clicking the first row, week names, week number column, or disabled dates displays the context menu. The context menu also contains a Show Today menu item, which scrolls the calendar to the current date.

Using the *DatePicker* Control

You can create a DatePicker using its default constructor; it uses null as the initial value. You can also pass a LocalDate to another constructor as the initial value, as in the following code:

```
// Create a DatePicker with null as its initial value
DatePicker birthDate1 = new DatePicker();

// Use September 19, 1969 as its initial value
DatePicker birthDate2 = new DatePicker(LocalDate.of(1969, 9, 19));
```

The value property of the control holds the current date in the control. You can use the property to set a date. When the control has a null value, the pop-up shows the dates for the current month. Otherwise, the pop-up shows the dates of the month of the current value, as with the following code:

```
// Get the current value
LocalDate dt = birthDate.getValue();

// Set the current value
birthDate.setValue(LocalDate.of(1969, 9, 19));
```

The DatePicker control provides a TextField to enter a date as text. Its editor property stores the reference of the TextField. The property is read-only. If you do not want users to enter a date, you can set the editable property of the DatePicker to false, as in the following code:

```
DatePicker birthDate = new DatePicker();

// Users cannot enter a date. They must select one from the popup.
birthDate.setEditable(false);
```

DatePicker has a converter property that uses a StringConverter to convert a LocalDate to a string and vice versa. Its value property stores the date as LocalDate and its editor displays it as a string, which is the formatted date. When you enter a date as text, the converter converts it to a LocalDate and stores it in the value property. When you pick a date from the calendar pop-up, the converter creates a LocalDate to store in the value property and it converts it to a string to display in the editor. The default converter uses the default Locale and chronology to format the date. When you enter a date as text, the default converter expects the text in the default Locale and chronology format.

Listing 12-24 contains the code for a LocalDateStringConverter class that is a StringConverter for LocalDate. By default, it formats dates in MM/dd/yyyy format. You can pass a different format in its constructor.

Listing 12-24. A StringConverter to Convert a LocalDate to a String and Vice Versa

```
// LocalDateStringConverter.java
package com.jdojo.control;

import javafx.util.StringConverter;
import java.time.LocalDate;
import java.time.format.DateTimeFormatter;

public class LocalDateStringConverter extends StringConverter<LocalDate> {
        private String pattern = "MM/dd/yyyy";
        private DateTimeFormatter dtFormatter;

        public LocalDateStringConverter() {
                dtFormatter = DateTimeFormatter.ofPattern(pattern);
        }

        public LocalDateStringConverter(String pattern) {
                this.pattern = pattern;
                dtFormatter = DateTimeFormatter.ofPattern(pattern);
        }

        @Override
        public LocalDate fromString(String text) {
                LocalDate date = null;
                if (text != null && !text.trim().isEmpty()) {
                        date = LocalDate.parse(text, dtFormatter);
                }
                return date;
        }
```

```
        @Override
        public String toString(LocalDate date) {
                String text = null;
                if (date != null) {
                        text = dtFormatter.format(date);
                }
                return text;
        }
}
```

To format the date in "MMMM dd, yyyy" format, for example, May 29, 2013, you would create and set the convert as follows:

```
DatePicker birthDate = new DatePicker();
birthDate.setConverter(new LocalDateStringConverter("MMMM dd, yyyy"));
```

You can configure the DatePicker control to work with a specific chronology instead of the default one. The following statement sets the chronology to Thai Buddhist chronology:

```
birthDate.setChronology(ThaiBuddhistChronology.INSTANCE);
```

You can change the default Locale for the current instance of the JVM and the DatePicker will use the date format and chronology for the default Locale:

```
// Change the default Locale to Canada
Locale.setDefault(Locale.CANADA);
```

Each day cell in the pop-up calendar is an instance of the DateCell class, which is inherited from the Cell<LocalDate> class. The dayCellFactory property of the DatePicker class lets you provide a custom day cell factory. The concept is the same as discussed earlier for providing the cell factory for the ListView control. The following statement creates a day cell factory. It changes the text color of weekend cells to blue and disables all future day cells. If you set this day cell factory to a DatePicker, the pop-up calendar will not let users select a future date because you will have disabled all future day cells:

```
Callback<DatePicker, DateCell> dayCellFactory =
        new Callback<DatePicker, DateCell>() {
                public DateCell call(final DatePicker datePicker) {
                        return new DateCell() {
                                @Override
                                public void updateItem(LocalDate item, boolean empty) {
                                        // Must call super
                                        super.updateItem(item, empty);

                                        // Disable all future date cells
                                        if (item.isAfter(LocalDate.now())) {
                                                this.setDisable(true);
                                        }
```

```
                                        // Show Weekends in blue
                                        DayOfWeek day = DayOfWeek.from(item);
                                        if (day == DayOfWeek.SATURDAY ||
                                            day == DayOfWeek.SUNDAY) {
                                                his.setTextFill(Color.BLUE);
                                        }
                                    }
                                };
                            }
                        };
```

The following snippet of code sets a custom day cell factory for a birth date DatePicker control. It also makes the control noneditable. The control will force the user to select a nonfuture date from the pop-up calendar:

```
DatePicker birthDate = new DatePicker();

// Set a day cell factory to disable all future day cells
// and show weekends in blue
birthDate.setDayCellFactory(dayCellFactory);

// Users must select a date from the popup calendar
birthDate.setEditable(false);
```

The DatePicker control fires an ActionEvent when its value property changes. The value property may change when a user enters a date, selects a date from the pop-up, or a date is set programmatically, as provided in the following code:

```
// Add an ActionEvent handler
birthDate.setOnAction(e -> System.out.println("Date changed to:" + birthDate.getValue()));
```

Listing 12-25 has a complete program showing how to use a DatePicker control. It uses most of the features of the DatePicker. It displays a window as shown in Figure 12-34. The control is noneditable, forcing the user to select a nonfuture date from the pop-up.

Listing 12-25. Using the DatePicker Control

```
// DatePickerTest.java
package com.jdojo.control;

import java.time.DayOfWeek;
import java.time.LocalDate;
import javafx.application.Application;
import javafx.scene.Scene;
import javafx.scene.control.DateCell;
import javafx.scene.control.DatePicker;
import javafx.scene.control.Label;
import javafx.scene.layout.HBox;
import javafx.scene.paint.Color;
import javafx.stage.Stage;
import javafx.util.Callback;
```

```java
public class DatePickerTest extends Application {
        public static void main(String[] args) {
                Application.launch(args);
        }

        public void start(Stage stage) {
                DatePicker birthDate = new DatePicker();
                birthDate.setEditable(false);

                // Print the new date on standard output
                birthDate.setOnAction(e ->
                        System.out.println("New Date:" + birthDate.getValue())));

                String pattern = "MM/dd/yyyy";
                birthDate.setConverter(new LocalDateStringConverter(pattern));
                birthDate.setPromptText(pattern.toLowerCase());

                // Create a day cell factory
                Callback<DatePicker, DateCell> dayCellFactory =
                new Callback<DatePicker, DateCell>() {
                        public DateCell call(final DatePicker datePicker) {
                                return new DateCell() {
                                        @Override
                                        public void updateItem(LocalDate item, boolean empty) {
                                                // Must call super
                                                super.updateItem(item, empty);

                                                // Disable all future date cells
                                                if (item.isAfter(LocalDate.now())) {
                                                        this.setDisable(true);
                                                }

                                                // Show Weekends in blue color
                                                DayOfWeek day = DayOfWeek.from(item);
                                                if (day == DayOfWeek.SATURDAY ||
                                                        day == DayOfWeek.SUNDAY) {
                                                        this.setTextFill(Color.BLUE);
                                                }
                                        }
                                };
                        }};

                // Set the day cell factory
                birthDate.setDayCellFactory(dayCellFactory);

                HBox root = new HBox(new Label("Birth Date:"), birthDate);
                root.setStyle("-fx-padding: 10;" +
                                "-fx-border-style: solid inside;" +
                                "-fx-border-width: 2;" +
                                "-fx-border-insets: 5;" +
                                "-fx-border-radius: 5;" +
                                "-fx-border-color: blue;");
```

```
                Scene scene = new Scene(root);
                stage.setScene(scene);
                stage.setTitle("Using DatePicker Control");
                stage.show();
                stage.sizeToScene();
        }
}
```

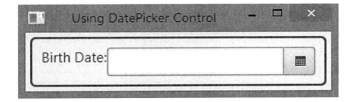

Figure 12-34. *A DatePicker control to select a nonfuture date*

Styling *DatePicker* with CSS

The default CSS style-class name for a DatePicker is date-picker, and for its pop-up, the class name is date-picker-popup. You can style almost every part of a DatePicker, for example, the month-year pane in the top area of the pop-up, day cells, week number cells, and current day cell. Please refer to the modena.css file for complete reference.

The CSS style-class name for day cell is day-cell. The day cell for the current date has the style-class name as today. The following styles display the current day number in bold and all day numbers in blue:

```
/* Display current day numbers in bolder font */
.date-picker-popup > * > .today {
        -fx-font-weight: bolder;
}

/* Display all day numbers in blue */
.date-picker-popup > * > .day-cell {
    -fx-text-fill: blue;
}
```

Understanding Text Input Controls

JavaFX supports text input controls that let users work with single line or multiple lines of plain text. I will discuss TextField, PasswordField, and TextArea text input controls in this section. All text input controls are inherited from the TextInputControl class. Please refer to Figure 12-1 for a class diagram for the text input controls.

▪ **Tip** JavaFX provides a rich text edit control named HTMLEditor. I will discuss HTMLEditor later in this chapter.

The TextInputControl class contains the properties and methods that apply to all types of text input controls. Properties and methods related to the current caret position and movement and text selection are in this class. Subclasses add properties and methods applicable to them. Table 12-5 lists the properties declared in the TextInputControl class.

Table 12-5. *Properties Declared in the TextInputControl Class*

Property	Type	Description
anchor	ReadOnlyIntegerProperty	It is the anchor of the text selection. It is at the opposite end of the caret position in the selection.
caretPosition	ReadOnlyIntegerProperty	It is the current position of the caret within the text.
editable	BooleanProperty	It is true if the control is editable. Otherwise, it is false.
font	ObjectProperty<Font>	It is the default font for the control.
length	ReadOnlyIntegerProperty	It is the number of characters in the control.
promptText	StringProperty	It is the prompt text. It is displayed in the control when control has no content.
selectedText	ReadOnlyStringProperty	It is the selected text in the control.
selection	ReadOnlyObjectProperty<IndexRange>	It is the selected text index range.
text	StringProperty	It is the text in the control.

Positioning and Moving Caret

All text input controls provide a caret. By default, a caret is a blinking vertical line when the control has focus. The current caret position is the target for the next input character from the keyboard. The caret position starts at zero, which is before the first character. Position 1 is after the first character and before the second character and so on. Figure 12-35 shows the caret positions in a text input control that has four characters. The number of characters in the text determines the valid range for the caret position, which is zero to the length of the text. Zero is the only valid caret position if the control does not contain text.

Figure 12-35. *Caret positions in a text input control having four characters*

Several methods take a caret position as an argument. Those methods clamp the argument value to the valid caret position range. Passing a caret position outside the valid range will not throw an exception. For example, if the control has four characters and you want to move the caret to position 10, the caret will be positioned at position 4.

The read-only `caretPosition` property contains the current caret position. Use the `positionCaret (int pos)` method to position the caret at the specified pos. The `backward()` and `forward()` methods move the caret one character backward and forward, respectively, if there is no selection. If there is a selection, they move the caret position to the beginning and end and clear the selection. The `home()` and `end()` methods move the caret before the first character and after the last character, respectively, and clear the selection. The `nextWord()` method moves the caret to the beginning of the next word and clears the selection. The `endOfNextWord()` method moves the caret to the end of the next word and clears the selection. The `previousWord()` method moves the caret to the beginning of the previous word and clears the selection.

Making Text Selection

The `TextInputControl` class provides a rich API through its properties and methods to deal with text selection. Using the selection API, you can select the entire or partial text and get the selection information.

The `selectedText` property contains the value of the selected text. Its value is an empty string if there is no selection. The `selection` property contains an `IndexRange` that holds the index range of the selection. The `getStart()` and `getEnd()` methods of the `IndexRange` class return the start index and end index of the selection, respectively, and its `getLength()` method returns the length of the selection. If there is no selection, the lower and upper limits of the range are the same and they are equal to the `caretPosition` value.

The `anchor` and `caretPosition` properties play a vital role in text selection. The value of these properties defines the selection range. The same value for both properties indicates no selection. Either property may indicate the start or end of the selection range. The `anchor` value is the caret position when the selection started. You can select characters by moving the caret backward or forward. For example, you can use the left or right arrow key with the Shift key pressed to select a range of characters. If you move the caret forward during the selection process, the `anchor` value will be less than the `caretPosition` value. If you move the caret backward during the selection process, the `anchor` value will be greater than the `caretPosition` value. Figure 12-36 shows the relation between the `anchor` and `caretPosition` values.

Figure 12-36. *Relation between the* `anchor` *and* `caretPosition` *properties of a text input control*

In Figure 12-36, the part labeled #1 shows a text input control with the text BLESSINGS. The `caretPosition` value is 1.The user selects four characters by moving the caret four positions forward, for example, by pressing Shift key and right arrow key or by dragging the mouse. The `selectedText` property, as shown in the part labeled #2, is LESS. The `anchor` value is 1 and the `caretPosition` value is 5. The selection property has an `IndexRange` of 1 to 5.

In the part labeled #3, the `caretPosition` value is 5. The user selects four characters by moving the caret backward as shown in the part labeled #4. The `selectedText` property, as shown in part labeled #4, is LESS. The `anchor` value is 5 and the `caretPosition` value is 1. The selection property has an `IndexRange` of 1 to 5. Notice that in the parts labeled #2 and #4, the `anchor` and `caretPosition` values are different and the `selectedText` and selection properties are the same.

Apart from the selection properties, the TextInputControl contains several useful selection-related methods:

- selectAll()
- deselect()
- selectRange(int anchor, int caretPosition)
- selectHome()
- selectEnd()
- extendSelection(int pos)
- selectBackward()
- selectForward()
- selectPreviousWord()
- selectEndOfNextWord()
- selectNextWord()
- selectPositionCaret(int pos)
- replaceSelection(String replacement)

Notice that you have a positionCaret(int pos) method and a selectPositionCaret(int pos) method. The former positions the caret at the specified position and clears the selection. The latter moves the caret to the specified pos and extends the selection if one exists. If no selection exists, it forms a selection by the current caret position as the anchor and moving the caret to the specified pos.

The replaceSelection(String replacement) method replaces the selected text by the specified replacement. If there is no selection, it clears the selection and inserts the specified replacement at the current caret position.

Modifying the Content

The text property of the TextInputControl class represents the textual content of text input controls. You can change the content using the setText(String text) method and get it using the getText() method. The clear() method sets the content to an empty string.

The insertText(int index, String text) method inserts the specified text at the specified index. It throws an IndexOutOfBoundsException if the specified index is outside the valid range (zero to the length of the content). The appendText(String text) method appends the specified text to the content. The deleteText() method lets you delete a range of characters from the content. You can specify the range as an IndexRange object or start and end index. The deleteNextChar() and deletePreviousChar() methods delete the next and previous character, respectively, from the current caret position if there is no selection. If there is a selection, they delete the selection. They return true if the deletion was successful. Otherwise, they return false.

The read-only length property represents the length of the content. It changes as you modify the content. Practically, the length value can be very big. There is no direct way to restrict the number of characters in a text input control. I will cover an example of restricting the length of text shortly.

Cutting, Copying, and Pasting Text

The text input controls supports cut, copy, and paste features programmatically, using the mouse and keyboard. To use these features using the mouse and keyboard, use the standard steps supported on your platform. Use the cut(), copy(), and paste() methods to use these features programmatically. The cut() method transfers the currently selected text to the clipboard and removes the current selection. The copy() method transfers the currently selected text to the clipboard without removing the current selection. The paste() method replaces the current selection with the content in the clipboard. If there is no selection, it inserts the clipboard content at the current caret position.

An Example

The program in Listing 12-26 demonstrates how the different properties of text input control change. It displays a window as shown in Figure 12-37. The program uses a TextField, which is a text input control, to display one line of text. Each property is displayed in a Label by binding the text properties to the properties of the TextField. After running the program, change the text in the name field, move the caret, and change the selection to see how the properties of the TextField change.

Listing 12-26. Using the Properties of Text Input Controls

```
// TextControlProperties.java
package com.jdojo.control;

import javafx.application.Application;
import javafx.scene.Scene;
import javafx.scene.control.Label;
import javafx.scene.control.TextField;
import javafx.scene.layout.GridPane;
import javafx.stage.Stage;

public class TextControlProperties extends Application {
        public static void main(String[] args) {
                Application.launch(args);
        }

        @Override
        public void start(Stage stage) {
                TextField nameFld = new TextField();
                Label anchorLbl = new Label("");
                Label caretLbl = new Label("");
                Label lengthLbl = new Label("");
                Label selectedTextLbl = new Label("");
                Label selectionLbl = new Label("");
                Label textLbl = new Label("");

                // Bind text property of the Labels to the properties of the TextField
                anchorLbl.textProperty().bind(nameFld.anchorProperty().asString());
                caretLbl.textProperty().bind(nameFld.caretPositionProperty().asString());
                lengthLbl.textProperty().bind(nameFld.lengthProperty().asString());
                selectedTextLbl.textProperty().bind(nameFld.selectedTextProperty());
                selectionLbl.textProperty().bind(nameFld.selectionProperty().asString());
                textLbl.textProperty().bind(nameFld.textProperty());
```

```
GridPane root = new GridPane();
root.setHgap(10);
root.setVgap(5);
root.addRow(0, new Label("Name:"), nameFld);
root.addRow(1, new Label("Anchor Position:"), anchorLbl);
root.addRow(2, new Label("Caret Postion:"), caretLbl);
root.addRow(3, new Label("Length:"), lengthLbl);
root.addRow(4, new Label("Selected Text:"), selectedTextLbl);
root.addRow(5, new Label("Selection:"), selectionLbl);
root.addRow(6, new Label("Text:"), textLbl);
root.setStyle("-fx-padding: 10;" +
              "-fx-border-style: solid inside;" +
              "-fx-border-width: 2;" +
              "-fx-border-insets: 5;" +
              "-fx-border-radius: 5;" +
              "-fx-border-color: blue;");

Scene scene = new Scene(root);
stage.setScene(scene);
stage.setTitle("Text Input Control Properties");
stage.show();
    }
}
```

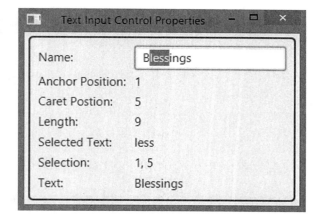

Figure 12-37. *Using properties of text input controls*

Styling *TextInputControl* with CSS

The TextInputControl class introduces a CSS pseudo-class named readonly, which applies when the control is not editable. It adds the following style properties:

- -fx-font
- -fx-text-fill
- -fx-prompt-text-fill

- `-fx-highlight-fill`
- `-fx-highlight-text-fill`
- `-fx-display-caret`

The `-fx-font` property is inherited from the parent by default. The value for the `-fx-display-caret` property could be true or false. When it is true, the caret is displayed when the control has focus. Otherwise, the caret is not displayed. Its default value is true. Most of the other properties affect background and text colors.

Understanding the *TextField* Control

`TextField` is a text input control. It inherits from the `TextInputControl` class. It lets the user enter a single line of plain text. If you need a control to enter multiline text, use `TextArea` instead. Newline and tab characters in the text are removed. Figure 12-38 shows a window with two `TextFields` having the text Layne and Estes.

Figure 12-38. *A window with two* `TextField` *controls*

You can create a `TextField` with an empty initial text or with a specified initial text, as shown in the following code:

```
// Create a TextField with an empty string as initial text
TextField nameFld1 = new TextField();

// Create a TextField with "Layne Estes" as an initial text
TextField nameFld2 = new TextField("Layne Estes");
```

As I have already mentioned, the text property of the `TextField` stores the textual content. If you are interested in handling the changes in a `TextField`, you need to add a `ChangeListener` to its text property. Most of the time you will be using its `setText(String newText)` method to set new text and the `getText()` method to get the text from it. `TextField` adds the following properties:

- `alignment`
- `onAction`
- `prefColumnCount`

The alignment property determines the alignment of the text within the TextField area when there is empty space. Its default value is CENTER_LEFT if the node orientation is LEFT_TO_RIGHT and CENTER_RIGHT if the node orientation is RIGHT_TO_LEFT. The onAction property is an ActionEvent handler, which is called when the Enter key is pressed in the TextField, as shown in the following code:

```
TextField nameFld = new TextField();
nameFld.setOnAction(e -> /* Your ActionEvent handler code...*/ );
```

The prefColumnCount property determines the width of the control. By default, its value is 12. A column is wide enough to display an uppercase letter W. If you set its value to 10, the TextField will be wide enough to display ten letter Ws, as shown in the following code:

```
// Set the preferred column count to 10
nameFld.setPrefColumnCount(10);
```

TextField provides a default context menu, as shown in Figure 12-39, that can be displayed by clicking the right mouse button. Menu items are enabled or disabled based on the context. You can replace the default context menu with a custom context menu. Currently, there is no way to customize the default context menu.

Figure 12-39. *The default context menu for TextField*

The following snippet of code sets a custom context menu for a TextField. It displays a menu item stating that the context menu is disabled. Selecting the menu item does nothing. You will need to add an ActionEvent handler to the menu items in context menu to perform some action.

```
ContextMenu cm = new ContextMenu();
MenuItem dummyItem = new MenuItem("Context menu is disabled");
cm.getItems().add(dummyItem);

TextField nameFld = new TextField();
nameFld.setContextMenu(cm);
```

The program in Listing 12-27 shows how to use TextField controls. It displays two TextFields. It shows adding ActionEvent handlers, a custom context menu, and ChangeListeners added to TextFields.

Listing 12-27. Using the TextField Control

```java
// TextFieldTest.java
package com.jdojo.control;

import javafx.application.Application;
import javafx.beans.value.ObservableValue;
import javafx.scene.Scene;
import javafx.scene.control.ContextMenu;
import javafx.scene.control.Label;
import javafx.scene.control.MenuItem;
import javafx.scene.control.TextField;
import javafx.scene.layout.GridPane;
import javafx.stage.Stage;

public class TextFieldTest extends Application {
        public static void main(String[] args) {
                Application.launch(args);
        }

        public void start(Stage stage) {
                // Create a TextFiled with an empty string as its initial text
                TextField firstNameFld = new TextField();
                TextField lastNameFld = new TextField();

                // Both fields should be wide enough to display 15 chars
                firstNameFld.setPrefColumnCount(15);
                lastNameFld.setPrefColumnCount(15);

                // Add a ChangeListener to the text property
                firstNameFld.textProperty().addListener(this::changed);
                lastNameFld.textProperty().addListener(this::changed);

                // Add a dummy custom context menu for the firstname field
                ContextMenu cm = new ContextMenu();
                MenuItem dummyItem = new MenuItem("Context menu is disabled");
                cm.getItems().add(dummyItem);
                firstNameFld.setContextMenu(cm);

                // Set ActionEvent handlers for both fields
                firstNameFld.setOnAction(e -> nameChanged("First Name"));
                lastNameFld.setOnAction(e -> nameChanged("Last Name"));

                GridPane root = new GridPane();
                root.setHgap(10);
                root.setVgap(5);
                root.addRow(0, new Label("First Name:"), firstNameFld);
```

```
            root.addRow(1, new Label("Last Name:"), lastNameFld);
            root.setStyle("-fx-padding: 10;" +
                        "-fx-border-style: solid inside;" +
                        "-fx-border-width: 2;" +
                        "-fx-border-insets: 5;" +
                        "-fx-border-radius: 5;" +
                        "-fx-border-color: blue;");

            Scene scene = new Scene(root);
            stage.setScene(scene);
            stage.setTitle("Using TextField Controls");
            stage.show();
        }

    public void nameChanged(String fieldName) {
            System.out.println("Action event fired on " + fieldName);
        }

    public void changed(ObservableValue<? extends String> prop,
                        String oldValue,
                        String newValue) {
            System.out.println("Old = " + oldValue + ", new = " + newValue);
        }
}
```

Styling *TextField* with CSS

The default CSS style-class name for a TextField is text-field. It adds an -fx-alignment property that is the alignment of its text within its content area. There is nothing special that needs to be said about styling TextField.

Understanding the *PasswordField* Control

PasswordField is a text input control. It inherits from TextField and it works much the same as TextField except it masks its text, that is, it does not display the actual characters entered. Rather, it displays an echo character for each character entered. The default echo character is a bullet. Figure 12-40 shows a window with a PasswordField.

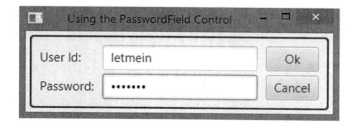

Figure 12-40. *A window using a PasswordField control*

The PasswordField class provides only one constructor, which is a no-args constructor. You can use the setText() and getText() methods to set and get, respectively, the actual text in a PasswordField, as in the following code. Typically, you do not set the password text. The user enters it.

```
// Create a PasswordField
PasswordField passwordFld = new PasswordField();
...
// Get the password text
String passStr = passwordFld.getText();
```

The PasswordField overrides the cut() and copy() methods of the TextInputControl class to make them no-op methods. That is, you cannot transfer the text in a PasswordField to the clipboard using the keyboard shortcuts or the context menu.

The default CSS style-class name for a PasswordField is password-field. It has all of the style properties of TextField. It does not add any style properties.

Understanding the *TextArea* Control

TextArea is a text input control. It inherits from the TextInputControl class. It lets the user enter multiline plain text. If you need a control to enter a single line of plain text, use TextField instead. If you want to use rich text, use the HTMLEditor control. Unlike the TextField, newline and tab characters in the text are preserved. A newline character starts a new paragraph in a TextArea. Figure 12-41 shows a window with a TextField and a TextArea. The user can enter a multiline résumé in the TextArea.

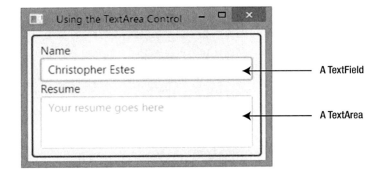

Figure 12-41. A window with a TextArea control

You can create a TextArea with an empty initial text or with a specified initial text using the following code:

```
// Create a TextArea with an empty string as its initial text
TextArea resume1 = new TextArea();

// Create a TextArea an initial text
TextArea resume2 = new TextArea("Years of Experience: 19");
```

As already discussed in the previous section, the text property of the TextArea stores the textual content. If you are interested in handling the changes in a TextArea, you need to add a ChangeListener to its text property. Most of the time, you will be using its setText(String newText) method to set new text and its getText() method to get the text from it.

TextArea adds the following properties:

- prefColumnCount
- prefRowCount
- scrollLeft
- scrollTop
- wrapText

The prefColumnCount property determines the width of the control. By default, its value is 32. A column is wide enough to display an uppercase letter W. If you set its value to 80, the TextArea will be wide enough to display 80 letter Ws. The following code accomplishes this:

```
// Set the preferred column count to 80
resume1.setPrefColumnCount(80);
```

The prefRowCount property determines the height of the control. By default, it is 10. The following code sets the row count to 20:

```
// Set the preferred row count to 20
resume.setPrefColumnCount(20);
```

If the text exceeds the number of columns and rows, the horizontal and vertical scroll panes are automatically displayed.

Like TextField, TextArea provides a default context menu. Please refer the "Understanding Text Input Controls" section for more detail on how to customize the default context menu.

The scrollLeft and scrollTop properties are the number of pixels that the text is scrolled to at the top and left. The following code sets it to 30px:

```
// Scroll the resume text by 30px to the top and 30 px to the left
resume.setScrollTop(30);
resume.setScrollLeft(30);
```

By default, TextArea starts a new line when it encounters a newline character in its text. A newline character also creates a new paragraph except for the first paragraph. By default, the text is not wrapped to the next line if it exceeds the width of the control. The wrapText property determines whether the text is wrapped to another line when its run exceeds the width of the control. By default, its value is false. The following code would set the default to true:

```
// Wrap the text if needed
resume.setWrapText(true);
```

The getParagraphs() method of the TextArea class returns an unmodifiable list of all paragraphs in its text. Each element in the list is a paragraph, which is an instance of CharSequence. The returned paragraph does not contain the newline characters. The following snippet of code prints the details, for example, paragraph number, and number of characters, for all paragraphs in the resume TextArea:

```
ObservableList<CharSequence> list = resume.getParagraphs();
int size = list.size();
System.out.println("Paragraph Count:" + size);
for(int i = 0; i < size; i++) {
        CharSequence cs = list.get(i);
        System.out.println("Paragraph #" + (i + 1) + ", Characters="  + cs.length());
        System.out.println(cs);
}
```

The program in Listing 12-28 shows how to use TextArea. It displays a window with a button to print the details of the text in the TextArea.

Listing 12-28. Using TextArea Controls

```
// TextAreaTest.java
package com.jdojo.control;

import javafx.application.Application;
import javafx.collections.ObservableList;
import javafx.scene.Scene;
import javafx.scene.control.Button;
import javafx.scene.control.Label;
import javafx.scene.control.TextArea;
import javafx.scene.control.TextField;
import javafx.scene.layout.VBox;
import javafx.stage.Stage;

public class TextAreaTest extends Application {
        public static void main(String[] args) {
                Application.launch(args);
        }

        @Override
        public void start(Stage stage) {
                TextField title = new TextField("Luci");
                title.setPromptText("Your poem title goes here");

                TextArea poem = new TextArea();
                poem.setPromptText("Your poem goes here");
                poem.setPrefColumnCount(20);
                poem.setPrefRowCount(10);
                poem.appendText("I told her this: her laughter light\n" +
                                "Is ringing in my ears:\n" +
                                "And when I think upon that night\n" +
                                "My eyes are dim with tears.");
```

```
            Button printBtn = new Button("Print Poem Details");
            printBtn.setOnAction(e -> print(poem));

            VBox root = new VBox(new Label("Title:"), title,
                            new Label("Poem:"), poem, printBtn);
            root.setStyle("-fx-padding: 10;" +
                            "-fx-border-style: solid inside;" +
                            "-fx-border-width: 2;" +
                            "-fx-border-insets: 5;" +
                            "-fx-border-radius: 5;" +
                            "-fx-border-color: blue;");

            Scene scene = new Scene(root);
            stage.setScene(scene);
            stage.setTitle("Using TextArea Controls");
            stage.show();
    }

    public void print(TextArea poem) {
            System.out.println("Poem Length: " + poem.getLength());
            System.out.println("Poem Text:\n" + poem.getText());
            System.out.println();

            ObservableList<CharSequence> list = poem.getParagraphs();
            int size = list.size();
            System.out.println("Paragraph Count:" + size);
            for(int i = 0; i < size; i++) {
                    CharSequence cs = list.get(i);
                    System.out.println("Paragraph #" + (i + 1) +
                                        ", Characters=" + cs.length());
                    System.out.println(cs);
            }
    }
}
```

Styling *TextArea* with CSS

The default CSS style-class name for a TextArea is text-area. It does not add any CSS properties to the ones present in its ancestor TextInputControl. It contains scroll-pane and content substructures, which are a ScrollPane and a Region, respectively. The scroll-pane is the scroll pane that appears when its text exceeds its width or height. The content is the region that displays the text.

The following styles set the horizontal and vertical scrollbar policies to always, so the scrollbars should always appear in TextArea. Padding for the content area is set to 10px:

```
.text-area > .scroll-pane {
        -fx-hbar-policy: always;
        -fx-vbar-policy: always;
}

.text-area .content {
        -fx-padding: 10;
}
```

528

■ Tip At the time of this writing, setting the scrollbar policy for the `scroll-pane` substructure is ignored by the `TextArea`.

Showing the Progress of a Task

When you have a long running task, you need to provide a visual feedback to the user about the progress of the task for a better user experience. JavaFX offers two controls to show the progress:

- `ProgressIndicator`
- `ProgressBar`

They differ in the ways they display the progress. The `ProgressBar` class inherits from the `ProgressIndicator` class. `ProgressIndicator` displays the progress in a circular control, whereas `ProgressBar` uses a horizontal bar. The `ProgressBar` class does not add any properties or methods. It just uses a different shape for the control. Figure 12-42 shows a `ProgressIndicator` in indeterminate and determinate states. Figure 12-43 shows a `ProgressBar` in indeterminate and determinate states. Both figures use the same progress values in the four instances of the determinate states.

Figure 12-42. A ProgressIndicator control in indeterminate and determinate states

Figure 12-43. A ProgressBar control in indeterminate and determinate states

The current progress of a task may be determined or not. If the progress cannot be determined, it is said to be in an indeterminate state. If the progress is known, it is said to be in a determinate state. The `ProgressIndicator` class declares two properties:

- `indeterminate`
- `progress`

The `indeterminate` property is a read-only `boolean` property. If it returns `true`, it means it is not possible to determine the progress. A `ProgressIndicator` in this state is rendered with some kind of repeated animation. The `progress` property is a `double` property. Its value indicates the progress between 0% and 100%. A negative value indicates that the progress is indeterminate. A value between 0 and 1.0 indicates a determinate state with a progress between 0% and 100%. A value greater than 1.0 is treated as 1.0 (i.e., 100% progress).

Both classes provide default constructors that create controls in indeterminate state, as shown in the following code:

```
// Create an indeterminate progress indicator and a progress bar
ProgressIndicator indeterminateInd = new ProgressIndicator();
ProgressBar indeterminateBar = new ProgressBar();
```

The other constructors that take the progress value create controls in the indeterminate or determinate state. If the progress value is negative, they create controls in indeterminate state. Otherwise, they create controls in determinate state, as shown in the following code:

```
// Create a determinate progress indicator with 10% progress
ProgressIndicator indeterminateInd = new ProgressIndicator(0.10);
```

```
// Create a determinate progress bar with 70% progress
ProgressBar indeterminateBar = new ProgressBar(0.70);
```

The program in Listing 12-29 shows how to use `ProgressIndicator` and `ProgressBar` controls. Clicking the Make Progress button increases the progress by 10%. Clicking the Complete Task button completes the indeterminate tasks by setting their progress to 100%. Typically, the progress properties of these controls are updated by a long running task when the task progresses to a milestone. You used a button to update the progress property to keep the program logic simple.

Listing 12-29. Using the `ProgressIndicator` and `ProgressBar` Controls

```
// ProgressTest.java
package com.jdojo.control;

import javafx.application.Application;
import javafx.scene.Scene;
import javafx.scene.control.Button;
import javafx.scene.control.Label;
import javafx.scene.control.ProgressBar;
import javafx.scene.control.ProgressIndicator;
import javafx.scene.layout.GridPane;
import javafx.stage.Stage;

public class ProgressTest extends Application {
        public static void main(String[] args) {
                Application.launch(args);
        }

        @Override
        public void start(Stage stage) {
                ProgressIndicator indeterminateInd = new ProgressIndicator();
                ProgressIndicator determinateInd = new ProgressIndicator(0);

                ProgressBar indeterminateBar = new ProgressBar();
                ProgressBar determinateBar = new ProgressBar(0);

                Button completeIndBtn = new Button("Complete Task");
                completeIndBtn.setOnAction(e -> indeterminateInd.setProgress(1.0));
```

```java
        Button completeBarBtn = new Button("Complete Task");
        completeBarBtn.setOnAction(e -> indeterminateBar.setProgress(1.0));

        Button makeProgresstIndBtn = new Button("Make Progress");
        makeProgresstIndBtn.setOnAction(e -> makeProgress(determinateInd));

        Button makeProgresstBarBtn = new Button("Make Progress");
        makeProgresstBarBtn.setOnAction(e -> makeProgress(determinateBar));

        GridPane root = new GridPane();
        root.setHgap(10);
        root.setVgap(5);
        root.addRow(0, new Label("Indeterminate Progress:"),
                      indeterminateInd, completeIndBtn);
        root.addRow(1, new Label("Determinate Progress:"),
                      determinateInd, makeProgresstIndBtn);
        root.addRow(2, new Label("Indeterminate Progress:"),
                      indeterminateBar, completeBarBtn);
        root.addRow(3, new Label("Determinate Progress:"),
                      determinateBar, makeProgresstBarBtn);
        root.setStyle("-fx-padding: 10;" +
                      "-fx-border-style: solid inside;" +
                      "-fx-border-width: 2;" +
                      "-fx-border-insets: 5;" +
                      "-fx-border-radius: 5;" +
                      "-fx-border-color: blue;");

        Scene scene = new Scene(root);
        stage.setScene(scene);
        stage.setTitle("Using ProgressIndicator and ProgressBar Controls");
        stage.show();
    }

    public void makeProgress(ProgressIndicator p) {
        double progress = p.getProgress();
        if (progress <= 0) {
            progress = 0.1;
        } else {
            progress = progress + 0.1;
            if (progress >= 1.0) {
                progress = 1.0;
            }
        }
        p.setProgress(progress);
    }
}
```

Styling *ProgressIndicator* with CSS

The default CSS style-class name for a ProgressIndicator is progress-indicator. ProgressIndicator supports determinate and indeterminate CSS pseudo-classes. The determinate pseudo-class applies when the indeterminate property is false. The indeterminate pseudo-class applies when the indeterminate property is true.

ProgressIndicator has a CSS style property named -fx-progress-color, which is the color of the progress. The following styles set the progress color to red for the indeterminate progress and blue for determinate progress:

```
.progress-indicator:indeterminate {
        -fx-progress-color: red;
}

.progress-indicator:determinate {
        -fx-progress-color: blue;
}
```

The ProgressIndicator contains four substructures:

- An indicator substructure, which is a StackPane

- A progress substructure, which is StackPane

- A percentage substructure, which is a Text

- A tick substructure, which is a StackPane

You can style all substructures of a ProgressIndicator. Please refer to the modena.css file for sample code.

Styling *ProgressIndicator* and Bar with CSS

The default CSS style-class name for a ProgressBar is progress-bar. It supports the CSS style properties:

- -fx-indeterminate-bar-length

- -fx-indeterminate-bar-escape

- -fx-indeterminate-bar-flip

- -fx-indeterminate-bar-animation-time

All properties apply to the bar that shows the indeterminate progress. The default bar length is 60px. Use the -fx-indeterminate-bar-length property to specify a different bar length.

When the -fx-indeterminate-bar-escape property is true, the bar starting edge starts at the starting edge of the track and the bar trailing edge ends at the ending edge of the track. That is, the bar is displayed beyond the track length. When this property is false, the bar moves within the track length. The default value is true.

The -fx-indeterminate-bar-flip property indicates whether the bar moves only in one direction or both. The default value is true, which means the bar moves in both directions by flipping its direction at the end of each edge.

The -fx-indeterminate-bar-animation-time property is the time in seconds that the bar should take to go from one edge to the other. The default value is 2.

The ProgressBar contains two substructures:

- A track substructure, which is a StackPane

- A bar substructure, which is a region

The following styles modify the background color and radius of the bar and track of ProgressBar control to give it a look as shown in Figure 12-44:

```
.progress-bar .track  {
        -fx-background-color: lightgray;
        -fx-background-radius: 5;
}

.progress-bar .bar  {
        -fx-background-color: blue;
        -fx-background-radius: 5;
}
```

Figure 12-44. *Customizing the bar and track of the* ProgressBar *control*

Understanding the *TitledPane* Control

TitledPane is a labeled control. The TitledPane class inherits from the Labeled class. A labeled control can have text and a graphic, so it can have a TitledPane. TitledPane displays the text as its title. The graphic is shown in the title bar.

Besides text and a graphic, a TitledPane has content, which is a Node. Typically, a group of controls is placed in a container and the container is added as the content for the TitledPane. TitledPane can be in a collapsed or expanded state. In the collapsed state, it displays only the title bar and hides the content. In the expanded state, it displays the title bar and the content. In its title bar, it displays an arrow that indicates whether it is expanded or collapsed. Clicking anywhere in the title bar expands or collapses the content. Figure 12-45 shows a TitledPane in both states along with all of its parts.

Figure 12-45. *A* TitledPane *in the collapsed and expanded states*

Use the default constructor to create a `TitledPane` without a title and content. You can set them later using the `setText()` and `setContent()` methods. Alternatively, you can provide the title and content as arguments to its constructor, using the following code:

```
// Create a TitledPane and set its title and content
TitledPane infoPane1 = new TitledPane();
infoPane1.setText("Personal Info");
infoPane1.setContent(new Label("Here goes the content."));

// Create a TitledPane with a title and content
TitledPane infoPane2 = new TitledPane("Personal Info", new Label("Content"));
```

You can add a graphic to a `TitledPane` using the `setGraphic()` method, which is declared in the `Labeled` class, as shown in the following code:

```
String imageStr = "resources/picture/privacy_icon.png";
URL imageUrl = getClass().getClassLoader().getResource(imageStr);
Image img = new Image(imageUrl.toExternalForm());
ImageView imgView = new ImageView(img);
infoPane2.setGraphic(imgView);
```

The `TitledPane` class declares four properties:

- animated
- collapsible
- content
- expanded

The animated property is a `boolean` property that indicates whether collapse and expand actions are animated. By default, it is true and those actions are animated. The `collapsible` property is a `boolean` property that indicates whether the `TitledPane` can collapse. By default, it is set to true and the `TitledPane` can collapse. If you do not want your `TitledPane` to collapse, set this property to false. A noncollapsible `TitledPane` does not display an arrow in its title bar. The content property is an `Object` property that stores the reference of any node. The content is visible when the control is in the expanded state. The expanded property is a `boolean` property. The `TitledPane` is in an expanded state when the property is true. Otherwise, it is in a collapsed state. By default, a `TitledPane` is in an expanded state. Use the `setExpanded()` method to expand and collapse the `TitledPane` programmatically, as shown in the following code:

```
// Set the state to expanded
infoPane2.setExpanded(true);
```

■ **Tip** Add a `ChangeListener` to its expanded property if you are interested in processing the expanded and collapsed events for a `TitledPane`.

Typically, `TitledPane` controls are used in a group in an `Accordion` control, which displays only one `TitledPane` from the group in the expanded state at a time to save space. You can also use a standalone `TitledPane` if you want to show controls in groups.

▪ **Tip**   Recall that the height of a TitledPane changes as it expands and collapses. Do not set its minimum, preferred, and maximum heights in your code. Otherwise, it may result in an unspecified behavior.

The program in Listing 12-30 shows how to use the TitledPane control. It displays a window with a TitledPane, which lets the user enter the first name, last name, and birth date of a person.

Listing 12-30.   Using the TitledPane Control

```
// TitledPaneTest.java
package com.jdojo.control;

import java.net.URL;
import javafx.application.Application;
import javafx.scene.Scene;
import javafx.scene.control.DatePicker;
import javafx.scene.control.Label;
import javafx.scene.control.TextField;
import javafx.scene.control.TitledPane;
import javafx.scene.image.Image;
import javafx.scene.image.ImageView;
import javafx.scene.layout.GridPane;
import javafx.scene.layout.HBox;
import javafx.stage.Stage;

public class TitledPaneTest extends Application {
        public static void main(String[] args) {
                Application.launch(args);
        }

        @Override
        public void start(Stage stage) {
                TextField firstNameFld = new TextField();
                firstNameFld.setPrefColumnCount(8);

                TextField lastNameFld = new TextField();
                lastNameFld.setPrefColumnCount(8);

                DatePicker dob = new DatePicker();
                dob.setPrefWidth(150);

                GridPane grid = new GridPane();
                grid.addRow(0, new Label("First Name:"), firstNameFld);
                grid.addRow(1, new Label("Last Name:"), lastNameFld);
                grid.addRow(2, new Label("DOB:"), dob);

                TitledPane infoPane = new TitledPane();
                infoPane.setText("Personal Info");
                infoPane.setContent(grid);
```

```
            String imageStr = "resources/picture/privacy_icon.png";
            URL imageUrl = getClass().getClassLoader().getResource(imageStr);
            Image img = new Image(imageUrl.toExternalForm());
            ImageView imgView = new ImageView(img);
            infoPane.setGraphic(imgView);

            HBox root = new HBox(infoPane);
            root.setSpacing(10);
            root.setStyle("-fx-padding: 10;" +
                          "-fx-border-style: solid inside;" +
                          "-fx-border-width: 2;" +
                          "-fx-border-insets: 5;" +
                          "-fx-border-radius: 5;" +
                          "-fx-border-color: blue;");

            Scene scene = new Scene(root);
            stage.setScene(scene);
            stage.setTitle("Using TitledPane Controls");
            stage.show();
        }
}
```

Styling *TitledPane* with CSS

The default CSS style-class name for a TitledPane is titled-pane. TitledPane adds two style properties of boolean type:

- -fx-animated
- -fx-collapsible

The default values for both properties are true. The -fx-animated property indicates whether the expanding and collapsing actions are animated. The -fx-collapsible property indicates whether the control can be collapsed.

TitledPane supports two CSS pseudo-classes:

- collapsed
- expanded

The collapsed pseudo-class applies when the control is collapsed and the expanded pseudo-class applies when it is expanded.

TitledPane contains two substructures:

- title
- Content

The title substructure is a StackPane that contains the content of the title bar. The title substructure contains text and arrow-button substructures. The text substructure is a Label and it holds the title text and the graphic. The arrow-button substructure is a StackPane that contains an arrow substructure, which is also a StackPane. The arrow substructure is an indicator that shows whether the control is in an expanded or collapsed state. The content substructure is a StackPane that contains the content of the control.

Let's look at an example of the effects of applying the four different styles to a `TitledPane` control, as presented in the following code:

```
/* #1 */
.titled-pane > .title  {
        -fx-background-color: lightgray;
        -fx-alignment: center-right;
}

/* #2 */
.titled-pane > .title > .text {
        -fx-font-size: 14px;
        -fx-underline: true;
}

/* #3 */
.titled-pane > .title > .arrow-button > .arrow {
        -fx-background-color: blue;
}

/* #4 */
.titled-pane > .content {
        -fx-background-color: burlywood;
        -fx-padding: 10;
}
```

Style #1 sets the background color of the title to light gray and places the graphic and title at the center right in the title bar. Style #2 changes the font size of the title text to 14px and underlines it. Setting the text color of the title using the -fx-text-fill property does not work at the time of this writing and setting the -fx-text-fill property on the TitledPane itself affects the text color of the content as well. Style #3 sets the background color of the arrow to blue. Style #4 sets the background color and padding of the content region. Figure 12-46 shows the same window as show in Figure 12-45 after applying the above styles.

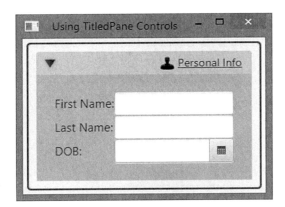

Figure 12-46. *Effects of applying styles to a* `TitledPane`

Understanding the *Accordion* Control

Accordion is a simple control. It displays a group of TitledPane controls where only one of them is in the expanded state at a time. Figure 12-47 shows a window with an Accordion, which contains three TitledPanes. The General TitledPane is expanded. The Address and Phone TitledPanes are collapsed.

Figure 12-47. An Accordion with three TitledPanes

The Accordion class contains only one constructor (a no-args constructor) to create its object:

```
// Create an Accordian
Accordion root = new Accordion();
```

Accordion stores the list of its TilePane controls in an ObservableList<TitledPane>. The getPanes() method returns the list of the TitledPane. Use the list to add or remove any TitledPane to the Accordion, as shown in the following code:

```
TitledPane generalPane = new TitledPane();
TitledPane addressPane = new TitledPane();
TitledPane phonePane = new TitledPane();
...
Accordion root = new Accordion();
root.getPanes().addAll(generalPane, addressPane, phonePane);
```

The Accordion class contains an expandedPane property, which stores the reference of the currently expanded TitledPane. By default, an Accordion displays all of its TitledPanes in a collapsed state, and this property is set to null. Click the title bar of a TitledPane or use the setExpandedPane() method to expand a TitledPane. Add a ChangeListener to this property if you are interested in when the expanded TitledPane changes. The program in Listing 12-31 shows how to create and populate an Accordion.

Listing 12-31. Using the TitledPane Control

```java
// AccordionTest.java
package com.jdojo.control;

import javafx.application.Application;
import javafx.scene.Scene;
import javafx.scene.control.Accordion;
import javafx.scene.control.DatePicker;
import javafx.scene.control.Label;
import javafx.scene.control.TextField;
import javafx.scene.control.TitledPane;
import javafx.scene.layout.GridPane;
import javafx.stage.Stage;

public class AccordionTest extends Application {
        public static void main(String[] args) {
                Application.launch(args);
        }

        @Override
        public void start(Stage stage) {
                TitledPane generalPane = this.getGeneralPane();
                TitledPane addressPane = this.getAddressPane();
                TitledPane phonePane = this.getPhonePane();

                Accordion root = new Accordion();
                root.getPanes().addAll(generalPane, addressPane, phonePane);
                root.setExpandedPane(generalPane);
                root.setStyle("-fx-padding: 10;" +
                                "-fx-border-style: solid inside;" +
                                "-fx-border-width: 2;" +
                                "-fx-border-insets: 5;" +
                                "-fx-border-radius: 5;" +
                                "-fx-border-color: blue;");

                Scene scene = new Scene(root);
                stage.setScene(scene);
                stage.setTitle("Using Accordion Controls");
                stage.show();
        }

        public TitledPane getGeneralPane() {
                GridPane grid = new GridPane();
                grid.addRow(0, new Label("First Name:"), new TextField());
                grid.addRow(1, new Label("Last Name:"), new TextField());
                grid.addRow(2, new Label("DOB:"), new DatePicker());

                TitledPane generalPane = new TitledPane("General", grid);
                return generalPane;
        }
```

```
        public TitledPane getAddressPane() {
                GridPane grid = new GridPane();
                grid.addRow(0, new Label("Street:"), new TextField());
                grid.addRow(1, new Label("City:"), new TextField());
                grid.addRow(2, new Label("State:"), new TextField());
                grid.addRow(3, new Label("ZIP:"), new TextField());

                TitledPane addressPane = new TitledPane("Address", grid);
                return addressPane;
        }

        public TitledPane getPhonePane() {
                GridPane grid = new GridPane();
                grid.addRow(0, new Label("Home:"), new TextField());
                grid.addRow(1, new Label("Work:"), new TextField());
                grid.addRow(2, new Label("Cell:"), new TextField());

                TitledPane phonePane = new TitledPane("Phone", grid);
                return phonePane;
        }
}
```

Styling *Accordion* with CSS

The default CSS style-class name for an Accordion is accordion. Accordion does not add any CSS properties. It contains a first-titled-pane substructure, which is the first TitledPane. The following style sets the background color and insets of the title bar of all TitledPanes:

```
.accordion > .titled-pane > .title {
    -fx-background-color: burlywood;
        -fx-background-insets: 1;
}
```

The following style sets the background color of the title bar of the first TitledPane of the Accordion:

```
.accordion > .first-titled-pane > .title {
    -fx-background-color: derive(red, 80%);
}
```

Understanding the *Pagination* Control

Pagination is used to display a large single content by dividing sections of it into smaller chunks called pages, for example, the results of a search. Figure 12-48 shows a Pagination control. A Pagination control has a page count, which is the number of pages in it. If the number of pages is not known, the page count may be indeterminate. Each page has an index, which starts at 0.

3/5

Figure 12-48. *A Pagination control*

A Pagination control is divided into two areas:

- Content area

- Navigation area

The content area displays the content of the current page. The navigation area contains parts to allow the user to navigate from one page to another. You can navigate between pages sequentially or randomly. The parts of a Pagination control are shown in Figure 12-49.

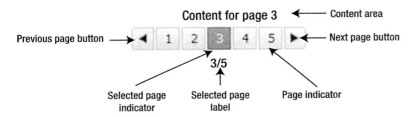

Figure 12-49. *Parts of a Pagination control*

The previous and next page arrow buttons let the user navigate to the previous and next pages, respectively. The previous page button is disabled when you are on the first page. The next page button is disabled when you are on the last page. Page indicators also let you navigate to a specific page by showing all of the page numbers. By default, page indicators use a tool tip to show the page number, which you have the option to disable using a CSS property. The selected page indicator shows the current page. The selected page label shows the current page selection details.

The Pagination class provides several constructors. They configure the control differently. The default constructor creates a control with an indeterminate page count and zero as the index for the selected page, as in the following code:

```
// Indeterminate page count and first page selected
Pagination pagination1 = new Pagination();
```

When the page count is indeterminate, the page indicator label displays x/..., where x is the current page index plus 1.

You use another constructor to specify a page count, as in the following code:

```
// 5 as the page count and first page selected
Pagination pagination2 = new Pagination(5);
```

You can use yet another constructor to specify the page count and the selected page index, as in the following code:

```
// 5 as the page count and second page selected (page index starts at 0)
Pagination pagination3 = new Pagination(5, 1);
```

The Pagination class declares an INDETERMINATE constant that can be used to specify an indeterminate page count, as in the following code:

```
// Indeterminate page count and second page selected
Pagination pagination4 = new Pagination(Pagination.INDETERMINATE, 1);
```

The Pagination class contains the following properties:

- currentPageIndex
- maxPageIndicatorCount
- pageCount
- pageFactory

The currentPageIndex is an integer property. Its value is the page index of the page to display. The default value is zero. You can specify its value using one of the constructors or using the setCurrentPageIndex() method. If you set its value to less than zero, the first page index, which is zero, is set as its value. If you set its value to greater than the page count minus 1, its value is set to page count minus 1. If you want to know when a new page is displayed, add a ChangeListener to the currentPageIndex property.

The maxPageIndicatorCount is an integer property. It sets the maximum number of page indicators to display. It defaults to 10. Its value remains unchanged if it is set beyond the page count range. If its value is set too high, the value is reduced so that the number of page indicators fits the control. You can set its value using the setMaxPageIndicatorCount() method.

The pageCount is an integer property. It is the number of pages in the Pagination control. Its value must be greater than or equal to 1. It defaults to indeterminate. Its value can be set in the constructors or using setPageCount() method.

The pageFactory is the most important property. It is an object property of the Callback<Integer, Node> type. It is used to generate pages. When a page needs to be displayed, the control calls the call() method of the Callback object passing the page index. The call() method returns a node that is the content of the page. The following snippet of code creates and sets a page factory for a Pagination control. The page factory returns a Label:

```
// Create a Pagination with an indeterminate page count
Pagination pagination = new Pagination();

// Create a page factory that returns a Label
Callback<Integer, Node> factory = pageIndex -> new Label("Content for page " + (pageIndex + 1));

// Set the page factory
pagination.setPageFactory(factory);
```

■ **Tip** The call() method of the page factory should return null if a page index does not exist. The current page does not change when the call() method returns null.

The program in Listing 12-32 shows how to use a Pagination control. It sets the page count to 5. The page factory returns a Label with text that shows the page number. It will display a window with a Pagination control similar to the one shown in Figure 12-48.

Listing 12-32. Using the Pagination Control

```java
// PaginationTest.java
package com.jdojo.control;

import javafx.application.Application;
import javafx.scene.Scene;
import javafx.scene.control.Label;
import javafx.scene.control.Pagination;
import javafx.scene.layout.VBox;
import javafx.stage.Stage;

public class PaginationTest extends Application {
        private static final int PAGE_COUNT = 5;

        public static void main(String[] args) {
                Application.launch(args);
        }

        @Override
        public void start(Stage stage) {
                Pagination pagination = new Pagination(PAGE_COUNT);

                // Set the page factory
                pagination.setPageFactory(this::getPage);

                VBox root = new VBox(pagination);
                root.setStyle("-fx-padding: 10;" +
                                "-fx-border-style: solid inside;" +
                                "-fx-border-width: 2;" +
                                "-fx-border-insets: 5;" +
                                "-fx-border-radius: 5;" +
                                "-fx-border-color: blue;");

                Scene scene = new Scene(root);
                stage.setScene(scene);
                stage.setTitle("Using Pagination Controls");
                stage.show();
        }

        public Label getPage(int pageIndex) {
                Label content = null;

                if (pageIndex >= 0 && pageIndex < PAGE_COUNT) {
                        content = new Label("Content for page " + (pageIndex + 1));
                }
                return content;
        }
}
```

The page indicators may be numeric buttons or bullet buttons. Numeric buttons are used by default. The Pagination class contains a String constant named STYLE_CLASS_BULLET, which is the style class for the control if you want to use bullet buttons. The following snippet of code creates a Pagination control and sets its style class to use bullet buttons as page indicators. Figure 12-50 shows a Pagination control with bullet buttons as page indicators.

```
Pagination pagination = new Pagination(5);

// Use bullet page indicators
pagination.getStyleClass().add(Pagination.STYLE_CLASS_BULLET);
```

Content for page 3

◀ ◯ ◯ ⬤ ◯ ◯ ▶

3/5

Figure 12-50. *A Pagination control using bullet buttons as page indicators*

Styling *Pagination* with CSS

The default CSS style-class name for a Pagination control is pagination. Pagination adds several CSS properties:

- -fx-max-page-indicator-count
- -fx-arrows-visible
- -fx-tooltip-visible
- -fx-page-information-visible
- -fx-page-information-alignment

The -fx-max-page-indicator-count property specifies the maximum number of page indicators to display. The default value is 10. The -fx-arrows-visible property specifies whether the previous and next page buttons are visible. The default value is true. The -fx-tooltip-visible property specifies whether a tool tip is displayed when the mouse hovers over a page indicator. The default value is true. The -fx-page-information-visible specifies whether the selected page label is visible. The default value is true. The -fx-page-information-alignment specifies the location of the selected page label relative to the page indicators. The possible values are top, right, bottom, and left. The default value is bottom, which displays the selected page indicator below the page indicators.

The Pagination control has two substructures of StackPane type:

- page
- pagination-control

The page substructure represents the content area. The `pagination-control` substructure represents the navigation area and it has the following substructures:

- `left-arrow-button`
- `right-arrow-Button`
- `bullet-button`
- `number-button`
- `page-information`

The `left-arrow-button` and `right-arrow-button` substructures are of the Button type. They represent the previous and next page buttons, respectively. The `left-arrow-button` substructure has a `left-arrow` substructure, which is a StackPane, and it represents the arrow in the previous page button. The `right-arrow-button` substructure has a `right-arrow` substructure, which is a StackPane, and it represents the arrow in the next page button. The `bullet-button` and `number-button` are of the ToggleButton type, and they represent the page indicators. The `page-information` substructure is a Label that holds the selected page information. The `pagination-control` substructure holds the previous and next page buttons and the page indicators in a substructure called `control-box`, which is an HBox.

The following styles make the selected page label invisible, set the page background to light gray, and draw a border around the previous, next, and page indicator buttons. Please refer to the `modena.css` file for more details on how to style a Pagination control.

```
.pagination  {
        -fx-page-information-visible: false;
}

.pagination > .page {
    -fx-background-color: lightgray;
}

.pagination  > .pagination-control > .control-box {
    -fx-padding: 2;
        -fx-border-style: dashed;
        -fx-border-width: 1;
        -fx-border-radius: 5;
        -fx-border-color: blue;
}
```

Understanding the Tool Tip Control

A tool tip is a pop-up control used to show additional information about a node. It is displayed when a mouse pointer hovers over the node. There is a small delay between when the mouse pointer hovers over a node and when the tool tip for the node is shown. The tool tip is hidden after a small period. It is also hidden when the mouse pointer leaves the control. You should not design a GUI application where the user depends on seeing tool tips for controls, as they may not be shown at all if the mouse pointer never hovers over the controls. Figure 12-51 shows a window with a tool tip, which displays Saves the data text.

Figure 12-51. *A window showing a tool tip*

A tool tip is represented by an instance of the Tooltip class, which inherits from the PopupControl class. A tool tip can have text and a graphic. You can create a tool tip using its default constructor, which has no text and no graphic. You can also create a tool tip with text using the other constructor, as in the following code:

```
// Create a Tooltip with No text and no graphic
Tooltip tooltip1 = new Tooltip();

// Create a Tooltip with text
Tooltip tooltip2 = new Tooltip("Closes the window");
```

A tool tip needs to be installed for a node using the install() static method of the Tooltip class. Use the uninstall() static method to uninstalled a tool tip for a node:

```
Button saveBtn = new Button("Save");
Tooltip tooltip = new Tooltip("Saves the data");

// Install a tooltip
Tooltip.install(saveBtn, tooltip);
...
// Uninstall the tooltip
Tooltip.uninstall(saveBtn, tooltip);
```

Tool tips are frequently used for UI controls. Therefore, installing tool tips for controls has been made easier. The Control class contains a tooltip property, which is an object property of the Tooltip type. You can use the setTooltip() method of the Control class to set a Tooltip for controls. If a node is not a control, for example, a Circle node, you will need to use the install() method to set a tool tip as shown above. The following snippet of code shows how to use the tooltip property for a button:

```
Button saveBtn = new Button("Save");

// Install a tooltip
saveBtn.setTooltip(new Tooltip("Saves the data"));
...
// Uninstall the tooltip
saveBtn.setTooltip(null);
```

■ **Tip**   A tool tip can be shared among multiple nodes. A tool tip uses a Label control to display its text and graphic. Internally, all content-related properties set on a tool tip are delegated to the Label control.

The Tooltip class contains several properties:

- text
- graphic
- contentDisplay
- textAlignment
- textOverrun
- wrapText
- graphicTextGap
- font
- activated

The text property is a String property, which is the text to be displayed in the tool tip. The graphic property is an object property of the Node type. It is an icon for the tool tip. The contentDisplay property is an object property of the ContentDisplay enum type. It specifies the position of the graphic relative to the text. The possible value is one of the constants in the ContentDisplay enum: TOP, RIGHT, BOTTOM, LEFT, CENTER, TEXT_ONLY, and GRAPHIC_ONLY. The default value is LEFT, which places the graphic left to the text.

The following snippet of code uses an icon for a tool tip and places it above the text. The icon is just a Label with X as its text. Figure 12-52 shows how the tool tip looks.

```
// Create and configure the Tooltip
Tooltip closeBtnTip = new Tooltip("Closes the window");
closeBtnTip.setStyle("-fx-background-color: yellow; -fx-text-fill: black;");

// Display the icon above the text
closeBtnTip.setContentDisplay(ContentDisplay.TOP);

Label closeTipIcon = new Label("X");
closeTipIcon.setStyle("-fx-text-fill: red;");
closeBtnTip.setGraphic(closeTipIcon);

// Create a Button and set its Tooltip
Button closeBtn = new Button("Close");
closeBtn.setTooltip(closeBtnTip);
```

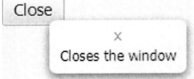

Figure 12-52. *Using an icon and placing it at the top of the text in a tool tip*

547

The textAlignment property is an object property of the TextAlignment enum type. If specifies the text alignment when the text spans multiple lines. The possible value is one of the constants in the TextAlignment enum: LEFT, RIGHT, CENTER, and JUSTIFY.

The textOverrun property is an object property of the OverrunStyle enum type. It specifies the behavior to use when there is not enough space in the tool tip to display the entire text. The default behavior is to use an ellipsis.

The wrapText is a boolean property. It specifies whether text should be wrapped onto another line if its run exceeds the width of the tool tip. The default value is false.

The graphicTextGap property is a double property that specifies the space between the text and graphic in pixel. The default value is 4. The font property is an object property of the Font type. It specifies the default font to use for the text. The activated property is a read-only boolean property. It is true when the tool tip is activated. Otherwise, it is false. A tool tip is activated when the mouse moves over a control, and it is shown after it is activated.

The program in Listing 12-33 shows how to create, configure, and set tool tips for controls. After you run the application, place the mouse pointer over the name field, Save button, and Close button. After a short time, their tool tips will be displayed. The tool tip for the Close button looks different from that of the Save button. It uses an icon and different background and text colors.

Listing 12-33. Using the Tooltip Control

```java
// TooltipTest.java
package com.jdojo.control;

import javafx.application.Application;
import javafx.scene.Scene;
import javafx.scene.control.Button;
import javafx.scene.control.ContentDisplay;
import javafx.scene.control.Label;
import javafx.scene.control.TextField;
import javafx.scene.control.Tooltip;
import javafx.scene.layout.HBox;
import javafx.stage.Stage;

public class TooltipTest extends Application {
        public static void main(String[] args) {
                Application.launch(args);
        }

        @Override
        public void start(Stage stage) {
                Label nameLbl = new Label("Name:");
                TextField nameFld = new TextField();
                Button saveBtn = new Button("Save");
                Button closeBtn = new Button("Close");

                // Set an ActionEvent handler
                closeBtn.setOnAction(e -> stage.close());

                // Add tooltips for Name field and Save button
                nameFld.setTooltip(new Tooltip("Enter your name\n(Max. 10 chars)"));
                saveBtn.setTooltip(new Tooltip("Saves the data"));
```

```java
// Create and configure the Tooltip for Close button
Tooltip closeBtnTip = new Tooltip("Closes the window");
closeBtnTip.setStyle("-fx-background-color: yellow; " +
                     " -fx-text-fill: black;");

// Display the icon above the text
closeBtnTip.setContentDisplay(ContentDisplay.TOP);

Label closeTipIcon = new Label("X");
closeTipIcon.setStyle("-fx-text-fill: red;");
closeBtnTip.setGraphic(closeTipIcon);

// Set its Tooltip for Close button
closeBtn.setTooltip(closeBtnTip);

HBox root = new HBox(nameLbl, nameFld, saveBtn, closeBtn);
root.setSpacing(10);
root.setStyle("-fx-padding: 10;" +
              "-fx-border-style: solid inside;" +
              "-fx-border-width: 2;" +
              "-fx-border-insets: 5;" +
              "-fx-border-radius: 5;" +
              "-fx-border-color: blue;");

Scene scene = new Scene(root);
stage.setScene(scene);
stage.setTitle("Using Tooltip Controls");
stage.show();
    }
}
```

Styling *Tooltip* with CSS

The default CSS style-class name for a Tooltip control is tooltip. Tooltip add several CSS properties:

- -fx-text-alignment
- -fx-text-overrun
- -fx-wrap-text
- -fx-graphic
- -fx-content-display
- -fx-graphic-text-gap
- -fx-font

All of the CSS properties correspond to the content-related properties in the Tooltip class. Please refer to the previous section for the description of all these properties. The following code sets the background color, text color, and the wrap text properties for Tooltip:

```
.tooltip {
        -fx-background-color: yellow;
        -fx-text-fill: black;
        -fx-wrap-text: true;
}
```

Providing Scrolling Features in Controls

JavaFX provides two controls named ScrollBar and ScrollPane that provide scrolling features to other controls. Typically, these controls are not used alone. They are used to support scrolling in other controls.

Understanding the *ScrollBar* Control

ScrollBar is a basic control that does not provide the scrolling feature by itself. It is represented as a horizontal or vertical bar that lets users choose a value from a range of values. Figure 12-53 shows a horizontal and a vertical scrollbar.

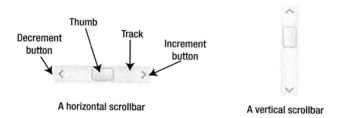

A horizontal scrollbar   A vertical scrollbar

Figure 12-53. *Horizontal and vertical scrollbars with their parts*

A ScrollBar control consists of four parts:

- An increment button to increase the value

- A decrement button to decrease the value

- A thumb (or knob) to show the current value

- A track where the thumb moves

The increment and decrement buttons in a vertical ScrollBar are on the bottom and top, respectively.

The ScrollBar class provides a default constructor that creates a horizontal scrollbar. You can set its orientation to vertical using the setOrientation() method:

```
// Create a horizontal scroll bar
ScrollBar hsb = new ScrollBar();

// Create a vertical scroll bar
ScrollBar vsb = new ScrollBar();
vsb.setOrientation(Orientation.VERTICAL);
```

The min and max properties represent the range of its value. Its value property is the current value. The default values for min, max, and value properties are 0, 100, and 0, respectively. If you are interested in knowing when the value property changes, you need to add a ChangeListener to it. The following code would set the value properties to 0, 200, and 150:

```
ScrollBar hsb = new ScrollBar();
hsb.setMin(0);
hsb.setMax(200);
hsb.setValue(150);
```

The current value of a scrollbar may be changed three different ways:

- Programmatically using the setValue(), increment(), and decrement() methods

- By the user dragging the thumb on the track

- By the user clicking the increment and decrement buttons

The blockIncrement and unitIncrement properties specify the amount to adjust the current value when the user clicks the track and the increment or decrement buttons, respectively. Typically, the block increment is set to a larger value than the unit increment.

The default CSS style-class name for a ScrollBar control is scroll-bar. ScrollBar supports two CSS pseudo-classes: horizontal and vertical. Some of its properties can be set using CSS.

ScrollBar is rarely used directly by developers. It is used to build complete controls that support scrolling, for example, the ScrollPane control. If you need to provide scrolling capability to a control, use the ScrollPane, which I will discuss in the next section.

Understanding the *ScrollPane* Control

A ScrollPane provides a scrollable view of a node. A ScrollPane consists of a horizontal ScrollBar, a vertical ScrollBar, and a content node. The node for which the ScrollPane provides scrolling is the content node. If you want to provide a scrollable view of multiple nodes, add them to a layout pane, for example, a GridPane, and then, add the layout pane to the ScrollPane as the content node. ScrollPane uses a scroll policy to specify when to show a specific scrollbar. The area through which the content is visible is known as *viewport*. Figure 12-54 shows a ScrollPane with a Label as its content node.

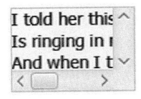

Figure 12-54. A ScrollPane with a Label as its content node

▪ **Tip**   Some of the commonly used controls that need scrolling capability, for example, a TextArea, provide a built-in ScrollPane, which is part of such controls.

You can use the constructors of the ScrollPane class to create an empty ScrollPane or a ScrollPane with a content node, as shown in the following code. You can set the content node later using the setContent() method.

```
Label poemLbl1 = ...
Label poemLbl2 = ...

// Create an empty ScrollPane
ScrollPane sPane1 = new ScrollPane();

// Set the content node for the ScrollPane
sPane1.setContent(poemLbl1);

// Create a ScrollPane with a content node
ScrollPane sPane2 = new ScrollPane(poemLbl2);
```

■ **Tip** The ScrollPane provides the scrolling for its content based on the layout bounds of the content. If the content uses effects or transformation, for example, scaling, you need to wrap the content in a Group and add the Group to the ScrollPane get proper scrolling.

The ScrollPane class contains several properties, most of which are commonly not used by developers:

- content
- pannable
- fitToHeight
- fitToWidth
- hbarPolicy
- vbarPolicy
- hmin
- hmax
- hvalue
- vmin
- vmax
- vvalue
- prefViewportHeight
- prefViewportWidth
- viewportBounds

The content property is an object property of the Node type and it specifies the content node. You can scroll the content using the scrollbars or by panning. If you use panning, you need to drag the mouse while left, right, or both buttons are pressed to scroll the content. By default, a ScrollPane is not pannable and you need to use the scrollbars to scroll through the content. The pannable property is a boolean property that specifies whether the ScrollPane is pannable. Use the setPannable(true) method to make a ScrollPane pannable.

The fitToHeight and fitToWidth properties specify whether the content node is resized to match the height and width of the viewport, respectively. By default, they are false. These properties are ignored if the content node is not resizable. Figure 12-55 shows the same ScrollPane as shown in Figure 12-54 with its fitToHeight and fitToWidth properties set to true. Notice that the Label content node has been resized to fit into the viewport.

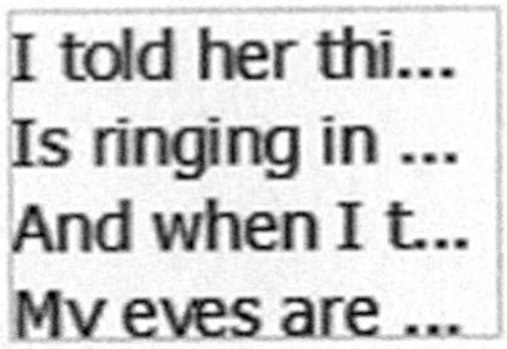

Figure 12-55. A ScrollPane with fitToHeight and fitToWidth properties set to true

The hbarPolicy and vbarPolicy properties are object properties of the ScrollPane.ScrollBarPolicy enum type. They specify when to show the horizontal and vertical scrollbars. The possible values are ALWAYS, AS_NEEDED, and NEVER. When the policy is set to ALWAYS, the scrollbar is shown all the time. When the policy is set to AS_NEEDED, the scrollbar is shown when required based on the size of the content. When the policy is set to NEVER, the scrollbar is never shown.

The hmin, hmax, and hvalue properties specify the min, max, and value properties of the horizontal scrollbar, respectively. The vmin, vmax, and vvalue properties specify the min, max, and value properties of the vertical scrollbar, respectively. Typically, you do not set these properties. They change based on the content and as the user scrolls through the content.

The prefViewportHeight and prefViewportWidth are the preferred height and width, respectively, of the viewport that is available to the content node.

The viewportBounds is an object property of the Bounds type. It is the actual bounds of the viewport. The program in Listing 12-34 shows how to use a ScrollPane. It sets a Label with four lines of text as its content. It also makes the ScrollPane pannable. That is, you can drag the mouse clicking its button to scroll through the text.

Listing 12-34. Using ScrollPane

```java
// ScrollPaneTest.java
package com.jdojo.control;

import javafx.application.Application;
import javafx.scene.Scene;
import javafx.scene.control.Label;
import javafx.scene.control.ScrollPane;
import javafx.scene.layout.HBox;
import javafx.stage.Stage;

public class ScrollPaneTest extends Application {
    public static void main(String[] args) {
        launch(args);
    }
```

```java
        @Override
        public void start(Stage stage) {
                Label poemLbl = new Label("I told her this; her laughter light\n" +
                                          "Is ringing in my ears;\n" +
                                          "And when I think upon that night\n" +
                                          "My eyes are dim with tears.");

                // Create a scroll pane with poemLbl as its content
                ScrollPane sPane = new ScrollPane(poemLbl);
                sPane.setPannable(true);

                HBox root = new HBox(sPane);
                root.setStyle("-fx-padding: 10;" +
                              "-fx-border-style: solid inside;" +
                              "-fx-border-width: 2;" +
                              "-fx-border-insets: 5;" +
                              "-fx-border-radius: 5;" +
                              "-fx-border-color: blue;");

                Scene scene = new Scene(root);
                stage.setScene(scene);
                stage.setTitle("Using ScrollPane Controls");
                stage.show();
        }
}
```

The default CSS style-class name for a ScrollPane control is scroll-pane. Please refer to the modena.css file for sample styles and the online *JavaFX CSS Reference Guide* for the complete list of CSS properties and pseudo-classes supported by the ScrollPane.

Keeping Things Separate

Sometimes you may want to place logically related controls side by side horizontally or vertically. For better appearance, controls are grouped using different types of separators. Sometimes using a border suffices; but sometimes you will use the TitledPane controls. The Separator and SplitPane controls are solely meant for visually separating two controls or two groups of controls.

Understanding the *Separator* Control

A Separator is a horizontal or vertical line that separates two groups of controls. Typically, they are used in menus or combo boxes. Figure 12-56 shows menu items of a restaurant separated by horizontal and vertical separators.

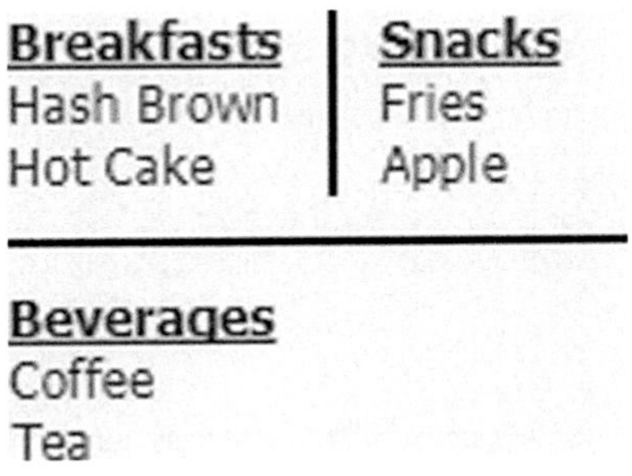

Breakfasts | **Snacks**
Hash Brown | Fries
Hot Cake | Apple

Beverages
Coffee
Tea

Figure 12-56. *Using horizontal and vertical separators*

The default constructor creates a horizontal Separator. To create a vertical Separator, you can specify a vertical orientation in the constructor or use the setOrientation() method, as shown in the following code:

```
// Create a horizontal separator
Separator separator1 = new Separator();

// Change the orientation to vertical
separator1.setOrientation(Orientation.VERTICAL);

// Create a vertical separator
Separator separator2 = new Separator(Orientation.VERTICAL);
```

A separator resizes itself to fill the space allocated to it. A horizontal Separator resizes horizontally and a vertical Separator resizes vertically. Internally, a Separator is a Region. You can change its color and thickness using a CSS.

The Separator class contains three properties:

- orientation
- halignment
- valignment

The orientation property specifies the orientation of the control. The possible values are one of the two constants of the Orientation enum: HORIZONTAL and VERTICAL. The halignment property specifies the horizontal alignment of the separator line within the width of a vertical separator. This property is ignored for a horizontal separator. The possible values are one of the constants of the HPos enum: LEFT, CENTER, and RIGHT. The default value is CENTER. The valignment property specifies the vertical alignment of the separator line within the height of a horizontal separator. This property is ignored for a vertical separator. The possible values are one of the constants of the VPos enum: BASELINE, TOP, CENTER, and BOTTOM. The default value is CENTER.

Styling *Separator* with CSS

The default CSS style-class name for a Separator control is separator. Separator contains CSS properties, which corresponds to its Java properties:

- -fx-orientation
- -fx-halignment
- -fx-valignment

Separator supports horizontal and vertical CSS pseudo-classes that apply to horizontal and vertical separators, respectively. It contains a line substructure that is a Region. The line you see in a separator is created by specifying the border for the line substructure. The following style was used to create the separators in Figure 12-56:

```
.separator > .line {
    -fx-border-style: solid;
    -fx-border-width: 1;
}
```

You can use an image as a separator. Set the appropriate width or height of the separator and use an image as the background image. The following code assumes that the separator.jpg image file exists in the same directory as the CSS file containing the style. The styles set the preferred height of the horizontal separator and the preferred width of the vertical separator to 10px.

```
.separator {
        -fx-background-image: url("separator.jpg");
        -fx-background-repeat: repeat;
        -fx-background-position: center;
        -fx-background-size: cover;
}

.separator:horizontal {
        -fx-pref-height: 10;
}

.separator:vertical {
        -fx-pref-width: 10;
}
```

Understanding the *SplitPane* Control

SplitPane arranges multiple nodes by placing them horizontally or vertically separated by a divider. The divider can be dragged by the user, so the node on one side of the divider expands and the node on the other side shrinks by the same amount. Typically, each node in a SplitPane is a layout pane containing some controls. However, you can use any node, for example, a Button. If you have used Windows Explorer, you are already familiar with using a SplitPane. In a Windows Explorer, the divider separates the tree view and the list view. Using the divider, you can resize the width of the tree view and the width of the list view resizes with the equal amount in the opposite direction. A resizable HTML frameset works similar to a SplitPane. Figure 12-57 shows a window with a horizontal SplitPane. The SplitPane contains two VBox layout panes, each of them contains a Label and a TextArea. Figure 12-57 shows the divider dragged to the right, so the left VBox gets more width than the right one.

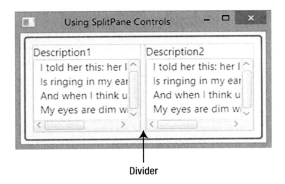

Divider

Figure 12-57. *A window with a horizontal SplitPane*

You can create a SplitPane using the default constructor of the SplitPane class:

```
SplitPane sp = new SplitPane();
```

The getItems() method of the SplitPane class returns the ObservableList<Node> that stores the list of nodes in a SplitPane. Add all your nodes to this list, as shown in the following code:

```
// Create panes
GridPane leftPane = new GridPane();
GridPane centerPane = new GridPane();
GridPane rightPane = new GridPane();

/* Populate the left, center, and right panes with controls here */

// Add panels to the a SplitPane
SplitPane sp = new SplitPane();
sp.getItems().addAll(leftPane, centerPane, rightPane);
```

By default, SplitPane places its nodes horizontally. Its orientation property can be used to specify the orientation:

```
// Place nodes vertically
sp.setOrientation(Orientation.VERTICAL);
```

A divider can be moved between the leftmost and rightmost edges or topmost and bottommost edges provided it does not overlap any other divider. The divider position can be set between 0 and 1. The position 0 means topmost or leftmost. The position 1 means bottommost or rightmost. By default, a divider is placed in the middle with its position set to 0.5. Use either of the following two methods to set the position of a divider:

- setDividerPositions(double... positions)
- setDividerPosition(int dividerIndex, double position)

The setDividerPositions() method takes the positions of multiple dividers. You must provide positions for all dividers from starting up to the one you want to set the positions.

If you want to set the position for a specific divider, use the setDividerPosition() method. The first divider has the index 0. Positions passed in for an index outside the range are ignored.

The getDividerPositions() method returns the positions of all dividers. It returns a double array. The index of dividers matches the index of the array elements.

By default, SplitPane resizes its nodes when it is resized. You can prevent a specific node from resizing with the SplitPane using the setResizableWithParent() static method:

```
// Make node1 non-resizable
SplitPane.setResizableWithParent(node1, false);
```

The program in Listing 12-35 shows how to use SplitPane. It displays a window as shown in Figure 12-57. Run the program and use the mouse to drag the divider to the left or right to adjust the spacing for the left and right nodes.

Listing 12-35. Using SplitPane Controls

```java
// SplitPaneTest.java
package com.jdojo.control;

import javafx.application.Application;
import javafx.scene.Scene;
import javafx.scene.control.Label;
import javafx.scene.control.SplitPane;
import javafx.scene.control.TextArea;
import javafx.scene.layout.HBox;
import javafx.scene.layout.VBox;
import javafx.stage.Stage;

public class SplitPaneTest extends Application {
        public static void main(String[] args) {
                Application.launch(args);
        }

        @Override
        public void start(Stage stage) {
                TextArea desc1 = new TextArea();
                desc1.setPrefColumnCount(10);
                desc1.setPrefRowCount(4);

                TextArea desc2 = new TextArea();
                desc2.setPrefColumnCount(10);
                desc2.setPrefRowCount(4);

                VBox vb1 = new VBox(new Label("Description1"), desc1);
                VBox vb2 = new VBox(new Label("Description2"), desc2);

                SplitPane sp = new SplitPane();
                sp.getItems().addAll(vb1, vb2);

                HBox root = new HBox(sp);
                root.setSpacing(10);
                root.setStyle("-fx-padding: 10;" +
                                "-fx-border-style: solid inside;" +
                                "-fx-border-width: 2;" +
```

```
                            "-fx-border-insets: 5;" +
                            "-fx-border-radius: 5;" +
                            "-fx-border-color: blue;");

            Scene scene = new Scene(root);
            stage.setScene(scene);
            stage.setTitle("Using SplitPane Controls");
            stage.show();
        }
    }
}
```

Styling *SplitPane* with CSS

The default CSS style-class name for a SplitPane control is split-pane. SplitPane contains -fx-orientation CSS properties, which determine its orientation. The possible values are horizontal and vertical.

SplitPane supports horizontal and vertical CSS pseudo-classes that apply to horizontal and vertical SplitPanes, respectively. The divider is a split-pane-divider substructure of the SplitPane, which is a StackPane. The following code sets a blue background color for dividers, 5px preferred width for dividers in a horizontal SplitPane, and 5px preferred height for dividers in a vertical SplitPane:

```
.split-pane > .split-pane-divider {
    -fx-background-color: blue;
}

.split-pane:horizontal > .split-pane-divider {
    -fx-pref-width: 5;
}

.split-pane:vertical > .split-pane-divider {
    -fx-pref-height: 5;
}
```

The split-pane-divider substructure contains a grabber substructure, which is a StackPane. Its CSS style-class name is horizontal-grabber for a horizontal SplitPane and vertical-grabber for a vertical SplitPane. The grabber is shown in the middle of the divider.

Understanding the *Slider* Control

A Slider lets the user select a numeric value from a numeric range graphically by sliding a thumb (or knob) along a track. A slider can be horizontal or vertical. Figure 12-58 shows a horizontal slider.

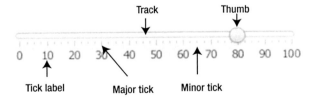

Figure 12-58. A horizontal Slider control and its parts

A slider has minimum and maximum values that determine the range of the valid selectable values. The thumb of the slider indicates its current value. You can slide the thumb along the track to change the current value. Major and minor tick marks shows the location of values along the track. You can also show tick labels. Custom labels are also supported.

The following code creates a Slider control using its default constructor that sets 0, 100, and 0 as the minimum, maximum, and current value, respectively. The default orientation is horizontal.

```
// Create a horizontal slider
Slider s1 = new Slider();
```

Use another constructor to specify the minimum, maximum, and current values:

```
// Create a horizontal slider with the specified min, max, and value
double min = 0.0;
double max = 200.0;
double value = 50.0;
Slider s2 = new Slider(min, max, value);
```

A Slider control contains several properties. I will discuss them by categories. The is horizontal. orientation property specifies the orientation of the slider:

```
// Create a vertical slider
Slider vs = new Slider();
vs.setOrientation(Orientation.VERTICAL);
```

The following properties are related to the current value and the range of values:

- min
- max
- value
- valueChanging
- snapToTicks

The min, max, and value properties are double properties, and they represent the minimum, maximum, and current values, respectively, of the slider. The current value of the slider can be changed by dragging the thumb on the track or using the setValue() method. The following snippet of code creates a slider and sets its min, max, and value properties to 0, 10, and 3, respectively:

```
Slider scoreSlider = new Slider();
scoreSlider.setMin(0.0);
scoreSlider.setMax(10.0);
scoreSlider.setValue(3.0);
```

Typically, you want to perform an action when the value property of the slider changes. You will need to add a ChangeListener to the value property. The following statement adds a ChangeListener using a lambda expression to the scoreSlider control and prints the old and new values whenever the value property changes:

```
scoreSlider.valueProperty().addListener(
        (ObservableValue<? extends Number> prop, Number oldVal, Number newVal) -> {
                System.out.println("Changed from " + oldVal + " to " + newVal);
});
```

The valueChanging property is a boolean property. It is set to true when the user presses the thumb and is set to false when the thumb is released. As the user drags the thumb, the value keeps changing and the valueChanging property is true. This property helps you avoid repeating an action if you want to take the action only once when the value changes.

The snapToTicks property is a boolean property, which is false by default. It specifies whether the value property of the slider is always aligned with the tick marks. If it is set to false, the value could be anywhere in the min to max range.

Be careful in using the valueChanging property inside a ChangeListener. The listener may be called several times for what the user sees as one change. Expecting that the ChangeListener will be notified when the valueChanging property changes from true to false, you wrap the main logic for the action inside an if statement:

```
if (scoreSlider.isValueChanging()) {
        // Do not perform any action as the value changes
} else {
        // Perform the action as the value has been changed
}
```

The logic works fine when the snapToTicks property is set to true. The ChangeListener for the value property is notified when the valueChanging property changes from true to false only when the snapToTicks property is set to true. Therefore, do not write the above logic unless you have set the snapToTicks property to true as well.

The following properties of the Slider class specify the tick spacing:

- majorTickUnit
- minorTickCount
- blockIncrement

The majorTickUnit property is a double property. It specifies the unit of distance between two major ticks. Suppose the min property is set to 0 and the majorTickUnit to 10. The slider will have major ticks at 0, 10, 20, 30, and so forth. An out-of-range value for this property disables the major ticks. The default value for the property is 25.

The minorTickCount property is an integer property. It specifies the number of minor ticks between two major ticks. The default value for the property is 3.

You can change the thumb position by using keys, for example, using left and right arrow keys in a horizontal slider and up and down arrow keys in a vertical slider. The blockIncrement property is a double property. It specifies the amount by which the current value of the slider is adjusted when the thumb is operating by using keys. The default value for the property is 10.

The following properties specify whether the tick marks and tick labels are shown; by default, they are set to false:

- showTickMarks
- showTickLabels

The labelFormatter property is an object property of the StringConverter<Double> type. By default, it is null and the slider uses a default StringConverter that displays the numeric values for the major ticks. The values for the major ticks are passed to the toString() method and the method is supposed to return a custom label for that value. The following snippet of code creates a slider with custom major tick labels, as shown in Figure 12-59:

```java
Slider scoreSlider = new Slider();
scoreSlider.setShowTickLabels(true);
scoreSlider.setShowTickMarks(true);
scoreSlider.setMajorTickUnit(10);
scoreSlider.setMinorTickCount(3);
scoreSlider.setBlockIncrement(20);
scoreSlider.setSnapToTicks(true);

// Set a custom major tick formatter
scoreSlider.setLabelFormatter(new StringConverter<Double>() {
        @Override
        public String toString(Double value) {
                String label = "";
                if (value == 40) {
                        label = "F";
                } else if (value == 70) {
                        label = "C";
                } else if (value == 80) {
                        label = "B";
                } else if (value == 90) {
                        label = "A";
                }

                return label;
        }

        @Override
        public Double fromString(String string) {
                return null; // Not used
        }
});
```

Figure 12-59. *A slider with custom major tick labels*

The program in Listing 12-36 shows how to use Slider controls. It adds a Rectangle, a Label, and three Slider controls to a window. It adds a ChangeListener to the Sliders. Sliders represent red, green, and blue components of a color. When you change the value for a slider, the new color is computed and set as the fill color for the rectangle.

Listing 12-36. Using the Slider Control

```java
// SliderTest.java
package com.jdojo.control;

import javafx.application.Application;
import javafx.beans.value.ObservableValue;
import javafx.scene.Scene;
import javafx.scene.control.Label;
import javafx.scene.control.Slider;
import javafx.scene.layout.GridPane;
import javafx.scene.paint.Color;
import javafx.scene.shape.Rectangle;
import javafx.stage.Stage;

public class SliderTest extends Application {
        Rectangle rect = new Rectangle(0, 0, 200, 50);
        Slider redSlider = getSlider();
        Slider greenSlider = getSlider();
        Slider blueSlider = getSlider();

        public static void main(String[] args) {
                Application.launch(args);
        }

        @Override
        public void start(Stage stage) {
                // Add a ChangeListener to all sliders
                redSlider.valueProperty().addListener(this::changed);
                greenSlider.valueProperty().addListener(this::changed);
                blueSlider.valueProperty().addListener(this::changed);

                GridPane root = new GridPane();
                root.setVgap(10);
                root.add(rect, 0, 0, 2, 1);
                root.add(new Label("Use sliders to change the fill color"), 0, 1, 2, 1);
                root.addRow(2, new Label("Red:"), redSlider);
                root.addRow(3, new Label("Green:"), greenSlider);
                root.addRow(4, new Label("Blue:"), blueSlider);

                root.setStyle("-fx-padding: 10;" +
                                "-fx-border-style: solid inside;" +
                                "-fx-border-width: 2;" +
                                "-fx-border-insets: 5;" +
                                "-fx-border-radius: 5;" +
                                "-fx-border-color: blue;");

                Scene scene = new Scene(root);
                stage.setScene(scene);
                stage.setTitle("Using Slider Controls");
                stage.show();
```

```
        // Adjust the fill color of the rectangle
        changeColor();
    }

    public Slider getSlider() {
        Slider slider = new Slider(0, 255, 125);
        slider.setShowTickLabels(true);
        slider.setShowTickMarks(true);
        slider.setMajorTickUnit(85);
        slider.setMinorTickCount(10);
        slider.setBlockIncrement(20);
        slider.setSnapToTicks(true);
        return slider;
    }

    // A change listener to track the change in color
    public void changed(ObservableValue<? extends Number> prop,
                        Number oldValue,
                        Number newValue) {
        changeColor();
    }

    public void changeColor() {
        int r = (int)redSlider.getValue();
        int g = (int)greenSlider.getValue();
        int b = (int)blueSlider.getValue();
        Color fillColor = Color.rgb(r, g, b);
        rect.setFill(fillColor);
    }
}
```

Styling *Slider* with CSS

The default CSS style-class name for a Slider control is slider. Slider contains the following CSS properties, each of them corresponds to its Java property in the Slider class:

- -fx-orientation
- -fx-show-tick-labels
- -fx-show-tick-marks
- -fx-major-tick-unit
- -fx-minor-tick-count
- -fx-show-tick-labels
- -fx-snap-to-ticks
- -fx-block-increment

Slider supports horizontal and vertical CSS pseudo-classes that apply to horizontal and vertical sliders, respectively. A Slider control contains three substructures that can be styled:

- axis
- track
- thumb

The axis substructure is a NumberAxis. It displays the tick marks and tick labels. The following code sets the tick label color to blue, major tick length to 15px, minor tick length to 5px, major tick color to red, and minor tick color to green:

```
.slider > .axis {
        -fx-tick-label-fill: blue;
        -fx-tick-length: 15px;
        -fx-minor-tick-length: 5px
}

.slider > .axis > .axis-tick-mark {
    -fx-stroke: red;
}

.slider > .axis > .axis-minor-tick-mark {
    -fx-stroke: green;
}
```

The track substructure is a StackPane. The following code changes the background color of track to red:

```
.slider > .track {
    -fx-background-color: red;
}
```

The thumb substructure is a StackPane. The thumb looks circular because it is given a background radius. If you remove the background radius, it will look rectangular, as shown in the following code:

```
.slider .thumb {
    -fx-background-radius: 0;
}
```

You can make an image like a thumb by setting the background of the thumb substructure to an image as follows (assuming that the thumb.jpg image file exists in the same directory as the CSS file containing the style):

```
.slider .thumb {
        -fx-background-image: url("thumb.jpg");
}
```

You can give the thumb any shape using the -fx-shape CSS property. The following code gives the thumb a triangular shape. The triangle is inverted for a horizontal slider and is pointed to the right for a vertical slider. Figure 12-60 shows a horizontal slider with the thumb.

```
/* An inverted triangle */
.slider > .thumb {
        -fx-shape: "M0, 0L10, 0L5, 10 Z";
}

/* A triangle pointing to the right*/
.slider:vertical > .thumb {
        -fx-shape: "M0, 0L10, 5L0, 10 Z";
}
```

Figure 12-60. *A slider with an inverted triangle thumb*

The following code gives the thumb a shape of a triangle placed beside a rectangle. The triangle is inverted for a horizontal slider and is pointed to the right for a vertical slider. Figure 12-61 shows a horizontal slider with the thumb.

```
/* An inverted triangle below a rectangle*/
.slider > .thumb {
        -fx-shape: "M0, 0L10, 0L10, 5L5, 10L0, 5 Z";
}

/* A triangle pointing to the right by the right side of a rectangle */
.slider:vertical > .thumb {
        -fx-shape: "M0, 0L5, 0L10, 5L5, 10L0, 10 Z";
}
```

Figure 12-61. *A slider with a thumb of an inverted triangle below a rectangle*

Understanding Menus

A menu is used to provide a list of actionable items to the user in a compact form. You can also provide the same list of items using a group of buttons, where each button represents an actionable item. It is a matter of preference which one you use: a menu or a group of buttons.

There is a noticeable advantage of a using a menu. It uses much less space on the screen, compared to a group of buttons, by folding (or nesting) the group of items under another item. For example, if you have used a file editor, the menu items such as New, Open, Save, and Print are nested under a top-level File menu. A user needs to click the File menu to see the list of items that are available under it. Typically, in cases of a group of buttons, all items are visible to the user all the time, and it is easy for users to know what actions are available. Therefore, there is little tradeoff between the amount of space and usability when you decide to use a menu or buttons. Typically, a menu bar is displayed at the top of a window.

■ **Tip** There is another kind of menu, which is called a *context menu* or *pop-up menu*, which is displayed on demand. I will discuss context menus in the next section.

A menu consists of several parts. Figure 12-62 shows a menu and its parts when the Save As submenu is expanded. A menu bar is the topmost part of the menu that holds menus. The menu bar is always visible. File, Edit, Options, and Help are the menu items shown in Figure 12-62. A menu contains menu items and submenus. In Figure 12-62, the File menu contains four menu items: New, Open, Save, and Exit; it contains two separator menu items and one Save As submenu. The Save As submenu contains two menu items: Text and PDF. A menu item is an actionable item. A separator menu item has a horizontal line that separates a group of related menu items from another group of items in a menu. Typically, a menu represents a category of items.

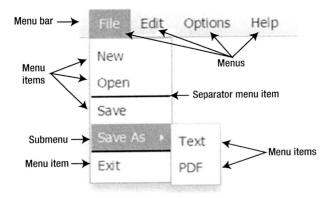

Figure 12-62. *A menu with a menu bar, menus, submenus, separators, and menu items*

Using a menu is a multistep process. The following sections describe the steps in detail. The following is the summary of steps:

1. Create a menu bar and add it to a container.

2. Create menus and add them to the menu bar.

3. Create menu items and add them to the menus.

4. Add `ActionEvent` handlers to the menu items to perform actions when they are clicked.

Using Menu Bars

A menu bar is a horizontal bar that acts as a container for menus. An instance of the `MenuBar` class represents a menu bar. You can create a `MenuBar` using its default constructor:

```
MenuBar menuBar = new MenuBar();
```

MenuBar is a control. Typically, it is added to the top part of a window. If you use a BorderPane as the root for a scene in a window, the top region is the usual place for a MenuBar:

```
// Add the MenuBar to the top region
BorderPane root = new BorderPane();
root.setBottom(menuBar);
```

The MenuBar class contains a useSystemMenuBar property, which is of boolean type. By default, it is set to false. When set to true, it will use the system menu bar if the platform supports it. For example, Mac supports a system menu bar. If you set this property to true on Mac, the MenuBar will use the system menu bar to display its items:

```
// Let the MenuBar use system menu bar
menuBar.setUseSystemMenuBar(true);
```

A MenuBar itself does not take any space unless you add menus to it. Its size is computed based on the details of the menus it contains. A MenuBar stores all of its menus in an ObservableList of Menu whose reference is returned by its getMenus() method:

```
// Add some menus to the MenuBar
Menu fileMenu = new Menu("File");
Menu editMenu = new Menu("Edit");
menuBar.getMenus().addAll(fileMenu, editMenu);
```

Using Menus

A menu contains a list of actionable items, which are displayed on demand, for example, by clicking it. The list of menu items is hidden when the user selects an item or moves the mouse pointer outside the list. A menu is typically added to a menu bar or another menu as a submenu.

An instance of the Menu class represents a menu. A menu displays text and a graphic. Use the default constructor to create an empty menu, and later, set the text and graphic:

```
// Create a Menu with an empty string text and no graphic
Menu aMenu = new Menu();
```

```
// Set the text and graphic to the Menu
aMenu.setText("Text");
aMenu.setGraphic(new ImageView(new Image("image.jpg")));
```

You can create a menu with its text, or text and a graphic, using other constructors:

```
// Create a File Menu
Menu fileMenu1 = new Menu("File");
```

```
// Create a File Menu
Menu fileMenu2 = new Menu("File", new ImageView(new Image("file.jpg")));
```

The Menu class is inherited from the MenuItem class, which is inherited from the Object class. Menu is not a node, and therefore, it cannot be added to a scene graph directly. You need to add it to a MenuBar. Use the getMenus() method to get the ObservableList<Menu> for the MenuBar and add instances of the Menu class to the list. The following snippet of code adds four Menu instances to a MenuBar:

```
Menu fileMenu = new Menu("File");
Menu editMenu = new Menu("Edit");
Menu optionsMenu = new Menu("Options");
Menu helpMenu = new Menu("Help");

// Add menus to a menu bar
MenuBar menuBar = new MenuBar();
menuBar.getMenus().addAll(fileMenu, editMenu, optionsMenu, helpMenu);
```

When a menu is clicked, typically its list of menu items are displayed, but no action is taken. The Menu class contains the following properties that can be set to handle when its list of options are showing, shown, hiding, and hidden, respectively:

- onShowing
- onShown
- onHiding
- onHidden
- showing

The onShowing event handler is called just before the menu items for the menu is shown. The onShown event handler is called after the menu items are displayed. The onHiding and onHidden event handlers are the counterparts of the onShowing and onShown event handlers, respectively.

Typically, you add an onShowing event handler that enables or disables its menu items based on some criteria. For example, suppose you have an Edit menu with Cut, Copy, and Paste menu items. In the onShowing event handler, you would enable or disable these menu items depending on whether the focus is in a text input control, if the control is enabled, or if the control has selection:

```
editMenu.setOnAction(e -> {/* Enable/disable menu items here */});
```

■ **Tip** Users do not like surprises when using a GUI application. For a better user experience, you should disable menu items instead of making them invisible when they are not applicable. Making them invisible changes the positions of other items and users have to relocate them.

The showing property is a read-only boolean property. It is set to true when the items in the menu are showing. It is set to false when they are hidden.

The program in Listing 12-37 puts this all together. It creates four menus, a menu bar, adds menus to the menu bar, and adds the menu bar to the top region of a BorderPane. Figure 12-63 shows the menu bar in the window. But you have not seen anything exciting about menus yet! You will need to add menu items to the menus to experience some excitement.

Listing 12-37. Creating a Menu Bar and Adding Menus to It

```java
// MenuTest.java
package com.jdojo.control;

import javafx.application.Application;
import javafx.scene.Scene;
import javafx.scene.control.Menu;
import javafx.scene.control.MenuBar;
import javafx.scene.layout.BorderPane;
import javafx.stage.Stage;

public class MenuTest extends Application {
        public static void main(String[] args) {
                Application.launch(args);
        }

        @Override
        public void start(Stage stage) {
                // Create some menus
                Menu fileMenu = new Menu("File");
                Menu editMenu = new Menu("Edit");
                Menu optionsMenu = new Menu("Options");
                Menu helpMenu = new Menu("Help");

                // Add menus to a menu bar
                MenuBar menuBar = new MenuBar();
                menuBar.getMenus().addAll(fileMenu, editMenu, optionsMenu, helpMenu);

                BorderPane root = new BorderPane();
                root.setTop(menuBar);
                root.setStyle("-fx-padding: 10;" +
                                "-fx-border-style: solid inside;" +
                                "-fx-border-width: 2;" +
                                "-fx-border-insets: 5;" +
                                "-fx-border-radius: 5;" +
                                "-fx-border-color: blue;");

                Scene scene = new Scene(root);
                stage.setScene(scene);
                stage.setTitle("Using Menus");
                stage.show();
        }
}
```

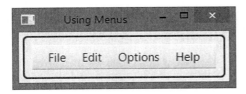

Figure 12-63. A menu bar with four menus

Using Menu Items

A menu item is an actionable item in a menu. The action associated with a menu item is performed by the mouse or keys. Menu items can be styled using a CSS.

An instance of the MenuItem class represents a menu item. The MenuItem class is not a node. It is inherited from the Object class and, therefore, cannot be added directly to a scene graph. You need to add it to a menu.

You can add several types of menu items to a menu. Figure 12-64 shows the class diagram for the MenuItem class and its subclasses that represent a specific type of menu item.

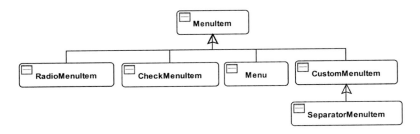

Figure 12-64. *A class diagram for the MenuItem class and its subclasses*

You can use the following types of menu items:

- A MenuItem for an actionable option

- A RadioMenuItem for a group of mutually exclusive options

- A CheckMenuItem for a toggle option

- A Menu, when used as a menu item and acts as a submenu that holds a list of menu items

- A CustomMenuItem for an arbitrary node to be used as an menu item

- A SeparatorMenuItem, which is a CustomMenuItem, to display a separator as a menu item

I will discuss all menu item types in details in the sections to follow.

Using a *MenuItem*

A MenuItem represents an actionable option. When it is clicked, the registered ActionEvent handlers are called. The following snippet of code creates an Exit MenuItem and adds an ActionEvent handler that exits the application:

```
MenuItem exitItem = new MenuItem("Exit");
exitItem.setOnAction(e -> Platform.exit());
```

A MenuItem is added to a menu. A menu stores the reference of its MenuItems in an ObservableList<MenuItem> whose reference can be obtained using the getItems() method:

```
Menu fileMenu = new Menu("File");
fileMenu.getItems().add(exitItem);
```

The MenuItem class contains the following properties that apply to all types of menu items:

- text
- graphic
- disable
- visible
- accelerator
- mnemonicParsing
- onAction
- onMenuValidation
- parentMenu
- parentPopup
- style
- id

The text and graphic properties are the text and graphics for the menu item, respectively, which are of String and Node types. The disable and visible properties are boolean properties. They specify whether the menu item is disabled and visible. The accelerator property is an object property of the KeyCombination type that specifies a key combination that can be used to execute the action associated with the menu item in one keystroke. The following snippet of code creates a Rectangle menu item and sets its accelerator to Alt + R. The accelerator for a menu item is shown next to it, as shown in Figure 12-65, so the user can learn about it by looking at the menu item. The user can activate the Rectangle menu item directly by pressing Alt + R.

```
MenuItem rectItem = new MenuItem("Rectangle");
KeyCombination kr = new KeyCodeCombination(KeyCode.R, KeyCombination.ALT_DOWN);
rectItem.setAccelerator(kr);
```

Rectangle   Alt+R

Figure 12-65. *A menu item with an accelerator Alt + R*

The mnemonicParsing property is a boolean property. It enables or disables text parsing to detect a mnemonic character. By default, it is set to true for menu items. If it is set to true, the text for the menu item is parsed for an underscore character. The character following the first underscore is added as the mnemonic for the menu item. Pressing the Alt key on Windows highlights mnemonics for all menu items. Typically, mnemonic characters are shown in underlined font style. Pressing the key for the mnemonic character activates the menu item.

```
// Create a menu item with x as its mnemonic character
MenuItem exitItem = new MenuItem("E_xit");
```

The onAction property is an ActionEvent handler that is called when the menu item is activated, for example, by clicking it with a mouse or pressing its accelerator key:

```
// Close the application when the Exit menu item is activated
exitItem.setOnAction(e -> Platform.exit());
```

The onMenuValidation property is an event handler that is called when a MenuItem is accessed using its accelerator or when the onShowing event handler for its menu (the parent) is called. For a menu, this handler is called when its menu items are shown.

The parentMenu property is a read-only object property of the Menu type. It is the reference of the Menu, which contains the menu item. Using this property and the items list returned by the getItems() method of the Menu class, you can navigate the menu tree from top to bottom and vice versa.

The parentPopup property is a read-only object property of the ContextMenu type. It is the reference of the ContextMenu in which the menu item appears. It is null for a menu item appearing in a normal menu.

The style and ID properties are included to support styling using a CSS. They represent the CSS style and ID.

Using a *RadioMenuItem*

A RadioMenuItem represents a mutually exclusive option. Typically, you add RadioMenuItem in multiples to a ToggleGroup, so only one item is selected. RadioMenuItem displays a check mark when selected. The following snippet of code creates three instances of RadioMenuItem and adds them to a ToggleGroup. Finally, they are all added to a File Menu. Typically, a RadioMenuItem in a group is selected by default. Figure 12-66 shows the group of RadioMenuItems: once when Rectangle is selected and once when Circle is selected.

```
// Create three RadioMenuItems
RadioMenuItem rectItem = new RadioMenuItem("Rectangle");
RadioMenuItem circleItem = new RadioMenuItem("Circle");
RadioMenuItem ellipseItem = new RadioMenuItem("Ellipse");

// Select the Rantangle option by default
rectItem.setSelected(true);

// Add them to a ToggleGroup to make them mutually exclusive
ToggleGroup shapeGroup = new ToggleGroup();
shapeGroup.getToggles().addAll(rectItem, circleItem, ellipseItem);

// Add RadioMenuItems to a File Menu
Menu fileMenu = new Menu("File");
fileMenu.getItems().addAll(rectItem, circleItem, ellipseItem);
```

Figure 12-66. RadioMenuItems in action

Add an ActionEvent handler to the RadioMenuItem if you want to perform an action when it is selected. The following snippet of code adds an ActionEvent handler to each RadioMenuItem, which calls a draw() method:

```
rectItem.setOnAction(e -> draw());
circleItem.setOnAction(e -> draw());
ellipseItem.setOnAction(e -> draw());
```

Using a *CheckMenuItem*

Use a CheckMenuItem to represent a boolean menu item that can be toggled between selected and unselected states. Suppose you have an application that draws shapes. You can have a Draw Stroke menu item as a CheckMenuItem. When it is selected, a stroke will be drawn for the shape. Otherwise, the shape will not have a stroke, as indicated in the following code. Use an ActionEvent handler to be notified when the state of the CheckMenuItem is toggled.

```
CheckMenuItem strokeItem = new CheckMenuItem("Draw Stroke");
strokeItem.setOnAction( e -> drawStroke());
```

When a CheckMenuItem is selected, a check mark is displayed beside it.

Using a Submenu Item

Notice that the Menu class is inherited from the MenuItem class. This makes it possible to use a Menu in place of a MenuItem. Use a Menu as a menu item to create a submenu. When the mouse hovers over a submenu, its list of options is displayed.

The following snippet of code creates a MenuBar, adds a File menu, adds New and Open MenuItems and a Save As submenu to the File menu, and adds Text and PDF menu items to the Save As submenu. It produces a menu as shown in Figure 12-67.

```
MenuBar menuBar = new MenuBar();
Menu fileMenu = new Menu("File");
menuBar.getMenus().addAll(fileMenu);

MenuItem newItem = new MenuItem("New");
MenuItem openItem = new MenuItem("Open");
Menu saveAsSubMenu = new Menu("Save As");

// Add menu items to the File menu
fileMenu.getItems().addAll(newItem, openItem, saveAsSubMenu);

MenuItem textItem = new MenuItem("Text");
MenuItem pdfItem = new MenuItem("PDF");
saveAsSubMenu.getItems().addAll(textItem, pdfItem);
```

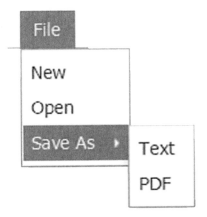

Figure 12-67. *A menu used as a submenu*

Typically, you do not add an ActionEvent handler for a submenu. Rather, you set an event handler to the onShowing property that is called before the list of items for the submenu is displayed. The event handler is used to enable or disable menu items.

Using a *CustomMenuItem*

CustomMenuItem is a simple yet powerful menu item type. It opens the door for all kinds of creativity for designing menu items. It lets you use any node. For example, you can use a Slider, a TextField, or an HBox as a menu item. The CustomMenuItem class contains two properties:

- content
- hideOnClick

The content property is an object property of Node type. Its value is the node that you want to use as the menu item.

When you click a menu item, all visible menus are hidden and only top-level menus in the menu bar stay visible. When you use a custom menu item that has controls, you do not want to hide menus when the user clicks it because the user needs to interact with the menu item, for example, to enter or select some data. The hideOnClick property is a boolean property that lets you control this behavior. By default, it is set to true, which means clicking a custom menu hides all showing menus.

The CustomMenuItem class provides several constructors. The default constructor creates a custom menu item setting the content property to null and the hideOnClick property to true, as shown in the following code:

```
// Create a Slider control
Slider slider = new Slider(1, 10, 1);

// Create a custom menu item and set its content and hideOnClick properties
CustomMenuItem cmi1 = new CustomMenuItem();
cmi1.setContent(slider);
cmi1.setHideOnClick(false);
```

```
// Create a custom menu item with a Slider content and
// set the hideOnClick property to false
CustomMenuItem cmi2 = new CustomMenuItem(slider);
cmi1.setHideOnClick(false);

// Create a custom menu item with a Slider content and false hideOnClick
CustomMenuItem cmi2 = new CustomMenuItem(slider, false);
```

The following snippet of code produces a menu as shown in Figure 12-68. One of the menu items is a CustomMenuItem, which uses a slider as its content.

```
CheckMenuItem strokeItem = new CheckMenuItem("Draw Stroke");
strokeItem.setSelected(true);

Slider strokeWidthSlider = new Slider(1, 10, 1);
strokeWidthSlider.setShowTickLabels(true);
strokeWidthSlider.setShowTickMarks(true);
strokeWidthSlider.setMajorTickUnit(2);
CustomMenuItem strokeWidthItem = new CustomMenuItem(strokeWidthSlider, false);

Menu optionsMenu = new Menu("Options");
optionsMenu.getItems().addAll(strokeItem, strokeWidthItem);

MenuBar menuBar = new MenuBar();
menuBar.getMenus().add(optionsMenu);
```

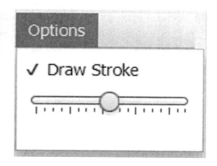

Figure 12-68. *A slider as a custom menu item*

Using a *SeparatorMenuItem*

There is nothing special to discuss about the SeparatorMenuItem. It inherits from the CustomMenuItem. It uses a horizontal Separator control as its content and sets the hideOnClick to false. It is used to separate menu items belonging to different groups, as shown in the following code. It provides a default constructor.

```
// Create a separator menu item
SeparatorMenuItem smi = SeparatorMenuItem();
```

Putting All Parts of Menus Together

Understanding the parts of menus is easy. However, using them in code is tricky because you have to create all parts separately, add listeners to them, and then assemble them.

The program in Listing 12-38 creates a shape drawing application using menus. It uses all types of menu items. The program displays a window with a BorderPane as the root of its scene. The top region contains a menu and the center region contains a canvas on which shapes are drawn.

Run the application and use the File menu to draw different types of shapes; clicking the Clear menu item clears the canvas. Clicking the Exit menu item closes the application.

Use the Options menu to draw or not to draw the strokes and set the stroke width. Notice that a slider is used as a custom menu item under the Options menu. When you adjust the slider value, the stroke width of the drawn shape is adjusted accordingly. The Draw Stroke menu item is a CheckMenuItem. When it is unselected, the slider menu item is disabled and the shape does not use a stroke.

Listing 12-38. Using Menus in a Shape Drawing Application

```java
// MenuItemTest.java
package com.jdojo.control;

import javafx.application.Application;
import javafx.application.Platform;
import javafx.beans.value.ObservableValue;
import javafx.scene.Scene;
import javafx.scene.canvas.Canvas;
import javafx.scene.canvas.GraphicsContext;
import javafx.scene.control.CheckMenuItem;
import javafx.scene.control.CustomMenuItem;
import javafx.scene.control.Menu;
import javafx.scene.control.MenuBar;
import javafx.scene.control.MenuItem;
import javafx.scene.control.RadioMenuItem;
import javafx.scene.control.SeparatorMenuItem;
import javafx.scene.control.Slider;
import javafx.scene.control.ToggleGroup;
import javafx.scene.input.KeyCode;
import javafx.scene.input.KeyCodeCombination;
import javafx.scene.input.KeyCombination;
import javafx.scene.layout.BorderPane;
import javafx.scene.paint.Color;
import javafx.stage.Stage;

public class MenuItemTest extends Application {
        // A canvas to draw shapes
        Canvas canvas = new Canvas(200, 200);

        // Create three RadioMenuItems for shapes
        RadioMenuItem rectItem = new RadioMenuItem("_Rectangle");
        RadioMenuItem circleItem = new RadioMenuItem("_Circle");
        RadioMenuItem ellipseItem = new RadioMenuItem("_Ellipse");

        // A menu item to draw stroke
        CheckMenuItem strokeItem = new CheckMenuItem("Draw _Stroke");
```

```java
// To adjust the stroke width
Slider strokeWidthSlider = new Slider(1, 10, 1);
CustomMenuItem strokeWidthItem = new CustomMenuItem(strokeWidthSlider, false);

public static void main(String[] args) {
        Application.launch(args);
}

@Override
public void start(Stage stage) {
        Menu fileMenu = getFileMenu();
        Menu optionsMenu = getOptionsMenu();

        MenuBar menuBar = new MenuBar();
        menuBar.getMenus().addAll(fileMenu, optionsMenu);

        // Draw the default shape, which is a Rectangle
        this.draw();

        BorderPane root = new BorderPane();
        root.setTop(menuBar);
        root.setCenter(canvas);
        root.setStyle("-fx-padding: 10;" +
                        "-fx-border-style: solid inside;" +
                        "-fx-border-width: 2;" +
                        "-fx-border-insets: 5;" +
                        "-fx-border-radius: 5;" +
                        "-fx-border-color: blue;");

        Scene scene = new Scene(root);
        stage.setScene(scene);
        stage.setTitle("Using Different Types of Menu Items");
        stage.show();
}

public void draw() {
        GraphicsContext gc = canvas.getGraphicsContext2D();
        gc.clearRect(0, 0, 200, 200); // First clear the canvas

        // Set drawing parameters
        gc.setFill(Color.TAN);
        gc.setStroke(Color.RED);
        gc.setLineWidth(strokeWidthSlider.getValue());

        String shapeType = getSelectedShape();
        switch(shapeType) {
                case "Rectangle":
                        gc.fillRect(0, 0, 200, 200);
                        if (strokeItem.isSelected()) {
                                gc.strokeRect(0, 0, 200, 200);
                        }
                        break;
```

```
                case "Circle":
                        gc.fillOval(10, 10, 180, 180);
                        if (strokeItem.isSelected()) {
                                gc.strokeOval(10, 10, 180, 180);
                        }
                        break;
                case "Ellipse":
                        gc.fillOval(10, 10, 180, 150);
                        if (strokeItem.isSelected()) {
                                gc.strokeOval(10, 10, 180, 150);
                        }
                        break;
                default:
                        clear(); // Do not know the shape type
        }
}

public void clear() {
        canvas.getGraphicsContext2D().clearRect(0, 0, 200, 200);
        this.rectItem.setSelected(false);
        this.circleItem.setSelected(false);
        this.ellipseItem.setSelected(false);
}

public Menu getFileMenu() {
        Menu fileMenu = new Menu("_File");

        // Make Rectangle the default option
        rectItem.setSelected(true);

        // Set Key Combinations for shapes
        KeyCombination kr =
                        new KeyCodeCombination(KeyCode.R, KeyCombination.ALT_DOWN);
        KeyCombination kc =
                        new KeyCodeCombination(KeyCode.C, KeyCombination.ALT_DOWN);
        KeyCombination ke =
                        new KeyCodeCombination(KeyCode.E, KeyCombination.ALT_DOWN);
        rectItem.setAccelerator(kr);
        circleItem.setAccelerator(kc);
        ellipseItem.setAccelerator(ke);

        // Add ActionEvent handler to all shape radio menu items
        rectItem.setOnAction(e -> draw());
        circleItem.setOnAction(e -> draw());
        ellipseItem.setOnAction(e -> draw());

        // Add RadioMenuItems to a ToggleGroup to make them mutually exclusive
        ToggleGroup shapeGroup = new ToggleGroup();
        shapeGroup.getToggles().addAll(rectItem, circleItem, ellipseItem);
```

```java
            MenuItem clearItem = new MenuItem("Cle_ar");
            clearItem.setOnAction(e -> clear());

            MenuItem exitItem = new MenuItem("E_xit");
            exitItem.setOnAction(e -> Platform.exit());

            // Add menu items to the File menu
            fileMenu.getItems().addAll(rectItem,
                                    circleItem, ellipseItem,
                                    new SeparatorMenuItem(),
                                    clearItem,
                                    new SeparatorMenuItem(),
                                    exitItem);
            return fileMenu;
    }

    public Menu getOptionsMenu() {
            // Draw stroke by default
            strokeItem.setSelected(true);

            // Redraw the shape when draw stroke option toggles
            strokeItem.setOnAction(e -> syncStroke());

            // Configure the slider
            strokeWidthSlider.setShowTickLabels(true);
            strokeWidthSlider.setShowTickMarks(true);
            strokeWidthSlider.setMajorTickUnit(2);
            strokeWidthSlider.setSnapToPixel(true);
            strokeWidthSlider.valueProperty().addListener(this::strokeWidthChanged);

            Menu optionsMenu = new Menu("_Options");
            optionsMenu.getItems().addAll(strokeItem, this.strokeWidthItem);

            return optionsMenu;
    }

    public void strokeWidthChanged (ObservableValue<? extends Number> prop,
                                    Number oldValue,
                                    Number newValue) {
            draw();
    }

    public String getSelectedShape() {
            if (rectItem.isSelected()) {
                    return "Rectangle";
            }
            else if (circleItem.isSelected()) {
                    return "Circle";
            }
            else if (ellipseItem.isSelected()) {
                    return "Ellipse";
```

```
            } else {
                    return "";
            }
    }

    public void syncStroke() {
            // Enable/disable the slider
            strokeWidthSlider.setDisable(!strokeItem.isSelected());
            draw();
    }
}
```

Styling Menus Using CSS

There are several components involved in using a menu. Table 12-6 lists the default CSS style-class names for components related to menus.

Table 12-6. *CSS Default Style-Class Names for Menu-Related Components*

Menu Component	Style-Class Name
MenuBar	menu-bar
Menu	menu
MenuItem	menu-item
RadioMenuItem	radio-menu-item
CheckMenuItem	check-menu-item
CustomMenuItem	custom-menu-item
SeparatorMenuItem	separator-menu-item

MenuBar supports an -fx-use-system-menu-bar property, which is set to false by default. It indicates whether to use a system menu for the menu bar. It contains a menu substructure that holds the menus for the menu bar. Menu supports a showing CSS pseudo-class, which applies when the menu is showing. RadioMenuItem and CheckMenuItem support a selected CSS pseudo-class, which applies when the menu items are selected.

You can style several components of menus. Please refer to the modena.css file for the sample styles.

Understanding the *ContextMenu* Control

ContextMenu is a pop-up control that displays a list of menu items on request. It is also known as a *context* or *pop-up* menu. By default, it is hidden. The user has to make a request, usually by right-clicking the mouse button, to show it. It is hidden once a selection is made. The user can dismiss a context menu by pressing the Esc key or clicking outside its bounds.

A context menu has a usability problem. It is difficult for users to know about its existence. Usually, nontechnical users are not accustomed to right-clicking the mouse and making selections. For those users, you can present the same options using toolbars or buttons instead. Sometimes, a text message is included on the screen stating that the user needs to right-click to view or show the context menu.

An object of the ContextMenu class represents a context menu. It stores the reference of its menu items in an ObservableList<MenuItem>. The getItems() method returns the reference of the observable list.

You will use the following three menu items in the examples presented below. Note that the menu items in a context menu could be an object of the MenuItem class or its subclasses. For the complete list of menu item types, please refer to the "Understanding Menus" section.

```
MenuItem rectItem = new MenuItem("Rectangle");
MenuItem circleItem = new MenuItem("Circle");
MenuItem ellipseItem = new MenuItem("Ellipse");
```

The default constructor of the ContextMenu class creates an empty menu. You need to add the menu items later:

```
ContextMenu ctxMenu = new ContextMenu();
ctxMenu.getItems().addAll(rectItem, circleItem, ellipseItem);
```

You can use the other constructor to create a context menu with an initial list of menu items:

```
ContextMenu ctxMenu = new ContextMenu(rectItem, circleItem, ellipseItem);
```

Typically, context menus are provided for controls for accessing their commonly used features, for example, Cut, Copy, and Paste features of text input controls. Some controls have default context menus. The control class makes it easy to display a context menu. It has a contextMenu property. You need to set this property to your context menu reference for the control. The following snippet of code sets the context menu for a TextField control:

```
ContextMenu ctxMenu = ...
TextField nameFld = new TextField();
nameFld.setContextMenu(ctxMenu);
```

When you right-click the TextField, your context menu will be displayed instead the default one.

■ **Tip** Activating an empty context menu does not show anything. If you want to disable the default context menu for a control, set its contextMenu property to an empty ContextMenu.

Nodes that are not controls do not have a contextMenu property. You need to use the show() method of the ContextMenu class to display the context menu for these nodes. The show() method gives you full control of the position where the context menu is displayed. You can use it for controls as well if you want to finetune the positioning of the context menu. The show() method is overloaded:

```
void show(Node anchor, double screenX, double screenY)
void show(Node anchor, Side side, double dx, double dy)
```

The first version takes the node for which the context menu is to be displayed with the x and y coordinates relative to the screen. Typically, you display a context menu in the mouse-clicked event where the MouseEvent object provides you the coordinates of the mouse pointer relative to the screen through the getScreenX() and getScreenY() methods.

The following snippet of code shows a context menu for a canvas at (100, 100) relative to the screen coordinate system:

```
Canvas canvas = ...
ctxMenu.show(canvas, 100, 100);
```

The second version lets you finetune the position of the context menu relative to the specified anchor node. The side parameter specifies on which side of the anchor node the context menu is displayed. The possible values are one of the constants—TOP, RIGHT, BOTTOM, and LEFT—of the Side enum. The dx and dy parameters specify the x and y coordinates, respectively, relative to the anchor node coordinate system. This version of the show() method requires a little more explanation.

The side parameter has an effect of shifting the x axis and y axis of the anchor node. The dx and dy parameters are applied after the axes are shifted. Note that the axes are shifted only for computing the position of the context menu when this version of the method is called. They are not shifted permanently, and the anchor node position does not change at all. Figure 12-69 shows an anchor node and its x and y axes for the values of the side parameter. The dx and dy parameters are the x and y coordinates of the point relative to the shifted x axis and y axis of the node.

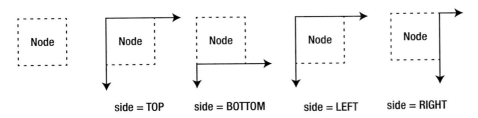

Figure 12-69. *Shifting the x axis and y axis of the anchor node with the side parameter value*

Note that the LEFT and RIGHT values for the side parameter are interpreted based on the node orientation of the anchor node. For a node orientation of RIGHT_TO_LEFT, the LEFT value means the right side of the node.

When you specify TOP, LEFT, or null for the side parameter, the dx and dy parameters are measured relative to the original x and y axes of the node. When you specify BOTTOM for the side parameter, the bottom of the node becomes the new x axis and the y axis remains the same. When you specify RIGHT for the side parameter, the right side of the node becomes the new y axis and the x axis remains the same.

The following call to the show() method displays a context menu at the upper left corner of the anchor node. The value of Side.LEFT or null for the side parameter would display the context menu at the same location:

```
ctxMenu.show(anchor, Side.TOP, 0, 0);
```

The following call to the show() method displays a context menu at the lower left corner of the anchor node:

```
ctxMenu.show(anchor, Side.BOTTOM, 0, 0);
```

Values for dx and dy can be negative. The following call to the show() method displays a context menu 10px above the upper left corner of the anchor node:

```
ctxMenu.show(myAnchor, Side.TOP, 0, -10);
```

The hide() method of the ContextMenu class hides the context menu, if it was showing. Typically, the context menu is hidden when you select a menu item. You need to use the hide() method when the context menu uses a custom menu item with hideOnClick property set to true.

Typically, an ActionEvent handler is added to the menu items of a context menu. The ContextMenu class contains an onAction property, which is an ActionEvent handler. The ActionEvent handler, if set, for a ContextMenu is called every time a menu item is activated. You can use this ActionEvent to execute a follow-up action when a menu item is activated.

The program in Listing 12-39 shows how to use a context menu. It displays a Label and a Canvas. When you right-click the canvas, a context menu with three menu items—Rectangle, Circle, and Ellipse—is displayed. Selecting one of the shapes from the menu items draws the shape on the canvas. The context menu is displayed when the mouse pointer is clicked.

Listing 12-39. Using the ContextMenu Control

```java
// ContextMenuTest.java
package com.jdojo.control;

import javafx.application.Application;
import javafx.scene.Scene;
import javafx.scene.canvas.Canvas;
import javafx.scene.canvas.GraphicsContext;
import javafx.scene.control.ContextMenu;
import javafx.scene.control.Label;
import javafx.scene.control.MenuItem;
import javafx.scene.input.MouseButton;
import javafx.scene.input.MouseEvent;
import javafx.scene.layout.BorderPane;
import javafx.scene.paint.Color;
import javafx.stage.Stage;

public class ContextMenuTest extends Application {
        // A canvas to draw shapes
        Canvas canvas = new Canvas(200, 200);

        public static void main(String[] args) {
                Application.launch(args);
        }

        @Override
        public void start(Stage stage) {
                // Add mouse click event handler to the canvas to show the context menu
                canvas.setOnMouseClicked(e -> showContextMenu(e));

                BorderPane root = new BorderPane();
                root.setTop(new Label("Right click below to display a context menu."));
                root.setCenter(canvas);
                root.setStyle("-fx-padding: 10;" +
                                "-fx-border-style: solid inside;" +
                                "-fx-border-width: 2;" +
                                "-fx-border-insets: 5;" +
                                "-fx-border-radius: 5;" +
                                "-fx-border-color: blue;");
```

```
                Scene scene = new Scene(root);
                stage.setScene(scene);
                stage.setTitle("Using Context Menus");
                stage.show();
        }

        public void showContextMenu(MouseEvent me) {
                // Show menu only on right click
                if (me.getButton() == MouseButton.SECONDARY) {
                        MenuItem rectItem = new MenuItem("Rectangle");
                        MenuItem circleItem = new MenuItem("Circle");
                        MenuItem ellipseItem = new MenuItem("Ellipse");
                        rectItem.setOnAction(e -> draw("Rectangle"));
                        circleItem.setOnAction(e -> draw("Circle"));
                        ellipseItem.setOnAction(e -> draw("Ellipse"));
                        ContextMenu ctxMenu =
                                   new ContextMenu(rectItem, circleItem, ellipseItem);
                        ctxMenu.show(canvas, me.getScreenX(), me.getScreenY());
                }
        }

        public void draw(String shapeType) {
                GraphicsContext gc = canvas.getGraphicsContext2D();
                gc.clearRect(0, 0, 200, 200); // clear the canvas first
                gc.setFill(Color.TAN);

                if (shapeType.equals("Rectangle")) {
                        gc.fillRect(0, 0, 200, 200);
                } else if (shapeType.equals("Circle")) {
                        gc.fillOval(0, 0, 200, 200);
                } else if (shapeType.equals("Ellipse")) {
                        gc.fillOval(10, 40, 180, 120);
                }
        }
}
```

Styling *ContextMenu* with CSS

The default CSS style-class name for a ContextMenu is context-menu. Please refer to the modena.css file
for sample styles for customizing the appearance of context menus. By default, a context menu uses a drop
shadow effect. The following style sets the font size to 8pt and removes the default effect:

```
.context-menu {
        -fx-font-size: 8pt;
        -fx-effect: null;
}
```

Understanding the *ToolBar* Control

ToolBar is used to display a group of nodes, which provide the commonly used action items on a screen. Typically, a ToolBar control contains the commonly used items that are also available through a menu and a context menu.

A ToolBar control can hold many types of nodes. The most commonly used nodes in a ToolBar are buttons and toggle buttons. Separators are used to separate a group of buttons from others. Typically, buttons are kept smaller by using small icons, preferably 16px by 16px in size.

If the items in a toolbar overflow, an overflow button appears to allow users to navigate to the hidden items. A toolbar can have the orientation of horizontal or vertical. A horizontal toolbar arranges the items horizontally in one row. A vertical toolbar arranges the items in one column. Figure 12-70 shows two toolbars: one has no overflow and one has an overflow. The one with an overflow displays an overflow button (>>). When you click the overflow button, the hidden toolbar items are displayed for selection.

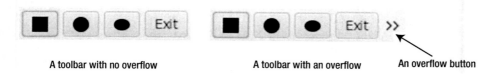

A toolbar with no overflow   A toolbar with an overflow   An overflow button

Figure 12-70. *A horizontal toolbar with three buttons*

You will use the following four ToolBar items in the examples in this chapter:

```
Button rectBtn = new Button("", new Rectangle(0, 0, 16, 16));
Button circleBtn = new Button("", new Circle(0, 0, 8));
Button ellipseBtn = new Button("", new Ellipse(8, 8, 8, 6));
Button exitBtn = new Button("Exit");
```

A ToolBar control stores the reference of items in an ObservableList<Node>. Use the getItems() method to get the reference of the observable list.

The default constructor of the ToolBar class creates an empty toolbar:

```
ToolBar toolBar = new ToolBar();
toolBar.getItems().addAll(circleBtn, ellipseBtn, new Separator(), exitBtn);
```

The ToolBar class provides another constructor that lets you add items:

```
ToolBar toolBar = new ToolBar(rectBtn, circleBtn, ellipseBtn,
                    new Separator(),
                    exitBtn);
```

The orientation property of the ToolBar class specifies its orientation: horizontal or vertical. By default, a toolbar uses the horizontal orientation. The following code sets it to vertical:

```
// Create a ToolBar and set its orientation to VERTICAL
ToolBar toolBar = new ToolBar();
toolBar.setOrientation(Orientation.VERTICAL);
```

■ **Tip** The orientation of a separator in a toolbar is automatically adjusted by the default CSS. It is good practice to provide tool tips for items in a toolbar, as they are small in size and typically do not use text content.

The program in Listing 12-40 shows how to create and use ToolBar controls. It creates a toolbar and adds four items. When you click one of the items with a shape, it draws the shape on a canvas. The Exit item closes the application.

Listing 12-40. Using the ToolBar Control

```
// ToolBarTest.java
package com.jdojo.control;

import javafx.application.Application;
import javafx.application.Platform;
import javafx.scene.Scene;
import javafx.scene.canvas.Canvas;
import javafx.scene.canvas.GraphicsContext;
import javafx.scene.control.Button;
import javafx.scene.control.Label;
import javafx.scene.control.Separator;
import javafx.scene.control.ToolBar;
import javafx.scene.control.Tooltip;
import javafx.scene.layout.BorderPane;
import javafx.scene.layout.VBox;
import javafx.scene.paint.Color;
import javafx.scene.shape.Circle;
import javafx.scene.shape.Ellipse;
import javafx.scene.shape.Rectangle;
import javafx.stage.Stage;

public class ToolBarTest  extends Application {
        // A canvas to draw shapes
        Canvas canvas = new Canvas(200, 200);

        public static void main(String[] args) {
                Application.launch(args);
        }

        public void start(Stage stage) {
                // Create ToolBar items
                Button rectBtn = new Button("", new Rectangle(0, 0, 16, 16));
                Button circleBtn = new Button("", new Circle(0, 0, 8));
                Button ellipseBtn = new Button("", new Ellipse(8, 8, 8, 6));
                Button exitBtn = new Button("Exit");
```

```
        // Set tooltips
        rectBtn.setTooltip(new Tooltip("Draws a rectangle"));
        circleBtn.setTooltip(new Tooltip("Draws a circle"));
        ellipseBtn.setTooltip(new Tooltip("Draws an ellipse"));
        exitBtn.setTooltip(new Tooltip("Exits application"));

        // Add ActionEvent handlers for items
        rectBtn.setOnAction(e -> draw("Rectangle"));
        circleBtn.setOnAction(e -> draw("Circle"));
        ellipseBtn.setOnAction(e -> draw("Ellipse"));
        exitBtn.setOnAction(e -> Platform.exit());

        ToolBar toolBar = new ToolBar(rectBtn, circleBtn, ellipseBtn,
                                      new Separator(),
                                      exitBtn);
        BorderPane root = new BorderPane();
        root.setTop(new VBox(new Label("Click a shape to draw."), toolBar));
        root.setCenter(canvas);
        root.setStyle("-fx-padding: 10;" +
                      "-fx-border-style: solid inside;" +
                      "-fx-border-width: 2;" +
                      "-fx-border-insets: 5;" +
                      "-fx-border-radius: 5;" +
                      "-fx-border-color: blue;");

        Scene scene = new Scene(root);
        stage.setScene(scene);
        stage.setTitle("Using ToolBar Controls");
        stage.show();
    }

    public void draw(String shapeType) {
        GraphicsContext gc = canvas.getGraphicsContext2D();
        gc.clearRect(0, 0, 200, 200); // First clear the canvas
        gc.setFill(Color.TAN);

        if (shapeType.equals("Rectangle")) {
            gc.fillRect(0, 0, 200, 200);
        } else if (shapeType.equals("Circle")) {
            gc.fillOval(0, 0, 200, 200);
        } else if (shapeType.equals("Ellipse")) {
            gc.fillOval(10, 40, 180, 120);
        }
    }
}
```

Styling a Toolbar with CSS

The default CSS style-class name for a ToolBar is tool-bar. It contains an -fx-orientation CSS property that specifies its orientation with the possible values of *horizontal* and *vertical*. It supports horizontal and vertical CSS pseudo-classes that apply when its orientation is horizontal and vertical, respectively.

A toolbar uses a container to arrange the items. The container is an HBox for a horizontal orientation and a VBox for a vertical orientation. The CSS style-class name for the container is container. You can use all CSS properties for the HBox and VBox for the container. The -fx-spacing CSS property specifies the spacing between two adjacent items in the container. You can set this property for the toolbar or the container. Both of the following styles have the same effect on a horizontal toolbar:

```
.tool-bar  {
        -fx-spacing: 2;
}

.tool-bar > .container  {
        -fx-spacing: 2;
}
```

A toolbar contains a tool-bar-overflow-button substructure to represent the overflow button. It is a StackPane. The tool-bar-overflow-button contains an arrow substructure to represent the arrow in the overflow button. It is also a StackPane.

Understanding TabPane and *Tab*

A window may not have enough space to display all of the pieces of information in one page view. JavaFX provides several controls to break down large content into multiple pages, for example, Accordion and Pagination controls. TabPane and Tab let you present information in a page much better. A Tab represents a page and a TabPane contains the Tab.

A Tab is not a control. An instance of the Tab class represents a Tab. The Tab class inherits from the Object class. However, the Tab supports some features as controls do, for example, they can be disabled, styled using CSS, and can have context menus and tool tips.

A Tab consists of a title and content. The title consists of text, an optional graphic, and an optional close button to close the tab. The content consists of controls. Typically, controls are added to a layout pane, which is added to the Tab as its content.

Typically, the titles of the Tab in a TabPane are visible. The content area is shared by all Tabs. You need to select a Tab, by clicking its title, to view its content. You can select only one tab at a time in a TabPane. If the titles of all tabs are not visible, a control button is displayed automatically that assists the user in selecting the invisible tabs.

Tabs in a TabPane may be positioned at the top, right, bottom, or left side of the TabPane. By default, they are positioned at the top.

Figure 12-71 shows two instances of a window. The window contains a TabPane with two tabs. In one instance, the General tab is selected, and in another, the Address tab is selected.

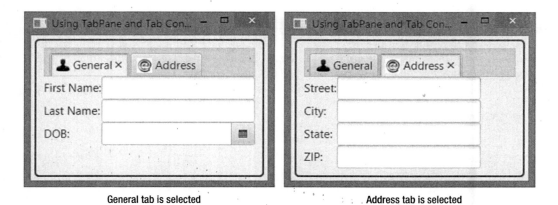

Figure 12-71. *A window with a TabPane, which contains two tabs*

A TabPane is divided into two parts: *header area* and *content area*. The header area displays the titles of tabs; the content area displays the content of the selected tab. The header area is subdivided into the following parts:

- Headers region
- Tab header background
- Control buttons tab
- Tab area

Figure 12-72 shows parts of the header area of a TabPane. The headers region is the entire header area. The tab header background is the area occupied by the titles of the tabs. The control buttons tab contains control buttons that are displayed when the width of the TabPane cannot display all of the tabs. The control button tab lets you select the tabs that are currently not visible. The tab area contains a Label and a close button (the X icon next to the tab label). The Label displays the text and icon for a tab. The close button is used to close a selected tab.

Figure 12-72. *Different parts of the header of a TabPane*

Creating Tabs

You can create a tab using the default constructor of the Tab class with an empty title:

```
Tab tab1 = new Tab();
```

Use the setText() method to set the title text for the tab:

```
tab1.setText("General");
```

The other constructor takes the title text as an argument:

```
Tab tab2 = new Tab("General");
```

Setting the Title and Content of Tabs

The Tab class contains the following properties that let you set the title and content:

- text

- graphic

- closable

- content

The text, graphic, and closable properties specify what appears in the title bar of a tab. The text property specifies a string as the title text. The graphic property specifies a node as the title icon. Notice that the type of the graphic property is Node, so you can use any node as a graphic. Typically, a small icon is set as the graphic. The text property can be set in the constructor or using the setText() method. The following snippet of code creates a tab with text and sets an image as its graphic (assuming the file resources/picture/address_icon.png is included in the package):

```
// Create an ImageView for graphic
String imagePath = "resources/picture/address_icon.png";
URL imageUrl = getClass().getClassLoader().getResource(imagePath);
Image img = new Image(imageUrl.toExternalForm());
ImageView icon = new ImageView(img);

// Create a Tab with "Address" text
Tab addressTab = new Tab("Address");

// Set the graphic
addressTab.setGraphic(icon);
```

The closable property is a boolean property that specifies whether the tab can be closed. If it is set to false, the tab cannot be closed. Closing of tabs is also controlled by the tab-closing policy of the TabPane. If the closable property is set to false, the tab cannot be closed by the user, irrespective of the tab-closing policy of the TabPane. You will learn about tab-closing policy when I discuss the TabPane later.

The content property is a node that specifies the content of the tab. The content of the tab is visible when the tab is selected. Typically, a layout pane with controls is set as the content of a tab. The following snippet of code creates a GridPane, adds some controls, and sets the GridPane as the content of a tab:

```
// Create a GridPane layout pane with some controls
GridPane grid = new GridPane();
grid.addRow(0, new Label("Street:"), streetFld);
grid.addRow(1, new Label("City:"), cityFld);
grid.addRow(2, new Label("State:"), stateFld);
grid.addRow(3, new Label("ZIP:"), zipFld);
```

591

```
Tab addressTab = new Tab("Address");
addressTab.setContent(grid); // Set the content
```

Creating *TabPanes*

The TabPane class provides only one constructor—the default constructor. When you create a TabPane, it has no tabs:

```
TabPane tabPane = new TabPane();
```

Adding Tabs to a *TabPane*

A TabPane stores the references of its tabs in an ObservableList<Tab>. The getTabs() method of the TabPane class returns the reference of the observable list. To add a tab to the TabPane, you need to add it to the observable list. The following snippet of code adds two tabs to a TabPane:

```
Tab generalTab = new Tab("General");
Tab addressTab = new Tab("Address");
...
TabPane tabPane = new TabPane();

// Add the two Tabs to the TabPane
tabPane.getTabs().addAll(generalTab, addressTab);
```

When a tab is not supposed to be part of a TabPane, you need to remove it from the observable list. The TabPane will update its view automatically:

```
// Remove the Address tab
tabPane.getTabs().remove(addressTab);
```

The read-only tabPane property of the Tab class stores the reference of the TabPane that contains the tab. If a tab has not yet been added to a TabPane, its tabPane property is null. Use the getTabPane() method of the Tab class to get the reference of the TabPane.

Putting *TabPanes* and *Tabs* Together

I have covered enough information to allow you to see a TabPane with Tabs in action. Typically, a tab is reused. Inheriting a class from the Tab class helps when reusing a tab. Listing 12-41 and Listing 12-42 create two Tab classes. You will use them as tabs in subsequent examples. The GeneralTab class contains fields to enter the name and birth date of a person. The AddressTab class contains fields to enter an address.

Listing 12-41. A GeneralTab Class that Inherits from the Tab Class

```
// GeneralTab.java
package com.jdojo.control;

import javafx.scene.Node;
import javafx.scene.control.DatePicker;
import javafx.scene.control.Label;
import javafx.scene.control.Tab;
```

```java
import javafx.scene.control.TextField;
import javafx.scene.layout.GridPane;

public class GeneralTab extends Tab {
        TextField firstNameFld = new TextField();
        TextField lastNameFld = new TextField();
        DatePicker dob = new DatePicker();

        public GeneralTab(String text, Node graphic) {
                this.setText(text);
                this.setGraphic(graphic);
                init();
        }

        public void init() {
                dob.setPrefWidth(200);
                GridPane grid = new GridPane();
                grid.addRow(0, new Label("First Name:"), firstNameFld);
                grid.addRow(1, new Label("Last Name:"), lastNameFld);
                grid.addRow(2, new Label("DOB:"), dob);
                this.setContent(grid);
        }
}
```

Listing 12-42. An AddressTab Class that Inherits from the Tab Class

```java
// AddressTab.java
package com.jdojo.control;

import javafx.scene.Node;
import javafx.scene.control.Label;
import javafx.scene.control.Tab;
import javafx.scene.control.TextField;
import javafx.scene.layout.GridPane;

public class AddressTab extends Tab {
        TextField streetFld = new TextField();
        TextField cityFld = new TextField();
        TextField stateFld = new TextField();
        TextField zipFld = new TextField();

        public AddressTab(String text, Node graphic) {
                this.setText(text);
                this.setGraphic(graphic);
                init();
        }

        public void init() {
                GridPane grid = new GridPane();
                grid.addRow(0, new Label("Street:"), streetFld);
                grid.addRow(1, new Label("City:"), cityFld);
```

```
                grid.addRow(2, new Label("State:"), stateFld);
                grid.addRow(3, new Label("ZIP:"), zipFld);
                this.setContent(grid);
        }
}
```

The program in Listing 12-43 creates two tabs. They are instances of the GeneralTab and AddressTab classes. They are added to a TabPane, which is added to center region of a BorderPane. The program displays a window as shown in Figure 12-71.

Listing 12-43. Using a TabPane and Tabs Together

```java
// TabTest.java
package com.jdojo.control;

import javafx.application.Application;
import javafx.scene.Scene;
import javafx.scene.control.TabPane;
import javafx.scene.image.Image;
import javafx.scene.image.ImageView;
import javafx.scene.layout.BorderPane;
import javafx.stage.Stage;

public class TabTest extends Application {
        public static void main(String[] args) {
                Application.launch(args);
        }

        @Override
        public void start(Stage stage) {
                ImageView privacyIcon = getImage("privacy_icon.png");
                GeneralTab generalTab = new GeneralTab("General", privacyIcon);

                ImageView addressIcon = getImage("address_icon.png");
                AddressTab addressTab = new AddressTab("Address", addressIcon);

                TabPane tabPane = new TabPane();
                tabPane.getTabs().addAll(generalTab, addressTab);

                BorderPane root = new BorderPane();
                root.setCenter(tabPane);
                root.setStyle("-fx-padding: 10;" +
                                "-fx-border-style: solid inside;" +
                                "-fx-border-width: 2;" +
                                "-fx-border-insets: 5;" +
                                "-fx-border-radius: 5;" +
                                "-fx-border-color: blue;");

                Scene scene = new Scene(root);
                stage.setScene(scene);
                stage.setTitle("Using TabPane and Tab Controls");
                stage.show();
        }
```

```
public ImageView getImage(String fileName) {
        ImageView imgView = null;
        try {
                String imagePath = "resources/picture/" + fileName;
                Image img = new Image(imagePath);
                imgView = new ImageView(img);
        }
        catch(Exception e) {
                e.printStackTrace();
        }
        return imgView;
    }
}
```

Understanding Tab Selection

TabPane supports single selection model, which allows selecting only one tab at a time. If a tab is selected by the user or programmatically, the previously selected tab is unselected. The Tab class provides the API to allow working with the selection state of an individual tab. The TabPane class provides API that allows working with the selection of all of its tabs.

The Tab class contains a read-only selected property of the boolean type. It is true when the tab is selected. Otherwise, it is false. Note that it is a property of the Tab, not the TabPane.

Tab lets you add event handlers that are notified when the tab is selected or unselected. The onSelectionChanged property stores the reference of such an event:

```
Tab generalTab = ...
generalTab.setOnSelectionChanged(e -> {
        if (generalTab.isSelected()) {
                System.out.println("General tab has been selected.");
        } else {
                System.out.println("General tab has been unselected.");
        }
});
```

TabPane tracks the selected tab and its index in the list of tabs. It uses a separate object, called *selection model*, for this purpose. The TabPane class contains a selectionModel property to store the tab selection details. The property is an object of the SingleSelectionModel class. You can use your own selection model, which is almost never needed. The selection model provides the selection-related functionalities:

- It lets you select a tab using the index of the tab. The first tab has an index of 0.

- It lets you select the first, next, previous, or last tab in the list.

- It lets you clear the selection. Note that this feature is available, but is not commonly used. A TabPane should always typically have a selected tab.

- The selectedIndex and selectedItem properties track the index and reference of the selected tab. You can add a ChangeListener to these properties to handle a change in tab selection in a TabPane.

By default, a TabPane selects its first tab. The following snippet of code selects the last Tab in a TabPane:

```
tabPane.getSelectionModel().selectLast();
```

Use the selectNext() method of the selection model to select the next tab from the list. Calling this method when the last tab is already selected has no effect.

Use the selectPrevious() and selectLast() methods to select the previous and the last tabs in the list. The select(int index) and select(T item) methods select a tab using the index and reference of the tab.

The program in Listing 12-44 adds two tabs to a TabPane. It adds a selection-changed event handler to both tabs. A ChangeListener is added to the selectedItem property of the selectionModel property of the TabPane. When a selection is made, a detailed message is printed on the standard output. Notice that a message is printed when you run the application because the TabPane selection model selects the first tab by default.

Listing 12-44. Tracking Tab Selection in a TabPane

```java
// TabSelection.java
package com.jdojo.control;

import javafx.application.Application;
import javafx.beans.value.ObservableValue;
import javafx.event.Event;
import javafx.scene.Scene;
import javafx.scene.control.Tab;
import javafx.scene.control.TabPane;
import javafx.scene.layout.HBox;
import javafx.stage.Stage;

public class TabSelection extends Application {
        public static void main(String[] args) {
                Application.launch(args);
        }

        @Override
        public void start(Stage stage) {
                GeneralTab generalTab = new GeneralTab("General", null);
                AddressTab addressTab = new AddressTab("Address", null);

                // Add selection a change listener to Tabs
                generalTab.setOnSelectionChanged(e -> tabSelectedChanged(e));
                addressTab.setOnSelectionChanged(e -> tabSelectedChanged(e));

                TabPane tabPane = new TabPane();

                // Add a ChangeListsner to the selection model
                tabPane.getSelectionModel().selectedItemProperty()
                        .addListener(this::selectionChanged);

                tabPane.getTabs().addAll(generalTab, addressTab);
```

```
            HBox root = new HBox(tabPane);
            root.setStyle("-fx-padding: 10;" +
                          "-fx-border-style: solid inside;" +
                          "-fx-border-width: 2;" +
                          "-fx-border-insets: 5;" +
                          "-fx-border-radius: 5;" +
                          "-fx-border-color: blue;");

            Scene scene = new Scene(root);
            stage.setScene(scene);
            stage.setTitle("TabPane Selection Model");
            stage.show();
    }

    public void selectionChanged(ObservableValue<? extends Tab> prop,
                                 Tab oldTab,
                                 Tab newTab) {
            String oldTabText = oldTab == null? "None": oldTab.getText();
            String newTabText = newTab == null? "None": newTab.getText();
            System.out.println("Selection changed in TabPane: old = " +
                               oldTabText + ", new = " + newTabText);
    }

    public void tabSelectedChanged(Event e) {
            Tab tab = (Tab)e.getSource();
            System.out.println("Selection changed event for " + tab.getText() +
                               " tab, selected = " + tab.isSelected());
    }
}
```

Closing Tabs in a *TabPane*

Sometimes the user needs to add tabs to a TabPane on demand and they should be able to close tabs as well. For example, all modern web browsers use tabs for browsing and let you open and close tabs. Adding tabs on demand requires some coding in JavaFX. However, closing tabs by the user is built in the Tab and TabPane classes.

Users can close Tabs in a TabPane using the close button that appears in the title bar of Tabs. The tab-closing feature is controlled by the following properties:

- The closable property of the Tab class

- The tabClosingPolicy property of the TabPane class

The closable property of a Tab class specifies whether the tab can be closed. If it is set to false, the tab cannot be closed, irrespective of the value for the tabClosingPolicy. The default value for the property is true. The tabClosingPolicy property specifies how the tab-closing buttons are available. Its value is one of the following constants of the TabPane.TabClosingPolicy enum:

- ALL_TABS

- SELECTED_TAB

- UNAVAILABLE

ALL_TABS means the close button is available for all tabs. That is, any tab can be closed at any time provided the closable property of the tab is true. SELECTED_TAB means the close button appears only for the selected tab. That is, only the selected tab can be closed at any time. This is the default tab-closing policy of a TabPane. UNAVAILABLE means the close button is not available for any tabs. That is, no tabs can be closed by the user, irrespective of their closable properties.

A distinction has to be made between:

- Closing tabs by the user using the close button

- Removing them programmatically by removing them from the observable list of Tabs of the TabPane

Both have the same effect, that Tabs are removed from the TabPane. The discussion in this section applies to closing tabs by the user.

The user action to closing tabs can be vetoed. You can add event handlers for the TAB_CLOSE_REQUEST_ EVENT event for a tab. The event handler is called when the user attempts to close the tab. If the event handler consumes the event, the closing operation is canceled. You can use the onCloseRequest property of the Tab class to set such an event:

```
Tab myTab = new Tab("My Tab");
myTab.setOnCloseRequest(e -> { if (SOME_CONDITION_IS_TRUE) {
                               // Cancel the close request
                               e.consume();
                           }
                       });
```

A tab also generates a closed event when it is closed by the user. Use the onClosed property of the Tab class to set a closed event handler for a tab. The event handler is typically used to release resources held by the tab:

```
myTab.setOnClosed(e -> {/* Release tab resources here */});
```

The program in Listing 12-45 shows how to use the tab-closing–related properties and events. It displays two tabs in a TabPane. A check box lets you veto the closing of tabs. Unless the check box is selected, an attempt to close tabs is vetoed on the close request event. If you close tabs, you can restore them using the Restore Tabs button. Use the tab-closing policy ChoiceBox to use a different tab-closing policy. For example, if you select UNAVAILABLE as the tab-closing policy, the close buttons will disappear from all tabs. When a tab is closed, a message is printed on the standard output.

Listing 12-45. Using Properties and Events Related to Closing Tabs by Users

```
// TabClosingTest.java
package com.jdojo.control;

import javafx.application.Application;
import javafx.beans.value.ObservableValue;
import javafx.collections.ObservableList;
import javafx.event.Event;
import javafx.scene.Scene;
import javafx.scene.control.Button;
import javafx.scene.control.CheckBox;
import javafx.scene.control.ChoiceBox;
import javafx.scene.control.Label;
```

```java
import javafx.scene.control.Tab;
import javafx.scene.control.TabPane;
import javafx.stage.Stage;
import javafx.scene.layout.BorderPane;
import javafx.scene.layout.GridPane;
import static javafx.scene.control.TabPane.TabClosingPolicy;

public class TabClosingTest extends Application {
        GeneralTab generalTab = new GeneralTab("General", null);
        AddressTab addressTab = new AddressTab("Address", null);
        TabPane tabPane = new TabPane();

        CheckBox allowClosingTabsFlag = new CheckBox("Are Tabs closable?");
        Button restoreTabsBtn = new Button("Restore Tabs");
        ChoiceBox<TabPane.TabClosingPolicy> tabClosingPolicyChoices = new ChoiceBox<>();

        public static void main(String[] args) {
                Application.launch(args);
        }

        @Override
        public void start(Stage stage) {
                // Add Tabs to the TabPane
                tabPane.getTabs().addAll(generalTab, addressTab);

                // Set a tab close request event handler for tabs
                generalTab.setOnCloseRequest(this::tabClosingRequested);
                addressTab.setOnCloseRequest(this::tabClosingRequested);

                // Set a closed event handler for the tabs
                generalTab.setOnClosed(e -> tabClosed(e));
                addressTab.setOnClosed(e -> tabClosed(e));

                // Set an action event handler for the restore button
                restoreTabsBtn.setOnAction(e -> restoreTabs());

                // Add choices to the choice box
                tabClosingPolicyChoices.getItems()
                                        .addAll(TabClosingPolicy.ALL_TABS,
                                                TabClosingPolicy.SELECTED_TAB,
                                                TabClosingPolicy.UNAVAILABLE);

                // Set the default value for the tab closing policy
                tabClosingPolicyChoices.setValue(tabPane.getTabClosingPolicy());


                // Bind the tabClosingPolicy of the tabPane to the value property of the
                // of the ChoiceBoxx
                tabPane.tabClosingPolicyProperty().bind(
                                                tabClosingPolicyChoices.valueProperty());
```

```
            BorderPane root = new BorderPane();
            GridPane grid = new GridPane();
            grid.setHgap(10);
            grid.setVgap(10);
            grid.setStyle("-fx-padding: 10;");
            grid.addRow(0, allowClosingTabsFlag, restoreTabsBtn);
            grid.addRow(1, new Label("Tab Closing Policy:"),
                            tabClosingPolicyChoices);
            root.setTop(grid);
            root.setCenter(tabPane);
            root.setStyle("-fx-padding: 10;" +
                            "-fx-border-style: solid inside;" +
                            "-fx-border-width: 2;" +
                            "-fx-border-insets: 5;" +
                            "-fx-border-radius: 5;" +
                            "-fx-border-color: blue;");

            Scene scene = new Scene(root);
            stage.setScene(scene);
            stage.setTitle("Closing Tabs");
            stage.show();
    }

    public void tabClosingRequested(Event e) {
            if (!allowClosingTabsFlag.isSelected()) {
                    e.consume(); // Closing tabs is not allowed
            }
    }

    public void tabClosed(Event e) {
            Tab tab = (Tab)e.getSource();
            String text = tab.getText();
            System.out.println(text + " tab has been closed.");
    }

    public void restoreTabs() {
            ObservableList<Tab> list = tabPane.getTabs();
            if (!list.contains(generalTab)) {
                    list.add(0, generalTab);
            }

            if (!list.contains(addressTab)) {
                    list.add(1, addressTab);
            }
    }

    public void closingPolicyChanged(
                        ObservableValue<? extends TabPane.TabClosingPolicy> prop,
                        TabPane.TabClosingPolicy oldPolicy,
                        TabPane.TabClosingPolicy newPolicy) {
            tabPane.setTabClosingPolicy(newPolicy);
    }
}
```

Positioning Tabs in a *TabPane*

Tabs in a TabPane may be positioned at the top, right, bottom, or left. The side property of the TabPane specifies the position of tabs. It is set to one of the constants of the Side enum:

- TOP

- RIGHT

- BOTTOM

- LEFT

The default value for the side property is Side.TOP. The following snippet of code creates a TabPane and sets the side property to Side.LEFT to position tabs on the left:

```
TabPane tabPane = new TabPane();
tabPane.setSide(Side.LEFT);
```

■ **Tip**   The actual placement of tabs also uses the node orientation. For example, if the side property is set to Side.LEFT and the node orientation of the TabPane is set to RIGHT_TO_LEFT, the tabs will be positioned on the right side.

The TabPane class contains a rotateGraphic property, which is a boolean property. The property is related to the side property. When the side property is Side.TOP or Side.BOTTOM, the graphics of all tabs in their title bars are in the upright position. By default, when the side property changes to Side.LEFT or Side.RIGHT, the title text is rotated, keeping the graphic upright. The rotateGraphic property specifies whether the graphic is rotated with the text, as shown in the following code. By default, it is set to false.

```
// Rotate the graphic with the text for left and right sides
tabPane.setRotateGraphic(true);
```

Figure 12-73 shows the title bar of a tab in a TabPane with the side property set to TOP and LEFT. Notice the effect on the graphics when the side property is LEFT and the rotateGraphic property is false and true. The rotateGraphic property has no effect when tabs are positioned at the top or bottom.

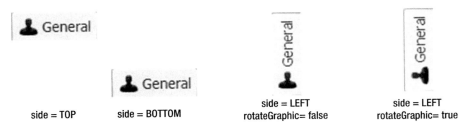

side = TOP	side = BOTTOM	side = LEFT rotateGraphic= false	side = LEFT rotateGraphic= true

Figure 12-73. *Effects of the side and* rotateGraphic *properties of the TabPane*

Sizing Tabs in a *TabPane*

TabPane divides its layout into two parts:

- Header area
- Content area

The header area displays the titles of tabs. The content area displays the content of the selected tab. The size of the content area is automatically computed based on the content of all tabs. TabPane contains the following properties that allow you to set the minimum and maximum sizes of the title bars of tabs:

- tabMinHeight
- tabMaxHeight
- tabMinWidth
- tabMaxWidth

The default values are zero for minimum width and height, and Double.MAX_VALUE for maximum width and height. The default size is computed based on the context of the tab titles. If you want all tab titles to be of a fixed size, set the minimum and maximum width and height to the same value. Note that for the fixed size tabs, the longer text in the title bar will be truncated.

The following snippet of code creates a TabPane and sets the properties, so all tabs are 100px wide and 30px tall:

```
TabPane tabPane = new TabPane();
tabPane.setTabMinHeight(30);
tabPane.setTabMaxHeight(30);
tabPane.setTabMinWidth(100);
tabPane.setTabMaxWidth(100);
```

Using Recessed and Floating *TabPanes*

A TabPane can be in recessed or floating mode. The default mode is recessed mode. In the recessed mode, it *appears* to be fixed. In floating mode, it appearance is changed to make it look like it is floating. In the floating mode, the background color of the header area is removed and a border around the content area is added. Here is a rule of thumb in deciding which mode to use:

- If you are using a TabPane along with other controls in a window, use floating mode.
- If the TabPane is the only one control on the window, use recessed mode.

Figure 12-74 shows two windows with the same TabPane: one in the recessed mode and one in the floating mode.

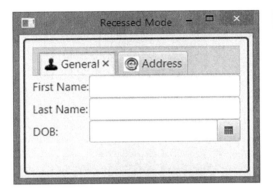 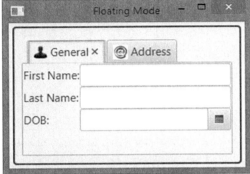

Figure 12-74. *A TabPane in recessed and floating modes*

The floating mode of a TabPane is specified by a style class. The TabPane class contains a STYLE_CLASS_FLOATING constant. If you add this style class to a TabPane, it is in the floating mode. Otherwise, it is in the recessed mode. The following snippet of code shows how to turn the floating mode for a TabPane on and off:

```
TabPane tabPane = new TabPane();

// Turn on the floating mode
tabPane.getStyleClass().add(TabPane.STYLE_CLASS_FLOATING);
...
// Turn off the floating mode
tabPane.getStyleClass().remove(TabPane.STYLE_CLASS_FLOATING);
```

Styling *Tab* and *TabPane* with CSS

The default CSS style-class name for a tab and for a TabPane is tab-pane. You can style Tabs directly using the tab style class or using the substructure of TabPane. The later approach is commonly used.

TabPane supports four CSS pseudo-classes, which correspond to the four values for its side property:

- top
- right
- bottom
- left

You can set the minimum and maximum sizes of the tab titles in a TabPane using the following CSS properties. They correspond to the four properties in the TabPane class. Please refer to the "Sizing Tabs in a *TabPane*" section for a detailed discussion of these properties.

- -fx-tab-min-width
- -fx-tab-max-width
- -fx-tab-min-height
- -fx-tab-max-height

A TabPane divides its layout bounds into two areas: header area and content area. Please refer to Figure 12-72 for the different subparts in the header area. The header area is called the tab-header-area substructure, which contains the following substructures:

- headers-region
- tab-header-background
- control-buttons-tab
- tab

The control-buttons-tab substructure contains a tab-down-button substructure, which contains an arrow substructure. The tab substructure contains tab-label and tab-close-button substructures. The tab-content-area substructure represents the content area of the TabPane. Substructures let you style different parts of TabPane.

The following code removes the background color for the header area as is done when the TabPane is in the floating mode:

```
.tab-pane > .tab-header-area > .tab-header-background {
    -fx-background-color: null;
}
```

The following code shows the text of the selected tab in boldface. Notice the use of the selected pseudo-class for the tab in the selector .tab:selected:

```
.tab-pane > .tab-header-area > .headers-region > .tab:selected > .tab-container > ,tab-label
{
        -fx-font-weight: bold;
}
```

The following code shows Tabs in a TabPane in blue background with 10pt white title text:

```
.tab-pane > .tab-header-area > .headers-region > .tab  {
    -fx-background-color: blue;
}
```

```
.tab-pane > .tab-header-area > .headers-region > .tab > .tab-container > .tab-label {
        -fx-text-fill: white;
        -fx-font-size: 10pt;
}
```

Use the floating style-class for the TabPane when styling it for the floating mode. The following style sets the border color to blue in floating mode:

```
.tab-pane.floating > .tab-content-area {
        -fx-border-color: blue;
}
```

Please refer to the modena.css file for the complete list of styles used for TabPane.

Understanding the *HTMLEditor* Control

The HTMLEditor control provides a rich text editing capability to JavaFX application. It uses HTML as its data model. That is, the formatted text in HTMLEditor is stored in HTML format. An HTMLEditor control can be used for entering formatted text in a business application, for example, product description, or comments. It can also be used to enter e-mail content in an e-mail client application. Figure 12-75 shows a window with an HTMLEditor control.

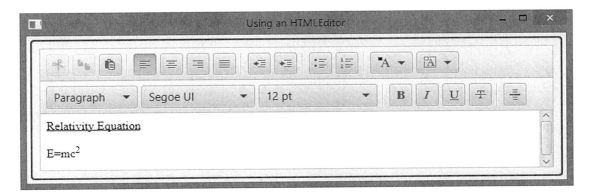

Figure 12-75. *An* HTMLEditor *control*

An HTMLEditor displays formatting toolbars with it. You cannot hide the toolbars. They can be styled using a CSS. Using the toolbars, you can:

- Copy, cut, and paste text using the system clipboard
- Apply text alignment
- Indent text
- Apply bulleted list and numbered list styles
- Set foreground and background colors
- Apply paragraph and heading styles with font family and font size
- Apply formatting styles such as bold, italic, underline, and strikethrough
- Add horizontal rulers

The control supports HTML5. Note that the toolbars do not allow you to apply all kinds of HTML. However, if you load a document that uses those styles, it allows you to edit them. For example, you cannot create an HTML table directly in the control. However, if you load HTML content having HTML tables into the control, you will be able to edit the data in the tables.

The HTMLEditor does not provide API to load HTML content from a file to save its content to a file. You will have to write your own code to accomplish this.

Creating an *HTMLEditor*

An instance of the HTMLEditor class represents an HTMLEditor control. The class is included in the javafx.scene.web package. Use the default constructor, which is the only constructor provided, to create an HTMLEditor:

```
HTMLEditor editor = new HTMLEditor();
```

Using an *HTMLEditor*

The HTMLEditor class has a very simple API that consists of only three methods:

- getHtmlText()
- setHtmlText(String htmlText)
- print(PrinterJob job)

The getHTMLText() method returns the HTML content as a string. The setHTMLText() method sets the content of the control to the specified HTML string. The print() method prints the content of the control.

The program in Listing 12-46 shows how to use an HTMLEditor. It displays an HTMLEditor, a TextArea, and two Buttons. You can use the buttons to convert text in the HTMLEditor to HTML code and vice versa.

Listing 12-46. Using the HTMLEditor Control

```java
// HTMLEditorTest.java
package com.jdojo.control;

import javafx.application.Application;
import javafx.scene.Scene;
import javafx.scene.control.Button;
import javafx.scene.control.TextArea;
import javafx.scene.layout.HBox;
import javafx.scene.layout.VBox;
import javafx.scene.web.HTMLEditor;
import javafx.stage.Stage;

public class HTMLEditorTest extends Application {
        public static void main(String[] args) {
                Application.launch(args);
        }

        @Override
        public void start(Stage stage) {
                HTMLEditor editor = new HTMLEditor();
                editor.setPrefSize(600, 300);

                TextArea html = new TextArea();
                html.setPrefSize(600, 300);
                html.setStyle("-fx-font-size:10pt; -fx-font-family: \"Courier New\";");

                Button htmlToText = new Button("Convert HTML to Text");
                Button textToHtml = new Button("Convert Text to HTML");
                htmlToText.setOnAction(e -> editor.setHtmlText(html.getText()));
                textToHtml.setOnAction(e -> html.setText(editor.getHtmlText()));
```

```
        HBox buttons = new HBox(htmlToText, textToHtml);
        buttons.setSpacing(10);

        VBox root = new VBox(editor, buttons, html);
        root.setSpacing(10);
        root.setStyle("-fx-padding: 10;" +
                      "-fx-border-style: solid inside;" +
                      "-fx-border-width: 2;" +
                      "-fx-border-insets: 5;" +
                      "-fx-border-radius: 5;" +
                      "-fx-border-color: blue;");

        Scene scene = new Scene(root);
        stage.setScene(scene);
        stage.setTitle("Using an HTMLEditor");
        stage.show();
    }
}
```

Styling *HTMLEditor* with CSS

The default CSS style-class name for an HTMLEditor is html-editor. The HTMLEditor uses styles of a Control such as padding, borders, and background color.

You can style each button in the toolbar separately. The following are the list of style-class names for the toolbar buttons. The names are self-explanatory, for example, html-editor-align-right and html-editor-hr are the style-class names for the toolbar buttons used to right align text and draw a horizontal ruler, respectively.

- html-editor-cut
- html-editor-copy
- html-editor-paste
- html-editor-align-left
- html-editor-align-center
- html-editor-align-right
- html-editor-align-justify
- html-editor-outdent
- html-editor-indent
- html-editor-bullets
- html-editor-numbers
- html-editor-bold
- html-editor-italic
- html-editor-underline
- html-editor-strike
- html-editor-hr

607

The following code sets a custom image for the Cut button in the toolbar:

```
.html-editor-cut {
        -fx-graphic: url("my_html_editor_cut.jpg");
}
```

Use the button and toggle-button style-class names if you want to apply styles to all toolbar buttons and toggle buttons:

```
/* Set the background colors for all buttons and toggle buttons */
.html-editor .button, .html-editor .toggle-button {
    -fx-background-color: lightblue;
}
```

The HTMLEditor shows two ColorPickers for users to select the background and foreground colors. Their style-class names are html-editor-background and html-editor-foreground. The following code shows the selected color labels in the ColorPickers:

```
.html-editor-background {
    -fx-color-label-visible: true;
}
```

```
.html-editor-foreground {
    -fx-color-label-visible: true;
}
```

Choosing Files and Directories

JavaFX provides the FileChooser and DirectoryChooser classes in the javafx.stage package that are used to show file and directory dialogs. The dialogs have a platform dependent look and feel and cannot be styled using JavaFX. They are *not* controls. I am discussing them in this chapter because they are typically used along with controls. For example, a file or directory dialog is displayed when a button is clicked. On some platforms, for example, some mobile and embedded devices, users may have access to the file systems. Using these classes to access files and directories on such devices does nothing.

The *FileChooser* Dialog

A FileChooser is a standard file dialog. It is used to let the user select files to open or save. Some of its parts, for example, the title, the initial directory, and the list of file extensions, can be specified before opening the dialogs. There are three steps in using a file dialog:

1. Create an object of the FileChooser class.

2. Set the initial properties for the file dialog.

3. Use one of the showXXXDialog() methods to show a specific type of file dialog.

Creating a File Dialog

An instance of the FileChooser class is used to open file dialogs. The class contains a no-args constructor to create its objects:

```
// Create a file dialog
FileChooser fileDialog = new FileChooser();
```

Setting Initial Properties of the Dialog

You can set the following initial properties of the file dialog:

- Title
- initialDirectory
- initialFileName
- Extension filters

The title property of the FileChooser class is a string, which represents the title of the file dialog:

```
// Set the file dialog title
fileDialog.setTitle("Open Resume");
```

The initialDirectory property of the FileChooser class is a File, which represents the initial directory when the file dialog is shown:

```
// Set C:\ as initial directory (on Windows)
fileDialog.setInitialDirectory(new File("C:\\"));
```

The initialFileName property of the FileChooser class is a string that is the initial file name for the file dialog. Typically, it is used for a file save dialog. Its effect depends on the platform if it is used for a file open dialog. For example, it is ignored on Windows:

```
// Set the initial file name
fileDialog.setInitialFileName("untitled.htm");
```

You can set a list of extension filters for a file dialog. Filters are displayed as a drop-down box. One filter is active at a time. The file dialog displays only those files that match the active extension filter. An extension filter is represented by an instance of the ExtensionFilter class, which is an inner static class of the FileChooser class. The getExtensionFilters() method of the FileChooser class returns an ObservableList<FileChooser.ExtensionFilter>. You add the extension filters to the list. An extension filter has two properties: a description and a list of file extension in the form *.<extension>:

```
import static javafx.stage.FileChooser.ExtensionFilter;
...
// Add three extension filters
fileDialog.getExtensionFilters().addAll(
        new ExtensionFilter("HTML Files", "*.htm", "*.html"),
        new ExtensionFilter("Text Files", "*.txt"),
        new ExtensionFilter("All Files", "*.*"));
```

By default, the first extension filter in the list is active when the file dialog is displayed. Use the selectedExtensionFilter property to specify the initial active filter when the file dialog is opened:

```
// Continuing with the above snippet of code, select *.txt filter by default
fileDialog.setSelectedExtensionFilter(fileDialog.getExtensionFilters().get(1));
```

The same selectedExtensionFilter property contains the extension filter that is selected by the user when the file dialog is closed.

Showing the Dialog

An instance of the FileChooser class can open three types of file dialogs:

- A file open dialog to select only one file
- A file open dialog to select multiple files
- A file save dialog

The following three methods of the FileChooser class are used to open three types of file dialogs:

- showOpenDialog(Window ownerWindow)
- showOpenMultipleDialog(Window ownerWindow)
- showSaveDialog(Window ownerWindow)

The methods do not return until the file dialog is closed. You can specify null as the owner window. If you specify an owner window, the input to the owner window is blocked when the file dialog is displayed.

The showOpenDialog() and showSaveDialog() methods return a File object, which is the selected file, or null if no file is selected. The showOpenMultipleDialog() method returns a List<File>, which contains all selected files, or null if no files are selected:

```
// Show a file open dialog to select multiple files
List<File> files = fileDialog.showOpenMultipleDialog(primaryStage);
if (files != null) {
        for(File f : files) {
                System.out.println("Selected file :" + f);
        }
} else {
        System.out.println("No files were selected.");
}
```

Use the selectedExtensionFilter property of the FileChooser class to get the selected extension filter at the time the file dialog was closed:

```
import static javafx.stage.FileChooser.ExtensionFilter;
...
// Print the selected extension filter description
ExtensionFilter filter = fileDialog.getSelectedExtensionFilter();
if (filter != null) {
    System.out.println("Selected Filter: " + filter.getDescription());
} else {
        System.out.println("No extension filter selected.");
}
```

Using a File Dialog

The program in Listing 12-47 shows how to use open and save file dialogs. It displays a window with an HTMLEditor and three buttons. Use the Open button to open an HTML file in the editor. Edit the content in the editor. Use the Save button to save the content in the editor to a file. If you chose an existing file in the Save Resume dialog, the content of the file will be overwritten. It is left to the reader as an exercise to enhance the program, so it will prompt the user before overwriting an existing file.

Listing 12-47. Using Open and Save File Dialogs

```java
// FileChooserTest.java
package com.jdojo.control;

import javafx.application.Application;
import java.io.File;
import java.io.IOException;
import java.nio.file.Files;
import javafx.geometry.Pos;
import javafx.scene.Scene;
import javafx.scene.control.Button;
import javafx.scene.layout.HBox;
import javafx.scene.layout.VBox;
import javafx.scene.web.HTMLEditor;
import javafx.stage.FileChooser;
import javafx.stage.Stage;
import static javafx.stage.FileChooser.ExtensionFilter;

public class FileChooserTest extends Application {
        private Stage primaryStage;
        private HTMLEditor resumeEditor;
        private final FileChooser fileDialog = new FileChooser();

        public static void main(String[] args) {
                Application.launch(args);
        }

        @Override
        public void start(Stage stage) {
                primaryStage = stage; // Used in file dialogs later
                resumeEditor = new HTMLEditor();
                resumeEditor.setPrefSize(600, 300);

                // Filter only HTML files
                fileDialog.getExtensionFilters()
                        .add(new ExtensionFilter("HTML Files", "*.htm", "*.html"));

                Button openBtn = new Button("Open");
                Button saveBtn = new Button("Save");
                Button closeBtn = new Button("Close");
                openBtn.setOnAction(e -> openFile());
                saveBtn.setOnAction(e -> saveFile());
                closeBtn.setOnAction(e -> stage.close());
```

```java
            HBox buttons = new HBox(20, openBtn, saveBtn, closeBtn);
            buttons.setAlignment(Pos.CENTER_RIGHT);
            VBox root = new VBox(resumeEditor, buttons);
            root.setSpacing(20);
            root.setStyle("-fx-padding: 10;" +
                          "-fx-border-style: solid inside;" +
                          "-fx-border-width: 2;" +
                          "-fx-border-insets: 5;" +
                          "-fx-border-radius: 5;" +
                          "-fx-border-color: blue;");

            Scene scene = new Scene(root);
            stage.setScene(scene);
            stage.setTitle("Editing Resume in HTML Format");
            stage.show();
    }

    private void openFile() {
            fileDialog.setTitle("Open Resume");
            File file = fileDialog.showOpenDialog(primaryStage);
            if (file == null) {
                    return;
            }

            try {
                    // Read the file and populate the HTMLEditor
                    byte[] resume = Files.readAllBytes(file.toPath());
                    resumeEditor.setHtmlText(new String(resume));
            }
            catch(IOException e) {
                    e.printStackTrace();
            }
    }

    private void saveFile() {
            fileDialog.setTitle("Save Resume");
            fileDialog.setInitialFileName("untitled.htm");
            File file = fileDialog.showSaveDialog(primaryStage);
            if (file == null) {
                    return;
            }

            try {
                    // Write the HTML contents to the file. Overwrite the existing file.
                    String html = resumeEditor.getHtmlText();
                    Files.write(file.toPath(), html.getBytes());
            }
            catch(IOException e) {
                    e.printStackTrace();
            }
    }
}
```

The *DirectoryChooser* Dialog

Sometimes you may need to let the user browse a directory from the available file systems on the computer. The DirectoryChooser class lets you display a platform-dependent directory dialog.

The DirectoryChooser class contains two properties:

- title
- initialDirectory

The title property is a string and it is the title of the directory dialog. The initialDirectory property is a File and it is the initial directory selected in the dialog when the dialog is shown.

Use the showDialog(Window ownerWindow) method of the DirectoryChooser class to open the directory dialog. When the dialog is opened, you can select at most one directory or close the dialog without selecting a directory. The method returns a File, which is the selected directory or null if no directory is selected. The method is blocked until the dialog is closed. If an owner window is specified, input to all windows in the owner window chain is blocked when the dialog is shown. You can specify a null owner window.

The following snippet of code shows how to create, configure, and display a directory dialog:

```
DirectoryChooser dirDialog = new DirectoryChooser();

// Configure the properties
dirDialog.setTitle("Select Destination Directory");
dirDialog.setInitialDirectory(new File("c:\\"));

// Show the directory dialog
File dir = dirDialog.showDialog(null);
if (dir != null) {
        System.out.println("Selected directory: " + dir);
} else {
        System.out.println("No directory was selected.");
}
```

Summary

A user interface is a means to exchange information in terms of input and output between an application and its users. Entering text using a keyboard, selecting a menu item using a mouse, and clicking a button are examples of providing input to a GUI application. The application displays output on a computer monitor using text, charts, dialog boxes, among others. Users interact with a GUI application using graphical elements called *controls* or *widgets*. Buttons, labels, text fields, text area, radio buttons, and check boxes are a few examples of controls. JavaFX provides a rich set of easy-to-use controls. Controls are added to layout panes that position and size them.

Each control in JavaFX is represented by an instance of a class. Control classes are included in the javafx.scene.control package. A control class in JavaFX is a subclass, direct or indirect, of the Control class, which in turn inherits from the Region class. Recall that the Region class inherits from the Parent class. Therefore, technically, a Control is also a Parent. A Parent can have children. However, control classes do not allow adding children. Typically, a control consists of multiple nodes that are internally maintained. Control classes expose the list of their internal unmodifiable children through the getChildrenUnmodifiable() method, which returns an ObservableList<Node>.

A labeled control contains a read-only textual content and optionally a graphic as part of its user interface. Label, Button, CheckBox, RadioButton, and Hyperlink are some examples of labeled controls in JavaFX. All labeled controls are inherited, directly or indirectly, from the Labeled class that, in turn, inherits from the Control class. The Labeled class contains properties common to all labeled controls, such as content alignment, positioning of text relative to the graphic, and text font.

JavaFX provides button controls that can be used to execute commands, make choices, or both. All button control classes inherit from the ButtonBase class. All types of buttons support the ActionEvent. Buttons trigger an ActionEvent when they are activated. A button can be activated in different ways, for example, by using a mouse, a mnemonic, an accelerator key, or other key combinations. A button that executes a command when activated is known as a command button. The Button, Hyperlink, and MenuButton classes represent command buttons. A MenuButton lets the user execute a command from a list of commands. Buttons used for presenting different choices to users are known as choice buttons. The ToggleButton, CheckBox, and RadioButton classes represent choice buttons. The third kind of button is a hybrid of the first two kinds. They let users execute a command or make choices. The SplitMenuButton class represents a hybrid button.

JavaFX provides controls that let users select an item(s) from a list of items. They take less space compared to buttons. Those controls are ChoiceBox, ComboBox, ListView, ColorPicker, and DatePicker. ChoiceBox lets users select an item from a small list of predefined items. ComboBox is an advanced version of ChoiceBox. It has many features, for example, an ability to be editable or changing the appearance of the items in the list, which are not offered in ChoiceBox. ListView provides users an ability to select multiple items from a list of items. Typically, all or more than one item in a ListView are visible to the user all of the time. ColorPicker lets users select a color from a standard color palette or define a custom color graphically. DatePicker lets users select a date from a calendar pop-up. Optionally, users can enter a date as text. ComboBox, ColorPicker, and DatePicker have the same superclass that is the ComboBoxBase class.

Text input controls let users work with single line or multiple lines of plain text. All text input controls are inherited from the TextInputControl class. There are three types of text input controls: TextField, PasswordField, and TextArea. TextField lets the user enter a single line of plain text; newlines and tab characters in the text are removed. PasswordField inherits from TextField. It works much the same as TextField, except it masks its text. TextArea lets the user enter multiline plain text. A newline character starts a new paragraph in a TextArea.

For a long running task, you need to provide visual feedback to the user indicating the progress of the task for a better user experience. The ProgressIndicator and ProgressBar controls are used to show the progress of a task. They differ in the ways they display the progress. The ProgressBar class inherits from the ProgressIndicator class. ProgressIndicator displays the progress in a circular control, whereas ProgressBar uses a horizontal bar.

TitledPane is a labeled control. It displays the text as its title. The graphic is shown in the title bar. Besides text and a graphic, it has content, which is a node. Typically, a group of controls is placed in a container and the container is added as the content for the TitledPane. TitledPane can be in a collapsed or expanded state. In the collapsed state, it displays only the title bar and hides the content. In the expanded state, it displays the title bar and the content.

Accordion is a control that displays a group of TitledPane controls where only one of them is in the expanded state at a time.

Pagination is a control that is used to display a large single content by dividing it into smaller chunks called pages, for example, the results of a search.

A tool tip is a pop-up control used to show additional information about a node. It is displayed when a mouse pointer hovers over the node. There is a small delay between when the mouse pointer hovers over a node and when the tool tip for the node is shown. The tool tip is hidden after a small period. It is also hidden when the mouse pointer leaves the control. You should not design a GUI application where the user depends on seeing tool tips for controls, as they may not be shown at all if the mouse pointer never hovers over the controls.

The ScrollBar and ScrollPane controls provide scrolling features to other controls. These controls are not used alone. They are always used to support scrolling in other controls.

Sometimes you want to place logically related controls side by side horizontally or vertically. For better appearance, controls are grouped using different types of separators. The Separator and SplitPane controls are used for visually separating two controls or two groups of controls.

The Slider control lets the user select a numeric value from a numeric range graphically by sliding a thumb (or knob) along a track. A Slider can be horizontal or vertical.

A menu is used to provide a list of actionable items to the user in a compact form. A menu bar is a horizontal bar that acts as a container for menus. An instance of the MenuBar class represents a menu bar. A menu contains a list of actionable items, which are displayed on demand, for example, by clicking it. The list of menu items is hidden when the user selects an item or moves the mouse pointer outside the list. A menu is typically added to a menu bar or another menu as a submenu. An instance of the Menu class represents a menu. A Menu displays text and a graphic. A menu item is an actionable item in a menu. The action associated with a menu item is performed by mouse or keys. Menu items can be styled using CSS. An instance of the MenuItem class represents a menu item. The MenuItem class is not a node. It is inherited from the Object class and, therefore, cannot be added directly to a scene graph. You need to add it to a Menu.

ContextMenu is a pop-up control that displays a list of menu items on request. It is known as a context or pop-up menu. By default, it is hidden. The user has to make a request, usually by right-clicking the mouse button, to show it. It is hidden once a selection is made. The user can dismiss a context menu by pressing the Esc key or clicking outside its bounds. An object of the ContextMenu class represents a context menu.

ToolBar is used to display a group of nodes, which provide the commonly used action items on a screen. Typically, a ToolBar contains the commonly used items that are also available through a menu and a context menu. A ToolBar can hold many types of nodes. The most commonly used nodes in a ToolBar are buttons and toggle buttons. Separators are used to separate a group of buttons from others. Typically, buttons are kept smaller by using small icons, preferably 16px by 16px in size.

A window may not have enough space to display all of the pieces of information in a one-page view. TabPanes and Tabs let you present information in a page much better. A Tab represents a page and a TabPane contains the tabs. A Tab is not a control. An instance of the Tab class represents a Tab. The Tab class inherits from the Object class. However, a Tab supports some features as controls do, for example, they can be disabled, styled using CSS, and have context menus and tool tips.

A Tab consists of a title and content. The title consists of text, an optional graphic, and an optional close button to close the tab. The content consists of controls. Typically, the titles of tabs in a TabPane are visible. The content area is shared by all tabs. Tabs in a TabPane may be positioned at the top, right, bottom, or left side of the TabPane. By default, they are positioned at the top.

The HTMLEditor control provides a rich text editing capability to JavaFX application. It uses HTML as its data model. That is, the formatted text in HTMLEditor is stored in HTML format.

JavaFX provides the FileChooser and DirectoryChooser classes in the javafx.stage package that are used to show file and directory dialogs, respectively. The dialogs have a platform dependent look and feel and cannot be styled using JavaFX. They are not controls. A FileChooser is a standard file dialog. It is used to let the user select files to open or save. A DirectoryChooser lets the user browse a directory from the available file systems on the machine.

The next chapter will discuss the TableView control that is used to display and edit data in tabular format.

CHAPTER 13

■ ■ ■

Understanding *TableView*

In this chapter, you will learn:

- What a TableView is
- How to create a TableView
- About adding columns to a TableView
- About populating a TableView with data
- About showing and hiding and reordering columns in a TableView
- About sorting and editing data in a TableView
- About adding and deleting rows in a TableView
- About resizing columns in a TableView
- About styling a TableView with CSS

What Is a *TableView*?

TableView is a powerful control to display and edit data in a tabular form from a data model. A TableView consists of rows and columns. A cell is an intersection of a row and a column. Cells contain the data values. Columns have headers that describe the type of data they contain. Columns can be nested. Resizing and sorting of column data have built-in support. Figure 13-1 shows a TableView with four columns that have the header text Id, First Name, Last Name, and Birth Date. It has five rows, with each row containing data for a person. For example, the cell in the fourth row and third column contains the last name Boyd.

Id	First Name	Last Name	Birth Date
1	Ashwin	Sharan	2012-10-11
2	Advik	Sharan	2012-10-11
3	Layne	Estes	2011-12-16
4	Mason	Boyd	2003-04-20
5	Babalu	Sharan	1980-01-10

Figure 13-1. A TableView showing a list of persons

TableView is a powerful, but not simple, control. You need to write a few lines of code to use even the simplest TableView that displays some meaningful data to users. There are several classes involved in working with TableView. I will discuss these classes in detail when I discuss the different features of the TableView:

- TableView

- TableColumn

- TableRow

- TableCell

- TablePosition

- TableView.TableViewFocusModel

- TableView.TableViewSelectionModel

The TableView class represents a TableView control. The TableColumn class represents a column in a TableView. Typically, a TableView contains multiple instances of TableColumn. A TableColumn consists of cells, which are instances of the TableCell class. A TableColumn uses two properties to populate cells and render values in them. It uses a cell value factory to extract the value for its cells from the list of items. It uses a cell factory to render data in a cell. You must specify a cell value factory for a TableColumn to see some data in it. A TableColumn uses a default cell factory that knows how to render text and a graphic node.

The TableRow class inherits from the IndexedCell class. An instance of TableRow represents a row in a TableView. You would almost never use this class in an application unless you want to provide a customized implementation for rows. Typically, you customize cells, not rows.

An instance of the TableCell class represents a cell in a TableView. Cells are highly customizable. They display data from the underlying data model for the TableView. They are capable of displaying data as well as graphics.

The TableColumn, TableRow, and TableCell classes contain a tableView property that holds the reference of the TableView that contains them. The tableView property contains null when the TableColumn does not belong to a TableView.

A TablePosition represents the position of a cell. Its getRow() and getColumn() methods return the indices of the row and column, respectively, to which the cell belongs.

The TableViewFocusModel class is an inner static class of the TableView class. It represents the focus model for the TableView to manage focus for rows and cells.

The TableViewSelectionModel class is an inner static class of the TableView class. It represents the selection model for the TableView to manage selection for rows and cells.

Like ListView and TreeView controls, TableView is virtualized. It creates just enough cells to display the visible content. As you scroll through the content, the cells are recycled. This helps keep the number of nodes in the scene graph to a minimum. Suppose you have ten columns and 1,000 rows in a TableView and only ten rows are visible at a time. An inefficient approach would be to create 10,000 cells, one cell for each piece of data. The TableView creates only 100 cells, so it can display ten rows with ten columns. As you scroll through the content, the same 100 cells will be recycled to show the other visible rows. Virtualization makes it possible to use TableView with a large data model without performance penalty for viewing the data in a chunk.

For examples in this chapter, I will use the Person class from Chapter 11 on MVC. The Person class is in the com.jdojo.mvc.model package. Before I start discussing the TableView control in detail, I will introduce a PersonTableUtil class, as shown in Listing 13-1. I will reuse it several times in the examples presented. It has static methods to return an observable list of persona and instances of the TableColumn class to represent columns in a TableView.

Listing 13-1. A PersonTableUtil Utility Class

```java
// PersonTableUtil.java
package com.jdojo.control;

import com.jdojo.mvc.model.Person;
import java.time.LocalDate;
import javafx.collections.FXCollections;
import javafx.collections.ObservableList;
import javafx.scene.control.TableColumn;
import javafx.scene.control.cell.PropertyValueFactory;

public class PersonTableUtil {
        /* Returns an observable list of persons */
        public static ObservableList<Person> getPersonList() {
                Person p1 = new Person("Ashwin", "Sharan", LocalDate.of(2012, 10, 11));
                Person p2 = new Person("Advik", "Sharan", LocalDate.of(2012, 10, 11));
                Person p3 = new Person("Layne", "Estes", LocalDate.of(2011, 12, 16));
                Person p4 = new Person("Mason", "Boyd", LocalDate.of(2003, 4, 20));
                Person p5 = new Person("Babalu", "Sharan", LocalDate.of(1980, 1, 10));
                return FXCollections.<Person>observableArrayList(p1, p2, p3, p4, p5);
        }

        /* Returns Person Id TableColumn */
        public static TableColumn<Person, Integer> getIdColumn() {
                TableColumn<Person, Integer> personIdCol = new TableColumn<>("Id");
                personIdCol.setCellValueFactory(new PropertyValueFactory<>("personId"));
                return personIdCol;
        }

        /* Returns First Name TableColumn */
        public static TableColumn<Person, String> getFirstNameColumn() {
                TableColumn<Person, String> fNameCol = new TableColumn<>("First Name");
                fNameCol.setCellValueFactory(new PropertyValueFactory<>("firstName"));
                return fNameCol;
        }

        /* Returns Last Name TableColumn */
        public static TableColumn<Person, String> getLastNameColumn() {
                TableColumn<Person, String> lastNameCol = new TableColumn<>("Last Name");
                lastNameCol.setCellValueFactory(new PropertyValueFactory<>("lastName"));
                return lastNameCol;
        }

        /* Returns Birth Date TableColumn */
        public static TableColumn<Person, LocalDate> getBirthDateColumn() {
                TableColumn<Person, LocalDate> bDateCol =
                                    new TableColumn<>("Birth Date");
                bDateCol.setCellValueFactory(new PropertyValueFactory<>("birthDate"));
                return bDateCol;
        }
}
```

Subsequent sections will walk you through the steps to display and edit data in a TableView.

Creating a *TableView*

In the following example, you will use the TableView class to create a TableView control. TableView is a parameterized class, which takes the type of items the TableView contains. Optionally, you can pass the model into its constructor that supplies the data. The constructor creates a TableView without a model. The following statement creates a TableView that will use objects of the Person class as its items:

```
TableView<Person> table = new TableView<>();
```

When you add the above TableView to a scene, it displays a placeholder, as shown in Figure 13-2. The placeholder lets you know that you need to add columns to the TableView. There must be at least one visible leaf column in the TableView data.

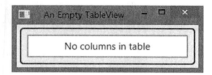

Figure 13-2. *A TableView with no columns and data showing a placeholder*

You would use another constructor of the TableView class to specify the model. It accepts an observable list of items. The following statement passes an observable list of Person objects as the initial data for the TableView:

```
TableView<Person> table = new TableView<>(PersonTableUtil.getPersonList());
```

Adding Columns to a *TableView*

An instance of the TableColumn class represents a column in a TableView. A TableColumn is responsible for displaying and editing the data in its cells. A TableColumn has a header that can display header text, a graphic, or both. You can have a context menu for a TableColumn, which is displayed when the user right-clicks inside the column header. Use the contextMenu property to set a context menu.

The TableColumn<S, T> class is a generic class. The S parameter is the items type, which is of the same type as the parameter of the TableView. The T parameter is the type of data in all cells of the column. For example, an instance of the TableColumn<Person, Integer> may be used to represent a column to display the ID of a Person, which is of int type; an instance of the TableColumn<Person, String> may be used to represent a column to display the *first name* of a person, which is of String type. The following snippet of code creates a TableColumn with First Name as its header text:

```
TableColumn<Person, String> fNameCol = new TableColumn<>("First Name");
```

A TableColumn needs to know how to get the value (or data) for its cells from the model. To populate the cells, you need to set the cellValueFactory property of the TableColumn. If the model for a TableView contains objects of a class that is based on JavaFX properties, you can use an object of the PropertyValueFactory class as the cell value factory, which takes the property name. It reads the property value from the model and populates all of the cells in the column, as in the following code:

```
// Use the firstName property of Person object to populate the column cells
PropertyValueFactory<Person, String> fNameCellValueFactory =
        new PropertyValueFactory<>("firstName");
fNameCol.setCellValueFactory(fNameCellValueFactory);
```

You need to create a TableColumn object for each column in the TableView and set its cell value factory property. The next section will explain what to do if your item class is not based on JavaFX properties or you want to populate the cells with computed values.

The last step in setting up a TableView is to add TableColumns to its list of columns. A TableView stores references of its columns in an ObservableList<TableColumn> whose reference can be obtained using the getColumns() method of the TableView:

```
// Add the First Name column to the TableView
table.getColumns().add(fNameCol);
```

That is all it takes to use a TableView in its simplest form, which is not so "simple" after all! The program in Listing 13-2 shows how to create a TableView with a model and add columns to it. It uses the PersonTableUtil class to get the list of persons and columns. The program displays a window as shown in Figure 13-3.

Listing 13-2. Using TableView in Its Simplest Form

```
// SimplestTableView.java
package com.jdojo.control;

import com.jdojo.mvc.model.Person;
import javafx.application.Application;
import javafx.scene.Scene;
import javafx.scene.control.TableView;
import javafx.scene.layout.VBox;
import javafx.stage.Stage;

public class SimplestTableView extends Application {
        public static void main(String[] args) {
                Application.launch(args);
        }

        @Override
        public void start(Stage stage) {
                // Create a TableView with a list of persons
                TableView<Person> table = new TableView<>(PersonTableUtil.getPersonList());

                // Add columns to the TableView
                table.getColumns().addAll(PersonTableUtil.getIdColumn(),
                                        PersonTableUtil.getFirstNameColumn(),
                                        PersonTableUtil.getLastNameColumn(),
                                        PersonTableUtil.getBirthDateColumn());
```

```
                VBox root = new VBox(table);
                root.setStyle("-fx-padding: 10;" +
                              "-fx-border-style: solid inside;" +
                              "-fx-border-width: 2;" +
                              "-fx-border-insets: 5;" +
                              "-fx-border-radius: 5;" +
                              "-fx-border-color: blue;");

                Scene scene = new Scene(root);
                stage.setScene(scene);
                stage.setTitle("Simplest TableView");
                stage.show();
        }
}
```

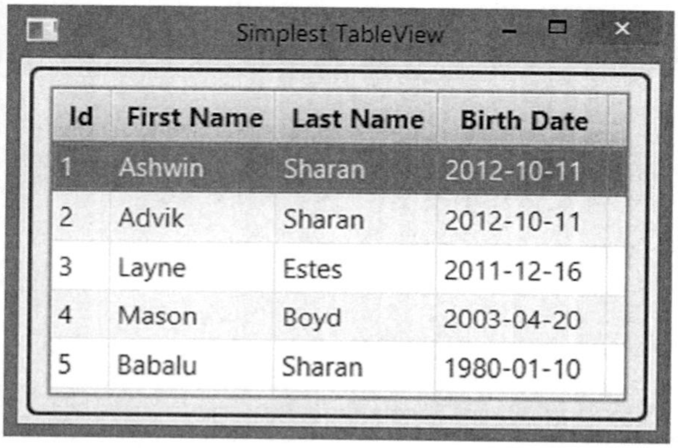

Figure 13-3. *A window with a TableView that displays four columns and five rows*

TableView supports nesting of columns. For example, you can have two columns, First and Last, nested inside a Name column. A TableColumn stores the list of nested columns in an observable list whose reference can be obtained using the getColumns() method of the TableColumn class. The innermost nested columns are known as *leaf columns*. You need to add the cell value factories for the leaf columns. Nested columns only provide visual effects. The following snippet of code creates a TableView and adds an Id column and two leaf columns, First and Last, that are nested in the Name column. The resulting TableView is shown in Figure 13-4. Note that you add the topmost columns to the TableView, not the nested columns. TableView takes care of adding all nested columns for the topmost columns. There is no limit on the level of column nesting.

```
// Create a TableView with data
TableView<Person> table = new TableView<>(PersonTableUtil.getPersonList());

// Create leaf columns - Id, First and Last
TableColumn<Person, String> idCol = new TableColumn<>("Id");
idCol.setCellValueFactory(new PropertyValueFactory<>("personId"));

TableColumn<Person, String> fNameCol = new TableColumn<>("First");
fNameCol.setCellValueFactory(new PropertyValueFactory<>("firstName"));
```

```
TableColumn<Person, String> lNameCol = new TableColumn<>("Last");
lNameCol.setCellValueFactory(new PropertyValueFactory<>("lastName"));

// Create Name column and nest First and Last columns in it
TableColumn<Person, String> nameCol = new TableColumn<>("Name");
nameCol.getColumns().addAll(fNameCol, lNameCol);

// Add columns to the TableView
table.getColumns().addAll(idCol, nameCol);
```

Id	Name	
	First	Last
1	Ashwin	Sharan
2	Advik	Sharan
3	Layne	Estes
4	Mason	Boyd
5	Babalu	Sharan

Figure 13-4. *A TableView with nested columns*

The following methods in the TableView class provide information about visible leaf columns:

```
TableColumn<S,?> getVisibleLeafColumn(int columnIndex)
ObservableList<TableColumn<S,?>> getVisibleLeafColumns()
int getVisibleLeafIndex(TableColumn<S,?> column)
```

The getVisibleLeafColumn() method returns the reference of the column for the specified column index. The column index is counted only for visible leaf column and the index starts at zero. The getVisibleLeafColumns() method returns an observable list of all visible leaf columns. The getVisibleLeafIndex() method returns the column reference for the specified column index of a visible leaf column.

Customizing *TableView* Placeholder

TableView displays a placeholder when it does not have any visible leaf columns or content. Consider the following snippet of code that creates a TableView and adds columns to it:

```
TableView<Person> table = new TableView<>();
table.getColumns().addAll(PersonTableUtil.getIdColumn(),
                          PersonTableUtil.getFirstNameColumn(),
                          PersonTableUtil.getLastNameColumn(),
                          PersonTableUtil.getBirthDateColumn());
```

Figure 13-5 shows the results of the above TableView. Columns and a placeholder are displayed, indicating that the TableView does not have data.

623

Id	First Name	Last Name	Birth Date
	No content in table		

Figure 13-5. *A TableView control with columns and no data*

You can replace the built-in placeholder using the placeholder property of the TableView. The value for the property is an instance of the Node class. The following statement sets a Label with a generic message as a placeholder:

```
table.setPlaceholder(new Label("No visible columns and/or data exist."));
```

You can set a custom placeholder to inform the user of the specific condition that resulted in showing no data in the TableView. The following statement uses binding to change the placeholder as the conditions change:

```
table.placeholderProperty().bind(
        new When(new SimpleIntegerProperty(0)
                .isEqualTo(table.getVisibleLeafColumns().size()))
            .then(new When(new SimpleIntegerProperty(0)
                        .isEqualTo(table.getItems().size()))
                    .then(new Label("No columns and data exist."))
                    .otherwise(new Label("No columns exist.")))
            .otherwise(new When(new SimpleIntegerProperty(0)
                        .isEqualTo(table.getItems().size()))
                    .then(new Label("No data exist."))
                    .otherwise((Label)null)));
```

Populating a *TableColumn* with Data

Cells in a row of a TableView contain data related to an item such as a person, a book, and so forth. Data for some cells in a row may come directly from the attributes of the item or they may be computed.

TableView has an items property of the ObservableList<S> type. The generic type S is the same as the generic type of the TableView. It is the data model for the TableView. Each element in the items list represents a row in the TableView. Adding a new item to the items list adds a new row to the TableView. Deleting an item from the items list deletes the corresponding row from the TableView.

■ **Tip** Whether updating an item in the items list updates the corresponding data in the TableView depends on how the cell value factory for the column is set up. I will discuss examples of both kinds in this section.

The following snippet of code creates a TableView in which a row represents a Person object. It adds data for two rows:

```
TableView<Person> table = new TableView<>();

Person p1 = new Person("John", "Jacobs", null);
Person p2 = new Person("Donna", "Duncan", null);
table.getItems().addAll(p1, p2);
```

624

Adding items to a TableView is useless unless you add columns to it. Among several other things, a TableColumn object defines:

- Header text and graphic for the column
- A cell value factory to populate the cells in the column

The TableColumn class gives you full control over how cells in a column are populated. The cellValueFactory property of the TableColumn class is responsible for populating cells of the column. A cell value factory is an object of the Callback class, which receives a TableColumn.CellDataFeatures object and returns an ObservableValue.

The CellDataFeatures class is a static inner class of the TableColumn class, which wraps the reference of the TableView, TableColumn, and the item for the row for which the cells of the column are being populated. Use the getTableView(), getTableColumn(), and getValue() methods of the CellDataFeatures class to get the reference of the TableView, TableColumn, and the item for the row, respectively.

When the TableView needs the value for a cell, it calls the call() method of the cell value factory object of the column to which the cell belongs. The call() method is supposed to return the reference of an ObservableValue object, which is monitored for any changes. The return ObservableValue object may contain any type of object. If it contains a node, the node is displayed as a graphic in the cell. Otherwise, the toString() method of the object is called and the retuned string is displayed in the cell.

The following snippet of code creates a cell value factory using an anonymous class. The factory returns the reference of the firstName property of the Person class. Note that a JavaFX property is an ObservableValue.

```
import static javafx.scene.control.TableColumn.CellDataFeatures;
...
// Create a String column with the header "First Name" for Person object
TableColumn<Person, String> fNameCol = new TableColumn<>("First Name");

// Create a cell value factory object
Callback<CellDataFeatures<Person, String>, ObservableValue<String>> fNameCellFactory =
new Callback<CellDataFeatures<Person, String>, ObservableValue<String>>() {
@Override
public ObservableValue<String> call(CellDataFeatures<Person, String> cellData) {
        Person p = cellData.getValue();
        return p.firstNameProperty();
}};

// Set the cell value factory
fNameCol.setCellValueFactory(fNameCellFactory);
```

Using a lambda expression to create and set a cell value factory comes in handy. The above snippet of code can be written as follows:

```
TableColumn<Person, String> fNameCol = new TableColumn<>("First Name");
fNameCol.setCellValueFactory(cellData -> cellData.getValue().firstNameProperty());
```

When a JavaFX property supplies values for cells in a column, creating the cell value factory is easier if you use an object of the PropertyValueFactory class. You need to pass the name of the JavaFX property to its constructor. The following snippet of code does the same as the code shown above. You would take this approach to create TableColumn objects inside the utility methods in the PersonTableUtil class.

```
TableColumn<Person, String> fNameCol = new TableColumn<>("First Name");
fNameCol.setCellValueFactory(new PropertyValueFactory<>("firstName"));
```

625

■ **Tip**   Using JavaFX properties as the value supplied for cells has a big advantage. The `TableView` keeps the value in the property and the cell in sync. Changing the property value in the model automatically updates the value in the cell.

TableColumn also supports POJO (Plain Old Java Object) as items in the `TableView`. The disadvantage is that when the model is updated, the cell values are not automatically updated. You use the same `PropertyValueFactory` class to create the cell value factory. The class will look for the public getter and setter methods with the property name you pass. If only the getter method is found, the cell will be read-only. For an xxx property, it tries looking for getXxx() and setXxx() methods using the JavaBeans naming conventions. If the type of xxx is boolean, it also looks for the isXxx() method. If a getter or a setter method is not found, a runtime exception is thrown. The following snippet of code creates a column with the header text Age Category:

```
TableColumn<Person, Person.AgeCategory> ageCategoryCol =
    new TableColumn<>("Age Category");
ageCategoryCol.setCellValueFactory(new PropertyValueFactory<>("ageCategory"));
```

It indicates that the items type is `Person` and the column type is `Person.AgeCategory`. It passes ageCategory as the property name into the constructor of the `PropertyValueFactory` class. First, the class will look for an ageCategory property in the `Person` class. The `Person` class does not have this property. Therefore, it will try using `Person` class as a POJO for this property. Then it will look for getAgeCategory() and setAgeCategory() methods in the `Person` class. It finds only the getter method, getAgeCategory(), and hence, it will make the column read-only.

The values in the cells of a column do not necessarily have to come from JavaFX or POJO properties. They can be computed using some logic. In such cases, you need to create a custom cell value factory and return a ReadOnlyXxxWrapper object that wraps the computed value. The following snippet of code creates an Age column that displays a computed age in years:

```
TableColumn<Person, String> ageCol = new TableColumn<>("Age");
ageCol.setCellValueFactory(cellData -> {
        Person p = cellData.getValue();
        LocalDate dob = p.getBirthDate();
        String ageInYear = "Unknown";
        if (dob != null) {
                long years = YEARS.between(dob, LocalDate.now());
                if (years == 0) {
                        ageInYear = "< 1 year";
                } else if (years == 1) {
                        ageInYear = years + " year";
                } else {
                        ageInYear = years + " years";
                }
        }
        return new ReadOnlyStringWrapper(ageInYear);
});
```

This completes the different ways of setting the cell value factory for cells of a column in a TableView. The program in Listing 13-3 creates cell value factories for JavaFX properties, a POJO property, and a computed value. It displays a window as shown in Figure 13-6.

Listing 13-3. Setting Cell Value Factories for Columns

```java
// TableViewDataTest.java
package com.jdojo.control;

import com.jdojo.mvc.model.Person;
import javafx.application.Application;
import javafx.beans.property.ReadOnlyStringWrapper;
import javafx.scene.Scene;
import javafx.scene.control.TableColumn;
import javafx.scene.control.TableView;
import javafx.scene.control.cell.PropertyValueFactory;
import java.time.LocalDate;
import javafx.scene.layout.HBox;
import javafx.stage.Stage;
import static java.time.temporal.ChronoUnit.YEARS;

public class TableViewDataTest extends Application {
        public static void main(String[] args) {
                Application.launch(args);
        }

        @Override
        @SuppressWarnings("unchecked")
        public void start(Stage stage) {
                // Create a TableView with data
                TableView<Person> table =
                                new TableView<>(PersonTableUtil.getPersonList());

                // Create an "Age" computed column
                TableColumn<Person, String> ageCol = new TableColumn<>("Age");
                ageCol.setCellValueFactory(cellData -> {
                                Person p = cellData.getValue();
                                LocalDate dob = p.getBirthDate();
                                String ageInYear = "Unknown";

                                if (dob != null) {
                                        long years = YEARS.between(dob, LocalDate.now());
                                        if (years == 0) {
                                                ageInYear = "< 1 year";
                                        } else if (years == 1) {
                                                ageInYear = years + " year";
                                        } else {
                                                ageInYear = years + " years";
                                        }
                                }
                                return new ReadOnlyStringWrapper(ageInYear);
                });
```

```
        // Create an "Age Cotegory" column
        TableColumn<Person, Person.AgeCategory> ageCategoryCol =
                        new TableColumn<>("Age Category");
        ageCategoryCol.setCellValueFactory(
                        new PropertyValueFactory<>("ageCategory"));

        // Add columns to the TableView
        table.getColumns().addAll(PersonTableUtil.getIdColumn(),
                                PersonTableUtil.getFirstNameColumn(),
                                PersonTableUtil.getLastNameColumn(),
                                PersonTableUtil.getBirthDateColumn(),
                                ageCol,
                                ageCategoryCol);

    HBox root = new HBox(table);
    root.setStyle("-fx-padding: 10;" +
                    "-fx-border-style: solid inside;" +
                    "-fx-border-width: 2;" +
                    "-fx-border-insets: 5;" +
                    "-fx-border-radius: 5;" +
                    "-fx-border-color: blue;");

    Scene scene = new Scene(root);
    stage.setScene(scene);
    stage.setTitle("Populating TableViews");
    stage.show();
    }
}
```

Id	First Name	Last Name	Birth Date	Age	Age Category
1	Ashwin	Sharan	2012-10-11	2 years	CHILD
2	Advik	Sharan	2012-10-11	2 years	CHILD
3	Layne	Estes	2011-12-16	3 years	CHILD
4	Mason	Boyd	2003-04-20	11 years	CHILD
5	Babalu	Sharan	1980-01-10	35 years	ADULT

Figure 13-6. A TableView having columns for JavaFX properties, POJO properties, and computed values

Cells in a TableView can display text and graphics. If the cell value factory returns an instance of the Node class, which could be an ImageView, the cell displays it as graphic. Otherwise, it displays the string returned from the toString() method of the object. It is possible to display other controls and containers in cells. However, a TableView is not meant for that and such uses are discouraged. Sometimes using a specific type of control in a cell, for example, a check box, to show or edit a boolean value provides a better user experience. I will cover such customization of cells shortly.

Using a *Map* as Items in a *TableView*

Sometimes data in a row for a TableView may not map to a domain object, for example, you may want to display the result set of a dynamic query in a TableView. The items list consists of an observable list of Map. A Map in the list contains values for all columns in the row. You can define a custom cell value factory to extract the data from the Map. The MapValueFactory class is especially designed for this purpose. It is an implementation of the cell value factory, which reads data from a Map for a specified key.

The following snippet of code creates a TableView of Map. It creates an Id column and sets an instance of the MapValueFactory class as its cell value factory specifying the idColumnKey as the key that contains the value for the Id column. It creates a Map and populates the Id column using the idColumnKey. You need to repeat these steps for all columns and rows.

```
TableView<Map> table = new TableView<>();

// Define the column, its cell value factory and add it to the TableView
String idColumnKey = "id";
TableColumn<Map, Integer> idCol = new TableColumn<>("Id");
idCol.setCellValueFactory(new MapValueFactory<>(idColumnKey));
table.getColumns().add(idCol);

// Create and populate a Map an item
Map row1 = new HashMap();
row1.put(idColumnKey, 1);

// Add the Map to the TableView items list
table.getItems().add(row1);
```

The program in Listing 13-4 shows how to use the MapValueFactory as the cell value factory for columns in a TableView. It displays the person's data returned by the getPersonList() method in the PersonTableUtil class.

Listing 13-4. Using MapValueFactory as a Cell Value Factory for Cells in a TableView

```
// TableViewMapDataTest.java
package com.jdojo.control;

import com.jdojo.mvc.model.Person;
import javafx.application.Application;
import javafx.scene.Scene;
import javafx.scene.control.TableColumn;
import javafx.scene.control.TableView;
import java.time.LocalDate;
import java.util.HashMap;
import java.util.Map;
import javafx.collections.FXCollections;
import javafx.collections.ObservableList;
import javafx.scene.control.cell.MapValueFactory;
import javafx.scene.layout.HBox;
import javafx.stage.Stage;
```

```java
public class TableViewMapDataTest  extends Application {
        private final String idColumnKey = "id";
        private final String firstNameColumnKey = "firstName";
        private final String lastNameColumnKey = "lastName";
        private final String birthDateColumnKey = "birthDate";

        public static void main(String[] args) {
                Application.launch(args);
        }

        @Override
        public void start(Stage stage) {
                TableView<Map> table = new TableView<>();
                ObservableList<Map<String, Object>> items = this.getMapData();
                table.getItems().addAll(items);
                this.addColumns(table);

                HBox root = new HBox(table);
                root.setStyle("-fx-padding: 10;" +
                                "-fx-border-style: solid inside;" +
                                "-fx-border-width: 2;" +
                                "-fx-border-insets: 5;" +
                                "-fx-border-radius: 5;" +
                                "-fx-border-color: blue;");

                Scene scene = new Scene(root);
                stage.setScene(scene);
                stage.setTitle("Using a Map as items in a TableView");
                stage.show();
        }

        public ObservableList<Map<String, Object>> getMapData() {
                ObservableList<Map<String, Object>> items =
                        FXCollections.<Map<String, Object>>observableArrayList();

                // Extract the person data, add the data to a Map, and add the Map to
                // the items list
                ObservableList<Person> persons = PersonTableUtil.getPersonList();
                for(Person p : persons) {
                        Map<String, Object> map = new HashMap<>();
                        map.put(idColumnKey, p.getPersonId());
                        map.put(firstNameColumnKey, p.getFirstName());
                        map.put(lastNameColumnKey, p.getLastName());
                        map.put(birthDateColumnKey, p.getBirthDate());
                        items.add(map);
                }

                return items;
        }
```

```java
@SuppressWarnings("unchecked")
public void addColumns(TableView table) {
        TableColumn<Map, Integer> idCol = new TableColumn<>("Id");
        idCol.setCellValueFactory(new MapValueFactory<>(idColumnKey));

        TableColumn<Map, String> firstNameCol = new TableColumn<>("First Name");
        firstNameCol.setCellValueFactory(new MapValueFactory<>(firstNameColumnKey));

        TableColumn<Map, String> lastNameCol = new TableColumn<>("Last Name");
        lastNameCol.setCellValueFactory(new MapValueFactory<>(lastNameColumnKey));

        TableColumn<Map, LocalDate> birthDateCol = new TableColumn<>("Birth Date");
        birthDateCol.setCellValueFactory(new MapValueFactory<>(birthDateColumnKey));

        table.getColumns().addAll(idCol, firstNameCol, lastNameCol, birthDateCol);
    }
}
```

Showing and Hiding Columns

By default, all columns in a TableView are visible. The TableColumn class has a visible property to set the visibility of a column. If you turn off the visibility of a parent column, a column with nested columns, all of its nested columns will also be invisible:

```java
TableColumn<Person, String> idCol = new TableColumn<>("Id");

// Make the Id column invisible
idCol.setVisible(false);
...
// Make the Id column visible
idCol.setVisible(true);
```

Sometimes you may want to let the user control the visibility of columns. The TableView class has a tableMenuButtonVisible property. If it is set to true, a menu button is displayed in the header area:

```java
// Create a TableView
TableView<Person> table = create the TableView here...

// Make the table menu button visible
table.setTableMenuButtonVisible(true);
```

Clicking the menu button displays a list of all leaf columns. Columns are displayed as radio menu items that can be used to toggle their visibility. Figure 13-7 shows a TableView with four columns. Its tableMenuButtonVisible property is set to true. The figure shows a menu with all column names with a check mark. The menu is displayed when the menu button is clicked. The check marks beside the column names indicate that the columns are visible. Clicking the column name toggles its visibility.

Id ▲4	First Name ▲	Last Name ▼	Birth Date ⁘
2	Advik	Sharan	2012-10-11
1	Ashwin	Sharan	2012-10-11
5	Babalu	Sharan	1980-01-10
3	Layne	Estes	2011-12-16
4	Mason	Boyd	2003-04-20

Figure 13-7. *A TableView with menu button to toggle the visibility of columns*

Reordering Columns in a *TableView*

You can rearrange columns in a TableView two ways:

- By dragging and dropping columns to a different position
- By changing their positions in the observable list of returned by the getColumns() method of the TableView class

The first option is available by default. The user needs to drag and drop a column at the new position. When a column is reordered, its position in the columns list is changed. The second option will reorder the column directly in the columns list.

There is no easy way to disable the default column-reordering feature. If you want to disable the feature, you would need to add a ChangeListener to the ObservableList returned by the getColumns() method of the TableView. When a change is reported, reset the columns so they are in the original order again.

Sorting Data in a TableView

TableView has built-in support for sorting data in columns. By default, it allows users to sort data by clicking column headers. It also supports sorting data programmatically. You can also disable sorting for a column or all columns in a TableView.

Sorting Data by Users

By default, data in all columns in a TableView can be sorted. Users can sort data in columns by clicking the column headers. The first click sorts the data in ascending order. The second click sorts the data in descending order. The third click removes the column from the sort order list.

By default, single column sorting is enabled. That is, if you click a column, the records in the TableView are sorted based on the data only in the clicked column. To enable multicolumn sorting, you need to press the Shift key while clicking the headers of the columns to be sorted.

TableView displays visual clues in the headers of the sorted columns to indicate the sort type and the sort order. By default, a triangle is displayed in the column header indicating the sort type. It points upward for ascending sort type and downward for descending sort type. The sort order of a column is indicated by dots or a number. Dots are used for the first three columns in the sort order list. A number is used for the fourth column onward. For example, the first column in the sort order list displays one dot, the second two dots, the third three dots, the fourth a number 4, the fifth a number 5, and so forth.

Figure 13-8 shows a TableView with four columns. The column headers are showing the sort type and sort orders. The sort types are descending for Last Name and ascending for others. The sort orders are 1, 2, 3, and 4 for Last Name, First Name, Birth Date, and Id, respectively. Notice that dots are used for the sort orders in the first three columns and a number 4 is used for the Id column because it is fourth on the sort order list. This sorting is achieved by clicking column headers in the following order: Last Name (twice), First Name, Birth Date, and Id.

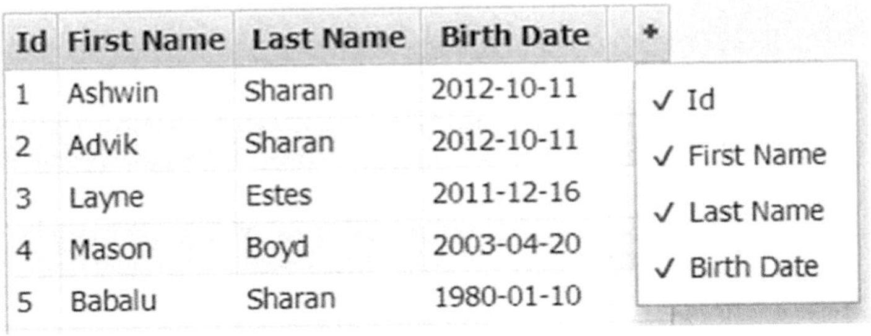

Id	First Name	Last Name	Birth Date	⁘
1	Ashwin	Sharan	2012-10-11	✓ Id
2	Advik	Sharan	2012-10-11	✓ First Name
3	Layne	Estes	2011-12-16	✓ Last Name
4	Mason	Boyd	2003-04-20	✓ Birth Date
5	Babalu	Sharan	1980-01-10	

Figure 13-8. *Column headers showing the sort type and sort order*

Sorting Data Programmatically

Data in columns can be sorted programmatically. The TableView and TableColumn classes provide a very powerful API for sorting. The sorting API consists of several properties and methods in the two classes. Every part and every stage of sorting are customizable. The following sections describe the API with examples.

Making a Column Sortable

The sortable property of a TableColumn determines whether the column is sortable. By default, it is set to true. Set it to false to disable the sorting for a column:

```
// Disable sorting for fNameCol column
fNameCol.setSortable(false);
```

Specifying the Sort Type of a Column

A TableColumn has a sort type, which can be ascending or descending. It is specified through the sortType property. The ASCENDING and DESCENDING constants of TableColumn.SortType enum represent the ascending and descending, respectively, sort types for columns. The default value for the sortType property is TableColumn.SortType.ASCENDING. The DESCENDING constant is set as follows:

```
// Set the sort type for fNameCol column to descending
fNameCol.setSortType(TableColumn.SortType.DESCENDING);
```

Specifying the *Comparator* for a Column

A TableColumn uses a Comparator to sort its data. You can specify the Comparator for a TableColumn using its comparator property. The comparator is passed in the objects in two cells being compared. A TableColumn uses a default Comparator, which is represented by the constant TableColumn.DEFAULT_COMPARATOR. The default comparator compares data in two cells using the following rules:

- It checks for null values. The null values are sorted first. If both cells have null, they are considered equal.

- If the first value being compared is an instance of the Comparable interface, it calls the compareTo() method of the first object passing the second object as an argument to the method.

- If neither of the above two conditions are true, it converts the two objects into strings calling their toString() methods and uses a Collator to compare the two String values.

In most cases, the default comparator is sufficient. The following snippet of code uses a custom comparator for a String column that compares only the first characters of the cell data:

```
TableColumn<Person, String> fNameCol = new TableColumn<>("First Name");
...
// Set a custom comparator
fNameCol.setComparator((String n1, String n2) -> {
        if (n1 == null && n2 == null) {
                return 0;
        }

        if (n1 == null) {
                return -1;
        }

        if (n2 == null) {
                return 1;
        }

        String c1 = n1.isEmpty()? n1:String.valueOf(n1.charAt(0));
        String c2 = n2.isEmpty()? n2:String.valueOf(n2.charAt(0));
        return c1.compareTo(c2);
});
```

Specifying the Sort Node for a Column

The TableColumn class contains a sortNode property, which specifies a node to display a visual clue in the column header about the current sort type and sort order for the column. The node is rotated by 180 degrees when the sort type is ascending. The node is invisible when the column is not part of the sort. By default, it is null and the TableColumn provides a triangle as the sort node.

Specifying the Sort Order of Columns

The TableView class contains several properties that are used in sorting. To sort columns, you need to add them to sort order list of the TableView. The sortOrder property specifies the sort order. It is an ObservableList of TableColumn. The order of a TableColumn in the list specifies the order of the column in the sort. Rows are sorted based on the first column in the list. If values in two rows in the column are equal, the second column in the sort order list is used to determine the sort order of the two rows and so on.

The following snippet of code adds two columns to a TableView and specifies their sort order. Notice that both columns will be sorted in ascending order, which is the default sort type. If you want to sort them in descending order, set their sortType property as follows:

```
// Create a TableView with data
TableView<Person> table = new TableView<>(PersonTableUtil.getPersonList());

TableColumn<Person, String> lNameCol = PersonTableUtil.getLastNameColumn();
TableColumn<Person, String> fNameCol = PersonTableUtil.getFirstNameColumn();

// Add columns to the TableView
table.getColumns().addAll(lNameCol, fNameCol );

// Add columns to the sort order to sort by last name followed by first name
table.getSortOrder().addAll(lNameCol, fNameCol);
```

The sortOrder property of the TableView is monitored for changes. If it is modified, the TableView is sorted immediately based on the new sort order. Adding a column to a sort order list does not guarantee inclusion of the column in sorting. The column must also be sortable to be included in sorting. The sortType property of the TableColumn is also monitored for changes. Changing the sort type of a column, which are in the sort order list, resorts the TableView data immediately.

Getting the Comparator for a *TableView*

TableView contains a read-only comparator property, which is a Comparator based on the current sort order list. You rarely need to use this Comparator in your code. If you pass two TableView items to the compare() method of the Comparator, it will return a negative integer, zero, or a positive integer indicating that the first item is less than, equal to, or greater than the second item, respectively.

Recall that TableColumn also has a comparator property, which is used to specify how to determine the order of values in the cells of the TableColumn. The comparator property of the TableView combines the comparator properties of all TableColumns in its sort order list.

Specifying the Sort Policy

A TableView has a sort policy to specify how the sorting is performed. It is a Callback object. The TableView is passed in as an argument to the call() method. The method returns true if the sorting successes. It returns false or null if the sorting fails.

The TableView class contains a DEFAULT_SORT_POLICY constant, which is used as a default sort policy for a TableView. It sorts the items list of the TableView using its comparator property. Specify a sort policy to take full charge of the sorting algorithm. The call() method of the sort policy Callback object will perform the sorting of the items of the TableView.

As a trivial example, setting the sort policy to null will disable the sorting, as no sorting will be performed when sorting is requested by the user or program:

```
TableView<Person> table = ...

// Disable sorting for the TableView
table.setSortPolicy(null);
```

Sometimes it is useful to disable sorting temporarily for performance reasons. Suppose you have a sorted TableView with a large number of items and you want to make several changes to the sort order list. Every change in the sort order list will trigger a sort on the items. In this case, you may disable the sorting by setting the sort policy to null, make all your changes, and enable the sorting by restoring the original sort policy. A change in the sort policy triggers an immediate sort. This technique will sort the items only once:

```
TableView<Person> table = ...
...
// Store the current sort policy
Callback<TableView<Person>, Boolean> currentSortPolicy = table.getSortPolicy();

// Disble the sorting
table.setSortPolicy(null)

// Make all changes that might need or trigger sorting
...

// Restore the sort policy that will sort the data once immediately
table.setSortPolicy(currentSortPolicy);
```

Sorting Data Manually

TableView contains a sort() method that sorts the items in the TableView using the current sort order list. You may call this method to sort items after adding a number of items to a TableView. This method is automatically called when the sort type of a column, the sort order, or sort policy changes.

Handling Sorting Event

TableView fires a SortEvent when it receives a request for sorting and just before it applies the sorting algorithm to its items. Add a SortEvent listener to perform any action before the actual sorting is performed:

```
TableView<Person> table = ...
table.setOnSort(e -> {/* Code to handle the sort event */});
```

If the SortEvent is consumed, the sorting is aborted. If you want to disable sorting for a TableView, consume the SortEvent as follows:

```
// Disable sorting for the TableView
table.setOnSort(e -> e.consume());
```

Disabling Sorting for a TableView

There are several ways you can disable sorting for a TableView.

- Setting the sortable property for a TableColumn disables sorting only for that column. If you set the sortable property to false for all columns in a TableView, the sorting for the TableView is disabled.

- You can set the sort policy for the TableView to null.

- You can consume the SortEvent for the TableView.

- Technically, it is possible, though not recommended, to override the sort() method of the TableView class and provide an empty body for the method.

The best way to disable sorting partially or completely for a TableView is to disable sorting for some or all of its columns.

Customizing Data Rendering in Cells

A cell in a TableColumn is an instance of the TableCell class, which displays the data in the cell. A TableCell is a Labeled control, which is capable of displaying text, a graphic, or both.

You can specify a cell factory for a TableColumn. The job of a cell factory is to render the data in the cell. The TableColumn class contains a cellFactory property, which is a Callback object. Its call() method is passed in the reference of the TableColumn to which the cell belongs. The method returns an instance of TableCell. The updateItem() method of the TableCell is overridden to provide the custom rendering of the cell data.

TableColumn uses a default cell factory if its cellFactory property is not specified. The default cell factory displays the cell data depending on the type of the data. If the cell data comprise a node, the data are displayed in the graphic property of the cell. Otherwise, the toString() method of the cell data is called and the retuned string is displayed in the text property of the cell.

Up to this point, you have been using a list of Person objects as the data model in the examples for displaying data in a TableView. The Birth Date column is formatted as yyyy-mm-dd, which is the default ISO date format return by the toString() method of the LocalDate class. If you would like to format birth dates in the mm/dd/yyyy format, you can achieve this by setting a custom cell factory for the Birth Date column:

```
TableColumn<Person, LocalDate> birthDateCol = ...;
birthDateCol.setCellFactory (col -> {
        TableCell<Person, LocalDate> cell = new TableCell<Person, LocalDate>() {
                @Override
                public void updateItem(LocalDate item, boolean empty) {
                        super.updateItem(item, empty);

                        // Cleanup the cell before populating it
                        this.setText(null);
                        this.setGraphic(null);
```

```
                        if (!empty) {
                            // Format the birth date in mm/dd/yyyy format
                            String formattedDob =
                                    DateTimeFormatter.ofPattern("MM/dd/yyyy").format(item);
                            this.setText(formattedDob);
                        }
                    }
            };
            return cell;
});
```

You can also use the above technique to display images in cells. In the updateItem() method, create an ImageView object for the image and display it using the setGraphic() method of the TableCell. TableCell contains tableColumn, tableRow, and tableView properties that store the references of its TableColumn, TableRow, and TableView, respectively. These properties are useful to access the item in the data model that represents the row for the cell.

If you replace the if statement in the above snippet of code with the following code, the Birth Date column displays the birth date and age category, for example, 10/11/2012 (BABY):

```
if (!empty) {
        String formattedDob = DateTimeFormatter.ofPattern("MM/dd/yyyy").format(item);

        if (this.getTableRow() != null ) {
                // Get the Person item for this cell
                int rowIndex = this.getTableRow().getIndex();
                Person p = this.getTableView().getItems().get(rowIndex);
                String ageCategory = p.getAgeCategory().toString();

                // Display birth date and age category together
                this.setText(formattedDob + " (" + ageCategory + ")" );
        }
}
```

The following are subclasses of TableCell that render cell data in different ways. For example, a CheckBoxTableCell renders cell data in a check box and a ProgressBarTableCell renders a number using a progress bar:

- CheckBoxTableCell
- ChoiceBoxTableCell
- ComboBoxTableCell
- ProgressBarTableCell
- TextFieldTableCell

The following snippet of code creates a column labeled Baby? and sets a cell factory to display the value in a CheckBoxTableCell. The forTableColumn(TableColumn<S, Boolean> col) method of the CheckBoxTableCell class returns a Callback object that is used as a cell factory:

```
// Create a "Baby?" column
TableColumn<Person, Boolean> babyCol = new TableColumn<>("Baby?");
babyCol.setCellValueFactory(cellData -> {
        Person p = cellData.getValue();
        Boolean v = (p.getAgeCategory() == Person.AgeCategory.BABY);
        return new ReadOnlyBooleanWrapper(v);
});

// Set a cell factory that will use a CheckBox to render the value
babyCol.setCellFactory(CheckBoxTableCell.<Person>forTableColumn(babyCol));
```

Please explore the API documentation for other subclasses of the TableCell and how to use them. For example, you can display a combo box with a list of choices in the cells of a column. Users can select one of the choices as the cell data.

Listing 13-5 has a complete program to show how to use custom cell factories. It displays a window as shown in Figure 13-9. The program uses a cell factory to format the birth date in mm/dd/yyyy format and a cell factory to display whether a person is a baby using a check box.

Listing 13-5. Using a Custom Cell Factory for a TableColumn

```
// TableViewCellFactoryTest.java
package com.jdojo.control;

import com.jdojo.mvc.model.Person;
import javafx.application.Application;
import java.time.LocalDate;
import javafx.scene.Scene;
import javafx.scene.control.TableCell;
import javafx.scene.control.TableColumn;
import javafx.scene.control.TableView;
import javafx.scene.layout.HBox;
import javafx.stage.Stage;
import java.time.format.DateTimeFormatter;
import javafx.beans.property.ReadOnlyBooleanWrapper;
import javafx.scene.control.cell.CheckBoxTableCell;

public class TableViewCellFactoryTest extends Application {
        public static void main(String[] args) {
                Application.launch(args);
        }

        @Override
        @SuppressWarnings("unchecked")
        public void start(Stage stage) {
                TableView<Person> table = new TableView<>(PersonTableUtil.getPersonList());
```

```
// Create the birth date column
TableColumn<Person, LocalDate> birthDateCol =
        PersonTableUtil.getBirthDateColumn();

// Set a custom cell factory for Birth Date column
birthDateCol.setCellFactory(col -> {
        TableCell<Person, LocalDate> cell = new TableCell<Person, LocalDate>() {
                @Override
                public void updateItem(LocalDate item, boolean empty) {
                        super.updateItem(item, empty);

                        // Cleanup the cell before populating it
                        this.setText(null);
                        this.setGraphic(null);

                        if (!empty) {
                                String formattedDob =
                                DateTimeFormatter.ofPattern("MM/dd/yyyy")
                                                .format(item);
                                this.setText(formattedDob);
                        }
                }
        };
        return cell;
});

// Create and configure the baby column
TableColumn<Person, Boolean> babyCol = new TableColumn<>("Baby?");
babyCol.setCellValueFactory(
                cellData -> {
                        Person p = cellData.getValue();
                        Boolean v =
                        (p.getAgeCategory() == Person.AgeCategory.BABY);
                        return new ReadOnlyBooleanWrapper(v);
                });

// Set a custom cell factory for the baby column
babyCol.setCellFactory(
                CheckBoxTableCell.<Person>forTableColumn(babyCol));

// Add columns to the table
table.getColumns().addAll(PersonTableUtil.getIdColumn(),
                PersonTableUtil.getFirstNameColumn(),
                PersonTableUtil.getLastNameColumn(),
                birthDateCol,
                babyCol);

HBox root = new HBox(table);
root.setStyle("-fx-padding: 10;" +
                "-fx-border-style: solid inside;" +
                "-fx-border-width: 2;" +
```

```
                              "-fx-border-insets: 5;" +
                              "-fx-border-radius: 5;" +
                              "-fx-border-color: blue;");

          Scene scene = new Scene(root);
          stage.setScene(scene);
          stage.setTitle("Using a Custom Cell Factory for a TableColumn");
          stage.show();
       }
}
```

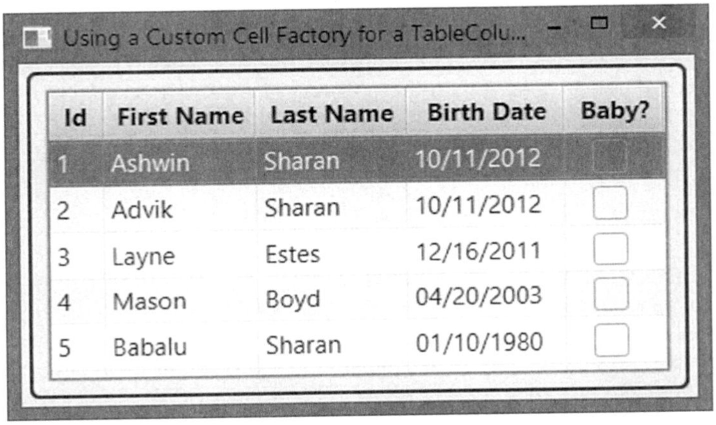

Id	First Name	Last Name	Birth Date	Baby?
1	Ashwin	Sharan	10/11/2012	☐
2	Advik	Sharan	10/11/2012	☐
3	Layne	Estes	12/16/2011	☐
4	Mason	Boyd	04/20/2003	☐
5	Babalu	Sharan	01/10/1980	☐

Figure 13-9. *Using custom cell factories to format data in cells and display cell data in check boxes*

Selecting Cells and Rows in a *TableView*

TableView has a selection model represented by its property selectionModel. A selection model is an instance of the TableViewSelectionModel class, which is an inner static class of the TableView class. The selection model supports cell-level and row-level selection. It also supports two selection modes: single and multiple. In the single-selection mode, only one cell or row can be selected at a time. In the multiple-selection mode, multiple cells or rows can be selected. By default, single-row selection is enabled. You can enable multirow selection, as follows:

```
TableView<Person> table = ...

// Turn on multiple-selection mode for the TableView
TableViewSelectionModel<Person> tsm = table.getSelectionModel();
tsm.setSelectionMode(SelectionMode.MULTIPLE);
```

The cell-level selection can be enabled by setting the cellSelectionEnabled property of the selection model to true, as in the following snippet of code. When the property is set to true, the TableView is put in cell-level selection mode and you cannot select an entire row. If multiple-selection mode is enabled, you can still select all cells in a row. However, the row itself is not reported as selected as the TableView is in the cell-level selection mode. By default, cell-level selection mode is false.

```
// Enable cell-level selection
tsm.setCellSelectionEnabled(true);
```

The selection model provides information about the selected cells and rows. The isSelected(int rowIndex) method returns true if the row at the specified rowIndex is selected. Use the isSelected(int rowIndex, TableColumn<S,?> column) method to know if a cell at the specified rowIndex and column is selected. The selection model provides several methods to select cells and rows and get the report of selected cells and rows:

- The selectAll() method selects all cells or rows.

- The select() method is overloaded. It selects a row, a row for an item, and a cell.

- The isEmpty() method returns true if there is no selection. Otherwise, it returns false.

- The getSelectedCells() method returns a read-only ObservableList<TablePosition> that is the list of currently selected cells. The list changes as the selection in the TableView changes.

- The getSelectedIndices() method returns a read-only ObservableList<Integer> that is the list of currently selected indices. The list changes as the selection in the TableView changes. If row-level selection is enabled, an item in the list is the row index of the selected row. If cell-level selection is enabled, an item in the list is the row index of the row in which one or more cells are selected.

- The getSelectedItems() method returns a read-only ObservableList<S> where S is the generic type of the TableView. The list contains all items for which the corresponding row or cells have been selected.

- The clearAndSelect() method is overloaded. It lets you clear all selections before selecting a row or a cell.

- The clearSelection() method is overloaded. It lets you clear selections for a row, a cell, or the entire TableView.

It is often a requirement to make some changes or take an action when a cell or row selection changes in a TableView. For example, a TableView may act as a master list in a master-detail data view. When the user selects a row in the master list, you want to refresh the data in the detail view. If you are interested in handling the selection change event, you need to add a ListChangeListener to one of the ObservableLists returned by the above listed methods that reports on the selected cells or rows. The following snippet of code adds a ListChangeListener to the ObservableList returned by the getSelectedIndices() method to track the row selection change in a TableView:

```
TableView<Person> table = ...
TableViewSelectionModel<Person> tsm = table.getSelectionModel();
ObservableList<Integer> list = tsm.getSelectedIndices();

// Add a ListChangeListener
list.addListener((ListChangeListener.Change<? extends Integer> change) -> {
        System.out.println("Row selection has changed");
});
```

Editing Data in a *TableView*

A cell in a TableView can be edited. An editable cell switches between editing and nonediting modes. In editing mode, cell data can be modified by the user. For a cell to enter editing mode, the TableView, TableColumn, and TableCell must be editable. All three of them have an editable property, which can be set to true using the setEditable(true) method. By default, TableColumn and TableCell are editable. To make cells editable in a TableView, you need make the TableView editable:

```
TableView<Person> table = ...
table.setEditable(true);
```

The TableColumn class supports three types of events:

- onEditStart
- onEditCommit
- onEditCancel

The onStartEdit event is fired when a cell in the column enters editing mode. The onEditCommit event is fired when the user successfully commits the editing, for example, by pressing the Enter key in a TextField. The onEditCancel event is fired when the user cancels the editing, for example, by pressing the Esc key in a TextField.

The events are represented by an object of the TableColumn.CellEditEvent class. The event object encapsulates the old and new values in the cell, the row object from the items list of the TableView, TableColumn, TablePosition indicating the cell position where the editing is happening, and the reference of the TableView. Use the methods of the CellEditEvent class to get these values.

Making a TableView editable does not let you edit its cell data. You need to do a little more plumbing before you can edit data in cells. Cell-editing capability is provided through specialized implementation of the TableCell class. the JavaFX library provides a few of these implementations. Set the cell factory for a column to use one of the following implementations of the TableCell to edit cell data:

- CheckBoxTableCell
- ChoiceBoxTableCell
- ComboBoxTableCell
- TextFieldTableCell

Editing Data Using a Check Box

A CheckBoxTableCell renders a check box inside the cell. Typically it is used to represent a boolean value in a column. The class provides a way to map other types of values to a boolean value using a Callback object. The check box is selected if the value is true. Otherwise, it is unselected. Bidirectional binding is used to bind the selected property of the check box and the underlying ObservableValue. If the user changes the selection, the underlying data are updated and vice versa.

You do not have a boolean property in the Person class. You must create a boolean column by providing a cell value factory, as shown in the following code. If a Person is a baby, the cell value factory returns true. Otherwise, it returns false.

```
TableColumn<Person, Boolean> babyCol = new TableColumn<>("Baby?");
babyCol.setCellValueFactory(cellData -> {
        Person p = cellData.getValue();
        Boolean v = (p.getAgeCategory() == Person.AgeCategory.BABY);
        return new ReadOnlyBooleanWrapper(v);
});
```

Getting a cell factory to use CheckBoxTableCell is easy. Use the forTableColumn()static method to get a cell factory for the column:

```
// Set a CheckBoxTableCell to display the value
babyCol.setCellFactory(CheckBoxTableCell.<Person>forTableColumn(babyCol));
```

A CheckBoxTableCell does not fire the cell-editing events. The selected property of the check box is bound to the ObservableValue representing the data in the cell. If you are interested in tracking the selection change event, you need to add a ChangeListener to the data for the cell.

Editing Data Using a Choice Box

A ChoiceBoxTableCell renders a choice box with a specified list of values inside the cell. The type of values in the list must match the type of the TableColumn. The data in a ChoiceBoxTableCell are displayed in a Label when the cell is not being edited. A ChoiceBox is used when the cell is being edited.

The Person class does not have a gender property. You want to add a Gender column to a TableView<Person>, which can be edited using a choice box. The following snippet of code creates the TableColumn and sets a cell value factory, which sets all cells to an empty string. You would set the cell value factory to use the gender property of the Person class if you had one.

```
// Gender is a String, editable, ComboBox column
TableColumn<Person, String> genderCol = new TableColumn<>("Gender");

// Use an appropriate cell value factory.
// For now, set all cells to an empty string
genderCol.setCellValueFactory(cellData -> new ReadOnlyStringWrapper(""));
```

You can create a cell factory that uses a choice box for editing data in cells using the forTableColumn() static method of the ChoiceBoxTableCell class. You need to specify the list of items to be displayed in the choice box.

```
// Set a cell factory, so it can be edited using a ChoiceBox
genderCol.setCellFactory(
        ChoiceBoxBoxTableCell.<Person, String>forTableColumn("Male", "Female"));
```

When an item is selected in the choice box, the item is set to the underlying data model. For example, if a column is based on a property in the domain object, the selected item will be set to the property. You can set an onEditCommit event handler that is fired when the user selects an item. The following snippet of code adds such a handler for the Gender column that prints a message on the standard output:

```
// Add an onEditCommit handler
genderCol.setOnEditCommit(e -> {
        int row = e.getTablePosition().getRow();
        Person person = e.getRowValue();
```

```
        System.out.println("Gender changed (" + person.getFirstName() + " " +
                            person.getLastName() + ")" + " at row " + (row + 1) +
                            ". New value = " + e.getNewValue());
});
```

Clicking a selected cell puts the cell into editing mode. Double-clicking an unselected cell puts the cell into editing mode. Changing the focus to another cell or selecting an item from the list puts the editing cell into nonediting mode and the current value is displayed in a Label.

Editing Data Using a Combo Box

A ComboBoxTableCell renders a combo box with a specified list of values inside the cells. It works similar to a ChoiceBoxTableCell. Please refer to the section "Editing Data Using a Choice Box" for more details.

Editing Data Using a *TextField*

A TextFieldTableCell renders a TextField inside the cell when the cell is being edited where the user can modify the data. It renders the cell data in a Label when the cell is not being edited.

Clicking a selected cell or double-clicking an unselected cell puts the cell into editing mode, which displays the cell data in a TextField. Once the cell is in editing mode, you need to click in the TextField (one more click!) to put the caret in the TextField so you can make changes. Notice that you need a minimum of three clicks to edit a cell, which is a pain for those users who have to edit a lot of data. Let's hope that the designers of the TableView API will make data editing less cumbersome in future releases.

If you are in the middle of editing a cell data, press the Esc key to cancel editing, which will return the cell to nonediting mode and reverts to the old data in the cell. Pressing the Enter key commits the data to the underlying data model if the TableColumn is based on a Writable ObservableValue.

If you are editing a cell using a TextFieldTableCell, moving the focus to another cell, for example, by clicking another cell, cancels the editing and puts the old value back in the cell. This is not what a user expects. At present, there is no easy solution for this problem. You will have to create a subclass of TableCell and add a focus change listener, so you can commit the data when the TextField loses focus.

Use the forTableColumn() static method of the TextFieldTableCell class to get a cell factory that uses a TextField to edit cell data. The following snippet of code shows how to do it for a First Name String column:

```
TableColumn<Person, String> fNameCol = new TableColumn<>("First Name");
fNameCol.setCellFactory(TextFieldTableCell.<Person>forTableColumn());
```

Sometimes you need to edit nonstring data using a TextField, for example, for a date. The date may be represented as an object of the LocalDate class in the model. You may want to display it in a TextField as a formatted string. When the user edits the date, you want to commit the data to the model as a LocalDate. The TextFieldTableCell class supports this kind of object-to-string and vice versa conversion through a StringConverter. The following snippet of code sets a cell factory for a Birth Date column with a StringConverter, which converts a string to a LocalDate and vice versa. The column type is LocalDate. By default, the LocalDateStringConverter assumes a date format of mm/dd/yyyy.

```
TableColumn<Person, LocalDate> birthDateCol = new TableColumn<>("Birth Date");
LocalDateStringConverter converter = new LocalDateStringConverter();
birthDateCol.setCellFactory(TextFieldTableCell.<Person, LocalDate>forTableColumn(converter));
```

The program in Listing 13-6 shows how to edit data in a TableView using different types of controls. The TableView contains Id, First Name, Last Name, Birth Date, Baby, and Gender columns. The Id column is noneditable. The First Name, Last Name, and Birth Date columns use TextFieldTableCell, so they can be edited using a TextField. The Baby column is a noneditable computed field and is not backed by the data model. It uses CheckBoxTableCell to render its values. The Gender column is an editable computed field. It is not backed by the data model. It uses a ComboBoxTableCell that presents the user a list of values (Male and Female) in editing model. When the user selects a value, the value is not saved to the data model. It stays in the cell. An onEditCommit event handler is added that prints the gender selection on the standard output. The program displays a window as shown in Figure 13-10, where it can be seen that you have already selected a gender value for all persons. The Birth Date value for the fifth row is being edited.

Listing 13-6. Editing Data in a TableView

```
// TableViewEditing.java
package com.jdojo.control;

import com.jdojo.mvc.model.Person;
import javafx.application.Application;
import javafx.beans.property.ReadOnlyBooleanWrapper;
import javafx.scene.Scene;
import javafx.scene.control.TableColumn;
import javafx.scene.control.TableView;
import javafx.scene.control.cell.TextFieldTableCell;
import javafx.scene.layout.HBox;
import javafx.stage.Stage;
import java.time.LocalDate;
import javafx.beans.property.ReadOnlyStringWrapper;
import javafx.scene.control.cell.CheckBoxTableCell;
import javafx.scene.control.cell.ComboBoxTableCell;

public class TableViewEditing extends Application {
        public static void main(String[] args) {
                Application.launch(args);
        }

        @Override
        public void start(Stage stage) {
                TableView<Person> table = new TableView<>(PersonTableUtil.getPersonList());

                // Make the TableView editable
                table.setEditable(true);

                // Add columns with appropriate editing features
                addIdColumn(table);
                addFirstNameColumn(table);
                addLastNameColumn(table);
                addBirthDateColumn(table);
                addBabyColumn(table);
                addGenderColumn(table);
```

```
        HBox root = new HBox(table);
        root.setStyle("-fx-padding: 10;" +
                       "-fx-border-style: solid inside;" +
                       "-fx-border-width: 2;" +
                       "-fx-border-insets: 5;" +
                       "-fx-border-radius: 5;" +
                       "-fx-border-color: blue;");

        Scene scene = new Scene(root);
        stage.setScene(scene);
        stage.setTitle("Editing Data in a TableView");
        stage.show();
}

public void addIdColumn(TableView<Person> table) {
        // Id column is non-editable
        table.getColumns().add(PersonTableUtil.getIdColumn());
}

public void addFirstNameColumn(TableView<Person> table) {
        // First Name is a String, editable column
        TableColumn<Person, String> fNameCol = PersonTableUtil.getFirstNameColumn();

        // Use a TextFieldTableCell, so it can be edited
        fNameCol.setCellFactory(TextFieldTableCell.<Person>forTableColumn());

        table.getColumns().add(fNameCol);
}

public void addLastNameColumn(TableView<Person> table) {
        // Last Name is a String, editable column
        TableColumn<Person, String> lNameCol = PersonTableUtil.getLastNameColumn();

        // Use a TextFieldTableCell, so it can be edited
        lNameCol.setCellFactory(TextFieldTableCell.<Person>forTableColumn());

        table.getColumns().add(lNameCol);
}

public void addBirthDateColumn(TableView<Person> table) {
        // Birth Date is a LocalDate, editable column
        TableColumn<Person, LocalDate> birthDateCol =
                PersonTableUtil.getBirthDateColumn();

        // Use a TextFieldTableCell, so it can be edited
        LocalDateStringConverter converter = new LocalDateStringConverter();
        birthDateCol.setCellFactory(
                TextFieldTableCell.<Person, LocalDate>forTableColumn(converter));

        table.getColumns().add(birthDateCol);
}
```

647

```java
    public void addBabyColumn(TableView<Person> table) {
            // Baby? is a Boolean, non-editable column
            TableColumn<Person, Boolean> babyCol = new TableColumn<>("Baby?");
            babyCol.setEditable(false);

            // Set a cell value factory
            babyCol.setCellValueFactory(cellData -> {
            Person p = cellData.getValue();
                    Boolean v =  (p.getAgeCategory() == Person.AgeCategory.BABY);
                    return new ReadOnlyBooleanWrapper(v);
            });

            // Use a CheckBoxTableCell to display the boolean value
            babyCol.setCellFactory(
                    CheckBoxTableCell.<Person>forTableColumn(babyCol));

            table.getColumns().add(babyCol);
    }

    public void addGenderColumn(TableView<Person> table) {
            // Gender is a String, editable, ComboBox column
            TableColumn<Person, String> genderCol = new TableColumn<>("Gender");
            genderCol.setMinWidth(80);

            // By default, all cells are have null values
            genderCol.setCellValueFactory(
                cellData -> new ReadOnlyStringWrapper(null));

            // Set a ComboBoxTableCell, so you can selects a value from a list
            genderCol.setCellFactory(
                    ComboBoxTableCell.<Person, String>forTableColumn("Male", "Female"));

            // Add an event handler to handle the edit commit event.
            // It displays the selected value on the standard output
            genderCol.setOnEditCommit(e -> {
                    int row = e.getTablePosition().getRow();
                    Person person = e.getRowValue();
                    System.out.println("Gender changed for " +
                                        person.getFirstName() + " " + person.getLastName() +
                                        " at row " + (row + 1) + " to " + e.getNewValue());
            });

            table.getColumns().add(genderCol);
    }
}
```

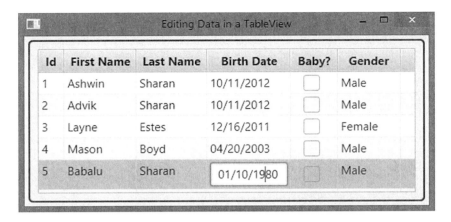

Figure 13-10. *A TableView with a cell in editing mode*

Editing Data in TableCell Using any Control

In the previous section, I discussed editing data in cells of a TableView using different controls, for example, TextField, CheckBox, and ChoiceBox. You can subclass TableCell to use any control to edit cell data. For example, you may want to use a DatePicker to select a date in cells of a date column or RadioButtons to select from multiple options. The possibilities are endless.

You need to override four methods of the TableCell class:

- startEdit()
- commitEdit()
- cancelEdit()
- updateItem()

The startEdit() method for the cell transitions from nonediting mode to editing mode. Typically, you set the control of your choice in the graphic property of the cell with the current data.

The commitEdit() method is called when the user action, for example, pressing the Enter key in a TextField, indicates that the user is done modifying the cell data and the data need to be saved in the underlying data model. Typically, you do not need to override this method as the modified data are committed to the data model if the TableColumn is based on a Writable ObservableValue.

The cancelEdit() method is called when the user action, for example, pressing the Esc key in a TextField, indicates that the user wants to cancel the editing process. When the editing process is canceled, the cell returns to nonediting mode. You need to override this method and revert the cell data to their old values.

The updateItem() method is called when the cell needs to be rendered again. Depending on the editing mode, you need to set the text and graphic properties of the cell appropriately.

Now let's develop a DatePickerTableCell class that inherits from the TableCell class. You can use instances of DatePickerTableCell when you want to edit cells of a TableColumn using a DatePicker control. The TableColumn must be of LocalDate. Listing 13-7 has the complete code for the DatePickerTableCell class.

Listing 13-7. The DatePickerTableCell Class to Allows Editing Table Cells Using a DatePicker Control

```java
// DatePickerTableCell.java
package com.jdojo.control;

import javafx.beans.value.ObservableValue;
import javafx.scene.control.DatePicker;
import javafx.scene.control.TableCell;
import javafx.beans.value.ChangeListener;
import javafx.scene.control.TableColumn;
import javafx.util.Callback;
import javafx.util.StringConverter;

@SuppressWarnings("unchecked")
public class DatePickerTableCell<S, T> extends TableCell<S, java.time.LocalDate> {
        private DatePicker datePicker;
        private StringConverter converter = null;
        private boolean datePickerEditable = true;

        public DatePickerTableCell() {
                this.converter = new LocalDateStringConverter();
        }

        public DatePickerTableCell(boolean datePickerEditable) {
            this.converter = new LocalDateStringConverter();
                this.datePickerEditable = datePickerEditable;
        }

        public DatePickerTableCell(StringConverter<java.time.LocalDate> converter) {
                this.converter = converter;
        }

        public DatePickerTableCell(StringConverter<java.time.LocalDate> converter,
                                boolean datePickerEditable) {
                this.converter = converter;
                this.datePickerEditable = datePickerEditable;
        }

        @Override
        public void startEdit() {
                // Make sure the cell is editable
                if (!isEditable() ||
                    !getTableView().isEditable() || !getTableColumn().isEditable()) {
                        return;
                }

                // Let the ancestor do the plumbing job
                super.startEdit();
```

```java
        // Create a DatePicker, if needed, and set it as the graphic for the cell
        if (datePicker == null) {
                this.createDatePicker();
        }

        this.setGraphic(datePicker);
}

@Override
public void cancelEdit() {
        super.cancelEdit();
        this.setText(converter.toString(this.getItem()));
        this.setGraphic(null);
}

@Override
public void updateItem(java.time.LocalDate item, boolean empty) {
        super.updateItem(item, empty);

        // Take actions based on whether the cell is being edited or not
        if (empty) {
                this.setText(null);
                this.setGraphic(null);
        } else {
                if (this.isEditing()) {
                        if (datePicker != null) {
                                datePicker.setValue((java.time.LocalDate)item);
                        }
                        this.setText(null);
                        this.setGraphic(datePicker);
                } else {
                        this.setText(converter.toString(item));
                        this.setGraphic(null);
                }
        }
}

private void createDatePicker() {
        datePicker = new DatePicker();
        datePicker.setConverter(converter);

        // Set the current value in the cell to the DatePicker
        datePicker.setValue((java.time.LocalDate)this.getItem());

        // Configure the DatePicker properties
        datePicker.setPrefWidth(this.getWidth() - this.getGraphicTextGap() * 2);
        datePicker.setEditable(this.datePickerEditable);
```

```
                    // Commit the new value when the user selects or enters a date
                    datePicker.valueProperty().addListener(new ChangeListener() {
                            @Override
                            public void changed(ObservableValue prop,
                                                Object oldValue,
                                                Object newValue) {
                                    if (DatePickerTableCell.this.isEditing()) {
                                            DatePickerTableCell.this.commitEdit(
                                            (java.time.LocalDate)newValue);
                                    }
                            }
                    });
            }

            public static <S> Callback<TableColumn<S, java.time.LocalDate>,
                            TableCell<S, java.time.LocalDate>> forTableColumn() {
                    return forTableColumn(true);
            }

            public static <S> Callback<TableColumn<S, java.time.LocalDate>,
                    TableCell<S, java.time.LocalDate>> forTableColumn(boolean
                    datePickerEditable) {
                    return (col -> new DatePickerTableCell<>(datePickerEditable));
            }

            public static <S> Callback<TableColumn<S, java.time.LocalDate>, TableCell<S,
            java.time.LocalDate>> forTableColumn(StringConverter<java.time.LocalDate> converter) {
                    return forTableColumn(converter, true);
            }

            public static <S> Callback<TableColumn<S, java.time.LocalDate>, TableCell<S,
            java.time.LocalDate>> forTableColumn(StringConverter<java.time.LocalDate> converter,
            boolean datePickerEditable) {
                    return (col -> new DatePickerTableCell<>(converter, datePickerEditable));
            }
}
```

The DatePickerTableCell class supports a StringConverter and the editable property value for the DatePicker. You can pass them to the constructors or the forTableColumn() methods. It creates a DatePicker control when the startEdit() method is called for the first time. A ChangeListener is added that commits the data when a new date is entered or selected. Several versions of the forTableColumn() static methods are provided that return cell factories. The following snippet of code shows how to use the DatePickerTableCell class:

```
TableColumn<Person, LocalDate> birthDateCol = ...

// Set a cell factory for birthDateCol. The date format is mm/dd/yyyy
// and the DatePicker is editable.
birthDateCol.setCellFactory(DatePickerTableCell.<Person>forTableColumn());
```

```
// Set a cell factory for birthDateCol. The date format is "Month day, year"
// and and the DatePicker is non-editable
StringConverter converter = new LocalDateStringConverter("MMMM dd, yyyy");
birthDateCol.setCellFactory(DatePickerTableCell.<Person>forTableColumn(converter, false));
```

The program in Listing 13-8 uses DatePickerTableCell to edit data in the cells of a Birth Date column. Run the application and then double-click a cell in the Birth Date column. The cell will display a DatePicker control. You cannot edit the date in the DatePicker, as it is noneditable. You will need to select a date from the pop-up calendar.

Listing 13-8. Using DatePickerTableCell to Edit a Dates in Cells

```java
// CustomTableCellTest.java
package com.jdojo.control;

import com.jdojo.mvc.model.Person;
import javafx.application.Application;
import javafx.scene.Scene;
import javafx.scene.control.TableColumn;
import javafx.scene.control.TableView;
import javafx.scene.layout.HBox;
import java.time.LocalDate;
import javafx.stage.Stage;
import javafx.util.StringConverter;

public class CustomTableCellTest extends Application {
        public static void main(String[] args) {
                Application.launch(args);
        }

        @Override
        @SuppressWarnings("unchecked")
        public void start(Stage stage) {
                TableView<Person> table = new TableView<>(PersonTableUtil.getPersonList());

                // Make sure teh TableView is editable
                table.setEditable(true);

                // Set up teh Birth Date column to use DatePickerTableCell
                TableColumn<Person, LocalDate> birthDateCol =
                        PersonTableUtil.getBirthDateColumn();
                StringConverter converter = new LocalDateStringConverter("MMMM dd, yyyy");
                birthDateCol.setCellFactory(
                        DatePickerTableCell.<Person>forTableColumn(converter, false));

                table.getColumns().addAll(PersonTableUtil.getIdColumn(),
                                        PersonTableUtil.getFirstNameColumn(),
                                        PersonTableUtil.getLastNameColumn(),
                                        birthDateCol);
```

```
                    HBox root = new HBox(table);
                    root.setStyle("-fx-padding: 10;" +
                                  "-fx-border-style: solid inside;" +
                                  "-fx-border-width: 2;" +
                                  "-fx-border-insets: 5;" +
                                  "-fx-border-radius: 5;" +
                                  "-fx-border-color: blue;");

                    Scene scene = new Scene(root);
                    stage.setScene(scene);
                    stage.setTitle("Using a Custom TableCell");
                    stage.show();
        }
}
```

Adding and Deleting Rows in a *TableView*

Adding and deleting rows in a TableView are easy. Note that each row in a TableView is backed by an item in the items list. Adding a row is as simple as adding an item in the items list. When you add an item to the items list, a new row appears in the TableView at the same index as the index of the added item in the items list. If the TableView is sorted, it may need to be resorted after adding a new row. Call the sort() method of the TableView to resort the rows after adding a new row.

You can delete a row by removing its item from the items list. An application provides a way for the user to indicate the rows that should be deleted. Typically, the user selects one or more rows to delete. Other options are to add a Delete button to each row or to provide a Delete check box to each row. Clicking the Delete button should delete the row. Selecting the Delete check box for a row indicates that the row is marked for deletion.

The program in Listing 13-9 shows how to add and delete rows to a TableView. It displays a window with three sections:

- The Add Person form at the top has three fields to add person details and an Add button. Enter the details for a person and click the Add button to add a record to the TableView. Error checking is skipped in the code.

- In the middle, you have two buttons. One button is used to restore the default rows in the TableView. Another button deletes the selected rows.

- At the bottom, a TableView is displayed with some rows. The multirow selection is enabled. Use the Ctrl or Shift key with the mouse to select multiple rows.

Listing 13-9. Adding and Deleting Rows in a TableView

```java
// TableViewAddDeleteRows.java
package com.jdojo.control;

import com.jdojo.mvc.model.Person;
import javafx.application.Application;
import javafx.collections.ObservableList;
import javafx.scene.Scene;
import javafx.scene.control.Button;
import javafx.scene.control.DatePicker;
import javafx.scene.control.Label;
```

```java
import javafx.scene.control.TableView;
import javafx.scene.control.TextField;
import javafx.scene.layout.GridPane;
import javafx.scene.layout.VBox;
import javafx.stage.Stage;
import java.util.Arrays;
import javafx.scene.control.SelectionMode;
import javafx.scene.layout.HBox;
import static javafx.scene.control.TableView.TableViewSelectionModel;

public class TableViewAddDeleteRows extends Application {
        // Fields to add Person details
        private final TextField fNameField = new TextField();
        private final TextField lNameField = new TextField();
        private final DatePicker dobField = new DatePicker();

        // The TableView
        TableView<Person> table = new TableView<>(PersonTableUtil.getPersonList());

        public static void main(String[] args) {
                Application.launch(args);
        }

        @Override
        @SuppressWarnings("unchecked")
        public void start(Stage stage) {
                // Turn on multi-row selection for the TableView
                TableViewSelectionModel<Person> tsm = table.getSelectionModel();
                tsm.setSelectionMode(SelectionMode.MULTIPLE);

                // Add columns to the TableView
                table.getColumns().addAll(PersonTableUtil.getIdColumn(),
                                        PersonTableUtil.getFirstNameColumn(),
                                        PersonTableUtil.getLastNameColumn(),
                                        PersonTableUtil.getBirthDateColumn());

                GridPane newDataPane  = this.getNewPersonDataPane();

                Button restoreBtn = new Button("Restore Rows");
                restoreBtn.setOnAction(e -> restoreRows());

                Button deleteBtn = new Button("Delete Selected Rows");
                deleteBtn.setOnAction(e -> deleteSelectedRows());

                VBox root = new VBox(newDataPane, new HBox(restoreBtn, deleteBtn), table);
                root.setSpacing(5);
                root.setStyle("-fx-padding: 10;" +
                                "-fx-border-style: solid inside;" +
                                "-fx-border-width: 2;" +
                                "-fx-border-insets: 5;" +
                                "-fx-border-radius: 5;" +
                                "-fx-border-color: blue;");
```

```java
        Scene scene = new Scene(root);
        stage.setScene(scene);
        stage.setTitle("Adding/Deleting Rows in a TableViews");
        stage.show();
    }

    public GridPane getNewPersonDataPane() {
        GridPane pane = new GridPane();
        pane.setHgap(10);
        pane.setVgap(5);
        pane.addRow(0, new Label("First Name:"), fNameField);
        pane.addRow(1, new Label("Last Name:"), lNameField);
        pane.addRow(2, new Label("Birth Date:"), dobField);

        Button addBtn = new Button("Add");
        addBtn.setOnAction(e -> addPerson());

        // Add the "Add" button
        pane.add(addBtn, 2, 0);

        return pane;
    }

    public void deleteSelectedRows() {
        TableViewSelectionModel<Person> tsm = table.getSelectionModel();
        if (tsm.isEmpty()) {
            System.out.println("Please select a row to delete.");
            return;
        }

        // Get all selected row indices in an array
        ObservableList<Integer> list = tsm.getSelectedIndices();
        Integer[] selectedIndices = new Integer[list.size()];
        selectedIndices = list.toArray(selectedIndices);

        // Sort the array
        Arrays.sort(selectedIndices);

        // Delete rows (last to first)
        for(int i = selectedIndices.length - 1; i >= 0; i--) {
            tsm.clearSelection(selectedIndices[i].intValue());
            table.getItems().remove(selectedIndices[i].intValue());
        }
    }

    public void restoreRows() {
        table.getItems().clear();
        table.getItems().addAll(PersonTableUtil.getPersonList());
    }
```

```
    public Person getPerson() {
            return new Person(fNameField.getText(),
                              lNameField.getText(),
                              dobField.getValue());
    }

    public void addPerson() {
            Person p = getPerson();
            table.getItems().add(p);
            clearFields();
    }

    public void clearFields() {
            fNameField.setText(null);
            lNameField.setText(null);
            dobField.setValue(null);
    }
}
```

Most of the logic in the code is simple. The deleteSelectedRows() method implements the logic to delete the selected rows. When you remove an item from the items list, the selection model does not remove its index. Suppose the first row is selected. If you remove the first item from the items list, the second row, which becomes the first row, is selected. To make sure that this does not happen, you clear the selection for the row before you remove it from the items list. You delete rows from last to first (higher index to lower index) because when you delete an item from the list, all of the items after the deleted items will have different indices. Suppose you have selected rows at indices 1 and 2. Deleting a row at index 1 first changes the index of the index 2 to 1. Performing deletion from last to first takes care of this issue.

Scrolling in a *TableView*

TableView automatically provides vertical and horizontal scrollbars when rows or columns fall beyond the available space. Users can use the scrollbars to scroll to a specific row or column. Sometimes you need programmatic support for scrolling. For example, when you append a row to a TableView, you may want the row visible to the user by scrolling it to the view. The TableView class contains four methods that can be used to scroll to a specific row or column:

- scrollTo(int rowIndex)
- scrollTo(S item)
- scrollToColumn(TableColumn<S,?> column)
- scrollToColumnIndex(int columnIndex)

The scrollTo() method scrolls the row with the specified index or item to the view. The scrollToColumn() and scrollToColumnIndex() methods scroll to the specified column and columnIndex, respectively.

TableView fires a ScrollToEvent when there is a request to scroll to a row or column using one of the above-mentioned scrolling methods. The ScrollToEvent class contains a getScrollTarget() method that returns the row index or the column reference depending on the scroll type:

```
TableView<Person> table = ...

// Add a ScrollToEvent for row scrolling
table.setOnScrollTo(e -> {
        int rowIndex = e.getScrollTarget();
        System.out.println("Scrolled to row " + rowIndex);
});

// Add a ScrollToEvent for column scrolling
table.setOnScrollToColumn(e -> {
        TableColumn<Person, ?> column = e.getScrollTarget();
        System.out.println("Scrolled to column " + column.getText());
});
```

■ **Tip** The ScrollToEvent is not fired when the user scrolls through the rows and columns. It is fired when you call one of the four scrolling-related methods of the TableView class.

Resizing a *TableColumn*

Whether a TableColumn is resizable by the user is specified by its resizable property. By default, a TableColumn is resizable. How a column in a TableView is resized is specified by the columnResizePolicy property of the TableView. The property is a Callback object. Its call() method takes an object of the ResizeFeatures class, which is a static inner class of the TableView class. The ResizeFeatures object encapsulates the delta by which the column is resized, the TableColumn being resized, and the TableView. The call() method returns true if the column was resized by the delta amount successfully. Otherwise, it returns false.

The TableView class provides two built-in resize policies as constants:

- CONSTRAINED_RESIZE_POLICY

- UNCONSTRAINED_RESIZE_POLICY

CONSTRAINED_RESIZE_POLICY ensures that the sum of the width of all visible leaf columns is equal to the width of the TableView. Resizing a column adjusts the width of all columns to the right of the resized column. When the column width is increased, the width of the rightmost column is decreased up to its minimum width. If the increased width is still not compensated, the width of the second rightmost column is decreased up to its minimum width and so on. When all columns to the right have their minimum widths, the column width cannot be increased any more. The same rule applies in the opposite direction when a column is resized to decrease its width.

When the width of a column is increased, UNCONSTRAINED_RESIZE_POLICY shifts all columns to its right by the amount the width is increased. When the width is decreased, columns to the right are shifted to the left by the same amount. If a column has nested columns, resizing the column evenly distributes the delta among the immediate children columns. This is the default column-resize policy for a TableView:

```
TableView<Person> table = ...;

// Set the column resize policy to constrained resize policy
table.setColumnResizePolicy(TableView.CONSTRAINED_RESIZE_POLICY);
```

You can also create a custom column resize policy. The following snippet of code will serve as a template. You will need to write the logic to consume the delta, which is the difference between the new and old width of the column:

```
TableView<Person> table = new TableView<>(PersonTableUtil.getPersonList());
table.setColumnResizePolicy(resizeFeatures -> {
        boolean consumedDelta = false; double delta = resizeFeatures.getDelta();
        TableColumn<Person, ?> column = resizeFeatures.getColumn();
        TableView<Person> tableView = resizeFeatures.getTable();

        // Adjust the delta here...

        return consumedDelta;
});
```

You can disable column resizing by setting a trivial callback that does nothing. Its call() simply returns true indicating that it has consumed the delta:

```
// Disable column resizing
table.setColumnResizePolicy(resizeFeatures -> true);
```

Styling a *TableView* with CSS

You can style a TableView and all its parts, for example, column headers, cells, placeholder, and so forth. Applying a CSS to TableView is very complex and broad in scope. This section covers a brief overview of CSS styling for TableView. The default CSS style-class name for a TableView is table-view. The default CSS style-classes for a cell, a row, and a column header are table-cell, table-row-cell, and column-header, respectively:

```
/* Set the font for the cells */
.table-row-cell {
        -fx-font-size: 10pt;
        -fx-font-family: Arial;
}

/* Set the font size and text color for column headers */
.table-view .column-header .label{
        -fx-font-size: 10pt;
        -fx-text-fill: blue;
}
```

TableView supports the following CSS pseudo-classes:

- cell-selection
- row-selection
- constrained-resize

The cell-selection pseudo-class is applied when the cell-level selection is enabled, whereas the row-selection pseudo-class is applied for row-level selection. The constrained-resize pseudo-class is applied when the column resize policy is CONSTRAINED_RESIZE_POLICY.

Alternate rows in a TableView are highlighted by default. The following code removes the alternate row highlighting. It sets the white background color for all rows:

```
.table-row-cell {
    -fx-background-color: white;
}

.table-row-cell .table-cell {
    -fx-border-width: 0.25px;
    -fx-border-color: transparent gray gray transparent;
}
```

TableView shows empty rows to fill its available height. The following code removes the empty rows. In fact, it makes them appear as removed:

```
.table-row-cell:empty {
    -fx-background-color: transparent;
}

.table-row-cell:empty .table-cell {
    -fx-border-width: 0px;
}
```

TableView contains several substructures that can be styled separately:

- column-resize-line
- column-overlay
- placeholder
- column-header-background

The column-resize-line substructure is a Region and is shown when the user tries to resize a column. The column-overlay substructure is a Region and is shown as an overlay for the column being moved. The placeholder substructure is a StackPane and is shown when the TableView does not have columns or data, as in the following code:

```
/* Make the text in the placeholder red and bold */
.table-view .placeholder .label {
    -fx-text-fill: red;
    -fx-font-weight: bold;
}
```

The `column-header-background` substructure is a `StackPane`, and it is the area behind the column headers. It contains several substructures. Its filler substructure, which is a `Region`, is the area between the rightmost column and the right edge of the `TableView` in the header area. Its show-hide-columns-button substructure, which is a `StackPane`, is the area that shows the menu button to display the list of columns to show and hide. Please refer to the `modena.css` file and the *JavaFX CSS Reference Guide* for a complete list of properties of `TableView` that can be styled. The following code sets the filler background to white:

```
/* Set the filler background to white*/
.table-view .column-header-background .filler {
        -fx-background-color: white;
}
```

Summary

`TableView` is a control that is used to display and edit data in a tabular form. A `TableView` consists of rows and columns. The intersection of a row and a column is called a cell. Cells contain the data values. Columns have headers that describe the type of data they contain. Columns can be nested. Resizing and sorting of column data have built-in support. The following classes are used to work with a `TableView` control: `TableView`, `TableColumn`, `TableRow`, `TableCell`, `TablePosition`, `TableView.TableViewFocusModel`, and `TableView.TableViewSelectionModel`. The `TableView` class represents a `TableView` control. The `TableColumn` class represents a column in a `TableView`. Typically, a `TableView` contains multiple instances of `TableColumn`. A `TableColumn` consists of cells, which are instances of the `TableCell` class. A `TableColumn` is responsible for displaying and editing the data in its cells. A `TableColumn` has a header that can display header text, a graphic, or both. You can have a context menu for a `TableColumn`, which is displayed when the user right-clicks inside the column header. Use the `contextMenu` property to set a context menu.

The `TableRow` class inherits from the `IndexedCell` class. An instance of `TableRow` represents a row in a `TableView`. You almost never use this class in your application unless you want to provide a customized implementation for rows. Typically, you customize cells, not rows.

An instance of the `TableCell` class represents a cell in a `TableView`. Cells are highly customizable. They display data from the underlying data model for the `TableView`. They are capable of displaying data as well as graphics. Cells in a row of a `TableView` contain data related to an item such as a person, a book, and so forth. Data for some cells in a row may come directly from the attributes of the item or they may be computed.

`TableView` has an `items` property of the `ObservableList<S>` type. The generic type S is the same as the generic type of the `TableView`. It is the data model for the `TableView`. Each element in the items list represents a row in the `TableView`. Adding a new item to the items list adds a new row to the `TableView`. Deleting an item from the items list deletes the corresponding row from the `TableView`.

The `TableColumn`, `TableRow`, and `TableCell` classes contain a `tableView` property that holds the reference of the `TableView` that contains them. The `tableView` property contains `null` when the `TableColumn` does not belong to a `TableView`.

A `TablePosition` represents the position of a cell. Its `getRow()` and `getColumn()` methods return the indices of rows and columns, respectively, to which the cell belongs.

The `TableViewFocusModel` class is an inner static class of the `TableView` class. It represents the focus model for the `TableView` to manage focus for rows and cells.

The `TableViewSelectionModel` class is an inner static class of the `TableView` class. It represents the selection model for the `TableView` to manage selection for rows and cells.

By default, all columns in a `TableView` are visible. The `TableColumn` class has a `visible` property to set the visibility of a column. If you turn off the visibility of a parent column, a column with nested columns, all of its nested columns will be invisible.

You can rearrange columns in a TableView in two ways: by dragging and dropping columns to a different position or by changing their positions in the observable list of returned by the getColumns() method of the TableView class. The first option is available by default.

TableView has built-in support for sorting data in columns. By default, it allows users to sort data by clicking column headers. It also supports sorting data programmatically. You can also disable sorting for a column or all columns in a TableView.

TableView supports customization at several levels. It lets you customize the rendering of columns, for example, you can display data in a column using a check box, a combo box, or a TextField. You can also style a TableView using CSS.

The next chapter will discuss the tree view control that is used to work with data representing a tree-like hierarchical structure.

CHAPTER 14

■ ■ ■

Understanding *TreeView*

In this chapter, you will learn:

- What a TreeView is
- How to create a TreeView
- How to hide the root node of a TreeView
- What a TreeItem is and how to handle TreeItem events in a TreeView
- How to customize cells in a TreeView
- How to edit data in a TreeView
- How to load a TreeItem in a TreeView on demand
- About the selection model of the TreeView
- How to style a TreeView using CSS

What Is a *TreeView*?

A TreeView is a control that displays hierarchical data in a tree-like structure, as shown in Figure 14-1. You can think of a TreeView as displaying a tree upside down—the root of the tree being at the top. Each item in a TreeView is an instance of the TreeItem class. TreeItems form parent-child relationships. In Figure 14-1, Departments, IS, and Doug Dyer are instances of a TreeItem.

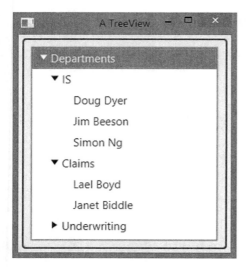

Figure 14-1. *A window with a* `TreeView` *control*

A `TreeItem` is also referred to as a *node*. The `TreeItem` class does not inherit from the Node class. Therefore, a `TreeItem` is not a JavaFX Node and it cannot be added to a scene graph.

A `TreeItem` is categorized as a *branch* or *leaf node*. If a `TreeItem` contains other instances of `TreeItem`, which are called its children, it is called a branch node. Otherwise, it is called a leaf node. In Figure 14-1, Departments, IS, and Claims are examples of branch nodes, whereas Doug Dyer and Lael Boyd are examples of leaf nodes. Notice that leaf nodes are those that occur at the tips of the tree hierarchy. A leaf node has a parent but no children. A branch node has a parent as well as children, except a special branch node, which is called the *root node*. The root node has no parent, but children only, and it is the first node in the TreeView. Departments is the root node in Figure 14-1.

A branch node can be in an *expanded* or *collapsed* state. In Figure 14-1, the Departments, IS, and Claims nodes are in the expanded state, whereas the Underwriting node is in the collapsed state. A triangle, which is called a *disclosure node*, is used to show the expanded and collapsed state of a branch node.

A `TreeItem` serves as the data model in a `TreeView`. Each `TreeItem` uses an instance of the `TreeCell` class to render its value. A `TreeCell` in a `TreeView` can be customized using a cell factory. By default, a `TreeCell` is not editable.

`TreeView` is a virtualized control. It creates only as many instances of `TreeCell` as needed to display the items for its current height. Cells are recycled as you scroll through items. Virtualization makes it possible to use `TreeView` for viewing very large number of items without using a large amount of memory. Note, however, that loading `TreeItems` always takes memory. Virtualization helps only in viewing the items by recycling the cells used in viewing them.

Creating a *TreeView*

An instance of the `TreeView<T>` class represents a `TreeView` control. The `TreeView` class takes a generic type, which is the type of the value contained in its `TreeItems`. The default constructor creates an empty `TreeView`:

```
// Create an empty TreeView whose TreeItems value type is String
TreeView<String> treeView = new TreeView<>();
```

Another constructor creates a TreeView with the root node:

```
// Create the root TreeItem
TreeItem<String> depts = new TreeItem<String>("Departments");

// Create a TreeView with depts as its root item
TreeView<String> treeView = new TreeView<>(depts);
```

The TreeView class contains a root property. Its type is TreeItem<T> and it represents the root node. You can create an empty TreeView and set its root node later using the setRoot() method:

```
// Create an empty TreeView whose TreeItems value is String
TreeView<String> treeView = new TreeView<>();
...
// Set the root node
treeView.setRoot(depts);
```

A TreeItem stores all its children in an ObservableList. The getChildren() method returns the reference of the list. The following snippet of code adds three children TreeItems to the root:

```
// Create children TreeItemsfor the root
TreeItem<String> isDept = new TreeItem<String>("IS");
TreeItem<String> claimsDept = new TreeItem<String>("Claims");
TreeItem<String> underwritingDept = new TreeItem<String>("Underwriting");

// Add children to the root
depts.getChildren().addAll(isDept, claimsDept, underwritingDept);
```

You can use the above logic to build a TreeView and add as many instances of TreeItem as you like. Notice that you add only the root node to the TreeView. All other nodes are added to the root node and its children.

You can use a TreeView with the same TreeItems several times. Let's look at the code to build a TreeView once and then reuse it. Listing 14-1 is a utility class. Its getTreeView() method shows how to create and populate a TreeView. It returns the reference of the TreeView. When you need a TreeView in an example, you will use this method.

Listing 14-1. A TreeView Utility Class that Builds a TreeView

```
// TreeViewUtil.java
package com.jdojo.control;

import javafx.scene.control.TreeItem;
import javafx.scene.control.TreeView;

public class TreeViewUtil {
        public static TreeView<String> getTreeView() {
                TreeItem<String> depts = new TreeItem<>("Departments");

                // Add items to depts
                TreeItem<String> isDept = new TreeItem<String>("IS");
                TreeItem<String> claimsDept = new TreeItem<String>("Claims");
                TreeItem<String> underwritingDept = new TreeItem<String>("Underwriting");
                depts.getChildren().addAll(isDept, claimsDept, underwritingDept);
```

```
                // Add employees for each dept
                isDept.getChildren().addAll(new TreeItem<String>("Doug Dyer"),
                                            new TreeItem<String>("Jim Beeson"),
                                            new TreeItem<String>("Simon Ng"));

                claimsDept.getChildren().addAll(new TreeItem<String>("Lael Boyd"),
                                                new TreeItem<String>("Janet Biddle"));

                underwritingDept.getChildren().addAll(new TreeItem<String>("Ken McEwen"),
                                                      new TreeItem<String>("Ken Mann"),
                                                      new TreeItem<String>("Lola Ng"));

                // Create a TreeView with depts as its root item
                TreeView<String> treeView = new TreeView<>(depts);

                return treeView;
        }
}
```

The program Listing 14-2 shows a `TreeView` control in a window. When you run the program, all nodes are collapsed, which is the default behavior for a `TreeView`. You will need to click the disclosure node (the triangle) for the root node to expand it and view its children. Repeat this to expand other nodes. Clicking the disclosure node for an expanded node hides its children.

■ **Tip** By default, a node is in the collapsed state. Call the `setExpanded(true)` method of a `TreeItem` to expand a node.

Listing 14-2. Creating a TreeView Control

```
// TreeViewTest.java
package com.jdojo.control;

import javafx.application.Application;
import javafx.scene.Scene;
import javafx.scene.control.TreeView;
import javafx.scene.layout.HBox;
import javafx.stage.Stage;

public class TreeViewTest extends Application {
        public static void main(String[] args) {
                Application.launch(args);
        }

        @Override
        public void start(Stage stage) {
                TreeView<String> treeView = TreeViewUtil.getTreeView();
                HBox root = new HBox(treeView);
```

```
        root.setStyle("-fx-padding: 10;" +
                      "-fx-border-style: solid inside;" +
                      "-fx-border-width: 2;" +
                      "-fx-border-insets: 5;" +
                      "-fx-border-radius: 5;" +
                      "-fx-border-color: blue;");

        Scene scene = new Scene(root);
        stage.setScene(scene);
        stage.setTitle("Creating a TreeView");
        stage.show();
    }
}
```

Hiding the Root Node

In a TreeView, you can hide the root node by setting the value for its showRoot property to false. By default, the root node is visible. Call setShowRoot(false) of the TreeView to hide the root node. Hiding root node makes traversing the TreeView a little easier as the user has one less level of indentation to traverse. Hiding the root node shows its child nodes at the first level. The following snippet of code will display a TreeView, as shown in Figure 14-2.

```
TreeView<String> treeView = TreeViewUtil.getTreeView();

// Hide the root node
treeView.setShowRoot(false);
```

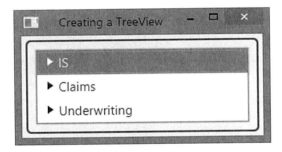

Figure 14-2. *A TreeView with with its root node hidden*

Understanding the *TreeItem*

A TreeItem supplies the data for a node. It has the following properties:

- expanded
- graphic
- leaf
- parent
- value

667

The expanded property indicates whether a TreeItem is expanded. It is true if the TreeItem is in the expanded state. Otherwise, it is false. You can expand a node using the setExpanded(true) method.

A TreeItem may optionally contain an icon represented by its graphic property. The type of the graphic property is Node, and therefore, you can use any node for the graphic property. Typically, a 16-by-16 image is used.

The leaf property indicates whether a TreeItem has children. It is true if the TreeItem has no children. Otherwise, it is false. It is a read-only property.

Every TreeItem in a TreeView, except the root TreeItem, has a parent TreeItem. The parent property is a read-only property that contains the parent of the TreeItem.

The value property stores the application-specific data for a TreeItem. Its type is the same as the generic type of the TreeItem class.

You can get the ObservableList of children of a TreeItem using the getChildren() method. You can traverse the tree up or down from a TreeItem using the getParent() and getChildren() methods recursively.

The TreeItem class provides several constructors to create an empty TreeItem, a TreeItem with a value, and a TreeItem with a value and graphic:

```
// Create an empty TreeItem and set the value
TreeItem<String> emptyItem = new TreeItem<>();
emptyItem.setValue("Departments");

// A TreeItem with a value
TreeItem<String> item2 = new TreeItem<>("Departments");

// A TreeItem with a value and an icon
ImageView icon = ...
TreeItem<String> item3 = new TreeItem<>("Departments", icon);
```

Handling *TreeItem* Events

A TreeItem fires events as it is modified, for example, by adding or removing children or expanding or collapsing. An instance of the TreeModificationEvent class, which is a static inner class of the TreeItem class, represents all kinds of modification events. Different types of events are represented by different event types. It is a little strange that the TreeItem class does not contain constants for those event types. Rather, it contains static methods that return those event types. For example, the TreeItem.branchCollapsedEvent() static method returns the event type of the event that is fired when a TreeItem is collapsed.

Event types are arranged in a hierarchy. The TreeNotification event type is at the top of the hierarchy. It is the parent of all event types for TreeItem. You can add an event handler for this event type to a TreeItem and it will listen for all event types for a TreeItem. The following three event types are the direct subtypes of the TreeNotification event type:

- ValueChanged
- GraphicChanged
- TreeItemCountChange

The ValueChanged and GraphicChanged event types are fired when the value and graphic properties, respectively, of the TreeItem change. The TreeItemCountChange event type is fired when the TreeItem is expanded, collapsed, or its children list is changed. It has three subtypes to handle the specific events:

- BranchExpanded
- BranchCollapsed
- ChildrenModification

You should add event handlers for specific type of events for better performance. When an event occurs on a TreeItem, all the registered listeners are called. The event bubbles up the TreeItem chain following the parent of the TreeItem until the root TreeItem is reached. Therefore, if you want to handle a specific event on all TreeItems, add an event handler only to the root TreeItem. The following snippet of code creates a TreeView with a root node. It adds BranchExpanded and BranchCollapsed event handlers to the root node. These event handlers will be called whenever any branch in the TreeView is expanded or collapsed. The handlers print a message on the standard output about the node being expanded or collapsed.

```
TreeItem<String> depts = new TreeItem<>("Departments");
TreeView<String> treeView = new TreeView<>(depts);

// Add BranchExpended event handler
depts.addEventHandler(TreeItem.<String>branchExpandedEvent(),
        e -> System.out.println("Node expanded: " + e.getSource().getValue()));

// Add BranchCollapsed event handler
depts.addEventHandler(TreeItem.<String>branchCollapsedEvent(),
 e -> System.out.println("Node collapsed: " + e.getSource().getValue()));
```

Adding and Removing Nodes

Adding and removing TreeItems is as easy as adding or removing them in the children list of their parents. Notice that the root node does not have a parent. To delete the root node, you need to set the root property of the TreeView to null.

The program in Listing 14-3 shows how to add and remove nodes in a TreeView. A TreeView with a root node is displayed in the left side of the window. The right side displays a TextField and an Add button. Enter a text and click the Add button; a new node will be added under the selected node. Click the Remove Selected Item button to remove the selected node from the TreeView. At the bottom of the window, a detailed message log is displayed in a TextArea. The program also shows how to handle TreeItem events.

Listing 14-3. Adding and Deleting Nodes in a TreeView

```
// TreeItemAddDeleteTest.java
package com.jdojo.control;

import javafx.application.Application;
import javafx.scene.Scene;
import javafx.scene.control.Button;
import javafx.scene.control.Label;
import javafx.scene.control.TreeItem;
import javafx.scene.control.TreeView;
import javafx.scene.layout.HBox;
import javafx.stage.Stage;
import javafx.scene.control.TextArea;
import javafx.scene.control.TextField;
import javafx.scene.layout.VBox;
```

```java
public class TreeItemAddDeleteTest  extends Application {
        private final TreeView<String> treeView = new TreeView<>();
        private final TextArea msgLogFld = new TextArea();

        public static void main(String[] args) {
                Application.launch(args);
        }

        @Override
        public void start(Stage stage) {
                // Select the root node
                treeView.getSelectionModel().selectFirst();

                // Create the root node and adds event handler to it
                TreeItem<String> depts = new TreeItem<>("Departments");
                depts.addEventHandler(TreeItem.<String>branchExpandedEvent(),
                                      this::branchExpended);
                depts.addEventHandler(TreeItem.<String>branchCollapsedEvent(),
                                      this::branchCollapsed);
                depts.addEventHandler(TreeItem.<String>childrenModificationEvent(),
                                      this::childrenModification);

                // Set the root node for the TreeViww
                treeView.setRoot(depts);

                VBox rightPane = getRightPane();

                HBox root = new HBox(treeView, rightPane);
                root.setSpacing(20);
                root.setStyle("-fx-padding: 10;" +
                              "-fx-border-style: solid inside;" +
                              "-fx-border-width: 2;" +
                              "-fx-border-insets: 5;" +
                              "-fx-border-radius: 5;" +
                              "-fx-border-color: blue;");

                Scene scene = new Scene(root);
                stage.setScene(scene);
                stage.setTitle("Creating a TreeView");
                stage.show();
        }

        public VBox getRightPane() {
                TextField itemFld = new TextField();

                Button addItemBtn = new Button("Add");
                addItemBtn.setOnAction(e -> this.addItem(itemFld.getText()));

                Button removeItemBtn = new Button("Remove Selected Item");
                removeItemBtn.setOnAction(e -> this.removeItem());
```

```
        msgLogFld.setPrefRowCount(15);
        msgLogFld.setPrefColumnCount(25);
        VBox box = new VBox(new Label("Select an item to add to or remove."),
                            new HBox(new Label("Item:"), itemFld, addItemBtn),
                            removeItemBtn,
                            new Label("Message Log:"),
                            msgLogFld);
        box.setSpacing(10);
        return box;
}

public void addItem(String value) {
        if (value == null || value.trim().equals("")) {
                this.logMsg("Item cannot be empty.");
                return;
        }

        TreeItem<String> parent = treeView.getSelectionModel().getSelectedItem();
        if (parent == null) {
                this.logMsg("Select a node to add this item to.");
                return;
        }

        // Check for duplicate
        for(TreeItem<String> child : parent.getChildren()) {
                if (child.getValue().equals(value)) {
                        this.logMsg(value + " already exists under " + parent.getValue());
                        return;
                }
        }

        TreeItem<String> newItem = new TreeItem<String>(value);
        parent.getChildren().add(newItem);
        if (!parent.isExpanded()) {
                parent.setExpanded(true);
        }
}

public void removeItem() {
        TreeItem<String> item = treeView.getSelectionModel().getSelectedItem();
        if (item == null) {
                this.logMsg("Select a node to remove.");
                return;
        }

        TreeItem<String> parent = item.getParent();
        if (parent == null ) {
                this.logMsg("Cannot remove the root node.");
        } else {
                parent.getChildren().remove(item);
        }

}
```

```
        public void branchExpended(TreeItem.TreeModificationEvent<String> e) {
                String nodeValue = e.getSource().getValue();
                this.logMsg("Event: " + nodeValue + " expanded.");
        }

        public void branchCollapsed(TreeItem.TreeModificationEvent<String> e) {
                String nodeValue = e.getSource().getValue();
                this.logMsg("Event: " + nodeValue + " collapsed.");
        }

        public void childrenModification(TreeItem.TreeModificationEvent<String> e) {
                if (e.wasAdded()) {
                        for(TreeItem<String> item : e.getAddedChildren()) {
                                this.logMsg("Event: " + item.getValue() + " has been added.");
                        }
                }

                if (e.wasRemoved()) {
                        for(TreeItem<String> item : e.getRemovedChildren()) {
                                this.logMsg("Event: " + item.getValue() + " has been removed.");
                        }
                }
        }

        public void logMsg(String msg) {
                this.msgLogFld.appendText(msg + "\n");
        }
}
```

Customizing Cells in a TreeView

TreeView uses a TreeCell to render a TreeItem. A TreeCell is an IndexedCell. You can visualize items in a TreeView from top to bottom arranged in rows. Each row has exactly one item. Each item is given a row index. The first item, which is the root item, has the index of zero. The row indices are given only to the visible items. TreeView contains a read-only expandedItemCount property that is the number of visible items. Use the getExpandedItemCount() method to get the number of visible items. If a node above an item is expanded or collapsed, the index of the item changes to reflect new visible items. The index of a TreeCell in a TreeView and the row index of an item are the same. Use the getIndex() method of the TreeCell or the getRow(TreeItem<T> item) method of the TreeView to get the row index of an item.

A TreeCell is a Labeled control. By default, it uses the following rules to render its TreeItem: If the value in the TreeItem is an instance of the Node class, the value is displayed using the graphic property of the cell. Otherwise, the toString() method of the value is called and the returned string is displayed using the text property of the cell.

You can take full control of how a TreeCell renders its TreeItem by providing a cell factory for the TreeView. The cellFactory property is a Callback instance, which takes the TreeView as an argument and returns a TreeCell. The following snippet of code shows how to sets a cell factory to a TreeView:

```
TreeView<String> treeView = new TreeView<>();
...
// Set a cell factory to prepend the row index to the TreeItem value
treeView.setCellFactory( (TreeView<String> tv) -> {
        TreeCell<String> cell = new TreeCell<String>() {
                @Override
                public void updateItem(String item, boolean empty) {
                        super.updateItem(item, empty);
                        /* Logic to render the cell goes here */
                }};
        return cell;
});
```

Listing 14-4 has a complete program that uses a cell factory for a TreeView. The cell displays the index of the cell followed with the value of the TreeItem. The program displays a window as shown in Figure 14-3.

Listing 14-4. Using a Cell Factory for a TreeView

```
// TreeViewCellFactory.java
package com.jdojo.control;

import javafx.application.Application;
import javafx.scene.Scene;
import javafx.scene.control.TreeCell;
import javafx.scene.control.TreeView;
import javafx.scene.layout.HBox;
import javafx.stage.Stage;

public class TreeViewCellFactory extends Application {
        public static void main(String[] args) {
                Application.launch(args);
        }

        @Override
        public void start(Stage stage) {
                TreeView<String> treeView = TreeViewUtil.getTreeView();

                // Set a cell factory to prepend the row index to the TreeItem value
                treeView.setCellFactory( (TreeView<String> tv) -> {
                        TreeCell<String> cell = new TreeCell<String>() {
                                @Override
                                public void updateItem(String item, boolean empty) {
                                        super.updateItem(item, empty);
                                        if (empty) {
                                                this.setText(null);
                                                this.setGraphic(null);
                                        }
```

```
                                  else {
                                      String value =
                                              this.getTreeItem().getValue();
                                      this.setText(
                                              this.getIndex() + ". " + value);
                                  }
                    }};
                return cell;
            });

            HBox root = new HBox(treeView);
            root.setSpacing(20);
            root.setStyle("-fx-padding: 10;" +
                    "-fx-border-style: solid inside;" +
                    "-fx-border-width: 2;" +
                    "-fx-border-insets: 5;" +
                    "-fx-border-radius: 5;" +
                    "-fx-border-color: blue;");

            Scene scene = new Scene(root);
            stage.setScene(scene);
            stage.setTitle("Using a Cell Factory in a TreeView");
            stage.show();
        }
}
```

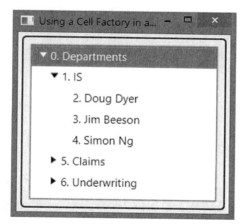

Figure 14-3. A TreeView showing the row index of its TreeItems

Editing Data in a *TreeView*

A cell in a TreeView can be editable. An editable cell may switch between editing and nonediting mode. In editing mode, cell data can be modified by the user. For a cell to enter editing mode, the TreeView must be editable. TreeView has an editable property, which can be set to true using the setEditable(true) method, as shown in the following code. By default, TreeView is not editable.

```
TreeView<Stirng> treeView = ...
treeView.setEditable(true);
```

TreeView supports three types of events:

- onEditStart
- onEditCommit
- onEditCancel

The onEditStart event is fired when a cell enters editing mode. The onEditCommit event is fired when the user successfully commits the editing, for example, by pressing the Enter key in a TextField. The onEditCancel event is fired when the user cancels the editing, for example, by pressing the Esc key in a TextField. The events are represented by an object of the TreeView.EditEvent class. The event object encapsulates the old and new values in the cell, the TreeItem being edited, and the reference of the TreeView. Use one of the methods of the EditEvent class to get these values.

Creating a TreeView does not let you edit its cells. Cell-editing capability is provided through specialized implementations of the TreeCell class. The JavaFX library provides some of these implementations. Set the cell factory for a TreeView, which is a Callback object, to use one of the following implementations of the TreeCell to make cells in a TreeView editable:

- CheckBoxTreeCell
- ChoiceBoxTreeCell
- ComboBoxTreeCell
- TextFieldTreeCell

TreeView has a read-only editingItem property that contains the reference of the TreeItem being edited. It is null when no TreeItem is being edited.

Editing Data using a Check Box

A CheckBoxTreeCell renders a check box in the cell. The following snippet of code sets the cell factory for a TreeView to use CheckBoxTreeCell:

```
TreeView<String> treeView = new TreeView<>();;

// Set a cell factory to use TextFieldTreeCell
treeView.setCellFactory(CheckBoxTreeCell.<String>forTreeView());
```

The above code will draw a check box in each cell of the TreeView, which can be selected and unselected. However, there is no way to know whether the check box for a TreeItem is selected or unselected because the TreeItem class does not provide access to the CheckBox state. CheckBoxTreeItem is a specialized implementation of TreeItem that should be used when you want to use CheckBoxTreeCell. It provides access to the selected state of the check box. It contains three boolean properties:

- independent
- indeterminate
- selected

The independent property represents the independent state of the CheckBoxTreeItem. By default, it is false. When a CheckBoxTreeItem is dependent, selecting or unselecting it affects the selected state of its children and its parent. For example, selecting or unselecting a dependent parent node selects or unselects all its children. If some, but not all, children are selected, a dependent parent node will be in an indeterminate state. If all children are selected, a dependent parent node will be selected. If all children are unselected, a dependent parent node will be unselected. The selected state of an independent CheckBoxTreeItem does not affect its parent and children.

■ **Tip**   The selection of an independent CheckBoxTreeItem does not affect is parent and children. However, the reverse is not true. That is, if a dependent parent is selected or unselected, all its children, dependent as well as independent, are selected or unselected.

The indeterminate property specifies the indeterminate state of the check box for the item. The selected property specifies the selected property of the check box for the item. Use the isIndeterminate() and isSelected() methods to determine the state of the check box of a CheckBoxTreeItem.

The program in Listing 14-5 shows how to use a cell factory to render a check box in each cell with a CheckBoxTreeItem. The initial part of the program is very similar to the first example you had for the TreeView. The only difference is that, this time, you have used CheckBoxTreeItem instead of a TreeItem. You have made the Claims item independent. That is, selecting and unselecting the Claims item does not affect the state of its parent and children. Select and unselect different items to see this effect.

Listing 14-5. Using CheckBoxTreeItem with a Check Box in a TreeCell

```java
// TreeViewCheckBoxTest.java
package com.jdojo.control;

import javafx.application.Application;
import javafx.scene.Scene;
import javafx.scene.control.CheckBoxTreeItem;
import javafx.scene.control.TreeView;
import javafx.scene.control.cell.CheckBoxTreeCell;
import javafx.scene.layout.HBox;
import javafx.stage.Stage;

public class TreeViewCheckBoxTest extends Application {
    public static void main(String[] args) {
        Application.launch(args);
    }

    @Override
    @SuppressWarnings("unchecked")
    public void start(Stage stage) {
        CheckBoxTreeItem<String> depts =
                new CheckBoxTreeItem<>("Departments");

        // Add items to depts
        CheckBoxTreeItem<String> isDept = new CheckBoxTreeItem<>("IS");
        CheckBoxTreeItem<String> claimsDept =
                new CheckBoxTreeItem<>("Claims");
```

```
CheckBoxTreeItem<String> underwritingDept =
            new CheckBoxTreeItem<>("Underwriting");
depts.getChildren().addAll(isDept, claimsDept, underwritingDept);

// Add employees for each dept
isDept.getChildren().addAll(new CheckBoxTreeItem<String>("Doug Dyer"),
                    new CheckBoxTreeItem<String>("Jim Beeson"),
                    new CheckBoxTreeItem<String>("Simon Ng"));

claimsDept.getChildren().addAll(
                    new CheckBoxTreeItem<String>("Lael Boyd"),
                    new CheckBoxTreeItem<String>("Janet Biddle"));

underwritingDept.getChildren().addAll(
                    new CheckBoxTreeItem<String>("Ken McEwen"),
                    new CheckBoxTreeItem<String>("Ken Mann"),
                    new CheckBoxTreeItem<String>("Lola Ng"));

// Make the claimsDept item independent
claimsDept.setIndependent(true);

// Create a TreeView with depts as its root item
TreeView<String> treeView = new TreeView<>(depts);

// Set the cell factory to draw a CheckBox in cells
treeView.setCellFactory(CheckBoxTreeCell.<String>forTreeView());

HBox root = new HBox(treeView);
root.setSpacing(20);
root.setStyle("-fx-padding: 10;" +
            "-fx-border-style: solid inside;" +
            "-fx-border-width: 2;" +
            "-fx-border-insets: 5;" +
            "-fx-border-radius: 5;" +
            "-fx-border-color: blue;");

Scene scene = new Scene(root);
stage.setScene(scene);
stage.setTitle("Using CheckBoxTreeItem");
stage.show();
    }
}
```

Editing Data Using a Choice Box

A ChoiceBoxTreeCell is rendered as a Label in nonediting mode and as a choice box in editing mode. Its forTreeView() static method returns a cell factory. The method is overloaded. You need to pass the list of items to be shown in the choice box. If the toString() method of the item does not return a user-friendly string for the user, use a string converter. The following snippet of code sets a cell factory for a TreeView that will use instances of ChoiceBoxTreeCell to render TreeItems. In editing mode, the choice box will display three items: Item-1, Item-2, and Item-3.

```
TreeView<String> treeView = new TreeView<>();
treeView.setCellFactory(ChoiceBoxTreeCell.<String>forTreeView("Item-1", "Item-2", "Item-3"));
```

When an item is selected in the choice box, the item is set to the TreeItem of the cell. You can set an onEditCommit event handler that is fired when the user selects an item. The following snippet of code adds such a handler for the TreeView that prints a message on the standard output:

```
// Add an onEditCommit handler
treeView.setOnEditCommit(e -> {
        System.out.println(e.getTreeItem() +  " changed." +
                           " old = " + e.getOldValue() +
                           ", new = " + e.getNewValue());
});
```

Clicking a selected cell puts the cell into editing mode. Double-clicking an unselected cell puts the cell into editing mode. Changing the focus to another cell or selecting an item from the list puts the editing cell into nonediting mode and the current value is displayed in a Label.

Editing Data Using a Combo Box

Editing data using a combo box works similar to the method used for a ChoiceBoxTreeCell. Please refer to the section "Editing Data Using a Choice Box" for more details.

A ComboBoxTreeCell is rendered as a Label in nonediting mode and as a combo box in editing mode. Its forTreeView() static method returns a cell factory. The method is overloaded. You need to pass the list of items to be shown in the combo box. If the toString() method of the item does not return a user-friendly string for the user, use a string converter. The following snippet of code sets a cell factory for a TreeView that will use instances of ComboBoxTreeCell to render TreeItems. In editing mode, the combo box will display three items: Item-1, Item-2, and Item-3.

```
TreeView<String> treeView = new TreeView<>();
treeView.setCellFactory(ComboBoxTreeCell.<String>forTreeView("Item-1", "Item-2", "Item-3"));
```

Editing Data Using a *TextField*

A TextFieldTreeCell is rendered as a Label in nonediting mode and as a TextField in editing mode. Its forTreeView() static method returns a cell factory. The method is overloaded. Use a string converter if the item type is not String. The following snippet of code sets a cell factory for a TreeView that will use instances of TextFieldTreeCell to render TreeItems. In editing mode, the TextField will display the item value.

```
TreeView<String> treeView = new TreeView<>();
treeView.setCellFactory(TextFieldTreeCell.forTreeView());
```

Clicking a selected cell or double-clicking an unselected cell puts the cell into editing mode, which displays the cell data in a TextField. Once the cell is in editing mode, you need to click in the TextField (one more click!) to put the caret in the TextField so you can make changes.

■ **Tip** Double-clicking a cell representing a branch node will not put the cell in editing mode. Rather, the cell is expanded or collapsed. The trick is to use two single clicks instead of a double-click on a branch node. Both a double-click and two single clicks put a cell of a leaf node in editing mode.

If you are in the middle of editing a cell data, press the Esc key to cancel editing, which will return the cell to nonediting mode and reverts to the old data in the cell. Pressing the Enter key commits the data to the TreeItem for the cell.

If you are editing a cell using a TextFieldTreeCell, moving the focus to another cell, for example, by clicking another cell, cancels the editing and puts the old value back in the cell. This is not what a user expects. At present, there is no easy solution to this problem. You will have to create a subclass of TreeCell and add a focus change listener so you can commit the data when the TextField loses focus.

The program in Listing 14-6 shows how to use TextFieldTreeCell to edit cell data in a TreeView. Run the application and click a cell two times to put the cell in editing mode. A TextField will display the cell data. Change the data and press the Enter key to commit the changes. The program adds edit-related event handlers to the TreeView that prints a message on the standard output when the events occur. Figure 14-4 shows the cell data being edited in a TextFieldTreeCell.

Listing 14-6. Using TextFieldTreeCell to Edit Cell Data in a TreeView

```java
// TreeViewEditingData.java
package com.jdojo.control;

import javafx.application.Application;
import javafx.scene.Scene;
import javafx.scene.control.TreeView;
import javafx.scene.control.cell.TextFieldTreeCell;
import javafx.scene.layout.HBox;
import javafx.stage.Stage;

public class TreeViewEditingData extends Application {
        public static void main(String[] args) {
                Application.launch(args);
        }

        @Override
        public void start(Stage stage) {
                TreeView<String> treeView = TreeViewUtil.getTreeView();

                // Make the TreeView editable
                treeView.setEditable(true);

                // Set a cell factory to use TextFieldTreeCell
                treeView.setCellFactory(TextFieldTreeCell.forTreeView());

                // Set editing related event handlers
                treeView.setOnEditStart(this::editStart);
                treeView.setOnEditCommit(this::editCommit);
                treeView.setOnEditCancel(this::editCancel);

                HBox root = new HBox(treeView);
                root.setStyle("-fx-padding: 10;" +
                                "-fx-border-style: solid inside;" +
                                "-fx-border-width: 2;" +
                                "-fx-border-insets: 5;" +
                                "-fx-border-radius: 5;" +
                                "-fx-border-color: blue;");
```

```
                Scene scene = new Scene(root);
                stage.setScene(scene);
                stage.setTitle("A Editing Cells in a TreeView");
                stage.show();
        }

        public void editStart(TreeView.EditEvent<String> e) {
                System.out.println("Started editng: " + e.getTreeItem() );
        }

        public void editCommit(TreeView.EditEvent<String> e) {
                System.out.println(e.getTreeItem() +  " changed." +
                                        " old = " + e.getOldValue() +
                                        ", new = " + e.getNewValue());
        }

        public void editCancel(TreeView.EditEvent<String> e) {
                System.out.println("Cancelled editng: " + e.getTreeItem() );
        }
}
```

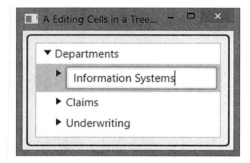

Figure 14-4. *A cell data being edited in a* `TextFieldTreeCell`

Loading *TreeItems* on Demand

So far in the examples, you have been loading all items in a `TreeView` at once. Sometimes the number of items is too big or unknown. In those cases, you would need to load the items when the user expands a node to make efficient use of memory. However, this approach is a little complex to implement. In this section, you will develop a file system browser that will create nodes on demand.

First, you need to create a class inheriting from the `TreeItem` class. Listing 14-7 has the code for this new class `PathTreeItem`, which inherits from `TreeItem<Path>`. The class needs to override the `getChildren()` and `isLeaf()` methods of the `TreeItem` class. The three instance variables are used to cache the results of the `isLeaf()` method call and flags indicating that the methods were called once. The constructor calls the constructor of the `TreeItem` class and sets an icon for the node depending on whether it is a file or a directory. The `populateChildren()` method contains the main logic for populating a node. The root directories for the default file system are added as children for the root node. A nonroot node is populated with its subdirectories and subfiles.

> ▪ **Note** This program will not refresh the items if they change in the file system after it loads them because you load children for a node only once. This task is left to you. As an exercise, you will need to modify the `PathTreeItem` class to implement the refresh functionality using the watch-service for root directories, which was introduced in Java 7. A trivial, inefficient implementation would be to load children every time the `getChildren()` method is called.

Listing 14-7. The `PathTreeItem` Class, as an Implementation of the `TreeItem<Path>` Class

```java
// PathTreeItem.java
package com.jdojo.control;

import java.io.IOException;
import java.nio.file.FileSystems;
import java.nio.file.Files;
import java.nio.file.Path;
import javafx.collections.ObservableList;
import javafx.scene.control.TreeItem;
import javafx.scene.image.Image;
import javafx.scene.image.ImageView;

public class PathTreeItem extends TreeItem<Path>{
        private boolean childrenLoaded = false;
        private boolean leafPropertyComputed = false;
        private boolean leafNode = false;

        public PathTreeItem(Path path) {
                super(path);
                ImageView icon = null;
                if (Files.isDirectory(path)) {
                        icon = getFolderIcon("folder.jpg");
                } else {
                        icon = getFolderIcon("file.jpg");
                }
                this.setGraphic(icon);
        }

        @Override
        public ObservableList<TreeItem<Path>> getChildren() {
                if (!childrenLoaded) {
                        childrenLoaded = true;
                        populateChildren(this);
                }
                return super.getChildren();
        }
```

```java
    @Override
    public boolean isLeaf() {
        if (!leafPropertyComputed) {
            leafPropertyComputed = true;
            Path path = this.getValue();
            leafNode = !Files.isDirectory(path);
        }
        return leafNode;
    }

    private void populateChildren(TreeItem<Path> item) {
        item.getChildren().clear();
        if (item.getParent() == null) {
            // Add root directories
            for (Path p : FileSystems.getDefault().getRootDirectories()) {
                item.getChildren().add(new PathTreeItem(p));
            }
        } else {
            Path path = item.getValue();
            // Populate sub-directories and files
            if (Files.isDirectory(path)) {
                try {
                    Files.list(path).forEach(
                            p -> item.getChildren().add(new PathTreeItem(p)));
                }
                catch(IOException e) {
                    e.printStackTrace();
                }
            }
        }
    }

    private ImageView getFolderIcon(String fileName) {
        ImageView imgView = null;
        try {
            String imagePath = "resources/picture/" + fileName;
            Image img = new Image(imagePath);
            imgView = new ImageView(img);
        }
        catch (Exception e) {
            e.printStackTrace();
        }
        return imgView;
    }
}
```

Once you have the PathTreeItem class, building a file system browser is easy. The program in Listing 14-8 creates a TreeView that lets you browse the default file system on your machine. It creates a root node with the current directory. You can create the root node for any directory, because you do not show the root node. The following snippet of code creates a TreeView with the current directory as its root node:

```
PathTreeItem rootNode = new PathTreeItem(Paths.get("."));
TreeView<Path> treeView = new TreeView<>(rootNode);
```

You would then hide the root node, so the user can start browsing the file system:

```
treeView.setShowRoot(false);
```

Then set a cell factory that displays only the name of the file instead of its path. If you want to see the path of all the files, you may comment the statement setting the cell factory:

```
// Set a cell factory to display only file name
treeView.setCellFactory(...);
```

Listing 14-8. A File System Browser

```
// FileSystemBrowser.java
package com.jdojo.control;

import java.nio.file.Path;
import java.nio.file.Paths;
import javafx.application.Application;
import javafx.scene.Scene;
import javafx.scene.control.TreeCell;
import javafx.scene.control.TreeView;
import javafx.scene.layout.HBox;
import javafx.stage.Stage;

public class FileSystemBrowser extends Application {
    public static void main(String[] args) {
        Application.launch(args);
    }

    @Override
    public void start(Stage stage) {
        // Create a root node using the current directory.
        PathTreeItem rootNode = new PathTreeItem(Paths.get("."));
        TreeView<Path> treeView = new TreeView<>(rootNode);
        treeView.setShowRoot(false);

        // Set a cell factory to display only file name
        treeView.setCellFactory((TreeView<Path> tv) -> {
            TreeCell<Path> cell = new TreeCell<Path>() {
                @Override
                public void updateItem(Path item, boolean empty) {
                    super.updateItem(item, empty);
                    if (item != null && !empty) {
                        Path fileName = item.getFileName();
```

```
                                            if (fileName == null) {
                                                    this.setText(item.toString());
                                            } else {
                                                    this.setText(fileName.toString());
                                            }
                                            this.setGraphic(
                                            this.getTreeItem().getGraphic());
                                } else {
                                            this.setText(null);
                                            this.setGraphic(null);
                                }
                        }
                };
                return cell;
        });

        HBox root = new HBox(treeView);
        root.setStyle("-fx-padding: 10;" +
                        "-fx-border-style: solid inside;" +
                        "-fx-border-width: 2;" +
                        "-fx-border-insets: 5;" +
                        "-fx-border-radius: 5;" +
                        "-fx-border-color: blue;");

        Scene scene = new Scene(root);
        stage.setScene(scene);
        stage.setTitle("File System Browser");
        stage.show();
    }
}
```

Scrolling to a *TreeItem*

TreeView automatically provides vertical and horizontal scrollbars when needed. Users can use the scrollbars to scroll to a specific item. Sometimes you may need programmatic support for scrolling. For example, when you add a TreeItem to a TreeView, you may want the TreeItem visible to the user by scrolling it to the view. Use the scrollTo(int rowIndex) method of the TreeView class to scroll the TreeItem at the specified rowIndex to the view. You can get the row index of a TreeItem using the getRow(TreeItem<T> item) method.

TreeView fires a ScrollToEvent when there is a request to scroll to a row index using the scrollTo() method. The ScrollToEvent class contains a getScrollTarget() method that returns the row index that was passed to the scrollTo() method.

■ **Tip** The ScrollToEvent is not fired when the user scrolls using the vertical scrollbar. It is fired when the scrollTo() method is used to scroll.

The following snippet of code sets a ScrollToEvent handler for a TreeView that prints the TreeItem and its row index to which the scrolling was requested:

```
TreeView<String> treeView = new TreeView<String>();
...
treeView.setOnScrollTo(e -> {
        int rowIndex = e.getScrollTarget();
        TreeItem<String> item = treeView.getTreeItem(rowIndex);
        System.out.println("Scrolled to: " + item.getValue() + at " + rowIndex);
});
```

TreeView Selection Model

TreeView uses a selection model to select one or multiple TreeItems. The selectionModel property represents the selection model. The default selection model is an instance of the abstract class MultipleSelectionModel. The following snippet of code enables multiple selection. Press the Ctrl or Shift key while clicking a node to select multiple nodes.

```
TreeView<String> treeView = new TreeView<>();;

// Enable mutiple selection for the TreeView
treeView.getSelectionModel().setSelectionMode(SelectionMode.MULTIPLE);
```

Please refer to the API documentation of the MultipleSelectionModel class for more details on how to select TreeItems and how to get the selected TreeItems.

Styling *TreeView* with CSS

The default CSS style-class name for a TreeView is tree-view. TreeView does not add any CSS pseudo-classes or properties. It inherits them from the Control.

A TreeView uses instances of TreeCell to display the TreeItems. Mostly you style the TreeCells in the TreeView. The default CSS style-class for TreeCell is tree-cell.

TreeCell contains an -fx-indent property, which is the amount of space to multiply by the level of the cell to get its left margin. The default value is 10px.

TreeCell supports two CSS pseudo-classes:

- expanded
- collapsed

The expanded pseudo-class is applied when the cell is expanded. The collapsed pseudo-class applies when the cell is not expanded.

The following style sets the text color to blue and font size to 10pt for a TreeCell:

```
.tree-cell {
        -fx-text-fill: blue;
        -fx-font-size: 10pt;
}
```

The style-class name for the disclosure node in a cell is `tree-disclosure-node`. It has a substructure named `arrow`, which is the triangle showing the expanded state of the node. You can change the triangle to a plus or minus sign icon using the following styles. The code assumes that the image files are in the same directory as the CSS file containing the styles:

```
.tree-cell .tree-disclosure-node .arrow {
        -fx-shape: null;
        -fx-background-color: null;
        -fx-background-image: url("plus_sign.jpg");
}

.tree-cell:expanded .tree-disclosure-node .arrow {
        -fx-shape: null;
        -fx-background-color: null;
        -fx-background-image: url("minus_sign.jpg");
}
```

You can also set the shape of the disclosure node in CSS using the SVG path. The following code sets plus and minus signs as the disclosure nodes for expanded and collapsed nodes, respectively. Figure 14-5 shows a TreeView using these styles.

```
.tree-cell .tree-disclosure-node .arrow {
        -fx-shape: "M0 -0.5 h2 v2 h1 v-2 h2 v-1 h-2 v-2 h-1 v2 h-2 v1z";
}

.tree-cell:expanded .tree-disclosure-node .arrow {
        -fx-shape: "M0 -0.5 h5 v-1 h-5 v1z";
        -fx-padding: 4 0.25 4 0.25;
}
```

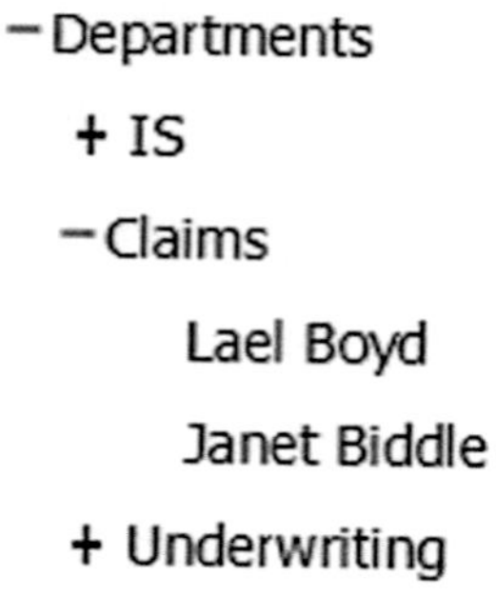

– Departments

    + IS

    – Claims

        Lael Boyd

        Janet Biddle

    + Underwriting

Figure 14-5. *A TreeView using plus and minus signs for expanded and collapsed disclosure nodes*

Summary

A TreeView is a control that displays hierarchical data in a tree-like structure. You can think of a TreeView as displaying a tree upside down—the root of the tree being at the top. Each item in a TreeView is an instance of the TreeItem class. TreeItems form parent-child relationships. A TreeItem is also referred to as a node. The TreeItem class does not inherit from the Node class. Therefore, a TreeItem is not a JavaFX Node and it cannot be added to a scene graph. A TreeItem is categorized as a branch or leaf node. If a TreeItem contains other instances of TreeItem, which are called its children, it is called a branch node. Otherwise, it is called a leaf node. A branch node can be in an expanded or collapsed state.

A TreeItem serves as the data model in a TreeView. Each TreeItem uses an instance of the TreeCell class to render its value. TreeCells in a TreeView can be customized using a cell factory. By default, a TreeCell is not editable.

TreeView is a virtualized control. It creates only as many instances of TreeCell as needed to display the items for its current height. Cells are recycled as you scroll through items. Virtualization makes it possible to use TreeView for viewing very large number of items without using a large amount of memory. Note, however, that loading TreeItems always takes memory. Virtualization helps only in viewing the items by recycling the cells used in viewing them.

The first item in a TreeView that does not have a parent is known as the root node. By default, the root node is visible. Calling the setShowRoot(false) method of the TreeView hides the root node. Hiding the root node makes traversing the TreeView a little easier because the user has one less level of indentation to traverse. Hiding the root node shows its child nodes at the first level.

A TreeItem fires events as it is modified, for example, by adding or removing children or expanding or collapsing. An instance of the TreeModificationEvent class, which is a static inner class of the TreeItem class, represents all kinds of modification events.

Adding and removing TreeItems is as easy as adding or removing them in the children list of their parents. The root node does not have a parent. To delete the root node, you need to set the root property of the TreeView to null.

TreeView uses a TreeCell to render a TreeItem. A TreeCell is an IndexedCell. You can visualize items in a TreeView from top to bottom arranged in rows. Each row has exactly one item. Each item is given a row index. The first item, which is the root item, has an index of zero. The row indices are given only to the visible items. TreeView contains a read-only expandedItemCount property that is the number of visible items. Use the getExpandedItemCount() method to get the number of visible items. If a node above an item is expanded or collapsed, the index of the item changes to reflect new visible items. The index of a TreeCell in a TreeView and the row index of an item are the same. Use the getIndex() method of the TreeCell or the getRow(TreeItem<T> item) method of the TreeView to get the row index of an item. A TreeCell is a Labeled control. By default, it uses the following rules to render its TreeItem: If the value in the TreeItem is an instance of the Node class, the value is displayed using the graphic property of the cell. Otherwise, the toString() method of the value is called and the returned string is displayed using the text property of the cell.

A cell in a TreeView can be editable. An editable cell may switch between editing and nonediting mode. In editing mode, cell data can be modified by the user. For a cell to enter editing mode, the TreeView must be editable. TreeView has an editable property, which can be set to true using the setEditable(true) method. By default, TreeView is not editable. Creating a TreeView does not let you edit its cells. Cell-editing capability is provided through specialized implementations of the TreeCell class. The JavaFX library provides some of these implementations. Set the cell factory for a TreeView, which is a Callback object, to use one of the following implementations of the TreeCell to make cells in a TreeView editable: CheckBoxTreeCell, ChoiceBoxTreeCell, ComboBoxTreeCell, or TextFieldTreeCell.

TreeView lets you load all items at once or items on demand. TreeView automatically provides vertical and horizontal scrollbars when needed. TreeView uses a selection model to select one or multiple TreeItems. The selectionModel property represents the selection model. TreeView supports styling using CSS.

The next chapter will discuss the control called TreeTableView.

CHAPTER 15

■ ■ ■

Understanding *TreeTableView*

In this chapter, you will learn:

- What a TreeTableView is
- How to set up the model for a TreeTableView
- How to create a TreeTableView, add columns to it, and populate it with data
- How to sort data in a TreeTableView
- How to show and hide columns in a TreeTableView
- How to customize cells in a TreeTableView
- How to use the selection model of a TreeTableView
- How to edit data and add or delete rows in a TreeTableView

If you are not already familiar with TableView and TreeView controls, I suggest you review that before proceeding with this chapter.

What Is a *TreeTableView*?

The TreeTableView control combines the features of the TableView and TreeView controls. It displays a TreeView inside a TableView. A TreeView is used to view hierarchical data; a TableView is used to view tabular data. A TreeTableView is used to view hierarchical data in a tabular form, as shown in Figure 15-1.

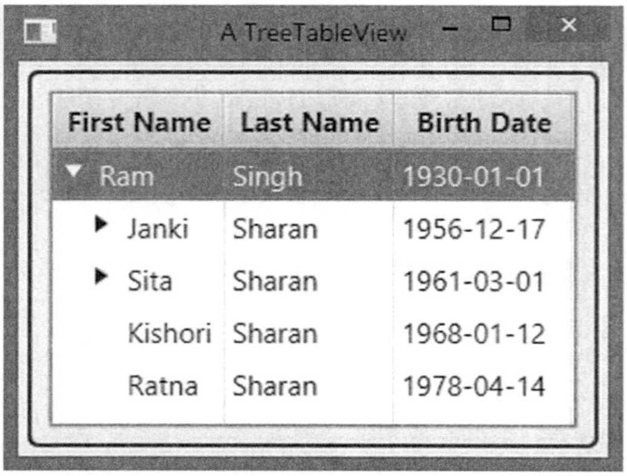

Figure 15-1. *A TreeTableView showing family hierarchy with details*

TreeTableView inherits from Control, not from TreeView or TableView. TreeTableView reuses most of the code used for TreeView and TableView. Most of the classes in the API are inherited from a common abstract base class for all three controls. For example, the TableColumn and TreeTableColumn classes are used to define columns in TableView and TreeTableView, respectively, and both are inherited from the TableColumnBase class.

TreeTableView API looks huge as it combines the APIs for both TreeView and TableView. However, if you are familiar with TreeView and TableView APIs, the TreeTableView API will look familiar to you. I will not discuss all features of TreeTableView, as they will be a repetition of what I have already discussed for TreeView and TableView. TreeTableView supports the following features:

- You can add multiple columns.

- You can have nested columns.

- You can resize columns at runtime.

- You can reorder columns at runtime.

- You can sort data on a single or multiple columns.

- You can add a context menu for columns.

- You can set a *cell value factory* for a column to populate its cells.

- You can set a *cell factory* for a column to customize its cells rendering.

- You can edit data in cells.

Model for *TreeTableView*

TreeItems provide the model in a TreeView. Each node in the TreeView derives its data from the corresponding TreeItem. Recall that you can visualize each node (or TreeItem) in a TreeView as a row with only one column.

An ObservableList provides the model in a TableView. Each item in the observable list provides data for a row in the TableView. A TableView can have multiple columns.

TreeTableView also uses a model for its data. Because it is a combination of TreeView and TableView, it has to decide which type of model it uses. It uses the model based on TreeView. That is, each row in a TreeTableView is defined by a TreeItem in a TreeView. TreeTableView supports multiple columns. Data for columns in a row are derived from the TreeItem for that row. Table 15-1 compares the model support for the three controls.

Table 15-1. *Comparing the Model Support for TreeView, TableView, and TreeTableView*

	TreeView	**TableView**	**TreeTableView**
Model	TreeItems	An ObservableList	TreeItems
Row	A TreeItem	An item from the ObservableList	A TreeItem
Column	Only one column	Multiple columns	Multiple columns

Creating a *TreeTableView*

An instance of the TreeTableView represents a TreeTableView control. The class takes a generic type argument, which is the type of the item contained in the TreeItems. Recall that TreeItems provide a model for a TreeTableView. The generic type of the controls and its TreeItems are the same.

The TreeTableView class provides two constructors. The default constructor creates a TreeTableView with no data. The following statement creates a TreeTableView of Person, which is shown in Figure 15-2. The control displays a placeholder, similar to the one shown by TableView. Like a TableView, TreeTableView contains a placeholder property, which is Node, and if you need to, you can supply your own placeholder:

```
// Create a TableView
TreeTableView<Person> treeTable = new TreeTableView<>();
```

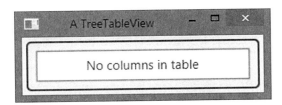

Figure 15-2. *A TreeTableView without a column and data*

An instance of the TreeTableColumn class represents a column in a TreeTableView. The getColumns() method of the TreeTableView class returns an ObservableList of TreeTableColumns, which are columns that are added to the TreeTableView. You need to add columns to this columns list. The following snippet of code creates three columns and adds them to the TreeTableView. The resulting TreeTableView is shown in Figure 15-3, which shows a placeholder stating that the content (or data/model) is missing.

```
// Create three columns
TreeTableColumn<Person, String> fNameCol = new TreeTableColumn<>("First Name");
TreeTableColumn<Person, String> lNameCol = new TreeTableColumn<>("Last Name");
TreeTableColumn<Person, String> bDateCol = new TreeTableColumn<>("Birth Date");

// Add columns to the TreeTableView
treeTable.getColumns().addAll(fNameCol, lNameCol, bDateCol);
```

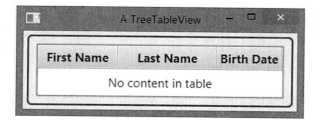

Figure 15-3. *A TreeTableView with three columns, but no content*

Now you need to supply data for the control. TreeTableView displays hierarchical data in tabular form. It requires you to construct a hierarchical model using TreeItems. You need to pass the root TreeItem to the TreeTableView. Like a TreeView, a TreeTableView contains a root property, which is the root TreeItem for the TreeView. The root property acts as a model for the TreeTableView to supply it data.

The following snippet of code creates a tree of some persons. The root TreeItem is set as the root of the TreeTableView. The resulting TreeTableView is shown in Figure 15-4.

```
// Create TreeItems
Person ram = new Person("Ram", "Singh", LocalDate.of(1930, 1, 1));
Person janki = new Person("Janki", "Sharan", LocalDate.of(1956, 12, 17));
Person sita = new Person("Sita", "Sharan", LocalDate.of(1961, 3, 1));
TreeItem<Person> rootNode =  new TreeItem<>(ram);
TreeItem<Person> jankiNode =  new TreeItem<>(janki);
TreeItem<Person> sitaNode =  new TreeItem<>(sita);

// Add children to the root node
rootNode.getChildren().addAll(jankiNode, sitaNode);

// Set the model for the TreeTableView
treeTable.setRoot(rootNode);
```

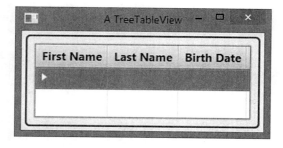

Figure 15-4. *A TreeTableView with columns, root node, but without cell value factory*

You have made progress! The placeholder has disappeared and you now see a disclosure node (a triangle) in the first column. However, you still do not see any data. You have columns and model (TreeItems). There is a missing link and the columns do not know how to extract data from the TreeItems. This is accomplished by setting the *cell value factory* for each column. Setting the cell value factory for a

TreeTableColumn is very similar to of the way you would for TableColumn. The following snippet of code sets the cell value factory for columns:

```
// Set the cell value factory for columns
fNameCol.setCellValueFactory(new TreeItemPropertyValueFactory<>("firstName"));
lNameCol.setCellValueFactory(new TreeItemPropertyValueFactory<>("lastName"));
bDateCol.setCellValueFactory(new TreeItemPropertyValueFactory<>("birthDate"));
```

A TreeItemPropertyValueFactory reads the specified property of the object stored in the value property of a TreeItem to populate the cells of the column. In the example, each TreeItem contains a Person object. The resulting TreeTableView is shown in Figure 15-5, after you expand the root node in the first column. The TreeTableView shows one row corresponding to each expanded TreeItem. If you collapse a node, the rows for its children nodes are hidden.

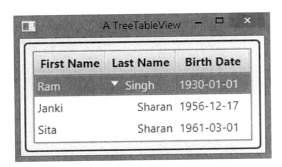

Figure 15-5. *A TreeTableView with data*

If you ignore the disclosure node and indentations in the first column, this is exactly how a TableView shows the data. The disclosure node and the indentations are features of the TreeView.

By default, a TreeTableView shows the disclosure node in the first column. You can show it in any other column using the treeColumn property. The following snippet of code shows the disclosure node in the Last Name column. The following snippet sets the treeColumn property to lNameCol, so the disclosure node is shown in the Last Name column, as shown in Figure 15-6.

```
// Show the disclosure node in the Last Name column
treeTable.setTreeColumn(lNameCol);
```

Figure 15-6. *A column other than the first column showing the disclosure node*

Another constructor of the TreeTableView class takes the value for its root property as an argument. You can use it as follows:

```
TreeTableView<Person> treeTable = new TreeTableView<Person>(rootNode);
```

You will be using data for a family tree as the model for most of the examples in this chapter. Let's use the reusable code for creating the mode and columns in a TreeTableUtil class as shown in Listing 15-1.The class consists of all static methods. The getModel() method constructs the family tree and returns the root node of the tree. All other methods create a column, set the cell value factory for the column, and return the column reference.

Listing 15-1. A Utility Class to Supply Model and Columns for a TreeTableView of Persons

```java
// TreeTableUtil.java
package com.jdojo.control;

import com.jdojo.mvc.model.Person;
import java.time.LocalDate;
import javafx.scene.control.TreeTableColumn;
import javafx.scene.control.TreeItem;
import javafx.scene.control.cell.TreeItemPropertyValueFactory;

public class TreeTableUtil {
    /* Returns a root TreeItem for a family members */
    @SuppressWarnings("unchecked")
    public static TreeItem<Person> getModel() {
        /* Create all persons */
        // First level
        Person ram = new Person("Ram", "Singh", LocalDate.of(1930, 1, 1));

        // Second level
        Person janki = new Person("Janki", "Sharan", LocalDate.of(1956, 12, 17));
        Person sita = new Person("Sita", "Sharan", LocalDate.of(1961, 3, 1));
        Person kishori = new Person("Kishori", "Sharan", LocalDate.of(1968, 1, 12));
        Person ratna = new Person("Ratna", "Sharan", LocalDate.of(1978, 4, 14));

        // Third level
        Person navin = new Person("Navin", "Sharan", LocalDate.of(1980, 5, 10));
        Person vandana = new Person("Vandana", "Sharan", LocalDate.of(1981, 3, 20));
        Person neeraj = new Person("Neeraj", "Sharan", LocalDate.of(1982, 6, 3));

        Person gaurav = new Person("Gaurav", "Sharan", LocalDate.of(1990, 8, 27));
        Person saurav = new Person("Saurav", "Sharan", LocalDate.of(1994, 5, 15));

        // Fourth level
        Person palak = new Person("Palak", "Sharan", LocalDate.of(2010, 6, 3));
        Person ashwin = new Person("Ashwin", "Sharan", LocalDate.of(2012, 10, 11));
        Person advik = new Person("Advik", "Sharan", LocalDate.of(2012, 10, 11));
```

```java
        // Build nodes
        TreeItem<Person> navinNode = new TreeItem<>(navin);
        navinNode.getChildren().addAll(new TreeItem<>(ashwin), new TreeItem<>(advik));
        TreeItem<Person> vandanaNode = new TreeItem<>(vandana);
        vandanaNode.getChildren().addAll(new TreeItem<>(palak));

        TreeItem<Person> jankiNode = new TreeItem<>(janki);
        jankiNode.getChildren().addAll(navinNode, new TreeItem<>(neeraj),vandanaNode);

        TreeItem<Person> sitaNode = new TreeItem<>(sita);
        sitaNode.getChildren().addAll(new TreeItem<>(gaurav), new TreeItem<>(saurav));

        TreeItem<Person> kishoriNode = new TreeItem<>(kishori);
        TreeItem<Person> ratnaNode = new TreeItem<>(ratna);

        // Create the root node and add children
        TreeItem<Person> rootNode = new TreeItem<>(ram);
        rootNode.getChildren().addAll(jankiNode, sitaNode, kishoriNode, ratnaNode);
        return rootNode;
}

/* Returns Person Id TreeTableColumn */
public static TreeTableColumn<Person, Integer> getIdColumn() {
        TreeTableColumn<Person, Integer> idCol = new TreeTableColumn<>("Id");
        idCol.setCellValueFactory(new TreeItemPropertyValueFactory<>("personId"));
        return idCol;
}

/* Returns First Name TreeTableColumn */
public static TreeTableColumn<Person, String> getFirstNameColumn() {
        TreeTableColumn<Person, String> fNameCol = new TreeTableColumn<>("First Name");
        fNameCol.setCellValueFactory(new TreeItemPropertyValueFactory<>("firstName"));
        return fNameCol;
}

/* Returns Last Name TreeTableColumn */
public static TreeTableColumn<Person, String> getLastNameColumn() {
        TreeTableColumn<Person, String> lNameCol = new TreeTableColumn<>("Last Name");
        lNameCol.setCellValueFactory(new TreeItemPropertyValueFactory<>("lastName"));
        return lNameCol;
}

/* Returns Birth Date TreeTableColumn */
public static TreeTableColumn<Person, LocalDate> getBirthDateColumn() {
        TreeTableColumn<Person, LocalDate> bDateCol =
                new TreeTableColumn<>("Birth Date");
        bDateCol.setCellValueFactory(new TreeItemPropertyValueFactory<>("birthDate"));
        return bDateCol;
}
```

```
        /* Returns Age Category TreeTableColumn */
        public static TreeTableColumn<Person, Person.AgeCategory> getAgeCategoryColumn() {
                TreeTableColumn<Person, Person.AgeCategory> bDateCol =
                        new TreeTableColumn<>("Age Category");
                bDateCol.setCellValueFactory(new TreeItemPropertyValueFactory<>("ageCategory"));
                return bDateCol;
        }
}
```

Listing 15-2 contains a complete program that shows how to create a TreeTableView. It uses the TreeTableUtil class to get the model and columns. Run the program and play with sorting, reordering, and resizing of the columns. Running the program results in a window as shown in Figure 15-7.

Listing 15-2. Using a TreeTableView

```java
// TreeTableViewTest.java
package com.jdojo.control;

import com.jdojo.mvc.model.Person;
import javafx.application.Application;
import javafx.scene.Scene;
import javafx.scene.control.TreeItem;
import javafx.scene.control.TreeTableView;
import javafx.scene.layout.HBox;
import javafx.stage.Stage;

public class TreeTableViewTest extends Application {
        public static void main(String[] args) {
                Application.launch(args);
        }

        @Override
        @SuppressWarnings("unchecked")
        public void start(Stage stage) {
                TreeItem<Person> rootNode = TreeTableUtil.getModel();
                rootNode.setExpanded(true);

                // Create a TreeTableView with model
                TreeTableView<Person> treeTable = new TreeTableView<>(rootNode);
                treeTable.setPrefWidth(400);

                // Add columns
                treeTable.getColumns().addAll(TreeTableUtil.getFirstNameColumn(),
                                        TreeTableUtil.getLastNameColumn(),
                                        TreeTableUtil.getBirthDateColumn(),
                                        TreeTableUtil.getAgeCategoryColumn());

                HBox root = new HBox(treeTable);
                root.setStyle("-fx-padding: 10;" +
                                "-fx-border-style: solid inside;" +
                                "-fx-border-width: 2;" +
```

```
                    "-fx-border-insets: 5;" +
                    "-fx-border-radius: 5;" +
                    "-fx-border-color: blue;");

        Scene scene = new Scene(root);
        stage.setScene(scene);
        stage.setTitle("Using a TreeTableView");
        stage.show();
    }
}
```

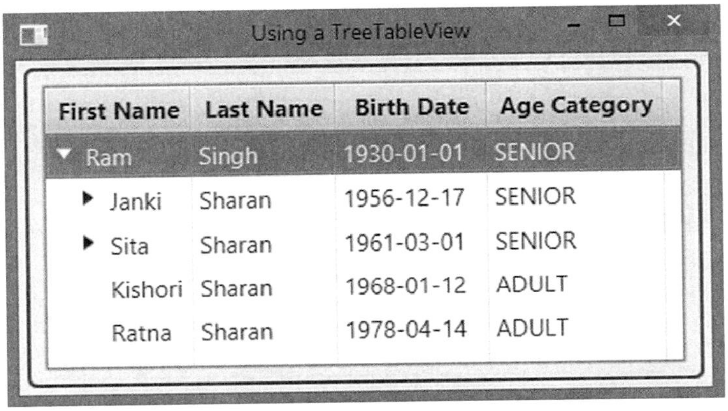

Figure 15-7. *A TreeTableView with its root node expanded*

Sorting Data in a *TreeTableView*

TreeTableView supports sorting the same way TableView supports sorting. Please refer to the sorting section of Chapter 14 for more in-depth discussion on sorting data. Note that the model for a TreeTableView is hierarchical. The hierarchy is always maintained whether or not the model is sorted. For example, the root node is always sorted at the top, irrespective of the sorting criteria used. Sorting in a TreeTableView is applied only to the immediate children of each branch node, thus maintaining the hierarchy.

Populating a *TreeTableColumn* with Data

The cellValueFactory property of the TreeTableColumn is responsible for populating cells in the column. It is a Callback object. The call() method receives an object of the CellDataFeatures class, which is an inner static class of the TreeTableColumn class, and returns an ObservableValue. The getValue() method of the CellDataFeatures class returns the reference of the TreeItem for the row. The following snippet of code creates an Age column and sets its cell value factory to compute the age in years of a Person using the birth date:

```
TreeTableColumn<Person, String> ageCol = new TreeTableColumn<>("Age");
ageCol.setCellValueFactory(cellData -> {
        Person p = cellData.getValue().getValue();
        LocalDate dob = p.getBirthDate();
        String ageInYear = "Unknown";
```

697

```
        if (dob != null) {
                long years = YEARS.between(dob, LocalDate.now());
                if (years == 0) {
                        ageInYear = "< 1 year";
                } else if (years == 1) {
                        ageInYear = years + " year";
                } else {
                        ageInYear = years + " years";
                }
        }
        return new ReadOnlyStringWrapper(ageInYear);
});
```

In Listing 15-1, you learned how to use a TreeItemPropertyValueFactory object to set a cell value factory if the values for a column come directly from a property of the TreeItem value. For an in-depth discussion of setting the cell value factory, please refer to Chapter 13, which discusses the TableView control.

Showing and Hiding Columns

Showing and hiding columns in a TreeTableView work the same way they do for TableView. By default, all columns in a TreeTableView are visible. The TreeTableColumn class has a visible property to set the visibility of a column. If you turn off the visibility of a parent column, a column with nested columns, all its nested columns will become invisible. The following code shows this:

```
TreeTableColumn<Person, String> idCol = new TreeTableColumn<>("Id");

// Make the Id column invisible
idCol.setVisible(false);
...
// Make the Id column visible
idCol.setVisible(true);
```

Sometimes you may want to let the user control the visibility of columns. The TreeTableView class has a tableMenuButtonVisible property. If it is set to true, a menu button is displayed in the header area. Clicking the Menu button displays a list of all leaf columns. Columns are displayed as radio menu items that can be used to toggle their visibility.

Customizing Data Rendering in Cells

A cell in a TreeTableColumn is an instance of the TreeTableCell class, which displays the data in the cell. A TreeTableCell is a Labeled control, which is capable of displaying text, a graphic, or both.

You can specify a cell factory for a TreeTableColumn. The job of a cell factory is to render the data in the cell. The TreeTableColumn class contains a cellFactory property, which is a Callback object. Its call() method is passed in the reference of the TreeTableColumn to which the cell belongs. The method returns an instance of TreeTableCell. The updateItem() method of the TreeTableCell is overridden to provide the custom rendering of the cell data.

TreeTableColumn uses a default cell factory if its cellFactory property is not specified. The default cell factory displays the cell data depending on the type of the data. If the cell data is a Node, the data are displayed in the graphic property of the cell. Otherwise, the toString() method of the cell data is called and the retuned string is displayed in the text property of the cell.

You can display formatted birth dates in the Birth Date column in the previous example. The Birth Date column is formatted as yyyy-mm-dd, which is the default ISO date format returned by the toString() method of the LocalDate class. You may want to format birth dates in the mm/dd/yyyy format. You can achieve this by setting a custom cell factory for the column, as shown in the following code:

```
TreeTableColumn<Person, LocalDate> birthDateCol = TreeTableUtil.getBirthDateColumn();
birthDateCol.setCellFactory (col -> {
        TreeTableCell<Person, LocalDate> cell = new TreeTableCell<Person, LocalDate>() {
                @Override
                public void updateItem(LocalDate item, boolean empty) {
                        super.updateItem(item, empty);

                        // Cleanup the cell before populating it
                        this.setText(null);
                        this.setGraphic(null);

                        if (!empty) {
                                // Format the birth date in mm/dd/yyyy format
                                String formattedDob =
                                DateTimeFormatter.ofPattern("MM/dd/yyyy").format(item);
                                this.setText(formattedDob);
                        }
                }
        };
        return cell;
});
```

You can use the above technique to display images in cells. In the updateItem() method, create an ImageView object for the image and display it using the setGraphic() method of the TreeTableCell.

TableCell contains tableColumn, tableRow, and tableView properties that store the references of its TableColumn, TableRow, and TableView, respectively. These properties are useful to access the item in the data model that represents the row for the TableCell.

TreeTableCell contains tableColumn, tableRow, and treeTableView properties that store the references of its TreeTableColumn, TreeTableRow, and TreeTableView, respectively. These properties are useful to access the item in the model that represents the row for the cell.

The following subclasses of TreeTableCell render cell data in different ways. For example, a CheckBoxTreeTableCell renders cell data in a CheckBox and a ProgressBarTreeTableCell renders a number using a ProgressBar:

- CheckBoxTreeTableCell

- ChoiceBoxTreeTableCell

- ComboBoxTreeTableCell

- ProgressBarTreeTableCell

- TextFieldTreeTableCell

The CheckBox, ChoiceBox, ComboBox, and TextField versions of the XxxTreeTableCell are used to edit data in cells. I will discuss how to edit data in a TreeTableCell shortly.

The following snippet of code creates a computed column. It sets the cell factory for the column to display a CheckBox. If the Person falls in the baby age category, the CheckBox is selected.

```
// Create a "Baby?" column
TreeTableColumn<Person, Boolean> babyCol = new TreeTableColumn<>("Baby?");
babyCol.setCellValueFactory(cellData -> {
        Person p = cellData.getValue().getValue();
        Boolean v =  (p.getAgeCategory() == Person.AgeCategory.BABY);
        return new ReadOnlyBooleanWrapper(v);
});

// Set a cell factory that will use a CheckBox to render the value
babyCol.setCellFactory(CheckBoxTreeTableCell.<Person>forTreeTableColumn(babyCol));
```

Selecting Cells and Rows in a *TreeTableView*

TreeTableView has a selection model represented by its property called selectionModel. A selection model is an instance of the TreeTableViewSelectionModel class, which is an inner static class of the TreeTableView class. The selection model supports cell-level and row-level selection. It also supports two selection modes: single and multiple. In the single selection mode, only one cell or row can be selected at a time. In the multiple-selection mode, multiple cells or rows can be selected. By default, single row selection is enabled. You can enable multirow selection using the following code:

```
TreeTableView<Person> treeTable = ...

// Turn on multiple-selection mode for the TreeTableView
TreeTableViewSelectionModel<Person> tsm = treeTable.getSelectionModel();
tsm.setSelectionMode(SelectionMode.MULTIPLE);
```

The cell-level selection can be enabled by setting the cellSelectionEnabled property of the selection model to true, as shown in the following snippet of code. When the property is set to true, the TreeTableView is put in cell-level selection mode and you cannot select an entire row. If multiple-selection mode is enabled, you can still select all cells in a row. However, the row itself is not reported as selected because the TreeTableView is in the cell-level selection mode. By default, cell-level selection mode is false.

```
// Enable cell-level selection
tsm.setCellSelectionEnabled(true);
```

The selection model provides information about the selected cells and rows. The isSelected(int rowIndex) method returns true if the row at the specified rowIndex is selected. Use the isSelected(int rowIndex, TableColumn<S,?> column) method to determine if a cell at the specified rowIndex and column is selected. The getModelItem(int rowIndex) method returns the TreeItem for the specified rowIndex.

The selection model provides several methods to select cells and rows and get the report of selected cells and rows. Please refer to the API documentation for the TreeTableViewSelectionModel class for more details.

It is often a requirement to make some changes or take an action when a cell or row selection changes in a TreeTableView. For example, a TreeTableView may act as a master list in a master-detail data view. When the user selects a row in the master list, you want the data in the detail view to refresh. Several methods of the TreeTableViewSelectionModel class return an ObservableList of selected indices and items. If you are interested in handling the selection change event, you need to add a ListChangeListener to one of those `ObservableLists`. The following snippet of code adds a `ListChangeListener` to the `ObservableList` returned by the `getSelectedIndices()` method to track the row selection change in a `TreeTableView`:

```
TreeTableViewSelectionModel<Person> tsm = treeTable.getSelectionModel();
ObservableList<Integer> list = tsm.getSelectedIndices();

// Add a ListChangeListener
list.addListener((ListChangeListener.Change<? extends Integer> change) -> {
        System.out.println("Row selection has changed");
});
```

Editing Data in a *TableView*

A cell in a `TreeTableView` can be editable. An editable cell switches between editing and nonediting modes. In editing mode, cell data can be modified by the user. In order for a cell to enter editing mode, the `TreeTableView`, `TreeTableColumn`, and `TreeTableCell` must be editable. All three of them have an editable property, which can be set to true using the `setEditable(true)` method. By default, `TreeTableColumn` and `TreeTableCell` are editable. To make cells editable in a `TreeTableView`, you need to make the `TreeTableView` editable, as shown in the following code:

```
TreeTableView<Person> treeTable = ...
treeTable.setEditable(true);
```

The `TreeTableColumn` class supports three types of events:

- `onEditStart`
- `onEditCommit`
- `onEditCancel`

The `onEditStart` event is fired when a cell in the column enters editing mode. The `onEditCommit` event is fired when the user successfully commits the editing, for example, by pressing the Enter key in a `TextField`. The `onEditCancel` event is fired when the user cancels the editing, for example, by pressing the Esc key in a `TextField`. The events are represented by an object of the `TreeTableColumn.CellEditEvent` class. The event object encapsulates the old and new values in the cell, the `TreeItem` of the model being edited, `TreeTableColumn`, the `TreeTablePosition` indicating the cell position where the editing is happening, and the reference of the `TreeTableView`. Use the methods of the `CellEditEvent` class to get these values.

Making a `TreeTableView` editable does not let you edit its cell data. You need to do a little more of a plumbing job before you can edit data in cells. Cell editing capability is provided through specialized implementations of the `TreeTableCell` class. JavaFX library provides a few of these implementations. Set the cell factory for a column to use one of the following implementations of the `TreeTableCell` to edit cell data:

- `CheckBoxTreeTableCell`
- `ChoiceBoxTreeTableCell`
- `ComboBoxTreeTableCell`
- `TextFieldTreeTableCell`

Now let's look at an example of editing data using a TextField. Please refer to the corresponding section for the TableView control for an in-depth discussion of editing data using various controls and handling editing related events. The only difference between editing cells in TableView and TreeTableView is the cell classes you will need to use: TableView uses subclasses of TableCell that are named as XxxTableCell; TreeTableView uses subclasses of TreeTableCell that are named as XxxTreeTableCell.

The following snippet of code sets the cell factory for the First Name column to use a TextField to edit data in its cells:

```
TreeTableColumn<Person, String> fNameCol = TreeTableUtil.getFirstNameColumn();
fNameCol.setCellFactory(TextFieldTreeTableCell.<Person>forTreeTableColumn());
```

When editing nonstring data in cell, you need to provide a StringConverter. The following snippet of code sets a cell factory for a Birth Date column with a StringConverter, which converts a String to a LocalDate and vice versa. The column type is LocalDate. By default, the LocalDateStringConverter assumes a date format of mm/dd/yyyy:

```
TreeTableColumn<Person, LocalDate> birthDateCol = TreeTableUtil.getBirthDateColumn();
LocalDateStringConverter converter = new LocalDateStringConverter();
birthDateCol.setCellFactory(
        TextFieldTreeTableCell.<Person, LocalDate>forTreeTableColumn(converter));
```

The program in Listing 15-3 shows how to make cells in a TreeTableView editable. Run the program and click a cell twice (using two single clicks) to start editing data. Figure 15-8 shows the First Name cell in the third row in edit mode. When you are done editing, press the Enter key to commit the changes or press the Esc key to cancel editing.

Listing 15-3. Editing Data in a TreeTableView

```
// TreeTableViewEditing.java
package com.jdojo.control;

import com.jdojo.mvc.model.Person;
import java.time.LocalDate;
import javafx.application.Application;
import javafx.scene.Scene;
import javafx.scene.control.TreeItem;
import javafx.scene.control.TreeTableColumn;
import javafx.scene.control.TreeTableView;
import javafx.scene.control.cell.TextFieldTreeTableCell;
import javafx.scene.layout.HBox;
import javafx.stage.Stage;

public class TreeTableViewEditing extends Application {
        public static void main(String[] args) {
                Application.launch(args);
        }
```

```java
@Override
@SuppressWarnings("unchecked")
public void start(Stage stage) {
        // Create the model
        TreeItem<Person> rootNode = TreeTableUtil.getModel();
        rootNode.setExpanded(true);

        // Create a TreeTableView with a model
        TreeTableView<Person> treeTable = new TreeTableView<Person>(rootNode);
        treeTable.setPrefWidth(400);

        // Must make the TreeTableView editable
        treeTable.setEditable(true);

        // Set appropariate cell factories for
        TreeTableColumn<Person, String> fNameCol = TreeTableUtil.
        getFirstNameColumn();
        fNameCol.setCellFactory(TextFieldTreeTableCell.<Person>forTreeTableColumn());

        TreeTableColumn<Person, String> lNameCol =
                TreeTableUtil.getLastNameColumn();
        lNameCol.setCellFactory(TextFieldTreeTableCell.<Person>forTreeTableColumn());

        TreeTableColumn<Person, LocalDate> birthDateCol =
                TreeTableUtil.getBirthDateColumn();
        LocalDateStringConverter converter = new LocalDateStringConverter();
        birthDateCol.setCellFactory(
        TextFieldTreeTableCell.<Person, LocalDate>forTreeTableColumn(converter));

        // Add Columns
        treeTable.getColumns().addAll(fNameCol, lNameCol, birthDateCol);

        HBox root = new HBox(treeTable);
        root.setStyle("-fx-padding: 10;" +
                      "-fx-border-style: solid inside;" +
                      "-fx-border-width: 2;" +
                      "-fx-border-insets: 5;" +
                      "-fx-border-radius: 5;" +
                      "-fx-border-color: blue;");

        Scene scene = new Scene(root);
        stage.setScene(scene);
        stage.setTitle("Editing Data in a TreeTableView");
        stage.show();
    }
}
```

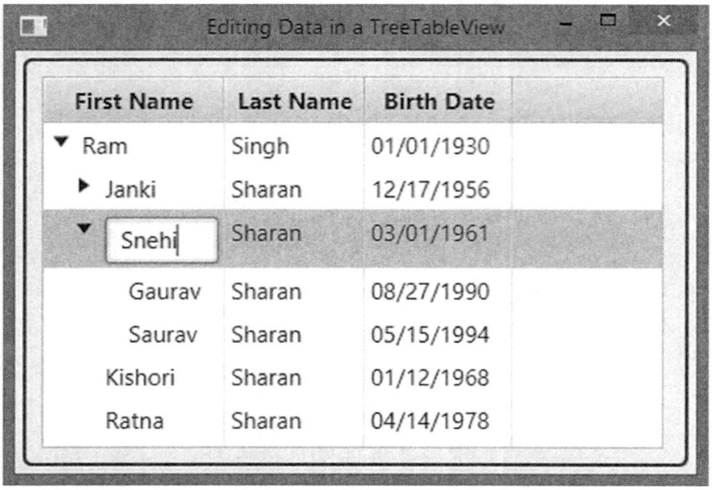

Figure 15-8. A cell in a TreeTableView *in edit mode*

Adding and Deleting Rows in a *TableView*

Each row in a TreeTableView is represented by a TreeItem in its model. Adding and deleting a row in a TreeTableView is as simple as adding and deleting TreeItems in the model.

The program in Listing 15-4 shows how to add and delete rows. It displays a prebuilt family hierarchy in a TreeTableView along with Add and Delete buttons, as shown in Figure 15-9. Clicking the Add button adds a new row as a child row for the selected row. If there is no row, a new root item is added to the tree. The new row is selected, scrolled to the view, and put in editing mode. The addRow() method contains the logic for adding a row. The Delete button deletes the selected row. Notice that all child rows of the selected row are deleted.

Listing 15-4. Adding and Deleting Rows in a TreeTableView

```java
// TreeTableViewAddDeleteRows.java
package com.jdojo.control;

import com.jdojo.mvc.model.Person;
import javafx.application.Application;
import javafx.scene.Scene;
import javafx.scene.control.Button;
import javafx.scene.control.TreeItem;
import javafx.scene.control.TreeTableColumn;
import javafx.scene.control.TreeTableView;
import javafx.scene.control.cell.TextFieldTreeTableCell;
import javafx.scene.layout.HBox;
import javafx.scene.layout.VBox;
import java.time.LocalDate;
import static javafx.scene.control.TreeTableView.TreeTableViewSelectionModel;
import javafx.scene.control.Label;
import javafx.stage.Stage;
```

```
public class TreeTableViewAddDeleteRows  extends Application {
        private final TreeTableView<Person> treeTable = new TreeTableView<>();

        public static void main(String[] args) {
                Application.launch(args);
        }

        @Override
        @SuppressWarnings("unchecked")
        public void start(Stage stage) {
                // Create the model
                TreeItem<Person> rootNode = TreeTableUtil.getModel();
                rootNode.setExpanded(true);
                treeTable.setRoot(rootNode);
                treeTable.setPrefWidth(400);
                treeTable.setEditable(true);
                treeTable.getSelectionModel().selectFirst();

                // Set appropariate cell factories for columns
                TreeTableColumn<Person, String> fNameCol = TreeTableUtil.getFirstNameColumn();
                fNameCol.setCellFactory(TextFieldTreeTableCell.<Person>forTreeTableColumn());

                TreeTableColumn<Person, String> lNameCol =
                                TreeTableUtil.getLastNameColumn();
                lNameCol.setCellFactory(TextFieldTreeTableCell.<Person>forTreeTableColumn());

                TreeTableColumn<Person, LocalDate> birthDateCol =
                                TreeTableUtil.getBirthDateColumn();
                LocalDateStringConverter converter = new LocalDateStringConverter();
                birthDateCol.setCellFactory(
                TextFieldTreeTableCell.<Person, LocalDate>forTreeTableColumn(converter));

                // Add Columns
                treeTable.getColumns().addAll(fNameCol, lNameCol, birthDateCol);

                // Add a placeholder to the TreeTableView.
                // It is displayed when the root node is deleted.
                treeTable.setPlaceholder(new Label("Click the Add button to add a row."));

                Label msgLbl = new Label("Please select a row to add/delete.");
                HBox buttons = this.getButtons();
                VBox root = new VBox(msgLbl, buttons, treeTable);
                root.setSpacing(10);
                root.setStyle("-fx-padding: 10;" +
                                "-fx-border-style: solid inside;" +
                                "-fx-border-width: 2;" +
                                "-fx-border-insets: 5;" +
                                "-fx-border-radius: 5;" +
                                "-fx-border-color: blue;");
```

```java
            Scene scene = new Scene(root);
            stage.setScene(scene);
            stage.setTitle("Adding/Deleting Rows in a TreeTableView");
            stage.show();
    }

    private HBox getButtons() {
            Button addBtn = new Button("Add");
            addBtn.setOnAction(e -> addRow());

            Button deleteBtn = new Button("Delete");
            deleteBtn.setOnAction(e -> deleteRow());

            return new HBox(20, addBtn, deleteBtn);
    }

    private void addRow() {
            if (treeTable.getExpandedItemCount() == 0 ) {
                    // There is no row in teh TreeTableView
                    addNewRootItem();
            } else if (treeTable.getSelectionModel().isEmpty()) {
                    System.out.println("Select a row to add.");
                    return;
            } else {
                    addNewChildItem();
            }
    }

    private void addNewRootItem() {
            // Add a root Item
            TreeItem<Person> item = new TreeItem<>(new Person("New", "New", null));
            treeTable.setRoot(item);

            // Edit the item
            this.editItem(item);
    }

    private void addNewChildItem() {
            // Prepare a new TreeItem with a new Person object
            TreeItem<Person> item = new TreeItem<>(new Person("New", "New", null));

            // Get the selection model
            TreeTableViewSelectionModel<Person> sm = treeTable.getSelectionModel();

            // Get the selected row index
            int rowIndex = sm.getSelectedIndex();

            // Get the selected TreeItem
            TreeItem<Person> selectedItem = sm.getModelItem(rowIndex);
```

```
            // Add the new item as children to the selected item
            selectedItem.getChildren().add(item);

            // Make sure the new item is visible
            selectedItem.setExpanded(true);

            // Edit the item
            this.editItem(item);
    }

    private void editItem(TreeItem<Person> item) {
            // Scroll to the new item
            int newRowIndex = treeTable.getRow(item);
            treeTable.scrollTo(newRowIndex);

            // Put the first column in editing mode
            TreeTableColumn<Person, ?> firstCol = treeTable.getColumns().get(0);
            treeTable.getSelectionModel().select(item);
            treeTable.getFocusModel().focus(newRowIndex, firstCol);
            treeTable.edit(newRowIndex, firstCol);
    }

    private void deleteRow() {
            // Get the selection model
            TreeTableViewSelectionModel<Person> sm = treeTable.getSelectionModel();
            if (sm.isEmpty()) {
                    System.out.println("Select a row to delete.");
                    return;
            }

            int rowIndex = sm.getSelectedIndex();
            TreeItem<Person> selectedItem = sm.getModelItem(rowIndex);

            TreeItem<Person> parent = selectedItem.getParent();
            if (parent != null) {
                    parent.getChildren().remove(selectedItem);
            } else {
                    // Must be deleting the root item
                    treeTable.setRoot(null);
            }
    }
}
```

Figure 15-9. *A TreeTableView allowing users to add or delete rows*

Scrolling in a *TreeTableView*

TreeTableView automatically provides vertical and horizontal scrollbars when rows or columns fall beyond the available space. Users can use the scrollbars to scroll to a specific row or column. Sometimes you may need to add programmatic support for scrolling. For example, when you append a row to a TreeTableView, you may want to scroll the new row to the view. The TreeTableView class contains three methods that can be used to scroll to a specific row or column:

- scrollTo(int rowIndex)
- scrollToColumn(TreeTableColumn<S,?> column)
- scrollToColumnIndex(int columnIndex)

The scrollTo() method scrolls the row with the specified rowIndex to the view. The scrollToColumn() and scrollToColumnIndex() methods scroll to the specified column and columnIndex, respectively.

TreeTableView fires a ScrollToEvent when there is a request to scroll to a row or column using one of the above-mentioned scrolling methods. The ScrollToEvent class contains a getScrollTarget() method that returns the row index or the column reference, depending on the scroll type, as shown in the following code:

```
TreeTableView<Person> treeTable = ...

// Add a ScrollToEvent for row scrolling
treeTable.setOnScrollTo(e -> {
        int rowIndex = e.getScrollTarget();
        System.out.println("Scrolled to row " + rowIndex);
});
```

```
// Add a ScrollToEvent for column scrolling
treeTable.setOnScrollToColumn(e -> {
        TreeTableColumn<Person, ?> column = e.getScrollTarget();
        System.out.println("Scrolled to column " + column.getText());
});
```

■ **Tip** The ScrollToEvent is not fired when the user scrolls through the rows and columns. It is fired when you call one of the scrolling-related methods of the TreeTableView class.

Styling *TreeTableView* with CSS

You can style a TreeTableView and all its parts, for example, column headers, cells, and placeholders. Applying the CSS to TreeTableView is very complex and broad in scope. This section covers a brief overview of CSS styling for TreeTableView. The default CSS style-class name for a TreeTableView is *tree-table-view*. The default CSS style-class names for a cell, a row, and a column header are *tree-table-cell*, *tree-table-row-cell*, and *column-header*, respectively. The following code shows how to set the font for cells and set the font size and text color for column headers in a TreeTableView:

```
/* Set the font for the cells */
.tree-table-row-cell {
        -fx-font-size: 10pt;
        -fx-font-family: Arial;
}

/* Set the font size and text color for column headers */
.tree-table-view .column-header .label {
        -fx-font-size: 10pt;
        -fx-text-fill: blue;
}
```

TreeTableView supports the following CSS pseudo-classes:

- cell-selection
- row-selection
- constrained-resize

The cell-selection pseudo-class is applied when the cell-level selection is enabled, whereas the row-selection pseudo-class is applied for row-level selection. The constrained-resize pseudo-class is applied when the column resize policy is CONSTRAINED_RESIZE_POLICY.

You can also set the shape of the disclosure node in CSS using the SVG path. The following styles set plus and minus signs as the disclosure nodes for expanded and collapsed nodes, respectively:

```
tree-table-row-cell .tree-disclosure-node .arrow {
        -fx-shape: "M0 -0.5 h2 v2 h1 v-2 h2 v-1 h-2 v-2 h-1 v2 h-2 v1z";
}

.tree-table-row-cell:expanded .tree-disclosure-node .arrow {
        -fx-shape: "M0 -0.5 h5 v-1 h-5 v1z";
        -fx-padding: 4 0.25 4 0.25;
}
```

A TreeTableView contains all substructures of a TableView. Please refer to the discussion on styling a TableView with CSS and Modena.css for more details.

Summary

The TreeTableView control combines the features of the TableView and TreeView controls. It displays a TreeView inside a TableView. A TreeView is used to view hierarchical data. A TableView is used to view tabular data. A TreeTableView is used to view hierarchical data in a tabular form. TreeTableView can be thought of as a nested table or a drill-down table.

An instance of the TreeTableColumn class represents a column in a TreeTableView. The getColumns() method of the TreeTableView class returns an ObservableList of TreeTableColumns, which are the columns added to the TreeTableView. You need to add columns to this columns list.

TreeItems act as models in a TreeView. Each node in the TreeView derives its data from the corresponding TreeItem. Recall that you can visualize each node (or TreeItem) in a TreeView as a row with only one column. An ObservableList provides the model in a TableView. Each item in the observable list provides data for a row in the TableView. A TableView can have multiple columns. TreeTableView also uses models for its data. Because it is a combination of TreeView and TableView, it has to decide which type of model it uses. It uses the model based on TreeView. That is, each row in a TreeTableView is defined by a TreeItem in a TreeView. TreeTableView supports multiple columns. Data for columns in a row are derived from the TreeItem for that row.

An instance of the TreeTableView represents a TreeTableView control. The class takes a generic type argument, which is the type of the item contained in the TreeItems. Recall that TreeItems provide the model for a TreeTableView. The generic type of the controls and its TreeItems are the same.

The TreeTableView class provides two constructors. The default constructor creates a TreeTableView with no data. The control displays a placeholder, similar to the one shown by TableView. Like a TableView, TreeTableView contains a placeholder property, which is Node, and if you need to, you can supply your own placeholder. You can add columns and data to a TreeTableView. TreeTableView supports sorting the same way TableView supports sorting.

Showing and hiding columns in a TreeTableView work the same way they do for TableView. By default, all columns in a TreeTableView are visible. The TreeTableColumn class has a visible property to set the visibility of a column. If you turn off the visibility of a parent column, a column with nested columns, all its nested columns will be invisible.

TreeTableView lets you customize rendering of its cells, using different selection models for its cells and rows. It also allows editing data in its cells and adding and deleting rows. You can also style TreeTableView using CSS.

The next chapter will discuss how to use the WebView node to browse web pages.

■ ■ ■

CHAPTER 16

Browsing Web Pages

In this chapter, you will learn:

- What WebView is
- What components are used with WebView
- How to create a web browser
- How to access the browsing history
- How to execute JavaScript code from JavaFX and vice versa
- How to access the web page DOM
- How to set User-Agent HTTP headers
- How to set a user style for the web page and how to style WebView with CSS

What Is a *WebView*?

JavaFX provides a web component that can be used as an embedded web browser in a JavaFX application. It is based on WebKit, which is an open source web browser engine. It supports:

- Viewing HTML5 content with CSS and JavaScript
- Access to the DOM of the HTML content
- Browsing history maintenance
- Executing JavaScript code from JavaFX and vice versa

The component handles most of the work of web browsing, for example, rendering the HTML content, maintaining a history of the visited web pages, navigating to a URL when links are clicked, displaying pop-up contents, among others. You would need to write code to handle other web-related features, for example, displaying an alert, prompt, or confirmation dialog using JavaScript. I will discuss all of the features of this component in this chapter.

The web browser component comprises a simple API consisting of a few classes in the javafx.scene.web package:

- WebView
- WebEngine
- WebHistory

- WebHistory.Entry
- WebEvent
- PopupFeatures
- PromptData

The WebView class inherits from the Parent class. It is a node, not a control. It is added to a scene graph for viewing web pages using local or remote URLs. A WebView displays one web page at a time and it can be styled using a CSS.

A WebView uses a WebEngine for the core processing of its content. A WebEngine manages one web page at a time. The WebView handles user input events such as mouse and keyboard events and other tasks, for example, loading the web page content, applying a CSS, and creating a DOM, that are performed by the WebEngine. When using a WebView component, you will be working with its WebEngine most of the time.

A WebEngine maintains the browsing history of all visited web pages for a session in an instance of the WebHistory class. An instance of the inner class WebHistory.Entry represents an entry in the browsing history. An instance of the WebEvent class represents an event generated by a WebEngine while it processes a web page. Examples of such events are a resized event that occurs when JavaScript running on a web page resizes or moves the window, an alert event that occurs when JavaScript running on the web page calls the window.alert() function, among others.

When JavaScript running on a web page opens a pop-up window, an instance of the PopupFeatures class encapsulates the details of the pop-up window The WebEngine lets you register a pop-up handler to handle the displaying of the pop-up window.

An instance of the PromptData class encapsulates the details of a prompt window (a message and an initial value) displayed by JavaScript code using the window.prompt() function. The WebEngine lets you register a prompt handler to handle the prompt. In the prompt handler, you can display a JavaFX dialog window to prompt the user for input. Figure 16-1 shows the architecture of the web browser component.

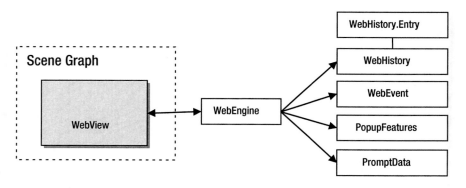

Figure 16-1. *Architecture of the web browser component*

Creating a Web Browser Component

An instance of the WebView class represents a web browser. The class contains only one constructor, which is a no-args constructor:

```
WebView webView = new WebView();
```

The constructor of the WebView class creates a WebEngine automatically and you cannot change it. The getEngine() method of the WebView class returns the reference of the WebEngine:

```
WebEngine webEngine = webView.getEngine();
```

A WebEngine can load content from a URL or a string in memory. You would use the load() method of the WebEngine class to load content from a URL. The URL is specified as a String. It can be a local or remote URL. You would use the reload() method of the WebEngine to reload the current page, as shown in the following code:

```
// Load the Google web page
webEngine.load("http://www.google.com");
```

You would use one of the loadContent() methods to load the content from a String:

- loadContent(String content)

- loadContent(String content, String contentType)

Typically, this method is used when the content is retrieved from a database or the content is constructed in memory. The first version assumes that the content type is "text/html".

```
// Load HTML Content
String html = "<html><head><title>Test</title></head>" +
              "<body><h1>Hello from WebView</h1></body></html>";
webEngine.loadContent(html);
```

```
// Load text content
String text = "WebView can display text content!";
webEngine.loadContent(text, "text/plain");
```

■ **Tip** The WebView component must be created in the JavaFX Application Thread. The load() and loadContent() methods of the WebEngine must also be called on the JavaFX Application Thread. Otherwise, a runtime exception is thrown.

WebEngine loads a web page asynchronously in the background threads using a Worker object. Submitting a request to load a web page before the previous request is fulfilled cancels the previous request. You can find the reference of the Worker object loading the web page using the getLoadWorker() method. You can observe the change in the state of the Worker by adding ChangeListener to its state property. The following snippet of code sets the title of a successfully loaded web page as the title of the stage showing the WebView:

```
import static javafx.concurrent.Worker.State;
...
Stage stage = ...
WebView webView = new WebView();
WebEngine webEngine = webView.getEngine();
```

```
// Set the title of the stage the same as the title of the loaded web page
webEngine.getLoadWorker().stateProperty().addListener(
        (ObservableValue<? extends State> p, State oldState,  State newState) -> {
            if (newState == State.SUCCEEDED) {
                    stage.setTitle(webView.getEngine().getTitle());
            }
});
```

The WebEngine class contains a title property, which is updated at some point while a web page is being loaded. You can achieve the same effect as above by listening to the change in the title property of the WebEngine:

```
webEngine.titleProperty().addListener(
        (ObservableValue<? extends String> p, String oldTitle, String newTitle) -> {
                stage.setTitle(newTitle);
});
```

The program in Listing 16-1 shows how to use a WebView component. The program is simple and uses the code that I have discussed so far. When you run the program, it opens the web page at http://www.google.com. Search for a keyword and click the links in the search result to navigate to different web pages. Notice that the title of the window changes as you navigate to different web pages. Navigating to other web pages by clicking links is a built-in feature of WebView.

Listing 16-1. Using a WebView to Display a Web Page

```
// WebViewTest.java
package com.jdojo.web;

import javafx.application.Application;
import javafx.beans.value.ObservableValue;
import javafx.scene.Scene;
import javafx.scene.layout.VBox;
import javafx.scene.web.WebView;
import javafx.stage.Stage;
import javafx.scene.web.WebEngine;

public class WebViewTest extends Application {
        public static void main(String[] args) {
                Application.launch(args);
        }

        @Override
        public void start(Stage stage) {
                WebView webView = new WebView();
                WebEngine webEngine = webView.getEngine();

                // Update the stage title when a new web page title is available
                webEngine.titleProperty().addListener((ObservableValue<? extends String> p,
                        String oldTitle, String newTitle) -> {
                                stage.setTitle(newTitle);
                });
```

```
                // Load the Google web page
                webEngine.load("http://www.google.com");

                VBox root = new VBox(webView);
                Scene scene = new Scene(root);
                stage.setScene(scene);
                stage.show();
        }
}
```

Setting Properties for a *WebView*

The WebView component comes with some built-in features. By default, it displays a context menu. The menu items in the context menu depend on the state of the component. For example, it shows a Go Back menu item when you have navigated to pages other than the first page and shows a Stop Loading menu item when the page is still being loaded. The standard text editing menu items (Cut, Copy, and Paste) are shown when text is selected or focus is in a text-editing field. You can set the contextMenuEnabled property to false to disable the context menu:

```
// Disable the context menu
webView.setContextMenuEnabled(false);
```

You can apply a scale factor for text using the fontScale property. It uses a double value number. For example, to make the text font 10% larger, set it to 1.10, and to make the text font 40% smaller, set it to 0.60. The default value is 1.0. Changing this property affects only the text in the web page, not images and other fixed-size elements. The following code would increase the font by 20%:

```
// Increase the text font size by 20%
webView.setFontScale(1.20);
```

You can apply a zoom factor to the content in the WebView using the zoom property. It also uses a double value number, as explained above. The default value is 1.0. Changing this property affects the entire content in WebView. The following code would change the zoom by 20%:

```
// Zoom 20%
webView.setZoom(1.20);
```

You can specify font smoothing of GRAY or LCD for onscreen text. The default value is LCD. The GRAY smoothing is suitable for graphics and animation. The LCD smoothing is suitable for small-sized text where legibility is important. A request for LCD text is treated as a hint, which may be ignored. The fontSmoothingType property specifies the font smoothing type. The property value is one of the constants (GRAY and LCD) of the FontSmoothingType enum, which is in the javafx.scene.text package. The following code sets font smoothing:

```
// Set font smoothing type to GRAY
webView.setFontSmoothingType(FontSmoothingType.GRAY);
```

The WebView class contains several other properties, which are related to setting its minimum, preferred, and maximum width and height.

Enhancing the Web Browser Application

In Listing 16-1, you had a very basic web browser. Let's enhance that browser to allow users to specify a URL and set options at runtime. The program in Listing 16-2 creates a WebOptionsMenu class for setting options for a WebView. It inherits from the MenuButton class. The constructor takes a WebView as an argument. Figure 16-2 shows an instance of the Options button showing the menu for the options. The class is simple to use; first create an instance for a WebView and add it to a layout pane:

```
WebView WebView = ...
MenuButton options = new WebOptionsMenu(webView);
```

Listing 16-2. Adding a MenuButton Containing Options for a WebView

```java
// WebOptionsMenu.java
package com.jdojo.web;

import javafx.beans.property.SimpleStringProperty;
import javafx.scene.control.CheckMenuItem;
import javafx.scene.control.Menu;
import javafx.scene.control.MenuButton;
import javafx.scene.control.MenuItem;
import javafx.scene.control.RadioMenuItem;
import javafx.scene.control.SeparatorMenuItem;
import javafx.scene.control.ToggleGroup;
import javafx.scene.web.WebView;
import static javafx.scene.text.FontSmoothingType.GRAY;
import static javafx.scene.text.FontSmoothingType.LCD;

public class WebOptionsMenu extends MenuButton {
        public WebOptionsMenu(WebView webView) {
                this.setText("Options");

                // Enabled Context Menu option
                CheckMenuItem ctxMenu = new CheckMenuItem("Enable Context Menu");
                ctxMenu.setSelected(true);
                webView.contextMenuEnabledProperty().bind(ctxMenu.selectedProperty());

                // Font Scale options
                Menu scalingMenu = new Menu("Font Scale");
                scalingMenu.textProperty().bind(
                                new SimpleStringProperty("Font Scale ")
                                .concat(webView.fontScaleProperty().multiply(100.0))
                                .concat("%"));
                MenuItem normalFontMenu = new MenuItem("Normal");
                MenuItem biggerFontMenu = new MenuItem("10% Bigger");
                MenuItem smallerFontMenu = new MenuItem("10% Smaller");
                normalFontMenu.setOnAction(e -> webView.setFontScale(1.0));
                biggerFontMenu.setOnAction(
                                e -> webView.setFontScale(webView.getFontScale() + 0.10));
```

```
smallerFontMenu.setOnAction(
                e -> webView.setFontScale(webView.getFontScale() - 0.10));
scalingMenu.getItems().addAll(normalFontMenu, biggerFontMenu, smallerFontMenu);

// Font Smoothing options
Menu smoothingMenu = new Menu("Font Smoothing");
RadioMenuItem grayMenu = new RadioMenuItem("GRAY");
grayMenu.setSelected(true);
RadioMenuItem lcdMenu = new RadioMenuItem("LCD");
grayMenu.setOnAction(e -> webView.setFontSmoothingType(GRAY));
lcdMenu.setOnAction(e -> webView.setFontSmoothingType(LCD));
new ToggleGroup().getToggles().addAll(lcdMenu, grayMenu);
smoothingMenu.getItems().addAll(grayMenu, lcdMenu);

// Zooming options
Menu zoomMenu = new Menu("Zoom");
zoomMenu.textProperty().bind(
                new SimpleStringProperty("Zoom ")
                .concat(webView.zoomProperty().multiply(100.0))
                .concat("%"));
MenuItem normalZoomMenu = new MenuItem("Normal");
MenuItem biggerZoomMenu = new MenuItem("10% Bigger");
MenuItem smallerZoomMenu = new MenuItem("10% Smaller");
normalZoomMenu.setOnAction(e -> webView.setZoom(1.0));
biggerZoomMenu.setOnAction(e -> webView.setZoom(webView.getZoom() + 0.10));
smallerZoomMenu.setOnAction(e -> webView.setZoom(webView.getZoom() - 0.10));
zoomMenu.getItems().addAll(normalZoomMenu, biggerZoomMenu, smallerZoomMenu);

// Enabled JavaScript option
CheckMenuItem scriptMenu = new CheckMenuItem("Enable JavaScript");
scriptMenu.setSelected(true);
webView.getEngine().javaScriptEnabledProperty()
                .bind(scriptMenu.selectedProperty());

// Add menus to the menu button
this.getItems().addAll(ctxMenu, scalingMenu,
                smoothingMenu, zoomMenu, new SeparatorMenuItem(), scriptMenu);
    }
}
```

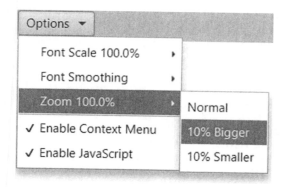

Figure 16-2. *A menu button showing options for a* WebView

Now let's create a reusable component for entering the URL of a new page. The code in Listing 16-3 creates a navigation bar, as shown in Figure 16-3. It boxes all the controls in an HBox. You need to pass the WebView for which the navigation will work, a home page URL, and a flag to indicate whether you want to navigate to the home page.

Listing 16-3. Adding a Navigation Bar with Navigation Options for a WebView

```java
// NavigationBar.java
package com.jdojo.web;

import java.io.File;
import java.net.MalformedURLException;
import javafx.beans.value.ObservableValue;
import javafx.scene.control.Button;
import javafx.scene.control.Label;
import javafx.scene.control.TextField;
import javafx.scene.layout.Priority;
import javafx.scene.layout.HBox;
import javafx.scene.web.WebEngine;
import javafx.scene.web.WebView;

import javafx.stage.FileChooser;
import javafx.stage.FileChooser.ExtensionFilter;

public class NavigationBar extends HBox {
        private FileChooser fileChooser = new FileChooser();

        public NavigationBar(WebView webView, String homePageUrl, boolean goToHomePage) {
                this.setSpacing(4);
                this.setStyle("-fx-background-color: lightblue;-fx-padding: 5;");

                WebEngine webEngine = webView.getEngine();
```

```java
TextField pageUrl = new TextField();
Button refreshBtn = new Button("Refresh");
Button goBtn = new Button("Go");
Button homeBtn = new Button("Home");
Button openBtn = new Button("Open");

// Let the TextField grow horizontallly
HBox.setHgrow(pageUrl, Priority.ALWAYS);

// Add an ActionListener to navigate to the entered URL
pageUrl.setOnAction(e -> webEngine.load(pageUrl.getText()));

// Update the URL in the TextField when user navigates to another page.
// for example, by clicking a link on the page
webEngine.locationProperty().addListener(
        (ObservableValue<? extends String> prop,
         String oldValue, String newValue) -> pageUrl.setText(newValue));

// Add an ActionListener for the Refresh button
refreshBtn.setOnAction(e -> webEngine.reload());

// Add an ActionListener for the Go Button
goBtn.setOnAction(e -> webEngine.load(pageUrl.getText()));

// Add an ActionListener for the Home Button
homeBtn.setOnAction(e -> webEngine.load(homePageUrl));

// Configure the FileChooser
fileChooser.setTitle("Open Web Content");
fileChooser.getExtensionFilters()
        .addAll(new ExtensionFilter("HTML Files", "*.html", "*.htm"));

// Add an ActionListener for the Open Button
openBtn.setOnAction(e -> {
    File selectedFile = fileChooser.showOpenDialog(webView.getScene().
    getWindow());
    if (selectedFile != null) {
            try {
                    webEngine.load(
                            selectedFile.toURI().toURL().toExternalForm());
            }
            catch(MalformedURLException e2) {
                    e2.printStackTrace();
            }
    }
});
```

```
                    this.getChildren().addAll(new Label("URL:"), pageUrl,
                                        goBtn, refreshBtn, homeBtn, openBtn);
                    if (goToHomePage) {
                            webEngine.load(homePageUrl);
                    }
            }
    }
}
```

Figure 16-3. *A web browser navigation bar*

The buttons on the navigation bar have the following functions:

- Enter a URL and press the Enter key to open the page or enter a URL and click the Go button to go to the page.

- Click the Refresh button to reload the current page.

- Click the Home button to go to the home page.

- Click the Open button to open an HTML file from the local file system.

With the NavigationBar and WebOptionsMenu classes, you can develop a basic web browser writing a few lines of code. The program in Listing 16-4 assembles the web browser components to build a basic web browser. It displays a window, as shown in Figure 16-4, with a navigation bar, options, and a WebView. You would use the navigation bar to open any local or remote web page. Later you will enhance this program to show the browsing history and add Back and Forward buttons.

Listing 16-4. Developing a Basic Web Browser with a Navigation Bar and an Options Menu

```
// BasicWebBrowser.java
package com.jdojo.web;

import javafx.application.Application;
import javafx.beans.value.ObservableValue;
import javafx.scene.Scene;
import javafx.scene.control.MenuButton;
import javafx.scene.layout.VBox;
import javafx.scene.web.WebView;
import javafx.stage.Stage;

public class BasicWebBrowser extends Application {
        public static void main(String[] args) {
                Application.launch(args);
        }

        @Override
        public void start(Stage stage) {
                WebView webView = new WebView();
```

```
        // Update the stage title when a new web page title is available
        webView.getEngine().titleProperty().addListener(
                (ObservableValue<? extends String> p, String oldTitle,
                 String newTitle) -> stage.setTitle(newTitle));

        // Load the Google web page
        String homePageUrl = "http://www.google.com";

        MenuButton options = new WebOptionsMenu(webView);
        NavigationBar navBar = new NavigationBar(webView, homePageUrl, true);
        navBar.getChildren().add(options);

        VBox root = new VBox(navBar, webView);
        Scene scene = new Scene(root);
        stage.setScene(scene);
        stage.show();
    }
}
```

Figure 16-4. *The window showing the basic web browser*

Accessing Browsing History

The WebEngine maintains the browsing history for a session. An instance of the WebHistory class represents the browsing history, which maintains an observable list of visited web pages as instances of the inner class WebHistory.Entry. You would use the getHistory() method of the WebEngine class to get its history object. The getEntries() method of a WebHistory returns an ObservableList<Entry>. The entries in the list are arranged from oldest to newest, that is, the first entry in the list is the page visited first.

An Entry provides the title, URL, and the last visited date of the visited page through its getTitle(), getUrl(), and getLastVisitedDate() methods, respectively. The following snippet of code prints the details of the browsing history of a WebEngine:

```
import javafx.scene.web.WebHistory;
import javafx.scene.web.WebHistory.Entry;
...
WebHistory history = webView.getEngine().getHistory();
ObservableList<Entry> entries = history.getEntries();
for(Entry entry : entries) {
        System.out.println("Title: " + entry.getTitle() +
                        ", URL: " + entry.getUrl() +
                        ", Last Visited: " + entry.getLastVisitedDate());
}
```

WebHistory has two properties:

- currentIndex

- maxSize

The currentIndex is a read-only int property that specifies the index of the current page in the list of visited pages. It changes as you visit different pages. The maxSize property specifies how many visited pages to keep in the history. The default is 100.

■ **Tip** Browsing history is maintained only for the current session. When you exit the JavaFX application, you lose the history. If you want to keep the history, you need to write code to save it to a file system or database.

The go(int offset) method of the WebHistory class navigates the WebEngine to the Entry object at the (currentIndex + offset) location in the list of visited web pages. For example, go(-1) and go(1) have the same effect as clicking the Back and Forward buttons, respectively, in a web browser. The go(0) call is ignored. The offset value must be between zero and (size - 1), which is the size of the number of entries in the WebHistory; otherwise, an IndexOutOfBoundsException is thrown. For example, if the currentIndex property is zero, you should not call go(-1) because the current web page is the last one visited.

The program in Listing 16-5 creates a component that can be used to browse the browsing history of a WebView. It creates a Back button, a Forward button, and a ComboBox to show the list of the titles of the visited pages. Figure 16-5 shows the added component. You can add this component to the navigation bar you developed in the previous section and you will then have a full browsing component for a WebView. The following snippet of code shows how to add the history-related controls to the navigation bar.

```
MenuButton options = new WebOptionsMenu(webView);
BrowserHistory historyComponent = new BrowserHistory(webView);
NavigationBar navBar = new NavigationBar(webView, homePageUrl, true);
navBar.getChildren().addAll(options, historyComponent);
```

Listing 16-5. Creating a Browsing History Navigation Component

```
// BrowserHistory.java
package com.jdojo.web;

import javafx.scene.control.Button;
import javafx.scene.control.ComboBox;
import javafx.scene.control.Label;
import javafx.scene.control.ListCell;
import javafx.scene.layout.HBox;
import javafx.scene.web.WebHistory;
import javafx.scene.web.WebHistory.Entry;
import javafx.scene.web.WebView;

public class BrowserHistory extends HBox {
        public BrowserHistory(WebView webView) {
                this.setSpacing(4);
                WebHistory history = webView.getEngine().getHistory();
                Button backBtn = new Button("Back");
                Button forwardBtn = new Button("Forward");
                backBtn.setDisable(true);
                forwardBtn.setDisable(true);

                // Add an ActionListener to the Back and Forward butons
                backBtn.setOnAction(e -> history.go(-1));
                forwardBtn.setOnAction(e -> history.go(1));

                // Add an  ChangeListener to the currentIndex property
                // to enable/disable Back and Forard buttons
                history.currentIndexProperty().addListener((p, oldValue, newValue) -> {
                        int currentIndex = newValue.intValue();
                        if (currentIndex <= 0) {
                                backBtn.setDisable(true);
                        } else {
                                backBtn.setDisable(false);
                        }

                        if (currentIndex >= history.getEntries().size()) {
                                forwardBtn.setDisable(true);
                        } else {
                                forwardBtn.setDisable(false);
                        }
                });
```

723

```
                    // Create the history list dropdown
                    ComboBox<Entry> historyList = new ComboBox<>();
                    historyList.setPrefWidth(150);
                    historyList.setItems(history.getEntries());

                    // Set a cell factory to to show only the page title in the history list
                    historyList.setCellFactory(entry -> {
                            ListCell<Entry> cell = new ListCell<Entry>() {
                                    @Override
                                    public void updateItem(Entry item, boolean empty) {
                                            super.updateItem(item, empty);
                                            if (empty) {
                                                    this.setText(null);
                                                    this.setGraphic(null);
                                            } else {
                                                    String pageTitle = item.getTitle();
                                                    this.setText(pageTitle);
                                            }
                                    }
                            };
                            return cell;
                    });

                    // Let the user navigate to a page using the history list
                    historyList.setOnAction(e -> {
                            int currentIndex = history.getCurrentIndex();
                            Entry selectedEntry = historyList.getValue();
                            int selectedIndex = historyList.getItems().indexOf(selectedEntry);
                            int offset = selectedIndex - currentIndex;
                            history.go(offset);
                    });

                    this.getChildren().addAll(backBtn, forwardBtn, new Label("History:"),
                    historyList);
            }
    }
```

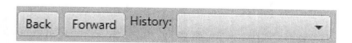

Figure 16-5. *The added browsing history component*

Handling JavaScript UI Requests

JavaScript running on a web page may request user interface operations, for example, open a pop-up window, change the status message, show an alert dialog, among others. For most of the requests, a WebEngine does not perform any action. You need to add a Callback or an event handler to the WebEngine for handling such operations. Table 16-1 shows the list of methods and properties of the window object in JavaScript and the corresponding properties of the WebEngine.

Table 16-1. *The JavaScript Operations on the window Object and the Corresponding WebEngine Handlers*

JavaScript *window* Object Method/Property	*WebEngine* Property	Comments
alert()	onAlert	Use a WebEvent<String> handler to show the alert.
confirm()	onConfirm	Use a Callback to show the confirmation dialog.
open()	createPopupHandler	Shows the pop-up web page in the same WebEngine. Use a Callback to show the pop-up window in a different WebEngine or block the pop-up.
open() and close()	onVisibilityChanged	Use a WebEvent<Boolean> handler to handle the visibility change of the JavaScript window.
prompt()	promptHandler	Use a Callback to show the prompt dialog.
status	onStatusChanged	Use a WebEvent<String> handler to handle the change in the status property.
innerWidth, innerHeight, outerWidth, outerHeight, screenX, screenY, screenLeft, screenTop	onResized	Use a WebEvent<Rectangle2D> handler to handle the change in the any of these properties.

When a method of the JavaScript window object is called, the WebEngine does nothing, except when a pop-up is shown using the window.open() method. The pop-up is displayed by the same WebEngine. If the WebEngine is associated with a WebView, the same WebView will display the pop-up content. You can set a Callback<PopupFeatures, WebEngine> object to the createPopupHandler property of the WebEngine to handle the pop-up. The returned WebEngine loads the pop-up. Return null to block the pop-up. The PopupFeatures object contains the details of the pop-up, for example, whether the pop-up has a menu, a toolbar, or a status bar and whether it is resizable. You can use its hadMenu(), hasToolbar(), hasStatus(), and isResizable() to display the details of the pop-up window. The following snippet of code sets a pop-up handler to a WebEngine to display the pop-up in a new window. It ignores the pop-up properties:

```
WebView webView = ...

// Create a popup handler
Callback<PopupFeatures, WebEngine> popupHandler = pFeatures -> {
        // Show a popup in a new window
        Stage stage = new Stage();
        stage.setTitle("Popup");
        WebView poupView = new WebView();
```

```
        VBox root = new VBox(poupView);
        Scene scene = new Scene(root);
        stage.setScene(scene);
        stage.show();
        return poupView.getEngine();
};
```

```
// Set the popup handler
webView.getEngine().setCreatePopupHandler(popupHandler);
```

The following snippet of code sets a pop-up handler that blocks all pop-ups:

```
webView.getEngine().setCreatePopupHandler(pFeatures -> null);
```

The following snippet of code adds an alert handler to show the alert in a dialog when the window.alert(msg) JavaScript function is called. The getData() method of the WebEvent returns the message passed to the window.alert(msg) function:

```
webView.getEngine().setOnAlert((WebEvent<String> e) -> {
        String alertMessage  = e.getData();
        // Display a modal dialog to show the alertMessage ...
});
```

Listing 16-6 creates reusable JavaScript command handlers that you will use in developing the advanced web browser.

Listing 16-6. A Factory to Create JavaScript Command Handlers

```
// JSHandlers.java
package com.jdojo.web;

import javafx.geometry.Pos;
import javafx.scene.Scene;
import javafx.scene.control.Button;
import javafx.scene.control.Label;
import javafx.scene.control.TextField;
import javafx.scene.layout.HBox;
import javafx.scene.layout.VBox;
import javafx.scene.web.PopupFeatures;
import javafx.scene.web.PromptData;
import javafx.scene.web.WebEngine;
import javafx.scene.web.WebEvent;
import javafx.scene.web.WebView;

import javafx.stage.Stage;
import javafx.util.Callback;
```

```java
public class JSHandlers {
        // Handles window.alert() call by displaying a dialog
        public static void alertHandler(WebEvent<String> e) {
                // Show an alert in a new window
                Stage stage = new Stage();
                stage.setTitle("Alert");

                Label msg = new Label(e.getData());
                Button okBtn = new Button("OK");
                okBtn.setOnAction(e2 -> stage.close());

                VBox root = new VBox(20, msg, okBtn);
                root.setAlignment(Pos.CENTER);
                Scene scene = new Scene(root);
                stage.setScene(scene);
                stage.showAndWait();
        }

        // Returns a Callback to handle window.prompt() call by displaying a dialog
        public static Callback<PromptData, String> getPromptHandler() {
                Callback<PromptData, String> handler = pData -> {
                        // Show a window to accept the user input
                        Stage stage = new Stage();
                        stage.setTitle("Prompt");

                        Label msgLbl = new Label(pData.getMessage());
                        TextField dataFld = new TextField();
                        dataFld.setText(pData.getDefaultValue());
                        Button okBtn = new Button("OK");
                        okBtn.setOnAction(e -> stage.close());

                        VBox root = new VBox(20, msgLbl, dataFld, okBtn);
                        root.setAlignment(Pos.CENTER);
                        Scene scene = new Scene(root);
                        stage.setScene(scene);
                        stage.showAndWait();

                        String userData = dataFld.getText();
                        return userData;
                };

                return handler;
        }

        // Returns a Callback to handle window.open() call by displaying the popup
        // in a separate window using a separate WebEngine
        public static Callback<PopupFeatures, WebEngine> getPopupHandler() {
                Callback<PopupFeatures, WebEngine> handler = pFeatures -> {
                        // Show a popup in a new window
                        Stage stage = new Stage();
                        stage.setTitle("Popup");
```

```
                    WebView poupView = new WebView();
                    VBox root = new VBox(poupView);
                    Scene scene = new Scene(root);
                    stage.setScene(scene);
                    stage.show();
                    return poupView.getEngine();
            };

            return handler;
    }

    // Returns a Callback to handle window.confirm() call by displaying a dialog
    public static Callback<String, Boolean> getConfirmHandler() {
            Callback<String, Boolean> handler = msg -> {
                    // Show a popup in a new window
                    Stage stage = new Stage();
                    stage.setTitle("Confirm");

                    Label msgLbl = new Label(msg);
                    Button okBtn = new Button("OK");
                    okBtn.setOnAction(e -> {
                            okBtn.getProperties().put("userPressed", true);
                            stage.close();
                    });

                    Button cancelBtn = new Button("Cancel");
                    cancelBtn.setOnAction(e -> stage.close());

                    HBox buttons = new HBox(20, okBtn, cancelBtn);
                    buttons.setAlignment(Pos.CENTER);

                    VBox root = new VBox(20, msgLbl, buttons);
                    Scene scene = new Scene(root);
                    stage.setScene(scene);
                    stage.showAndWait();

                    Boolean userSelection = (Boolean)okBtn.getProperties()
                                                    .get("userPressed");
                    userSelection = (userSelection == null? false: true);
                    return userSelection;
            };

            return handler;
    }
}
```

Now you can create a reusable complete web browser component using the code in Listing 16-7. The class name is BrowserPane, which inherits from the BorderPane class. It adds a WebView in the center region, a navigation bar in the top region, and a status bar in the bottom region. It also adds commonly used JavaScript command handlers to the WebEngine associated with the WebView. Constructors allow you to customize the component.

Listing 16-7. A Web Browser Component

```java
// BrowserPane.java
package com.jdojo.web;

import javafx.scene.control.Label;
import javafx.scene.control.MenuButton;
import javafx.scene.layout.BorderPane;
import javafx.scene.web.WebView;
import javafx.stage.Stage;
import javafx.stage.Window;

public class BrowserPane extends BorderPane {
        private static String DEFAULT_HOME_PAGE = "http://www.google.com";
        private WebView webView;

        public BrowserPane(Window ownerWindow) {
                this(null, ownerWindow);
        }

        public BrowserPane(String homePageUrl, Window ownerWindow) {
                this(homePageUrl, true, true, true, ownerWindow);
        }

        public BrowserPane(String homePageUrl,
                           boolean enableNavigationBar,
                           boolean enableStatusBar,
                           boolean enableJSHandlers,
                           Window ownerWindow) {

                // Create the WebView
                webView = new WebView();
                this.setCenter(webView);

                if (homePageUrl == null) {
                        homePageUrl = DEFAULT_HOME_PAGE;
                }

                if (enableNavigationBar) {
                        this.addNavigationBar(homePageUrl);
                }

                if (enableStatusBar) {
                        this.addStatusBar();
                }

                if (enableJSHandlers) {
                        this.addJSHandlers(ownerWindow);
                }
        }
```

729

```java
    private void addNavigationBar(String homePageUrl) {
            MenuButton options = new WebOptionsMenu(webView);
            BrowserHistory historyComponent = new BrowserHistory(webView);
            NavigationBar navBar = new NavigationBar(webView, homePageUrl, true);
            navBar.getChildren().addAll(options, historyComponent);
            this.setTop(navBar);
    }

    private void addStatusBar() {
            Label statusLbl = new Label();

            // Configure the status bar
            statusLbl.setStyle("-fx-background-color: lightgray;");
            statusLbl.prefWidthProperty().bind(webView.widthProperty());

            // If the Worker object reports a message, display it in the status bar
            webView.getEngine().getLoadWorker().messageProperty().addListener(
                    (prop, oldMsg,  newMsg) -> statusLbl.setText(newMsg));

            // Update the status bar when window.status proeprty changes
            webView.getEngine().setOnStatusChanged(
                            e -> statusLbl.setText(e.getData())));

            this.setBottom(statusLbl);
    }

    private void addJSHandlers(Window ownerWindow) {
            webView.getEngine().setPromptHandler(JSHandlers.getPromptHandler());
            webView.getEngine().setCreatePopupHandler(JSHandlers.getPopupHandler());
            webView.getEngine().setOnAlert(JSHandlers::alertHandler);
            webView.getEngine().setConfirmHandler(JSHandlers.getConfirmHandler());
            if (ownerWindow instanceof Stage) {
                    Stage stage = (Stage) ownerWindow;

                    // Sync the title of the stage with the title of the loaded web page
                    webView.getEngine().titleProperty().addListener(
                            (prop, oldTitle, newTitle) -> stage.setTitle(newTitle));
            }
    }

    public WebView getWebView() {
            return webView;
    }
}
```

You will need an HTML page with some JavaScript code to test what you have covered in this section. Listing 16-8 shows the HTML content of a jshandlers.html file. It displays an HTML page with some buttons. Clicking the buttons executes the JavaScript commands.

Listing 16-8. An HTML Page to Test JavaScript Command Handlers of the WebEngine

```
<!-- jshandlers.html -->
<html>
<head>
<title>Browsing Web Pages Using Jqva FX WebView</title>
<script type="text/javascript">
        function promptUser() {
                var userMsg = window.prompt("Please enter a message:","Your message");
                document.getElementById("prompt_msg").innerHTML= userMsg;
        }

        function showPopup() {
                window.open("http://www.oracle.com");
        }

        function showAlert() {
                window.alert("This is an alert!");
        }

        function showConfirm() {
                var userResponse = window.confirm("Are you sure you want to learn FX?");
                if (userResponse == true) {
                        document.getElementById("confirm_msg").innerHTML = "You pressed OK.";
                }
                else {
                        document.getElementById("confirm_msg").innerHTML =
                                "You pressed Cancel.";
                }
        }
        </script>
</head>
<body>
        <h1>Using a WebView node to view webpages in JavaFX</h1>

        <p>Go to: <a href="http://www.yahoo.com">Yahoo!</a>    
        <a href="http://www.google.com">Google</a>    
        <a href="http://www.oracle.com">Oracle</a> <br/><br/>

        <b>Your message:</b> <span id="prompt_msg" style="color:red;"></span>
        <input type="button" name="prompt_btn" value="Enter a Message" onclick="promptUser()"/>

        <p>Let us try showing a confirmation window. <span id="confirm_msg"
        style="color:red;"></span>
        <input type="button" name="confirm_btn" value="Show a Confirmation Dialog"
        onclick="showConfirm()"/>
        </p>

        <p>Let us try using a popup window.
        <input type="button" name="popup_btn" value="Show a Popup" onclick="showPopup()"/>
        </p>
```

731

```
    <p>Let us try showing an alert.
            <input type="button" name="popup_btn" value="Show an Alert"
            onclick="showAlert()"/>
    </p>

    <p>Let us try showing current date in the status bar
    <input type="button" name="status_btn" value="Show Current Date"
    onclick="window.status=new Date()"/>
    </p>
</body>
</html>
```

You will need one more program to test what you have covered in this section. The program in Listing 16-9 shows how to open the jshandlers.html page in a WebView. If this page is not displayed, use the Open button in the navigation bar to open the file, which is located in resources\html directory in the source directory. Click each button on the page to test the JavaScript command handlers in JavaFX.

Listing 16-9. Testing JavaScript Command Handlers in the WebEngine

```
// JSCommandTest.java
package com.jdojo.web;

import java.net.URL;
import javafx.application.Application;
import javafx.scene.Scene;
import javafx.stage.Stage;

public class JSCommandTest extends Application {
        private final String DEFAULT_HOME_PAGE = "resources\\html\\jshandlers.html";
        public static void main(String[] args) {
                Application.launch(args);
        }

        @Override
        public void start(Stage stage) {
                String homePageUrl = getDefaultHomePageUrl();
                BrowserPane root = new BrowserPane(homePageUrl, stage);
                Scene scene = new Scene(root);
                stage.setScene(scene);
                stage.show();
        }

        public String getDefaultHomePageUrl() {
                String pageUrl = "http://www.google.com";
                URL url = this.getClass().getClassLoader()
                                .getResource(DEFAULT_HOME_PAGE);
                if (url == null) {
                        System.out.println(
                                "Could not find " + DEFAULT_HOME_PAGE + " in CLASSPATH. " +
                                "Using " + pageUrl + " as the default home page." );
                }
```

```
        else {
                pageUrl = url.toExternalForm();
        }
        return pageUrl;
    }
}
```

Executing JavaScript Code from JavaFX

A WebEngine lets you execute JavaScript code from JavaFX using the executeScript() method. The method takes the JavaScript code in a string as an argument and returns the results in an object. The method uses the following rules to convert the results, which is a JavaScript value, to a Java object:

- JavaScript null is returned as Java null.

- JavaScript boolean is returned as Java Boolean.

- JavaScript Int32 is returned as Java Integer.

- JavaScript numbers are returned as Java Double.

- JavaScript string is returned as Java String.

- JavaScript objects are returned as Java netscape.javascript.JSObject.

- JavaScript JSNode objects are mapped to instances of the Java netscape.javascript. JSObject class that implement the org.w3c.dom.Node interface. If the JavaScript result is a JavaRuntimeObject, the original Java value is returned.

Listing 16-10 shows the content of an HTML page, which contains three JavaScript functions:

- The showTime() function displays the current local time.

- The startShowingTIme() function starts a timer to update the displayed time every second.

- The stopShowingTime() function stops the timer and clears the displayed time.

The two functions to start and stop the timer will be called from JavaFX code.

Listing 16-10. The Contents of of an HTML Page with JavaScript Code

```
<!-- javafx_to_javascript.html -->
<html>
<head>
<title>JavaFX to JavaSCript</title>
        <script type="text/javascript">
                function showTime() {
                        var currDt = new Date();
                        var localTime = currDt.toLocaleTimeString();
                        document.getElementById("current_time").innerHTML = localTime;
                }
```

```
                function startShowingTime() {
                        // Update the time every second
                        var timerId = window.setInterval(showTime, 1000);
                        return timerId;
                }

                function stopShowingTime(timerId) {
                        window.clearInterval(timerId);
                        document.getElementById("current_time").innerHTML = "";
                }
        </script>
</head>
<body>
        <h1>Executing JavaScript Code from JavaFX</h1>

        <p>Current Time: <b><span id="current_time" style="color:blue;"></span></b></p>
</body>
</html>
```

The program in Listing 16-11 shows how to execute JavaScript code from JavaFX. It displays a window with two buttons and a web browser. The web browser should display the content of the javafx_to_javascript.html file. If it does not, you need to open this file using the Open button. Clicking the Start Showing Time button executes the startShowingTime() JavaScript function, which starts a timer and shows the current time in the web page. The function returned a timer ID, which is an Integer. You save the timer ID in an instance variable, so you can use it to stop the timer later. Clicking the Stop Showing Time button executes the stopShowingTime() JavaScript function, which stops the timer and clears the current time in the web page. If the web browser is not showing the correct HTML content, which has these JavaScript functions, clicking the buttons logs an error message on the standard output.

Listing 16-11. A JavaFX Program Executing JavaScript Code

```java
// JavaFXToJavaScript.java
package com.jdojo.web;

import java.net.URL;
import javafx.application.Application;
import javafx.scene.Scene;
import javafx.scene.control.Button;
import javafx.scene.layout.HBox;
import javafx.scene.layout.VBox;
import javafx.scene.web.WebEngine;
import javafx.stage.Stage;

public class JavaFXToJavaScript  extends Application {
        private final String HOME_PAGE = "resources\\html\\javafx_to_javascript.html";
        private Integer jsTimerId = null;
        private WebEngine webEngine;

        public static void main(String[] args) {
                Application.launch(args);
        }
```

```java
@Override
public void start(Stage stage) {
        String homePageUrl = getHomePageUrl();
        BrowserPane browser = new BrowserPane(homePageUrl, stage);

        // Save the web engine reference to call JavaScript code later
        webEngine = browser.getWebView().getEngine();

        Button startTimeBtn = new Button("Start Showing Time");
        startTimeBtn.setOnAction(e -> startJSTimer());

        Button stopTimeBtn = new Button("Stop Showing Time");
        stopTimeBtn.setOnAction(e -> stopJSTimer());

        HBox buttons = new HBox(10, startTimeBtn, stopTimeBtn);
        VBox root = new VBox(10, buttons, browser);
        Scene scene = new Scene(root);
        stage.setScene(scene);
        stage.show();
}

public void startJSTimer() {
        try {
                jsTimerId = (Integer)webEngine.executeScript("startShowingTime()");
        }
        catch(Exception e) {
                System.out.println(e.getMessage());
        }
}

public void stopJSTimer() {
        if (jsTimerId != null) {
                String script = "stopShowingTime(" + jsTimerId + ")";
                webEngine.executeScript(script);
                jsTimerId = null;
        }
}

public String getHomePageUrl() {
        String pageUrl = null;
        URL url = this.getClass().getClassLoader().getResource(HOME_PAGE);
        if (url == null) {
                System.out.println("Could not find " + HOME_PAGE + " in CLASSPATH." +
                        " Use the OPen button in the navigation bar to open it." );
        }
        else {
                pageUrl = url.toExternalForm();
        }
        return pageUrl;
}
}
```

The following snippet of code does the same job as the Back and Forward buttons in the browsing history bar examples:

```
// Go back
webEngine.executeScript("history.back()");

// Go forward
webEngine.executeScript("history.forward()");
```

The following snippet of code calls the window.eval() JavaScript function to add two numbers:

```
Object sum = webEngine.executeScript("window.eval(10 + 20)");
```

Executing JavaFX Code from JavaScript

A WebEngine lets you execute JavaFX code from JavaScript. First, you need to make the JavaScript aware of the JavaFX object whose public methods and properties need to be accessed from JavaScript. The following snippet of code is an FXAdder class, which has an add() method to add two numbers:

```
public class FXAdder {
        public double add(double n1, double n2) {
                return n1 + n2;
                }
        }
```

The following snippet of code accesses the window JavaScript object. It sets a member named fxAdder in the window object. The fxAdder object is an instance of the FXAdder class:

```
JSObject jsWindow = (JSObject)webEngine.executeScript("window");
jsWindow.setMember("fxAdder", new FXAdder());
```

Now, JavaScript can use window.fxAdder.add(n1, n2) to add two numbers. The call will execute the add() method of the FXAdder class and return the sum of two numbers.

JavaFX has a bug that loses the members set in a JavaScript object if the member is set before the document is loaded. To avoid that, you can replace the above code with the following code, which does the same thing, but sets the member after the document has been loaded:

```
webEngine.getLoadWorker().stateProperty().addListener(
        (prop, oldState, newState) -> {
        if (newState == Worker.State.SUCCEEDED) {
                JSObject jsWindow = (JSObject)webEngine.executeScript("window");
                jsWindow.setMember("fxAdder", new FXAdder());
        }
});
```

Listing 16-12 has the web content that displays an HTML form to enter two numbers. When the Add button is clicked, the addNumbers() JavaScript function is called, which in turn calls a JavaFX method to add two numbers. The value returned from JavaFX is displayed in the Sum field:

Listing 16-12. The Contents of a Web Page that Executes JavaFX Code

```html
<!-- javascript_to_javafx.html -->
<html>
<head>
<title>JavaScript to JavaFX</title>
        <script type="text/javascript">
                function addNumbers() {
                        var n1 = Number(document.adder_form.num1.value);
                        var n2 = Number(document.adder_form.num2.value);

                        // Call the JavaFX method to add two numbers
                        var n3 = window.fxAdder.add(n1, n2);
                        document.adder_form.sum.value = n3;
                }
        </script>
</head>
<body>
        <h1>Executing JavaScript Code from JavaFX</h1>
        Enter two numbers and click the Add button to add them.
        <form name="adder_form">
                Number-1: <input type="number" name="num1" value="20" /> <br/>
                Number-2: <input type="number" name="num2" value="80" /> <br/>
                Sum from JavaFX: <input type="number" name="sum" disabled />
                <input type="button" name="add_btn" value="Add" onClick="addNumbers();"/>
        </form>
</body>
</html>
```

The program in Listing 16-13 shows how to set up a Java object to the JavaScript window object as a member, so its method can be called from JavaScript. It is set up to open the javascript_to_javafx.html file, which is located in the resources\html directory. If this file is not loaded automatically, use the Open button to load it. Add two numbers in the number fields and click the Add button. The JavaScript will call the add() method of the FXAdder class and display the results.

The JSObject class is in the netscape.javascript package, which is not part of the standard Java development library. It is part of the plugin.jar file, which is located in the JRE_HOME\lib directory. You need to add the plugin.jar file to the CLASSPATH if you are compiling the program in Listing 16-13.

Listing 16-13. Executing JavaFX Code from JavaScript

```java
// JavaScriptToJavaFX.java
package com.jdojo.web;

import java.net.URL;
import javafx.application.Application;
import javafx.concurrent.Worker;
import javafx.scene.Scene;
import javafx.scene.layout.VBox;
import javafx.scene.web.WebEngine;
import javafx.stage.Stage;
import netscape.javascript.JSObject; // Add plugin.jar to CLASSPATH
```

```java
public class JavaScriptToJavaFX extends Application {
        // An inner class
        public class FXAdder {
                public double add(double n1, double n2) {
                        return n1 + n2;
                }
        }

        private String HOME_PAGE = "resources\\html\\javascript_to_javafx.html";

        public static void main(String[] args) {
                Application.launch(args);
        }

        @Override
        public void start(Stage stage) {
                String homePageUrl = getHomePageUrl();
                BrowserPane browser = new BrowserPane(homePageUrl, stage);

                VBox root = new VBox(browser);
                Scene scene = new Scene(root);
                stage.setScene(scene);
                stage.show();

                // Let JavaScript know about the FXAdder object
                WebEngine webEngine = browser.getWebView().getEngine();

                // Set the member for the window object after the document loads
                 webEngine.getLoadWorker().stateProperty().addListener(
                        (prop, oldState, newState) -> {
                                if (newState == Worker.State.SUCCEEDED) {
                                        JSObject jsWindow =
                                                (JSObject)webEngine.executeScript("window");
                                        jsWindow.setMember("fxAdder", new FXAdder());
                                }
                });
        }

        public String getHomePageUrl() {
                String pageUrl = null;
                URL url = this.getClass().getClassLoader().getResource(HOME_PAGE);
                if (url == null) {
                        System.out.println("Could not find " + HOME_PAGE + " in CLASSPATH." +
                                        "Use the Open button in the navigation bar to open it." );
                }
                else {
                        pageUrl = url.toExternalForm();
                }
                return pageUrl;
        }
}
```

Accessing the DOM

The WebEngine creates a DOM of the web pages it loads. You can access the DOM through the read-only document property of the WebEngine class. The property is an object of the class org.w3c.dom.Document or null if the page fails to load. You can access and modify the DOM using the Java DOM API in the org.w3c.dom package. The following snippet of code accesses the body element of the HTML page and sets its style to change the background color of the page to light gray:

```
import org.w3c.dom.Document;
import org.w3c.dom.Element;
...
Document doc = webEngine.getDocument();
Element bodyElement = (Element)doc.getElementsByTagName("body").item(0);
bodyElement.setAttribute("style", "background-color: lightgray;");
```

Setting the User-Agent HTTP Header

An HTTP request identifies the client software making the request using a User-Agent header. All browsers use a different User-Agent header to identify themselves uniquely. Sometimes you will generate specific HTML content on the server depending on which browser has requested the content.

The WebEngine class contains a userAgent property, which defaults to a system-dependent value. For example, the value of the userAgent property on Windows is:

```
Mozilla/5.0 (Windows NT 5.1) AppleWebKit/537.44 (KHTML, like Gecko) JavaFX/8.0 Safari/537.44
```

Typically, you will not need to change the User-Agent property for your browser. However, if you want to identify your web browser differently, you can do so using the following code:

```
webEngine.setUserAgent("Who knows!!!");
```

Setting a User Style Sheet

A web browser can have style sheets defined at three levels:

- Web browser
- User
- Author

The web content is styled using the styles specified by the author of the content. If the author does not provide styles for some elements, the user-specified style sheets are looked up. If user style sheets are not provided or they do not contain styles for the elements, the default styles are always provided by the web browser. Therefore, the priorities of style sheets, from lowest to highest, are web browser, user, and author.

You can specify the location of a user style sheet using the userStyleSheetLocation property of the WebEngine class. The location is specified in a String URL. The URL must be local using a file, data, or jar protocol. The following snippet of code sets the location of the user style sheet on Windows using the file protocol:

```
webEngine.setUserStyleSheetLocation("file://C:/mystyles.css");
```

Styling a *WebView* with CSS

The default CSS style-class name for a WebView is *web-view*. Apart from size-related CSS properties, it has three properties that can be set in CSS:

- `-fx-context-menu-enabled`
- `-fx-font-smoothing-type`
- `-fx-font-scale`

The `-fx-context-menu-enabled` property specifies whether the context menu is enabled. It is true by default. The `-fx-font-smoothing-type` property specifies the font smoothing type, which could be gray or lcd. The default is lcd. The `-fx-font-scale` property specifies the font scale, which is 1.0 by default.

The following style disables the context menu, sets the font smoothing type to gray, and sets the font scale to 110%:

```
.web-view {
        -fx-context-menu-enabled: false;
        -fx-font-smoothing-type: gray;
        -fx-font-scale: 1.1;
}
```

Summary

JavaFX provides a web component that can be used as an embedded web browser in a JavaFX application. It is based on WebKit, which is an open source web browser engine. The component handles most of the work of web browsing, for example, rendering the HTML content, maintaining a history of the visited web pages, navigating to a URL when links are clicked, displaying pop-up contents, among others. Code is written to handle other web-related features, for example, displaying an alert, prompt, or confirmation dialog using JavaScript.

The web browser component comprises a simple API consisting of the following classes in the javafx.scene.web package: WebView, WebEngine, WebHistory, WebHistory.Entry, WebEvent, PopupFeatures, and PromptData.

The WebView class inherits from the Parent class. It is a node, not a control. It is added to a scene graph for viewing web pages using local or remote URLs. A WebView displays one web page at a time and can be styled using a CSS.

A WebView uses a WebEngine for core processing of its content. A WebEngine manages one web page at a time. The WebView handles user input events such as mouse and keyboard events and other functions, for example, loading the web page content, applying the CSS, and creating DOM, which are performed by the WebEngine. When using a WebView component, you will be working with its WebEngine most of the time.

A WebEngine maintains the browsing history of all visited web pages for a session in an instance of the WebHistory class. An instance of the inner class WebHistory.Entry represents an entry in the browsing history. An instance of the WebEvent class represents an event generated by a WebEngine while it processes a web page. Examples of such events are a resized event that occurs when JavaScript running on a web page resizes or moves the window, an alert event that occurs when JavaScript running on the web page calls the window.alert() function, among others.

When JavaScript running on a webpage opens a pop-up window, an instance of the PopupFeatures class encapsulates the details of the pop-up window. The WebEngine lets you register a pop-up handler to handle the displaying of the pop-up window.

An instance of the PromptData class encapsulates the details of a prompt window (a message and an initial value) displayed by JavaScript code using the window.prompt() function. The WebEngine lets you register a prompt handler to handle the prompt. In the prompt handler, you can display a JavaFX dialog window to prompt the user for input.

The next chapter will discuss how to draw and style 2D shapes.

CHAPTER 17

■ ■ ■

Understanding 2D Shapes

In this chapter, you will learn:

- What 2D shapes are and how they are represented in JavaFX

- How to draw 2D shapes

- How to draw complex shapes using the Path class

- How to draw shapes using the Scalable Vector Graphics (SVG)

- How to combine shapes to build another shape

- How to use strokes for a shape

- How to style shapes using Cascading Style Sheets (CSS)

What Are 2D Shapes?

Any shape that can be drawn in a two-dimensional plane is called a 2D shape. JavaFX offers variety nodes to draw different types of shapes (lines, circles, rectangles, etc.). You can add shapes to a scene graph.

Shapes can be two-dimensional or three-dimensional. In this chapter, I will discuss 2D shapes. Chapter 19 discusses 3D shapes.

All shape classes are in the `javafx.scene.shape` package. Classes representing 2D shapes are inherited from the abstract Shape class as shown in Figure 17-1.

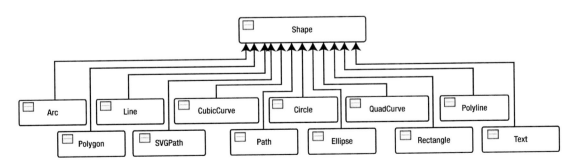

Figure 17-1. A class diagram for classes representing 2D shapes

A shape has a size and a position, which are defined by their properties. For example, the width and height properties define the size of a rectangle; the radius property defines the size of a circle, the x and y properties define the position of the upper-left corner of a rectangle, the centerX and centerY properties define the center of a circle, etc.

Shapes are not resized by their parents during layout. The size of a shape changes only when its size-related properties are changed. You may find a phrase like "JavaFX shapes are non-resizable." It means shapes are non-resizable by their parent during layout. They can be resized only by changing their properties.

Shapes have an interior and a stroke. The properties for defining the interior and stroke of a shape are declared in the Shape class. The fill property specifies the color to fill the interior of the shape. The default fill is Color.BLACK. The stroke property specifies the color for the outline stroke, which is null by default, except for Line, Polyline, and Path, which have Color.BLACK as the default stroke. The strokeWidth property specifies the width of the outline, which is 1.0px by default. The Shape class contains other stroke-related properties that I will discuss in the section "Understanding the Stroke of a Shape".

The Shape class contains a smooth property, which is true by default. Its true value indicates that an antialiasing hint should be used to render the shape. If it is set to false, the antialiasing hint will not be used, which may result in the edges of shapes being not crisp.

The program in Listing 17-1 creates two circles. The first circle has a light gray fill and no stroke, which is the default. The second circle has a yellow fill and a 2.0px wide black stroke. Figure 17-2 shows the two circles.

Listing 17-1. Using fill and stroke Properties of the Shape Class

```
// ShapeTest.java
package com.jdojo.shape;

import javafx.application.Application;
import javafx.scene.Scene;
import javafx.scene.layout.HBox;
import javafx.scene.paint.Color;
import javafx.scene.shape.Circle;
import javafx.stage.Stage;

public class ShapeTest extends Application {
        public static void main(String[] args) {
                Application.launch(args);
        }

        @Override
        public void start(Stage stage) {
                // Create a circle with a light gray fill and no stroke
                Circle c1 = new Circle(40, 40, 40);
                c1.setFill(Color.LIGHTGRAY);

                // Create a circle with an yellow fill and a black stroke of 2.0px
                Circle c2 = new Circle(40, 40, 40);
                c2.setFill(Color.YELLOW);
                c2.setStroke(Color.BLACK);
                c2.setStrokeWidth(2.0);

                HBox root = new HBox(c1, c2);
                root.setSpacing(10);
                root.setStyle("-fx-padding: 10;" +
```

```
                              "-fx-border-style: solid inside;" +
                              "-fx-border-width: 2;" +
                              "-fx-border-insets: 5;" +
                              "-fx-border-radius: 5;" +
                              "-fx-border-color: blue;");

            Scene scene = new Scene(root);
            stage.setScene(scene);
            stage.setTitle("Using Shapes");
            stage.show();
        }
}
```

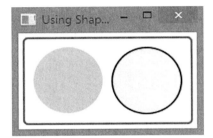

Figure 17-2. *Two circles with different fills and strokes*

Drawing 2D Shapes

The following sections describe in detail how to use the JavaFX classes representing 2D shapes to draw those shapes.

Drawing Lines

An instance of the Line class represents a line node. A Line has no interior. By default, its fill property is set to null. Setting fill has no effects. The default stroke is Color.BLACK and the default strokeWidth is 1.0. The Line class contains four double properties.

- startX
- startY
- endX
- endY

The Line represents a line segment between (startX, startY) and (endX, endY) points. The Line class has a no-args constructor, which defaults all its four properties to zero resulting in a line from (0, 0) to (0, 0), which represents a point. Another constructor takes values for startX, startY, endX, and endY. After you create a Line, you can change its location and length by changing any of the four properties.

The program in Listing 17-2 creates some Lines and sets their stroke and strokeWidth properties. The first Line will appear as a point. Figure 17-3 shows the line.

Listing 17-2. Using the Line Class to Create Line Nodes

```java
// LineTest.java
package com.jdojo.shape;

import javafx.application.Application;
import javafx.scene.Scene;
import javafx.scene.layout.HBox;
import javafx.scene.paint.Color;
import javafx.scene.shape.Line;
import javafx.stage.Stage;

public class LineTest extends Application {
        public static void main(String[] args) {
                Application.launch(args);
        }

        @Override
        public void start(Stage stage) {
                // It will be just a point at (0, 0)
                Line line1 = new Line();

                Line line2 = new Line(0, 0, 50, 0);
                line2.setStrokeWidth(1.0);

                Line line3 = new Line(0, 50, 50, 0);
                line3.setStrokeWidth(2.0);
                line3.setStroke(Color.RED);

                Line line4 = new Line(0, 0, 50, 50);
                line4.setStrokeWidth(5.0);
                line4.setStroke(Color.BLUE);

                HBox root = new HBox(line1, line2, line3, line4);
                root.setSpacing(10);
                root.setStyle("-fx-padding: 10;" +
                                "-fx-border-style: solid inside;" +
                                "-fx-border-width: 2;" +
                                "-fx-border-insets: 5;" +
                                "-fx-border-radius: 5;" +
                                "-fx-border-color: blue;");

                Scene scene = new Scene(root);
                stage.setScene(scene);
                stage.setTitle("Using Lines");
                stage.show();
        }
}
```

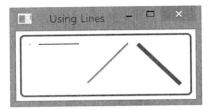

Figure 17-3. *Using line nodes*

Drawing Rectangles

An instance of the Rectangle class represents a rectangle node. The class uses six properties to define the rectangle.

- x
- y
- width
- height
- arcWidth
- arcHeight

The x and y properties are the x and y coordinates of the upper-left corner of the rectangle in the local coordinate system of the node. The width and height properties are the width and height of the rectangle, respectively. Specify the same width and height to draw a square.

By default, the corners of a rectangle are sharp. A rectangle can have rounded corners by specifying the arcWidth and arcHeight properties. You can think of one of the quadrants of an ellipse positioned at the four corners to make them round. The arcWidth and arcHeight properties are the horizontal and vertical diameters of the ellipse. By default, their values are zero, which makes a rectangle have sharp corners. Figure 17-4 shows two rectangles—one with sharp corners and one with rounded corners. The ellipse is shown to illustrate the relationship between the arcWidth and arcHeight properties for a rounded rectangle.

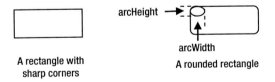

Figure 17-4. *Rectangles with sharp and rounded corners*

The Rectangle class contains several constructors. They take various properties as arguments. The default values for x, y, width, height, arcWidth, and arcHeight properties are zero. The constructors are

- Rectangle()

- Rectangle(double width, double height)

- Rectangle(double x, double y, double width, double height)

- Rectangle(double width, double height, Paint fill)

You will not see effects of specifying the values for the x and y properties for a Rectangle when you add it to most of the layout panes as they place their children at (0, 0). A Pane uses these properties. The program in Listing 17-3 adds two rectangles to a Pane. The first rectangle uses the default values of zero for the x and y properties. The second rectangle specifies 120 for the x property and 20 for the y property. Figure 17-5 shows the positions of the two rectangles inside the Pane. Notice that the upper-left corner of the second rectangle (on the right) is at (120, 20).

Listing 17-3. Using the Rectangle Class to Create Rectangle Nodes

```java
// RectangleTest.java
package com.jdojo.shape;

import javafx.application.Application;
import javafx.scene.Scene;
import javafx.scene.layout.Pane;
import javafx.scene.paint.Color;
import javafx.scene.shape.Rectangle;
import javafx.stage.Stage;

public class RectangleTest extends Application {
        public static void main(String[] args) {
                Application.launch(args);
        }

        @Override
        public void start(Stage stage) {
                // x=0, y=0, width=100, height=50, fill=LIGHTGRAY, stroke=null
                Rectangle rect1 = new Rectangle(100, 50, Color.LIGHTGRAY);

                // x=120, y=20, width=100, height=50, fill=WHITE, stroke=BLACK
                Rectangle rect2 = new Rectangle(120, 20, 100, 50);
                rect2.setFill(Color.WHITE);
                rect2.setStroke(Color.BLACK);
                rect2.setArcWidth(10);
                rect2.setArcHeight(10);

                Pane root = new Pane();
                root.getChildren().addAll(rect1, rect2);
                Scene scene = new Scene(root);
                stage.setScene(scene);
                stage.setTitle("Using Rectangles");
                stage.show();
        }
}
```

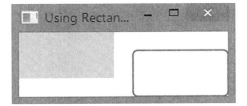

Figure 17-5. *Rectangles inside a Pane, which uses the x and y properties to posiiton them*

Drawing Circles

An instance of the Circle class represents a circle node. The class uses three properties to define the circle.

- centerX
- centerY
- radius

The centerX and centerY properties are the x and y coordinates of the center of the circle in the local coordinate system of the node. The radius property is the radius of the circle. The default values for these properties are zero.

The Circle class contains several constructors.

- Circle()
- Circle(double radius)
- Circle(double centerX, double centerY, double radius)
- Circle(double centerX, double centerY, double radius, Paint fill)
- Circle(double radius, Paint fill)

The program in Listing 17-4 adds two circles to an HBox. Notice that the HBox does not use centerX and centerY properties of the circles. Add them to a Pane to see the effects. Figure 17-6 shows the two circles.

Listing 17-4. Using the Circle Class to Create Circle Nodes

```java
// CircleTest.java
package com.jdojo.shape;

import javafx.application.Application;
import javafx.scene.Scene;
import javafx.scene.layout.HBox;
import javafx.scene.paint.Color;
import javafx.scene.shape.Circle;
import javafx.stage.Stage;

public class CircleTest extends Application {
        public static void main(String[] args) {
                Application.launch(args);
        }
```

```
@Override
public void start(Stage stage) {
        // centerX=0, centerY=0, radius=40, fill=LIGHTGRAY, stroke=null
        Circle c1 = new Circle(0, 0, 40);
        c1.setFill(Color.LIGHTGRAY);

        // centerX=10, centerY=10, radius=40. fill=YELLOW, stroke=BLACK
        Circle c2 = new Circle(10, 10, 40, Color.YELLOW);
        c2.setStroke(Color.BLACK);
        c2.setStrokeWidth(2.0);

        HBox root = new HBox(c1, c2);
        root.setSpacing(10);
        root.setStyle("-fx-padding: 10;" +
                      "-fx-border-style: solid inside;" +
                      "-fx-border-width: 2;" +
                      "-fx-border-insets: 5;" +
                      "-fx-border-radius: 5;" +
                      "-fx-border-color: blue;");

        Scene scene = new Scene(root);
        stage.setScene(scene);
        stage.setTitle("Using Circle");
        stage.show();
    }
}
```

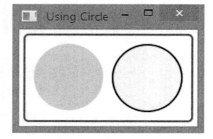

Figure 17-6. *Using circle nodes*

Drawing Ellipses

An instance of the Ellipse class represents an ellipse node. The class uses four properties to define the ellipse.

- centerX
- centerY
- radiusX
- radiusY

The centerX and centerY properties are the x and y coordinates of the center of the circle in the local coordinate system of the node. The radiusX and radiusY are the radii of the ellipse in the horizontal and vertical directions. The default values for these properties are zero. A circle is a special case of an ellipse when radiusX and radiusY are the same.

The Ellipse class contains several constructors.

- Ellipse()

- Ellipse(double radiusX, double radiusY)

- Ellipse(double centerX, double centerY, double radiusX, double radiusY)

The program in Listing 17-5 creates three instances of the Ellipse class. The third instance draws a circle as the program sets the same value for the radiusX and radiusY properties. Figure 17-7 shows the three ellipses.

Listing 17-5. Using the Ellipse Class to Create Ellipse Nodes

```
// EllipseTest.java
package com.jdojo.shape;

import javafx.application.Application;
import javafx.scene.Scene;
import javafx.scene.layout.HBox;
import javafx.scene.paint.Color;
import javafx.scene.shape.Ellipse;
import javafx.stage.Stage;

public class EllipseTest extends Application {
        public static void main(String[] args) {
                Application.launch(args);
        }

        @Override
        public void start(Stage stage) {
                Ellipse e1 = new Ellipse(50, 30);
                e1.setFill(Color.LIGHTGRAY);

                Ellipse e2 = new Ellipse(60, 30);
                e2.setFill(Color.YELLOW);
                e2.setStroke(Color.BLACK);
                e2.setStrokeWidth(2.0);

                // Draw a circle using the Ellipse class (radiusX=radiusY=30)
                Ellipse e3 = new Ellipse(30, 30);
                e3.setFill(Color.YELLOW);
                e3.setStroke(Color.BLACK);
                e3.setStrokeWidth(2.0);
```

```
            HBox root = new HBox(e1, e2, e3);
            root.setSpacing(10);
            root.setStyle("-fx-padding: 10;" +
                          "-fx-border-style: solid inside;" +
                          "-fx-border-width: 2;" +
                          "-fx-border-insets: 5;" +
                          "-fx-border-radius: 5;" +
                          "-fx-border-color: blue;");

            Scene scene = new Scene(root);
            stage.setScene(scene);
            stage.setTitle("Using Ellipses");
            stage.show();
        }
    }
```

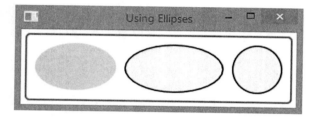

Figure 17-7. *Using ellipse nodes*

Drawing Polygons

An instance of the Polygon class represents a polygon node. The class does not define any public properties. It lets you draw a polygon using an array of (x, y) coordinates defining the vertices of the polygon. Using the Polygon class, you can draw any type of geometric shape that is created using connected lines (triangles, pentagons, hexagons, parallelograms, etc.).

The Polygon class contains two constructors.

- Polygon()

- Polygon(double... points)

The no-args constructor creates an empty polygon. You need add the (x, y) coordinates of the vertices of the shape. The polygon will draw a line from the first vertex to the second vertex, from the second to the third, and so on. Finally, the shape is closed by drawing a line from the last vertex to the first vertex.

The Polygon class stores the coordinates of the vertices in an ObservableList<Double>. You can get the reference of the observable list using the getPoints() method. Notice that it stores the coordinates in a list of Double, which is simply a number. It is your job to pass the numbers in pairs, so they can be used as (x, y) coordinates of vertices. If you pass an odd number of numbers, no shape is created. The following snippet of code creates two triangles—one passes the coordinates of the vertices in the constructor and another adds them to the observable list later. Both triangles are geometrically the same.

```
// Create an empty triangle and add vertices later
Polygon triangle1 = new Polygon();
triangle1.getPoints().addAll(50.0, 0.0,
                              0.0, 100.0,
                              100.0, 100.0);

// Create a triangle with vertices
Polygon triangle2 = new Polygon(50.0, 0.0,
                                0.0, 100.0,
                                100.0, 100.0);
```

The program in Listing 17-6 creates a triangle, a parallelogram, and a hexagon using the Polygon class as shown in Figure 17-8.

Listing 17-6. Using the Polygon Class to Create a Triangle, a Parallelogram, and a Hexagon

```
// PolygonTest.java
package com.jdojo.shape;

import javafx.application.Application;
import javafx.scene.Scene;
import javafx.scene.layout.HBox;
import javafx.scene.paint.Color;
import javafx.scene.shape.Polygon;
import javafx.stage.Stage;

public class PolygonTest extends Application {
        public static void main(String[] args) {
                Application.launch(args);
        }

        @Override
        public void start(Stage stage) {
                Polygon triangle1 = new Polygon();
                triangle1.getPoints().addAll(50.0, 0.0,
                                             0.0, 50.0,
                                             100.0, 50.0);
                triangle1.setFill(Color.WHITE);
                triangle1.setStroke(Color.RED);

                Polygon parallelogram = new Polygon();
                parallelogram.getPoints().addAll(30.0, 0.0,
                                                 130.0, 0.0,
                                                 100.00, 50.0,
                                                 0.0, 50.0);
                parallelogram.setFill(Color.YELLOW);
                parallelogram.setStroke(Color.BLACK);
```

```
                    Polygon hexagon = new Polygon(100.0, 0.0,
                                                  120.0, 20.0,
                                                  120.0, 40.0,
                                                  100.0, 60.0,
                                                  80.0, 40.0,
                                                  80.0, 20.0);
                    hexagon.setFill(Color.WHITE);
                    hexagon.setStroke(Color.BLACK);

                    HBox root = new HBox(triangle1, parallelogram, hexagon);
                    root.setSpacing(10);
                    root.setStyle("-fx-padding: 10;" +
                                "-fx-border-style: solid inside;" +
                                "-fx-border-width: 2;" +
                                "-fx-border-insets: 5;" +
                                "-fx-border-radius: 5;" +
                                "-fx-border-color: blue;");

                    Scene scene = new Scene(root);
                    stage.setScene(scene);
                    stage.setTitle("Using Polygons");
                    stage.show();
        }
}
```

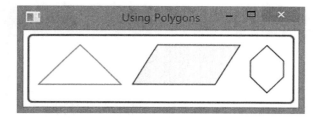

Figure 17-8. *Using polygon nodes*

Drawing Polylines

A polyline is similar to a polygon, except that it does not draw a line between the last and first points. That is, a polyline is an open polygon. However, the fill color is used to fill the entire shape as if the shape was closed.

An instance of the Polyline class represents a polyline node. The class does not define any public properties. It lets you draw a polyline using an array of (x, y) coordinates defining the vertices of the polyline. Using the Polyline class, you can draw any type of geometric shape that is created using connected lines (triangles, pentagons, hexagons, parallelograms, etc.).

The Polyline class contains two constructors.

- Polyline()

- Polyline(double... points)

The no-args constructor creates an empty polyline. You need add (x, y) coordinates of the vertices of the shape. The polygon will draw a line from the first vertex to the second vertex, from the second to the third, and so on. Unlike a Polygon, the shape is not closed automatically. If you want to close the shape, you need to add the coordinates of the first vertex as the last pair of numbers.

If you want to add coordinates of vertices later, add them to the ObservableList<Double> returned by the getPoints() method of the Polyline class. The following snippet of code creates two triangles with the same geometrical properties using different methods. Notice that the first and the last pairs of numbers are the same in order to close the triangle.

```
// Create an empty triangle and add vertices later
Polygon triangle1 = new Polygon();
triangle1.getPoints().addAll(50.0, 0.0,
                             0.0, 100.0,
                             100.0, 100.0,
                             50.0, 0.0);

// Create a triangle with vertices
Polygon triangle2 = new Polygon(50.0, 0.0,
                                0.0, 100.0,
                                100.0, 100.0,
                                50.0, 0.0);
```

The program in Listing 17-7 creates a triangle, an open parallelogram, and a hexagon using the Polyline class as shown in Figure 17-9.

Listing 17-7. Using the Polyline Class to Create a Triangle, an Open Parallelogram, and a Hexagon

```
// PolylineTest.java
package com.jdojo.shape;

import javafx.application.Application;
import javafx.scene.Scene;
import javafx.scene.layout.HBox;
import javafx.scene.paint.Color;
import javafx.scene.shape.Polyline;
import javafx.stage.Stage;

public class PolylineTest extends Application {
        public static void main(String[] args) {
                Application.launch(args);
        }

        @Override
        public void start(Stage stage) {
                Polyline triangle1 = new Polyline();
                triangle1.getPoints().addAll(50.0, 0.0,
                                            0.0, 50.0,
                                            100.0, 50.0,
                                            50.0, 0.0);
                triangle1.setFill(Color.WHITE);
                triangle1.setStroke(Color.RED);
```

```
// Create an open parallelogram
Polyline parallelogram = new Polyline();
parallelogram.getPoints().addAll(30.0, 0.0,
                                 130.0, 0.0,
                                 100.00, 50.0,
                                 0.0, 50.0);
parallelogram.setFill(Color.YELLOW);
parallelogram.setStroke(Color.BLACK);

Polyline hexagon = new Polyline(100.0, 0.0,
                                120.0, 20.0,
                                120.0, 40.0,
                                100.0, 60.0,
                                80.0, 40.0,
                                80.0, 20.0,
                                100.0, 0.0);
hexagon.setFill(Color.WHITE);
hexagon.setStroke(Color.BLACK);

HBox root = new HBox(triangle1, parallelogram, hexagon);
root.setSpacing(10);
root.setStyle("-fx-padding: 10;" +
              "-fx-border-style: solid inside;" +
              "-fx-border-width: 2;" +
              "-fx-border-insets: 5;" +
              "-fx-border-radius: 5;" +
              "-fx-border-color: blue;");

Scene scene = new Scene(root);
stage.setScene(scene);
stage.setTitle("Using Polylines");
stage.show();
    }
}
```

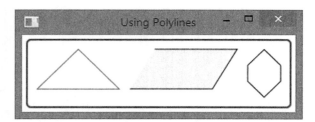

Figure 17-9. *Using polyline nodes*

Drawing Arcs

An instance of the Arc class represents a sector of an ellipse. The class uses seven properties to define the ellipse.

- centerX
- centerY
- radiusX
- radiusY
- startAngle
- length
- type

The first four properties define an ellipse. Please refer to the section "Drawing Ellipses" for how to define an ellipse. The last three properties define a sector of the ellipse that is the Arc node. The startAngle property specifies the start angle of the section in degrees measured counterclockwise from the positive x-axis. It defines the beginning of the arc. The length is an angle in degrees measured counterclockwise from the start angle to define the end of the sector. If the length property is set to 360, the Arc is a full ellipse. Figure 17-10 illustrates the properties.

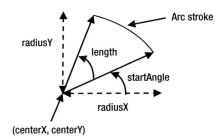

Figure 17-10. *Properties defining an Arc*

The type property specifies the way the Arc is closed. It is one of the constants, OPEN, CHORD, and ROUND, defined in the ArcType enum.

- The ArcType.OPEN does not close the arc.
- The ArcType.CHORD closes the arc by joining the starting and ending points by a straight line.
- The ArcType.ROUND closes the arc by joining the starting and ending point to the center of the ellipse.

Figure 17-11 shows the three closure types for an arc. The default type for an Arc is ArcType.OPEN. If you do not apply a stroke to an Arc, both ArcType.OPEN and ArcType.CHORD look the same.

OPEN   CHORD   ROUND

Figure 17-11. *Closure types of an arc*

The Arc class contains two constructors:

- `Arc()`

- `Arc(double centerX, double centerY, double radiusX, double radiusY, double startAngle, double length)`

The program in Listing 17-8 shows how to create Arc nodes. The resulting window is shown in Figure 17-12.

Listing 17-8. Using the Arc Class to Create Arcs, Which Are Sectors of Ellipses

```java
// ArcTest.java
package com.jdojo.shape;

import javafx.application.Application;
import javafx.scene.Scene;
import javafx.scene.layout.HBox;
import javafx.scene.paint.Color;
import javafx.scene.shape.Arc;
import javafx.scene.shape.ArcType;
import javafx.stage.Stage;

public class ArcTest extends Application {
        public static void main(String[] args) {
                Application.launch(args);
        }

        @Override
        public void start(Stage stage) {
                // An OPEN arc with a fill
                Arc arc1 = new Arc(0, 0, 50, 100, 0, 90);
                arc1.setFill(Color.LIGHTGRAY);

                // An OPEN arc with no fill and a stroke
                Arc arc2 = new Arc(0, 0, 50, 100, 0, 90);
                arc2.setFill(Color.TRANSPARENT);
                arc2.setStroke(Color.BLACK);

                // A CHORD arc with no fill and a stroke
                Arc arc3 = new Arc(0, 0, 50, 100, 0, 90);
                arc3.setFill(Color.TRANSPARENT);
                arc3.setStroke(Color.BLACK);
                arc3.setType(ArcType.CHORD);
```

```
                // A ROUND arc with no fill and a stroke
                Arc arc4 = new Arc(0, 0, 50, 100, 0, 90);
                arc4.setFill(Color.TRANSPARENT);
                arc4.setStroke(Color.BLACK);
                arc4.setType(ArcType.ROUND);

                // A ROUND arc with a gray fill and a stroke
                Arc arc5 = new Arc(0, 0, 50, 100, 0, 90);
                arc5.setFill(Color.GRAY);
                arc5.setStroke(Color.BLACK);
                arc5.setType(ArcType.ROUND);

                HBox root = new HBox(arc1, arc2, arc3, arc4, arc5);
                root.setSpacing(10);
                root.setStyle("-fx-padding: 10;" +
                              "-fx-border-style: solid inside;" +
                              "-fx-border-width: 2;" +
                              "-fx-border-insets: 5;" +
                              "-fx-border-radius: 5;" +
                              "-fx-border-color: blue;");

                Scene scene = new Scene(root);
                stage.setScene(scene);
                stage.setTitle("Using Arcs");
                stage.show();
        }
}
```

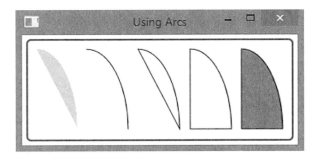

Figure 17-12. *Using Arc nodes*

Drawing Quadratic Curves

Bezier curves are used in computer graphics to draw smooth curves. An instance of the QuadCurve class represents a quadratic Bezier curve segment intersecting two specified points using a specified Bezier control point. The QuadCurve class contains six properties to specify the three points.

- startX

- startY

- controlX

- controlY

- endX

- endY

The QuadCurve class contains two constructors.

- QuadCurve()

- QuadCurve(double startX, double startY, double controlX, double controlY, double endX, double endY)

The program in Listing 17-9 draws the same quadratic Bezier curve twice—once with a stroke and a transparent fill and once with no stroke and a light gray fill. Figure 17-13 shows the two curves.

Listing 17-9. Using the QuadCurve Class to Draw Quadratic BezierCurve

```java
// QuadCurveTest.java
package com.jdojo.shape;

import javafx.application.Application;
import javafx.scene.Scene;
import javafx.scene.layout.HBox;
import javafx.scene.paint.Color;
import javafx.scene.shape.QuadCurve;
import javafx.stage.Stage;

public class QuadCurveTest extends Application {
        public static void main(String[] args) {
                Application.launch(args);
        }

        @Override
        public void start(Stage stage) {
                QuadCurve qc1 = new QuadCurve(0, 100, 20, 0, 150, 100);
                qc1.setFill(Color.TRANSPARENT);
                qc1.setStroke(Color.BLACK);

                QuadCurve qc2 = new QuadCurve(0, 100, 20, 0, 150, 100);
                qc2.setFill(Color.LIGHTGRAY);

                HBox root = new HBox(qc1, qc2);
                root.setSpacing(10);
                root.setStyle("-fx-padding: 10;" +
                                "-fx-border-style: solid inside;" +
                                "-fx-border-width: 2;" +
                                "-fx-border-insets: 5;" +
                                "-fx-border-radius: 5;" +
                                "-fx-border-color: blue;");
```

```
            Scene scene = new Scene(root);
            stage.setScene(scene);
            stage.setTitle("Using QuadCurves");
            stage.show();
        }
}
```

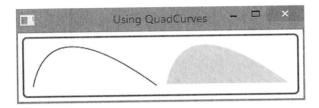

Figure 17-13. *Using quadratic Bezier curves*

Drawing Cubic Curves

An instance of the CubicCurve class represents a cubic Bezier curve segment intersecting two specified points using two specified Bezier control points. Please refer to the Wikipedia article at http://en.wikipedia.org/wiki/Bezier_curves for a detailed explanation and demonstration of Bezier curves. The CubicCurve class contains eight properties to specify the four points.

- startX
- startY
- controlX1
- controlY1
- controlX2
- controlY2
- endX
- endY

The CubicCurve class contains two constructors.

- CubicCurve()
- CubicCurve(double startX, double startY, double controlX1, double controlY1, double controlX2, double controlY2, double endX, double endY)

The program in Listing 17-10 draws the same cubic Bezier curve twice—once with a stroke and a transparent fill and once with no stroke and a light gray fill. Figure 17-14 shows the two curves.

Listing 17-10. Using the CubicCurve Class to Draw Cubic Bezier Curve

```java
// CubicCurveTest.java
package com.jdojo.shape;

import javafx.application.Application;
import javafx.scene.Scene;
import javafx.scene.layout.HBox;
import javafx.scene.paint.Color;
import javafx.scene.shape.CubicCurve;
import javafx.stage.Stage;

public class CubicCurveTest extends Application {
        public static void main(String[] args) {
                Application.launch(args);
        }

        @Override
        public void start(Stage stage) {
                CubicCurve cc1 = new CubicCurve(0, 50, 20, 0, 50, 80, 50, 0);
                cc1.setFill(Color.TRANSPARENT);
                cc1.setStroke(Color.BLACK);

                CubicCurve cc2 = new CubicCurve(0, 50, 20, 0, 50, 80, 50, 0);
                cc2.setFill(Color.LIGHTGRAY);

                HBox root = new HBox(cc1, cc2);
                root.setSpacing(10);
                root.setStyle("-fx-padding: 10;" +
                                "-fx-border-style: solid inside;" +
                                "-fx-border-width: 2;" +
                                "-fx-border-insets: 5;" +
                                "-fx-border-radius: 5;" +
                                "-fx-border-color: blue;");

                Scene scene = new Scene(root);
                stage.setScene(scene);
                stage.setTitle("Using CubicCurves");
                stage.show();
        }
}
```

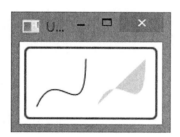

Figure 17-14. *Using cubic Bezier curves*

Building Complex Shapes Using the Path Class

I discussed several shape classes in the previous sections. They are used to draw simple shapes. It is not convenient to use them for complex shapes. You can draw complex shapes using the Path class. An instance of the Path class defines the path (outline) of a shape. A path consists of one or more subpaths. A subpath consists of one or more path elements. Each subpath has a starting point and an ending point.

A path element is an instance of the PathElement abstract class. The following subclasses of the PathElement class exist to represent specific type of path elements:

- MoveTo
- LineTo
- HLineTo
- VLineTo
- ArcTo
- QuadCurveTo
- CubicCurveTo
- ClosePath

Before you see an example, let us outline the process of creating a shape using the Path class. The process is similar to drawing a shape on a paper with a pencil. First, you place the pencil on the paper. You can restate it, "You move the pencil to a point on the paper." Regardless of what shape you want to draw, moving the pencil to a point must be the first step. Now, you start moving your pencil to draw a path element (e.g., a horizontal line). The starting point of the current path element is the same as the ending point of the previous path element. Keep drawing as many path elements as needed (e.g., a vertical line, an arc, and a quadratic Bezier curve). At the end, you can end the last path element at the same point where you started or somewhere else.

The coordinates defining a PathElement can be absolute or relative. By default, coordinates are absolute. It is specified by the absolute property of the PathElement class. If it is true, which is the default, the coordinates are absolute. If it is false, the coordinates are relative. The absolute coordinates are measured relative to the local coordinate system of the node. Relative coordinates are measured treating the ending point of the previous PathElement as the origin.

The Path class contains three constructors.

- Path()
- Path(Collection<? extends PathElement> elements)
- Path(PathElement... elements)

The no-args constructor creates an empty shape. The other two constructors take a list of path elements as arguments. A Path stores path elements in an ObservableList<PathElement>. You can get the reference of the list using the getElements() method. You can modify the list of path elements to modify the shape. The following snippet of code shows two ways of creating shapes using the Path class:

```
// Pass the path elements to the constructor
Path shape1 = new Path(pathElement1, pathElement2, pathElement3);

// Create an empty path and add path elements to the elements list
Path shape2 = new Path();
shape2.getElements().addAll(pathElement1, pathElement2, pathElement3);
```

■ **Tip** An instance of the `PathElement` may be added as a path element to `Path` objects simultaneously. A `Path` uses the same `fill` and `stroke` for all its path elements.

The MoveTo Path Element

A `MoveTo` path element is used to make the specified x and y coordinates as the current point. It has the effect of lifting and placing the pencil at the specified point on the paper. The first path element of a `Path` object must be a `MoveTo` element and it must not use relative coordinates. The `MoveTo` class defines two `double` properties that are the x and y coordinates of the point.

- x

- y

The `MoveTo` class contains two constructors. The no-args constructor sets the current point to (0.0, 0.0). The other constructor takes the x and y coordinates of the current point as arguments.

```
// Create a MoveTo path element to move the current point to (0.0, 0.0)
MoveTo mt1 = new MoveTo();

// Create a MoveTo path element to move the current point to (10.0, 10.0)
MoveTo mt2 = new MoveTo(10.0, 10.0);
```

■ **Tip** A path must start with a `MoveTo` path element. You can have multiple `MoveTo` path elements in a path. A subsequent `MoveTo` element denotes the starting point of a new subpath.

The LineTo Path Element

A `LineTo` path element draws a straight line from the current point to the specified point. It contains two `double` properties that are the x and y coordinates of the end of the line:

- x

- y

The `LineTo` class contains two constructors. The no-args constructor sets the end of the line to (0.0, 0.0). The other constructor takes the x and y coordinates of the end of the line as arguments.

```
// Create a LineTo path element with its end at (0.0, 0.0)
LineTo lt1 = new LineTo();

// Create a LineTo path element with its end at (10.0, 10.0)
LineTo lt2 = new LineTo(10.0, 10.0);
```

With the knowledge of the MoveTo and LineTo path elements, you can construct shapes that are made of lines only. The following snippet of code creates a triangle as shown in Figure 17-15. The figure shows the triangle and its path elements. The arrows show the flow of the drawing. Notice that the drawing starts at (0.0) using the first MoveTo path element.

```
Path triangle = new Path(new MoveTo(0, 0),
                         new LineTo(0, 50),
                         new LineTo(50, 50),
                         new LineTo(0, 0));
```

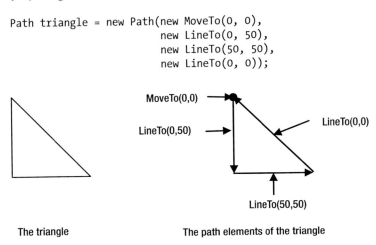

The triangle   The path elements of the triangle

Figure 17-15. *Creating a triangle using the MoveTo and LineTo path elements*

The ClosePath path element closes a path by drawing a straight line from the current point to the starting point of the path. If multiple MoveTo path elements exist in a path, a ClosePath draws a straight line from the current point to the point identified by the last MoveTo. You can rewrite the path for the previous triangle example using a ClosePath.

```
Path triangle = new Path(new MoveTo(0, 0),
                         new LineTo(0, 50),
                         new LineTo(50, 50),
                         new ClosePath());
```

The program in Listing 17-11 creates two Path nodes: one triangle and one with two inverted triangles to give it a look of a star as shown in Figure 17-16. In the second shape, each triangle is created as a subpath—each subpath starting with a MoveTo element. Notice the two uses of the ClosePath elements. Each ClosePath closes its subpath.

Listing 17-11. Using the Path Class to Create a Triangle and a Star

```java
// PathTest.java
package com.jdojo.shape;

import javafx.application.Application;
import javafx.scene.Scene;
import javafx.scene.layout.HBox;
import javafx.scene.shape.ClosePath;
import javafx.scene.shape.LineTo;
import javafx.scene.shape.MoveTo;
import javafx.scene.shape.Path;
import javafx.stage.Stage;

public class PathTest extends Application {
        public static void main(String[] args) {
                Application.launch(args);
        }

        @Override
        public void start(Stage stage) {
                Path triangle = new Path(new MoveTo(0, 0),
                                        new LineTo(0, 50),
                                        new LineTo(50, 50),
                                        new ClosePath());

                Path star = new Path();
                star.getElements().addAll(new MoveTo(30, 0),
                                        new LineTo(0, 30),
                                        new LineTo(60, 30),
                                        new ClosePath(),/* new LineTo(30, 0), */
                                        new MoveTo(0, 10),
                                        new LineTo(60, 10),
                                        new LineTo(30, 40),
                                        new ClosePath() /*new LineTo(0, 10)*/);

                HBox root = new HBox(triangle, star);
                root.setSpacing(10);
                root.setStyle("-fx-padding: 10;" +
                                "-fx-border-style: solid inside;" +
                                "-fx-border-width: 2;" +
                                "-fx-border-insets: 5;" +
                                "-fx-border-radius: 5;" +
                                "-fx-border-color: blue;");

                Scene scene = new Scene(root);
                stage.setScene(scene);
                stage.setTitle("Using Paths");
                stage.show();
        }
}
```

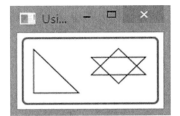

Figure 17-16. *Shapes based on path elements*

The HLineTo and VLineTo Path Elements

The HLineTo path element draws a horizontal line from the current point to the specified x coordinate. The y coordinate of the ending point of the line is the same as the y coordinate of the current point. The x property of the HLineTo class specifies the x coordinate of the ending point.

```
// Create an horizontal line from the current point (x, y) to (50, y)
HLineTo hlt = new HLineTo(50);
```

The VLineTo path element draws a vertical line from the current point to the specified y coordinate. The x coordinate of the ending point of the line is the same as the x coordinate of the current point. The y property of the VLineTo class specifies the y coordinate of the ending point.

```
// Create a vertical line from the current point (x, y) to (x, 50)
VLineTo vlt = new VLineTo(50);
```

■ **Tip** The LineTo path element is the generic version of HLineTo and VLineTo.

The following snippet of code creates the same triangle as discussed in the previous section. This time, you use HLineTo and VLineTo path elements to draw the base and height sides of the triangle instead of the LineTo path elements.

```
Path triangle = new Path(new MoveTo(0, 0),
                         new VLineTo(50),
                         new HLineTo(50),
                         new ClosePath());
```

The ArcTo Path Element

An ArcTo path element defines a segment of ellipse connecting the current point and the specified point. It contains the following properties:

- radiusX
- radiusY
- x
- y

765

- XAxisRotation
- largeArcFlag
- sweepFlag

The radiusX and radiusY properties specify the horizontal and vertical radii of the ellipse. The x and y properties specify the x and y coordinates of the ending point of the arc. Note that the starting point of the arc is the current point of the path.

The XAxisRotation property specifies the rotation of the x-axis of the ellipse in degrees. Note that the rotation is for the x-axis of the ellipse from which the arc is obtained, not the x-axis of the coordinate system of the node. A positive value rotates the x-axis counterclockwise.

The largeArcFlag and sweepFlag properties are Boolean type, and by default, they are set to false. Their uses need a detailed explanation. Two ellipses can pass through two given points as shown in Figure 17-17 giving us four arcs to connect the two points.

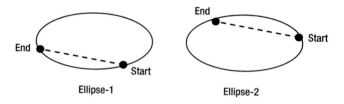

Figure 17-17. *Effects of the largeArcFlag and sweepFlag properties on an ArcTo path element*

Figure 17-17 shows starting and ending points labeled Start and End, respectively. Two points on an ellipse can be traversed through the larger arc or smaller arc. If the largeArcFlag is true, the larger arc is used. Otherwise, the smaller arc is used.

When it is decided that the larger or smaller arc is used, you still have two choices: which ellipse of the two possible ellipses will be used? This is determined by the sweepFlag property. Try drawing the arc from the starting point to the point ending point using two selected arcs—the two larger arcs or the two smaller arcs. For one arc, the traversal will be clockwise and for the other counterclockwise. If the sweepFlag is true, the ellipse with the clockwise traversal is used. If the sweepFlag is false, the ellipse with the counterclockwise traversal is used. Table 17-1 shows which type of arc from which ellipse will be used based on the two properties.

Table 17-1. *Choosing the Arc Segment and the Ellipse Based on the largeArcFlag and sweepFlag Properties*

largeArcFlag	sweepFlag	Arc Type	Ellipse
true	true	Larger	Ellipse-2
true	false	Larger	Ellipse-1
false	true	Smaller	Ellipse-1
false	false	Smaller	Ellipse-2

The program in Listing 17-12 uses an ArcTo path element to build a Path object. The program lets the user change properties of the ArcTo path element. Run the program and change largeArcFlag, sweepFlag, and other properties to see how they affect the ArcTo path element.

Listing 17-12. Using ArcTo Path Elements

```java
// ArcToTest.java
package com.jdojo.shape;

import javafx.application.Application;
import javafx.scene.Scene;
import javafx.scene.control.CheckBox;
import javafx.scene.control.Label;
import javafx.scene.control.Slider;
import javafx.scene.layout.BorderPane;
import javafx.scene.layout.GridPane;
import javafx.scene.shape.ArcTo;
import javafx.scene.shape.HLineTo;
import javafx.scene.shape.MoveTo;
import javafx.scene.shape.Path;
import javafx.scene.shape.VLineTo;
import javafx.stage.Stage;

public class ArcToTest extends Application {
        private ArcTo arcTo;

        public static void main(String[] args) {
                Application.launch(args);
        }

        @Override
        public void start(Stage stage) {
                // Create the ArcTo path element
                arcTo = new ArcTo();

                // Use the arcTo element to build a Path
                Path path = new Path(new MoveTo(0, 0),
                                     new VLineTo(100),
                                     new HLineTo(100),
                                     new VLineTo(50),
                                     arcTo);

                BorderPane root = new BorderPane();
                root.setTop(this.getTopPane());
                root.setCenter(path);
                root.setStyle("-fx-padding: 10;" +
                              "-fx-border-style: solid inside;" +
                              "-fx-border-width: 2;" +
                              "-fx-border-insets: 5;" +
                              "-fx-border-radius: 5;" +
                              "-fx-border-color: blue;");
```

767

```java
                Scene scene = new Scene(root);
                stage.setScene(scene);
                stage.setTitle("Using ArcTo Path Elements");
                stage.show();
        }

        private GridPane getTopPane() {
                CheckBox largeArcFlagCbx = new CheckBox("largeArcFlag");
                CheckBox sweepFlagCbx = new CheckBox("sweepFlag");
                Slider xRotationSlider = new Slider(0, 360, 0);
                xRotationSlider.setPrefWidth(300);
                xRotationSlider.setBlockIncrement(30);
                xRotationSlider.setShowTickMarks(true);
                xRotationSlider.setShowTickLabels(true);

                Slider radiusXSlider = new Slider(100, 300, 100);
                radiusXSlider.setBlockIncrement(10);
                radiusXSlider.setShowTickMarks(true);
                radiusXSlider.setShowTickLabels(true);

                Slider radiusYSlider = new Slider(100, 300, 100);
                radiusYSlider.setBlockIncrement(10);
                radiusYSlider.setShowTickMarks(true);
                radiusYSlider.setShowTickLabels(true);

                // Bind ArcTo properties to the control data
                arcTo.largeArcFlagProperty().bind(largeArcFlagCbx.selectedProperty());
                arcTo.sweepFlagProperty().bind(sweepFlagCbx.selectedProperty());
                arcTo.XAxisRotationProperty().bind(xRotationSlider.valueProperty());
                arcTo.radiusXProperty().bind(radiusXSlider.valueProperty());
                arcTo.radiusYProperty().bind(radiusYSlider.valueProperty());

                GridPane pane = new GridPane();
                pane.setHgap(5);
                pane.setVgap(10);
                pane.addRow(0, largeArcFlagCbx, sweepFlagCbx);
                pane.addRow(1, new Label("XAxisRotation"), xRotationSlider);
                pane.addRow(2, new Label("radiusX"), radiusXSlider);
                pane.addRow(3, new Label("radiusY"), radiusYSlider);

                return pane;
        }
}
```

The QuadCurveTo Path Element

An instance of the QuadCurveTo class draws a quadratic Bezier curve from the current point to the specified ending point (x, y) using the specified control point (controlX, controlY). It contains four properties to specify the ending and control points.

- x

- y

- controlX

- controlY

The x and y properties specify the x and y coordinates of the ending point. The controlX and controlY properties specify the x and y coordinates of the control point.

The QuadCurveTo class contains two constructors.

- QuadCurveTo()

- QuadCurveTo(double controlX, double controlY, double x, double y)

The following snippet of code uses a QuadCurveTo with the (10, 100) control point and (0, 0) ending point. Figure 17-18 shows the resulting path.

```
Path path = new Path(new MoveTo(0, 0),
                     new VLineTo(100),
                     new HLineTo(100),
                     new VLineTo(50),
                     new QuadCurveTo(10, 100, 0, 0));
```

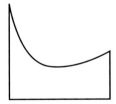

Figure 17-18. *Using a QuadCurveTo path element*

The CubicCurveTo Path Element

An instance of the CubicCurveTo class draws a cubic Bezier curve from the current point to the specified ending point (x, y) using the specified control points (controlX1, controlY1) and (controlX2, controlY2). It contains six properties to specify the ending and control points:

- x

- y

- controlX1

- controlY1

- controlX2

- controlY2

769

The x and y properties specify the x and y coordinates of the ending point. The controlX1 and controlY1 properties specify the x and y coordinates of the first control point. The controlX2 and controlY2 properties specify the x and y coordinates of the second control point.

The CubicCurveTo class contains two constructors:

- CubicCurveTo()

- CubicCurveTo(double controlX1, double controlY1, double controlX2, double controlY2, double x, double y)

The following snippet of code uses a CubicCurveTo with the (10, 100) and (40, 80) as control points, and (0, 0) as the ending point. Figure 17-19 shows the resulting path.

```
Path path = new Path(new MoveTo(0, 0),
                     new VLineTo(100),
                     new HLineTo(100),
                     new VLineTo(50),
                     new CubicCurveTo(10, 100, 40, 80, 0, 0));
```

Figure 17-19. *Using a QuadCurveTo path element*

The ClosePath Path Element

The ClosePath path element closes the current subpath. Note that a Path may consist of multiple subpaths, and, therefore, it is possible to have multiple ClosePath elements in a Path. A ClosePath element draws a straight line from the current point to the initial point of the current subpath and ends the subpath. A ClosePath element may be followed by a MoveTo element, and in that case, the MoveTo element is the starting point of the next subpath. If a ClosePath element is followed by a path element other than a MoveTo element, the next subpath starts at the starting point of the subpath that was closed by the ClosePath element.

The following snippet of code creates a Path object, which uses two subpaths. Each subpath draws a rectangle. The subpaths are closed using ClosePath elements. Figure 17-20 shows the resulting shape.

```
Path p1 = new Path(new MoveTo(50, 0),
                   new LineTo(0, 50),
                   new LineTo(100, 50),
                   new ClosePath(),
                   new MoveTo(90, 15),
                   new LineTo(40, 65),
                   new LineTo(140, 65),
                   new ClosePath());
p1.setFill(Color.LIGHTGRAY);
```

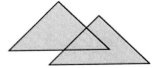

Figure 17-20. *A shape using two subpaths and ClosePath element*

The Fill Rule for a Path

A Path can be used to draw very complex shapes. Sometimes, it is hard to determine whether a point is inside or outside the shape. The Path class contains a fillRule property that is used to determine whether a point is inside a shape. Its value could be one of the constants of the FillRule enum: NON_ZERO and EVEN_ODD. If a point is inside the shape, it will be rendered using the fill color. Figure 17-21 shows two triangles created by a Path and a point in area common to both triangles. I will discuss whether the point is considered inside the shape.

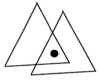

Figure 17-21. *A shape made of two triangular subpaths*

The direction of the stroke is the vital factor in determining whether a point is inside a shape. The shape in Figure 17-21 can be drawn using strokes in different directions. Figure 17-22 shows two of them. In Shape-1, both triangles use counterclockwise strokes. In Shape-2, one triangle uses a counterclockwise stroke and another uses a clockwise stroke.

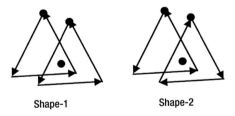

Shape-1   Shape-2

Figure 17-22. *A shape made of two triangular subpaths using different stroke directions*

The fill rule of a Path draws rays from the point to infinity, so they can intersect all path segments. In the NON_ZERO fill rule, if the number of path segments intersected by rays is equal in counterclockwise and clockwise directions, the point is outside the shape. Otherwise, the point is inside the shape. You can understand this rule by using a counter, which starts with zero. Add one to the counter for every ray intersecting a path segment in the counterclockwise direction. Subtract one from the counter for every ray intersecting a path segment in the clockwise direction. At the end, if the counter is non-zero, the point is inside; otherwise, the point is outside. Figure 17-23 shows the same two paths made of two triangular

771

subpaths with their counter values when the NON_ZERO fill rule is applied. The rays drawn from the point are shown in dashed lines. The point in the first shape scores six (a non-zero value) and it is inside the path. The point in the second shape scores zero and it is outside the path.

Like the NON_ZERO fill rule, the EVEN_ODD fill rule also draws rays from a point in all directions extending to infinity, so all path segments are intersected. It counts the number of intersections between the rays and the path segments. If the number is odd, the point is inside the path. Otherwise, the point is outside the path. If you set the fillRule property to EVEN_ODD for the two shapes shown in Figure 17-23, the point is outside the path for both shapes because the number of intersections between rays and path segments is six (an even number) in both cases. The default value for the fillRule property of a Path is FillRule.NON_ZERO.

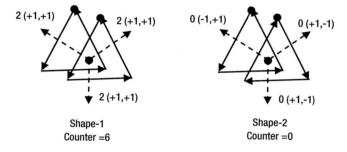

Figure 17-23. *Applying the NON_ZERO fill rule to two triangular subpaths*

The program in Listing 17-13 is an implementation of the examples discussed in this section. It draws four paths: the first two (counting from the left) with NON_ZERO fill rules and the last two with EVEN_ODD fill rules. Figure 17-24 shows the paths. The first and third paths use a counterclockwise stroke for drawing both triangular subpaths. The second and fourth paths are drawn using a counterclockwise stroke for one triangle and a clockwise stroke for another.

Listing 17-13. Using Fill Rules for Paths

```java
// PathFillRule.java
package com.jdojo.shape;

import javafx.application.Application;
import javafx.scene.Scene;
import javafx.scene.layout.HBox;
import javafx.scene.paint.Color;
import javafx.scene.shape.FillRule;
import javafx.scene.shape.LineTo;
import javafx.scene.shape.MoveTo;
import javafx.scene.shape.Path;
import javafx.scene.shape.PathElement;
import javafx.stage.Stage;

public class PathFillRule extends Application {
    public static void main(String[] args) {
        Application.launch(args);
    }
```

```java
@Override
public void start(Stage stage) {
        // Both triangles use a couterclockwise stroke
        PathElement[] pathEleemnts1 = {new MoveTo(50, 0),
                                       new LineTo(0, 50),
                                       new LineTo(100, 50),
                                       new LineTo(50, 0),
                                       new MoveTo(90, 15),
                                       new LineTo(40, 65),
                                       new LineTo(140, 65),
                                       new LineTo(90, 15)};

        // One traingle uses a clockwise stroke and
        // another uses a couterclockwise stroke
        PathElement[] pathEleemnts2 = {new MoveTo(50, 0),
                                       new LineTo(0, 50),
                                       new LineTo(100, 50),
                                       new LineTo(50, 0),
                                       new MoveTo(90, 15),
                                       new LineTo(140, 65),
                                       new LineTo(40, 65),
                                       new LineTo(90, 15)};

        /* Using the NON-ZERO fill rule by default */
        Path p1 = new Path(pathEleemnts1);
        p1.setFill(Color.LIGHTGRAY);

        Path p2 = new Path(pathEleemnts2);
        p2.setFill(Color.LIGHTGRAY);

        /* Using the EVEN_ODD fill rule */
        Path p3 = new Path(pathEleemnts1);
        p3.setFill(Color.LIGHTGRAY);
        p3.setFillRule(FillRule.EVEN_ODD);

        Path p4 = new Path(pathEleemnts2);
        p4.setFill(Color.LIGHTGRAY);
        p4.setFillRule(FillRule.EVEN_ODD);

        HBox root = new HBox(p1, p2, p3, p4);
        root.setSpacing(10);
        root.setStyle("-fx-padding: 10;" +
                      "-fx-border-style: solid inside;" +
                      "-fx-border-width: 2;" +
                      "-fx-border-insets: 5;" +
                      "-fx-border-radius: 5;" +
                      "-fx-border-color: blue;");

        Scene scene = new Scene(root);
        stage.setScene(scene);
        stage.setTitle("Using Fill Rules for Paths");
        stage.show();
    }
}
```

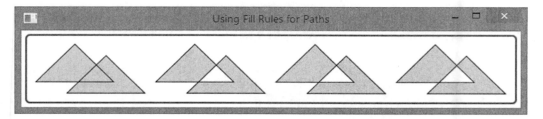

Figure 17-24. *Paths using different fill rules*

Drawing Scalable Vector Graphics

An instance of the SVGPath class draws a shape from path data in an encoded string. You can find the SVG specification at http://www.w3.org/TR/SVG. You can find the detailed rules of constructing the path data in string format at http://www.w3.org/TR/SVG/paths.html. JavaFX partially supports SVG specification.

The SVGPath class contains a no-args constructor to create its object.

```
// Create a SVGPath object
SVGPath sp = new SVGPath();
```

The SVGPath class contains two properties.

- content
- fillRule

The content property defines the encoded string for the SVG path. The fillRule property specifies the fill rule for the interior of the shape, which could be FillRule.NON_ZERO or FilleRule.EVEN_ODD. The default value for the fillRule property is FillRule.NON_ZERO. Please refer to the section "The Fill Rule for a Path" for more details on fill rules. Fill rule for a Path and a SVGPath work the same.

The following snippet of code sets "M50, 0 L0, 50 L100, 50 Z" encoded string as the content for a SVGPath object to draw a triangle as shown in Figure 17-25:

```
SVGPath sp2 = new SVGPath();
sp2.setContent("M50, 0 L0, 50 L100, 50 Z");
sp2.setFill(Color.LIGHTGRAY);
sp2.setStroke(Color.BLACK);
```

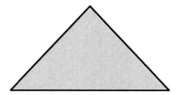

Figure 17-25. *A triangle using a SVGPath*

The content of a SVGPath is an encoded string following some rules:

- The string consists of a series of commands.

- Each command name is exactly one-letter long.

- A command is followed by its parameters.

- Parameter values for a command are separated by a comma or a space. For example, "M50, 0 L0, 50 L100, 50 Z" and "M50 0 L0 50 L100 50 Z" represent the same path. For readability, you will use a comma to separate two values.

- You do not need to add spaces before or after the command character. For example, "M50 0 L0 50 L100 50 Z" can be rewritten as "M50 0L0 50L100 50Z".

Let us consider the SVG content used in the previous example.

```
M50, 0 L0, 50 L100, 50 Z
```

The content consists of four commands.

- M50, 0
- L0, 50
- L100, 50
- Z

Comparing the SVG path commands with the Path API, the first command is "MoveTo (50, 0)"; the second command is "LineTo(0, 50)"; the third command is "LineTo(100, 50)" and the fourth command is "ClosePath".

■ **Tip** The command name in SVGPath content is the first letter of the classes representing path elements in a Path object. For example, an absolute MoveTo in the Path API becomes M in SVGPath content, an absolute LineTo becomes L, and so on.

The parameters for the commands are coordinates, which can be absolute or relative. When the command name is in uppercase (e.g., M), its parameters are considered absolute. When the command name is in lowercase (e.g., m), its parameters are considered relative. The "closepath" command is Z or z. Because the "closepath" command does take any parameters, both uppercase and lowercase versions behave the same.

Consider the content of two SVG paths:

- M50, 0 L0, 50 L100, 50 Z
- M50, 0 l0, 50 l100, 50 Z

The first path uses absolute coordinates. The second path uses absolute and relative coordinates. Like a Path, a SVGPath must start with a "moveTo" command, which must use absolute coordinates. If a SVGPath starts with a relative "moveTo" command (e.g., "m 50, 0"), its parameters are treated as absolute coordinates. In the foregoing SVG paths, you can start the string with "m50, 0" and the result will be the same.

The previous two SVG paths will draw two different triangles, as shown in Figure 17-26, even though both use the same parameters. The first path draws the triangle on the left and the second one draws the triangle on the right. The commands in the second path are interpreted as follows:

- Move to (50, 0)

- Draw a line from the current point (50, 0) to (50, 50). The ending point (50, 50) is derived by adding the x and y coordinates of the current point to the relative "lineto" command (l) parameters. The ending point becomes (50, 50).

- Draw a line from the current point (50, 50) to (150, 100). Again, the coordinates of the ending point are derived by adding the x and y coordinates of the current point (50, 50) to the command parameter "l100, 50" (The first character in "l100, 50" is the lowercase L. not the digit 1).

- The close the path (Z)

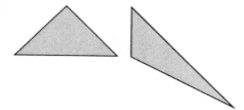

Figure 17-26. *Using absolute and relative coordinates in SVG paths*

Table 17-2 lists the commands used in the content of the SVGPath objects. It also lists the equivalent classes used in the Path API. The table lists the command, which uses absolute coordinates. The relative versions of the commands use lowercase letters. The plus sign (+) in the parameter column indicates that multiple parameters may be used.

Table 17-2. *List of SVG Path Commands*

Command	Parameter	Command Name	Path API Class
M	(x, y)+	moveto	MoveTo
L	(x, y)+	lineto	LineTo
H	x+	lineto	HLineTo
V	y+	lineto	VLineTo
A	(rx, ry, x-axis-rotation, large-arc-flag, sweep-flag, x, y)+	arcto	ArcTo
Q	(x1, y1, x, y)+	Quadratic Bezier curveto	QuadCurveTo
T	(x, y)+	Shorthand/smooth quadratic Bezier curveto	QuadCurveTo
C	(x1, y1, x2, y2, x, y)+	curveto	CubicCurveTo
S	(x2, y2, x, y)+	Shorthand/smooth curveto	CubicCurveTo
Z	None	closePath	ClosePath

The "moveTo" Command

The "moveTo" command M starts a new subpath at the specified (x, y) coordinates. It may be followed by one or multiple pairs of coordinates. The first pair of coordinates is considered the x and y coordinates of the point, which the command will make the current point. Each additional pair is treated as a parameter for a "lineto" command. If the "moveTo" command is relative, the "lineto" command will be relative. If the "moveTo" command is absolute, the "lineto" command will be absolute. For example, the following two SVG paths are the same:

```
M50, 0 L0, 50 L100, 50 Z
M50, 0, 0, 50, 100, 50 Z
```

The "lineto" Commands

There are three "lineto" commands: L, H, and V. They are used to draw straight lines.

The command L is used to draw a straight line from the current point to the specified (x, y) point. If you specify multiple pairs of (x, y) coordinates, it draws a polyline. The final pair of the (x, y) coordinate becomes the new current point. The following SVG paths will draw the same triangle. The first one uses two L commands and the second one uses only one.

- M50, 0 L0, 50 L100, 50 L50, 0

- M50, 0 L0, 50, 100, 50, 50, 0

The H and V commands are used to draw horizontal and vertical lines from the current point. The command H draws a horizontal line from the current point (cx, cy) to (x, cy). The command V draws a vertical line from the current point (cx, cy) to (cx, y). You can pass multiple parameters to them. The final parameter value defines the current point. For example, "M0, 0H200, 100 V50Z" will draw a line from (0, 0) to (200, 0), from (200, 0) to (100, 0). The second command will make (100, 0) as the current point. The third command will draw a vertical line from (100, 0) to (100, 50). The z command will draw a line from (100, 50) to (0, 0). The following snippet of code draws a SVG path as shown in Figure 17-27:

```
SVGPath p1 = new SVGPath();
p1.setContent("M0, 0H-50, 50, 0 V-50, 50, 0, -25 L25, 0");
p1.setFill(Color.LIGHTGRAY);
p1.setStroke(Color.BLACK);
```

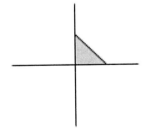

Figure 17-27. Using multiple parameters to "lineto" commands

The "arcto" Command

The "arcto" command A draws an elliptical arc from the current point to the specified (x, y) point. It uses rx and ry as the radii along x-axis and y-axis. The x-axis-rotation is a rotation angle in degrees for the x-axis of the ellipse. The large-arc-flag and sweep-flag are the flags used to select one arc out of four possible arcs. Use 0 and 1 for flag values, where 1 means true and 0 means false. Please refer to the section "The ArcTo Path Element" for a detailed explanation of all its parameters. You can pass multiple arcs parameters, and in that case, the ending point of an arc becomes the current point for the subsequent arc. The following snippet of code draws two SVG paths with arcs. The first path uses one parameter for the "arcTo" command and the second path uses two parameters. Figure 17-28 shows the paths.

```
SVGPath p1 = new SVGPath();

// rx=150, ry=50, x-axis-rotation=0, large-arc-flag=0,
// sweep-flag 0, x=-50, y=50
p1.setContent("M0, 0 A150, 50, 0, 0, 0, -50, 50 Z");
p1.setFill(Color.LIGHTGRAY);
p1.setStroke(Color.BLACK);

// Use multiple arcs in one "arcTo" command
SVGPath p2 = new SVGPath();

// rx1=150, ry1=50, x-axis-rotation1=0, large-arc-flag1=0,
// sweep-flag1=0, x1=-50, y1=50
// rx2=150, ry2=10, x-axis-rotation2=0, large-arc-flag2=0,
// sweep-flag2=0, x2=10, y2=10
p2.setContent("M0, 0 A150 50 0 0 0 -50 50, 150 10 0 0 0 10 10 Z");
p2.setFill(Color.LIGHTGRAY);
p2.setStroke(Color.BLACK);
```

Figure 17-28. *Using "arcTo" commands to draw elliptical arc paths*

The "Quadratic Bezier curveto" Command

Both commands Q and T are used to draw quadratic Bezier curve.

The command Q draws a quadratic Bezier curve from the current point to the specified (x, y) point using the specified (x1, y1) as the control point.

The command T draws a quadratic Bezier curve from the current point to the specified (x, y) point using a control point that is the reflection of the control point on the previous command. The current point is used as the control point if there was no previous command or the previous command was not Q, q, T, or t.

The command Q takes the control point as parameters whereas the command T assumes the control point. The following snippet of code uses the commands Q and T to draw quadratic Bezier curves as shown in Figure 17-29:

```
SVGPath p1 = new SVGPath();
p1.setContent("M0, 50 Q50, 0, 100, 50");
p1.setFill(Color.LIGHTGRAY);
p1.setStroke(Color.BLACK);

SVGPath p2 = new SVGPath();
p2.setContent("M0, 50 Q50, 0, 100, 50 T200, 50");
p2.setFill(Color.LIGHTGRAY);
p2.setStroke(Color.BLACK);
```

Figure 17-29. *Using Q and T commands to draw quadratic Bezier curves*

The "Cubic Bezier curveto" Command

The commands C and S are used to draw cubic Bezier curves.

The command C draws a cubic Bezier curve from the current point to the specified point (x, y) using the specified controls points (x1, y1) and (x2, y2).

The command S draws a cubic Bezier curve from the current point to the specified point (x, y). It assumes the first control point to be the reflection of the second control point on the previous command. The current point is used as the first control point if there was no previous command or the previous command was not C, c, S, or s. The specified point (x2, y2) is the second control point. Multiple sets of coordinates draw a polybezier.

The following snippet of code uses the commands C and S to draw cubic Bezier curves as shown in Figure 17-30. The second path uses the command S to use the reflection of the second control point of the previous command C as its first control point.

```
SVGPath p1 = new SVGPath();
p1.setContent("M0, 0 C0, -100, 100, 100, 100, 0");
p1.setFill(Color.LIGHTGRAY);
p1.setStroke(Color.BLACK);

SVGPath p2 = new SVGPath();
p2.setContent("M0, 0 C0, -100, 100, 100, 100, 0 S200 100 200, 0");
p2.setFill(Color.LIGHTGRAY);
p2.setStroke(Color.BLACK);
```

Figure 17-30. *Using C and S commands to draw cubic Bezier curves*

The "closepath" Command

The "closepath" commands Z and z draw a straight line from the current point to the starting point of the current subpath and ends the subpath. Both uppercase and lowercase versions of the command work the same.

Combining Shapes

The Shape class provides three static methods that let you perform union, intersection and subtraction of shapes.

- union(Shape shape1, Shape shape2)
- intersect(Shape shape1, Shape shape2)
- subtract(Shape shape1, Shape shape2)

The methods return a new Shape instance. They operate on the areas of the input shapes. If a shape does not have a fill and a stroke, its area is zero. The new shape has a stroke and a fill. The union() method combines the areas of two shapes. The intersect() method uses the common areas between the shapes to create the new shape. The subtract() method creates a new shape by subtracting the specified second shape from the first shape.

The program in Listing 17-14 combines two circles using the union, intersection, and subtraction operations. Figure 17-31 shows the resulting shapes.

Listing 17-14. Combining Shapes to Create New Shapes

```java
// CombiningShapesTest.java
package com.jdojo.shape;

import javafx.application.Application;
import javafx.scene.Scene;
import javafx.scene.layout.HBox;
import javafx.scene.paint.Color;
import javafx.scene.shape.Circle;
import javafx.scene.shape.Shape;
import javafx.stage.Stage;

public class CombiningShapesTest extends Application {
    public static void main(String[] args) {
        Application.launch(args);
    }
```

```
@Override
public void start(Stage stage) {
        Circle c1 = new Circle (0, 0, 20);
        Circle c2 = new Circle (15, 0, 20);

        Shape union = Shape.union(c1, c2);
        union.setStroke(Color.BLACK);
        union.setFill(Color.LIGHTGRAY);

        Shape intersection = Shape.intersect(c1, c2);
        intersection.setStroke(Color.BLACK);
        intersection.setFill(Color.LIGHTGRAY);

        Shape subtraction = Shape.subtract(c1, c2);
        subtraction.setStroke(Color.BLACK);
        subtraction.setFill(Color.LIGHTGRAY);

        HBox root = new HBox(union, intersection, subtraction);
        root.setSpacing(20);
        root.setStyle("-fx-padding: 10;" +
                    "-fx-border-style: solid inside;" +
                    "-fx-border-width: 2;" +
                    "-fx-border-insets: 5;" +
                    "-fx-border-radius: 5;" +
                    "-fx-border-color: blue;");

        Scene scene = new Scene(root);
        stage.setScene(scene);
        stage.setTitle("Combining Shapes");
        stage.show();
    }
}
```

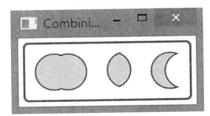

Figure 17-31. *Shapes created by combining two circles*

781

Understanding the Stroke of a Shape

Stroking is the process of painting the outline of a shape. Sometimes, the outline of a shape is also known as stroke. The Shape class contains several properties to define the appearance of the stroke of a shape.

- stroke
- strokeWidth
- strokeType
- strokeLineCap
- strokeLineJoin
- strokeMiterLimit
- strokeDashOffset

The stroke property specifies the color of the stroke. The default stroke is set to null for all shapes except Line, Path and Polyline, which have Color.BLACK as their default stroke.

The strokeWidth property specifies the width of the stroke. It is 1.0px by default.

The stroke is painted along the boundary of a shape. The strokeType property specifies the distribution of the width of the stroke on the boundary. Its value is one of the three constants, CENTERED, INSIDE, and OUTSIDE, the StrokeType enum. The default value is CENTERED. The CENTERED stroke type draws a half of the stroke width outside and half inside the boundary. The INSIDE stroke type draws the stroke inside the boundary. The OUTSIDE stroke draws the stroke outside the boundary. The stroke width of a shape is included in its layout bounds.

The program in Listing 17-15 creates four rectangles as shown in Figure 17-32. All rectangles have the same width and height (50px and 50px). The first rectangle, counting from the left, has no stroke and it has layout bounds of 50px X 50px. The second rectangle uses a stroke of width 4px and an INSIDE stroke type. The INSIDE stroke type is drawn inside the width and height boundary, the rectangle has the layout bounds of 50px X 50px. The third rectangle uses a stroke width 4px and a CENTERED stroke type, which is the default. The stroke is drawn 2px inside the boundary and 2px outside the boundary. The 2px outside stroke is added to the dimensions of all four making the layout bounds to 54px X 54px. The fourth rectangle uses a 4px stroke width and an OUTSIDE stroke type. The entire stroke width falls outside the width and height of the rectangle making the layouts to 58px X 58px.

Listing 17-15. Effects of Applying Different Stroke Types on a Rectangle

```java
// StrokeTypeTest.java
package com.jdojo.shape;

import javafx.application.Application;
import javafx.geometry.Pos;
import javafx.scene.Scene;
import javafx.scene.layout.HBox;
import javafx.scene.paint.Color;
import javafx.scene.shape.Rectangle;
import javafx.scene.shape.StrokeType;
import javafx.stage.Stage;

public class StrokeTypeTest extends Application {
    public static void main(String[] args) {
        Application.launch(args);
    }
```

```
@Override
public void start(Stage stage) {
        Rectangle r1 = new Rectangle(50, 50);
        r1.setFill(Color.LIGHTGRAY);

        Rectangle r2 = new Rectangle(50, 50);
        r2.setFill(Color.LIGHTGRAY);
        r2.setStroke(Color.BLACK);
        r2.setStrokeWidth(4);
        r2.setStrokeType(StrokeType.INSIDE);

        Rectangle r3 = new Rectangle(50, 50);
        r3.setFill(Color.LIGHTGRAY);
        r3.setStroke(Color.BLACK);
        r3.setStrokeWidth(4);

        Rectangle r4 = new Rectangle(50, 50);
        r4.setFill(Color.LIGHTGRAY);
        r4.setStroke(Color.BLACK);
        r4.setStrokeWidth(4);
        r4.setStrokeType(StrokeType.OUTSIDE);

        HBox root = new HBox(r1, r2, r3, r4);
        root.setAlignment(Pos.CENTER);
        root.setSpacing(10);
        root.setStyle("-fx-padding: 10;" +
                      "-fx-border-style: solid inside;" +
                      "-fx-border-width: 2;" +
                      "-fx-border-insets: 5;" +
                      "-fx-border-radius: 5;" +
                      "-fx-border-color: blue;");

        Scene scene = new Scene(root);
        stage.setScene(scene);
        stage.setTitle("Using Different Stroke Types for Shapes");
        stage.show();
    }
}
```

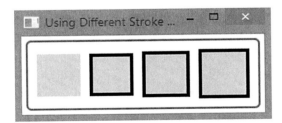

Figure 17-32. *Rectangles using different types of strokes*

The strokeLineCap property specifies the ending decoration of a stroke for unclosed subpaths and dash segments. Its value is one of the constants of the StrokeLineCap enum: BUTT, SQUARE, and ROUND. The default is BUTT. The BUTT line cap adds no decoration to the end of a subpath; the stroke starts and ends exactly at the starting and ending points. The SQUARE line cap extends the end by half the stroke width. The ROUND line cap adds a round cap to the end. The round cap uses a radius equal to half the stroke width. Figure 17-33 shows three lines, which are unclosed subpaths. All lines are 100px wide using 10px stroke width. The figure shows the strokeLineCap they use. The width of the layout bounds of the line using the BUTT line cap remains 100px. However, for other two lines, the width of the layout bounds increases to 110px—increasing by 10px at both ends.

Figure 17-33. *Different line cap style for strokes*

Note that the strokeLineCap properties are applied to the ends of a line segment of *unclosed* subpaths. Figure 17-34 shows three triangles created by unclosed subpaths. They use different stroke line caps. The SVG path data "M50, 0L0, 50 M0, 50 L100, 50 M100, 50 L50, 0" was used to draw the triangles. The fill was set to null and the stroke width to 10px.

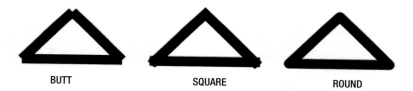

Figure 17-34. *Triangles using unclosed subpaths using different stroke line caps*

The strokeLineJoin property specifies how two successive path elements of a subpath are joined. Its value is one of the constants of the StrokeLineJoin enum: BEVEL, MITER, and ROUND. The default is MITER. The BEVEL line join connects the outer corners of path elements by a straight line. The MITER line join extends the outer edges of two path elements until they meet. The ROUND line join connects two path elements by rounding their corners by half the stroke width. Figure 17-35 shows three triangles created with the SVG path data "M50, 0L0, 50 L100, 50 Z". The fill color is null and the stroke width is 10px. The triangles use different line joins as shown in the figure.

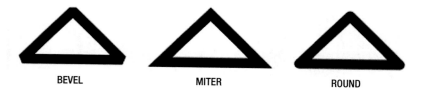

Figure 17-35. *Triangles using different stroke line join types*

A MITER line join joins two path elements by extending their outer edges. If the path elements meet at a smaller angle, the length of the join may become very big. You can limit the length of the join using the strokeMiterLimit property. It specifies the ratio of the miter length and the stroke width. The miter length is the distance between the most inside point and the most outside point of the join. If the two path elements cannot meet by extending their outer edges within this limit, a BEVEL join is used instead. The default value is 10.0. That is, by default, the miter length may be up to ten times the stroke width.

The following snippet of code creates two triangles as shown in Figure 17-36. Both use MITER line join by default. The first triangle uses 2.0 as the miter limit. The second triangle uses the default miter limit, which is 10.0. The stroke width is 10px. The first triangle tries to join the corners by extending two lines up to 20px, which is computed by multiplying the 10px stroke width by the miter limit of 2.0. The corners cannot be joined using the MITER join within 20px, so a BEVEL join is used.

```
SVGPath t1 = new SVGPath();
t1.setContent("M50, 0L0, 50 L100, 50 Z");
t1.setStrokeWidth(10);
t1.setFill(null);
t1.setStroke(Color.BLACK);
t1.setStrokeMiterLimit(2.0);

SVGPath t2 = new SVGPath();
t2.setContent("M50, 0L0, 50 L100, 50 Z");
t2.setStrokeWidth(10);
t2.setFill(null);
t2.setStroke(Color.BLACK);
```

Figure 17-36. *Triangles using different stroke miter limits*

By default, the stroke draws a solid outline. You can also have a dashed outline. You need to provide a dashing pattern and a dash offset. The dashing pattern is an array of double that is stored in an ObservableList<Double>. You can get the reference of the list using the getStrokeDashArray() method of the Shape class. The elements of the list specify a pattern of dashes and gaps. The first element is the dash length, the second gap, the third dash length, the fourth gap, and so on. The dashing pattern is repeated to draw the outline. The strokeDashOffset property specifies the offset in the dashing pattern where the stroke begins.

The following snippet of code creates two instances of Polygon as shown in Figure 17-37. Both use the same dashing patterns but a different dash offset. The first one uses the dash offset of 0.0, which is the default. The stroke of the first rectangle starts with a 15.0px dash, which is the first element of the dashing pattern, which can be seen in the dashed line drawn from the (0, 0) to (100, 0). The second Polygon uses a dash offset of 20.0, which means the stroke will start 20.0px inside the dashing pattern. The first two elements 15.0 and 3.0 are inside the dash offset 20.0. Therefore, the stroke for the second Polygon starts at the third element, which is a 5.0px dash.

```
Polygon p1 = new Polygon(0, 0, 100, 0, 100, 50, 0, 50, 0, 0);
p1.setFill(null);
p1.setStroke(Color.BLACK);
p1.getStrokeDashArray().addAll(15.0, 5.0, 5.0, 5.0);
```

785

```
Polygon p2 = new Polygon(0, 0, 100, 0, 100, 50, 0, 50, 0, 0);
p2.setFill(null);
p2.setStroke(Color.BLACK);
p2.getStrokeDashArray().addAll(15.0, 5.0, 5.0, 5.0);
p2.setStrokeDashOffset(20.0);
```

Figure 17-37. *Two polygons using dashing patterns for their outline*

Styling Shapes with CSS

All shapes do not have a default style-class name. If you want to apply styles to shapes using CSS, you need to add style-class names to them. All shapes can use the following CSS properties:

- -fx-fill
- -fx-smooth
- -fx-stroke
- -fx-stroke-type
- -fx-stroke-dash-array
- -fx-stroke-dash-offset
- -fx-stroke-line-cap
- -fx-stroke-line-join
- -fx-stroke-miter-limit
- -fx-stroke-width

All CSS properties correspond to the properties in the Shape class, which I have discussed at length in the previous section. Rectangle supports two additional CSS properties to specify arc width and height for rounded rectangles:

- -fx-arc-height
- -fx-arc-width

The following snippet of code creates a Rectangle and adds *rectangle* as its style-class name:

```
Rectangle r1 = new Rectangle(200, 50);
r1.getStyleClass().add("rectangle");
```

The following style will produce a rectangle as shown in Figure 17-38:

```
.rectangle {
        -fx-fill: lightgray;
        -fx-stroke: black;
        -fx-stroke-width: 4;
```

```
    -fx-stroke-dash-array: 15 5 5 10;
    -fx-stroke-dash-offset: 20;
    -fx-stroke-line-cap: round;
    -fx-stroke-line-join: bevel;
}
```

Figure 17-38. *Applying CSS styles to a rectangle*

Summary

Any shape that can be drawn in a two-dimensional plane is called a 2D shape. JavaFX offers various nodes to draw different types of shapes (lines, circles, rectangles, etc.). You can add shapes to a scene graph. All shape classes are in the javafx.scene.shape package. Classes representing 2D shapes are inherited from the abstract Shape class. A shape can have a stroke that defines the outline of the shape. A shape may have a fill.

An instance of the Line class represents a line node. A Line has no interior. By default, its fill property is set to null. Setting fill has no effect. The default stroke is Color.BLACK and the default strokeWidth is 1.0.

An instance of the Rectangle class represents a rectangle node. The class uses six properties to define the rectangle: x, y, width, height, arcWidth, and arcHeight. The x and y properties are the x and y coordinates of the upper-left corner of the rectangle in the local coordinate system of the node. The width and height properties are the width and height of the rectangle, respectively. Specify the same width and height to draw a square. By default, the corners of a rectangle are sharp. A rectangle can have rounded corners by specifying the arcWidth and arcHeight properties.

An instance of the Circle class represents a circle node. The class uses three properties to define the circle: centerX, centerY, and radius. The centerX and centerY properties are the x and y coordinates of the center of the circle in the local coordinate system of the node. The radius property is the radius of the circle. The default values for these properties are zero.

An instance of the Ellipse class represents an ellipse node. The class uses four properties to define the ellipse: centerX, centerY, radiusX, radiusY. The centerX and centerY properties are the x and y coordinates of the center of the circle in the local coordinate system of the node. The radiusX and radiusY are the radii of the ellipse in the horizontal and vertical directions. The default values for these properties are zero. A circle is a special case of an ellipse when radiusX and radiusY are the same.

An instance of the Polygon class represents a polygon node. The class does not define any public properties. It lets you draw a polygon using an array of (x, y) coordinates defining the vertices of the polygon. Using the Polygon class, you can draw any type of geometric shape that is created using connected lines (triangles, pentagon, hexagon, parallelogram, etc.).

A polyline is similar to a polygon, except that it does not draw a line between the last and first points. That is, a polyline is an open polygon. However, the fill color is used to fill the entire shape as if the shape was closed. An instance of the Polyline class represents a polyline node.

An instance of the Arc class represents a sector of an ellipse. The class uses seven properties to define the ellipse: centerX, centerY, radiusX, radiusY, startAngle, length, and type. The first four properties define an ellipse. The last three properties define a sector of the ellipse that is the Arc node. The startAngle property specifies the start angle of the section in degrees measured counterclockwise from the positive x-axis. It defines the beginning of the arc. The length is an angle in degrees measured counterclockwise from the start angle to define the end of the sector. If the length property is set to 360, the Arc is a full ellipse.

Bezier curves are used in computer graphics to draw smooth curves. An instance of the QuadCurve class represents a quadratic Bezier curve segment intersecting two specified points using a specified Bezier control point.

An instance of the CubicCurve class represents a cubic Bezier curve segment intersecting two specified points using two specified Bezier control points.

You can draw complex shapes using the Path class. An instance of the Path class defines the path (outline) of a shape. A path consists of one or more subpaths. A subpath consists of one or more path elements. Each subpath has a starting point and an ending point. A path element is an instance of the PathElement abstract class. Several subclasses of the PathElement class exist to represent specific type of path elements; those classes are MoveTo, LineTo, HLineTo, VLineTo, ArcTo, QuadCurveTo, CubicCurveTo, and ClosePath.

JavaFX partially supports SVG specification. An instance of the SVGPath class draws a shape from path data in an encoded string.

JavaFX lets you create a shape by combining multiple shapes. The Shape class provides three static methods named union(), intersect(), and subtract() that let you perform union, intersection, and subtraction of two shapes that are passed as the arguments to these methods. The methods return a new Shape instance. They operate on the areas of the input shapes. If a shape does not have a fill and a stroke, its area is zero. The new shape has a stroke and a fill. The union() method combines the areas of two shapes. The intersect() method uses the common areas between the shapes to create the new shape. The subtract() method creates a new shape by subtracting the specified second shape from the first shape.

Stroking is the process of painting the outline of a shape. Sometimes, the outline of a shape is also known as stroke. The Shape class contains several properties such as stroke, strokeWidth, and so on to define the appearance of the stroke of a shape.

JavaFX lets you style 2D shapes with CSS.

CHAPTER 18

■ ■ ■

Understanding Text Nodes

In this chapter, you will learn:

- What a Text node is and how to create it
- The coordinate system used for drawing Text nodes
- How to display multiline text in a Text node
- How to set fonts for a Text node
- How to access installed fonts and how to install custom fonts
- How to set the fill and stroke for Text nodes
- How to apply decoration such as underline and strikethrough to Text nodes
- How to apply font smoothing
- How to style Text nodes using CSS

What Is a Text Node?

A text node is an instance of the Text class that is used to render text. The Text class contains several properties to customize the appearance of text. The Text class and all its related classes – for example, the Font class, the TextAlignment enum, the FontWeight enum, etc. – are in the javafx.scene.text package.

The Text class inherits from the Shape class. That is, a Text is a Shape, which allows you to use all properties and methods of the Shape class on a Text node. For example, you can apply a fill color and a stroke to a Text node. Because Text is a node, you can use features of the Node class: for example, applying effects and transformations. You can also set text alignment, font family, font size, text wrapping style, etc., on a Text node.

Figure 18-1 shows three text nodes. The first one (from the left) is a simple text node. The second one uses bold text in a bigger font size. The third one uses the Reflection effect, a bigger font size, a stroke, and a fill.

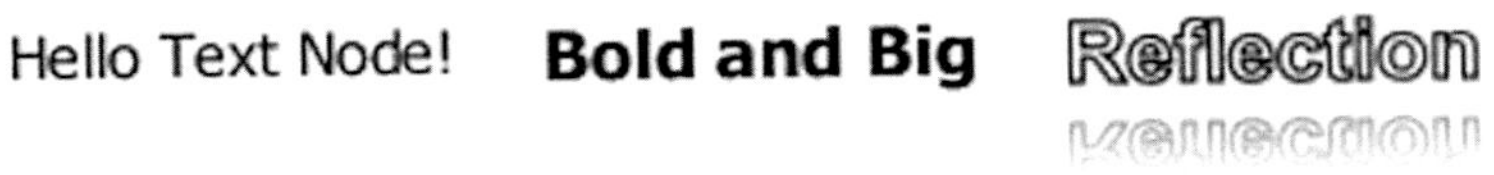

Hello Text Node! **Bold and Big** Reflection

Figure 18-1. A window showing three Text nodes

Creating a Text Node

An instance of the Text class represents a Text node. A Text node contains text and properties to render the text. You can create a Text node using one of the constructors of the Text class:

- `Text()`
- `Text(String text)`
- `Text(double x, double y, String text)`

The no-args constructor creates a Text node with an empty string as its text. Other constructors let you specify the text and position the node.

The text property of the Text class specifies the text (or content) of the Text node. The x and y properties specify the x and y coordinates of the text origin, which are described in the next section.

```
// Create an empty Text Node and later set its text
Text t1 = new Text();
t1.setText("Hello from the Text node!");

// Create a Text Node with initial text
Text t2 = new Text("Hello from the Text node!");

// Create a Text Node with initial text and position
Text t3 = new Text(50, 50, "Hello from the Text node!");
```

■ **Tip** The width and height of a text node are automatically determined by its font. By default, a Text node uses a system default font to render its text.

The program in Listing 18-1 creates three Text nodes, sets their different properties, and adds them to an HBox. The Text nodes are displayed as shown in Figure 18-1.

Listing 18-1. Creating Text Nodes

```
// TextTest.java
package com.jdojo.shape;

import javafx.application.Application;
import javafx.scene.Scene;
import javafx.scene.effect.Reflection;
import javafx.scene.layout.HBox;
import javafx.scene.paint.Color;
import javafx.scene.text.Font;
import javafx.scene.text.FontWeight;
import javafx.scene.text.Text;
import javafx.stage.Stage;

public class TextTest extends Application {
        public static void main(String[] args) {
                Application.launch(args);
        }
```

```
@Override
public void start(Stage stage) {
        Text t1 = new Text("Hello Text Node!");

        Text t2 = new Text("Bold and Big");
        t2.setFont(Font.font("Tahoma", FontWeight.BOLD, 16));

        Text t3 = new Text("Reflection");
        t3.setEffect(new Reflection());
        t3.setStroke(Color.BLACK);
        t3.setFill(Color.WHITE);
        t3.setFont(Font.font("Arial", FontWeight.BOLD, 20));

        HBox root = new HBox(t1, t2, t3);
        root.setSpacing(20);
        root.setStyle("-fx-padding: 10;" +
                        "-fx-border-style: solid inside;" +
                        "-fx-border-width: 2;" +
                        "-fx-border-insets: 5;" +
                        "-fx-border-radius: 5;" +
                        "-fx-border-color: blue;");

        Scene scene = new Scene(root);
        stage.setScene(scene);
        stage.setTitle("Using Text Nodes");
        stage.show();
    }
}
```

Understanding the Text Origin

Apart from the local and parent coordinate system, a Text node has an additional coordinate system. It is the coordinate system used for drawing the text. Three properties of the Text class define the text coordinate system:

- x

- y

- textOrigin

The x and y properties define the x and y coordinates of the text origin. The textOrigin property is of type VPos. Its value could be VPos.BASELINE, VPos.TOP, VPos.CENTER, and VPos.BOTTOM. The default is VPos.BASELINE. It defines where the x-axis of the text coordinate system lies within the text height. Figure 18-2 shows the local and text coordinate systems of a text node. The local coordinate axes are in solid lines. The text coordinate axes are in dashed lines.

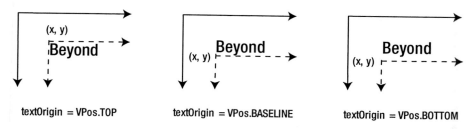

textOrigin = VPos.TOP   textOrigin = VPos.BASELINE   textOrigin = VPos.BOTTOM

Figure 18-2. Effects of the textOrigin property on the vertical location of text drawing

When the textOrigin is VPos.TOP, the x-axis of the text coordinate system is aligned with the top of the text. That is, the y property of the Text node is the distance between the x-axis of the local coordinate system and the top of the displayed text. A font places its characters on a line called the *baseline*. The VPos.BASELINE aligns the x-axis of the text coordinate system with the baseline of the font. Note that some characters (e.g., g, y, j, p, etc.) are extended below the baseline. The VPos.BOTTOM aligns the x-axis of the text coordinate system with the bottom of the displayed text accounting for the descent for the font. The VPos.CENTER (not shown in the figure) aligns the x-axis of the text coordinate system in the middle of the displayed text, accounting for the ascent and descent for the font.

■ **Tip** The Text class contains a read-only baselineOffset property. Its value is the vertical distance between the top and baseline of the text. It is equal to the max ascent of the font.

Most of the time, you need not worry about the textOrigin property of the Text node, except when you need to align it vertically relative to another node. Listing 18-2 shows how to center a Text node horizontally and vertically in a scene. To center the node vertically, you must set the textOrigin property to VPos.TOP. The text is displayed as shown in Figure 18-3. If you do not set the textOrigin property, its y-axis is aligned with its baseline and it appears above the centerline of the scene.

Listing 18-2. Centering a Text Node in a Scene

```java
// TextCentering.java
package com.jdojo.shape;

import javafx.application.Application;
import javafx.geometry.VPos;
import javafx.scene.Group;
import javafx.scene.Scene;
import javafx.scene.text.Text;
import javafx.stage.Stage;

public class TextCentering extends Application {
        public static void main(String[] args) {
                Application.launch(args);
        }
```

```
        @Override
        public void start(Stage stage) {
                Text msg = new Text("A Centered Text Node");

                // Must set the textOrigian to VPos.TOP to center
                // the text node vertcially within the scene
                msg.setTextOrigin(VPos.TOP);

                Group root = new Group();
                root.getChildren().addAll(msg);
                Scene scene = new Scene(root, 200, 50);
                msg.layoutXProperty().bind(scene.widthProperty().subtract(
                                msg.layoutBoundsProperty().get().getWidth()).divide(2));
                msg.layoutYProperty().bind(scene.heightProperty().subtract(
                                msg.layoutBoundsProperty().get().getHeight()).divide(2));

                stage.setTitle("Centering a Text Node in a Scene");
                stage.setScene(scene);
                stage.sizeToScene();
                stage.show();
        }
}
```

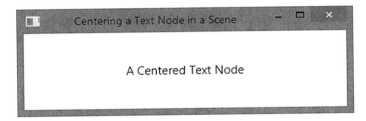

Figure 18-3. *A Text node centered in a scene*

Displaying Multiline Text

A Text node is capable of displaying multiple lines of text. It creates a new line in two cases:

- A newline character '\n' in the text creates a new line causing the characters following the newline to wrap to the next line.

- The Text class contains a wrappingWidth property, which is 0.0 by default. Its value is specified in pixels, not characters. If it is greater than zero, the text in each line is wrapped to at the specified value.

The lineSpacing property specifies the vertical spacing in pixels between two lines. It is 0.0 by default.

The textAlignment property specifies the horizontal alignment of the text lines in the bounding box. The widest line defines the width of the bounding box. Its value has no effect in a single line Text node. Its value can be one of the constants of the TextAlignment enum: LEFT, RIGHT< CENTER, and JUSTIFY. The default is TextAlignment.LEFT.

The program in Listing 18-3 creates three multiline Text nodes as shown in Figure 18-4. The text for all nodes is the same. The text contains three newline characters. The first node uses the default LEFT text alignment and a line spacing of 5px. The second node uses RIGHT text alignment with the default line spacing of 0px. The third node uses a wrappingWidth of 100px. A new line is created at 100px as well as a newline character '\n'.

Listing 18-3. Using Multiline Text Nodes

```java
// MultilineText.java
package com.jdojo.shape;

import javafx.application.Application;
import javafx.scene.Scene;
import javafx.scene.layout.HBox;
import javafx.scene.text.Text;
import javafx.scene.text.TextAlignment;
import javafx.stage.Stage;

public class MultilineText extends Application {
        public static void main(String[] args) {
                Application.launch(args);
        }

        @Override
        public void start(Stage stage) {
                String text = "Strange fits of passion have I known: \n" +
                              "And I will dare to tell, \n" +
                              "But in the lover's ear alone, \n" +
                              "What once to me befell.";

                Text t1 = new Text(text);
                t1.setLineSpacing(5);

                Text t2 = new Text(text);
                t2.setTextAlignment(TextAlignment.RIGHT);

                Text t3 = new Text(text);
                t3.setWrappingWidth(100);

                HBox root = new HBox(t1, t2, t3);
                root.setSpacing(20);
                root.setStyle("-fx-padding: 10;" +
                              "-fx-border-style: solid inside;" +
                              "-fx-border-width: 2;" +
                              "-fx-border-insets: 5;" +
                              "-fx-border-radius: 5;" +
                              "-fx-border-color: blue;");

                Scene scene = new Scene(root);
                stage.setScene(scene);
                stage.setTitle("Using Multiline Text Nodes");
                stage.show();
        }
}
```

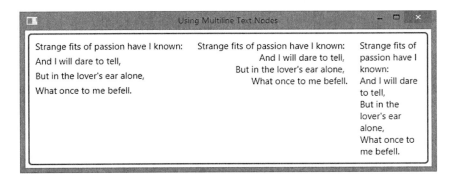

Figure 18-4. *Multiline Text nodes*

Setting Text Fonts

The font property of the Text class defines the font for the text. The default font used is from "System" font family with the "Regular" style. The size of the default font is dependent on the platform and the desktop settings of the user.

A font has a *family* and a *family name*. A font family is also known as a *typeface*. A font family defines shapes (or glyphs) for characters. The same characters appear differently when displayed using fonts belonging to different font families. Variants of a font are created by applying styles. Each variant of the font has a name that consists of the family name and the style names. For example, "Arial" is a family name of a font whereas "Arial Regular," "Arial Bold," and "Arial Bold Italic" are names of the variants of the "Arial" font.

Creating Fonts

An instance of the Font class represents a font. The Font class provides two constructors:

- Font(double size)
- Font(String name, double size)

The first constructor creates a Font object of the specified size that belongs to the "System" font family. The second one creates a Font object of the specified full name of the font and the specified size. The size of the font is specified in points. The following snippet of code creates some font objects of the "Arial" family. The getFamily(), getName(), and getSize() methods of the Font class return the family name, full name, and size of the font, respectively.

```
// Arial Plain
Font f1 = new Font("Arial", 10);

// Arial Italic
Font f2 = new Font("Arial Italic", 10);

// Arial Bold Itailc
Font f3 = new Font("Arial Bold Italic", 10);

// Arial Narrow Bold
Font f4 = new Font("Arial Narrow Bold", 30);
```

If the full font name is not found, the default "System" font will be created. It is hard to remember or know the full names for all variants of a font. To address this, the Font class provides factory methods to create fonts using a font family name, styles, and size:

- `font(double size)`
- `font(String family)`
- `font(String family, double size)`
- `font(String family, FontPosture posture, double size)`
- `font(String family, FontWeight weight, double size)`
- `font(String family, FontWeight weight, FontPosture posture, double size)`

The font() methods let you specify the family name, font weight, font posture, and font size. If only the family name is provided, the default font size is used, which depends on the platform and the desktop setting of the user.

The font weight specifies how bold the font is. Its value is one of the constants of the FontWeight enum: THIN, EXTRA_LIGHT, LIGHT, NORMAL, MEDIUM, SEMI_BOLD, BOLD, EXTRA_BOLD, BLACK. The constant THIN represents the thinnest font and the constant BLOCK the thickest font.

The posture of a font specifies whether it is italicized. It is represented by one of the two constants of the FontPosture enum: REGULAR and ITALIC.

The following snippet of code creates fonts using the factory methods of the Font class.

```
// Arial Regular
Font f1 = Font.font("Arial", 10);

// Arial Bold
Font f2 = Font.font("Arial", FontWeight.BOLD, 10);

// Arial Bold Italic
Font f3 = Font.font("Arial", FontWeight.BOLD, FontPosture.ITALIC, 10);

// Arial THIN
Font f4 = Font.font("Arial", FontWeight.THIN, 30);
```

■ **Tip** Use the getDefault() static method of the Font class to get the system default font.

The program in Listing 18-4 creates Text nodes and sets their font property. The first Text node uses the default font. Figure 18-5 shows the Text nodes. The text for the Text nodes is the String returned from the toString() method of their Font objects.

Listing 18-4. Setting Fonts for Text Nodes

```
// TextFontTest.java
package com.jdojo.shape;

import javafx.application.Application;
import javafx.scene.Scene;
import javafx.scene.layout.VBox;
import javafx.scene.text.Font;
import javafx.scene.text.FontPosture;
```

```
import javafx.scene.text.FontWeight;
import javafx.scene.text.Text;
import javafx.stage.Stage;

public class TextFontTest extends Application {
        public static void main(String[] args) {
                Application.launch(args);
        }

        @Override
        public void start(Stage stage) {
                Text t1 = new Text();
                t1.setText(t1.getFont().toString());

                Text t2 = new Text();
                t2.setFont(Font.font("Arial", 12));
                t2.setText(t2.getFont().toString());

                Text t3 = new Text();
                t3.setFont(Font.font("Arial", FontWeight.BLACK, 12));
                t3.setText(t2.getFont().toString());

                Text t4 = new Text();
                t4.setFont(Font.font("Arial", FontWeight.THIN, FontPosture.ITALIC, 12));
                t4.setText(t2.getFont().toString());

                VBox root = new VBox(t1, t2, t3, t4);
                root.setSpacing(10);
                root.setStyle("-fx-padding: 10;" +
                                "-fx-border-style: solid inside;" +
                                "-fx-border-width: 2;" +
                                "-fx-border-insets: 5;" +
                                "-fx-border-radius: 5;" +
                                "-fx-border-color: blue;");

                Scene scene = new Scene(root);
                stage.setScene(scene);
                stage.setTitle("Setting Fonts for Text Nodes");
                stage.show();
        }
}
```

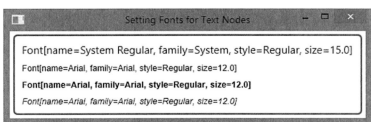

Figure 18-5. *Text nodes using variants of the "Arial" font family*

Accessing Installed Fonts

You can get the list of installed fonts on your machine. You can get the list of font family names, full font names, and full font names for a specified family name for all installed fonts. The following static methods in the Font class provide these lists.

- List<String> getFamilies()

- List<String> getFontNames()

- List<String> getFontNames(String family)

The following snippet of code prints the family names of all installed fonts on a machine. The output was generated on Windows. A partial output is shown:

```
// Print the family names of all installed fonts
for(String familyName: Font.getFamilies()) {
        System.out.println(familyName);
}
```

```
Agency FB
Algerian
Arial
Arial Black
Arial Narrow
Arial Rounded MT Bold
...
```

The following snippet of code prints the full names of all installed fonts on a machine. The output was generated on Windows. A partial output is shown:

```
// Print the full names of all installed fonts
for(String fullName: Font.getFontNames()) {
        System.out.println(fullName);
}
```

```
Agency FB
Agency FB Bold
Algerian
Arial
Arial Black
Arial Bold
Arial Bold Italic
Arial Italic
Arial Narrow
Arial Narrow Bold
Arial Narrow Bold Italic
More output goes here...
```

The following snippet of code prints the full names of all installed fonts for the "Times New Roman" family:

```
// Print the full names of "Times New Roman" family
for(String fullName: Font.getFontNames("Times New Roman")) {
        System.out.println(fullName);
}
```

```
Times New Roman
Times New Roman Bold
Times New Roman Bold Italic
Times New Roman Italic
```

Using Custom Fonts

You can load custom fonts from external sources: for example, from a file from the local file system or from a URL. The loadFont() static method in the Font class loads a custom font.

- loadFont(InputStream in, double size)

- loadFont(String urlStr, double size)

Upon successfully loading of the custom font, the loadFont() method registers font with JavaFX graphics engine, so a font can be created using the constructors and factory methods of the Font class. The method also creates a Font object of the specified size and returns it. Therefore, the size parameter exists for loading the font and creating its object in the same method call. If the method cannot load the font, it returns null.

The program in Listing 18-5 shows how to load a custom font from a local file system. The font file name is *4starfac.ttf*. The file was downloaded free from http://www.fontfile.com. The file is assumed to be in the CLASSPATH under *resources\font* directory. After the font is loaded successfully, it is set for the first Text node. A new Font object is created for its family name and set for the second Text node. If the font file does not exist or the font cannot be loaded, an appropriate error message is displayed in the window. Figure 18-6 shows the window when the font is loaded successfully.

Listing 18-5. Loading and Using Custom Fonts Using the Font Class

```
// TextCustomFont.java
package com.jdojo.shape;

import java.net.URL;
import javafx.application.Application;
import javafx.scene.Scene;
import javafx.scene.layout.HBox;
import javafx.scene.text.Font;
import javafx.scene.text.FontPosture;
import javafx.scene.text.FontWeight;
import javafx.scene.text.Text;
import javafx.stage.Stage;
```

```java
public class TextCustomFont extends Application {
        public static void main(String[] args) {
                Application.launch(args);
        }

        @Override
        public void start(Stage stage) {
                Text t1 = new Text();
                t1.setLineSpacing(10);

                Text t2 = new Text("Another Text node");

                // Load the custom font
                String fontFile = "resources/font/4starfac.ttf";
                URL url = this.getClass().getClassLoader().getResource(fontFile);
                if (url != null) {
                        String urlStr = url.toExternalForm();
                        Font customFont = Font.loadFont(urlStr, 16);
                        if (customFont != null ) {
                                // Set the custom font  for the first Text node
                                t1.setFont(customFont);

                                // Set the text and line spacing
                                t1.setText("Hello from the custom font!!! \nFont Family: " +
                                        customFont.getFamily());

                                // Create an object of the custom font and use it
                                Font font2 = Font.font(customFont.getFamily(), FontWeight.BOLD,
                                        FontPosture.ITALIC, 24);

                                // Set the custom font for the second Text node
                                t2.setFont(font2);
                        } else {
                                t1.setText("Could not load the custom font from " + urlStr);
                        }
                } else {
                        t1.setText("Could not find the custom font file " +
                                fontFile + " in CLASSPATH. Used the default font.");
                }

                HBox root = new HBox(t1, t2);
                root.setSpacing(20);
                root.setStyle("-fx-padding: 10;" +
                                "-fx-border-style: solid inside;" +
                                "-fx-border-width: 2;" +
                                "-fx-border-insets: 5;" +
                                "-fx-border-radius: 5;" +
                                "-fx-border-color: blue;");
```

```
                    Scene scene = new Scene(root);
                    stage.setScene(scene);
                    stage.setTitle("Loading and Using Custom Font");
                    stage.show();
            }
}
```

Figure 18-6. *Text nodes using custom fonts*

Setting Text Fill and Stroke

A Text node is a shape. Like a shape, it can have a fill and a stroke. By default, a Text node has null stroke and Color.BLACK fill. The Text class inherits properties and methods for setting its stroke and fill from the Shape class. I have discussed them at length in Chapter 17.

The Program in Listing 18-6 shows how to set stroke and fill for Text nodes. Figure 18-7 shows two Text nodes. The first one uses a red stroke and a white fill. The second one uses a black stroke and white fill. The stroke style for the second one uses a dashed line.

Listing 18-6. Using Stroke and Fill for Text Nodes

```
// TextFillAndStroke.java
package com.jdojo.shape;

import javafx.application.Application;
import javafx.scene.Scene;
import javafx.scene.layout.HBox;
import javafx.scene.paint.Color;
import javafx.scene.text.Font;
import javafx.scene.text.Text;
import javafx.stage.Stage;

public class TextFillAndStroke extends Application {
        public static void main(String[] args) {
                Application.launch(args);
        }

        @Override
        public void start(Stage stage) {
                Text t1 = new Text("Stroke and fill!");
                t1.setStroke(Color.RED);
                t1.setFill(Color.WHITE);
                t1.setFont(new Font(36));
```

```
        Text t2 = new Text("Dashed Stroke!");
        t2.setStroke(Color.BLACK);
        t2.setFill(Color.WHITE);
        t2.setFont(new Font(36));
        t2.getStrokeDashArray().addAll(5.0, 5.0);

        HBox root = new HBox(t1, t2);
        root.setSpacing(20);
        root.setStyle("-fx-padding: 10;" +
                      "-fx-border-style: solid inside;" +
                      "-fx-border-width: 2;" +
                      "-fx-border-insets: 5;" +
                      "-fx-border-radius: 5;" +
                      "-fx-border-color: blue;");

        Scene scene = new Scene(root);
        stage.setScene(scene);
        stage.setTitle("Using Stroke and Fill for Text Nodes");
        stage.show();
    }
}
```

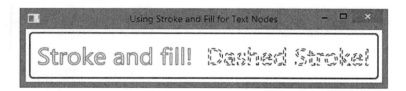

Figure 18-7. *Text nodes using strokes and fills*

Applying Text Decorations

The Text class contains two boolean properties to apply text decorations to its text:

- strikethrough
- underline

By default, both properties are set to false. If the strikethrough is set to true, a line is drawn through each line of text. If the underline is set to true, a line is drawn below each line of text. The following snippet of code uses the decorations for Text nodes. The nodes are shown in Figure 18-8.

```
Text t1 = new Text("It uses the \nunderline decoaration.");
t1.setUnderline(true);

Text t2 = new Text("It uses the \nstrikethrough decoration.");
t2.setStrikethrough(true);
```

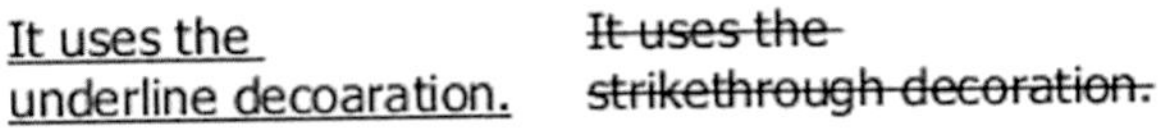

It uses the
underline decoaration.

~~It uses the~~
~~strikethrough decoration.~~

Figure 18-8. *Text nodes using the underline and strikethrough decorations*

Applying Font Smoothing

The Text class contains a fontSmoothingType property, which can be used to apply a gray or LCD font smoothing. Its value is one of the constants of the FontSmoothingType enum: GRAY and LCD. The default-smoothing type is fontSmoothingType.GRAY. The LCD smoothing type is used as a hint. The following snippet of code creates two Text nodes: one uses LCD and one GRAY font-smoothing type. The Text nodes have been shown in Figure 18-9.

```
Text t1 = new Text("Hello world in LCD.");
t1.setFontSmoothingType(FontSmoothingType.LCD);

Text t2 = new Text("Hello world in GRAY.");
t2.setFontSmoothingType(FontSmoothingType.GRAY);
```

Hello world in LCD.   Hello world in GRAY.

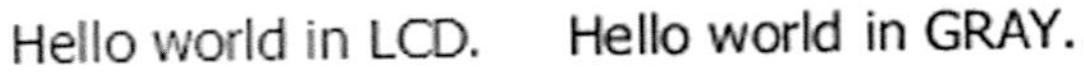

Figure 18-9. *Text nodes using LCD and GRAY font-smoothing types*

Styling a Text Node with CSS

A Text node does not have a default CSS style-class name. In addition to all CSS properties of the Shape, a Text node supports the following CSS properties:

- -fx-font
- -fx-font-smoothing-type
- -fx-text-origin
- -fx-text-alignment
- -fx-strikethrough
- -fx-underline

I have discussed all properties in the previous sections. The -fx-font property is inherited from the parent. If the parent does not set the property, the default system font is used. The valid values for the -fx-font-smoothing-type property are lcd and gray. The valid values for the -fx-text-origin property are baseline, top, and bottom. Let us create a style named *my-text* as follows. It sets a font and a linear gradient fill. The fill starts as a light gray color and ends as black.

```
.my-text {
        -fx-font: 36 Arial;
        -fx-fill: linear-gradient(from 0% 0% to 100% 0%, lightgray 0%, black 100%);
        -fx-font-smoothing-type: lcd;
        -fx-underline: true;
}
```

The following snippet of code creates a Text node and sets it style-class name to *my-text*. Figure 18-10 shows the Text node with its styled applied to it.

```
Text t1 = new Text("Styling Text Nodes!");
t1.getStyleClass().add("my-text");
```

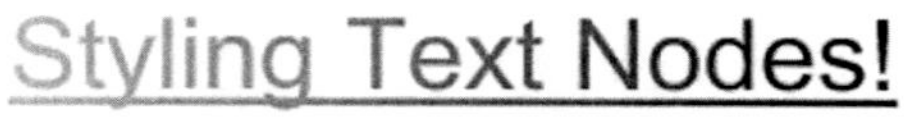

Styling Text Nodes!

Figure 18-10. *A Text node using CSS styles*

Summary

A text node is an instance of the Text class that is used to render text. The Text class contains several properties to customize the appearance of text. The Text class and all its related classes are in the javafx.scene.text package. The Text class inherits from the Shape class. That is, a Text is a Shape, which allows you to use all properties and methods of the Shape class on a Text node. A Text node is capable of displaying multiple lines of text.

A Text node contains text and properties to render the text. You can create a Text node using one of the three constructors of the Text class. You can specify the text or text and position of the text while creating the node. The no-args constructor creates a text node with an empty text and is located at $(0, 0)$.

The no-args constructor creates a Text node with an empty string as its text. Other constructors let you specify the text and position the node. The width and height of a text node are automatically determined by its font. By default, a Text node uses a system default font to render its text.

Apart from the local and parent coordinate system, a Text node has an additional coordinate system. It is the coordinate system used for drawing the text. The x, y, and textOrigin properties of the Text class define the text coordinate system: The x and y properties define the x and y coordinates of the text origin. The textOrigin property is of type VPos. Its value could be VPos.BASELINE, VPos.TOP, VPos.CENTER, and VPos.BOTTOM. The default is VPos.BASELINE. It defines where the x-axis of the text coordinate system lies within the text height.

The font property of the Text class defines the font for the text. The default font used is from "System" font family with the "Regular" style. The size of the default font is dependent on the platform and the desktop settings of the user. An instance of the Font class represents a font. The Font class contains several static methods that let you access the installed fonts on your computer and load custom fonts from font files.

A Text node is a shape. Like a shape, it can have a fill and a stroke. By default, a Text node has null stroke and Color.BLACK fill.

The strikethrough and underline properties of the Text class lets you text decorations to the text. By default, both properties are set to false.

The Text class contains a fontSmoothingType property, which can be used to apply a gray or LCD font smoothing. Its value is one of the constants of the FontSmoothingType enum: GRAY and LCD. The default-smoothing type is fontSmoothingType.GRAY. The LCD-smoothing type is used as a hint.

You can style Text nodes using CSS. Setting font, text alignment, font smoothing, and decorations are supported through CSS.

The next chapter will discuss how to draw 3D shapes in JavaFX.

■ ■ ■

CHAPTER 19

Understanding 3D Shapes

In this chapter, you will learn:

- About 3D shapes and the classes representing 3D shapes in JavaFX
- How to check whether your machine supports 3D
- About the 3D coordinate system used in JavaFX
- About the rendering order of nodes
- How to draw predefined 3D shapes
- About the different types of cameras and how to use them to render scenes
- How to use light sources to view 3D objects in scenes
- How to create and use subscenes
- How to draw user-defined 3D shapes in JavaFX

What Are 3D Shapes?

Any shape, drawn in a three-dimensional space, having three dimensions (length, width, and depth) is known as a 3D shape. Cubes, spheres, and pyramids are examples.

Although it was possible to have 2D nodes with 3D effects before, JavaFX 8 offers real 3D shapes as nodes. Before Java FX 8, the 3D effects were achieved using transformations in 3D space. JavaFX 8 offers two types of 3D shapes.

- Predefined shapes
- User-defined shapes

Box, sphere, and cylinder are three predefined 3D shapes that you can readily use in your JavaFX applications. You can also create any type of 3D shapes using a triangle mesh.

Figure 19-1 shows a class diagram of classes representing JavaFX 3D shapes. The 3D-shape classes are in the javafx.scene.shape package. The Box, Sphere, and Cylinder classes represent the three predefined shapes. The MeshView class represents a user-defined 3D shape in a scene.

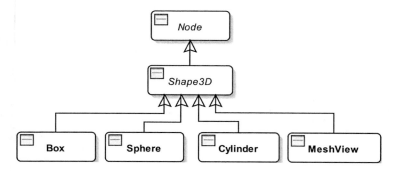

Figure 19-1. *A class diagram for classes representing 3D shapes*

The 3D visualization in JavaFX is accomplished using lights and cameras. Lights and cameras are also nodes, which are added to the scene. You add 3D nodes to a scene, light it with lights, and view it using a camera. The positions of lights and cameras in the space determine the lighted and viewable areas of the scene. Figure 19-2 shows a 3D box, which is created using an instance of the Box class.

Figure 19-2. *An example of a 3D box shape*

Checking Support for 3D

JavaFX 3D support is a conditional feature. If it is not supported on your platform, you get a warning message on the console when you run a program that attempts to use 3D features. Run the program in Listing 19-1 to check if your machine supports JavaFX 3D. The program will print a message stating whether the 3D support is available.

Listing 19-1. Checking JavaFX 3D Support on Your Machine

```
// Check3DSupport.java
package com.jdojo.shape3d;

import javafx.application.ConditionalFeature;
import javafx.application.Platform;

public class Check3DSupport {
    public static void main(String[] args) {
        boolean supported = Platform.isSupported(ConditionalFeature.SCENE3D);
```

```
        if (supported) {
            System.out.println("3D is supported on your machine.");
        } else {
            System.out.println("3D is not supported on your machine.");
        }
    }
}
```

The 3D Coordinate System

A point in the 3D space is represented by (x, y, z) coordinates. A 3D object has three dimensions: x, y, and z. Figure 19-3 shows the 3D coordinate system used in JavaFX.

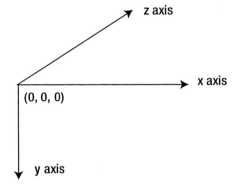

Figure 19-3. *The 3D coordinate system used in JavaFX*

The positive direction of the x-axis points to the right from the origin; the positive direction of the y-axis points down; the positive direction of the z-axis points into the screen (away from the viewer). The negative directions on the axes, which are not shown, extend in the opposite directions at the origin.

Rendering Order of Nodes

Suppose you are looking at two overlapping objects at a distance. The object closer to you always overlaps the object farther from you, irrespective of the sequence in which they appeared in the view. When dealing with 3D objects in JavaFX, you would like them to appear the same way.

In JavaFX, by default, nodes are rendered in the order they are added to the scene graph. Consider the following snippet of code:

```
Rectangle r1 = new Rectangle(0, 0, 100, 100);
Rectangle r2 = new Rectangle(50, 50, 100, 100);
Group group = new Group(r1, r2);
```

Two rectangles are added to a group. The rectangle r1 is rendered first followed by rectangle r2. The overlapping area will show only the area of r2, not r1. If the group was created as new Group(r2, r1), the rectangle r2 will be rendered first followed with rectangle r1. The overlapping area will show the area of r1, not r2. Let us add the z coordinates for the two rectangles as follows:

```
Rectangle r1 = new Rectangle(0, 0, 100, 100);
r1.setTranslateZ(10);

Rectangle r2 = new Rectangle(50, 50, 100, 100);
r2.setTranslateZ(50);

Group group = new Group(r1, r2);
```

The foregoing snippet of code will produce the same effect as before. The rectangle r1 will be rendered first followed by the rectangle r2. The z values for the rectangles are ignored. In this case, you would like to render the rectangle r1 last as it is closer to the viewer (z=10 is closer than z=50).

The previous rendering behavior is not desirable in a 3D space. You expect the 3D objects to appear the same way as they would appear in a real world. You need to do two things two achieve this.

- When creating a Scene object, specify that it needs to have a depth buffer.

- Specify in the nodes that their z coordinate values should be used during rendering. That is, they need to be rendered according to their depth (the distance from the viewer).

When you create a Scene object, you need to specify the depthBuffer flag, which is set to false by default.

```
// Create a Scene object with depthBuffer set to true
double width = 300;
double height = 200;
boolean depthBuffer = true;
Scene scene = new Scene(root, width, height, depthBuffer);
```

The depthBuffer flag for a scene cannot be changed after the scene is created. You can check whether a scene has a depthBuffer using the isDepthBuffer() method of the Scene object.

The Node class contains a depthTest property, which is available for all nodes in JavaFX. Its value is one of the constants of the javafx.scene.DepthTest enum:

- ENABLE

- DISABLE

- INHERIT

The ENABLE value for the depthTest indicates that the z coordinate values should be taken into account when the node is rendered. When the depth testing is enabled for a node, its z coordinate is compared with all other nodes with depth testing enabled, before rendering.

The DISABLE value indicates that the nodes are rendered in the order they are added to the scene graph.

The INHERIT value indicates that the depthTest property for a node is inherited from its parent. If a node has null parent, it is the same as ENABLE.

The program in Listing 19-2 demonstrates the concepts of using the depth buffer for a scene and the depth test for nodes. It adds two rectangles to a group. The rectangles are filled with red and green colors. The z coordinates for the red and green rectangles are 400px and 300px, respectively. The green rectangle is added to the group first. However, it is rendered first as it is closer to the viewer. You have added a camera to the scene, which is needed to view objects having depth (the z coordinate). The CheckBox is used to enable and disable the depth test for the rectangles. When the depth test is disabled, the rectangles are rendered in the order they are added to the group: the green rectangle followed with the red rectangle. Figure 19-4 shows rectangles in both states.

Listing 19-2. Enabling/Disabling DepthTest Property for Nodes

```java
// DepthTestCheck.java
package com.jdojo.shape3d;

import javafx.application.Application;
import javafx.scene.Group;
import javafx.scene.PerspectiveCamera;
import javafx.scene.Scene;
import javafx.scene.control.CheckBox;
import javafx.scene.layout.BorderPane;
import javafx.scene.paint.Color;
import javafx.scene.shape.Rectangle;
import javafx.scene.DepthTest;
import javafx.stage.Stage;

public class DepthTestCheck  extends Application {
        public static void main(String[] args) {
                Application.launch(args);
        }

        @Override
        public void start(Stage stage) {
                // Create two rectangles and add then to a Group
                Rectangle red = new Rectangle(100, 100);
                red.setFill(Color.RED);
                red.setTranslateX(100);
                red.setTranslateY(100);
                red.setTranslateZ(400);

                Rectangle green = new Rectangle(100, 100);
                green.setFill(Color.GREEN);
                green.setTranslateX(150);
                green.setTranslateY(150);
                green.setTranslateZ(300);

                Group center = new Group(green, red);

                CheckBox depthTestCbx = new CheckBox("DepthTest for Rectangles");
                depthTestCbx.setSelected(true);
                depthTestCbx.selectedProperty().addListener(
                                (prop, oldValue, newValue) -> {
                        if (newValue) {
                                red.setDepthTest(DepthTest.ENABLE);
                                green.setDepthTest(DepthTest.ENABLE);
                        }
```

```
                else {
                        red.setDepthTest(DepthTest.DISABLE);
                        green.setDepthTest(DepthTest.DISABLE);
                }
        });

        // Create a BorderPane as the root node for the scene. Need to
        // set the background transparent, so the cemera can view the
        // rectangles behind the surface of the BorderPane
        BorderPane root = new BorderPane();
        root.setStyle("-fx-background-color: transparent;");
        root.setTop(depthTestCbx);
        root.setCenter(center);

        // Create a scene with depthBuffer enabled
        Scene scene = new Scene(root, 200, 200, true);

        // Need to set a camera to look into the 3D space of the scene
        scene.setCamera(new PerspectiveCamera());

        stage.setScene(scene);
        stage.setTitle("Depth Test");
        stage.show();
    }
}
```

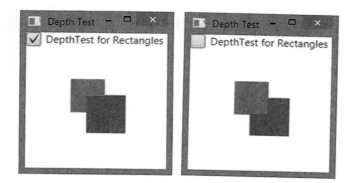

Figure 19-4. *Effects of depthTest property on rendering nodes*

Using Predefined 3D Shapes

JavaFX 8 provides the following three built-in 3D geometric shapes:

- Box
- Sphere
- Cylinder

The shapes are represented by instances of the Box, Sphere, and Cylinder classes. The classes inherit from the Shape3D class, which contains three properties that are common to all types of 3D shapes.

- Material

- Draw mode

- Cull face

I will discuss these properties in detail in subsequent sections. If you do not specify these properties for a shape, reasonable defaults are provided.

The properties specific to a shape type are defined in the specific class defining the shape. For example, properties for a box are defined in the Box class. All shapes are nodes. Therefore, you can apply transformations to them. You can position them at any point in the 3D space using the translateX, translateY, and translateZ transformations

---

■ **Tip**   The center of a 3D shape is located at the origin of the local coordinate system of the shape.

A Box is defined by the following three properties:

- width

- height

- depth

The Box class contains two constructors:

- Box()

- Box(double width, double height, double depth)

The no-args constructor creates a Box with width, height, and depth of 2.0 each. The other constructor lets you specify the dimensions of the Box. The center of the Box is located at the origin of its local coordinate system.

```
// Create a Box with width=10, height=20, and depth=50
Box box = new Box(10, 20, 50);
```

A Sphere is defined by only one property named radius. The Sphere class contains three constructors:

- Sphere()

- Sphere(double radius)

- Sphere(double radius, int divisions)

The no-args constructor creates a sphere of radius 1.0.
The second constructor lets you specify the radius of the sphere.
The third constructor lets you specify the radius and divisions. A 3D sphere is made up of many divisions, which are constructed from connected triangles. The value of the number of divisions defines the resolution of the sphere. The higher the number of divisions, the smoother the sphere looks. By default, a value of 64 is used for the divisions. The value of divisions cannot be less than 1.

```
// Create a Sphere with radius =50
Sphere sphere = new Sphere(50);
```

A Cylinder is defined by two properties:

- radius

- height

The radius of the cylinder is measured on the XZ plane. The axis of the cylinder is measured along the y-axis. The height of the cylinder is measured along its axis. The Cylinder class contains three constructors:

- Cylinder()

- Cylinder(double radius, double height)

- Cylinder(double radius, double height, int divisions)

The no-args constructor creates a Cylinder with a 1.0 radius and a 2.0 height.

The second constructor lets you specify the radius and height properties.

The third constructor lets you specify the number of divisions, which defines the resolution of the cylinder. The higher the number of divisions, the smoother the cylinder looks. Its default value is 15 along the x-axis and z-axis each. Its value cannot be less than 3. If a value less than 3 is specified, a value of 3 is used. Note that the number of divisions does not apply along the y-axis. Suppose the number of divisions is 10. It means that the vertical surface of the cylinder is created using 10 triangles. The height of the triangle will extend the entire height of the cylinder. The base of the cylinder will be created using 10 triangles.

```
// Create a cylinder with radius=40 and height=120
Cylinder cylinder = new Cylinder(40, 120);
```

The program in Listing 19-3 shows how to create 3D shapes. Figure 19-5 shows the shapes.

Listing 19-3. Creating 3D Primitive Shapes: Box, Sphere, and Cylinder

```
// PreDefinedShapes.java
package com.jdojo.shape3d;

import javafx.application.Application;
import javafx.scene.Group;
import javafx.scene.PerspectiveCamera;
import javafx.scene.PointLight;
import javafx.scene.Scene;
import javafx.scene.shape.Box;
import javafx.scene.shape.Cylinder;
import javafx.scene.shape.Sphere;
import javafx.stage.Stage;

public class PreDefinedShapes extends Application {
        public static void main(String[] args) {
                Application.launch(args);
        }

        @Override
        public void start(Stage stage) {
                // Create a Box
                Box box = new Box(100, 100, 100);
                box.setTranslateX(150);
                box.setTranslateY(0);
                box.setTranslateZ(400);
```

```
            // Create a Sphere
            Sphere sphere = new Sphere(50);
            sphere.setTranslateX(300);
            sphere.setTranslateY(-5);
            sphere.setTranslateZ(400);

            // Create a cylinder
            Cylinder cylinder = new Cylinder(40, 120);
            cylinder.setTranslateX(500);
            cylinder.setTranslateY(-25);
            cylinder.setTranslateZ(600);

            // Create a light
            PointLight light = new PointLight();
            light.setTranslateX(350);
            light.setTranslateY(100);
            light.setTranslateZ(300);

            // Add shapes and a light to the group
            Group root = new Group(box, sphere, cylinder, light);

            // Create a Scene with depth buffer enabled
            Scene scene = new Scene(root, 300, 100, true);

            // Set a camera to view the 3D shapes
            PerspectiveCamera camera = new PerspectiveCamera(false);
            camera.setTranslateX(100);
            camera.setTranslateY(-50);
            camera.setTranslateZ(300);
            scene.setCamera(camera);

            stage.setScene(scene);
            stage.setTitle("Using 3D Shapes: Box, Sphere and Cylinder");
            stage.show();
        }
}
```

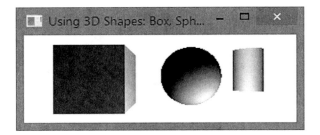

Figure 19-5. *Primitive 3D shapes: a box, a sphere, and a cylinder*

The program creates the three shapes and positions them in the space. It creates a light, which is an instance of the PointLight, and positions it in the space. Note that a light is also a Node. The light is used to light the 3D shapes. All shapes and the light are added to a group, which is added to the scene.

To view the shapes, you need to add a camera to the scene. The program adds a PerspectiveCamera to the scene. Note that you need to position the camera as its position and orientation in the space determine what you see. The origin of the local coordinate system of the camera is located at the center of the scene. Try resizing the window after you run the program. You will notice that the view of the shapes changes as you resize the window. It happens because the center of the scene is changing when you resize the window, which in turn repositions the camera, resulting in the change in the view.

Specifying the Shape Material

A material is used for rendering the surface of shapes. You can specify the material for the surface of 3D objects using the material property, which is defined in the Shape3D class. The material property is an instance of the abstract class Material. JavaFX provides the PhongMaterial class as the only concrete implementation of Material. Both classes are in the javafx.scene.paint package. An instance of the PhongMaterial class represents Phong shaded material. Phong shaded material is based on Phong shading and the Phong reflection model (also known as Phong illumination and Phong lighting), which were developed at the University of Utah by Bui Tuong Phong as part of his Ph.D. dissertation in 1973. A complete discussion of the Phong model is beyond the scope of this book. The model provides an empirical formula to compute the color of a pixel on the geometric surface in terms of the following properties defined in the PhongMaterial class:

- diffuseColor
- diffuseMap
- specularColor
- specularMap
- selfIlluminationMap
- specularPower
- bumpMap

The PhongMaterial class contains three constructors:

- PhongMaterial()
- PhongMaterial(Color diffuseColor)
- PhongMaterial(Color diffuseColor, Image diffuseMap, Image specularMap, Image bumpMap, Image selfIlluminationMap)

The no-args constructor creates a PhongMaterial with the diffuse color as Color.WHITE. The other two constructors are used to create a PhongMaterial with the specified properties.

When you do not provide a material for a 3D shape, a default material with a diffuse color of Color.LIGHTGRAY is used for rendering the shape. All shapes in our previous example in Listing 19-3 used the default material.

The following snippet of code creates a Box, creates a PhongMaterial with tan diffuse color, and sets the material to the box:

```
Box box = new Box(100, 100, 100);
PhongMaterial material = new PhongMaterial();
material.setDiffuseColor(Color.TAN);
box.setMaterial(material);
```

You can use an Image as the diffuse map to have texture for the material, as shown in the following code:

```
Box boxWithTexture = new Box(100, 100, 100);
PhongMaterial textureMaterial = new PhongMaterial();
Image randomness = new Image("resources/picture/randomness.jpg");
textureMaterial.setDiffuseMap(randomness);
boxWithTexture.setMaterial(textureMaterial);
```

The program in Listing 19-4 shows how to create and set material for shapes. It creates two boxes. It sets the diffuse color for one box and the diffuse map for other. The image used for the diffuse map provides the texture for the surface of the second box. The two boxes look as shown in Figure 19-6.

Listing 19-4. Using the Diffuse Color and Diffuse Map to Create PhongMaterial

```
// MaterialTest.java
package com.jdojo.shape3d;

import javafx.application.Application;
import javafx.scene.Group;
import javafx.scene.PerspectiveCamera;
import javafx.scene.PointLight;
import javafx.scene.Scene;
import javafx.scene.image.Image;
import javafx.scene.paint.Color;
import javafx.scene.paint.PhongMaterial;
import javafx.scene.shape.Box;
import javafx.stage.Stage;

public class MaterialTest extends Application {
    public static void main(String[] args) {
        Application.launch(args);
    }

    @Override
    public void start(Stage stage) {
        // Create a Box
        Box box = new Box(100, 100, 100);

        // Set the material for the box
        PhongMaterial material = new PhongMaterial();
        material.setDiffuseColor(Color.TAN);
        box.setMaterial(material);
```

815

```
        // Place the box in the space
        box.setTranslateX(250);
        box.setTranslateY(0);
        box.setTranslateZ(400);

        // Create a Box with texture
        Box boxWithTexture = new Box(100, 100, 100);
        PhongMaterial textureMaterial = new PhongMaterial();
        Image randomness = new Image("resources/picture/randomness.jpg");
        textureMaterial.setDiffuseMap(randomness);
        boxWithTexture.setMaterial(textureMaterial);

        // Place the box in the space
        boxWithTexture.setTranslateX(450);
        boxWithTexture.setTranslateY(-5);
        boxWithTexture.setTranslateZ(400);

        PointLight light = new PointLight();
        light.setTranslateX(250);
        light.setTranslateY(100);
        light.setTranslateZ(300);

        Group root = new Group(box, boxWithTexture);

        // Create a Scene with depth buffer enabled
        Scene scene = new Scene(root, 300, 100, true);

        // Set a camera to view the 3D shapes
        PerspectiveCamera camera = new PerspectiveCamera(false);
        camera.setTranslateX(200);
        camera.setTranslateY(-50);
        camera.setTranslateZ(325);
        scene.setCamera(camera);

        stage.setScene(scene);
        stage.setTitle("Using Material Color and Texture for 3D Surface");
        stage.show();
    }
}
```

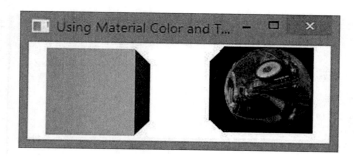

Figure 19-6. *Two boxes: one with a tan diffuse color and one with texture using a diffuse map*

Specifying the Draw Mode of Shapes

A 3D shape surface consists of many connected polygons made up of triangles. For example, a Box is made up of 12 triangles—each side of the Box using two triangles. The drawMode property in the Shape3D class specifies how the surface of 3D shapes is rendered. Its value is one of the constants of the DrawMode enum.

- DrawMode.FILL

- DrawMode.LINE

The DrawMode.FILL is the default and it fills the interior of the triangles. The DrawMode.LINE draws only the outline of the triangles. That is, it draws only lines connecting the vertices of the consecutive triangles.

```
// Create a Box with outline only
Box box = new Box(100, 100, 100);
box.setDrawMode(DrawMode.LINE);
```

The program in Listing 19-5 shows how to draw only the outline of 3D shapes. Figure 19-7 shows the shapes. The program is similar to the one shown in Listing 19-3. The program sets the drawMode property of all shapes to DrawMode.LINE. The program specifies the divisions of creating the Sphere and Cylinder. Change the value for divisions to a lesser value. You will notice that the number of triangles used to create the shapes decreases, making the shape less smooth.

Listing 19-5. Drawing Only Lines for 3D Shapes

```
// DrawModeTest.java
package com.jdojo.shape3d;

import javafx.application.Application;
import javafx.scene.Group;
import javafx.scene.PerspectiveCamera;
import javafx.scene.PointLight;
import javafx.scene.Scene;
import javafx.scene.shape.Box;
import javafx.scene.shape.Cylinder;
import javafx.scene.shape.DrawMode;
import javafx.scene.shape.Sphere;
import javafx.stage.Stage;

public class DrawModeTest extends Application {
    public static void main(String[] args) {
        Application.launch(args);
    }

    @Override
    public void start(Stage stage) {
        // Create a Box
        Box box = new Box(100, 100, 100);
        box.setDrawMode(DrawMode.LINE);
        box.setTranslateX(150);
        box.setTranslateY(0);
        box.setTranslateZ(400);
```

```
// Create a Sphere: radius = 50, divisions=20
Sphere sphere = new Sphere(50, 20);
sphere.setDrawMode(DrawMode.LINE);
sphere.setTranslateX(300);
sphere.setTranslateY(-5);
sphere.setTranslateZ(400);

// Create a cylinder: radius=40, height=120, divisions=5
Cylinder cylinder = new Cylinder(40, 120, 5);
cylinder.setDrawMode(DrawMode.LINE);
cylinder.setTranslateX(500);
cylinder.setTranslateY(-25);
cylinder.setTranslateZ(600);

PointLight light = new PointLight();
light.setTranslateX(350);
light.setTranslateY(100);
light.setTranslateZ(300);

Group root = new Group(box, sphere, cylinder, light);

// Create a Scene with depth buffer enabled
Scene scene = new Scene(root, 300, 100, true);

// Set a camera to view the 3D shapes
PerspectiveCamera camera = new PerspectiveCamera(false);
camera.setTranslateX(100);
camera.setTranslateY(-50);
camera.setTranslateZ(300);
scene.setCamera(camera);

stage.setScene(scene);
stage.setTitle("Drawing Only Lines");
stage.show();
    }
}
```

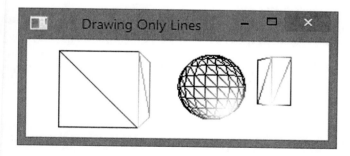

Figure 19-7. *Drawing the outline of 3D shapes*

Specifying the Face Culling for Shapes

A 3D object is never visible entirely. For example, you can never see an entire building at once. When you change the viewing angle, you see different parts of the building. If you face the front of the building, you see only the front part of the building. Standing in front, if you move to the right, you see the front and right sides of the building.

The surface of 3D objects is made of connected triangles. Each triangle has two faces: the exterior face and the interior face. You see the exterior face of the triangles when you look at the 3D objects. Not all triangles are visible all the time. Whether a triangle is visible depends on the position of the camera. There is a simple rule to determine the visibility of triangles making up the surface of a 3D object. Draw a line coming out from the plane of the triangle and the line is perpendicular to the plane of a triangle. Draw another line from the point where the first line intersects the plane of the triangle to the viewer. If the angle between two lines is greater than 90 degrees, the face of the triangle is not visible to the view. Otherwise, the face of the triangle is visible to the viewer. Note that not both faces of a triangle are visible at the same time.

Face culling is a technique of rendering 3D geometry based on the principle that the nonvisible parts of an object should not be rendered. For example, if you are facing a building from the front, there is no need to render the sides, top, and bottom of the building, as you cannot see them.

▪ Tip   Face culling is used in 3D rendering to enhance performance.

The Shape3D class contains a `cullFace` property that specifies the type of culling applied in rendering the shape. Its value is one of the constants of the `CullFace` enum:

- BACK
- FRONT
- NONE

The `CullFace.BACK` specifies that all triangles that cannot be seen through the camera in its current position should be culled (i.e., not rendered). That is, all triangles whose exterior faces are not facing the camera should be culled. If you are facing the front of a building, this setting will render only the front part of the building. This is the default.

The `CullFace.FRONT` specifies that the all triangles whose exterior faces are facing the camera should be culled. If you are facing the front of a building, this setting will render all parts of the building, except the front part.

The `CullFace.NONE` specifies that no face culling should be applied. That is, all triangles making up the shape should be rendered.

```
// Create a Box with no face culling
Box box = new Box(100, 100, 100);
Box.setCullFace(CullFace.NONE);
```

It is easy to see the effect of face culling when you draw the shape using the drawMode as DrawMode.LINE. I will draw only nonculled triangles. Figure 19-8 shows the same Box using three different face cullings. The first Box (from left) uses the back-face culling, the second front-face culling, and the third one uses no culling. Notice that the first picture of the Box shows the front, right, and top faces whereas these faces are culled in the second Box. In the second picture, you see the back, left, and bottom faces. Note that when you use front-face culling, you see the interior faces of the triangles as the exterior faces are hidden from the view.

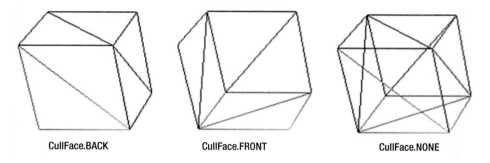

CullFace.BACK   CullFace.FRONT   CullFace.NONE

Figure 19-8. *A box using different cullFace properties*

Using Cameras

Cameras are used to render the scene. Two types of cameras are available.

- Perspective camera

- Parallel camera

The names of the cameras suggest the projection type they use to render the scene. Cameras in JavaFX are nodes. They can be added to the scene graph and positioned like other nodes.

The abstract base class Camera represents a camera. Two concrete subclasses of the Camera class exist: PerspectiveCamera and ParallelCamera. The three classes are in the javafx.scene package.

■ **Tip**   Before Java 8, camera classes were inherited from the Object class and they were not nodes. In JavaFX 8, they inherit from the Node class.

A PerspectiveCamera defines the viewing volume for a perspective projection, which is a truncated right pyramid as shown in Figure 19-9. The camera projects the objects contained within the near and far clipping planes onto the projection plane. Therefore, any objects outside the clipping planes are not visible.

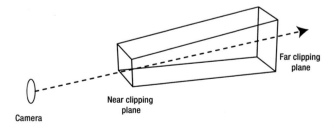

Far clipping
plane

Near clipping
plane

Camera

Figure 19-9. *The viewing volume of a perspective camera defined by the near clip and far clip planes*

The content that the camera will project onto the projection plane is defined by two properties in the Camera class.

- nearClip

- farClip

The nearClip is the distance between the camera and the near clipping plane. Objects closer to the camera than the nearClip are not rendered. The default value is 0.1.

The farClip is the distance between the camera and the far clipping plane. Objects farther from the camera than the farClip are not rendered. The default value is 100.

The PerspectiveCamera class contains two constructors.

- PerspectiveCamera()

- PerspectiveCamera(boolean fixedEyeAtCameraZero)

The no-args constructor creates a PerspectiveCamera with the fixedEyeAtCameraZero flag set to false, which makes it behave more or less like a parallel camera where the objects in the scene at Z=0 stay the same size when the scene is resized. The second constructor lets you specify this flag. If you want to view 3D objects with real 3D effects, you need to set this flag to true. Setting this flag to true will adjust the size of the projected images of the 3D objects as the scene is resized. Making the scene smaller will make the objects look smaller as well.

```
// Create a perspective camera for viewing 3D objects
PerspectiveCamera camera = new PerspectiveCamera(true);
```

The PerspectiveCamera class declares two additional properties.

- fieldOfView

- verticalFieldOfView

The fieldOfView is measured in degrees and it is the view angle of the camera. Its default value is 30 degrees.

The verticalFieldOfView property specifies whether the fieldOfView property applies to the vertical dimension of the projection plane. By default, its value is true. Figure 19-10 depicts the camera, its view angle, and field of view.

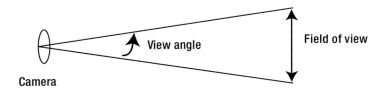

Figure 19-10. *The view angle and field of view for a perspective camera*

An instance of the ParallelCamera specifies the viewing volume for a parallel projection, which is a rectangular box. The ParallelCamera class does not declare any additional properties. It contains a no-args constructor.

```
ParallelCamera camera = new ParallelCamera();
```

You can set a camera for a scene using the setCamera() method of the Scene class.

```
Scene scene = create a scene....
PerspectiveCamera camera = new PerspectiveCamera(true);
scene.setCamera(camera);
```

Because a camera is a node, you can add it to the scene graph.

```
PerspectiveCamera camera = new PerspectiveCamera(true);
Group group = new Group(camera);
```

You can move and rotate the camera as you move and rotate nodes. To move it to a different position, use the translateX, translateY, and translateZ properties. To rotate, use the Rotate transformation.

The program in Listing 19-6 uses a PerspectiveCamera to view a Box. You have used two lights: one to light the front and the top faces and one to light the bottom face of the box. The camera is animated by rotating it indefinitely along the x-axis. As the camera rotates, it brings different parts of the box into the view. You can see the effect of the two lights when the bottom of the box comes into the view. The bottom is shown in green whereas the top and front are in red.

Listing 19-6. Using a PerspectiveCamera as a Node

```
// CameraTest.java
package com.jdojo.shape3d;

import javafx.animation.Animation;
import javafx.animation.RotateTransition;
import javafx.application.Application;
import javafx.scene.Group;
import javafx.scene.PerspectiveCamera;
import javafx.scene.PointLight;
import javafx.scene.Scene;
import javafx.scene.paint.Color;
import javafx.scene.shape.Box;
import javafx.scene.shape.CullFace;
import javafx.scene.transform.Rotate;
import javafx.stage.Stage;
import javafx.util.Duration;

public class CameraTest extends Application {
        public static void main(String[] args) {
                Application.launch(args);
        }

        @Override
        public void start(Stage stage) {
                Box box = new Box(100, 100, 100);
                box.setCullFace(CullFace.NONE);
                box.setTranslateX(250);
                box.setTranslateY(100);
                box.setTranslateZ(400);
```

```
        PerspectiveCamera camera = new PerspectiveCamera(false);
        camera.setTranslateX(100);
        camera.setTranslateY(-50);
        camera.setTranslateZ(300);

        // Add a Rotation animation to the camera
        RotateTransition rt = new RotateTransition(Duration.seconds(2), camera);
        rt.setCycleCount(Animation.INDEFINITE);
        rt.setFromAngle(0);
        rt.setToAngle(90);
        rt.setAutoReverse(true);
        rt.setAxis(Rotate.X_AXIS);
        rt.play();

        PointLight redLight = new PointLight();
        redLight.setColor(Color.RED);
        redLight.setTranslateX(250);
        redLight.setTranslateY(-100);
        redLight.setTranslateZ(250);

        PointLight greenLight = new PointLight();
        greenLight.setColor(Color.GREEN);
        greenLight.setTranslateX(250);
        greenLight.setTranslateY(300);
        greenLight.setTranslateZ(300);

        Group root = new Group(box, redLight, greenLight);
        root.setRotationAxis(Rotate.X_AXIS);
        root.setRotate(30);

        Scene scene = new Scene(root, 500, 300, true);
        scene.setCamera(camera);
        stage.setScene(scene);
        stage.setTitle("Using camaras");
        stage.show();
    }
}
```

Using Light Sources

Similar to the real world, you need a light source to view the 3D objects in a scene. An instance of the abstract base class LightBase represents a light source. Its two concrete subclasses, AmbientLight and PointLight, represent an ambient light and a point light. Light source classes are in the javafx.scene package. The LightBase class inherits from the Node class. Therefore, a light source is a node and it can be added to the scene graph as any other nodes.

A light source has three properties: light color, on/off switch, and a list of affected nodes. The LightBase class contains the following two properties:

- color
- lightOn

823

The color specifies the color of the light. The lightOn specifies whether the light is on. The getScope() method of the LightBase class returns an ObservableList<Node>, which is the hierarchical list of nodes affected by this light source. If the list is empty, the scope of the light source is universe, which means that it affects all nodes in the scene.

An instance of the AmbientLight class represents an ambient light source. An ambient light is a nondirectional light that seems to come from all directions. Its intensity is constant on the surface of the affected shapes.

```
// Create a red ambient light
AmbientLight redLight = new AmbientLight(Color.RED);
```

An instance of the PointLight class represents a point light source. A point light source is a fixed point in space and radiates lights equally in all directions. The intensity of a point light decreases as the distance of the of the lighted point increases from the light source.

```
// Create a Add the point light to a group
PointLight redLight = new PointLight(Color.RED);
redLight.setTranslateX(250);
redLight.setTranslateY(-100);
redLight.setTranslateZ(290);
Group group = new Group(node1, node2, redLight);
```

Creating Subscenes

A scene can use only one camera. Sometimes, you may want to view different parts of a scene using multiple cameras. JavaFX 8 introduces the concept as subscenes. A subscene is a container for a scene graph. It can have its own width, height, fill color, depth buffer, antialiasing flag, and camera. An instance of the SubScene class represents a subscene. The SubScene inherits from the Node class. Therefore, a subscene can be used wherever a node can be used. A subscene can be used to separate 2D and 3D nodes in an application. You can use a camera for the subscene to view 3D objects that will not affect the 2D nodes in the other part of the main scene. The following snippet of code creates a SubScene and sets a camera to it:

```
SubScene ss = new SubScene(root, 200, 200, true, SceneAntialiasing.BALANCED);
PerspectiveCamera camera = new PerspectiveCamera(false);
ss.setCamera(camera);
```

■ **Tip** If a SubScene contains Shape3D nodes having a light node, a head light with a PointLight with Color.WHITE light source is provided. The head light is positioned at the camera position.

The program in Listing 19-7 shows how to use subscenes. The getSubScene() method creates a SubScene with a Box, a PerspectiveCamera, and a PointLight. An animation is set up to rotate the camera along the specified axis. The start() method creates two subscenes and adds them to an HBox. One subscene swings the camera along the y-axis and another along the x-axis. The HBox is added to the main scene.

Listing 19-7. Using Subscenes

```java
// SubSceneTest.java
package com.jdojo.shape3d;

import javafx.animation.Animation;
import javafx.animation.RotateTransition;
import javafx.application.Application;
import javafx.geometry.Point3D;
import javafx.scene.Group;
import javafx.scene.PerspectiveCamera;
import javafx.scene.PointLight;
import javafx.scene.Scene;
import javafx.scene.SceneAntialiasing;
import javafx.scene.SubScene;
import javafx.scene.layout.HBox;
import javafx.scene.paint.Color;
import javafx.scene.shape.Box;
import javafx.scene.shape.CullFace;
import javafx.scene.transform.Rotate;
import javafx.stage.Stage;
import javafx.util.Duration;

public class SubSceneTest extends Application {
        public static void main(String[] args) {
                Application.launch(args);
        }

        @Override
        public void start(Stage stage) {
                SubScene ySwing = getSubScene(Rotate.Y_AXIS);
                SubScene xSwing = getSubScene(Rotate.X_AXIS);
                HBox root = new HBox(20, ySwing, xSwing);
                Scene scene = new Scene(root, 500, 300, true);
                stage.setScene(scene);
                stage.setTitle("Using Sub-Scenes");
                stage.show();
        }

        private SubScene getSubScene(Point3D rotationAxis) {
                Box box = new Box(100, 100, 100);
                box.setCullFace(CullFace.NONE);
                box.setTranslateX(250);
                box.setTranslateY(100);
                box.setTranslateZ(400);

                PerspectiveCamera camera = new PerspectiveCamera(false);
                camera.setTranslateX(100);
                camera.setTranslateY(-50);
                camera.setTranslateZ(300);
```

825

```
                    // Add a Rotation animation to the camera
                    RotateTransition rt = new RotateTransition(Duration.seconds(2), camera);
                    rt.setCycleCount(Animation.INDEFINITE);
                    rt.setFromAngle(-10);
                    rt.setToAngle(10);
                    rt.setAutoReverse(true);
                    rt.setAxis(rotationAxis);
                    rt.play();

                    PointLight redLight = new PointLight(Color.RED);
                    redLight.setTranslateX(250);
                    redLight.setTranslateY(-100);
                    redLight.setTranslateZ(290);

                    // If you remove the redLight from the following group,
                    // a default head light will be provided by the SubScene.
                    Group root = new Group(box, redLight);
                    root.setRotationAxis(Rotate.X_AXIS);
                    root.setRotate(30);

                    SubScene ss = new SubScene(root, 200, 200, true, SceneAntialiasing.BALANCED);
                    ss.setCamera(camera);
                    return ss;
            }
    }
```

Creating User-Defined Shapes

JavaFX lets you define a 3D shape using a mesh of polygons. An instance of the abstract Mesh class represents the mesh data. The TriangleMesh class is concrete subclass of the Mesh class. A TriangleMesh represents a 3D surface consisting of a mesh of triangles.

▪ **Tip** In 3D modeling, a mesh of different types of polygons can be used to construct a 3D object. JavaFX supports only a mesh of triangles.

An instance of the MeshView class represents a 3D surface. The data for constructing a MeshView is specified as an instance of the Mesh.

Supplying the mesh data by hand is not an easy task. The problem is complicated by the way you need to specify the data. I will make it easier by demonstrating the mesh usage from a very simple user case to a more complex one.

A TriangleMesh needs to supply data for three aspects of a 3D object.

- Points

- Texture coordinates

- Faces

■ **Note**   If you have not worked with 3D objects using a mesh of triangles before, the explanation may seem a little complex. You need to be patient and learn a step at a time to understand the process of creating a 3D object using a mesh of triangles.

Points are the vertices of the triangles in the mesh. You need to specify the (x, y, z) coordinates of vertices in an array. Suppose v0, v1, v2, v3, v4, and so on are the points in 3D space that represent the vertices of the triangles in a mesh. Points in a TriangleMesh are specified as an array of floats.

The texture of a 3D surface is provided as an image that is a 2D object. Texture coordinates are points in a 2D plane, which are mapped to the vertices of triangles. You need to think of the triangles in a mesh unwrapped and placed onto a 2D plane. Overlay the image that supplies the surface texture for the 3D shape onto the same 2D plane. Map the vertices of the triangles to the 2D coordinates of the image to get a pair of (u, v) coordinates for each vertex in the mesh. The array of such (u, v) coordinates is the texture coordinate. Suppose t0, t1, t2, t3, t4, and so on are the texture coordinates.

Faces are the planes created by joining the three edges of the triangles. Each triangle has two faces: a front face and a back face. A face is specified in terms of indices in the points and texture coordinates arrays. A face is specified as v0, t0, v1, t1, v2, t2, and so on, where v1 is the index of the vertex in the points array and t1 is the index of the vertex in the texture coordinates array.

Consider the box shown in Figure 19-11.

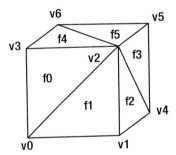

Figure 19-11. *A box made of 12 triangles*

A box consists of six sides. Each side is a rectangle. Each rectangle consists of two triangles. Each triangle has two faces: a front face and a back face. A box has eight vertices. You have named vertices as v0, v1, v2, and so on, and the faces as f0, f1, f2, and so on in the figure. You do not see the numberings for the vertices and faces that are not visible in the current orientation of the box. Each vertex is defined by a triple (x, y, z), which is the coordinate of the vertex in the 3D space. When you use the term *vertex v1*, you, technically, mean its coordinates (x1, y1, z1) for the vertex.

To create a mesh of triangles, you need to specify all vertices making up the 3D object. In the case of a box, you need to specify the eight vertices. In the TriangleMesh class, the vertices are known as points and they are specified as an observable array of float. The following pseudo-code creates the array of vertices. The first array is for understanding purpose only. The actual array specifies the coordinates of the vertices.

```
// For understanding purpose only
float[] points = {v0,
                  v1,
                  v2,
                  ...
                  v7};
```

```
// The actual array contain (x, y, z) coordinates of all vertices
float[] points = {x0, y0, z0, // v0
                  x1, y1, z1, // v1
                  x2, y2, z2, // v2
                  ...
                  x7, y7, z7  // v7
                  };
```

In the points array, the indices 0 to 2 contain coordinates of the first vertex, indices 3 to 5 contain the coordinates of the second vertex, and so on. How do you number the vertices? That is, which vertex is #1 and which one is #2, and so on? There is no rule to specify the order to vertices. It is all up to you how you number them. JavaFX cares about only one thing: you must include all vertices making up the shape in the points array. You are done with generating the points array. You will use it later.

Now, you need to create an array containing coordinates of 2D points. Creating this array is a little tricky. Beginners have hard time understanding this. Consider the figure shown in Figure 19-12.

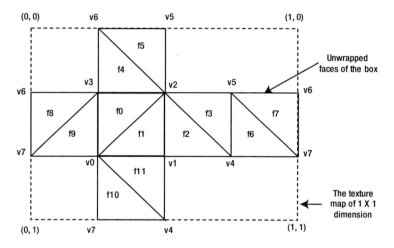

Figure 19-12. *Surface of a box mapped onto a 2D plane*

Figure 19-11 and Figure 19-12 are two views of the surface of the same box. Figure 19-12 mapped the surface from the 3D space to a 2D plane. Think of the box as a 3D object made of 12 triangular pieces of paper. Figure 19-11 shows those 12 pieces of paper put together as a 3D box whereas Figure 19-12 shows the same pieces of paper put side by side on the floor (a 2D plane).

■ **Tip** It is up to you to decide how you want to map the surface of a 3D object into a 2D plane. For example, in Figure 19-12, you could have also mapped the bottom side of the box into the lower, left, or top of the unit square.

Think of an image that you want to use as the texture for your box. The image will not have the third dimension (z dimension). The image needs to be applied on the surface of the box. JavaFX needs to know how the vertices on the box are mapped to the points on the image. You provide this information in terms of mapping of box vertices to the points on the image.

Now, think of a unit square (a 1 x 1 square) that represents the texture image. Overlay the unit square on the unwrapped faces of the box. The unit square is shown in dotted outline in Figure 19-12. The upper-left corner of the square has the coordinates (0, 0); the lower-left corner has the coordinates (0, 1); the upper-right corner has the coordinates (1, 0); the lower-left corner has the coordinates (1, 1).

In Figure 19-12, when you opened the surface of the box to put it onto a 2D plane, some of the vertices had to be split into multiple vertices. The box has eight vertices. The mapped box into the 2D plane has 14 vertices. The figure shows some of the vertices having the same number as those vertices representing the same vertex in the 3D box. Each vertex mapped into 2D plane (in Figure 19-12) becomes an element in the texture coordinates array. Figure 19-13 shows those 14 texture points; they are numbered as t0, t1, t2, and so on. You can number the vertices of the box onto the 2D plane in any order you want. The x and y coordinates of a texture point will be between 0 and 1. The actual mapping of these coordinates to the actual image size is performed by JavaFX. For example, (0.25, 0.) may be used for the coordinates of the vertex t9 and (0.25, 0.25) for the vertex t10.

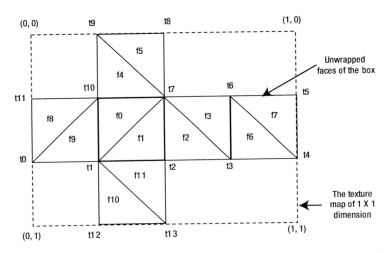

Figure 19-13. *A box surface mapped onto a 2D plane with texture coordinates*

You can create the texture coordinates array as shown in the following code. Like the points array, following is the pseudo-code. The first array is for understanding the concept and the second array is the actual one that is used in code.

```
// For understanding purpose-only
float[] texCoords = {t0,
                     t1,
                     t2,
                     ...
                     t14};
```

```
// The actual texture coordinates of vertices
float[] texCoords = {x0, y0, // t0
                     x1, y1, // t1
                     x2, y2, // t2
                     ...
                     x13, y13 // t13
                     };
```

The third piece of information that you need to specify is an array of faces. Note that each triangle has two faces. In our figures, you have shown only the front faces of the triangles. Specifying faces is the most confusing step in creating a TriangleMesh object. A face is specified using the points array and texture coordinates array. You use the indices of the vertices in the point array and the indices of the texture points in the texture coordinates array to specify a face. A face is specified in using six integers in the following formats:

ivo, ito, iv1, it1, iv2, it2

Here,

- ivo is the index of the vertex v0 in the points array and ito is the index of the point t0 in the texture coordinates array

- iv1 and it1 are the indices of the vertex v1 and point t1 in the points and texture coordinates arrays

- iv2 and it2 are the indices of the vertex v2 and point t2 in the points and texture coordinates arrays

Figure 19-14 shows only two triangles, which make up the front side of the box.

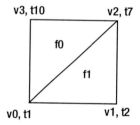

Figure 19-14. *Two triangles of the box with their vertices in points and texture coordinates arrays*

Figure 19-14 is the superimposition of the figures shown in Figure 19-12 and Figure 19-13. The figure shows the vertex number and their corresponding texture coordinate point number. To specify the f0 in the faces array, you can specify the vertices of the triangle in two ways: counterclockwise and clockwise.

ivo, it1, iv2, it7, iv3, it10 (Counterclockwise)
ivo, it1, iv3, it10, iv2, it7 (Clockwise)

The starting vertex does not matter in specifying a face. You can start with any vertex and go in a clockwise or a counterclockwise direction. When the vertices for a face are specified in the counterclockwise direction, it is considered the front face. Otherwise, it is considered the back face. The following series of numbers will specify the face f1 in our figure:

ivo, it1, iv1, it2, iv2, it7 (Counterclockwise: front-face)
ivo, it1, iv2, it7, iv1, it2 (Clockwise: back-face)

To determine whether you are specifying front face or back face, apply the following rules as illustrated in Figure 19-15:

- Draw a line perpendicular to the surface of the triangle going outward.

- Imagine you are looking into the surface by aligning your view along the line.

- Try traversing the vertices in counterclockwise. The sequence of vertices will give you front face. If you traverse the vertices clockwise, the sequence will give you back face.

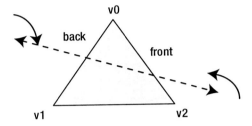

Figure 19-15. *Winding order of vertices of a triangle*

The following pseudo-code illustrates how to create an int array for specifying faces. The int values are the array indices from the points and texture coordinates arrays.

```
int[] faces = new int[] {
ivo, it1, iv2, it7, iv3, it10, // f0: front-face
ivo, it1, iv3, it10, iv2, it7, // f0: back-face
ivo, it1, iv1, it2, iv2, it7,  // f1: front-face
ivo, it1, iv2, it7, iv1, it2   // f1: back-face
...
};
```

Once you have the points, texture coordinates, and faces arrays, you can construct a TriangleMesh object as follows:

```
TriangleMesh mesh = new TriangleMesh();
mesh.getPoints().addAll(points);
mesh.getTexCoords().addAll(texCoords);
mesh.getFaces().addAll(faces);
```

A TriangleMesh provides the data for constructing a user-defined 3D object. A MeshView object creates the surface for the object with a specified TriangleMesh.

```
// Create a MeshView
MeshView meshView = new MeshView();
meshView.setMesh(mesh);
```

Once you have a MeshView object, you need to add it to a scene graph to view it. You can view it the same you have been viewing the predefined 3D shapes Boxes, Spheres, and Cylinders.

In the next few sections, you will create 3D objects using a TriangleMesh. You will start with the simplest 3D object, which is a triangle.

Creating a 3D Triangle

You may argue that a triangle is a 2D shape, not a 3D shape. It is agreed that a triangle is a 2D shape. You will create a triangle in a 3D space using a TriangleMesh. The triangle will have two faces. This example is chosen because it is the simplest shape you can create with a mesh of triangles. In case of a triangle, the mesh consists of only one triangle. Figure 19-16 shows a triangle in the 3D space and its vertices mapped into a 2D plane.

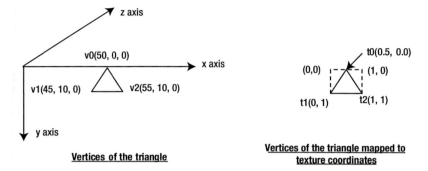

Figure 19-16. *Vertices of a triangle in the 3D space and mapped onto a 2D plane*

The triangle can be created using a mesh of one triangle. Let us create the points array for the TriangleMesh object.

```
float[] points = {50, 0, 0,  // v0 (iv0 = 0)
                  45, 10, 0, // v1 (iv1 = 1)
                  55, 10, 0  // v2 (iv2 = 2)
                 };
```

The second part of the figure, shown on the right, maps the vertices of the triangle to a unit square. You can create the texture coordinates array as follows:

```
float[] texCoords = {0.5f, 0.5f,  // t0 (it0 = 0)
                     0.0f, 1.0f,  // t1 (it1 = 1)
                     1.0f, 1.0f   // t2 (it2 = 2)
                    };
```

Using the points and texture coordinates arrays, you can specify the faces array as follows:

```
int[] faces = { 0, 0, 2, 2, 1, 1,  // iv0, it0, iv2, it2, iv1, it1 (front face)
                0, 0, 1, 1, 2, 2   // iv0, it0, iv1, it1, iv2, it2 back face
              };
```

Listing 19-8 contains the complete program to create a triangle using a TriangleMesh. It adds two different lights to light the two faces of the triangle. An animation rotates the camera, so you can view both sides of the triangle in different colors. The createMeshView() method has the coordinate values and logic to create the MeshView.

Listing 19-8. Creating a Triangle Using a TriangleMesh

```java
// TriangleWithAMesh.java
package com.jdojo.shape3d;

import javafx.animation.Animation;
import javafx.animation.RotateTransition;
import javafx.application.Application;
import javafx.scene.Group;
import javafx.scene.PerspectiveCamera;
import javafx.scene.PointLight;
import javafx.scene.Scene;
import javafx.scene.paint.Color;
import javafx.scene.shape.MeshView;
import javafx.scene.shape.TriangleMesh;
import javafx.scene.transform.Rotate;
import javafx.stage.Stage;
import javafx.util.Duration;

public class TriangleWithAMesh extends Application {
        public static void main(String[] args) {
                Application.launch(args);
        }

        @Override
        public void start(Stage stage) {
                // Create a MeshView and position ity in the space
                MeshView meshView = this.createMeshView();
                meshView.setTranslateX(250);
                meshView.setTranslateY(100);
                meshView.setTranslateZ(400);

                // Scale the Meshview to make it look bigger
                meshView.setScaleX(10.0);
                meshView.setScaleY(10.0);
                meshView.setScaleZ(10.0);

                PerspectiveCamera camera = new PerspectiveCamera(false);
                camera.setTranslateX(100);
                camera.setTranslateY(-50);
                camera.setTranslateZ(300);

                // Add a Rotation animation to the camera
                RotateTransition rt = new RotateTransition(Duration.seconds(2), camera);
                rt.setCycleCount(Animation.INDEFINITE);
                rt.setFromAngle(-30);
                rt.setToAngle(30);
                rt.setAutoReverse(true);
                rt.setAxis(Rotate.Y_AXIS);
                rt.play();
```

```java
        // Front light is red
        PointLight redLight = new PointLight();
        redLight.setColor(Color.RED);
        redLight.setTranslateX(250);
        redLight.setTranslateY(150);
        redLight.setTranslateZ(300);

        // Back light is green
        PointLight greenLight = new PointLight();
        greenLight.setColor(Color.GREEN);
        greenLight.setTranslateX(200);
        greenLight.setTranslateY(150);
        greenLight.setTranslateZ(450);

        Group root = new Group(meshView, redLight, greenLight);

        // Rotate the triangle with its lights to 90 degrees
        root.setRotationAxis(Rotate.Y_AXIS);
        root.setRotate(90);

        Scene scene = new Scene(root, 400, 300, true);
        scene.setCamera(camera);
        stage.setScene(scene);
        stage.setTitle("Creating a Triangle using a TriangleMesh");
        stage.show();
    }

    public MeshView createMeshView() {
        float[] points = {50, 0, 0,  // v0 (iv0 = 0)
                          45, 10, 0, // v1 (iv1 = 1)
                          55, 10, 0  // v2 (iv2 = 2)
                         };

        float[] texCoords = { 0.5f, 0.5f, // t0 (it0 = 0)
                              0.0f, 1.0f, // t1 (it1 = 1)
                              1.0f, 1.0f  // t2 (it2 = 2)
                            };

        int[] faces = {
            0, 0, 2, 2, 1, 1, // iv0, it0, iv2, it2, iv1, it1 (front face)
            0, 0, 1, 1, 2, 2  // iv0, it0, iv1, it1, iv2, it2 (back face)
        };

        // Create a TriangleMesh
        TriangleMesh mesh = new TriangleMesh();
        mesh.getPoints().addAll(points);
        mesh.getTexCoords().addAll(texCoords);
        mesh.getFaces().addAll(faces);
```

```
                // Create a NeshView
                MeshView meshView = new MeshView();
                meshView.setMesh(mesh);

                return meshView;
            }
    }
```

Creating a 3D Rectangle

In this section, you will create a rectangle using a mesh of two triangles. This will give us an opportunity to use what you have learned so far. Figure 19-17 shows a rectangle in the 3D space and its vertices mapped into a 2D plane.

Vertices of the rectangle

Vertices of the rectangle mapped to texture coordinates

Figure 19-17. Vertices of a rectangle in the 3D space and mapped into a 2D plane

The rectangle consists of two triangles. Both triangles have two faces. In the figure, I have shown only two faces f0 and f1. The following is the points array for the four vertices of the rectangle.

```
float[] points = {50, 0, 0,   // v0 (iv0 = 0)
                  50, 10, 0,  // v1 (iv1 = 1)
                  60, 10, 0,  // v2 (iv2 = 2)
                  60, 0, 0    // v3 (iv3 = 3)
                 };
```

The texture coordinate array can be constructed as follows:

```
float[] texCoords = {0.0f, 0.0f,   // t0 (it0 = 0)
                     0.0f, 1.0f,   // t1 (it1 = 1)
                     1.0f, 1.0f,   // t2 (it2 = 2)
                     1.0f, 0.0f    // t3 (it3 = 3)
                    };
```

You will specify the four faces as follows:

```
int[] faces =
        { 0, 0, 3, 3, 1, 1,   // iv0, it0, iv3, it3, iv1, it1 (f0 front face)
          0, 0, 1, 1, 3, 3,   // iv0, it0, iv1, it1, iv3, it3 (f0 back face)
          1, 1, 3, 3, 2, 2,   // iv1, it1, iv3, it3, iv2, it2 (f1 front face)
          1, 1, 2, 2, 3, 3    // iv1, it1, iv2, it2, iv3, it3 (f1 back face)
        };
```

If you plug the aforementioned three arrays into the createMeshView() method in Listing 19-8, you will get a rotating rectangle.

Creating a Tetrahedron

Now, you are prepared to create a little complex 3D object. You will create a tetrahedron. Figure 19-18 shows the top view of a tetrahedron.

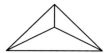

Figure 19-18. *A tetrahedron*

A tetrahedron consists of four triangles. It has four vertices. Three triangles meet at a point. Figure 19-19 shows the two views of the tetrahedron. On the left, you have numbered the four vertices as v0, v1, v2, and v3 and four faces as f0m f1, f2, and f3. Note that the face f3 is the face of the triangle at the base and it is not visible from the top view. The second view has unwrapped the four triangles giving rise to eight vertices on the 2D plane. The dotted rectangle is the unit square into which the eight vertices will be mapped.

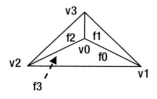 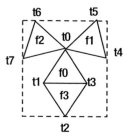

Vertices of the tetrahedron

Vertices of the tetrahedron mapped to texture coordinates

Figure 19-19. *Vertices of a tetrahedron in the 3D space and mapped into a 2D plane*

You can create the points, faces, and texture coordinates arrays as follows:

```
float[] points = {10, 10, 10, // v0 (iv0 = 0)
                  20, 20, 0,  // v1 (iv1 = 1)
                  0, 20, 0,   // v2 (iv2 = 2)
                  10, 20, 20  // v3 (iv3 = 3)
                 };

float[] texCoords = {
        0.50f, 0.33f, // t0 (it0 = 0)
        0.25f, 0.75f, // t1 (it1 = 1)
        0.50f, 1.00f, // t2 (it2 = 2)
        0.66f, 0.66f, // t3 (it3 = 3)
```

```
        1.00f, 0.35f, // t4 (it4 = 4)
        0.90f, 0.00f, // t5 (it5 = 5)
        0.10f, 0.00f, // t6 (it6 = 6)
        0.00f, 0.35f  // t7 (it7 = 7)
};

int[] faces = {
        0, 0, 2, 1, 1, 3, // f0 front-face
        0, 0, 1, 3, 2, 1, // f0 back-face
        0, 0, 1, 4, 3, 5, // f1 front-face
        0, 0, 3, 5, 1, 4, // f1 back-face
        0, 0, 3, 6, 2, 7, // f2 front-face
        0, 0, 2, 7, 3, 6, // f2 back-face
        1, 3, 3, 2, 2, 1, // f3 front-face
        1, 3, 2, 1, 3, 2  // f3 back-face
};
```

Listing 19-9 contains a complete program to show how to construct a tetrahedron using a TriangleMesh. The tetrahedron is rotated along y-axis, so you can view two of its vertical faces. Figure 19-20 shows the window with the tetrahedron.

Listing 19-9. Creating a Tetrahedron Using a TriangleMesh

```java
// Tetrahedron.java
package com.jdojo.shape3d;

import javafx.application.Application;
import javafx.scene.Group;
import javafx.scene.PerspectiveCamera;
import javafx.scene.PointLight;
import javafx.scene.Scene;
import javafx.scene.paint.Color;
import javafx.scene.shape.MeshView;
import javafx.scene.shape.TriangleMesh;
import javafx.scene.transform.Rotate;
import javafx.stage.Stage;

public class Tetrahedron extends Application {
        public static void main(String[] args) {
                Application.launch(args);
        }

        @Override
        public void start(Stage stage) {
                MeshView meshView = this.createMeshView();
                meshView.setTranslateX(250);
                meshView.setTranslateY(50);
                meshView.setTranslateZ(400);

                meshView.setScaleX(10.0);
                meshView.setScaleY(20.0);
                meshView.setScaleZ(10.0);
```

```
            PerspectiveCamera camera = new PerspectiveCamera(false);
            camera.setTranslateX(100);
            camera.setTranslateY(0);
            camera.setTranslateZ(100);

            PointLight redLight = new PointLight();
            redLight.setColor(Color.RED);
            redLight.setTranslateX(250);
            redLight.setTranslateY(-100);
            redLight.setTranslateZ(250);

            Group root = new Group(meshView, redLight);
            root.setRotationAxis(Rotate.Y_AXIS);
            root.setRotate(45);

            Scene scene = new Scene(root, 200, 150, true);
            scene.setCamera(camera);
            stage.setScene(scene);
            stage.setTitle("A Tetrahedron using a TriangleMesh");
            stage.show();
    }

    public MeshView createMeshView() {
            float[] points = {10, 10, 10, // v0 (iv0 = 0)
                              20, 20, 0,  // v1 (iv1 = 1)
                              0, 20, 0,   // v2 (iv2 = 2)
                              10, 20, 20  // v3 (iv3 = 3)
                             };

            float[] texCoords = {
                    0.50f, 0.33f, // t0 (it0 = 0)
                    0.25f, 0.75f, // t1 (it1 = 1)
                    0.50f, 1.00f, // t2 (it2 = 2)
                    0.66f, 0.66f, // t3 (it3 = 3)
                    1.00f, 0.35f, // t4 (it4 = 4)
                    0.90f, 0.00f, // t5 (it5 = 5)
                    0.10f, 0.00f, // t6 (it6 = 6)
                    0.00f, 0.35f  // t7 (it7 = 7)
            };

            int[] faces = {
                    0, 0, 2, 1, 1, 3, // f0 front-face
                    0, 0, 1, 3, 2, 1, // f0 back-face
                    0, 0, 1, 4, 3, 5, // f1 front-face
                    0, 0, 3, 5, 1, 4, // f1 back-face
                    0, 0, 3, 6, 2, 7, // f2 front-face
                    0, 0, 2, 7, 3, 6, // f2 back-face
                    1, 3, 3, 2, 2, 1, // f3 front-face
                    1, 3, 2, 1, 3, 2, // f3 back-face
            };
```

```
            TriangleMesh mesh = new TriangleMesh();
            mesh.getPoints().addAll(points);
            mesh.getTexCoords().addAll(texCoords);
            mesh.getFaces().addAll(faces);

            MeshView meshView = new MeshView();
            meshView.setMesh(mesh);

            return meshView;
        }
    }
```

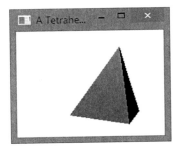

Figure 19-20. *A tetrahedron using a TriangleMesh*

Summary

Any shape, drawn in a three-dimensional space, having three dimensions (length, width, and depth), is known as a 3D shape such as cubes, spheres, pyramids, and so on. JavaFX 8 provides 3D shapes as nodes. JavaFX 8 offers two types of 3D shapes: predefined shapes and user-defined shapes.

Box, sphere, and cylinder are three predefined 3D shapes that you can readily use in your JavaFX applications. You can create any type of 3D shapes using a triangle mesh. The Box, Sphere, and Cylinder classes represent the three predefined shapes. The MeshView class represents a user-defined 3D shape in a scene. The 3D shape classes are in the javafx.scene.shape package.

JavaFX 3D support is a conditional feature. If it is not supported on your platform, you get a warning message on the console when you run a program that attempts to use 3D features. The method Platform.isSupported(ConditionalFeature.SCENE3D) returns true if 3D is supported on your platform.

When dealing with 3D objects in JavaFX, you would like the object closer to you to overlap the object farther from you. In JavaFX, by default, nodes are rendered in the order they are added to the scene graph. In order for 3D shapes to appear as they would appear in the real world, you need to specify two things. First, when you create a Scene object, specify that it needs to have a depth buffer, and second, specify that the nodes' z coordinate values should be used when they are rendered.

Cameras are used to render the scene. Cameras in JavaFX are nodes. They can be added to the scene graph and positioned like other nodes. Perspective camera and parallel camera are two types of cameras used in JavaFX and they are represented by the PerspectiveCamera and ParallelCamera classes. A perspective camera defines the viewing volume for a perspective projection, which is a truncated right pyramid. The camera projects the objects contained within the near and far clipping planes onto the projection plane. Therefore, any objects outside the clipping planes are not visible. A parallel camera specifies the viewing volume for a parallel projection, which is a rectangular box.

Similar to the real world, you need a light source to view the 3D objects in a scene. An instance of the abstract base class LightBase represents a light source. Its two concrete subclasses, AmbientLight and PointLight represent an ambient light and a point light.

A scene can use only one camera. Sometimes, you may want to view different parts of a scene using multiple cameras. JavaFX 8 introduces the concept as subscenes. A subscene is a container for a scene graph. It can have its own width, height, fill color, depth buffer, antialiasing flag, and camera. An instance of the SubScene class represents a subscene. The SubScene inherits from the Node class.

The next chapter will discuss how to apply different types of effects to nodes in a scene graph.

CHAPTER 20

■ ■ ■

Applying Effects

In this chapter, you will learn:

- What an effect is
- How to chain effects
- What different types of effects are
- How to use perspective transformation effect

What Is an Effect?

An effect is a filter that accepts one or more graphical inputs, applies an algorithm on the inputs, and produces an output. Typically, effects are applied to nodes to create visually appealing user interfaces. Examples of effects are shadow, blur, warp, glow, reflection, blending, different types of lighting, among others. The JavaFX library provides several effect-related classes. Effects are conditional features. They are applied to nodes and will be ignored if they are not available on a platform. Figure 20-1 shows four Text nodes using the drop shadow, blur, glow, and bloom effects.

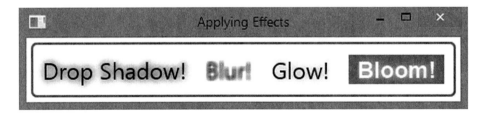

Figure 20-1. *Text nodes with different effects*

The Node class contains an effect property that specifies the effect applied to the node. By default, it is null. The following snippet of code applies a drop shadow effect to a Text node:

```
Text t1 = new Text("Drop Shadow");
t1.setFont(Font.font(24));
t1.setEffect(new DropShadow());
```

An instance of the Effect class represents an effect. The Effect class is the abstract base for all effect classes. All effect classes are included in the javafx.scene.effect package.

The program in Listing 20-1 creates Text nodes and applies effects to them. These nodes are the ones shown in Figure 20-1. I will explain the different types of effects and their usages in subsequent sections.

Listing 20-1. Applying Effects to Nodes

```java
// EffectTest.java
package com.jdojo.effect;

import javafx.application.Application;
import javafx.scene.Scene;
import javafx.scene.effect.Bloom;
import javafx.scene.effect.BoxBlur;
import javafx.scene.effect.DropShadow;
import javafx.scene.effect.Glow;
import javafx.scene.layout.HBox;
import javafx.scene.layout.StackPane;
import javafx.scene.paint.Color;
import javafx.scene.shape.Rectangle;
import javafx.scene.text.Font;
import javafx.scene.text.FontWeight;
import javafx.scene.text.Text;
import javafx.stage.Stage;

public class EffectTest extends Application {
        public static void main(String[] args) {
                Application.launch(args);
        }

        @Override
        public void start(Stage stage) {
                Text t1 = new Text("Drop Shadow!");
                t1.setFont(Font.font(24));
                t1.setEffect(new DropShadow());

                Text t2 = new Text("Blur!");
                t2.setFont(Font.font(24));
                t2.setEffect(new BoxBlur());

                Text t3 = new Text("Glow!");
                t3.setFont(Font.font(24));
                t3.setEffect(new Glow());

                Text t4 = new Text("Bloom!");
                t4.setFont(Font.font("Arial", FontWeight.BOLD, 24));
                t4.setFill(Color.WHITE);
                t4.setEffect(new Bloom(0.10));

                // Stack the Text node with bloom effect over a Reactangle
                Rectangle rect = new Rectangle(100, 30, Color.GREEN);
                StackPane spane = new StackPane(rect, t4);
```

```
            HBox root = new HBox(t1, t2, t3, spane);
            root.setSpacing(20);
            root.setStyle("-fx-padding: 10;" +
                          "-fx-border-style: solid inside;" +
                          "-fx-border-width: 2;" +
                          "-fx-border-insets: 5;" +
                          "-fx-border-radius: 5;" +
                          "-fx-border-color: blue;");

            Scene scene = new Scene(root);
            stage.setScene(scene);
            stage.setTitle("Applying Effects");
            stage.show();
        }
}
```

■ **Tip** An effect applied to a Group is applied to all its children. It is also possible to chain multiple effects where the output of one effect becomes the input for the next effect in the chain. The layout bounds of a node are not affected by the effects applied to it. However, the local bounds and bounds in parent are affected by the effects.

Chaining Effects

Some effects can be chained with other effects when they are applied in sequence. The output of the first effect becomes the input for the second effect and so on, as shown in Figure 20-2.

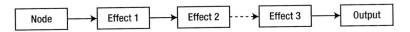

Figure 20-2. *A chain of effects applied on a node*

Effect classes that allow chaining contain an input property to specify the effect that precedes it. If the input is null, the effect is applied to the node on which this effect is set instead of being applied to the preceding input effect. By default, the input is null. The following snippet of code creates two chains of effects on Text nodes, as shown in Figure 20-3:

```
// Effect Chain: Text >> Reflection >> Shadow
DropShadow dsEffect = new DropShadow();
dsEffect.setInput(new Reflection());
Text t1 = new Text("Reflection and Shadow");
t1.setEffect(dsEffect);

// Effect Chain: Text >> Shadow >> Reflection
Reflection reflection = new Reflection();
reflection.setInput(new DropShadow());
Text t2 = new Text("Shadow and Reflection");
t2.setEffect(reflection);
```

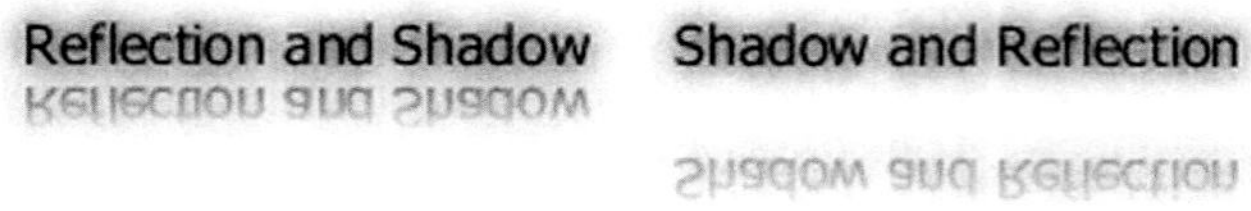

Reflection and Shadow   Shadow and Reflection

Figure 20-3. *Chaining a DropShadow effect with a Reflection effect*

In Figure 20-3, a Reflection effect followed by a DropShadow is applied to the text on the left; a DropShadow followed by a Reflection effect is applied to the text on the right. Notice the sequence of effects makes a difference in the output. The second chain of effects produces a taller output as the reflection also includes the shadow.

If an effect allows chaining, it will have an input property. In subsequent sections, I will list the input property for the effect classes, but not discuss it.

Shadowing Effects

A shadowing effect draws a shadow and applies it to an input. JavaFX supports three types of shadowing effects:

- DropShadow
- InnerShadow
- Shadow

The *DropShadow* Effect

The DropShadow effect draws a shadow (a blurred image) behind the input, so the input seems to be raised. It gives the input a 3D look. The input can be a node or an effect in a chain of effects.

An instance of the DropShadow class represents a DropShadow effect. The size, location, color, and quality of the effect are controlled by several properties of the DropShadow class:

- offsetX
- offsetY
- color
- blurType
- radius
- spread
- width
- height
- input

The DropShadow class contains several constructors that let you specify the initial values for the properties:

- DropShadow()

- DropShadow(BlurType blurType, Color color, double radius, double spread, double offsetX, double offsetY)

- DropShadow(double radius, Color color)

- DropShadow(double radius, double offsetX, double offsetY, Color color)

The offsetX and offsetY properties control the position of the shadow in pixels relative to the input. By default, their values are zero. The positive values of offsetX and offsetY move the shadow in the positive x axis and y axis directions, respectively. The negative values move the shadow in the reverse directions.

The following snippet of code creates a DropShadow object with the offsetX and offsetY of 10px. The third rectangle from the left in Figure 20-4 shows the rectangle with the effect using the same rectangle with a DropShadow effect and different x and y offsets. For the fourth from the left rectangle, the shadow is positioned at the lower right corner of the rectangle as the rectangle size (50, 25) matches the offsets (50, 25).

```
DropShadow dsEffect = new DropShadow();
dsEffect.setOffsetX(10);
dsEffect.setOffsetY(10);

Rectangle rect = new Rectangle(50, 25, Color.LIGHTGRAY);
rect.setEffect(dsEffect);
```

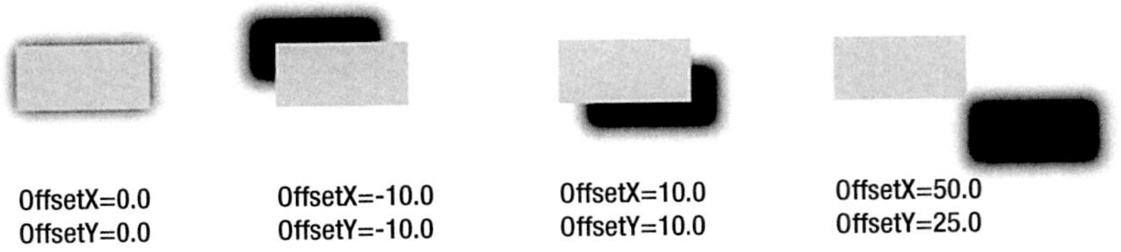

| OffsetX=0.0 | OffsetX=-10.0 | OffsetX=10.0 | OffsetX=50.0 |
| OffsetY=0.0 | OffsetY=-10.0 | OffsetY=10.0 | OffsetY=25.0 |

Figure 20-4. *Effects of the offsetX and offsetY properties on a DropShadow effect*

The color property specifies the color of the shadow. By default, it is Color.BLACK. The following code would set the color to red:

```
DropShadow dsEffect = new DropShadow();
dsEffect.setColor(Color.RED);
```

The blurring in the shadow can be achieved using different algorithms. The blurType property specifies the type of blurring algorithm for the shadow. Its value is one of the following constants of the BlurType enum:

- ONE_PASS_BOX

- TWO_PASS_BOX

- THREE_PASS_BOX

- GAUSSIAN

The ONE_PASS_BOX uses a single pass of the box filter to blur the shadow. The TWO_PASS_BOX uses two passes of the box filter to blur the shadow. The THREE_PASS_BOX uses three passes of the box filter to blur the shadow. The GAUSSIAN uses a Gaussian blur kernel to blur the shadow. The blur quality of the shadow is the least in ONE_PASS_BOX and the best in GAUSSIAN. The default is THREE_PASS_BOX, which is very close to GAUSSIAN in quality. The following snippet of code sets the GAUSSIAN blur type:

```
DropShadow dsEffect = new DropShadow();
dsEffect.setBlurType(BlurType.GAUSSIAN);
```

The radius property specifies the distance the shadow is spread on each side of the source pixel. If the radius is zero, the shadow has sharp edges. Its value can be between 0 and 127. The default value is 10. The blurring outside the shadow region is achieved by blending the shadow color and the background color. The blur color fades out over the radius distance from the edges.

Figure 20-5 shows a rectangle twice with a DropShadow effect. The one on the left uses the radius of 0.0, which results in sharp edges of the shadow. The one on the right uses the default radius of 10.0 that spreads the shadow 10px around the edges. The following snippet of code produces the first rectangle in the figure that has sharp edges of the shadow:

```
DropShadow dsEffect = new DropShadow();
dsEffect.setOffsetX(10);
dsEffect.setOffsetY(10);
dsEffect.setRadius(0);

Rectangle rect = new Rectangle(50, 25, Color.LIGHTGRAY);
rect.setEffect(dsEffect);
```

radius=0.0   radius=10.0

Figure 20-5. Effects of the radius property of a DropShadow effect

The spread property specifies the portion of the radius, which has the same color as the shadow. The color for the remaining portion of the radius is determined by the blur algorithm. Its value is between 0.0 and 1.0. The default is 0.0.

Suppose you have a DropShadow with a radius 10.0 and a spread value of 0.60 and the shadow color is black. In this case, the blur color will be black up to 6px around the source pixel. It will start fading out from the seventh pixel to the tenth pixel. If you specify the spread value as 1.0, there would be no blurring of the shadow. Figure 20-6 shows three rectangles with a DropShadow using a radius of 10.0. The three DropShadow effects use different spread values. The spread of 0.0 blurs fully along the radius. The spread of 0.50 spreads the shadow color in the first half of the radius and blurs the second half. The spread of 1.0 spreads the shadow color fully along the radius and there is no blurring. The following snippet of code produces the middle rectangle in Figure 20-6:

```
DropShadow dsEfefct = new DropShadow();
dsEfefct.setOffsetX(10);
dsEfefct.setOffsetY(10);
dsEfefct.setRadius(10);
dsEfefct.setSpread(.50);
```

```
Rectangle rect = new Rectangle(50, 25, Color.LIGHTGRAY);
rect.setEffect(dsEfefct);
```

spread=0.0   spread=0.5   spread=1.0

Figure 20-6. *Effects of the spread property of a DropShadow effect*

The width and height properties specify the horizontal and vertical distances, respectively, from the source pixel up to where the shadow color is spread. Their values are between 0 and 255. Setting their values is equivalent to setting the radius property, so they are equal to (2 * radius + 1). Their default value is 21.0. When you change the radius, the width and height properties are adjusted using the formula if they are not bound. However, setting the width and height changes the radius value, so the average of the width and height is equal to (2 * radius + 1). Figure 20-7 shows four rectangles with a DropShadow effects. Their width and height properties were set as shown under each rectangle. Their radius properties were adjusted automatically. The fourth from the left rectangle was produced using the following snippet of code:

```
DropShadow dsEffect = new DropShadow();
dsEffect.setOffsetX(10);
dsEffect.setOffsetY(10);
dsEffect.setWidth(20);
dsEffect.setHeight(20);

Rectangle rect = new Rectangle(50, 25, Color.LIGHTGRAY);
rect.setEffect(dsEffect);
```

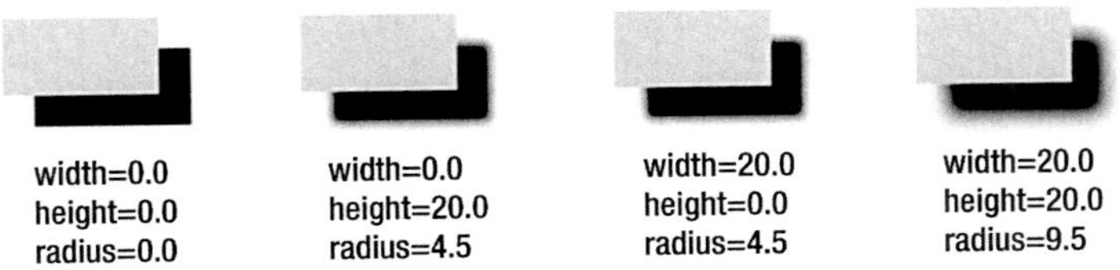

width=0.0   width=0.0   width=20.0   width=20.0
height=0.0   height=20.0   height=0.0   height=20.0
radius=0.0   radius=4.5   radius=4.5   radius=9.5

Figure 20-7. *Effects of setting width and height of a DropShadow*

The program in Listing 20-2 lets you experiment with properties of the DropShadow effect. It displays a window as shown in Figure 20-8. Change the properties to see their effects in action.

Listing 20-2. Experimenting with DropShadow Properties

```
// DropShadowTest.java
package com.jdojo.effect;

import javafx.application.Application;
import javafx.scene.Scene;
import javafx.scene.control.ColorPicker;
import javafx.scene.control.ComboBox;
import javafx.scene.control.Label;
```

847

```java
import javafx.scene.control.Slider;
import javafx.scene.effect.BlurType;
import javafx.scene.effect.DropShadow;
import javafx.scene.layout.BorderPane;
import javafx.scene.layout.GridPane;
import javafx.scene.paint.Color;
import javafx.scene.shape.Rectangle;
import javafx.stage.Stage;

public class DropShadowTest extends Application {
        public static void main(String[] args) {
                Application.launch(args);
        }

        @Override
        public void start(Stage stage) {
                Rectangle rect = new Rectangle(100, 50, Color.GRAY);
                DropShadow dsEffect = new DropShadow();
                rect.setEffect(dsEffect);

                GridPane controllsrPane = this.getControllerPane(dsEffect);
                BorderPane root = new BorderPane();
                root.setCenter(rect);
                root.setBottom(controllsrPane);
                root.setStyle("-fx-padding: 10;" +
                                "-fx-border-style: solid inside;" +
                                "-fx-border-width: 2;" +
                                "-fx-border-insets: 5;" +
                                "-fx-border-radius: 5;" +
                                "-fx-border-color: blue;");

                Scene scene = new Scene(root);
                stage.setScene(scene);
                stage.setTitle("Experimenting with DropShadow Effect");
                stage.show();
        }

        private GridPane getControllerPane(final DropShadow dsEffect) {
                Slider offsetXSlider = new Slider(-200, 200, 0);
                dsEffect.offsetXProperty().bind(offsetXSlider.valueProperty());

                Slider offsetYSlider = new Slider(-200, 200, 0);
                dsEffect.offsetYProperty().bind(offsetYSlider.valueProperty());

                Slider radiusSlider = new Slider(0, 127, 10);
                dsEffect.radiusProperty().bind(radiusSlider.valueProperty());

                Slider spreadSlider = new Slider(0.0, 1.0, 0);
                dsEffect.spreadProperty().bind(spreadSlider.valueProperty());
```

```
ColorPicker colorPicker = new ColorPicker(Color.BLACK);
dsEffect.colorProperty().bind(colorPicker.valueProperty());

ComboBox<BlurType> blurTypeList = new ComboBox<>();
blurTypeList.setValue(dsEffect.getBlurType());
blurTypeList.getItems().addAll(BlurType.ONE_PASS_BOX,
                               BlurType.TWO_PASS_BOX,
                               BlurType.THREE_PASS_BOX,
                               BlurType.GAUSSIAN);
dsEffect.blurTypeProperty().bind(blurTypeList.valueProperty());

GridPane pane = new GridPane();
pane.setHgap(5);
pane.setVgap(10);
pane.addRow(0, new Label("OffsetX:"), offsetXSlider);
pane.addRow(1, new Label("OffsetY:"), offsetYSlider);
pane.addRow(2, new Label("Radius:"), radiusSlider,
               new Label("Spread:"), spreadSlider);
pane.addRow(3, new Label("Color:"), colorPicker,
               new Label("Blur Type:"), blurTypeList);

return pane;
    }
}
```

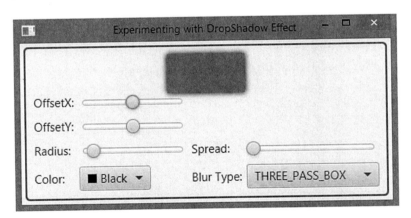

Figure 20-8. *A window that allows you to change the properties of a DropShadow effect at runtime*

The *InnerShadow* Effect

The InnerShadow effect works very similar to the DropShadow effect. It draws a shadow (a blurred image) of an input inside the edges of the input, so the input seems to have depth or a 3D look. The input can be a node or an effect in a chain of effects.

An instance of the InnerShadow class represents an InnerShadow effect. The size, location, color, and quality of the effect are controlled by several properties of the InnerShadow class:

- offsetX
- offsetY
- color
- blurType
- radius
- choke
- width
- height
- input

The number of properties of the InnerShadow class is equal to that for the DropShadow class. The spread property in the DropShadow class is replaced by the choke property in the InnerShadow class, which works similar to the spread property in the DropShadow class. Please refer to the previous section "The *DropShadow* Effect" for a detailed description and examples of these properties.

The DropShadow class contains several constructors that let you specify the initial values for the properties:

- InnerShadow()
- InnerShadow(BlurType blurType, Color color, double radius, double choke, double offsetX, double offsetY)
- InnerShadow(double radius, Color color)
- InnerShadow(double radius, double offsetX, double offsetY, Color color)

The program in Listing 20-3 creates a Text node and two Rectangle nodes. An InnerShadow is applied to all three nodes. Figure 20-9 shows the results for these nodes. Notice that the shadow is not spread outside the edges of the nodes. You need to set the offsetX and offsetY properties to see a noticeable effect.

Listing 20-3. Using InnerShadow Class

```java
// InnerShadowTest.java
package com.jdojo.effect;

import javafx.application.Application;
import javafx.geometry.Pos;
import javafx.scene.Scene;
import javafx.scene.effect.InnerShadow;
import javafx.scene.layout.HBox;
import javafx.scene.layout.VBox;
import javafx.scene.paint.Color;
import javafx.scene.shape.Rectangle;
import javafx.scene.shape.Shape;
import javafx.scene.text.Font;
import javafx.scene.text.FontWeight;
import javafx.scene.text.Text;
import javafx.stage.Stage;
```

```java
public class InnerShadowTest extends Application {
        public static void main(String[] args) {
                Application.launch(args);
        }

        @Override
        public void start(Stage stage) {
                InnerShadow is1 = new InnerShadow();
                is1.setOffsetX(3);
                is1.setOffsetY(6);

                Text t1 = new Text("Inner Shadow");
                t1.setEffect(is1);
                t1.setFill(Color.RED);
                t1.setFont(Font.font(null, FontWeight.BOLD, 36));

                InnerShadow is2 = new InnerShadow();
                is2.setOffsetX(3);
                is2.setOffsetY(3);
                is2.setColor(Color.GRAY);
                Rectangle rect1 = new Rectangle(100, 50, Color.LIGHTGRAY);
                rect1.setEffect(is2);

                InnerShadow is3 = new InnerShadow();
                is3.setOffsetX(-3);
                is3.setOffsetY(-3);
                is3.setColor(Color.GRAY);
                Rectangle rect2 = new Rectangle(100, 50, Color.LIGHTGRAY);
                rect2.setEffect(is3);

                HBox root = new HBox(wrap(t1, is1),  wrap(rect1, is2), wrap(rect2, is3));
                root.setSpacing(10);
                root.setStyle("-fx-padding: 10;" +
                                "-fx-border-style: solid inside;" +
                                "-fx-border-width: 2;" +
                                "-fx-border-insets: 5;" +
                                "-fx-border-radius: 5;" +
                                "-fx-border-color: blue;");

                Scene scene = new Scene(root);
                stage.setScene(scene);
                stage.setTitle("Applying InnerShadow Effect");
                stage.show();
        }
```

```
        private VBox wrap(Shape s, InnerShadow in) {
                Text t = new Text ("offsetX=" + in.getOffsetX() + "\n" +
                                   "offsetY=" + in.getOffsetY());
                t.setFont(Font.font(10));

                VBox box =  new VBox(10, s, t);
                box.setAlignment(Pos.CENTER);
                return box;
        }
}
```

Figure 20-9. *A Text and two Rectangle nodes using InnerShadow effects*

The *Shadow* Effect

The Shadow effect creates a shadow with blurry edges of its input. Unlike DropShadow and InnerShadow, it modifies the original input itself to convert it into a shadow. Typically, a Shadow effect is combined with the original input to create a higher-level shadowing effect:

- You can apply a Shadow effect with a light color to a node and superimpose it on a duplicate of the original node to create a glow effect.

- You can create a Shadow effect with a dark color and place it behind the original node to create a DropShadow effect.

An instance of the Shadow class represents a Shadow effect. The size, color, and quality of the effect are controlled by several properties of the Shadow class:

- color
- blurType
- radius
- width
- height
- input

These properties work the same way they work in the DropShadow. Please refer to the section "The *DropShadow* Effect" for a detailed description and examples of these properties.

The Shadow class contains several constructors that let you specify the initial values for the properties:

- Shadow()
- Shadow(BlurType blurType, Color color, double radius)
- Shadow(double radius, Color color)

The program in Listing 20-4 demonstrates how to use the Shadow effect. It creates three Text nodes. A shadow is applied to all three nodes. The output of the first shadow is displayed. The output of the second shadow is superimposed on the original node to achieve a glow effect. The output of the third shadow is placed behind its original node to achieve a DropShadow effect. Figure 20-10 shows these three nodes.

Listing 20-4. Using a Shadow Effect and Creating High-Level Effects

```java
// ShadowTest.java
package com.jdojo.effect;

import javafx.application.Application;

import javafx.scene.Scene;
import javafx.scene.effect.Shadow;
import javafx.scene.layout.HBox;
import javafx.scene.layout.StackPane;
import javafx.scene.paint.Color;
import javafx.scene.text.Font;
import javafx.scene.text.Text;
import javafx.stage.Stage;

public class ShadowTest extends Application {
        public static void main(String[] args) {
                Application.launch(args);
        }

        @Override
        public void start(Stage stage) {
                // Create a Shadow of a Text node
                Text t1 = new Text("Shadow");
                t1.setFont(Font.font(36));
                t1.setEffect(new Shadow());

                // Create a Glow effect using a Shadow
                Text t2Original = new Text("Glow");
                t2Original.setFont(Font.font(36));
                Text t2 = new Text("Glow");
                t2.setFont(Font.font(36));
                Shadow s2 = new Shadow();
                s2.setColor(Color.YELLOW);
                t2.setEffect(s2);
                StackPane glow = new StackPane(t2Original, t2);
```

```
                    // Create a DropShadow effect using a Shadow
                    Text t3Original = new Text("DropShadow");
                    t3Original.setFont(Font.font(36));
                    Text t3 = new Text("DropShadow");
                    t3.setFont(Font.font(36));
                    Shadow s3 = new Shadow();
                    t3.setEffect(s3);
                    StackPane dropShadow = new StackPane(t3, t3Original);

                    HBox root = new HBox(t1, glow, dropShadow);
                    root.setSpacing(20);
                    root.setStyle("-fx-padding: 10;" +
                                "-fx-border-style: solid inside;" +
                                "-fx-border-width: 2;" +
                                "-fx-border-insets: 5;" +
                                "-fx-border-radius: 5;" +
                                "-fx-border-color: blue;");

                    Scene scene = new Scene(root);
                    stage.setScene(scene);
                    stage.setTitle("Using Shadow Effect");
                    stage.show();
        }
}
```

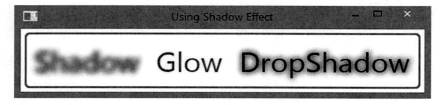

Figure 20-10. *Applying a shadow to a Text node and creating Glow and DropShadow effects*

Blurring Effects

A blurring effect produces a blurred version of an input. JavaFX lets you apply different types of blurring effects, which differ in the algorithms used to create these effect.

The *BoxBlur* Effect

The BoxBlur effect uses a box filter kernel to produce a blurring effect. An instance of the BoxBlur class represents a BoxBlur effect. The size and quality of the effect can be configured using these properties of the class:

- width
- height
- iterations
- input

The width and height properties specify the horizontal and vertical size of the effect, respectively. Imagine a box defined by the width and height centered on a pixel of the input. The color information of the pixel is spread within the box during the blurring process. The values of these properties are between 5.0 and 255.0. The default values are 5.0. A value of less than or equal to 1.0 does not produce the blurring effect in the corresponding direction.

The iterations property specifies the number of times the blurring effect is applied. A higher value produces a better quality blur. Its value can be between 0 and 3. The default is 1. The value of 3 produces the blur quality comparable to the Gaussian blur, discussed in the next section. The value of zero produces no blur at all.

The BoxBlur class contains two constructors:

- BoxBlur()

- BoxBlur(double width, double height, int iterations)

The no-args constructor creates a BoxBlur object with the width and height of 5.0 pixels and iterations of 1. The other constructor lets you specify the initial value for the width, height, and iterations properties, as in the following section of code:

```
// Create a BoxBlur with defaults: width=5.0, height=5.0, iterations=1
BoxBlur bb1 = new BoxBlur();

// Create a BoxBlur with width=10.0, height=10.0, iterations=3
BoxBlur bb2 = new BoxBlur(10, 10, 3);
```

The following snippet of code creates four Text nodes and applies BoxBlur effects of various qualities. Figure 20-11 show the results of these Text nodes. Notice that the last Text node does not have any blur effect as the iterations property is set to zero.

```
Text t1 = new Text("Box Blur");
t1.setFont(Font.font(24));
t1.setEffect(new BoxBlur(5, 10, 1));

Text t2 = new Text("Box Blur");
t2.setFont(Font.font(24));
t2.setEffect(new BoxBlur(10, 5, 2));

Text t3 = new Text("Box Blur");
t3.setFont(Font.font(24));
t3.setEffect(new BoxBlur(5, 5, 3));

Text t4 = new Text("Box Blur");
t4.setFont(Font.font(24));
t4.setEffect(new BoxBlur(5, 5, 0)); // Zero iterations = No blurring
```

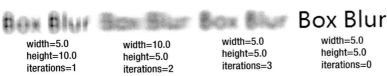

width=5.0   width=10.0   width=5.0   width=5.0
height=10.0   height=5.0   height=5.0   height=5.0
iterations=1   iterations=2   iterations=3   iterations=0

Figure 20-11. *Text nodes with BoxBlur effects of varying qualities*

The *GaussianBlur* Effect

The GaussianBlur effect uses a Gaussian convolution kernel to produce a blurring effect. An instance of the GaussianBlur class represents a GaussianBlur effect. The effect can be configured using two properties of the class:

- radius

- input

The radius property controls the distribution of the blur in pixels from the source pixel. The greater this value, the more the blur effect. Its value can be between 0.0 and 63.0. The default value is 10.0. A radius of zero pixels produces no blur effect.

The GaussianBlur class contains two constructors:

- GaussianBlur()

- GaussianBlur(double radius)

The no-args constructor creates a GaussianBlur object with a default radius of 10.0px. The other constructor lets you specify the initial value for the radius, as in the following code:

```
// Create a GaussianBlur with a 10.0 pixels radius
GaussianBlur gb1 = new GaussianBlur();

// Create a GaussianBlur with a 20.0 pixels radius
GaussianBlur gb2 = new GaussianBlur(20);
```

The following snippet of code creates four Text nodes and applies GaussianBlur effects of different radius values. Figure 20-12 show the results of these Text nodes. Notice that the last Text node does not have any blur effect as the radius property is set to zero.

```
Text t1 = new Text("Gaussian Blur");
t1.setFont(Font.font(24));
t1.setEffect(new GaussianBlur(5));

Text t2 = new Text("Gaussian Blur");
t2.setFont(Font.font(24));
t2.setEffect(new GaussianBlur(10));

Text t3 = new Text("Gaussian Blur");
t3.setFont(Font.font(24));
t3.setEffect(new GaussianBlur(15));

Text t4 = new Text("Gaussian Blur");
t4.setFont(Font.font(24));
t4.setEffect(new GaussianBlur(0)); // radius = 0 means no blur
```

radius=5.0	radius=10.0	radius=15.0	radius=0.0

Figure 20-12. *Text nodes with GaussianBlur effects of varying sizes*

The *MotionBlur* Effect

The MotionBlur effect produces a blurring effect by motion. The input looks as if you are seeing it while it is moving. A Gaussian convolution kernel is used with a specified angle to produce the effect. An instance of the MotionBlur class represents a MotionBlur effect. The effect can be configured using the three properties of the class:

- radius
- angle
- input

The radius and input properties work the same as respective properties for the GaussianBlur class, as described in the previous section. The angle property specifies the angle of the motion in degrees. By default, the angle is zero.

The MotionBlur class contains two constructors:

- MotionBlur()
- MotionBlur(double angle, double radius)

The no-args constructor creates a MotionBlur object with a default radius of 10.0px and an angle of 0.0 degrees. The other constructor lets you specify the initial value for the angle and radius, as shown in the following code:

```
// Create a MotionBlur with a 0.0 degrees angle and a 10.0 pixels radius
MotionBlur mb1 = new MotionBlur();

// Create a MotionBlur with a 30.0 degrees angle and a 20.0 pixels radius
MotionBlur mb1 = new MotionBlur(30.0, 20.0);
```

The program in Listing 20-5 shows how to use the MotionBlur effect on a Text node, with the results shown in Figure 20-13. The two sliders let you change the radius and angle properties.

Listing 20-5. Using the MotionBlur Effect on a Text Node

```java
// MotionBlurTest.java
package com.jdojo.effect;

import javafx.application.Application;
import javafx.scene.Scene;
import javafx.scene.control.Label;
import javafx.scene.control.Slider;
import javafx.scene.effect.MotionBlur;
import javafx.scene.layout.BorderPane;
import javafx.scene.layout.HBox;
import javafx.scene.text.Font;
import javafx.scene.text.FontWeight;
import javafx.scene.text.Text;
import javafx.stage.Stage;

public class MotionBlurTest extends Application {
    public static void main(String[] args) {
        Application.launch(args);
    }

    @Override
    public void start(Stage stage) {
        Text t1 = new Text("Motion Blur");
        t1.setFont(Font.font(null, FontWeight.BOLD, 36));
        MotionBlur mbEffect = new MotionBlur();
        t1.setEffect(mbEffect);

        Slider radiusSlider = new Slider(0.0, 63.0, 10.0);
        radiusSlider.setMajorTickUnit(10);
        radiusSlider.setShowTickLabels(true);
        mbEffect.radiusProperty().bind(radiusSlider.valueProperty());

        Slider angleSlider = new Slider(0.0, 360.0, 0);
        angleSlider.setMajorTickUnit(10);
        angleSlider.setShowTickLabels(true);
        mbEffect.angleProperty().bind(angleSlider.valueProperty());

        HBox pane = new HBox(10, new Label("Radius:"), radiusSlider,
                                 new Label("Angle:"), angleSlider);

        BorderPane root = new BorderPane();
        root.setCenter(t1);
        root.setBottom(pane);
        root.setStyle("-fx-padding: 10;" +
                      "-fx-border-style: solid inside;" +
                      "-fx-border-width: 2;" +
                      "-fx-border-insets: 5;" +
                      "-fx-border-radius: 5;" +
                      "-fx-border-color: blue;");
```

```
                        Scene scene = new Scene(root);
                        stage.setScene(scene);
                        stage.setTitle("Using the MotionBlur Effect");
                        stage.show();
                }
        }
}
```

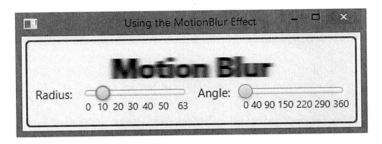

Figure 20-13. *Text nodes with GaussianBlur effects of varying sizes*

The *Bloom* Effect

The Bloom effect adds a glow to the pixels of its input that have a luminosity greater than or equal to a specified limit. Note that not all pixels in a Bloom effect are made to glow.

An instance of the Bloom class represents a Bloom effect. It contains two properties:

- threshold
- input

The threshold property is a number between 0.0 and 1.0. Its default value is 0.30. All pixels in the input having a luminosity greater than or equal to the threshold property are made to glow. The brightness of a pixel is determined by its luminosity. A pixel with a luminosity of 0.0 is not bright at all. A pixel with a luminosity of 1.0 is 100% bright. By default, all pixels having a luminosity greater than or equal to 0.3 are made to glow. A threshold of 0.0 makes all of the pixels glow. A threshold of 1.0 makes almost no pixels glow.

The Bloom class contains two constructors:

- Bloom()
- Bloom(double threshold)

The no-args constructor creates a Bloom object with a default threshold of 0.30. The other constructor lets you specify the threshold value, as shown in the following code:

```
// Create a Bloom with threshold 0.30
Bloom b1 = new Bloom();

// Create a Bloom with threshold 0.10 - more pixels will glow.
Bloom b2 = new Bloom(0.10);
```

Figure 20-14 shows four Text nodes with Bloom effects that have different threshold values. A Text node is laid over a rectangle using a StackPane. Notice that the lower the threshold value, the higher the blooming effect. The following snippet of code created the first Text node and Rectangle pair from the left in Figure 20-14:

```
Text t1 = new Text("Bloom");
t1.setFill(Color.YELLOW);
t1.setFont(Font.font(null, FontWeight.BOLD, 24));
t1.setEffect(new Bloom(0.10));
Rectangle r1 = new Rectangle(100, 50, Color.GREEN);
StackPane sp1 = new StackPane(r1, t1);
```

| threshold=0.1 | threshold=0.3 | threshold=0.7 | threshold=1.0 |

Figure 20-14. Text nodes with Bloom effects

The *Glow* Effect

The Glow effect makes the bright pixels of the input brighter. An instance of the Glow class represents a Glow effect. It contains two properties:

- level
- input

The level property specifies the intensity of the Glow effect. It is a number between 0.0 and 1.0, and its default value is 0.30. A level of 0.0 adds no glow and a level of 1.0 adds the maximum glow.

The Glow class contains two constructors:

- Glow()
- Glow(double level)

The no-args constructor creates a Glow object with a default level of 0.30. The other constructor lets you specify the level value, as shown in the following code:

```
// Create a Glow with level 0.30
Glow g1 = new Glow();

// Create a Glow with level 0.90 - more glow.
Glow g2 = new Glow(0.90);
```

Figure 20-15 shows four Text nodes with Glow effects with different level values. A Text node is laid over a rectangle using a StackPane. Notice that the higher the level value, the higher the glowing effect. The following snippet of code created the first Text node and Rectangle pair from the left in Figure 20-15:

```
Text t1 = new Text("Glow");
t1.setFill(Color.YELLOW);
t1.setFont(Font.font(null, FontWeight.BOLD, 24));
t1.setEffect(new Glow(0.10));
Rectangle r1 = new Rectangle(100, 50, Color.GREEN);
StackPane sp1 = new StackPane(r1, t1);
```

| level=0.1 | level=0.3 | level=0.7 | level=1.0 |

Figure 20-15. *Text nodes with Glow effects*

The *Reflection* Effect

The Reflection effect adds a reflection of the input below the input. An instance of the Reflection class represents a reflection effect. The position, size, and opacity of the reflection are controlled by various properties:

- topOffset
- fraction
- topOpacity
- bottomOpacity
- input

The topOffset specifies the distance in pixels between the bottom of the input and the top of the reflection. By default, it is 0.0. The fraction property specifies the faction of the input height that is visible in the reflection. It is measured from the bottom. Its value can be between 0.0 and 1.0. A value of 0.0 means no reflection. A value of 1.0 means the entire input is visible in the reflection. A value of 0.25 means 25% of the input from the bottom is visible in the reflection. The default value is 0.75. The topOpacity and bottomOpacity properties specify the opacity of the reflection at its top and bottom extremes. Their values can be between 0.0 and 1.0. The default value is 0.50 for the topOpacity and 0.0 for the bottomOpacity.

The Reflection class contains two constructors:

- Reflection()
- Reflection(double topOffset, double fraction, double topOpacity, double bottomOpacity)

The no-args constructor creates a Reflection object with the default initial values for its properties. The other constructor lets you specify the initial values for the properties, as shown in the following code:

```
// Create a Reflection with default values
Reflection g1 = new Reflection();

// Create a Reflection with topOffset=2.0, fraction=0.90,
// topOpacity=1.0, and bottomOpacity=1.0
Reflection g2 = new Reflection(2.0, 0.90, 1.0, 1.0);
```

Figure 20-16 shows four Text nodes with Reflection effects configured differently. The following snippet of code creates the second Text node from the left, which shows the full input as the reflection:

```
Text t2 = new Text("Chatar");
t2.setFont(Font.font(null, FontWeight.BOLD, 24));
t2.setEffect(new Reflection(0.0, 1.0, 1.0, 1.0));
```

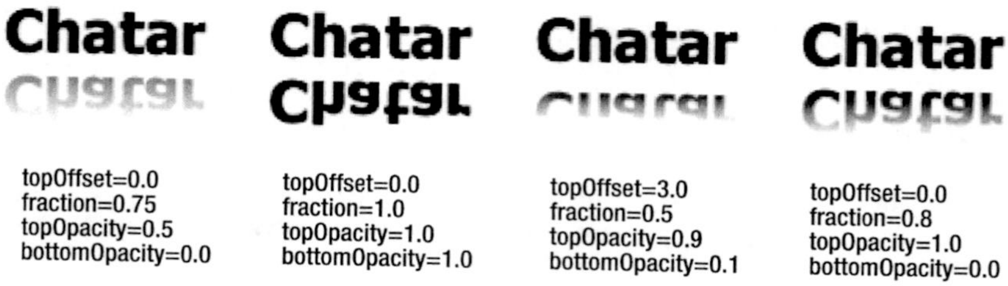

Figure 20-16. Text nodes with Reflection effects

The SepiaTone Effect

Sepia is a reddish-brown color. Sepia toning is performed on black-and-white photographic prints to give them a warmer tone. An instance of the SepiaTone class represents a SepiaTone effect. It contains two properties:

- level

- input

The level property specifies the intensity of the SepiaTone effect. It is a number between 0.0 and 1.0. Its defaults value is 1.0. A level of 0.0 adds no sepia toning and a level of 1.0 adds the maximum sepia toning. The SepiaTone class contains two constructors:

- SepiaTone ()

- SepiaTone (double level)

The no-args constructor creates a SepiaTone object with a default level of 1.0. The other constructor lets you specify the level value, as shown in the following code:

```
// Create a SepiaTone with level 1.0
SepiaTone g1 = new SepiaTone ();
```

```
// Create a SepiaTone with level 0.50
SepiaTone g2 = new SepiaTone(0.50);
```

The following snippet of code creates two Text nodes with the results shown in Figure 20-17. Notice that the higher the level value, the higher the sepia toning effect:

```
Text t1 = new Text("SepiaTone");
t1.setFill(Color.WHITE);
t1.setFont(Font.font(null, FontWeight.BOLD, 24));
1.setEffect(new SepiaTone(0.50));
Rectangle r1 = new Rectangle(150, 50, Color.BLACK);
r1.setOpacity(0.50);
StackPane sp1 = new StackPane(r1, t1);

Text t2 = new Text("SepiaTone");
t2.setFill(Color.WHITE);
t2.setFont(Font.font(null, FontWeight.BOLD, 24));
t2.setEffect(new SepiaTone(1.0));
Rectangle r2 = new Rectangle(150, 50, Color.BLACK);
r2.setOpacity(0.50);
StackPane sp2 = new StackPane(r2, t2);
```

level=0.5   level=1.0

Figure 20-17. Text nodes with SepiaTone effect

The *DisplacementMap* Effect

The DisplacementMap effect shifts each pixel in the input to produce an output. The name has two parts: "Displacement" and "Map." The first part implies that the effect displaces the pixels in the input. The second part implies that the displacement is based on a map that provides a displacement factor for each pixel in the output.

An instance of the DisplacementMap class represents a DisplacementMap. The class contains several properties to configure the effect:

- mapData
- scaleX
- scaleY
- offsetX
- offsetY
- wrap
- input

The mapData property is an instance of the FloatMap class. A FloatMap is a data structure that stores up to four values for each point in a rectangular area represented by its width and height properties. For example, you can use a FloatMap to store four components of the color (red, green, blue, and alpha) for each pixel in a two-dimensional rectangle. Each of the four values associated with a pair of numbers in the FloatMap are said to be in a band numbered 0, 1, 2, and 3. The actual meaning of the values in each band is context dependent. The following code provides an example of setting the FloatMap width and height:

```
// Create a FloatMap (width = 100, height = 50)
FloatMap map = new FloatMap(100, 50);
```

Now you need to populate the FloatMap with band values for each pair of numbers. You can use one of the following methods of the FloatMap class to populate it with the data:

- setSample(int x, int y, int band, float value)

- setSamples(int x, int y, float s0)

- setSamples(int x, int y, float s0, float s1)

- setSamples(int x, int y, float s0, float s1, float s2)

- setSamples(int x, int y, float s0, float s1, float s2, float s3)

The setSample() method sets the specified value in the specified band for the specified (x, y) location. The setSamples() methods sets the specified values in the bands determined by the positions of the values in the method call. That is, the first value is set for band 0, the second value for band 1, and so forth:

```
// Set 0,50f for band 0 and band 1 for each point in the map
for (int i = 0; i < 100; i++) {
        for (int j = 0; j < 50; j++) {
                map.setSamples(i, j, 0.50f, 0.50f);
        }
}
```

The DisplacementMap class requires that you set the mapData property to a FloatMap that contains values for band 0 and band 1 for each pixel in the output.

The scaleX, scaleY, offsetX, and offsetY are double properties. They are used in the equation (described shortly) to compute the displacement of the pixels. The scaleX and scaleY properties have 1.0 as their default values. The offsetX and offsetY properties have 0.0 as their default values.

The following equation is used to compute the pixel at (x, y) coordinates in the output. The abbreviations dst and src in the equation represent the destination and source, respectively:

```
dst[x,y] = src[x + (offsetX + scaleX * mapData[x,y][0]) * srcWidth,
              y + (offsetY + scaleY * mapData[x,y][1]) * srcHeight]
```

If the above equation looks very complex, don't be intimidated. In fact, the equation is very simple once you read the explanation that follows. The mapData[x,y][0] and mapData[x,y][1] parts in the equation refer to the values at band 0 and band 1, respectively, in the FloatMap for the location at (x, y).

Suppose you want to get the pixel for the (x, y) coordinates in the output, that is, you want to know which pixel from the input will be moved to (x, y) in the output. First, make sure you get the starting point right. To repeat, the equation starts with a point (x, y) in the output and finds the pixel at (x1, y1) in the input that will move to (x, y) in the output.

■ **Tip** Many will get the equation wrong by thinking that you start with a pixel in the input and then find its location in the output. This is not true. The equation works the other way around. It picks a point (x, y) in the output and then finds which pixel in the input will move to this point.

Below are the steps to fully explain the equation:

- You want to find the pixel in the input that will be moved to the point (x, y) in the output.

- Get the values (band 0 and band 1) from the mapData for (x, y).

- Multiply the mapData values by the scale (scaleX for x coordinate and scaleY for y coordinate).

- Add the corresponding offset values to the values computed in the previous step.

- Multiply the previous step values with the corresponding dimensions of the input. This gives you the offset values along the x and y coordinate axes from the output (x, y) from where the pixels in the input will be moving to the (x, y) in the output.

- Add the values in the previous step to the x and y coordinates of the point in the output. Suppose these values are (x1, y1). The pixel at (x1, y1) in the input moves to the point (x, y) in the output.

If you still have problem understanding the pixel-shifting logic, you can break the above equation into two parts:

```
x1 = x + (offsetX + scaleX * mapData[x,y][0]) * srcWidth
y1 = y + (offsetY + scaleY * mapData[x,y][1]) * srcHeight
```

You can read these equations as "The pixel at (x, y) in the output is obtained by moving the pixel at (x1, y1) in the input to (x, y)."

If you leave the scale and offset values to their default:

- Use a positive value in band 0 to move the input pixels to the left.

- Use a negative value in band 0 to move the input pixels to the right.

- Use a positive value in band 1 to move the input pixels up.

- Use a negative value in band 1 to move the input pixels down.

The program in Listing 20-6 creates a Text node and adds a DisplacementMap effect to the node. In the mapData, it sets values, so all pixels in the top half of the input are moved to the right by 1 pixel, and all pixels in the bottom half of the input are moved to the left by 1 pixel. The Text node will look like the one shown in Figure 20-18.

Listing 20-6. Using the DisplacementMap Effect

```java
// DisplacementmapTest.java
package com.jdojo.effect;

import javafx.application.Application;
import javafx.scene.Scene;
import javafx.scene.effect.DisplacementMap;
import javafx.scene.effect.FloatMap;
import javafx.scene.layout.HBox;
import javafx.scene.text.Font;
import javafx.scene.text.Text;
import javafx.stage.Stage;

public class DisplacementmapTest extends Application {
        public static void main(String[] args) {
                Application.launch(args);
        }

        @Override
        public void start(Stage stage) {
                // Create a FloatMap
                int width = 250;
                int height = 50;
                FloatMap map = new FloatMap(width, height);

                double xDisplacement = 1.0;
                for (int i = 0; i < width; i++) {
                        for (int j = 0; j < height; j++) {
                                double u = xDisplacement;
                                if (j < height / 2) {
                                        // Move the top-half pixels to the right
                                        // (a nagative value)
                                        u = -1.0 * (u * xDisplacement / width);
                                } else {
                                        // Move the bottom-half pixels to the
                                        // left.(a positive value)
                                        u = u * xDisplacement / width;
                                }

                                // Set values for band 0 and 1 (x and y axes
                                // displacements factors).
                                // Always use 0.0f for y-axis displacement factor.
                                // map.setSamples(i, j, (float)u, 0.0f);
                        }
                }

                Text t1 = new Text("Displaced Text");
                t1.setFont(Font.font(36));
```

```
            DisplacementMap effect1 = new DisplacementMap();
            effect1.setMapData(map);
            t1.setEffect(effect1);

            HBox root = new HBox(t1);
            root.setStyle("-fx-padding: 10;" +
                          "-fx-border-style: solid inside;" +
                          "-fx-border-width: 2;" +
                          "-fx-border-insets: 5;" +
                          "-fx-border-radius: 5;" +
                          "-fx-border-color: blue;");

            Scene scene = new Scene(root);
            stage.setScene(scene);
            stage.setTitle("Applying the DisplacementMap Effect");
            stage.show();
        }
}
```

Figure 20-18. *A* Text *node with* DisplacementMap *effect*

The DisplacementMap class contains a wrap property, which is set to false by default. A pixel in the output is a pixel in the input that is moved to a new location. The location of the pixel in the input that needs to move to a new location is computed by the equation. It is possible that for some locations in the output, you do not have available pixels in the input. Suppose you have a 100px wide by 50px tall rectangle and you apply a DisplacementMap effect to move all pixels to the left by 50px. The points at x = 75 in the output will get the pixel at x = 125 in the input. The input is only 100px wide. Therefore, for all points x > 50 in the output, you will not have available pixels in the input. If the wrap property is set to true, when the locations of the pixels in the input to be moved are outside the input bounds, the locations are computed by taking their modulus with the corresponding dimension (width along the x axis and height for along the y axis) of the input. In the example, x = 125 will be reduced to 125 % 100, which is 25 and the pixels at x = 25 in the input will be moved to x = 75 in the output. If the wrap property is false, the pixels in the output are left transparent.

Figure 20-19 shows two Text nodes with DisplacementMap effects. Pixels in both nodes are moved 100px to the left. The Text node at the top has the wrap property set to false, whereas the Text node at the bottom has the wrap property set to true. Notice that output for the bottom node is filled by wrapping the input. The program in Listing 20-7 is used to apply the wrapping effects.

Figure 20-19. *Effects of using the* wrap *property in* DisplacementMap

Listing 20-7. Using the wrap Property in DisplacementMap Effect

```java
// DisplacementMapWrap.java
package com.jdojo.effect;

import javafx.application.Application;
import javafx.scene.Scene;
import javafx.scene.effect.DisplacementMap;
import javafx.scene.effect.FloatMap;
import javafx.scene.layout.VBox;
import javafx.scene.text.Font;
import javafx.scene.text.Text;
import javafx.stage.Stage;

public class DisplacementMapWrap extends Application {
        public static void main(String[] args) {
                Application.launch(args);
        }

        @Override
        public void start(Stage stage) {
                // Create a FloatMap
                int width = 200;
                int height = 25;

                FloatMap map = new FloatMap(width, height);
                for (int i = 0; i < width; i++) {
                        for (int j = 0; j < height; j++) {
                                // Move all pixels 100 pixels to the left
                                double u = 100.0/width;
                                map.setSamples(i, j, (float)u, 0.0f);
                        }
                }

                Text t1 = new Text("Displaced Text");
                t1.setFont(Font.font(24));
                DisplacementMap effect1 = new DisplacementMap();
                effect1.setMapData(map);
                t1.setEffect(effect1);
```

```
            Text t2 = new Text("Displaced Text");
            t2.setFont(Font.font(24));
            DisplacementMap effect2 = new DisplacementMap();
            effect2.setWrap(true);
            effect2.setMapData(map);
            t2.setEffect(effect2);

            VBox root = new VBox(t1, t2);
            root.setSpacing(5);
            root.setStyle("-fx-padding: 10;" +
                          "-fx-border-style: solid inside;" +
                          "-fx-border-width: 2;" +
                          "-fx-border-insets: 5;" +
                          "-fx-border-radius: 5;" +
                          "-fx-border-color: blue;");

            Scene scene = new Scene(root);
            stage.setScene(scene);
            stage.setTitle("Using the warps proeprty in DisplacementMap");
            stage.show();
        }
    }
```

The *ColorInput* Effect

The ColorInput effect is a simple effect that fills (floods) a rectangular region with a specified paint. Typically, it is used as an input to another effect.

An instance of the ColorInput class represents the ColorInput effect. The class contains five properties that define the location, size, and the paint for the rectangular region:

- x
- y
- width
- height
- paint

Creating a ColorInput object is similar to creating a rectangle filled with the paint of the ColorInput. The x and y properties specify the location of the upper left corner of the rectangular region in the local coordinate system. The width and height properties specify the size of the rectangular region. The default value for x, y, width, and height is 0.0. The paint property specifies the fill paint. The default value for paint is Color.RED.

You can use the following constructors to create an object of the ColorInput class:

- ColorInput()
- ColorInput(double x, double y, double width, double height, Paint paint)

The following snippet of code creates a ColorInput effect and applies it to a rectangle. The rectangle with the effect applied is shown in Figure 20-20. Note that when you apply the ColorInput effect to a node, all you see is the rectangular area generated by the ColorInput effect. As stated earlier, the ColorInput effect is not applied directly on nodes. Rather it is used as an input to another effect.

```
ColorInput effect = new ColorInput();
effect.setWidth(100);
effect.setHeight(50);
effect.setPaint(Color.LIGHTGRAY);

// Size of the Rectangle does not matter to the rectangular area
// of the ColorInput
Rectangle r1 = new Rectangle(100, 50);
r1.setEffect(effect);
```

Figure 20-20. *A ColorInput effect applied to a rectangle*

The *ColorAdjust* Effect

The ColorAdjust effect adjusts the hue, saturation, brightness, and contrast of pixels by the specified delta amount. Typically, the effect is used on an ImageView node to adjust the color of an image.

An instance of the ColorAdjust class represents the ColorAdjust effect. The class contains five properties that define the location, size, and the paint for the rectangular region:

- hue
- saturation
- brightness
- contrast
- input

The hue, saturation, brightness, and contrast properties specify the delta amount by which these components are adjusted for all pixels. They range from -1.0 to 1.0. Their default values are 0.0.

The program in Listing 20-8 shows how to use the ColorAdjust effect on an image. It displays an image and four sliders to change the properties of the ColorAdjust effect. Adjust their values using the sliders to see the effects. If the program does not find the image, it prints a message and displays a Text node overlaying a rectangle in a StackPane and the effect is applied to the StackPane.

Listing 20-8. Using the ColorAdjust Effect to Adjust the Color of Pixels in an Image

```
// ColorAdjustTest.java
package com.jdojo.effect;

import java.net.URL;
import javafx.application.Application;
import javafx.scene.Node;
import javafx.scene.Scene;
import javafx.scene.control.Label;
import javafx.scene.control.Slider;
import javafx.scene.effect.ColorAdjust;
```

```java
import javafx.scene.image.ImageView;
import javafx.scene.layout.BorderPane;
import javafx.scene.layout.GridPane;
import javafx.scene.layout.StackPane;
import javafx.scene.paint.Color;
import javafx.scene.shape.Rectangle;
import javafx.scene.text.Text;
import javafx.stage.Stage;

public class ColorAdjustTest extends Application {
        public static void main(String[] args) {
                Application.launch(args);
        }

        @Override
        public void start(Stage stage) {
                ColorAdjust effect = new ColorAdjust();

                Node node = getImageNode();
                node.setEffect(effect);

                GridPane controller = getController(effect);

                BorderPane root = new BorderPane();
                root.setCenter(node);
                root.setBottom(controller);
                root.setStyle("-fx-padding: 10;" +
                                "-fx-border-style: solid inside;" +
                                "-fx-border-width: 2;" +
                                "-fx-border-insets: 5;" +
                                "-fx-border-radius: 5;" +
                                "-fx-border-color: blue;");

                Scene scene = new Scene(root);
                stage.setScene(scene);
                stage.setTitle("Applying the ColorAdjust Effect");
                stage.show();
        }

        private Node getImageNode() {
                Node node = null;
                String path = "\\resources\\picture\\randomness.jpg";
                URL url = getClass().getClassLoader().getResource(path);

                if (url != null) {
                        node = new ImageView(url.toExternalForm());
                } else {
                        System.out.println("Missing image file " + path);
                        node = new StackPane(new Rectangle(100, 50, Color.LIGHTGRAY),
                                        new Text("Color Adjust"));
                }
                return node;
        }
```

```
private GridPane getController(ColorAdjust effect) {
        Slider hueSlider = new Slider(-1.0, 1.0, 0.0);
        effect.hueProperty().bind(hueSlider.valueProperty());

        Slider saturationSlider = new Slider(-1.0, 1.0, 0.0);
        effect.saturationProperty().bind(saturationSlider.valueProperty());

        Slider brightnessSlider = new Slider(-1.0, 1.0, 0.0);
        effect.brightnessProperty().bind(brightnessSlider.valueProperty());

        Slider contrastSlider = new Slider(-1.0, 1.0, 0.0);
        effect.contrastProperty().bind(contrastSlider.valueProperty());

        Slider[] sliders = new Slider[] {hueSlider, saturationSlider,
                                    brightnessSlider, contrastSlider};
        for (Slider s : sliders) {
                s.setPrefWidth(300);
                s.setMajorTickUnit(0.10);
                s.setShowTickMarks(true);
                s.setShowTickLabels(true);
        }

        GridPane pane = new GridPane();
        pane.setHgap(5);
        pane.setVgap(10);
        pane.addRow(0, new Label("Hue:"), hueSlider);
        pane.addRow(1, new Label("Saturation:"), saturationSlider);
        pane.addRow(2, new Label("Brightness:"), brightnessSlider);
        pane.addRow(3, new Label("Contrast:"), contrastSlider);

        return pane;
    }
}
```

The *ImageInput* Effect

The ImageInput effect works like the ColorInput effect. It passes the given image as an input to another effect. The given image is not modified by this effect. Typically, it is used as an input to another effect, not as an effect directly applied to a node.

An instance of the ImageInput class represents the ImageInput effect. The class contains three properties that define the location and the source of the image:

- x

- y

- source

The x and y properties specify the location of the upper left corner of the image in the local coordinate system of the content node on which the effect is finally applied. Their default values are 0.0. The source property specifies the Image object to be used.

You can use the following constructors to create an object of the ColorInput class:

- ImageInput()

- ImageInput(Image source)

- ImageInput(Image source, double x, double y)

The program in Listing 20-9 shows how to use the ImageInput effect. It passes an ImageInput as an input to a DropShadow effect, which is applied on a rectangle, as shown in Figure 20-21.

Listing 20-9. Using an ImageInput Effect as an Input to a DropShadow Effect

```
// ImageInputTest.java
package com.jdojo.effect;

import java.net.URL;
import javafx.application.Application;
import javafx.scene.Node;
import javafx.scene.Scene;
import javafx.scene.effect.GaussianBlur;
import javafx.scene.effect.ImageInput;
import javafx.scene.image.Image;
import javafx.scene.layout.HBox;
import javafx.scene.shape.Rectangle;
import javafx.scene.text.Text;
import javafx.stage.Stage;

public class ImageInputTest extends Application {
        public static void main(String[] args) {
                Application.launch(args);
        }

        @Override
        public void start(Stage stage) {
                String path = "\\resources\\picture\\randomness.jpg";
                URL url = getClass().getClassLoader().getResource(path);

                Node node = null;
                if (url == null) {
                        node = new Text("Missing image file " + path + " in classpath.");
                }
                else {
                        ImageInput imageInputEffect = new ImageInput();
                        double requestedWidth = 100;
                        double requestedHeight = 50;
                        boolean preserveRation = false;
                        boolean smooth = true;
                        Image image = new Image(url.toExternalForm(),
                                                requestedWidth,
                                                requestedHeight,
                                                preserveRation,
                                                smooth);
                        imageInputEffect.setSource(image);
```

873

```
            node = new Rectangle(100, 50);
            GaussianBlur dsEffect = new GaussianBlur();
            dsEffect.setInput(imageInputEffect);
            node.setEffect(dsEffect);
        }

        HBox root = new HBox(node);
        root.setStyle("-fx-padding: 10;" +
                      "-fx-border-style: solid inside;" +
                      "-fx-border-width: 2;" +
                      "-fx-border-insets: 5;" +
                      "-fx-border-radius: 5;" +
                      "-fx-border-color: blue;");

        Scene scene = new Scene(root);
        stage.setScene(scene);
        stage.setTitle("Applying the ImageInput Effect");
        stage.show();
    }
}
```

Figure 20-21. An *ImageInput* effect with a *DropShadow* effect applied to a rectangle

The *Blend* Effect

Blending combines two pixels at the same location from two inputs to produce one composite pixel in the output. The Blend effect takes two input effects and blends the overlapping pixels of the inputs to produce an output. The blending of two inputs is controlled by a blending mode.

An instance of the Blend class represents the Blend effect. The class contains properties to specify the:

- topInput
- bottomInput
- mode
- opacity

The topInput and bottomInput properties specify the top and bottom effects, respectively. They are null by default. The mode property specifies the blending mode, which is one of the constants defined in the BlendMode enum. The default is BlendMode.SRC_OVER. JavaFX provides 17 predefined blending modes. Table 20-1 lists all of the constants in the BlendMode enum with a brief description of each. All blending modes use the SRC_OVER rules to blend the alpha components. The opacity property specifies the opacity to be applied to the top input before the blending is applied. The opacity is 1.0 by default.

Table 20-1. *The Constants in the BlendMode Enum with Their Descriptions*

BlendMode Enum Constant	Description
ADD	It adds the color (red, green, and blue) and alpha values for the pixels in the top and bottom inputs to get the new component value.
MULTIPLY	It multiplies the color components from two inputs.
DIFFERENCE	It subtracts the darker color components from any inputs from the lighter color components of the other input to get the resulting color components.
RED	It replaces the red component of the bottom input with the red component of the top input, leaving all other color components unaffected.
BLUE	It replaces the blue component of the bottom input with the blue component of the top input, leaving all other color components unaffected.
GREEN	It replaces the green component of the bottom input with the green component of the top input, leaving all other color components unaffected.
EXCLUSION	It multiplies the color components of the two inputs and doubles the result. The value thus obtained is subtracted from the sum of the color components of the bottom input to get the resulting color component.
COLOR_BURN	It divides the inverse of the bottom input color components by the top input color components and inverts the result.
COLOR_DODGE	It divides the bottom input color components by the inverse of the top input color.
LIGHTEN	It uses the lighter of the color components from the two inputs.
DARKEN	It uses the darker of the color components from the two inputs.
SCREEN	It inverts the color components from both inputs, multiplies them, and inverts the result.
OVERLAY	Depending on the bottom input color, it multiplies or screens the input color components.
HARD_LIGHT	Depending on the top input color, it multiplies or screens the input color components.
SOFT_LIGHT	Depending on the top input color, it darkens or lightens the input color components.
SRC_ATOP	It keeps the bottom input for the nonoverlapping area and the top input for the overlapping area.
SRC_OVER	The top input is drawn over the bottom input. Therefore, the overlapping area shows the top input.

The program in Listing 20-10 creates two ColorInput effects of the same size. Their x and y properties are set in such a way that they overlap. These two effects are used as top and bottom inputs to the Blend effect. A combo box and a slider are provided to select the blending mode and the opacity of the top input. Figure 20-22 shows the window that results from running this code. Run the program and try selecting different blending modes to see the Blend effect in action.

Listing 20-10. Using the Blend Effect

```java
// BlendTest.java
package com.jdojo.effect;

import javafx.application.Application;
import javafx.scene.Scene;
import javafx.scene.control.ComboBox;
import javafx.scene.control.Label;
import javafx.scene.control.Slider;
import javafx.scene.effect.Blend;
import javafx.scene.effect.BlendMode;
import javafx.scene.effect.ColorInput;
import javafx.scene.layout.GridPane;
import javafx.scene.layout.HBox;
import javafx.scene.paint.Color;
import javafx.scene.shape.Rectangle;
import javafx.stage.Stage;

public class BlendTest extends Application {
        public static void main(String[] args) {
                Application.launch(args);
        }

        @Override
        public void start(Stage stage) {
                ColorInput topInput = new ColorInput(0, 0, 100, 50, Color.LIGHTGREEN);
                ColorInput bottomInput = new ColorInput(50, 25, 100, 50, Color.PURPLE);

                // Create the Blend effect
                Blend effect = new Blend();
                effect.setTopInput(topInput);
                effect.setBottomInput(bottomInput);

                Rectangle rect = new Rectangle(150, 75);
                rect.setEffect(effect);

                GridPane controller = this.getController(effect);

                HBox root = new HBox(rect, controller);
                root.setSpacing(30);
                root.setStyle("-fx-padding: 10;" +
                              "-fx-border-style: solid inside;" +
                              "-fx-border-width: 2;" +
                              "-fx-border-insets: 5;" +
                              "-fx-border-radius: 5;" +
                              "-fx-border-color: blue;");
```

```
            Scene scene = new Scene(root);
            stage.setScene(scene);
            stage.setTitle("Applying the Blend Effect");
            stage.show();
    }

    private GridPane getController(Blend effect) {
            ComboBox<BlendMode> blendModeList = new ComboBox<>();
            blendModeList.setValue(effect.getMode());
            blendModeList.getItems().addAll(BlendMode.values());
            effect.modeProperty().bind(blendModeList.valueProperty());

            Slider opacitySlider = new Slider (0, 1.0, 1.0);
            opacitySlider.setMajorTickUnit(0.10);
            opacitySlider.setShowTickMarks(true);
            opacitySlider.setShowTickLabels(true);
            effect.opacityProperty().bind(opacitySlider.valueProperty());

            GridPane pane = new GridPane();
            pane.setHgap(5);
            pane.setVgap(10);
            pane.addRow(0, new Label("Blend Mode:"), blendModeList);
            pane.addRow(1, new Label("Opacity:"), opacitySlider);

            return pane;
    }
}
```

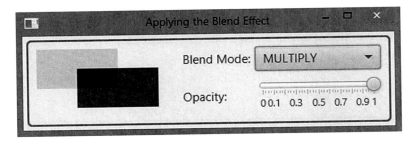

Figure 20-22. *The Blend effect*

The *Lighting* Effect

The Lighting effect, as the name suggests, simulates a light source shining on a specified node in a scene to give the node a 3D look. A Lighting effect uses a light source, which is an instance of the Light class, to produce the effect. Different types of configurable lights are available. If you do not specify a light source, the effect uses a default light source.

An instance of the Lighting class represents a Lighting effect. The class contains two constructors:

- Lighting()
- Lighting(Light light)

The no-args constructor uses a default light source. The other constructor lets you specify a light source.

Applying a Lighting effect to a node may be a simple or complex task depending on the type of effect you want to achieve. Let's look at a simple example. The following snippet of code applies a Lighting effect to a Text node to give it a 3D look, as shown in Figure 20-23:

```
// Create a Text Node
Text text = new Text("Chatar");
text.setFill(Color.RED);
text.setFont(Font.font(null, FontWeight.BOLD, 72));
HBox.setMargin(text, new Insets(10));

// Set a Lighting effect to the Text node
text.setEffect(new Lighting());
```

Chatar

Figure 20-23. *A Text node with a Lighting effect using the default for the light source*

In the above example, adding the Lighting effect is as simple as creating an object of the Lighting class and setting it as the effect for the Text node. I will discuss some complex Lighting effects later. The Lighting class contains several properties to configure the effect:

- contentInput
- surfaceScale
- bumpInput
- diffuseConstant
- specularConstant
- specularExponent
- light

If you use a chain of effects, the contentInput property specifies the input effect to the Lighting effect. This property is named as input in all other effects discussed earlier. I will not discuss this property further in this section. Please refer to the section "Chaining Effects" for more details on how to use this property.

Customizing the Surface Texture

The surfaceScale and bumpInput properties are used to provide texture to a 2D surface to make it look like a 3D surface. Pixels, based on their opacity, look high or low to give the surface a texture. Transparent pixels appear low and opaque pixels appear raised.

The surfaceScale property lets you control the surface roughness. Its value ranges from 0.0 to 10.0. The default is 1.5. For a higher surfaceScale, the surface appears rougher, giving it a more 3D look.

You can pass an Effect as an input to the Lighting effect using its bumpInput property. The opacity of the pixels in the bumpInput is used to obtain the height of the pixels of the lighted surface, and then the surfaceScale is applied to increase the roughness. If bumpInput is null, the opacity of the pixels from the node on which the effect is applied is used to generate the roughness of the surface. By default, a Shadow effect with a radius of 10 is used as the bumpInput. You can use an ImageInput, a blur effect, or any other effect as the bumpInput for a Lighting effect.

The program in Listing 20-11 displays a Text node with a Lighting effect. The bumpInput is set to null. It provides a check box to set a GaussianBlur effect as the bumpInput and a slider to adjust the surfaceScale value. Figure 20-24 shows two screenshots: one without a bump input and another with a bump input. Notice the difference in the surface texture.

Listing 20-11. Using the surfaceScale and bumpInput Properties

```java
// SurfaceTexture.java
package com.jdojo.effect;

import javafx.application.Application;
import javafx.scene.Scene;
import javafx.scene.control.CheckBox;
import javafx.scene.control.Slider;
import javafx.scene.effect.GaussianBlur;
import javafx.scene.effect.Lighting;
import javafx.scene.layout.VBox;
import javafx.scene.paint.Color;
import javafx.scene.text.Font;
import javafx.scene.text.FontWeight;
import javafx.scene.text.Text;
import javafx.scene.text.TextBoundsType;

import javafx.stage.Stage;

public class SurfaceTexture extends Application {
        public static void main(String[] args) {
                Application.launch(args);
        }

        @Override
        public void start(Stage stage) {
                Text text = new Text();
                text.setText("Texture");
                text.setFill(Color.RED);
                text.setFont(Font.font(null, FontWeight.BOLD, 72));
                text.setBoundsType(TextBoundsType.VISUAL);

                Lighting effect = new Lighting();
                effect.setBumpInput(null); // Remove the default bumpInput
                text.setEffect(effect);
```

```
// Let the user choose to use a bumpInput
CheckBox bumpCbx = new CheckBox("Use a GaussianBlur Bump Input?");
bumpCbx.selectedProperty().addListener((prop, oldValue,newValue) -> {
        if (newValue) {
                effect.setBumpInput(new GaussianBlur(20));
        } else {
                effect.setBumpInput(null);
        }
});

// Let the user select a surfaceScale
Slider scaleSlider = new Slider(0.0, 10.0, 1.5);
effect.surfaceScaleProperty().bind(scaleSlider.valueProperty());
scaleSlider.setShowTickLabels(true);
scaleSlider.setMajorTickUnit(2.0);
scaleSlider.setShowTickMarks(true);

VBox root = new VBox(10, text, bumpCbx, scaleSlider);
root.setStyle("-fx-padding: 10;" +
                "-fx-border-style: solid inside;" +
                "-fx-border-width: 2;" +
                "-fx-border-insets: 5;" +
                "-fx-border-radius: 5;" +
                "-fx-border-color: blue;");
Scene scene = new Scene(root);
stage.setScene(scene);
stage.setTitle("Using Surface Scale and Bump Input");
stage.show();
    }
}
```

Figure 20-24. *The effects of surfaceScale and bumpInput on a Lighting effect on a Text node*

Understanding Reflection Types

When light falls on an opaque surface, part of light is absorbed, part is transmitted, and some is reflected. A 3D look is achieved by showing part of the surface brighter and part shadowy. You see the reflected light from the surface. The 3D look varies depending on the light source and the way the node surface reflects the light. The structure of the surface at the microscopic level defines the details of the reflection, such as the intensity and directions. Among several reflection types, two types are worth mentioning at this point: diffuse reflection and specular reflection.

In a *diffuse* reflection, the surface reflects an incident ray of light at many angles. That is, a diffuse reflection scatters a ray of light by reflecting it in all directions. A perfect diffuse reflection reflects light equally in all directions. The surface using a diffuse reflection appears to be equally bright from all directions. This does not mean that the entire diffuse surface is visible. The visibility of an area on a diffuse surface depends on the direction of the light and the orientation of the surface. The brightness of the surface depends on the surface type itself and the intensity of the light. Typically, a rough surface, for example, clothing, paper, or plastered walls, reflects light using a diffuse reflection. Surfaces may appear smooth to the eyes, for example, paper or clothing, but they are rough at the microscopic level, and they reflect light diffusively.

In a *specular* reflection, the surface reflects a ray of light in exactly one direction. That is, there is a single reflected ray for one incident ray. A smooth surface at the microscopic level, for example, mirrors or polished marbles, produces a specular reflection. Some smooth surfaces may not be 100% smooth at the microscopic level, and they may reflect part of the light diffusively as well. Specular reflection produces a brighter surface compared to diffuse reflection. Figure 20-25 depicts the ways light is reflected in diffuse and specular reflections.

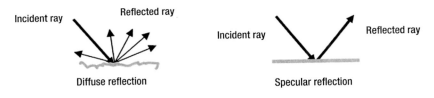

Figure 20-25. *Diffuse and specular reflection type*

Three properties of the Lighting class are used to control the size and intensity of the reflection:

- diffuseConstant
- specularConstant
- specularExponent

The properties are of the double type. The diffuseConstant is used for diffuse reflection. The specularConstant and specularExponent are used for specular reflection. The diffuseConstant property specifies a multiplier for the diffuse reflection intensity. Its value ranges from 0.0 to 2.0 with a default of 1.0. A higher value makes the surface brighter. The specularConstant property specifies the fraction of the light to which the specular reflection applies. Its value ranges from 0.0 to 2.0 with a default value of 0.30. A higher value means a bigger-sized specular highlight. The specularExponent specifies the shininess of the surface. A higher value means a more intense reflection and the surface looks shinier. The specularExponent ranges from 0.0 to 40.0 with a default value of 20.0.

Listing 20-12 contains the code for a utility class that binds the properties of the Lighting class to some controls that will be used to control the properties in the examples discussed later.

Listing 20-12. A Utility Class that Creates a Set of Controls Bound to the Properties of a Lighting Instance

```java
// LightingUtil.java
package com.jdojo.effect;

import javafx.beans.property.DoubleProperty;
import javafx.scene.control.Label;
import javafx.scene.control.Slider;
import javafx.scene.effect.Lighting;
import javafx.scene.layout.GridPane;

public class LightingUtil {
        public static GridPane getPropertyControllers(Lighting effect) {
                Slider surfaceScaleSlider = getSlider(0.0, 10.0,
                        effect.getSurfaceScale(), effect.surfaceScaleProperty());
                Slider diffuseConstantSlider = getSlider(0.0, 2.0,
                        effect.getDiffuseConstant(), effect.diffuseConstantProperty());
                Slider specularConstantSlider = getSlider(0.0, 2.0,
                        effect.getSpecularConstant(), effect.specularConstantProperty());
                Slider specularExponentSlider = getSlider(0.0, 40.0,
                        effect.getSpecularExponent(), effect.specularExponentProperty());

                GridPane pane = new GridPane();
                pane.setHgap(5);
                pane.setVgap(5);
                pane.addRow(0, new Label("Surface Scale:"), surfaceScaleSlider);
                pane.addRow(1, new Label("Diffuse Constant:"), diffuseConstantSlider);
                pane.addRow(2, new Label("Specular Constant:"), specularConstantSlider);
                pane.addRow(3, new Label("Specular Exponent:"), specularExponentSlider);

                return pane;
        }

        public static Slider getSlider(double min, double max, double value,
                        DoubleProperty prop) {
                Slider slider = new Slider(min, max, value);
                slider.setShowTickMarks(true);
                slider.setShowTickLabels(true);
                slider.setMajorTickUnit(max / 4.0);
                prop.bind(slider.valueProperty());
                return slider;
        }
}
```

The program in Listing 20-13 uses the utility class to bind the properties of a Lighting effect to UI controls. It displays a window as shown in Figure 20-26. Change the reflection properties using the sliders to see their effects.

Listing 20-13. Controlling Reflection's Details

```java
// ReflectionTypeTest.java
package com.jdojo.effect;

import javafx.application.Application;
import javafx.scene.Scene;
import javafx.scene.effect.Lighting;
import javafx.scene.layout.BorderPane;
import javafx.scene.layout.GridPane;
import javafx.scene.layout.StackPane;
import javafx.scene.paint.Color;
import javafx.scene.shape.Rectangle;
import javafx.scene.text.Font;
import javafx.scene.text.FontWeight;
import javafx.scene.text.Text;
import javafx.scene.text.TextBoundsType;
import javafx.stage.Stage;

public class ReflectionTypeTest extends Application {
        public static void main(String[] args) {
                Application.launch(args);
        }

        @Override
        public void start(Stage stage) {
                Text text = new Text();
                text.setText("Chatar");
                text.setFill(Color.RED);
                text.setFont(Font.font("null", FontWeight.BOLD, 72));
                text.setBoundsType(TextBoundsType.VISUAL);

                Rectangle rect = new Rectangle(300, 100);
                rect.setFill(Color.LIGHTGRAY);

                // Set the same Lighting effect to both Rectangle and Text nodes
                Lighting effect = new Lighting();
                text.setEffect(effect);
                rect.setEffect(effect);

                StackPane sp = new StackPane(rect, text);

                GridPane controllsrPane = LightingUtil.getPropertyControllers(effect);
                BorderPane root = new BorderPane();
                root.setCenter(sp);
                root.setRight(controllsrPane);
                root.setStyle("-fx-padding: 10;" +
                                "-fx-border-style: solid inside;" +
                                "-fx-border-width: 2;" +
                                "-fx-border-insets: 5;" +
                                "-fx-border-radius: 5;" +
                                "-fx-border-color: blue;");
```

```
            Scene scene = new Scene(root);
            stage.setScene(scene);
            stage.setTitle("Controlling Reflection Details");
            stage.show();
        }
    }
```

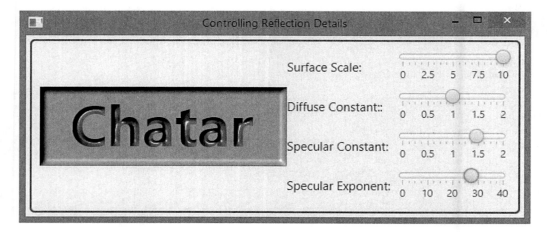

Figure 20-26. *Effects of reflection properties on lighting nodes*

Understanding the Light Source

JavaFX provides three built-in light sources: distant light, point light, and spot light. A *distant* light is also known as a *directional* or *linear* light. A distant light source emanates parallel rays of light in a *specific direction* on the entire surface uniformly. The sun is a perfect example of a distant light source for the lighted surface of an object on the earth. The light source is so distant from the lighted object that the rays are almost parallel. A distant light source lights a surface uniformly, irrespective of its distance from the surface. This does not mean that the entire object is lighted. For example, when you stand in sunlight, not all parts of your body are lighted. However, the lighted part of your body has uniform light. The lighted part of an object depends on the direction of the light. Figure 20-27 shows a distant light hitting some part of the surface of an object. Notice that the rays of light are seen, not the light source itself, because, for a distant light, only the direction of the light is important, not the distance of the light source from the lighted object.

Figure 20-27. *A distant light hitting the surface of an object*

A *point* light source emanates rays of light in all directions from an infinitesimally small point in a 3D space. Theoretically, the light source has no dimension. It emanates light uniformly in all directions. Therefore, unlike the distant light, the direction of the point light source relative to the lighted object is immaterial. Bare light bulbs, stars (excluding the sun, which serves like a distant light), and candlelight are examples of point light sources. The intensity of a point light hitting a surface decreases with the square of the distance between the surface and the point light source. If a point light is very close to the surface, it creates a hotspot, which is a very bright point on the surface. To avoid hotspots, you need to move the light source a little away from the surface. A point light source is defined at a specific point in a 3D space, for example, using x, y, and z coordinates of the point. Figure 20-28 shows a point light radiating rays in all directions. The point on the object surface closest to the light will be illuminated the most.

Figure 20-28. *A point light hitting the surface of an object*

A *spot* light is a special type of a point light. Like a point light, it emanates rays of light radially from an infinitesimally small point in a 3D space. Unlike a point light, the radiation of light rays is confined to an area defined by a cone—the light source being at the vertex of the cone emanating light toward its base, as shown in Figure 20-29. Examples of spot lights are car headlights, flashlights, spotlights, and desk lights with lampshades. A spot light is aimed at a point on the surface, which is the point on the surface where the cone axis is located. The cone axis is the line joining the vertex of the cone to the center of the base of the cone. In Figure 20-29, the cone axis is shown with a dashed arrow. The effect of a spot light is defined by the position of the vertex of the cone, the cone angle, and the rotation of the cone. The rotation of the cone determines the point on the surface that is intersected by the cone axis. The angle of the cone controls the area of the lighted area. The intensity of a spot light is highest along the cone axis. You can simulate a distant light using a spot light if you pull the spot light "far" back, so the rays of light reaching the surface are parallel.

Figure 20-29. *A spot light hitting the surface of an object*

A light source is an instance of the abstract Light class. A light has a color, which is specified by using the color property of the Light class. For example, using a red color Light will make a Text node with a white fill look red.

There are three subclasses of the Light class to represent specific types of light source. The subclasses are static inner classes of the Light class:

- Light.Distant
- Light.Point
- Light.Spot

A class diagram for classes representing light sources is shown in Figure 20-30. The Light.Spot class inherits from the Light.Point class. Classes define properties to configure the specific type of light sources.

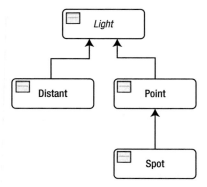

Figure 20-30. *A class diagram for classes representing a light source*

■ **Tip**   When you do not provide a light source for a lighting effect, a distant light is used, which is an instance of the Light.Distant class.

Using a Distant Light Source

An instance of the Light.Distant class represents a distant light source. The class contains two properties to specify the direction of the light source:

- azimuth
- elevation

Both properties are of the double type. Their values are specified in degrees. Both properties are used together to position the light source in a 3D space in a specific direction. By default, their values are 45 degrees. They do not have maximum and minimum values. Their values are computed using modulo 360. For example, an azimuth value of 400 is effectively 40 (400 modulo 360 = 40).

The azimuth property specifies the direction angle in the XY plane. A positive value is measured clockwise and a negative value is measured counterclockwise. A 0 value for the azimuth is located at the 3 o'clock position, 90 at 6 o'clock, 180 at 9 o'clock, 270 at 12 o'clock, and 360 at 3 o'clock. An azimuth of -90 will be located at 12 o'clock. Figure 20-31 shows the location of the distant light in the XY plane for different azimuth values.

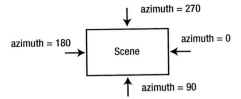

Figure 20-31. *Determining the direction of the distant light in the XY plane using the azimuth value*

The elevation property specifies the direction angle of the light source in the YZ plane. The elevation property values of 0 and 180 make the light source stay on the XY plane. An elevation of 90 puts the light source in front of the scene and the entire scene is lighted. An elevation greater than 180 and less than 360 puts the light source behind the scene making it appear dark (without light).

The Light.Distant class contains two constructers:

- Light.Distant()

- Light.Distant(double azimuth, double elevation, Color color)

The no-args constructor uses 45.0 degrees for azimuth and elevation and Color.WHITE as the light color. The other constructor lets you specify these properties.

The program in Listing 20-14 shows how to use a Light.Distant light. It displays a window that lets you set the direction for a distant light shining on a rectangle and a Text node. Figure 20-32 shows an example of a text and rectangle with a distant light.

Listing 20-14. Using a Distant Light Source

```java
// DistantLightTest.java
package com.jdojo.effect;

import javafx.application.Application;
import javafx.geometry.Insets;
import javafx.scene.Scene;
import javafx.scene.control.Label;
import javafx.scene.control.Slider;
import javafx.scene.effect.Light;
import javafx.scene.effect.Lighting;
import javafx.scene.layout.BorderPane;
import javafx.scene.layout.GridPane;
import javafx.scene.layout.StackPane;
import javafx.scene.paint.Color;
import javafx.scene.shape.Rectangle;
import javafx.scene.text.Font;
import javafx.scene.text.FontWeight;
import javafx.scene.text.Text;
import javafx.scene.text.TextBoundsType;
import javafx.stage.Stage;
```

```java
public class DistantLightTest extends Application {
        public static void main(String[] args) {
                Application.launch(args);
        }

        @Override
        public void start(Stage stage) {
                // Create a light source and position it in the space
                Light.Distant light = new Light.Distant(45.0, 60.0, Color.WHITE);

                // Create a Lighting effect with the light source
                Lighting effect = new Lighting();
                effect.setLight(light);
                effect.setSurfaceScale(8.0);

                Text text = new Text();
                text.setText("Distant");
                text.setFill(Color.RED);
                text.setFont(Font.font("null", FontWeight.BOLD, 72));
                text.setBoundsType(TextBoundsType.VISUAL);

                Rectangle rect = new Rectangle(300, 100);
                rect.setFill(Color.LIGHTGRAY);

                // Set the same Lighting effect to both Rectangle and Text nodes
                text.setEffect(effect);
                rect.setEffect(effect);

                StackPane sp = new StackPane(rect, text);
                BorderPane.setMargin(sp, new Insets(5));
                GridPane lightDirectionController = this.getDistantLightUI(light);
                GridPane controllsrPane = LightingUtil.getPropertyControllers(effect);

                BorderPane root = new BorderPane();
                root.setCenter(sp);
                root.setRight(controllsrPane);
                root.setBottom(lightDirectionController);
                root.setStyle("-fx-padding: 10;" +
                                "-fx-border-style: solid inside;" +
                                "-fx-border-width: 2;" +
                                "-fx-border-insets: 5;" +
                                "-fx-border-radius: 5;" +
                                "-fx-border-color: blue;");

                Scene scene = new Scene(root);
                stage.setScene(scene);
                stage.setTitle("Configuring a Distant Light");
                stage.show();
        }
}
```

```
    private GridPane getDistantLightUI(Light.Distant light) {
            Slider azimuthSlider = LightingUtil.getSlider(0.0, 360.0,
                            light.getAzimuth(), light.azimuthProperty());
            Slider elevationSlider = LightingUtil.getSlider(0.0, 360.0,
                            light.getElevation(), light.elevationProperty());

            GridPane pane = new GridPane();
            pane.setHgap(5);
            pane.setVgap(5);
            pane.addRow(0, new Label("Azimuth:"), azimuthSlider);
            pane.addRow(1, new Label("Elevation:"), elevationSlider);

            return pane;
    }
}
```

Figure 20-32. *A distant light lighting a Text node and a rectangle*

Using a Point Light Source

An instance of the Light.Point class represents a point light source. The class contains three properties to specify the position of the light source in space: x, y, and z. The x, y, and z properties are the x, y, and z coordinates of point where the point light is located in the space. If you set the z property to 0.0, the light source will be in the plane of the scene showing as a very tiny bright point lighting a very small area. As the z value increases, the light source moves away from the scene plane, lighting more area on the scene. A negative value of z will move the light source behind the scene, leaving it with no light, and the scene will look completely dark.

The Light.Point class contains two constructers:

- Light.Point()

- Light.Point(double x, double y, double z, Color color)

The no-args constructor places the point light at (0, 0, 0) and uses a Color.WHITE color for the light. The other constructor lets you specify the location and the color of the light source.

The program in Listing 20-15 shows how to use a Light.Point light. It displays a window with sliders at the bottom to change the location of the point light source. As the point light source moves away from the scene, some area on the scene will be brighter than the other area. Figure 20-33 shows an example of a Text node overlaid on a rectangle being lighted by a point light.

Listing 20-15. Using a Point Light Source

```java
// PointLightTest.java
package com.jdojo.effect;

import javafx.application.Application;
import javafx.geometry.Insets;
import javafx.scene.Scene;
import javafx.scene.control.Label;
import javafx.scene.control.Slider;
import javafx.scene.effect.Light;
import javafx.scene.effect.Lighting;
import javafx.scene.layout.BorderPane;
import javafx.scene.layout.GridPane;
import javafx.scene.layout.StackPane;
import javafx.scene.paint.Color;
import javafx.scene.shape.Rectangle;
import javafx.scene.text.Font;
import javafx.scene.text.FontWeight;
import javafx.scene.text.Text;
import javafx.scene.text.TextBoundsType;
import javafx.stage.Stage;

public class PointLightTest extends Application {
        public static void main(String[] args) {
                Application.launch(args);
        }

        @Override
        public void start(Stage stage) {
                // Create a light source and position it in the space
                Light.Point light = new Light.Point(150.0, 50.0, 50.0, Color.WHITE);

                // Create a Lighting effect with the light source
                Lighting effect = new Lighting();
                effect.setLight(light);
                effect.setSurfaceScale(8.0);

                Text text = new Text();
                text.setText("Point");
                text.setFill(Color.RED);
                text.setFont(Font.font("null", FontWeight.BOLD, 72));
                text.setBoundsType(TextBoundsType.VISUAL);

                Rectangle rect = new Rectangle(300, 100);
                rect.setFill(Color.LIGHTGRAY);

                // Set the same Lighting effect to both Rectangle and Text nodes
                text.setEffect(effect);
                rect.setEffect(effect);
```

```
        StackPane sp = new StackPane(rect, text);
        BorderPane.setMargin(sp, new Insets(5));
        GridPane lightDirectionController = this.getPointLightUI(light);
        GridPane controllsrPane = LightingUtil.getPropertyControllers(effect);

        BorderPane root = new BorderPane();
        root.setCenter(sp);
        root.setRight(controllsrPane);
        root.setBottom(lightDirectionController);
        root.setStyle("-fx-padding: 10;" +
                    "-fx-border-style: solid inside;" +
                    "-fx-border-width: 2;" +
                    "-fx-border-insets: 5;" +
                    "-fx-border-radius: 5;" +
                    "-fx-border-color: blue;");

        Scene scene = new Scene(root);
        stage.setScene(scene);
        stage.setTitle("Configuring a Point Light");
        stage.show();
    }

    private GridPane getPointLightUI(Light.Point light) {
        Slider xSlider = LightingUtil.getSlider(-200.0, 200.0,
            light.getX(), light.xProperty());
        Slider ySlider = LightingUtil.getSlider(-200.0, 200.0,
            light.getY(), light.yProperty());
        Slider zSlider = LightingUtil.getSlider(-200.0, 200.0,
            light.getZ(), light.zProperty());

        GridPane pane = new GridPane();
        pane.setHgap(5);
        pane.setVgap(5);
        pane.addRow(0, new Label("x:"), xSlider);
        pane.addRow(1, new Label("y:"), ySlider);
        pane.addRow(2, new Label("z:"), zSlider);

        return pane;
    }
}
```

Figure 20-33. *A point light lighting a Text node and a rectangle*

Using a Spot Light Source

An instance of the Light.Spot class represents a spot light source. The class inherits from the Light.Point class. The inherited properties (x, y, and z) from the Light.Point class specify the location of the light source, which coincides with the vertex of the cone. The Light.Spot class contains four properties to specify the position of the light source in space:

- pointsAtX
- pointsAtY
- pointsAtZ
- specularExponent

The pointsAtX, pointsAtY, and pointsAtY properties specify a point in the space to set the direction of the light. A line starting from (x, y, z) and going toward (pointsAtX, pointsAtY, pointsAtZ) is the cone axis, which is also the direction of the light. By default, they are set to 0.0. The specularExponent property defines the focus of the light (the width of the cone), which ranges from 0.0 to 4.0. The default is 1.0. The higher the value for the specularExponent, the narrower the cone is and the more focused light will be on the scene.

The Light.Spot class contains two constructers:

- Light.Spot()
- Light.Spot(double x, double y, double z, double specularExponent, Color color)

The no-args constructor places the light at (0, 0, 0) and uses a Color.WHITE color for the light. Because the default values for pointsAtX, pointsAtY, and pointsAtZ are 0.0, the light does not have a direction. The other constructor lets you specify the location and the color of the light source. The cone axis will pass from the specified (x, y, x) to (0, 0, 0).

The program in Listing 20-16 shows how to use a Light.Spot light. It displays a window that lets you configure the location, direction, and focus of the light using sliders at the bottom. Figure 20-34 shows an example of a Light.Spot light focused almost in the middle of the rectangle.

Listing 20-16. Using a Spot Light Source

```
// SpotLightTest.java
package com.jdojo.effect;

import javafx.application.Application;
import javafx.geometry.Insets;
import javafx.scene.Scene;
import javafx.scene.control.Label;
import javafx.scene.control.Slider;
import javafx.scene.effect.Light;
import javafx.scene.effect.Lighting;
import javafx.scene.layout.BorderPane;
import javafx.scene.layout.GridPane;
import javafx.scene.layout.StackPane;
import javafx.scene.paint.Color;
import javafx.scene.shape.Rectangle;
import javafx.scene.text.Font;
```

```
import javafx.scene.text.FontWeight;
import javafx.scene.text.Text;
import javafx.scene.text.TextBoundsType;
import javafx.stage.Stage;

public class SpotLightTest extends Application {
        public static void main(String[] args) {
                Application.launch(args);
        }

        @Override
        public void start(Stage stage) {
                // Create a light source and position it in the space
                Light.Spot light = new Light.Spot(150.0, 50.0, 50.0, 1.0, Color.WHITE);

                // Create a Lighting effect with the light source
                Lighting effect = new Lighting();
                effect.setLight(light);
                effect.setSurfaceScale(8.0);

                Text text = new Text();
                text.setText("Spot");
                text.setFill(Color.RED);
                text.setFont(Font.font("null", FontWeight.BOLD, 72));
                text.setBoundsType(TextBoundsType.VISUAL);

                Rectangle rect = new Rectangle(300, 100);
                rect.setFill(Color.LIGHTGRAY);

                // Set the same Lighting effect to both Rectangle and Text nodes
                text.setEffect(effect);
                rect.setEffect(effect);

                StackPane sp = new StackPane(rect, text);
                BorderPane.setMargin(sp, new Insets(5));
                GridPane lightDirectionController = this.getPointLightUI(light);
                GridPane controllsrPane = LightingUtil.getPropertyControllers(effect);

                BorderPane root = new BorderPane();
                root.setCenter(sp);
                root.setRight(controllsrPane);
                root.setBottom(lightDirectionController);
                root.setStyle("-fx-padding: 10;" +
                                "-fx-border-style: solid inside;" +
                                "-fx-border-width: 2;" +
                                "-fx-border-insets: 5;" +
                                "-fx-border-radius: 5;" +
                                "-fx-border-color: blue;");
```

```
            Scene scene = new Scene(root);
            stage.setScene(scene);
            stage.setTitle("Configuring a Spot Light");
            stage.show();
    }

    private GridPane getPointLightUI(Light.Spot light) {
            Slider xSlider = LightingUtil.getSlider(-200.0, 200.0,
                    light.getX(), light.xProperty());
            Slider ySlider = LightingUtil.getSlider(-200.0, 200.0,
                    light.getY(), light.yProperty());
            Slider zSlider = LightingUtil.getSlider(-200.0, 200.0,
                    light.getZ(), light.zProperty());

            Slider pointsAtXSlider = LightingUtil.getSlider(-200.0, 200.0,
                    light.getPointsAtX(), light.pointsAtXProperty());
            Slider pointsAtYSlider = LightingUtil.getSlider(-200.0, 200.0,
                    light.getPointsAtY(), light.pointsAtYProperty());
            Slider pointsAtZSlider = LightingUtil.getSlider(-200.0, 200.0,
                    light.getPointsAtZ(), light.pointsAtZProperty());

            Slider focusSlider = LightingUtil.getSlider(0.0, 4.0,
                    light.getSpecularExponent(), light.specularExponentProperty());

            GridPane pane = new GridPane();
            pane.setHgap(5);
            pane.setVgap(5);
            pane.addRow(0, new Label("x:"), xSlider);
            pane.addRow(1, new Label("y:"), ySlider);
            pane.addRow(2, new Label("z:"), zSlider);
            pane.addRow(3, new Label("PointsAtX:"), pointsAtXSlider);
            pane.addRow(4, new Label("PointsAtY:"), pointsAtYSlider);
            pane.addRow(5, new Label("PointsAtZ:"), pointsAtZSlider);
            pane.addRow(6, new Label("Focus:"), focusSlider);

            return pane;
    }
}
```

Figure 20-34. *A spot light lighting a Text node and a rectangle*

The *PerspectiveTransform* Effect

A PerspectiveTransform effect gives a 2D node a 3D look by mapping the corners to different locations. The straight lines in the original nodes remain straight. However, parallel lines in the original nodes may not necessarily remain parallel.

An instance of the PerspectiveTransform class represents a PerspectiveTransform effect. The class contains eight properties to specify the x and y coordinates of four corners:

- ulx

- uly

- urx

- ury

- lrx

- lry

- llx

- lly

The first letter in the property names (u or l) indicates upper and lower. The second letter in the property names (l or r) indicates left and right. The last letter in the property names (x or y) indicates the x or y coordinate of a corner. For example, urx indicates the x coordinate of the upper right corner.

▪ **Tip** The PerspectiveTransform class also contains an input property to specify the input effect to it in a chain of effects.

The PerspectiveTransform class contains two constructors:

- PerspectiveTransform()

- PerspectiveTransform(double ulx, double uly, double urx, double ury, double lrx, double lry, double llx, double lly)

The no-args constructor creates a PerspectiveTransform object with all new corners at (0, 0). If you set the object as an effect to a node, the node will be reduced to a point, and you will not be able to see the node. The other constructor lets you specify the new coordinates for the four corners of the node.

The program in Listing 20-17 creates two sets of a Text node and a rectangle. It adds two sets to two different groups. It applies a PerspectiveTransform effect on the second group. Both groups are shown in Figure 20-35. The group on the left shows the original nodes; the group on the right has the effect applied to it.

Listing 20-17. Using the PerspectiveTransform Effect

```java
// PerspectiveTransformTest.java
package com.jdojo.effect;

import javafx.application.Application;
import javafx.scene.Group;
import javafx.scene.Scene;
import javafx.scene.effect.PerspectiveTransform;
import javafx.scene.layout.HBox;
import javafx.scene.paint.Color;
import javafx.scene.shape.Rectangle;
import javafx.scene.text.Font;
import javafx.scene.text.FontWeight;
import javafx.scene.text.Text;
import javafx.stage.Stage;

public class PerspectiveTransformTest extends Application {
        public static void main(String[] args) {
                Application.launch(args);
        }

        @Override
        public void start(Stage stage) {
                // Create the efefct and set the mapping for the corners
                PerspectiveTransform effect = new PerspectiveTransform();
                effect.setUlx(0.0);
                effect.setUly(0.0);
                effect.setUrx(250.0);
                effect.setUry(20.0);
                effect.setLrx(310.0);
                effect.setLry(60.0);
                effect.setLlx(20.0);
                effect.setLly(60.0);

                // Create two rectangles and two Text nodes. Apply effects
                // to one set and show another set without effect
                Rectangle rect1 = new Rectangle(200, 60, Color.LIGHTGRAY);
                Rectangle rect2 = new Rectangle(200, 60, Color.LIGHTGRAY);

                Text text1 = new Text();
                text1.setX(20);
                text1.setY(40);
                text1.setText("Welcome");
                text1.setFill(Color.RED);
                text1.setFont(Font.font(null, FontWeight.BOLD, 36));

                System.out.println(text1.getLayoutBounds());
```

```
        Text text2 = new Text();
        text2.setX(20);
        text2.setY(40);
        text2.setText("Welcome");
        text2.setFill(Color.RED);
        text2.setFont(Font.font(null, FontWeight.BOLD, 36));

        // Group the original nodes
        Group group1 = new Group(rect1, text1);

        // Group the nodes with the effect
        Group group2 = new Group(rect2, text2);
        group2.setEffect(effect);
        group2.setCache(true); // A hint to cache the bitmap for the group

        HBox root = new HBox(group1, group2);
        root.setSpacing(20);
        root.setStyle("-fx-padding: 10;" +
                      "-fx-border-style: solid inside;" +
                      "-fx-border-width: 2;" +
                      "-fx-border-insets: 5;" +
                      "-fx-border-radius: 5;" +
                      "-fx-border-color: blue;");

        Scene scene = new Scene(root, 600, 100);
        stage.setScene(scene);
        stage.setTitle("Applying the PerspectiveTransform Effect");
        stage.show();
    }
}
```

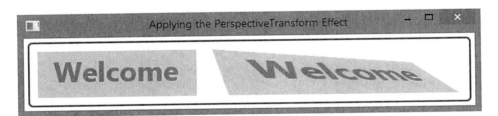

Figure 20-35. Text and Rectangle nodes with a PerspectiveTransform effect

Summary

An effect is a filter that accepts one or more graphical inputs, applies an algorithm on the inputs, and produces an output. Typically, effects are applied to nodes to create visually appealing user interfaces. Examples of effects are shadow, blur, warp, glow, reflection, blending, and different types of lighting. The JavaFX library provides several effect-related classes. Effect is a conditional feature. Effects applied to nodes will be ignored if it is not available on a platform. The Node class contains an effect property that specifies the effect applied to the node. By default, it is null. An instance of the Effect class represents an effect. The Effect class is the abstract base for all effect classes. All effect classes are included in the javafx.scene.effect package.

Some effects can be chained with other effects. The effects are applied in sequence. The output of the first effect becomes the input for the second effect and so on. Effect classes that allow chaining contain an input property to specify the effect that precedes it. If the input property is null, the effect is applied to the node on which this effect is set. By default, the input property is null.

A shadowing effect draws a shadow and applies it to an input. JavaFX supports three types of shadowing effects: DropShadow, InnerShadow, and Shadow.

A blurring effect produces a blurred version of an input. JavaFX lets you apply different types of blurring effects, which differ in the algorithms they use to create the effect. Three types of blurring effects are BoxBlur, GaussianBlur, and MotionBlur.

The Bloom effect adds glow to the pixels of its input that have a luminosity greater than or equal to a specified limit. Note that not all pixels in a Bloom effect are made to glow. An instance of the Bloom class represents a Bloom effect.

The Glow effect makes the bright pixels of the input brighter. An instance of the Glow class represents a Glow effect.

The Reflection effect adds a reflection of the input below the input. An instance of the Reflection class represents a reflection effect.

Sepia is a reddish-brown color. Sepia toning is performed on black-and-white photographic prints to give them a warmer tone. An instance of the SepiaTone class represents a SepiaTone effect.

The DisplacementMap effect shifts each pixel in the input to produce an output. The name has two parts: Displacement and Map. The first part implies that the effect displaces the pixels in the input. The second part implies that the displacement is based on a map that provides a displacement factor for each pixel in the output. An instance of the DisplacementMap class represents a DisplacementMap.

The ColorInput effect is a simple effect that fills (floods) a rectangular region with a specified paint. Typically, it is used as an input to another effect. An instance of the ColorInput class represents the ColorInput effect.

The ImageInput effect works like the ColorInput effect. It passes the given image as an input to another effect. The given image is not modified by this effect. Typically, it is used as an input to another effect, not as an effect directly applied to a node. An instance of the ImageInput class represents the ImageInput effect.

Blending combines two pixels at the same location from two inputs to produce one composite pixel in the output. The Blend effect takes two input effects and blends the overlapping pixels of the inputs to produce an output. The blending of two inputs is controlled by a blending mode. JavaFX provides 17 predefined blending modes. An instance of the Blend class represents the Blend effect.

The Lighting effect, as the name suggests, simulates a light source shining on a specified node in a scene to give the node a 3D look. A Lighting effect uses a light source, which is an instance of the Light class, to produce the effect.

A PerspectiveTransform effect gives a 2D node a 3D look by mapping the corners to different locations. The straight lines in the original nodes remain straight. However, parallel lines in the original nodes may not necessarily remain parallel. An instance of the PerspectiveTransform class represents a PerspectiveTransform effect.

The next chapter will discuss how to apply different types of transformations to nodes.

■ ■ ■

CHAPTER 21

Understanding Transformations

In this chapter, you will learn:

- What a transformation is
- What are translation, rotation, scale, and shear transformations and how to apply them to nodes
- How to apply multiple transformations to a node

What Is a Transformation?

A transformation is a mapping of points in a coordinate space to themselves preserving distances and directions between them. Several types of transformations can be applied to points in a coordinate space. JavaFX supports the following types of transformation:

- Translation
- Rotation
- Shear
- Scale
- Affine

An instance of the abstract Transform class represents a transformation in JavaFX. The Transform class contains common methods and properties used by all types of transformations on nodes. It contains factory methods to create specific types of transformations. Figure 21-1 shows a class diagram for the classes representing different types of transformations. The name of the class matches with the type of transformation the class provides. All classes are in the javafx.scene.transform package.

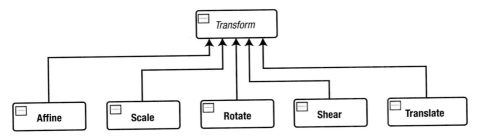

Figure 21-1. *A class diagram for transform-related classes*

An affine transformation is the generalized transformation that preserves the points, straight lines, and planes. The parallel lines remain parallel after the transformation. It may not preserve the angles between lines or the distances between points. However, the ratios of distances between points on a straight line are preserved. Translation, scale, homothetic transformation, similarity transformation, reflection, rotation, shear, and so on are examples of the affine transformation.

An instance of the Affine class represents an affine transformation. The class is not easy to use for beginners. Its use requires advanced knowledge of mathematics such as matrix. If you need a specific type of transformation, use the specific subclasses such as Translate, Shear, and so on, rather than using the generalized Affine class. You can also combine multiple individual transformations to create a more complex one .We will not discuss this class in this book.

Using transformations is easy. However, sometimes it is confusing because there are multiple ways to create and apply them.

There are two ways to create a Transform instance.

- Use one of the factory methods of the Transform class—for example, the translate() method for creating a Translate object, the rotate() method to create a Rotate object, etc.

- Use the specific class to create a specific type of transform—for example, the Translate class for a translation, the Rotate class for a rotation, etc.

Both of the following Translate objects represent the same translation:

```
double tx = 20.0;
double ty = 10.0;

// Using the factory method in the Transform class
Translate translate1 = Transform.translate(tx, ty);

// Using the Translate class constructor
Translate translate2 = new Translate(tx, ty);
```

There are two ways to apply a transformation to a node.

- Use the specific properties in the Node class. For example, use the translateX, translateY, and translateZ properties of the Node class to apply a translation to a node. Note that you cannot apply a shear transformation this way.

- Use the transforms sequence of a node. The getTransforms() method of the Node class returns an ObservableList<Transform>. Populate this list with all the Transform objects. The Transforms will be applied in sequence. You can apply a shear transformation only using this method.

The two methods of applying Transforms work little differently. We will discuss the differences when we discuss the specific types of transformation. Sometimes, it is possible to use both of the foregoing methods to apply transformations, and in that case, the transformations in the transforms sequence are applied before the transformation set on the properties of the node.

The following snippet of code applies three transformations to a rectangle: shear, scale, and translation:

```
Rectangle rect = new Rectangle(100, 50, Color.LIGHTGRAY);

// Apply transforms using the transforms sequence of the Rectangle
Transform shear = Transform.shear(2.0, 1.2);
Transform scale = Transform.scale(1.1, 1.2);
rect.getTransforms().addAll(shear, scale);
```

```
// Apply a translation using the translatex and translateY
// properties of the Node class
rect.setTranslateX(10);
rect.setTranslateY(10);
```

The shear and scale are applied using the transforms sequence. The translation is applied using the translateX and translateY properties of the Node class. The transformations in the transforms sequence, shear and scale, are applied in sequence followed by the translation.

The Translation Transformation

A translation moves every point of a node by a fixed distance in a specified direction relative to its parent coordinate system. It is achieved by shifting the origin of the local coordinate system of the node to a new location. Computing the new locations of points is easy—just add a triplet of numbers to the coordinates of each point in a 3D space. In a 2D space, add a pair of numbers to the coordinates of each point.

Suppose you want to apply translation to a 3D coordinate space by (tx, ty, tz). If a point had coordinates (x, y, z) before the translation, after the translation its coordinates would be (x + tx, y + ty, z + tz).

Figure 21-2 shows an example of a translation transformation. Axes before the transformations are shown in solid lines. Axes after the transformations are shown in dashed lines. Note that the coordinates of the point P remains the same (4, 3) in the translated coordinate spaces. However, the coordinates of the point relative to the original coordinate space change after the transformation. The point in the original coordinate space is shown in a solid black fill color, and in the transformed coordinate space, it is shown without a fill color. The origin of the coordinate system (0, 0) has been shifted to (3, 2). The coordinates of the point P (the shifted point) in the original coordinate space become (7, 5), which is computed as (4+3, 3+2).

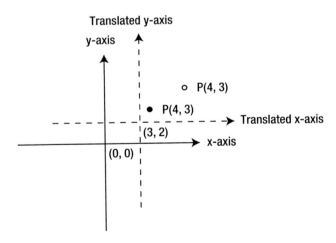

Figure 21-2. *An example of a translation transformation*

An instance of the Translate class represents a translation. It contains three properties.

- x

- y

- z

The properties specify the x, y, and z coordinates of the new origin of the local coordinate system of the node after translation. The default values for the properties are 0.0.

The Translate class provides three constructors.

- `Translate()`
- `Translate(double x, double y)`
- `Translate(double x, double y, double z)`

The no-args constructor creates a Translate object with the default values for the x, y, and z properties, which, in essence, represents no translation. The other two constructors let you specify the translation distance along the three axes. A transformation to a Group is applied to all the nodes in the Group.

Compare the use of the layoutX and layoutY properties of the Node class with the translateX and translateY properties. The layoutX and layoutY properties position the node in its local coordinate system without transforming the local coordinate system whereas the translateX and translateY properties transform the local coordinate system of the node by shifting the origin. Typically, layoutX and layoutY are used to place a node in a scene whereas translation is used for moving a node in an animation. If you set both properties for a node, its local coordinate system will be transformed using the translation, and, then, the node will be placed in the new coordinate system using its layoutX and layoutY properties.

The program in Listing 21-1 creates three rectangles. By default, they are placed at (0, 0). It applies a translation to the second and third rectangles. Figure 21-3 shows the rectangles after the translation.

Listing 21-1. Applying Translations to Nodes

```java
// TranslateTest.java
package com.jdojo.transform;

import javafx.application.Application;
import javafx.scene.Scene;
import javafx.scene.layout.Pane;
import javafx.scene.paint.Color;
import javafx.scene.shape.Rectangle;
import javafx.scene.transform.Translate;
import javafx.stage.Stage;

public class TranslateTest extends Application {
    public static void main(String[] args) {
        Application.launch(args);
    }

    @Override
    public void start(Stage stage) {
        Rectangle rect1 = new Rectangle(100, 50, Color.LIGHTGRAY);
        rect1.setStroke(Color.BLACK);

        Rectangle rect2 = new Rectangle(100, 50, Color.YELLOW);
        rect2.setStroke(Color.BLACK);

        Rectangle rect3 = new Rectangle(100, 50, Color.STEELBLUE);
        rect3.setStroke(Color.BLACK);

        // Apply a translation on rect2 using the transforms sequence
        Translate translate1 = new Translate(50, 10);
        rect2.getTransforms().addAll(translate1);
```

```
            // Apply a translation on rect3 using the translateX
            // and translateY proeprties
            rect3.setTranslateX(180);
            rect3.setTranslateY(20);

            Pane root = new Pane(rect1, rect2, rect3);
            root.setPrefSize(300, 80);
            Scene scene = new Scene(root);
            stage.setScene(scene);
            stage.setTitle("Applying the Translation Transformation");
            stage.show();
        }
}
```

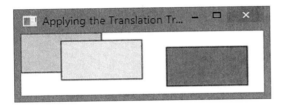

Figure 21-3. Rectangles with translations

The Rotation Transformation

In a rotation transformation, the axes are rotated around a pivot point in the coordinate space and the coordinates of points are mapped to the new axes. Figure 21-4 shows the axes of a coordinate system in a 2D plane rotated by an angle of 30 degrees. The axis of rotation is z-axis. The origin of the original coordinate system is used as the pivot point of rotation. The original axes are shown in solid lines and the rotated axes in dashed lines. The point P in the original coordinate system is shown in a black fill and in the rotated coordinate system with no fill.

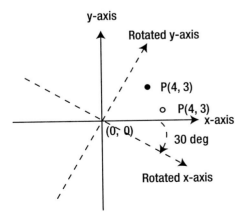

Figure 21-4. An example of a rotation transformation

An instance of the Rotate class represents a rotation transformation. It contains five properties to describe the rotation:

- angle
- axis
- pivotX
- pivotY
- pivotZ

The angle property specifies the angle of rotation in degrees. The default is 0.0 degrees. A positive value for the angle is measured clockwise.

The axis property specifies the axis of rotation at the pivot point. Its value can be one of the constants, X_AXIS, Y_AXIS, and Z_AXIS, defined in the Rotate class. The default axis of rotation is Rotate.Z_AXIS.

The pivotX, pivotY, and pivotZ properties are the x, y, and z coordinates of the pivot point. The default values for the properties are 0.0.

The Rotate class contains several constructors:

- Rotate()
- Rotate(double angle)
- Rotate(double angle, double pivotX, double pivotY)
- Rotate(double angle, double pivotX, double pivotY, double pivotZ)
- Rotate(double angle, double pivotX, double pivotY, double pivotZ, Point3D axis)
- Rotate(double angle, Point3D axis)

The no-args constructor creates an identity rotation, which does not have any effect on the transformed node. The other constructors let you specify the details.

The program in Listing 21-2 creates two rectangles and places them at the same location. The opacity of the second rectangle is set to 0.5, so we can see through it. The coordinate system of the second rectangle is rotated by 30 degrees in the clockwise direction using the origin as the pivot point. Figure 21-5 shows the rotated rectangle.

Listing 21-2. Using a Rotation Transformation

```java
// RotateTest.java
package com.jdojo.transform;

import javafx.application.Application;
import javafx.scene.Scene;
import javafx.scene.layout.Pane;
import javafx.scene.paint.Color;
import javafx.scene.shape.Rectangle;
import javafx.scene.transform.Rotate;
import javafx.stage.Stage;

public class RotateTest extends Application {
        public static void main(String[] args) {
                Application.launch(args);
        }
```

```
        @Override
        public void start(Stage stage) {
                Rectangle rect1 = new Rectangle(100, 50, Color.LIGHTGRAY);
                rect1.setStroke(Color.BLACK);

                Rectangle rect2 = new Rectangle(100, 50, Color.LIGHTGRAY);
                rect2.setStroke(Color.BLACK);
                rect2.setOpacity(0.5);

                // Apply a rotation on rect2. The rotation angle is 30 degree clockwise
                // (0, 0) is the pivot point
                Rotate rotate = new Rotate(30, 0, 0);
                rect2.getTransforms().addAll(rotate);

                Pane root = new Pane(rect1, rect2);
                root.setPrefSize(300, 80);
                Scene scene = new Scene(root);
                stage.setScene(scene);
                stage.setTitle("Applying the Rotation Transformation");
                stage.show();
        }
}
```

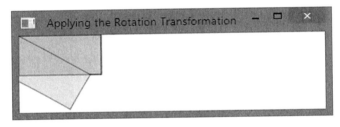

Figure 21-5. *A Rectangle using a rotation transformation*

It is easy to visualize the effect of a rotation when the pivot point is the origin of the local coordinate system of the node and the upper-left corner of a node is located at the origin as well. Let us consider the following snippet of code that rotates a rectangle as shown in Figure 21-6.

```
Rectangle rect1 = new Rectangle(100, 50, Color.LIGHTGRAY);
rect1.setY(20);
rect1.setStroke(Color.BLACK);
Rectangle rect2 = new Rectangle(100, 50, Color.LIGHTGRAY);
rect2.setY(20);
rect2.setStroke(Color.BLACK);
rect2.setOpacity(0.5);
// Apply a rotation on rect2. The rotation angle is 30 degree anticlockwise
// (100, 0) is the pivot point.
Rotate rotate = new Rotate(-30, 100, 0);
rect2.getTransforms().addAll(rotate);
```

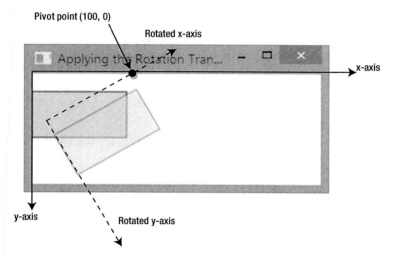

Figure 21-6. *Rotating a Rectangle using a pivot point other than the origin of its local coordinate system*

The coordinates of the upper-left of the rectangles are set to (0, 20). A point at (100, 0) is used as the pivot point to rotate the second rectangle. The pivot point is located on the x-axis of the rectangle. The coordinate system of the second rectangle is pinned at (100, 0), and then, rotated by 30 degree in the anticlockwise direction. Notice that the second rectangle maintains its location (0, 20) in the rotated coordinate space.

You can also apply a rotation to a node using the rotate and rotationAxis properties of the Node class. The rotate property specifies the angle of rotation in degrees. The rotationAxis property specifies the axis of rotation. The center of the untransformed layout bounds of the node is used as the pivot point.

■ **Tip**   The default pivot point used in a transforms sequence is the origin of the local coordinate system of the node whereas the rotate property of the Node class uses the center of the untransformed layout bounds of the node as the pivot point.

The program in Listing 21-3 creates two rectangles similar to the ones in Listing 21-2. It uses the rotate property of the Node class to rotate the rectangle by 30 degrees. Figure 21-7 shows the rotated rectangle. Compare the rotated rectangles in Figure 21-5 and Figure 21-7. The former uses the origin of the local coordinate system as the pivot point and the latter uses the center of the rectangle as the pivot point.

Listing 21-3. Using the rotate Property of the Node Class to Rotate a Rectangle

```java
// RotatePropertyTest.java
package com.jdojo.transform;

import javafx.application.Application;
import javafx.scene.Scene;
import javafx.scene.layout.Pane;
import javafx.scene.paint.Color;
import javafx.scene.shape.Rectangle;
import javafx.stage.Stage;
```

```java
public class RotatePropertyTest extends Application {
        public static void main(String[] args) {
                Application.launch(args);
        }

        @Override
        public void start(Stage stage) {
                Rectangle rect1 = new Rectangle(100, 50, Color.LIGHTGRAY);
                rect1.setStroke(Color.BLACK);

                Rectangle rect2 = new Rectangle(100, 50, Color.LIGHTGRAY);
                rect2.setStroke(Color.BLACK);
                rect2.setOpacity(0.5);

                // Use the rotate proeprty of the node class
                rect2.setRotate(30);

                Pane root = new Pane(rect1, rect2);
                root.setPrefSize(300, 80);
                Scene scene = new Scene(root);
                stage.setScene(scene);
                stage.setTitle("Applying the Rotation Transformation");
                stage.show();
        }
}
```

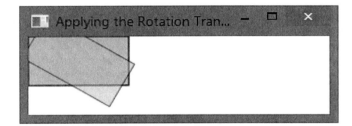

Figure 21-7. *A Rectangle rotated using the rotate property of the Node class*

The Scale Transformation

A scale transformation scales the unit of measurement along axes of a coordinate system by a scale factor. This causes the dimensions of a node to change (stretch or shrink) by the specified scale factors along axes. The dimension along an axis is multiplied by the scale factor along that axis. The transformation is applied at a pivot point whose coordinates remain the same after the transformation.

An instance of the Scale class represents a scale transformation. It contains the following six properties to describe the transformation:

- x
- y
- z
- pivotX
- pivotY
- pivotZ

The x, y, and z properties specify the scale factors long the x-axis, y-axis, and z-axis. They are 1.0 by default. The pivotX, pivotY, and pivotZ properties are the x, y, and z coordinates of the pivot point. The default values for the properties are 0.0.

The Scale class contains several constructors.

- Scale()
- Scale(double x, double y)
- Scale(double x, double y, double z)
- Scale(double x, double y, double pivotX, double pivotY)
- Scale(double x, double y, double z, double pivotX, double pivotY, double pivotZ)

The no-args constructor creates an identity scale transformation, which does not have any effect on the transformed node. The other constructors let you specify the scale factors and the pivot point.

You can use an object of the Scale class or the scaleX, scaleY, and scaleX properties of the Node class to apply a scale transformation. By default, the pivot point used by the Scale class is at (0, 0, 0). The properties of the Node class use the center of the node as the pivot point.

The program in Listing 21-4 creates two rectangles. Both are placed at the same location. One of them is scaled and the other not. The opacity of the not scaled rectangle is set to 0.5, so we can see through it. Figure 21-8 shows the rectangles. The scaled rectangle is smaller. The coordinate system of the second rectangle is scaled by 0.5 along the x-axis and 0.50 along the y-axis. The scaleX and scaleY properties are used to apply the transformation, which uses the center of the rectangles as the pivot point making the rectangles shrunk, but keeping it at the same location.

Listing 21-4. Using Scale Transformations

```
// ScaleTest.java
package com.jdojo.transform;

import javafx.application.Application;

import javafx.scene.Scene;
import javafx.scene.layout.Pane;
import javafx.scene.paint.Color;
import javafx.scene.shape.Rectangle;
import javafx.stage.Stage;
```

```java
public class ScaleTest extends Application {
        public static void main(String[] args) {
                Application.launch(args);
        }

        @Override
        public void start(Stage stage) {
                Rectangle rect1 = new Rectangle(100, 50, Color.LIGHTGRAY);
                rect1.setStroke(Color.BLACK);
                rect1.setOpacity(0.5);

                Rectangle rect2 = new Rectangle(100, 50, Color.LIGHTGRAY);
                rect2.setStroke(Color.BLACK);

                // Apply a scale on rect2. Center of the Rectangle is the pivot point.
                rect2.setScaleX(0.5);
                rect2.setScaleY(0.5);

                Pane root = new Pane(rect1, rect2);
                root.setPrefSize(150, 60);
                Scene scene = new Scene(root);
                stage.setScene(scene);
                stage.setTitle("Applying the Scale Transformation");
                stage.show();
        }
}
```

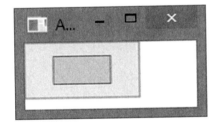

Figure 21-8. *Two Rectangles using scale transformations*

If the pivot point is not the center of the node, the scale transformation may move the node. The program in Listing 21-5 creates two rectangles. Both are placed at the same location. One of them is scaled and the other not. The opacity of the not scaled rectangle is set to 0.5, so we can see through it. Figure 21-9 shows the rectangles. The scaled rectangle is smaller. A Scale object with the transforms sequence is used to apply the transformation, which uses the upper-left corner of the rectangle as the pivot point making the rectangle shrink, but moving it to the left to keep the coordinates of its upper-left corner the same (150, 0) in the transformed coordinate system. The scaled rectangles shrinks by half (scale factor = 0.50) in both directions and moves half the distance to the left.

Listing 21-5. Using Scale Transformations

```java
// ScalePivotPointTest.java
package com.jdojo.transform;
import javafx.application.Application;
import javafx.scene.Scene;
import javafx.scene.layout.Pane;
import javafx.scene.paint.Color;
import javafx.scene.shape.Rectangle;

import javafx.scene.transform.Scale;
import javafx.stage.Stage;

public class ScalePivotPointTest extends Application {
        public static void main(String[] args) {
                Application.launch(args);
        }

        @Override
        public void start(Stage stage) {
                Rectangle rect1 = new Rectangle(100, 50, Color.LIGHTGRAY);
                rect1.setX(150);
                rect1.setStroke(Color.BLACK);
                rect1.setOpacity(0.5);

                Rectangle rect2 = new Rectangle(100, 50, Color.LIGHTGRAY);
                rect2.setX(150);
                rect2.setStroke(Color.BLACK);

                // Apply a scale on rect2. The origin of the local coordinate system
                // of rect4 is the pivot point
                Scale scale = new Scale(0.5, 0.5);
                rect2.getTransforms().addAll(scale);

                Pane root = new Pane(rect1, rect2);
                root.setPrefSize(300, 60);
                Scene scene = new Scene(root);
                stage.setScene(scene);
                stage.setTitle("Applying the Scale Transformation");
                stage.show();
        }
}
```

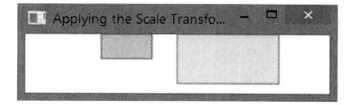

Figure 21-9. *Two Rectangles using scale transformations*

The Shear Transformation

A shear transformation rotates axes of the local coordinate system of the node around a pivot point, so the axes are no longer perpendicular. A rectangular node becomes a parallelogram after the transformation.

An instance of the Shear class represents a shear transformation. It contains four properties to describe the transformation.

- x
- y
- pivotX
- pivotY

The x property specifies a multiplier by which the coordinates of points are shifted along the positive x-axis by a factor of the y coordinate of the point. The default is 0.0.

The y property specifies a multiplier by which the coordinates of points are shifted along the positive y-axis by a factor of the x coordinate of the point. The default is 0.0.

The pivotX, and pivotY properties are the x and y coordinates of the pivot point about which the shear occurs. The default values for them are 0.0. The pivot point is not shifted by the shear. By default, the pivot point is the origin of the untransformed coordinate system.

Suppose you have a point (x1, y1) inside a node, and by the shear transformation, the point is shifted to (x2, y2). You can use the following formula to compute (x2, y2):

```
x2 = pivotX + (x1 - pivotX) + x * (y1 - pivotY)
y2 = pivotY + (y1 - pivotY) + y * (x1 - pivotX)
```

All coordinates (x1, y1, x2, and y2) in the previous formula are in the untransformed local coordinate system of the node. Notice that if (x1, y1) is the pivot point, the foregoing formula computes the shifted point (x2, y2), which is the same as (x1, y1). That is, the pivot point is not shifted.

The Shear class contains several constructors.

- Shear()
- Shear(double x, double y)
- Shear(double x, double y, double pivotX, double pivotY)

The no-args constructor creates an identity shear transformation, which does not have any effect on the transformed node. The other constructors let you specify the shear multipliers and the pivot point.

■ **Tip** You can apply a shear transformation to a node using only a Shear object in the transforms sequence. Unlike for other types of transformations, the Node class does not contain a property allowing you to apply shear transformation.

The program in Listing 21-6 applies a Shear to a rectangle as shown in Figure 21-10. The original rectangle is also shown. A multiplier of 0.5 is used along both axes. Note that the pivot point is (0, 0), which is the default.

Listing 21-6. Using the Shear Transformation

```
// ShearTest.java
package com.jdojo.transform;

import javafx.application.Application;
import javafx.scene.Group;
import javafx.scene.Scene;
import javafx.scene.paint.Color;
import javafx.scene.shape.Rectangle;
import javafx.scene.transform.Shear;
import javafx.stage.Stage;

public class ShearTest extends Application {
        public static void main(String[] args) {
                Application.launch(args);
        }

        @Override
        public void start(Stage stage) {
                Rectangle rect1 = new Rectangle(100, 50, Color.LIGHTGRAY);
                rect1.setStroke(Color.BLACK);

                Rectangle rect2 = new Rectangle(100, 50, Color.LIGHTGRAY);
                rect2.setStroke(Color.BLACK);
                rect2.setOpacity(0.5);

                // Apply a shear on rect2. The x and y multipliers are 0.5 and
                // (0, 0) is the pivot point.
                Shear shear = new Shear(0.5, 0.5);
                rect2.getTransforms().addAll(shear);

                Group root = new Group(rect1, rect2);
                Scene scene = new Scene(root);
                stage.setScene(scene);
                stage.setTitle("Applying the Shear Transformation");
                stage.show();
        }
}
```

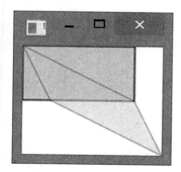

Figure 21-10. *A Rectangle with a shear transformation using (0, 0) as the pivot point*

Let us use a pivot point other than (0, 0) for a Shear transformation. Consider the following snippet of code:

```
Rectangle rect1 = new Rectangle(100, 50, Color.LIGHTGRAY);
rect1.setX(100);
rect1.setStroke(Color.BLACK);
Rectangle rect2 = new Rectangle(100, 50, Color.LIGHTGRAY);
rect2.setX(100);
rect2.setStroke(Color.BLACK);
rect2.setOpacity(0.5);

// Apply a shear on rect2. The x and y multipliers are 0.5 and
// (100, 50) is the pivot point.
Shear shear = new Shear(0.5, 0.5, 100, 50);
rect2.getTransforms().addAll(shear);
```

The code is similar to the one shown in Listing 21-6. The upper-left corners of the rectangles are placed at (100, 0), so we can see the sheared rectangle fully. We have used (100, 50), which is the lower-left corner of the rectangle, as the pivot point. Figure 21-11 shows the transformed rectangle. Notice that the transformation did not shift the pivot point.

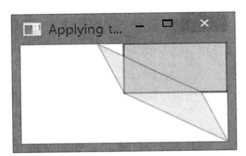

Figure 21-11. *A Rectangle with a shear transformation using (100, 50) as the pivot point*

Let us apply our formula to validate the coordinates of the upper-right corner, which is originally at (200, 0) relative to the untransformed coordinate system of the rectangle.

```
x1 = 200
y1 = 0
pivotX = 100
pivotY = 50
x = 0.5
y = 0.5

x2 = pivotX + (x1 - pivotX) + x * (y1 - pivotY)
   = 100 + (200 - 100) + 0.5 * (0 - 50)
   = 175

y2 = pivotY + (y1 - pivotY) + y * (x1 - pivotX)
   = 50 + (0 -50) + 0.5 * (200 - 100)
   = 50
```

Therefore, (175, 50) is the shifted location of the upper-right corner in the untransformed coordinate system of the rectangle.

Applying Multiple Transformations

You can apply multiple transformations to a node. As mentioned previously, the transformations in the transforms sequence are applied before the transformation set on the properties of the node. When properties of the Node class are used, translation, rotation, and scale are applied in sequence. When the transforms sequence is used, transformations are applied in the order they are stored in the sequence.

The program in Listing 21-7 creates three rectangles and positions them at the same location. It applies multiple transformations to the second and third rectangles in different order. Figure 21-12 shows the result. The first rectangle is shown at its original position, as we did not apply any transformation to it. Notice that two rectangles ended up at different locations. If you change the order of the transformation for the third rectangle as shown next, both rectangles will overlap.

```
rect3.getTransforms().addAll(new Translate(100, 0),
                             new Rotate(30, 50, 25),
                             new Scale(1.2, 1.2, 50, 25));
```

Listing 21-7. Using Multiple Transformations on a Node

```java
// MultipleTransformations.java
package com.jdojo.transform;

import javafx.application.Application;
import javafx.scene.Group;
import javafx.scene.Scene;
import javafx.scene.layout.Pane;
import javafx.scene.paint.Color;
import javafx.scene.shape.Rectangle;
import javafx.scene.transform.Rotate;
import javafx.scene.transform.Scale;
import javafx.scene.transform.Translate;
import javafx.stage.Stage;

public class MultipleTransformations extends Application {
        public static void main(String[] args) {
                Application.launch(args);
        }

        @Override
        public void start(Stage stage) {
                Rectangle rect1 = new Rectangle(100, 50, Color.LIGHTGRAY);
                rect1.setStroke(Color.BLACK);

                Rectangle rect2 = new Rectangle(100, 50, Color.LIGHTGRAY);
                rect2.setStroke(Color.BLACK);
                rect2.setOpacity(0.5);

                Rectangle rect3 = new Rectangle(100, 50, Color.LIGHTCYAN);
                rect3.setStroke(Color.BLACK);
                rect3.setOpacity(0.5);
```

```
            // apply transformations to rect2
            rect2.setTranslateX(100);
            rect2.setTranslateY(0);
            rect2.setRotate(30);
            rect2.setScaleX(1.2);
            rect2.setScaleY(1.2);

            // Apply the same transformation as on rect2, but in a different order
            rect3.getTransforms().addAll(new Scale(1.2, 1.2, 50, 25),
                                         new Rotate(30, 50, 25),
                                         new Translate(100, 0));

            Group root = new Group(rect1, rect2, rect3);
            Scene scene = new Scene(root);
            stage.setScene(scene);
            stage.setTitle("Applying Multiple Transformations");
            stage.show();
        }
}
```

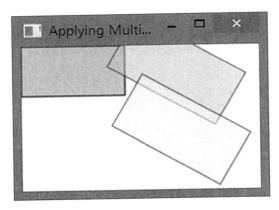

Figure 21-12. *Rectangles with multiple transformations*

Summary

A transformation is a mapping of points in a coordinate space to themselves preserving distances and directions between them. Several types of transformations can be applied to points in a coordinate space. JavaFX supports the following types of transformation: translation, rotation, shear, scale, and affine.

An instance of the abstract Transform class represents a transformation in JavaFX. The Transform class contains common methods and properties used by all types of transformations on nodes. It contains factory methods to create specific types of transformations. All transformation classes are in the javafx.scene.transform package.

An affine transformation is the generalized transformation that preserves the points, lines, and planes. The parallel lines remain parallel after the transformation. The affine transformation may not preserve the angles between lines and the distances between points. However, the ratios of distances between points on a straight line are preserved. Translation, scale, homothetic transformation, similarity transformation, reflection, rotation, and shear are examples of the affine transformation. An instance of the Affine class represents an affine transformation.

There are two ways to apply a transformation to a node: using the specific properties in the Node class and using the transforms sequence of a node.

A translation moves every point of a node by a fixed distance in a specified direction relative to its parent coordinate system. It is achieved by shifting the origin of the local coordinate system of the node to a new location. An instance of the Translate class represents a translation.

In a rotation transformation, the axes are rotated around a pivot point in the coordinate space and the coordinates of points are mapped to the new axes. An instance of the Rotate class represents a rotation transformation.

A scale transformation scales the unit of measurement along axes of a coordinate system by a scale factor. This causes the dimensions of a node to change (stretch or shrink) by the specified scale factors along axes. The dimension along an axis is multiplied by the scale factor along that axis. The transformation is applied at a pivot point whose coordinates remain the same after the transformation. An instance of the Scale class represents a scale transformation.

A shear transformation rotates axes of the local coordinate system of the node around a pivot point, so the axes are no longer perpendicular. A rectangular node becomes a parallelogram after the transformation. An instance of the Shear class represents a shear transformation.

You can apply multiple transformations to a node. The transformations in the transforms sequence are applied before the transformation set on the properties of the node. When properties of the Node class are used, translation, rotation, and scale are applied in order. When the transforms sequence is used, transformations are applied in the order they are stored in the sequence.

The next chapter will discuss how to apply animation to nodes.

CHAPTER 22

Understanding Animation

In this chapter, you will learn:

- What animation is in JavaFX
- About classes in JavaFX that are used in performing animation in JavaFX
- How to perform a timeline animation and how to set up cue points on a timeline animation
- How to control animation such as playing, reversing, pausing, and stopping
- How to perform animation using transitions
- About different types of interpolators and their roles in animation

What Is Animation?

In real world, *animation* implies some kind of motion, which is generated by displaying images in quick succession. For example, when you watch a movie, you are watching images, which change so quickly that you get an illusion of motion.

In JavaFX, animation is defined as changing the property of a node over time. If the property that changes determines the location of the node, the animation in JavaFX will produce an illusion of motion as found in movies. Not all animations have to involve motion; for example, changing the fill property of a shape over time is an animation in JavaFX that does not involve motion.

To understand how animation is performed, it is important to understand some key concepts.

- Timeline
- Key frame
- Key value
- Interpolator

Animation is performed over a period of time. A *timeline* denotes the progression of time during animation with an associated key frame at a given instant. A *key frame* represents the state of the node being animated at a specific instant on the timeline. A key frame has associated key values. A *key value* represents the value of a property of the node along with an interpolator to be used.

Suppose you want to move a circle in a scene from left to right horizontally in 10 seconds. Figure 22-1 shows the circle at some positions. . . . The thick horizontal line represents a timeline. Circles with a solid outline represent the key frames at specific instants on the timeline. The key values associated with key frames are shown at the top line. For example, the value for translateX property of the circle for the key frame at the fifth second is 500, which is shown as tx=500 in the figure.

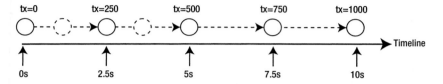

Figure 22-1. *Animating a circle along a horizontal line using a timeline*

The developer provides timelines, key frames, and key values. In this example, there are five key frames. If JavaFX shows only five key frames at the five respective instants, the animation will look jerky. To provide a smooth animation, JavaFX needs to interpolate the position of the circle at any instant on the timeline. That is, JavaFX needs to create intermediate key frames between two consecutive provided key frames. JavaFX does this with the help of an *interpolator*. By default, it uses a *linear interpolator*, which changes the property being animated linearly with time. That is, if the time on the timeline passes x%, the value of the property will be x% between the initial and final target values. Circles with the dashed outline are created by JavaFX using an interpolator.

Understating Animation Classes

Classes providing animation in JavaFX are in the javafx.animation package, except the Duration class, which is in the javafx.util package. Figure 22-2 shows a class diagram for most of the animation-related classes.

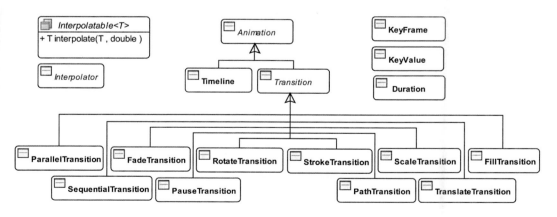

Figure 22-2. *A class diagram for core classes used in animation*

The abstract Animation class represents an Animation. It contains common properties and methods used by all types of animation.

JavaFX supports two types of animations.

- Timeline animations

- Transitions

In a timeline animation, you create a timeline and add key frames to it. JavaFX creates the intermediate key frames using an interpolator. An instance of the Timeline class represents a timeline animation. This type of animation requires a little more code, but it gives you more control.

Several types of animations are commonly performed (moving a node along a path, changing the opacity of a node over time, etc.). These types of animations are known as transitions. They are performed using an internal timeline. An instance of the Transition class represents a transition animation. Several subclasses of the Transition class exist to support specific types of transitions. For example, the FadeTransition class implements a fading effect animation by changing the opacity of a node over time. You create an instance of the Transition class (typically, an instance of one of its subclasses), specify the initial and final values for the property to be animated and the duration for the animation. JavaFX takes care of creating the timeline and performing the animation. This type of animation is easier to use.

Sometimes, you may want to perform multiple transitions sequentially or simultaneously. The SequentialTransition and ParallelTransition classes let you perform a set of transitions sequentially and simultaneously, respectively.

Understanding Utility Classes

Before discussing the details of JavaFX animation, I will discuss a few utility classes that are used in implementing animations. The following sections will discuss those classes.

Understanding the Duration Class

The Duration class is in the javafx.util package. It represents a duration of time in milliseconds, seconds, minutes, and hours. It is an immutable class. A Duration represents the amount of time for each cycle of an animation. A Duration can represent a positive or negative duration.

You can create a Duration object in three ways.

- Using the constructor

- Using factory methods

- Using the valueOf() method from a duration in String format

The constructor takes the amount of time in milliseconds.

```
Duration tenMillis = new Duration(10);
```

Factory methods create Duration objects for different units of time. They are millis(), seconds(), minutes(), and hours().

```
Duration tenMillis = Duration.millis(10);
Duration tenSeconds = Duration.seconds(10);
Duration tenMinutes = Duration.minutes(10);
Duration tenHours = Duration.hours(10);
```

The valueOf() static method takes a String argument containing the duration of time and returns a Duration object. The format of the argument is "number[ms|s|m|h]", where number is the amount of time, and ms, s, m, and h denote milliseconds, seconds, minutes, and hours, respectively.

```
Duration tenMillis = Duration.valueOf("10.0ms");
Duration tenMililsNeg = Duration.valueOf("-10.0ms");
```

You can also represent a duration of an unknown amount of time and an indefinite time using the UNKNOWN and INDEFINITE constants of the Duration class, respectively. You can use the isIndefinite() and isUnknown() methods to check if a duration represents an indefinite or unknown amount of time. | The class declares two more constants, ONE and ZERO, that represent durations of 1 millisecond and 0 (no time), respectively.

The Duration class provides several methods to manipulate durations (adding a duration to another duration, dividing and multiplying a duration by a number, comparing two durations, etc.). Listing 22-1 shows how to use the Duration class.

Listing 22-1. Using the Duration Class

```
// DurationTest.java
package com.jdojo.animation;

import javafx.util.Duration;

public class DurationTest {
        public static void main(String[] args) {
                Duration d1 = Duration.seconds(30.0);
                Duration d2 = Duration.minutes(1.5);
                Duration d3 = Duration.valueOf("35.25ms");
                System.out.println("d1  = " + d1);
                System.out.println("d2  = " + d2);
                System.out.println("d3  = " + d3);

                System.out.println("d1.toMillis() = " + d1.toMillis());
                System.out.println("d1.toSeconds() = " + d1.toSeconds());
                System.out.println("d1.toMinutes() = " + d1.toMinutes());
                System.out.println("d1.toHours() = " + d1.toHours());

                System.out.println("Negation of d1  = " + d1.negate());
                System.out.println("d1 + d2 = " + d1.add(d2));
                System.out.println("d1 / 2.0 = " + d1.divide(2.0));

                Duration inf = Duration.millis(1.0/0.0);
                Duration unknown = Duration.millis(0.0/0.0);
                System.out.println("inf.isIndefinite() = " + inf.isIndefinite());
                System.out.println("unknown.isUnknown() = " + unknown.isUnknown());
        }
}
```

```
d1   = 30000.0 ms
d2   = 90000.0 ms
d3   = 35.25 ms
d1.toMillis() = 30000.0
d1.toSeconds() = 30.0
d1.toMinutes() = 0.5
d1.toHours() = 0.008333333333333333
Negation of d1   = -30000.0 ms
d1 + d2 = 120000.0 ms
d1 / 2.0 = 15000.0 ms
inf.isIndefinite() = true
unknown.isUnknown() = true
```

Understating the KeyValue Class

An instance of the KeyValue class represents a key value that is interpolated for a particular interval during animation. It encapsulates three things.

- A target
- An end value for the target
- An interpolator

The target is a WritableValue, which qualifies all JavaFX properties to be a target. The end value is the value for the target at the end of the interval. The interpolator is used to compute the intermediate key frames.

A key frame contains one or more key values and it defines a specific point on a timeline. Figure 22-3 shows an interval on a timeline. The interval is defined by two instants: *instant1* and *instant2*. Both instants have an associated key frame; each key frame contains a key value. An animation may progress forward or backward on the timeline. When an interval starts, the end value of the target is taken from the key value of the end key frame of the interval and its interpolator is used to compute the intermediate key frames. Suppose, in the figure, the animation is progressing in the forward direction and instant1 occurs before instant2. From instant1 to instant2, the interpolator of the key-value2 will be used to compute the key frames for the interval. If the animation is progressing in the backward direction, the interpolator of the key-value1 will be used to compute the intermediate key frames from instant2 to instant1.

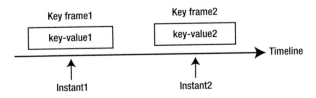

***Figure 22-3.** Key frames at two instants on a timeline*

The KeyValue class is immutable. It provides two constructors.

- KeyValue(WritableValue<T> target, T endValue)

- KeyValue(WritableValue<T> target, T endValue, Interpolator interpolator)

The Interpolator.LINEAR is used as the default interpolator that interpolates the animated property linearly with time. I will discuss different types of interpolators later.

The following snippet of code creates a Text object and two KeyValue objects. The translateX property is the target. 0 and 100 are the end values for the target. The default interpolator is used.

```
Text msg = new Text("JavaFX animation is cool!");
KeyValue initKeyValue = new KeyValue(msg.translateXProperty(), 0.0);
KeyValue endKeyValue = new KeyValue(msg.translateXProperty(), 100.0);
```

The following snippet of code is similar to the one shown above. It uses the Interpolator.EASE_BOTH interpolator, which slows down the animation in the start and toward the end.

```
Text msg = new Text("JavaFX animation is cool!");
KeyValue initKeyValue = new KeyValue(msg.translateXProperty(), 0.0, Interpolator.EASE_BOTH);
KeyValue endKeyValue = new KeyValue(msg.translateXProperty(), 100.0, Interpolator.EASE_BOTH);
```

Understanding the KeyFrame Class

A key frame defines the target state of a node at a specified point on the timeline. The target state is defined by the key values associated with the key frame.

A key frame encapsulates four things.

- An instant on the timeline

- A set of KeyValues

- A name

- An ActionEvent handler

The instant on the timeline with which the key frame is associated is defined by a Duration, which is an offset of the key frame on the timeline.

- The set of KeyValues defines the end value of the target for the key frame.

A key frame may optionally have a name that can be used as a cue point to jump to the instant defined by it during an animation. The getCuePoints() method of the Animation class returns a Map of cue points on the Timeline.

Optionally, you can attach an ActionEvent handler to a KeyFrame. The ActionEvent handler is called when the time for the key frame arrives during animation.

An instance of the KeyFrame class represents a key frame. The class provides several constructors:

- KeyFrame(Duration time, EventHandler<ActionEvent> onFinished, KeyValue... values)

- KeyFrame(Duration time, KeyValue... values)

- KeyFrame(Duration time, String name, EventHandler<ActionEvent> onFinished, Collection<KeyValue> values)

- KeyFrame(Duration time, String name, EventHandler<ActionEvent> onFinished, KeyValue... values)

- KeyFrame(Duration time, String name, KeyValue... values)

The following snippet of code creates two instances of KeyFrame that specify the translateX property of a Text node at 0 seconds and 3 seconds on a timeline:

```
Text msg = new Text("JavaFX animation is cool!");
KeyValue initKeyValue = new KeyValue(msg.translateXProperty(), 0.0);
KeyValue endKeyValue = new KeyValue(msg.translateXProperty(), 100.0);

KeyFrame initFrame = new KeyFrame(Duration.ZERO, initKeyValue);
KeyFrame endFrame = new KeyFrame(Duration.seconds(3), endKeyValue);
```

Understating the Timeline Animation

A timeline animation is used for animating any properties of a node. An instance of the Timeline class represents a timeline animation. Using a timeline animation involves the following steps:

- Construct key frames

- Create a Timeline object with key frames

- Set the animation properties

- Use the play() method to run the animation

You can add key frames to a Timeline at the time of creating it or after. The Timeline instance keeps all key frames in an ObservableList<KeyFrame> object. The getKeyFrames() method returns the list. You can modify the list of key frames at any time. If the timeline animation is already running, you need to stop and restart it to pick up the modified list of key frames.

The Timeline class contains several constructors.

- Timeline()

- Timeline(double targetFramerate)

- Timeline(double targetFramerate, KeyFrame... keyFrames)

- Timeline(KeyFrame... keyFrames)

The no-args constructor creates a Timeline with no key frames with animation running at the optimum rate. Other constructors let you specify the target frame rate for the animation, which is the number of frames per second, and the key frames.

Note that the order in which the key frames are added to a Timeline is not important. Timeline will order them based on their time offset.

The program in Listing 22-2 starts a timeline animation that scrolls a text horizontally from right to left across the scene forever. Figure 22-4 shows a screenshot of the animation.

Listing 22-2. Scrolling Text Using a Timeline Animation

```java
// ScrollingText.java
package com.jdojo.animation;

import javafx.animation.KeyFrame;
import javafx.animation.KeyValue;
import javafx.animation.Timeline;
import javafx.application.Application;
import javafx.geometry.VPos;
import javafx.scene.Scene;
import javafx.scene.layout.Pane;
import javafx.scene.text.Font;
import javafx.scene.text.Text;
import javafx.stage.Stage;
import javafx.util.Duration;

public class ScrollingText extends Application {
        public static void main(String[] args) {
                Application.launch(args);
        }

        @Override
        public void start(Stage stage) {
                Text msg = new Text("JavaFX animation is cool!");
                msg.setTextOrigin(VPos.TOP);
                msg.setFont(Font.font(24));

                Pane root = new Pane(msg);
                root.setPrefSize(500, 70);
                Scene scene = new Scene(root);

                stage.setScene(scene);
                stage.setTitle("Scrolling Text");
                stage.show();

                /* Set up a Timeline animation */
                // Get the scene width and the text width
                double sceneWidth = scene.getWidth();
                double msgWidth = msg.getLayoutBounds().getWidth();

                // Create the initial and final key frames
                KeyValue initKeyValue =
                                new KeyValue(msg.translateXProperty(), sceneWidth);
                KeyFrame initFrame = new KeyFrame(Duration.ZERO, initKeyValue);

                KeyValue endKeyValue =
                                new KeyValue(msg.translateXProperty(), -1.0 * msgWidth);
                KeyFrame endFrame = new KeyFrame(Duration.seconds(3), endKeyValue);

                // Create a Timeline object
                Timeline timeline = new Timeline(initFrame, endFrame);
```

```
        // Let the animation run forever
        timeline.setCycleCount(Timeline.INDEFINITE);

        // Start the animation
        timeline.play();
    }
}
```

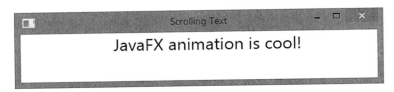

Figure 22-4. *Scrolling text using a timeline animation*

The logic to perform the animation is in the start() method. The method starts with creating a Text object, a Pane with the Text object, and setting up a scene for the stage. After showing the stage, it sets up an animation.

It gets the width of the scene and the Text object.

```
double sceneWidth = scene.getWidth();
double msgWidth = msg.getLayoutBounds().getWidth();
```

Two key frames are created: one for time = 0 seconds and one for time = 3 seconds. The animation uses the translateX property of the Text object to change its horizontal position to make it scroll. At 0 seconds, the Text is positioned at the scene width, so it is invisible. At 3 seconds, it is placed to the left of the scene at a distance equal to its length, so again it is invisible.

```
KeyValue initKeyValue = new KeyValue(msg.translateXProperty(), sceneWidth);
KeyFrame initFrame = new KeyFrame(Duration.ZERO, initKeyValue);

KeyValue endKeyValue = new KeyValue(msg.translateXProperty(), -1.0 * msgWidth);
KeyFrame endFrame = new KeyFrame(Duration.seconds(3), endKeyValue);
```

A Timeline object is created with two key frames.

```
Timeline timeline = new Timeline(initFrame, endFrame);
```

By default, the animation will run only one time. That is, the Text will scroll from right to left once and the animation will stop. You can set the cycle count for an animation, which is the number of times the animation needs to run. You run the animation forever by setting the cycle count to Timeline.INDEFINITE.

```
timeline.setCycleCount(Timeline.INDEFINITE);
```

Finally, the animation is started by calling the play() method.

```
timeline.play();
```

Our example has a flaw. The scrolling the text does not update its initial horizontal position when the width of the scene changes. You can rectify this problem by updating the initial key frame whenever the scene width changes. Append the following statement to the start() method of Listing 22-2. It adds a ChangeListener for the scene width that updates key frames and restarts the animation.

```
scene.widthProperty().addListener( (prop, oldValue , newValue) -> {
        KeyValue kv = new KeyValue(msg.translateXProperty(), scene.getWidth());
        KeyFrame kf = new KeyFrame(Duration.ZERO, kv);
        timeline.stop();
        timeline.getKeyFrames().clear();
        timeline.getKeyFrames().addAll(kf, endFrame);
        timeline.play();
});
```

It is possible to create a Timeline animation with only one key frame. The key frame is treated as the last key frame. The Timeline synthesizes an initial key frame (for time = 0 seconds) using the current values for the WritableValue being animated. To see the effect, let us replace the statement

```
Timeline timeline = new Timeline(initFrame, endFrame);
```

in Listing 22-2 with the following

```
Timeline timeline = new Timeline(endFrame);
```

The Timeline will create an initial key frame with the current value of translateX property of the Text object, which is 0.0. This time, the Text scrolls differently. The scrolling starts by placing the Text at 0.0 and scrolling it to the left, so it goes beyond the scene.

Controlling an Animation

The Animation class contains properties and methods that can be used to control animation in various ways. The following sections will explain those properties and methods and how to use them to | control animation.

Playing an Animation

The Animation class contains four methods to play an animation.

- play()
- playFrom(Duration time)
- playFrom(String cuePoint)
- playFromStart()

The play() method plays an animation from its current position. If the animation was never started or stopped, it will play from the beginning. If the animation was paused, it will play from the position where it was paused. You can use the jumpTo(Duration time) and jumpTo(String cuePoint) methods to set the current position of the animation to a specific duration or a cue point, before calling the play() method. Calling the play() method is asynchronous. The animation may not start immediately. Calling the play() method while animation is running has no effect.

The playFrom() method plays an animation from the specified duration or the specified cue point. Calling this method is equivalent to setting the current position using the jumpTo() method and then calling the play() method.

The playFromStart() method plays the animation from the beginning (duration = 0).

Delaying the Start of an Animation

You can specify a delay in starting the animation using the delay property. The value is specified in Duration. By default, it is 0 milliseconds.

```
Timeline timeline = ...

// Deplay the start of the animation by 2 seconds
timeline.setDelay(Duration.seconds(2));

// Play the animation
timeline.play();
```

Stopping an Animation

Use the stop() method to stop a running animation. The method has no effect if the animation is not running. The animation may not stop immediately when the method is called as the method executes asynchronously. The method resets the current position to the beginning. That is, calling play() after stop() will play the animation from the beginning.

```
Timeline timeline = ...
...
timeline.play();
...
timeline.stop();
```

Pausing an Animation

Use the pause() method to pause an animation. Calling this method when animation is not running has no effect. This method executes asynchronously. Calling the play() method when the animation is paused plays it from the current position. If you want to play the animation from the start, call the playFromStart() method.

Knowing the State of an Animation

An animation can be one of the following three states:

- Running
- Paused
- Stopped

The three states are represented by RUNNING, STOPPED, and PAUSED constants of the Animation.Status enum. You do not change the state of an animation directly. It is changed by calling one of the methods of the Animation class. The class contains a read-only status property that can be used to know the state of the animation at any time.

```
Timeline timeline = ...
...
Animation.Status status = timeline.getStatus();
switch(status) {
        case RUNNING:
                System.out.println("Running");
                break;
        case STOPPED:
                System.out.println("Stopped");
                break;
        case PAUSED:
                System.out.println("Paused");
                break;
}
```

Looping an Animation

An animation can cycle multiple times, even indefinitely. The cycleCount property specifies the number of cycles in an animation, which defaults to 1. If you want to run the animation in an infinite loop, specify Animation.INDEFINITE as the cycleCount. The cycleCount must be set to a value greater than zero. If the cycleCount is changed while the animation is running, the animation must be stopped and restarted to pick up the new value.

```
Timeline timeline1 = ...
Timeline1.setCycleCount(Timeline.INDEFINITE); // Run the animation forever

Timeline timeline2 = ...
Timeline2.setCycleCount(2); // Run the animation for two cycles
```

Auto Reversing an Animation

By default, an animation runs only in the forward direction. For example, our scrolling text animation scrolled the text from right to left in one cycle. In the next cycle, the scrolling occurs again from right to left.

Using the autoReverse property, you can define whether the animation is performed in the reverse direction for alternating cycles. By default, it is set to false. Set it to true to reverse the direction of the animation.

```
Timeline timeline = ...
timeline.setAutoReverse(true); // Reverse direction on alternating cycles
```

If you change the autoReverse, you need to stop and restart the animation for the new value to take effect.

Attaching an onFinished Action

You can execute an `ActionEvent` handler when an animation finishes. Stopping the animation or terminating the application while the animation is running will not execute the handler. You can specify the handler in the `onFinished` property of the `Animation` class. The following snippet of code sets the `onFinished` property to an `ActionEvent` handler that prints a message on the standard output:

```
Timeline timeline = ...
timeline.setOnFinished(e -> System.out.print("Animation finished."));
```

Note that an animation with an `Animation.INDEFINITE` cycle count will not finish and attaching such an action to the animation will never execute.

Knowing the Duration of an Animation

An animation involves two types of durations.

- Duration to play one cycle of the animation

- Duration to play all cycles of the animation

These durations are not set directly. They are set using other properties of the animation (cycle count, key frames, etc.).

The duration for one cycle is set using key frames. The key frame with the maximum duration determines the duration for one cycle when the animation is played at the rate 1.0. The read-only `cycleDuration` property of the `Animation` class reports the duration for one cycle.

The total duration for an animation is reported by the read-only `totalDuration` property. It is equal to `cycleCount * cycleDuration`. If the `cycleCount` is set to `Animation.INDEFINITE`, the `totalDuration` is reported as `Duration.INDEFINITE`.

Note that the actual duration for an animation depends on its play rate represented by the `rate` property. Because the play rate can be changed while animation is running, there is no easy way to compute the actual duration of an animation.

Adjusting the Speed of an Animation

The `rate` property of the `Animation` class specifies the direction and the speed for the animation. The sign of its value indicates the direction. The magnitude of the value indicates the speed. A positive value indicates the play in the forward direction. A negative value indicates the play in the backward direction. A value of 1.0 is considered the normal rate of play, a value of 2.0 double the normal rate, 0.50 half the normal rate, and so on. A rate of 0.0 stops the play.

It is possible to invert the `rate` of a running animation. In that case, the animation is played in the reverse direction from the current position for the duration that has already elapsed. Note that you cannot start an animation using a negative `rate`. An animation with a negative `rate` will not start. You can change the `rate` to be negative only when the animation has played for a while.

```
Timeline timeline = ...

// Play the animation at double the normal rate
Timeline.setRate(2.0);
...
timeline.play();
...
```

```
// Invert the rate of the play
timeline.setRate(-1.0 * timeline.getRate());
```

The read-only currentRate property indicates the current rate (the direction and speed) at which the animation is playing. The values for the rate and currentRate properties may not be equal. The rate property indicates the rate at which the animation is expected to play when it runs, whereas the currentRate indicates the rate at which the animation is being played. When the animation is stopped or paused, the currentRate value is 0.0. If the animation reverses its direction automatically, the currentRate will report a different direction during reversal; for example, if the rate is 1.0, the currentRate reports 1.0 for the forward play cycle and -1.0 for the reverse play cycle.

Understanding Cue Points

You can set up cue points on a timeline. Cue points are named instants on the timeline. An animation can jump to a cue point using the jumpTo(String cuePoint) method. An animation maintains an ObservableMap<String,Duration> of cue points. The key in the map is the name of the cue points and the values are the corresponding duration on the timeline. Use the getCuePoints() method to get the reference of the cue points map.

There are two ways to add cue points to a timeline.

- Giving a name to the KeyFrame you add to a timeline that adds a cue point in the cue point map

- Adding name-duration pairs to the map returned by the getCuePoints() method of the Animation class

---

■ **Tip**   Every animation has two predefined cue points: "start" and "end." They are set at the start and end of the animation. The two cue points do not appears in the map returned by the getCuePoints() method.

The following snippet of code creates a KeyFrame with a name "midway." When it is added to a timeline, a cue point named "midway" will added to the timeline automatically. You can jump to this KeyFrame using jumpTo("midway").

```
// Create a KeyFrame with name "midway"
KeyValue midKeyValue = ...
KeyFrame midFrame = new KeyFrame(Duration.seconds(5), "midway", midKeyValue);
```

The following snippet of code adds two cue points directly to the cue point map of a timeline:

```
Timeline timeline = ...
timeline.getCuePoints().put("3 seconds", Duration.seconds(3));
timeline.getCuePoints().put("7 seconds", Duration.seconds(7));
```

The program in Listing 22-3 shows how to add and use cue points on a timeline. It adds a KeyFrame with a "midway" name, which automatically becomes cue point. It adds two cue points, "3 seconds" and "7 seconds," directly to the cue point map. The list of available cue points is shown in a ListView on the left side of the screen. A Text object scrolls with a cycle duration of 10 seconds. The program displays a window as shown in Figure 22-5. Select a cue point from the list and the animation will start playing from that point.

Listing 22-3. Using Cue Points in Animation

```java
// CuePointTest.java
package com.jdojo.animation;

import java.util.Map;
import java.util.SortedMap;
import java.util.TreeMap;
import java.util.Comparator;
import javafx.animation.KeyFrame;
import javafx.animation.KeyValue;
import javafx.animation.Timeline;
import javafx.application.Application;
import javafx.geometry.VPos;
import javafx.scene.Scene;
import javafx.scene.control.ListView;
import javafx.scene.layout.BorderPane;
import javafx.scene.layout.Pane;
import javafx.scene.text.Font;
import javafx.scene.text.Text;
import javafx.stage.Stage;
import javafx.util.Duration;

public class CuePointTest extends Application {
        Text msg = new Text("JavaFX animation is cool!");
        Pane pane;
        ListView<String> cuePointsListView;
        Timeline timeline;

        public static void main(String[] args) {
                Application.launch(args);
        }

        @Override
        public void start(Stage stage) {
                msg.setTextOrigin(VPos.TOP);
                msg.setFont(Font.font(24));

                BorderPane root = new BorderPane();
                root.setPrefSize(600, 150);

                cuePointsListView = new ListView<>();
                cuePointsListView.setPrefSize(100, 150);
                pane = new Pane(msg);

                root.setCenter(pane);
                root.setLeft(cuePointsListView);

                Scene scene = new Scene(root);
                stage.setScene(scene);
                stage.setTitle("Cue Points");
                stage.show();
```

```java
            this.setupAnimation();
            this.addCuePoints();
    }

    private void setupAnimation() {
            double paneWidth = pane.getWidth();
            double msgWidth = msg.getLayoutBounds().getWidth();

            // Create the initial and final key frames
            KeyValue initKeyValue = new KeyValue(msg.translateXProperty(), paneWidth);
            KeyFrame initFrame = new KeyFrame(Duration.ZERO, initKeyValue);

            // A KeyFrame with a name "midway" that defines a cue point this name
            KeyValue midKeyValue = new KeyValue(msg.translateXProperty(), paneWidth / 2);
            KeyFrame midFrame = new KeyFrame(Duration.seconds(5), "midway", midKeyValue);

            KeyValue endKeyValue = new KeyValue(msg.translateXProperty(), -1.0 * msgWidth);
            KeyFrame endFrame = new KeyFrame(Duration.seconds(10), endKeyValue);

            timeline = new Timeline(initFrame, midFrame, endFrame);
            timeline.setCycleCount(Timeline.INDEFINITE);
            timeline.play();
    }

    private void addCuePoints() {
            // Add two cue points directly to the map
            timeline.getCuePoints().put("3 seconds", Duration.seconds(3));
            timeline.getCuePoints().put("7 seconds", Duration.seconds(7));

            // Add all cue points from the map to the ListView in the order
            // of their durations
            SortedMap<String, Duration> smap = getSortedCuePoints(timeline.getCuePoints());
            cuePointsListView.getItems().addAll(smap.keySet());

            // Add the special "start" and "end" cue points
            cuePointsListView.getItems().add(0, "Start");
            cuePointsListView.getItems().add("End");

            // Jusp to the cue point when the user selects it
            cuePointsListView.getSelectionModel().selectedItemProperty().addListener(
                            (prop, oldValue, newValue) -> {
                                    timeline.jumpTo(newValue);
                            });
    }

    // Sort the cue points based on their durations
    private SortedMap<String, Duration> getSortedCuePoints(
                    Map<String, Duration> map) {
            Comparator<String> comparator = (e1, e2) -> map.get(e1).compareTo(map.get(e2));
            SortedMap<String, Duration> smap = new TreeMap<>(comparator);
            smap.putAll(map);
            return smap;
    }
}
```

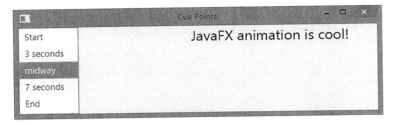

Figure 22-5. *Scrolling text with the list of cue points*

Understanding Transitions

In the previous sections, you saw animations using a timeline that involved setting up key frames on the timeline. Using timeline animation is not easy in all cases. Consider moving a node in a circular path. Creating key frames and setting up a timeline to move the node on the circular path are not easy. JavaFX contains a number of classes (known as *transitions*) that let you animate nodes using predefined properties.

All transition classes inherit from the Transition class, which, in turn, inherits from the Animation class. All methods and properties in the Animation class are also available for use in creating transitions. The transition classes take care of creating the key frames and setting up the timeline. You need to specify the node, duration for the animation, and end values that are interpolated. Special transition classes are available to combine multiple animations that may run sequentially or in parallel.

The Transition class contains an interpolator property that specifies the interpolator to be used during animation. By default, it uses Interpolator.EASE_BOTH, which starts the animation slowly, accelerates it, and slows it down toward the end.

Understanding the Fade Transition

An instance of the FadeTransition class represents a fade-in or fade-out effect for a node by gradually increasing or decreasing the opacity of the node over the specified duration. The class defines the following properties to specify the animation:

- duration
- node
- fromValue
- toValue
- byValue

The duration property specifies the duration for one cycle of the animation.
The node property specifies the node whose opacity property is changed.
The fromValue property specifies the initial value for the opacity. If it is not specified, the current opacity of the node is used.
The toValue property specifies the opacity end value. The opacity of the node is updated between the initial value and the toValue for one cycle of the animation.

The byValue property lets you specify the opacity end value differently using the formula

opacity_end_value = opacity_initial_value + byValue

The byValue lets you set the opacity end value by incrementing or decrementing the initial value by an offset. If both toValue and byValue are specified, the toValue is used.

Suppose you want to set the initial and end opacity of a node between 1.0 and 0.5 in an animation. You can achieve it by setting the fromValue and toValue to 1.0 and 0.50 or by setting fromValue and byValue to 1.0 and -0.50.

The valid opacity value for a node is between 0.0 and 1.0. It is possible to set FadeTransition properties to exceed the range. The transition takes care of clamping the actual value in the range.

The following snippet of code sets up a fade-out animation for a Rectangle by changing its opacity from 1.0 to 0.20 in 2 seconds:

```
Rectangle rect = new Rectangle(200, 50, Color.RED);
FadeTransition fadeInOut = new FadeTransition(Duration.seconds(2), rect);
fadeInOut.setFromValue(1.0);
fadeInOut.setToValue(.20);
fadeInOut.play();
```

The program in Listing 22-4 creates a fade-out and fade-in effect in an infinite loop for a Rectangle.

Listing 22-4. Creating a Fading Effect Using the FadeTransition Class

```
// FadeTest.java
package com.jdojo.animation;

import javafx.animation.FadeTransition;
import javafx.application.Application;
import javafx.scene.Scene;
import javafx.scene.layout.HBox;
import javafx.scene.paint.Color;
import javafx.scene.shape.Rectangle;
import javafx.stage.Stage;
import javafx.util.Duration;

public class FadeTest extends Application {
        public static void main(String[] args) {
                Application.launch(args);
        }

        @Override
        public void start(Stage stage) {
                Rectangle rect = new Rectangle(200, 50, Color.RED);
                HBox root = new HBox(rect);
                Scene scene = new Scene(root);
                stage.setScene(scene);
                stage.setTitle("Fade-in and Fade-out");
                stage.show();
```

```
                    // Set up a fade-in and fade-out animation for the rectangle
                    FadeTransition fadeInOut = new FadeTransition(Duration.seconds(2), rect);
                    fadeInOut.setFromValue(1.0);
                    fadeInOut.setToValue(.20);
                    fadeInOut.setCycleCount(FadeTransition.INDEFINITE);
                    fadeInOut.setAutoReverse(true);
                    fadeInOut.play();
            }
    }
```

Understanding the Fill Transition

An instance of the FillTransition class represents a fill transition for a shape by gradually transitioning the fill property of the shape between the specified range and duration. The class defines the following properties to specify the animation:

- duration
- shape
- fromValue
- toValue

The duration property specifies the duration for one cycle of the animation.

The shape property specifies the Shape whose fill property is changed.

The fromValue property specifies the initial fill color. If it is not specified, the current fill of the shape is used.

The toValue property specifies the fill end value.

The fill of the shape is updated between the initial value and the toValue for one cycle of the animation. The fill property in the Shape class is defined as a Paint. However, the fromValue and toValue are of the type Color. That is, the fill transition works for two Colors, not two Paints.

The following snippet of code sets up a fill transition for a Rectangle by changing its fill from blue violet to azure in 2 seconds:

```
FillTransition fillTransition = new FillTransition(Duration.seconds(2), rect);
fillTransition.setFromValue(Color.BLUEVIOLET);
fillTransition.setToValue(Color.AZURE);
fillTransition.play();
```

The program in Listing 22-5 creates a fill transition to change the fill color of a Rectangle from blue violet to azure in 2 seconds in an infinite loop.

Listing 22-5. Creating a Fill Transition Using the FillTransition Class

```
// FillTest.java
package com.jdojo.animation;

import javafx.animation.FillTransition;
import javafx.application.Application;
import javafx.scene.Scene;
import javafx.scene.layout.HBox;
```

```
import javafx.scene.paint.Color;
import javafx.scene.shape.Rectangle;
import javafx.stage.Stage;
import javafx.util.Duration;

public class FillTest extends Application {
        public static void main(String[] args) {
                Application.launch(args);
        }

        @Override
        public void start(Stage stage) {
                Rectangle rect = new Rectangle(200, 50, Color.RED);
                HBox root = new HBox(rect);
                Scene scene = new Scene(root);
                stage.setScene(scene);
                stage.setTitle("Fill Transition");
                stage.show();

                // Set up a fill transition for the rectangle
                FillTransition fillTransition = new FillTransition(Duration.seconds(2), rect);
                fillTransition.setFromValue(Color.BLUEVIOLET);
                fillTransition.setToValue(Color.AZURE);
                fillTransition.setCycleCount(FillTransition.INDEFINITE);
                fillTransition.setAutoReverse(true);
                fillTransition.play();
        }
}
```

Understanding the Stroke Transition

An instance of the StrokeTransition class represents a stroke transition for a shape by gradually transitioning the stroke property of the shape between the specified range and duration. The stroke transition works the same as the fill transition, except that it interpolates the stroke property of the shape rather than the fill property. The StrokeTransition class contains the same properties as the FillTransition class. Please refer to the section "Understanding the Fill Transition" for more details. The following snippet of code starts animating the stroke of a Rectangle in an infinite loop. The stroke changes from red to blue in a cycle duration of 2 seconds.

```
Rectangle rect = new Rectangle(200, 50, Color.WHITE);
StrokeTransition strokeTransition = new StrokeTransition(Duration.seconds(2), rect);
strokeTransition.setFromValue(Color.RED);
strokeTransition.setToValue(Color.BLUE);
strokeTransition.setCycleCount(StrokeTransition.INDEFINITE);
strokeTransition.setAutoReverse(true);
strokeTransition.play();
```

Understanding the Translate Transition

An instance of the TranslateTransition class represents a translate transition for a node by gradually changing the translateX, translateY, and translateZ properties of the node over the specified duration. The class defines the following properties to specify the animation:

- duration
- node
- fromX
- fromY
- fromZ
- toX
- toY
- toZ
- byX
- byY
- byZ

The duration property specifies the duration for one cycle of the animation.

The node property specifies the node whose translateX, translateY, and translateZ properties are changed.

The initial location of the node is defined by the (fromX, fromY, fromZ) value. If it is not specified, the current (translateX, translateY, translateZ) value of the node is used as the initial location.

The (toX, toY, toZ) value specifies the end location.

The (byX, byY, byZ) value lets you specify the end location using the following formula:

```
translateX_end_value = translateX_initial_value + byX
translateY_end_value = translateY_initial_value + byY
translateZ_end_value = translateZ_initial_value + byZ
```

If both (toX, toY, toZ) and (byX, byY, byZ) values are specified, the former is used.

The program in Listing 22-6 creates a translate transition in an infinite loop for a Text object by scrolling it across the width of the scene. The program in Listing 22-2 created the same animation using a Timeline object with one difference. They use different interpolators. By default, timeline-based animations use the Interpolator.LINEAR interpolator whereas transition-based animation uses the Interpolator.EASE_BOTH interpolator. When you run the program in Listing 22-6, the text starts scrolling slow in the beginning and end, whereas in Listing 22-2, the text scrolls with a uniform speed all the time.

Listing 22-6. Creating a Translate Transition Using the TranslateTransition Class

```
// TranslateTest.java
package com.jdojo.animation;

import javafx.animation.TranslateTransition;
import javafx.application.Application;
import javafx.geometry.VPos;
import javafx.scene.Scene;
```

```
import javafx.scene.layout.Pane;
import javafx.scene.text.Font;
import javafx.scene.text.Text;
import javafx.stage.Stage;
import javafx.util.Duration;

public class TranslateTest extends Application {
        public static void main(String[] args) {
                Application.launch(args);
        }

        @Override
        public void start(Stage stage) {
                Text msg = new Text("JavaFX animation is cool!");
                msg.setTextOrigin(VPos.TOP);
                msg.setFont(Font.font(24));

                Pane root = new Pane(msg);
                root.setPrefSize(500, 70);
                Scene scene = new Scene(root);

                stage.setScene(scene);
                stage.setTitle("Scrolling Text using a Translate Transition");
                stage.show();

                // Set up a translate transition for the Text object
                TranslateTransition tt = new TranslateTransition(Duration.seconds(2), msg);
                tt.setFromX(scene.getWidth());
                tt.setToX(-1.0 * msg.getLayoutBounds().getWidth());
                tt.setCycleCount(TranslateTransition.INDEFINITE);
                tt.setAutoReverse(true);
                tt.play();
        }
}
```

Understanding the Rotate Transition

An instance of the RotateTransition class represents a rotation transition for a node by gradually changing its rotate property over the specified duration. The rotation is performed around the center of the node along the specified axis. The class defines the following properties to specify the animation:

- duration
- node
- axis
- fromAngle
- toAngle
- byAngle

The duration property specifies the duration for one cycle of the animation.

The node property specifies the node whose rotate property is changed.

The axis property specifies the axis of rotation. If it is unspecified, the value for the rotationAxis property, which defaults to Rotate.Z_AXIS, for the node is used. The possible values are Rotate.X_AXIS, Rotate.Y_AXIS, and Rotate.Z_AXIS.

The initial angle for the rotation is specified by fromAngle property. If it is unspecified, the value for the rotate property of the node is used as the initial angle.

The toAngle specifies the end rotation angle.

The byAngle lets you specify the end rotation angle using the following formula:

```
rotation_end_value = rotation_initial_value + byAngle
```

If both toAngle and byAngle values are specified, the former is used. All angles are specified in degrees. Zero degrees correspond to the 3 o'clock position. Positive values for angles are measured clockwise.

The program in Listing 22-7 creates a rotate transition in an infinite loop for a Rectangle. It rotates the Rectangle in clockwise and anticlockwise directions in alternate cycles.

Listing 22-7. Creating a Rotate Transition Using the RotateTransition Class

```
// RotateTest.java
package com.jdojo.animation;

import javafx.animation.RotateTransition;
import javafx.application.Application;
import javafx.geometry.Insets;
import javafx.scene.Scene;
import javafx.scene.layout.HBox;
import javafx.scene.paint.Color;
import javafx.scene.shape.Rectangle;
import javafx.stage.Stage;
import javafx.util.Duration;

public class RotateTest extends Application {
        public static void main(String[] args) {
                Application.launch(args);
        }

        @Override
        public void start(Stage stage) {
                Rectangle rect = new Rectangle(50, 50, Color.RED);
                HBox.setMargin(rect, new Insets(20));
                HBox root = new HBox(rect);
                Scene scene = new Scene(root);
                stage.setScene(scene);
                stage.setTitle("Rotate Transition");
                stage.show();
```

```
                    // Set up a rotate transition the rectangle
                    RotateTransition rt = new RotateTransition(Duration.seconds(2), rect);
                    rt.setFromAngle(0.0);
                    rt.setToAngle(360.0);
                    rt.setCycleCount(RotateTransition.INDEFINITE);
                    rt.setAutoReverse(true);
                    rt.play();
        }
}
```

Understanding the Scale Transition

An instance of the ScaleTransition class represents a scale transition for a node by gradually changing its scaleX, scaleY, and scaleZ properties over the specified duration. The class defines the following properties to specify the animation:

- duration
- node
- fromX
- fromY
- fromZ
- toX
- toY
- toZ
- byX
- byY
- byZ

The duration property specifies the duration for one cycle of the animation.

The node property specifies the node whose scaleX, scaleY, and scaleZ properties are changed.

The initial scale of the node is defined by the (fromX, fromY, fromZ) value. If it is not specified, the current (scaleX, scaleY, scaleZ) value of the node is used as the initial scale.

The (toX, toY, toZ) value specifies the end scale.

The (byX, byY, byZ) value lets you specify the end scale using the following formula:

```
scaleX_end_value = scaleX_initial_value + byX
scaleY_end_value = scaleY_initial_value + byY
scaleZ_end_value = scaleZ_initial_value + byZ
```

If both (toX, toY, toZ) and (byX, byY, byZ) values are specified, the former is used.

The program in Listing 22-8 creates a scale transition in an infinite loop for a Rectangle by changing its width and height between 100% and 20% of their original values in 2 seconds.

Listing 22-8. Creating a Scale Transition Using the ScaleTransition Class

```java
// ScaleTest.java
package com.jdojo.animation;

import javafx.animation.ScaleTransition;
import javafx.application.Application;
import javafx.scene.Scene;
import javafx.scene.layout.HBox;
import javafx.scene.paint.Color;
import javafx.scene.shape.Rectangle;
import javafx.stage.Stage;
import javafx.util.Duration;

public class ScaleTest extends Application {
        public static void main(String[] args) {
                Application.launch(args);
        }

        @Override
        public void start(Stage stage) {
                Rectangle rect = new Rectangle(200, 50, Color.RED);
                HBox root = new HBox(rect);
                Scene scene = new Scene(root);
                stage.setScene(scene);
                stage.setTitle("Scale Transition");
                stage.show();

                // Set up a scale transition for the rectangle
                ScaleTransition st = new ScaleTransition(Duration.seconds(2), rect);
                st.setFromX(1.0);
                st.setToX(0.20);
                st.setFromY(1.0);
                st.setToY(0.20);
                st.setCycleCount(ScaleTransition.INDEFINITE);
                st.setAutoReverse(true);
                st.play();
        }
}
```

Understanding the Path Transition

An instance of the PathTransition class represents a path transition for a node by gradually changing its translateX and translateY properties to move it along a path over the specified duration. The path is defined by the outline of a Shape. The class defines the following properties to specify the animation:

- duration
- node
- path
- orientation

The duration property specifies the duration for one cycle of the animation.

The node property specifies the node whose rotate property is changed.

The path property defines the path along which the node is moved. It is a Shape. You can use an Arc, a Circle, a Rectangle, an Ellipse, a Path, a SVGPath, and so on as the path.

The moving node may maintain the same upright position or it may be rotated to keep it perpendicular to the tangent of the path at any point along the path. The orientation property specifies the upright position of the node along the path. Its value is one of the constants (NONE and ORTHOGONAL_TO_TANGENT) of the PathTransition.OrientationType enum. The default is NONE, which maintains the same upright position. The ORTHOGONAL_TO_TANGENT value keeps the node perpendicular to the tangent of the path at any point. Figure 22-6 shows the positions of a Rectangle moving along a Circle using a PathTransition. Notice the way the Rectangle is rotated along the path when the ORTHPGONAL_TO_TANGENT orientation is used.

NONE   ORTHOGONAL_TO_TANGENT

Figure 22-6. *Effect of using the orientation property of the PathTransition class*

You can specify the duration, path, and node for the path transition using the properties of the PathTransition class or in the constructors. The class contains the following constructors:

- PathTransition()

- PathTransition(Duration duration, Shape path)

- PathTransition(Duration duration, Shape path, Node node)

The program in Listing 22-9 creates a path transition in an infinite loop for a Rectangle. It moves the Rectangle along a circular path defined by the outline of a Circle.

Listing 22-9. Creating a Path Transition Using the PathTransition Class

```java
// PathTest.java
package com.jdojo.animation;

import javafx.animation.PathTransition;
import javafx.application.Application;
import javafx.scene.Group;
import javafx.scene.Scene;
import javafx.scene.paint.Color;
import javafx.scene.shape.Circle;
import javafx.scene.shape.Rectangle;
import javafx.stage.Stage;
import javafx.util.Duration;

public class PathTest extends Application {
        public static void main(String[] args) {
                Application.launch(args);
        }
```

```
        @Override
        public void start(Stage stage) {
                // Create the node
                Rectangle rect = new Rectangle(20, 10, Color.RED);

                // Create the path
                Circle path = new Circle(100, 100, 100);
                path.setFill(null);
                path.setStroke(Color.BLACK);

                Group root = new Group(rect, path);
                Scene scene = new Scene(root);
                stage.setScene(scene);
                stage.setTitle("Path Transition");
                stage.show();

                // Set up a path transition for the rectangle
                PathTransition pt = new PathTransition(Duration.seconds(2), path, rect);
                pt.setOrientation(PathTransition.OrientationType.ORTHOGONAL_TO_TANGENT);
                pt.setCycleCount(PathTransition.INDEFINITE);
                pt.setAutoReverse(true);
                pt.play();
        }
}
```

Understanding the Pause Transition

An instance of the PauseTransition class represents a pause transition. It causes a delay of the specified duration. Its use is not obvious. It is not used alone. Typically, it is used in a sequential transition to insert a pause between two transitions. It defines a duration property to specify the duration of the delay.

A pause transition is also useful if you want to execute an ActionEvent handler after a specified duration when a transition is finished. You can achieve this by setting its onFinished property, which is defined in the Animation class.

```
// Create a pause transition of 400 milliseconds that is the default duration
PauseTransition pt1 = new PauseTransition();

// Change the duration to 10 seconds
pt1.setDuration(Duration.seconds(10));

// Create a pause transition of 5 seconds
PauseTransition pt2 = new PauseTransition(Duration.seconds(5));
```

If you change the duration of a running pause transition, you need to stop and restart the transition to pick up the new duration. You will have an example when I discuss the sequential transition.

Understanding the Sequential Transition

An instance of the SequentialTransition class represents a sequential transition. It executes a list of animations in sequential order. The list of animation may contain timeline-based animations, transition-based animations, or both.

The SequentialTransition class contains a node property that is used as the node for animations in the list if the animation does not specify a node. If all animations specify a node, this property is not used.

A SequentialTransition maintains the animations in an ObservableList<Animation>. The getChildren() method returns the reference of the list.

The following snippet of code creates a fade transition, a pause transition, and a path transition. Three transitions are added to a sequential transition. When the sequential transition is played, it will play the fade transition, pause transition, and the path transition in sequence.

```
FadeTransition fadeTransition = ...
PauseTransition pauseTransition = ...
PathTransition pathTransition = ...

SequentialTransition st = new SequentialTransition();
st.getChildren().addAll(fadeTransition, pauseTransition, pathTransition);
st.play();
```

■ **Tip** The SequentialTransition class contains constructors that let you specify the list of animations and node.

The program in Listing 22-10 creates a scale transition, a fill transition, a pause transition, and a path transition, which are added to a sequential transition. The sequential transition runs in an infinite loop. When the program runs

- It scales up the rectangle to double its size, and then down to the original size.

- It changes the fill color of the rectangle from red to blue, and then, back to red.

- It pauses for 200 milliseconds, and then, prints a message on the standard output.

- It moves the rectangle along the outline of a circle.

- The foregoing sequence of animations is repeated indefinitely.

Listing 22-10. Creating a Sequential Transition Using the SequentialTransition Class

```
// SequentialTest.java
package com.jdojo.animation;

import javafx.animation.FillTransition;
import javafx.animation.PathTransition;
import javafx.animation.PauseTransition;
import javafx.animation.ScaleTransition;
import javafx.animation.SequentialTransition;
import javafx.application.Application;
import javafx.scene.Scene;
```

```java
import javafx.scene.layout.Pane;
import javafx.scene.paint.Color;
import javafx.scene.shape.Circle;
import javafx.scene.shape.Rectangle;
import javafx.stage.Stage;
import javafx.util.Duration;
import static javafx.animation.PathTransition.OrientationType.ORTHOGONAL_TO_TANGENT;

public class SequentialTest extends Application {
        public static void main(String[] args) {
                Application.launch(args);
        }

        @Override
        public void start(Stage stage) {
                // Create the node to be animated
                Rectangle rect = new Rectangle(20, 10, Color.RED);

                // Create the path
                Circle path = new Circle(100, 100, 75);
                path.setFill(null);
                path.setStroke(Color.BLACK);

                Pane root = new Pane(rect, path);
                root.setPrefSize(200, 200);
                Scene scene = new Scene(root);
                stage.setScene(scene);
                stage.setTitle("Sequential Transition");
                stage.show();

                // Set up a scale transition
                ScaleTransition scaleTransition = new ScaleTransition(Duration.seconds(1));
                scaleTransition.setFromX(1.0);
                scaleTransition.setToX(2.0);
                scaleTransition.setFromY(1.0);
                scaleTransition.setToY(2.0);
                scaleTransition.setCycleCount(2);
                scaleTransition.setAutoReverse(true);

                // Set up a fill transition
                FillTransition fillTransition = new FillTransition(Duration.seconds(1));
                fillTransition.setFromValue(Color.RED);
                fillTransition.setToValue(Color.BLUE);
                fillTransition.setCycleCount(2);
                fillTransition.setAutoReverse(true);

                // Set up a pause transition
                PauseTransition pauseTransition = new PauseTransition(Duration.millis(200));
                pauseTransition.setOnFinished(e -> System.out.println("Ready to circle..."));
```

945

```
                    // Set up a path transition
                    PathTransition pathTransition = new PathTransition(Duration.seconds(2), path);
                    pathTransition.setOrientation(ORTHOGONAL_TO_TANGENT);

                    // Create a sequential transition
                    SequentialTransition st = new SequentialTransition();

                    // Rectangle is the node for all animations
                    st.setNode(rect);

                    // Add animations to the list
                    st.getChildren().addAll(scaleTransition,
                                            fillTransition,
                                            pauseTransition,
                                            pathTransition);
                    st.setCycleCount(PathTransition.INDEFINITE);
                    st.play();
            }
}
```

Understanding the Parallel Transition

An instance of the ParallelTransition class represents a parallel transition. It executes a list of animations simultaneously. The list of animations may contain timeline-based animations, transition-based animations, or both.

The ParallelTransition class contains a node property that is used as the node for animations in the list if the animation does not specify a node. If all animations specify a node, this property is not used.

A ParallelTransition maintains the animations in an ObservableList<Animation>. The getChildren() method returns the reference of the list.

The following snippet of code creates a fade transition and a path transition. They transitions are added to a parallel transition. When the sequential transition is played, it will apply the fading effect and move the node at the same time.

```
FadeTransition fadeTransition = ...
PathTransition pathTransition = ...

ParallelTransition pt = new ParallelTransition();
pt.getChildren().addAll(fadeTransition, pathTransition);
pt.play();
```

■ **Tip**   The ParallelTransition class contains constructors that let you specify the list of animations and node.

The program in Listing 22-11 creates a fade transition and a rotate transition. It adds them to a parallel transition. When the program is run, the rectangle rotates and fades in/out at the same time.

Listing 22-11. Creating a Parallel Transition Using the ParallelTransition Class

```java
// ParallelTest.java
package com.jdojo.animation;

import javafx.animation.FadeTransition;
import javafx.animation.ParallelTransition;
import javafx.animation.PathTransition;
import javafx.animation.RotateTransition;
import javafx.application.Application;
import javafx.geometry.Insets;
import javafx.scene.Scene;
import javafx.scene.layout.HBox;
import javafx.scene.paint.Color;
import javafx.scene.shape.Rectangle;
import javafx.stage.Stage;
import javafx.util.Duration;

public class ParallelTest extends Application {
        public static void main(String[] args) {
                Application.launch(args);
        }

        @Override
        public void start(Stage stage) {
                Rectangle rect = new Rectangle(100, 100, Color.RED);
                HBox.setMargin(rect, new Insets(20));

                HBox root = new HBox(rect);
                Scene scene = new Scene(root);
                stage.setScene(scene);
                stage.setTitle("Parallel Transition");
                stage.show();

                // Set up a fade transition
                FadeTransition fadeTransition = new FadeTransition(Duration.seconds(1));
                fadeTransition.setFromValue(0.20);
                fadeTransition.setToValue(1.0);
                fadeTransition.setCycleCount(2);
                fadeTransition.setAutoReverse(true);

                // Set up a rotate transitione
                RotateTransition rotateTransition =
                        new RotateTransition(Duration.seconds(2));
                rotateTransition.setFromAngle(0.0);
                rotateTransition.setToAngle(360.0);
                rotateTransition.setCycleCount(2);
                rotateTransition.setAutoReverse(true);

                // Create and start a sequential transition
                ParallelTransition pt = new ParallelTransition();
```

```
        // Rectangle is the node for all animations
        pt.setNode(rect);
        pt.getChildren().addAll(fadeTransition, rotateTransition);
        pt.setCycleCount(PathTransition.INDEFINITE);
        pt.play();
    }
}
```

Understanding Interpolators

An interpolator is an instance of the abstract Interpolator class. An interpolator plays an important role in an animation. Its job is to compute the key values for the intermediate key frames during animation. Implementing a custom interpolator is easy. You need to subclass the Interpolator class and override its curve() method. The curve() method is passed the time elapsed for the current interval. The time is normalized between 0.0 and 1.0. The start and end of the interval have the value of 0.0 and 1.0, respectively. The value passed to the method would be 0.50 when half of the interval time has elapsed. The return value of the method indicates the fraction of change in the animated property.

The following interpolator is known as a linear interpolator whose curve() method returns the passed in argument value:

```
Interpolator linearInterpolator = new Interpolator() {
        @Override
        protected double curve(double timeFraction) {
                return timeFraction;
        }
};
```

The linear interpolator mandates that the percentage of change in the animated property is the same as the progression of the time for the interval.

Once you have a custom interpolator, you can use it in constructing key values for key frames in a timeline-based animation. For a transition-based animation, you can use it as the interpolator property of the transition classes.

The animation API calls the interpolate() method of the Interpolator. If the animated property is an instance of Number, it returns

```
startValue + (endValue - startValue) * curve(timeFraction)
```

Otherwise, if the animated property is an instance of the Interpolatable, it delegates the interpolation work to the interpolate() method of the Interpolatable. Otherwise, the interpolator defaults to a discrete interpolator by returning 1.0 when the time fraction is 1.0, and 0.0 otherwise.

JavaFX provides some standard interpolators that are commonly used in animations. They are available as constants in the Interpolator class or as its static methods.

- Linear interpolator

- Discrete interpolator

- Ease-in interpolator

- Ease-out interpolator

- Ease-both interpolator
- Spline interpolator
- Tangent interpolator

Understanding the Linear Interpolator

The Interpolator.LINEAR constant represents a linear interpolator. It interpolates the value of the animated property of a node linearly with time. The percentage change in the property for an interval is the same as the percentage of the time passed.

Understanding the Discrete Interpolator

The Interpolator.DISCRETE constant represents a discrete interpolator. A discrete interpolator jumps from one key frame to the next, providing no intermediate key frame. The curve() method of the interpolator returns 1.0 when the time fraction is 1.0, and 0.0 otherwise. That is, the animated property value stays at its initial value for the entire duration of the interval. It jumps to the end value at the end of the interval. The program in Listing 22-12 uses discrete interpolators for all key frames. When you run the program, it moves text jumping from key frame to another. Compare this example with the scrolling text example, which used a linear interpolator. The scrolling text example moved the text smoothly whereas this example created a jerk in the movement.

Listing 22-12. Using a Discrete Interpolator to Animate Hopping Text

```java
// HoppingText.java
package com.jdojo.animation;

import javafx.animation.Interpolator;
import javafx.animation.KeyFrame;
import javafx.animation.KeyValue;
import javafx.animation.Timeline;
import javafx.application.Application;
import javafx.geometry.VPos;
import javafx.scene.Scene;
import javafx.scene.layout.Pane;
import javafx.scene.text.Font;
import javafx.scene.text.Text;
import javafx.stage.Stage;
import javafx.util.Duration;

public class HoppingText extends Application {
        public static void main(String[] args) {
                Application.launch(args);
        }

        @Override
        public void start(Stage stage) {
                Text msg = new Text("Hopping text!");
                msg.setTextOrigin(VPos.TOP);
                msg.setFont(Font.font(24));
```

```
              Pane root = new Pane(msg);
              root.setPrefSize(500, 70);
              Scene scene = new Scene(root);

              stage.setScene(scene);
              stage.setTitle("Hopping Text");
              stage.show();

              // Setup a Timeline animation
              double start = scene.getWidth();
              double end = -1.0 * msg.getLayoutBounds().getWidth();

              KeyFrame[] frame = new KeyFrame[11];
              for(int i = 0; i <= 10; i++) {
                      double pos = start - (start - end) * i / 10.0;

                      // Set 2.0 seconds as the cycle duration
                      double duration = i/5.0;

                      // Use a discrete interpolator
                      KeyValue keyValue = new KeyValue(msg.translateXProperty(),
                                                       pos ,
                                                       Interpolator.DISCRETE);
                      frame[i] = new KeyFrame(Duration.seconds(duration), keyValue);
              }

              Timeline timeline = new Timeline();
              timeline.getKeyFrames().addAll(frame);
              timeline.setCycleCount(Timeline.INDEFINITE);
              timeline.setAutoReverse(true);
              timeline.play();
      }
}
```

Understanding the Ease-In Interpolator

The Interpolator.EASE_IN constant represents an ease-in interpolator. It starts the animation slowly for the first 20% of the time interval and accelerates afterward.

Understanding the Ease-Out Interpolator

The Interpolator.EASE_OUT constant represents an ease-out interpolator. It plays animation at a constant speed up to 80% of the time interval and slows down afterwards.

Understanding the Ease-Both Interpolator

The Interpolator.EASE_BOTH constant represents an ease-both interpolator. Its plays the animation slower in the first 20% and the last 20% of the time interval and maintains a constant speed otherwise.

Understanding the Spline Interpolator

The `Interpolator.SPLINE(double x1, double y1, double x2, double y2)` static method returns a spline interpolator. It uses a cubic spline shape to compute the speed of the animation at any point in the interval. The parameters (x1, y1) and (x2, y2) define the control points of the cubic spline shape with (0, 0) and (1, 1) as implicit anchor points. The values of the parameters are between 0.0 and 1.0.

The slope at a given point on the cubic spline shape defines the acceleration at that point. A slope approaching the horizontal line indicates deceleration whereas a slope approaching the vertical line indicates acceleration. For example, using (0, 0, 1, 1) as the parameters to the SPLINE method creates an interpolator with a constant speed whereas the parameters (0.5, 0, 0.5, 1.0) will create an interpolator that accelerates in the first half and decelerates in the second half. Please refer to `http://www.w3.org/TR/SMIL/smil-animation.html#animationNS-OverviewSpline` for more details.

Understanding the Tangent Interpolator

The `Interpolator.TANGENT` static method returns a tangent interpolator, which defines the behavior of an animation before and after a key frame. All other interpolators interpolate data between two key frames. If you specify a tangent interpolator for a key frame, it is used to interpolate data before and after the key frame. The animation curve is defined in terms of a tangent, which is known as in-tangent, at a specified duration before the key frame and a tangent, which is called an out-tangent, at a specified duration after the key frame. This interpolator is used only in timeline-based animations as it affects two intervals.

The TANGENT static method is overloaded.

- `Interpolator TANGENT(Duration t1, double v1, Duration t2, double v2)`

- `Interpolator TANGENT(Duration t, double v)`

In the first version, the parameters t1 and t2 are the duration before and after the key frame, respectively. The parameters v1 and v2 are the in-tangent and out-tangent values. That is, v1 is the tangent value at duration t1 and v2 is the tangent value at duration t2. The second version specifies the same value for both pairs.

Summary

In JavaFX, animation is defined as changing the property of a node over time. If the property that changes determines the location of the node, the animation in JavaFX will produce an illusion of motion. Not all animations have to involve motion; for example, changing the fill property of a Shape over time is an animation in JavaFX that does not involve motion.

Animation is performed over a period of time. A *timeline* denotes the progression of time during animation with an associated key frame at a given instant. A *key frame* represents the state of the node being animated at a specific instant on the timeline. A key frame has associated key values. A *key value* represents the value of a property of the node along with an interpolator to be used.

A timeline animation is used for animating any properties of a node. An instance of the Timeline class represents a timeline animation. Using a timeline animation involves the following steps: constructing key frames, creating a Timeline object with key frames, setting the animation properties, and using the play() method to run the animation. You can add key frames to a Timeline at the time of creating it or after. The Timeline instance keeps all key frames in an ObservableList<KeyFrame> object. The getKeyFrames() method returns the list. You can modify the list of key frames at any time. If the timeline animation is already running, you need to stop and restart it to pick up the modified list of key frames.

The Animation class contains several properties and methods to control animation such as playing, reversing, pausing, and stopping.

You can set up cue points on a timeline. Cue points are named instants on the timeline. An animation can jump to a cue point using the jumpTo(String cuePoint) method.

Using timeline animation is not easy in all cases. JavaFX contains a number of classes (known as *transitions*) that let you animate nodes using predefined properties. All transition classes inherit from the Transition class, which, in turn, inherits from the Animation class. The transition classes take care of creating the key frames and setting up the timeline. You need to specify the node, duration for the animation, and end values that are interpolated. Special transition classes are available to combine multiple animations that may run sequentially or in parallel. The Transition class contains an interpolator property that specifies the interpolator to be used during animation. By default, it uses Interpolator.EASE_BOTH, which starts the animation slowly, accelerates it, and slows it down toward the end.

An interpolator is an instance of the abstract Interpolator class. Its job is to compute the key values for the intermediate key frames during animation. JavaFX provides several built-in interpolators such as linear, discrete, ease-in, and ease-out. You can also implement a custom interpolator easily. You need to subclass the Interpolator class and override its curve() method. The curve() method is passed the time elapsed for the current interval. The time is normalized between 0.0 and 1.0. The return value of the method indicates the fraction of change in the animated property.

The next chapter will discuss how to incorporate different types of charts in a JavaFX application.

■ ■ ■

CHAPTER 23

Understanding Charts

In this chapter, you will learn

- What a chart is
- What the Chart API is in JavaFX
- How to create different types of charts using the Chart API
- How to style charts with CSS

What Is a Chart?

A chart is a graphical representation of data. Charts provide an easier way to analyze large volume of data visually. Typically, they are used for reporting purposes. Different types of charts exist. They differ in the way they represent the data. Not all types of charts are suitable for analyzing all types of data. For example, a line chart is suitable for understanding the comparative trend in data whereas a bar chart is suitable for comparing data in different categories.

JavaFX supports charts, which can be integrated in a Java application by writing few lines of code. It contains a comprehensive, extensible Chart API that provides built-in support for several types of charts.

Understating the Chart API

The Chart API consists of a number of predefined classes in the `javafx.scene.chart` package. Figure 23-1 shows a class diagram for classes representing different types of charts.

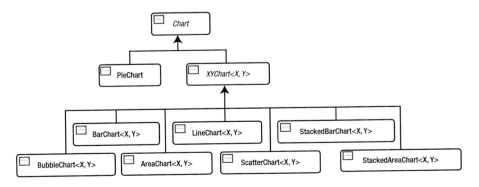

Figure 23-1. *A class diagram for the classes representing charts in JavaFX*

The abstract Chart is the base class for all charts. It inherits the Node class. Charts can be added to a scene graph. They can also be styled with CSS as any other nodes. I will discuss styling charts in the sections that discuss specific type of charts. The Chart class contains properties and methods common to all type of charts.

JavaFX divides charts into two categories:

- Charts having no-axis

- Charts having an x-axis and a y-axis

The PieChart class falls into the first category. It has no axis, and it is used to draw a pie chart.

The XYChart class falls into the second category. It is the abstract base class for all charts having two axes. Its subclasses, for example, LineChart, BarChart, etc., represent specific type of charts.

Every chart in JavaFX has three parts:

- A title

- A legend

- Content (or data)

Different types of charts define their data differently. The Chart class contains the following properties that are common to all types of charts:

- title

- titleSide

- legend

- legendSide

- legendVisible

- animated

The title property specifies the title for a chart. The titleSide property specifies the location of the title. By default, the title is placed above the chart content. Its value is one of the constants of the Side enum: TOP (default), RIGHT, BOTTOM, and LEFT.

Typically, a chart uses different types of symbols to represent data in different categories. A legend lists symbols with their descriptions. The legend property is a Node and it specifies the legend for the chart. By default, a legend is placed below the chart content. The legendSide property specifies the location of the legend, which is one of the constants of the Side enum: TOP, RIGHT, BOTTOPM (default), and LEFT. The legendVisible property specifies whether the legend is visible. By default, it is visible.

The animated property specifies whether the change in the content of the chart is shown with some type of animation. By default, it is true.

Styling Charts with CSS

You can style all types of charts. The Chart class defines properties common to all types of charts. The default CSS style-class name for a chart is *chart*. You can specify the legendSide, legendVisible, and titleSide properties for all charts in a CSS as shown:

```
.chart {
        -fx-legend-side: top;
        -fx-legend-visible: true;
        -fx-title-side: bottom;
}
```

Every chart defines two substructures:

- chart-title
- chart-content

The chart-title is a Label and the chart-content is a Pane. The following styles sets the background color for all charts to yellow and the title font to Arial 16px bold.

```
.chart-content {
        -fx-background-color: yellow;
}

.chart-title {
        -fx-font-family: "Aeial";
        -fx-font-size: 16px;
        -fx-font-weight: bold;
}
```

The default style-class name for legends is *chart-legend*. The following style sets the legend background color to light gray.

```
.chart-legend {
        -fx-background-color: lightgray;
}
```

Every legend has two substructures:

- chart-legend-item
- chart-legend-item-symbol

The chart-legend-item is a Label, and it represents the text in the legend. The chart-legend-item-symbol is a Node, and it represents the symbol next to the label, which is a circle by default. The following style sets the font size for the labels in legends to 10px and the legend symbols to an arrow.

```
.chart-legend-item {
        -fx-font-size: 16px;
}

.chart-legend-item-symbol {
        -fx-shape: "M0 -3.5 v7 l 4 -3.5z";
}
```

■ **Note** Many examples in this chapter use external resources such as CSS files. You will need to include the resources directory and its contents in CLASSPATH for all programs to work correctly. The resources directory is located under the src directory in the source code bundle that you can download from www.apress.com/source-code.

Data Used in Chart Examples

I will discuss different types of charts shortly. Charts will use data from Table 23-1, which has the actual and estimated population of some countries in the world. The data has been taken from the report published by the United Nations at http://www.un.org. The population values have been rounded.

Table 23-1. *Current and Estimated Populations (in Millions) of Some Countries in the World*

	1950	2000	2050	2100	2150	2200	2250	2300
China	555	1275	1395	1182	1149	1201	1247	1285
India	358	1017	1531	1458	1308	1304	1342	1372
Brazil	54	172	233	212	202	208	216	223
UK	50	59	66	64	66	69	71	73
USA	158	285	409	437	453	470	483	493

Understanding the PieChart

A pie chart consists of a circle divided into sectors of different central angles. Typically, a pie is circular. The sectors are also known as *pie pieces* or *pie slices*. Each sector in the circle represents a quantity of some kind. The central angle of the area of a sector is proportional to the quantity it represents. Figure 23-2 shows a pie chart that displays the population of five countries in the year 2000.

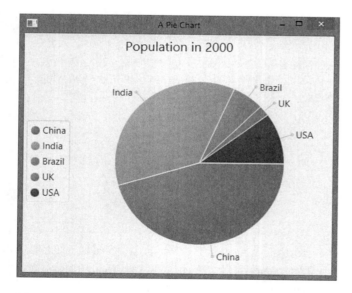

Figure 23-2. *A pie chart showing population of five countries in 2000*

An instance of the PieChart class represents a pie chart. The class contains two constructors:

- PieChart()
- PieChart(ObservableList<PieChart.Data> data)

The no-args constructor creates a pie chart with no content. You can add the content later using its data property. The second constructor creates a pie chart with the specified data as its content.

```
// Create an empty pie chart
PieChart chart = new PieChart();
```

A slice in a pie chart is specified as an instance of the PieChart.Data class. A slice has a name (or a label) and a pie value represented by the name and pieValue properties of the PieChart.Data class, respectively. The following statement creates a slice for a pie chart. The slice name is "China," and the pie value is 1275.

```
PieChar.Data chinaSlice = new PieChart.Data("China", 1275);
```

The content of a pie chart (all slices) is specified in an ObservableList<PieChart.Data>. The following snippet of code creates an ObservableList<PieChart.Data> and adds three pie slices to it.

```
ObservableList<PieChart.Data> chartData = FXCollections.observableArrayList();
chartData.add(new PieChart.Data("China", 1275));
chartData.add(new PieChart.Data("India", 1017));
chartData.add(new PieChart.Data("Brazil", 172));
```

Now, you can use the second constructor to create a pie chart by specifying the chart content:

```
// Create a pie chart with content
PieChart charts = new PieChart(chartData);
```

You will use populations of different countries in 2050 as the data for all our pie charts. Listing 23-1 contains a utility class. Its getChartData() method returns an ObservableList of PieChart.Data to be used as data for a pie chart. You will use this class in our examples in this section.

Listing 23-1. A Utility Class to Generate Data for Pie Charts

```
// PieChartUtil.java
package com.jdojo.chart;

import javafx.collections.FXCollections;
import javafx.collections.ObservableList;
import javafx.scene.chart.PieChart;

public class PieChartUtil {
        public static ObservableList<PieChart.Data> getChartData() {
                ObservableList<PieChart.Data> data = FXCollections. observableArrayList();
                data.add(new PieChart.Data("China", 1275));
                data.add(new PieChart.Data("India", 1017));
                data.add(new PieChart.Data("Brazil", 172));
                data.add(new PieChart.Data("UK", 59));
                data.add(new PieChart.Data("USA", 285));
                return data;
        }
}
```

The PieChart class contains several properties:

- data
- startAngle
- clockwise
- labelsVisible
- labelLineLength

The data property specifies the content for the chart in an ObservableList<PieChart.Data>.

The startAngle property specifies the angle an degrees to start the first pie slice. By default, it is zero degrees, which corresponds to three o'clock position. A positive startAngle is measured anticlockwise. For example, a 90-degree startAngle will start at the 12 o'clock position.

The clockwise property specifies whether the slices are placed clockwise starting at the startAngle. By default, it is true.

The labelsVisible property specifies whether the labels for slices are visible. Labels for slices are displayed close to the slice and they are placed outside the slices. The label for a slice is specified using the name property of the PieChart.Data class. In Figure 23-2, "China," India," Brazil,, etc., are labels for slices.

Labels and slices are connected through straight lines. The labelLineLength property specifies the length of those lines. Its default value is 20.0 pixels.

The program in Listing 23-2 uses a pie chart to display the population for five countries in 2000. The program creates an empty pie chart and sets its title. The legend is placed on the left side. Later, it sets the data for the chart. The data is generated in the getChartData() method, which returns an ObservableList<PieChart.Data> containing the name of the countries as the labels for pie slices and their populations as pie values. The program displays a window as shown in Figure 23-2.

Listing 23-2. Using the PieChart Class to Create a Pie Chart

```java
// PieChartTest.java
package com.jdojo.chart;

import javafx.application.Application;
import javafx.collections.ObservableList;
import javafx.geometry.Side;
import javafx.scene.Scene;
import javafx.scene.chart.PieChart;
import javafx.scene.layout.StackPane;
import javafx.stage.Stage;

public class PieChartTest extends Application {
        public static void main(String[] args) {
                Application.launch(args);
        }

        @Override
        public void start(Stage stage) {
                PieChart chart = new PieChart();
                chart.setTitle("Population in 2000");

                // Place the legend on the left side
                chart.setLegendSide(Side.LEFT);
```

```
            // Set the data for the chart
            ObservableList<PieChart.Data> chartData = PieChartUtil.getChartData();
            chart.setData(chartData);

            StackPane root = new StackPane(chart);
            Scene scene = new Scene(root);

            stage.setScene(scene);
            stage.setTitle("A Pie Chart");
            stage.show();
        }
}
```

Customizing Pie Slices

Each pie slice data is represented by a Node. The reference to the Node can be obtained using the getNode() method of the PieChart.Data class. The Node is created when the slices are added to the pie chart. Therefore, you must call the getNode() method on the PieChart.Data representing the slice after adding it to the chart. Otherwise, it returns null. The program in Listing 23-3 customizes all pie slices of a pie chart to add a tooltip to them. The tooltip shows the slice name, pie value, and percent pie value. The addSliceTooltip() method contains the logic to accessing the slice Nodes and adding the tooltips. You can customize pie slices to animate them, let the user drag them out from the pie using the mouse, etc.

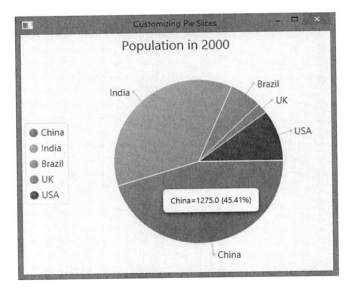

Figure 23-3. *A pie slice showing a tooltip with its pie value and percent of the total pie*

Listing 23-3. Adding Tooltips to Pie Slices

```java
// PieSliceTest.java
package com.jdojo.chart;

import javafx.application.Application;
import javafx.collections.ObservableList;
import javafx.geometry.Side;
import javafx.scene.Node;
import javafx.scene.Scene;
import javafx.scene.chart.PieChart;
import javafx.scene.control.Tooltip;
import javafx.scene.layout.StackPane;
import javafx.stage.Stage;

public class PieSliceTest extends Application {
        public static void main(String[] args) {
                Application.launch(args);
        }

        @Override
        public void start(Stage stage) {
                PieChart chart = new PieChart();
                chart.setTitle("Population in 2000");

                // Place the legend on the left side
                chart.setLegendSide(Side.LEFT);

                // Set the data for the chart
                ObservableList<PieChart.Data> chartData = PieChartUtil.getChartData();
                chart.setData(chartData);

                // Add a Tooltip to all pie slices
                this.addSliceTooltip(chart);

                StackPane root = new StackPane(chart);
                Scene scene = new Scene(root);
                stage.setScene(scene);
                stage.setTitle("Customizing Pie Slices");
                stage.show();
        }

        private void addSliceTooltip(PieChart chart) {
                // Compute the total pie value
                double totalPieValue = 0.0;
                for (PieChart.Data d : chart.getData()) {
                        totalPieValue += d.getPieValue();
                }
```

```
                    // Add a tooltip to all pie slices
                    for (PieChart.Data d : chart.getData()) {
                            Node sliceNode = d.getNode();
                            double pieValue = d.getPieValue();
                            double percentPieValue = (pieValue / totalPieValue) * 100;

                            // Create and install a Tooltip for the slice
                            String msg = d.getName() + "=" + pieValue +
                                        " (" + String.format("%.2f", percentPieValue) + "%)";
                            Tooltip tt = new Tooltip(msg);
                            tt.setStyle("-fx-background-color: yellow;" +
                                        "-fx-text-fill: black;");
                            Tooltip.install(sliceNode, tt);
                    }
            }
    }
}
```

Styling the PieChart with CSS

All properties, except the data property, defined in the PieChart class, can be styled using CSS as shown below.

```
.chart {
        -fx-clockwise: false;
        -fx-pie-label-visible: true;
        -fx-label-line-length: 10;
        -fx-start-angle: 90;
}
```

Four style classes are added to each pie slice added to a pie chart:

- chart-pie
- data<i>
- default-color<j>
- negative

The <i> in the style-class name data<i> is the slice index. The first slice has the class data0, the second data1, the third data2, etc.

The <j> in the style-class name default-color<j> is the color index of the series. In a pie chart, you can think of each slice as a series. The default CSS (Modena.css) defines eight series colors. If your pie slice has more than eight slices, the slice color will be repeated. The concept of series in a chart will be more evident when I discuss two-axis charts in the next section.

The *negative* style-class is added only when the data for the slice is negative.

Define a style for *chart-pie* style-class-name if you want that style to apply to all pie slices. The following style will set a white border with 2px of background insets for all pie slices. It will show a wider gap between two slices as you have set 2px insets.

```
.chart-pie {
        -fx-border-color: white;
        -fx-background-insets: 2;
}
```

You can define colors for pie slices using the following styles. It defines colors for only five slices. Slices beyond the sixth one will use default colors.

```
.chart-pie.default-color0 {-fx-pie-color: red;}
.chart-pie.default-color1 {-fx-pie-color: green;}
.chart-pie.default-color2 {-fx-pie-color: blue;}
.chart-pie.default-color3 {-fx-pie-color: yellow;}
.chart-pie.default-color4 {-fx-pie-color: tan;}
```

Using More Than Eight Series Colors

It is quite possible that you will have more than eight series (slices in a pie chart) in a chart and you do not want to repeat the colors for the series. The technique is discussed for a pie chart. However, it can be used for a 2-axis chart as well.

Suppose you want to use a pie that will display populations of ten countries. If you use the code for this pie chart, the colors for the ninth and tenth slices will be the same as the colors for the first and second slices, respectively. First, you need to define the colors for the ninth and tenth slices as shown in Listing 23-4.

Listing 23-4. Additional Series Colors

```
/* additional_series_colors.css */
.chart-pie.default-color8 {
        -fx-pie-color: gold;
}

.chart-pie.default-color9 {
        -fx-pie-color: khaki;
}
```

The pie slices and the legend symbols will be assigned style-class names such as default-color0, default-color2... default-color7. You need to identify the nodes for the slices and legend symbols associated with data items with index greater than 7 and replace their default-color <j> style-class name with the new ones. For example, for the ninth and tenth slices, the style-class names are default-color0 and default-color1 as the color series number is assigned as (dataIndex % 8). You will replace them with default-color9 and default-color10.

The program in Listing 23-5 shows how to change the colors for the slices and legend symbols. It adds ten slices to a pie chart. The setSeriesColorStyles() method replaces the style-class names for the slice nodes for the ninth and tenth slices and for their associated legend symbols. Figure 23-4 shows the pie chart. Notice the colors for "Germany" and "Indonesia" are gold and khaki as set in the CSS. Comment the last statement in the start() method, which is a call to the setSeriesColorStyles() and you will find that the colors for "Germany" and "Indonesia" will be the same as the colors for "China" and "India."

Listing 23-5. A Pie Chart Using Color Series up to Index 10

```
// PieChartExtraColor.java
package com.jdojo.chart;

import javafx.application.Application;
import javafx.collections.ObservableList;
import javafx.geometry.Side;
import javafx.scene.Node;
```

```
import javafx.scene.Scene;
import javafx.scene.chart.PieChart;
import javafx.scene.layout.StackPane;
import javafx.stage.Stage;

public class PieChartExtraColor extends Application {
        public static void main(String[] args) {
                Application.launch(args);
        }

        @Override
        public void start(Stage stage) {
                PieChart chart = new PieChart();
                chart.setTitle("Population in 2000");

                // Place the legend on the left side
                chart.setLegendSide(Side.LEFT);

                // Set the data for the chart
                ObservableList<PieChart.Data> chartData = PieChartUtil.getChartData();
                this.addData(chartData);
                chart.setData(chartData);

                StackPane root = new StackPane(chart);
                Scene scene = new Scene(root);
                scene.getStylesheets()
                    .add("resources/css/additional_series_colors.css");
                stage.setScene(scene);
                stage.setTitle("A Pie Chart with over 8 Slices");
                stage.show();

                // Override the default series color style-class-name for slices over 8.
                // Works only when you set it after the scene is visible
                this.setSeriesColorStyles(chart);
        }

        private void addData(ObservableList<PieChart.Data> data) {
                data.add(new PieChart.Data("Bangladesh", 138));
                data.add(new PieChart.Data("Egypt", 68));
                data.add(new PieChart.Data("France", 59));
                data.add(new PieChart.Data("Germany", 82));
                data.add(new PieChart.Data("Indonesia", 212));
        }

        private void setSeriesColorStyles(PieChart chart) {
                ObservableList<PieChart.Data> chartData = chart.getData();
                int size = chartData.size();
                for (int i = 8; i < size; i++) {
                        String removedStyle = "default-color" + (i % 8);
                        String addedStyle = "default-color" + (i % size);
```

```
                    // Reset the pie slice colors
                    Node node = chartData.get(i).getNode();
                    node.getStyleClass().remove(removedStyle);
                    node.getStyleClass().add(addedStyle);

                    // Reser the legend colors
                    String styleClass = ".pie-legend-symbol.data" + i +
                                         ".default-color" + (i % 8);
                    Node legendNode = chart.lookup(styleClass);
                    if (legendNode != null) {
                            legendNode.getStyleClass().remove(removedStyle);
                            legendNode.getStyleClass().add(addedStyle);
                    }
                }
            }
        }
}
```

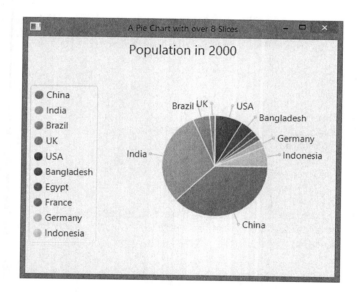

Figure 23-4. *A pie chart using over 8 slice colors*

Using Background Images for Pie Slices

You can also use a background image in a pie slice. The following style defines the background image for the first pie slice.

```
.chart-pie.data0 {
        -fx-background-image: url("china_flag.jpg");
}
```

Listing 23-6 contains the content of a CSS file named pie_slice.css. It defines styles that specify the background images used for pie slices, the preferred size of the legend symbols, and the length of the line joining the pie slices and their labels.

964

Listing 23-6. A CSS for Customizing Pie Slices

```
// pie_slice.css
/* Set a background image for pie slices */
.chart-pie.data0 {-fx-background-image: url("china_flag.jpg");}
.chart-pie.data1 {-fx-background-image: url("india_flag.jpg");}
.chart-pie.data2 {-fx-background-image: url("brazil_flag.jpg");}
.chart-pie.data3 {-fx-background-image: url("uk_flag.jpg");}
.chart-pie.data4 {-fx-background-image: url("usa_flag.jpg");}

/* Set the preferred size for legend symbols */
.chart-legend-item-symbol {
        -fx-pref-width: 100;
        -fx-pref-height: 30;
}

.chart {
        -fx-label-line-length: 10;
}
```

The program in Listing 23-7 creates a pie chart. It uses the same data as you have been using in our previous examples. The difference is that it sets a CSS defined in a *pie_slice.css* file.

```
// Set a CSS for the scene
scene.getStylesheets().addAll("resources/css/pie_slice.css");
```

The resulting window is shown in Figure 23-5. Notice that slices and legend symbols show the flags of the countries. It is important to keep in mind that you have matched the index of the chart data and the index in the CSS file to match countries and their flags.

■ **Tip**   It is also possible to style the shape of the line joining the pie slices and their labels, labels for the pie slices, and the legend symbols in a pie chart.

Listing 23-7. Using Pie Slices with a Background Image

```
// PieChartCustomSlice.java
package com.jdojo.chart;

import javafx.application.Application;
import javafx.collections.ObservableList;
import javafx.geometry.Side;
import javafx.scene.Scene;
import javafx.scene.chart.PieChart;
import javafx.scene.layout.StackPane;
import javafx.stage.Stage;

public class PieChartCustomSlice extends Application {
        public static void main(String[] args) {
                Application.launch(args);
        }
```

```
        @Override
        public void start(Stage stage) {
                PieChart chart = new PieChart();
                chart.setTitle("Population in 2000");

                // Place the legend on the left side
                chart.setLegendSide(Side.LEFT);

                // Set the data for the chart
                ObservableList<PieChart.Data> chartData = PieChartUtil.getChartData();
                chart.setData(chartData);

                StackPane root = new StackPane(chart);
                Scene scene = new Scene(root);

                // Set a CSS for the scene
                scene.getStylesheets().addAll("resources/css/pie_slice.css");

                stage.setScene(scene);
                stage.setTitle("Custom Pie Slices");
                stage.show();
        }
}
```

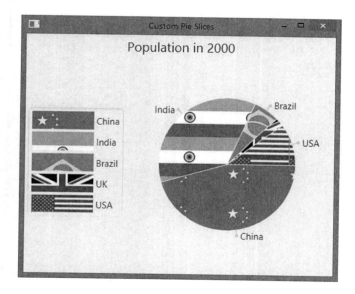

Figure 23-5. *A pie chart using a background image for its slices*

Understating the XYChart

An instance of a concrete subclass of the abstract XYChart<X,Y> class defines a two-axis chart. The generic type parameters X and Y are the data type of values plotted along x-axis and y-axis, respectively.

Representing Axes in an XYChart

An instance of a concrete subclass of the abstract Axis<T> class defines an axis in the XYChart. Figure 23-6 shows a class diagram for the classes representing axes.

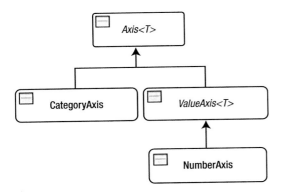

Figure 23-6. A class diagram for classes representing axes in an XYChart

The abstract Axis<T> class is the base class for all classes representing axes. The generic parameter T is the type of the values plotted along the axis, for example, String, Number, etc. An axis displays ticks and tick labels. The Axis<T> class contains properties to customize the ticks and tick labels. An axis can have a label, which is specified in the label property.

The concrete subclasses CategoryAxis and NumberAxis are used for plotting String and Number data values along an axis, respectively. They contain properties specific to the data values. For example, NumberAxis inherits ValueAxis<T> 's lowerBound and upperBound properties, which specify the lower and upper bounds of the data plotted on the axis. By default, the range of the data on an axis is automatically determined based on the data. You can turn off this feature by setting the autoRanging property in the Axis<T> class to false. The following snippet of code creates an instance of the CategoryAxis and NumberAxis and sets their labels.

```
CategoryAxis xAxis = new CategoryAxis();
xAxis.setLabel("Country");
NumberAxis yAxis = new NumberAxis();
yAxis.setLabel("Population (in millions)");
```

■ **Tip** Use a CategoryAxis to plot String values along an axis, and use a NumberAxis to plot numeric values along an axis.

Adding Data to an XYChart

Data in an XYChart represents points in the 2D plane defined by the x-axis and y-axis. A point in a 2D plane is specified using the x and y coordinates, which are values along the x-axis and y-axis, respectively. The data in an XYChart is specified as an ObservableList of named series. A series consists of multiple data items, which are points in the 2D plane. How the points are rendered depends on the chart type. For example, a scatter chart shows a symbol for a point whereas a bar chart shows a bar for a point.

An instance of the nested static XYChart.Data<X,Y> class represents a data item in a series. The class defines the following properties:

- XValue

- YValue

- extraValue

- node

- The XValue and YValue are the values for the data item along the x-axis and y-axis, respectively. Their data types need to match the data type of the x-axis and y-axis for the chart. The extraValue is an Object, which can be used to store any additional information for the data item. Its use depends of the chart type. If the chart does not use this value, you can use it for any other purpose: for example, to store the tooltip value for the data item. The node specifies the node to be rendered for the data item in the chart. By default, the chart will create a suitable node depending on the chart type.

Suppose both axes of an XYChart plot numeric values. The following snippet of code creates some data items for the chart. The data items are the population of China in 1950, 2000, and 2050.

```
XYChart.Data<Number, Number> data1 = new XYChart.Data<>(1950, 555);
XYChart.Data<Number, Number> data2 = new XYChart.Data<>(2000, 1275);
XYChart.Data<Number, Number> data3 = new XYChart.Data<>(2050, 1395);
```

An instance of the nested static XYChart.Series<X,Y> class represents a series of data items. The class defines the following properties:

- name

- data

- chart

- node

The name is the name of the series. The data is an ObservableList of XYChart.Data<X,Y>. The chart is a read-only reference to the chart to which the series belong. The node is a Node to display for this series. A default node is automatically created based on the chart type. The following snippet of code creates a series, sets its name, and adds data items to it.

```
XYChart.Series<Number, Number> seriesChina = new XYChart.Series<>();
seriesChina.setName("China");
seriesChina.getData().addAll(data1, data2, data3);
```

The data property of the XYChart class represents the data for the chart. It is an ObservableList of XYChart.Series class. The following snippet of code creates and adds the data for an XYChart chart assuming the data series seriesIndia and seriesUSA exists.

```
XYChart<Number, Number> chart = ...
chart.getData().addAll(seriesChina, seriesIndia, seriesUSA);
```

How the data items for a series are displayed depends on the specific chart type. Every chart type has a way to distinguishes one series from another.

You will reuse the same series of data items representing the population of some counties in some years several times. Listing 23-8 has code for a utility class. The class consists of two static methods that generate and return XYChart data. The getCountrySeries() method returns the list of series that plots the years along the x-axis and the corresponding populations along the y-axis. The getYearSeries() method returns a list of series that plots the countries along the x-axis and the corresponding populations along the y-axis. You will be calling these methods to get data for our XYCharts in subsequent sections.

Listing 23-8. A Utility Class to Generate Data Used in XYCharts

```
// XYChartDataUtil.java
package com.jdojo.chart;

import javafx.collections.FXCollections;
import javafx.collections.ObservableList;
import javafx.scene.chart.XYChart;

@SuppressWarnings("unchecked")
public class XYChartDataUtil {
        public static ObservableList<XYChart.Series<Number, Number>> getCountrySeries() {
                XYChart.Series<Number, Number> seriesChina = new XYChart.Series<>();
                seriesChina.setName("China");
                seriesChina.getData().addAll(new XYChart.Data<>(1950, 555),
                                        new XYChart.Data<>(2000, 1275),
                                        new XYChart.Data<>(2050, 1395),
                                        new XYChart.Data<>(2100, 1182),
                                        new XYChart.Data<>(2150, 1149));

                XYChart.Series<Number, Number> seriesIndia = new XYChart.Series<>();
                seriesIndia.setName("India");
                seriesIndia.getData().addAll(new XYChart.Data<>(1950, 358),
                                        new XYChart.Data<>(2000, 1017),
                                        new XYChart.Data<>(2050, 1531),
                                        new XYChart.Data<>(2100, 1458),
                                        new XYChart.Data<>(2150, 1308));

                XYChart.Series<Number, Number> seriesUSA = new XYChart.Series<>();
                seriesUSA.setName("USA");
                seriesUSA.getData().addAll(new XYChart.Data<>(1950, 158),
                                        new XYChart.Data<>(2000, 285),
                                        new XYChart.Data<>(2050, 409),
                                        new XYChart.Data<>(2100, 437),
                                        new XYChart.Data<>(2150, 453));
```

```
                ObservableList<XYChart.Series<Number, Number>> data =
                        FXCollections.<XYChart.Series<Number, Number>>observableArrayList();
                data.addAll(seriesChina, seriesIndia, seriesUSA);
                return data;
        }

        public static ObservableList<XYChart.Series<String, Number>> getYearSeries() {
                XYChart.Series<String, Number> series1950 = new XYChart.Series<>();
                series1950.setName("1950");
                series1950.getData().addAll(new XYChart.Data<>("China", 555),
                                            new XYChart.Data<>("India", 358),
                                            new XYChart.Data<>("Brazil", 54),
                                            new XYChart.Data<>("UK", 50),
                                            new XYChart.Data<>("USA", 158));

                XYChart.Series<String, Number> series2000 = new XYChart.Series<>();
                series2000.setName("2000");
                series2000.getData().addAll(new XYChart.Data<>("China", 1275),
                                            new XYChart.Data<>("India",1017),
                                            new XYChart.Data<>("Brazil", 172),
                                            new XYChart.Data<>("UK", 59),
                                            new XYChart.Data<>("USA", 285));

                XYChart.Series<String, Number> series2050 = new XYChart.Series<>();
                series2050.setName("2050");
                series2050.getData().addAll(new XYChart.Data<>("China", 1395),
                                            new XYChart.Data<>("India",1531),
                                            new XYChart.Data<>("Brazil", 233),
                                            new XYChart.Data<>("UK", 66),
                                            new XYChart.Data<>("USA", 409));

                ObservableList<XYChart.Series<String, Number>> data =
                        FXCollections.<XYChart.Series<String, Number>>observableArrayList();
                data.addAll(series1950, series2000, series2050);
                return data;
        }
}
```

Understating the BarChart

A bar chart renders the data items as horizontal or vertical rectangular bars. The lengths of the bars are proportional to the value of the data items.

An instance of the BarChart class represents a bar chart. In a bar chart, one axis must be a CategoryAxis and the other a ValueAxis/NumberAxis. The bars are drawn vertically or horizontally, depending on whether the CategoryAxis is the x-axis or the y-axis.

The BarChart contain two properties to control the distance between two bars in a category and the distance between two categories:

- barGap

- categoryGap

The default value is 4 pixels for the barGap and 10 pixels for the categoryGap.

The BarChart class contains three constructors to create bar charts by specifying axes, data, and gap between two categories.

- BarChart(Axis<X> xAxis, Axis<Y> yAxis)

- BarChart(Axis<X> xAxis, Axis<Y> yAxis, ObservableList<XYChart. Series<X,Y>> data)

- BarChart(Axis<X> xAxis, Axis<Y> yAxis, ObservableList<XYChart. Series<X,Y>> data, double categoryGap)

Notice that you must specify at least the axes when you create a bar chart. The following snippet of code creates two axes and a bar chart with those axes.

```
CategoryAxis xAxis = new CategoryAxis();
xAxis.setLabel("Country");

NumberAxis yAxis = new NumberAxis();
yAxis.setLabel("Population (in millions)");

// Create a bar chart
BarChart<String, Number> chart = new BarChart<>(xAxis, yAxis);
```

The bars in the chart will appear vertically as the category axis is added as the x-axis. You can populate the chart with data using its setData() method.

```
// Set the data for the chart
chart.setData(XYChartDataUtil.getYearSeries());
```

The program in Listing 23-9 shows how to create and populate a vertical bar chart as shown in Figure 23-7.

Listing 23-9. Creating a Vertical Bar Chart

```
// VerticalBarChart.java
package com.jdojo.chart;

import javafx.application.Application;
import javafx.collections.ObservableList;
import javafx.scene.Scene;
import javafx.scene.chart.BarChart;
import javafx.scene.chart.CategoryAxis;
import javafx.scene.chart.NumberAxis;
import javafx.scene.chart.XYChart;
import javafx.scene.layout.StackPane;
import javafx.stage.Stage;

public class VerticalBarChart extends Application {
        public static void main(String[] args) {
                Application.launch(args);
        }
```

```
        @Override
        public void start(Stage stage) {
                CategoryAxis xAxis = new CategoryAxis();
                xAxis.setLabel("Country");

                NumberAxis yAxis = new NumberAxis();
                yAxis.setLabel("Population (in millions)");

                BarChart<String, Number> chart = new BarChart<>(xAxis, yAxis);
                chart.setTitle("Population by Country and Year");

                // Set the data for the chart
                ObservableList<XYChart.Series<String,Number>> chartData =
                                                XYChartDataUtil.getYearSeries();
                chart.setData(chartData);

                StackPane root = new StackPane(chart);
                Scene scene = new Scene(root);
                stage.setScene(scene);
                stage.setTitle("A Vertical Bar Chart");
                stage.show();
        }
}
```

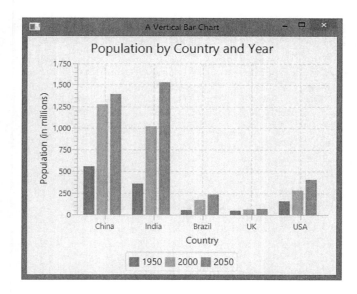

Figure 23-7. *A vertical bar chart*

The program in Listing 23-10 shows how to create and populate a horizontal bar chart as shown in Figure 23-8. The program needs to supply data to the chart in an ObservableList of XYChart. Series<Number,String>. The getYearSeries() method in the XYChartDataUtil class returns XYChart. Series<String,Number>. The getChartData() method in the program converts the series data from <String,Number> to <Number,String> format as needed to create a horizontal bar chart.

Listing 23-10. Creating a Horizontal Bar Chart

```java
// HorizontalBarChart.java
package com.jdojo.chart;

import javafx.application.Application;
import javafx.collections.FXCollections;
import javafx.collections.ObservableList;
import javafx.scene.Scene;
import javafx.scene.chart.BarChart;
import javafx.scene.chart.CategoryAxis;
import javafx.scene.chart.NumberAxis;
import javafx.scene.chart.XYChart;
import javafx.scene.layout.StackPane;
import javafx.stage.Stage;

public class HorizontalBarChart extends Application {
        public static void main(String[] args) {
                Application.launch(args);
        }

        @Override
        public void start(Stage stage) {
                NumberAxis xAxis = new NumberAxis();
                xAxis.setLabel("Population (in millions)");

                CategoryAxis yAxis = new CategoryAxis();
                yAxis.setLabel("Country");

                // Use a category axis as the y-axis for a horizontal bar chart
                BarChart<Number, String> chart = new BarChart<>(xAxis, yAxis);
                chart.setTitle("Population by Country and Year");

                // Set the data for the chart
                ObservableList<XYChart.Series<Number,String>> chartData =
                                this.getChartData(XYChartDataUtil.getYearSeries());
                chart.setData(chartData);

                StackPane root = new StackPane(chart);
                Scene scene = new Scene(root);
                stage.setScene(scene);
                stage.setTitle("A Horizontal Bar Chart");
                stage.show();
        }

        private ObservableList<XYChart.Series<Number,String>> getChartData(
                        ObservableList<XYChart.Series<String,Number>> oldData) {
                ObservableList<XYChart.Series<Number, String>> newData =
                        FXCollections.observableArrayList();
```

```
// Read (String, Number) from old data and convert it into
// (Nubmer, String) in new data
for(XYChart.Series<String, Number> oldSeries: oldData) {
        XYChart.Series<Number, String> newSeries = new XYChart.Series<>();
        newSeries.setName(oldSeries.getName());

        for(XYChart.Data<String, Number> oldItem: oldSeries.getData()) {
                XYChart.Data<Number, String> newItem =
                        new XYChart.Data<>(oldItem.getYValue(),
                                                oldItem.getXValue());
                newSeries.getData().add(newItem);
        }
        newData.add(newSeries);
}
return newData;
    }
}
```

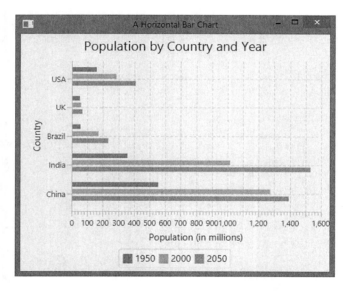

Figure 23-8. *A horizontal bar chart*

■ **Tip** Each bar in a bar chart is represented with a node. The user can interact with the bars in a bar chart, by adding event handlers to the nodes representing the data items. Please refer to the section on the pie chart for an example in which you added tooltips for the pie slices.

Styling the BarChart with CSS

By default, a BarChart is given style-class names: *chart* and *bar-chart*.

The following style sets the default values for the barGap and categoryGap properties for all bar charts to 0px and 20px. The bars in the same category will be placed next to each other.

```
.bar-chart {
        -fx-bar-gap: 0;
        -fx-category-gap: 20;
}
```

You can customize the appearance of the bars for each series or each data item in a series. Each data item in a BarChart is represented by a node. The node gets four default style-class names:

- chart-bar
- series<i>
- data<j>
- default-color<k>
- negative

In series<i>, <i> is the series index. For example, the first series is given the style-class name as series0, the second as series1, etc.

In data<j>, <j> is the index of the data item within a series. For example, the first data item in each series gets a style-class name as data0, the second as data1, etc.

In default-color<k>, <k> is the series color index. For example, each data item in the first series will get a style-class name as default-color0, in the second series default-color1, etc. The default CS defines only eight series colors. The value for <k> is equal to (i%8), where i is the series index. That is, series colors will repeat if you have more than eight series in a bar chart. Please refer to the pie chart section on how to use unique colors for series with index greater than eight. The logic will be similar to the one used for a pie chart, with a difference that, this time, you will be looking up the bar-legend-symbol within a series instead of a pie-legend-symbol.

The negative class is added if the data value is negative.

Each legend item in a bar chart is given the following style-class names:

- chart-bar
- series<i>
- bar-legend-symbol
- default-color<j>

In series<i>, <i> is the series index. In default-color<j>, <j> is the color index of the series. The legend color will repeat, as the bar colors do, if the number of series exceeds 8.

The following style defines the color of the bars for the all data items in series with series index 0, 8, 16, 24, etc., as blue.

```
.chart-bar.default-color0 {
        -fx-bar-fill: blue;
}
```

Understating the StackedBarChart

A stacked bar chart is a variation of the bar chart. In a stacked bar chart, the bars in a category are stacked. Except for the placement of the bars, it works the same way as the bar chart.

An instance of the StackedBarChart class represents a stacked bar chart. The bars can be placed horizontally or vertically. If the x-axis is a CategoryAxis, the bars are placed vertically. Otherwise, they are placed horizontally. Like the BarChart, one of the axes must be a CategoryAxis and the other a ValueAxis/NumberAxis.

The StackedBarChart class contains a categoryGap property that defines the gap between bars in adjacent categories. The default gap is 10px. Unlike the BarChart class, the StackedBarChart class does not contain a barGap property, as the bars in one category are always stacked.

The constructors of the StackedBarChart class are similar to the ones for the BarChart class. They let you specify the axes, chart data, and category gap.

There is one notable difference in a creating the CategoryAxis for the BarChart and the StackedBarChart. The BarChart reads the categories values from the data whereas you must explicitly add all category values to the CategoryAxis for a StackedBarChart.

```
CategoryAxis xAxis = new CategoryAxis();
xAxis.setLabel("Country");

// Must set the categories in a StackedBarChart explicitly. Otherwise,
// the chart will not show bars.
xAxis.getCategories().addAll("China," "India," "Brazil," "UK," "USA");

NumberAxis yAxis = new NumberAxis();
yAxis.setLabel("Population (in millions)");

StackedBarChart<String, Number> chart = new StackedBarChart<>(xAxis, yAxis);
```

The program in Listing 23-11 shows how to create a vertical stacked bar chart. The chart is shown in Figure 23-9. To create a horizontal stacked bar chart, use a CategoryAxis as the y-axis.

Listing 23-11. Creating a Vertical Stacked Bar Chart

```
// VerticalStackedBarChart.java
package com.jdojo.chart;

import javafx.application.Application;
import javafx.collections.ObservableList;
import javafx.scene.Scene;
import javafx.scene.chart.CategoryAxis;
import javafx.scene.chart.NumberAxis;
import javafx.scene.chart.StackedBarChart;
import javafx.scene.chart.XYChart;
import javafx.scene.layout.StackPane;
import javafx.stage.Stage;

public class VerticalStackedBarChart extends Application {
    public static void main(String[] args) {
        Application.launch(args);
    }
```

```java
@Override
public void start(Stage stage) {
        CategoryAxis xAxis = new CategoryAxis();
        xAxis.setLabel("Country");

        // Must set the categories in a StackedBarChart explicitly. Otherwise,
        // the chart will not show any bars.
        xAxis.getCategories().addAll("China," "India," "Brazil," "UK," "USA");

        NumberAxis yAxis = new NumberAxis();
        yAxis.setLabel("Population (in millions)");

        StackedBarChart<String, Number> chart =
                new StackedBarChart<>(xAxis, yAxis);
        chart.setTitle("Population by Country and Year");

        // Set the data for the chart
        ObservableList<XYChart.Series<String, Number>> chartData =
                XYChartDataUtil.getYearSeries();
        chart.setData(chartData);

        StackPane root = new StackPane(chart);
        Scene scene = new Scene(root);
        stage.setScene(scene);
        stage.setTitle("A Vertical Stacked Bar Chart");
        stage.show();
    }
}
```

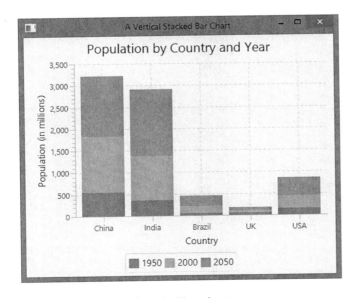

Figure 23-9. *A vertical stacked bar chart*

Styling the StackedBarChart with CSS

By default, a StackedBarChart is given style-class names: *chart* and *stacked-bar-chart*.

The following style sets the default value for the categoryGap properties for all stacked bar charts to 20px. The bars in a category will be placed next to each other.

```
.stacked-bar-chart {
        -fx-category-gap: 20;
}
```

In a stacked bar chart, the style-class names assigned to the nodes representing bars and legend items are the same as that of a bar chart. Please refer to the section *Styling the BarChart with CSS* for more details.

Understanding the ScatterChart

A bar chart renders the data items as symbols. All data items in a series use the same symbol. The location of the symbol for a data item is determined by the values on the data item along the x-axis and y-axis.

An instance of the ScatterChart class represents a scatter chart. You can use any type of Axis for the x-axis and y-axis. The class does not define any additional properties. It contains constructors that allow you to a create scatter chart by specifying axes and data.

- ScatterChart(Axis<X> xAxis, Axis<Y> yAxis)

- ScatterChart(Axis<X> xAxis, Axis<Y> yAxis, ObservableList<XYChart.
  Series<X,Y>> data)

Recall that the autoRanging for an Axis is set to true by default. If you are using numeric values in a scatter chart, make sure to set the autoRanging to false. It is important to set the range of the numeric values appropriately to get uniformly distributed points in the chart. Otherwise, the points may be located densely in a small area and it will be hard to read the chart.

The program in Listing 23-12 shows how to create and populate a scatter chart as shown in Figure 23-10. Both axes are numeric axes. The x-axis is customized. The autoRanging is set to false; reasonable lower and upper bounds are set. The tick unit is set to 50. If you do not customize these properties, the ScatterChart will automatically determine them and the chart data will be hard to read.

```
NumberAxis xAxis = new NumberAxis();
xAxis.setLabel("Year");
xAxis.setAutoRanging(false);
xAxis.setLowerBound(1900);
xAxis.setUpperBound(2300);
xAxis.setTickUnit(50);
```

Listing 23-12. Creating a Scatter Chart

```
// ScatterChartTest.java
package com.jdojo.chart;

import javafx.application.Application;
import javafx.collections.ObservableList;
import javafx.scene.Scene;
import javafx.scene.chart.NumberAxis;
```

```java
import javafx.scene.chart.ScatterChart;
import javafx.scene.chart.XYChart;
import javafx.scene.layout.StackPane;
import javafx.stage.Stage;

public class ScatterChartTest extends Application {
        public static void main(String[] args) {
                Application.launch(args);
        }

        @Override
        public void start(Stage stage) {
                NumberAxis xAxis = new NumberAxis();
                xAxis.setLabel("Year");

                // Customize the x-axis, so points are scattred uniformly
                xAxis.setAutoRanging(false);
                xAxis.setLowerBound(1900);
                xAxis.setUpperBound(2300);
                xAxis.setTickUnit(50);

                NumberAxis yAxis = new NumberAxis();
                yAxis.setLabel("Population (in millions)");

                ScatterChart<Number,Number> chart = new ScatterChart<>(xAxis, yAxis);
                chart.setTitle("Population by Year and Country");

                // Set the data for the chart
                ObservableList<XYChart.Series<Number,Number>> chartData =
                        XYChartDataUtil.getCountrySeries();
                chart.setData(chartData);

                StackPane root = new StackPane(chart);
                Scene scene = new Scene(root);
                stage.setScene(scene);
                stage.setTitle("A Scatter Chart");
                stage.show();
        }
}
```

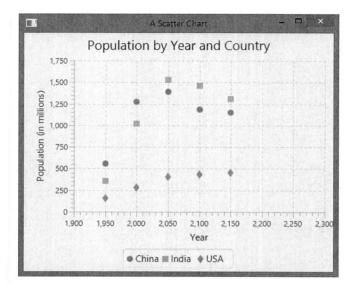

Figure 23-10. *A scatter chart*

■ **Tip**   You can use the node property for data items to specify symbols in a ScatterChart.

Styling the ScatterChart with CSS

The ScatterChart is not assigned any additional style-class name other than *chart*.

You can customize the appearance of the symbols for each series or each data item in a series. Each data item in a ScatterChart is represented by a node. The node gets four default style-class names:

- chart-symbol
- series<i>
- data<j>
- default-color<k>
- negative

Please refer to the section *Styling the BarChart with CSS* for more details on the meanings of <i>, <j>, and <k> in these style-class names.

Each legend item in a scatter chart is given the following style-class names:

- chart-symbol
- series<i>
- data<j>
- default-color<k>

The following style will display the data items in the first series as triangles filled in blue. Note that only eight color series are defined. After that, colors are repeated as discussed at length in the section on the pie chart.

```
.chart-symbol.default-color0 {
        -fx-background-color: blue;
        -fx-shape: "M5, 0L10, 5L0, 5z";
}
```

Understanding the LineChart

A line chart displays the data items in a series by connecting them by line segments. Optionally, the data points themselves may be represented by symbols. You can think of a line chart as a scatter chart with symbols in a series connected by straight line segments. Typically, a line chart is used to view the trend in data change over time or in a category.

An instance of the LineChart class represents a line chart. The class contains a createSymbols property, which is set to true by default. It controls whether symbols are created for the data points. Set it to false to show only straight lines connecting the data points in a series.

The LineChart class contains two constructors to create line charts by specifying axes and data.

- LineChart(Axis<X> xAxis, Axis<Y> yAxis)
- LineChart(Axis<X> xAxis, Axis<Y> yAxis, ObservableList<XYChart. Series<X,Y>> data)

The program in Listing 23-13 shows how to create and populate a line chart as shown in Figure 23-11. The program is the same as for using the scatter chart, except that it uses the LineChart class. The chart displays circles as symbols for data items. You can remove the symbols by using the following statement, after you create the line chart.

```
// Do not create the symbols for the data items
chart.setCreateSymbols(false);
```

Listing 23-13. Creating a Line Chart

```
// LineChartTest.java
package com.jdojo.chart;

import javafx.application.Application;
import javafx.collections.ObservableList;
import javafx.scene.Scene;
import javafx.scene.chart.LineChart;
import javafx.scene.chart.NumberAxis;
import javafx.scene.chart.XYChart;
import javafx.scene.layout.StackPane;
import javafx.stage.Stage;

public class LineChartTest extends Application {
        public static void main(String[] args) {
                Application.launch(args);
        }
```

```
@Override
public void start(Stage stage) {
        NumberAxis xAxis = new NumberAxis();
        xAxis.setLabel("Year");

        // Customize the x-axis, so points are scattred uniformly
        xAxis.setAutoRanging(false);
        xAxis.setLowerBound(1900);
        xAxis.setUpperBound(2300);
        xAxis.setTickUnit(50);

        NumberAxis yAxis = new NumberAxis();
        yAxis.setLabel("Population (in millions)");

        LineChart<Number,Number> chart = new LineChart<>(xAxis, yAxis);
        chart.setTitle("Population by Year and Country");

        // Set the data for the chart
        ObservableList<XYChart.Series<Number,Number>> chartData =
                        XYChartDataUtil.getCountrySeries();
        chart.setData(chartData);

        StackPane root = new StackPane(chart);
        Scene scene = new Scene(root);
        stage.setScene(scene);
        stage.setTitle("A Line Chart");
        stage.show();
    }
}
```

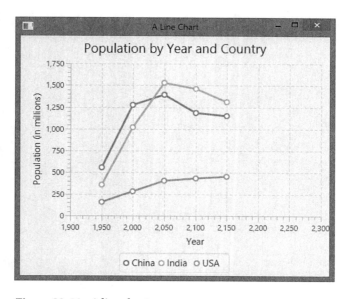

Figure 23-11. *A line chart*

Styling the LineChart with CSS

The LineChart is not assigned any additional style-class name other than *chart*. The following style specifies that the LineChart should not create symbols.

```
.chart {
        -fx-create-symbols: false;
}
```

The LineChart creates a Path node to show the lines connecting all data points for a series. A line for a series is assigned the following style-class names:

- chart-series-line
- series<i>
- default-color<j>

Here, <i> is the series index and <j> is the color index of the series.

If the createSymbols property is set to true, a symbol is created for each data point. Each symbol node is assigned the following style-class name:

- chart-line-symbol
- series<i>
- data<j>
- default-color<k>

Here, <i> is the series index, <j> is the data item index within a series, and <k> is the color index of the series.

Each series is assigned a legend item, which gets the following style-class names:

- chart-line-symbol
- series<i>
- default-color<j>

The following styles set the line stroke for the color index 0 of series to blue. The symbol is for the series is also shown in blue.

```
.chart-series-line.default-color0 {
        -fx-stroke: blue;
}

.chart-line-symbol.default-color0 {
        -fx-background-color: blue, white;
}
```

Understating the BubbleChart

A bubble chart is very similar to a scatter chart, except that it has the ability to represent three values for a data point. A bubble is used to represent a data items in series. You can set the radius of the bubble to represent the third value for the data point.

An instance of the BubbleChart class represents a bubble chart. The class does not define any new properties. A bubble chart uses the extraValue property of the XYChart.Data class to get the radius of the bubble. The bubble is an ellipse whose radii are scaled based on the scale used for the axes. Bubbles look more like a circle (or less stretched on one direction) if the scales for x-axis and y-axis are almost equal.

■ **Tip**   The bubble radius is set by default, which is scaled using the scale factor of the axes. You may not see the bubbles if the scale factor for axes are very small. To see the bubbles, set the extraValue in data items to a high value or use a higher scale factors along the axes.

The BubbleChart class defines two constructors:

- BubbleChart(Axis<X> xAxis, Axis<Y> yAxis)

- BubbleChart(Axis<X> xAxis, Axis<Y> yAxis, ObservableList<XYChart.
  Series<X,Y>> data)

The program in Listing 23-14 shows how to create a bubble chart as shown in Figure 23-12. The chart data is passed to the setBubbleRadius() method, which explicitly sets the extraValue for all data points to 20px. If you want to use the radii of bubbles to represent another dimension of data, you can set the extraValue accordingly.

Listing 23-14.   Creating a Bubble Chart

```java
// BubbleChartTest.java
package com.jdojo.chart;

import javafx.application.Application;
import javafx.collections.ObservableList;
import javafx.scene.Scene;
import javafx.scene.chart.BubbleChart;
import javafx.scene.chart.NumberAxis;
import javafx.scene.chart.XYChart;
import javafx.scene.layout.StackPane;
import javafx.stage.Stage;

public class BubbleChartTest extends Application {
        public static void main(String[] args) {
                Application.launch(args);
        }

        @Override
        public void start(Stage stage) {
                NumberAxis xAxis = new NumberAxis();
                xAxis.setLabel("Year");

                // Customize the x-axis, so points are scattred uniformly
                xAxis.setAutoRanging(false);
                xAxis.setLowerBound(1900);
                xAxis.setUpperBound(2300);
                xAxis.setTickUnit(50);

                NumberAxis yAxis = new NumberAxis();
                yAxis.setLabel("Population (in millions)");
```

```java
BubbleChart<Number,Number> chart = new BubbleChart<>(xAxis, yAxis);
chart.setTitle("Population by Year and Country");

// Get the data for the chart
ObservableList<XYChart.Series<Number,Number>> chartData =
        XYChartDataUtil.getCountrySeries();

// Set the bubble radius
setBubbleRadius(chartData);

// Set the data for the chart
chart.setData(chartData);

StackPane root = new StackPane(chart);
Scene scene = new Scene(root);
stage.setScene(scene);
stage.setTitle("A Bubble Chart");
stage.show();
}

private void setBubbleRadius(ObservableList<XYChart.Series<Number,Number>>
chartData) {
        for(XYChart.Series<Number,Number> series: chartData) {
                for(XYChart.Data<Number,Number> data : series.getData()) {
                        data.setExtraValue(20); // Bubble radius
                }
        }
}
}
```

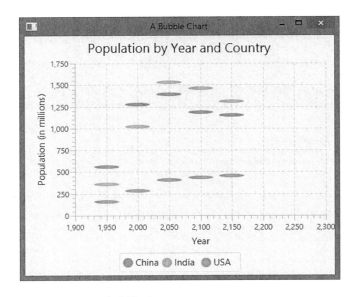

Figure 23-12. *A bubble chart*

Styling the BubbleChart with CSS

The BubbleChart is not assigned any additional style-class name other than *chart*.

You can customize the appearance of the bubbles for each series or each data item in a series. Each data item in a BubbleChart is represented by a node. The node gets four default style-class names:

- chart-bubble
- series<i>
- data<j>
- default-color<k>

Here, <i> is the series index, <j> is the data item index within a series, and <k> is the color index of the series.

Each series is assigned a legend item, which gets the following style-class names:

- chart-bubble
- series<i>
- bubble-legend-symbol
- default-color<k>

Here, <i> and <k> have the same meanings as described above.

The following style sets the fill color for the series color index 0 to blue. The bubbles and legend symbols for the data items in the first series will be displayed in blue. The color will repeat for series index 8, 16, 24, etc.

```
.chart-bubble.default-color0 {
    -fx-bubble-fill: blue;
}
```

Understating the AreaChart

The area chart is a variation of the line chart. It draws lines connecting all data items in a series and, additionally, fills the area between where the line and the x-axis is painted. Different colors are used to paint areas for different series.

An instance of the AreaChart represents an area chart. Like the LineChart, class, the class contains a createSymbols property to control whether symbols are drawn at the data points. By default, it is set to true. The class contains two constructors:

- AreaChart(Axis<X> xAxis, Axis<Y> yAxis)
- AreaChart(Axis<X> xAxis, Axis<Y> yAxis, ObservableList<XYChart. Series<X,Y>> data)

The program in Listing 23-15 shows how to create an area chart as shown in Figure 23-13. There is nothing new in the program, except that you have used the AreaChart class to create the chart. Notice that the area for a series overlays the area for the preceding series.

Listing 23-15. Creating an Area Chart

```java
// AreaChartTest.java
package com.jdojo.chart;

import javafx.application.Application;
import javafx.collections.ObservableList;
import javafx.scene.Scene;
import javafx.scene.chart.AreaChart;
import javafx.scene.chart.NumberAxis;
import javafx.scene.chart.XYChart;
import javafx.scene.layout.StackPane;
import javafx.stage.Stage;

public class AreaChartTest extends Application {
        public static void main(String[] args) {
                Application.launch(args);
        }

        @Override
        public void start(Stage stage) {
                NumberAxis xAxis = new NumberAxis();
                xAxis.setLabel("Year");

                // Customize the x-axis, so points are scattred uniformly
                xAxis.setAutoRanging(false);
                xAxis.setLowerBound(1900);
                xAxis.setUpperBound(2300);
                xAxis.setTickUnit(50);

                NumberAxis yAxis = new NumberAxis();
                yAxis.setLabel("Population (in millions)");

                AreaChart<Number,Number> chart = new AreaChart<>(xAxis, yAxis);
                chart.setTitle("Population by Year and Country");

                // Set the data for the chart
                ObservableList<XYChart.Series<Number,Number>> chartData =
                                XYChartDataUtil.getCountrySeries();
                chart.setData(chartData);

                StackPane root = new StackPane(chart);
                Scene scene = new Scene(root);
                stage.setScene(scene);
                stage.setTitle("An Area Chart");
                stage.show();
        }
}
```

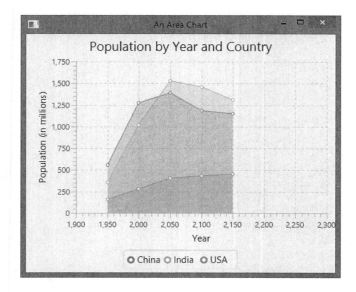

Figure 23-13. *An area chart*

Styling the AreaChart with CSS

The AreaChart is not assigned any additional style-class name other than *chart*. The following style specifies that the AreaChart should not create symbols for representing the data points.

```
.chart {
        -fx-create-symbols: false;
}
```

Each series in an AreaChart is represented by a Group containing two Path nodes. One Path represents the line segment connecting all data points in the series, and another Path represents the area covered by the series. The Path node representing the line segment for a series is assigned the following style-class names:

- chart-series-area-line
- series<i>
- default-color<j>

Here, <i> is the series index and <j> is the color index of the series.
The Path node representing the area for a series is assigned the following style-class names:

- chart-series-area-fill
- series<i>
- default-color<j>

Here, <i> is the series index and <j> is the color index of the series.

If the `createSymbols` property is set to true, a symbol is created for each data point. Each symbol node is assigned the following style-class name:

- `chart-area-symbol`
- `series<i>`
- `data<j>`
- `default-color<k>`

Here, `<i>` is the series index, `<j>` is the data item index within a series, and `<k>` is the color index of the series.

Each series is assigned a legend item, which gets the following style-class names:

- `chart-area-symbol`
- `series<i>`
- `area-legend-symbol`
- `default-color<j>`

Here, `<i>` is the series index and `<j>` is the color index of the series.

The following style sets the area fill color for the color index 0 for the series to blue with 20% opacity. Make sure to set transparent colors for the area fills as areas overlap in an `AreaChart`.

```
.chart-series-area-fill.default-color0 {
        -fx-fill: rgba(0, 0, 255, 0.20);
}
```

The following styles set the blue as the color for symbols, line segment, and legend symbol for the color index 0 for the series.

```
/* Data point symbols color */
.chart-area-symbol.default-color0. {
        -fx-background-color: blue, white;
}

/* Series line segment color */
.chart-series-area-line.default-color0 {
        -fx-stroke: blue;
}

/* Series legend symbol color */
.area-legend-symbol.default-color0 {
        -fx-background-color: blue, white;
}
```

Understanding the StackedAreaChart

The stacked area chart is a variation of the area chart. It plots data items by painting an area for each series. Unlike the area chart, areas for series do not overlap; they are stacked.

An instance of the StackedAreaChart represents a stacked area chart. Like the AreaChart class, the class contains a createSymbols property. The class contains two constructors:

- StackedAreaChart(Axis<X> xAxis, Axis<Y> yAxis)

- StackedAreaChart(Axis<X> xAxis, Axis<Y> yAxis, ObservableList<XYChart.Series<X,Y>> data)

The program in Listing 23-16 shows how to create a stacked area chart as shown in Figure 23-14. The program is the same as the one that created an AreaChart, except that you have used the StackedAreaChart class to create the chart.

Listing 23-16. Creating a Stacked Area Chart

```java
// StackedAreaChartTest.java
package com.jdojo.chart;

import javafx.application.Application;
import javafx.collections.ObservableList;
import javafx.scene.Scene;
import javafx.scene.chart.StackedAreaChart;
import javafx.scene.chart.NumberAxis;
import javafx.scene.chart.XYChart;
import javafx.scene.layout.StackPane;
import javafx.stage.Stage;

public class StackedAreaChartTest extends Application {
        public static void main(String[] args) {
                Application.launch(args);
        }

        @Override
        public void start(Stage stage) {
                NumberAxis xAxis = new NumberAxis();
                xAxis.setLabel("Year");

                // Customize the x-axis, so points are scattred uniformly
                xAxis.setAutoRanging(false);
                xAxis.setLowerBound(1900);
                xAxis.setUpperBound(2300);
                xAxis.setTickUnit(50);

                NumberAxis yAxis = new NumberAxis();
                yAxis.setLabel("Population (in millions)");

                StackedAreaChart<Number,Number> chart = new StackedAreaChart<>(xAxis, yAxis);
                chart.setTitle("Population by Year and Country");
```

```
        // Set the data for the chart
        ObservableList<XYChart.Series<Number,Number>> chartData =
                XYChartDataUtil.getCountrySeries();
        chart.setData(chartData);

        StackPane root = new StackPane(chart);
        Scene scene = new Scene(root);
        stage.setScene(scene);
        stage.setTitle("A Stacked Area Chart");
        stage.show();
    }
}
```

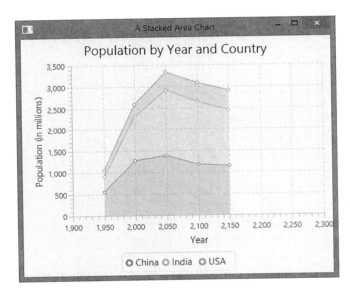

Figure 23-14. *A stacked area chart*

Styling the StackedAreaChart with CSS

Styling a StackedAreaChart is the same as styling an AreaChart. Please refer to the section *Styling the AreaChart with CSS* for more details.

Customizing XYChart Appearance

You have seen how to apply chart-specific CSS styles to customize the appearance of charts. In this section, you will look at some more ways to customize XYChart plot and axes. The XYChart class contains several boolean properties to change the chart plot appearance:

- alternativeColumnFillVisible
- alternativeRowFillVisible
- horizontalGridLinesVisible

- verticalGridLinesVisible
- horizontalZeroLineVisible
- verticalZeroLineVisible

The chart area is divided into a grid of columns and rows. Horizontal lines are drawn passing through major ticks on the y-axis making up rows. Vertical lines are drawn passing through major ticks on the x-axis making up columns.

Setting Alternate Row/Column Fill

The alternativeColumnFillVisible and alternativeRowFillVisible control whether alternate columns and rows in the grid are filled. By default, alternativeColumnFillVisible is set to false and alternativeRowFillVisible is set to true.

As of time of this writing, setting the alternativeColumnFillVisible and alternativeRowFillVisible properties do not have any effects in JavaFX 8, which uses Modena CSS by default. There are two solutions. You can use the Caspian CSS for your application using the following statement:

```
Application.setUserAgentStylesheet(Application.STYLESHEET_CASPIAN);
```

The other solution is to include the following styles in your application CSS.

```
.chart-alternative-column-fill {
        -fx-fill: #eeeeee;
        -fx-stroke: transparent;
        -fx-stroke-width: 0;
}

.chart-alternative-row-fill {
        -fx-fill: #eeeeee;
        -fx-stroke: transparent;
        -fx-stroke-width: 0;
}
```

These styles are taken from Caspian CSS. These styles set the fill and stroke properties to null in Modena CSS.

Showing Zero Line Axes

The axes for a chart may not include zero lines. Whether zero lines are includes depends on the lower and upper bounds represented by the axes. The horizontalZeroLineVisible and verticalZeroLineVisible control whether zero lines should be visible. By default, they are visible. Note that the zero line for an axis is visible only when the axis has both positive and negative data to plot. If you have negative and positive values along the y-axis, an additional horizontal axis will appear indicating the zero value along the y-axis. The same rule applies for values along the x-axis. If the range for an axis is set explicitly using its lower and upper bounds, the visibility of the zero line depends on whether zero falls in the range.

Showing Grid Lines

The horizontalGridLinesVisible and verticalGridLinesVisible specify whether the horizontal and vertical grid lines are visible. By default, both are set to true.

Formatting Numeric Tick Labels

Sometimes, you may want to format the values displayed on a numeric axis. You want to format the labels for the numeric axis for different reasons:

- You want to add prefixes or suffixes to the tick labels. For example, you may want to display a number 100 as $100 or 100M.

- You may be supplying the chart scaled data to get an appropriate scale value for the axis. For example, for the actual value 100, you may be supplying 10 to the chart. In this case, you would like to display the actual value 100 for the label.

The ValueAxis class contains a tickLabelFormatter property, which is a StringConverter and it is used to format tick labels. By default, tick labels for a numeric axis are formatted using a default formatter. The default formatter is an instance of the static inner class NumberAxis.DefaultFormatter.

In our examples of XYChart, you had set the label for the y-axis to "Population (in millions)" to indicate that the tick values on the axis are in millions. You can use a label formatter to append "M" to the tick values to indicate the same meaning. The following snippet of code will accomplish this.

```
NumberAxis yAxis = new NumberAxis();
yAxis.setLabel("Population");

// Use a formatter for tick labels on y-axis to apend
// M (for millioms) to the population value
yAxis.setTickLabelFormatter(new StringConverter<Number>() {
        @Override
        public String toString(Number value) {
                // Append M to the value
                return Math.round(value.doubleValue()) + "M";
        }

        @Override
        public Number fromString(String value) {
                // Strip M from the value
                value = value.replaceAll("M", "");
                return Double.parseDouble(value);
        }
});
```

The NumberAxis.DefaultFormatter works better for adding a prefix or suffix to tick labels. This formatter is kept in sync with the autoRanging property for the axis. You can pass a prefix and a suffix to the constructor. The following snippet of code accomplishes the same thing as the above snippet of code.

```
NumberAxis yAxis = new NumberAxis();
yAxis.setLabel("Population");
yAxis.setTickLabelFormatter(new NumberAxis.DefaultFormatter(yAxis, null, "M"));
```

You can customize several visual aspects of an Axis. Please refer to the API documentation for the Axis class and its subclasses for more details.

The program in Listing 23-17 shows how to customize a line chart. The chart is shown in Figure 23-15. It formats the tick labels on the y-axis to append "M" to the label value. It hides the grid lines and shows the alternate column fills.

Listing 23-17. Formatting Tick Labels and Customizing Chart Plot

```java
// CustomizingCharts.java
package com.jdojo.chart;

import javafx.application.Application;
import javafx.scene.Scene;
import javafx.scene.chart.LineChart;
import javafx.scene.chart.NumberAxis;
import javafx.scene.layout.StackPane;
import javafx.stage.Stage;

public class CustomizingCharts extends Application {
        public static void main(String[] args) {
                Application.launch(args);
        }

        @Override
        public void start(Stage stage) {
                // Set caspian CSS to get alternate column fills
                // until modena CSS is fixed
                Application.setUserAgentStylesheet(Application.STYLESHEET_CASPIAN);

                NumberAxis xAxis = new NumberAxis();
                xAxis.setLabel("Year");

                // CUstomize the x-axis, so points are scattred uniformly
                xAxis.setAutoRanging(false);
                xAxis.setLowerBound(1900);
                xAxis.setUpperBound(2300);
                xAxis.setTickUnit(50);

                NumberAxis yAxis = new NumberAxis();
                yAxis.setLabel("Population");

                // Use a formatter for tick labels on y-axis to append
                // M (for millioms) to the population value
                yAxis.setTickLabelFormatter(new NumberAxis.DefaultFormatter(yAxis, null, "M"));

                LineChart<Number, Number> chart = new LineChart<>(xAxis, yAxis);
                chart.setTitle("Population by Year and Country");

                // Set the data for the chart
                chart.setData(XYChartDataUtil.getCountrySeries());
```

```
            // Show alternate column fills
            chart.setAlternativeColumnFillVisible(true);
            chart.setAlternativeRowFillVisible(false);

            // Hide grid lines
            chart.setHorizontalGridLinesVisible(false);
            chart.setVerticalGridLinesVisible(false);

            StackPane root = new StackPane(chart);
            Scene scene = new Scene(root);
            stage.setScene(scene);
            stage.setTitle("Customizing Tick Labels and Chart Plot");
            stage.show();
        }
    }
```

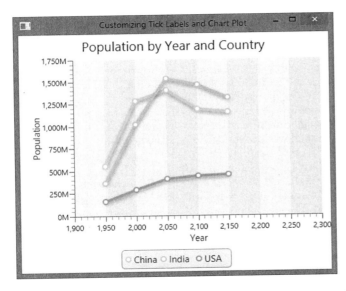

Figure 23-15. *A line chart with formatted tick labels and customized plot*

Summary

A chart is a graphical representation of data. Charts provide an easier way to analyze large volume of data visually. Typically, they are used for reporting purposes. Different types of charts exist. They differ in the way they represent the data. Not all types of charts are suitable for analyzing all types of data. For example, a line chart is suitable for understanding the comparative trend in data whereas a bar chart is suitable for comparing data in different categories.

JavaFX supports charts, which can be integrated in a Java application by writing few lines of code. It contains a comprehensive, extensible Chart API that provides built-in support for several types of charts. The Chart API consists of a number of predefined classes in the javafx.scene.chart package. Few of those classes are Chart, XYChart, PieChart, BarChart and LineChart.

The abstract Chart is the base class for all charts. It inherits the Node class. Charts can be added to a scene graph. They can also be styled with CSS as any other nodes. Every chart in JavaFX has three parts: a title, a legend, and data. Different types of charts define their data differently. The Chart class contains the properties to deal with the title and legend.

A chart can be animated. The animated property in the Chart class specifies whether the change in the content of the chart is shown with some type of animation. By default, it is true.

A pie chart consists of a circle divided into sectors of different central angles. Typically, a pie is circular. The sectors are also known as *pie pieces* or *pie slices*. Each sector in the circle represents a quantity of some kind. The central angle of the area of a sector is proportional to the quantity it represents. An instance of the PieChart class represents a pie chart.

A bar chart renders the data items as horizontal or vertical rectangular bars. The lengths of the bars are proportional to the value of the data items. An instance of the BarChart class represents a bar chart.

A stacked bar chart is a variation of the bar chart. In a stacked bar chart, the bars in a category are stacked. Except for the placement of the bars, it works the same way as the bar chart. An instance of the StackedBarChart class represents a stacked bar chart.

A scatter chart renders the data items as symbols. All data items in a series use the same symbol. The location of the symbol for a data item is determined by the values on the data item along the x-axis and y-axis. An instance of the ScatterChart class represents a scatter chart.

A line chart displays the data items in a series by connecting them by line segments. Optionally, the data points themselves may be represented by symbols. You can think of a line chart as a scatter chart with symbols in a series connected by straight line segments. Typically, a line chart is used to view the trend in data change over time or in a category. An instance of the LineChart class represents a line chart.

A bubble chart is very similar to a scatter chart, except that it has ability to represent three values for a data point. A bubble is used to represent a data items in series. You can set the radius of the bubble to represent the third value for the data point. An instance of the BubbleChart class represents a bubble chart.

The area chart is a variation of the line chart. It draws lines connecting all data items in a series and, additionally, fills the area between where the line and the x-axis is painted. Different colors are used to paint areas for different series. An instance of the AreaChart represents an area chart.

The stacked area chart is a variation of the area chart. It plots data items by painting an area for each series. Unlike the area chart, areas for series do not overlap; they are stacked. An instance of the StackedAreaChart represents a stacked area chart.

Besides using CSS to customize the appearance of charts, the Chart API provides several properties and methods to customize charts' appearance such as adding alternate row/column fills, showing zero line axes, showing grid lines, and formatting numeric tick labels.

The next chapter will discuss how to work with images in JavaFX using the Image API.

■ ■ ■

CHAPTER 24

Understanding the Image API

In this chapter, you will learn:

- What the Image API is
- How to load an image
- How to view an image in an `ImageView` node
- How to perform image operations such as reading/writing pixels, creating an image from scratch, and saving the image to the file system
- How to take the snapshot of nodes and scenes

What Is the Image API?

JavaFX provides the Image API that lets you load and display images, and read/write raw image pixels. A class diagram for the classes in the image API is shown in Figure 24-1. All classes are in the `javafx.scene.image` package. The API lets you

- Load an image in memory
- Display an image as a node in a scene graph
- Read pixels from an image
- Write pixels to an image
- Convert a node in a scene graph to an image and save it to the local file system

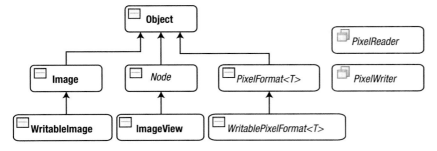

Figure 24-1. *A class diagram for classes in the image API*

An instance of the Image class represents an image in memory. You can construct an image in a JavaFX application by supplying pixels to a WritableImage instance.

An ImageView is a Node. It is used to display an Image in a scene graph. If you want to display an image in an application, you need to load the image in an Image and display the Image in an ImageView.

Images are constructed from pixels. Data for pixels in an image may be stored in different formats. A PixelFormat defines how the data for a pixel for a given format is stored. A WritablePixelFormat represents a destination format to write pixels with full pixel color information.

The PixelReader and PixelWriter interfaces define methods to read from an Image and write data to a WritableImage. Besides an Image, you can read pixels from and write pixels to any surface that contain pixels.

I will cover examples of using these classes in the sections to follow.

Loading an Image

An instance of the Image class is an in-memory representation of an image. The class supports BMP, PNG, JPEG, and GIF image formats. It loads an image from a source, which can be specified as a string URL or an InputStream. It can also scale the original image while loading.

The Image class contains several constructors that let you specify the properties for the loaded image:

- Image(InputStream is)

- Image(InputStream is, double requestedWidth, double requestedHeight, boolean preserveRatio, boolean smooth)

- Image(String url)

- Image(String url, boolean backgroundLoading)

- Image(String url, double requestedWidth, double requestedHeight, boolean preserveRatio, boolean smooth)

- Image(String url, double requestedWidth, double requestedHeight, boolean preserveRatio, boolean smooth, boolean backgroundLoading)

There is no ambiguity of the source of the image if an InputStream is specified as the source. If a string URL is specified as the source, it could be a valid URL or a valid path in the CLASSPATH. If the specified URL is not a valid URL, it is used as a path and the image source will be searched on the path in the CLASSPATH.

```
// Load an image from local machine using an InputStream
String sourcePath = "C:\\mypicture.png";
Image img = new Image(new FileInputStream(sourcePath));
```

```
// Load an image from a URL
Image img = new Image("http://jdojo.com/wp-content/uploads/2013/03/randomness.jpg");
```

```
// Load an image from the CLASSPATH. The image is located in the resources.picture package
Image img = new Image("resources/picture/randomness.jpg");
```

In the above statement, the specified URL resources/picture/randomness.jpg is not a valid URL. The Image class will treat it as a path expecting it to exist in the CLASSPATH. It treats the resource.picture as a package and the randomness.jpg as a resource in that package.

Specifying the Image-Loading Properties

Some constructors let you specify some image-loading properties to controls the quality of the image and the loading process:

- requestedWidth
- requestedHeight
- preserveRatio
- smooth
- backgroundLoading

The requestedWidth and requestedHeight properties specify the scaled width and height of the image. By default, an image is loaded in its original size.

The preserveRatio property specifies whether to preserve the aspect ratio of the image while scaling. By default, it is false.

The smooth property specifies the quality of the filtering algorithm to be used in scaling. By default, it is false. If it is set to true, a better quality filtering algorithm is used, which slows down the image-loading process a bit.

The backgroundLoading property specifies whether to load the image asynchronously. By default, the property is set to false and the image is loaded synchronously. The loading process starts when the Image object is created. If this property is set to true, the image is loaded asynchronously in a background thread.

Reading the Loaded-Image Properties

The Image class contains the following read-only properties:

- width
- height
- progress
- error
- exception

The width and height properties are the width and height of the loaded image, respectively. They are zero if the image failed to load.

The progress property indicates the progress in loading the image data. It is useful to know the progress when the backgroundLoading property is set to true. Its value is between 0.0 and 1.0 where 0.0 indicates zero percent loading and 1.0 indicates hundred percent loading. When the backgroundLoading property is set to false (the default), its value is 1.0. You can add a ChangeListener to the progress property to know the progress in image loading. You may display a text as a placeholder for an image while it is loading and update the text with the current progress in the ChangeListener.

```
// Load an image in the background
String imagePath = "resources/picture/randomness.jpg";
Boolean backgroundLoading = true;
Image image = new Image(imagePath, backgroundLoading);

// Print the loading progress on the standard output
image.progressProperty().addListener((prop, oldValue, newValue) -> {
        System.out.println("Loading:" + Math.round(newValue.doubleValue() * 100.0) + "%");
});
```

The error property indicates whether an error occurred while loading the image. If it is true, the exception property specifies the Exception that caused the error. At the time of this writing, TIFF image format is not supported on Windows. The following snippet of code attempts to load a TIFF image on Windows XP and it produces an error. The code contains an error handling logic that adds a ChangeListener to the error property if backgroundLoading is true. Otherwise, it checks for the value of the error property.

```
String imagePath = "resources/picture/test.tif";
Boolean backgroundLoading = false;
Image image = new Image(imagePath, backgroundLoading);

// Add a ChangeListener to the error property for background loading and
// check its value for non-backgroudn loading
if (image.isBackgroundLoading()) {
        image.errorProperty().addListener((prop, oldValue, newValue) -> {
                if (newValue) {
                        System.out.println("An error occurred while loading the image.\n" +
                                "Error message: " + image.getException().getMessage());
                }
        });
}
else if (image.isError()) {
        System.out.println("An error occurred while loading the image.\n" +
                        "Error message: " + image.getException().getMessage());
}
```

```
An error occurred while loading the image.
Error message: No loader for image data
```

Viewing an Image

An instance of the ImageView class is used to display an image loaded in an Image object. The ImageView class inherits from the Node class, which makes an ImageView suitable to be added to a scene graph. The class contains several constructors:

- ImageView()

- ImageView(Image image)

- ImageView(String url)

The no-args constructor creates an ImageView without an image. Use the image property to set an image. The second constructor accepts the reference of an Image. The third constructor lets you specify the URL of the image source. Internally, it creates an Image using the specified URL.

```
// Create an empty ImageView and set an Image for it later
ImageView imageView = new ImageView();
imageView.setImage(new Image("resources/picture/randomness.jpg"));
```

```
// Create an ImageView with an Image
ImageView imageView = new ImageView(new Image("resources/picture/randomness.jpg"));

// Create an ImageView with the URL of the image source
ImageView imageView = new ImageView("resources/picture/randomness.jpg");
```

The program in Listing 24-1 shows how to display an image in a scene. It loads an image in an Image object. The image is scaled without preserving the aspect ratio. The Image object is added to an ImageView, which is added to an HBox. Figure 24-2 shows the window.

Listing 24-1. Displaying an Image in an ImageView Node

```
// ImageTest.java
package com.jdojo.image;

import javafx.application.Application;
import javafx.scene.Scene;
import javafx.scene.image.Image;
import javafx.scene.image.ImageView;
import javafx.scene.layout.HBox;
import javafx.stage.Stage;

public class ImageTest extends Application {
        public static void main(String[] args) {
                Application.launch(args);
        }

        @Override
        public void start(Stage stage) {
                String imagePath = "resources/picture/randomness.jpg";

                // Scale the iamge to 200 X 100
                double requestedWidth = 200;
                double requestedHeight = 100;
                boolean preserveRatio = false;
                boolean smooth = true;
                Image image = new Image(imagePath,
                                        requestedWidth,
                                        requestedHeight,
                                        preserveRatio,
                                        smooth);
                ImageView imageView = new ImageView(image);

                HBox root = new HBox(imageView);
                Scene scene = new Scene(root);
                stage.setScene(scene);
                stage.setTitle("Displaying an Image");
                stage.show();
        }
}
```

Figure 24-2. *A window with an image*

Multiple Views of an Image

An Image loads an image in memory from its source. You can have multiple views of the same Image. An ImageView provides one of the views.

You have an option to resize the original image while loading, displaying, or at both times. Which option you choose to resize an image depends on the requirement at hand.

- Resizing an image in an Image object resizes the image permanently in memory and all views of the image will use the resized image. Once an Image is resized, its size cannot be altered. You may want to reduce the size of an image in an Image object to save memory.

- Resizing an image in an ImageView resizes the image only for this view. You can resize the view of an image in an ImageView even after the image has been displayed.

We have already discussed how to resize an image in an Image object. In this section, we will discuss resizing an image in an ImageView.

Similar to the Image class, the ImageView class contains the following four properties to control the resizing of view of an image.

- fitWidth
- fitHeight
- preserveRatio
- smooth

The fitWidth and fitHeight properties specify the resized width and height of the image, respectively. By default, they are zero, which means that the ImageView will use the width and height of the loaded image in the Image.

The preserveRatio property specifies whether to preserve the aspect ratio of the image while resizing. By default, it is false.

The smooth property specifies the quality of the filtering algorithm to be used in resizing. Its default value is platform dependent. If it is set to true, a better quality filtering algorithm is used.

The program in Listing 24-2 loads an image in an Image object in original size. It creates three ImageView objects of the Image specifying different sizes. Figure 24-3 shows the three images. The image shows a junk school bus and a junk car. The image is used with a permission from Richard Castillo (http://www.digitizedchaos.com).

Listing 24-2. Displaying the Same Image in Different ImageView in Different Sizes

```java
// MultipleImageViews.java
package com.jdojo.image;

import javafx.application.Application;
import javafx.scene.Scene;
import javafx.scene.image.Image;
import javafx.scene.image.ImageView;
import javafx.scene.layout.HBox;
import javafx.stage.Stage;

public class MultipleImageViews extends Application {
        public static void main(String[] args) {
                Application.launch(args);
        }

        @Override
        public void start(Stage stage) {
                // Load an image in its original size
                String imagePath = "resources/picture/school_bus.jpg";
                Image image = new Image(imagePath);

                // Create three views of different sizes of the same image
                ImageView view1 = getImageView(image, 100, 50, false);
                ImageView view2 = getImageView(image, 100, 50, true);
                ImageView view3 = getImageView(image, 100, 100, true);

                HBox root = new HBox(10, view1, view2, view3);
                Scene scene = new Scene(root);
                stage.setScene(scene);
                stage.setTitle("Multiple Views of an Image");
                stage.show();
        }

        private ImageView getImageView(Image image,
                                       double fitWidth,
                                       double fitHeight,
                                       boolean preserveRation) {
                ImageView view = new ImageView(image);
                view.setFitWidth(fitWidth);
                view.setFitHeight(fitHeight);
                view.setPreserveRatio(preserveRation);
                view.setSmooth(true);
                return view;
        }
}
```

Figure 24-3. *Three views of the same image*

Viewing an Image in a Viewport

A viewport is a rectangular region to view part of a graphics. It is common to use scrollbars in conjunction with a viewport. As the scrollbars are scrolled, the viewport shows different part of the graphics.

An ImageView lets you define a viewport for an image. In JavaFX, a viewport is an instance of the javafx.geometry.Rectangle2D object. A Rectangle2D is immutable. It is defined in terms of four properties: minX, minY, width, and height. The (minX, minY) value defines the location of the upper-left corner of the rectangle. The width and height properties specify its size. You must specify all properties in the constructor.

```
// Create a viewport located at (0, 0) and of isze 200 X 100
Rectangle2D viewport = new Rectangle2D(0, 0, 200,100);
```

The ImageView class contains a viewport property, which provides a viewport into the image displayed in the ImageView. The viewport defines a rectangular region in the image. The ImageView shows only the region of the image that falls inside the viewport. The location of the viewport is defined relative to the image, not the ImageView. By default, the viewport of an ImageView is null and the ImageView shows the whole image.

The following snippet of code loads an image in its original size in an Image. The Image is set as the source for an ImageView. A viewport 200 X 100 in size is set for the ImageView. The viewport is located at (0, 0). This shows in the ImageView the top-left 200 X 100 region of the image

```
String imagePath = "resources/picture/school_bus.jpg";
Image image = new Image(imagePath);
imageView = new ImageView(image);
Rectangle2D viewport = new Rectangle2D(0, 0, 200, 100);
imageView.setViewport(viewport);
```

The following snippet of code will change the view port to show the 200 X 100 lower-right region of the image.

```
double minX = image.getWidth() - 200;
double minY = image.getHeight() - 100;
Rectangle2D viewport2 = new Rectangle2D(minX, minY, 200, 100);
imageView.setViewport(viewport2);
```

■ **Tip**   The Rectangle2D class is immutable. Therefore, you need to create a new viewport every time you want to move the viewport into the image.

The program in Listing 24-3 loads an image into an ImageView. It sets a viewport for the ImageView. You can drag the mouse, while pressing the left, right, or both buttons, to scroll to the different parts of the image into the view.

Listing 24-3. Using a Viewport to View Part of an Image

```java
// ImageViewPort.java
package com.jdojo.image;

import javafx.application.Application;
import javafx.geometry.Rectangle2D;
import javafx.scene.Scene;
import javafx.scene.image.Image;
import javafx.scene.image.ImageView;
import javafx.scene.input.MouseEvent;
import javafx.scene.layout.HBox;
import javafx.stage.Stage;

public class ImageViewPort extends Application {
        private static final double VIEWPORT_WIDTH = 300;
        private static final double VIEWPORT_HEIGHT = 200;
        private double startX;
        private double startY;
        private ImageView imageView;

        public static void main(String[] args) {
                Application.launch(args);
        }

        @Override
        public void start(Stage stage) {
                // Load an image in its original size
                String imagePath = "resources/picture/school_bus.jpg";
                Image image = new Image(imagePath);
                imageView = new ImageView(image);

                // Set a viewport for the ImageView
                Rectangle2D viewport = new Rectangle2D(0, 0, VIEWPORT_WIDTH, VIEWPORT_HEIGHT);
                imageView.setViewport(viewport);

                // Set the mouse pressed and mouse dragged event hanlders
                imageView.setOnMousePressed(this::handleMousePressed);
                imageView.setOnMouseDragged(this::handleMouseDragged);

                HBox root = new HBox(imageView);
                Scene scene = new Scene(root);
                stage.setScene(scene);
                stage.setTitle("Viewing an Image in a Viewport");
                stage.show();
        }
```

```
    private void handleMousePressed(MouseEvent e) {
        startX = e.getX();
        startY = e.getY();
    }

    private void handleMouseDragged(MouseEvent e) {
        // How far the mouse was dragged
        double draggedDistanceX = e.getX() - startX;
        double draggedDistanceY = e.getY() - startY;

        // Reset the starting point for the next drag
        // if the user keeps the mouse pressed and drags again
        startX = e.getX();
        startY = e.getY();

        // Get the minX and minY of the current viewport
        double curMinX = imageView.getViewport().getMinX();
        double curMinY = imageView.getViewport().getMinY();

        // Move the new viewport by the dragged distance
        double newMinX = curMinX + draggedDistanceX;
        double newMinY = curMinY + draggedDistanceY;

        // Make sure the viewport does not fall outside the image area
        newMinX = clamp(newMinX, 0, imageView.getImage().getWidth() - VIEWPORT_WIDTH);
        newMinY = clamp(newMinY, 0, imageView.getImage().getHeight() - VIEWPORT_HEIGHT);

        // Set a new viewport
        imageView.setViewport(
                new Rectangle2D(newMinX, newMinY, VIEWPORT_WIDTH, VIEWPORT_HEIGHT));
    }

    private double clamp(double value, double min, double max) {
        if (value < min) {
            return min;
        } else if (value > max) {
            return max;
        }

        return value;
    }
}
```

The program declares a few class and instance variables. The VIEWPORT_WIDTH and VIEWPORT_HEIGHT are constants holding the width and height of the viewport. The startX and startY instance variables will hold the x and y coordinates of the mouse when the mouse is pressed or dragged. The ImageView instance variable holds the reference of the ImageView. We need this reference in the mouse dragged event handler.

The starting part of the start() method is simple. It creates an Image, an ImageView, and sets a viewport for the ImageView. Then, it sets the mouse pressed and dragged event handlers to the ImageView.

```
// Set the mouse pressed and mouse dradded event hanlders
imageView.setOnMousePressed(this::handleMousePressed);
imageView.setOnMouseDragged(this::handleMouseDragged);
```

In the handleMousePressed() method, we store the coordinates of the mouse in the startX and startY instance variables. The coordinates are relative to the ImageView.

```
startX = e.getX();
startY = e.getY();
```

The handleMousePressed() method computes the new location of the viewport inside the image because of the mouse drag and sets a new viewport at the new location. First, it computes the dragged distance for the mouse along the x-axis and y-axis.

```
// How far the mouse was dragged
double draggedDistanceX = e.getX() - startX;
double draggedDistanceY = e.getY() - startY;
```

You reset the startX and startY values to mouse location that triggered the current mouse dragged event. This is important to get the correct dragged distance when the user keeps the mouse pressed, drags it, stops without releasing the mouse, and drags it again.

```
// Reset the starting point for the next drag
// if the user keeps the mouse pressed and drags again
startX = e.getX();
startY = e.getY();
```

You compute the new location of the upper-left corner of the viewport. You always have a viewport in the ImageView. The new viewport will be located at the dragged distance from the old location.

```
// Get the minX and minY of the current viewport
double curMinX = imageView.getViewport().getMinX();
double curMinY = imageView.getViewport().getMinY();

// Move the new viewport by the dragged distance
double newMinX = curMinX + draggedDistanceX;
double newMinY = curMinY + draggedDistanceY;
```

It is fine to place the viewport outside the region of the image. The viewport simply displays an empty area when it falls outside the image area. To restrict the viewport inside the image area, we clamp the location of the viewport.

```
// Make sure the viewport does not fall outside the image area
newMinX = clamp(newMinX, O, imageView.getImage().getWidth() - VIEWPORT_WIDTH);
newMinY = clamp(newMinY, O, imageView.getImage().getHeight() - VIEWPORT_HEIGHT);
```

Finally, we set a new viewport using the new location.

```
// Set a new viewport
imageView.setViewport(new Rectangle2D(newMinX, newMinY, VIEWPORT_WIDTH, VIEWPORT_HEIGHT));
```

■ **Tip**   It is possible to scale or rotate the ImageView and set a viewport to view the region of the image defined by the viewport.

Understanding Image Operations

JavaFX supports reading pixels from an image, writing pixels to an image, and creating a snapshot of the scene. It supports creating an image from scratch. If an image is writable, you can also modify the mage in memory and save it to the file system. The image API provides access to each pixel in the image. It supports reading and writing one pixel or a chunk of pixel at a time. This section will discuss operations supported by the image API with simple examples.

Pixel Formats

The image API in JavaFX gives you access to each pixel in an image. A pixel stores information about its color (red, green, blue) and opacity (alpha). The pixel information can be stored in several formats.

An instance the PixelFormat<T extends Buffer> represents the layout of data for a pixel. You need to know the pixel format when you read the pixels from an image. You need to specify the pixel format when you write pixels to an image. The WritablePixelFormat class inherits from the PixelFormat class and its instance represents a pixel format that can store full color information. An instance of the WritablePixelFormat class is used when writing pixels to an image.

Both class PixelFormat and its subclass WritablePixelFormat are abstract. The PixelFormat class provides several static methods to obtain instances to PixelFormat and WritablePixelFormat abstract classes. Before we discuss how to get an instance of the PixelFormat, let us discuss types of storage formats available for storing the pixel data.

A PixelFormat has a type that specifies the storage format for a single pixel. The constants of the PixelFormat.Type enum represent different type of storage formats:

- BYTE_RGB

- BYTE_BGRA

- BYTE_BGRA_PRE

- BYTE_INDEXED

- INT_ARGB

- INT_ARGB_PRE

In the BYTE_RGB format, the pixels are assumed opaque. The pixels are stored in adjacent byes as red, green, and blue, in order.

In the BYTE_BGRA format, pixels are stored in adjacent byes as blue, green, red, and alpha in order. The color values (red, green, and blue) are not pre-multiplied with the alpha value.

The BYTE_BGRA_PRE type format is similar to BYTE_BGRA, except that in BYTE_BGRA_PRE the stored color component values are pre-multiplied by the alpha value.

In the BYTE_INDEXED format, a pixel is as a single byte. A separate lookup list of colors is provided. The single byte value for the pixel is used as an index in the lookup list to get the color value for the pixel.

In the INT_ARGB format, each pixel is stored in a 32-bit integer. Bytes from the most significant byte (MSB) to the least significant byte (LSB) store alpha, red, green, and blue values. The color values (red, green, and blue) are not pre-multiplied with the alpha value. The following snippet of code shows how to extract components from a pixel value in this format.

```
int pixelValue = get the value for a pixel...
int alpha = (pixelValue >> 24) & 0xff;
int red   = (pixelValue >> 16) & 0xff;
int green = (pixelValue >>  8) & 0xff;
int blue  = pixelValue & 0xff;
```

The INT_ARGB_PRE format is similar to the INT_ARGB format, except that INT_ARGB_PRE stores the color values (red, green, and blue) pre-multiplied with the alpha value.

Typically, you need to create a WritablePixelFormat when you write pixels to create a new image. When you read pixels from an image, the pixel reader will pride you a PixelFormat instance that will tell you how the color information in the pixels are stored. The following snippet of code creates some instances of WritablePixelFormat class:

```
import javafx.scene.image.PixelFormat;
import javafx.scene.image.WritablePixelFormat;
import java.nio.ByteBuffer;
import java.nio.IntBuffer;
...
// BYTE_BGRA Format type
WritablePixelFormat<ByteBuffer> format1 = PixelFormat.getByteBgraInstance();

// BYTE_BGRA_PRE Format type
WritablePixelFormat<ByteBuffer> format2 = PixelFormat.getByteBgraPreInstance();

// INT_ARGB Format type
WritablePixelFormat<IntBuffer> format3 = PixelFormat.getIntArgbInstance();

// INT_ARGB_PRE Format type
WritablePixelFormat<IntBuffer> format4 = PixelFormat.getIntArgbPreInstance();
```

Pixel format classes are not useful without pixel information. After all, they describes layout of information in a pixel! We will use these classes when we read and write image pixels in the sections to follow. Their use will be obvious in the examples.

Reading Pixels from an Image

An instance of the PixelReader interface is used to read pixels from an image. Use the getPixelReader() method of the Image class to obtains a PixelReader. The PixelReader interface contains the following methods:

- int getArgb(int x, int y)
- Color getColor(int x, int y)

- Void getPixels(int x, int y, int w, int h,
  WritablePixelFormat<ByteBuffer> pixelformat, byte[] buffer, int offset,
  int scanlineStride)

- void getPixels(int x, int y, int w, int h,
  WritablePixelFormat<IntBuffer> pixelformat, int[] buffer, int offset,
  int scanlineStride)

- <T extends Buffer> void getPixels(int x, int y, int w, int h,
  WritablePixelFormat<T> pixelformat, T buffer, int scanlineStride)

- PixelFormat getPixelFormat()

The PixelReader interface contains methods to read one pixel or multiple pixels at a time. Use the getArgb() and getColor() methods to read the pixel at the specified (x, y) coordinate. Use the getPixels() method to read pixels in bulk. Use the getPixelFormat() method to get the PixelFormat that best describes the storage format for the pixels in the source.

The getPixelReader() method of the Image class returns a PixelReader only if the image is readable. Otherwise, it returns null. Am image may not be readable if it is not fully loaded yet, it had an error during loading, or its format does not support reading pixels.

```
Image image = new Image("resources/picture/ksharan.jpg");

// Get the pixel reader
PixelReader pixelReader = image.getPixelReader();
if (pixelReader == null) {
        System.out.println("Connot read pixels from the image");
} else {
        // Read image pixels
}
```

Once you have a PixelReader, you can read pixels invoking one of its methods. The program in Listing 24-4 shows how to read pixels from an image. The code is self-explanatory.

- The start() method creates an Image. The Image is loaded synchronously.

- The logic to read the pixels is in the readPixelsInfo() method. The method receives a fully loaded Image. It uses the getColor() method of the PixelReader to get the pixel at a specified location. It prints the colors for all pixels. At the end, it prints the pixel format, which is BYTE_RBG.

Listing 24-4. Reading Pixels from an Image

```
// ReadPixelInfo.java
package com.jdojo.image;

import javafx.application.Application;
import javafx.scene.Scene;
import javafx.scene.image.Image;
import javafx.scene.image.ImageView;
import javafx.scene.image.PixelFormat;
import javafx.scene.image.PixelReader;
import javafx.scene.layout.HBox;
import javafx.scene.paint.Color;
import javafx.stage.Stage;
```

```java
public class ReadPixelInfo extends Application {
        public static void main(String[] args) {
                Application.launch(args);
        }

        @Override
        public void start(Stage stage) {
                String imagePath = "resources/picture/ksharan.jpg";
                Image image = new Image(imagePath);
                ImageView imageView = new ImageView(image);
                HBox root = new HBox(imageView);
                Scene scene = new Scene(root);
                stage.setScene(scene);
                stage.setTitle("Reading Pixels from an Image");
                stage.show();

                // Read pixels from the image
                this.readPixelsInfo(image);
        }

        private void readPixelsInfo(Image image) {
                // Obtain the pixel reader from the image
                PixelReader pixelReader = image.getPixelReader();
                if (pixelReader == null) {
                        System.out.println("Connot read pixels from the image");
                        return;
                }

                // Get image width and height
                int width = (int)image.getWidth();
                int height = (int)image.getHeight();

                // Read all pixels
                for(int y = 0; y < height; y++) {
                        for(int x = 0; x < width; x++) {
                                Color color = pixelReader.getColor(x, y);
                                System.out.println("Color at (" + x + ", " + y + ") = " +
                                                color);
                        }
                }

                PixelFormat format = pixelReader.getPixelFormat();
                PixelFormat.Type formatType = format.getType();
                System.out.println("Pixel format type: " + formatType);
        }
}
```

```
Color at (0, 0) = 0xb5bb41ff
Color at (1, 0) = 0xb0b53dff
...
Color at (233, 287) = 0x718806ff
Color at (234, 287) = 0x798e0bff
Pixel format type: BYTE_RGB
```

Reading pixels in bulk is little more difficult than reading one pixel at a time. The difficulty arises from the setup information that you have to provide to the getPixels() method. We will repeat the above example by reading all pixels in bulk using the following method of the PixelReader.

```
void getPixels(int x, int y,
               int width, int height,
               WritablePixelFormat<ByteBuffer> pixelformat,
               byte[] buffer,
               int offset,
               int scanlineStride)
```

The method reads the pixels from rows in order. The pixels in the first row are read, then the pixels from the second row, and so on. It is important that you understand the meaning of all parameters to the method:

The method reads the pixels of a rectangular region in the source.

The x and y coordinates of the upper-left corner of the rectangular region are specified in the x and y arguments.

The width and height arguments specify the width and height of the rectangular region.

The pixelformat specifies the format of the pixel that should be used to store the read pixels in the specified buffer.

The buffer is a byte array in which the PixelReader will store the read pixels. The length of the array must be big enough to store all read pixels.

The offset specifies the starting index in the buffer array to store the first pixel data. Its value of zero indicates that the data for the first pixel will start at index 0 in the buffer.

The scanlineStride specify the distance between the start of one row of data In the buffer to the start of the next row of data. Suppose you have two pixels in a row and you want to read in the BYTE_BGRA format taking four bytes for a pixel. One row of data can be stored in eight bytes. If you specify 8 as the argument value, the data for the next row will start in the buffer just after the data for the previous row data ends. If you specify the argument value 10, last two bytes will be empty for each row of data. The first row pixels will be stored from index 0 to 7. The indexes 8 and 9 will be empty (or not written). Indexes 10 to 17 will store pixel data for the second row leaving indexes 19 and 19 empty. You may want to specify a bigger value for the agrument than needed to store one row of pixel data if you want to fill the empty slots with yor won values later. Specifying avlaue less than needed will overwrite part of the data in the previous row.

The following snippet of code shows hwo to real all pixels from am image in a byte array.in BYTE_BGRA format.

```
Image image = ...
PixelReader pixelReader = image.getPixelReader();

int x = 0;
int y = 0;
int width = (int)image.getWidth();
int height = (int)image.getHeight();
```

```
int offset = 0;
int scanlineStride = width * 4;
byte[] buffer = new byte[width * height * 4];

// Get a WritablePixelFormat for the BYTE_BGRA format type
WritablePixelFormat<ByteBuffer> pixelFormat = PixelFormat.getByteBgraInstance();

// Read all pixels at once
pixelReader.getPixels(x, y,
                        width, height,
                        pixelFormat,
                        buffer,
                        offset,
                        scanlineStride);
```

The x and y coordinates of the upper-left corner of the rectangular region to be read are set to zero. The width and height of the region are set to the width and height of the image. This sets up the arguments to read the entire image.

You want to read the pixel data into the buffer starting at index 0, so you set the offset argument to 0.

You want to read the pixel data in BYTE_BGRA format type, which takes 4 bytes to store data for one pixel. We have set the scanlineStride argument value, which is the length of a row data, to width * 4, so a row data starts at the next index from where the previous row data ended.

You get an instance of the WritablePixelFormat to read the data in the BYTE_BGRA format type. Finally, we call the getPixels() method of the PixelReader to read the pixel data. The buffer will be filled with the pixel data when the getPixels() method returns.

■ **Tip** Setting the value for the scanlineStride argument and the length of the buffer array depends on the pixelFormat argument. Other versions of the getPixels() method allows reading pixel data in different formats.

The program in Listing 24-5 has the complete source code to read pixels in bulk. After reading all pixels, it decodes the color components in the byte array for the pixel at (0, 0). It reads the pixel at (0, 0) using the getColor() method. The pixel data at (0, 0) obtained through both methods are printed on the standard output.

Listing 24-5. Reading Pixels from an Image in Bulk

```
// BulkPixelReading.java
package com.jdojo.image;

import java.nio.ByteBuffer;
import javafx.application.Application;
import javafx.scene.Scene;
import javafx.scene.image.Image;
import javafx.scene.image.ImageView;
import javafx.scene.image.PixelFormat;
import javafx.scene.image.PixelReader;
import javafx.scene.image.WritablePixelFormat;
```

```java
import javafx.scene.layout.HBox;
import javafx.scene.paint.Color;
import javafx.stage.Stage;

public class BulkPixelReading extends Application {
        public static void main(String[] args) {
                Application.launch(args);
        }

        @Override
        public void start(Stage stage) {
                String imagePath = "resources/picture/ksharan.jpg";
                Image image = new Image(imagePath);
                ImageView imageView = new ImageView(image);

                HBox root = new HBox(imageView);
                Scene scene = new Scene(root);
                stage.setScene(scene);
                stage.setTitle("Reading Pixels in Bulk");
                stage.show();

                // Read pixels in bulk from the image
                this.readPixelsInfo(image);
        }

        private void readPixelsInfo(Image image) {
                // Obtain the pixel reader from the image
                PixelReader pixelReader = image.getPixelReader();
                if (pixelReader == null) {
                        System.out.println("Connot read pixels from the image");
                        return;
                }

                // Read all pixels in a byte array in one go
                int x = 0;
                int y = 0;
                int width = (int)image.getWidth();
                int height = (int)image.getHeight();
                int offset = 0;
                int scanlineStride = width * 4;
                byte[] buffer = new byte[width * height * 4];

                // Get a WritablePixelFormat
                WritablePixelFormat<ByteBuffer> pixelFormat = PixelFormat.getByteBgraInstance();

                // Read all pixels at once
                pixelReader.getPixels(x, y,
                                        width, height,
                                        pixelFormat,
                                        buffer,
                                        offset,
                                        scanlineStride);
```

```
            // Read the color of the pixel at (0, 0)
            int blue = (buffer[0] & 0xff);
            int green = (buffer[1] & 0xff);
            int red = (buffer[2] & 0xff);
            int alpha = (buffer[3] & 0xff);
            System.out.println("red=" + red +  ", green=" + green +
                               ", blue=" + blue +  ", alpha=" + alpha);

            // Get the color of the pixel at (0, 0)
            Color c = pixelReader.getColor(0, 0);
            System.out.println("red=" + (int)(c.getRed() * 255) +
                               ", green=" + (int)(c.getGreen() * 255) +
                               ", blue=" + (int)(c.getBlue() * 255) +
                               ", alpha=" + (int)(c.getOpacity() * 255));
        }
}
```

```
red=181, green=187, blue=65, alpha=255
red=181, green=187, blue=65, alpha=255
```

Writing Pixels to an Image

You can write pixels to an image or any surface that supports writing pixels. For example, you can write pixels to a WritableImage and a Canvas.

■ **Tip**   An Image is a read-only pixel surface. You can read pixels from an Image. However, you cannot write pixels to an Image. If you want to write to an image or create an image from scratch, use a WritableImage.

An instance of the PixelWriter interface is used to write pixels to a surface. A PixelWriter is provided by the writable surface. For example, you can use the getPixelWriter() method of the Canvas and WritableImage to obtain a PixelWriter for them.

The PixelWriter interface contains methods to write pixels to a surface and obtain the pixel format supported by the surface:

- PixelFormat getPixelFormat()

- void setArgb(int x, int y, int argb)

- void setColor(int x, int y, Color c)

- void setPixels(int x, int y, int w, int h, PixelFormat<ByteBuffer> pixelformat, byte[] buffer, int offset, int scanlineStride)

- void setPixels(int x, int y, int w, int h, PixelFormat<IntBuffer> pixelformat, int[] buffer, int offset, int scanlineStride)

- <T extends Buffer> void setPixels(int x, int y, int w, int h, PixelFormat<T> pixelformat, T buffer, int scanlineStride)

- void setPixels(int dstx, int dsty, int w, int h, PixelReader reader, int srcx, int srcy)

The getPixelFormat() method returns the pixel format in which the pixels can be written to the surface. The setArgb() and setColor() methods allow for writing one pixel at the specified (x, y) location in the destination surface. The setArgb() method accepts the pixel data in an integer in the INT_ARGB format whereas the setColor() method accepts a Color object. The setPixels() methods allow for bulk pixel writing.

You can use an instance of the WritableImage to create an image from scratch. The class contains three constructors:

- WritableImage(int width, int height)

- WritableImage(PixelReader reader, int width, int height)

- WritableImage(PixelReader reader, int x, int y, int width, int height)

The first constructor creates an empty image of the specified width and height.

```
// Create a new empty image of 200 X 100
WritableImage newImage = new WritableImage(200, 100);
```

The second constructor creates an image of the specified width and height. The specified reader is used to fill the image with pixels. An ArrayIndexOutOfBoundsException is thrown if the reader reads from a surface that does not have the necessary number of rows and columns to fill the new image. Use this constructor to copy the whole or part of an image. The following snippet of code creates a copy of an image.

```
String imagePath = "resources/picture/ksharan.jpg";
Image image = new Image(imagePath, 200, 100, true, true);

int width = (int)image.getWidth();
int height = (int)image.getHeight();

// Create a copy of the image
WritableImage newImage = new WritableImage(image.getPixelReader(), width, height);
```

The third constructor lets you copy a rectangular region from a surface. The (x, y) value is coordinates of the upper-left corner of the rectangular region. The (width, height) value is the dimension of the rectangular region to be read using the reader and the desired dimension of the new image. An ArrayIndexOutOfBoundsException is thrown if the reader reads from a surface that does not have the necessary number of rows and columns to fill the new image.

The WritableImage is a read-write image. Its getPixelWriter() method returns a PixelWriter to write pixels to the image. It inherits the getPixelReader() method that returns a PixelReader to read data from the image.

The following snippet of code creates an Image and an empty WritableImage. It reads one pixel at a time from the Image, makes the pixel darker, and writes the same pixel to the new WritableImage. At the end, we have created a darker copy of the original image.

```
Image image = new Image("resources/picture/ksharan.jpg";);
PixelReader pixelReader = image.getPixelReader();
int width = (int)image.getWidth();
int height = (int)image.getHeight();

// Create a new, empty WritableImage
WritableImage darkerImage = new WritableImage(width, height);
PixelWriter darkerWriter = darkerImage.getPixelWriter();
```

```
// Read one pixel at a time from the source and
// write it to the destinations - one darker and one brighter
for(int y = 0; y < height; y++) {
        for(int x = 0; x < width; x++) {
                // Read the pixel from the source image
                Color color = pixelReader.getColor(x, y);

                // Write a darker pixel to the new image at the same location
                darkerWriter.setColor(x, y, color.darker());
        }
}
```

The program in Listing 24-6 creates an Image. It creates three instances of the WritableImage and copies the pixels from the original image to them. The copied pixels are modified before they written to the destination. For one destination, pixels are darkened: for one brightened, and for one, made semi-transparent. All four images are displayed in ImageViews as shown in Figure 24-4.

Listing 24-6. Writing Pixels to an Image

```
// CopyingImage.java
package com.jdojo.image;

import javafx.application.Application;
import javafx.scene.Scene;
import javafx.scene.image.Image;
import javafx.scene.image.ImageView;
import javafx.scene.image.PixelReader;
import javafx.scene.image.PixelWriter;
import javafx.scene.image.WritableImage;
import javafx.scene.layout.HBox;
import javafx.scene.layout.VBox;
import javafx.scene.paint.Color;
import javafx.scene.text.Text;
import javafx.stage.Stage;

public class CopyingImage extends Application {
        public static void main(String[] args) {
                Application.launch(args);
        }

        @Override
        public void start(Stage stage) {
                String imagePath = "resources/picture/ksharan.jpg";
                Image image = new Image(imagePath, 200, 100, true, true);

                int width = (int)image.getWidth();
                int height = (int)image.getHeight();

                // Create three WritableImage instances
                // one will be a darker, one brighter, and one semi-transparent
                WritableImage darkerImage = new WritableImage(width, height);
                WritableImage brighterImage = new WritableImage(width, height);
                WritableImage semiTransparentImage = new WritableImage(width, height);
```

```java
                // Copy source pixels to the destinations
                this.createImages(image,
                                darkerImage,
                                brighterImage,
                                semiTransparentImage,
                                width,
                                height);

        ImageView imageView = new ImageView(image);
        ImageView darkerView = new ImageView(darkerImage);
        ImageView brighterView = new ImageView(brighterImage);
        ImageView semiTransparentView = new ImageView(semiTransparentImage);

        HBox root = new HBox(10,
                new VBox(imageView, new Text("Original")),
                new VBox(darkerView, new Text("Darker")),
                new VBox(brighterView, new Text("Brighter")),
                new VBox(semiTransparentView, new Text("Semi-Transparent")));

        Scene scene = new Scene(root);
        stage.setScene(scene);
        stage.setTitle("Writing Pixels to an Image");
        stage.show();
    }

    private void createImages(Image image,
                                WritableImage darkerImage,
                                WritableImage brighterImage,
                                WritableImage semiTransparentImage,
                                int width, int height) {
    // Obtain the pixel reader from the image
    PixelReader pixelReader = image.getPixelReader();
    PixelWriter darkerWriter = darkerImage.getPixelWriter();
    PixelWriter brighterWriter = brighterImage.getPixelWriter();
    PixelWriter semiTransparentWriter = semiTransparentImage.getPixelWriter();

        // Read one pixel at a time from the source and
        // write it to the destinations
        for(int y = 0; y < height; y++) {
                for(int x = 0; x < width; x++) {
                        Color color = pixelReader.getColor(x, y);

                        // Write a darker pixel to the new image
                        darkerWriter.setColor(x, y, color.darker());

                        // Write a brighter pixel to the new image
                        brighterWriter.setColor(x, y, color.brighter());
```

```
                    // Write a semi-transparent pixel to the new image
                    semiTransparentWriter.setColor(x, y,
                            Color.color(color.getRed(),
                                        color.getGreen(),
                                        color.getBlue(),
                                        0.50));
                }
            }
        }
}
```

***Figure 24-4.** Original image and modified images*

■ **Tip**   It is easy to crop an image in JavaFX. Use one of the `getPixels()` methods of the `PixelReader` to read the needed area of the image in a buffer and write the buffer to a new image. This gives you a new image that is the cropped version of the original image.

Creating an Image from Scratch

In the previous section, we created new images by copying pixels from another image. We had altered the color and opacity of the original pixels before writing them to the new image. That was easy because we were working on one pixel at a time and we received a pixel as a `Color` object. It is also possible to create pixels from scratch then use them to create a new image. Anyone would admit that creating a new, meaningful image by defining its each pixel in code is not an easy task. However, JavaFX has made the process of doing so easy.

In this section, we will create a new image with a pattern of rectangles placed in a grid-like fashion. Each rectangle will be divided into two parts using the diagonal connecting the upper-left and lower-right corners. The upper triangle is painted in painted in green and the lower in red. A new image will be created and filled with the rectangles.

Creating an image from scratch involves three steps:

- Create an instance of the `WritableImage`.

- Create buffer (a `byte` array, an `int` array, etc.) and populate it with pixel data depending on the pixel format you want to use for the pixels data.

- Write the pixels in the buffer to the image.

Let us write the code that creates the pixels for our rectangular region. Let us declare constants for the width and height of the rectangle.

```
static final int RECT_WIDTH = 20;
static final int RECT_HEIGHT = 20;
```

We need to define a buffer (a byte array) big enough to hold data for all pixels. Each pixel in BYTE_RGB format takes 2 bytes.

```
byte[] pixels = new byte[RECT_WIDTH * RECT_HEIGHT * 3];
```

If the region is rectangular, we need to know the height to width ration to divide the region into upper and lower rectangles.

```
double ratio = 1.0 * RECT_HEIGHT/RECT_WIDTH;
```

The following snippet of code populates the buffer.

```
// Generate pixel data
for (int y = 0; y < RECT_HEIGHT; y++) {
        for (int x = 0; x < RECT_WIDTH; x++) {
                int i = y * RECT_WIDTH * 3 + x * 3;
                if (x <= y/ratio) {
                        // Lower-half
                        pixels[i] = -1;   // red -1 means 255 (-1 & 0xff = 255)
                        pixels[i+1] = 0; // green = 0
                        pixels[i+2] = 0; // blue = 0
                } else {
                        // Upper-half
                        pixels[i] = 0;     // red = 0
                        pixels[i+1] = -1; // Green 255
                        pixels[i+2] = 0;  // blue = 0
                }
        }
}
```

Pixels are stored in the buffer in the row first order. The variable i inside the loop computes the position in the buffer where the 3-byte data starts for a pixel. For example, the data for the pixel at (0, 0) starts at the index 0; the data for the pixel at (0, 1) starts at index 3, etc. The 3 bytes for a pixel stores red, green, and blue values in order of increasing index. Encoded values for the color components are stored in the buffer, so that the expression "byteValue & 0xff" will produce the actual color component value between 0 and 255. If you want a red pixel, you need to set -1 for the red component as "-1 & 0xff" produces 255. For a red color, the green and blue components will be set to zero. A byte array initializes all elements to zero. However, we have explicitly set them to zero in our code. For the lower-half triangle, we set the color to green. The condition "x =<= y/ratio" is used to determine the position of a pixel whether it falls in the upper-half triangle or the lower-half triangle. If the y/ratio is not an integer, the division of the rectangle into two triangles may be a little off at the lower-right corner.

Once we get the pixel data, we need to write them to a `WritableImage`. The following snippet of code writes the pixels for the rectangle, once at the upper-left corner of the image.

```
WritableImage newImage = new WritableImage(350, 100);
PixelWriter pixelWriter = newImage.getPixelWriter();
byte[] pixels = generate pixel data...

// Our data is in BYTE_RGB format
PixelFormat<ByteBuffer> pixelFormat = PixelFormat.getByteRgbInstance();
Int xPos 0;
int yPos =0;
int offset = 0;
int scanlineStride = RECT_WIDTH * 3;
pixelWriter.setPixels(xPos, yPos,
                      RECT_WIDTH, RECT_HEIGHT,
                      pixelFormat,
                      pixels, offset,
                      scanlineStride);
```

The program in Listing 24-7 creates an image from scratch. It creates a pattern by writing row pixels for the rectangular region to fill the image. Figure 24-5 shows the image.

Listing 24-7. Creating an Image from Scratch

```
// CreatingImage.java
package com.jdojo.image;

import java.nio.ByteBuffer;
import javafx.application.Application;
import javafx.scene.Scene;
import javafx.scene.image.ImageView;
import javafx.scene.image.PixelFormat;
import javafx.scene.image.PixelWriter;
import javafx.scene.image.WritableImage;
import javafx.scene.layout.HBox;
import javafx.stage.Stage;

public class CreatingImage extends Application {
        private static final int RECT_WIDTH = 20;
        private static final int RECT_HEIGHT = 20;

        public static void main(String[] args) {
                Application.launch(args);
        }

        @Override
        public void start(Stage stage) {
                WritableImage newImage = new WritableImage(350, 100);

                // Get the pixels data
                byte[] pixels = getPixelsData();
```

```
            // Write pixels data to the image
            this.writePattern(newImage, pixels);

            // Display the new image in an ImageView
            ImageView newImageView = new ImageView(newImage);

            HBox root = new HBox(newImageView);
            Scene scene = new Scene(root);
            stage.setScene(scene);
            stage.setTitle("Creating an Image from Scratch");
            stage.show();
    }

    private byte[] getPixelsData() {
            // Each pixel takes 3 bytes
            byte[] pixels = new byte[RECT_WIDTH * RECT_HEIGHT * 3];

            // Height to width ratio
            double ratio = 1.0 * RECT_HEIGHT/RECT_WIDTH;

            // Generate pixels data
            for (int y = 0; y < RECT_HEIGHT; y++) {
                    for (int x = 0; x < RECT_WIDTH; x++) {
                            int i = y * RECT_WIDTH * 3 + x * 3;
                            if (x <= y/ratio) {
                                    pixels[i] = -1;   // red -1 means 255 (-1 & 0xff = 255)
                                    pixels[i+1] = 0; // green = 0
                                    pixels[i+2] = 0; // blue = 0
                            } else {
                                    pixels[i] = 0;    // red = 0
                                    pixels[i+1] = -1; // Green 255
                                    pixels[i+2] = 0;  // blue = 0
                            }
                    }
            }

            return pixels;
    }

    private void writePattern(WritableImage newImage, byte[] pixels) {
            PixelWriter pixelWriter = newImage.getPixelWriter();

            // Our data is in BYTE_RGB format
            PixelFormat<ByteBuffer> pixelFormat = PixelFormat.getByteRgbInstance();

            int spacing = 5;
            int imageWidth = (int)newImage.getWidth();
            int imageHeight = (int)newImage.getHeight();

            // Roughly compute the number of rows and columns
            int rows = imageHeight/(RECT_HEIGHT + spacing);
            int columns = imageWidth/(RECT_WIDTH + spacing);
```

```
                    // Write the pixels to the image
                    for (int y = 0; y < rows; y++) {
                        for (int x = 0; x < columns; x++) {
                            // Compute the current location inside the image where
                            // the rectangular region to be written
                            int xPos = x * (RECT_WIDTH + spacing);
                            int yPos = y * (RECT_HEIGHT + spacing);

                            // Write the pixels data at he current location
                            // defined by xPos and yPos
                            pixelWriter.setPixels(xPos, yPos,
                                            RECT_WIDTH, RECT_HEIGHT,
                                            pixelFormat,
                                            pixels, 0,
                                            RECT_WIDTH * 3);
                        }
                    }
                }
}
```

Figure 24-5. *An image created from scratch*

Saving a New Image to a FileSystem

Saving an Image to the file system is easy:

- Convert the Image to a BufferedImage using the fromFXImage() method of the SwingFXUtils class.

- Pass the BufferedImage to the write() method of the ImageIO class.

Notice that we have to use two classes – BufferedImage and ImageIO – that are part of the standard Java library, not the JavaFX library. The following snippet of code shows the outline of the steps involved in saving an image to a file in the PNG format.

```
import java.awt.image.BufferedImage;
import java.io.File;
import java.io.IOException;
import javafx.embed.swing.SwingFXUtils;
import javafx.scene.image.Image;
import javax.imageio.ImageIO;
...
```

```
Image image = create an image...
BufferedImage bImage = SwingFXUtils.fromFXImage(image, null);

// Save the image to the file
File fileToSave = ...
String imageFormat = "png";
try {
        ImageIO.write(bImage, imageFormat, fileToSave);
}
catch (IOException e) {
        throw new RuntimeException(e);
}
```

The program in Listing 24-8 has code for a utility class ImageUtil. Its static saveToFile(Image image) method can be used to save an Image to a local file system. The method asks for a file name. The user can select a PNG or a JPEG format for the image.

Listing 24-8. A Utility Class to Save an Image to a File

```
// ImageUtil.java
package com.jdojo.image;

import java.awt.image.BufferedImage;
import java.io.File;
import java.io.IOException;
import javafx.embed.swing.SwingFXUtils;
import javafx.scene.image.Image;
import javafx.stage.FileChooser;
import static javafx.stage.FileChooser.ExtensionFilter;
import javax.imageio.ImageIO;

public class ImageUtil {
        public static void saveToFile(Image image) {
                // Ask the user for the file name
                FileChooser fileChooser = new FileChooser();
                fileChooser.setTitle("Select an image file name");
                fileChooser.setInitialFileName("untitled");
                ExtensionFilter pngExt = new ExtensionFilter("PNG Files", "*.png");
                ExtensionFilter jpgExt =
                                new ExtensionFilter("JPEG Files", "*.jpg", "*.jpeg");
                fileChooser.getExtensionFilters().addAll(pngExt, jpgExt);

                File outputFile = fileChooser.showSaveDialog(null);
                if (outputFile == null) {
                        return;
                }

                ExtensionFilter selectedExt = fileChooser.getSelectedExtensionFilter();
                String imageFormat = "png";
                if (selectedExt == jpgExt) {
                        imageFormat = "jpg";
                }
```

```
            // Check for the file extension. Add oen, iff not specified
            String fileName = outputFile.getName().toLowerCase();
            switch (imageFormat) {
                    case "jpg":
                            if (!fileName.endsWith(".jpeg") && !fileName.endsWith(".jpg")) {
                                    outputFile = new File(outputFile.getParentFile(),
                                                            outputFile.getName() + ".jpg");
                            }
                            break;
                    case "png":
                            if (!fileName.endsWith(".png")) {
                                    outputFile = new File(outputFile.getParentFile(),
                                                            outputFile.getName() + ".png");
                            }
            }

            // Convert the image to a buffered image
            BufferedImage bImage = SwingFXUtils.fromFXImage(image, null);

            // Save the image to the file
            try {
                    ImageIO.write(bImage, imageFormat, outputFile);
            }
            catch (IOException e) {
                    throw new RuntimeException(e);
            }
        }
    }
}
```

The program in Listing 24-9 shows how to save an image to a file. Click the Save Image button to save the picture to a file. It opens a file chooser dialog to let you select a file name. If you cancel the file chooser dialog, the saving process is aborted.

Listing 24-9. Saving an Image to a File

```
// SaveImage.java
package com.jdojo.image;

import javafx.application.Application;
import javafx.scene.Scene;
import javafx.scene.control.Button;
import javafx.scene.image.Image;
import javafx.scene.image.ImageView;
import javafx.scene.layout.VBox;
import javafx.stage.Stage;

public class SaveImage  extends Application {
        public static void main(String[] args) {
                Application.launch(args);
        }
```

```
        @Override
        public void start(Stage stage) {
                String imagePath = "resources/picture/ksharan.jpg";
                Image image = new Image(imagePath);
                ImageView imageView = new ImageView(image);

                Button saveBtn = new Button("Save Image");
                saveBtn.setOnAction(e -> ImageUtil.saveToFile(image));

                VBox root = new VBox(10, imageView, saveBtn);
                Scene scene = new Scene(root);
                stage.setScene(scene);
                stage.setTitle("Saving an Image to a File");
                stage.show();
        }
}
```

Taking the Snapshot of a Node and a Scene

JavaFX allows you to take a snapshot of a Node and a Scene as they will appear in the next frame. You get the snapshot in a WritableImage, which means you can perform all pixel-level operations after you take the snapshot. The Node and Scene classes contain a snapshot() method to accomplish this.

Taking the Snapshot of a Node

The Node class contains an overloaded snapshot() method:

- WritableImage snapshot(SnapshotParameters params, WritableImage image)

- void snapshot(Callback<SnapshotResult,Void> callback, SnapshotParameters params, WritableImage image)

The first version of the snapshot() method is synchronous whereas the second one is asynchronous. The method lets you specify an instance of the SnapshotParameters class that contains the rendering attributes for the snapshot. If this is null, default values will be used. You can set the following attributes for the snapshot:

- A fill color

- A transform

- A viewport

- A camera

- A depth buffer

By default, the fill color is white; no transform and viewport are used; a ParallelCamera is used; and, the depth buffer is set to false. Note that these attributes are used on the node only while taking its snapshot.

You can specify a WritableImage in the snapshot() method that will hold the snapshot of the node. If this is null, a new WritableImage is created. If the specified WritableImage is smaller than the node, the node will be clipped to fit the image size.

The first version of the snapshot() method returns the snapshot in a WritableImage. The image is either the one that is passed as the parameter or a new one created by the method.

The second, asynchronous version of the snapshot() method accepts a Callback object whose call() method is called. A SnapshotResult object is passed to the call() method, which can be used to obtain the snapshot image, the source node, and the snapshot parameters using the following methods:

- WritableImage getImage()
- SnapshotParameters getSnapshotParameters()
- Object getSource()

■ **Tip** The snapshot() method takes the snapshot of the node using the boundsInParent property of the node. That is, the snapshot contains all effects and transformations applied to the node. If the node is being animated, the snapshot will include the animated state of the node at the time it is taken.

The program in Listing 24-10 shows how to take a snapshot of a TextField node. It displays a Label, a TextField, and two Buttons in a GridPane. Buttons are used to take the snapshot of the TextField synchronously and asynchronously. Click one of the Buttons to take a snapshot. A file save dialog appears for you to enter the file name for the saved snapshot. The syncSnapshot() and asyncSnapshot() methods contain the logic to take the snapshot. For the snapshot, the fill is set to red, and a Scale and a Rotate transforms are applied. Figure 24-6 shows the snapshot.

Listing 24-10. Taking a Snapshot of a Node

```java
// NodeSnapshot.java
package com.jdojo.image;

import javafx.application.Application;
import javafx.scene.Node;
import javafx.scene.Scene;
import javafx.scene.SnapshotParameters;
import javafx.scene.SnapshotResult;
import javafx.scene.control.Button;
import javafx.scene.control.Label;
import javafx.scene.control.TextField;
import javafx.scene.image.WritableImage;
import javafx.scene.layout.GridPane;
import javafx.scene.paint.Color;
import javafx.scene.transform.Rotate;
import javafx.scene.transform.Scale;
import javafx.scene.transform.Transform;
import javafx.stage.Stage;
import javafx.util.Callback;

public class NodeSnapshot extends Application {
    public static void main(String[] args) {
        Application.launch(args);
    }
```

```java
        @Override
        public void start(Stage stage) {
                GridPane root = new GridPane();

                Label nameLbl = new Label("Name:");
                TextField nameField = new TextField("Prema");

                Button syncSnapshotBtn = new Button("Synchronous Snapshot");
                syncSnapshotBtn.setOnAction(e -> syncSnapshot(nameField));

                Button asyncSnapshotBtn = new Button("Asynchronous Snapshot");
                asyncSnapshotBtn.setOnAction(e -> asyncSnapshot(nameField));

                root.setHgap(10);
                root.addRow(0, nameLbl, nameField, syncSnapshotBtn);
                root.add(asyncSnapshotBtn, 2, 1);

                Scene scene = new Scene(root);
                stage.setScene(scene);
                stage.setTitle("Taking the Snapshot of a Node");
                stage.show();
        }

        private void syncSnapshot(Node node) {
                SnapshotParameters params = getParams();
                WritableImage image = node.snapshot(params, null);
                ImageUtil.saveToFile(image);
        }

        private void asyncSnapshot(Node node) {
                // Create a Callback. Its call() method is called when
                // the snapshot is ready. The getImage() method returns the snapshot
                Callback<SnapshotResult, Void> callback = (SnapshotResult result) -> {
                        WritableImage image = result.getImage();
                        ImageUtil.saveToFile(image);
                        return null;
                };

                SnapshotParameters params = getParams();
                node.snapshot(callback, params, null);
        }

        private SnapshotParameters getParams() {
                // Set the fill to red and rotate the node by 30 degrees
                SnapshotParameters params = new SnapshotParameters();
                params.setFill(Color.RED);
                Transform tf = new Scale(0.8, 0.8);
                tf = tf.createConcatenation(new Rotate(10));
                params.setTransform(tf);
                return params;
        }
}
```

Figure 24-6. *The snapshot of a node*

Taking the Snapshot of a Scene

The Scene class contains an overloaded `snapshot()` method:

- `WritableImage snapshot(WritableImage image)`
- `void snapshot(Callback<SnapshotResult,Void> callback, WritableImage image)`

Compare the `snapshot()` methods of the Scene class with that of the Node class. The only difference is that the `snapshot()` method in the Scene class does not contain the `SnapshotParameters` argument. This means that you cannot customize the scene snapshot. Except this, the method works the same way as it works for the Node class, as discussed in the previous section.

The first version of the `snapshot()` method is synchronous whereas the second one is asynchronous. You can specify a `WritableImage` to the method that will hold the snapshot of the node. If this is `null`, a new `WritableImage` is created. If the specified `WritableImage` is smaller than the scene, the scene will be clipped to fit the image size.

The program in Listing 24-11 shows how to take a snapshot of a scene. The main logic in the program is essentially the same as that of the program in Listing 24-10, except that, this time, it takes a snapshot of a scene. Figure 24-7 shows the snapshot.

Listing 24-11. Taking a Snapshot of a Scene

```
// SceneSnapshot.java
package com.jdojo.image;

import javafx.application.Application;
import javafx.scene.Scene;
import javafx.scene.control.Button;
import javafx.scene.control.Label;
import javafx.scene.control.TextField;
import javafx.scene.image.WritableImage;
import javafx.scene.layout.GridPane;;
import javafx.scene.SnapshotResult;
import javafx.util.Callback;
import javafx.stage.Stage;

public class SceneSnapshot extends Application {
        public static void main(String[] args) {
                Application.launch(args);
        }
```

```
        @Override
        public void start(Stage stage) {
                GridPane root = new GridPane();
                Scene scene = new Scene(root);

                Label nameLbl = new Label("Name:");
                TextField nameField = new TextField("Prema");

                Button syncSnapshotBtn = new Button("Synchronous Snapshot");
                syncSnapshotBtn.setOnAction(e -> syncSnapshot(scene));

                Button asyncSnapshotBtn = new Button("Asynchronous Snapshot");
                asyncSnapshotBtn.setOnAction(e -> asyncSnapshot(scene));

                root.setHgap(10);
                root.addRow(0, nameLbl, nameField, syncSnapshotBtn);
                root.add(asyncSnapshotBtn, 2, 1);

                stage.setScene(scene);
                stage.setTitle("Taking the Snapshot of a Scene");
                stage.show();
        }

        private void syncSnapshot(Scene scene) {
                WritableImage image = scene.snapshot(null);
                ImageUtil.saveToFile(image);
        }

        private void asyncSnapshot(Scene scene) {
                // Create a Callback. Its call() method is called when
                // the snapshot is ready. The getImage() method returns the snapshot
                Callback<SnapshotResult, Void> callback = (SnapshotResult result) -> {
                        WritableImage image = result.getImage();
                        ImageUtil.saveToFile(image);
                        return null;
                };

                scene.snapshot(callback, null);
        }
}
```

Name:	Prema	Synchronous Snapshot
		Asynchronous Snapshot

Figure 24-7. *The snapshot of a scene*

Summary

JavaFX provides the Image API that lets you load and display images, and read/write raw image pixels. All classes in the API are in the javafx.scene.image package. The API lets you perform the following operations on images: load an image in memory, display an image as a node in a scene graph, read pixels from an image, write pixels to an image, and convert a node in a scene graph to an image and save it to the local file system.

An instance of the Image class is an in-memory representation of an image. You can also construct an image in a JavaFX application by supplying pixels to a WritableImage instance. The Image class supports BMP, PNG, JPEG, and GIF image formats. It loads an image from a source, which can be specified as a string URL or an InputStream. It can also scale the original image while loading.

An instance of the ImageView class is used to display an image loaded in an Image object. The ImageView class inherits from the Node class, which makes an ImageView suitable to be added to a scene graph.

Images are constructed from pixels. JavaFX supports reading pixels from an image, writing pixels to an image, and creating a snapshot of the scene. It supports creating an image from scratch. If an image is writable, you can also modify the mage in memory and save it to the file system. The image API provides access to each pixel in the image. It supports reading and writing one pixel or a chunk of pixel at a time.

Data for pixels in an image may be stored in different formats. A PixelFormat defines how the data for a pixel for a given format is stored. A WritablePixelFormat represents a destination format to write pixels with full pixel color information.

The PixelReader and PixelWriter interfaces define methods to read data from an Image and write data to a WritableImage. Besides an Image, you can read pixels from and write pixels to any surface that contain pixels.

JavaFX allows you to take a snapshot of a Node and a Scene as they will appear in the next frame. You get the snapshot in a WritableImage, which means you can perform all pixel-level operations after you take the snapshot. The Node and Scene classes contain a snapshot() method to accomplish this.

The next chapter will discuss how to draw on a canvas using the Canvas API.

CHAPTER 25

Drawing on a Canvas

In this chapter, you will learn:

- What the Canvas API is
- How to create a canvas
- How to draw on a canvas such as basic shapes, text, paths, and images
- How to clear the canvas area
- How to save and restore the drawing states in a GraphicsContext

What Is the Canvas API?

Through the javafx.scene.canvas package, JavaFX provides the Canvas API that offers a drawing surface to draw shapes, images, and text using drawing commands. The API also gives pixel-level access to the drawing surface where you can write any pixels on the surface. The API consists of only two classes:

- Canvas
- GraphicsContext

A canvas is a bitmap image, which is used as a drawing surface. An instance of the Canvas class represents a canvas. It inherits from the Node class. Therefore, a canvas is a node. It can be added to a scene graph, and effects and transformations can be applied to it.

A canvas has a graphics context associated with it that is used to issue drawing commands to the canvas. An instance of the GraphicsContext class represents a graphics context.

Creating a Canvas

The Canvas class has two constructors. The no-args constructor creates an empty canvas. Later, you can set the size of the canvas using its width and height properties. The other constructor takes the width and height of the canvas as parameters:

```
// Create a Canvas of zero width and height
Canvas canvas = new Canvas();
```

```
// Set the canvas size
canvas.setWidth(400);
canvas.setHeight(200);

// Create a 400X200 canvas
Canvas canvas = new Canvas(400, 200);
```

Drawing on the Canvas

Once you create a canvas, you need to get its graphics context using the getGraphicsContext2D() method, as in the following snippet of code:

```
// Get the graphics context of the canvas
GraphicsContext gc = canvas.getGraphicsContext2D();
```

All drawing commands are provided in the GraphicsContext class as methods. Drawings that fall outside the bounds of the canvas are clipped. The canvas uses a buffer. The drawing commands push necessary parameters to the buffer. It is important to note that you should use the graphics context from any one thread before adding the Canvas to the scene graph. Once the Canvas is added to the scene graph, the graphics context should be used only on the JavaFX Application Thread. The GraphicsContext class contains methods to draw the following types of objects:

- Basic shapes
- Text
- Paths
- Images
- Pixels

Drawing Basic Shapes

The GraphicsContext class provides two types of methods to draw the basic shapes. The method fillXxx() draws a shape Xxx and fills it with the current fill paint. The method strokeXxx() draws a shape Xxx with the current stroke. Use the following methods for drawing shapes:

- fillArc()
- fillOval()
- fillPolygon()
- fillRect()
- fillRoundRect()
- strokeArc()
- strokeLine()
- strokeOval()

- strokePolygon()

- strokePolyline()

- strokeRect()

- strokeRoundRect()

The following snippet of code draws a rectangle. The stroke color is red and the stroke width is 2px. The upper-left corner of the rectangle is at (0, 0). The rectangle is 100px wide and 50px high.

```
Canvas canvas = new Canvas(200, 100);
GraphicsContext gc = canvas.getGraphicsContext2D();
gc.setLineWidth(2.0);
gc.setStroke(Color.RED);
gc.strokeRect(0, 0, 100, 50);
```

Drawing Text

You can draw text using the fillText() and strokeText() methods of the GraphicsContext using the following snippets of code:

- void strokeText(String text, double x, double y)

- void strokeText(String text, double x, double y, double maxWidth)

- void fillText(String text, double x, double y)

- void fillText(String text, double x, double y, double maxWidth)

Both methods are overloaded. One version lets you specify the text and its position. The other version lets you specify the maximum width of the text as well. If the actual text width exceeds the specified maximum width, the text is resized to fit the specified the maximum width. The following snippet of code draws two strings. Figure 25-1 shows the two strings on the canvas.

```
Canvas canvas = new Canvas(200, 50);
GraphicsContext gc = canvas.getGraphicsContext2D();
gc.setLineWidth(1.0);
gc.setStroke(Color.BLACK);
gc.strokeText("Drawing Text", 10, 10);
gc.strokeText("Drawing Text", 100, 10, 40);
```

Drawing Text   Drawing Text

Figure 25-1. *Drawing text on a canvas*

Drawing Paths

Use can use path commands and SVG path strings to create a shape of your choice. A path consists of multiple subpaths. The following methods are used to draw paths:

- beginPath()
- lineTo(double x1, double y1)
- moveTo(double x0, double y0)
- quadraticCurveTo(double xc, double yc, double x1, double y1)
- appendSVGPath(String svgpath)
- arc(double centerX, double centerY, double radiusX, double radiusY, double startAngle, double length)
- arcTo(double x1, double y1, double x2, double y2, double radius)
- bezierCurveTo(double xc1, double yc1, double xc2, double yc2, double x1, double y1)
- closePath()
- stroke()
- fill()

The beginPath() and closePath() methods start and close a path, respectively. Methods such as arcTo() and lineTo() are the path commands to draw a specific type of subpath. Do not forget to call the stroke() or fill() method at the end, which will draw an outline or fill the path. The following snippet of code draws a triangle, as shown in Figure 25-2.

```
Canvas canvas = new Canvas(200, 50);
GraphicsContext gc = canvas.getGraphicsContext2D();
gc.setLineWidth(2.0);
gc.setStroke(Color.BLACK);

gc.beginPath();
gc.moveTo(25, 0);
gc.appendSVGPath("L50, 25L0, 25");
gc.closePath();
gc.stroke();
```

Figure 25-2. *Drawing a triangle*

Drawing Images

You can draw an image on the canvas using the drawImage() method. The method has three versions:

- void drawImage(Image img, double x, double y)

- void drawImage(Image img, double x, double y, double w, double h)

- void drawImage(Image img, double sx, double sy, double sw, double sh, double dx, double dy, double dw, double dh)

You can draw the whole or part of the image. The drawn image can be stretched or shortened on the canvas. The following snippet of code draws the whole image in its original size on the canvas at (10, 10):

```
Image image = new Image("your_image_URL");
Canvas canvas = new Canvas(400, 400);
GraphicsContext gc = canvas.getGraphicsContext2D();
gc.drawImage(image, 10, 10);
```

The following statement will draw the whole image on the canvas by resizing it to fit in a 100px wide by 150px high area. Whether the image is stretched or shortened depends on its original size.

```
// Draw the whole image in 100X150 area at (10, 10)
gc.drawImage(image, 10, 10, 100, 150);
```

The following statement will draw part of an image on the canvas. Here it is assumed that the source image is bigger than 100px by 150px. The image part being drawn is 100px wide and 150px high and its upper left corner is at (0, 0) in the source image. The part of the image is drawn on the canvas at (10, 10) and it is stretched to fit 200px wide and 200px high area on the canvas.

```
// Draw part of the image in 200X200 area at (10, 10)
gc.drawImage(image, 0, 0, 100, 150, 10, 10, 200, 200);
```

Writing Pixels

You can also directly modify pixels on the canvas. The getPixelWriter() method of the GraphicsContext object returns a PixelWriter that can be used to write pixels to the associated canvas:

```
Canvas canvas = new Canvas(200, 100);
GraphicsContext gc = canvas.getGraphicsContext2D();
PixelWriter pw = gc.getPixelWriter();
```

Once you get a PixelWriter, you can write pixels to the canvas. Chapter 24 presented more details on how to write pixels using a PixelWriter.

Clearing the Canvas Area

The canvas is a transparent area. Pixels will have colors and opacity depending on what is drawn at those pixels. Sometimes you may want to clear the whole or part of the canvas so the pixels are transparent again. The clearRect() method of the GraphicsContext lets you clears a specified area on the canvas:

```
// Clear the top-left 100X100 rectangular area from the canvas
gc.clearRect(0, 0, 100, 100);
```

Saving and Restoring the Drawing States

The current settings for the GraphicsContext are used for all subsequent drawing. For example, if you set the line width to 5px, all subsequent strokes will be 5px in width. Sometimes you may want to modify the state of the graphics context temporarily, and after some time, restore the state that existed before the modification.

The save() and restore() methods of the GraphicsContext object let you save the current state and restore it afterward, respectively. Before you use these methods, let's discuss its need. Suppose you want to issue the following commands to the GraphicsContext object in order:

- Draw a rectangle without any effects

- Draw a string with a reflection effect

- Draw a rectangle without any effects

The following is the first (and incorrect) attempt of achieving this:

```
Canvas canvas = new Canvas(200, 120);
GraphicsContext gc = canvas.getGraphicsContext2D();
gc.strokeRect(10, 10, 50, 20);
gc.setEffect(new Reflection());
gc.strokeText("Chatar", 70, 20);
gc.strokeRect(120, 10, 50, 20);
```

Figure 25-3 shows the drawing of the canvas. Notice that the reflection effect was also applied to the second rectangle, which was not wanted.

Figure 25-3. *Drawing shapes and text*

You can fix the problem by setting the Effect to null after you draw the text. You had modified several properties for the GraphicsContext then had to restore them all manually. Sometimes a GraphicsContext may be passed to your code but you do not want to modify its existing state.

The save() method stores the current state of the GraphicsContext on a stack. The restore() method restores the state of the GraphicsContext to the last saved state. Figure 25-4 shows the results of this. You can fix the problem using the following methods:

```
Canvas canvas = new Canvas(200, 120);
GraphicsContext gc = canvas.getGraphicsContext2D();

gc.strokeRect(10, 10, 50, 20);

// Save the current state
gc.save();

// Modify the current state to add an effect and darw the text
gc.setEffect(new Reflection());
gc.strokeText("Chatar", 70, 20);
```

```
// Restore the state what it was when the last save() was called and draw the second rectangle
gc.restore();
gc.strokeRect(120, 10, 50, 20);
```

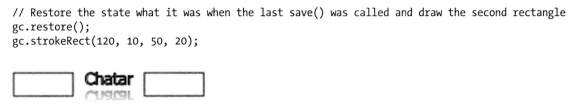

Figure 25-4. *Drawing shapes and text using save() and restore() methods*

A Canvas Drawing Example

The program in Listing 25-1 shows how to draw basic shapes, text, images, and row pixels to a canvas. Figure 25-5 shows the resulting canvas with all drawings.

Listing 25-1. Drawing on a Canvas

```java
// CanvasTest.java
package com.jdojo.canvas;

import java.nio.ByteBuffer;
import javafx.application.Application;
import javafx.scene.Scene;
import javafx.scene.canvas.Canvas;
import javafx.scene.canvas.GraphicsContext;
import javafx.scene.image.Image;
import javafx.scene.image.PixelFormat;
import javafx.scene.image.PixelWriter;
import javafx.scene.layout.Pane;
import javafx.scene.paint.Color;
import javafx.stage.Stage;

public class CanvasTest extends Application {
        private static final int RECT_WIDTH = 20;
        private static final int RECT_HEIGHT = 20;

        public static void main(String[] args) {
                Application.launch(args);
        }

        @Override
        public void start(Stage stage) {
                Canvas canvas = new Canvas(400, 100);
                GraphicsContext gc = canvas.getGraphicsContext2D();

                // Set line width and fill color
                gc.setLineWidth(2.0);
                gc.setFill(Color.RED);

                // Draw a rounded rectangle
                gc.strokeRoundRect(10, 10, 50, 50, 10, 10);
```

```java
        // Fill an oval
        gc.fillOval(70, 10, 50, 20);

        // Draw text
        gc.strokeText("Hello Canvas", 10, 85);

        // Draw an Image
        String imagePath = "resources/picture/ksharan.jpg";
        Image image = new Image(imagePath);
        gc.drawImage(image, 130, 10, 60, 80);

        // Write custom pixels to create a pattern
        writePixels(gc);

        Pane root = new Pane();
        root.getChildren().add(canvas);
        Scene scene = new Scene(root);
        stage.setScene(scene);
        stage.setTitle("Drawing on a Canvas");
        stage.show();
    }

    private void writePixels(GraphicsContext gc) {
        byte[] pixels = this.getPixelsData();
        PixelWriter pixelWriter = gc.getPixelWriter();

        // Our data is in BYTE_RGB format
        PixelFormat<ByteBuffer> pixelFormat = PixelFormat.getByteRgbInstance();

        int spacing = 5;
        int imageWidth = 200;
        int imageHeight = 100;

        // Roughly compute the number of rows and columns
        int rows = imageHeight/(RECT_HEIGHT + spacing);
        int columns = imageWidth/(RECT_WIDTH + spacing);

        // Write the pixels to the canvas
        for (int y = 0; y < rows; y++) {
            for (int x = 0; x < columns; x++) {
                int xPos = 200 + x * (RECT_WIDTH + spacing);
                int yPos = y * (RECT_HEIGHT + spacing);
                pixelWriter.setPixels(xPos, yPos,
                                      RECT_WIDTH, RECT_HEIGHT,
                                      pixelFormat,
                                      pixels, 0,
                                      RECT_WIDTH * 3);
            }
        }
    }
```

```
private byte[] getPixelsData() {
    // Each pixel in the w X h region will take 3 bytes
    byte[] pixels = new byte[RECT_WIDTH * RECT_HEIGHT * 3];

    // Height to width ration
    double ratio = 1.0 * RECT_HEIGHT/RECT_WIDTH;

    // Generate pixel data
    for (int y = 0; y < RECT_HEIGHT; y++) {
        for (int x = 0; x < RECT_WIDTH; x++) {
            int i = y * RECT_WIDTH * 3 + x * 3;
            if (x <= y/ratio) {
                pixels[i] = -1;    // red -1 means 255 (-1 & 0xff = 255)
                pixels[i+1] = 0; // green = 0
                pixels[i+2] = 0; // blue = 0
            } else {
                pixels[i] = 0;     // red = 0
                pixels[i+1] = -1; // Green 255
                pixels[i+2] = 0;   // blue = 0
            }
        }
    }
    return pixels;
}
}
```

Figure 25-5. *A canvas with shapes, text, images, and raw pixels on drawn on it*

Summary

Through the javafx.scene.canvas package, JavaFX provides the Canvas API that offers a drawing surface to draw shapes, images, and text using drawing commands. The API also gives pixel-level access to the drawing surface where you can write any pixels on the surface. The API consists of only two classes: Canvas and GraphicsContext. A canvas is a bitmap image, which is used as a drawing surface. An instance of the Canvas class represents a canvas. It inherits from the Node class. Therefore, a canvas is a node. It can be added to a scene graph, and effects and transformations can be applied to it. A canvas has a graphics context associated with it that is used to issue drawing commands to the canvas. An instance of the GraphicsContext class represents a graphics context.

The Canvas class contains a getGraphicsContext2D() method that returns an instance of the GraphicsContext class. After obtaining the GraphicsContext of a canvas, you issue drawing commands to the GraphicsContext that performs the drawing.

Drawings falling outside the bounds of the canvas are clipped. The canvas uses a buffer. The drawing commands push necessary parameters to the buffer. The GraphicsContext of a canvas can be used from any one thread before the canvas is added to the scene graph. Once the canvas is added to the scene graph, the graphics context should be used only on the JavaFX Application Thread. The GraphicsContext class contains methods to draw the following types of objects: basic shapes, text, paths, images, and pixels.

The next chapter will discuss how to use the drag-and-drop gesture to transfer data between nodes in the same JavaFX application, between two different JavaFX applications, and between a JavaFX application and a native application.

CHAPTER 26

■ ■ ■

Understanding Drag and Drop

In this chapter, you will learn:

- What a press-drag-release gesture is
- How to use a dragboard to facilitate data transfers
- How to initiate and detect a drag-and-drop gesture
- How to transfer data from the source to the target using a drag-and-drop gesture
- How to transfer images using a drag-and-drop gesture
- How to transfer custom data between the source and the target using a drag-and-drop gesture

What Is a Press-Drag-Release Gesture?

A press-drag-release gesture is a user action of pressing a mouse button, dragging the mouse with the pressed button, and releasing the button. The gesture can be initiated on a scene or a node. Several nodes and scenes may participate in a single press-drag-release gesture. The gesture is capable of generating different types of events and delivering those events to different nodes. The type of generated events and nodes receiving the events depends on the purpose of the gesture. A node can be dragged for different purposes:

- You may want to change the shape of a node by dragging its boundaries or move it by dragging it to a new location. In this case, the gesture involves only one node: the node on which the gesture was initiated.

- You may want to drag a node and drop it onto another node to connect them in some fashion, for example, connecting two nodes with a symbol in a flow chart. In this case, the drag gesture involves multiple nodes. When the source node is dropped onto the target node, an action takes place.

- You can drag a node and drop it onto another node to transfer data from the source node to the target node. In this case, the drag gesture involves multiple nodes. A data transfer occurs when the source node is dropped.

JavaFX supports three types of drag gestures:

- A simple press-drag-release gesture
- A full press-drag-release gesture
- A drag-and-drop gesture

This chapter will focus mainly on the third type of gesture: the drag-and-drop gesture. It is essential to understand the first two types of gestures to gain full insight into the drag-and-drop gesture. I will discuss the first two types of gestures briefly with a simple example of each type.

A Simple Press-Drag-Release Gesture

The *simple press-drag-release* gesture is the default drag gesture. It is used when the drag gesture involves only one node—the node on which the gesture was initiated. During the drag gesture, all MouseDragEvent types—mouse-drag entered, mouse-drag over, mouse-drag exited, mouse, and mouse-drag released—are delivered only to the gesture source node. In this case, when the mouse button is pressed, the topmost node is picked and all subsequent mouse events are delivered to that node until the mouse button is released. When the mouse is dragged onto another node, the node on which the gesture was started is still under the cursor and, therefore, no other nodes receive the events until the mouse button is released.

The program in Listing 26-1 demonstrates a case of the simple press-drag-release gesture. It adds two TextFields to a scene: one is called the source node and the other the target node. Event handlers are added to both nodes. The target node adds MouseDragEvent handlers to detect any mouse-drag event on it. Run the program, press the mouse button on the source node, drag it onto the target node, and, finally, release the mouse button. The output that follows shows that the source node receives all mouse-drag events. The target node does not receive any mouse-drag events. This is the case of a simple press-drag-release gesture where the node initiating the drag gesture receives all mouse-drag events.

Listing 26-1. Demonstrating a Simple Press-Drag-Release Gesture

```
// SimplePressDragRelease.java
package com.jdojo.dnd;

import javafx.application.Application;
import javafx.scene.Scene;
import javafx.scene.control.Label;
import javafx.scene.control.TextField;
import javafx.scene.layout.GridPane;
import javafx.stage.Stage;

public class SimplePressDragRelease extends Application {
        TextField sourceFld = new TextField("Source Node");
        TextField targetFld = new TextField("Target node");

        public static void main(String[] args) {
                Application.launch(args);
        }

        @Override
        public void start(Stage stage) {
                // Build the UI
                GridPane root = getUI();

                // Add event handlers
                this.addEventHanders();
```

```
            Scene scene = new Scene(root);
            stage.setScene(scene);
            stage.setTitle("A simple press-drag-release gesture");
            stage.show();
    }

    private GridPane getUI() {
            GridPane pane = new GridPane();
            pane.setHgap(5);
            pane.setVgap(20);
            pane.addRow(0, new Label("Source Node:"), sourceFld);
            pane.addRow(1, new Label("Target Node:"), targetFld);
            return pane;
    }

    private void addEventHanders() {
            // Add mouse event handlers for the source
            sourceFld.setOnMousePressed(e -> print("Source: pressed"));
            sourceFld.setOnMouseDragged(e -> print("Source: dragged"));
            sourceFld.setOnDragDetected(e -> print("Source: dragged detected"));
            sourceFld.setOnMouseReleased(e -> print("Source: released"));

            // Add mouse event handlers for the target
            targetFld.setOnMouseDragEntered(e -> print("Target: drag entered"));
            targetFld.setOnMouseDragOver(e -> print("Target: drag over"));
            targetFld.setOnMouseDragReleased(e -> print("Target: drag released"));
            targetFld.setOnMouseDragExited(e -> print("Target: drag exited"));
    }

    private void print(String msg) {
            System.out.println(msg);
    }
}
```

```
Source: Mouse pressed
Source: Mouse dragged
Source: Mouse dragged detected
Source: Mouse dragged
Source: Mouse dragged
...
Source: Mouse released
```

Note that the drag-detected event is generated once after the mouse is dragged. The MouseEvent object has a dragDetect flag, which can be set in the mouse-pressed and mouse-dragged events. If it is set to true, the subsequent event that is generated is the drag-detected event. The default is to generate it after the mouse-dragged event. If you want to generate it after the mouse-pressed event, not the mouse-dragged event, you need to modify the event handlers:

```
sourceFld.setOnMousePressed(e -> {
        print("Source: Mouse pressed");

        // Generate drag detect event after the current mouse pressed event
        e.setDragDetect(true);
});

sourceFld.setOnMouseDragged(e -> {
        print("Source: Mouse dragged");

        // Suppress the drag detected default event generation after mouse dragged
        e.setDragDetect(false);
});
```

A Full Press-Drag-Release Gesture

When the source node of a drag gesture receives the drag-detected event, you can start a *full press-drag-release* gesture by calling the startFullDrag() method on the source node. The startFullDrag() method exists in both Node and Scene classes, allowing you to start a full press-drag-release gesture for a node and a scene. I will simply use only the term node during this discussion.

■ **Tip** The startFullDrag() method can only be called from the drag-detected event handler. Calling this method from any other place throws an IllegalStateException.

You need to do one more set up to see the full press-drag-release gesture in action. The source node of the drag gesture will still receive all mouse-drag events as it is under the cursor when a drag is happening. You need to set the mouseTransparent property of the gesture source to false so the node below it will be picked and mouse-drag events will be delivered to that node. Set this property to true in the mouse-pressed event and set it back to false in the mouse-released event.

The program in Listing 26-2 demonstrates a full press-drag-release gesture. The program is similar to the one show in Listing 26-1, except for the following:

- In the mouse-pressed event handler for the source node, the mouseTransparent property for the source node is set to false. It is set back to true in the mouse-released event handler.

- In the drag-detected event handler, the startFullDrag() method is called on the source node.

Run the program, press the mouse button on the source node, drag it onto the target node, and, finally, release the mouse button. The output that follows shows that the target node receives mouse-drag events as the mouse is dragged inside its bounds. This is the case of a full press-drag-release gesture where the node over which the mouse drag takes place receives the mouse-drag events.

Listing 26-2. Demonstrating a Full Press-Drag-Release Gesture

```java
// FullPressDragRelease.java
package com.jdojo.dnd;

import javafx.application.Application;
import javafx.scene.Scene;
import javafx.scene.control.Label;
import javafx.scene.control.TextField;
import javafx.scene.layout.GridPane;
import javafx.stage.Stage;

public class FullPressDragRelease extends Application {
        TextField sourceFld = new TextField("Source Node");
        TextField targetFld = new TextField("Target node");

        public static void main(String[] args) {
                Application.launch(args);
        }

        @Override
        public void start(Stage stage) {
                // Build the UI
                GridPane root = getUI();

                // Add event handlers
                this.addEventHanders();

                Scene scene = new Scene(root);
                stage.setScene(scene);
                stage.setTitle("A full press-drag-release gesture");
                stage.show();
        }

        private GridPane getUI() {
                GridPane pane = new GridPane();
                pane.setHgap(5);
                pane.setVgap(20);
                pane.addRow(0, new Label("Source Node:"), sourceFld);
                pane.addRow(1, new Label("Target Node:"), targetFld);
                return pane;
        }

        private void addEventHanders() {
                // Add mouse event handlers for the source
                sourceFld.setOnMousePressed(e -> {
                        // Make sure the node is not picked
                        sourceFld.setMouseTransparent(true);
                        print("Source: Mouse pressed");
                });

                sourceFld.setOnMouseDragged(e -> print("Source: Mouse dragged"));
```

```
                    sourceFld.setOnDragDetected(e -> {
                            // Start a full press-drag-release gesture
                            sourceFld.startFullDrag();
                            print("Source: Mouse dragged detected");
                    });

                    sourceFld.setOnMouseReleased(e -> {
                            // Make sure the node is picked
                            sourceFld.setMouseTransparent(false);
                            print("Source: Mouse released");
                    });

                    // Add mouse event handlers for the target
                    targetFld.setOnMouseDragEntered(e -> print("Target: drag entered"));
                    targetFld.setOnMouseDragOver(e -> print("Target: drag over"));
                    targetFld.setOnMouseDragReleased(e -> print("Target: drag released"));
                    targetFld.setOnMouseDragExited(e -> print("Target: drag exited"));
            }

            private void print(String msg) {
                    System.out.println(msg);
            }
    }
```

```
Source: Mouse pressed
Source: Mouse dragged
Source: Mouse dragged
Source: Mouse dragged detected
Source: Mouse dragged
Source: Mouse dragged
Target: drag entered
Target: drag over
Source: Mouse dragged
Target: drag over
Target: drag released
Source: Mouse released
Target: drag exited
```

A Drag-and-Drop Gesture

The third type of drag gesture is called a *drag-and-drop* gesture, which is a user action combining the mouse movement with a pressed mouse button. It is used to transfer data from the *gesture source* to a *gesture target*. A drag-and-drop gesture allows transferring data from:

- One node to another node

- A node to a scene

- One scene to another scene

- A scene to a node

The source and target can be in the same Java or JavaFX application or two different Java or JavaFX applications. A JavaFX application and a native application may also participate in the gesture, for example:

- You can drag text from a Microsoft Word application to a JavaFX application to populate a TextArea and vice versa.

- You can drag an image file from Windows Explorer and drop it onto an ImageView in a JavaFX application. The ImageView can display the image.

- You can drag a text file from Windows Explorer and drop it onto a TextArea in a JavaFX application. The TextArea will read the file and display its content.

Several steps are involved in performing a drag-and-drop gesture:

- A mouse button is pressed on a node.

- The mouse is dragged with the button pressed.

- The node receives a drag-detected event.

- A drag-and-drop gesture is started on the node by calling the startDragAndDrop() method, making the node a the gesture source. The data from the source node is placed in a dragboard.

- Once the system switches to a drag-and-drop gesture, it stops delivering MousEvents and starts delivering DragEvents.

- The gesture source is dragged onto the potential gesture target. The potential gesture target checks whether it accepts the data placed in the dragboard. If it accepts the data, it may become the actual gesture target. The node indicates whether it accepts the data in one of its DragEvent handlers.

- The user releases the pressed button on the gesture target, sending it a drag-dropped event.

- The gesture target uses the data from the dragboard.

- A drag-done event is sent to the gesture source indicating that the drag-and-drop gesture is complete.

I will discuss all of these steps in detail in the sections that follow. The classes supporting the drag-and-drop gesture are included in the javafx.scene.input package.

Understanding the Data Transfer Modes

In a drag-and-drop gesture, the data can be transferred in three modes:

- Copy
- Move
- Link

The *copy* mode indicates that the data will be copied from the gesture source to the gesture target. You may drag a TextField and drop it onto another TextField. The latter gets a copy of the text contained in the former.

The *move* mode indicates that the data will be moved from the gesture source to the gesture target. You may drag a TextField and drop it onto another TextField. The text in the former is then moved to the latter.

The *link* mode indicates that the gesture target will create a link (or reference) to the data being transferred. The actual meaning of "link" depends on the application. You may drag and drop a URL to a WebView in the link mode. The WebView then loads the URL content.

The three data transfer modes are represented by the following three constants in the TransferMode enum:

- TransferMode.COPY

- TransferMode.MOVE

- TransferMode.LINK

Sometimes you may need a combination of the three transfer modes. The TransferMode enum contains three convenience static fields that are arrays of its enum constants:

- TransferMode[] ANY

- TransferMode[] COPY_OR_MOVE

- TransferMode[] NONE

The ANY field is an array of COPY, MOVE, and LINK enum constants. The COPY_OR_MOVE field is an array of the COPY and MOVE enum constants. The NONE constant is an empty array.

Every drag-and-drop gesture includes the use of the TransferMode enum constants. The gesture source specifies the transfer modes that it supports for the data transfer. The gesture target specifies the modes in which it accepts the data transfer.

Understanding the *Dragboard*

In a drag-and-drop data transfer, the gesture source and the gesture target do not know each other. In fact, they may belong to two different applications: two JavaFX applications, or one JavaFX and one native. How does the data transfer take place between the gesture source and target if they do not know each other? In the real world, an intermediary is needed to facilitate a transaction between two unknown parties. In a drag-and-drop gesture, an intermediary is also used to facilitate the data transfer.

A dragboard acts as an intermediary between the gesture source and gesture target. A dragboard is the storage device that holds the data being transferred. The gesture source places the data into a dragboard; the dragboard is made available to the gesture target, so it can inspect the type of content that is available for transfer. When the gesture target is ready to transfer the data, it gets the data from the dragboard. Figure 26-1 shows the roles played by a dragboard.

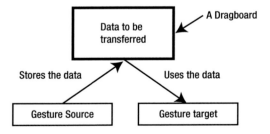

Figure 26-1. *Data transfer mechanism in a drag-and-drop gesture*

An instance of the Dragboard class represents a dragboard. The class is inherited from the Clipboard class. An instance of the Clipboard class represents an operating system clipboard. Typically, an operating system uses a clipboard to store data during cut, copy, and paste operations. You can get the reference of the general clipboard of the operating system using the static getSystemClipboard() method of the Clipboard class:

```
Clipboard systemClipboard = Clipboard.getSystemClipboard();
```

You can place data in the system clipboard that will be accessible to all applications in the system. You can read the data placed in the system clipboard, which can be placed there by any application. A clipboard can store different types of data, for example, rich text format (RTF) text, plain text, HTML, URL, images, or files. The class contains several methods to check if data in a specific format are available in the clipboard. These methods return true if the data in the specific format are available. For example, the hasString() method returns true if the clipboard contains a plain string; the hasRtf() method returns true for text in rich text format. The class contains methods to retrieve data in the specific format. For example, the getString() method returns data in plain text format; the getHtml() returns HTML text; the getImage() returns an image, and so forth. The clear() method clears the clipboard.

■ **Tip** You cannot create an instance of the Clipboard class directly. The clipboard is meant to store one *conceptual* item. The term conceptual means that the data in the clipboard may be stored in different formats representing the same item. For example, you may store RTF text and its plain text version. In this case, the clipboard has two copies of the same item in different formats.

The clipboard is not limited to store only a fixed number of data types. Any serializable data can be stored on the clipboard. Data stored on the clipboard has an associated data format. An instance of the DataFormat class represents a data format. The DataFormat class contains six static fields to represent the commonly used data formats:

- FILES
- HTML
- IMAGE
- PLAIN_TEXT
- RTF
- URL

The FILES represents a list of java.io.File objects. The HTML represents an HTML-formatted string. The IMAGE represents a platform-specific image type. The PLAIN_TEXT represents a plain text string. The RTF represents an RTF-formatted string. The URL represents a URL encoded as a string.

You may want to store data in the clipboard in a format other than those listed above. You can create a DataFormat object to represent any arbitrary format. You need to specify a list of mime types for your data format. The following statement creates a DataFormat with jdojo/person and jdojo/personlist as the mime types:

```
DataFormat myFormat = new DataFormat("jdojo/person", "jdojo/person");
```

The Clipboard class provides the following methods to work with the data and its format:

- `boolean setContent(Map<DataFormat,Object> content)`
- `Object getContent(DataFormat dataFormat)`

The content of the clipboard is a map with the DataFormat as keys and data as values. The getContent() method returns null if data in the specific data format are not available in the clipboard. The following snippet of code stores HTML and plain text version of data, and later, retrieves the data in both formats:

```
// Store text in HTML and plain-text formats in the system clipboard
Clipboard clipboard = Clipboard.getSystemClipboard();

Map<DataFormat,Object> data = new HashMap<>();
data.put(DataFormat.HTML, "<b>Yahoo!</b>");
data.put(DataFormat.PLAIN_TEXT, "Yahoo!");
clipboard.setContent(data);
...

// Try reading HTML text and plain text from the clipboard
If (clipboard.hasHtml()) {
        String htmlText = (String)clipboard.getContent(DataFormat.HTML);
        System.out.println(htmlText);
}

If (clipboard.hasString()) {
        String plainText = (String)clipboard.getContent(DataFormat.PLAIN_TEXT);
        System.out.println(plainText);
}
```

Preparing data to store in the clipboard requires writing a little bloated code. An instance of the ClipboardContent class represents the content of the clipboard, and it makes working with the clipboard data a little easier. The class inherits from the HashMap<DataFormat,Object> class. It provides convenience methods in the form putXxx() and getXxx() for commonly used data types. The following snippet of code rewrites the above logic to store data into the clipboard. The logic to retrieve the data remains the same.

```
Clipboard clipboard = Clipboard.getSystemClipboard();
ClipboardContent content = new ClipboardContent();
content.putHtml("<b>Yahoo!</b>");
content.putString("Yahoo!");
clipboard.setContent(content);
```

The Dragboard class contains all the methods available in the Clipboard class. It adds the following methods:

- `Set<TransferMode> getTransferModes()`
- `void setDragView(Image image)`
- `void setDragView(Image image, double offsetX, double offsetY)`
- `void setDragViewOffsetX(double offsetX)`
- `void setDragViewOffsetY(double offsetY)`

- Image getDragView()

- Double getDragViewOffsetX()

- double getDragViewOffsetY()

The getTransferModes() method returns the set of transfer modes supported by the gesture target. The setDragView() method sets an image as the drag view. The image is shown when the gesture source is dragged. The offsets are the x and y positions of the cursor over the image. Other methods involve getting the drag-view image and the cursor offsets.

Tip A dragboard is a special system clipboard used for the drag-and-drop gesture. You cannot create a dragboard explicitly. Whenever it is necessary to work with the dragboard, its reference is made available as the returned value from methods or the property of the event object. For example, the DragEvent class contains a getDragboard() method that returns the reference of the Dragboard containing the data being transferred.

The Example Application

In the following sections I will discuss the steps in a drag-and-drop gesture in detail, and you will build an example application. The application will have two TextFields displayed in a scene. One text field is called the source node and the other the target node. The user can drag and drop the source node over to the target node. Upon completion of the gesture, the text from source node is transferred (copied or moved) to the target node. I will refer to those nodes in the discussion. They are declared as follows:

```
TextField sourceFld = new TextField("Source node");
TextField targetFld = new TextField("Target node");
```

Initiating the Drag-and-Drop Gesture

The first step in a drag-and-drop gesture is to convert a simple press-drag-release gesture into a drag-and-drop gesture. This is accomplished in the mouse-drag detected event handler for the gesture source. Calling the startDragAndDrop() method on the gesture source initiates a drag-and-drop gesture. The method is available in the Node and Scene classes, so a node and a scene can be the gesture source of a drag-and-drop gesture. The method signature is:

```
Dragboard startDragAndDrop(TransferMode... transferModes)
```

The method accepts the list of supported transfer modes by the gesture source and returns a dragboard. The gesture source needs to populate the dragboard with the data it intends to transfer. The following snippet of code initiates a drag-and-drop gesture, copies the source TextField text to the dragboard, and consumes the event. The drag-and-drop gesture is initiated only when the TextField contains text.

```
sourceFld.setOnDragDetected((MouseEvent e) -> {
        // User can drag only when there is text in the source field
        String sourceText = sourceFld.getText();
        if (sourceText == null || sourceText.trim().equals("")) {
                e.consume();
                return;
        }
```

```
        // Initiate a drag-and-drop gesture
        Dragboard dragboard = sourceFld.startDragAndDrop(TransferMode.COPY_OR_MOVE);

        // Add the source text to the Dragboard
        ClipboardContent content = new ClipboardContent();
        content.putString(sourceText);
        dragboard.setContent(content);

        e.consume();
});
```

Detecting a Drag Gesture

Once the drag-and-drop gesture has been initiated, you can drag the gesture source over to any other node. The gesture source has already put the data in the dragboard declaring the transfer modes that it supports. It is now time for the potential gesture targets to declare whether they accept the data transfer offered by the gesture source. Note that there could be multiple potential gesture targets. One of them will become the actual gesture target when the gesture source is dropped on it.

The potential gesture target receives several types of drag events:

- It receives a drag-entered event when the gesture source enters its bounds.

- It receives a drag-over event when the gesture source is dragged around within its bounds.

- It receives a drag-exited event when the gesture source exits its bounds.

- It receives a drag-dropped event when the gesture source is dropped over it by releasing the mouse button.

In a drag-over event handler, the potential gesture target needs to declare that it intends to participate in the drag-and-drop gesture by calling the acceptTransferModes(TransferMode... modes) method of the DragEvent. Typically, the potential target checks the content of the dragboard before declaring whether it accepts the transfer modes. The following snippet of code accomplishes this. The target TextField checks the dragboard for plain text. It contains plain text, so the target declares that it accepts COPY and MOVE transfer modes.

```
targetFld.setOnDragOver((DragEvent e) -> {
        // If drag board has a string, let the event know that the target accepts
        // copy and move transfer modes
        Dragboard dragboard = e.getDragboard();

        if(dragboard.hasString()) {
                e.acceptTransferModes(TransferMode.COPY_OR_MOVE);
        }

        e.consume();
});
```

Dropping the Source onto the Target

If the potential gesture target accepts the transfer mode supported by the gesture source, the gesture source can be dropped on the target. The dropping is accomplished by releasing the mouse button while the gesture source is still over the target. When the gesture source is dropped onto a target, the target becomes the actual gesture target. The actual gesture target receives the drag-dropped event. You need to add a drag-drop event handler for the gesture target in which it performs two tasks:

- It accesses the data in the dragboard.

- It calls the setDropCompleted(boolean isTransferDone) method of the DragEvent object.

Passing true to the method indicates that the data transfer was successful. Passing false indicates that the data transfer was unsuccessful. The dragboard cannot be accessed after calling this method.

The following snippet of code performs the data transfer and sets the appropriate completion flag:

```
targetFld.setOnDragDropped((DragEvent e) -> {
        // Transfer the data to the target
        Dragboard dragboard = e.getDragboard();
        if(dragboard.hasString()) {
                String text = dragboard.getString();
                targetFld.setText(text);

                // Data transfer is successful
                e.setDropCompleted(true);
        } else {
                // Data transfer is not successful
                e.setDropCompleted(false);
        }

        e.consume();
});
```

Completing the Drag-and-Drop Gesture

After the gesture source has been dropped, it receives a drag-done event. The DragEvent object contains a getTransferMode() method. When it is called from the drag-done event handler, it returns the transfer mode used for the data transfer. Depending on the transfer mode, you can clear or keep the content of the gesture source. For example, if the transfer mode is MOVE, it is better to clear the source content to give the user a real feel of the data move.

You may wonder what determines the data transfer mode. In this example, both the gesture source and the target support COPY and MOVE. When the target accessed the data from the dragboard in the drag-dropped event, it did not set any transfer mode. The system determines the data transfer mode depending on the state of certain keys and the source and target. For example, when you drag a TextField and drop it onto another TextField, the default data transfer mode is MOVE. When the same drag and drop is performed with the Ctrl key pressed, the COPY mode is used.

If the getTransferMode() method returns null or TransferMode.ONE, it indicates that no data transfer happened. The following snippet of code handles the drag-done event for the source TextField. The source text is cleared if the data transfer mode was MOVE.

```
sourceFld.setOnDragDone((DragEvent e) -> {
        // Check how the data transfer happened. If it was moved, clear the text in the source.
        TransferMode modeUsed = e.getTransferMode();

        if (modeUsed == TransferMode.MOVE) {
                sourceFld.setText("");
        }

        e.consume();
});
```

This completes handling of a drag-and-drop gesture. If you need more information about the parties participating in the drag-and-drop gesture, please refer to the API documentation for the DragEvent class. For example, use the getGestureSource() and getGestureTarget() methods to get the reference of the gesture source and target, respectively.

Providing Visual Clues

There are several ways to provide visual clues during a drag-and-drop gesture:

- The system provides an icon under the cursor during the drag gesture. The icon changes depending on the transfer mode determined by the system and whether the drag target is a potential target for the drag-and-drop gesture.

- You can write code for the drag-enter and drag-exited events for the potential targets by changing its visual appearance. For example, in the drag-entered event handler, you can change the background color of the potential target to green if it allows the data transfer and to red if it does not. In the drag-exited event handler, you can change the background color back to normal.

- You can set a drag view in the dragboard in the drag-detected event handler for the gesture. The drag view is an image. For example, you can take a snapshot of the node or part of the node being dragged and set it as the drag view.

A Complete Drag-and-Drop Example

The program in Listing 26-3 has the complete source code for this example. It displays a window as shown in Figure 26-2. You can drag the gesture source TextField and drop it onto the target TextField. The text from the source will be copied or moved to the target. The transfer mode depends on the system. For example, on Windows, pressing the Ctrl key while dropping will copy the text, and dropping without pressing the Ctrl key will move the text. Notice that the drag icon is changed during the drag action. The icon gives you a clue as to what kind of data transfer is going to happen when you drop the source. For example, when you drag the source on a target that does not accept the data transfer offered by the source, a "not-allowed" icon, a circle with a diagonal solid line, is displayed.

Listing 26-3. Performing a Drag-and-Drop Gesture

```java
// DragAndDropTest.java
package com.jdojo.dnd;

import javafx.application.Application;
import javafx.scene.Scene;
import javafx.scene.control.Label;
import javafx.scene.control.TextField;
import javafx.scene.input.ClipboardContent;
import javafx.scene.input.DragEvent;
import javafx.scene.input.Dragboard;
import javafx.scene.input.MouseEvent;
import javafx.scene.input.TransferMode;
import javafx.scene.layout.GridPane;
import javafx.stage.Stage;

public class DragAndDropTest extends Application {
        TextField sourceFld = new TextField("JavaFX");
        TextField targetFld = new TextField("Drag and drop the source text here");

        public static void main(String[] args) {
                Application.launch(args);
        }

        @Override
        public void start(Stage stage) {
                // Build UI
                GridPane root = getUIs();

                // Add event handlers for the source and target
                this.addDnDEventHanders();

                root.setStyle("-fx-padding: 10;" +
                                "-fx-border-style: solid inside;" +
                                "-fx-border-width: 2;" +
                                "-fx-border-insets: 5;" +
                                "-fx-border-radius: 5;" +
                                "-fx-border-color: blue;");
                Scene scene = new Scene(root);
                stage.setScene(scene);
                stage.setTitle("Performing a Drag-and-Drop Gesture");
                stage.show();
        }

        private GridPane getUIs() {
                // Set prompt text
                sourceFld.setPromptText("Enter text to drag");
                targetFld.setPromptText("Drag the source text here");
```

```java
            GridPane pane = new GridPane();
            pane.setHgap(5);
            pane.setVgap(20);
            pane.add(new Label("Drag and drop the source text field" +
                              " onto the target text field."), 0, 0, 2, 1);
            pane.addRow(1, new Label("DnD Gesture Source:"), sourceFld);
            pane.addRow(2, new Label("DnD Gesture Target:"), targetFld);
            return pane;
    }

    private void addDnDEventHanders() {
            sourceFld.setOnDragDetected(this::dragDetected);
            targetFld.setOnDragOver(this::dragOver);
            targetFld.setOnDragDropped(this::dragDropped);
            sourceFld.setOnDragDone(this::dragDone);
    }

    private void dragDetected(MouseEvent e) {
            // User can drag only when there is text in the source field
            String sourceText = sourceFld.getText();
            if (sourceText == null || sourceText.trim().equals("")) {
                    e.consume();
                    return;
            }

            // Initiate a drag-and-drop gesture
            Dragboard dragboard =
                    sourceFld.startDragAndDrop(TransferMode.COPY_OR_MOVE);

            // Add the source text to the Dragboard
            ClipboardContent content = new ClipboardContent();
            content.putString(sourceText);
            dragboard.setContent(content);

            e.consume();
    }

    private void dragOver(DragEvent e) {
            // If drag board has a string, let the event know that
            // the target accepts copy and move transfer modes
            Dragboard dragboard = e.getDragboard();
            if (dragboard.hasString()) {
                    e.acceptTransferModes(TransferMode.COPY_OR_MOVE);
            }

            e.consume();
    }

    private void dragDropped(DragEvent e) {
            // Transfer the data to the target
            Dragboard dragboard = e.getDragboard();
```

```
            if (dragboard.hasString()) {
                    String text = dragboard.getString();
                    targetFld.setText(text);

                    // Data transfer is successful
                    e.setDropCompleted(true);
            } else {
                    // Data transfer is not successful
                    e.setDropCompleted(false);
            }

            e.consume();
    }

    private void dragDone(DragEvent e) {
            // Check how data was transfered to the target. If it was moved, clear the
            // text in the source.
            TransferMode modeUsed = e.getTransferMode();

            if (modeUsed == TransferMode.MOVE) {
                    sourceFld.setText("");
            }

            e.consume();
    }
}
```

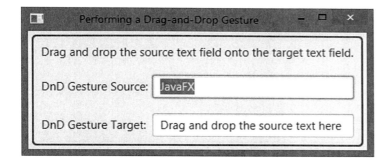

Figure 26-2. *A scene letting transfer text from a* TextField *to another using a drag-and-drop gesture*

Transferring an Image

The drag-and-drop gesture allows you to transfer an image. The image can be placed on the dragboard. You can also place a URL or a file on the dragboard that refers to the image location. Let's develop a simple application to demonstrate an image data transfer. To transfer an image, the user can drag and drop the following to a scene:

- An image

- An image file

- A URL pointing to an image

The program in Listing 26-4 opens a window with a text message, an empty ImageView, and a button. The ImageView will display the dragged and dropped image. Use the button to clear the image.

The entire scene is a potential target for a drag-and-drop gesture. A drag-over event handler is set for the scene. It checks whether the dragboard contains an image, a list of files, or a URL. If it finds one of these data types in the dragboard, it reports that it will accept ANY data transfer mode. In the drag-dropped event handler for the scene, the program attempts to read the image data, list of files, and the URL in order. If it is a list of files, you look at the mime type of each file to see if the name starts with image/. You use the first file with an image mime type and ignore the rest. If it is a URL, you simply try creating an Image object from it. You can play with the application in different ways:

- Run the program and open the HTML file drag_and_drop.html in a browser. The file is included in the src/resources\html directory. The HTML file contains two links: one pointing to a local image file and the other to a remote image file. Drag and drop the links onto the scene. The scene will show the images referred to by the links. Drag and drop the image from the web page. The scene will display the image. (Dragging and dropping of the image worked fine in Mozilla and Google Chrome browsers, but not in Windows Explorer.)

- Open a file explorer, for example, Windows Explorer on Windows. Select an image file and drag and drop the file onto the scene. The scene will display the image from the file. You can drop multiple files, but the scene will display only an image from one of those files.

You can enhance the application by allowing the user to drag multiple files onto the scene and showing them all in a TilePane. You can also add more error checks and feedbacks to the user about the drag-and-drop gesture.

Listing 26-4. Transferring an Image Using a Drag-and-Drop Gesture

```java
// ImageDragAndDrop.java
package com.jdojo.dnd;

import java.io.File;
import java.io.IOException;
import java.nio.file.Files;
import java.util.List;
import javafx.application.Application;
import javafx.scene.Scene;
import javafx.scene.control.Button;
import javafx.scene.control.Label;
import javafx.scene.image.Image;
import javafx.scene.image.ImageView;
import javafx.scene.input.DragEvent;
import javafx.scene.input.Dragboard;
import javafx.scene.input.TransferMode;
import javafx.scene.layout.VBox;
import javafx.stage.Stage;

public class ImageDragAndDrop extends Application {
        ImageView imageView = new ImageView();
        Button clearBtn = new Button("Clear Image");
        Scene scene;
```

```java
public static void main(String[] args) {
        Application.launch(args);
}

@Override
public void start(Stage stage) {
        // Build UI
        VBox root = getUIs();
        scene = new Scene(root);
        stage.setScene(scene);

        // Add event handlers for the source and target
        this.addDnDEventHanders();

        root.setStyle("-fx-padding: 10;" +
                    "-fx-border-style: solid inside;" +
                    "-fx-border-width: 2;" +
                    "-fx-border-insets: 5;" +
                    "-fx-border-radius: 5;" +
                    "-fx-border-color: blue;");
        stage.setTitle("Performing a Drag-and-Drop Gesture");
        stage.show();
}

private VBox getUIs() {
        Label msgLbl = new Label(
                "Drag and drop an image, an image file, or an image URL below.");

        // Set the size for the image view
        imageView.setFitWidth(300);
        imageView.setFitHeight(300);
        imageView.setSmooth(true);
        imageView.setPreserveRatio(true);

        clearBtn.setOnAction(e -> imageView.setImage(null));

        VBox box = new VBox(20, msgLbl, imageView, clearBtn);
        return box;
}

private void addDnDEventHanders() {
        scene.setOnDragOver(this::dragOver);
        scene.setOnDragDropped(this::dragDropped);
}

private void dragOver(DragEvent e) {
        // You can drag an image, a URL or a file
        Dragboard dragboard = e.getDragboard();

        if (dragboard.hasImage() || dragboard.hasFiles() || dragboard.hasUrl()) {
                e.acceptTransferModes(TransferMode.ANY);
        }

        e.consume();
}
```

```java
        private void dragDropped(DragEvent e) {
                boolean isCompleted = false;

                // Transfer the data to the target
                Dragboard dragboard = e.getDragboard();

                if (dragboard.hasImage()) {
                        this.transferImage(dragboard.getImage());
                        isCompleted = true;
                } else if (dragboard.hasFiles()) {
                        isCompleted = this.transferImageFile(dragboard.getFiles());
                } else if (dragboard.hasUrl()) {
                   isCompleted = this.transferImageUrl(dragboard.getUrl());
                } else {
                        System.out.println("Dragboard does not contain an image" +
                                            " in the expected format: Image, File, URL");
                }

                // Data transfer is not successful
                e.setDropCompleted(isCompleted);

                e.consume();
        }

        private void transferImage(Image image) {
                imageView.setImage(image);
        }

        private boolean transferImageFile(List<File> files) {
                // Look at the mime typeof all file.
                // Use the first file having the mime type as "image/xxx"
                for(File file : files) {
                        String mimeType;
                        try {
                                mimeType = Files.probeContentType(file.toPath());
                                if (mimeType != null && mimeType.startsWith("image/")) {
                                        this.transferImageUrl(file.toURI().toURL().
                                        toExternalForm());
                                        return true;
                                }
                        }
                        catch (IOException e) {
                                System.out.println(e.getMessage());
                        }
                }

                return false;
        }
```

```java
        private boolean transferImageUrl(String imageUrl) {
                try {
                        imageView.setImage(new Image(imageUrl));
                        return true;
                }
                catch(Exception e) {
                        System.out.println(e.getMessage());
                }

                return false;
        }
}
```

Transferring Custom Data Types

You can transfer data in any format using the drag-and-drop gesture provided the data is Serializable. In this section, I will demonstrate how to transfer custom data. You will transfer an ArrayList<Item>. The Item class is shown in Listing 26-5; it is Serializable. The class is very simple. It contains one private field with its getter and setter methods.

Listing 26-5. Using a Custom Data Type in Data Transfer

```java
// Item.java
package com.jdojo.dnd;

import java.io.Serializable;

public class Item implements Serializable {
        private String name = "Unknown";

        public Item(String name) {
                this.name = name;
        }

        public String getName() {
                return name;
        }

        public void setName(String name) {
                this.name = name;
        }

        @Override
        public String toString() {
                return name;
        }
}
```

The program in Listing 26-6 shows how to use a custom data format in a drag-and-drop gesture. It displays a window as shown in Figure 26-3. The window contains two ListViews. Initially, only one of the ListViews is populated with a list of items. Both ListViews support multiple selection. You can select items in one ListView and drag and drop them into another ListView. The selected items will be copied or moved depending on the system-determined transfer mode. For example, on Windows, items will be moved by default. If you press the Ctrl key while dropping, the items will be copied instead.

Listing 26-6. Transferring Custom Data Using a Drag-and-Drop Gesture

```java
// CustomDataTransfer.java
package com.jdojo.dnd;

import java.util.ArrayList;
import java.util.List;
import javafx.application.Application;
import javafx.collections.FXCollections;
import javafx.collections.ObservableList;
import javafx.scene.Scene;
import javafx.scene.control.Label;
import javafx.scene.control.ListView;
import javafx.scene.control.SelectionMode;
import javafx.scene.input.ClipboardContent;
import javafx.scene.input.DataFormat;
import javafx.scene.input.DragEvent;
import javafx.scene.input.Dragboard;
import javafx.scene.input.MouseEvent;
import javafx.scene.input.TransferMode;
import javafx.scene.layout.GridPane;
import javafx.stage.Stage;

public class CustomDataTransfer extends Application {
        ListView<Item> lv1 = new ListView<>();
        ListView<Item> lv2 = new ListView<>();

        // Our custom Data Format
        static final DataFormat ITEM_LIST = new DataFormat("jdojo/itemlist");

        public static void main(String[] args) {
                Application.launch(args);
        }

        @Override
        public void start(Stage stage) {
                // Build the UI
                GridPane root = getUIs();

                // Add event handlers for the source and target
                // text fields of the the DnD operation
                this.addDnDEventHanders();
```

```
        root.setStyle("-fx-padding: 10;" +
                     "-fx-border-style: solid inside;" +
                     "-fx-border-width: 2;" +
                     "-fx-border-insets: 5;" +
                     "-fx-border-radius: 5;" +
                     "-fx-border-color: blue;");
        Scene scene = new Scene(root);
        stage.setScene(scene);
        stage.setTitle("Drag-and-Drop Test");
        stage.show();
    }

    private GridPane getUIs() {
        Label msgLbl = new Label("Select one or more items from a list, " +
                                 "drag and drop them to another list");

        lv1.setPrefSize(200, 200);
        lv2.setPrefSize(200, 200);
        lv1.getItems().addAll(this.getList());

        // Allow multi-select in lists
        lv1.getSelectionModel().setSelectionMode(SelectionMode.MULTIPLE);
        lv2.getSelectionModel().setSelectionMode(SelectionMode.MULTIPLE);

        GridPane pane = new GridPane();
        pane.setHgap(10);
        pane.setVgap(10);
        pane.add(msgLbl, 0, 0, 3, 1);
        pane.addRow(1, new Label("List 1:" ), new Label("List 2:" ));
        pane.addRow(2, lv1, lv2);
        return pane;
    }

    private ObservableList<Item> getList() {
        ObservableList<Item> list = FXCollections.<Item>observableArrayList();
        list.addAll(new Item("Apple"), new Item("Orange"),
                    new Item("Papaya"), new Item("Mango"),
                    new Item("Grape"), new Item("Guava"));
        return list;
    }

    private void addDnDEventHanders() {
        lv1.setOnDragDetected(e -> dragDetected(e, lv1));
        lv2.setOnDragDetected(e -> dragDetected(e, lv2));

        lv1.setOnDragOver(e -> dragOver(e, lv1));
        lv2.setOnDragOver(e -> dragOver(e, lv2));

        lv1.setOnDragDropped(e -> dragDropped(e, lv1));
        lv2.setOnDragDropped(e -> dragDropped(e, lv2));
```

```java
                lv1.setOnDragDone(e -> dragDone(e, lv1));
                lv2.setOnDragDone(e -> dragDone(e, lv2));
        }

        private void dragDetected(MouseEvent e, ListView<Item> listView) {
                // Make sure at least one item is selected
                int selectedCount = listView.getSelectionModel().getSelectedIndices().
                                    size();
                if (selectedCount == 0) {
                        e.consume();
                        return;
                }

                // Initiate a drag-and-drop gesture
                Dragboard dragboard = listView.startDragAndDrop(TransferMode.COPY_OR_MOVE);

                // Put the the selected items to the dragboard
                ArrayList<Item> selectedItems = this.getSelectedItems(listView);
                ClipboardContent content = new ClipboardContent();
                content.put(ITEM_LIST, selectedItems);
                dragboard.setContent(content);

                e.consume();
        }

        private void dragOver(DragEvent e, ListView<Item> listView) {
                // If drag board has an ITEM_LIST and it is not being dragged
                // over itself, we accept the MOVE transfer mode
                Dragboard dragboard = e.getDragboard();

                if (e.getGestureSource() != listView &&
                        dragboard.hasContent(ITEM_LIST)) {
                        e.acceptTransferModes(TransferMode.COPY_OR_MOVE);
                }

                e.consume();
        }

        @SuppressWarnings("unchecked")
        private void dragDropped(DragEvent e, ListView<Item> listView) {
                boolean dragCompleted = false;

                // Transfer the data to the target
                Dragboard dragboard = e.getDragboard();

                if(dragboard.hasContent(ITEM_LIST)) {
                        ArrayList<Item> list = (ArrayList<Item>)dragboard.getContent
                                        (ITEM_LIST);
                        listView.getItems().addAll(list);
```

```
                // Data transfer is successful
                dragCompleted = true;
        }

        // Data transfer is not successful
        e.setDropCompleted(dragCompleted);

        e.consume();
    }

    private void dragDone(DragEvent e, ListView<Item> listView) {
        // Check how data was transfered to the target
        // If it was moved, clear the selected items
        TransferMode tm = e.getTransferMode();

        if (tm == TransferMode.MOVE) {
                removeSelectedItems(listView);
        }

        e.consume();
    }

    private ArrayList<Item> getSelectedItems(ListView<Item> listView) {
        // Return the list of selected item in an ArratyList, so it is
        // serializable and can be stored in a Dragboard.
        ArrayList<Item> list =
                new ArrayList<>(listView.getSelectionModel().getSelectedItems());
        return list;
    }

    private void removeSelectedItems(ListView<Item> listView) {
        // Get all selected items in a separate list to avoid the shared list issue
        List<Item> selectedList = new ArrayList<>();
        for(Item item : listView.getSelectionModel().getSelectedItems()) {
                selectedList.add(item);
        }

        // Clear the selection
        listView.getSelectionModel().clearSelection();

        // Remove items from the selected list
        listView.getItems().removeAll(selectedList);
    }
}
```

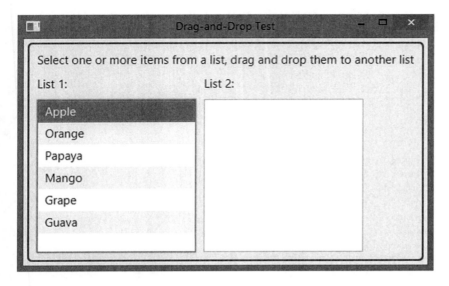

Figure 26-3. *Transferring a list of selected items between two* ListViews

Most of the program is similar to what you have seen before. The difference is in how you store and retrieve the ArrayList<Item> in the dragboard.

You define a new data format for this data transfer because the data do not fit into any of the categories available as the constants in the DataFormat class. You have to define the data as constants, as in the following code:

```
// Our custom Data Format
static final DataFormat ITEM_LIST = new DataFormat("jdojo/itemlist");
```

Now you have given a unique mime type jdojo/itemlist for the data format.

In the drag-detected event, you need to store the list of selected items onto the dragboard. The following snippet of code in the dragDetected() method stores the job. Notice that you have used the new data format while storing the data on the dragboard.

```
ArrayList<Item> selectedItems = this.getSelectedItems(listView);
ClipboardContent content = new ClipboardContent();
content.put(ITEM_LIST, selectedItems);
dragboard.setContent(content);
```

In the drag-over event, if the ListView is not being dragged over itself and the dragboard contains data in the ITEM_LIST data format, the ListView declares that it accepts a COPY or MOVE transfer. The following snippet of code in the dragOver() method does the job:

```
Dragboard dragboard = e.getDragboard();
if (e.getGestureSource() != listView && dragboard.hasContent(ITEM_LIST)) {
        e.acceptTransferModes(TransferMode.COPY_OR_MOVE);
}
```

Finally, you need to read the data from the dragboard when the source is dropped on the target. You need to use the getContent() method of the dragboard specifying the ITEM_LIST as the data format. The returned result needs to be cast to the ArrayList<Item>. The following snippet of code in the dragDropped() method does the job:

```
Dragboard dragboard = e.getDragboard();
if(dragboard.hasContent(ITEM_LIST)) {
        ArrayList<Item> list = (ArrayList<Item>)dragboard.getContent(ITEM_LIST);
        listView.getItems().addAll(list);

        // Data transfer is successful
        dragCompleted = true;
}
```

Finally, in the drag-done event handler, which is implemented in the dragDone() method, you remove the selected items from the source ListView if MOVE was used as the transfer mode. Notice that you have used an ArrayList<Item>, as both the ArrayList and Item classes are serializable.

Summary

A press-drag-release gesture is a user action of pressing a mouse button, dragging the mouse with the pressed button, and releasing the button. The gesture can be initiated on a scene or a node. Several nodes and scenes may participate in a single press-drag-release gesture. The gesture is capable of generating different types of events and delivering those events to different nodes. The type of generated events and the nodes receiving the events depend on the purpose of the gesture.

JavaFX supports three types of drag gestures: a simple press-drag-release gesture, a full press-drag-release gesture, and a drag-and-drop gesture.

The simple press-drag-release gesture is the default drag gesture. It is used when the drag gesture involves only one node—the node on which the gesture was initiated. During the drag gesture, all MouseDragEvent types—mouse-drag entered, mouse-drag over, mouse-drag exited, mouse, and mouse-drag released—are delivered only to the gesture source node.

When the source node of a drag gesture receives the drag-detected event, you can start a full press-drag-release gesture by calling the startFullDrag() method on the source node. The startFullDrag() method exists in both Node and Scene classes, allowing you to start a full press-drag-release gesture for a node and a scene.

The third type of drag gesture is called a drag-and-drop gesture, which is a user action combining the mouse movement with a pressed mouse button. It is used to transfer data from the gesture source to a gesture target. In a drag-and-drop gesture, the data can be transferred in three modes: Copy, Move, and Link. The copy mode indicates that the data will be copied from the gesture source to the gesture target. The move mode indicates that the data will be moved from the gesture source to the gesture target. The link mode indicates that the gesture target will create a link (or reference) to the data being transferred. The actual meaning of "link" depends on the application.

In a drag-and-drop data transfer, the gesture source and the gesture target do not know each other—they may even belong to two different applications. A dragboard acts as an intermediary between the gesture source and the gesture target. A dragboard is the storage device to hold the data being transferred. The gesture source places the data onto a dragboard; the dragboard is made available to the gesture target, so it can inspect the type of content that is available for the transfer. When the gesture target is ready to transfer the data, it gets the data from the dragboard.

Using a drag-and-drop gesture, the data transfer takes place in three steps: initiating the drag-and-drop gesture by the source, detecting the drag gesture by the target, and dropping the source onto the target. Different types of events are generated for the source and target nodes during this gesture. You can also provide visual clues by showing icons during the drag-and-drop gesture. The drag-and-drop gesture supports transferring of any type of data, provided the data are serializable.

The next chapter discusses how to handle concurrent operations in JavaFX.

CHAPTER 27

∎ ∎ ∎

Understanding Concurrency in JavaFX

In this chapter, you will learn:

- Why you need a concurrency framework in JavaFX
- How the Worker<V> interface represents a concurrent task
- How to run a one-time task
- How to run a reusable task
- How to run a scheduled task

The Need for a Concurrency Framework

Java (including JavaFX) GUI (graphical user interface) applications are inherently multithreaded. Multiple threads perform different tasks to keep the UI in sync with the user actions. JavaFX, like Swing and AWT, uses a single thread, called JavaFX Application Thread, to process all UI events. The nodes representing UI in a scene graph are not thread-safe. Designing nodes that are not thread-safe has advantages and disadvantages. They are faster, as no synchronization is involved. The disadvantage is that they need to be accessed from a single thread to avoid being in an illegal state. JavaFX puts a restriction that a live scene graph must be accessed from one and only one thread, the JavaFX Application Thread. This restriction indirectly imposes another restriction that a UI event should not process a long-running task, as it will make the application unresponsive. The user will get the impression that the application is hung.

The program in Listing 27-1 displays a window as shown in Figure 27-1. It contains three controls.

- A Label to display the progress of a task
- A *Start* button to start the task
- An *Exit* button to exit the application

Listing 27-1. Performing a Long-Running Task in an Event Handler

```java
// UnresponsiveUI.java
package com.jdojo.concurrent;

import javafx.application.Application;
import javafx.scene.Scene;
import javafx.scene.control.Button;
import javafx.scene.control.Label;
import javafx.scene.layout.HBox;
import javafx.scene.layout.VBox;
import javafx.stage.Stage;

public class UnresponsiveUI extends Application {
        Label statusLbl = new Label("Not Started...");
        Button startBtn = new Button("Start");
        Button exitBtn = new Button("Exit");

        public static void main(String[] args) {
                Application.launch(args);
        }

        @Override
        public void start(Stage stage) {
                // Add event handlers to the buttons
                startBtn.setOnAction(e -> runTask());
                exitBtn.setOnAction(e -> stage.close());

                HBox buttonBox = new HBox(5, startBtn, exitBtn);
                VBox root = new VBox(10, statusLbl, buttonBox);
                Scene scene = new Scene(root);
                stage.setScene(scene);
                stage.setTitle("An Unresponsive UI");
                stage.show();
        }

        public void runTask() {
                for(int i = 1; i <= 10; i++) {
                        try {
                                String status = "Processing " + i + " of " + 10;
                                statusLbl.setText(status);
                                System.out.println(status);
                                Thread.sleep(1000);
                        }
                        catch (InterruptedException e) {
                                e.printStackTrace();
                        }
                }
        }
}
```

Figure 27-1. *An example of an unresponsive UI*

The program is very simple. When you click the *Start* button, a task lasting for 10 seconds is started. The logic for the task is in the `runTask()` method, which simply runs a loop ten times. Inside the loop, the task lets the current thread, which is the JavaFX Application Thread, sleep for 1 second. The program has two problems.

Click the *Start* button and immediately try to click the *Exit* button. Clicking the *Exit* button has no effect until the task finishes. Once you click the *Start* button, you cannot do anything else on the window, except to wait for 10 seconds for the task to finish. That is, the application becomes unresponsive for 10 seconds. This is the reason you named the class `UnresponsiveUI`.

Inside the loop in the `runTask()` method, the program prints the status of the task on the standard output and displays the same in the `Label` in the window. You see the status updated on the standard output, but not in the `Label`.

It is repeated to emphasize that all UI event handlers in JavaFX run on a single thread, which is the JavaFX Application Thread. When the *Start* button is clicked, the `runTask()` method is executed in the JavaFX Application Thread. When the *Exit* button is clicked while the task is running, an `ActionEvent` event for the *Exit* button is generated and queued on the JavaFX Application Thread. The `ActionEvent` handler for the *Exit* button is run on the same thread after the thread is done running the `runTask()` method as part of the `ActionEvent` handler for the *Start* button.

A pulse event is generated when the scene graph is updated. The pulse event handler is also run on the JavaFX Application Thread. Inside the loop, the `text` property of the `Label` was updated ten times, which generated the pulse events. However, the scene graph was not refreshed to show the latest text for the `Label`, as the JavaFX Application Thread was busy running the task and it did not run the pulse event handlers.

Both problems arise because there is only one thread to process all UI event handlers and you ran a long-running task in the `ActionEvent` handler for the *Start* button.

What is the solution? You have only one option. You cannot change the single-threaded model for handling the UI events. You must not run long-running tasks in the event handlers. Sometimes, it is a business need to process a big job as part of a user action. The solution is to run the long-running tasks in one or more background threads, instead of in the JavaFX Application Thread.

The program in Listing 27-2 is your first, incorrect attempt to provide a solution. The `ActionEvent` handler for the `Start` button calls the `startTask()` method, which creates a new thread and runs the `runTask()` method in the new thread.

Listing 27-2. A Program Accessing a Live Scene Graph from a Non-JavaFX Application Thread

```
// BadUI.java
package com.jdojo.concurrent;

import javafx.application.Application;
import javafx.scene.Scene;
import javafx.scene.control.Button;
```

```java
import javafx.scene.control.Label;
import javafx.scene.layout.HBox;
import javafx.scene.layout.VBox;
import javafx.stage.Stage;

public class BadUI extends Application {
        Label statusLbl = new Label("Not Started...");
        Button startBtn = new Button("Start");
        Button exitBtn = new Button("Exit");

        public static void main(String[] args) {
                Application.launch(args);
        }

        @Override
        public void start(Stage stage) {
                // Add event handlers to the buttons
                startBtn.setOnAction(e -> startTask());
                exitBtn.setOnAction(e -> stage.close());

                HBox buttonBox = new HBox(5, startBtn, exitBtn);
                VBox root = new VBox(10, statusLbl, buttonBox);
                Scene scene = new Scene(root);
                stage.setScene(scene);
                stage.setTitle("A Bad UI");
                stage.show();
        }

        public void startTask() {
                // Create a Runnable
                Runnable task = () -> runTask();

                // Run the task in a background thread
                Thread backgroundThread = new Thread(task);

                // Terminate the running thread if the application exits
                backgroundThread.setDaemon(true);

                // Start the thread
                backgroundThread.start();
        }

        public void runTask() {
                for(int i = 1; i <= 10; i++) {
                        try {
                                String status = "Processing " + i + " of " + 10;
                                statusLbl.setText(status);
                                System.out.println(status);
                                Thread.sleep(1000);
                        }
```

```
                    catch (InterruptedException e) {
                            e.printStackTrace();
                    }
            }
        }
}
```

Run the program and click the *Start* button. A runtime exception is thrown. The partial stack trace of the exception is as follows:

```
Exception in thread "Thread-4" java.lang.IllegalStateException: Not on FX application
thread; currentThread = Thread-4
        at com.sun.javafx.tk.Toolkit.checkFxUserThread(Toolkit.java:209)
        at com.sun.javafx.tk.quantum.QuantumToolkit.checkFxUserThread(QuantumToolkit.java:393)...
at com.jdojo.concurrent.BadUI.runTask(BadUI.java:47)...
```

The following statement in the `runTask()` method generated the exception

```
statusLbl.setText(status);
```

The JavaFX runtime checks that a live scene must be accessed from the JavaFX Application Thread. The `runTask()` method is run on a new thread, named Thread-4 as shown in the stack trace, which is not the JavaFX Application Thread. The foregoing statement sets the `text` property for the `Label`, which is part of a live scene graph, from the thread other than the JavaFX Application Thread, which is not permissible.

How do you access a live scene graph from a thread other than the JavaFX Application Thread? The simple answer is that you cannot. The complex answer is that when a thread wants to access a live scene graph, it needs to run the part of the code that accesses the scene graph in the JavaFX Application Thread. The `Platform` class in the `javafx.application` package provides two static methods to work with the JavaFX application Thread.

- `public static boolean isFxApplicationThread()`
- `public static void runLater(Runnable runnable)`

The `isFxApplicationThread()` method returns true if the thread calling this method is the JavaFX Application Thread. Otherwise, it returns false.

The `runLater()` method schedules the specified `Runnable` to be run on the JavaFX Application Thread at some unspecified time in future.

■ **Tip** If you have experience working with Swing, the `Platform.runLater()` in JavaFX is the counterpart of the `SwingUtilities.invokeLater()` in Swing.

Let us fix the problem in the BadUI application. The program in Listing 27-3 is the correct implementation of the logic to access the live scene graph. Figure 27-2 shows a snapshot of the window displayed by the program.

Listing 27-3. A Responsive UI That Runs Long-Running Tasks in a Background Thread

```java
// ResponsiveUI.java
package com.jdojo.concurrent;

import javafx.application.Application;
import javafx.application.Platform;
import javafx.scene.Scene;
import javafx.scene.control.Button;
import javafx.scene.control.Label;
import javafx.scene.layout.HBox;
import javafx.scene.layout.VBox;
import javafx.stage.Stage;

public class ResponsiveUI extends Application {
        Label statusLbl = new Label("Not Started...");
        Button startBtn = new Button("Start");
        Button exitBtn = new Button("Exit");

        public static void main(String[] args) {
                Application.launch(args);
        }

        @Override
        public void start(Stage stage) {
                // Add event handlers to the buttons
                startBtn.setOnAction(e -> startTask());
                exitBtn.setOnAction(e -> stage.close());

                HBox buttonBox = new HBox(5, startBtn, exitBtn);
                VBox root = new VBox(10, statusLbl, buttonBox);
                Scene scene = new Scene(root);
                stage.setScene(scene);
                stage.setTitle("A Responsive UI");
                stage.show();
        }

        public void startTask() {
                // Create a Runnable
                Runnable task = () -> runTask();

                // Run the task in a background thread
                Thread backgroundThread = new Thread(task);

                // Terminate the running thread if the application exits
                backgroundThread.setDaemon(true);

                // Start the thread
                backgroundThread.start();
        }
```

```java
public void runTask() {
    for(int i = 1; i <= 10; i++) {
        try {
            String status = "Processing " + i + " of " + 10;

            // Update the Label on the JavaFx Application Thread
            Platform.runLater(() -> statusLbl.setText(status));

            System.out.println(status);
            Thread.sleep(1000);
        }
        catch (InterruptedException e) {
            e.printStackTrace();
        }
    }
}
}
```

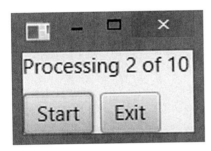

Figure 27-2. *A UI that runs a task in a background thread and updates the live scene graph correctly*

The program replaces the statement

```java
statusLbl.setText(status);
```

in the BadUI class with the statement

```java
// Update the Label on the JavaFx Application Thread
Platform.runLater(() -> statusLbl.setText(status));
```

Now, setting the text property for the Label takes place on the JavaFX Application Thread. The ActionEvent handler of the *Start* button runs the task in a background thread, thus freeing up the JavaFX Application Thread to handle user actions. The status of the task is updated in the Label regularly. You can click the *Exit* button while the task is being processed.

Did you overcome the restrictions imposed by the event-dispatching threading model of the JavaFX? The answer is yes and no. You used a trivial example to demonstrate the problem. You have solved the trivial problem. However, in a real world, performing a long-running task in a GUI application is not so trivial. For example, your task-running logic and the UI are tightly coupled as you are referencing the Label inside the runTask() method, which is not desirable in a real world. Your task does not return a result, nor does it have a reliable mechanism to handle errors that may occur. Your task cannot be reliably cancelled, restarted, or scheduled to be run at a future time.

The JavaFX concurrency framework has answers to all these questions. The framework provides a reliable way of running a task in one or multiple background threads and publishing the status and the result of the task in a GUI application. The framework is the topic of discussion in this chapter. I have taken several pages just to make the case for a concurrency framework in JavaFX. If you understand the background of the problem as presented in this section, understanding the framework will be easy.

Understating the Concurrent Framework API

Java 5 added a comprehensive concurrency framework to the Java programming language through the libraries in the java.util.concurrent package. The JavaFX concurrency framework is very small. It is built on top of the Java language concurrency framework keeping in mind that it will be used in a GUI environment. Figure 27-3 shows a class diagram of the classes in the JavaFX concurrency framework.

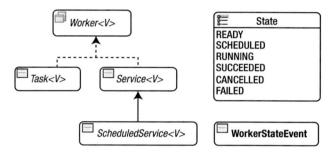

Figure 27-3. *A class diagram for classes in the JavaFX Concurrency Framework*

The framework consists of one interface, four classes, and one enum.

An instance of the Worker interface represents a task that needs to be performed in one or more background threads. The state of the task is observable from the JavaFX Application Thread.

The Task, Service, and ScheduledService classes implement the Worker interface. They represent different types of tasks. They are abstract classes. An instance of the Task class represents a one-shot task. A Task cannot be reused. An instance of the Service class represents a reusable task. The ScheduledService class inherits from the Service class. A ScheduledService is a task that can be scheduled to run repeatedly after a specified interval.

The constants in the Worker.State enum represent different states of a Worker.

An instance of the WorkerStateEvent class represents an event that occurs as the state of a Worker changes. You can add event handlers to all three types of tasks to listen to the change in their states.

Understanding the Worker<V> Interface

The Worker<V> interface provides the specification for any task performed by the JavaFX concurrency framework. A Worker is a task that is performed in one or more background threads. The generic parameter V is the data type of the result of the Worker. Use Void as the generic parameter if the Worker does not produce a result. The state of the task is observable. The state of the task is published on the JavaFX Application Thread, making it possible for the task to communicate with the scene graph, as is commonly required in a GUI application.

State Transitions for a Worker

During the life cycle, a Worker transitions through different states. The constants in the Worker.State enum represent the valid states of a Worker.

- Worker.State.READY
- Worker.State.SCHEDULED
- Worker.State.RUNNING
- Worker.State.SUCCEEDED
- Worker.State.CANCELLED
- Worker.State.FAILED

Figure 27-4 shows the possible state transitions of a Worker with the Worker.State enum constants representing the states.

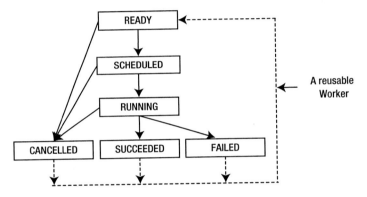

Figure 27-4. *Possible state transition paths for a Worker*

When a Worker is created, it is in the READY state. It transitions to the SCHEDULED state, before it starts executing. When it starts running, it is in the RUNNING state. Upon successful completion, a Worker transitions from the RUNNING state to the SUCCEEDED state. If the Worker throws an exception during its execution, it transitions to the FAILED state. A Worker may be cancelled using the cancel() method. It may transition to the CANCELLED state from the READY, SCHEDULED, and RUNNING states. These are the normal state transitions for a one-shot Worker.

A reusable Worker may transition from the CANCELLED, SUCCEEDED, and FAILED states to the READY state as shown in the figure by dashed lines.

Properties of a Worker

The Worker interface contains nine read-only properties that represent the internal state of the task.

- title
- message
- running
- state

- progress

- workDone

- totalWork

- value

- exception

When you create a Worker, you will have a chance to specify these properties. The properties can also be updated as the task progresses.

The title property represents the title for the task. Suppose a task generates prime numbers. You may give the task a title "Prime Number Generator."

The message property represents a detailed message during the task processing. Suppose a task generates several prime numbers; you may want to give feedback to the user at a regular interval or at appropriate times with a message such as "Generating X of Y prime numbers."

The running property tells whether the Worker is running. It is true when the Worker is in the SCHEDULED or RUNNING states. Otherwise, it is false.

The state property specifies the state of the Worker. Its value is one of the constants of the Worker.State enum.

The totalWork, workDone, and progress properties represent the progress of the task. The totalWork is the total amount of work to be done. The workDone is the amount of work that has been done. The progress is the ratio of workDone and totalWork. They are set to -1.0 if their values are not known.

The value property represents the result of the task. Its value is non-null only when the Worker finishes successfully reaching the SUCCEEDED state. Sometimes, a task may not produce a result. In those cases, the generic parameter V would be Void and the value property will always be null.

A task may fail by throwing an exception. The exception property represents the exception that is thrown during the processing of the task. It is non-null only when the state of the Worker is FAILED. It is of the type Throwable.

Typically, when a task is in progress, you want to display the task details in a scene graph. The concurrency framework makes sure that the properties of a Worker are updated on the JavaFX Application Thread. Therefore, it is fine to bind the properties of the UI elements in a scene graph to these properties. You can also add Invalidation and ChangeListener to these properties and access a live scene graph from inside those listeners.

In subsequent sections, you will discuss specific implementations of the Worker interface. Let us create a reusable GUI to use in all examples. The GUI is based on a Worker to display the current values of its properties.

Utility Classes for Examples

Let us create the reusable GUI and non-GUI parts of the programs to use in examples in the subsequent sections. The WorkerStateUI class in Listing 27-4 builds a GridPane to display all properties of a Worker. It is used with a Worker<ObservableList<Long>>. It displays the properties of a Worker by UI elements to them. You can bind properties of a Worker to the UI elements by passing a Worker to the constructor or calling the bindToWorker() method.

Listing 27-4. A Utility Class to Build UI Displaying the Properties of a Worker

```java
// WorkerStateUI.java
package com.jdojo.concurrent;

import javafx.beans.binding.When;
import javafx.collections.ObservableList;
import javafx.concurrent.Worker;
import javafx.scene.control.Label;
import javafx.scene.control.ProgressBar;
import javafx.scene.control.TextArea;
import javafx.scene.layout.GridPane;
import javafx.scene.layout.HBox;

public class WorkerStateUI extends GridPane {
        private final Label title = new Label("");
        private final Label message = new Label("");
        private final Label running = new Label("");
        private final Label state = new Label("");
        private final Label totalWork = new Label("");
        private final Label workDone = new Label("");
        private final Label progress = new Label("");
        private final TextArea value = new TextArea("");
        private final TextArea exception = new TextArea("");
        private final ProgressBar progressBar = new ProgressBar();

        public WorkerStateUI() {
                addUI();
        }

        public WorkerStateUI(Worker<ObservableList<Long>> worker) {
                addUI();
                bindToWorker(worker);
        }

        private void addUI() {
                value.setPrefColumnCount(20);
                value.setPrefRowCount(3);
                exception.setPrefColumnCount(20);
                exception.setPrefRowCount(3);
                this.setHgap(5);
                this.setVgap(5);
                addRow(0, new Label("Title:"), title);
                addRow(1, new Label("Message:"), message);
                addRow(2, new Label("Running:"), running);
                addRow(3, new Label("State:"), state);
                addRow(4, new Label("Total Work:"), totalWork);
                addRow(5, new Label("Work Done:"), workDone);
                addRow(6, new Label("Progress:"), new HBox(2, progressBar, progress));
                addRow(7, new Label("Value:"), value);
                addRow(8, new Label("Exception:"), exception);
        }
```

```java
    public void bindToWorker(final Worker<ObservableList<Long>> worker) {
        // Bind Labels to the properties of the worker
        title.textProperty().bind(worker.titleProperty());
        message.textProperty().bind(worker.messageProperty());
        running.textProperty().bind(worker.runningProperty().asString());
        state.textProperty().bind(worker.stateProperty().asString());
        totalWork.textProperty().bind(new When(worker.totalWorkProperty().isEqualTo(-1))
                .then("Unknown")
                .otherwise(worker.totalWorkProperty().asString()));
        workDone.textProperty().bind(new When(worker.workDoneProperty().isEqualTo(-1))
                .then("Unknown")
                .otherwise(worker.workDoneProperty().asString()));
        progress.textProperty().bind(new When(worker.progressProperty().isEqualTo(-1))
                .then("Unknown")
                .otherwise(worker.progressProperty().multiply(100.0)
                                .asString("%.2f%%")));
        progressBar.progressProperty().bind(worker.progressProperty());
        value.textProperty().bind(worker.valueProperty().asString());

        // Display the exception message when an exception occurs in the worker
        worker.exceptionProperty().addListener((prop, oldValue, newValue) -> {
            if (newValue != null) {
                    exception.setText(newValue.getMessage());
            } else {
                    exception.setText("");
            }
        });
    }
}
```

The PrimeUtil class in Listing 27-5 is a utility class to check whether a number is a prime number.

Listing 27-5. A Utility Class to Work with Prime Numbers

```java
// PrimeUtil.java
package com.jdojo.concurrent;

public class PrimeUtil {
    public static boolean isPrime(long num) {
        if (num <= 1 || num % 2 == 0) {
            return false;
        }

        int upperDivisor = (int)Math.ceil(Math.sqrt(num));
        for (int divisor = 3; divisor <= upperDivisor; divisor += 2) {
            if (num % divisor == 0) {
                    return false;
            }
        }
        return true;
    }
}
```

Using the Task<V> Class

An instance of the Task<V> class represents a one-time task. Once the task is completed, cancelled, or failed, it cannot be restarted. The Task<V> class implements the Worker<V> interface. Therefore, all properties and methods specified by the Worker<V> interface are available in the Task<V> class.

The Task<V> class inherits from the FutureTask<V> class, which is part of the Java concurrency framework. The FutureTask<V> implements the Future<V>, RunnableFuture<V>, and Runnable interfaces. Therefore, a Task<V> also implements all these interfaces.

Creating a Task

How do you create a Task<V>? Creating a Task<V> is easy. You need to subclass the Task<V> class and provide an implementation for the abstract method call(). The call() method contains the logic to perform the task. The following snippet of code shows the skeleton of a Task implementation:

```
// A Task that produces an ObservableList<Long>
public class PrimeFinderTask extends Task<ObservableList<Long>> {
        @Override
        protected ObservableList<Long>> call() {
                // Implement the task logic here...
        }
}
```

Updating Task Properties

Typically, you would want to update the properties of the task as it progresses. The properties must be updated and read on the JavaFX Application Thread, so they can be observed safely in a GUI environment. The Task<V> class provides special methods to update some of its properties.

- protected void updateMessage(String message)
- protected void updateProgress(double workDone, double totalWork)
- protected void updateProgress(long workDone, long totalWork)
- protected void updateTitle(String title)
- protected void updateValue(V value)

You provide the values for the workDone and the totalWork properties to the updateProgress() method. The progress property will be set to workDone/totalWork. The method throws a runtime exception if the workDone is greater than the totalWork or both are less than -1.0.

Sometimes, you may want to publish partial results of a task in its value property. The updateValue() method is used for this purpose. The final result of a task is the return value of its call() method.

All updateXxx() methods are executed on the JavaFX application Thread. Their names indicate the property they update. They are safe to be called from the call() method of the Task. If you want to update the properties of the Task from the call() method directly, you need to wrap the code inside a Platform.runLater() call.

Listening to Task Transition Events

The Task class contains the following properties to let you set event handlers for its state transitions:

- onCancelled
- onFailed
- onRunning
- onScheduled
- onSucceeded

The following snippet of code adds an onSucceeded event handler, which would be called when the task transitions to the SUCCEEDED state:

```
Task<ObservableList<Long>> task = create a task...
task.setOnSucceeded(e -> {
        System.out.println("The task finished. Let us party!")
});
```

Cancelling a Task

Use one of the following two cancel() methods to cancel a task:

- public final boolean cancel()
- public boolean cancel(boolean mayInterruptIfRunning)

The first version removes the task from the execution queue or stops its execution. The second version lets you specify whether the thread running the task be interrupted. Make sure to handle the InterruptedException inside the call() method. Once you detect this exception, you need to finish the call() method quickly. Otherwise, the call to cancel(true) may not cancel the task reliably. The cancel() method may be called from any thread.

The following methods of the Task are called when it reaches a specific state:

- protected void scheduled()
- protected void running()
- protected void succeeded()
- protected void cancelled()
- protected void failed()

Their implementations in the Task class are empty. They are meant to be overridden by the subclasses.

Running a Task

A Task is Runnable as well as a FutureTask. To run it, you can use a background thread or an ExecutorService.

```
// Schedule the task on a background thread
Thread backgroundThread = new Thread(task);
backgroundThread.setDaemon(true);
backgroundThread.start();

// Use the executor service to schedule the task
ExecutorService executor = Executors.newSingleThreadExecutor();
executor.submit(task);
```

A Prime Finder Task Example

It is time to see a Task in action. The program in Listing 27-6 is an implementation of the Task<ObservableList<Long>>. It checks for prime numbers between the specified lowerLimit and upperLimit. It returns all the numbers in the range. Notice that the task thread sleeps for a short time before checking a number for a prime number. This is done to give the user an impression of a long-running task. It is not needed in a real world application. The call() method handles an InterruptedException and finishes the task if the task was interrupted as part of a cancellation request.

The call to the method updateValue() needs little explanation.

```
updateValue(FXCollections.<Long>unmodifiableObservableList(results));
```

Every time a prime number is found, the results list is updated. The foregoing statement wraps the results list in an unmodifiable observable list and publishes it for the client. This gives the client access to the partial results of the task. This is a quick and dirty way of publishing the partial results. If the call() method returns a primitive value, it is fine to call the updateValue() method repeatedly.

■ **Tip** In this case, you are creating a new unmodifiable list every time you find a new prime number, which is not acceptable in a production environment for performance reasons. The efficient way of publishing the partial results would be to declare a read-only property for the Task; update the read-only property regularly on JavaFX Application Thread; let the client bind to the read-only property to see the partial results.

Listing 27-6. Finding Prime Numbers Using a Task<Long>

```java
// PrimeFinderTask.java
package com.jdojo.concurrent;

import javafx.collections.FXCollections;
import javafx.collections.ObservableList;
import javafx.concurrent.Task;

public class PrimeFinderTask extends Task<ObservableList<Long>> {
        private long lowerLimit = 1;
        private long upperLimit = 30;
        private long sleepTimeInMillis = 500;

        public PrimeFinderTask() {
        }

        public PrimeFinderTask(long lowerLimit, long upperLimit) {
                this.lowerLimit = lowerLimit;
                this.upperLimit = upperLimit;
        }

        public PrimeFinderTask(long lowerLimit,
                               long upperLimit,
                               long sleepTimeInMillis) {
                this(lowerLimit, upperLimit);
                this.sleepTimeInMillis = sleepTimeInMillis;
        }
```

```java
        // The task implementation
        @Override
        protected ObservableList<Long> call() {
                // An observable list to represent the results
                final ObservableList<Long> results =
                                FXCollections.<Long>observableArrayList();

                // Update the title
                this.updateTitle("Prime Number Finder Task");

                long count = this.upperLimit - this.lowerLimit + 1;
                long counter = 0;

                // Find the prime numbers
                for (long i = lowerLimit; i <= upperLimit; i++) {
                        // Check if the task is cancelled
                        if (this.isCancelled()) {
                                break;
                        }

                        // Increment the counter
                        counter++;

                        // Update message
                        this.updateMessage("Checking " + i + " for a prime number");

                        // Sleep for some time
                        try {
                                Thread.sleep(this.sleepTimeInMillis);
                        }
                        catch (InterruptedException e) {
                                // Check if the task is cancelled
                                if (this.isCancelled()) {
                                        break;
                                }
                        }

                        // Check if the number is a prime number
                        if (PrimeUtil.isPrime(i)) {
                                // Add to the list
                                results.add(i);

                                // Publish the read-only list to give the GUI access to the
                                // partial results
                                updateValue(
                                        FXCollections.<Long>unmodifiableObservableList(
                                                results));
                        }
```

```
                        // Update the progress
                        updateProgress(counter, count);
                }

                return results;
        }

        @Override
        protected void cancelled() {
                super.cancelled();
                updateMessage("The task was cancelled.");
        }

        @Override
        protected void failed() {
                super.failed();
                updateMessage("The task failed.");
        }

        @Override
        public void succeeded() {
                super.succeeded();
                updateMessage("The task finished successfully.");
        }
}
```

The program in Listing 27-7 contains the complete code to build a GUI using your PrimeFinderTask class. Figure 27-5 shows the window when the task is running. You will need to click the *Start* button to start the task. Clicking the *Cancel* button cancels the task. Once the task finishes, it is cancelled or it fails; you cannot restart it and both the Start and Cancel buttons are disabled. Notice that when the task finds a new prime number, it is displayed on the window immediately.

Listing 27-7. Executing a Task in GUI Environment

```java
// OneShotTask.java
package com.jdojo.concurrent;

import javafx.application.Application;
import javafx.scene.Scene;
import javafx.scene.control.Button;
import javafx.scene.layout.BorderPane;
import javafx.scene.layout.GridPane;
import javafx.scene.layout.HBox;
import javafx.stage.Stage;
import static javafx.concurrent.Worker.State.READY;
import static javafx.concurrent.Worker.State.RUNNING;
```

```java
public class OneShotTask extends Application {
        Button startBtn = new Button("Start");
        Button cancelBtn = new Button("Cancel");
        Button exitBtn = new Button("Exit");

        // Create the task
        PrimeFinderTask task = new PrimeFinderTask();

        public static void main(String[] args) {
                Application.launch(args);
        }

        @Override
        public void start(Stage stage) {
                // Add event handlers to the buttons
                startBtn.setOnAction(e -> startTask());
                cancelBtn.setOnAction(e -> task.cancel());
                exitBtn.setOnAction(e -> stage.close());

                // Enable/Disable the Start and Cancel buttons
                startBtn.disableProperty().bind(task.stateProperty().isNotEqualTo(READY));
                cancelBtn.disableProperty().bind(task.stateProperty().isNotEqualTo(RUNNING));
                GridPane pane = new WorkerStateUI(task);
                HBox buttonBox = new HBox(5, startBtn, cancelBtn, exitBtn);
                BorderPane root = new BorderPane();
                root.setCenter(pane);
                root.setBottom(buttonBox);
                root.setStyle("-fx-padding: 10;" +
                                "-fx-border-style: solid inside;" +
                                "-fx-border-width: 2;" +
                                "-fx-border-insets: 5;" +
                                "-fx-border-radius: 5;" +
                                "-fx-border-color: blue;");
                Scene scene = new Scene(root);
                stage.setScene(scene);
                stage.setTitle("A Prime Number Finder Task");
                stage.show();
        }

        public void startTask() {
                // Schedule the task on a background thread
                Thread backgroundThread = new Thread(task);
                backgroundThread.setDaemon(true);
                backgroundThread.start();
        }
}
```

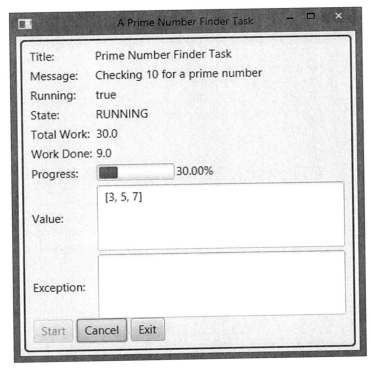

Figure 27-5. A window using the prime number finder Task

Using the Service<V> Class

The Service<V> class is an implementation of the Worker<V> interface. It encapsulates a Task<V>. It makes the Task<V> reusable by letting it be started, cancelled, reset, and restarted.

Creating the Service

Remember that a Service<V> encapsulates a Task<V>. Therefore, you need a Task<V> to have a Service<V>. The Service<V> class contains an abstract protected createTask() method that returns a Task<V>. To create a service, you need to subclass the Service<V> class and provide an implementation for the createTask() method.

The following snippet of code creates a Service that encapsulates a PrimeFinderTask, which you have created earlier:

```
// Create a service
Service<ObservableList<Long>> service = new Service<ObservableList<Long>>() {
        @Override
        protected Task<ObservableList<Long>> createTask() {
                // Create and return a Task
                return new PrimeFinderTask();
        }
};
```

The createTask() method of the service is called whenever the service is started or restarted.

Updating Service Properties

The Service class contains all properties (title, message, state, value, etc.) that represent the internal state of a Worker. It adds an executor property, which is a java.util.concurrent.Executor. The property is used to run the Service. If it is not specified, a daemon thread is created to run the Service.

Unlike the Task class, the Service class does not contain updateXxx() methods for updating its properties. Its properties are bound to the corresponding properties of the underlying Task<V>. When the Task updates its properties, the changes are reflected automatically to the Service and to the client.

Listening to Service Transition Events

The Service class contains all properties for setting the state transition listeners as contained by the Task class. It adds an onReady property. The property specifies a state transition event handler, which is called when the Service transitions to the READY state. Note that the Task class does not contain an onReady property as a Task is in the READY state when it is created and it never transitions to the READY state again. However, a Service can be in the READY state multiple times. A Service transitions to the READY state when it is created, reset, and restarted. The Service class also contains a protected ready() method, which is intended to be overridden by subclasses. The ready() method is called when the Service transitions to the READY state.

Cancelling the Service

Use the cancel() methods to cancel a Service: the method sets the state of the Service to CANCELLED.

Starting the Service

Calling the start() method of the Service class starts a Service. The method calls the createTask() method to get a Task instance and runs the Task. The Service must be in the READY state when its start() method is called.

```
Service<ObservableList<Long>> service = create a service
...
// Start the service
service.start();
```

Resetting the Service

Calling the reset() method of the Service class resets the Service. Resetting puts all the Service properties back to their initial states. The state is set to READY. Resetting a Service is allowed only when the Service is in one of the finish states: SUCCEEDED, FAILED, CANCELLED, or READY. Calling the reset() method throws a runtime exception if the Service is in the SCHEDULED or RUNNING state.

Restarting the Service

Calling the restart() method of the Service class restarts a Service. It cancels the task if it exists, resets the service, and starts it. It calls the three methods on the Service object in sequence.

- cancel()
- reset()
- start()

The Prime Finder Service Example

The program in Listing 27-8 shows how to use a Service. The Service object is created and stored as an instance variable. The Service object manages a PrimeFinderTask object, which is a Task to find prime numbers between two numbers. Four buttons are added: *Start/Restart, Cancel, Reset,* and *Exit.* The *Start* button is labeled Restart after the Service is started for the first time. The buttons do what their labels indicate. Buttons are disabled when they are not applicative. Figure 27-6 shows a screenshot of the window after the *Start* button is clicked.

Listing 27-8. Using a Service to Find Prime Numbers

```java
// PrimeFinderService.java
package com.jdojo.concurrent;

import javafx.application.Application;
import javafx.application.Platform;
import javafx.beans.binding.Bindings;
import javafx.collections.ObservableList;
import javafx.concurrent.Service;
import javafx.concurrent.Task;
import static javafx.concurrent.Worker.State.RUNNING;
import static javafx.concurrent.Worker.State.SCHEDULED;
import javafx.scene.Scene;
import javafx.scene.control.Button;
import javafx.scene.layout.BorderPane;
import javafx.scene.layout.GridPane;
import javafx.scene.layout.HBox;
import javafx.stage.Stage;

public class PrimeFinderService extends Application {
    Button startBtn = new Button("Start");
    Button cancelBtn = new Button("Cancel");
    Button resetBtn = new Button("Reset");
    Button exitBtn = new Button("Exit");
    boolean onceStarted = false;

    // Create the service
    Service<ObservableList<Long>> service = new Service<ObservableList<Long>>() {
        @Override
        protected Task<ObservableList<Long>> createTask() {
            return new PrimeFinderTask();
        }
    };

    public static void main(String[] args) {
        Application.launch(args);
    }

    @Override
    public void start(Stage stage) {
        // Add event handlers to the buttons
        addEventHandlers();
```

```java
                // Enable disable buttons based on the service state
                bindButtonsState();

                GridPane pane = new WorkerStateUI(service);
                HBox buttonBox = new HBox(5, startBtn, cancelBtn, resetBtn, exitBtn);
                BorderPane root = new BorderPane();
                root.setCenter(pane);
                root.setBottom(buttonBox);
                root.setStyle("-fx-padding: 10;" +
                              "-fx-border-style: solid inside;" +
                              "-fx-border-width: 2;" +
                              "-fx-border-insets: 5;" +
                              "-fx-border-radius: 5;" +
                              "-fx-border-color: blue;");
                Scene scene = new Scene(root);
                stage.setScene(scene);
                stage.setTitle("A Prime Number Finder Service");
                stage.show();
        }

        public void addEventHandlers() {
                // Add event handlers to the buttons
                startBtn.setOnAction(e -> {
                        if (onceStarted) {
                                service.restart();
                        } else {
                                service.start();
                                onceStarted = true;
                                startBtn.setText("Restart");
                        }
                });

                cancelBtn.setOnAction(e -> service.cancel());
                resetBtn.setOnAction(e -> service.reset());
                exitBtn.setOnAction(e -> Platform.exit());
        }

        public void bindButtonsState() {
                cancelBtn.disableProperty().bind(service.stateProperty().isNotEqualTo(RUNNING));
                resetBtn.disableProperty().bind(
                        Bindings.or(service.stateProperty().isEqualTo(RUNNING),
                                        service.stateProperty().isEqualTo(SCHEDULED)));
        }
}
```

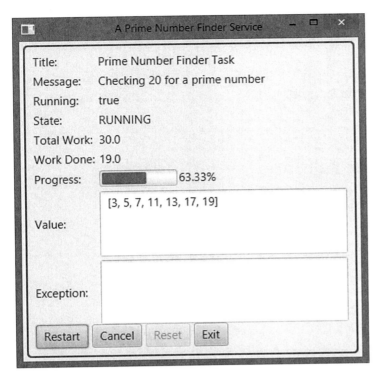

Figure 27-6. *A window using a Service to find prime numbers*

Using the ScheduledService<V> Class

The ScheduledService<V> is a Service<V>, which automatically restarts. It can restart when it finishes successfully or when it fails. Restarting on a failure is configurable. The ScheduledService<V> class inherits from the Service<V> class. The ScheduledService is suitable for tasks that use polling. For example, you may use it to refresh the score of a game or the weather report from the Internet after every 10 minutes.

Creating the ScheduledService

The process of creating a ScheduledService is the same as that of creating a Service. You need to subclass the ScheduledService<V> class and provide an implementation for the createTask() method.

The following snippet of code creates a ScheduledService that encapsulates a PrimeFinderTask, which you have created earlier:

```
// Create a scheduled service
ScheduledService<ObservableList<Long>> service =
                    new ScheduledService <ObservableList<Long>>() {
        @Override
        protected Task<ObservableList<Long>> createTask() {
                // Create and return a Task
                return new PrimeFinderTask();
        }
};
```

The createTask() method of the service is called when the service is started or restarted manually or automatically. Note that a ScheduledService is automatically restarted. You can start and restart it manually by calling the start() and restart() methods.

■ **Tip** Starting, cancelling, resetting, and restarting a ScheduledService work the same way as these operations on a Service.

Updating ScheduledService Properties

The ScheduledService<ScheduledService> class inherits properties from the Service<V> class. It adds the following properties that can be used to configure the scheduling of the service.

- lastValue
- delay
- period
- restartOnFailure
- maximumFailureCount
- backoffStrategy
- cumulativePeriod
- currentFailureCount
- maximumCumulativePeriod

A ScheduledService<V> is designed to run several times. The current value computed by the service is not very meaningful. Your class adds a new property lastValue, which is of the type V, and it is the last value computed by the service.

The delay is a Duration, which specifies a delay between when the service is started and when it begins running. The service stays in the SCHEDULED state for the specified delay. The delay is honored only when the service is started manually calling the start() or restart() method. When the service is restarted automatically, honoring the delay property depends on the current state of the service. For example, if the service is running behind its periodic schedule, it will rerun immediately, ignoring the delay property. The default delay is zero.

The period is a Duration, which specifies the minimum amount of time between the last run and the next run. The default period is zero.

The restartOnFailure specifies whether the service restarts automatically when it fails. By default, it is set to true.

The currentFailureCount is the number of times the scheduled service has failed. It is reset to zero when the scheduled service is restarted manually.

The maximumFailureCount specifies the maximum number of times the service can fail before it is transitioned into the FAILED state and it is not automatically restarted again. Note that you can restart a scheduled service any time manually. By default, it is set to Integer.MAX_VALUE.

The backoffStrategy is a Callback<ScheduledService<?>,Duration> that computes the Duration to add to the period on each failure. Typically, if a service fails, you want to slow down before retrying it. Suppose a service runs every 10 minutes. If it fails for the first time, you may want to restart it after 15 minutes. If it fails for the second time, you want to increase the rerun time to 25 minutes, and so on. The ScheduledService class provides three built-in backoff strategies as constants.

- EXPONENTIAL_BACKOFF_STRATEGY

- LINEAR_BACKOFF_STRATEGY

- LOGARITHMIC_BACKOFF_STRATEGY

The rerun gaps are computed based on the non-zero period and the current failure count. The time between consecutive failed runs increases exponentially in the exponential backoffStrategy, linearly in the linear backoffStrategy, and logarithmically in the logarithmic backoffStrategy. The LOGARITHMIC_BACKOFF_STRATEGY is the default. When the period is zero, the following formulas are used. The computed duration is in milliseconds.

- Exponential: Math.exp(currentFailureCount)

- Linear: currentFailureCount

- Logarithmic: Math.log1p(currentFailureCount)

The following formulas are used for the non-null period:

- Exponential: period + (period * Math.exp(currentFailureCount))

- Linear: period + (period * currentFailureCount)

- Logarithmic: period + (period * Math.log1p(currentFailureCount))

The cumulativePeriod is a Duration, which is the time between the current failed run and the next run. Its value is computed using the backoffStrategy property. It is reset upon a successful run of the scheduled service. Its value can be capped using the maximumCumulativePeriod property.

Listening to ScheduledService Transition Events

The ScheduledService goes through the same transition states as the Service. It goes through the READY, SCHEDULED, and RUNNING states automatically after a successful run. Depending on how the scheduled service is configured, it may go through the same state transitions automatically after a failed run.

You can listen to the state transitions and override the transition-related methods (ready(), running(), failed(), etc.) as you can for a Service. When you override the transition-related methods in a ScheduledService subclass, make sure to call the super method to keep your ScheduledService working properly.

The Prime Finder ScheduledService Example

Let us use the PrimeFinderTask with a ScheduledService. Once started, the ScheduledService will keep rerunning forever. If it fails five times, it will quit by transitioning itself to the FAILED state. You can cancel and restart the service manually any time.

The program in Listing 27-9 shows how to use a ScheduledService. The program is very similar to the one shown in Listing 27-8, except at two places. The service is created by subclassing the ScheduledService class.

```java
// Create the scheduled service
ScheduledService<ObservableList<Long>> service = new ScheduledService<ObservableList<Long>>() {
        @Override
        protected Task<ObservableList<Long>> createTask() {
                return new PrimeFinderTask();
        }
};
```

The ScheduledService is configured in the beginning of the start() method, setting the delay, period, and maximumFailureCount properties.

```java
// Configure the scheduled service
service.setDelay(Duration.seconds(5));
service.setPeriod(Duration.seconds(30));
service.setMaximumFailureCount(5);
```

Figure 27-7, Figure 27-8, and Figure 27-9 show the state of the ScheduledService when it is not started, when it is observing the delay period in the SCHEDULED state, and when it is running. Use the *Cancel* and Reset buttons to cancel and reset the service. Once the service is cancelled, you can restart it manually by clicking the Restart button.

Listing 27-9. Using a ScheduledService to Run a Task

```java
// PrimeFinderScheduledService.java
package com.jdojo.concurrent;

import javafx.application.Application;
import javafx.application.Platform;
import javafx.beans.binding.Bindings;
import javafx.collections.ObservableList;
import javafx.concurrent.ScheduledService;
import javafx.concurrent.Task;
import static javafx.concurrent.Worker.State.RUNNING;
import static javafx.concurrent.Worker.State.SCHEDULED;
import javafx.scene.Scene;
import javafx.scene.control.Button;
import javafx.scene.layout.BorderPane;
import javafx.scene.layout.GridPane;
import javafx.scene.layout.HBox;
import javafx.stage.Stage;
import javafx.util.Duration;

public class PrimeFinderScheduledService extends Application {
        Button startBtn = new Button("Start");
        Button cancelBtn = new Button("Cancel");
        Button resetBtn = new Button("Reset");
        Button exitBtn = new Button("Exit");
        boolean onceStarted = false;

        // Create the scheduled service
```

```java
ScheduledService<ObservableList<Long>> service =
            new ScheduledService<ObservableList<Long>>() {
        @Override
        protected Task<ObservableList<Long>> createTask() {
                return new PrimeFinderTask();
        }
};

public static void main(String[] args) {
        Application.launch(args);
}

@Override
public void start(Stage stage) {
        // Configure the scheduled service
        service.setDelay(Duration.seconds(5));
        service.setPeriod(Duration.seconds(30));
        service.setMaximumFailureCount(5);

        // Add event handlers to the buttons
        addEventHandlers();

        // Enable disable buttons based on the service state
        bindButtonsState();

        GridPane pane = new WorkerStateUI(service);
        HBox buttonBox = new HBox(5, startBtn, cancelBtn, resetBtn, exitBtn);
        BorderPane root = new BorderPane();
        root.setCenter(pane);
        root.setBottom(buttonBox);
        root.setStyle("-fx-padding: 10;" +
                        "-fx-border-style: solid inside;" +
                        "-fx-border-width: 2;" +
                        "-fx-border-insets: 5;" +
                        "-fx-border-radius: 5;" +
                        "-fx-border-color: blue;");
        Scene scene = new Scene(root);
        stage.setScene(scene);
        stage.setTitle("A Prime Number Finder Scheduled Service");
        stage.show();
}

  public void addEventHandlers() {
        // Add event handlers to the buttons
        startBtn.setOnAction(e -> {
                if (onceStarted) {
                        service.restart();
                } else {
                        service.start();
                        onceStarted = true;
```

```
                                    startBtn.setText("Restart");
                    }
            });

            cancelBtn.setOnAction(e -> service.cancel());
            resetBtn.setOnAction(e -> service.reset());
            exitBtn.setOnAction(e -> Platform.exit());
    }

    public void bindButtonsState() {
            cancelBtn.disableProperty().bind(service.stateProperty().isNotEqualTo(RUNNING));
            resetBtn.disableProperty().bind(
                    Bindings.or(service.stateProperty().isEqualTo(RUNNING),
                            service.stateProperty().isEqualTo(SCHEDULED)));
    }
}
```

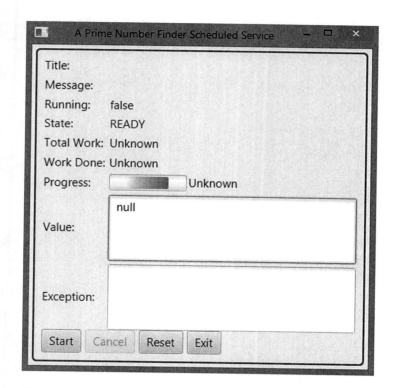

Figure 27-7. *The ScheduledService is not started*

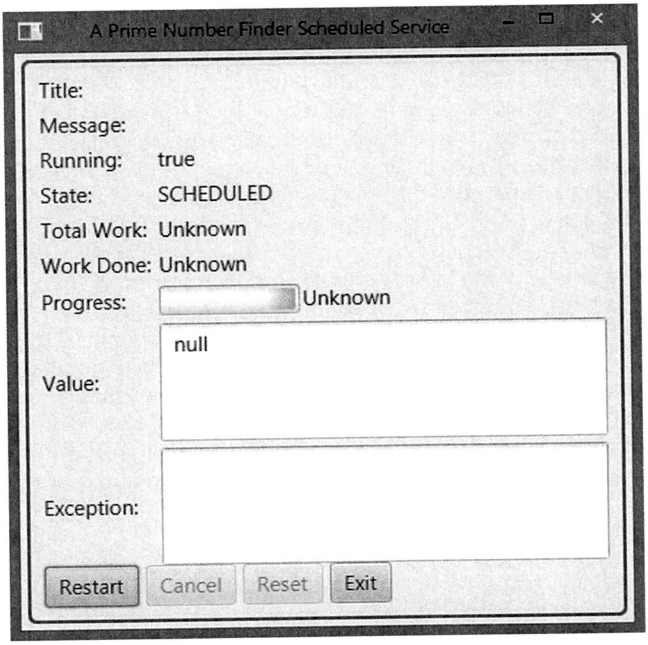

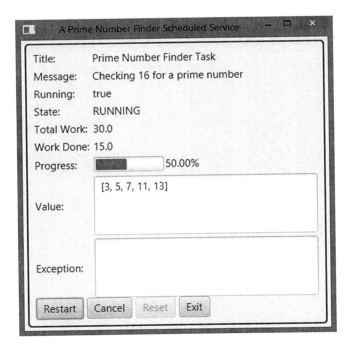

Figure 27-8. *The ScheduledService is started for the first time and it is observing the delay period*

Figure 27-9. *The ScheduledService is started and running*

Summary

Java (including JavaFX) GUI applications are inherently multithreaded. Multiple threads perform different tasks to keep the UI in sync with the user actions. JavaFX, like Swing and AWT, uses a single thread, called JavaFX Application Thread, to process all UI events. The nodes representing UI in a scene graph are not thread-safe. Designing nodes that are not thread-safe has advantages and disadvantages. They are faster, as no synchronization is involved. The disadvantage is that they need to be accessed from a single thread to avoid being in an illegal state. JavaFX puts a restriction that a live scene graph must be accessed from one and only one thread, the JavaFX Application Thread. This restriction indirectly imposes another restriction that a UI event should not process a long-running task, as it will make the application unresponsive. The user will get the impression that the application is hung. The JavaFX concurrency framework is built on top of the Java language concurrency framework keeping in mind that it will be used in a GUI environment. The framework consists of one interface, four classes, and one enum. It provides a way to design a multithreaded JavaFX application that can perform long-running tasks in worker threads, keeping the UI responsive.

An instance of the Worker interface represents a task that needs to be performed in one or more background threads. The state of the task is observable from the JavaFX Application Thread. The Task, Service, and ScheduledService classes implement the Worker interface. They represent different types of tasks. They are abstract classes.

An instance of the Task class represents a one-shot task. A Task cannot be reused.

An instance of the Service class represents a reusable task.

The ScheduledService class inherits from the Service class. A ScheduledService is a task that can be scheduled to run repeatedly after a specified interval.

The constants in the Worker.State enum represent different states of a Worker. An instance of the WorkerStateEvent class represents an event that occurs as the state of a Worker changes. You can add event handlers to all three types of tasks to listen to the change in their states.

The next chapter will discuss how to incorporate audios and videos in JavaFX applications.

CHAPTER 28

■ ■ ■

Playing Audios and Videos

In this chapter, you will learn:

- What the Media API is

- How to play short audio clips

- How to playback media (audios and videos) and how to track different aspects of the playback such as playback rate, volume, playback time, repeating the playback, and media errors

Understanding the Media API

JavaFX supports playing audio and video through the JavaFX Media API. HTTP live streaming of static media files and live feeds are also supported. A number of media formats are supported, including AAC, AIFF, WAV, and MP3. FLV containing VP6 video and MP3 audio and MPEG-4 multimedia container with H.264/AVC video formats are also supported. The support for a specific media format is platform dependent. Some media playback features and formats do not require any addition installations; some require third-party software to be installed. Please refer to the web page at http://docs.oracle.com/javafx/release-documentation.html for details on the system requirements and supported media formats in JavaFX.

The Media API consists of several classes. Figure 28-1 shows a class diagram that includes only the core classes in the Media API. All classes in the API are included in the javafx.scene.media package.

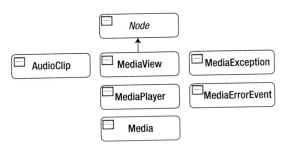

Figure 28-1. *A class diagram for core classes in the Media API*

AudioClip is used to play a short audio clip with minimal latency. Typically, this is useful for sound effects, which are usually short audio clips. Use the Media, MediaPlayer, and MediaView classes for playing audios and videos of longer length.

The Media and MediaPlayer classes are used to play audios as well as videos. An instance of the Media class represents a media resource, which could be an audio or video. It provides the information about the media, for example, the duration of the media. An instance of the MediaPlayer class provides controls for playing a media.

An instance of the MediaView class provides the view of a media being played by a MediaPlayer. A MediaView is used for viewing a video.

Several things can go wrong when you attempt to play a media, for example, the media format may not be supported or the media content may be corrupt. An instance of the MediaException class represents a specific type of media error that may occur during media playback. When a media-related error occurs, a MediaErrorEvent is generated. You can handle the error by adding an appropriate event handler to the media objects.

I will cover the details of using these classes and other supporting classes in the Media API in this chapter.

Playing Short Audio Clips

An instance of the AudioClip class is used to play a short audio clip with minimal latency. Typically, this is useful for playing short audio clips, for example, a beep sound when the user makes an error or producing short sound effects in gaming applications.

The AudioClip class provides only one constructor that takes a URL in string form, which is the URL of the audio source. The audio clip is immediately loaded into memory in raw, uncompressed form. This is the reason why you should not use this class for long-playing audio clips. The source URL could use the HTTP, file, and JAR protocols. This means that you can play an audio clip from the Internet, the local file system, and a JAR file.

The following snippet of code creates an AudioClip using the HTTP protocol:

```
String clipUrl = "http://www.jdojo.com/myaudio.wav";
AudioClip audioClip = new AudioClip(clipUrl);
```

When an AudioClip object is created, the audio data are loaded into the memory and they are ready to be played immediately. Use the play() method to play the audio and the stop() method to stop the playback:

```
// Play the audio
audioClip.play();
...
// Stop the playback
audioClip.stop();
```

The program in Listing 28-1 shows how to play an audio clip using the AudioClip class. It declares an instance variable to store the AudioClip reference. The AudioClip is created in the init() method to make sure the clip is ready to be played when the window is shown in the start() method. You could have also created the AudioClip in the constructor. The start() method adds Start and Stop buttons. Their action event handlers start and stop the playback, respectively.

Listing 28-1. Playing Back an Audio Clip Using an AudioClip Instance

```java
// AudioClipPlayer.java
package com.jdojo.media;

import java.net.URL;
import javafx.application.Application;
import javafx.scene.Scene;
import javafx.scene.control.Button;
import javafx.scene.layout.HBox;
import javafx.scene.media.AudioClip;
import javafx.stage.Stage;

public class AudioClipPlayer extends Application {
        private AudioClip audioClip;

        public static void main(String[] args) {
                Application.launch(args);
        }

        @Override
        public void init() {
                URL mediaUrl = this.getClass()
                                .getClassLoader()
                                .getResource("resources/media/chimes.wav");

                // Create an AudioClip, which loads the audio data synchronously
                audioClip = new AudioClip(mediaUrl.toExternalForm());
        }

        @Override
        public void start(Stage stage) {
                Button playBtn = new Button("Play");
                Button stopBtn = new Button("Stop");

                // Set event handlers for buttons
                playBtn.setOnAction(e -> audioClip.play());
                stopBtn.setOnAction(e -> audioClip.stop());

                HBox root = new HBox(5, playBtn, stopBtn);
                root.setStyle("-fx-padding: 10;");
                Scene scene = new Scene(root);
                stage.setScene(scene);
                stage.setTitle("Playing Short Audio Clips");
                stage.show();
        }
}
```

The AudioClip class supports setting some audio properties when the clip is played:

- cycleCount
- volume
- rate
- balance
- pan
- priority

All of the above properties, except the cycleCount, can be set on the AudioClip class. Subsequent calls to the play() method will use them as defaults. The play() method may also override the defaults for a specific playback. The cycleCount property must be specified on the AudioClip and all subsequent playbacks will use the same value.

The cycleCount specifies the number of times the clip is played when the play() method is called. It defaults to 1, which plays the clip only once. You can use one of the following three INDEFINITE constants as the cycleCount to play the AudioClip loop until stopped:

- AudioClip.INDEFINITE
- MediaPlayer.INDEFINITE
- Animation.INDEFINITE

The following snippet of code shows how to play an audio clip five times and indefinitely:

```
// Play five times
audioClip.setCycleCount(5);
...
// Loop forever
audioClip.setCycleCount(AudioClip.INDEFINITE);
```

The volume specifies the relative volume of the playback. The valid range is 0.0 to 1.0. A value of 0.0 represented muted, whereas 1.0 represents full volume.

The rate specifies the relative speed at which the audio is played. The valid range is 0.125 to 8.0. A value of 0.125 means the clip is played eight times slower, and the value of 8.0 means the clip will play eight times faster. The rate affects the playtime and the pitch. The default rate is 1.0, which plays the clip at the normal rate.

The balance specifies the relative volume for the left and right channels. The valid range is -1.0 to 1.0. A value of -1.0 sets the playback in the left channel at normal volume and mutes the right channel. A value of 1.0 sets the playback in the right channel at normal volume and mutes the left channel. The default value is 0.0, which sets the playback in both channels at normal volume.

The pan specifies distribution of the clip between the left and right channels. The valid range is -1.0 to 1.0. A value of -1.0 shifts the clip entirely to the left channel. A value of 1.0 shifts the clip entirely to the right channel. The default value is 0.0, which plays the clip normally. Setting the value for pan for a mono clip has the same effect of setting the balance. You should change the default for this property only for audio clips using stereo sound.

The priority specifies the priority of the clip relative to other clips. It is used only when the number of playing clips exceeds the system limits. The playing clips with the lower priority will be stopped. It can be set to any integer. The default priority is set to zero.

The play() method is overloaded. It has three versions:

- Void play()
- void play(double volume)
- void play(double volume, double balance, double rate, double pan, int priority)

The no-args version of the method uses all of the properties set on the AudioClip. The other two versions can override the specified properties for a specific playback. Suppose the volume for the AudioClip is set to 1.0. Calling play() will play the clip at the volume 1.0 and calling play(0.20) will play the clip at volume 0.20, leaving the volume property for the AudioClip unchanged at 1.0. That is, the play() method with parameters allows you to override the AudioClip properties on a per-playback basis.

The AudioClip class contains an isPlaying() method to check if the clip is still playing. It returns true is the clip is playing. Otherwise, it returns false.

Playing Media

JavaFX provides a unified API to work with audio and videos. You use the same classes to work with both. The Media API internally treats them as two different types of media that is transparent to the API users. From here onward, I will use the term media to mean both audio and video, unless specified otherwise.

The Media API contains three core classes to play back media:

- Media
- MediaPlayer
- MediaView

Creating a Media Object

An instance of the Media class represents a media resource, which could be an audio or a video. It provides the information related to the media, for example, the duration, metadata, data, and so forth. If the media is a video, it provides the width and height of the video. A Media object is immutable. It is created by supplying a string URL of the media resource, as in the following code:

```
// Create a Media
String mediaUrl = "http://www.jdojo.com/mymusic.wav";
Media media = new Media(mediaUrl);
```

The Media class contains the following properties, all (except onError) of which are read-only:

- duration
- width
- height
- error
- onError

The duration specifies the duration of the media in seconds. It is a Duration object. If the duration is unknown, it is Duration.UNKNOWN.

The width and height give the width and height of the source media in pixels, respectively. If the media does not have width and height, they are set as zero.

The error and onError properties are related. The error property represents the MediaException that occurs during the loading of the media. The onError is a Runnable object that you can set to get notified when an error occurs. The run() method of the Runnable is called when an error occurs:

```
// When an error occurs in loading the media, print it on the console
media.setOnError(() -> System.out.println(player.getError().getMessage()));
```

Creating a *MediaPlayer* Object

A MediaPlayer provides the controls, for example, play, pause, stop, seek, play speed, volume adjustment, for playing the media. The MediaPlayer provides only one constructor that takes a Media object as an argument:

```
// Create a MediaPlayer
MediaPlayer player = new MediaPlayer(media);
```

You can get the reference of the media from the MediaPlayer using the getMedia() method of the MediaPlayer class.

Like the Media class, the MediaPlayer class also contains error and onError properties to report errors. When an error occurs on the MediaPlayer, the same error is also reported on the Media object.

The MediaPlayer class contains many properties and methods. I will discuss them in subsequent sections.

Creating a *MediaView* Node

A MediaView is a node. It provides the view of a media being played by a MediaPlayer. Note that an audio clip does not have visuals. If you try creating a MediaView for an audio content, it would be empty. To watch a video, you create a MediaView and add it to a scene graph.

The MediaView class provides two constructors: one no-args constructor and one that takes a MediaPlayer as an argument:

- public MediaView()
- public MediaView(MediaPlayer mediaPlayer)

The no-args constructor creates a MediaView that is attached to any MediaPlayer. You will need to set a MediaPlayer using the setter for the mediaPlayer property:

```
// Create a MediaView with no MediaPlayer
MediaView mediaView = new MediaView();
mediaView.setMediaPlayer(player);
```

The other constructor lets you specify a MediaPlayer for the MediaView:

```
// Create a MediaView
MediaView mediaView = new MediaView(player);
```

Combining *Media, MediaPlayer,* and *MediaView*

The content of a media can be used simultaneously by multiple Media objects. However, one Media object can be associated with only one media content in its lifetime.

A Media object can be associated with multiple MediaPlayer objects. However, a MediaPlayer is associated with only one Media in its lifetime.

A MediaView may optionally be associated with a MediaPlayer. Of course, a MediaView that is not associated with a MediaPlayer does not have any visuals. The MediaPlayer for a MediaView can be changed. Changing the MediaPlayer for a MediaView is similar to changing the channel on a television. The view for the MediaView is provided by its current MediaPlayer. You can associate the same MediaPlayer with multiple MediaViews: Different MediaViews may display different parts of the same media during the playback. This relationship between the three types of objects involved in a media playback is shown in Figure 28-2.

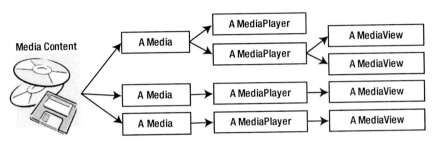

Figure 28-2. *Roles of different media-related objects in a media playback and relation among them*

A Media Player Example

You now have enough background to understand the mechanism used to play an audio and a video. The program in Listing 28-2 plays a video clip from the CLASSPATH. The program uses a video file resources/media/gopro.mp4. You will need to have this file in the CLASSPATH. This file is not included in the source code because it is approximately 50MB. You can substitute your own media file in this program if it is in a format supported by JavaFX.

Listing 28-2. Using the Media, MediaPlayer, and MediaView Classes to Play a Media

```
// QuickMediaPlayer.java
package com.jdojo.media;

import java.net.URL;
import javafx.application.Application;
import javafx.scene.Scene;
import javafx.scene.control.Button;
import javafx.scene.layout.BorderPane;
import javafx.scene.layout.HBox;
import javafx.scene.media.Media;
import javafx.scene.media.MediaPlayer;
import javafx.scene.media.MediaView;
import javafx.stage.Stage;
import static javafx.scene.media.MediaPlayer.Status.PLAYING;
```

```java
public class QuickMediaPlayer extends Application {
        public static void main(String[] args) {
                Application.launch(args);
        }

        @Override
        public void start(Stage stage) {
                // Locate the media content in the CLASSPATH
                String mediaPath = "resources/media/gopro.mp4";
                URL mediaUrl = getClass().getClassLoader().getResource(mediaPath);
                String mediaStringUrl = mediaUrl.toExternalForm();

                // Create a Media
                Media media = new Media(mediaStringUrl);

                // Create a Media Player
                MediaPlayer player = new MediaPlayer(media);

                // Automatically begin the playback
                player.setAutoPlay(true);

                // Create a 400X300 MediaView
                MediaView mediaView = new MediaView(player);
                mediaView.setFitWidth(400);
                mediaView.setFitHeight(300);

                // Create Play and Stop player control buttons and add action
                // event handlers to them
                Button playBtn = new Button("Play");
                playBtn.setOnAction(e -> {
                        if (player.getStatus() == PLAYING) {
                                player.stop();
                                player.play();
                        } else {
                                player.play();
                        }
                });

                Button stopBtn = new Button("Stop");
                stopBtn.setOnAction(e -> player.stop());

                // Add an error handler
                player.setOnError(() -> System.out.println(player.getError().getMessage()));

                HBox controlBox = new HBox(5, playBtn, stopBtn);
                BorderPane root = new BorderPane();

                // Add the MediaView and player controls to the scene graph
                root.setCenter(mediaView);
                root.setBottom(controlBox);
```

```
                  Scene scene = new Scene(root);
                  stage.setScene(scene);
                  stage.setTitle("Playing Media");
                  stage.show();
          }
}
```

The first three statements in the start() method prepare a string URL for the media file. The media path is assumed to exist in the application CLASSPATH:

```
// Locate the media content in the CLASSPATH
String mediaPath = "resources/media/beach.flv";
URL mediaUrl = getClass().getClassLoader().getResource(mediaPath);
String mediaStringUrl = mediaUrl.toExternalForm();
```

If you want to play a media from your local file system, you can replace the above three statements with a string URL using the file protocol. The following statement uses a URL on the Windows file system:

```
String mediaStringUrl = "file:///C:/myvideo.flv";
```

If you want to play a media from the Internet, you can replace the three statements with a statement similar to the following:

```
String mediaStringUrl = "http://www.jdojo.com/video.flv";
```

The program creates a Media, a MediaPlayer, and a MediaView. It sets the autoPlay property for the MediaPlayer to true, which will start playing the media as soon as possible:

```
// Automatically begin the playback
player.setAutoPlay(true);
```

The size of the MediaView is set 400px wide by 300px tall. If the media is a video, the video will be scaled to fit in this size. You will see an empty area for the audios. You can enhance the MediaView later, so it will take as much space as the media needs.

The Play and Stop buttons are created. Event handlers are added to them. They can be used to begin and stop the playback, respectively. When the media is already playing, clicking the Play button stops the playback and plays the media again.

A number of things can go wrong when playing a media. The program sets the onError property for the MediaPlayer, which is a Runnable. Its run() method is called when an error occurs. The run() method prints the error message on the console:

```
// Add an error handler
player.setOnError(() -> System.out.println(player.getError().getMessage()));
```

When you run the program the video should play automatically. You can stop and replay it using the buttons at the bottom of the screen. If there is an error, you will see an error message on the console.

■ **Tip**   The QuickMediaPlayer class can play audios as well as videos. All you need to do is change the URL of the source to point to the media you want to play.

Handling Playback Errors

An instance of the MediaException class, which inherits from the RuntimeException class, represents a media error that may occur in a Media, MediaPlayer, and MediaView. Media playback may fail for a number of reasons. The API users should be able to identify specific errors. The MediaException class defines a static enum MediaException.Type whose constants identify the type of error. The MediaException class contains a getType() method that returns one of the constants of the MediaException.Type enum.

The constants in the MediaException.Type enum are listed below:

- MEDIA_CORRUPTED

- MEDIA_INACCESSIBLE

- MEDIA_UNAVAILABLE

- MEDIA_UNSPECIFIED

- MEDIA_UNSUPPORTED

- OPERATION_UNSUPPORTED

- PLAYBACK_HALTED

- PLAYBACK_ERROR

- UNKNOWN

The MEDIA_CORRUPTED error type indicates that the media is corrupted or invalid. The MEDIA_INACCESSIBLE error type indicates that the media is inaccessible. However, the media may exist. The MEDIA_UNAVAILABLE error type indicates that that media does not exist or it is unavailable. The MEDIA_UNSPECIFIED error type indicates that the media has not been specified. The MEDIA_UNSUPPORTED error type indicates that the media is not supported by the platform. The OPERATION_UNSUPPORTED error type indicates that the operation performed on the media is not supported by the platform. The PLAYBACK_HALTED error type indicates an unrecoverable error that has halted the playback. The PLAYBACK_ERROR error type indicates a playback error that does not fall into any other described categories. The UNKNOWN error type indicates that an unknown error has occurred.

The Media and MediaPlayer classes contain an error property that is a MediaException. All three classes—Media, MediaPlayer, and MediaView—contain an onError property, which is an event handler that is invoked when an error occurs. The types of the onError properties in these classes are not consistent. It is a Runnable for the Media and MediaPlayer classes and the MediaErrorEvent for the MediaView class. The following snippet of code shows how to handle errors on a Media, MediaPlayer, and MediaView. They print the error details on the console:

```
player.setOnError(() -> {
        System.out.println(player.getError().getMessage());
});

media.setOnError(() -> {
        System.out.println(player.getError().getMessage());
});
```

```
mediaView.setOnError((MediaErrorEvent e) -> {
        MediaException error = e.getMediaError();
        MediaException.Type errorType = error.getType();
        String errorMsg = error.getMessage();
        System.out.println("Error Type:" + errorType + ", error mesage:" + errorMsg);
});
```

Media error handlers are invoked on the JavaFX Application Thread. Therefore, it is safe to update the scene graph from the handlers.

It is recommended that you enclose the creation of the Media, MediaPlayer, and MediaView objects in a try-catch block and handle the exception appropriately. The onError handlers for these objects are involved after the objects are created. If an error occurs during the creation of these objects, those handlers will not be available. For example, if the media type you are trying to use is not supported, creating the Media object results in an error:

```
try {
        Media media = new Media(mediaStringUrl);
        ...
}
catch (MediaException e) {
        // Handle errors here
}
```

State Transitions of the *MediaPlayer*

A MediaPlayer always has a status. The current status of a MediaPlayer is indicated by the read-only status property. The status changes when an action is performed on the MediaPlayer. It cannot be set directly. The status of a MediaPlayer is defined by one of the eight constants in the MediaPlayer.Status enum:

- UNKNOWN
- READY
- PLAYING
- PAUSED
- STALLED
- STOPPED
- HALTED
- DISPOSED

The MediaPlayer transitions from one status to another when one of the following methods is called:

- play()
- pause()
- stop()
- dispose()

Figure 28-3 shows the status transition for a MediaPlayer. Figure 28-3 excludes the HALTED and DISPOSED statuses as these two statuses are terminal statuses.

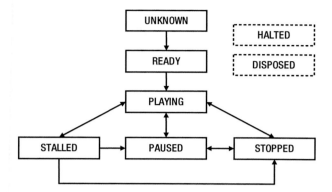

Figure 28-3. *Statuses of a MediaPlayer and the transition among them*

When a MediaPlayer is created, its status is UNKNOWN. Once the media is prerolled and it is ready to be played, the MediaPlayer transitions from UNKNOWN to READY. Once the MediaPlayer exits the UNKNOWN status, it cannot reenter it in its lifetime.

The MediaPlayer transitions to the PLAYING status when the play() method is called. This status indicates that the media is playing. Note if the autoPlay property is set to true, the MediaPlayer may enter the PLAYING status without calling the play() method explicitly after it is created.

When the MediaPlayer is playing, it may enter the STALLED status if it does not have enough data in its buffer to play. This status indicates that the MediaPlayer is buffering data. When enough data are buffered, it goes back to the PLAYING status. When a MediaPlayer is stalled, calling the pause() and stop() methods, it transitions to the PAUSED and STOPPED status, respectively. In that case, the buffering continues; however, the MediaPlayer does not transition to the PLAYING status once enough data are buffered. Rather, it stays in the PAUSED or STOPPED status.

Calling the paused() method transitions the MediaPlayer to the PAUSED status. Calling the stop() method transitions the MediaPlayer to the STOPPED status.

In cases of an unrecoverable error, the MediaPlayer transitions to the HALTED terminal status. This status indicates that the MediaPlayer cannot be used again. You must create a new MediaPlayer if you want to play the media again.

The dispose() method frees all of the resources associated with the MediaPlayer. However, the Media object used by the MediaPlayer can still be used. Calling the dispose() method transitions the MediaPlayer to the terminal status DISPOSED.

It is common to display the status of the MediaPlayer in an application. Add a ChangeListener to the status property to listen for any status changes.

■ **Tip** Before Java 8, the status property of the MediaPlayer was updated on a thread other than the JavaFX Application Thread. Therefore, it was not safe to update the scene graph from the status change listeners. In JavaFX 8, the status change notifications are sent on the JavaFX Application Thread, and, therefore, you can update the scene graph from the status change listeners or bind the status property to UI elements.

Typically, you will be interested in receiving a notification when the status of the MediaPlayer changes. There are two ways to get the notifications:

- By adding a ChangeListener to the status property

- By setting status change handlers

The first method is suitable if you are interested in listening for any type of status change. The following snippet of code shows this method:

```
MediaPlayer player = new MediaPlayer(media);

// Add a ChangeListener to the player
player.statusProperty().addListener((prop, oldStatus, newStatus) -> {
        System.out.println("Status changed from " + oldStatus + " to " + newStatus);
});
```

The second method is suitable if you are interested in handling a specific type of status change. The MediaPlayer class contains the following properties that can be set to Runnable objects:

- onReady

- onPlaying

- onRepeat

- onStalled

- onPaused

- onStopped

- onHalted

The run() method of the Runnable object is called when the MediaPlayer enters into the specific status. For example, the run() method of the onPlaying handler is called when the player enters the PLAYING status. The following snippet of code shows how to set handlers for a specific type of status change:

```
// Add a handler for PLAYING status
player.setOnPlaying(() -> {
        System.out.println("Playing...");
});

// Add a handler for STOPPED status
player.setOnStopped(() -> {
        System.out.println("Stopped...");
});
```

Repeating Media Playback

A media can be played repeatedly for a specified number of times or even indefinitely. The cycleCount property specifies the number of times a playback will be repeated. By default, it is set to 1. Set it to MediaPlayer.INDEFINITE to repeat the playback indefinitely until the player is paused or stopped. The read-only currentCount property is set to the number of completed playback cycles. It is set to 0 when the media is playing the first cycle. At the end of the first cycle, it is set to 1; it is incremented to 2 at the end of second cycle, and so on. The following code would set a playback cycle of four times:

```
// The playback should repeat 4 times
player.setCycleCount(4);
```

You can receive a notification when the end of media for a cycle in playback is reached. Set a Runnable for the onEndOfMedia property of the MediaPlayer class to get the notification. Note that if a playback continues for four cycles, the end of media notification will be sent four times.

```
player.setOnEndOfMedia(() -> {
        System.out.println("End of media...");
});
```

You can add an onRepeat event handler that is called when the end of media for a playback cycle is reached and the playback is going to repeat. It is called after the onEndOfMedia event handler:

```
player.setOnRepeat(() -> {
        System.out.println("Repeating...");
});
```

Tracking Media Time

Displaying the media duration and the elapsed time for a playback are important feedback for the audience. A good understanding of these duration types is important in developing a good media playback dashboard. Different types of duration can be associated with a media:

- The current duration of a media playing media

- The duration of the media playback

- The duration of the media play for one cycle

- The start offset time

- The end offset time

By default, a media plays for its original duration. For example, if the duration of the media is 30 minutes, the media will play for 30 minutes in one cycle. The MediaPlayer lets you specify the length of the playback, which can be anywhere in the duration of the media. For example, for each playback cycle, you can specify that only the middle 10 minutes (11th to 12th) of the media should be played. The length of the media playback is specified by the following two properties of the MediaPlayer class:

- startTime

- stopTime

Both properties are of the Duration type. The startTime and stopTime are the time offsets where the media should start and stop playing for each cycle, respectively. By default, the startTime is set to Duration.ZERO and the stopTime is set to the duration of the media. The following snippet of code sets these properties, so the media will be played from the 10th minute to the 21st minute:

```
player.setStartTime(Duration.minutes(10));
player.setStartTime(Duration.minutes(21));
```

The following constrains are applicable to the startTime and stopTime values:

```
0 ≤ startTime < stopTime
startTime < stopTime ≤ Media.duration
```

The read-only currentTime property is the current time offset in the media playback. The read-only cycleDuration property is the difference between the stopTime and startTime. It is the length of playback for each cycle. The read-only totalDuration property specifies the total duration of the playback if the playback is allowed to continue until finished. Its value is the cycleDuration multiplied by the cycleCount. If the cycleCount is INDEFINITE, the totalDuration will be INDEFINITE. If the media duration is UNKNOWN, the totalDuration will be UNKNOWN.

When you play a media from the network, the MediaPlayer may get stalled because it does not have enough data to continue the playback. The read-only bufferProgressTime property gives you the duration for which the media can be played without stalling.

Controlling the Playback Rate

The rate property of the MediaPlayer specifies the rate of the playback. The valid range is 0.0 to 8.0. For example, a rate of 2.0 plays the media two times faster than the normal rate. The default value is 1.0, which plays the media at the normal rate. The read-only currentRate property is the current rate of playback. The following code would set the rate at three times the normal rate:

```
// Play the media at 3x
player.setRate(3.0);
```

Controlling the Playback Volume

Three properties in the MediaPlayer class control the volume of the audio in the media:

- volume
- mute
- balance

The volume specifies the volume of the audio. The range is 0.0 to 1.0. A value of 0.0 makes the audio inaudible, whereas a value of 1.0 plays it at full volume. The default value is 1.0.

The mute specifies whether the audio is produced by the MediaPlayer. By default, its value is false and the audio is produced. Setting it to true does not produce audio. Note that setting the mute property does not affect the volume property. Suppose the volume is set to 1.0 and the muted is set to true. There is no audio being produced. When the mute is set to false, the audio will use the volume property that is 1.0 and it will play at full volume. The following code would set the volume at half:

```
// Play the audio at half the full volumne
player.setVolumne(0.5);
...
// Mute the audio
player.setMute(true)
```

The balance specifies the relative volume for the left and right channels. The valid range is -1.0 to 1.0. A value of -1.0 sets the playback in the left channel at normal volume and mutes the right channel. A value of 1.0 sets the playback in the right channel at normal volume and mutes the left channel. The default value is 0.0, which sets the playback in both channels at normal volume.

Positioning the *MediaPlayer*

You can position a MediaPlayer at a specific playback time using the seek(Duration position) method:

```
// Position the media at the fifth minutes play time
player.seek(Duration.minutes(5.0));
```

Calling the seek() method has no effect if:

- The MediaPlayer is in the STOPPED status

- The media duration is Duration.INDEFINITE

- You pass null or Duration.UNKNOWN to the seek() method

- In all other cases, the position is clamped between the startTime and stopTime of the MediaPlayer.

Marking Positions in the Media

You can associate markers with specific point on the media timeline. Markers are simply text that are useful in a number of ways. You can use them to insert advertisements. For example, you can insert a URL as the marker text. When the marker is reached, you can pause playing the media and play another media. Note that playing another media involves creating new Media and MediaPlayer objects. You can reuse a MediaView. When you are playing the advertisement video, associate the MediaView with the new MediaPlayer. When the advertisement playback is finished, associate the MediaView back to the main MediaPlayer.

The Media class contains a getMarkers() method that returns an ObservableMap<String, Duration>. You need to add the (key, value) pairs in the map to add markers. The following snippet of code adds three markers to a media:

```
Media media = ...
ObservableMap<String, Duration> markers = media.getMarkers();
markers.put("START", Duration.ZERO);
markers.put("INTERVAL", media.getDuration().divide(2.0));
markers.put("END", media.getDuration());
```

The MediaPlayer fires a MediaMarkerEvent when a marker is reached. You can register a handler for this event in the onMarker property of the MediaPlayer. The following snippet of code shows how to handle the MediaMarkerEvent. The getMarker() method of the event returns a Pair<String, Duration> whose key and value are the marker text and marker duration, respectively.

```
// Add a marker event handler
player.setOnMarker((MediaMarkerEvent e) -> {
        Pair<String, Duration> marker = e.getMarker();
        String markerText = marker.getKey();
        Duration markerTime = marker.getValue();
        System.out.println("Reached the marker " + markerText + " at " + markerTime);
});
```

Showing Media Metadata

Some metadata may be embedded into a media that describe the media. Typically, the metadata contains the title, artist name, album name, genre, year, and so forth. The following snippet of code displays the metadata for the media when the MediaPlayer enters the READY status. Do not try reading the metadata just after creating the Media object, as the metadata may not be available.

```
Media media = ...
MediaPlayer player = new MediaPlayer(media);

// Display the metadata data on the console
player.setOnReady(() -> {
        ObservableMap<String, Object> metadata = media.getMetadata();
        for(String key : metadata.keySet()) {
                System.out.println(key + " = " + metadata.get(key));
        }
});
```

You cannot be sure whether there are metadata in a media or the type of metadata a media may contain. In your application, you can just look for the title, artist, album, and year. Alternatively, you could read all of the metadata and display them in a two-column table. Sometimes the metadata may contain an embedded image of the artist. You would need to check the class name of the value in the map to use the image.

Customizing the *MediaView*

If the media has a view (e.g., a video), you can customize the size, area, and quality of the video using the following properties:

- fitHeight
- fitWidth
- preserveRatio
- smooth
- viewport
- x
- y

The fitWidth and fitHeight properties specify the resized width and height of the video, respectively. By default, they are zero, which means that the original width and height of the media will be used.

The preserveRatio property specifies whether to preserve the aspect ratio of the media while resizing. By default, it is false.

The smooth property specifies the quality of the filtering algorithm to be used in resizing the video. The default value is platform dependent. If it is set to true, a better-quality filtering algorithm is used. Note that a better-quality filtering takes more processing time. For smaller-sized videos, you may set it to false. For bigger-sized videos, it is recommended to set the property to true.

A viewport is a rectangular region to view part of a graphic. The viewport, x, and y properties together let you specify the rectangular area in the video that will be shown in the MediaView. The viewport is a Rectangle2D that is specified in the coordinate system of the original media frame. The x and y properties are the coordinates of the upper left corner of the viewport. Recall that you can have multiple MediaViews associated with a MediaPlayer. Using multiple MediaViews with viewports, you can give the audience the impression of splitting the video. Using one MediaView with a viewport, you can let the audience view only part of the viewable area of the video.

A MediaView is a node. Therefore, to give a better visual experience to the audience, you can also apply effects and transformations to the MediaView.

Developing a Media Player Application

It requires a careful design to develop a good-looking, customizable media player application. I have covered most of the features offered by the Media API in JavaFX. Combining your knowledge of developing a user interface and the Media API, you can design and develop your own media player application. Keep the following points in mind while developing the application:

- The application should have the ability to specify a media source.
- The application should provide a UI to control the media playback.
- When the media source changes, you will need to create a new Media object and a MediaPlayer. You can reuse the MediaView by setting the new MediaPlayer using its setMediaPlayer() method.

Summary

JavaFX supports playing audio and video through the JavaFX Media API. HTTP live streaming of static media files and live feeds are also supported. A number of media formats are supported, such as AAC, AIFF, WAV, and MP3. FLV containing VP6 video and MP3 audio and MPEG-4 multimedia container with H.264/AVC video formats are supported. The support for a specific media format is platform dependent. Some media playback features and formats do not require any addition installations; but some require third-party software to be installed. The Media API consists of several classes. All classes in the API are included in the javafx.scene.media package.

An AudioClip is used to play a short audio clip with minimal latency. Typically, this is useful for sound effects, which are usually short audio clips. Use the Media, MediaPlayer, and MediaView classes for playing audios and videos of longer length.

The Media and MediaPlayer classes are used to play audios as well as videos. An instance of the Media class represents a media resource, which could be an audio or video. It provides the information about the media, for example, the duration of the media. An instance of the MediaPlayer class provides controls for playing a media. A MediaPlayer always indicates the status of the playback. The current status of a MediaPlayer is indicated by the read-only status property. The status changes when an action is performed on the MediaPlayer. The status can be unknown, ready, playing, paused, stalled, stopped, halted, or disposed.

An instance of the MediaView class provides the view of a media being played by a MediaPlayer. A MediaView is used for viewing a video.

Several things can go wrong when you attempt to play a media, for example, the media format may not be supported or the media content may be corrupt. An instance of the MediaException class represents a specific type of media error that may occur during media playback. When a media-related error occurs, a MediaErrorEvent is generated. You can handle the error by adding an appropriate event handler to the media objects.

The next chapter will discuss FXML, which is an XML-based language to build user interfaces for a JavaFX application

CHAPTER 29

▓ ▓ ▓

Understanding FXML

In this chapter, you will learn:

- What FXML is
- How to edit an FXML document
- The structure of an FXML document
- How to create objects in an FXML document
- How to specify the location of resources in FXML documents
- How to use resource bundles in FXML documents
- How to refer to other FXML documents from an FXML document
- How to refer to constants in FXML documents
- How to refer to other elements and how to copy elements in FXML documents
- How to bind properties in FXML documents
- How to create custom controls using FXML

What Is FXML?

FXML is an XML-based language designed to build the user interface for JavaFX applications. You can use FXML to build an entire scene or part of a scene. FXML allows application developers to separate the logic for building the UI from the business logic. If the UI part of the application changes, you do not need to recompile the JavaFX code. Instead you can change the FXML using a text editor and rerun the application. You still use JavaFX to write business logic using the Java language. An FXML document is an XML document. A basic knowledge of XML is required to understand this chapter.

A JavaFX scene graph is a hierarchical structure of Java objects. XML format is well suited for storing information representing some kind of hierarchy. Therefore, using FXML to store the scene-graph is very intuitive. It is common to use FXML to build a scene graph in a JavaFX application. However, the use of FXML is not limited to building only scene graphs. It can build a hierarchical object-graph of Java objects. In fact, it can be used to create just one object, such as an object of a Person class.

Let's get a quick preview of what an FXML document looks like. First, create a simple UI, which consists of a VBox with a Label and a Button. Listing 29-1 contains the JavaFX code to build the UI, which is familiar to you. Listing 29-2 contains the FXML version for building the same UI.

Listing 29-1. A Code Snippet to Build an Object-Graph in JavaFX

```
import javafx.scene.layout.VBox;
import javafx.scene.control.Label;
import javafx.scene.control.Button;

VBox root = new VBox();
root.getChildren().addAll(new Label("FXML is cool"), new Button("Say Hello"));
```

Listing 29-2. A Code Snippet to Build an Object-Graph in FXML

```
<?xml version="1.0" encoding="UTF-8"?>

<?import javafx.scene.layout.VBox?>
<?import javafx.scene.control.Label?>
<?import javafx.scene.control.Button?>

<VBox>
        <children>
                <Label text="FXML is cool"/>
                <Button text="Say Hello"/>
        </children>
</VBox>
```

The first line in FXML is the standard XML declaration that is used by XML parsers. It is optional in FXML. If it is omitted, the version and encoding are assumed to be 1 and UTF-8, respectively. The next three lines are import statements that correspond to the import statements in Java code. Elements representing UI, such as VBox, Label, and Button, have the same name as the JavaFX classes. The `<children>` tag specifies the children of the VBox. The text property for the Label and Button are specified using the text attributes of the respective elements.

Editing FXML Documents

An FXML document is simply a text file. Typically, the file name has a .fxml extension (e.g., hello.fxml). For example, you can use Notepad to create an FXML document in Windows. If you have used XML, you know that it is not easy to edit a large XML document in a text editor. Oracle Corporation provides a visual editor called *Scene Builder* for editing FXML documents. Scene Builder is open source. You can download its latest version from www.oracle.com/technetwork/java/javase/downloads/index.html. Scene Builder can also be integrated into NetBeans IDE, so you can edit FXML documents using Scene Builder from inside the NetBeans IDE. Scene Builder is not discussed in this book.

FXML Basics

This section covers the basics of FXML. You will develop a simple JavaFX application, which consists of the following:

- A VBox
- A Label
- A Button

The spacing property for the VBox is set to 10px. The text properties for the Label and Button are set to "FXML is cool!" and "Say Hello". When the Button is clicked, the text in the Label changes to "Hello from FXML!". Figure 29-1 shows two instances of the window displayed by the application.

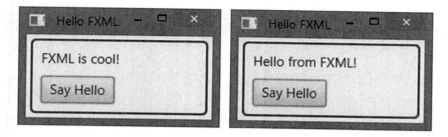

Figure 29-1. Two instances of a window whose scene graphs are created using FXML

The program in Listing 29-3 is the JavaFX implementation of the example application. The program should be easy if you have made it up to this chapter in the book.

Listing 29-3. The JavaFX Version of the FXML Example Application

```java
// HelloJavaFX.java
package com.jdojo.fxml;

import javafx.application.Application;
import javafx.event.ActionEvent;
import javafx.scene.Scene;
import javafx.scene.control.Button;
import javafx.scene.control.Label;
import javafx.scene.layout.VBox;
import javafx.stage.Stage;

public class HelloJavaFX extends Application {
        private final Label msgLbl = new Label("FXML is cool!");
        private final Button sayHelloBtn = new Button("Say Hello");

        public static void main(String[] args) {
                Application.launch(args);
        }

        @Override
        public void start(Stage stage) {
                // Set the preferred width of the label
                msgLbl.setPrefWidth(150);

                // Set the ActionEvent handler for the button
                sayHelloBtn.setOnAction(this::sayHello);

                VBox root = new VBox(10);
                root.getChildren().addAll(msgLbl, sayHelloBtn);
                root.setStyle("-fx-padding: 10;" +
```

```
                              "-fx-border-style: solid inside;" +
                              "-fx-border-width: 2;" +
                              "-fx-border-insets: 5;" +
                              "-fx-border-radius: 5;" +
                              "-fx-border-color: blue;");
            Scene scene = new Scene(root);
            stage.setScene(scene);
            stage.setTitle("Hello FXML");
            stage.show();
    }

    public void sayHello(ActionEvent e) {
            msgLbl.setText("Hello from FXML!");
    }
}
```

Creating the FXML File

Let's create an FXML file sayhello.fxml. Store the file in the resources/fxml directory where the resources directory will be included in the CLASSPATH for the application.

Adding UI Elements

The root element of the FXML document is the top-level object in the object-graph. Your top-level object is a VBox. Therefore, the root element of your FXML would be

```
<VBox>
</VBox>
```

How do you know that to represent a VBox in the object-graph, you need to use a <VBox> tag in FXML? It is both difficult and easy. It is difficult because there is no documentation for FXML tags. It is easy because FXML has a few rules explaining what constitutes a tag name. For example, if a tag name is the simple or full-qualified name of a class, the tag will create an object of that class. The above element will create an object of the VBox class. The above FXML can be rewritten using the fully qualified class name:

```
<javafx.scene.layout.VBox>
</javafx.scene.layout.VBox>
```

In JavaFX, layout panes have children. In FXML, layout panes have children as their child elements. You can add a Label and a Button to the VBox as follows.

```
<VBox>
        <Label></Label>
        <Button></Button>
</VBox>
```

This defines the basic structure of the object-graph for this example application. It will create a VBox with a Label and a Button. The rest of the discussion will focus on adding details, for example, adding text for controls and setting styles for the VBox.

The above FXML shows that the Label and Button are children of the VBox. In the GUI sense, that is true. However, technically, they belong to the children property of the VBox object, not directly to the VBox. To be more technical (and a little verbose), you can rewrite the above FXML as shown below.

```
<VBox>
        <children>
                <Label></Label>
                <Button></Button>
        <children>
</VBox>
```

How do you know that you can ignore the <children> tag in the above FXML and still get the same results? The JavaFX library contains an annotation DefaultProperty in the javafx.beans package. It can be used to annotate classes. It contains a value element of the String type. The element specifies the property of the class, which should be treated as the default property in FXML. If a child element in FXML does not represent a property of its parent element, it belongs to the default property of the parent. The VBox class inherits from the Pane class, whose declaration is as follows.

```
@DefaultProperty(value="children")
public class Pane extends Region {...}
```

The annotation on the Pane class makes the children property the default property in FXML. The VBox inherits this annotation from the Pane class. This is the reason that the <children> tag can be omitted in the above FXML. If you see the DefaultProperty annotation on a class, it means you can omit the tag for the default property in FXML.

Importing Java Types in FXML

To use the simple names of Java classes in FXML, you must import the classes as you do in Java programs. There is one exception. In Java programs, you do not need to import classes from the java.lang package. However, in FXML, you need to import classes from all packages, including the java.lang package. An import processing instruction is used to import a class or all classes from a package. The following processing instructions import the VBox, Label, and Button classes.

```
<?import javafx.scene.layout.VBox?>
<?import javafx.scene.control.Label?>
<?import javafx.scene.control.Button?>
```

The following import processing instructions import all classes from the javafx.scene.control and java.lang packages:

```
<?import javafx.scene.control.*?>
<?import java.lang.*?>
```

Importing static members is not supported in FXML. Note that the import statement does not use a trailing semi-colon.

Setting Properties in FXML

You can set properties for Java objects in FXML. A property for an object can be set in FXML if the property declaration follows the JavaBean conventions. There are two ways to set properties:

- Using attributes of an FXML element
- Using property elements

The attribute name or the property element name is the same as the name of the property being set. The following FXML creates a Label and sets its text property using an attribute.

```
<Label text="FXML is cool!"/>
```

The following FXML achieves the same using a property element.

```
<Label>
        <text>FXML is cool!</text>
</Label>
```

The following FXML creates a Rectangle, and sets its x, y, width, height, and fill properties using attributes.

```
<Rectangle x="10" y="10" width="100" height="40" fill="red"/>
```

FXML specifies values for attributes as Strings. Appropriate conversion is automatically applied to convert the String values to the required types. In the above case, the value "red" for the fill property will be automatically converted to a Color object; the value "100" for the width property will be converted to a double value, and so on.

Using property elements to set object properties is more flexible. Attributes can be used when the automatic type conversion from String is possible. Suppose you want set an object of a Person class to a property of an object. It can be done using a property element. The following FXML sets the person property of an object of the class MyCls.

```
<MyCls>
        <person>
                <Person>
                        <!-- Configure the Person object here -->
                </Person>
        </person>
</MyCls>
```

A read-only property is a property that has a getter, but no setter. Two special types of read-only properties can be set in FXML using a property element:

- A read-only List property
- A read-only Map property

Use a property element for setting a read-only List property. All children of the property element will be added to the List returned by the getter of the property. The following FXML sets the read-only children property of a VBox.

```
<VBox>
        <children>
                <Label/>
                <Button/>
        <children>
</VBox>
```

You can use attributes of the property element to add entries to a read-only Map property. The names and values of the attributes become the keys and the values in the Map. The following snippet of code declares a class Item, which has a read-only map property.

```
public class Item {
        private Map<String, Integer> map = new HashMap<>();
        public Map getMap() {
                return map;
        }
}
```

The following FXML creates an Item object and sets its map property with two entries ("n1", 100) and ("n2", 200). Notice that the names of the attributes n1 and n2 become the keys in the Map.

```
<Item>
        <map n1="100" n2="200"/>
</Item>
```

There is one special type of property for Java objects known as static property. The static property is not declared on the class of the object. Rather, it is set using a static method of another class. Suppose you want to set the margin for a Button that will be placed in a VBox. The JavaFX code is shown below.

```
Button btn = new Button("OK");
Insets insets = new Insets(20.0);;
VBox.setMargin(btn, insets);
VBox vbox = new VBox(btn);
```

You can achieve the same in FXML by setting a VBox.margin property for the Button.

```
<?import javafx.scene.layout.VBox?>
<?import javafx.scene.control.Button?>
<?import javafx.geometry.Insets?>

<VBox>
        <Button text="OK">
                <VBox.margin>
                        <Insets top="20.0" right="20.0" bottom="20.0" left="20.0"/>
                </VBox.margin>
        </Button>
</VBox>
```

You cannot create an Insets object from a String, and therefore, you cannot use an attribute to set the margin property. You need to use a property element to set it. When you use a GridPane in FXML, you can set the rowIndex and columnIndex static as shown below.

```
<?import javafx.scene.layout.GridPane?>
<?import javafx.scene.control.Button?>

<GridPane>
        <Button text="OK">
                <GridPane.rowIndex>0</GridPane.rowIndex>
                <GridPane.columnIndex>0</GridPane.columnIndex>
        </Button>
</GridPane>
```

Because the rowIndex and columnIndex properties can also be represented as Strings, you can use attributes to set them.

```
<GridPane>
        <Button text="OK" GridPane.rowIndex="0" GridPane.columnIndex="0"/>
</GridPane>
```

Specifying FXML Namespace

FXML does not have an XML schema. It uses a namespace that needs to be specified using the namespace prefix "fx". For the most part, the FXML parser will figure out the tag names such as tag names that are classes, properties of the classes, and so on. FXML uses special elements and attribute names, which must be qualified with the "fx" namespace prefix. The following FXML declares the "fx" namespace prefix.

```
<VBox xmlns:fx="http://javafx.com/fxml">...</VBox>
```

Optionally, you can append the version of the FXML in the namespace URI. The FXML parser will verify that it can parse the specified. At the time of this writing, the only supported version is 1.0.

```
<VBox xmlns:fx="http://javafx.com/fxml/1.0">...</VBox>
```

The FXML version can include dots, underscores, and dashes. Only the numbers before the first occurrence of the underscores and dashes are compared. All of the following three declarations specify the FXML version as 1.0.

```
<VBox xmlns:fx="http://javafx.com/fxml/1">...</VBox>
<VBox xmlns:fx="http://javafx.com/fxml/1.0-ea">...</VBox>
<VBox xmlns:fx="http://javafx.com/fxml/1.0-rc1-2014_03_02">...</VBox>
```

The following FXML uses the "fx" namespace prefix to define a block of script that defines a sayHello() function.

```
<?language JavaScript?>
<?import javafx.scene.layout.VBox?>

<VBox xmlns:fx="http://javafx.com/fxml">
        <fx:script>
                function sayHello() {
                        java.lang.System.out.println("Hello from FXML");
                }
        </fx:script>
</VBox>
```

FXML needs to specify the name of the scripting language for the script using a language processing instruction. The above FXML specifies *javascript* as the scripting language. You can use any other scripting languages such as Python, Ruby, and Groovy. You can use any scripting language to define a block of script in an FXML document.

Assigning an Identifier to an Object

An object created in FXML can be referred to somewhere else in the same document. It is common to get the reference of UI objects created in FXML inside the JavaFX code. You can achieve this by first identifying the objects in FXML with an fx:id attribute. The value of the fx:id attribute is the identifier for the object. If the object type has an id property, the value will be also set for the property. Note that each Node in JavaFX has an id property that can be used to refer to them in CSS. The following is an example of specifying the fx:id attribute for a Label.

```
<Label fx:id="msgLbl" text="FXML is cool!"/>
```

Now, you can refer to the Label using the msgLbl. The following FXML has a block of script written in JavaScript to set the text property for the Label, assuming that both the Label and the script elements exist in the same FXML.

```
<fx:script>
        function sayHello() {
                msgLbl.setText("Hello from FXML!");
        }
</fx:script>
```

The fx:id attribute has several uses. It is also used to inject the reference of UI elements into the instance variables of a JavaFX class at the time FXML is loaded. I will discuss other uses in separate sections.

Adding Event Handlers

You can set event handlers for nodes in FXML. Setting an event handler is similar to setting any other properties. JavaFX classes define onXxx properties to set an event handler for Xxx event. For example, the Button class contains an onAction property to set an ActionEvent handler. In FXML, you can specify two types of event handlers:

- Script Event Handlers

- Controller Event Handlers

The script event handler is used when the event handler is defined in a scripting language. The value of the attribute is the script itself, such as a function call or one or more statements. The following snippet of FXML sets the ActionEvent handler for a Button that calls the f1() function defined using JavaScript.

```
<?language JavaScript?>
<?import javafx.scene.control.Button?>

<fx:script>
        function f1() {
                java.lang.System.out.println("f1");
        };
```

```
        function f2() {
                java.lang.System.out.println("f2");
        };
</fx:script>
<Button text="Close" onAction="f1();"/>
```

If you want to execute both functions f1() and f2() when the button is clicked, you can set the event handler as

```
<Button text="Close" onAction="f1(); f2();"/>
```

The following snippet of FXML is the shorter version of the one shown above. It prints a string on the console when the button is clicked. The call to the println() function is made directly as part of the onAction attribute value.

```
<?language javascript?>
<?import javafx.scene.control.Button?>

<Button text="Close" onAction="java.lang.System.out.println(&quot;f1&quot;);"/>
```

Note the use of " in the attribute value. It is an XML entity reference to represent double quotes. You can use single quotes instead.

```
<Button text="Close" onAction="java.lang.System.out.println('f1');"/>
```

I will discuss how to specify controller event handlers in the section *Using a Controller in FXML*.

Listing 29-4 is the FXML document for this example. It will create the root element for the scene shown in Figure 29-1.

Listing 29-4. The Contents of the sayhello.fxml File

```
<?xml version="1.0" encoding="UTF-8"?>
<?language javascript?>
<?import javafx.scene.Scene?>
<?import javafx.scene.layout.VBox?>
<?import javafx.scene.control.Label?>
<?import javafx.scene.control.Button?>

<VBox spacing="10" xmlns:fx="http://javafx.com/fxml">
        <Label fx:id="msgLbl" text="FXML is cool!" prefWidth="150"/>
        <Button fx:id="sayHelloBtn" text="Say Hello" onAction="sayHello()"/>
        <style>
                -fx-padding: 10;
                -fx-border-style: solid inside;
                -fx-border-width: 2;
                -fx-border-insets: 5;
                -fx-border-radius: 5;
                -fx-border-color: blue;
        </style>
```

```
    <fx:script>
          function sayHello() {
                msgLbl.setText("Hello from FXML!");
          }
    </fx:script>
</VBox>
```

You have set the spacing property for the VBox, the fx:id attribute for the Label and Button controls. You have set the style property of the VBox using a <style> property element. You had an option to set the style using a style attribute or a property element. You chose to use a property element because the style value is a big string and it is more readable to write them in multiple lines. The <fx:script> element defines a script block with one function sayHello(). The function sets the text property of the Label identifies by the msgLbl fx:id attribute.

Loading FXML Documents

An FXML document defines the view (the GUI) part of a JavaFX application. You need to load the FXML document to get the object-graph it represents. Loading an FXML is performed by an instance of the FXMLLoader class, which is in the javafx.fxml package.

The FXMLLoader class provides several constructors that let you specify the location, charset, resource bundle, and other elements to be used for loading the document. You need to specify at least the location of the FXML document, which is a URL. The class contains load() methods to perform the actual loading of the document. The following snippet of code loads an FXML document from a local file system in Windows:

```
String fxmlDocUrl = "file:///C:/resources/fxml/test.fxml";
URL fxmlUrl = new URL(fxmlDocUrl);
FXMLLoader loader = new FXMLLoader();
loader.setLocation(fxmlUrl);
VBox root = loader.<VBox>load();
```

The load() method has a generic return type. In the above snippet of code, you have made your intention clear in the call to the load() method (loader.<VBox>load()) that you are expecting a VBox instance from the FXML document. If you prefer, you may omit the generic parameter.

```
// Will work
VBox root = loader.load();
```

FXMLLoader supports loading a FXML document using an InputStream. The following snippet of code loads the same FXML document using an InputStream.

```
FXMLLoader loader = new FXMLLoader();
String fxmlDocPath = " C:\\resources\\fxml\\test.fxml ";
FileInputStream fxmlStream = new FileInputStream(fxmlDocPath);
VBox root = loader.<VBox>load(fxmlStream);
```

Internally, the FXMLLoader reads the document using streams, which may throw an IOException. All versions of the load() method in FXMLLoader class throw IOException. You have omitted the exception-handling code in this sample code above. In your application, you will need to handle the exception.

The FXMLLoader class contains several versions of the load() method. Some of them are instance methods and some static methods. You need to create an FXMLLoader instance and use the instance load() method, if you want to retrieve more information from the loader, such as the controller reference, resource bundle, the location, charset, and root object. If you just want to load an FXML document without regard for any other details, you need to use the static load() methods. The following snippet of code uses a static load() method to load an FXML document.

```
String fxmlDocUrl = "file:///C:/resources/fxml/test.fxml";
URL fxmlUrl = new URL(fxmlDocUrl);
VBox root = FXMLLoader.<VBox>load(fxmlUrl);
```

What do you do next after loading an FXML document? At this point, the role of FXML is over and your JavaFX code should take over. I will discuss the loader later in the text.

The program in Listing 29-5 has the JavaFX code for this example. It loads the FXML document stored in the *sayHello.fxml* file. The program loads the document from the CLASSPATH. The loader returns a VBox, which is set as the root for the scene. The rest of the code is the same as you have been using except for one difference in the declaration of the start() method. The method declares that it may throw an IOException, which you had to add because you have called the load() method of the FXMLLoader inside the method. When you run the program, it displays a window as shown in Figure 29-1. Click the button and the text for the Label will change.

Listing 29-5. Using FXML to Build the GUI

```java
// SayHelloFXML.java
package com.jdojo.fxml;

import javafx.application.Application;
import javafx.fxml.FXMLLoader;
import java.io.IOException;
import java.net.URL;
import javafx.scene.Scene;
import javafx.scene.layout.VBox;
import javafx.stage.Stage;

public class SayHelloFXML extends Application {
        public static void main(String[] args) {
                Application.launch(args);
        }

        @Override
        public void start(Stage stage) throws IOException {
                // Construct a URL for the FXML document
                URL fxmlUrl = this.getClass()
                                .getClassLoader()
                                .getResource("resources/fxml/sayhello.fxml");

                // Load the FXML document
                VBox root = FXMLLoader.<VBox>load(fxmlUrl);
                Scene scene = new Scene(root);
                stage.setScene(scene);
                stage.setTitle("Hello FXML");
                stage.show();
        }
}
```

You have completed the example that you started in the beginning of this section. You need to note a few points about this implementation:

- The FXML built the UI and it also provided the event handling code in JavaScript.

- You do not have references to the UI elements such as the Label and Button in your JavaFX code. References to UI elements are needed to hookup event handling code and bind the UI to the model.

In short, you are missing the link between UI and JavaFX code. You can create this link by specifying a controller in FXML, which is discussed in the next section.

Using a Controller in FXML

A controller is simply a class name whose object is created by FXML and used to initialize the UI elements. FXML lets you specify a controller on the root element using the fx:controller attribute. Note that only one controller is allowed per FXML document, and if specified, it must be specified on the root element.
The following FXML specifies a controller for the VBox element.

```
<VBox fx:controller="com.jdojo.fxml.SayHelloController"
      xmlns:fx="http://javafx.com/fxml">
</VBox>
```

A controller needs to conform to some rules and it can be used for different reasons:

- The controller is instantiated by the FXML loader.

- The controller must have a public no-args constructor. If it does not exist, the FXML loader will not be able to instantiate it, which will throw an exception at the load time.

- The controller can have accessible methods, which can be specified as event handlers in FXML. Please refer to the discussion below for the meaning of "accessible".

- The FXML loader will automatically look for accessible instance variables of the controller. If the name of an accessible instance variable matches the fx:id attribute of an element, the object reference from FXML is automatically copied into the controller instance variable. This feature makes the references of UI elements in FXML available to the controller. The controller can use them later, such as binding them to model.

- The controller can have an accessible initialize() method, which should take no arguments and have a return type of void. The FXML loader will call the initialize() method after the loading of the FXML document is complete.

Listing 29-6 shows the code for a controller class that you will use for this example.

Listing 29-6. A Controller Class

```
// SayHelloController.java
package com.jdojo.fxml;

import java.net.URL;
import java.util.ResourceBundle;
import javafx.fxml.FXML;
import javafx.scene.control.Label;
```

```java
public class SayHelloController {
        // The reference of msgLbl will be injected by the FXML loader
        @FXML
        private Label msgLbl;

        // location and resources will be automatically injected by the FXML loader
        @FXML
        private URL location;

        @FXML
        private ResourceBundle resources;

        // Add a public no-args constructor explicitly just to
        // emphasize that it is needed for a controller
        public SayHelloController() {
        }

        @FXML
        private void initialize() {
                System.out.println("Initializing SayHelloController...");
                System.out.println("Location = " + location);
                System.out.println("Resources = " + resources);
        }

        @FXML
        private void sayHello() {
                msgLbl.setText("Hello from FXML!");
        }
}
```

The controller class uses a @FXML annotation on some members. The @FXML annotation can be used on fields and methods. It cannot be used on classes and constructors. By using a @FXML annotation on a member, you are declaring that the FXML loader can access the member even if it is private. A public member used by the FXML loader does not need to be annotated with @FXML. However, annotating a public member with @FXML is not an error. It is better to annotate all members, public and private, used by the FXML loader with @FXML annotation. This tells the reader of your code how the members are being used.

The following FXML sets the sayHello() method of the controller class as the event handler for the Button.

```xml
<VBox fx:controller="com.jdojo.fxml.SayHelloController"
      xmlns:fx="http://javafx.com/fxml">
    <Button fx:id="sayHelloBtn" text="Say Hello" onAction="#sayHello"/>
...
</VBox>
```

There two special instance variables that can be declared in the controller and they are automatically injected by the FXML loader:

- @FXML private URL location;

- @FXML private ResourceBundle resources;

The location is the location of the FXML document. The resources is the reference of the ResourceBundle used, if any, in the FXML.

When the event handler attribute value starts with a hash symbol (#), it indicates to the FXML loader that sayHello is the method in the controller, not in a script. The event handler method in the controller should conform to some rules:

- The method may take no arguments or a single argument. If it takes an argument, the argument type must be a type assignment compatible with the event it is supposed to handle.

- It is not an error to have both versions of the method: one that takes no arguments and with a single argument. In such a case, the method with a single argument is used.

- Conventionally, the method return type should be void, because there is no taker of the returned value.

- The method must be accessible to the FXML loader: make it public or annotate it with @FXML.

When the FXML loader is done loading the FXML document, it calls the initialize() method of the controller. The method should not take any argument. It should be accessible to the FXML loader. In the controller, you used the @FXML annotation to make it accessible to the FXML loader.

The FXMLLoader class lets you set a controller for the root element in the code using the setController() method. Use the getController() method to get the reference of the controller from the loader. Developers make a common mistake in getting the reference of the controller. The mistake is made because of the way the load() method is designed. There are seven overloaded versions of the load() method: two of them are instance methods and five are static methods. To use the getController() method, you must create an object of the FXMLLoader class and make sure that you use one of the instance methods of the class to load the document. Below is an example of the common mistake.

```
URL fxmlUrl = new URL("file:///C:/resources/fxml/test.fxml");

// Create an FXMLLoader object - a good start
FXMLLoader loader = new FXMLLoader();

// Load the document -- mistake
VBox root = loader.<VBox>load(fxmlUrl);

// loader.getController() will return null
Test controller = loader.getController();
// controller is null here
```

The above code creates an object of the FXMLLoader class. However, the load(URL url) method that is called in the loader variable is the static load() method, not the instance load() method. Therefore, the loader instance never got a controller and when you ask it for a controller, it returns null. To clear the confusion, below are the instance and static versions of the load() method of which only the first two versions are instance methods:

- `<T> T load()`

- `<T> T load(InputStream inputStream)`

- `static <T> T load(URL location)`

- `static <T> T load(URL location, ResourceBundle resources)`

- static <T> T load(URL location, ResourceBundle resources, BuilderFactory builderFactory)

- static <T> T load(URL location, ResourceBundle resources, BuilderFactory builderFactory, Callback<Class<?>,Object> controllerFactory)

- static <T> T load(URL location, ResourceBundle resources, BuilderFactory builderFactory, Callback<Class<?>,Object> controllerFactory, Charset charset)

The following snippet of code is the correct way of using the load() method, so you can get the reference of the controller in JavaFX code.

```
URL fxmlUrl = new URL("file:///C:/resources/fxml/test.fxml");

// Create an FXMLLoader object - a good start
FXMLLoader loader = new FXMLLoader();
loader.setLocation(fxmlUrl);

// Calling the no-args instance load() method - Correct
VBox root = loader.<VBox>load();

// loader.getController() will return the controller
Test controller = loader.getController();
```

You now have the controller for this example application. Let's modify the FXML to match the controller. Listing 29-7 shows the modified FXML. It is saved in the sayhellowithcontroller.fxml file under the *resources/fxml* directory.

Listing 29-7. The Contents of the sayhellowithcontroller.fxml File

```
<?xml version="1.0" encoding="UTF-8"?>
<?language javascript?>

<?import javafx.scene.Scene?>
<?import javafx.scene.layout.VBox?>
<?import javafx.scene.control.Label?>
<?import javafx.scene.control.Button?>

<VBox fx:controller="com.jdojo.fxml.SayHelloController" spacing="10" xmlns:fx="http://
javafx.com/fxml">
        <Label fx:id="msgLbl" text="FXML is cool!" prefWidth="150"/>
        <Button fx:id="sayHelloBtn" text="Say Hello" onAction="#sayHello"/>
        <style>
                -fx-padding: 10;
                -fx-border-style: solid inside;
                -fx-border-width: 2;
                -fx-border-insets: 5;
                -fx-border-radius: 5;
                -fx-border-color: blue;
        </style>
</VBox>
```

The program in Listing 29-8 is the JavaFX application for this example. The code is very similar to the one shown in Listing 29-5. The main difference is the FXML document that uses a controller. When the document is loaded, the initialize() method of the controller is called by the loader. The method prints a message, the location and the resource bundle the reference. When you click the button, the sayHello() method of the controller is called that sets the text in the Label. Note that the Label reference is automatically injected into the controller by the FXML loader.

Listing 29-8. A JavaFX Application Class using FXML and a Controller

```
// SayHelloFXMLMain.java
package com.jdojo.fxml;

import java.io.IOException;
import java.net.URL;
import javafx.application.Application;
import javafx.fxml.FXMLLoader;
import javafx.scene.Scene;
import javafx.scene.layout.VBox;
import javafx.stage.Stage;

public class SayHelloFXMLMain extends Application {
        public static void main(String[] args) {
                Application.launch(args);
        }

        @Override
        public void start(Stage stage) throws IOException {
                // Construct a URL for the FXML document
                String stringUrl = "resources/fxml/sayhellowithcontroller.fxml";
                URL fxmlUrl = this.getClass()
                                .getClassLoader()
                                .getResource(stringUrl);

                VBox root = FXMLLoader.<VBox>load(fxmlUrl);
                Scene scene = new Scene(root);
                stage.setScene(scene);
                stage.setTitle("Hello FXML");
                stage.show();
        }
}
```

Creating Objects in FXML

The main purpose of using FXML is creating an object-graph. Objects of all classes are not created the same way. For example, some classes provide constructors to create their objects, some static valueOf() method and some factory methods. FXML should be able to create objects of all classes, or at least it should give you some control over deciding how to create those objects. In the following sections, I will discuss different ways of creating objects in FXML.

Using the no-args Constructor

Using the no-args constructor to create objects in FXML is easy. If an element name is a class name, which has a no-args constructor, the element will create an object of that class. The following element creates a VBox object as the VBox class has a no-args constructor.

```
<VBox>
        ...
</VBox>
```

Using the static valueOf() Method

Sometimes, immutable classes provide a valueOf() method to construct an object. If the valueOf() method is declared static; it can accept a single String argument, and returns an object. You can use the fx:value attribute to create an object using the method. Suppose you have an Xxx class, which contains a static valueOf(String s) method. The following is the Java code:

```
Xxx x = Xxx.valueOf("a value");
```

You can do the same in FXML as

```
<Xxx fx:value="a value"/>
```

Note that you have stated that the valueOf() method should be able to accept a String argument, which qualifies both of the following methods in this category.

- `public static Xxx valueOf(String arg)`
- `public static Xxx valueOf(Object arg)`

The following elements create Long and String objects with 100 and "Hello" as their values.

```
<Long fx:value="100"/>
<String fx:value="Hello"/>
```

Note that the String class contains a no-args constructor that creates an empty string. If you need a String object with an empty string as the content, you can still use the no-args constructor:

```
<!-- Will create a String object with "" as the content -->
<String/>
```

Do not forget to import classes, Long and String when you use the above elements as FXML does not automatically import classes from the java.lang package.

It is worth noting that the object type the fx:value attribute creates is the type of the returned object from the valueOf() object, not of the class type of the element. Consider the following method declaration for a class Yyy.

```
public static Zzz valueOf(String arg);
```

What type of object will the following element create?

```
<Yyy fx:value="hello"/>
```

If your answer is Yyy, it is wrong. It is commonly thought that the element name is Yyy, so it creates a Yyy type object. The above element is the same as invoking Yyy.valueOf("Hello"), which returns an object of Zzz type. Therefore, the above element creates an object of Zzz type, not Yyy type. Although it is possible to have this use case, this is a confusing way to design your class. Typically, a valueOf() method in the class Xxx returns an object of the Xxx type.

Using a Factory Method

Sometimes, a class provides factory methods to create its object. If a class contains a static, no-args method that returns an object, you can use the method with the fx:factory attribute. The following element creates a LocalDate in FXML using the now() factory method of the LocalDate class.

```
<?import java.time.LocalDate?>
<LocalDate fx:factory="now"/>
```

Sometimes, you need to create JavaFX collections in FXML. The FXCollections class contains several factory methods to create collections. The following snippet of FXML creates an ObservableList<String> that adds four fruit names to the list.

```
<?import java.lang.String?>
<?import javafx.collections.FXCollections?>
<FXCollections fx:factory="observableArrayList">
        <String fx:value="Apple"/>
        <String fx:value="Banana"/>
        <String fx:value="Grape"/>
        <String fx:value="Orange"/>
</FXCollections>
```

The FXML in Listing 29-9 is an example of using the fx:factory attribute to create an ObservableList. The list is used to set the items property of a ComboBox. The value "Orange" from the list is set as the default value. The VBox will show a Label and a ComboBox with the list of four fruit names.

Listing 29-9. Creating a ComboBox, Populating It, and Selecting an Item

```
<?import javafx.scene.layout.VBox?>
<?import javafx.scene.control.Label?>
<?import javafx.scene.control.Button?>
<?import javafx.scene.control.ComboBox?>
<?import java.lang.String?>
<?import javafx.collections.FXCollections?>

<VBox xmlns:fx="http://javafx.com/fxml">
        <Label text="List of Fruits"/>
        <ComboBox>
                <items>
                        <FXCollections fx:factory="observableArrayList">
                                <String fx:value="Apple"/>
                                <String fx:value="Banana"/>
                                <String fx:value="Grape"/>
                                <String fx:value="Orange"/>
                        </FXCollections>
                </items>
```

```
            <value>
                    <String fx:value="Orange"/>
            </value>
        </ComboBox>
</VBox>
```

Using Builders

If the FXMLLoader cannot create an object of a class, it looks for a builder that can create the object. A builder is an implementation of the Builder interface. The interface is in the javafx.util package and it contains one method build().

```
public interface Builder<T> {
    public T build();
}
```

A Builder knows how to build an object of a specific type. A Builder is used with a BuilderFactory, which is another interface in the same package.

```
public interface BuilderFactory {
    public Builder<?> getBuilder(Class<?> type);
}
```

The FXMLLoader allows you to use a BuilderFactory. When it cannot create the object of a class using all other methods, it calls the getBuilder() method of the BuilderFactory by passing the type of the object as the method argument. If the BuilderFactory returns a non-null Builder, the loader sets all the properties of the object being created in the Builder. Finally, it calls the build() method of the Builder to get the object. The FXMLLoader class uses an instance of the JavaFXBuilderFactory as a default BuilderFactory.

FXMLLoader supports two types of Builders:

- If the Builder implements the Map interface, the put() method is used to pass the object properties to the Builder. The put() method is passed the name and value of the property.

- If the Builder does not implement the Map interface, the Builder should contain the getter and setter methods, based on the JavaBeans convention, for all properties specified in the FXML.

Consider the declaration of the Item class in Listing 29-10. By default, FXML will not be able to create an Item object as it does not have a no-args constructor. The class has two properties, id and name.

Listing 29-10. An Item Class That Does Not Have a no-args Constructor

```
// Item.java
package com.jdojo.fxml;

public class Item {
        private Long id;
        private String name;

        public Item(Long id, String name) {
                this.id = id;
                this.name = name;
        }
```

```java
    public Long getId() {
            return id;
    }

    public void setId(Long id) {
            this.id = id;
    }

    public String getName() {
            return name;
    }

    public void setName(String name) {
            this.name = name;
    }

    @Override
    public String toString() {
            return "id=" + id + ", name=" + name;
    }
}
```

Listing 29-11 contains the content of an FXML file items.fxml. It creates an ArrayList with three objects of the Item class. If you load this file using FXMLLoader, you would receive an error that the loader cannot instantiate the Item class.

Listing 29-11. FXML to create a list of Item objects

```xml
<!-- items.fxml -->
<?import com.jdojo.fxml.Item?>
<?import java.util.ArrayList?>
<ArrayList>
        <Item name="Kishori" id="100"/>
        <Item name="Ellen" id="200"/>
        <Item name="Kannan" id="300"/>
</ArrayList>
```

Let's create a Builder to build object of the Item class. The ItemBuilder class in Listing 29-12 is the Builder for the Item class. It declares id and name instance variables. As the FXMLLoader comes across these properties, the loader will call the corresponding setters. The setters store the values in the instance variable. When the loader needs the object, it calls the build() method, which builds and returns an Item object.

Listing 29-12. A Builder for the Item Class That Uses Properties Setters to Build an Object

```java
// ItemBuilder.java
package com.jdojo.fxml;

import javafx.util.Builder;

public class ItemBuilder implements Builder<Item> {
        private Long id;
        private String name;
```

```
        public Long getId() {
                return id;
        }

        public String getName() {
                return name;
        }

        public void setId(Long id) {
                this.id = id;
        }

        public void setName(String name) {
                this.name = name;
        }

        @Override
        public Item build() {
                return new Item(id, name);
        }
}
```

Now, you need to create a BuilderFactory for the Item type. The ItemBuilderFactory class shown in Listing 29-13 implements the BuilderFactory interface. When the getBuilder() is passed the Item type, it returns an ItemBuilder object. Otherwise, it returns the default JavaFX builder.

Listing 29-13. A BuilderFactory to Get a Builder for Item Type

```
// ItemBuilderFactory.java
package com.jdojo.fxml;

import javafx.util.Builder;
import javafx.util.BuilderFactory;
import javafx.fxml.JavaFXBuilderFactory;

public class ItemBuilderFactory implements BuilderFactory {
        private final JavaFXBuilderFactory fxFactory = new JavaFXBuilderFactory();

        @Override
        public Builder<?> getBuilder(Class<?> type) {
                // You supply a Builder only for Item type
                if (type == Item.class) {
                        return new ItemBuilder();
                }

                // Let the default Builder do the magic
                return fxFactory.getBuilder(type);
        }
}
```

Listings 29-14 and 29-15 have code for the Builder and BuilderFactory implementation for Item type. This time, the Builder implements the Map interface by extending the AbstractMap class. It overrides the put() method to read the passed in properties and their values. The entrySet() method needs to be overridden as it is defined as abstract in the AbstractMap class. You do not have any useful implementation for it. You just throw a runtime exception. The build() method creates and returns an object of the Item type. The BuilderFactory implementation is similar to the one in Listing 29-13, except that it returns a ItemBuilderMap as the Builder for the Item type.

Listing 29-14. A Builder for the Item Class That Implements the Map Interface

```java
// ItemBuilderMap.java
package com.jdojo.fxml;

import java.util.AbstractMap;
import java.util.Map;
import java.util.Set;
import javafx.util.Builder;

public class ItemBuilderMap extends AbstractMap<String, Object> implements Builder<Item> {
        private String name;
        private Long id;

        @Override
        public Object put(String key, Object value) {
                if ("name".equals(key)) {
                        this.name = (String)value;
                } else if ("id".equals(key)) {
                        this.id = Long.valueOf((String)value);
                } else {
                        throw new IllegalArgumentException("Unknown Item property: " + key);
                }

                return null;
        }

        @Override
        public Set<Map.Entry<String, Object>> entrySet() {
                throw new UnsupportedOperationException();
        }

        @Override
        public Item build() {
                return new Item(id, name);
        }
}
```

Listing 29-15. Another BuilderFactory to Get a Builder for Item Type

```java
// ItemBuilderFactoryMap.java
package com.jdojo.fxml;

import javafx.fxml.JavaFXBuilderFactory;
import javafx.util.Builder;
import javafx.util.BuilderFactory;

public class ItemBuilderFactoryMap implements BuilderFactory {
        private final JavaFXBuilderFactory fxFactory = new JavaFXBuilderFactory();

        @Override
        public Builder<?> getBuilder(Class<?> type) {
                if (type == Item.class) {
                        return new ItemBuilderMap();
                }
                return fxFactory.getBuilder(type);
        }
}
```

Let's test both Builders for the Item class. The program in Listing 29-16 uses both Builders for the Item class. It loads the list of Items from the items.fxml file, assuming that the file is located in the CLASSPATH in the resources/fxml directory.

Listing 29-16. Using Builders to Instantiate Item Objects in FXML

```java
// BuilderTest.java
package com.jdojo.fxml;

import java.io.IOException;
import java.net.URL;
import java.util.ArrayList;
import javafx.fxml.FXMLLoader;
import javafx.util.BuilderFactory;

public class BuilderTest {
        public static void main(String[] args) throws IOException {
            // Use the Builder with property getter and setter
            loadItems(new ItemBuilderFactory());

            // Use the Builder with Map
                loadItems(new ItemBuilderFactoryMap());
        }

        public static void loadItems(BuilderFactory builderFactory) throws IOException {
            URL fxmlUrl = BuilderTest.class
                            .getClassLoader()
                            .getResource("resources/fxml/items.fxml");
```

```
        FXMLLoader loader = new FXMLLoader();
        loader.setLocation(fxmlUrl);
        loader.setBuilderFactory(builderFactory);
        ArrayList items = loader.<ArrayList>load();
        System.out.println("List:" + items);
    }
}
```

```
List:[id=100, name=Kishori, id=200, name=Ellen, id=300, name=Kannan]
List:[id=100, name=Kishori, id=200, name=Ellen, id=300, name=Kannan]
```

■ **Tip** The BuilderFactory you supply to the FXMLLoader replaces the default BuilderFactory. You need to make sure that your BuilderFactory returns a specific Builder for your custom type and returns the default Builder for the rest. Currently, FXMLLoader does not allow using more than one BuilderFactory.

Creating Reusable Objects in FXML

Sometimes, you need to create objects that are not directly part of the object-graph. However, they may be used somewhere else in the FXML document. For example, you may want to create an Insets or a Color once and reuse them in several places. Using a ToggleGroup is a typical use case. A ToggleGroup is created once and used with several RadioButton objects.

You can create an object in FXML without making it part of the object-group using the <fx:define> block. You can refer to the objects created in the <fx:define> block by their fx:id in the attribute value of other elements. The attribute value must be prefixed with a dollar symbol ($).

```
<?import javafx.scene.layout.VBox?>
<?import javafx.scene.control.Label?>
<?import javafx.scene.control.Button?>
<?import javafx.geometry.Insets?>
<?import javafx.scene.control.ToggleGroup?>
<?import javafx.scene.control.RadioButton?>

<VBox fx:controller="com.jdojo.fxml.Test" xmlns:fx="http://javafx.com/fxml">
        <fx:define>
                <Insets fx:id="margin" top="5.0" right="5.0" bottom="5.0" left="5.0"/>
                <ToggleGroup fx:id="genderGroup"/>
        </fx:define>
        <Label text="Gender" VBox.margin="$margin"/>
        <RadioButton text="Male" toggleGroup="$genderGroup"/>
        <RadioButton text="Female" toggleGroup="$genderGroup"/>
        <RadioButton text="Unknown" toggleGroup="$genderGroup" selected="true"/>
        <Button text="Close" VBox.margin="$margin"/>
</VBox>
```

The above FXML creates two objects, an Insets and a ToggleGroup, in a <fx:define> block. They are given an fx:id of "margin" and "genderGroup". They are referred to in controls, which are part of the object-graph, by "$margin" and "$genderGroup".

■ **Tip** If the value of an attribute starts with a $ symbol, it is considered a reference to an object. If you want to use a leading $ symbol as part of the value, escape it with a backslash ("\$hello").

Specifying Locations in Attributes

An attribute value starting with a @ symbol refers to a location. If the @ symbol is followed by a forward slash (@/), the location is considered relative to the CLASSPATH. If the @ symbol is not followed by a forward slash, the location is considered relative to the location of the FXML file being processed.

In the following FXML, the image URL will be resolved relative to the location of the FXML file that contains the element.

```
<ImageView>
        <Image url="@resources/picture/ksharan.jpg"/>
</ImageView>
```

In the following FXML, the image URL will be resolved relative to the CLASSPATH.

```
<ImageView>
        <Image url="@/resources/picture/ksharan.jpg"/>
</ImageView>
```

If you want to use a leading @ symbol as part of the attribute value, escape it with a backward slash ("\@not-a-location").

Using Resource Bundles

Using a ResourceBundle in FXML is much easier than using it in Java code. Specifying the keys from a ResourceBundle in attribute values uses the corresponding values for the default Locale. If an attribute value starts with a % symbol, it is considered as the key name from the resource bundle. At runtime, the attribute value will come from the specified ResourceBundle in the FXMLLoader. If you want to use a leading % symbol in an attribute value, escape it with a backward slash (e.g., "\%hello").

Consider the FXML content in Listing 29-17. It uses "%greetingText" as the value for the text property of the Label. The attribute value starts with a % symbol. The FXMLLoader will look up the value of the "greetingText" in the ResourceBundle and use it for the text property. It is all done for you without writing even a single line of code!

Listing 29-17. The Contents of the greetings.fxml File

```
<?import javafx.scene.control.Label?>
<Label text="%greetingText"/>
```

Listings 29-18 and 29-19 have contents for ResourceBundle files: one for default Locale named greetings.properties, and one for Indian Locale named greetings_hi.properties. The suffix _hi in the file name means the Indian language Hindi.

Listing 29-18. The Contents of the greetings.properties File

```
# The default greeting
greetingText = Hello
```

Listing 29-19. The Contents of the greetings_hi.properties File

```
# The Indian greeting
greetingText = Namaste
```

The program in Listing 29-20 uses a ResourceBundle with the FXMLLoader. The ResourceBundle is loaded from resources/resourcebundles directory in CLASSPATH. The FXML file is loaded from the resources/fxml/greetings.fxml in CLASSPATH. The program loads the Label from the FXML file twice: once for the default Locale US and once by change the default Locale to India Hindi. Both Labels are displayed in the VBox as shown in Figure 29-2.

Listing 29-20. Using a Resource Bundle With the FXMLLoader

```java
// ResourceBundleTest.java
package com.jdojo.fxml;

import java.io.IOException;
import java.net.URL;
import java.util.Locale;
import java.util.ResourceBundle;
import javafx.application.Application;
import javafx.fxml.FXMLLoader;
import javafx.scene.Scene;
import javafx.scene.control.Label;
import javafx.scene.layout.VBox;
import javafx.stage.Stage;

public class ResourceBundleTest extends Application {
        public static void main(String[] args) {
                Application.launch(args);
        }

        @Override
        public void start(Stage stage) throws IOException {
                URL fxmlUrl = this.getClass()
                                .getClassLoader()
                                .getResource("resources/fxml/greetings.fxml");

                // Create a ResourceBundle to use in FXMLLoader
                String resourcePath = "resources/resourcebundles/greetings";
                ResourceBundle resourceBundle = ResourceBundle.getBundle(resourcePath);

                // Load the Label for default Locale
                Label defaultGreetingLbl = FXMLLoader.<Label>load(fxmlUrl, resourceBundle);

                // Change the default Locale and load the Label again
                Locale.setDefault(new Locale("hi", "in"));
```

```
        // We need to recreate the ResourceBundler to pick up the new default Locale
        resourceBundle = ResourceBundle.getBundle(resourcePath);

        Label indianGreetingLbl = FXMLLoader.<Label>load(fxmlUrl, resourceBundle);

        // Add both Labels to a Vbox
        VBox root = new VBox(5, defaultGreetingLbl, indianGreetingLbl);
        Scene scene = new Scene(root);
        stage.setScene(scene);
        stage.setTitle("Using a ResourceBundle in FXML");
        stage.show();
    }
}
```

Figure 29-2. *Labels using a resource bundle to populate their text properties*

Including FXML Files

An FXML document can include another FXML document using the <fx:include> element. The object-graph generated by the nested document is included at the position where the nested document occurs in the containing document. The <fx:include> element takes a source attribute whose value is the path of the nested document.

```
<fx:include source="nested_document_path"/>
```

If the nested document path starts with a leading forward slash, the path is resolved relative to the CLASSPATH. Otherwise, it is resolved related to the containing document path.

The <fx:include> element can have the fx:id attribute and all attributes that are available for the included object. The attributes specified in the containing document override the corresponding attributes in the included document. For example, if you include an FXML document, which creates a Button, you can specify the text property in the included document as well as the containing document. When the containing document is loaded, the text property from the containing document will be used.

An FXML document may optionally specify a controller using the fx:controller attribute for the root element. The rule is that you can have maximum of one controller per FXML document. When you nest documents, each document can have its own controller. FXMLLoader lets you inject the nested controller reference into the controller of the main document. You need to follow a naming convention to inject the nested controller. The controller for the main document should have an accessible instance variable with the name as:

```
Instance variable name = "fx:id of the fx:include element" + "Controller"
```

If the fx:id for the <fx:include> element is "xxx", the instance variable name should be xxxController.

Consider the two FXML documents shown in Listings 29-21 and 29-22. The closebutton.fxml file creates a Button, sets its text property to Close, and attaches an action event handler. The event handler uses the JavaScript language. It closes the containing window.

The maindoc.fxml includes the closebutton.fxml, assuming that both files are in the same directory. It specifies text and fx:id attributes for the <fx:include> element. Note that the included FXML specifies "Close" as the test property and the maindoc.fxml overrides it and sets it to "Close".

Listing 29-21. An FXML Document That Creates a Close Button to Close the Containing Window

```
<!-- closebutton.fxml -->
<?language javascript?>
<?import javafx.scene.control.Button?>
<Button fx:controller="com.jdojo.fxml.CloseBtnController" text="Close" fx:id="closeBtn"
onAction="closeWindow()" xmlns:fx="http://javafx.com/fxml">
        <fx:script>
                function closeWindow() {
                        var scene = closeBtn.getScene();
                        if (scene != null) {
                                scene.getWindow().hide();
                        }
                }
        </fx:script>
</Button>
```

Listing 29-22. An FXML Document Using a <fx:include> Element

```
<!-- maindoc.fxml -->
<?import javafx.scene.layout.VBox?>
<?import javafx.scene.control.Label?>

<VBox fx:controller="com.jdojo.fxml.MainDocController" xmlns:fx="http://javafx.com/fxml">
        <Label text="Testing fx:include"/>

        <!-- Override the text property of the included Button -->
        <fx:include source="closebutton.fxml" fx:id="includedCloseBtn" text="Hide"/>
</VBox>
```

Both FXML documents specify a controller listed in Listings 29-23 and 29-24. Note that the controller for the main document declares two instance variables: one will refer to the included Button and the other will refer to the controller of the included document. Note that the reference of the Button will also be included in the controller of the nested document.

Listing 29-23. The ControllerClass for the FXML Defining the Close Button

```
// CloseBtnController.java
package com.jdojo.fxml;

import javafx.fxml.FXML;
import javafx.scene.control.Button;
```

```java
public class CloseBtnController {
        @FXML
        private Button closeBtn;

        @FXML
        public void initialize() {
                System.out.println("CloseBtnController.initialize()");
        }
}
```

Listing 29-24. The Controller Class for the Main Document

```java
// MainDocController.java
package com.jdojo.fxml;

import javafx.fxml.FXML;
import javafx.scene.control.Button;

public class MainDocController {
        @FXML
        private Button includedCloseBtn;

        @FXML
        private CloseBtnController includedCloseBtnController;

        @FXML
        public void initialize() {
                System.out.println("MainDocController.initialize()");
                // You can use the nested controller here
        }
}
```

The program in Listing 29-25 loads the maindoc.fxml and adds the loaded VBox to the scene. It displays a window with the *Hide* button from the closebutton.fxml file. Clicking the Hide button will close the window.

Listing 29-25. Loading and Using a Nested FXML Documents

```java
// FxIncludeTest.java
package com.jdojo.fxml;

import java.io.IOException;
import java.net.MalformedURLException;
import java.net.URL;

import javafx.application.Application;
import javafx.fxml.FXMLLoader;
import javafx.scene.Scene;
import javafx.scene.layout.VBox;
import javafx.stage.Stage;
```

```java
public class FxIncludeTest extends Application {
        public static void main(String[] args) {
                Application.launch(args);
        }

        @Override
        public void start(Stage stage) throws MalformedURLException, IOException {
                URL fxmlUrl = this.getClass()
                                        .getClassLoader()
                                        .getResource("resources/fxml/maindoc.fxml");

                FXMLLoader loader = new FXMLLoader();
                loader.setLocation(fxmlUrl);
                VBox root = loader.<VBox>load();
                Scene scene = new Scene(root);
                stage.setScene(scene);
                stage.setTitle("Nesting Documents in FXML");
                stage.show();
        }
}
```

Using Constants

Classes, interfaces, and enums may define constants, which are static, final variables. You can refer to those constants using the fx:constant attribute. The attribute value is the name of the constant. The name of the element is the name of the type that contains the constant. For example, for Long.MAX_VALUE, you can use the following element.

```
<Long fx:constant="MAX_VALUE"/>
```

Note that all enum constants belong to this category and they can be accessed using the fx:constant attribute. The following element accesses the Pos.CENTER enum constant.

```
<Pos fx:constant="CENTER"/>
```

The following FXML content accesses constants from the Integer and Long classes, and the Pos enum. It sets the alignment property of a VBox to Pos.CENTER.

```xml
<?import javafx.scene.layout.VBox?>
<?import javafx.scene.control.TextField?>
<?import java.lang.Integer?>
<?import java.lang.Long?>
<?import javafx.scene.text.FontWeight?>
<?import javafx.geometry.Pos?>

<VBox xmlns:fx="http://javafx.com/fxml">
        <fx:define>
                <Integer fx:constant="MAX_VALUE" fx:id="minInt"/>
        </fx:define>
        <alignment><Pos fx:constant="CENTER"/></alignment>
        <TextField text="$minInt"/>
```

```
        <TextField>
                <text><Long fx:constant="MIN_VALUE"/></text>
        </TextField>
</VBox>
```

Referencing Another Element

You can reference another element in the document using the `<fx:reference>` element. The `fx:id` attribute specifies the `fx:id` of the referred element.

```
<fx:reference source="fx:id of the source element"/>
```

The following FXML content uses an `<fx:reference>` element to refer to an Image.

```
<?import javafx.scene.layout.VBox?>
<?import javafx.scene.image.Image?>
<?import javafx.scene.image.ImageView?>
<VBox xmlns:fx="http://javafx.com/fxml">
        <fx:define>
                <Image url="resources/picture/ksharan.jpg" fx:id="myImg"/>
        </fx:define>
        <ImageView>
                <image>
                        <fx:reference source="myImg"/>
                </image>
        </ImageView>
</VBox>
```

Note that you can also rewrite the above FXML content using the variable dereferencing method as follows:

```
<VBox xmlns:fx="http://javafx.com/fxml">
        <fx:define>
                <Image url="resources/picture/ksharan.jpg" fx:id="myImg"/>
        </fx:define>
        <ImageView image="$myImg"/>
</VBox>
```

Copying Elements

Sometimes, you want to copy an element. Copying in this context is creating a new object by copying the attributes of the source object. You can do so using the `<fx:copy>` element.

```
<fx:copy source="fx:id of the source object" />
```

To copy an object, the class must provide a copy constructor. A copy constructor takes an object of the same class. Suppose you have an Item class that contains a copy constructor.

```
public class Item {
        private Long id;
        private String name;

        public Item() {
        }

        // The copy constructor
        public Item(Item source) {
                this.id = source.id + 100;
                this.name = source.name + " (Copied)";
        }
        ...
}
```

The following FXML document creates an Item object inside the <fx:define> block. It copies the Item object several times and adds them to the items list for a ComboBox. Note that the source Item itself is added to the items list using a <fx:reference> element.

```
<?import javafx.scene.layout.VBox?>
<?import javafx.scene.control.ComboBox?>
<?import javafx.collections.FXCollections?>
<?import com.jdojo.fxml.Item?>

<VBox xmlns:fx="http://javafx.com/fxml">
        <fx:define>
                <Item name="Kishori" id="100" fx:id="myItem"/>
        </fx:define>
        <ComboBox value="$myItem">
                <items>
                        <FXCollections fx:factory="observableArrayList">
                                <fx:reference source="myItem"/>
                                <fx:copy source="myItem" />
                                <fx:copy source="myItem" />
                                <fx:copy source="myItem" />
                                <fx:copy source="myItem" />
                        </FXCollections>
                </items>
        </ComboBox>

</VBox>
```

Binding Properties in FXML

FXML supports simple property bindings. You need to use an attribute for the property to bind it to the property of another element or a document variable. The attribute value starts with a $ symbol, which is followed with a pair of curly braces. The following FXML content creates a VBox with two TextFields. The text property of the mirrorText field is bound to the text property of the mainText field.

```
<?import javafx.scene.layout.VBox?>
<?import javafx.scene.control.TextField?>

<VBox xmlns:fx="http://javafx.com/fxml">
        <TextField fx:id="mainText" text="Hello"/>
        <TextField fx:id="mirrorText" text="${mainText.text}" disable="true"/>
</VBox>
```

Creating Custom Controls

You can create custom controls using FXML. Let's create a log in form with two Labels, a TextField, a PasswordField, and two Buttons. Listing 29-26 contains the FXML content for the form. Note that the root element is a <fx:root>. The <fx:root> element creates a reference to the previously created element. The value for the <fx:root> element is set in the FXMLLoader using the setRoot() method. The type attribute specifies the type of the root that will be injected.

Listing 29-26. The FXML contents for a custom login form

```
<!-- login.fxml -->
<?import javafx.scene.layout.GridPane?>
<?import javafx.scene.control.Label?>
<?import javafx.scene.control.Button?>
<?import javafx.scene.control.TextField?>
<?import javafx.scene.control.PasswordField?>

<fx:root type="javafx.scene.layout.GridPane" xmlns:fx="http://javafx.com/fxml">
        <Label text="User Id:" GridPane.rowIndex="0" GridPane.columnIndex="0"/>
        <TextField fx:id="userId" GridPane.rowIndex="0" GridPane.columnIndex="1"/>
        <Label text="Password:" GridPane.rowIndex="1" GridPane.columnIndex="0"/>
        <PasswordField fx:id="pwd" GridPane.rowIndex="1" GridPane.columnIndex="1"/>
        <Button fx:id="okBtn" text="OK" onAction="#okClicked" GridPane.rowIndex="0"
                    GridPane.columnIndex="2"/>
        <Button fx:id="cancelBtn" text="Cancel" onAction="#cancelClicked"
                    GridPane.rowIndex="1" GridPane.columnIndex="2"/>
</fx:root>
```

The class in Listing 29-27 represents the JavaFX part of the custom control. You will create an object of the LogInControl class and use it as any other standard control. This class is also used as a controller for the login.fxml. In the constructor, the class loads the FXML content. Before loading the content, it sets itself as the root and the controller in the FXMLLoader. Instance variables allow for the userId and pwd controls injection in the class. When the Buttons are clicked, you simply print a message on the console. This control needs more work, if you want to use it in a real-world application. You will need to provide a way for the users to hook event notification when the *OK* and *Cancel* buttons are clicked.

Listing 29-27. A Class Implementing the Custom Control

```
// LoginControl.java
package com.jdojo.fxml;

import java.io.IOException;
import java.net.URL;
import javafx.fxml.FXML;
```

```java
import javafx.fxml.FXMLLoader;
import javafx.scene.control.PasswordField;
import javafx.scene.control.TextField;
import javafx.scene.layout.GridPane;

public class LoginControl extends GridPane {
        @FXML
        private TextField userId;

        @FXML
        private PasswordField pwd;

        public LoginControl() {
                // Load the FXML
                URL fxmlUrl = this.getClass()
                                    .getClassLoader()
                                    .getResource("resources/fxml/login.fxml");
                FXMLLoader loader = new FXMLLoader();
                loader.setLocation(fxmlUrl);
                loader.setRoot(this);
                loader.setController(this);
                try {
                        loader.load();
                }
                catch (IOException exception) {
                    throw new RuntimeException(exception);
                }
        }

        @FXML
        private void initialize() {
                // Do some work
        }

        @FXML
        private void okClicked() {
                System.out.println("Ok clicked");
        }

        @FXML
        private void cancelClicked() {
            System.out.println("Cancel clicked");
        }

        public String getUserId() {
                return userId.getText();
        }

        public String getPassword() {
                return pwd.getText();
        }
}
```

The program in Listing 29-28 shows how to use the custom control. Using the custom control is as easy as creating a Java object. The custom control extends the GridPane, therefore, it can be used as a GridPane. Using the control in FXML is no different than using other controls. The control provides a no-args constructor, which will allow creating it in FXML by using an element with the class name <LoginControl>.

Listing 29-28. Using the Custom Control

```
// LoginTest.java
package com.jdojo.fxml;

import javafx.application.Application;
import javafx.scene.Scene;
import javafx.scene.layout.GridPane;
import javafx.stage.Stage;

public class LoginTest extends Application {
        public static void main(String[] args) {
                Application.launch(args);
        }

        @Override
        public void start(Stage stage) {
                // Create the Login custom control
                GridPane root = new LoginControl();
                Scene scene = new Scene(root);
                stage.setScene(scene);
                stage.setTitle("Using FXMl Custom Control");
                stage.show();
        }
}
```

Summary

FXML is an XML-based language to build a user interface for a JavaFX application. You can use FXML to build an entire scene or part of a scene. FXML allows application developers to separate the logic for building the UI from the business logic. If the UI part of the application changes, you do not need to recompile the JavaFX code: change the FXML using a text editor and rerun the application. You still use JavaFX to write business logic using the Java language. An FXML document is an XML document.

It is common to use FXML to build a scene graph in a JavaFX application. However, the use of FXML is not limited to building only scene graphs. It can build a hierarchical object-graph of Java objects. In fact, it can be used to create just one object, such as an object of a Person class.

An FXML document is simply a text file. Typically, the file name has a .fxml extension (e.g., hello.fxml). You can use any text editor to edit an FXML document. Oracle Corporation provides an open-source visual editor called *Scene Builder* for editing FXML documents. You can download its latest version from the link www.oracle.com/technetwork/java/javase/downloads/index.html. Scene Builder can also be integrated into NetBeans IDE, so you can edit FXML documents using Scene Builder from inside the NetBeans IDE.

FXML lets you create an object using the no-args constructor, the valueOf() method, a factory method and a builder.

1155

Sometimes, you need to create objects that are not directly part of the object-graph. However, they may be used somewhere else in the FXML document. You can create an object in FXML without making it part of the object-group using the <fx:define> block. You can refer to the objects created in the <fx:define> block by their fx:id in the attribute value of other elements. The attribute value must be prefixed with a dollar symbol ($).

FXML lets you refer to resources by specifying their locations. An attribute value starting with a @ symbol refers to a location. If the @ symbol is followed with a forward slash (@/), the location is considered relative to the CLASSPATH. If the @ symbol is not followed by a forward slash, the location is considered relative to the location of the FXML file being processed.

Using a ResourceBundle in FXML is much easier than using it in Java code. Specifying the keys from a ResourceBundle in attribute values uses the corresponding values for the default Locale. If an attribute value starts with a % symbol, it is considered as the key name from the resource bundle. At runtime, the attribute value will come from the specified ResourceBundle in the FXMLLoader. If you want to use a leading % symbol in an attribute value, escape it with a backward slash (e.g., "\%hello").

An FXML document can include another FXML document using the <fx:include> element. The object-graph generated by the nested document is included at the position where the nested document occurs in the containing document.

Classes, interfaces, and enums may define constants, which are static, final variables. You can refer to those constants using the fx:constant attribute. The attribute value is the name of the constant. The name of the element is the name of the type that contains the constant. For example, for Long.MAX_VALUE, you can use the element <Long fx:constant="MAX_VALUE"/>.

You can reference another element in the document using the <fx:reference> element. The fx:id attribute specifies the fx:id of the referred element. You can copy an element using the <fx:copy> element. It will create a new object by copying the attributes of the source object.

FXML supports simple property bindings. You need to use an attribute for the property to bind it to the property of another element or a document variable. The attribute value starts with a $ symbol, which is followed with a pair of curly braces. You can create custom controls using FXML. The next chapter will discuss Printing API in JavaFX that lets you configure printers and print nodes in JavaFX applications.

CHAPTER 30

■ ■ ■

Understanding the Print API

In this chapter, you will learn:

- What the Print API is
- How to obtain the list of available printers
- How to get the default printer
- How to print nodes
- How to show the page setup and print dialog to users
- How to customize the setting for the printer jobs
- How to setup the page layout for printing
- How to print webpages displayed in a `WebView`

What is the Printing API?

JavaFX 8 added support for printing nodes through the Print API in the `javafx.print` package. The API consists of the following classes and a number of enums (not listed):

- `Printer`
- `PrinterAttributes`
- `PrintResolution`
- `PrinterJob`
- `JobSettings`
- `Paper`
- `PaperSource`
- `PageLayout`
- `PageRange`

Instances of the above-listed classes represent different parts of the printing process. For example, a `Printer` represents a printer that can be used for printing jobs; a `PrinterJob` represents a print job that can be sent to a `Printer` for printing; and a `Paper` represents the paper sizes available on printers.

The Print API provides support for printing nodes that may or may not be attached to a scene graph. It is a common requirement to print the content of a webpage, not the WebView node that contains the webpage. The javafx.scene.web.WebEngine class contains a print(PrinterJob job) method that prints the contents of the webpage, not the WebView node.

If a node is modified during the printing process, the printed node may not appear correct. Note that the printing of a node may span multiple pulse events resulting in concurrent change in the content being printed. To ensure correct printing, please make sure that the node being printed is not modified during the print process.

Nodes can be printed on any thread including the JavaFX Application Thread. It is recommended that large, time-consuming print jobs be submitted on a background thread to keep the UI responsive.

Classes in the Print API are final as they represent existing printing device properties. Most of them do not provide any public constructor as you cannot make up a printing device. Rather, you obtain their references using factory methods in various classes.

■ **Note** The Print API provides the basic printing support only to print nodes and webpages. You will not be able to use it to print reports in JavaFX applications.

Listing Available Printers

The Printer.getAllPrinters() static method returns an observable list of installed printers on the machine. Note that the list of printers returned by the method may change over time as new printers are installed or old printers are removed. Use the getName() method of the Printer to get the name of the printer. The following snippet of code lists all installed printers on the machine running the code. You may get a different output.

```
import javafx.collections.ObservableSet;
import javafx.print.Printer;
...
ObservableSet<Printer> allPrinters = Printer.getAllPrinters();
for(Printer p : allPrinters) {
        System.out.println(p.getName());
}
```

```
ImageRight Printer
Microsoft XPS Document Writer
PDF995
Sybase DataWindow PS
\\pro-print1\IS-CANON1
\\pro-print1\IS-HP4000
\\pro-print1\IS-HP4015
\\pro-print1\IS-HP4050
\\pro-print1\IS-HP4650
\\pro-print1\IS-HP4650(Color)
```

Getting the Default Printer

The Printer.getDefaultPrinter() method returns the default Printer. The method may return null if no printer is installed. The default printer may be changed on a machine. Therefore, the method may return different printers from call to call, and the printer returned may not be valid after some time. The following snippet of code shows how to get the default printer.

```
Printer defaultprinter = Printer.getDefaultPrinter();
if (defaultprinter != null) {
        String name = defaultprinter.getName();
        System.out.println("Default printer name: " + name);
} else {
        System.out.println("No printers installed.");
}
```

Printing Nodes

Printing a node is easy: create a PrinterJob and call its printPage() method passing the node to be printed. Printing a node using the default printer with all default settings takes only three lines of code:

```
PrinterJob printerJob = PrinterJob.createPrinterJob();
printerJob.printPage(node); // node is the node to be printed
printerJob.endJob();
```

In a real-world application, you want to handle the errors. You can rewrite the code to handle errors as follows:

```
// Create a printer job for the default printer
PrinterJob printerJob = PrinterJob.createPrinterJob();
if (printerJob!= null) {
        // Print the node
        boolean printed = printerJob.printPage(node);
        if (printed) {
                // End the printer job
                printerJob.endJob();
        } else {
                System.out.println("Printing failed.");
        }
} else {
        System.out.println("Could not create a printer job.");
}
```

You can use the createPrinterJob() static method of the PrinterJob class to create a printer job:

- `public static PrinterJob createPrinterJob()`
- `public static PrinterJob createPrinterJob(Printer printer)`

The method with no-args creates a printer job for the default printer. You can use the other version of the method to create a printer job for the specified printer.

You can change the printer for a `PrinterJob` by calling its `setPrinter()` method. If the current printer job settings are not supported by the new printer, the settings are reset automatically for the new printer.

```
// Set a new printer for the printer job
printerJob.setPrinter(myNewPrinter);
```

Setting a `null` printer for the job will use the default printer.
Use one of the following `printPage()` methods to print a node:

- `boolean printPage(Node node)`

- `boolean printPage(PageLayout pageLayout, Node node)`

The first version of the method takes only the node to be printed as the parameter. It uses the default page layout for the job for printing.

The second version lets you specify a page layout for printing the node. The specified `PageLayout` will override the `PageLayout` for the job and it will be used only for printing the specified node. For subsequent printing, the default `PageLayout` for the job will be used. You can create a `PageLayout` using the `Printer` class. I will discuss an example of this kind later.

The `printPage()` method returns true if the printing was successful. Otherwise, it returns false. When you are done printing, call the `endJob()` method. The method returns true if the job can be successfully spooled to the printer queue. Otherwise, it returns false, which may indicate that the job could not be spooled or it was already completed. After successful completion of the job, the job can no longer be reused.

■ **Tip** You can call the `printPage()` method on a `PrinterJob` as many times as you want. Calling the `endJob()` method tells the job that no more printing will be performed. The method transitions the job status to DONE and the job should no longer be reused.

You can cancel a print job using the `cancelJob()` method of the `PrinterJob`. The printing may not be cancelled immediately, for example, when a page is in the middle of printing. The cancellation occurs as soon as possible. The method does not have any effect if

- The job has already been requested to be cancelled.

- The job is already completed.

- The job has an error.

A `PrinterJob` has a read-only status, which is defined by one of the constants of the `PrinterJob.JobStatus` enum:

- `NOT_STARTED`

- `PRINTING`

- `CANCELED`

- `DONE`

- `ERROR`

The `NOT_STARTED` status indicates a new job. In this status, the job can be configured and printing can be initiated. The `PRINTING` status indicates that the job has requested to print at least one page and it has not terminated printing. In this status, the job cannot be configured.

The other three statuses, CANCELED, DONE, and ERROR, indicate the termination state of the job. Once the job is in one of these statuses, it should not be reused. There is no need to call the endJob() method when the status goes to CANCELED or ERROR. The DONE status is entered when the printing was successful and the endJob() method was called. The PrinterJob class contains a read-only jobStatus property that indicates the current status of the print job.

The program in Listing 30-1 shows how to print nodes. It displays a TextArea where you can enter text. Two Buttons are provided: one prints the TextArea node and the other the entire scene. When printing is initiated, the print job status is displayed in a Label. The code in the print() method is the same as previously discussed. The method includes the logic to display the job status in the Label. The program displays the window shown in Figure 30-1. Run the program; enter text in the TextArea; and click one of the two buttons to print.

Listing 30-1. Printing Nodes

```java
// PrintingNodes.java
package com.jdojo.print;

import javafx.application.Application;
import javafx.print.PrinterJob;
import javafx.scene.Node;
import javafx.scene.Scene;
import javafx.scene.control.Button;
import javafx.scene.control.Label;
import javafx.scene.control.TextArea;
import javafx.scene.layout.HBox;
import javafx.scene.layout.VBox;
import javafx.stage.Stage;

public class PrintingNodes  extends Application {
        private Label jobStatus = new Label();

        public static void main(String[] args) {
                Application.launch(args);
        }

        @Override
        public void start(Stage stage) {
                VBox root = new VBox(5);

                Label textLbl = new Label("Text:");
                TextArea text = new TextArea();
                text.setPrefRowCount(10);
                text.setPrefColumnCount(20);
                text.setWrapText(true);

                // Button to print the TextArea node
                Button printTextBtn = new Button("Print Text");
                printTextBtn.setOnAction(e -> print(text));
```

```
                    // Button to print the entire scene
                    Button printSceneBtn = new Button("Print Scene");
                    printSceneBtn.setOnAction(e -> print(root));

                    HBox jobStatusBox = new HBox(5, new Label("Print Job Status:"), jobStatus);
                    HBox buttonBox = new HBox(5, printTextBtn, printSceneBtn);

                    root.getChildren().addAll(textLbl, text, jobStatusBox, buttonBox);
                    Scene scene = new Scene(root);
                    stage.setScene(scene);
                    stage.setTitle("Printing Nodes");
                    stage.show();
            }

        private void print(Node node) {
                    jobStatus.textProperty().unbind();
                    jobStatus.setText("Creating a printer job...");

                    // Create a printer job for the default printer
                    PrinterJob job = PrinterJob.createPrinterJob();
                    if (job != null) {
                            // Show the printer job status
                            jobStatus.textProperty().bind(job.jobStatusProperty().asString());

                            // Print the node
                            boolean printed = job.printPage(node);
                            if (printed) {
                                    // End the printer job
                                    job.endJob();
                            } else {
                                    jobStatus.textProperty().unbind();
                                    jobStatus.setText("Printing failed.");
                            }
                    } else {
                            jobStatus.setText("Could not create a printer job.");
                    }
            }
    }
}
```

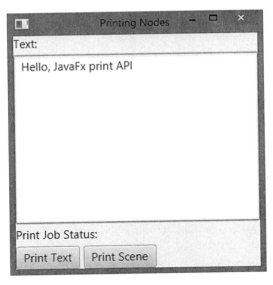

Figure 30-1. *A window letting the user print text in a TextArea and the scene*

Showing the Page Setup and Print Dialogs

The Print API allows users to interact with the printing process. Users can change the printer settings interactively before the printing is initiated. The API lets you show Page Setup and Print Setup dialogs for setting the page properties and printer settings for the job.

You can let the user configure the page layout by showing a Page Setup dialog. Use the showPageSetupDialog(Window owner) method of the PrinterJob to show a Page Setup dialog. The user can set the page size, source, orientation, and margin. The dialog may allow the user to access other printing properties such as the list of printers. Once the user confirms the settings on the dialog, the PrinterJob has the new settings. The method returns true if the user confirms the settings on the dialog. It returns false if the user cancels the dialog. It also returns false if the dialog cannot be displayed, such as when the job is not in the NOT_STARTED state.

The owner parameter to the method is the window that will be the owner of the dialog box. It can be null. If specified, the inputs to the window will be blocked while the dialog is displayed.

```
PrinterJob job = PrinterJob.createPrinterJob();

// Show the page setup dialog
boolean proceed = job.showPageSetupDialog(null);
if (proceed) {
        // Start printing here or you can print later
}
```

You can use the showPrintDialog(Window owner) method to show a Print dialog where the user can modify the printer and settings for the PrinterJob. The return value and parameter of this method have meanings similar to that of the showPageSetupDialog() method.

```
PrinterJob job = PrinterJob.createPrinterJob();

// Show the print setup dialog
boolean proceed = job.showPrintDialog(null);
if (proceed) {
        // Start printing here or you can print later
}
```

The program in Listing 30-2 shows a similar window as shown by the program in Listing 30-1. This time, clicking the print buttons displays a Page Setup and Print Setup dialogs (as shown in Figure 30-2). Once the user confirms the settings on the dialogs, the text in the TextArea is printed. Notice that even though you create a PrinterJob for the default printer before showing the dialogs, you can change the printer using the dialogs, and the text will print using the changed printer.

Listing 30-2. Showing the Page Setup and Print Dialogs to the User

```
// PrintDialogs.java
package com.jdojo.print;

import javafx.application.Application;
import javafx.print.PrinterJob;
import javafx.scene.Node;
import javafx.scene.Scene;
import javafx.scene.control.Button;
import javafx.scene.control.Label;
import javafx.scene.control.TextArea;
import javafx.scene.layout.HBox;
import javafx.scene.layout.VBox;
import javafx.stage.Stage;

public class PrintDialogs extends Application {
        private final Label jobStatus = new Label();

        public static void main(String[] args) {
                Application.launch(args);
        }

        @Override
        public void start(Stage stage) {
                Label textLbl = new Label("Text:");
                TextArea text = new TextArea();
                text.setPrefRowCount(10);
                text.setPrefColumnCount(20);
                text.setWrapText(true);

                // Button to print the TextArea node
                Button pageSetupBtn = new Button("Page Setup and Print");
                pageSetupBtn.setOnAction(e -> pageSetup(text, stage));
```

```
            // Button to print the entire scene
            Button printSetupBtn = new Button("Print Setup and Print");
            printSetupBtn.setOnAction(e -> printSetup(text, stage));

            HBox jobStatusBox = new HBox(5, new Label("Print Job Status:"), jobStatus);
            HBox buttonBox = new HBox(5, pageSetupBtn, printSetupBtn);

            VBox root = new VBox(5, textLbl, text, jobStatusBox, buttonBox);
            Scene scene = new Scene(root);
            stage.setScene(scene);
            stage.setTitle("Showing Print Dialogs");
            stage.show();
    }

    private void pageSetup(Node node, Stage owner) {
            PrinterJob job = PrinterJob.createPrinterJob();
            if (job == null) {
                    return;
            }

            // Show the page setup dialog
            boolean proceed = job.showPageSetupDialog(owner);
            if (proceed) {
                    print(job, node);
            }
    }

    private void printSetup(Node node, Stage owner) {
            PrinterJob job = PrinterJob.createPrinterJob();
            if (job == null) {
                    return;
            }

            // Show the print setup dialog
            boolean proceed = job.showPrintDialog(owner);
            if (proceed) {
                    print(job, node);
            }
    }

    private void print(PrinterJob job, Node node) {
            jobStatus.textProperty().bind(job.jobStatusProperty().asString());

            boolean printed = job.printPage(node);
            if (printed) {
                    job.endJob();
            }
    }
}
```

Figure 30-2. A window letting users use print dialogs to customize the printer settings

Customizing PrinterJob Settings

The Print API contains two classes that are related to printer and printer job settings:

- `PrinterAttributes`
- `JobSettings`

A printer has attributes, which indicate the printing capabilities of the printer. Examples of printer attributes are default paper size, supported paper sizes, maximum number of copies, and default collation. A `PrinterAttributes` object encapsulates the attributes of a printer. The Print API does not let you change the printer attributes as you cannot change the capabilities of a printer. You can only use its capabilities. You cannot create a `PrinterAttributes` object directly. You need to get it from a `Printer` object using the `getPrinterAttributes()` method. The following snippet of code prints some attributes of the default printer in the machine: You may get a different output.

```
import javafx.print.Collation;
import javafx.print.PageOrientation;
import javafx.print.PrintSides;
import javafx.print.Printer;
import javafx.print.PrinterAttributes;
...
Printer printer = Printer.getDefaultPrinter();
PrinterAttributes attribs = printer.getPrinterAttributes();

// Read some printer attributes
int maxCopies = attribs.getMaxCopies();
PrintSides printSides = attribs.getDefaultPrintSides();
Set<PageOrientation> orientations = attribs.getSupportedPageOrientations();
Set<Collation> collations = attribs.getSupportedCollations();
```

```
// Print the printer attributes
System.out.println("Max. Copies: " + maxCopies);
System.out.println("Print Sides: " + printSides);
System.out.println("Supported Orientation: " + orientations);
System.out.println("Supported Collations: " + collations);
```

```
Max. Copies: 999
Print Sides: ONE_SIDED
Supported Orientation: [PORTRAIT, LANDSCAPE, REVERSE_LANDSCAPE]
Supported Collations: [UNCOLLATED, COLLATED]
```

■ **Tip** A `PrinterAttributes` is an immutable object. It contains the default and supported attributes of a printer. You obtain `PrinterAttributes` from a `Printer` object.

A `JobSettings` contains the printer attributes to be used for a print job for a specific printer. You can obtain the `JobSettings` of a print job using the `getJobSettings()` method of the `PrinterJob` object. A `JobSettings` is a mutable object. It contains a property for each printer attribute that can be set for a print job. By default, its properties are initialized to the default properties of the printer. You can change the property that will be used for the current print job. If you change the property of a `JobSettings` that is not supported by the printer, the property reverts to the default value for the printer. The following snippet of code sets the `printSides` property to `DUPLEX`. In this case, the printer supports only `ONE_SIDED` printing. Therefore, the `printSides` property is set to `ONE_SIDED`, which is the default, and only supported `printSides` value by the printer. You may get a different output.

```
// Create a printer job for the default printer
PrinterJob job = PrinterJob.createPrinterJob();

// Get the JobSettings for the print job
JobSettings jobSettings = job.getJobSettings();
System.out.println(jobSettings.getPrintSides());

// Set the printSides to DUPLEX
jobSettings.setPrintSides(PrintSides.DUPLEX);
System.out.println(jobSettings.getPrintSides());
```

```
ONE_SIDED
ONE_SIDED
```

For a print job, you can specify the page ranges using the pageRanges property of the `JobSettings`. The pageRanges property is an array of PageRange. A PageRange has startPage and endPage properties that define the range. The following snippet of code sets the page ranges for a job to 1-5 and 20-25.

```
PrinterJob job = PrinterJob.createPrinterJob();
JobSettings jobSettings = job.getJobSettings();
jobSettings.setPageRanges(new PageRange(1, 5), new PageRange(20, 25));
```

Most of the printer attributes are represented by enum constants. For example, the collation attribute is represented by Collation.COLLATED and Collation.UNCOLLATED constants. Some attributes, such as number of copies to be printed, are specified as an int. Please refer the list of properties in the JobSettings class that you can set for a print job.

Setting Page Layout

An instance of the PageLayout class represents the page setup for a print job. By default, it is set to the printer default value. You have already seen setting up the page layout using the Page Setup dialog. A PageLayout encapsulates three things:

- The paper size

- The page orientation

- The page margins

A PageLayout is used to configure the printable area of the page, which must lie within the printable area of the hardware. If a page is rendered outside the printable area of the hardware, the content is clipped.

You cannot create a PageLayout object directly. You need to use one of the createPageLayout() methods of the Printer to get a PageLayout.

- PageLayout createPageLayout(Paper paper, PageOrientation orient, double lMargin, double rMargin, double tMargin, double bMargin)

- PageLayout createPageLayout(Paper paper, PageOrientation orient, Printer.MarginType mType)

The margins can be specified as numbers or as one of the following constants of the Printer.MarginType enum.

- DEFAULT

- EQUAL

- EQUAL_OPPOSITES

- HARDWARE_MINIMUM

The DEFAULT margin type requests default 0.75 inch on all sides.

The EQUAL margin type uses the largest of the four hardware margins on all four sides, so the margins are equal on all four sides.

The EQUAL_OPPOSITES margin type uses the larger of left and right hardware margins for the left and right sides, and the larger of the top and bottom hardware margins for the top and bottom sides.

The HARDWARE_MINIMUM requests that the minimum hardware allowed margins should be set on all sides.

The following snippet of code creates a PageLayout for A4 size paper, LANDSCAPE page orientation, and equal margins on all sides. The PageLayout is set to a print job.

```
import javafx.print.JobSettings;
import javafx.print.PageLayout;
import javafx.print.PageOrientation;
import javafx.print.Paper;
import javafx.print.Printer;
import javafx.print.PrinterJob;
...
```

```
PrinterJob job = PrinterJob.createPrinterJob();
Printer printer = job.getPrinter();
PageLayout pageLayout = printer.createPageLayout(Paper.A4,
                                         PageOrientation.LANDSCAPE,
                                         Printer.MarginType.EQUAL);

JobSettings jobSettings = job.getJobSettings();
jobSettings.setPageLayout(pageLayout);
```

Sometimes, you want to know the size of the printable area on the page. You can get it using the getPrintableWidth() and getPrintableHeight() methods of the PageLayout. This is useful if you want to resize a node before printing, so it fits the printable area. The following snippet of code prints an Ellipse that fits the printable area.

```
PrinterJob job = PrinterJob.createPrinterJob();
JobSettings jobSettings = job.getJobSettings();
PageLayout pageLayout = jobSettings.getPageLayout();
double pgW = pageLayout.getPrintableWidth();
double pgH = pageLayout.getPrintableHeight();

// Make the Ellipse fit the printable are of the page
Ellipse node = new Ellipse(pgW/2, pgH/2, pgW /2, pgH/2);
node.setFill(null);
node.setStroke(Color.BLACK);
node.setStrokeWidth(1);

boolean printed = job.printPage(node);
if (printed) {
        // End the printer job
        job.endJob();
}
```

Printing a Webpage

There is a special way to print the contents of a webpage. Use the print(PrinterJob job) method of the WebEngine class to print the webpage loaded by the engine. The method does not modify the specified job. The job can be used for more printing after the print() method call.

```
WebView webView = new WebView();
WebEngine webEngine = webView.getEngine();
...
PrinterJob job = PrinterJob.createPrinterJob();
webEngine.print(job);
```

The program in Listing 30-3 shows how to print webpages. There is nothing new in the program that you have not already covered. If you have not used a WebView before, please refer to *Chapter 16: Browsing Webpages*. The program displays a window with a URL field, a *Go* button, a *Print* button, and a WebView. The Print button is enabled when a webpage is successfully loaded. You can enter a webpage URL and click the *Go* button to navigate to the page. Click the *Print* button to print the webpage.

Listing 30-3. Printing a Webpage

```java
// PrintingWebPage.java
package com.jdojo.print;

import javafx.application.Application;
import javafx.concurrent.Worker;
import javafx.geometry.Insets;
import javafx.print.PrinterJob;
import javafx.scene.Scene;
import javafx.scene.control.Button;
import javafx.scene.control.Label;
import javafx.scene.control.TextField;
import javafx.scene.layout.BorderPane;
import javafx.scene.layout.HBox;
import javafx.scene.web.WebEngine;
import javafx.scene.web.WebView;
import javafx.stage.Stage;

public class PrintingWebPage extends Application {
        String HOME_PAGE = "http://www.yahoo.com";

        TextField urlFld = new TextField();
        Button goBtn = new Button("Go");
        Button printBtn = new Button("Print");
        WebView webView = new WebView();
        WebEngine webEngine = webView.getEngine();

        public static void main(String[] args) {
                Application.launch(args);
        }

        @Override
        public void start(Stage stage) {
                // Add event handlers
                addEventHandlers(stage);

                BorderPane root = new BorderPane();
                HBox top = new HBox(5, new Label("URL"), urlFld,  goBtn, printBtn);
                top.setPadding(new Insets(2, 5, 10, 5));
                root.setTop(top);

                root.setCenter(webView);
                Scene scene = new Scene(root);
                stage.setScene(scene);
                stage.show();

                // Load the Home Page
                webEngine.load(HOME_PAGE);
        }
```

```java
    private void addEventHandlers(Stage stage) {
        // Update the stage title when a new web page title is available
        webEngine.titleProperty().addListener((prop, oldTitle, newTitle) -> {
            stage.setTitle(newTitle);
        });

        // Add event handler for GO button
        goBtn.setOnAction(e -> {
            webEngine.load(urlFld.getText());
        });

        printBtn.setOnAction(e -> print(stage));

        // Enable the print button and sync the URL
        webEngine.getLoadWorker().stateProperty().addListener(
                (prop, oldState, newState) -> {
            if (newState == Worker.State.SUCCEEDED) {
                String newLocation = webEngine.getLocation();
                urlFld.setText(newLocation);
                printBtn.setDisable(false);
            } else {
                printBtn.setDisable(true);
            }
        });
    }

    private void print(Stage stage) {
        PrinterJob job = PrinterJob.createPrinterJob();
        if (job == null) {
            return;
        }

        // Show the print setup dialog
        boolean proceed = job.showPrintDialog(stage);
        if (proceed) {
            webEngine.print(job);
            job.endJob();
        }
    }
}
```

Summary

JavaFX 8 added support for printing nodes through the Print API in the javafx.print package. The API consists of a few classes and a number of enums. The Print API provides support for printing nodes that may or may not be attached to a scene graph. It is a common requirement to print the content of a webpage, not the WebView node that contains the webpage. The javafx.scene.web.WebEngine class contains a print(PrinterJob job) method that prints the contents of the webpage, not the WebView node.

If a node is modified during the printing process, the printed node may not appear correct. Note that the printing of a node may span multiple pulse events resulting in concurrent change in the content being printed. To ensure correct printing, make sure that the node being printed is not modified during the print process.

Nodes can be printed on any thread including the JavaFX Application Thread. It is recommended that large, time-consuming print jobs be submitted on a background thread to keep the UI responsive.

Classes in the Print API are final as they represent existing printing device properties. Most of them do not provide any public constructor as you cannot make up a printing device. Rather, you obtain their references using factory methods in various classes.

An instance of the `Printer` class represents a printer. The `Printer.getAllPrinters()` static method returns an observable list of installed printers on the machine. Note that the list of printers returned by the method may change over time as new printers are installed or old printers are removed. Use the `getName()` method of the `Printer` to get the name of the printer.

The `Printer.getDefaultPrinter()` method returns the default `Printer`. The method may return `null` if no printer is installed. The default printer may be changed on a machine. Therefore, the method may return different printers from call to call, and the printer returned may not be valid after some time.

You can create a printer job by calling the `PrinterJob.createPrinterJob()` method. It returns an object of the `PrinterJob` class. Once you get a `PrinterJob` object, call its `printPage()` method to print a node. The node to be printed is passed as an argument to the method.

The Print API allows users to interact with the printing process. Users can change the printer settings interactively before the printing is initiated. The API lets you show Page Setup and Print Setup dialogs for setting the page properties and printer settings for the job. You can let the user configure the page layout by showing a Page Setup dialog. Use the `showPageSetupDialog(Window owner)` method of the `PrinterJob` to show a Page Setup dialog. The user can set the page size, source, orientation, and margins. The dialog may allow the user to access other printing properties such as the list of printers.

The Print API lets you customize the printer job settings. The API contains two classes that are related to printer and printer job settings: `PrinterAttributes` and `JobSettings` classes. A printer has attributes, which indicate the printing capabilities of the printer such as default paper size, supported paper sizes, maximum number of copies, and default collation. A `PrinterAttributes` object encapsulates the attributes of a printer. The Print API does not let you change the printer attributes as you cannot change the capabilities of a printer. You cannot create a `PrinterAttributes` object directly. You need to get it from a `Printer` object using the `getPrinterAttributes()` method.

An instance of the `PageLayout` class represents the page setup for a print job. By default, it is set to the printer default value. A `PageLayout` is used to configure the printable area of the page, which must lie within the printable area of the hardware. If a page is rendered outside the printable area of the hardware, the content is clipped. You cannot create a `PageLayout` object directly. You need to use one of the `createPageLayout()` methods of the `Printer` to get a `PageLayout`.

There is a special way to print the contents of a webpage. Use the `print(PrinterJob job)` method of the `WebEngine` class to print the webpage loaded by the engine. The method does not modify the specified job. The job can be used for more printing after the `print()` method call.

Index